STATISTICAL ANALYSIS FOR BUSINESS AND ECONOMICS:
CONCEPTS AND PRACTICE

Willbann D. Terpening
Mirjeta Beqiri
Sarah Schwering

Gonzaga University

Copyright © 2013
HERCHER Publishing Inc
Naperville, Il 60564

ISBN 978-1-939297-09-9

Preface To Instructors

This text offers a sound introduction to statistics appropriate for either the undergraduate or introductory MBA level. We hope you'll find the writing style clear and concise. Each chapter begins with learning objectives and an opening vignette of a business situation or problem that introduces the topics in a creative way. Within the chapters, abundant figures, charts, and drawings have been designed to enhance the learning process. Key concepts, definitions and formulas are highlighted, examples are clearly outlined, and exercises and problems of varying difficulty are provided.

Every textbook reflects the philosophy and pedagogical approach of the authors and this text is no different. Therefore, it would be helpful to state the elements of that philosophy and how they shape the text upfront:

(1) We believe that there is merit in adopting a process point of view in the teaching of statistics. This view imparts the idea that the data come from somewhere, e.g., a process, and that the primary business challenge is in understanding and managing that process. The process point of view is most heavily emphasized in Chapter 1 but is reinforced throughout the text.

(2) We believe that the ability of students to learn and apply statistical thinking to improve business processes is often impeded by a focus on the nuts and bolts of formulas and calculations. Therefore, when students have completed the course they know how to plug numbers into formulas, but have no idea what to do with a set of data in a real-life situation; however, we also believe that there is merit in understanding the underlying logic of the calculations. For this reason, we have divided the material in most chapters into two major sections called Concepts and Practice. The concepts section provides the formulas and logic of the procedures and has one or two examples illustrating the calculations involved. The practice section focuses on the use of computer software to perform those calculations more easily and accurately than by hand. This will also give the students a feel for how statistics is actually done in practice. In this text, we emphasize the use of Excel and the XLDataAnalyst software because of the near universal availability of Excel in the business world. Excel templates that accompany the text can be used by the student to perform calculations to see how the computational techniques can be implemented in Excel.

(3) We believe that short story problems in traditional texts with data already summarized do not adequately teach the student how statistics can be used in the real world. For this reason, we have provided computer-oriented exercises in each chapter to provide experience in dealing with realistic data. We have also included four detailed datasets at the end of the text. These datasets correspond to problems in each chapter and provide continuity throughout the text.

In addition, most chapters begin with an opening vignette that describes a particular decision-making situation. Usually, the vignettes involve a dataset of some kind. The opening vignette is revisited at the end of each chapter to apply the techniques learned in that chapter to solve the problem.

(4) During our careers we have seen many examples of statistical techniques applied to data that were inappropriate for that type of analysis. We have also attempted, usually unsuccessfully, in our classes to reach that last chapter on nonparametric techniques to deal with some of the measurement issues. For this reason, we stress throughout the text that all statistical methods make certain assumptions about the level of measurement of the data and cover techniques appropriate to all levels of measurement in each chapter. In other words, nonparametric

techniques are integrated throughout the text. We hope that students will have a good grasp on when to apply a particular method or technique and when such techniques may be inappropriate.

(5) We believe that statistics is a powerful tool that can be used to deceive as well as enlighten and that students should be made aware of the ways is which statistics can be misused. To that end, we discuss ethical issues in the use of statistics throughout the text.

(6) We also believe that audio tools can be essential to learning in addition to visuals. To that end, we have included a number of Screencasts with the text. These Screencasts show the student how to install and use the XLDataAnalyst software and how to use the templates that accompany the text. Also, the PowerPoint slides that accompany the text have two versions. One simply provides the traditional slides that accompany most texts. The other provides Screencasts of the PowerPoint presentations along with a voiceover narrative explaining the material in each slide. MP3 files of the Chapter glossaries are also provided to aid in the process of learning statistical terminology.

Although we firmly believe in these pedagogical principles, we have tried to be flexible in the organization of the text for those who may want to employ different approaches. For example, in each chapter there are numerous traditional exercises where the student will need to perform calculations as well as a number of computer exercises. These traditional exercises can be performed using formulas and a calculator, or by using the Excel templates provided with the text at the discretion of the instructor. For instructors wishing to use tables rather than Excel functions, an Excel file with the traditional tables will be provided on request.

The computer exercises can generally be addressed using only the built-in tools in Excel, or using the Excel templates accompanying the text, or with the XLDataAnalyst software. Some of the computer exercises require the use of XLDataAnalyst as they cannot be solved using Excel alone.

PREFACE TO STUDENTS

Statistics is a fascinating subject–but sometimes students find it relatively difficult. The purpose of this book is to increase your interest in statistics while easing the learning process with a clear, organized, and intuitively understandable presentation of the material. We would like you to appreciate the valuable role of statistics in the analysis of business problems and in your daily life. As H.G. Wells once said, "Statistical thinking will one day be as necessary for efficient citizenship as the ability to read or write." We believe that this is the day. You are constantly surrounded by statistical facts and statistical reasoning, much of it inaccurate. A lack of statistical knowledge in this era is dangerous.

Our aim is to help you develop your analytical skills to where you will feel confident using statistical methods in decision-making situations. Thousands of managers already use a broad spectrum of statistical methods every day. These same statistical skills can prove useful to you as well.

We recognize the difficulties of a formal mathematical approach to statistics. We believe that you can learn the essential statistical concepts without embroiling yourself too deeply in the mathematical details. After all, you certainly will not perform statistical analyses by hand in the real world. Our approach has been to make this book as clear and understandable to students as possible. Mathematical symbols are used where necessary, but are omitted when a concept can be presented verbally or in graphs with equal clarity and conciseness. If you have a reasonable understanding of algebra, you should have no difficulty with the mathematics in this book. We also stress using computer software to perform most calculations. It can perform them much faster, and more importantly, more accurately than by hand.

Statistical methods do require analytical thought patterns best developed through consistent practice over time. You may have a fine instructor and a good book, but that is not enough. Nor will cramming material prior to a quiz or exam serve you well. Independent and group study on a regular basis is essential. Form study groups and work together with your instructor's permission. Nothing aids learning like trying to explain something to someone else. We have found that one way of learning this material is to (1) read the assigned materials before class and view the screencast for that chapter, (2) take notes of key points from class, (3) complete a good selection of problems, and (4) summarize all your notes in condensed form. The last step may be the most important. Your summary should be a well-organized breakdown of the most important points from each chapter; it should include the items especially emphasized by your instructor, as well as the cogent points from the homework. Learning is something you do for yourself. No one can "teach" you something; they can merely help you learn. Good luck in your journey through the world of statistics.

Willbann D. Terpening

Mirjeta Beqiri

Sarah Schwering

CONTENTS

Chapter 1:

Introduction to Statistics

Why Study Statistics?
Concepts and Practice
A Process View
What is Statistics?
- Descriptive Statistics
- Inferential Statistics

Statistical Terminology
- Census and Sample Data
- Parameters and Statistics
- Point and Interval Estimates
- Sampling Error
- Nonsampling Error

Steps in a Statistical Study
Collecting Data
- Collecting Primary Data
- Surveys and Observation
- Experimental and Nonexperimental Studies
- A Classification of Data Gathering Situations

Overview of the Text
Ethical Issues in Statistics
Computers and Statistical Analysis
- Built-In Excel Tools
- XLDataAnalyst
- Special Purpose Statistical Software

Summary
Chapter Glossary
Questions and Problems
Database Problems
Appendix
- Government Sources
- Trade and Periodical Data

Chapter 1 Learning Objectives

When you finish this chapter you should be able to:

1. **Explain why we study statistics**

2. **Explain the process view of an organization**

3. **Define the terms statistics, population, sample and estimate**

4. **Distinguish between descriptive and inferential statistics**

5. **Explain the concept of sampling error**

6. **Describe the steps in a statistical study**

7. **Describe the use of Excel and other software in statistics**

According to Hossein Eslambolchi, CIO, CTO and President of Global Network Technologies, AT&T is no longer a voice company, it is a data company.[1] Internet Protect Services is one of the recent products announced by AT&T. New features added to this service perform stochastic analysis of internet data using a technique called smart sampling. Using this technology, AT&T claims to be able to detect patterns in the 1,700 terabytes of Internet traffic processed by the AT&T IP network each day that indicate a virus or other Internet attack before it hits on a large scale. According to Eslambolchi, AT&T identified the SQL Slammer attack three weeks before it hit full scale on the Internet. Increasingly, these and other data-mining techniques are being used, not only for network security, but also to help companies improve their relationships with important customers and other vital activities. Sophisticated analysis of the massive amounts of data that are available can reveal undiscovered patterns and other valuable information to help make a firm more profitable. With the increasing flow of information on the Internet and from other sources, data-mining and other statistical techniques will only become more important in the future.

Why Study Statistics?

As the above paragraph illustrates, with the advent of the Internet and new techniques for gathering data, the amount of information in the modern business is exploding. Most organizations realize that there is great potential value in this information but still struggle to use this information in any meaningful way. As described by Eslambolchi, companies, such as AT&T, are turning to more sophisticated statistical analysis of this information to try and uncover patterns in the data that will give them a competitive edge.

Statistical analysis is part of the growing field of *business analytics.* Analytics derives from the Greek word "analutiká" pertaining to mathematical or logical analysis. Google uses the term to describe the analysis of information gathered from the web which is a big part of their business[2]. Software companies such as SAS, SPSS, and Oracle tout their analytics products under the broad umbrella of *business intelligence* (BI); however, our use of analytics is much broader than tracking web statistics or even statistical analysis. A recent book by Davenport and Harris on the topic defined analytics as "the

---

[1] The World According to AT&T, Ephraim Schwartz, Infoworld, November 22, 2004.
[2] www.google/analytics

extensive use of data, statistical and quantitative analysis, explanatory and predictive models, and fact based management to drive decisions and actions.[3]" The authors cite many diverse companies such as Harrah's Entertainment Inc., Netflix, and the Boston Red Sox baseball team as examples of analytical businesses.

It is apparent that statistical analysis has become an increasingly important tool in the business arsenal. As Davenport and Harris put it, "Organizations (and people) that make good use of statistical methods are likely to be more successful than those which do not[3]". That is why it is so important for business students to have a basic fundamental knowledge of statistical reasoning.

Studying statistics helps ensure that you will make better decisions as a manager. Statistical *What we do with it* ← methodologies enable managers to identify problems, make comparisons, perform tests, and decide on the best course of action to take. It doesn't guarantee correct decisions, but it does help reduce the chance of making serious mistakes. After decisions are implemented, statistical analysis is also used to evaluate the results of those decisions.

In summary, statistics is important because:

- #1 Statistics is the factual language of business and is required to communicate effectively and efficiently within business.

- #2 Statistical methods describe data that relate to the status of all aspects of the business and its relationships with other entities.

- #3 Statistics can be used to gain new knowledge by uncovering hidden relationships in the massive amounts of data collected by most modern businesses.

- #4 Statistical methodologies support conclusions, inferences, and the decision-making processes that are the prime responsibility of management.

The importance of statistics is not limited to the field of business. Statistics is an important, and often required, course in many fields of study. If you have friends majoring in psychology, sociology, education, biology, or even anthropology, chances are that they also are required to take a course in statistics with topics very similar to those discussed in this text. In addition, other professional fields such as medicine and engineering use statistical analysis extensively.

Concepts and Practice

You will notice that most of the later chapters in the text are divided into two sections. These sections are labeled "Concepts" and "Practice" respectively. It is important to keep in mind that you can understand a subject such as statistics at many different levels. In the case of statistics, we can postulate at least three different levels of understanding.

1. Standard statistical software can analyze data, but not provide the understanding of underlying calculations or logic involved. Software is like a black box that "spits out answers."

2. You can understand the logic behind the calculations and understand the conceptual underpinnings of statistical analysis. You can explain to your colleagues the basic idea behind the "black box" and can determine when certain techniques should be used and when they should not be used.

---

[3] Thomas H. Davenport and Jeanne G. Harris, Competing on Analytics: The New Science of Winning, 2007, Cambridge Mass.: Harvard Business School Press.

3. You can perform all of the calculations necessary in statistical analysis and can devise algorithms and programs to perform the calculations.

The first level of understanding is a very dangerous level. Modern statistical packages are readily available and are becoming more and more user-friendly and easy-to-use. This encourages the use of the software without understanding the underlying concepts behind the calculations. Unfortunately, computer software will "crunch the numbers" no matter if it is appropriate to utilize a particular technique or not. The computer does not understand the logical underpinnings of statistics, but assumes that you do. Just because the computer gives you an answer does not necessarily mean that it is an appropriate or meaningful answer or even relevant to your original problem.

The second understanding implies that you know statistical terminology and understand the basic logic of statistical inference. That will tell when it is appropriate to apply different techniques to certain questions. But, even if you understand the logic, you may not necessarily be able to perform the calculations yourself.

The third level of understanding assumes that you recognize the techniques and theory behind them and can perform all necessary calculations. In essence, you understand the methods well enough to create solution algorithms and perform the relevant calculations.

Traditional textbooks in Business Statistics aim for at least a level two combined with a level three understanding, in terms of manual calculations. To that end, they present a number of equations and provide practice exercises, oriented toward the manual calculations of results. They may also discuss the use of computer software to solve these problems as well. There is some value in understanding the manual calculations involved in statistics because it aids in understanding the logic behind the calculations; however, in actual practice, analysts and managers almost never perform statistical calculations manually so it is important that you be able to use tools to perform the calculations and know when to apply those tools.

Therefore, most of the later chapters in this text are divided into two sections: **concepts** and **practices**. The first section on "Concepts" introduces the logic behind the techniques. Equations are introduced and examples are provided with solutions for you to see the logic behind the exercises. There will also be problems for you to practice those concepts. The "Practice" section of each chapter will assume that you understand the basic logic of the techniques presented in the "Concepts" section and will focus on the use of computer programs to perform the calculations. Software will be used throughout this text as the primary calculation platform because it is almost universally available in the business world and widely used by managers and analysts to analyze data[4]. The problems in this section will be more realistic of situations you may encounter in a business environment and will use raw data as input for the analysis. Each chapter will describe the built-in Excel tools that can be used along with more specialized software (XLDataAnalyst) to solve problems. We will describe some of these tools at the end of this chapter.

A Process View

Historically, business organizations were viewed as a set of functions that must be performed. There were "Marketing", "Operations", "Financial", "Human Resource" functions, and so on. This view of a business was also reflected in the organizational structure of the firm which was divided into departments based on

---

[4] Excel 2007 (Version 12) will be used in this text. All screenshots will be taken from this version of Excel; however, all of the data files are available for older versions of Excel and all software used in this text is also available for older versions of Excel.

those functions. After World War II, W. Edwards Deming began developing a different view of the business enterprise in Japan. Since that time, various management movements, such as total quality management and Six Sigma have begun to change the business process landscape. At its simplest level, a process takes inputs and transforms them into outputs as shown in Figure 1-1.

Figure 1-1   A Process as Transformation

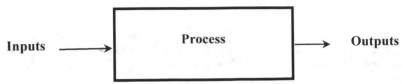

An example of a process is a manufacturing operation that takes raw materials and parts and produces physical goods as outputs, such as automobiles, refrigerators or computers; however, such processes are not restricted to manufacturing. For example, hiring processes take inputs of applicants and produce trained employees for the organization. Or advertising campaigns transform digital information into a communication message to increase brand awareness. In fact, the process view of an organization asserts that all work of any type goes through a process. As Deming once said, "If you can't describe what you do as a process, you don't know what you are doing."

Statistical thinking is based on the process view of the organization and helps ensure organizational objectives are met using statistics[5].

> *Statistical thinking* is a philosophy of learning and action based on three fundamental principles:
>
> 1. All work consists of a system of interconnected processes
> 2. Variability exists in all processes
> 3. Understanding and reducing variability are the keys to improving a process

Understanding variability is the heart of statistical thinking. At its simplest level, variability can be conceptualized as a deviation from an average or expected value. Therefore, stating that variability exists in all processes implies things may not always remain the same from one time to the next. One of the keys to understanding process variability is to realize that there are two kinds of variability: **common cause** and **special cause**[6].

Common cause variability is inherent in the process itself and is due to small causes that are unpredictable, given the current state of knowledge. It needs to be measured, but requires no special action. Rather, it is simply the expected random variability of the process.

Special cause variability, on the other hand, indicates that something has changed about the process or that an outside force is affecting the process. Special cause variability requires managerial action to correct the process and restore it to its proper functioning. For example, suppose a major credit card company has developed a sophisticated system to predict total individual credit card purchases on a

---

[5] *Statistical Thinking: Improving Business Performance*, Hoerl, R. and Snee, R.D, Duxbury, 2002.
[6] These terms were popularized by Dr. W. Edwards Deming. Walter Shewhart, who inspired many of the ideas popularized by Deming, originally used the terms chance and assignable cause respectively.

monthly basis. To monitor the performance of this system, the company tracks the difference between the predicted and actual values each month. Ideally, this difference (the error in prediction) should be zero but it is rarely exactly zero. Moreover, the difference varies from month to month due to idiosyncrasies in the model and the vagaries of individual consumer decisions; however, if the prediction process is working properly the average difference should be zero and the variations around this difference should be random. But suppose that the onset of a recent recession has caused consumers to cut back on their purchases. This could cause the model to suddenly over predict consumer expenditures on many of the cards leading to a significant spike in the differences between predicted and actual. This is not a reflection of the normal variation in the process but is due to a special variation and will require the company to take action to modify the prediction system to take into account the changing economic environment.

The key to successful process control is to be able to distinguish between common cause and special cause variability. Measuring common cause variability is the first step as it indicates how much variability is to be expected. Variability outside this range will be due to special cause variation. In a very real sense, statistics is about distinguishing between common cause and special cause variability.

As a more everyday life example, suppose that you hear on the news one night that juvenile crime is up 7 percent this year in the town where you live. What does this increase mean? Is there a crime wave? Do the police and local city government need to take action? We cannot adequately address these questions without knowing something about the common cause variability. Juvenile crime is a result of a process, albeit a very complex socioeconomic process. For this reason, we would expect some natural variability in crime rates from year to year even if there was no change in the underlying factors that lead to reported crimes. If we knew that juvenile crime rates typically fluctuated by 10 percent each year, then we would not be too alarmed by the 7 percent increase this year. On the other hand, if we know that juvenile crime rates typically vary by only 1 or 2 percent each year, then the 7 percent increase would be quite alarming. Without an awareness of the normal or common cause variability, we cannot interpret a deviation or variation from the expected. Ignorance about variability would have us constantly react to random variations, as if they were important. This can lead to a great deal of stress, expense, and many other unintended consequences. Sadly we do this all too often in public policy and even in the business environment.

As we will see later, comparing a deviation or sample result to the expected or normal variability is essentially the process of statistical inference. Making inferences in statistics can be reduced to the question of, "Are the data that we observe within the range of common cause variability and therefore due to chance, or are they outside that range and therefore indicative of something important?" It will help you to better appreciate the role of statistics in business if you understand that all data arise from a process, that the outputs of a process are inherently variable, and that managers must make decisions about the process and what steps to take based on that data. Statistics helps managers make more informed and better decisions.

What is Statistics?

Managerial success today depends heavily on the availability of valid, timely, and relevant data. No matter the business function, up-to-date information is critical to making business decisions:

- An auditor needs a sample of accounts receivable to determine whether the stated amounts in the company's accounting statements are materially correct.

- A Human Resource manager wants an estimate of the average salary for Java programmers in the local area.

- A marketing manager wants to chart sales by product line for his next presentation.

- A purchasing manager needs an estimate of the average time it takes to get parts from a particular supplier to plan lead times for materials.

Each example requires unique data. The goal of an effective information system is to supply the needed data at the appropriate times. Statistical theory and procedures help ensure that the data are in the proper form and can be used to make the most effective decisions.

> *Statistics* is the body of methods for the collection, analysis, presentation, interpretation and the use of data.

Although there are a wide variety of methods included in the field of statistics, almost all of them begin with the distinction between a population and a sample. In statistical analysis, a *population* is the entire collection of elements in a particular study. The elements could be people (employees, customers, voters, etc.), groups (companies, sales regions, etc.) or things (products, services, political positions, etc.). A *sample* is any part of the population. *(Note: a good sample should be representative of the population.)* Statistical methods are sometimes divided into two branches: (1) descriptive and (2) inferential.

Descriptive Statistics

Descriptive statistics describes data by classifying, summarizing, and displaying either population or sample data. In other words, descriptive statistics can be applied to either a population or a sample. In Chapter 2, we will see how data can be summarized using tables, charts, and graphs. For example, suppose that a personnel manager of an airline company is faced with negotiating a new wage contract. Charts and summary measures of the current wages of pilots, mechanics, flight attendants, and other employee groups would provide the negotiators a composite overview, or summary, of wage levels and differences among workers. It's true—a picture is worth a thousand words! *funny!*

In Chapter 3 we will turn to numerical values that summarize particular characteristics of the data, such as central tendency or the variability (dispersion). Often, we need to use descriptive measures for other purposes, such as making financial projections or building financial models. Although pictures can be helpful, they are difficult to incorporate into a financial spreadsheet.

Descriptive statistics simply describe the data and do not make inferences on the basis of that information.

Inferential Statistics

Inferential statistics involve making inferences that go beyond the known data. Statistical inference takes one of two forms: (1) deduction or (2) induction. Figure 1-2 illustrates the difference.

Figure 1-2   *Statistical Inferential Procedures*

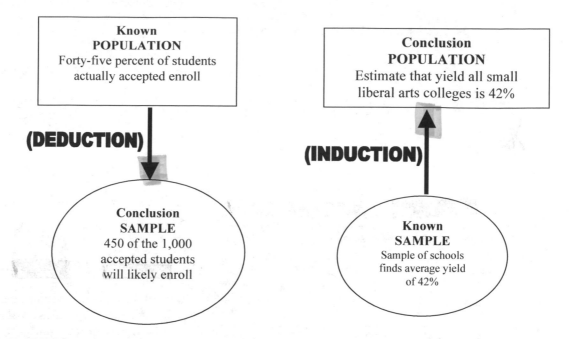

Deduction is the logical process of taking general population knowledge to draw a conclusion about a specific element or sample taken from that population. As we will see in Chapters 4 and 5, some probability statements use deductive logic. For example, a small liberal arts college knows that historically 45% of the students accepted for admission to the college actually enroll the following fall semester. They can use this knowledge about the "yield" rate to estimate (deduce) the likelihood of having more than 500 students enroll next fall on the basis of this year's acceptances or the probability of more than 50% of the accepted students enrolling in the fall.

Induction is the logical process of taking specific knowledge about a sample to infer something about the population as a whole. There is significant value in induction as we can make estimations about a population using sample data. We use inference procedures extensively in Chapters 6 through 11 to estimate population values and test whether assumptions about populations are supported by sample data. For example, our small liberal arts college wanted to know what the average yield rate was for all such colleges they might take a random sample of similar schools and finding an average yield in the sample of 42% might estimate that the average yield of all such schools was 42%.

Statistical Terminology

Statistics, like most fields of study, has its own terminology. In order to understand statistics, it is important to "learn the language." In this section, we will introduce you to some basic terminology that will be used throughout our study of statistics. Don't worry if you do not comprehend all of the nuances of the terms at this point. We will discuss these terms in more detail in coming chapters. It is easiest to introduce these terms within the context of an example:

Suppose you are a management trainee for a local grocery firm. Your supervisor has just learned that a bank is auctioning a warehouse of nonperishable goods next week because a competitor declared bankruptcy. She has asked you to review the data and recommend whether your firm should bid on the warehouse goods. The advertisement says that there are 513,711 cases in the warehouse, but it doesn't specifically say what they are and you don't know their total value[7]; however, the bank conducting the sale has collected a representative sample of 100 cases of goods and placed them in a truck for public inspection. You price the truckload of 100 cases and estimate their value at $708.00. Figure 1-3 illustrates the situation.

Figure 1-3   Population and Sample Data

Population	**Sample**
Warehouse	Truckload of Goods
513, 711 items	100 items
Unknown Value	Value $708.00

Census and Sample

A *census* is the collection of data on every element in the entire population, whereas a sample describes only part of the population. In Figure 1-3, the population consists of all 513,711 items in the warehouse while a sample would be the 100 items in the truck. In order to determine the precise value of all 513,711 items in the warehouse, you would have to complete a population study; however, that information is not available, so the sample data will have to be used to make the bid decision. In many, if not most, business situations, completing a census is difficult to justify because of the length of time and cost it would require. This means that in the world of business we are often utilizing sample information. Nevertheless, we often need estimates of population values to make decisions.

Parameters and Statistics

A *population parameter* is a descriptive measure of the population, whereas a *sample statistic* is a descriptive measure of a sample. In this text, population parameters will always be designated by Greek symbols, while we will use English symbols for sample statistics. In Figure 1-3, the population parameter is unknown (which is often the case), but one sample statistic (the sample mean) is known to be $7.08 per case. We designate the sample mean as $\bar{X}$ (pronounced *x-bar*), so we would say $\bar{X}$ = $7.08.

The word "statistic" also has another meaning. People often refer to any single item of quantitative data as a statistic, and to collections of such items as statistics. We will use the term **data** to refer to raw numbers and reserve the term **statistics** for values we gather by doing further analysis of raw data.

Point and Interval Estimates

A *point estimate* is a single value, from a sample, used to estimate some characteristic of a population. For example, suppose we want to make a point estimate of the total value of the groceries in the warehouse from Figure 1-3.

---

[7] Economists call this situation a common value auction where there is a true but unknown value for the items up for bid but the bidders do not know this value.

Assuming that the 100 cases in the sample are representative of all the items in the warehouse from the sample we know that:

Average unit value = \$708.00 ÷ 100 cases = \$7.08 per case

We could then estimate that for the population:

Estimated total value = (\$7.08 per case) x (513,711 cases) = \$3,637,074

This example uses a form of induction. We reason from our knowledge of the sample (truckload) to a point estimate of the population value (warehouse); however, point estimates, although sometimes very close, are almost always not exactly correct.

For this reason, statisticians frequently use intervals to express their estimates. *Interval estimates* provide the bounds within which the population value is believed to lie. For example, an interval estimate around the \$7.08 sample average might be a range from \$6.83 to \$7.33 per item. This would yield an estimated total value in the range of \$3,508,646 to \$3,765,502. Using statistical theory (from Chapter 6), you could also determine how strongly we believe that this range really does include the true, but unknown population value.

Sampling Error

Firms apply statistical sampling to everything from inspecting raw materials to auditing accounts or assessing customer satisfaction with their products. In each case, only part of the population is inspected or measured as a sample. But, that limited information is used to make a decision about the entire population, such as whether the warehouse of groceries is worth \$3,637,074, from the previous example. There is some risk of making a mistake because the decision is made on the basis of partial information. Recall from Figure 1-2, where we took a sample of memory chips and determined the number of defects. If we gathered a sample with an unusually large number of defects, this would result in our estimation of a higher process defect rate than necessary.

> *Sampling error* is the deviation that exists whenever a sample statistic differs from the population parameter due to a sample failing to perfectly represent the population from which it is taken.

Sampling error is due to chance (the "luck of the draw") and is a characteristic of statistical analysis. If the selected sampling approach is inaccurate or biased, sampling error can occur. As a result, we can expect it and must account for it in our analysis. In fact, the analysis of sampling error is a trademark of inferential statistics.

Nonsampling Error

Statistical investigations can contain errors not due to sampling error. These *nonsampling errors* or bias can arise from the nature of the estimator used, or from unrecognized systematic causes, such as unskilled interviewers or inaccurate measuring devices. For example, if the sample of grocery products in Figure 1-3 was taken from only one type of canned goods (e.g., peaches and other canned fruits), or from easy-to-load items, the sample would be biased. Biased sample statistics do not accurately represent population values because they are consistently off the mark, much like a speedometer that always registers too low or a bathroom scale that reads too high. If you don't know about the bias, you may be in for a surprise.

But, if you do know the amount and direction of bias, you can correct for it. In a perfect world, we will always want to eliminate bias, if at all possible.

Bias or systematic errors can occur for many reasons. For example, suppose that a company has 10 molding machines that make parts fed onto an assembly line at regular intervals. If a worker samples every tenth item (or multiples of 10), he may (unwittingly) be gathering all observations from one machine. Nonsampling errors arise from administrative procedures and the tasks associated with gathering, recording, or reporting data. **Moreover, nonsampling errors can occur in both census and sample data.** In fact, if there are large masses of data, the nonsampling error may be so large that a smaller sample may be more accurate in estimating the population value than an entire census. This is one argument that some have proposed for using sample data rather than completing a census every 10 years.

Accuracy, however, is not the only criterion of a good sample. A sample of two items can be very "accurate" in the sense of no systematic bias, but may be too small to provide a reliable estimate of the population parameter. The sample must be large enough to ensure that it is representative of the total population. Although a sample of two items may not have any individual inaccuracies, a decision-maker would feel more confident using a sample of 1,000 to provide an indication of the population parameter.

Steps in a Statistical Study

Statistical studies are one of the more "scientific" and systematic activities of business. Although they are not always conducted in the same way, these studies generally encompass the steps shown in Figure 1-4.

Step 1 - Identify Problem: Careful identification of the problem ensures that the question or hypothesis is clearly stated in a way that will allow us to draw valid conclusions. Care must be taken to abstract the relevant variables from the problem environment. The question should be stated in such a way that the results of the study address the real question rather than support or fail to support decisions to be made. The expected costs and benefits of conducting the study are also relevant in this initial step.

Step 2 – Establish Criteria for Solution: The criteria for solution are the standards by which the results will be judged. They include the type of statistical test to be performed, computational procedures to follow, and the amount of precision expected in the results. These are considerations we will discuss throughout this text.

Step 3 – Collect Data: The data collection phase (often a random sampling process) refers to all activities related to acquisition of data to solve the problem in step 1. This may include an investigation of related studies to determine what has already been done in the problem area (referred to as secondary data). Here, we are concerned with the amount and type of data to be used in the analysis.

Data may come from internal company sources, such as accounting or operating records, from external sources, such as periodicals, trade associations, and government agencies, or they may be gathered through customer interviews or surveys. In the next section, we will discuss this step in more detail.

Extreme care must be taken when using any data from other sources that do not provide the terms used or how the data were collected, classified, and recorded. For example, if University enrollment is reported to be 6,500 students, does this mean 6,500 full-time students or is it the equivalent of 6,500 full-time students? How many credit hours constitute a full-time student? Are executives who attend a two-week conference counted as students? Is the number exactly 6,500, or has it been rounded to the nearest hundred? These are all important questions to ask when using secondary data.

Step 4 – Analyze and Test Data: Analyzing and testing the data is often completed with the aid of computer software, such as Microsoft Excel. At other times, a specialized statistical package, such as SPSS or SAS may be required. In any case, both descriptive and inferential procedures are used to discover the meaning of the data and explore significant relationships.

Step 5 – Draw Conclusions: Conclusions may be stated verbally or in tabular, graphic, or numerical forms. Chapter 2 provides tables and graphic presentations of data and Chapter 3 discusses numerical summaries of data. The conclusions should be qualified by any assumptions or limitations that could influence the findings. This last step usually also includes recommended actions and guidelines for making appropriate decisions based on the data.

important Chart

Figure 1-4   5 Steps in a Statistical Study

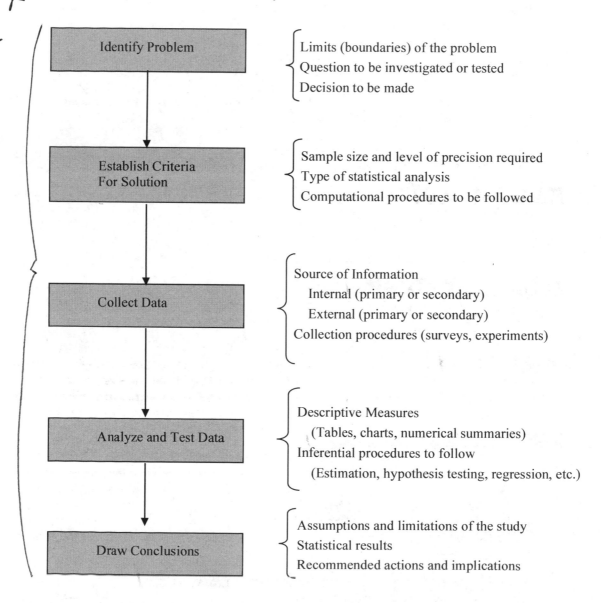

Identify Problem
- Limits (boundaries) of the problem
- Question to be investigated or tested
- Decision to be made

Establish Criteria For Solution
- Sample size and level of precision required
- Type of statistical analysis
- Computational procedures to be followed

Collect Data
- Source of Information
  - Internal (primary or secondary)
  - External (primary or secondary)
- Collection procedures (surveys, experiments)

Analyze and Test Data
- Descriptive Measures
  - (Tables, charts, numerical summaries)
- Inferential procedures to follow
  - (Estimation, hypothesis testing, regression, etc.)

Draw Conclusions
- Assumptions and limitations of the study
- Statistical results
- Recommended actions and implications

Most of this text will be concerned with Steps 4 and 5, analyzing the data and drawing conclusions, which presumes that the data is already available; however, it is important to remember that the data collection step determines the quality of the data, and therefore, the quality of the inferences we draw from the data and the derived conclusions.

As Figure 1-4 makes clear, data are gathered for a purpose: to shed light on a particular problem that has been identified. In a business context, there are four basic types of problems for which statistical analysis is normally used:

- **Problem 1: Estimating a Value**
    - What percent of consumers shop online on a regular basis?
    - What is the average salary of a college graduate with a degree in Philosophy?
- **Problem 2: Making a Comparison Between Groups**
    - Are women more likely to use coupons when shopping than men?
    - Are the dividends paid in the electronics industry greater than those paid by companies in the hospitality industry?
- **Problem 3: Studying Relationships Between Variables**
    - Is there a relationship between employee job satisfaction and employee turnover?
    - What is the relationship between advertising expenditures and monthly sales in the brewing industry?
- **Problem 4: Detecting Change**
    - Is the process working properly or is there a problem that needs to be corrected?
    - Has the recession changed how often people eat out at restaurants in our area?

We cannot always neatly divide statistical techniques into these four categories, but the chapters in this text will each explore these problem areas individually.

Collecting Data

As mentioned before, the quality of the conclusions, derived from a statistical study, depend on the quality of the data used in the analysis. Therefore, we will try to highlight some key issues in data collection that have important ramifications for the total quality of the investigation.

No matter what business issue is being addressed, the first major question is whether there are existing data that would be adequate for our needs or if we need to collect additional data ourselves. Remember that data that already exists, but were gathered for another purpose, is called *secondary data*. Data gathered for the purpose of the current study is called *primary data.* There are two principle sources of secondary data for any business: (1) the firm's internal records and resources, and (2) the external data outside the organization.

The firm's own records and data files are often its most useful sources of information. For example, the grocery warehouse example from Figure 1-3 would undoubtedly have electronic invoices and computer inventory records showing the types and quantities of items on hand, as well as costs, selling prices, customer lists, sales volumes, and inventory turnover rates. This data is typically gathered as a consequence of monitoring and documenting everyday business activities and not for the purposes of a statistical study. Other common forms of data, typically maintained by organizations, include personnel records and accounting information.

Data of this type, however, may also be very useful for other purposes. For example, a Montana lawn care company could find that late summer sales were strongly associated with customers that had sprinkler systems. Although the sales and sprinkler data were not originally gathered to address this issue, a decision to expand the services of the company to include sprinkler installation with a service contract could be justified on this evidence and could increase future sales. Organizations, large and small, use well-designed information systems to provide a variety of data about past and present operations. Modern organizations often purchase Business Intelligence software to mine the vast array of collected information to help manage operations more effectively and gain a competitive advantage over other businesses.

In many cases, data comes from unrelated studies, conducted by other organizations. For example, the United States Census Bureau routinely publishes information regarding the characteristics of the population and domestic economic activity from each of its census studies. Other government units routinely publish volumes of data ranging from information about species of animals, to import and export data. Not too surprisingly, the billions of dollars spent each year by the government offers businesses valuable data concerning their customers' buying habits and competition's practices. External secondary data are readily available, but there can be problems with this information. The data may have been transcribed incorrectly, be too out-of-date to be useful, or only peripherally address the important issues. Although external secondary data should be used with caution, it can sometimes provide the necessary information at a very modest cost. Some popular sources of external secondary data are national and regional government agencies and trade and periodical publications and databases. The appendix to this chapter lists some common sources of governmental and other data, both online and in published documents.

Collecting Primary Data

The obvious advantage of secondary data is the lowered cost of gathering the information; often, we can even get the information we need without the direct costs of gathering it ourselves. Another advantage of secondary data is that we can usually get the information very quickly; however, there are a number of potentially negative issues with secondary information.

Potential Questions to Ask with Secondary Data:

- Are there errors in the data?

- Do the definitions and measures used in the study correspond to the needs of our study?

- Are the data current?

- Was the data gathered in an appropriate manner?

The potential problems with secondary data are based on the fact that we have no control over how the data was gathered and reported. For example, there are a variety of secondary sources of productivity data in different industries; but, there are many different ways of defining productivity and different sources may use slightly different definitions. Using this data for other purposes can be problematic. Issues around measurement and definition can also arise with internal data. For example, with internal information we can often find data that closely, but not exactly, matches our needs. A common instance of this is attempting to forecast demand for the firm's products and services. The data that we are likely to find in the firm's records are past sales data; however, sales and demand are not the same thing. One reason that they can differ is that there are times when a customer wants to purchase a product or service (there is a demand) but for one reason or another our business is not able to provide the product or service; we do not have the product in inventory or we are at our maximum capacity for providing the service. This demand may never be recorded as a sale if the customer goes to a competitor to buy the product or service, or the sale may occur during a different time period than the original demand even if the customer is willing to wait. In either event, sales data does not equal demand.

Given these issues with secondary data, it may be well worth the time and expense of gathering our own data for a statistical investigation. There is an old saying, "When you want something done right, do it yourself." This is often good advice when it comes to primary versus secondary data.

Should we decide to collect our own data, there are a number of questions that arise. Most of these questions revolve around four key issues:

> **Key Issues in Collecting Data**
>
> - Who are we going to gather the data from and how do we select them?
>
> - What should our sample size be?
>
> - How are we going to get the data?
>
> - How much control are we going to exercise over the situation when the data are collected?

The first two issues will be dealt with in more detail in later chapters when we talk about sampling and estimation. We will explore the last two issues in this chapter. The third issue relates to how we collect the data. To gather the data, we could either ask the respondents through a *survey*, or we could *observe* the data through behaviors and choices. For example, we could ask individuals which set of multimedia advertisements are the most attention-getting (survey) or we could observe them as they watch the ads and do other tasks (observation).

Surveys and Observation

Surveys and observation are ways of obtaining data about the elements of a population. *Surveys* typically ask for responses from the elements of the population and with *observation* we simply observe the behavior of interest. Examples of surveys might be an employee survey of attitudes toward current benefits packages (as illustrated in the MegaCorp dataset in Appendix A) or a consultant's survey of customers and potential customers regarding preferences for particular product features. One example of using observation to obtain data might be the use of "mystery shoppers" that some retail firms employ where they send trained personnel into their stores to pose as shoppers and gather data on employee behavior. Another example of using observation might be a bank using student interns to record waiting times of customers waiting in line for tellers.

The major problem with observation is that people often react differently when they know that they are being watched. This means that we often need to observe them without their knowing that they are being observed which can bring up ethical issues and potential privacy concerns. A second issue with observation is that there is potential for observer bias. Since the observers are usually human, their observations are potentially subject to their own experiences and preferences. It's necessary to ensure that the observers are objective and that those being observed do not alter their behavior in response to the situation. In addition, there are three conditions that must be satisfied before we can use observational data effectively:

- The phenomenon we are interested in must be something that is observable. For example, we cannot use the observation method to study employee attitudes attitudes are not directly observable.

- The phenomenon must be one that occurs frequently. For example, it would be difficult to use observation to study industrial accidents since such accidents would be fairly rare and it would take a long time to gather even a few observations.

- The phenomenon must occur over a fairly short timeframe. For example, studying the potential effects of a change in benefits on long-term retention of key employees would be difficult because so many other conditions would change over that time span that it would be difficult to attribute the changes solely to the change in benefits.

Even with these issues, observation can provide high-quality data that hasn't been biased by socially-desirable behavior or faulty measurement devices. If any of these issues cannot be resolved however, you would probably be better off asking someone a direct question in a survey.

Surveys, directly asking the respondents for information, can be done through interviews or questionnaires. Interviews, whether in-person or over the phone, require a trained interviewer asking written questions of a respondent and recording the response on a standard form. Response rates are typically higher than with mail or Internet questionnaires because of the physical presence of the interviewer. More detailed information can also be obtained because questions can be explained in more detail and clarified as needed.

In-person interviews are expensive, sometimes costing hundreds of dollars per respondent. For example, according to CensusScope, the 2000 U.S. Census cost approximately $6.5 billion, or $56 per housing unit. Phone interviews are less expensive and widely-used method of obtaining data through personal interviews. Phone interviews are becoming increasingly difficult because of things like Caller ID and the national do-not-call list.

Questionnaires involve providing each respondent the same preset questions to answer. They have traditionally been administered through the mail, but increasingly the Internet is being used to administer web-based surveys (through tools like SurveyMonkey and Zoomerang). Questionnaires are a relatively impersonal means of collecting external statistical data. Great care must be exercised in designing both types of questionnaires to avoid misunderstandings, to eliminate questions that could yield biased results, and to ensure that the needed data can be obtained and tabulated quickly and accurately.

Inexperienced analysts frequently mail a lengthy questionnaire to several thousand potential respondents, only to find that they have failed to ask for vital information (e.g., income level, product preferences, etc.) or have too many unusable responses.

For example, suppose that you are surveying the production managers of oil companies in an attempt to forecast the price of oil two years from now. Assume that you have used the categories of:

- o   Under $80 per barrel
- o $80 to under $89.99 per barrel
- o $90 to under $99.99 per barrel
- o $100 to under $109.99 per barrel
- o $110 per barrel or more

If 85% of your respondents checked the category of $110 per barrel or more, you may still not have adequately narrowed down the price question. Perhaps, the majority feels it will be over $130 per barrel! Open-ended intervals such as this are limiting because they do not allow the researcher to calculate the principal measures used to summarize data. Pre-testing the questionnaire and completing "dry runs" of the data analysis can help avoid some of these problems.

Well-designed questions, on the other hand, elicit short responses that can be numerically coded for easy processing with statistical software. Multiple-choice questions should be clear, relevant, easy to answer, and contain sufficient alternatives to cover all possibilities. Open-ended questions often require special attention to avoid biasing the respondent or suggesting a desired response.

Another potential problem with surveys is the possibility of nonresponse bias. Rarely, if ever, do all respondents that have received a survey provide a completed survey. Often a positive response rate of 35% is considered good. If those that do respond differ in some important respect from those that do not respond, the results of the survey may be biased. One way to gauge the potential impact of nonresponse bias is to complete a second or even third follow-up to those who did not respond to the first survey distribution. If those who respond to the second or third solicitation do not differ significantly from those who responded in the first round, then we can feel more comfortable that those who failed to respond are also similar in most respects. Figure 1-5 illustrates a clear response bias since those responding to later follow-ups are clearly different that those responding to the first solicitation:

Figure 1-5   Indication of Nonresponse Bias

Characteristics of Respondents who Responded Initially or to Follow-Up Calls			
	First Call	**Second Call**	**Third Call**
Income over $50,000	31.5%	48.0%	64.8%
Male	36.8%	41.2%	57.1%
Democrat	40.8%	34.1%	19.6%
Approve of President's Economic Policies	40.1%	43.9%	57.1%
Recall a Presidential Advertisement	24.1%	27.2%	37.5%

Experimental and Non-experimental Studies

Another fundamental issue in gathering primary data relates to how much control the researcher exercises over the situation. In *experiments,* the researcher actively controls at least some of the factors involved. For example, in a taste test to discover preference among different brands of soft drinks, all brand-identifying marks would be carefully hidden to prevent the bias of brand recognition. Or we might physically change the point-of-sale displays in a sample of stores to observe the impact on sales. In *non-experimental situations,* the researcher takes the factors as they exist in the environment. The primary advantage of experiments over non-experimental studies is in demonstrating causality. The active manipulation of experimental factors is crucial to the demonstration of causality. It is virtually impossible to argue causality from non-experimental tests because we cannot rule out other plausible environmental factors as having caused the relationship(s) between variables or differences between groups. Experiments where some factors are directly controlled and others controlled through randomization are crucial to arguing for causal influence.

A Classification of Data-Gathering Situations

We can combine the data-gathering situations into four different types as depicted in Figure 1-6. It should be noted that a study can use a combination of these methods. For example, in a given study we might control some variables (experiment), but simply take others as they exist (post-hoc), We may ask respondents for some information (survey) and observe other data (observation).

In a business context, much of the data we deal with is historical (such as sales, expenses, and other performance measures); however, some areas often deal with survey data. For example, the marketing department often deals with survey data obtained from customers that incorporate post-hoc variables, but may also include experimental control as well.

Figure 1-6   Examples of Data-Gathering Situations

	Survey (self-report)	Observation
Experiment	Two groups of volunteers are shown different films: one group with violent content and another group mild content. They are then asked their opinions on capital punishment.	One group of workers is organized in teams and another group consists of individuals who work alone. We observe their productivity (units of output).
Non-experiment	A survey is conducted with a group of consumers about their shopping habits to look at the differences between those who are married and those who are single.	Observing a number of shoppers and whether or not they stop and look at an in-store display. We also note their gender and whether or not they have children with them.

Overview of the Text

At this point, it would be good to present an overview of the coming chapters in the text. Our goal is to ultimately discuss the process of making inferences about an unknown population based on sample data. Before we can carry out that task, however, we need a great deal of background information. The chapters leading up to and introducing inferential statistics are shown in Figure 1-7.

As Figure 1-7 indicates, in the next two chapters we will discuss descriptive statistics in terms of tables and graphs and single numerical summary measures. Descriptive statistics can be used either for populations or for samples. Recall that summary measures of population values are called population parameters and summary measures of sample values are called sample statistics. Before we discuss inferential statistics, we first need to talk about probabilities and sampling distributions. We need information about probabilities because we can never say for sure what we will observe when we take a random sample from a population; however, we can predict, in probability terms, what we can expect to observe. A sampling distribution allows us to "deduce" what we are likely to observe when taking samples from a population with known parameters. This is deductive reasoning, moving from a known population to an unknown sample. Of course, this is the reverse of where we take a sample from a population so that we know the characteristics of the sample (sample statistics) and want to "infer" something about the unknown population parameters (inferential statistics). As we will see, the process of statistical inference depends critically on the notion of sampling distributions from Chapter 5. Sampling distributions provide the "bridge" to make inferences about an unknown population based on a known sample.

Figure 1-7   Overview of Text Through Chapter 7

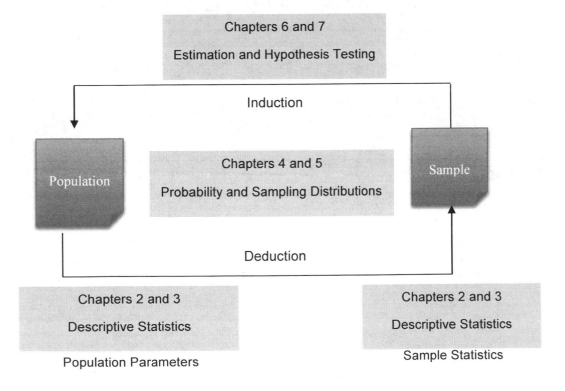

Once we have the basics of inferential statistics (Chapters 6 and 7), we will apply that knowledge to comparisons between two or more groups in Chapters 8 and 9 and to examining relationships between variables in Chapters 10 and 11. We will close out the text discussing the applications of statistical methods to two common application areas in business: analyzing time series data in Chapter 12.

Ethical Issues in Statistics

As we will see, statistics can be a very powerful tool in the business world. Strong statistical evidence can sway judges and juries in a court of law, change political opinions and policies, and influence public opinion. As with any tool, statistics can be misused. Although we may well not view such misuse as a terrible act, the consequences can be severe. In other cases, statistics may be used deliberately to deceive. Such attempts are obviously unethical to most people and hopefully this course will enable to detect such deceptions; however, ethical issues still arise where some might argue that a slight deception in the service of a greater good is acceptable. This utilitarian view of ethics has come under criticism from most ethicists. In general, statistical ethics would dictate that any deliberate use of statistics to deceive is unethical; however, in many cases, there are grey areas that are not clear-cut.

An interesting example of ethical issues can be found in the distinction we made between experiments and post-hoc studies. Remember that experiments are vital to the demonstration of causality; however, in many areas, like the medical research field, the use of experimentation poses ethical dilemmas. Most would agree that it would be unethical to take one group of young people and make them smoke the rest of their lives while forcing another group to never smoke in order to investigate the effects of smoking on lung cancer. That is why most medical studies with human subjects are post-hoc in nature and this makes the demonstration of causality difficult.

Consider another situation which is not so obvious. In testing the efficacy of drugs, it is common to have a control group that receives a placebo and a group that receives the drug being tested. The *placebo group* receives what appears to be a treatment but is really not, for example a sugar pill instead of the real drug. Although placebo groups are crucial to demonstrate the causal effects of a drug, there are certainly ethical implications of giving one group a placebo treatment instead of the real drug once the drug has been shown to be effective in treating the disease. That is why most studies of life-saving drugs usually have a cutoff option so that when it becomes apparent that the drug is effective, the placebo group will begin to receive the drug as well.

Even though statistics is based on mathematics, the use of statistical analysis involves many subjective judgments. In important matters, where competing interests are at stake, ethical issues can become major considerations. Ethics in statistics has become an important enough issue that many countries have established policies on ethical principles for organizations engaged in the gathering of statistical data (See the line for Finland in Table 1-1). We will attempt to highlight ethical issues in this text when we encounter situations in which ethical questions might arise. This will help you to be more aware of these issues and be able to deal with these situations in the future. Several general sources of ethical material related to statistics are given in Table 1-1.

Table 1-1   *Web Sources of Material on Ethics in Statistics*

Description	Website
American Statistical Association's Committee on Professional Ethics	http://www.tcnj.edu/~ethcstat/index.html
American Statistical Association Ethical Guidelines for Statistical Practice	http://www.amstat.org/profession/index.cfm?fuseaction=ethicalstatistics
Vardeman, S.B. & Morris, M.D. Statistics and Ethics: Some Advice for Young Statisticians, The American Statistician, 2003, 57, 1, 21-26	http://www.tcnj.edu/~ethcstat/varmor.pdf
Statistics Finland: Guide to Professional Ethics	http://www.stat.fi/tk/tt/laatuatilastoissa/lm010102/su_en.html
International Statistical Institute Declaration on Professional Ethics	http://www.cbs.nl/isi/ethics.htm

Computers and Statistical Analysis

When computers were first introduced into businesses about 60 years ago, they were used to automate well-established data processing procedures, such as wage and salary calculations. Different departments gradually automated their own records (e.g., marketing computerized sales records, operations put inventory records on computers, etc.); however, all corporate data files were not linked together or widely accessible. Files were often duplicated in two or three departments, and they were not always consistent with each other.

Today, enterprise information systems usually operate from a common database. That is, information is centrally-stored and is accessible via the network throughout the organization or even over mobile devices outside organizational walls. This means that the same current (online) information is available almost instantaneously to anyone in the organization. Of course, not all data in the organization necessarily resides in a central database. Some of the data is often still stored in spreadsheets, electronic documents and personal databases throughout the organization.

We cannot duplicate a corporate database here, nor would it be worthwhile to do so; however, there is great value in using larger sets of data and computers to practice some statistical procedures we will study in this book. When you have graduated and started on your career path, you will not find any daily problems packaged in a neat one-paragraph description with the relevant data already summarized. Rather, you will have to obtain relevant information stored in a corporate database or seek primary data which is both time-consuming and expensive. In any case, you will usually be faced with a large set of numbers, often in spreadsheets, that must be analyzed to make necessary decisions.

To illustrate this more realistic situation, we have included four larger datasets in the appendices. These datasets are referenced throughout the book and are designed to provide a consistent problem-solving environment. We have selected one of these datasets for the problems with answers in the back of the text. In this way, you can use the same dataset throughout the course and always have the answers to the chapter questions. We have also provided more extensive data for at least some of the problems in each chapter along with some shorter, more traditional problems, typically found in statistics textbooks. Problems that lend themselves to solution via Excel or standard statistical computer programs are marked with an icon ( ) and the data for these problems is provided on the website for this text. Microsoft Excel will be used throughout this text because it is almost universally available in the business world and widely-used by managers and analysts to analyze data[8]. You can utilize Excel in different ways for statistical analysis and the way you choose to use it is often a matter of personal preference. There are built-in tools in Excel, most notably, the available functions that can be used to perform some of the calculations involved in statistical analysis; however, there are limitations as to what you can do with these simple functions. There are more advanced tools available that work within the Excel environment to go beyond what can be accomplished with the built-in functions.

Built-In Excel Tools

There are several built-in tools within Excel for statistical analysis. We will utilize four different types in this text:

 Functions and the Function Wizard

Some of the most useful statistical tools are in the form of functions that can be directly entered into cells in the spreadsheet or pasted in to a cell using the function wizard. Figure 1-8 shows the function wizard and some of the built-in statistical functions in Excel. We will cover a number of Excel's statistical functions in the text; however, these functions are best used for quick answers to a probability question or calculating a small number of descriptive measures like averages or standard deviations. More sophisticated analysis requires either a great deal of work in setting up spreadsheets or the use of specialized software.

Figure 1-8   Excel Function Wizard

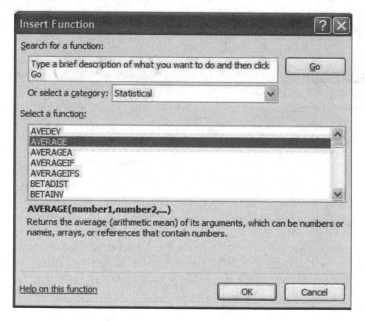

---

[8] Excel 2007 (Version 12) or later will be used in this text. All screenshots will be taken from Excel 2007 or 2010; however, all of the data files are available for older versions of Excel and all software used in this text will also work in older versions of Excel. In fact, at least some of the functions in this text will also work in available alternative to Microsoft Excel such as Open Office.

#2 The Data Analysis ToolPak

There are a number of statistical packages that have been especially designed to work closely with Excel as add-ins. An Excel add-in is a program designed to integrate with Excel and operate as a part of the software. Several add-ins come with the Excel software, including one for statistical analysis, the *Data Analysis ToolPak*. Although the Data Analysis add-in comes with Excel, it may or may not be installed on your computer. To see if it is installed on your particular machine, start Excel and then select Data from the ribbon[9]. You should see an item entitled Data Analysis at the end of the ribbon. If it is not yet installed, you can install the add-in using the Add-in Manager. Appendix B explains how to use the add-in manager in more detail. If the Data Analysis add-in was not installed initially with Excel, you may need to install it manually from your Microsoft Office CD. See Excel help for more details.

Assuming the add-in is properly installed, the Data Analysis ToolPak is started by selecting Data—Data Analysis from the main Excel ribbon. The main dialog is shown in Figure 1-9. The Data Analysis add-in contains a variety of tools for performing statistical analysis and can carry out many of the statistical calculations described in this textbook; however, it is not always easy to use and is incomplete in terms of the common statistical techniques discussed in this text. For example, chi-square analysis is not included in the add-in. For this reason, there have been a variety of add-ins developed for Excel that are designed to be more complete and easier to use. We will discuss one of these add-ins that comes with the textbook shortly. The Data Analysis Toolpak will be illustrated throughout the textbook where it can be used.

Figure 1-9 Data Analysis Dialog

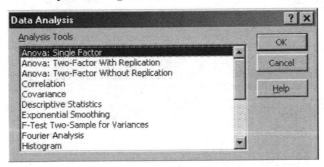

#3 Excel Charts

In Chapter 2, we will discuss the graphing and charting of data to summarize a large set of numbers. Excel contains very good charting tools and can be used directly to create many of the charts we will discuss. A little creativity in using the chart functions in Excel can produce virtually all of the charts we will discuss in this textbook. In fact, many Excel add-ins, including the one included with this textbook, actually use these built-in charting tools to produce their graphs.

#4 Pivot Tables

Pivot tables are a widely used tool in Excel that can help summarize data and perform calculations involved in some statistical techniques. We will discuss the use of pivot tables in Chapter 2, as well.

---

[9] In earlier versions of Excel go to the Tools menu and look for Data Analysis as an option in that menu.

XLDataAnalyst

As we have described above, there are built-in tools in Excel for performing many of the calculations we will need in this textbook; however, these tools are often somewhat cumbersome and difficult to use. They also have limitations in terms of the types of problems they can address. For this reason, a variety of add-ins have been developed for performing statistical analysis, using data organized in an Excel spreadsheet. One such add-in is included with this textbook and can be accessed at the textbook's website. This add-in is called XLDataAnalyst and will be used throughout the text to illustrate statistical calculations[10]. XLDataAnalyst can be used for datasets with up to 16,384 variables and up to 20,000 observations. This is certainly large enough for any of the calculations in this textbook. The installation and the general use of XLDataAnalyst is described in Appendix B. We will illustrate specific uses of XLDataAnalyst in each chapter where it is used.

Special Purpose Statistical Software

More sophisticated data analysis may require the use of special statistical packages that contain advanced statistical methods and can operate with larger datasets. Three well-developed statistical programs that you may encounter in the business world are SAS, JMP, and SPSS. These packages are available for most computers and operating systems. They are very powerful, but also contain many options and techniques that a beginning statistics student may find them quite overwhelming. That is why we will use Excel and XLDataAnalyst throughout this text. Once you are comfortable with performing data analysis using these tools, you will find it quite easy to graduate to more powerful statistical software. Most statistical software will also directly import Excel files for data analysis.

---

[10] There is a Mac version for XLDataAnalyst available as well.

Summary

Statistics is the body of methods used for the collection, analysis, presentation, and interpretation of data. As a language of business, statistics enables us to describe data and make inferences for decision-making purposes. Deductive inference moves from general to specific knowledge, whereas inductive inference proceeds from specific knowledge to general conclusions.

A population is a total collection of elements and is described by parameters, whereas a sample is a part of a population and is described by statistics. We use point and interval estimates from samples to make inferences about population values; however, sample statistics are not expected to perfectly represent population parameters due to sampling error. But, we do try to reduce bias through eliminating all sources of nonsampling error.

Statistical studies entail (1) identifying the problem, (2) establishing the criteria for solution, (3) collecting data, (4) analyzing and testing the data, and (5) drawing conclusions. Every step is important. Data are obtained either from internal sources, such as corporate databases and records, or external sources, such as national, regional, trade, and periodical data. Field studies generally use a type of direct observation, personal interview or questionnaire.

The data collection phase requires important decisions regarding the use of primary or secondary data, internal versus external sources, surveys versus observations, and experimental versus post-hoc studies. Ethical issues often arise in some of these choices as well as in many other aspects of a statistical study.

As societies become more affluent and knowledgeable, information systems and databases become even more important. Excel and specialized software is often used for performing the calculations required for statistical analysis. Appendix A contains four datasets that we will use to practice some of the statistical methods in this textbook using Excel and XLDataAnalyst.

Chapter Glossary

Census	The collection of data from an entire population.
Common Cause Variability	Random variability in the process that arises from many small causes which are not predictable. It does not require action unless we are going to change the entire process to reduce this variability.
Descriptive Statistic	Concerned with summarizing, displaying and describing a set of numbers. It does not involve any inference that goes beyond the given data.
Experiments	Involves the deliberate control and manipulation of some variables when studying a sample or population.
Inferential Statistic	Making inferences about unknown values based on known information.
Interval Estimate	Gives the end points that bound an interval of values that is thought to contain a population value.
Nonsampling Error	Errors due to ways that a statistical study is conducted that can occur in a population as well as in a sample.
Observation	Gathering data without the direct questioning of the participants in the study. Usually involves visual or auditory information.
Placebo Group	A group that appears to receive a treatment such as a pill, but in fact is given something that should have no effect, such as a sugar pill.
Point Estimate	A single value derived from sample data that is used to estimate a characteristic of a population.
Population	The set of all elements that we are interested in for a particular study.
Population Parameter	A measured characteristic of a population such as an average value.
Post-hoc	A study that takes the measures of variables and other factors as they exist without any active manipulation.
Primary Data	Data gathered for the particular purpose of a statistical study.
Sample	A subset of the population.
Sample Statistic	A measured characteristic of a sample such as an average or a proportion.
Sampling Error	The difference between a sample statistic and a population parameter that is due to the chance failure of the sample to be exactly representative of the population.
Secondary Data	Data used in a statistical study that was originally gathered for some other purpose.
Special Cause Variability	Nonrandom variability introduced into the process by a specific identifiable cause either from outside the process or because of a change in the process itself.

Statistical Thinking	The philosophy of learning and action based on the principles that (1) all work consists of a system of interconnected processes, (2) variability exists in all processes and (3) understanding and reducing variability is the key to improving a process.
Statistics	The body of methods for the collection, analysis, presentation, and interpretation and use of data.
Survey	A process of gathering information about a population or sample by asking questions.

Questions and Problems

1. Define (a) statistics; (b) population; and (c) sample.

2. A friend of yours from high school has gone to work for a bank and claims that you are wasting your time studying statistics in college. How might you respond to him that your time (hopefully) is well-spent?

3. Distinguish between the following: (a) descriptive and inferential statistics; (b) deduction and induction; and (c) census data and sample data.

4. Indicate whether each of the following represents deductive or inductive reasoning:

    (a) You receive a recall notice to return your 2005 model car to an authorized shop for correction of a possible steering problem.

    (b) A marketing representative in a supermarket encourages you to taste a new chicken chili that is on special today.

    (c) You decide to purchase a state lottery ticket because you believe you have a good chance of winning $1.5 million.

    (d) First National Bank sends you a questionnaire explaining that they are trying to obtain a regional estimate of student income and loan amounts.

5. Give an example of (a) a point estimate and (b) an interval estimate.

6. Explain the difference between sampling error and nonsampling error.

7. Nationwide Car Rental Co. has just announced that a survey of 100 customer records revealed that their customers drove an average of 22.6 miles per day for work transportation, and between 6,100 and 6,500 miles per year total. (a) Indicate whether this is (i) sample or population data, (ii) internal or external data, (iii) a point or interval estimate. (b) Why would Nationwide want this information and what type of inference would they be likely to use it for? (c) Are Nationwide's conclusions likely to be accurate? Explain.

8. Allfresh Baking Co. supplies loaves of bread to supermarkets in Missouri. They use the previous week's data, together with "intuition," to decide how many loaves to deliver; however, some supermarket managers have complained that the number of loaves is "usually too many, sometimes not enough, and rarely just right!" Use the concepts of uncertainty, sampling error, and bias to explain what might be the problem.

9. Baxter Pharmaceuticals has developed a new drug, TPC, designed to maintain a certain viral blood cell count at 600 points plus or minus a few percent. In support of their application to distribute the drug nationally, Baxter submitted sample data to the Food and Drug Administration (FDA) on 125 of the 3,000 patients who used the drug on a trial basis. For the 125 patients tested, the average viral count was 560; however, the FDA withheld permission to distribute the drug because the 560 was 40 points below the 600 expected. To gain approval, Baxter decided to phone the attending physicians of all 3,000 patients who were using the drug on the trial basis. Upon receiving all these data they found that the average viral count was 596. Baxter summarized the results of the survey, sent the data to the FDA, and ultimately received their approval.

    (a) What are the respective values of the parameter and statistic in this study?

(b) How would you explain the difference between the population value and the sample statistic—assuming the population value was correct and the sampling procedure was appropriate?

(c) Identify some possible sources of error in the population and sample data.

10. Suppose you wished to determine if the rate of change in a representative sample of retail food prices in your city is exceeding the rate of change in the national consumer price index. You must do this by comparing values on a monthly basis over a designated future time (e.g., six months). Briefly outline what procedure you would follow to complete this investigation.

11. Suppose that you had to conduct a study to determine the cost of producing plywood in the United States. How would you go about it?

12. A competitor claims (on TV) that their product is superior to your firm's product. Explain how you might conduct a study to determine whether your competitor's claim is justified by the facts or is merely unsubstantiated propaganda.

13. Suppose that you wanted to locate recent data concerning the U.S. money supply and the unemployment rate. What national data sources would yield this type of information?

Database Problems

Corporate Statistical Database

14. Using only the data on banking and insurance companies in the database, determine (a) how many firms are located in Ohio, and (b) in which states are the two firms with the largest number of employees located, (c) what was the total cost of advertising and public relations for all the banking and insurance firms listed?

15. For the database as a whole:

(a) Which (specific) organizations have employees of the oldest and youngest average age, respectively?

(b) Which types (categories) of organizations are most heavily involved in exporting their products?

(c) What is the total value of export sales of electronics firms located in Massachusetts?

16. For the database as a whole:

(a) What percent of the organizations are utilities?

(b) What percent of the organizations have profit sharing?

(c) What are the export sales of Advanced Computer Co.?

17. For the utility company data in the database:

(a) Use a summation function to show the total sales (millions of dollars) of the 20 companies.

(b) Use a summation function to show the total dividends (dollars) of the 20 companies.

(c) Use the "average" function in Excel to find the average sales of the 20 companies.

18. For the utility company data in database

   (a) Sort the data so that the corporate names appear in alphabetical order.

   (b) Sort the data on the variable "sales," listing those firms with the largest sales first.

   (c) Use Excel to identify the company with the smallest number of employees.

MegaCorp Employee Survey Database

19. For the data in the database:

   (a) What percent of the sample employees are married?

   (b) What percent of the sample employees are female?

   (c) How many of the sample employees are in management?

20. For the data in the database:

   (a) Which subsidiaries have employees of the oldest and youngest average age, respectively?

   (b) Which subsidiary has the highest average salary?

   (c) What is the average salary of nonmanagement personnel in the Snackrite subsidiary?

21. For the Entron subsidiary of the database:

   (a) Use a summation function to show the total salaries of the 20 employees.

   (b) Use an average function to show the average age of the 20 employees.

   (c) Use the average function to find the average number of years with the firm for the 20 employees.

Alaska Sport Fishing Survey

22. For the Alaska Fishing Survey database:

   (a) What is total number of trips taken by the respondents to Alaska over the last five years?

   (b) What is the total amount spent by the respondents in their last fishing trip to Alaska?

   (c) How many of the respondents were single?

23. For the Alaska Fishing Survey database:

   (a) What percent of the respondents stayed in a lodge or motel on their last trip?

   (b) What percent of the respondents stayed with a friend or relative on their last trip?

   (c) How many of the respondents are female?

Appendix

This appendix contains some key sources of existing data, both governmental and trade associations. This is not intended to be an exhaustive list, but a starting point to find the data that you need.

Government Sources

The Statistical Abstract of the United States published annually by the U.S. Bureau of the Census. (www.census.gov/statab/www/)

Survey of Current Business, published monthly by the U.S. Bureau of the Census, Office of Business Economics.(www.bea.doc.gov/bea/pubs.htm)

Federal Reserve Bulletin, published monthly by the Board of Governors of the Federal Reserve System.(www.federalreserve.gov/pubs/bulletin/default.htm)

Monthly Labor Review, published monthly by the U.S. Department of Labor. (www.bls.gov/opub/mlr/mlrhome.htm)

Bureau of the Census Catalog, published quarterly by the U.S. Bureau of the Census or available online at www.census.gov/prod/www/abs/catalogs.html

The U.S. Bureau of the Census also publishes a useful *County and City Data Book*. (www.census.gov/statab/www/ccdb.html) It contains information on income, housing, labor, banking, vital statistics, population, and other facts.

Trade and Periodical Data

Trade associations publish data on lumber, steel, automotive, insurance, savings and loan, and numerous other industries that can be useful in analyzing industry trends and performance information. Much of this data is now online and available in formats conducive to statistical analysis using tools such as Excel.

The *Business Conditions Digest* (http://scolar.vsc.edu:8006/VSCCAT/ABQ-3248), *Federal Reserve Bulletin*, the *Life Insurance Fact Book* (www.acli.com/ACLI/About%20ACLI%20nonmember/Industry%20Facts/Life%20Insurers%20Fact%20 Book%202003), and *Sales and Marketing Management* are periodicals that provide extensive summaries of external secondary data. Current information of a statistical nature can also be obtained from *The Wall Street Journal* (http://online.wsj.com/public/us), *U.S.A. Today* (http://www.usatoday.com/), *New York Times* (www.nytimes.com/), *Newsweek* (www.msnbc.msn.com/id/3032542/site/newsweek/), *Time* (www.time.com/time/), *The Economist* (www.economist.com/), *U.S. News and World Report* (www.usnews.com/usnews/home.htm), *Fortune* (www.fortune.com/fortune/), *Business Week* (www.businessweek.com/), and other publications.

A number of guides and indexes are also useful references, although they contain no data themselves. Examples of these include the *Business Periodical Index* and *The Wall Street Journal Index*.

Chapter 2:

Organizing and Displaying Data

Opening Vignette
Introduction
Classifying Data
Quantitative and Qualitative Data
- Discrete and Continuous Variables
- Scales of Measurement

Statistical Tables
- Tables for Qualitative Data
- Tables for Quantitative Data
- Frequency Distributions for Quantitative Variables
- Relative and Cumulative Frequency Distributions

Graphical Presentations of Qualitative Data
Graphic Presentation of Quantitative Data
- Histogram
- Frequency Polygon
- Cumulative Frequency Distribution (Ogive)
- Stem-and-Leaf Diagrams
- Dot Plots
- Line Charts

Looking at Relationships
- Scatter Diagrams
- Contingency Tables

Ethical Issues in Displaying Data
- Problems with Bar Charts
- Misleading Line Charts

Excel List Structures
Excel Pivot Tables
Using Excel and XLDataAnalyst to Display Data
- Using Excel
- The Excel Template
- Using XLDataAnalyst

Opening Vignette Revisited
Summary
Chapter Glossary
Questions and Problems

Chapter 2 Objectives

When you finish this chapter you should be able to:

1. **Distinguish between different types of variables**
2. **Understand the different scales of measurement and their properties**
3. **Construct and interpret statistical tables**
4. **Construct and interpret frequency distributions**
5. **Produce histograms and frequency polygons**
6. **Develop and interpret stem-and-leaf displays and dot plots**
7. **Construct and interpret scatter plots and contingency tables**
8. **Understand the Excel list structure and its role in computer datasets**
9. **Construct pivot tables in Excel**
10. **Display statistical data using Excel and XLDataAnalyst**

Opening Vignette

Sarah is a senior manager of First Inland Northwest (FIN), a large financial institution that has been in business for over 60 years. Currently, her main concerns are increasing profits and market share. Market research shows that First Nova, a new competitor, has quickly become very successful, stealing customers. The research also indicates that the average age of the customers at First Nova was about 33 years old.

The next morning, Sarah reads an article about the buying behaviors of young people and how they view the companies that they do business with. The article states that many young people prefer newer companies or those that have "cutting edge" images. After reading the article, Sarah began to think that FIN's younger customers may not view the company in this way and perhaps that is the reason why they are leaving to work with the competition.

Realizing the value of lifetime customers and the necessity of attracting and retaining new young customers, Sarah asks her assistant to prepare customer data based on age to either confirm or refute her intuition. The next day her assistant emails her a spreadsheet with the requested data on customer ages at FIN along with an age profile of First Nova's customers. The data are shown in the Excel screen shot below.

What can Sarah conclude from this information? Are her suspicions correct? Does the data indicate that First Inland Northwest has a problem? One difficulty in answering these questions is that there is too much data to digest the information or draw conclusions. A way to summarize and present the data is needed to understand the situation and develop appropriate strategies.

Customer	Age		Customer	Age		Customer	Age		Customer	Age
1	39		24	22		47	45		70	52
2	37		25	46		48	38		71	48
3	57		26	37		49	48		72	37
4	29		27	42		50	31		73	42
5	40		28	43		51	22		74	32
6	56		29	49		52	33		76	47
7	37		30	44		53	56		77	42
8	27		31	28		54	36		78	49
9	42		32	55		55	45		79	34
10	47		33	41		56	31		80	46
11	43		34	43		57	58		81	43
12	35		35	48		58	56		82	17
13	40		36	31		59	30		83	41
14	39		37	36		60	48		84	35
15	48		38	37		61	38		85	47
16	45		39	36		62	14		86	53
17	55		40	38		63	27		87	34
18	40		41	28		64	46		88	61
19	34		42	41		65	29		89	19
20	25		43	44		66	48		90	49
21	36		44	49		67	45		91	42
22	27		45	30		68	45		92	23
23	39		46	51		69	29		93	36

Introduction

Like most developed countries, the United States is becoming a knowledge economy. Fifty years ago most workers were part of the manufacturing industry. Today, more than two thirds of the jobs are in information or "knowledge" activities and that percentage is growing. These occupations range from collecting market research data to conveying legal, investment, and health advice. The chances that your future work will involve generating, controlling, and using information are now very high. For accounting, finance, marketing and other managers, this information takes the form of numbers (or data) that describe the flow of economic activities. Data are used to describe nearly every facet of business and government operations—from the number of olives produced in California to the budget for the Department of Defense; however, our understanding of data is often inversely related to the amount of data we are trying to comprehend. In other words, we can easily be overwhelmed by too much information. We often need ways of organizing and summarizing data.

In this chapter, we will first draw distinctions in the types of data you will likely encounter in business. Then, we will review two visual forms of organizing and presenting data: tables and graphs or charts. The material is largely descriptive and not conceptually difficult, but very essential for those who work with statistical data.

Classifying Data

There are numerous ways to classify data. Some widely used bases for grouping data are by size, type, time and place. For example, sales reports of a book publishing company might reveal data classified as follows:

Classification Basis	Data Type Examples
Quantitatively *(amount)*	Total yearly (unit) sales of each product line
Qualitatively *(type)*	Classification of books sold as texts, novels, and technical publications
Chronologically *(time)*	Sales ($) during each month of the year
Geographically *(place)*	Sales ($) in East, Midwest, West and South

Quantitative and Qualitative Data

Although chronological and geographical classifications are common, for statistical purposes the most important distinction to make is between qualitative and quantitative data. We are all familiar with *quantitative data*, like total unit sales of a product, or data on income or employment levels. Quantitative variables are inherently **numerical** in value[1]. Qualitative variables, on the other hand, are inherently **non-numerical** and are the types of data that we ordinarily treat as text. The type of sale (text, novel or technical publication) would be a *qualitative* variable and a report may show the number or percent of total sales that come from the each category. Although the distinction between quantitative and qualitative data is the most important for our purposes, chronological data are also important in statistics and, in fact, Chapter 12 is devoted largely to chronological or time series data.

Discrete and Continuous Variables

Insofar as the value of each data point can vary from one location, person, or time period to another, data points are referred to as the values of a variable. A *variable* is a common attribute that can differ from one observation to the next. For example, the number of books sold by a bookstore will vary from month to month. In statistics, we often let the letter **X**, represent the (unspecified) value of a variable. It is necessary to distinguish between discrete and continuous variables because, as we will see later, the types of statistical procedures we use will depend upon the type of variable we are working with.

> *Discrete variables* - Variables that can assume only separate and distinct (countable) values are referred to as discrete. Although there are exceptions, in general, discrete variables have integer values and do not assume fractional values.
>
> *Continuous variables* - Variables that can take on any value in a range of (measurable) values are referred to as continuous. In general, continuous values can take on any integer or fractional value.

You can usually differentiate between the variables by asking yourself whether they can be counted (discrete) or measured (continuous). Discrete variables can assume only a finite number of values within any interval. Continuous variables, on the other hand, can take on an infinite number of values within an interval, depending on the precision of measurement. Figure 2-1 gives some examples of this range. Variables are designated by the letter "X" and the subscripts (e.g., 1, 2 and 3) further specify the variables. For example, a firm may have $XB_{1B} = 205$ employees (discrete) and their average age may be $XB_{4B} = 42$ years of age. If we wanted to be more precise, we could refine the average age to be $XB_{4B} = 42.2$ years, or 42.23 years, or 42.234 years, and so on. In theory, there is no limit to the precision with which we could measure age. In other words, it is continuous and can take on any value greater than zero; however, we cannot further refine the variable XB_{1B} to a higher level of precision and it cannot be fractional (e.g., we cannot have 205.5 employees). Therefore, this variable is discrete because it can only take on certain values.

---

[1] There are few instances where the variable may incorporate numbers but is not in fact quantitative (for example, an area's zip code or a student's GPA).

Figure 2-1   *Examples of Discrete and Continuous Variables*

Discrete Variables	Continuous Variables
XB_{1B} = Number of Employees	XB_{4B} = Age of Employees
XB_{2B} = Number of Units Sold	XB_{5B} = Time Required to Serve a Customer
XB_{3B} = Number of Defective Units	XB_{6B} = Weight of Product Being Shipped

Although the distinction between discrete and continuous variables is a dichotomy (a variable is either one or the other, it cannot be both), it is often useful to view the situation more as a continuum from a pure discrete variable to a pure continuous variable. Suppose we are studying the number of hammers sold each month at Home Depot. Although this variable can only take on a finite number of values, the number of possible values is so large that we might treat it as continuous. The best way to think of this distinction is that discrete variables are those that can take on only a few values while continuous variables can take on a very large number of values. The distinction can be subjective in terms of the appropriate statistical methods to use.

Four Scales of Measurement

Statistics deals with data. Data are measured on scales, and we can classify data by the properties of each scale. It is important to know the type of scale because the kinds of operations you can perform on the data will depend on the properties of the underlying scale. For example, addition and subtraction aren't appropriate for certain types of scales. For other scales, addition and subtraction may be fine, but ratios would not be not appropriate. Four scale categories are commonly distinguished: (1) nominal, (2) ordinal, (3) interval, and (4) ratio scales.

Nominal Scales

A *nominal scale* is used to describe data that are **categorical or qualitative** in nature. For example, residents of an area may be classified by the type of automobile they drive or their religious affiliation. In a previous section, we classified items as texts, novels, or periodicals. This is an example of a nominal scale. Nominal scale data are the types that we ordinarily treat as text. For example, the type of car might be classified as Ford, Chevrolet, Chrysler, Toyota, Nissan, etc. If numbers are assigned to represent the different values, and they often are, the numbers have limited meaning. The only meaning in the numbers is to indicate that the cars come from the same or different manufacturers. Table 2-1 illustrates a small set of nominal scale data by the type of auto. Although the values in the third column are numbers, it wouldn't make sense to perform arithmetic operations. For example, it wouldn't make much sense to ask, "What is the average value for the third column of numbers?" Nominal data is sometimes easiest to collect, but often provides the least value of information of the four scales. The order of the numbers is meaningless for a nominal scale. In closing, the values in Table 2-1 do not imply that one car is somehow "better" than another.

Ordinal Scales

An *ordinal scale* is used for **ranked** observations according to some order of preference, where the rankings convey a relative position (e.g., on a scale from high to low or low to high). For example, a supermarket survey may show that consumers rank dessert preferences as cheesecake (1P[st]P), ice cream (2P[nd]P), pie (3P[rd]P), cake (4P[th]P), cookies (5P[th]P), and pudding (6P[th]P). Ordinal data may begin as qualitative data and then transition to quantitative data using such tools as likert scales. An ordinal ranking conveys more information than a nominal classification in that the order of the values carries more meaning; however, it does not imply anything about the equality of the differences between ranks. Thus, the preferential difference between the first two items (cheesecake and ice cream) is not necessarily the same as the difference between the last two (cookies and pudding). This also means that addition and subtraction are not acceptable operations for ordinal scales. Therefore, asking for the average ranking is not a meaningful question; however, asking, what is the middle value, such that half of the values are above and half below, would make sense because the overall order has meaning.

Table 2-1   ***Nominal Scale Data for Type of Automobile***

Observation	Type	Numerical Assignment
1	Toyota	1
2	Chrysler	2
3	Chrysler	2
4	Chevrolet	3
5	Ford	4
6	Chevrolet	3
7	Nissan	5
8	Dodge	6
9	Ford	4
10	Toyota	1

Interval Scales

An *interval scale* describes data that have a constant unit of measure, but **not necessarily a natural zero point**. For example, assume the temperature in Phoenix is 110° and in Anchorage is 55°F. We could say the temperature in Phoenix if 55 degrees higher than in Anchorage because each degree is a known (constant) increment; however, we could not say that Phoenix is twice as warm as Anchorage. This is because zero on the Fahrenheit scale is not an absolute zero (absolute zero, where there is no heat, is at -460°F). The zero points on the Fahrenheit and Celsius scales are in a sense arbitrary. Therefore, a ratio of 2:1 on the Fahrenheit scale is not a ratio of 2:1 on the Celsius scale[2]T

While temperature is an obvious example of an interval scale, other measures are not so obvious and can be debated. Consider, for example, the common five to seven point response items found on questionnaires and student course evaluations. Often these are analyzed as if they were interval scale items by, for example, calculating average or mean values. There is considerable doubt as to whether or not these are interval scales. Many have argued that they are only ordinal in nature. Similarly, consider common teacher evaluation forms used at universities at the end of a term. These questions are often on a point scale, say from 1 to 7 where 1 is the most negative evaluation and 7 is the most positive. That means that a value of 4 would serve as a neutral or zero point value. Treating this as an interval scale implies that the differences between the numbers are constant so that the difference between the ratings of 4 and 5 are the same as the differences between the ratings of 5 and 6; however, this is often a doubtful assumption. The difference between a rating of 4 (neutral) and 5 (positive) may be, in fact, much larger than the difference between 5 and 6, which are two positive ratings. Although researchers often treat such data as if it were interval in nature, this practice can be misleading. Many modern statistical software packages, such as JMP from SAS Inc., make a clear distinction between ordinal and interval data and classify ordinal data as being more similar to nominal scale data than to interval scale.

---

[2]The Kelvin scale, on the other hand, does have an absolute zero point and is therefore a ratio not an interval scale.

Ratio Scales

A *ratio scale* describes data that not only has a constant unit of measure, so that one can talk about differences, but also **has a natural zero point** so that we can also talk about ratios of values. For example, $100,000 of profit is indeed twice as much as a $50,000 profit. This ratio will be the same no matter what currency the profits are measured in. If we convert the currencies to Euros or the Chinese Yuan the ratio will still be 2:1. This is because there is a natural zero point. Zero money is zero money no matter whether measured in dollars, pounds, Euros, Yuan, or any other currency. Data that has ratio scale properties contain the most information and are the most useful for statistical purposes. We can perform any kind of arithmetic operations on ratio scales.

It is important that you understand the level of measurement for the data being analyzed. Otherwise you may calculate values and perform arithmetic operations that are not appropriate for the data. For example, people using the common rating scales discussed above routinely calculate averages for the responses; however, averages are not appropriate unless the measurements are interval or ratio scales. Unfortunately the computer will let you do anything you want to the data; it is up to the analyst to know what is appropriate and what is not.

Exercises I

1. Indicate whether the following are discrete or continuous variables:

    (a) Mileage on company car C

    (b) Number of books in library D

    (c) Flight time to Boston C

    (d) Number of unionized employees D

    (e) Tons of wheat in a warehouse C

2. For the following situations, indicate whether the variable is measured on a nominal, ordinal, interval, or ratio scale:

    (a) NCAA Basketball rankings O

    (b) Majors within the School of Business N

    (c) Classification as Freshman, Sophomore, Junior or Senior N

    (d) Accounts receivable of a firm RS

    (e) Daily high temperatures at the local airport IS

3. Describe the difference between an interval and ratio scale. What types of mathematical operations are appropriate for each type of scale? Ratio has a natural zero point

4. Some philosophers have argued that nominal and ordinal scales are not really measurements at all and that we cannot say that something is "measured" unless we have at least an interval scale. Comment on this argument.

    True, doesn't really help understand data, just organizes it

Statistical Tables

We now want to turn to ways of describing a set of data. For example, in our opening vignette, how can Sarah's assistant describe this set of numbers since it is so large? We will describe both tabular and graphical methods of summarizing data in this chapter beginning with *tables*.

A table is data presented in rows and columns. Tables are ubiquitous in our daily lives. For many people, tables are what they think of when they think of statistics. They can be used for qualitative or quantitative data and are often used to show comparisons or relationships between variables. We will include several examples of tables in our discussions below.

Tables for Qualitative Data

Since qualitative data are inherently non-numerical, tables for qualitative data are almost always frequency tables e.g., tables of counts. Table 2-2 illustrates an example. It shows the primary causes of accidents in worldwide commercial aviation from 1950 through 2010. The primary variable in the table is the cause of the accident (qualitative variable) and the numerical data in the table are simple counts or frequencies (quantitative variable). Such a table is often called a *frequency distribution*. Frequency distributions are tables that show the number (or percent) of data grouped into non-overlapping classes.

Table 2-2   ***Primary Causes of Commercial Airline Accidents***

Cause of Accident	Number of Accidents
Pilot Error	539
Other Human Error	74
Mechanical /Maintenance Problem	237
Weather	128
Sabotage	95
Other	12

Source: Estimated from information at http://planecrashinfo.com/cause.htm

Frequency distributions and tables are also often cross-classified by other qualitative variables. For example, managers in the hospital, insurance, and health care industries use research data on mortality to help guide their strategic and tactical decisions. Table 2-3 shows the 12 leading causes of death in the United States cross-classified by gender in the columns. The table quickly makes it apparent that diseases of the heart and cancers (malignant neoplasms) are the prime causes of mortality for both men and women; however, the table also shows some interesting differences between males and females regarding causes of death. For example, accidents and chronic liver disease are almost twice as prevalent among males versus females while the opposite is true for hypertension and Alzheimer's deaths.

Tables for Quantitative Data

Summary tables of quantitative variables are common in business and economics. These tables compare quantitative variables classified by other variables over time. Table 2-4 illustrates both uses with gross domestic product of the U.S. over a 10-year period broken down by sectors. Here, you can clearly see that GDP increases over time and that the government portion of GDP was larger than the households and institutions sector in the first two years, but has been close to the same since then.

Table 2-3   **Leading Causes of Death in the United States 2005 Data**

	Male	Female	Total
Diseases of the heart	322,841	329,250	652,091
Malignant neoplasms	290,422	268,890	559,312
Cerebrovascular diseases	56,586	86,993	143,579
Chronic lower respiratory diseases	62,435	68,498	130,933
Alzheimer's disease	20,559	51,040	71,599
Accidents (unintentional injuries)	76,375	41,434	117,809
Diabetes mellitus	36,538	38,581	75,119
Influenza and pneumonia	28,052	34,949	63,001
Nephritis, nephrotic syndrome and nephrosis	21,268	22,663	43,901
Septicemia	15,322	18,814	34,136
Essential (primary) hypertension and	9,458	15,444	24,902
Chronic liver disease and cirrhosis	17,937	9,593	27,530
Total	**957,793**	**986,119**	**1,943,912**

Source: National Center for Health Statistics:
http://www.cdc.gov/nchs/data/nvsr/nvsr52/nvsr5203.pdf

Table 2-4   **GDP From 1998 – 2007 Broken Down into Sectors**

Gross value added by sector, 1997–2007
[Billions of dollars; quarterly data at seasonally adjusted annual rates]

Year	Gross domestic product	Business Total	Business Nonfarm	Business Farm	Households and institutions Total	Households	Nonprofit institutions serving households	General government Total	Federal	State and local
1998.	8,747.0	6,827.1	6,748.2	78.9	949.7	538.0	411.7	970.3	293.1	677.2
1999.	9,268.4	7,243.4	7,174.7	68.8	1,012.3	576.4	435.9	1,012.7	300.9	711.8
2000.	9,817.0	7,666.7	7,595.1	71.5	1,080.7	615.6	465.1	1,069.6	315.4	754.2
2001.	10,128.0	7,841.2	7,768.0	73.1	1,160.4	662.0	498.4	1,126.4	325.7	800.8
2002.	10,469.6	8,040.5	7,969.7	70.8	1,227.3	687.7	539.6	1,201.8	352.9	848.9
2003.	10,960.8	8,411.5	8,323.2	88.3	1,269.2	699.9	569.3	1,280.1	383.9	896.2
2004.	11,685.9	8,987.5	8,872.8	114.7	1,350.0	744.9	605.1	1,348.4	412.6	935.8
2005.	12,421.9	9,591.8	9,487.7	104.1	1,405.2	772.3	632.9	1,424.9	438.2	986.6
2006.	13,178.4	10,183.8	10,092.6	91.1	1,497.3	834.5	662.8	1,497.3	460.1	1,037.2
2007.	13,807.5	10,642.3	10,505.1	137.3	1,582.0	882.1	699.9	1,583.2	484.2	1,099.0

Frequency Distributions for Quantitative Variables

Frequency distributions can also be generated for quantitative variables, but there often arises the issue of a large number of values with each value having a small frequency of occurrence (e.g., 1 or 2). On the other hand, with qualitative variables, there are usually only a few values of the variable to list. Since the purpose of a frequency distribution is to give a clearer impression of the range and composition of the data, a simple frequency distribution is often of little help for quantitative variables. Therefore, we often have to group values into classes to obtain a meaningful frequency distribution. An example will help illustrate the concept.

Example 2-1

Sam Davis is the Operations Manager at Lucky 7, a chain of convenience stores in Texas and Oklahoma. He is trying to determine staffing requirements for the stores during different times of the day. The data shown below are for the hour just before closing and consist of a count of the number of customers entering a store during the hour before closing. There are 100 observations in the data which are also contained in the file Example 2-1.xlsx.

39	22	35	45	30	14	31	24	22	41	12	30	50	43	47	31	17	27	21	47
32	29	34	32	59	37	21	17	24	31	23	11	45	39	32	30	11	43	20	28
49	38	38	24	44	24	29	13	23	42	53	14	37	54	30	60	37	21	39	33
33	50	41	44	24	32	31	48	42	49	25	17	50	49	25	35	32	12	59	44
21	14	25	48	15	13	43	37	35	52	32	26	28	32	18	64	21	36	63	39

If you sort the data and complete a count of the different values you will find that the numbers range from 11 to 64 and that the frequencies of each number range from zero to 7. The resulting frequency distribution is shown in Table 2-5. As you can see, this table hardly summarizes the data at all. It does give us the range of the data (from 11 to 64), but tells us little else. For example, it doesn't really tell us where most of the values lie or how they are distributed. To get a better summary picture of the data we must group the values together into class intervals and count the frequencies in each of those intervals.

Table 2-5   *Simple Frequency Distribution of the Example 2-1 Data*

Value	Frequency
11	2
12	2
13	2
14	4
15	1
16	0
17	3
18	1
19	0
20	1
21	5
22	2
23	2
24	5
25	3
26	1
27	1
28	2
29	1
30	4
31	4
32	7
33	2
34	1
35	3
36	1
37	4
38	2
39	3
40	0
41	2
42	2
43	3
44	3
45	2
46	0
47	2
48	2
49	3
50	3
51	0
52	1
53	1
54	1
55	0
56	0
57	0
58	0
59	3
60	1
61	0
62	0
63	1
64	1

Table 2-6   *Frequency Distribution of Number of Convenience Store Customers*

No. Customers	Frequency
10 to under 20	14
20 to under 30	24
30 to under 40	32
40 to under 50	19
50 to under 60	8
60 to under 70	3
Total	*100*

Notice that we lose information when we group values into intervals in the frequency distribution. For example, we know that there are 14 observations in the 10 to under 20 range, but we have no idea what the individual values are or if they are clustered at one end of the interval or spread evenly throughout the interval. Therefore, the ability to summarize data in a frequency distribution comes at a price for quantitative variables. We will later describe some graphical techniques that do not suffer from this problem.

We can summarize the procedure for constructing frequency distributions in the form of the guidelines in Figure 2-2. It is important to keep in mind that these are merely guidelines. The purpose of frequency distributions is to reveal the underlying pattern of the data. Thus, the number and the size of the classes should be more a function of the actual data than of any specific rules. With fewer than five classes, the patterns may remain hidden. But, more than 15 or 20 classes can obscure any benefits of grouping the data. **Six to 10 intervals** are common and can serve as a good starting point. There are also rules of thumb that can be used in determining the number of classes. One such rule is to use the square root of the number of observations as a starting point for establishing the number of classes. Most statistical software has built-in rules for establishing the number and size of the class intervals.

Figure 2-2   *Steps in Constructing a Frequency Distribution*

1. Find the range (maximum – minimum) of values from the raw data.

2. Determine a preliminary *class interval* by choosing a reasonable number of classes (usually between 5 and 20) and divide the range by the number of classes.

3. Set the stated class interval by adjusting the preliminary value upward to a common or convenient width (e.g., 10 or 20). Avoid fractional or odd-numbered interval widths, if possible.

4. Record the number of observations that fall into each class.

Relative and Cumulative Frequency Distributions

The frequency distributions shown to this point have been absolute frequency distributions because the frequency for each class represented the actual number of data points or observations in that class. *Relative frequency distributions* show the class frequencies expressed as a **proportion** or percent of the total number of observations. They are especially useful for analyzing the relative percentage of different classes. Table 2-7 shows the frequency distribution from Table 2-6 as relative frequencies.

Table 2-7   ***Relative Frequency Distribution of Number of Convenience Store Customers***

No. Customers	Relative Frequency
10 to under 20	(14/100) = .14
20 to under 30	(24/100) = .24
30 to under 40	(32/100) = .32
40 to under 50	(19/100) = .19
50 to under 60	(8/100) = .08
60 to under 70	(3/100) = .03
TOTAL	**(100/100) = 1.0***

Note: This total should always equal 1.0

Either absolute frequency or relative frequency distributions can also be presented as cumulative distributions. *Cumulative frequency distributions* show the number (absolute) or percentage (relative) of data points falling at or below various class boundaries of the distribution. Table 2-8 shows a cumulative frequency distribution for the data in Table 2-6.

Table 2-8   ***Cumulative Frequency Distribution of Number of Convenience Store Customers***

No. Customers	Frequency
10 to under 20	(.14*100) = 14
20 to under 30	(.24*100) + 14 = 38
30 to under 40	(.32*100) + 38 = 70
40 to under 50	(.19*100) + 70 = 89
50 to under 60	(.08*100) + 89 = 97
60 to under 70	(.03*100) + 97 = 100

Exercises II

5.   The following represents the number of passengers boarding at some large hub airports (in millions of passengers) as recorded (for 1988) and projected (for 2000) by the Federal Aviation Administration: Chicago (29, 42), Dallas/F.W. (23, 35), Denver (15, 33), Atlanta (24, 31), Kennedy (19, 27), Los Angeles (22, 26), San Francisco (15, 19), Miami (14, 18), and Boston (12, 17). Prepare a table of their data with geographical locations on the vertical dimension and the chronological classification on the horizontal scale. Arrange the vertical classification in alphabetical order and include a column showing the estimated percent changes over the 12-year period 1988-2000. *(Source: The Wall Street Journal, June 2, 1990, p. B1)*

6.   A travel agent has collected the following information concerning the minimum mileage required for two round-trip tickets under the airlines "frequent flyer" programs. The numbers in parentheses after the airline name indicate the minimum mileage required (000 miles) for two round-trip tickets (1) on

domestic routes, (2) to Hawaii, and (3) to Europe, respectively: Continental (35, 45, 55), Delta (60, 70, 110), Northwest (40, 60, 60), Alaska (40, 40, 60), United (40, 60, 80), and TWA (40, 80, 90). Arrange the data in a table with destinations on the vertical scale and airlines across the top as columns. Include an extra column to show the average mileage required for all the listed airlines

7. Use your library or the web to locate a cross-classified table. Describe the two types of classification and indicate whether each is qualitative or quantitative and the type of scale for each variable.

8. A government banking committee is concerned about the effect of uninsured bank failures upon the elderly. In an effort to better identify the age distribution of customers, examiners have randomly selected 60 accounts from failed savings and loan institutions (S & L's) and recorded the ages of customers as follows (the data are also contained in the file Exercise 2-8.xlsx):

27	83	75	91	54	60	49	86	66	44	59	25	96	87	46
79	62	32	87	95	79	64	88	82	77	07	79	80	78	76
03	77	43	87	78	86	14	82	99	69	79	83	62	91	77
62	94	32	10	76	48	80	78	70	86	65	55	88	70	41

(a) Before you do any summarization, glance at the data and estimate the age level beyond which 50% of the observations lie. (That is, 50% of the customers are older than what age?)

(b) Develop a frequency distribution where the first class interval is $0 < 15$ years.

9. Use the data of Problem 8 and let your first class interval be $0 < 15$ years.

(a) Formulate a cumulative distribution with one column showing the class frequencies and another showing the cumulative frequencies.

(b) How many customers are in the "$45 < 75$ year" age classification? Using your distribution only (e.g., not the raw data), can you tell how many of the customers surveyed are:

(i)   Less than 60 years old,

(ii)   Less than 50 years old? Explain.

10. Use the data of Problem 8 and let your first class interval be $0 < 15$ years.

(a) Formulate a relative frequency distribution.

(b) What percent of the customers are 60 to less than 75 years old?

(c) What percent are greater than 75 years old? Greater than 90?

(d) Do the data tend to support the concern that elderly people would be more affected by failures of uninsured S & L's?

Graphical Presentation of Qualitative Data

Tables like frequency distributions are useful, but graphs and charts have several advantages over tables: (1) graphs are more likely to attract attention than would the same data presented in table form, (2) graphs can sometimes present the data more succinctly than a table, and (3) graphs enable the analyst and the reader to spot trends or relationships that would be less obvious in a table. Business organizations often use many different types of graphs to describe financial, marketing, and other activities because graphs are such an excellent means of communication.

Qualitative variables are usually displayed either as bar charts or pie charts. *Bar charts* are commonly used to convey frequency information for qualitative variables where the bars represent the frequency or relative frequency for that value of the qualitative variable. The values of the qualitative variable can be displayed along the X-axis in a vertical bar chart or along the Y-axis for a horizontal bar chart. Figure 2-3 shows a bar chart of the data in Table 2-2 on airline accidents.

Figure 2-3   ***Bar Chart of Commercial Jets Accident Causes***

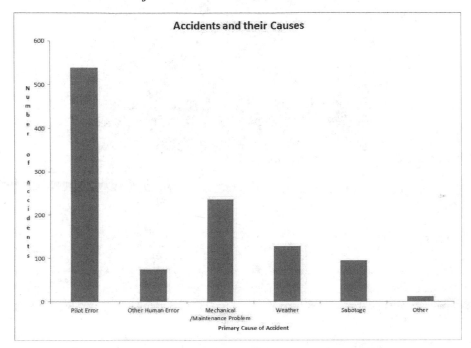

Pie charts are another way to present qualitative data. Pie charts are used exclusively with relative frequency distributions and have an intuitive appeal because they show proportional effects and convey relative frequencies. Figure 2-4 shows a pie chart of the data in Table 2-2.

Figure 2-4   Pie Chart of Airline Accident Data

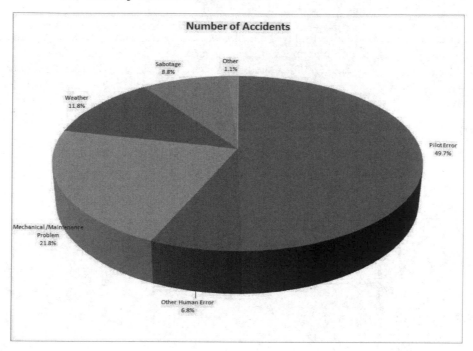

Exercises III

11. One of the world's largest food companies, The Unilever Group, which markets products ranging from detergents and toiletries to Lipton tea and Ragu pasta sauces, had sales last year (in billions) of $20.6 in Europe, $7.4 in North America, and $6.4 in other locations. Prepare a pie chart showing the percentage of sales by region.

12. Use an appropriate graph to illustrate the number of new business starts in River City since an industrial park was formed:

Years since park	0	1	2	3	4	5	6	7
New businesses	12	7	4	10	18	28	32	25

13. Use the data from Table 2-3 to draw a pie chart to depict the four leading causes of death in the United States for females. [*Note*: Use a category called "other" for the remaining six causes.

14. Use the data from Table 2-3 to prepare a bar chart comparing the number of male and female deaths from accidents, cancer, heart disease and diabetes. [*Note*: Show two bars for each category of death, but distinguish them by different colors or patterns.]

15. Using online data, find and *graph* (in an appropriate manner) one of the following: (1) a representative price of gold over the past eight years, (2) the rate of unemployment in the United States over the past five years, or (3) the earnings per share of Boeing stock for the past five years.

Graphic Presentation of Quantitative Data

Quantitative data can also be very effectively presented in graphs. Graphs of quantitative frequency distributions often take the form of (1) histograms, (2) frequency polygons, or (3) ogives.

Histogram

A *histogram* is a vertical bar graph of a frequency distribution, where the x-axis shows the class intervals of the variable of interest and the y-axis details the number of observations in that class interval. As with frequency distributions, histograms can be used to show either actual frequencies or relative frequencies and therefore can be used with either frequency or relative frequency distributions. If equal intervals are used, the bars are of equal width and the height of each bar is determined directly by the frequency of the interval.

Example 2-2

The study of the number of customers entering the convenience store in the hour before closing (Example 2-1) resulted in the frequency distribution repeated below. Use these data to construct a histogram.

No. Customers	Frequency (No. days)
10 to under 20	14
20 to under 30	24
30 to under 40	32
40 to under 50	19
50 to under 60	8
60 to under 70	3

Solution

The histogram for this frequency distribution is shown below:

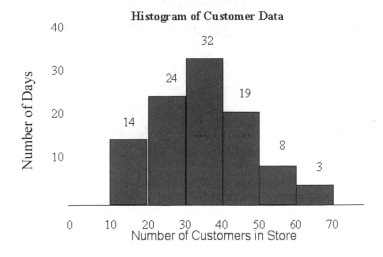

Histograms are similar to the bar charts that we discussed for qualitative data. The only difference between the two, besides the fact that one represents a quantitative variable and the other a qualitative variable, is that histograms do not have any gaps between the columns and bar charts do. The reason there are no gaps in the histogram is because the value on the axis is continuous and we have arbitrarily divided it into groups.

Frequency Polygon

A *frequency polygon* is a (many-sided) line graph that portrays the data of a frequency distribution. It has the same height (and approximately the same spread) as a histogram. The height of each plotted point is again determined by the frequency of the respective class interval; however, polygons are formed by using straight lines to connect the **midpoints** at the top of each bar. The lines on each end are anchored to the horizontal axis at the midpoints of what "would be" the next-lower interval (on the left) and higher interval (on the right). The x-axis scale can show either the class limits or the class midpoints.

Example 2-3

Use the data from Example 2-1 to construct a frequency polygon.

Solution

Figure 2-5 shows the frequency polygon. The dashed lines show the histogram for reference (only) so you can see how the polygon lines cross the column midpoint values.

Figure 2-5   *Frequency Polygon of Customer Data*

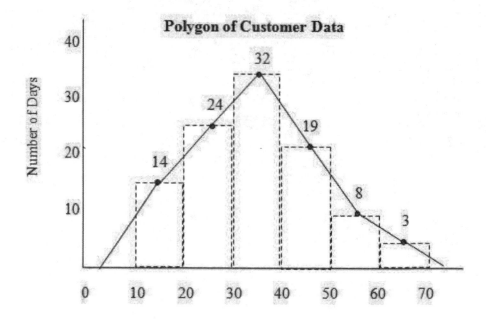

The polygon depicted in Example 2-3 shows the actual frequencies and is an absolute frequency polygon. If the vertical scale had shown the percent of days for each class, the figure would be referred to as a relative frequency polygon.

Cumulative Frequency Distribution (Ogive)

An *ogive* (pronounced oh-jive) is a graph of a **cumulative frequency** distribution with points connected by straight lines. It is constructed by plotting the cumulative frequency (*y*-axis) that corresponds to each class interval boundary (*x*-axis). The cumulative function starts at zero and rises to the top of the graph. As with other frequency polygons, the cumulative graphs can be absolute or relative cumulative frequency distributions, depending upon whether the cumulative frequencies are expressed in numbers or in percents.

Example 2-4

(a) Use the data from Example 2-1 to construct an ogive showing the number of days when less than 20, 30, . . ., 70 customers entered the convenience store.

(b) What would be required to make the ogive show the relative (e.g., %) values as well?

Solution

The frequency distribution values of Example 2-1 are repeated below along with the cumulative values which are needed for this example.

Class Interval	10 to under 20	20 to under 30	30 to under 40	40 to under 50	50 to under 60	60 to under 70
Frequency	14	24	32	19	8	3
Cumulative Frequency	14	38	70	89	97	100

As with the frequency polygon, we begin on the axis at what would be the upper class boundary of the next lower class (e.g., 10) (Figure 2-6). The first plotted point will then be at a cumulative frequency (*Y* value) of 14 that corresponds to the upper class boundary (or *X* value) of 20. Then, the next point is at *Y* = 38 and *X* = 30. This means that on 38 of the days (observations), there were fewer than 30 customers in the store during the last hour.

Figure 2-6   ***Cumulative Frequency of an Ogive for the Data from Example 2-1***

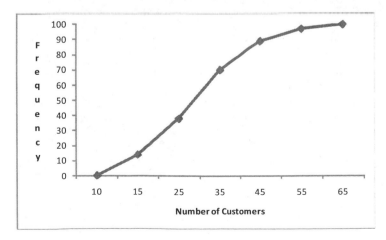

Percentage or relative frequency values are easy to show, for we simply let the total number of observations be 100% and apportion the other values accordingly. The percentage scale in the above example would be the same as the absolute scale because there happen to be exactly 100 observations—this is an unusual case.

Several useful statistics can be obtained from the ogive. The point on the x-axis that lies directly below the intersection of the curve and a line at the 50% point is the value above and below which exactly half of the data points lie. This point is the median value that we will discuss in the next chapter. If a percent scale is shown on the chart, the percent of observations lying above and below other points is also easy to determine. The point that separates the bottom one-quarter from the top three-quarters of the observations is called the first-quartile (QB_{1B}). Next is the median (QB_{2B}), and the point that separates the top one-quarter from the bottom three-quarters is the third-quartile (QB_{3B}). The points that divide the scores into 10 equal groups (deciles) are also sometimes useful. We will discuss these concepts further in the next chapter and while all of these points can be located mathematically, the ogive clarifies the meaning of the values.

Stem-and-Leaf Diagrams

Stem-and-leaf diagrams display data that incorporates aspects of both tabular and charting concepts. One problem with frequency distributions for quantitative variables is that information is lost in the process. For example, in Example 2-1 we know that the frequency for between 10 and 20 people entered the store in the last hour is 14, but we have no idea if most of these values were around 10, around 20 or spread evenly throughout that range. Stem-and-leaf displays are visually much like a histogram, but preserve all of the original data in their visual.

Constructing a stem-and-leaf diagram requires that the value of each observation be divided into a "stem" and a "leaf." Stems are leading digits (on the left) and leaves are trailing digits (which extend out to the right). An example of a stem-and leaf display would be:

- The observations 47, 42, and 45 all have a leading digit of 4 and the trailing digits are 7, 2, and 5, respectively. These would be displayed as:

$$4 \mid 7 \ 2 \ 5$$

- The values 50 and 58 would be shown as:

$$5 \mid 0 \ 8$$

Example 2-5
Construct a stem-and-leaf diagram using the first five columns of raw data from Example 2-1.

Solution

The first two values of 39 and 32 customers both belong to the stem "3" (shown in boldface type in Figure 2-6a). Continue on until all 25 values are located on the diagram. Normally, the leaves are arranged in numerical order, as shown in Figure 2-6b. This ordered arrangement of the individual values gives the viewer an even better feeling for any clustering effects within the given leaves.

Stem-and-leaf diagrams are easily constructed and convey a surprising amount of information about the data. If the diagrams were rotated 90° counterclockwise, they would resemble histograms. Unlike the data displayed in an ordinary histogram, however, all the values of the individual observations are preserved in a stem-and-leaf diagram so that no information is lost. Yet, the pattern of the data is clearly presented. By viewing Figure 2-7, one gets a clear impression that the observations are distributed symmetrically around the mid-30's.

Figure 2-7 **Stem and Leaf Diagrams for Example 2-1**

```
1  | 4 5                          1  | 4 5
2  | 1 2 9 5 4 4                  2  | 1 2 4 4 5 9
3  | 9 2 3 8 5 4 8 2 0            3  | 0 2 2 3 4 5 8 8 9
4  | 9 1 5 4 8 4                  4  | 1 4 4 5 8 9
5  | 0 9                          5  | 0 9
```

Figure 2-7a   **Figure 2-7b**

Sometimes decisions must be made in constructing stem-and-leaf diagrams. For example, with four-digit numbers, the first three would normally be used as the stem and the fourth as the leaf. For example, the number 6325 would be displayed as 632 | 5; however, if the final digit is not really meaningful, it might be dropped, as in 63 | 2. But if any modifications such as these are made, they should be very clearly noted. Also, if there is too high a concentration in some of the stems to get a meaningful representation, the stems can be divided into two portions, a low portion (e.g., for the digits 0 to 4) and high portion (the digits 5 to 9). Thus, the revised portion of the number in the 40s in Figure 2-6 might be given as:

$$4 | 1 \; 4 \; 4$$
$$4 | 5 \; 8 \; 9$$

Most statistical software will automatically make these adjustments for you to best use the available data.

Dot plots are line graphs where a dot is placed above the X-axis for each observation. Dot plots have one of the same advantages as stem-and-leaf plots in that all of the original data are retained. Although all of the original values are included in the plot, these values are more difficult to recover in a dot plot than in a stem and-leaf diagram; however, such plots are very useful for comparing two different groups of data. To illustrate this, Figure 2-8 shows a dot plot of salaries by gender[3].

Figure 2-8 **A Dot Plot of Salaries by Gender**

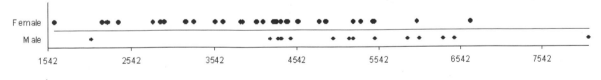

Dot Plots for Current Sal by Gender

As you can see, the salaries for females are spread out over the entire range while the salaries for the males tend to be clustered in the upper half of the range. Such a pattern would be very difficult to detect from a frequency distribution or separate stem-and-leaf plots of each gender, but is readily apparent from a dot plot.

[3] This data is from Example 2-8 later in this chapter

Line and Area Charts

Line charts and *area charts* are frequently used to **depict data over time**, with the time scale being on the horizontal axis. They are effective for comparing one time period (hour, month, year) with the next and for presenting long-term trends in the series of data. As with all charts, scales that do not begin at zero must be clearly marked so as not to mislead the reader. Although the Y-axis normally contains the original scale of the variable, logarithmic vertical scales are sometimes better for presenting data that have been increasing (or decreasing) at an almost constant rate or for comparing fluctuations in two series that have vastly different magnitudes.

Example 2-6

The Burritos and More Restaurant has kept track of the sales of its SuperMex dinners for the last 8 weeks. The data are provided in the table below. Construct a line chart of the data. What can you infer about sales of the SuperMex dinners?

Week	1	2	3	4	5	6	7	8
Sales	121	142	137	164	173	194	203	210

Solution

Figure 2-9 contains the resulting line chart produced using Excel. As you can see from the chart, sales of the SuperMex dinners have been generally increasing over the last 8 weeks. This is a good trend if you are the owner of the restaurant.

Figure 2-9   ***Line Chart of the SuperMex Dinner Sales***

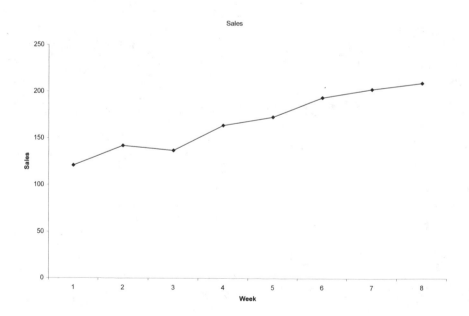

Area charts are most often used to contrast the changes in two different time series. For example, suppose that we also have data on the MiniMex dinner sales at the Burritos and More Restaurant as shown below:

Week	1	2	3	4	5	6	7	8
SuperMex	121	142	137	164	173	194	203	210
MiniMex	101	124	133	145	154	161	178	190

An area chart of these data is shown in Figure 2-9. The area chart is a line chart for the two variables with the areas shaded in. This is useful for comparing the relative values or gaps between two variables. Figure 2-10 shows the gap between sales of the SuperMex and MiniMex dinners has been growing over the past 8 weeks. The same data could just as well be presented with a line chart with separate lines representing each type of dinner; however, the area chart is sometimes more useful in conveying the relative growth rates for two sets of data.

Figure 2-10   *Area Chart for Two Sets of Data*

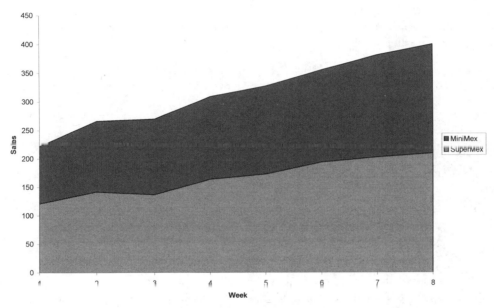

Exercises IV

16. Construct a histogram showing the annual wages ($000) of the following applicants who applied for loans at a bank during one week in June.

Wage interval	0 to under 20	20 to under 40	40 to under 60	60 to under 80	80 to under 100
No. applicants	35	20	90	45	10

17. Using the raw data shown below and contained in the file Exercise 2-17.xlsx, construct a histogram with the classes of 5 to under 15, 15 to under 25, . . . 55 to under 65.

18. The data shown below represent battery lifetimes in hours for a sample of batteries produced by the Everbright Battery Company. For these data, construct (a) a histogram, and (b) a frequency polygon.

Class interval	5—9	10—14	15—19	20—24	25—29	30—34	35—39	40--44
Frequency	1	5	13	19	30	17	9	6

19. For the Everbright Battery data in problem 18 construct an ogive showing the cumulative number of observations *less than* the upper class boundary.

Use the following data concerning the number of DVDs rented per year to answer Problems 20 and 21.

No. DVDs rented	0	1—4	5—9	10—19	20—29	30—39	40—49	50—60
% of households	27	5	8	17	16	9	3	15

20. Using the data above, construct a histogram showing the number of DVD rentals. [*Note*: Let the *x*-axis be the number of DVDs rented, and combine the first three classes.]

21. For the DVD rental data shown above, (a) construct a cumulative ogive showing the cumulative percent of households greater than the lower class boundary. (b) What would be your estimate of the number of tapes rented by the median (50th percentile) household? (c) What is the maximum number of tapes rented by any household?

22. In Exercise 8 you were asked to construct a frequency distribution for the ages of S & L customers. Construct (a) a histogram and (b) a "less than" ogive of those data.

23. Construct a stem-and-leaf diagram using the second set of five columns of raw data from Example 2-1. Rearrange the data so that the digits are in ascending order.

24. Present the first two rows of raw data from Exercise 8 in the form of a stem-and-leaf diagram. Does this sample of data tend to suggest that the bulk of S & L customers are in their younger years or their older years?

Looking at Relationships

In this section, we investigate methods for exploring the relationship between two variables. This can be a situation of evaluating relationships between two qualitative variables (e.g., gender and participation in a health plan) or qualitative and quantitative variables (e.g., gender and age). We will first look at the relationship between two quantitative variables measured on an interval or ratio scale and we will then look at ways of exploring qualitative variables measured on nominal, or ordinal, scales.

Scatter Plots

Scatter plots are familiar to you if you have worked with Excel's charting feature. In Excel, they are sometimes also called XY plots. *Scatter plots* graph paired observations in a two-dimensional space defined by the X and Y variables, both of which are quantitative in nature.

Example 2-7

Example 2-8 discussed later in this chapter contains a number of quantitative and qualitative variables. Two of the quantitative variables in that data are current salary and beginning salary. Suppose, we are interested in the relationship between these two quantitative variables. Logically, we would probably expect a positive relationship between these two variables. In other words, the higher the starting salary, the higher the current salary is likely to be. We can look at this relationship with a scatter plot of the data.

Solution

Figure 2-11 shows the resulting scatter plot. From the figure you can see that as the beginning salary increases, the current salary also tends to increase, indicating a positive relationship between the two variables. You can also see that the relationship is not a perfect one. In other words, for a given beginning salary there may be several current salaries, not just one. Therefore, we cannot perfectly predict current salary from beginning salary. In Chapter 10 we will detail a numerical measure to indicate the strength of this relationship called a correlation.

Figure 2-11   ***Scatter Plot With Beginning Salary on the X-Axis and Current Salary on the Y-Axis***

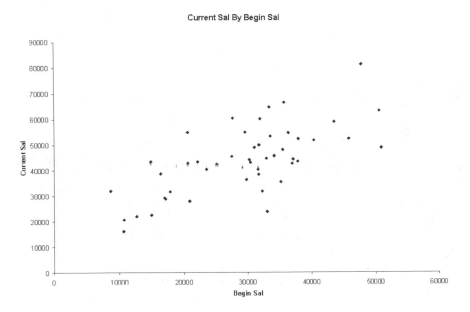

Contingency Tables and Mosaic Plots

When we deal with nominal or ordinal scale data, we should not display relationships between variables as a scatter plot since they assume at least an interval scale of measurement[4]. To explore relationships between nominal or ordinal scale data, the correct technique is to use a contingency table. A *contingency table* is a table of frequencies or counts where the rows and columns of the table are the nominal or ordinal scale categories. The data in Example 2-8, later in this chapter, contain information on gender and whether or not the employee participated in the company health care plan. Since these are nominal scale measures, a contingency table would be the appropriate means of exploring the relationship between the two variables. Table 2-9 illustrates the contingency table for this example.

---

[4] There is nothing in Excel that will prevent you from producing a scatter plot with nominal scale or ordinal scale data but it is not appropriate to do so.

Table 2-9   ***Contingency Table for the Gender and Health Care Variables of Example 2-7***

Health Plan

		Yes	No	Totals
	Male	11	4	15
Gender	Female	17	18	35
	Totals	28	22	50

As you can see, there tends to be a relationship between gender and the use of the health plan in that males overwhelmingly use the health plan, but females are almost evenly split on whether or not they use the plan. In other words, based on these data, it appears that the two variables are not independent of one another. Whether or not one uses the company health plan tends to depend on gender. We will make further use of contingency tables in Chapter 8, 9 and 10 to explore the effects of nominal scale variables.

This table is very similar to a pivot table, which we will discuss later in this chapter. In fact, a contingency table can be transformed very quickly into a pivot table with the row and column variables being the two nominal scale variables. The trick is to place any variable you want in the data section of the pivot table and then change the measure for the data to a count instead of a sum or an average. This will produce the desired frequencies.

A contingency table can also be displayed graphically as a mosaic plot. A mosaic plot begins with a square area that is first divided into two parts based on the relative frequencies of the first categorical variable. Each of these two areas are then split into two parts based on the relative frequencies of the second categorical variable within each category of the first variable. The mosaic plot for the data in Table 2-9 is shown in Figure 2-11. To understand the mosaic plot it is helpful to calculate a few relative frequencies from Table 2-9. The mosaic plot is first divided by gender. In Table 2-9, 15 out of the 50 employees or 30% are male and 35 out of 50 or 70% are female. The square area on the left is divided with 30% on the left and 70% on the right. Then within the males, 11 out of 15 or 73.3% are on the health plan and 4 out of 15 or 26.7% are not. The first column is divided into areas based on these relative frequencies. Similarly, within the second column, 17 out of the 35 or 49% of the females are on the health plan and 18 out of 35 or 51% are not. The second column is divided based on these relative frequencies. The final column simply shows the overall relative frequencies of those on the health plan (28 out of 50 = 56%) and those not on the health plan (22 out of 50 = 44%). As you can see from Figure 2-12 it is clear that a larger percentage of males are on the health plan than females.

Figure 2-12   ***Mosaic Plot of the Data in Table 2-9***

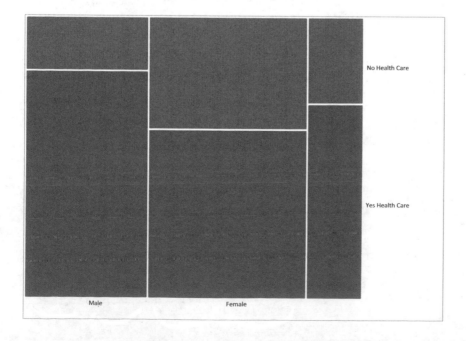

Ethical Issues in Displaying Data

Graphic displays can be powerful tools to summarize and condense large sets of numbers and convey the essential information contained in the data; however, there are a variety of ways in which graphical displays can mislead and misinform. Sometimes, these techniques may be deliberately used to deceive the reader. At other times, ignorance of graphical techniques can produce graphs that tend to mislead rather than enlighten. We will explore several "don'ts" in this section about the graphical displays of data so that you are aware of some of the potential problems in using graphs.

Problems with Bar Charts

Bar charts may not seem capable of deception, but they can unintentionally mislead a reader. The issue relates to the human tendency to pay attention to areas beyond just height or width. Consider the bar chart of sales over the past three years depicted in Figure 2-12. Notice two things about this chart: (1) Sales have increased by $10,000 units each year and, (2) the width of each bar is the same. The information about the quantity is contained in the height of the bar, not its width. The problem arises when images other than bars are used in a chart. Many people like to replace bars in a chart with images that convey the essence of what is being measured, such as a picture of a dollar bill or bag of money as shown in Figure 2-13. When working with images, most software locks the aspect ratio when the images are resized. That means that as the height is increased so is the width. Therefore, when we double the height of an image we also tend to double the width which makes the image four times as large area-wise. Since people would tend to perceive the increase in area, the chart makes the change seem twice as big as it really was. Figure 2-14 shows a similar figure where the width was maintained at the same value. You can see that the increases "look" much larger in Figure 2-13 than in 2-14.

Figure 2-12   ***Sales Figures Over the Past Three Years***

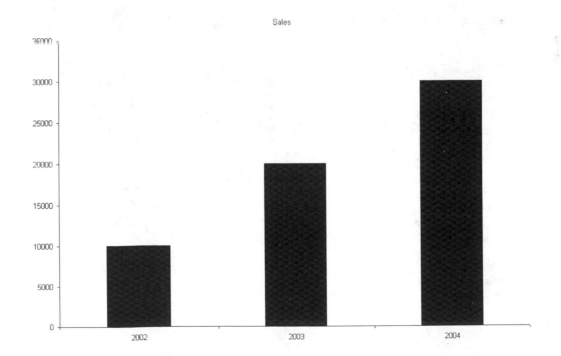

Figure 2-13   ***Same Sales Chart with Images, not Bars***

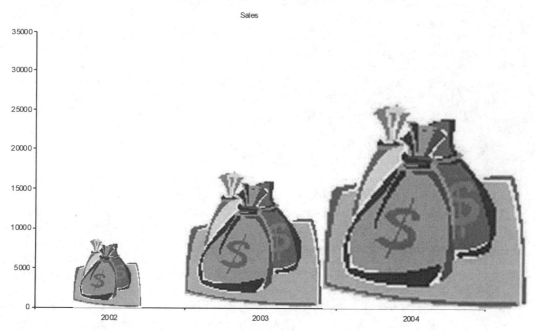

Figure 2-14   ***Same Sales Chart With Width Held Constant***

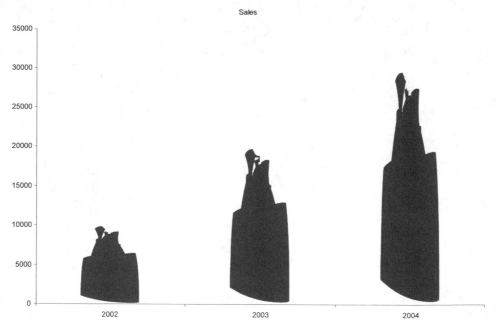

Misleading Line Charts

Line charts can look at changes or trends over time. Such graphs can also mislead the reader, if not done properly. Consider the data in Figure 2-15(a) which plots the average retail price of gas in the U.S. for the years 1995 to 2004. The same data are shown again in Figure 2-15(b). Notice that the perceived increase in prices is much higher in graph (b) than in graph (a). The reason is that the Y-axis does not start at 0 in

Figure 2-15(b), but starts at 100. Any graph where the axis starts at a value other than zero accentuates the trend. This may be useful for zooming in on the data and highlighting trends as long as one is aware of what is going on.

Figure 2-15   Average Retail Gas Prices from 1995 to 2004

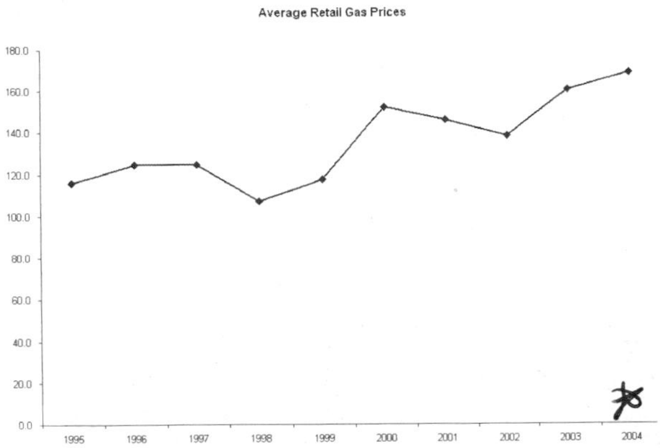

Figure 2-15(a) 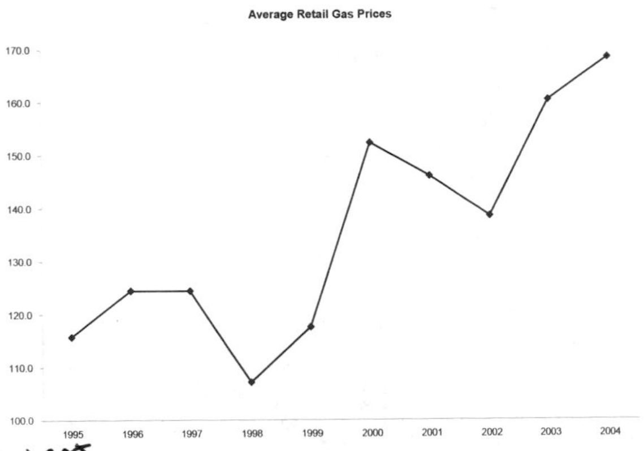   Figure 2-15(b)

However, presenting a graph such as this without warning the reader is misleading. When you are looking at line charts based on data over time make sure that you pay attention to the axes. When either axis of a graph starts at a value other than zero this fact should be called to the reader's attention.

Practice

Excel List Structures

In this text we will be using Excel extensively to analyze data, especially with the XLDataAnalyst add-in. XLDataAnalyst, Excel functions, and other statistical software for analyzing data, usually assume that the data is in the form of a "list structure." In Excel, a list structure is a table of values where the first row of the table is a "header" row that contains text representing the names of the variables in the dataset. Each additional row under the header row contains an observation in the dataset with numerical values for each variable. Thus a list structure will have one row for each observation in the data and a header row, or n+1 rows in total, where n is the number of observations in the data. Figure 2-16 shows an example list structure that has a large number of observations[5].

---

[5] You may notice that the data in the introductory figure for this chapter is not a well structured list. A list structure for this data would have only two columns, one for customer number and the other for age. The data in this figure was rearranged for convenient display rather than for analysis.

Figure 2-16   ***Example of Data in an Excel List Structure***

	A	B	C	D	E	F	G	H	I	J	K	L
1	Observ	BeginSal	CurrentSal	Gender	Seniorty	Age	Educate	PriorExp	Management			
2	17	5280	8760	1	98	557	8	190	0			
3	18	5280	8040	1	88	745	8	90	0			
4	28	5220	7860	1	70	671	8	120	0			
5	29	5100	9660	1	66	554	8	96	0			
6	30	4380	9600	1	92	305	8	6.25	0			
7	34	5400	8640	1	65	603	8	173	0			
8	36	4500	12540	1	96	366	8	52	0			
9	41	5400	8640	1	66	771	8	228	0			
10	48	4800	8340	1	79	602	8	70	0			
11	51	4980	8700	1	74	718	8	318	0			
12	74	6000	8940	0	78	659	8	320	0			
13	90	4380	10020	1	93	313	8	7.5	0			
14	8	6000	10140	0	82	363	12	32	0			
15	11	6900	10920	0	89	481	12	175	0			
16	16	4800	8580	1	98	774	12	381	0			
17	19	4800	9000	1	77	505	12	63	0			
18	20	4800	8820	1	76	482	12	6	0			
19	22	5520	9600	1	82	558	12	97	0			
20	23	5400	8940	1	88	338	12	26	0			
21	24	5700	9000	1	76	667	12	90	0			
22	25	3900	8760	1	98	327	12	0	0			
23	26	4800	9780	1	75	619	12	144	0			
24	27	6120	9360	1	78	624	12	208.5	0			

Note that the value for a variable can be expressed qualitatively if it is a categorical or nominal scale variable; however, most software, including XLDataAnalyst works best with numbers. You can always associate text with the numbers in XLDataAnalyst. The software will use the text in all output to make the results easier to interpret. The Appendix on using XLDataAnalyst describes how you can do this easily. There should always be a blank column to the right of the list structure and a blank row below it. If the list structure does not start in the first row there should also be a blank row above the list structure. In other words, the list structure should be like an island and have nothing else "touching" it. In this text, unless explicitly stated otherwise, we will assume that any data to be analyzed is in the form of an Excel list structure. XLDataAnalyst further assumes that the list structure starts in the first column. It does not have to start in the first row, however.

Excel Pivot Tables

Excel has a very powerful tool, pivot tables, for developing and manipulating summary tables of data. They are easy to produce using the pivot table wizard in Excel. The pivot table wizard expects your data to be in the form of a list structure, as defined in the last section. Example 2-8 will be used to illustrate the use of pivot tables.

Example 2-8

The dataset in the Excel file Example 2-8.xlsx contains sample data from 60 employees of a large national bank. Table 2-10 shows the variables represented in the data.

Table 2-10   ***Variables in the Dataset***

Variable	Description
Observation	Sequential observation number
Begin Sal	Beginning salary at the bank
Current Sal	Current salary at the bank
Seniority	Seniority at the bank in months
Age	Age in months
Education	Years of education
Management	0=non-management 1=management
Health	0=not on health plan 1=on health plan
Gender	0=male 1=female

Solution

To generate a pivot table, select Pivot Table from the Insert tab on the ribbon. You should then see something like the dialog box shown in Figure 2-17. The dialog asks you to identify the list structure that you want to use. If you have organized the data into a proper list structure as described earlier, Excel may already have identified it and selected the data so that the appropriate range will appear in the dialog box as shown in Figure 2-17. If Excel has not properly identified your data, simply enter the relevant range into this dialog or outline the data in the spreadsheet with your mouse. After identifying the data, click the OK button and Excel will create a new worksheet like that shown in Figure 2-18.

Figure 2-17   ***Pivot Table Wizard Dialog***

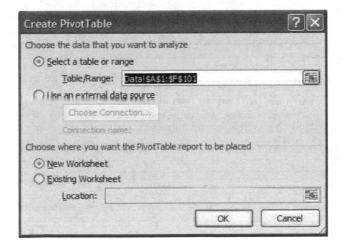

Figure 2-18   *Blank Pivot Table Sheet*

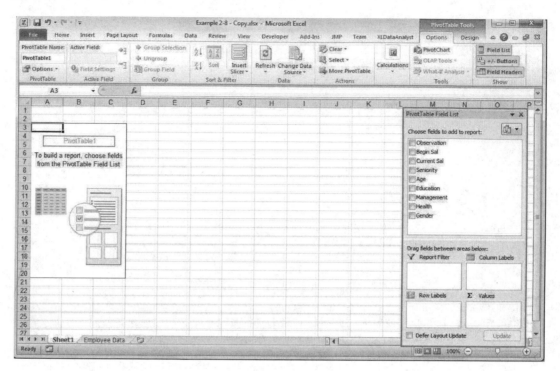

The exact appearance of the new worksheet depends on the version of Excel that you are using and the options that have been set for pivot tables. The worksheet shown in Figure 2-18 is the default in Excel 2007 or later. Earlier versions of Excel had a different layout that can be used in newer versions of Excel by selecting a special option for pivot tables. The outline where the pivot table will go is shown on the left side of the screen with a listing of the variables in the list structure in a toolbar on the right side of the screen. To create the pivot table, you must select the row and column variables and the data items that go in the table. Select the fields in the list and drag them into the Column Labels, Row Labels, or Σ Values section, as appropriate. As with the statistical tables in an earlier section, the rows and columns of tables must be discrete values and are therefore typically qualitative or nominal scale variables. At the very least, they should be discrete quantitative variables, such as years of education above, or continuous variables that are grouped into categories.

To illustrate the process, we will use the Management variable for the columns and the Gender variable for the rows from Example 2-8. Your table should resemble that of Figure 2-19. This table shows the sum of the current salaries as indicated in the upper left hand corner. This is not usually what we want to show. If you double click the area that says "Sum of Current Sal" in that title you will see a list of available options, including one for the average value. Select the average to show the average values in the main table. You will now have a table of average salaries classified by gender and whether or not employees are management personnel. You will likely also want to further format the table to make it look better. You can use the normal formatting options to format the table entries as currency for example, and you will likely want to enter the appropriate text in the relevant cells instead of the 0's and 1's now given in the row and column headers. With a little formatting you should end up with a table like that shown in Figure 2-20.

Figure 2-19   ***Rough Unfinished Pivot Table***

	A	B	C	D	E
1		Drop Page Fields Here			
2					
3	Sum of CurrentSal	Management ▾			
4	Gender ▾	0	1	Grand Total	
5	0	1186700	810980	1997680	
6	1	2849520	141060	2990580	
7	Grand Total	4036220	952040	4988260	
8					
9					

Figure 2-20   ***Final Pivot Table for Example 2-8***

2				
3	Average of CurrentSal	Management ▾		
4	Gender ▾	Nonmanagemen	Management	Grand Total
5	Male	$ 53,940.91	$ 81,098.00	$ 62,427.50
6	Female	$ 48,296.95	$ 70,530.00	$ 49,025.90
7	Grand Total	$ 49,829.88	$ 79,336.67	$ 53,637.20
8				
9				

From this table, you can see that males make more on average than females and that management personnel makes more than non-management employees. You can also see that males make more than females in both management and non-management categories.

Pivot tables are an extremely useful tool for summarizing data in Excel. You can also add multiple variables in the rows or in the columns. In Excel versions prior to 2007, you can "pivot" the table by dragging a variable name and moving it to another section. For example, if you drag the Management variable down to the row section, then both Gender and Management will appear in the rows and there will be only one column. If you then drag the Gender variable to the columns section you will effectively transpose the pivot table so that the columns are defined by Gender and the rows by Management. To do this in versions of Excel 2007 or later you will have to set the option for the classic pivot table layout. Select Options from the Options tab of the Pivot Table section of the ribbon. Select the Display tab of the dialog and check the box labeled "Classic Pivot Table Layout" (enables dragging of fields in the grid). Experiment with the pivot table until you get more comfortable with its operation. Make liberal use of the Help feature to assist you in learning how the pivot table operates.

We could easily turn our pivot table in Figure 2-20 into a contingency table by double clicking on the title "Average of Current Sal" and changing the average to the Count function.

Using Excel and XLDataAnalyst to Display Data

Using Excel

Microsoft Excel can produce a wide variety of charts and graphs and, in fact, its charting capabilities have long been one of the noted strengths of the software. We will discuss two different tools in Excel for producing frequency distributions, charts and graphs.

The Histogram Tool

The histogram tool is part of the Data Analysis Toolpak with Excel and can produce frequency distributions, histograms, and ogives. In the Data tab of the ribbon select Data Analysis and then select Histogram from the resulting list of techniques[6]. The dialog box in Figure 2-21 will then appear on the screen.[7] P You must specify the Input Range for the data either by entering the address of the range in the dialog box (in this case B1:B41) or by using the mouse to highlight the range in the spreadsheet. You can specify the class intervals and widths to use for the frequency distribution or you can let Excel formulate the intervals. If you specify the intervals yourself you must enter the Bin Range in the appropriate box. The bin range should specify the upper limit of the class interval for each class. Excel uses the square root rule noted earlier to determine the class intervals, if you do not specify them. You can also specify where the output is to be placed by specifying the appropriate output options. The default is to place the output on a new worksheet.

The histogram tool will automatically create a frequency distribution. Checking the box labeled Chart Output will also produce a histogram. Selecting the box labeled Cumulative Percentage will create an ogive for the data.

Figure 2-21   *Histogram Tool Dialog Box*

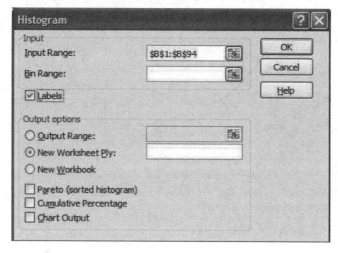

Example 2-9

Use the Histogram tool of the Data Analysis Toolpak to formulate a histogram describing the current earnings per share (EPSC) of the utility, transportation, and retail firms included in the Corporate Statistical Database of Appendix A.

---

[6] In versions of Excel prior to 2007 Select Tools—Data Analysis from the Excel menu and then select Histogram from the list of techniques in the Data Analysis dialog box.

[7] This assumes that the Data Analysis Toolpak has been loaded as an add-in. See the discussion of this tool in Chapter 1 for details.

Solution

The relevant data are provided below. Enter this data in a single column in an Excel worksheet with an appropriate header in the first row. You may also want to create another column with an identifier for the company. Part of an example worksheet is given in Figure 2-22. The data are also contained in the file Example 2-9.xlsx.

4.04	3.13	2.98	2.21	1.92	2.26	1.95	2.35	4.30	2.20	2.15	2.30	3.42
4.25	4.60	3.20	2.95	5.85	2.55	3.21	4.00	1.45	5.00	2.70	3.70	2.15
0.81	1.25	6.90	2.00	2.30	0.95	2.00	4.95	6.20	4.10	2.65	2.25	5.00

Using the Histogram tool and letting Excel chose the class intervals results in the output shown in Figure 2-23. Excel divides the data into 6 class intervals with the upper interval being open ended. If you would prefer more natural intervals that end in even numbers you will need to specify your own class intervals in the Histogram dialog. You may also notice that the resulting histogram has gaps between the bars. This is typical of bar charts produced by Excel but histograms usually do not have such gaps in them. To eliminate the gaps in the chart right click on one of the bars of the chart and select Format Data Series from the menu. Select the Series Options tab from the resulting dialog and set the Gap Width to 0. This will result in a more traditional chart with the gaps eliminated. You might also want to enlarge the chart to get a clearer picture of the data.

Figure 2-22 Excel Worksheet With Data for Example 2-9

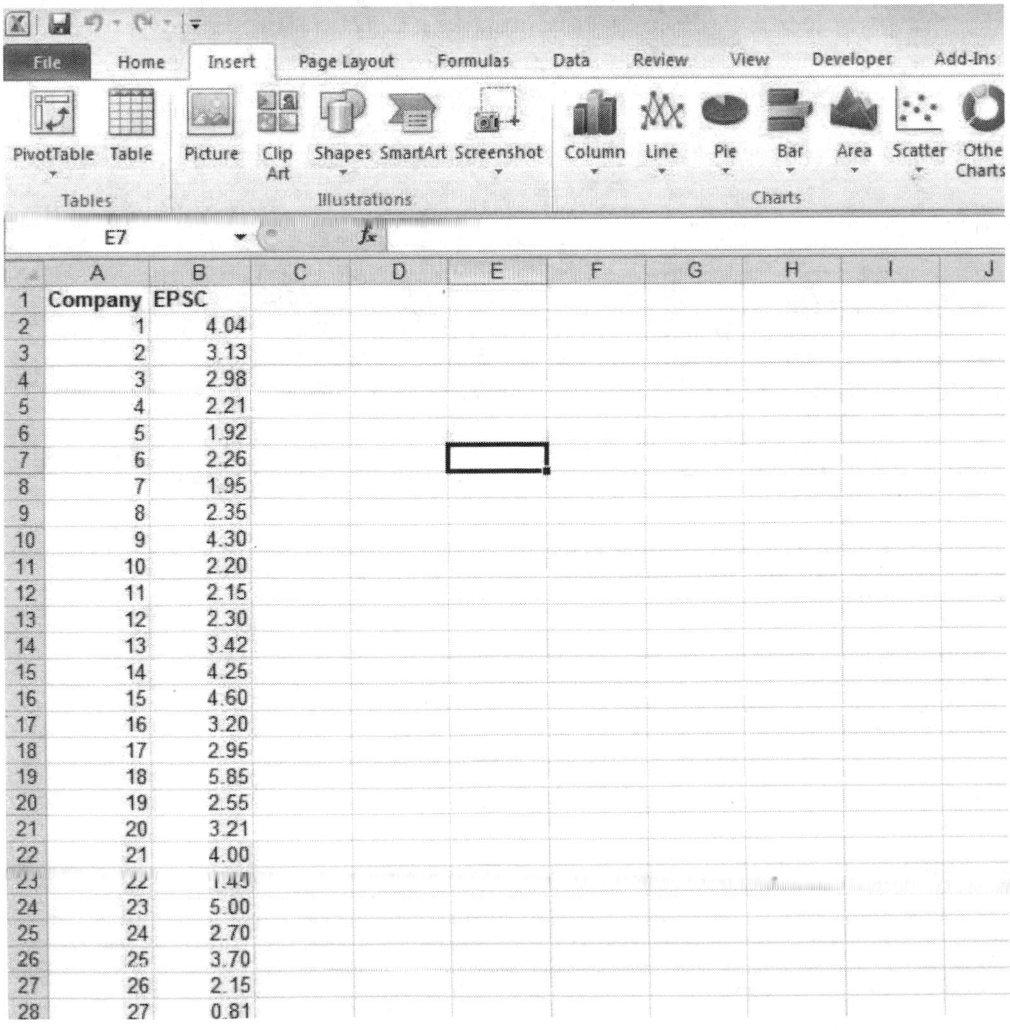

	A	B
1	Company	EPSC
2	1	4.04
3	2	3.13
4	3	2.98
5	4	2.21
6	5	1.92
7	6	2.26
8	7	1.95
9	8	2.35
10	9	4.30
11	10	2.20
12	11	2.15
13	12	2.30
14	13	3.42
15	14	4.25
16	15	4.60
17	16	3.20
18	17	2.95
19	18	5.85
20	19	2.55
21	20	3.21
22	21	4.00
23	22	1.45
24	23	5.00
25	24	2.70
26	25	3.70
27	26	2.15
28	27	0.81

Figure 2-23   ***Output from the Histogram Tool***

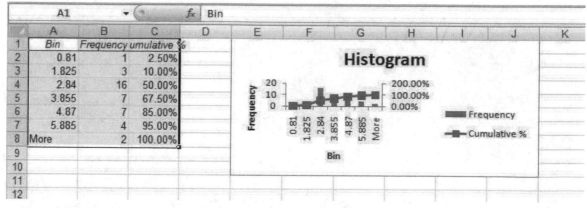

Excel Chart Tools

We have discussed a variety of charts in this chapter and Excel can produce most of them using the built-in chart tools. A detailed discussion of charting in Excel is beyond the scope of this book (entire books are published on charts in Excel). We will illustrate the use of the chart tools to produce a pie chart of the accident data from Example 2-1.

First, create a worksheet with the causes of the accident in column A and the frequencies in column B. Of course, you should create headers for the data, as usual. Once the data is entered, highlight the entire range of data, including the headers, and select the Insert tab of the ribbon. Then, select Pie from the Chart group as shown in Figure 2-24 and then select the appropriate type of pie chart. The resulting output using the three dimensional option is shown in Figure 2-25.

Figure 2-24   *Chart Tools in the Insert Tab*

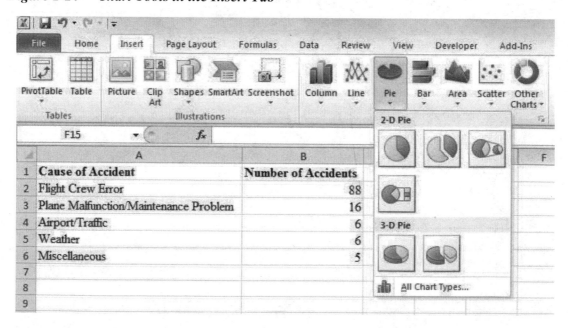

Figure 2-25   ***Pie Chart of Accident Data***

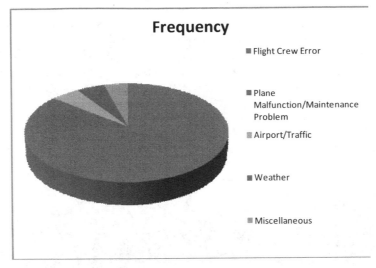

Excel can produce a variety of different charts and there are several subtypes with each type of chart. This means that many of the charts can be produced with Excel; however, you must do some preparatory work in advance. For example, you can produce histograms and ogives, but you must prepare the frequency distribution in advance. To produce an ogive, prepare the frequency distribution with the midpoints of the interval in one column of the data and the frequencies in another. Then select the Line Chart in the chart wizard to produce the ogive. Explore the "Help" function in Excel to learn more about the charting options in Excel.

The Excel Template

The Excel template for Chapter 2 is called Graphs and Charts.xlsx. This template contains four different worksheets for creating charts and graphs from raw data. The first worksheet is shown in Figure 2-26 with the data from Example 2-1.

Figure 2-26   ***The Graphs and Charts Template***

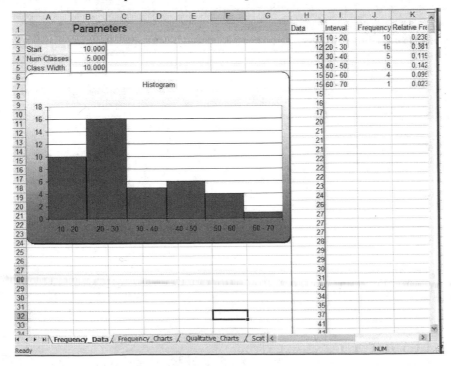

This worksheet is for frequency distributions of quantitative variables and will produce a frequency distribution and histogram of the raw data contained in Column H. Note that you also need to specify the starting value of the first interval, the number of classes and the class width in Column B before the template can produce the frequency distribution and histogram. The second worksheet produces the various charts such as frequency polygons and ogives from the data in the first worksheet. The results for our example are shown in Figure 2-27. The template produces both frequency and relative frequency histograms and polygons. It also produces an ogive of the frequencies. These charts are produced any time you enter data and set the appropriate values in the first worksheet.

Figure 2-27   Charts For Quantitative Frequency Distributions

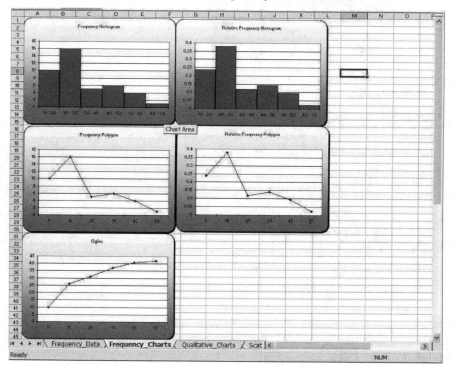

The third worksheet in the template produces bar charts and pie charts for qualitative data. To use this worksheet, simply insert the values of the qualitative variable in Column H of the worksheet and the frequencies of each category in Column I. Figure 2-28 shows this worksheet with the data from Table 2-1 entered into the worksheet.

Figure 2-28   *The Worksheet for Qualitative Charts*

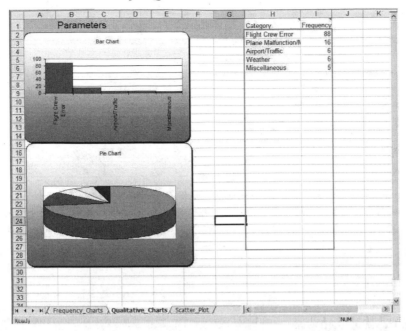

The final worksheet in the template produces scatter plots for two quantitative variables. This worksheet can utilize up to four different quantitative variables entered in columns H through K. To change the variables that are graphed enter the number of the variable (1 through 4) you want for the X-axis in Cell B3 and the number of the variable (1 through 4) for the Y-axis in cell B4. The results for two sample variables are shown in Figure 2-29.

Figure 2-29   *Worksheet for Scatter Plots*

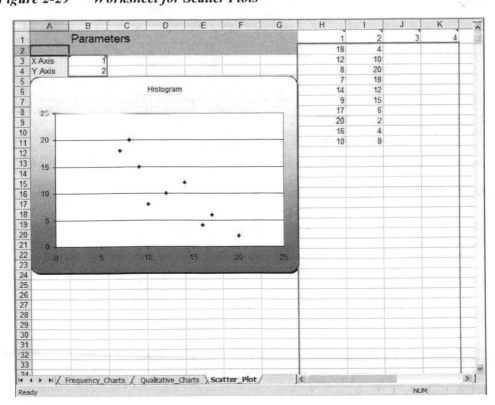

Using XLDataAnalyst

The XLDataAnalyst software is capable of producing the tables and graphs discussed in this chapter. Most of the tables described in this chapter can be produced easily with the pivot table wizard described above. The exception is the frequency distribution table for quantitative variables. This can be produced using XLDataAnalyst.

Frequency Distributions

To illustrate the creation of a frequency distribution we will consider the same data that we used in Example 2-9.

Example 2-10
Use XLDataAnalyst to formulate a frequency distribution describing the current earnings per share (EPSC) of the utility, transportation, and retail firms included in the Corporate Statistical Database of Appendix A (same data as Example 2-9).

Solution

From the XLDataAnalyst ribbon select Frequency Distribution from the Descriptive Statistics group. This will result in the dialog box shown in Figure 2-30. You first need to select the variable to be used for the frequency distribution, in this case the variable EPS. There are also options for how to set up the class intervals. The default is for the program to set the number of class intervals and interval width although you can override the default and set your own. Figure 2-31 shows the results using the default settings.

Figure 2-30   **XLDataAnalyst Dialog for a Frequency Distribution**

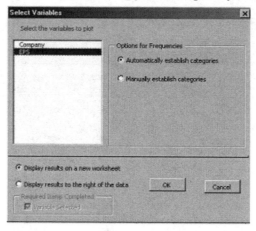

Figure 2-31   **The Frequency Distribution for Example 2-10**

Frequency Tables

EPSC

Interval	Frequency
0.75-1.75	4
1.75-2.75	16
2.75-3.75	7
3.75-4.75	7
4.75-5.75	3
5.75-6.75	2
6.75-7.75	1

Note that the beginning interval at .75 and the interval width of $1.00 was calculated automatically by the program; however, you can set the beginning interval and interval width yourself by selecting the option to manually establish the categories. You will then need to provide the necessary information yourself. One useful strategy is to first let the software select the intervals and then fine-tune the results, if need be.

Graphs and XLDataAnalyst

XLDataAnalyst can also produce most of the graphs described in this chapter. The graphic choices are all located under the Graphs menu in the Descriptive Statistics group of the XLDataAnalyst ribbon. Figure 2-32 shows the submenus of the Graphs menu. As you can see, XLDataAnalyst can produce a wide variety of graphs. Table 2-11 provides a brief description of each of these options.

Figure 2-32   *The Graphic Menu Options in XLDataAnalyst*

Table 2-11   *Graphing Options in XLDataAnalyst*

Menu Option	Type of Chart
Box Plot	Creates box plots of quantitative data
Dot Plot	Similar to histograms, but use dots. Useful for comparing groups
Frequency Polygon	Creates a frequency polygon for quantitative data
Histogram	Creates a histogram of quantitative data
Ogive	Creates a cumulative frequency polygon or ogive
Pie Chart	Creates a pie chart for qualitative data
Scatter Plot	Creates a scatter plot of two quantitative variables
Stem and Leaf	Creates a stem-and-leaf diagram of a quantitative variable
Time Series Plot	Plots a quantitative variable versus a time scale

Histograms

To produce a histogram in XLDataAnalyst select the Histograms option from the graphic menu options. You will see the same dialog as the dialog for Frequency distributions shown in Figure 2-31. The histogram for Example 2-10 is shown in Figure 2-33.

Figure 2-33   Histogram for the Data from Example 2-10

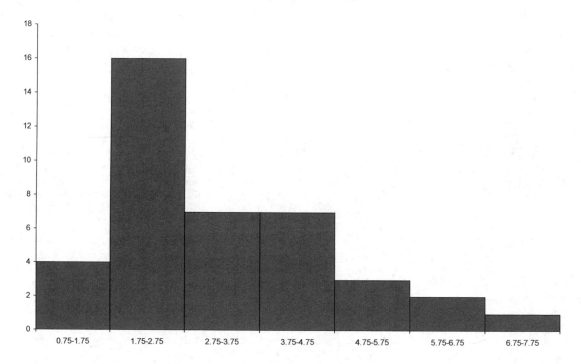

Stem-and-Leaf Diagram

Stem-and-Leaf diagrams can also be produced by XLDataAnalyst using the Stem-and-Leaf option from the graphics options shown in Figure 2-32. The resulting dialog box will ask you to select a variable to diagram. Select the EPSC variable. There is an option to force plotting of extreme values. Leave it unchecked for this example. The results are presented in Figure 2-34.

Figure 2-34   Stem-and-leaf Display of the EPSC Data

```
EPSC
Unit = 0.1
1 | 2 represents  1.2
     0     0|
     1     0|8
     3     1|03
     5     1|59
    17     2|000222233334
    (3)    2|677
    20     3|001224
    14     3|7
    13     4|001133
     7     4|6
     6     5|000
     3     5|9
     2     6|2
     1     6|
          Hi   69
```

The top portion of the output shows you how to interpret the numbers. The unit refers to the leaf and is equal to .1. Thus a 1 for the stem and a 2 for the leaf represent the value 1.2. Therefore, the smallest value in the data is 0.8 and the largest value is 6.9. Notice that the 6.9 value is printed separately from the other values since it is a very large value, e.g., a possible outlier. You can force the plotting of such extreme values by checking the appropriate box in the Stem-and-Leaf dialog box. The left column of values gives the cumulative frequency (less than) going down the column until the group that contains the middle or median value. That group is indicated by the actual group frequency in parentheses, in this case (3). Thus, the middle value is about 2.7. After the middle group this column displays the cumulative frequency in a greater than direction.

XLDataAnalyst also has easy-to-use options for constructing frequency polygons and ogives along with a variety of other graphic options. Explore the various submenus under the Graphs menu by creating different kinds of graphs using the dataset created in Example 2-9 and other data from this chapter.

Exercises V

25. Using the data from Example 2-8 create a pivot table for average age classified by Gender and Health, the health plan variable. What conclusions can you draw from this table?

26. Using the data from Example 2-8 create a pivot table for the average beginning salary classified by Gender and Management. What conclusions can you draw from this table?

27. A government banking committee is concerned about the effect of uninsured bank failures upon the elderly. In an effort to better identify the age distribution of customers, examiners have randomly selected 60 accounts from failed savings and loan institutions (S & L's) and recorded the ages of customers. The data are contained in the file Exercise 2-27.xlsx.

    (a) Develop a frequency distribution for the customer ages. Where do they seem to be concentrated? About how old is the average customer?

    (b) Develop a stem-and-leaf plot of the data. Where does the middle value fall?

28. Management of the Yokes Fresh Market supermarket chain have recently been advised by a consultant that excessive time spent waiting in line is the number one reason that customers give for changing from one supermarket to another. The managers have hired you to monitor wait times at random times in a randomly selected number of their supermarkets. You gather data on wait times for 100 different shoppers and that data are contained in the file Exercise 2-28.

    (a) Develop a frequency distribution, histogram and ogive for this data.

    (b) What can you say about the distribution of wait times for Yokes customers?

    (c) Develop a stem-and-leaf plot of the data. Does this change your answer to part b?

29. The Association of Realtors in Hidden Lakes has conducted a survey of 50 local homeowners. One of the questions asked was how far would interest rates (in percentage points) have to drop before you would consider refinancing your house. They also asked the residents to indicate how many bedrooms their current house had and the assessed value of the house. The data from the survey are contained in the file Exercise 2-29.xlsx.

    (a) Construct a frequency polygon of the assessed value.

(b)   Where do the assessed values seem to be concentrated?

(c)   Draw a pie chart of the number of bedrooms in the survey. What is the most common number of bedrooms?

(d)   Develop a stem-and-leaf plot of the indicated interest rate values? What can you deduce from this plot?

30.   You have recently read an article that discussed possible labor shortages in the years ahead as the "baby boomers" near retirement age. As manager of a large department store this got you thinking about your employees and their characteristics. The next day you have your assistant extract information on your employees from the corporate database. You request information on age, department, whether they are hourly or salary, and total salary for the recently completed fiscal year. Your assistant returns with the data given in the file Exercise 2-30.

(a)   Construct a frequency polygon of the age and salary data. What impressions can you derive from these graphs?

(b)   Construct a pie chart of the employees by department. Which department has the largest number of employees?

(c)   Construct a stem-and-leaf diagram of the age data. What percentage of your employees are currently 50 years or older?

Opening Vignette Revisited

Sarah recognizes that the data her assistant gave her is not in an appropriate format to analyze with Excel or XLDataAnalyst since it is not a proper list structure. Sarah rearranges the data into two columns, one for customer number and the other for age. The resulting data are contained in the file Chapter 2 Vignette.xlsx. After rearranging the data, Sarah decides first to use XLDataAnalyst to develop a histogram (shown below). Sarah suspects that the customers at First Inland Northwest are somewhat older than the 35 years reported, as most of the ages are above 35. It appears that more than half of the ages at FIN are above 35.5 years. Based on this information, Sarah decides to bring the topic up at the next board meeting so the bank can begin to devise a strategy to appeal to younger customers. She can use the histogram in her report so that the board can better understand the situation.

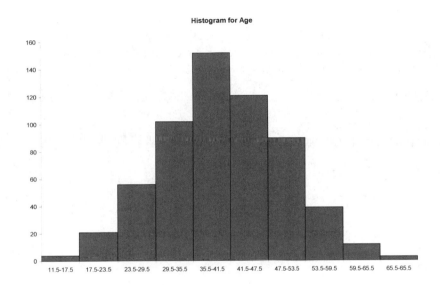

Summary

Data are numbers that are classified by type, size (amount), time, or place, and by the scale of measurement: nominal, ordinal, interval or ratio. Discrete data are countable, whereas continuous data are measurable. Frequency distributions are among the most important tabular devices for summarizing or presenting qualitative data. A frequency distribution shows the number of data points that were observed in each category of a qualitative variable. Frequency distributions can also be used with quantitative data but the quantitative variable has to first be divided into mutually exclusive classes.

Graphs and charts provide a more visual interpretation of data. Qualitative data are typically presented in bar or pie charts. Quantitative data can be presented in histograms or frequency polygons. Cumulative graphs (or ogives) are also useful for showing the number (or proportion) of observations that are greater than or less than designated class boundaries.

Stem-and-Leaf diagrams are similar to histograms, but do not lose the original information as with frequency distributions and histograms. Dot plots are similar in that the original values are retained, but are more useful for comparing different groups of data.

Relationships between variables can be explored by using scatter plots or diagrams for interval and ratio data, or contingency tables for nominal and ordinal data. Computer software, such as Excel and XLDataAnalyst is available to analyze raw data and print virtually any form of chart or graph used in business. These include area charts, bar graphs, column charts, line graphs, and pie charts.

Chapter Glossary

Bar Chart	A graphical display of quantitative information or counts where each bar of the chart represents a value of a categorical (nominal or ordinal scale) variable or a quantitative variable divided into classes.
Class Interval	The width of a class in a frequency distribution; the difference between the upper and lower limits of the class.
Class Midpoint	The middle of a class in a frequency distribution; the average of the upper and lower limits of the class.
Contingency Table	A table of counts or frequencies where the rows and columns of the table are categorical or nominal scale variables.
Continuous Variable	A variable that can take on any value within a range of values. These variables can typically take on fractional values.
Cumulative Frequency Distribution	A frequency distribution where the count or percentage for each class is the total number of observations (or relative percentage) in that class or lower. The count for the last class must be the total number of observations or 1.0 for a relative cumulative frequency distribution.
Discrete Variable	A variable that can only assume certain values. Discrete variables are usually integer values such as counts.
Dot Plot	A plot of all of the observations in a set of data where each dot is plotted above the numerical value on the horizontal axis.
Frequency Distribution	A table of counts for a quantitative variable where the variable is divided into numerical classes.
Frequency Polygon	A line chart of the same data contained in a histogram. The frequencies for each class are represented by a point above the midpoint for that class and these points are connected by lines.
Histogram	A vertical bar chart of a frequency distribution where the height of the bar represents a count or relative frequency and the horizontal axis represents the classes of the quantitative variable.
Ogive	A cumulative frequency polygon.
Pie Chart	Circular charts of count or frequency data where the area of a slice represents the relative proportion of that category of the total.
Pivot Table	Special tables produced in Excel that summarize data classified by different qualitative variables.
Stem-and-Leaf Display	Display of all of the observations of a set of data in a graph where the stem represents the significant digits of the number and the leaf represents the last digit.

Real Class Limits	The values actually used to classify the variable into classes for a frequency distribution. Also called class boundaries.
Relative Frequency Distribution	A frequency distribution where the counts are divided by the total number of frequencies to represent the proportion of observations in each class.
Scatter Plot	A plot of each paired observation for two quantitative variables where one quantitative variable is represented on the X-axis and the other on the Y-axis; used to explore the relationship between two quantitative variables; also called scatter diagrams.
Variable	An attribute that can take on different values so that it can vary from one observation to the next.

Questions and Problems

31. Compare or contrast (a) a histogram versus a frequency polygon; (b) a bar chart versus a histogram; (c) a bar chart versus a pie chart.

32. The following data show the amounts of money ($ billions) given by four charitable sectors over the five consecutive years prior to 2012: by individuals ($217.79, 211.77, 227.41, 229.3, 229.03), by foundations ($41.67, 41.00, 38.44, 41.2, 38.52), by corporations ($14.55, 15.29, 14.1, 14.5, 15.69), and by bequest ($24.41, 22.83, 23.8, 22.7, 23.15).

    (a) Arrange the data in a statistical table with time on the horizontal scale. Add an additional row to show the total charitable gifts for each year.

    (b) Compute the percentage change for each category over the five-year period and compare the pattern (trend) in donations from individuals and corporations.

    (*Source*: Data from reports from the *Giving USA* annual surveys http://www.givingusareports.org/)

33. The following represents the amount of money ($ billions) given to the listed charity sectors by individuals, corporations, and other sources for two consecutive years where P = previous year, and C = current year: religion (P = 48.1, C = 54.3), education (P = 10.2, C = 10.7), health (P = 9.8, C = 10.0), human services (P = 10.5, C = 11.4), arts/culture (P = 6.8, C = 7.5), public benefit (P = 3.2, C = 3.6), other (P = 15.5, C = 17.2).

    (a) Prepare a table of these data showing the charity sector on the vertical dimension and a chronological classification on the horizontal scale. Arrange the vertical classification in alphabetical order and include two additional columns to show the actual billion-dollar change in giving, and the percent change over the one-year period.

    (b) Which charity sector had the largest dollar increase?

    (c) Which two charity sectors had the smallest percentage increases?

    (d) What percent of the total money was given to the combined category of health and human services in the current year?

34. Following are U.S. Census Bureau estimates of selected state populations by age group (data in thousands of people with ages reported to last birthday)

	< 5 yr	5-17	18-24	25-44	45-64	> 64
Maine	82	225	142	328	220	149
Mississippi	226	573	336	697	451	303
Wyoming	53	107	63	168	83	40
Hawaii	89	195	142	324	185	89

    (a) Construct a *histogram* showing the Maine population.

    (b) Construct a *frequency polygon* showing the Mississippi population?

    (c) Construct an *ogive* showing the number of people "greater than" a given age in the state of Hawaii.

    (d) Construct *some form of chart* that will highlight any proportional differences in the different age groups for Maine and Wyoming

35. The data below represent the weights (pounds) of boxes of canned goods collected for a food bank by a service club in their Christmas drive.

Interval	Frequency
10—19	6
20—29	18
30—39	20
40—49	14
50—59	12
60—69	6
70—79	4
Total	80

(a) Are the data discrete or continuous?

(b) Were the observations (e.g., weight measurements) most likely made to the nearest one-tenth of a pound? How do you know?

(c) How many class intervals were used to present these data?

(d) What is the size of the class intervals?

(e) What are the stated class limits of the interval having the highest frequency?

36. Use the data from Problem 35 to prepare the following graphs: (a) a histogram; (b) a frequency polygon; (c) an ogive.

37. Use the data from Problem 35 to prepare:

(a) A relative frequency distribution.

(b) An ogive showing absolute values of $F > LCB$.

(c) Add a relative scale on the right of your distribution in part (b).

(d) Find the X values exceeded by 25%, 50%, and 75% of the observations. What are these values called?

(e) What is the ordinate (Y-value) of your ogive at 29.5 on the X scale?

38. Using the last five columns of data from Example 2-2, (a) construct an ordered list, and (b) construct a stem-and-leaf display of these data.

39. For the last two rows of raw data in Exercise 8, (a) estimate the middle point or median value (before you do any data summarization), and (b) form a stem-and-leaf display with the data in an ascending order. (c) Which value represents the median point?

40. A survey of 30 economists from banks, brokerage institutions, and universities yielded the following forecast of interest rates one year into the future (The data are also in file Exercise 2-40).

4.49	4.86	4.00	4.72	5.09	5.23	4.31	3.55	3.77	4.42
4.06	5.08	3.35	4.87	5.36	3.61	4.87	4.42	4.19	4.54

3.80   3.99   3.90   4.23   3.30   4.88   3.59   4.01   4.16   3.47

(a) Present the data in the form of a stem-and-leaf display, with each stem representing one-half percentage point.

(b) What does your diagram suggest about the extent of agreement among the economists?

41. Using the data from Exercise 8 that is contained in the file Exercise 2-8.xlsx:

(a) Use XLDataAnalyst to develop a frequency distribution.

(b) Which class interval has the largest frequency?

(c) Construct a stem-and-leaf display of the data. What is the middle value approximately?

42. A cellular phone company wants to know how long their customers tend to talk during each call. They gather data on 100 calls which are contained in the file Exercise 2-42.xlsx.

(a) Use XLDataAnalyst to develop a frequency distribution from the data.

(b) Approximately what is the average call length?

43. Using the data from Exercise 17 that is contained in the file Exercise 2-17:

(a) Use XLDataAnalyst to develop a frequency distribution.

(b) Which class interval has the largest frequency?

(c) Construct a stem-and-leaf display of the data. What is the middle value approximately?

44. Who are the major consumers of soft drinks? The results of a study by MRCA Information Services as reported in *The Wall Street Journal* (Dec. 9, 1988, p. B1) are as follows. Data show the age group, followed by the percentage of total soft drink consumption (in parentheses): 1 to 5 years (6.5%), 6 to 12 years (9.3%), 13 to 17 years (6.4%), 18 to 34 years (25.4%), 35 to 54 years (28.4%), 55 to 64 years (12.7%), and 65 years and over (11.2%).

(a) Use Excel to prepare a pie chart or a column chart to illustrate the data.

(b) Comment on the age classification system used to present these data.

(c) Do the data suggest that people in the 35 to 54 age group consume more soft drinks per capita than people in other age groups?

45. Use Excel or XLDataAnalyst to develop a histogram describing the interest rate estimates of the economists provided in Exercise 40.

46. Use XLDataAnalyst to develop a stem-and-leaf diagram describing the interest rate estimates of the economists given in Exercise 40.

Database Problems

Corporate Statistical Database

47. Construct a frequency distribution of the years of operation data using an interval width of 10 years. Start with the class 0 < 10.

(a) How many class intervals result?

(b) Which class interval includes the most number of companies?

(c) How many of the companies have been in operation for 50 years or more?

(d) Using the same data, reconstruct the frequency distribution using an interval width of 20 years. Now, how many class intervals result using such an interval width?

(e) Suppose that you wished to determine the number of companies that had been in operation for 50 years or more from this new distribution. What problem do you encounter?

(f) What generalization concerning the number of classes versus the amount of information can you draw from this comparison?

48. Construct a dot plot of years of operation by industry code. What conclusions can you draw from this graph?

49. Construct a scatter plot price per share on the Y-axis and annual dividend on the X-axis. What can you say about the relationship between these two variables?

50. Construct the following graphs for the number of employees: (1) a *histogram*, (2) a *frequency polygon*, (3) an *ogive*, and (4) a *stem-and-leaf diagram*.

51. Construct a *pie chart* showing the proportion of firms in the various industry classifications (e.g., banking, chemical, electrical, retail, transportation, and utility).

MegaCorp Employee Survey Database

52. Construct a histogram for the following variables (a) employee salaries (b) age

53. Construct a dot plot of salaries by gender. What can you say about the salary structure at Megacorp?

54. Construct the following graphs for salaries: (1) a *histogram*, (2) a *frequency polygon*, (3) an *ogive*, and (4) a *stem-and-leaf diagram*.

55. Construct a scatter plot current salary on the Y-axis and years with the company on the X-axis. What can you say about the relationship between these two variables?

56. Construct a pie chart showing the proportion of employees in the different subsidiaries.

57. Construct a contingency table of management level by gender. What does this table tell you about the company?

Alaska Sport Fishing Survey

58. Construct a histogram for the following variables: (a) number of fishing trips taken to Alaska, (b) amount spent on the last fishing trip to Alaska.

59. Construct a dot plot of amount spent by gender. Can you draw any inferences from this plot?

60. Construct the following graphs for amount spent on the last trip: (1) a *histogram*, (2) a *frequency polygon*, (3) an *ogive*, and (4) a *stem-and-leaf diagram*.

61. Construct a scatter plot with amount spent on the X-axis and number of trips on the Y-axis. What can you say about the relationship between these two variables?

62. Construct a pie chart showing the proportion of respondents in the different education levels.

63. Construct a contingency table of where the respondent stayed by gender. Can you draw any conclusions from this table?

Chapter 3:
Summary Measures of Data

Opening Vignette
Introduction
Measures of Central Tendency
- Arithmetic Mean and Weighted Mean
- Median
- Quartiles and Percentiles
- Mode
- Other Special-Purpose Measures
- Box Plots (Box and Whisker Plots)

Measures of Dispersion/Variability
- Range and Interquartile Range
- Mean Absolute Deviation
- Variance and Standard Deviation
- The Coefficient of Variation

Interpretation and Use of the Standard Deviation
- Standard Scores
- Chebyshev's Theorem
- Empirical Rule
- Identifying Outliers

Shapes of Distributions: Skewness
> *Practice*

Finding Numerical Measures in Excel and XLDataAnalyst
- Excel Functions
- The Analysis Toolpak
- The Excel Template
- Summary Measures in XLDataAnalyst

Opening Vignette Revisited
Summary
Chapter Glossary
Questions and Problems

Chapter 3 Objectives

When you finish this chapter you should be able to:

- Compute summary measures of central tendency
- Compute percentile measures and box plots for the graphical description of data
- Understand the concept of variability and develop the summary measures of variability
- Understand the key role of the standard deviation as a measure of variability
- Understand standard scores, Chebyshev's theorem, and the Empirical Rule as they relate to a set of observations
- Describe the shape of a distribution of values and measures of shape
- Use Excel and XLDataAnalyst to compute these summary measures

Opening Vignette

Sue Myers is a recently hired accountant for B&B Distributing, a local beer and wine distributor. The distributor is attempting to borrow money from Bonanza Bank and the bank has asked for information on the firm's accounts receivable. Managers at the bank are concerned that bills may not be paid in a timely fashion thereby creating cash flow problems for the distributor that may impact their ability to pay on the loan. Sue's boss, Mike Mason, assured the bank that, on average, B&B's invoices were paid within 10 days, but the bank would like some hard data to support that claim. Sue asked her assistant, Bob Young, for information on accounts receivable so Bob provided Sue the below graph of accounts receivables from a recent budget presentation. What inferences can you draw from this graph? Are Mike Mason's assurances to the bank correct? Will this convince the loan officers at the bank?

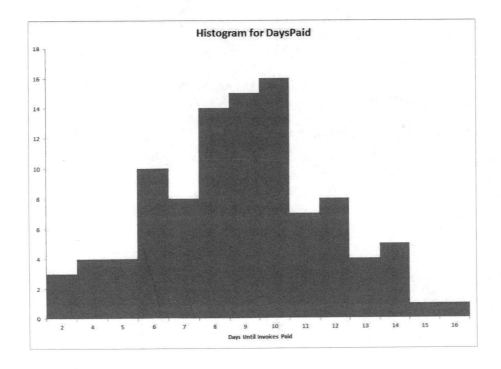

Introduction

The news bombards us every day with data. Fortunately, many of the statistics we get are already summarized in one way or another, making them easier to understand. Often, statistics are in the form of numerical values that are even more condensed than the tables and graphs we worked with in Chapter 2. In this chapter, we will study numerical measures including: (1) measures of location (or central tendency), (2) measures of ranks or percentiles, (3) measures of dispersion/variability, (4) box plots (which give us a graphical representation of location and dispersion), and (5) measures of shape (that tell us about how the data values are arranged around the central tendency). We will also discuss why standard deviation is so important as a measure of dispersion/variability. These summary measures are not conceptually difficult and Excel and XLDataAnalyst can very quickly extract these measures from a set of data; however, it is important to be aware of the underlying measurement scale of the given data (nominal, ordinal, interval or ratio) when calculating summary measures. Certain operations, such as addition and subtraction, are not appropriate for nominal and ordinal scales and therefore summary measures that utilize these operations are not meaningful for these scale types. At the end of this chapter, you should feel comfortable working with any of these measures and know when it is appropriate to use them.

Measures of Central Tendency

Measures of central tendency develop numbers that describe the typical value (or location) of a variable. These measures result in values around which the other observations tend to be clustered. Recall the introductory scenario with Sue and B&B Distributing where Sue had her assistant develop data based on the accounts receivables for the company. The data that he developed were measures of central tendency. The company was looking for a "typical" or average value for the number of days it took to receive payment. We will now discuss how to calculate such a value.

Arithmetic Mean

The *arithmetic mean* is the most widely used and important of all statistical averages. In fact, the words "average" or "mean" usually refer to the arithmetic mean unless stated otherwise. The arithmetic mean is calculated summing all the individual values of the variable (X), and dividing by the total number of observations. If the data are from a sample of size n, the equation for the sample mean, $\overline{X}$ (pronounced x bar) is:

$$\overline{X} = \frac{X_1 + X_2 + X_3 + \cdots X_n}{n}$$

which means to find the sum of the values of X_1 to X_n and divide by n. We will shorten this to:

$$\overline{X} = \frac{\sum X}{n} \tag{3-1}$$

When using population data, the definition of the population mean is similar to that of the sample. If the X values constitute a population of size N, the population mean is designated as μ (pronounced mu):

$$\mu = \frac{\sum X}{N} \tag{3-2}$$

Example 3-1

Computer Graphics Ltd. has 300 sales representatives in England. The numbers of sales calls made by a sample of five representatives last week were 12, 4, 9, 0, and 5. What is the mean number of calls made?

Solution

The sum of all of the X values (our numerator) is 30. Our total sample size is 5. Because this is a sample, we designate the mean as $\bar{X}$:

$$\bar{X} = \frac{\Sigma X}{n} = \frac{30}{5} = 6 \text{ calls}$$

The mean is the central or middle value in the sense that it represents the balance point around which the observations are centered as illustrated in Figure 3-1 below. As a point of balance, the sum of the deviations of the points away from the mean in the positive and negative directions offset each other. Referring to Example 3-1:

Negative Deviations	Positive Deviations
$(0-6) + (4-6) + (5-6)$	$(9-6) + (12-6)$
- 9	+ 9

Stated another way, **the sum of the deviations of each of the values away from the mean is <u>always</u> <u>zero</u>** for any set of numbers:

$$\Sigma(X - \bar{X}) = 0 \text{ and } \Sigma(X - \mu) = 0$$

Figure 3-1   Mean As A Balance Point

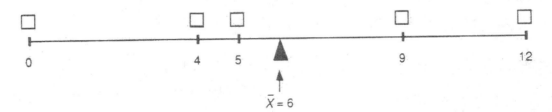

$\bar{X} = 6$

Weighted Mean

The arithmetic mean automatically assigns equal weight to each observation; however, in some instances, we may wish to assign different weights to different values by a measure of their individual importance. This is called the weighted mean. Grade point averages (GPAs) are a good example of weighted averages. In the calculation of grade point averages, the letter grades (A, B, C, D) are assigned points (4.0, 3.0, 2.0, 1.0 respectively) and the grade points are then weighted by the number of credit hours to calculate the grade point average.

The weighted mean is calculated by multiplying the individual values (X) by their assigned weight (w) and dividing it by the total sum of the weights:

$$\bar{X}_w = \frac{\Sigma wX}{\Sigma w} \tag{3-3}$$

Example 3-2

A student received the following semester grades. All were 3-credit-hour courses except statistics (4 credits) and P.E. (1 credit). Compute the student's GPA for the term given the following weights: A = 4, B = 3, C = 2, and D = 1

English	B
Logic	A
Statistics	A
Psychology	B
History	C
P.E.	A

Solution

		Value	Weight (credits)	
Course	Grade	X	W	wX
English	B	3	3	9
Logic	A	4	3	12
Statistics	A	4	4	16
Psychology	B	3	3	9
History	C	2	3	6
P.E.	A	4	1	4
Total			17 (credits)	56 (points)

$$\bar{X}_w = \frac{\sum wX}{\sum w} = \frac{56}{17} = 3.29$$

Another example of a weighted average would be calculating the average cost per item when you purchase different items with different prices at the store. In that case, you would weigh the number of items of each type purchased by their price and divide the sum by the total number of items purchased to calculate the average cost of the items. The weighted mean would then be equal to the arithmetic mean where the observations would be grouped into frequencies (e.g., a frequency distribution).

For example, suppose we purchased 4 items that cost \$2.00, 3 items that cost \$4.00 and 2 items that cost \$5.00. The weighted average would be:

$$\bar{X}_w = \frac{\sum wX}{\sum w} = \frac{(4)(2)+(3)(4)+(2)(5)}{4+3+2} = \frac{27}{9} = \$3.00$$

If we looked at the individual items and calculated the arithmetic mean, we would find the average cost per item would be:

$$\bar{X} = \frac{\sum X}{n} = \frac{2+2+2+2+4+4+4+5+5}{9} = \frac{27}{9} = \$3.00$$

In the above example, the prices per item were the weights used to calculate the weighted mean.

Median

The *median* is the value such that an equal number of data values lie above it and below it. It is typically the "halfway" point in the data when the data are sorted in numerical order, such that half of the scores will be below the median and half will be above the median. We will designate the population median with the Greek symbol η and the sample median with the letter M[1]. Calculating the position of the median in a range of values depends on whether there are an odd or even number of total values or data points:

Odd Number of Values:

To find the median for an odd number of data points, arrange the data in ascending or descending order and select the middle number; this value is the median. An equation for the position of the median in a set of n data points is:

$$\text{Position of median: } \frac{n+1}{2}$$

For example, if we were to arrange the five observations from Example 3-1 in order, we would have 0, 4, 5, 9, and 12 calls. The median is the $(n + 1)/2$ position, which is the $(5 + 1)/2$ or 3rd position. The median is therefore the third value, or 5.

Even Number of Values:

If the total number of observations is even, the median is assumed to be halfway between the two middle numbers. Suppose that there were six observations in the sample, and the array of values was 0, 4, 4, 5, 9, and 12. In that case the median would be the $(6 + 1)/2 = 3.5^{th}$ position, which would the average of the two middle numbers; therefore, a value of $(4 + 5)/2$ or 4.5.

Because the median is not based on the sum of the values of X, it is not affected by the extreme items (outliers) and at times may be a better measure of central tendency or typical value than the mean. For example, if the "12" in the previous array of values was replaced by 38, the mean would be 10. A mean of 10 may not be as good a standard for comparing performance of the salespersons as the median, which would be 4.5.

The median is also an appropriate measure of central tendency for ordinal data where a mean would not be meaningful. For ordinal data, the median and the mode (defined later) are the only measures of central tendency that have meaning.

Quartiles and Percentiles

Closely related to the median are the concepts of quartiles, deciles, and percentiles. Whereas the median is the "center" of an array of values and divides the data into two equal halves, quartiles divide the data into quarters, deciles into tenths, and percentiles into one hundredths. These measures are all special cases

---

[1] There is no standard conventional symbol for the population median; this is the symbol that will be used throughout this text.

of a more general concept called quantiles. *Quantiles* are numbers between 0 and 1 that apportion ordered data on the basis of the proportion of scores that lie above or below them. Quantiles are defined on the basis of the number of values below that quantile.

Quartiles divide data sets into four equal parts. The first quartile, Q_1, is the value below which 25% of the data points lie (and above which 75% lie). To determine Q_1, use the formula $(n+1)/4$ to find the data point's position. Next comes the median, or second quartile, Q_2, below which 50% of the data points lie. The third quartile, Q_3, is the value below which lie 75% of the data points.

Percentiles are quantiles that divide the data into 100 equal subgroups. They are most appropriate for large data sets where a simple percentage can be applied to the number of observations. For example, a survey of several hundred workers may yield earnings data that show 42% of factory workers earn less than $9.50 per hour. In that example, $9.50 would be the 42nd percentile. Similarly, 85% of the observations would be less than (or to the left of) the 85th percentile, and so on. We can find the location of any percentile with the following equation where the subscript $(_p)$ denotes a positional value:

$$L_p = (n+1)p \qquad (3-4)$$

When a small number of discrete values are involved, the percentile locations do not always coincide with a specific data point. For example, suppose that an array of data had only five observations: 6, 9, 13, 14, and 22. As this is an odd number of data values, the median (Q_2) is the value of the third observation, or 13. Q_1 should be the value of the data point in the $(n + 1)/4$, or $(5 + 1)/4 = 1.5^{th}$ position, but there is no data point in that position. For the purposes of this text we shall calculate the difference between the two closest points. In the previous example, the first and second observations were 6 and 9 with the difference between them being $9 - 6 = 3$ units. The value of the 1.5^{th} position (Q_1) would be computed by using the value of the first position (6) plus 50% of the distance between the first and second, or $.50(3) = 1.5$. Therefore, 7.5 would be the first quartile. In fact, this is the same calculation that we would use to find the median if there were an even number of values.

When using Excel to calculate quartiles, caution should be taken. The QUARTILE function can be used to approximate the interquartile range.

Example 3-3

The data set shown below represents the number of patients per day seeking care at the emergency room of a city hospital over 12 consecutive days. Find Q_1 and Q_3.

$$25 \quad 20 \quad 30 \quad 22 \quad 21 \quad 38 \quad 60 \quad 32 \quad 25 \quad 29 \quad 23 \quad 35$$

Solution

First, rearrange the 12 data points in numerical order:

$$20 \quad 21 \quad 22 \quad 23 \quad 25 \quad 25 \quad 29 \quad 30 \quad 32 \quad 35 \quad 38 \quad 60$$

Second, determine the positions of the first and third quartiles from the locational expressions:

$$Q_{1p} = (n + 1)(.25) = (13)(.25) = \qquad 3.25^{th} \text{ position}$$

$$Q_{3p} = (13)(.75) = \qquad\qquad 9.75^{th} \text{ position}$$

Third, look between the neighboring values to find the values of the quartiles. Q_1 consists of the value of the third observation plus 25% of the interval between the third and fourth:

$$Q_1 = 22 + .25(23 - 22) = 22.25 \qquad\qquad Q3 = 32 + .75(35 - 32) = 34.25$$

Quartiles

Although we cannot have 22.25 patients or 34.25 patients, we can still work with these numbers as useful descriptors of the data. Later, we will look at the difference between these two quartiles as a measure of dispersion called the interquartile range. Also note that quartiles, percentiles and deciles only utilize the order information of the data and are therefore appropriate for ordinal scale data as well as interval and ratio scale values. As in the case of median, percentiles are also very useful measures when there are extremely large or extremely small values (outliers) in the data set.

Mode

The *mode* is the most frequently occurring value(s) in a data set. A mode is simple to identify after the data have been ordered. For example, the mode of a data set consisting of 0, 4, 4, 5, 9, and 12 is 4. If this array had only one 4, it would not have a mode (we call that "no mode"). If the set had two 9s as well as two 4s, it would have two modes (we refer to it as "bimodal"). If a data set has more than two modes, we refer to it as "multimodal."

The mode is the least important of the three measures of central tendency, but it does help identify a prominent feature of a data set. For example, the modal (most commonly occurring) P/E ratio of the 100 firms in the Corporate Statistical Database (Appendix A) is 12 because the greatest number of firms (14 firms) has a P/E ratio of 12. The mode is also a useful measure for qualitative variables measured on a nominal scale. For example, the most common religious affiliation of students on a college campus, or the most popular (best-selling) brand of shoe in a shoe store would be a modal value. Typically, we use the mode for nominal scale data. As discussed earlier, mean and median are not used in such case.

Comparison of Mean, Median, and Mode

Although the mean, median, and mode are all "averages" (or typical) values, they do differ. The mean is affected by every data point and is influenced by extreme values. For example, if a set of salaries has a few extremely high values, the mean tends to be higher than the median.[2] The median, being the middle value, is not influenced by the magnitude of other data points. It may be more representative of the center of the observations, but it conveys less information than the mean and is not as useful for purposes of statistical inference; however, for ordinal data, the median is the most useful measure of central tendency. The mode is even less useful, but it does indicate where a major cluster of data lies and is the only meaningful measure for nominal scale data.

An additional consideration is the level of measurement for the data. Calculating a mean requires interval or ratio scale data. If we have data from a rating scale that we are not sure satisfies the properties of an interval scale, we should use the median as the measure of central tendency. Of course, for nominal scale data only the mode is appropriate as a measure of central tendency.

Other Special-Purpose Measures

In addition to the measures of central tendency discussed above, two special-purpose measures (harmonic mean and geometric mean) have been developed for special situations:

The *harmonic mean* is sometimes used to compute an average of quantities per unit of time when the times per unit vary. For example, if workers A, B, and C took 10, 12, and 20 minutes per unit, respectively, to assemble a product, the average assembly time *would not be* (10 + 12 + 20)/3, or 14 min./unit because the number of units produced in a given time would vary by worker. In essence, the arithmetic average would fail to account for the fact that only 10 minutes of worker A's time would be incorporated in the average, whereas 20 minutes of worker C's time would be included. This situation involves times per unit that vary from worker to worker. Harmonic mean problems can often be solved by

---

[2] A value that is far removed from the bulk of the values is known as an *outlier*. Outliers sometimes stem from recording errors, and, though noted, are not always included in graphs of the data.

restating them in a common time period, such as output per hour. For example, the output per hour of worker A is 60 minutes/hour divided by 10 minutes/unit, or 6 units/hour. Workers B and C would then be 5 and 3 units/hour, respectively. Once the data are in a more consistent format, we can calculate the workers average as $(6 + 5 + 3) \div 3$, or 4.67 units/hour. Dividing this into 60 minutes would yield the correct average of 12.86 minutes per unit.

The *geometric mean* is used to find the average rate of change in a series of percentages where the individual percentage rates are known, but there is not a common base. The geometric mean is calculated as the nth root of the product of the n values:

$$\bar{X}_G = \sqrt[n]{(X_1)(X_2)(X_3) \ldots (X_n)} \tag{3-5}$$

The geometric mean is useful for averaging growth rates such as sales or productivity.

Example 3-4

Sales of ABC Video increased 10% the first year, decreased 5% the second, increased 40% the third, and increased 20% the fourth. What is the average rate of increase?

Solution

Since each rate is based on the preceding year, the percentages do not have a common base. The 10% increase in the first year is 110% of the preceding year, so our first value in the equation is 1.10. Stating each year as a multiple of the preceding year, the geometric mean would be:

$$\bar{X}_G = \sqrt[4]{(1.10)(0.95)(1.40)(1.20)} = 1.15$$

Therefore, the average growth rate is .15 or 15%.

Recall that taking the nth root of a number is the same as raising the number to the power of $1/n$, which in the case of the example above would be to the ¼ power.

Box Plots (Box and Whisker Plots)

Whereas the mean, median, and mode are all "numbers," a more intuitive feeling for the location and concentration of data can be gained by using a graph like a box plot (also called a box and whisker plot). A *box plot* conveys the relative positions of the majority of the data by using the three quartiles (Q_1, Q_2, and Q_3). The graphic representation of a box plot is illustrated in Figure 3-2. All box plots base the sides of the "box" on quartiles Q_1 and Q_3 making the box encompass 50% of the data. In Figure 3-2, the first quartile is close to 20 and the third quartile is at roughly 60. Therefore, 50% of the values are between 20 and 60. The median is usually represented as a vertical line within the box and sometimes the mean is represented by a dot within the box. In the previous figure, the median is close to 35 and the mean is not pictured.

Figure 3-2   *Example Box Plot*

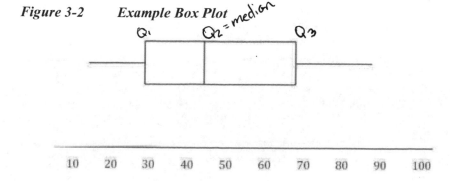

The major differences in approaches of these graphs relate to the placement of the "whiskers." Some draw a line from the box to the minimum and maximum values for the whiskers. This has the advantage of directly indicating the range of the values; however, this approach also means that extremely large or small values (or *outliers*) cannot be readily identified in the data. A second approach is to calculate *upper* and *lower fences* which are calculated as follows:

$$\text{Lower Fence} = Q_1 - 1.5*(Q_3 - Q_1) \tag{3-6}$$

$$\text{Upper Fence} = Q_3 + 1.5*(Q_3 - Q_1)$$

The smallest value in the data greater than the lower fence and the largest value less than the upper fence are called *adjacent values*. In the box plot, the whiskers connect the box with the upper and lower adjacent values. Outliers are then defined as values outside the upper and lower fences and are usually plotted as small boxes or points beyond the whiskers.

Example 3-5

Use a box plot to illustrate the emergency room patient data points of Example 3-3 (repeated below):

20   21   22   23   25   25   29   30   32   35   38   60

Solution

The median of these 12 values is the average of the 6th and 7th values or:

$$\text{Median} = (25+29)/2 = 27$$

The first and third quartiles we calculated earlier were:

$$Q_1 = 22.25 \text{ and } Q_3 = 34.25$$

The interquartile range (or the difference between the third and the first quartile) is $Q_3 - Q_1 = 34.25 - 22.25 = 12$. The upper and lower fences are then:

$$\text{Lower Fence} = Q_1 - 1.5*(Q_3 - Q_1) = 22.25 - 1.5*(12) = 4.25$$

$$\text{Upper Fence} = Q_3 + 1.5*(Q_3 - Q_1) = 34.25 + 1.5*(12) = 52.25$$

The lowest adjacent value is the value just above the lower fence, or in this case 20, the minimum value in the data set. This will always be true if there are no outliers on the lower end. The upper adjacent value is the largest value less than or equal to the upper fence, or in this case 38. This is not the maximum value so there is one outlier, in this case 60. The box plot for this example is shown in Figure 3-3.

Figure 3-3   Box Plot of Hospital Emergency Room Patient Load per Days

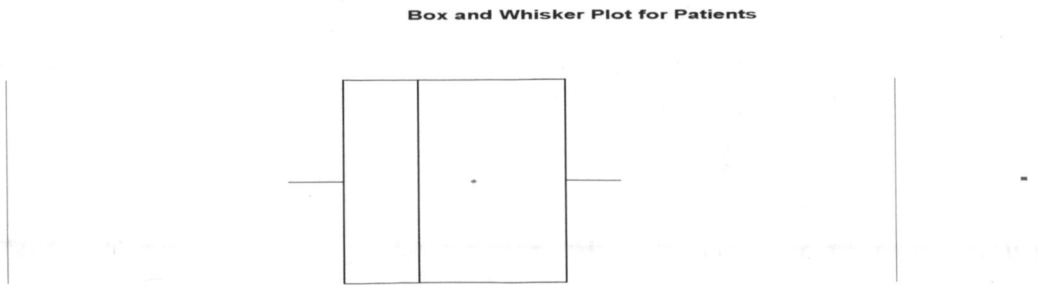

Box and Whisker Plot for Patients

Box plots can provide useful insights about the distribution of data points. The box plot in Example 3-5 suggests that although the number of emergency cases ranges from a low of 20 to a high of 60, about 50% of the time the hospital can reasonably expect between about 22.25 and 34.25 (22 and 34/35) patients. The data points are more concentrated at the low end of the scale (e.g., fewer emergency patients) and are not symmetrically distributed around the median of 27 patients. There is one outlier (60 patients in one day). The analyst would want to investigate further and determine the cause of this unusually large value. Something outside the ordinary may have occurred on that particular day.

Exercises I

1. What type of average would be most appropriate for determining (a) the average income of employees of Sacred Heart Hospital; (b) a course grade where projects count 15%, quizzes 30%, and exams 55%; (c) the average growth rate in productivity over a five-year period?

2. A telephone service technician installed the following number of phones on successive days: 4, 7, 5, 8, 5, 6, 3, 6, 4 and 5. Find the (a) mean, (b) median, and (c) mode.

3. A group of recent marketing graduates from a small liberal arts university have jobs ranging from selling shoes at $18,000/yr. to playing professional basketball at $1.5 million/yr. Current salaries for the 22 graduates are (in $000): 24, 20, 32, 36, 18, 28, 42, 37, 20, 27, 52, 31, 45, 33, 20, 1500, 23, 38, 27, 31, 36, 40.

    (a) What is the mean salary for these graduates?
    (b) Suppose the university wished to publish a brochure for prospective students, and include some indication of the average salary of recent graduates in various disciplines. Compute the average that best represents the central tendency of the data on marketing graduates.
    (c) Explain your choice of one average over other averages for the data.

4. A study of 10 managers in two comparably-sized firms revealed the following number of years of within-company experience:

U.S. firm	10	6	7	24	5	43	6	46	2	3
Japanese firm	9	22	16	26	34	11	20	14	4	16

    (a) Compute the mean, median, and mode of both sets of data.

    (b) Compute the first and third quartiles for both sets of data.

    (c) Compare the two sets of data and summarize your conclusions.

    (d) Prepare a box plot for the Japanese firm's data set. What implication does the plot suggest about the long-run viability of managerial talent in this firm?

5. Evergreen Nursery purchased 1,100 fruit trees from an Iowa supplier at the costs shown below. Find the (weighted) average cost per tree:

Date	No. Trees	Cost per Tree	Invoice Cost
Mar. 10	200	$5.00	$1,000
Apr. 12	500	4.00	2,000
May 17	100	6.00	600
Oct. 30	300	4.50	1,350

6. As a professor of Business at the State University, you have an annual policy of awarding the top 27% of your students with a gift card. Using data on the final student grades in your MBA finance course, determine the lowest grade that would qualify for a gift card.

Final Grades	85	87	93	84	89	86	83	95	95	84	81	86	95	83	92	83

7. The following data represents the monthly costs ($) for an 800-number service as billed by a phone company to 15 of its customers:

34	22	72	30	24	30	25	76
20	28	26	80	66	24	32	

   (a) What is the mean cost paid by 800-number customers?

   (b) Prepare a box plot of the data.

   (c) Comment on any difference in the results from parts (a) and (b).

8. As of January 1st, 2010, shareholders of Netflix (Ticker: NFLX) had experienced 3 years of significant share appreciation when shares rose 24%, 81%, and 220% respectively in 2008, 2009, and 2010; however, shares saw a net decrease of 61% in 2011, following a management decision to increase subscription fees. What is the average percent change in share price from the beginning of 2008 to the end of 2011?

9. Company XYZ's share price decreased from $800 at the beginning of year 1 to $500 at the beginning of year 3. What is the average percentage decrease in share price per year?

10. Economists have said increased productivity leads to better economic performance and increased standards of living. The Bureau of Labor Statistics productivity table below lists the actual % change in output per hour compared to the previous year. a) What is the average percentage change in productivity in Quarter 1 over the past 11 years? b) What is the average percentage change in Annual Productivity over the past 11 years?

Labor Productivity (Output Per Hour) % Change					
Year	Qtr1	Qtr2	Qtr3	Qtr4	Annual
2001	-1.3	7.4	2.5	5.8	2.9
2002	8.8	0.5	3.8	-0.2	4.6
2003	3.7	5.5	9.5	1.5	3.7
2004	0.6	3.3	0.7	0.5	2.6
2005	4.2	-0.8	3.1	-0.2	1.6
2006	2.5	0.4	-2.2	2.7	0.9
2007	-0.2	3.4	4.8	1.9	1.5
2008	-2.6	2.4	-0.8	-3.4	0.6
2009	1.3	8.3	6.4	5.3	2.3
2010	4.5	1.2	1.8	1.8	4.0
2011	-1.0	-0.3	1.8	0.9	0.4

11. Over the past four years, a New York mutual fund specializing in international investments experienced the following growth in its share price from the prior year. What is the average rate of change in the share price of this mutual fund?

First year = 18% increase	Third year = 4% decrease
Second year = 12% increase	Fourth year = 35% increase

Measures of Dispersion/Variability

Business processes vary over time and all business data exhibit variability. Bicycle rim diameters vary from one rim to the next, surgeries for different patients take different amounts of time, cans and bottles contain slightly different amounts. We usually do not know why these differences exist; rather, we simply accept them as "inherent variability" in the process (previously referred to as common cause variability). Sometimes, however, a process or situation will produce results that are outside the normal parameters of the process indicating that something has changed (also known as "special cause" or "assignable cause variability" from Chapter 1). Much of what we will review later in inferential statistics will try to distinguish between common cause and special cause variability.

To talk about variability, we must first have a measure of it. For example, suppose you are managing a project that involves the construction of a 10-story office building, as shown in Figure 3-4. Your company hired a contractor to do the work, but you still have overall responsibility for the project. Your contractor has proposed to lift a 100,000-lb. roof section with a cable, having an average lift strength of 120,000 lb. The cable is made of hundreds of small strands of steel wire twisted into a ropelike cord. You would probably feel more comfortable knowing the strength of the cables varied between only plus or minus ($\pm$) 5,000 lb., rather than $\pm$ 25,000 lb.

Figure 3-4   Cables with the Same Mean and Different Dispersion

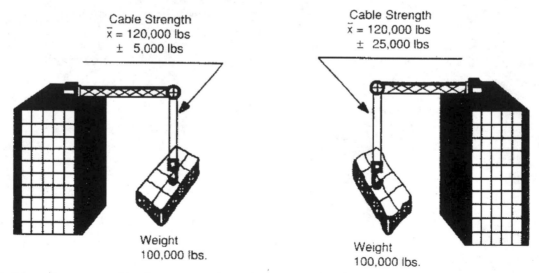

In this section, we consider four commonly used measures of variability: (1) range, (2) mean absolute deviation, (3) variance, and (4) standard deviation. Our discussion will utilize the data in Table 3-1, which represents the individual breaking strength (pounds) of a sample of 10 wire strands used in a steel cable, such as in Figure 3-4. The strength measurements on the strands have been arranged in increasing value from left to right:

Table 3-1   ***Strength of Sample of Ten Strands of Steel Wire***

Strand (no.)	1	2	3	4	5	6	7	8	9	10
Strength (lbs.)	54	62	63	65	68	71	73	78	82	84

#1 Range and Interquartile Range

The *range* is the difference between the largest and smallest values in the data set. In Table 3-1, the range is 84–54, or 30 lbs. Ranges are used in financial analysis, quality control work, and personnel reports because they provide us with an overall sense of the data and are easy to calculate; however, the downfall is that a single extreme data point (outlier) can cause a distorted picture of the dispersion. For example, suppose that one weakened strand of wire exhibited a test strength of only 4 lbs. The range of 80 lbs. (84 − 4) would not represent the bulk of the data in Table 3-1. Although the range is simple to calculate, it fails to make full use of the data as it only uses two values (the highest and the lowest).

The *interquartile range* eliminates the issue of extremes by computing the difference between the first and the third quartile of the data rather than the difference of the highest and lowest values. That is, it starts at the 25th percentile and ends at the 75th percentile. For example, using the data in Table 3-1, the first quartile is at $Q_1 = 62 + .75(63-62) = 62.75$ and the third quartile is at $Q_3 = 78 + .25(82-78) = 79$. The interquartile range, IQR, therefore is:

$$IQR = Q_3 - Q_1 = 79 - 62.75 = 16.25 \text{ lbs.}$$

#2 Deviations

The remaining measures of dispersion or variability are based on deviations. Remember that a *deviation* is the difference between a data value and an expected (or average) value. For sample data, a deviation is expressed as $(X - \overline{X})$ and for population data it is expressed as (X - m). A useful measure of dispersion might be the average deviation:

$$\frac{\sum(X-\overline{X})}{n} \quad or \quad \frac{\sum(X-\mu)}{N}$$

This measure, unlike range or interquartile range, uses all of the information in the data set; however, there is a problem with this measure. Recall that with a mean value, the positive and negative deviations offset each other; consequently, the sum of the deviations as well as the average deviation will always be zero for any set of numbers. This is not a very useful property for a measure of variability, but there are two common ways of getting around this problem. The first one is to calculate the absolute values of the deviations. The second (which we will cover later), and more useful statistically, is to square the deviations.

#3 Mean Absolute Deviation

The *mean absolute deviation (MAD)* is the average of the absolute deviations of values from the mean and is calculated by adding all of the absolute deviations together and dividing by the total number of data values, *n* (note: an analogous equation would hold for a population):

$$\text{MAD:} \quad \frac{\sum|X-\overline{X}|}{n}$$

(3-7)

Example 3-6

Find MAD for the data from Table 3-2.

Solution

First, we must determine the data mean:

$$\overline{X} = \frac{\Sigma X}{n} = \frac{700}{10} = 70 \text{ lbs.}$$

Next, compute the individual deviations and absolute deviations from the mean:

Strength	54	62	63	65	68	71	73	78	82	84
Deviations	-16	-8	-7	-5	-2	1	3	8	12	14
Absolute Deviations	16	8	7	5	2	1	3	8	12	14

Finally, compute the MAD:

$$MAD = \frac{16 + 8 + 7 + ... + 14}{10} = \frac{76}{10} = 7.6$$

MAD is frequently used in forecasting and inventory control activities to assess the extent to which current demand (X) for a product deviates from past average demand ($\overline{X}$) or as a measure of forecast error. If MAD is too large, the firm's forecasting or control systems are not functioning adequately and costs may be too high. While the MAD was more useful when measures were calculated by hand, it is not as useful today with the prevalence of statistical software.

Variance and Standard Deviation

Two of the most useful statistical measures of variability are the variance and the standard deviation. These measures provide information about the uniformity of a data set and about the reliability of statistics obtained from samples. The relationship between the two is simple; therefore, if you compute one, it is easy to calculate the other:

> The *variance* is the average of the squared deviations of values from the mean.
>
> The *standard deviation* is the square root of the *variance*.

When calculating the variance and the standard deviation, there is a slight difference between population and sample values. A population variance is designated by the Greek lowercase letter **sigma squared**, σ^2, and is computed by subtracting the mean (μ) from each data value (X), squaring the difference, adding the squared values, and dividing by the total number of observations, N:

$$\textbf{Population variance: } \sigma^2 = \frac{\Sigma(X - \mu)^2}{N} \tag{3-8}$$

The population standard deviation, designated by the Greek lowercase letter **sigma**, σ, is the square root of the population variance:

Population standard deviation: $\sigma = \sqrt{\dfrac{\Sigma(X - \mu)^2}{N}}$ (3-9)

Since the only way to calculate population variance and standard deviation is by collecting data from an entire population, these values are seldom calculated. That is, in order to calculate these parameters, we must first know the true mean, μ, of the data. Nevertheless, even though we rarely know or calculate either μ or σ, these values do exist for every population.

More typically, in business situations, variances and standard deviations are calculated with sample data; however, because sample information is always incomplete, we must make a minor adjustment to the formulas above when using sample data. This is partly because the deviations of data points about a sample mean ($\overline{X}$) tend to be smaller than the deviations about the true (but unknown) population mean (μ). We correct for this bias by using **n − 1** in the denominator instead of N used for the population equation. This yields an unbiased estimate of the population variance.

The **sample variance, s², is** then:

$$s^2 = \frac{\Sigma(X - \overline{X})^2}{n-1}$$ (3-10)

and the **sample standard deviation, s, is:**

$$s = \sqrt{s^2} = \sqrt{\frac{\Sigma(X - \overline{X})^2}{n-1}}$$ (3-11)

The difficulty with the variance as a useful measure is that, unlike the mean, it is no longer measured in the original units of the data. This means that our measure of central tendency (mean) and the measure of variability (variance) are measured in different units. For example, if the original values were in pounds or dollars, then the variance would be in terms of (dollars)^2 or (pounds)^2. By taking the square root of the variance, the equation for the standard deviation returns the measure of variability back to the same units of the original variable and the mean. For example, the standard deviation, as a measure of dispersion, is more easily grasped in units such as dollars or pounds, instead of (dollars)^2 or (pounds)^2.

Example 3-7

Compute the (a) *variance* and (b) *standard deviation* of the sample data given in Table 3-2.

Solution

We previously found the mean ($\overline{X} = 70$) and the deviations from the mean. Now, we must square the deviations, sum them, and divide by $n − 1$ to obtain the sample variance:

Score X	Deviation from $\overline{X}$ $(X - \overline{X})$	Deviation Squared $(X - \overline{X})^2$
54	-16	256
62	-8	64
63	-7	49
65	-5	25
68	-2	4
71	1	1
73	3	9
78	8	64
82	12	144
84	14	196
Total 700	0	812

(a) *Variance*
$$s^2 = \frac{\Sigma(X - \overline{X})^2}{n-1} = \frac{812}{10-1} = 90.22 \, \text{lb.}^2$$

(b) *Standard deviation*
$$s = \sqrt{\frac{\Sigma(X - \overline{X})^2}{n-1}} = \sqrt{\frac{812}{10-1}} = \sqrt{90.22} = 9.50 \, \text{lb.}$$

While sample standard deviation is the widely used measure of variability, variance is often used for comparing two or more data sets. Since each measure has its advantages and disadvantages, we will use the standard deviation when it is most useful and the variance when it is called for.

The standard deviation is expressed in the same units as the data (e.g., pounds) and is used to express the amount of variability in a set of data and also as a reference or standard to locate a specific data point relative to the mean of the data set. For example, the standard deviation of the data set above is 9.5 lbs. The largest value in the data set (84 lbs.) is approximately 1.5 standard deviations above the mean of 70 lbs. All of the points in this set of data happen to be within ±2 standard deviations of the mean. We can use the standard deviation as a unit of measure to make statements about the location and distribution of values in a set of data.

The Coefficient of Variation

It is difficult to compare absolute measures of variability unless both sets of data are in the same terms and have approximately equal means. This is because the absolute value of the variance and the standard deviation depends on the magnitude of the numerical values and is related to the mean. To deal with this issue, the coefficient of variation offers a unitless measure that can be used to compare different sets of data. It should be noted, however, that the coefficient of variation is highly affected by the mean and so its usefulness can be questionable.

> The *coefficient of variation* (*CV*) is a relative measure that compares the variability of sets of data by expressing each standard deviation relative to the mean of its data. It is frequently expressed as a percentage.

The CV for sample data is calculated as:

$$CV = \frac{s}{\overline{X}}(100)$$

(3-12)

(Note: with population data, use μ and σ as the parameter symbols)

Example 3-8

Clear Lens International produces lens-cleaning fluid in two different plants. One plant is in Paris and produces an 18-ml bottle with σ = .9 ml, and the other is in Cleveland and produces a 3.5-oz. bottle with σ = .3 oz. The quality control manager is concerned that the filling machine controls in the Paris plant are not "tight" enough. Compare the relative dispersions at the two locations, and comment.

Solution

In this problem, one measure is in milliliters and the other in ounces. The coefficient of variation can accommodate this difference in units. Moreover, because we are using population values, we can use σ and μ instead of s and $\overline{X}$:

Paris: $\qquad CV = \frac{\sigma}{\mu}(100) = \frac{.9}{18}(100) = 5.0\%$

Cleveland: $\qquad CV = \frac{\sigma}{\mu}(100) = \frac{.3}{3.5}(100) = 8.6\%$

The dispersions are relatively close, but the Paris plant is under closer control. It has less variation in the amount of fill relative to the amount of fluid in the bottle.

Exercises II

12. Boxes of bulk candy are supposed to weigh within 4 oz. of 28 lb. (a) Which measures of dispersion would tell, on average, how much weight deviation exists? (b) What would the significance be of a sample standard deviation of zero?

13. In the 2011-2012 season, Gonzaga University men's basketball team listed 15 team members in its roster. Players' height information is listed below in inches:

Height	84	76	77	73	73	78	71	84	75	80	79	79	77	78	81

What is the mean and standard deviation of team members' height? Show work when calculating standard deviation. To check your answer, use =stdevp() in Excel.

14. A population of N = 425 pieces of airline luggage has a mean weight of μ = 43 lbs. and σ = 12 lbs. If a constant 5 lbs. of weight is added to each piece of luggage, what would be the effect on μ and σ?

15. Compute the range and interquartile range for the following data: 5, 9, 8, 3, 6, 10, 4, 7, 2 and 6. Interpret your findings.

16. Compute (a) MAD, (b) the variance, and (c) the standard deviation for the population in Problem 18. Interpret your findings.

17. The number of sales calls made by a sample of five marketing representatives were: 12, 4, 9, 0, and 5. For this data, compute the (a) range, (b) mean absolute deviation, (c) variance, and (d) standard deviation. Interpret your findings.

18. As an intern at the Midland Savings Association (MSA) you want to analyze your customers' membership information. You collect sample data from a sample of 10 customers. Calculate the sample mean and standard deviation of the number of years as a member. Show work when calculating the standard deviation. To check your answer, use =stdev() in Excel.

Last Name	First Name	Years With MSA
Collier	Courtney.	8
Collins	Erich	10
Berry	Amy	7
Goodman	Sebastian	7
House	Sigourney.	9
Curry	Byron.	\3
Spencer	Ignacia	9
Fitzgerald	Vernon	4
Reese	Silas.	9
Chan	Selma	13

19. Coast-to-Coast Car Rental has obtained sample data on the costs of operating a specific model car in several different cities. Monthly fixed costs include depreciation and insurance, whereas the cost per mile includes gas, oil, and repairs. The firm uses 15,000 miles as a basis for computing annual costs.

Location (city)	Monthly Fixed Cost	Cost per Mile	Location (city)	Monthly Fixed Cost	Cost per Mile
Chicago	$255	$.104	Philadelphia	$301	$.097
Denver	225	.089	Phoenix	251	.085
El Paso	231	.083	San Diego	230	.107
Gainesville	209	.075	San Francisco	282	.112

(a) What is the mean monthly cost for the eight cities?

(b) Computer the variance and standard deviation for the monthly fixed cost.

(c) Compare the total annual costs for operating the car in San Francisco versus Gainesville.

20. The following represent the heights of the 8 leading players of the 15 member State University Basketball team. What is the sample mean and standard deviation? Show work when calculating the standard deviation. To check your answer, use =stdev() in Excel.

Height	84	75	80	79	79	77	78	81

21. As a volunteer at the local humane society you have been involved in an experiment with nutrition supplements used with cats and dogs to make them bigger and stronger. You have just finished weighing 10 cats and 10 dogs involved in the experiment. The cats and dogs were selected to be similar in initial

height and weight. The weights gains in pounds are shown below. Your supervisor is interested in whether or not the supplement leads to more consistent increases in one type of animal or the other   Find the coefficient of variation for each type of animal. Which group has a higher coefficient of variation?

	Weight Gain									
Cats	4.1	4.0	5.0	4.8	4.6	4.3	4.7	6.0	4.1	4.1
Dogs	18.0	22.0	17.0	14.0	15.0	20.0	18.0	18.0	19.0	18.0

22.   As the HR manager at TradeBigger, a securities investing and trading firm, you have one portfolio manager position to fill and you have narrowed the list of candidates down to two people: Lisa and Jackie. Both candidates have spent the last 7 months interning at your firm, and have equally excellent qualifications. Given the similar average monthly returns, you decide to hire the person with the most steady investment performance because most customers prefer to see steady returns. Use the coefficient of variation (CV) to compare the variability in the two candidates' investment returns.

	Month 1	Month 2	Month 3	Month 4	Month 5	Month 6	Month 7	Avg Monthly Return
Lisa	0.5%	0.8%	0.2%	0.3%	0.4%	0.7%	1.5%	0.63%
Jackie	0.8%	0.9%	0.2%	0.2%	0.3%	0.5%	1.6%	0.64%

Interpretation and Use of the Standard Deviation

The standard deviation is a widely used unit of measure allowing for the comparison of values from different scales and also to make statements about the location and distribution of values in a set of data. We will explore these uses in this section and utilize these concepts in later chapters.

Standard Scores

Sometimes, we may want to compare values that are measured on different scales[3]. We can accomplish this by using the standard deviation as a unit of measure since all sets of numbers have a standard deviation no matter their original units. Standard scores (also called "z-scores") are the distance of the score from the mean relative to the standard deviation. The formula for the standard score in a population is:

$$\text{Standard Score: } Z = \frac{X - \mu}{\sigma} \qquad\qquad (3\text{-}13)$$

A similar formula applies to sample data. For example, imagine that you are the parent of three children who recently took standardized tests at their schools. You have the three test scores in front of you and are wondering how to interpret the results:

Child	Test	Score
Angie	A	80
Tom	B	70
Melissa	C	450

---

[3] This is referring to comparing items measured on different scales such as comparing one item measured in feet to another object measured in pounds.

In terms of the test scores alone, Melissa has scored much higher than Tom or Angie. But does this automatically mean that Melissa did better on the test than the other two children? Realizing that you need more information, you go online and access the websites for the different tests. At these sites, you find the average scores for each of the tests being 100, 50, and 400 respectively. With these values, you can see that Angie scored below average and that Tom and Melissa both scored above average. But, there is still no way of comparing Tom and Melissa. Going back online, you find the standard deviations of each test, which are 20, 10, and 30 respectively. You can now calculate the *z-scores* of the test scores, as shown below:

Child	Test	Score	Mean	Standard Deviation	Z
Angie	A	80	100	20	-1.00
Tom	B	70	50	10	+2.00
Melissa	C	450	400	30	+1.67

By interpreting the z-scores, Angie scored one standard deviation below the mean, Tom's score was two standard deviations above the mean and Melissa's score was 1.67 standard deviations above the mean. Thus, Tom's performance was higher than Melissa's relative to others that took the same tests. Now, we can compare scores on different tests by translating them into another scale where the zero point of the scale is the mean and the unit of measure is the standard deviation. As we will see, we can also make additional statements about scores on this scale.

Chebyshev's[4] Theorem

One of the most famous theorems in statistics is Chebyshev's Theorem (or Chebyshev's Inequality). Although in one sense Chebyshev's Theorem is relatively weak, the fact that it applies to any set of numbers makes it a very powerful statement:

> ### Chebyshev's Theorem
>
> For any set of numbers, at least $(1-1/k^2)$% of the data must be within k standard deviations of the mean, where $k \geq 1$. In other words, at least $(1-1/k^2)$% of the values must have z-values between -k and +k and only $1/k^2$ can be outside this range.

Value of k	Chebyshev's Inequality
1	$(1-1/1^2) = .00 = 0\%$
2	$(1-1/2^2) = .75 = 75\%$
3	$(1-1/3^2) = .89 = 89\%$

[handwritten margin note: remarkable? How? →]

Notice that for k = 1, Chebyshev's Theorem really doesn't say anything at all but if k = 2, Chebyshev's Theorem says that at least $(1-1/2^2)$% = .75 or 75% of the values will lie within 2 standard deviations of the mean. This is a rather remarkable statement since it applies to any set of data. At least 89% of the values must be within 3 standard deviations of the mean.

Empirical Rule

If we can make a further assumption about the shape of the distribution of values, we can make stronger statements about their values. If the distribution of values is relatively symmetrical and bell-shaped[5] then we can state the following empirical rule:

---

[4] You may see this name spelled in different ways in different sources. Other common spellings are Chebychev, Tchebyshev, and Tchebychev.

> **Empirical Rule**
>
> If the data has a symmetrical bell-shaped distribution, then:
>
> 1. Approximately 68.6% of the values will be within **1** standard deviation of the mean
>
> 2. Approximately 95.54% of the values will be within **2** standard deviations of the mean
>
> 3. Virtually all (99.97%) of the values will be within **3** standard deviations of the mean

In considering "k" values (the number of standard deviations) in relation to the empirical rule, we would have:

Value of k	Empirical Rule
1	68%
2	95%
3	Almost 100%

The empirical rule makes a more powerful statement than Chebyshev's Theorem. Recall the previous example about the three children taking the school exams. The mean of the test that Tom took was 50 and the standard deviation was 10. The empirical rule would then tell us the following:

- Approximately 68% of the test scores will be between 40 and 60
- Approximately 95% of the test scores will be between 30 and 70
- Almost all of the test scores will be between 20 and 80

Identifying Outliers

For any set of data, it is always good to look for unusually large or small values, or outliers. Unusual values can occur because of data-recording errors or because of sampling errors. In a case of data-recording errors, the values should be corrected or possibly omitted from the total set of numbers before drawing any conclusions about the data. Even if the unusual values cannot be omitted, they should always be noted and their possible influence on the conclusions acknowledged before making inferences about the data. As we discussed earlier, box plots can help in identifying outliers. The empirical rule and standard scores give us another basis for identifying unusual values or outliers in a set of data.

For data that have a reasonably symmetric and bell-shaped distribution, we can use the empirical rule to determine where the majority of the data lie. The empirical rule states that almost all of the values should lie within **three** standard deviation units of the mean. This means that values outside this range (values with z-scores less than −3.0 or greater than +3.0) are by definition unusual values. Therefore, the first step in identifying outliers is to convert the values to z-scores and look for values less than -3.0 or greater than +3.0. Values outside this range are definitely outliers and values outside the range of -2.0 and +2.0 are somewhat marginal and probably should be examined as well.

Exercises III

23. The data from Example 3-7 are shown again in the table below. The mean of the sample was calculated to be 70 and the standard deviation was 9.50:

---

[5] In Chapter 5 we will call such a distribution a "Normal distribution." The Normal distribution is the most significant distribution in statistics.

Score	54	62	63	65	68	71	73	78	82	84

24. Using the data from problem 26:

   (a)   Calculate the z-scores for this set of data. Do there appear to be any outliers?

   (b)   According to the empirical rule, 68.6% of the data should be between what two values?

25. In 2011, over 1.6 million students took the SAT exam. On average, students scored 514 out of 800 (with a standard deviation of 117) on the math portion of the exam[6]. Recent data show over 616,000 people taking the GMAT exam each year. On average, test-takers scored 37 out of 60 (with a standard deviation of 10.5) on the quantitative portion of the exam. If Matt took the SAT exam and scored 700 on the math portion, and Jenna took the GMAT exam and scored a 55 on the quantitative portion, who performed better relative others who took the same tests? Use z-scores to standardize the comparisons with the two different populations.

26. The total sales for 10 regional sales reps for the past month are given in the table below:

Sales Rep	1	2	3	4	5	6	7	8	9	10
Sales	25	18	32	10	17	35	20	24	16	28

   (a)   Calculate the mean and standard deviation for this data.

   (b)   Calculate the z-scores for this data. Do there appear to be any outliers?

   (c)   According to the empirical rule, 68% of the data should be within +/- 19 sales of the mean. Is this the case for this data?

27. You work as a manager at HROS, a tableware manufacturer. You operate two different production lines producing different products. One production line makes plates and the other production line makes bowls. Demand for tableware is high and both production lines are lagging far behind customer orders. Based on the last 5 years' production records and engineering analysis, the plates production line should be producing 250 plates a day with a 50 plate standard deviation. The bowls production line should be producing 112 bowls a day with a 15 bowl standard deviation; however, the plate production line is only producing 210 plates a day and the bowl production line is only producing 80 bowls a day. About which process should worry you more? In other words, which process is doing worse off compared to its target production rate?

28. Hourly salaries for a sample of 12 carpenters in the South Bend, Indiana area are shown in the table below:

Carpenter	1	2	3	4	5	6	7	8	9	10	11	12
Salary	$17.50	15.00	14.50	18.75	20.50	22.00	16.50	18.00	15.25	14.75	20.25	23.00

   (a)   Calculate the mean and standard deviation for this data.

   (b)   Calculate the z-scores for this data. Do there appear to be any outliers?

   (c)   According to the empirical rule, 99.97%% of the data should be within what two values?

---

[6] http://professionals.collegeboard.com/profdownload/cbs2011_total_group_report.pdf

29. SlapDot.com employees analyzed their extensive database of fulfillment information. They found that 95% of the orders took between 100 and 140 minutes to fill with an average of 120 minutes. Assuming that the empirical rule applies, what was the standard deviation of the times?

30. A national sleep researcher has collected a large amount of data on how long people sleep at night. According to the researcher, 68% of all people sleep between 430 and 530 minutes with an average of 480 minutes. Assuming that the empirical rule applies, what was the standard deviation of the sleep times?

Shapes of Distributions: Skewness

In many situations, such as with the empirical rule, we may want to make some kind of statement about the shape of the value distribution as well as the central tendency and variability. Suppose that you wish to convey some information about the average income of residents in a city. The arithmetic mean alone may not be a satisfactory measure, because a few individuals with high incomes may distort the mean. In such a situation, it may be wise to say something about the shape of the income distribution.

Skewness is a departure from symmetry and its distributions appear lopsided and do not have a symmetrical concentration of data. This asymmetry stems from the presence of extreme scores (outliers) on either the high or low end of the data that pull the mean away from the center of the data.

Figure 3-5 shows the approximate effects of skewness on the relative location of the mean, median, and mode of the data. The mean is the most affected by extreme values, then the median, while the mode is not affected at all by extreme values since it is simply the most frequent value. The relationship between the mean and the median is the most useful and can usually provide us an indication of the broader shape of the distribution. Following are the rules of symmetry:

- When the mean is greater than the median, the data fall to the right or are *positively* skewed
- When the mean is less than the median, the data fall to the left or are *negatively* skewed[7]
- When the mean is equal to the median, the distribution is *symmetrical*

Figure 3-5   ***Effect of Skewness on Relative Location of Mean, Median, and Mode***

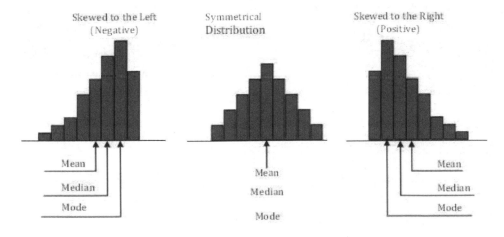

---

[7] This rule of thumb is a generalization that is not always correct. It is most often violated with discrete data, but can also be violated by continuous data in certain circumstances. See for example the article by von Hippel in the Journal of Statistics Education, 2005, 13 (2): http://www.amstat.org/publications/jse/v13n2/vonhippel.html.

One measure of skewness is defined as follows[8]:

$$Sk_M = \frac{n}{(n-1)(n-2)} \sum \left(\frac{X - \overline{X}}{s} \right)^3$$

Skewness: (3-14)

We will call this measure *moment skewness*. The problem with this method is that it is difficult to interpret the resulting value. If the skewness equals zero, the distribution is symmetrical and lacks skewness; however, that rarely occurs. So, how large does the value have to be to indicate a significant amount of skewness? The magnitude of the skewness measure depends on the magnitude of the numbers. The best way to determine if a given value of skewness represents a "significant" amount of skewness is to divide the skewness measure by the square root of 6 divided by n. In other words, calculate the value:

$$\frac{Sk_M}{\sqrt{\frac{6}{n}}}$$ (3-15)

If the result is 2.0 or more in absolute value, then that is an indication of significant skewness in the data. Values less than 2.0 do not indicate significant skewness.

A simpler measure of skewness is the *Pearson Skewness Coefficient*. This measure relies on the distance between the mean and the median relative to the standard deviation of the data. Recall that the mean is influenced by extreme values; hence, a skewed distribution would have some extreme values that would pull the mean in one direction or the other in relation to the median, which is relatively unaffected by extreme values. The formula for this skewness measure is[9]:

Pearson Skewness Coefficient: $$Sk_P = \frac{3(\overline{X} - M)}{s}$$ (3-16)

The normal range for this measure is from -3.0 to +3.0. This measure can be interpreted as follows:

- Values between 0.0 and 1.0 in absolute value indicate little skewness
- Values greater than 1.0 but less than 2.0 indicate moderate skewness
- Values greater than 2.0 indicate severe skewness

A final measure of skewness, *Bowley Skewness*, can be used with ordinal data since it depends only on the first and third quartiles and the median of the data. This measure is calculated as:

Bowley Skewness: $$Sk_B = \frac{(Q_3 - Q_2) - (Q_2 - Q_1)}{(Q_3 - Q_1)}$$ (3-17)

Example 3-9

Using the data in Example 3-8 and Table 3-1 shown below, calculate the three skewness measures:

---

[8] For all of the skewness measures use μ and σ if the values are from a population.

[9] There are three different Pearson Skewness measures. This one is the most commonly used. The population equation would use the corresponding population symbols for the mean, median, and standard deviation.

	Score X	Deviation from $\overline{X}$ $(X - \overline{X})$	$\left(\dfrac{X - \overline{X}}{s}\right)^3$
	54	-16	-4.77737
	62	-8	-0.59717
	63	-7	-0.40006
	65	-5	-0.14579
	68	-2	-0.00933
	71	1	0.001166
	73	3	0.031491
	78	8	0.597172
	82	12	2.015454
	84	14	3.200467
Total	700	0	-0.08398

Solution

We previously calculated the mean as 70 and the standard deviation as 9.5. The calculations for the cubed deviation are then:

$$Sk_M = \frac{n}{(n-1)(n-2)}\sum\left(\frac{X-\overline{X}}{s}\right)^3 = \frac{10}{(9)(8)}(-0.08398) = -0.01167$$

Since there are 10 values, the median is the average of the 5th and 6th value or $(68+71)/2 = 69.5$. The Pearson Skewness is then:

$$Sk_P = \frac{3(\overline{X} - M)}{s} = \frac{3(70 - 69.5)}{9.5} = 0.157895$$

Notice that these two skewness measures are not equal and in fact, are of the opposite sign. This can happen when the skewness is very close to zero.

Using equation 3-4, the positions of the first and third quartiles are:

$$L_{.25} = (10+1)(.25) = 2.75 \text{ and } L_{.75} = (10+1)(.75) = 8.25$$

Then $Q_1 = 62 + .75(63\text{-}62) = 62.75$ and $Q_3 = 78 + .25(82\text{-}78) = 79$ and the Bowley Skewness measure is:

$$Sk_B = \frac{(Q_1 - 2M + Q_3)}{(Q_3 - Q_1)} = \frac{62.75 - 2(69.5) + 79}{(79 - 62.75)} = \frac{2.75}{16.25} = 0.169231$$

Skewness is one of the factors that can invalidate the application of the empirical rule. Usually, the empirical rule can still be applied if there is only a small or moderate amount of skewness. If there is severe skewness, however, the rule should not be used.

Practice

Finding Numerical Measures with Excel and XLDataAnalyst

Excel Functions

Most of the statistical measures discussed in this chapter can be readily computed in Excel using the built in functions under the **Statistical** category. Bear in mind that when calculating the variance and standard deviation in Excel there are two different formulas depending on whether you are calculating a population variance (or standard deviation) or a sample variance (or standard deviation). Table 3-2 shows the most commonly used functions in Excel.

There are several things that should be noted about the Excel functions:

- There is no direct function to calculate the coefficient of variation but you can easily use Excel to calculate these values.
- The caution noted earlier on the use of Excel's Quartile and Percentile functions applies here as well.
- The skewness measure calculated by the Excel SKEW function is the moment skewness measure.

Using the Data Analysis Toolpak

The Data Analysis Toolpak in Excel can also be used to find summary measures. To find summary measures with the Data Analysis Toolpak, select the Insert tab of the Ribbon and select the Data Analysis from the Analysis group[10]. The dialogue shown in Figure 3-6 will appear on the screen. Select the **Descriptive Statistics** option from the list. The dialogue shown in Figure 3-7 will appear on the screen. Indicate the location of the input data on the worksheet and where you want to place the output. You can also use the mouse to highlight the range for the input data and the output range. If you have labels that you want to appear in the output make sure that they are included in the input range and check the box for Labels in First Row. Also, make sure that you check the box labeled Summary Statistics or no output will be produced.

Table 3-2   Excel Functions for Summary Measures

Measures of Central Tendency		
Measure	**Excel Function**	**Example**
Mean	AVERAGE(range)	=AVERAGE(A2:A30)
Median	MEDIAN(range)	=MEDIAN(A2:A30)
Mode	MODE(range)	=MODE(A2:A30)
Geometric Mean	GEOMEAN(range)	=GEOMEAN(A2:A8)
Harmonic Mean	HARMEAN(range)	=HARMEAN(A2:A8)
Quartiles	QUARTILE(range,quartile)	=QUARTILE(A2:A30,3)
		=PERCENTILE(A2:A30,.90)
Percentiles	PERCENTILE(range,percentile)	

---

[10] In Excel versions prior to 2007 select Tools--Data Analysis from the Excel menu.

Measures of Dispersion		
Range	Use MAX(range) and MIN(range) functions	=MAX(A2:A30) – MIN(A2:A30)
Interquartile Range	Use QUARTILE(range,quartile) function to get the quartiles[11]	=QUARTILE(A2:A30,3) – QUARTILE(A2:A30,1)
Mean Absolute Deviation	AVEDEV(range)	=AVEDEV(A2:A30)
Sample Variance	VAR(range)	=VAR(A2:A30)
Population Variance	VARP(range)	=VARP(A2:A30)
Sample Standard Deviation	STDEV(range)	=STDEV(A2:A30)
Population Standard Deviation	STDEVP(range)	=STDEVP(A2:A30)
Other Measures		
Skewness	SKEW(range)	=SKEW(A2:A30)
Standardize	STANDARDIZE(x,mean,standard_dev)	=STANDARDIZE(A2, 100, 10)
Kurtosis	KURT(range)	=KURT(A2:A30)

Figure 3-6   *List of Routines in the Analysis Toolpak*

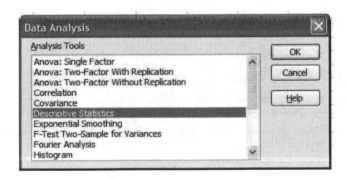

---

[11] Note the prior cautions on the QUARTILE function however. Nonetheless, the QUARTILE function can be used to approximate the interquartile range.

Figure 3-7   ***Data Analysis Toolpak Descriptive Statistics Dialog Box***

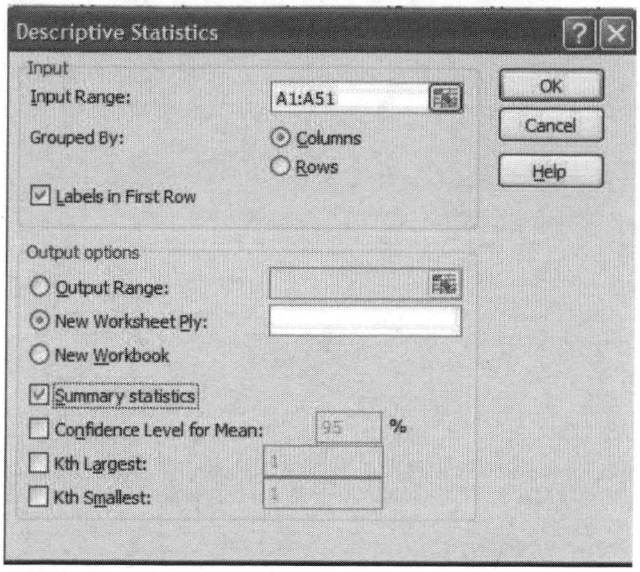

Example 3-10

Coast-to-Coast Transport Co. has a fleet of trucks and uses a large number of tires each year. The brand of tire that they have traditionally used traveled an average of 30,000 miles with a standard deviation of 5,000 miles before having to be replaced (when the center tread depth was worn to 1/16 in.). A competitor has presented a proposal to Coast-to-Coast that claims their tires will last longer and therefore save Coast-to-Coast money. They have provided Coast-to-Coast a sample of 50 tires to test. Engineers at Coast-to-Coast have run the sample tires on a machine that simulates highway driving until the tire is worn to replacement depth. The number of simulated miles for each tire is contained in the file Example 3-10.xlsx. Use the Data Analysis Toolpak to summarize the data.

Solution

The output results from using the Data Analysis Toolpak are shown in Figure 3-8 (Note: in the original output, the first column is too narrow to read the labels so that you need to expand the first column). The average number of miles before replacement for these 50 tires is approximately 32,572 miles with a standard deviation of approximately 4,654 miles. This seems to indicate that the competitor's tires do last longer than the current 30,000 miles; however, to make a definitive decision about the meaning of these sample results requires the methods of inferential statistics that will be discussed in Chapter 7.

The empirical rule would say that 95% of the values should then be between $32,572 \pm 2*2,654$ miles or between 23,264 miles and 41,888 miles. In the data, only one value (42, 503) is outside this range so 98% fall within that interval. The skewness measure of .343 indicates very little skewness in the data. As with the Excel function, the skewness measure reported by the Data Analysis Toolpak is the moment skewness measure.

Figure 3-8   *Output of Summary Measures From the Analysis Toolpak*

Miles	
Mean	32571.94
Standard Error	658.139
Median	31700.5
Mode	#N/A
Standard Deviation	4653.746
Sample Variance	21657349
Kurtosis	-0.50809
Skewness	0.342943
Range	18237
Minimum	24266
Maximum	42503
Sum	1628597
Count	50

The Excel Template

The Excel template named Descriptive Stats.xlsx that accompanies the text can also be used to find various summary measures of a set of data and also produces a box and whisker plot. This template consists of a single worksheet as shown in Figure 3-9. To use the template you need to paste the data you want to analyze in Column H starting in row 2. It is always a good idea to delete the old data before entering new values. In this way, you will not have extraneous values left over at the bottom of the data if the new data set has fewer observations than what is now in the template. The data shown in Figure 3-9 is from the data file used in Example 3-10. The summary measures and the box and whisker plot are shown in Figure 3-9 and mirror the values found with the Analysis Toolpak above.

Figure 3-9   **The Descriptive Stats Template**

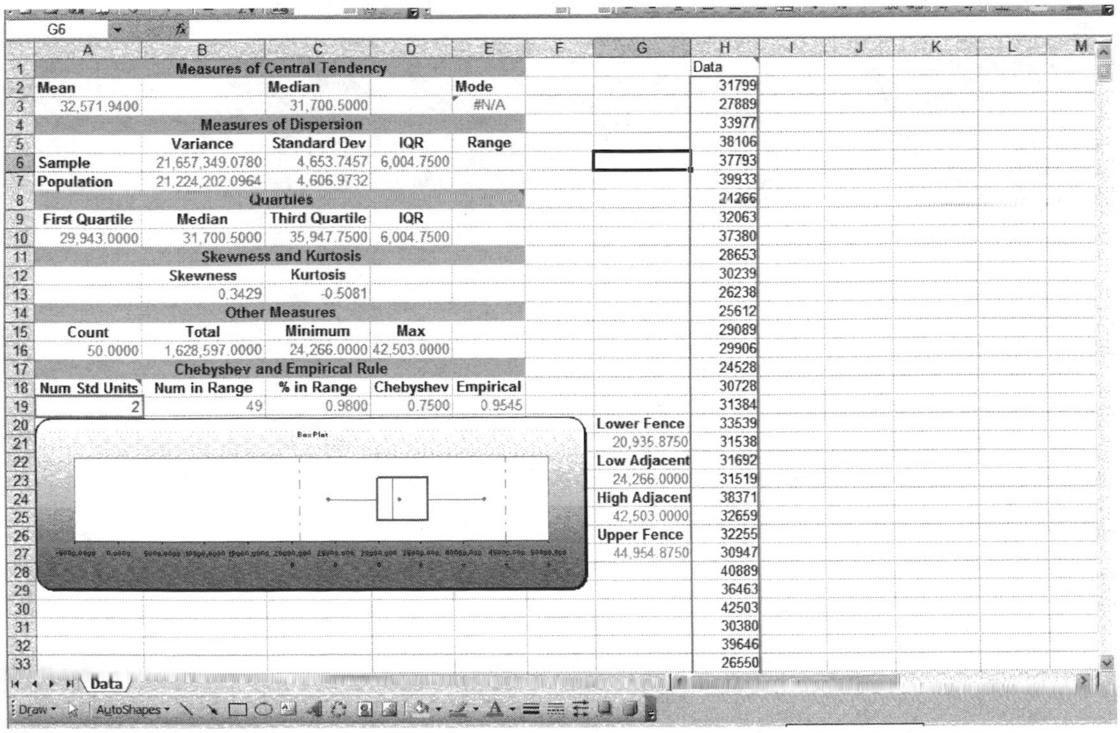

Summary Measures in XLDataAnalyst

XLDataAnalyst can also be used to obtain descriptive measures. Select Summary from the Descriptive Statistics section of the XLDataAnalyst ribbon. This will bring up the dialogue box shown in Figure 3-10. Select the variables you wish to analyze from the list of variables on the left. Then select the summary measures you want to calculate by checking the appropriate boxes on the right. If you have a categorical variable in the dataset you can also derive summary measures by each value of the categorical or nominal scale variable. To do this, check the "Summarize By" checkbox and selecting the appropriate grouping variable from a list that will appear to the right of the box. For example, if we had three different hospitals we could calculate the summary measures separately for each hospital. Figure 3-11 shows the XLDataAnalyst output for a variety of summary measures for the Example 3-12 data.

Figure 3-10   *Dialog Box for Summary Measures in XLDataAnalyst*

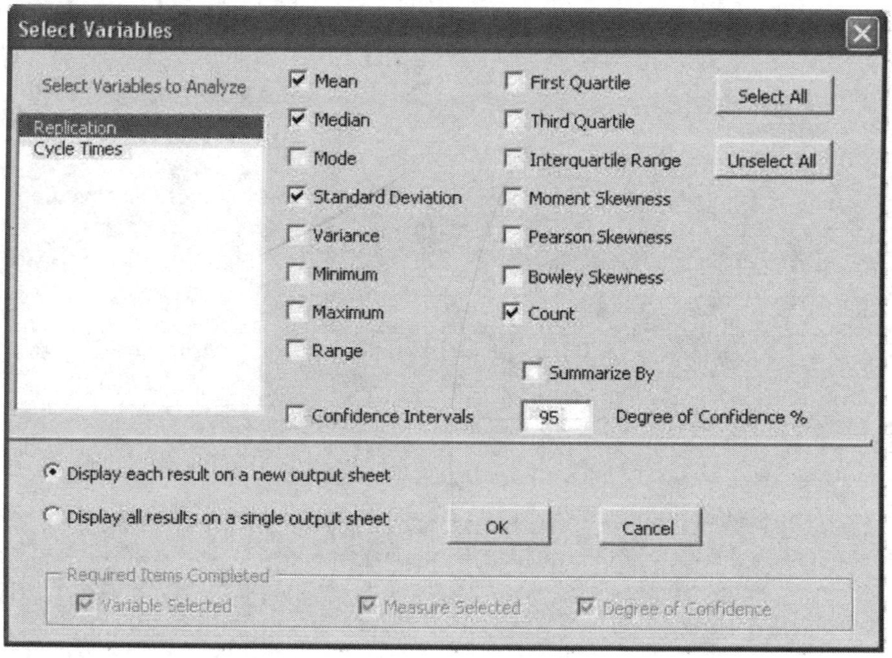

Figure 3-11   *XLDataAnalyst Output for Tire Data in Example 3-10*

Summary Measures

	Miles
Mean	32,571.939
Median	31,700.500
Standard Deviation	4,653.746
Variance	21,657,349.078
Minimum	24,266.000
Maximum	42,503.000
Range	18,237.000
Interquartile Range	6,004.750
Skewness	0.343
Count	50.000

We get much the same output from XLDataAnalyst as we did from the Data Analysis Toolpak. We can also obtain a box plot with XLDataAnalyst. From the Graphs menu in the Descriptive Statistics section of the ribbon select Box Plot. A dialogue similar to that shown in Figure 3-12 will appear (this is the dialogue for the data in the file Example 3-10.xlsx). Select the variable that you want to plot (in this case there is only one). If your data also contains categorical variables you can plot separate box plots by each value of the categorical variable as illustrated later in Example 3-13. Figure 3-13 shows the resulting box plot for the data in Example 3-12.

The box plot indicates that there are no outliers in this data. The mean (plotted as a red dot) is somewhat larger than the median (the blue line within the box) indicating a slight bit of positive skewness that we saw in the descriptive measures.

Figure 3-12   ***XLDataAnalyst Dialog for Box Plots***

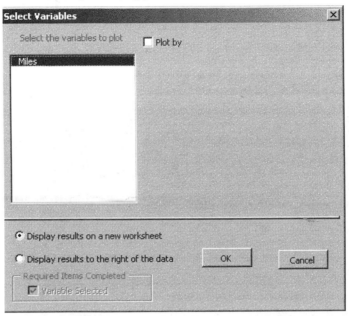

Figure 3-13   ***XLDataAnalyst Box Plot of Example 3-12 Data***

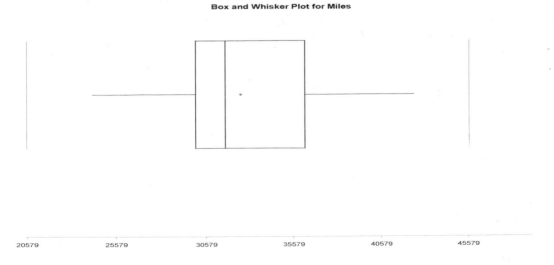

XLDataAnalyst can also produce box plots for each level of a qualitative or discrete variable. This is helpful when you want to compare different groups on another variable. The next example illustrates this.

Example 3-11

The data in the file Example 3-11.xlsx are monthly salaries for employees at a particular firm along with their gender (0 is Male, 1 is Female). Generate a box plot for salaries plotted by gender.

Solution

Select Box Plot from the Graphs menu. Then select Salary from the variable list as the variable to plot. Next check the box labeled Plot by and another list of discrete or qualitative variables will appear on the right side of the dialog box as shown in Figure 3-14. Select Gender as the variable to plot by and then click on the OK button. The box plot shown in Figure 3-15 will be the result. As you can see from the figure, males earn more, in general, than females do. There is also one outlier in the male data and several outliers in the female data. Both distributions are relatively symmetrical.

Figure 3-14   *New Box Plot Dialog for Example 3-11*

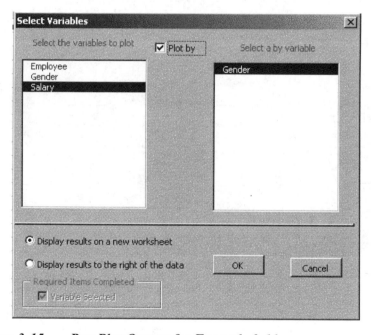

Figure 3-15   *Box Plot Output for Example 3-11*

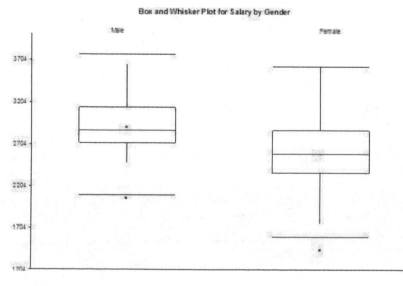

Exercises IV

31. The following unemployment rate data were obtained from the US Bureau of Labor Statistics. Find the mean and median unemployment rate in February 2012 (ignore population differences between states). Solve for the Pearson Skewness Coefficient, and explain what your answer suggests. *Hint: Absolute value Pearson results between 0 and 1 indicate little skewness, values between 1 and 2 indicate moderate skewness, and values greater than 2 indicate severe skewness.*

Unemployment Rates for States		
February 2012 Seasonally Adjusted		
Rank	State	Rate
1	NORTH DAKOTA	3.1
2	NEBRASKA	4.0
3	SOUTH DAKOTA	4.3
4	VERMONT	4.9
5	NEW HAMPSHIRE	5.2
6	IOWA	5.3
7	WYOMING	5.4
8	MINNESOTA	5.7
8	UTAH	5.7
8	VIRGINIA	5.7
11	OKLAHOMA	6.0
12	KANSAS	6.1
13	MONTANA	6.2
14	HAWAII	6.4
15	MARYLAND	6.5
16	MASSACHUSETTS	6.9
17	WISCONSIN	6.9
18	DELAWARE	7.0
18	LOUISIANA	7.0
20	ALASKA	7.1
20	MAINE	7.1
20	TEXAS	7.1
23	NEW MEXICO	7.2
23	WEST VIRGINIA	7.2
25	MISSOURI	7.4
26	ALABAMA	7.6
26	ARKANSAS	7.6
26	OHIO	7.6
26	PENNSYLVANIA	7.6
30	COLORADO	7.8
30	CONNECTICUT	7.8
32	IDAHO	8.0

32	TENNESSEE	8.0
34	WASHINGTON	8.2
35	INDIANA	8.4
36	NEW YORK	8.5
37	ARIZONA	8.7
37	KENTUCKY	8.7
39	MICHIGAN	8.8
39	OREGON	8.8
41	NEW JERSEY	9.0
42	GEORGIA	9.1
42	ILLINOIS	9.1
42	SOUTH CAROLINA	9.1
45	FLORIDA	9.4
46	MISSISSIPPI	9.5
47	DISTRICT OF COLUMBIA	9.9
47	NORTH CAROLINA	9.9
49	CALIFORNIA	10.9
50	RHODE ISLAND	11.0
51	NEVADA	12.3

32. The following data on uninsured Americans in 2009 are provided by the US Census Bureau. 1) Find the mean and median percent uninsured in 2009. 2) Find the Pearson Skewness Coefficient. 3) Explain what your answer suggests. What is causing the skewness if there is skewness? *Hint: Absolute value Pearson results between 0 and 1 indicate little skewness, values between 1 and 2 indicate moderate skewness, and values greater than 2 indicate severe skewness.*

	Total	Uninsured	
		Number	Percent Uninsured
Total (USA)	**304,280,000**	**50,674,000**	**0.1665**
Under 18 years	75,040,000	7,513,000	0.1001
18 to 24 years	29,313,000	8,923,000	0.3044
25 to 34 years	41,085,000	11,963,000	0.2912
35 to 44 years	40,447,000	8,759,000	0.2166
45 to 64 years	79,782,000	12,840,000	0.1609
65 years and over	38,613,000	676,000	0.0175

33. The Luck Penny Silver Mine has developed a new technology to extract silver from older mines that no longer use traditional technologies. If the new technology works, Luck Penny could reopen some old mines and acquire additional inactive mines. The finance department has calculated that the new technology would need to extract 100 ounces of silver per ton or ore to break even. If the new technology cannot extract at least this much, it is not economically viable. Engineers take 40 samples using the new technologies from various locations in older inactive mines and the data are contained in the file Exercises 3-33.xlsx.

(a) Find the mean and median number of ounces extracted. Does the new technology appear to be viable?

(b) Find the variance, standard deviation, and range of number of ounces extracted. What is the coefficient of variation for this data?

34. The data for the opening vignette in this chapter is contained in the file Chapter 3 Vignette.xlsx.

(a) Find the mean, median, mode, standard deviation and skewness for the number of days to receive payment.

(b) Calculate the z-scores for each observation. Are there any outliers?

(c) What percentage of the observations fall within two standard deviations of the mean? How does this compare with the empirical rule?

(d) Prepare a box plot of the data. Does the box plot indicate any outliers?

(e) Calculate the skewness and Pearson skewness measures. Do the two measures agree?

35. The Riverpoint Pharmacy produces a compound used by cats with a thyroid condition. The compound is designed to contain 6 milligrams of an essential active ingredient. Samples of 30 compounds were taken and the amount of active ingredient in each is measured. The results are contained in the file Exercises 3-35.xlsx.

(a) Find the mean and median milligrams of active ingredient.

(b) Prepare a box plot of the data. Are there any outliers?

(c) What percentage of the observations fall within two standard deviations of the mean? How does this compare with the empirical rule?

(d) What is the coefficient of determination for the active ingredient?

(e) Calculate the skewness and Pearson skewness measures. Do the two measures agree?

36. In the first six months of 2004, consumer complaints against U.S. Airlines were as follows[12] (this data also is in the file Exercise3-36.xlsx):

Airlines (Alphabetical Order)	Complaints
Air Wisconsin	79
Airtran Airways	73
Alaska Airlines	51
Aloha Airlines	21
America West Airlines	112
American Airlines	384
American Eagle Airlines	39
Ata Airlines	37
Atlantic Coast Airlines	47
Atlantic Southeast Airlines	17
Comair	56

---

[12] Department of Transportation, Aviation Consumer Protection Division.
http://airconsumer.ost.dot.gov/reports/atcr04.htm

Continental Airlines	161
Delta Air Lines	364
Executive Airlines	11
Frontier Airlines	17
Hawaiian Airlines	16
Horizon Airlines	11
Jetblue Airways	14
Mesa Airlines	63
Mesaba Aviation	26
North American Airlines	14
Northwest Airlines	268
Pan Am Airways	11
Pinnacle Airlines	11
Psa Airlines	13
Piedmont Airlines	11
Ryan International Airlines	14
Skywest Airlines	35
Southeast Airlines	15
Southwest Airlines	76
Spirit Airlines	22
United Airlines	325
United Express	14
Us Airways	193
Usa3000	23
World Airways	41
Other U.S. Airlines	115

(a)   For this data, determine the median number of complains received, the first and third quartiles, and explain the meaning of Q_3.

(b)   Develop a box plot for the complaint data. Are there any outliers?

(c)   Calculate the mean, standard deviation and coefficient of variation for the complaints. What does this value mean?

Opening Vignette Revisited

To better understand the collected data, Sue Myers decides to do some further analysis. Since the data that Bob Young gathered had the amounts of the accounts receivable as well as how long it took to receive the money, Sue decided to analyze both variables. She used XLDataAnalyst to derive the summary measures. The results are shown in Figure 3-5. From the results, Sue could see that the average accounts receivable is about $298.00 and that the amounts range from $243.80 to $348.44. The data appear to be very symmetrical since all of the skewness measures are approximately zero. The average days to payment is $8.91 which is indeed less than 10 days as Mike Mason had stated. Sue also notes that 75% of the payments are made in 11 days or less. The payment times also appear to be symmetrical with little evidence of skewness.

Figure 3-16   **Summary Measures of the Vignette Data**

Summary Measures

	Amount	DaysPaid
Mean	298.535	8.910
Median	298.590	9.000
Standard Deviation	18.366	2.906
Variance	337.328	8.446
Minimum	243.800	2.000
Maximum	348.440	16.000
Range	104.640	14.000
First Quartile	285.905	7.000
Third Quartile	309.823	11.000
Skewness	0.011	-0.075
Pearson Skewness	-0.009	-0.093
Bowley Skewness	-0.061	0.000
Count	100.000	100.000

Summary

Some of the key characteristics of the measures we studied in the chapter are listed in Table 3-3. In addition to these numerical measures, this chapter also discussed box plots, quartiles and percentiles. Box plots are based on quartiles and provide a graphical representation of data showing the range, quartiles, and location of the median. The use and interpretation of the standard deviation for standard scores, Chebyshev's inequality, the empirical rule and the concept outliers was also discussed. The coefficient of variation is a ratio of the standard deviation to the mean of a data set, and it is a method of comparing the relative dispersion in two different sets of data.

Table 3-3   ***Characteristics of Summary Measures***

	CENTRAL TENDENCY	
Measure	**Advantages**	**Disadvantages**
Mean		
Arithmetic	• Most widely used and easily computed • Includes every value of data set • Good statistical properties (balances points so $\sum(X - \bar{X}) = 0$) • Can be weighted	• Affected by extreme values • Cannot be used on open-ended distributions
Harmonic **Geometric**	• Applied to quantities when times per unit vary • Applied to percentages that are a function of previous period	• Not widely recognized • Need to know how to take nth root
Median	• Widely understood and easily computed • Influenced by the number of observations as opposed to the values of the observations • Can be used on open-ended distributions • Good measure for highly skewed distributions	• Identifies center of data only • Doesn't reflect any importance of individual value • Not as widely used for statistical inference
Mode	• Easy to find (if it exists) • Identifies main concentration of data • Can be used on highly skewed distributions • Can be used for nominal data	• Not always unique • May be more than one • Not widely used • Lacks good statistical properties

	VARIABILITY	
Measure	**Advantages**	**Disadvantages**
Range	• Widely used and understood • Easily computed	• Cannot be determined for open-ended data • Uses extreme cnd points of data only • Doesn't reflect dispersion of individual values • Has limited value for statistical inference
Interquartile Range	• Avoids influence of extreme values • Can be used on open-ended distributions • Can be used on highly skewed distributions	• Still doesn't reflect dispersion of individual values • Has limited value for statistical inference
Coefficient of Variation	• Compares the variability of sets of data by expressing each standard deviation relative to the mean of its data • Frequently expressed as a percentage	• Highly influenced by the mean
MAD	• Best intuitive measure of "average" deviation • Easily understood, and used • Influenced by every value of the data set	• Required more calculation than range • Has limited value for statistical inference
Standard Deviation	• Widely used measure of dispersion • Very good properties for statistical inference • Influenced by every value of the data set • In same units as the variable of interest	• Not as easily understood as MAD • Extreme values can distort it because deviations are squared • Reasons for using n versus $n - 1$ frequently not understood • Requires more calculation than MAD
Variance	• Similar to standard deviation • Excellent properties for inference *(variances are additive whereas standard deviations are not)*	• Units not same as original variable

Two other topics considered in this chapter were the concepts of *skewness* and *kurtosis*. Skewness reflects the presence of extreme scores that pull the mean (most) and the median (next) away from the mode of the data. Kurtosis refers to how peaked the values are.

Chapter Glossary

Adjacent Values	The lower adjacent value is the smallest value in the data greater than the lower fence. The upper adjacent value is the largest value less than the upper fence in a box plot.
Box Plot	A graph that conveys the relative positions of the majority of the data as well as the three quartiles. Can also be used to identify outliers.
Coefficient of Variation	A measure that compares the relative amount of dispersion in two or more sets of data. Calculated as the ratio of the standard deviation to the mean.
Deciles	Values that divide the data into tenths.
Empirical Rule	By using the standard deviation as a unit of measure, it states that approximately 68% of the values in a data set will be within one standard deviation of the mean, 95% within two standard deviations, and virtually all of the values will lie within three standard deviations.
Fences	The lower fence is calculated as the first quartile of the data minus 1.5 times the interquartile range. The upper fence is the third quartile plus 1.5 times the interquartile range.
Geometric Mean	Used to find the average rate of change in a series of percentages where the individual percentage rates are known.
Harmonic Mean	Used to compute an average of quantities per unit of time when the times per unit vary.
Index Numbers	The ratio of two summary measures of the same data at different points in time.
Interquartile Range	The difference between the first and third quartiles. A measure of dispersion.
Mean	Calculated by adding the individual values and dividing the sum by the total number of observations.
Mean Absolute Deviation	The average of the absolute deviations of values from the mean calculated by adding all of the absolute deviations and dividing the sum by the total number of values.
Measure of Central Tendency	A representative point in the set of numbers around which the other observations tend to be clustered. A typical value of the data set.
Median	A value in the data such that an equal number of the scores lie above and below it.
Mode	The most frequently occurring value in a data set.
Outliers	Values in a set of data that lie outside the normal range of values in the data, e.g., they are extremely large or extremely small relative to the other data.
Percentiles	Divide data into one hundredths. A generalization of quartiles and deciles.

Quantiles
Numbers between 0 and 1 that divide ordered data on the basis of the proportion of scores that lie above them or below them.

Quartiles
Values that divide the data into four equal groups, e.g., the 25th, 50th and 75th percentiles.

Range
The difference between the largest and smallest values in the data set. A measure of dispersion.

Skewness
A measure of the symmetry or lack of symmetry in a set of data.

Standard Deviation
The square root of the variance. A measure of dispersion.

Variance
The average of the squared deviations of values from their mean. A measure of dispersion.

Questions and Problems

37. Identify (a) three measures of central tendency, (b) four measures of dispersion, and (c) one term that describe the shape of a distribution.

38. For the following values, find the (a) mean, (b) median, and (c) mode.

$$23, 13, 17, 19, 20, 21, 16, 18, 17, 20$$

39. For the following population values, find the (a) range, (b) interquartile range, (c) MAD, (d) standard deviation, and (e) variance. (f) Do the quartiles suggest significant skewness? 23, 30, 15, 26, 14, 29, 15, 10, 17, 22, 28, 16, 25, 14, 16

40. On a Monday, four workers in a factory in Jakarta produced 700 pairs of shoes, some of which required rework as shown below. What is the average percent requiring rework?

Employee	Number Produced	Percent Requiring Rework
Sam	120	10.0
Aki	100	5.2
Dang	180	6.0
Jose	300	15.0

41. Valley Lumber Company management is concerned about the financial viability of the independently-owned retail lumberyards it serves. A survey of the current ratios (e.g., current assets ÷ current liabilities) of 15 yards resulted in the following data:

Company	A	B	C	D	E	F	G	H	I	J	K	L	M	N	O
Current Ratio	1.6	1.7	1.9	1.9	1.9	2.0	2.0	2.1	2.2	2.4	2.9	3.1	3.8	4.6	7.2

Find the (a) range of current ratios, (b) mode, (c) median, (d) arithmetic mean, and (e) mean of the middle nine scores; that is, the mean if the highest three scores and the lowest three scores are discarded. Which of these measures are averages and which are measures of dispersion?

42. This problem calls for a comparison of the arithmetic mean, the median, and the mode as measures of central tendency. Values of X are:

$$2, 15, 32, 8, 14, 9, 75, 10, 12, 16, 15, 88, 33, 42, 57, 8$$

(a) Compare the arithmetic mean, median, and mode.

(b) Why is the mode said to be an erratic measure of central tendency?

(c) If the 16 observations are weights (in pounds), explain why the mean may be a better average than the median.

43. The following represents the stock price and the total shares held (e.g., a *population*) by an investor on the closing day of the year:

Company Designation	A	B	C	D	E	F
Stock Price (nearest $)	16	9	20	14	4	9
# of shares held	100	100	400	100	200	100

(a)   For the stock prices only, find the (1) mean, (2) median, and (3) mode.

(b)   Calculate the *population* (1) variance and (2) standard deviation of stock prices.

(c)   Using the number of shares as weights, compute the weighted mean value of stock price for shares held by this investor.

44.   O'Malley's Auto Parts Centers has several parts stores, and their accounting department bills each store on the basis of the average cost per unit of inventory acquired during the month. During the month of October, the Boone Avenue Store received the following number of quarts of motor oil:

Date Received	# Quarts	Price	Total
October 3	500	$1.26	$630
October 18	300	1.32	396
October 26	200	1.36	272

a)   What is the average cost per quart that should be used for accounting purposes?

b)   Suppose that each store is also billed a "loading" charge of 8% of the total purchase price to cover freight, sales, tax, and handling costs. What total would the Boone Avenue Store be billed for the 1,000 quarts?

45.   Keytop Corporation has three plastic molding machines producing keys for computer keyboards. The machines operate at different speeds, but their output flows onto a common conveyor belt. The output rates and defect rates are as follows:

Machine	Keys/Hour Produced	Percent Defective
A	16,000	4.0
B	12,000	5.2
C	18,000	3.6
Total	46,000	

(a) Find the average number of defects per 1,000 keys produced.

(b) What kind of mean did you use and why?

46.   Management Services Corporation provides cleaning and laundry facilities to an office building in Atlanta. Over the past four years, their sales as a percent of the preceding year have been 110%, 106%, 92%, and 124% respectively. (a) What is their average annual rate of increase in sales? (b) Why can you not use an arithmetic mean?

47.   Use the U.S. and Japanese data from Problem 4:

(a)   Prepare box plots of the U.S. Japanese firm data.

(b)   Compare the two box plots and describe your conclusions.

48.   Chuck, of Chuck's Gelato, is trying to decide if extending business hours during the week will be profitable. In order to justify extended hours to cover all the expenses he will incur during the extended hours, the shop must bring in at least $3,000 per week during those hours. Chuck decides to experiment

with the extended hours for 30 days. The resulting daily sales during the extended hours are contained in the file Exercise 3-48.xlsx:

    (a)   Based on the average daily sales, can Chuck make enough money during the extended hours to cover expenses (assume they are open 6 days a week)?

    (b)   What is the standard deviation of the daily sales? Using the empirical rule, between what two values should 95% of the daily sales fall? If daily sales actually fall at the lower limit of this range, will Chuck be able to cover expenses?

    (c)   Prepare a box plot of the data. Are there any outliers?

49. New Mexico, *The Magazine*, distributes issues to five major cities throughout New Mexico, Albuquerque, Santa Fe, Roswell, Taos and Gallup. *The Magazine* is considering expanding to a sixth location, Truth or Consequences. To determine the level of interest, *The Magazine's* Public Relations Editor took a survey from a random sample of 100 citizens from Truth or Consequences. The survey asked for gender, annual household income, number of years they had lived in Truth or Consequences, and whether or not they would subscribe to The Magazine if it were available in Truth or Consequences (Yes or No). The data are contained in the file Exercise 3-49.xlsx

    (a)   What is the mean, standard deviation and skewness of the age data? Is the distribution of ages reasonably symmetrical?

    (b)   What is the proportion of females in the sample. What is the proportion of the sample that would subscribe to *The Magazine* if it were available?

    (c)   Prepare a box plot of the income data. Are there any outliers?

50. Fidelity periodically posts performance information about its mutual funds on its' web site at www.fidelity.com. The file Exercise 3-50.xlsx contains data on its' domestic stock funds posted on Jun 30, 2012. The data contains information on market capitalization (large, mid and small cap and index funds) , their investment strategy (growth, value, or blend), the year to date (YTD) return, and their 1year, 5 year, and 10 year average returns. The data also includes performance data on indexed funds.

    (a)   Calculate the mean, standard deviation, and relative variability (coefficient of variation) of the 1 year, 5 year and 10 year return across all categories. What can you conclude from these calculations?

    (b)   Calculate the mean and standard deviation of one year returns separately by market capitalization. What can you conclude from these measures?

51. Using the data from Exercise 50,

    (a)   Prepare a box plot for 5 year returns by market capitalization category. What can you conclude from these graphs? Are there any outliers?

    (b)   Prepare a box plot of 5 year returns by investment strategy. What can you conclude from these graphs? Are there any outliers?

52. Calculate the mean and standard deviation of the 1 year, 3 year, and 5 year returns for the data in Exercise 50. What can you conclude from this data?

53. Calculate the mean, standard deviation, and three skewness measures for the 5 year return data in Exercise 50.

    (a)   Is the distribution relatively symmetrical?

(b)   Calculate the lower and upper bounds for the empirical rule. How well does this data fit the empirical rule?

Database Problems

Corporate Statistical Database

 54.   Using the price/earnings ratio data, find the (a) mean, (b) median, and (c) mode.

 55.   Using the same price/earnings data, find the (a) range, (b) interquartile range, (c) variance, and (d) standard deviation.

 56.   Using only the first 20 companies in the database,

    (a)   Find the mean, median, and mode of the average annual salary of employees.

    (b)   Weight the average salaries of each of the 20 companies by the number of employees in the company, and find the weighted mean salary of the 20 companies.

 57.   Using the average annual salary data, find the (a) range and (b) variance, and (c) standard deviation.

 58.   Calculate the average salary and the standard deviation of the salaries. (b) Count the number of companies within two standard deviations of the mean. (c) How does your answer compare with the empirical rule? (d) How does your answer compare with Chebyshev's Theorem

 59.   We wish to compare the relative dispersion in the price/earnings ratio of the 20 chemical and drug companies with the 20 electrical utilities. Compute and state the coefficient of variation for each. Which group of companies has a greater relative dispersion?

 60.   Using the average annual salary data (a) prepare a box plot of the data. (b) Use your box plot to estimate the first and third quartiles of the data. (c) Does the distribution appear to be fairly symmetrical about the median? Explain.

MegaCorp Employee Survey Database

 61.   Find the mean, median and mode for the following variables (a) current salary, (b) years with the company, and (c) overall satisfaction with the benefits. Do employees appear to be satisfied with their benefits?

 62.   Find the range, variance and standard deviation (a) current salary, (b) years with the company, and (c) overall satisfaction with the benefits. (d) Compute the coefficient of variation for current salary and years with the company. Which has the largest relative variability?

 63.   Calculate the average salary and the standard deviation of the salaries. (b) Count the number of employees within two standard deviations of the mean. (c) How does your answer compare with the empirical rule? (d) How does your answer compare with Chebyshev's Theorem

 64.   (a) Prepare a box plot of the employee salaries by subsidiary. (b) What do the plots tell you about the salaries in the different subsidiaries?

 65.   (a) Calculate the average salary separately for each subsidiary. Using the number of employees in each subsidiary as the weight, calculate the weighted average salary of all employees in MegaCorp. (b) Calculate the average salary for all employees in the database. (c) Compare your answers for parts (a) and (b). Are they equal? Should they be?

Alaska Sport Fishing Survey

 66. Find the mean, median and mode for the following variables (a) number of trips, (b) money spent on last trip, and (c) days stayed on last trip.

 67. Find the range, variance and standard deviation (a) number of trips, (b) money spent on last trip, and (c) days stayed on last trip. (d) Compute the coefficient of variation for money spent and days stayed. Which has the largest relative variability?

 68. (a) Prepare a box plot of money spent on the last trip. (b) Does the distribution appear to be fairly symmetrical? (c) Calculate the skewness measure. What does it tell you about the skewness?

 69. (a) Create a new variable for the age of each respondent. Calculate the average age and the standard deviation of the ages. (b) Count the number of respondents within two standard deviations of the mean. (c) How does your answer compare with the empirical rule? (d) How does your answer compare with Chebyshev's Theorem?

Chapter 4:
Probability Distributions

Opening Vignette
Introduction
- Meaning of Probability
- Random Variables
- Probability Distributions and Expected Values
- Overview of Theoretical Probability Distributions

The Binomial Distribution
- Using the Binomial Equation
- Using Excel for Binomial Probabilities
- Binomial Distribution Graphs
- Mean and Standard Deviation of the Binomial Distribution

The Poisson Distribution
- When to Use the Poisson Distribution
- Using the Poisson Equation
- Using Excel for Poisson Probabilities

The Normal Distribution
- Characteristics of the Normal Distribution
- The Importance of the Normal Distribution
- The Standard Normal Distribution
- Using Excel Functions for Normal Distributions

Other Continuous Distributions Related to the Normal
- The Student t-distribution
- The Chi-Square (c^2) Distribution
- The F-Distribution

Opening Vignette Revisited
Summary
Chapter Glossary
Questions and Problems
Optional: The Normal and Poisson as Approximations to the Binomial

Chapter 4 Objectives

When you finish this chapter you should be able to:

1. **Explain the three definitions of probability**
2. **Explain the terms probability distribution and expected value**
3. **Compute binomial probabilities**
4. **Compute Poisson probabilities**
5. **Compute normal probabilities**
6. **Explain the relationships between the normal, student t and chi-square distributions**
7. **Use the binomial, Poisson, and normal distributions to solve problems**

Opening Vignette

Gail Tweedy, chief aroma scientist at Ramone Fragrances, has developed a new perfume that she thinks will do well against a popular competing brand. Bob Moore, the Vice-President of Marketing, wants to do preliminary tests before investing money and resources in producing and marketing the product. He asks that the new fragrance be tested with a consumer panel to get their reactions. A panel of 30 consumers is selected from a pool of consumer panelists. The 30 individuals are asked to sample both the new fragrance and the competing brand and indicate their preference. Of the 30 panelists, 22 indicated that they preferred the new fragrance that Gail developed. Gail knows that Ramone Fragrances doesn't like to bring a product to market unless it is likely to take at least 60% of a competitor's market share. Gail thinks that the consumer panel results are certainly favorable toward the new fragrance, but isn't sure that it will convince Bob Moore.

Introduction

People say nothing is as unpredictable as the weather; however, it is still important to try and predict natural phenomena, such as hurricanes, since they can have such large impact. Hurricane Andrew swept through Florida and Louisiana in 1992, causing approximately $10 billion in property losses. The economic impact of Hurricane Katrina in 2005 has been estimated at over $100 billion with untold human costs. In addition to trying to predict natural disasters as best we can, we still need to take steps to deal with the uncertainty, such as buying insurance. These two points constitute a good lesson for managers who work in a competitive business environment. First, uncertainty exists in the business environment just as it does in nature. Second, it is best to assess uncertainty and take it into account. Ignoring it can have disastrous consequences.

You are already somewhat familiar with the concept of probabilities. Probabilities are values we use to measure and describe the degree of uncertainty of an event. We often speak of statistical experiments or events determined by chance when talking about probabilities. We'll try to lend a little more structure to the understanding of probabilities and probability distributions.

We begin the chapter by distinguishing between different meanings of the term "probability." We then introduce the concept of a random variable from which we can define the concept of a probability distribution. We will see that the type of variable affects our calculation of probabilities. In particular, probability calculations differ depending on whether the random variable is discrete or continuous.

It is often most convenient to compute probabilities using a theoretical probability distribution that closely resembles the actual situation. In this chapter, we introduce several theoretical probability distributions, such as the Binomial, Poisson and Normal distributions, and show how we can calculate probabilities in business situations. At the end of this chapter, you should have a good grasp of the principles of probability needed for inferential and statistical decision-making. Goal

Defining Probability

We spoke earlier of probability as a means of describing the level of uncertainty of an "event." More specifically, probabilities are expressed as numbers, and the event can be any uncertain occurrence (e.g., a 60% chance of the event "rain").

> *Probabilities* are decimals or fractions used to express the likelihood of the occurrence of an uncertain or chance event. Probabilities range from **zero** (event will definitely not occur) to **1** (event will occur for certain), and are sometimes expressed as percentages.

Following the initial development of mathematical probability in the seventeenth century, three methods of assigning probabilities have emerged. The first two methods are considered "objective," whereas the third is often classified as "subjective."

Classical probabilities are probabilities based on equally likely outcomes (assuming random selection) that can be calculated prior to an event on the basis of mathematical logic. Classical probability calculations yield theoretically correct probabilities (as opposed to historical or subjective probabilities):

$$P(A) = \frac{Number\ of\ ways\ to\ obtain\ outcome\ A}{Total\ number\ of\ possible\ outcomes} \tag{4-1}$$

Example 4-1

We know that one light bulb in a package of eight is burned out (B), but we don't know which one it is. Assuming equal likelihoods of outcomes, if a bulb is randomly selected from the package, what is the probability of it being burned out?

Solution

$$P(B) = (1\ burned\ out\ bulb)/(8\ bulbs\ total) = 1/8 = .125$$

Classical probabilities concerned with gambling situations (rolling dice, tossing coins, and playing cards) were the first to receive rigorous investigation. They represented a logical situation and probabilities could be calculated before the action was taken. For example, the probability of rolling a 5 on a six-sided die is 1/6, and the probability of drawing any one of four aces from a deck of 52 playing cards is 4/52.

Since these early beginnings, classical probabilities have been applied to business and social situations where all the possible outcomes of an event have an equally likely chance of occurring. The difficulty with this definition of probability is that rarely, at least outside of gambling games, does the "equally likely" assumption hold.

Relative frequency probabilities are probabilities based on historical frequencies or empirical evidence, i.e. experiments. The probability of an event is the relative frequency with which it occurs:

from past experience

$$P(A) = \frac{Number\ of\ times\ outcome\ A\ occured}{Total\ number\ of\ observations} \tag{4-2}$$

Example 4-2

Records show that 360 of the last 500 customers at a fast food restaurant ordered the Big Billy burger (B). Estimate the probability of the next customer ordering a Big Billy burger.

Solution

$$P(B) = (360\ burgers\ ordered)/(500\ customers\ total) = .72$$

Relative frequency probability requires that an event be repeatable so that we can observe the relative frequency with which it occurs. Such frequencies, in the form of actuarial tables, are extensively used in the insurance industry.

The relative frequency approach assumes that what happened in the past will continue in the future. Some events of interest are repeatable, but many others are not. This probability relies on the notion that in the long run, as a sample increases in size, it will take on the same characteristics as a population. A larger sample tends to yield a better estimate than a smaller sample. This is why an auto insurance company with several years of experience is in a better position to estimate the probability you will have an auto accident than is a newly-formed company.

Subjective probabilities are probabilities based on personal beliefs or judgment. For example, a personnel manager may assess the probability of a labor strike at 40%, or a financial manager may feel there is a .90 probability of securing a needed line of credit. Ultimately, a manager will have to rely on her own judgment about the likelihood of events.

Subjective probabilities are unique as they allow the decision maker to inject his or her own professional judgment into the situation. They do not necessarily rely on long history and can even be applied to one-time situations. For example, they can be used to describe the likelihood of success of a new product or the chance of having the low bid in a sealed-bid competition for a construction project. For example, demand for an entirely new kind of product is not something that can be based on historical frequencies. When Apple first introduced the iPad, historical frequencies would have been of no help in predicting future sales of this new type of machine.

Insofar as business decisions frequently relate to specific one-time situations, some managers make fairly extensive use of subjective probabilities. Nevertheless, we must remember that subjective probabilities often represent only one person's assessment—and quantifying such values does not automatically make them correct. On the other hand, as many "subjectivists" have pointed out, all probabilities are ultimately subjective in that we have to accept that the historical information still applies for relative frequency probabilities or that the assumption of equally likely events will fit the current situation for classical probabilities.

Probabilities are a point of philosophical debate and have implications for statistical inference. Traditional statistical inference is based on a relative frequency view of probabilities. This means that in statistics we can only discuss probabilities for repeatable events. Probabilities for unique, one-of-a-kind, events have no meaning. It also does not, from this point-of-view, make sense to assess probabilities of population parameters that are not repeatable events. This has implications for how we discuss the outcomes of statistical inference, as we will see in Chapters 6 and 7.

Random Variables

We have been using the term "random" since Chapter 1 referring to outcomes determined by chance. We now want to give the term more specific meaning in the context of probability distributions.

> A *random variable* is a variable whose value is determined by chance. We frequently use the capital letter X to represent a random variable.

Suppose a state lottery provides first round winners with $10,000 times the value that surfaces from the roll of a die. By the classical definition of probability, each of the six sides of the die has an equal chance (1/6) of landing face up. We cannot predict for certain which value will emerge, so the outcome is truly a chance event. The numerical value assigned by the random variable X would be one of the outcomes of $10,000, $20,000, $30,000, $40,000, $50,000 or $60,000.

Many of the variables affecting marketing, operations, finance, and other business decisions can be considered as random variables. For example, the number of customers entering a store may be considered a random variable, as might the number of defects from a production line, or the time required to handle a banking transaction.

[handwritten margin note: Random Variable Examples]

Probability Distributions and Expected Values

All random variables have an associated probability distribution. In this chapter, we will establish the basics properties of probability distributions and introduce some standard distributions that are particularly useful in statistics. First, we need to formally define what we mean by a probability distribution.

> A *probability distribution* of a random variable shows all possible values of the variable and the associated probability of each value[1].

Any legitimate distribution must have certain properties in order to be called a probability distribution:

> 1. The values of the random variable must be mutually exclusive and exhaustive
>
> 2. All probabilities must be between 0 and 1, inclusively
>
> 3. Since the outcomes of the random variable are exhaustive, the sum of the probabilities must be 1.0

As with any other variable, a random variable and its associated probability distribution also has a mean. The mean of a random variable, sometimes called *expected value E(X)*, is the weighted average of the values of the random variable (where the probabilities are the weights). It is computed by multiplying each of the n possible values of the random variable (X) by their probability of occurrence (P(X) and summing these products. For discrete random variables:

Expected Value of a Random Variable: $\qquad E(X) = \sum_i P(X_i)X_i$ $\qquad\qquad$ (4-3)

The mean of a probability distribution is also called the expected value because it is the average value we would expect to observe if we repeated the experiment (i.e., generated the value of the random variable) a large number of times.

In Chapter 3 we discussed the variance as the average of the squared deviations around the mean. Similarly, the variance of a random variable, V(X), is computed as the weighted average of the squared deviations about the expected value:

Variance of a Random Variable: $\qquad V(X) = \sum_i P(X_i)(X_i - E(X))^2$ $\qquad\qquad$ (4-4)

Just like before, the standard deviation is the square root of the variance:

Standard Deviation of a Random Variable: $\qquad S(X) = \sqrt{V(X)}$ $\qquad\qquad$ (4-5)

Example 4-3

A medical clinic has kept track of the wait times for patients at the clinic. The frequency distribution of the last 500 times rounded to 5 minute intervals are shown below. (a) Convert the frequencies to a probability distribution for the wait time of the next person to enter the clinic. (b) Compute the expected value, the variance, and the standard deviation of the distribution.

Time	Frequency
0	75
5	250
10	125
15	40
20	10
Total	500

---

[1] Technically this definition applies only to discrete probability distributions. We will discuss the differences for continuous distribution later in this chapter.

Solution

Probability Distribution				
Random Variable (X)	Probability	X*P(X)	$[X-E(X)]^2$	$[X-E(X)]^2 P(X)$
0	.15	0.0	43.56	6.534
5	.50	2.5	2.56	1.28
10	.25	2.5	11.56	2.89
15	.08	1.2	70.56	5.6448
20	.02	0.4	179.56	3.5912
Sum	1.0	6.6		19.94

(a) $E(X) = \sum_i P(X_i) X_i = 6.6$ Minutes

(b) $V(X) = \sum_i P(X_i)(X_i - E(X))^2 = 19.94$

(c) $S(X) = \sqrt{V(X)} = \sqrt{19.94} = 4.465$ Minutes

Overview of Theoretical Probability Distributions

In this section, we will provide a brief overview of some standard probability distributions, both discrete and continuous. All probability distributions satisfy the requirements that (1) individual event probabilities must be between 0 and 1, and (2) the sum of the probabilities must equal 1.0; however, the calculation of individual probabilities of a distribution differs depending on whether the variable is *discrete* or *continuous*. For example, the number of hammers purchased at a particular Home Depot store today is a discrete random variable; the shipping weight of all the hammers purchased is a continuous random variable.

> *Discrete Probability Distributions* are often **based on counts** and show the probability of each discrete event. Two types of discrete distributions are binomial probability distributions and Poisson probability distributions.
>
> *Continuous Probability Distributions* are **based on measurements** (e.g., quantitative variables) and describe the probability of events that occupy some interval on a continuum. Two types of continuous distributions are normal probability distributions and exponential probability distributions.

Figure 4-1 gives an overview of several probability distributions and graphically shows differences between discrete and continuous distributions. Recall from Chapter 2 the use of bar and pie charts (discrete distributions) and relative frequency histograms (continuous distributions). Discrete distributions depend on the addition of individual (discrete) probabilities to determine the probability of compound events. Continuous distributions are computed as areas under a probability function, with different functions yielding different probability distributions.

Figure 4-1   **Characteristics of Probability Distributions**

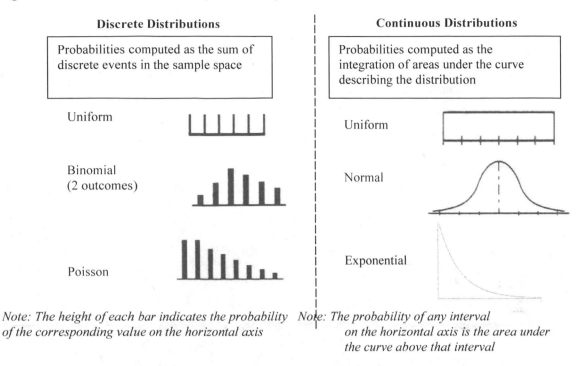

Discrete Distributions

Probabilities computed as the sum of discrete events in the sample space

Uniform

Binomial (2 outcomes)

Poisson

Continuous Distributions

Probabilities computed as the integration of areas under the curve describing the distribution

Uniform

Normal

Exponential

Note: The height of each bar indicates the probability of the corresponding value on the horizontal axis

Note: The probability of any interval on the horizontal axis is the area under the curve above that interval

Although all the distributions in Figure 4–1 are useful in the analysis of business data, the figure includes more distributions than we will cover. Our primary focus will be limited to the binomial, Poisson, and normal distributions and a few additional continuous distributions related to the normal distribution.

Uniform Distribution

Uniform distribution describes situations where each value of the random variable has the same probability. Uniform distribution is the only distribution that applies to both discrete and continuous variables; however, the nature of the probability calculations still differs between the discrete and continuous versions.

Example 4–1 was a discrete uniform distribution because only a discrete number of dots could come up on the die, and each number had the same probability of occurrence (1/6). If the random variable is related to the time interval of an event (e.g., the time between customer arrivals) and all times were equally likely, that would be a continuous uniform distribution. The parameters of uniform distribution differ for discrete and continuous variables. Although we will not take the time to explore the difference in any depth, the equations for the mean and variance are provided here. For a discrete uniform random variable consisting of *n* values:

Discrete Uniform Variable Mean: $\qquad\qquad \mu = \frac{n+1}{2}$ *(4-6)*

Discrete Uniform Variable Variance: $\qquad \sigma^2 = \frac{n^2-1}{12}$ *(4-7)*

As we saw in Example 4-3, the number of dots resulting from the roll of a die would be a discrete uniform random variable, with mean $\mu = (6 + 1) \div 2 = 3.5$ dots, and a variance of $\sigma^2 = (6^2 - 1) \div 12 = 2.9$. The mean is the expected value of the distribution, $E(X)$, but the expected value itself may not be a feasible event as the long-run average value from the roll of a die may be 3.5 dots, but you could never actually get 3.5 dots on one roll.

For a continuous uniform distribution having values ranging from a low of *a* to a high of *b*:

Continuous Uniform Variable Mean: $\qquad \mu = \frac{a+b}{2}$ $\hspace{2cm}$ *(4-8)*

Continuous Uniform Variable Variance: $\qquad \sigma^2 = \frac{(b-a)^2}{12}$ $\hspace{1.5cm}$ *(4-9)*

For example, assume that the time between the successive arrivals of cars at a car wash is uniformly distributed, with a minimum inter-arrival time of 2 minutes and a maximum inter-arrival time of 10 minutes. The mean inter-arrival time would be $\mu = (2 + 10) \div 2 = 6$ minutes, and the variance $\sigma^2 = (10 - 2)^2 / 12 = 5.33/\text{minutes}^2$.

Exponential Distribution

Exponential distribution is a continuous distribution related to the discrete Poisson distribution, discussed later in this chapter. For example, if the Poisson random variable describes the number of arrivals at a restaurant in a given time period, the exponential distribution can be used to describe the time between arrivals. This is similar to the above discussion of discrete and continuous uniform distributions. Both the exponential and Poisson distributions are used extensively in describing queuing or waiting line situations.

Exercises I

1. Identify whether or not these probability distributions are discrete or continuous:

    (a) Number of forest fires on a timber company's land each year

    (b) Acres of trees burned in forest fires each year

    (c) Ounces per bottle of dishwashing liquid

    (d) Number of service calls made by a repair person on Tuesdays

2. What kind of probability distribution (discrete or continuous) would be represented by data from:

    (a) The number of customers using post office fax machines on weekdays in selected cities

    (b) The time required by service technicians to repair phone systems, where the probabilities are equal for taking 1, 2, or 3 hours

    (c) Air pressure in front tires of a fleet of rental cars, where pressures of 30, 31, and 32 are equally probable

    (d) The weekly attendance at Sunday church services in Tulsa over a one-year period

3. An oil well drilling firm is equally likely to strike oil on any of the five workdays of the week. The random variable is the day on which oil is struck. (a) What type of probability distribution would describe this situation? (b) Would the distribution be discrete or continuous?

4. A production supervisor has some assembly jobs that take the following times to complete:

Assembly job	A	B	C	D	E	F	G
Time required (hour)	5	4	6	6	9	5	3

    The supervisor wants to be fair to everyone so plans to assign the jobs to the workers on a random basis. Let the random variable be the time required for a particular individual to do the assigned job. (a) What type of probability distribution would apply? (b) Construct the probability distribution showing the random variable (X) and $P(X)$. (c) Compute $E(X)$.

5. You need to make a management decision on whether or not to accept project X. Project X will cost $20,000. If you decide to pursue the project, you will not have enough money to pursue project Y, which is a sure bet to provide $21,000 profit. You determine that there is a 70% chance of Project X

being successful. If the project is successful, you will earn $60,000 in revenue. If the project is not successful you will earn $0.

   (a) Should you accept project X or project Y?

   (b) Should you go with a project that has a 70% chance of earning $120 profit or a project with a 90% chance of earning $95 profit, all else equal?

6.   A computer is being used to simulate the number of trucks on a bridge at one time. If the computer assigns 1 to 12 trucks on the bridge on an equally likely basis, compute the (a) mean and (b) variance of the resulting probability distribution.

7.   A car rental agency has the following cars in stock, which are assigned to governmental employees on a random basis, without regard to model:

Model	AX10	BX11	CX12	DX13
No. cars	4	10	2	4
Miles per gallon	36	50	28	30

Suppose that we let the random variable be X = miles per gallon and our interest lies in the average mileage from the inventory of the 20 cars. (a) Construct the resulting probability distribution. (b) What is $E(X)$?

The Binomial Distribution

Binomial distributions are the most widely-used discrete distribution in business applications. They are probabilities of independent events, categorized "dichotomously" (e.g., into two mutually exclusive and exhaustive classes). For example, employees may be classified into those who favor a new union contract and those who do not; products may be classified as good or defective; and sales calls as successful or unsuccessful. With binomial distributions, only two categories exist and all elements of the population can be classified into one of these two categories. only 2 options

Population Proportions

Statisticians usually denote the population proportion of a binomial distribution with the Greek lowercase letter pi (π)[2]. We will use π to designate the *proportion of successes* and $(1-\pi)$ to designate the *proportion of failures* in a population. Therefore, if the proportion of successful sales call is $\pi = .8$, the proportion of unsuccessful ones or failures is $(1 - \pi)$ or $(1 - .8) = .2$. We are using the notion of "success" here in a generic sense; it does not translate to the definition of the word "success" and it does not matter which category we designate as success. The important point is to categorize the data into two classes and to maintain that distinction between the two throughout the analysis.

Sample Proportions

For sample proportions, we use the English letter p to represent the proportion of successes in a sample. Thus, p and $(1-p)$ of sample data will correspond with π and $(1 - \pi)$ of population data; however, this designation is not universal. Some statistics texts, and even some computer packages such as MINITAB, use p to designate the population parameter while we are using π.

---

[2] Note: this variable does not equal the mathematical constant pi (3.14….). We will use the Greek letter π to represent a population proportion. Here, it represents the probability of a success on any one trial of the binomial experiment.

Binomial Probabilities

Binomial probabilities arise from what is known as a *Bernoulli process*. This process generates one of two possible outcomes; one designated a "success," the other a "failure," where the probability of a success, as stated earlier, is denoted by π. A binomial distribution is a sequence of Bernoulli trials that satisfy the following:

Binomial Probability Distribution Conditions
1. Each of *n* trials has only *two* possible outcomes (e.g., success or failure)
2. The probabilities of success and failure remain *constant* from trial to trial
3. Each trial is *independent* of any previous trials

The binomial distribution will show the probabilities of $X = 0, 1, 2$, up to *n* successes in *n* trials, when the probability of success on any one trial is equal to some known (or assumed) population proportion, π. In a binomial random variable distribution, the desired random variable equals the number of successful outcomes in "n" trials. This distribution is theoretically correct for describing any process that satisfies the above conditions. In addition, it offers a useful approximation if probabilities change only slightly over a series of trials.

Using the Binomial Equation

Calculating binomial probabilities can be performed using the binomial equation. Letting *X* take on a value in the range of $X = 1, 2, \ldots, n$, following is the binomial equation:

Binomial Equation: $\qquad P(x|n, \pi) = \frac{n!}{x!(n-x)!} \pi^x (1 - \pi)^{n-x} \qquad$ (for x = 0, 1, ...n) $\qquad$ *(4-10)*

Equation (4–10) provides the probability of *exactly x* successes in *n* trials, given the population proportion, π.

Example 4-4

A crystal manufacturing process consistently produces 10% defective wine glasses because of unavoidable dust particles in an acid bath. Suppose that a sample of four glasses is shipped (without inspection) to a customer. Find the probability that one of the glasses is defective.

Solution

$$P(X = 1|n = 4, \pi = .10) = \frac{4!}{1!(4-1)!}(.10)^1(.90)^3 = .2916$$

Recall that a probability distribution must show all the values that a random variable can take on, and the probability of each. A complete binomial probability distribution would also include the probability of 0, 2, 3, and all 4 glasses being defective as well. Table 4–1 shows the complete binomial distribution for $P(X \mid n = 4, \pi = .10)$. Remember that the probability distribution accounts for all combinations of events, so that $\Sigma P(X)$ equals 1; but, unless it is asked for in the problem, it is usually unnecessary to compute the entire probability distribution.

Table 4-1   ***Binomial Distribution for n = 4, π = .10***

No. Defectives X	Probability $P(X)$
0	.6561
1	.2916
2	.0486
3	.0036
4	.0001
Total	1.0000

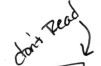

Using Excel for Binomial Probabilities

Even one example should be enough to convince you that calculating binomial probabilities can often be a tedious process. Fortunately, Excel can simplify the calculations with its built-in function for calculating binomial probabilities—BINOM.DIST(). The BINOM.DIST function has four elements:

1. x, the number of successes (i.e., the value of the random variable)
2. n, the number of trials
3. π, the probability of a success
4. cumulative, either TRUE or FALSE depending on whether you want an exact value (FALSE) or the cumulative probability through that value of x (TRUE)[3]

The use of this function is illustrated in the next example:

Example 4-5

Use Excel to find the following probabilities:

    (a) $P(X = 4 \mid n = 8, \pi = .30)$
    (b) $P(X = 0 \mid n = 8, \pi = .10)$
    (c) $P(X \le 3 \mid n = 8, \pi = .25)$
    (d) $P(X \ge 7 \mid n = 8, \pi = .50)$

Solution

    (a)   Enter the following formula into a cell in an Excel worksheet
           =BINOM.DIST(4,8,0.3,FALSE) This will result in the value 0.136137

    (b)   BINOM.DIST(0,8,0.1,FALSE) gives 0.430467

    (c) $P(X \le 3 \mid n = 8, \pi = .25)$ BINOM.DIST(3,8,0.25,TRUE) gives the result 0.886185

    (d) $P(X \ge 7 \mid n = 8, \pi = .50) = P(X = 7) + P(X = 8)$
           Using BINOM.DIST, we know that we can find $P(X \le 6)$ and if we subtract that from 1.0 we will have the desired probability: 1 - BINOM.DIST(6,8,0.5,TRUE) = 1 - 0.964844 = 0.035156

---

[3] Although the Excel functions and some of the arguments will be in all capital letters to highlight them, you do not have to use capital letters when you enter the functions in Excel. The capitalization here is only to identify them as Excel functions and arguments.

Binomial Distribution Graphs

Binomial distribution graphs can be constructed using BINOM.DIST and the Excel graphing capabilities. Figure 4-2 compares the graphs for sample sizes of $n = 6$ for the different proportions of π equal to .10, .25, .50, and .90. Note that (a) all graphs are *unimodal* (has one mode or peak) and (b) they are *symmetric when $\pi = .50$*. As π deviates from .50, the distribution is skewed positively (when $\pi < .50$) or negatively (when $\pi > .50$).

Figure 4-2   *Graphs of Binomial Distributions for n = 6*

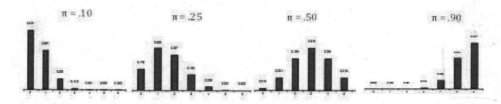

Binomial Distribution Mean and Standard Deviation

The two most important summary characteristics of the binomial distribution are its expected value, or mean (μ) and its standard deviation (σ). They are easy to compute and can be expressed either in terms of the *proportion* of successes or the *number* of successes (because multiplying the proportion of values, π, by the number of items, n, equals the number of successes).

Expressed as a proportion:

Binomial Distribution Mean: $\qquad\qquad\qquad\qquad \mu = \pi$ $\qquad\qquad\qquad$ *(4-11)*

Binomial Distribution Standard Deviation: $\qquad \sigma = \sqrt{\dfrac{\pi(1-\pi)}{n}}$ $\qquad\qquad$ *(4-12)*

Expressed as the number of successes:

Binomial Distribution Mean: $\qquad\qquad\qquad\qquad \mu = n\pi$ $\qquad\qquad\qquad$ *(4-13)*

Binomial Distribution Standard Deviation: $\qquad \sigma = \sqrt{n\pi(1-\pi)}$ $\qquad\qquad$ *(4-14)*

Example 4-6

A shipment of 500 crystal wine glasses is to be produced on equipment that generates 10% defectives in the population. Estimate the mean and standard deviation of the binomial distribution for both (a) the proportion of successes, and (b) the number of successes in the shipment.

Solution

As a proportion:

Mean: $\qquad\qquad\qquad\qquad \mu = \pi = .10$

Standard Deviation: $\qquad\qquad \sigma = \sqrt{\dfrac{\pi(1-\pi)}{n}} = \sqrt{\dfrac{.1(1-.1)}{500}} = .013$

The expected (or mean) proportion of defectives is .10, and the standard deviation is .013, or 1.3% defectives.

As "the number of successes":

Mean: $\qquad\qquad\qquad\qquad \mu = n\pi = (500)(.10) = 50$ glasses

Standard Deviation: $\quad \sigma = \sqrt{n\pi(1 - \pi)} = \sqrt{500(.1)(1 - .9)} = 6.7$ glasses

In terms of numbers, one could expect 50 defective glasses in a sample of 500, when the population is 10% defective.

Proportions are long-run expected values. If they are multiplied by the sample size (500 in the above case), we can gather the specific number of successes (of 50 and 6.7 glasses allowing for rounding error). The values are readily convertible from one to another. Moreover, the standard deviation for any given binomial distribution is determined by the proportion of successes and the sample size. As the equation and graphs suggest, the standard deviation is the largest when $\pi = .50$.

Exercises II

8. What conditions need to be present in a situation to use the binomial distribution?

9. Determine the following probabilities:

    (a) Probability of 3 or more successes when n = 12 and π = .30

    (b) Probability of 2 or 3 successes in a sample of 10 and π = .40

10. A telemarketing representative promoting the sale of storm doors considers a call "successful" if she can convince her phone respondents to accept a home visit from a company salesperson. Her historical success rate is 15%. Assuming that this average holds, determine the probability that in the next 18 calls she will get (a) no respondents to accept a home visit; (b) fewer than five successes; (c) five or more successes.

11. Forty percent of the companies in a mutual fund portfolio are engaged in international business. If 10 companies are randomly selected from the portfolio, what is the probability that (a) exactly four are engaged in international business; (b) more than one is engaged in international business?

12. Records show that 80% of the Crown Exploration Co. employees have subscribed to a company health insurance plan. If a team of 14 workers is randomly selected to go to Venezuela on an oil drilling job, what is the probability that (a) all of the workers will have company health insurance; (b) exactly 10 of the workers will have company health insurance; (c) at least 10 of the workers will have company health insurance?

13. Silk handkerchiefs are produced in a Korean textile plant where 30% are classified as premium grade and 70% are standard. Premium handkerchiefs sell for $20, but the standard grade ones sell for only $8 each. If a prospective buyer randomly samples 12 handkerchiefs, what is the probability that exactly (a) one will be a $20 handkerchief; (b) one will be an $8 handkerchief; (c) half will be $8 handkerchiefs?

14. A Space Lab experiment requires 12 acceptable solar cells; however, past experience has shown that approximately 10% of all solar cells are not satisfactory. If a shipment of 15 solar cells is received, what is the probability that it will contain enough satisfactory cells to do the experiment?

15. Cancer statistics show that approximately 20% of all deaths in the United States are attributed to cancer. What is the probability that from a group of six randomly selected people, (a) none will die of cancer; (b) all will die of cancer?

16. European Insurance Company has purchased six new Zolta automobiles at a good price. They are also aware that 25% of the Zolta cars require some factory attention during the first year. Construct a binomial distribution graph to show the probability that none, one ... up to all six of their cars will require factory attention.

17. Given the following binomial probability distributions:

    $n = 100, \pi = .40$

$n = 20, \pi = .05$

For both distributions, compute the mean and standard deviation for (a) the proportion of successes, and (b) the number of successes.

The Poisson Distribution

Poisson is a discrete distribution used to describe the pattern of discrete events over a continuous dimension of measurement, such as time or space. It applies where the probabilities of the events, $P(X)$, are based on prior knowledge about the average number of occurrences. For example, Poisson distribution may describe the probability of a specific number of patient arrivals at a hospital (based on the mean number of arrivals per hour) or a specific number of defects in a sheet of aluminum (based on the average number of defects per square foot).

Insofar as Poisson probabilities are completely defined by the average or the mean number of occurrences, the Poisson is referred to as a single parameter distribution. We assume that the random variable X can take on nonnegative integer values ranging from zero to infinity. But, the probability of an event's occurrence during a small interval of the time or space is usually very low. Hence, Poisson is also referred to as a *rare event* distribution. In fact, the Poisson distribution provides a very good approximation to the Binomial when the probability of a success is very small (rare) and the sample size is very large.

The parameter that completely defines Poisson distribution is its mean, which is designated by the Greek lowercase letter lambda (λ). Moreover, the variance of a Poisson distribution also equals λ, so Poisson standard deviation is the square root of lambda, or $\sqrt{\lambda}$.

There are three conditions that must be satisfied in order to apply Poisson distribution:

1. There are multiple discrete outcomes over a continuous space

2. The probability of any single outcome is *low and constant* from trial to trial

3. Each trial is *independent* of any previous trial

Poisson also offers a useful approximation to binomial probabilities, when π is small and n is large.

Using the Poisson Equation

For random variables that are distributed according to the Poisson distribution with mean λ, the probability of any given number of occurrences, X, is:

Poisson Equation: $P(X|\lambda) = \frac{\lambda^X e^{-\lambda}}{X!}$ for X – 0, 1, 2, ...∞   *(4-15)*

where λ = mean or the expected number of occurrences

e = 2.7183 (the base of the natural logarithms)

Remember that $e^{-\lambda}$ is equivalent to $\frac{1}{e^{\lambda}}$. So, for example:

$$e^{-2} = \frac{1}{(2.7183)^2} = .1353$$

Example 4-7

Telephone calls arrive at an emergency (911) number at an average rate of 2 per hour. Assuming that the call probabilities can be described by a Poisson distribution, what is the probability of (a) no calls during any given hour, and (b) three calls during any given hour?

Solution

(a)

$$P(X=0|\lambda=2) = \frac{\lambda^X e^{-\lambda}}{X!} = \frac{(2)^0 e^{-2}}{0!} = \frac{(1)(2.7183)^{-2}}{1} = \frac{1}{(2.7183)^2} = .1353$$

(b)

$$P(X=3|\lambda=2) = \frac{\lambda^X e^{-\lambda}}{X!} = \frac{(2)^3 e^{-2}}{3!} = \frac{(8)(2.7183)^{-2}}{6} = \frac{1}{6(2.7183)^2} = .1804$$

It is always necessary to express the probability being calculated (X) and the parameter being used (λ) in the same continuous units, such as hours, pounds, and so on.

Using Excel for Poisson Probabilities

don't Read →

Excel can perform the necessary calculations with the built-in POISSON.DIST function. The arguments for this function are the value of X, the mean of the distribution and a cumulative parameter which if TRUE returns the probability of X or less, and if it is set to FALSE returns the probability of exactly X values.

Example 4-8

In Example 4-7, telephone calls arrived at an average rate of 2 per hour. Assuming that the call probabilities can be described by a Poisson distribution, what is the probability of (a) no calls during any given hour, and (b) three or fewer calls during any given hour?

Solution

(a) $P(X = 0|\lambda = 2) = $ POISSON.DIST(0,2,FALSE) = .135335

(b) $P(X \leq 3|\lambda = 2) = $ POISSON.DIST(3,2,TRUE) = .857123

Example 4-9

A truck assembly plant in Michigan uses welding robots that produce truck body welds with only 4 minor defects per 100 ft. of weld. If one of the robots does 2.5 ft. of welding on each truck body, what is the probability of that robot working on 10 truck bodies without producing any defects?

Solution

This is a "defect per unit of distance" problem, and we must first clarify the X and λ values. The 2.5 ft. of welding on 10 truck bodies equals 25 ft. of weld, so we are concerned with the probability of zero defects in 25 ft. of weld. Next, we must establish λ as the mean number of defects in 25 ft of weld. The rate of 4 defects per 100 ft. can be stated in a smaller common unit rate of 4/100 or .04 defect/ft. Then, in 25 ft., the mean rate would be (.04) (25) = 1 defect.

$$P(X=0| \lambda = 1) = \text{POISSON.DIST}(0,1,\text{FALSE}) = .36788$$

Exercises III

18. Under what conditions does the Poisson distribution apply?

19. The customer billing printers at a credit card center in St. Louis historically malfunction on average about six times per 8-hr shift. Using the Poisson distribution, determine the probability that there will be no malfunction during a critical 4-hr period.

20. An oil refinery has averaged three pump failures per year. What is the probability of fewer than the average number of pump failures this year?

21. In the manufacture of aluminum, the shutdown of a pot line is an expensive affair. Suppose that a particular pot line averages four emergency shutdowns per year. Find the probability of having (a) no shutdowns in a year, and (b) two shutdowns during a six-month period. Assume that the Poisson distribution applies.

22. Wheat trucks arrive at Midwest Grain Elevators at an average rate of 24 per hour. (a) Use the *Poisson equation* to estimate the probability of receiving no trucks in a 5-minute period, and (b) no trucks in a 10-minute period. (c) Use the *Poisson tables* to estimate the probability of receiving more than 4 trucks in a 10-minute period.

23. International Glass Co. supplies hospitals with glass tubing that has, on average, one scratch or other defect in every 20 ft. All sales are in 60-ft.length packages.

    (a) *Graph* the Poisson probability distribution to show the probability of zero, one, two, and so on, defects in the 60-ft. length packages.

    (b) What are the *mean* and *standard deviation* of the distribution?

    (c) What is the probability of two or fewer defects in a 60-ft. length package?

24. Employee absences can seriously affect productivity. For one large corporation, employees are absent from work an average of 2.6 weeks of the 52-week work-year. Assuming that the absences follow a Poisson distribution, what is the probability that during any given week (a) no workers will be absent; (b) one worker will be absent; (c) two or more workers will be absent?

The Normal Distribution

Both the binomial and Poisson distributions are *discrete* as they assign probabilities to events on the basis of a *count* of the number of occurrences of some specified outcome. Normal distributions, on the other hand, are continuous distributions. Continuous distributions differ from discrete distributions in several ways. When a random variable is assigned a value that can take on any real number (decimal or non-counting value) within a range, the variable is said to be continuous. A continuous scale has an infinite number of real number values—depending on how precise the measurement is. Any point along the measurement scale represents a potential value for the random variable; however, insofar as a "mathematical point" has no width, the probability at any point is undefined for continuous variables. Thus, the probability of any point, for analytical purposes, is equal to zero.

Probabilities for continuous variables must be determined as the area under the curve. This, of course, relies on the integration of a function over an interval of values. For example, the probability of getting through a supermarket checkout counter in exactly 2.25 minutes is zero. But, the probability of getting through the line between 2.00 and 3.00 minutes (or even 2.20 to 3.30) can be estimated—despite the fact that the probability of any one of the infinite number of points between these two values is zero ($P(X = x) = 0$).

The mathematical functions used for continuous probability distributions are referred to as *density functions* and are fundamentally different from the equations for discrete probability distributions. Density functions do not calculate the probability of observing a particular value of the random variable, but calculate the height of the curve at that value. In statistics, one very important such function is the normal density function which describes the normal probability distribution.[4]

Characteristics of the Normal Distribution

The *normal distribution* is described by a continuous, unimodal, symmetrical, bell-shaped curve. As illustrated in Figure 4-3, the probability (area) under the curve is equal to 1.00. As sample sizes increase, distributions begin to reflect a normal distribution. The curve approaches the *x*-axis in both directions, although it (theoretically) never actually touches it. This is because the range of the normal density function is from minus infinity to plus infinity. For practical purposes, however, the area under the curve outside of plus and minus 3 standard deviations away from the mean is extremely small.

Figure 4-3   **Graphic Presentation of a Normal Distribution**

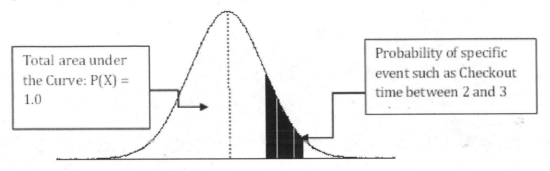

The normal distribution is completely defined by its mean (μ) and standard deviation (σ). There are as many normal distributions as there are values of μ and σ. The proportion of area under a normal curve between a mean and any value X is a function of the number of standard deviations the value X is located away from the mean. Figure 4-4 shows the approximate proportions for any normal distribution. About 68.3% of the area lies within ±1 standard deviation of the mean, 95.5% within 2 σ, and 99.7% within 3 σ. You may remember these approximate values as the *empirical rule* that was described in Chapter 3.

Figure 4-4   **Areas Under the Normal Curve**

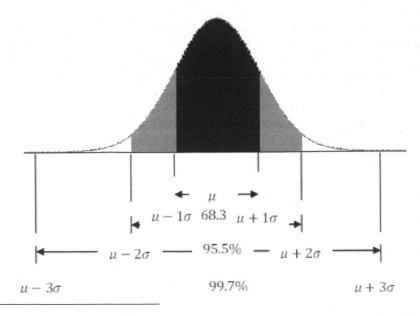

---

[4] The normal density function is $f(X) = \dfrac{e^{-\left(\frac{1}{2}\right)\left(\frac{X-\mu}{\sigma}\right)^2}}{\sigma\sqrt{2\pi}}$ where f(X) is the ordinate of the curve at point X, π is the constant 3.146, e is the constant 2.7183, μ is the true mean, and σ is the standard deviation of the X values. This is presented for reference only.

The Importance of the Normal Distribution

The normal distribution is sometimes called the Gaussian distribution after Carl Gauss (1777–1855), who was one of the first individuals to describe its mathematical properties[5]. During his time, scientists observed that repeated measurements of some physical quantities, such as the distance to the moon, did not result in exactly the same value each time; rather, the measurements tended to cluster around their mean, and the farther a value was from the mean, the less likely that value was to occur. Because the distribution represented the normal error in repeated measurements, the graph of the distribution was called the *normal curve of error* and later became known as the *normal curve.*

Today, the normal distribution is probably the most important probability distribution in inferential statistics for several reasons. First, a large number of natural measurements are at least approximately normal, from the weights of cereal boxes to gasoline mileage estimates for new cars. Second, and even more significant, it forms the basis for much of statistical inference. This is because most of the distributions that we actually use for statistical inference are closely related to the normal distribution. Finally, the normal distribution is useful as an approximation for discrete distributions such as the binomial and Poisson, especially as the sample size becomes large. This idea is further discussed at the end of this chapter.

The Standard Normal Distribution

As we noted before, there are an infinite number of normal distributions with different values of μ and σ; however, there is one normal distribution that has special status in many textbooks on statistics. This special distribution is called the *standard normal distribution.* Any set of data can be expressed in a standardized (Z) format that allows us to express any point in the distribution in terms of its distance (in standard deviation units) from the mean of the distribution. This is similar to our discussion of standard z-scores in Chapter 3.

The standardized (Z) value of an observation is an expression of the number of standard deviations a value is from the mean of the distribution. It is computed by taking the difference between the value X and the mean μ, divided by the standard deviation:

$$Z = \frac{X-\mu}{\sigma}$$

(4-16)

If we do this with all of the values, we will arrive at a normal distribution with a mean of zero and a standard deviation of 1. This is the standard normal distribution. Figure 4-5 shows both the X-scale and the standardized Z-scale for a distribution where $\mu = 500$ and $\sigma = 30$. Note that the mean of the distribution is at 500 on the X-scale, and the Z-value for 500 is zero because the Z-scale measures the deviation from the mean. The X-scale value of 530 has a corresponding Z-scale value of 1.00, because $Z = (X - \mu)/\sigma = (530 - 500)/30 = 1.00$, and the X-value at 560 is equivalent to a Z-value of 2.00, since $(560 - 500)/30 = 2.00$. All other Z-scale values are obtained in similar manner.

---

[5] Historians note that the first descriptions of the distribution were published by Abraham de Moivre in 1733.

Figure 4-5   *Normal Distribution with μ = 500 and σ = 30*

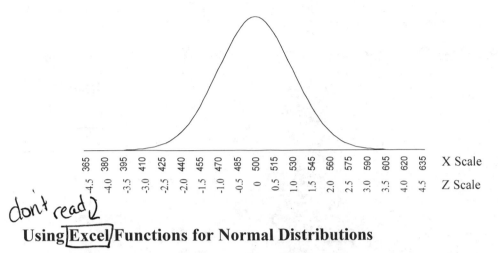

don't read↓

Using Excel Functions for Normal Distributions

Excel has built-in functions for the normal distribution that we can use to reliably calculate the required values. In fact, there are four such functions as shown in Table 4-2. Since the standard normal distribution is just like any other normal distribution, except that it has a mean of 0 and a standard deviation of 1, we really do not need the function for the standard normal distribution. Therefore, we will work only with the NORM.DIST and NORM.INV functions.

Table 4-2 Normal Distribution Functions in Excel

Function	Arguments	Distribution Type	What It Returns
NORM.DIST	X, Mean, Std, Cumulative	Any Normal	Area or to the left of X (i.e. P (x<X))
NORM.INV	Probability, Mean, Std	Any Normal	Value of X such that area to the left is equal to the Probability value
NORMS.DIST	Z	Standard Normal	Area to left of Z (i.e. P (z<Z))
NORMS.INV	Probability	Standard Normal	Value of Z such that the area to the left is equal to Probability value

There is one parameter in the NORM.DIST function that deserves clarification. The Cumulative parameter is set to either TRUE or FALSE. If Cumulative is TRUE, then the function returns the area to the left of X, the cumulative probability. If Cumulative is FALSE, then the function returns the density function value, i.e., the height of the curve. Since we will always want areas rather than the value of the density function, we should always set the Cumulative argument to TRUE as illustrated in the following examples:

Example 4-10

What is the probability that an element selected at random from the normal distribution with a mean of 500 and a standard deviation of 30 will have a value between 475 and 530? The distribution is shown below:

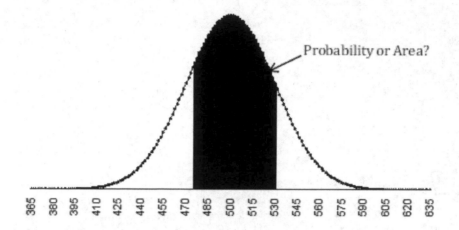

Solution

Since the NORM.DIST function returns the area to the left of a value, to find that area between two values we simply need to find the area to the left of the larger value and subtract from that value the area to the left of the smaller value.

$$NORM.DIST(530,500,30,TRUE) = .841345$$

$$NORM.DIST(475,500,30,TRUE) = .202328$$

so that the area we want is .841345 - .202328 = .639016

Example 4-11

What is the area to the right of a given value; for example, what percentage of the values will weigh more than 525 lbs.?

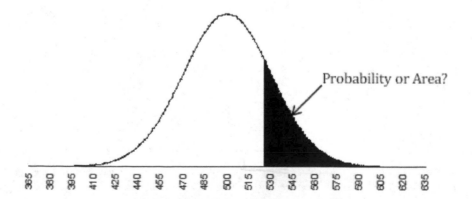

Solution

Since the total area under the curve is 1.0, we must find the area to the left and subtract from 1.0.

$$\text{NORM.DIST}(525,500,30,\text{TRUE}) = .797672$$

so that 1 - .797672 = .202328 is the desired area.

Another question that can be asked for probability distribution is what is the number such that a certain percentage of the values fall below that value. This number is called a *percentile*. For example, the 95th percentile would be the value such that 95% of the probability distribution lies below that value. Percentile questions can be solved using the inverse function for the Normal distribution, NORINV.

Example 4-12

What is the value such that 95% of the distribution lies above this value? If 95% of the distribution lies above this value, then 5% must be below so the question is asking for the fifth percentile of the distribution.

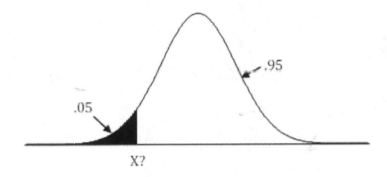

Solution

Since this problem gives us the desired area and asks for the value of X, we must use the inverse function NORM.INV. The area that we want is .05 and NORM.INV(.05,500,30) = 450.6544 so that 95% of the pallets should weigh 450.7 lbs. or more.

Example 4-13

Between what symmetrical limits will a given percent of the area lie? For example, find symmetrical limits within which the middle 95% of the values will lie.

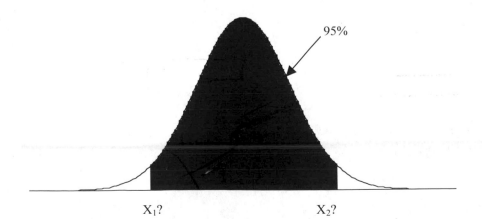

Solution

Since we want .05 total in both tails, we want .05/2 = .025 in each tail. This means that the upper value should have 97.5% of the distribution to the left of that value and the lower value should have 2.5% of the area to the left.

NORM.INV(.975,300,20) = 339.1992 and NORM.INV(.025,300,20) = 260.8008 so that ninety-five percent of the boxes should weigh between 260.80 and 339.20 lbs.

Example 4-14

The lowest given percent will lie below what *X*-value? For example, what is the value such that only 1% of the values lie below this value?

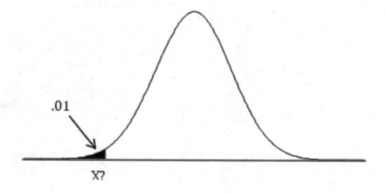

Solution

Since we want the area to the left to be .01, we use NORM.INV(.01,300,20) = 253.4732

Exercises IV

25.   In a normal distribution, what probability is associated with:

(a)   Any particular point on the *X*-scale?

(b)   The area within ± 1 σ of the mean?

(c)   The area within ± 2 σ of the mean?

26.   For normal distribution with $\mu = 400$ and $\sigma = 20$, find the area:

(a)   Below 400, [e.g., P(X < 400)]

(b)   Between 400 and 420

(c)   Above 420, [e.g., P(X > 420)]

(d)   Between 340 and 460

27.   A variable is normally distributed with $\mu = 250$ and $\sigma = 20$.

(a)   What percent of the area lies between the following pairs of points?

i.   250 and 290

    ii.   230 and 270
   iii.   270 and 280
   iv.   0 and 280
    v.   100 and 400
   vi.   270 and 600

28.   For a normally distributed variable with $\mu = 250$ and $\sigma = 20$, (a) the middle 95% of the scores lie between what two points? (b) the middle 99% of the scores lie between what two points?

29.   The time required to service customers at a Rapid-Cut Hair Care center is normally distributed with a mean of 12.4 minutes and a standard deviation of 2 minutes. The firm usually makes $3 profit on each haircut, but if the service takes more than 16 minutes, it is free.

    (a)   What percent of the customers would be finished in no more than 10 minutes?

    (b)   If 150 customers were serviced in one day, about how many would receive their haircut free?

    (c)   Estimate the weekly cost (in lost profits) for 500 customers/week.

30.   The scores on a sales aptitude test are normally distributed with a mean of 80 points and standard deviation of 8 points. If 50 independent applicants took the test, what is the probability that two (or more) received scores of higher than 90 points?

31.   A state consumer protection agency has extensively tested a new model car from a major American manufacturer and has found that the highway gas mileage varies under different conditions, but the average is 37 mpg with a standard deviation of 4 mpg.   Assuming that this distribution follows a normal distribution

    (a)   What is the probability that you will get less than 32 mpg on your next highway trip if you own such a vehicle?

    (b)   What is the probability that you will get more than 40 mpg on an upcoming trip?

    (c)   What is the probability that your mileage will be between 34 and 38 mpg?

    (d)   95% of the time, cars of this type will get less than what gas mileage on a highway trip?

    32.   Gus runs a small convenience store in Seattle. One of his most popular items is a high energy drink called PowerAide which comes in individual 12 ounce cans. Gus has determined that the weekly demand for PowerAide follows a normal distribution with an average of 750 cans and a standard deviation of 25 cans.

    (a)   What is the probability that demand in a given week will exceed 800 cans?

    (b)   Gus is reluctant to run out of PowerAide since it is a big seller. The distributor will deliver only once a week so Gus has to order enough to last. How much should Gus order so that there is only a 5% chance that he will run out of PowerAide during a given week.

Other Continuous Distributions Related to the Normal

Although the normal distribution is very important to the theoretical development of statistical inference, most actual statistical work involves other continuous probability distributions derived from the normal distribution. Although we will not solve very many problems with these distributions, they will become critical to our discussions of statistical inference later on.

t-distribution

A continuous probability distribution closely related to the normal is the Student t or just t-distribution. The t-distribution is often associated with small samples (n of fewer than 30) because of its origins. W.S.

Gossett worked as a quality control expert at the Guinness Brewery in Dublin. Needing a distribution to describe certain characteristics of small samples taken from a population with a normal distribution, he developed the t-distribution based on the normal distribution. In fact, as the sample size gets very large, the t-distribution becomes the normal distribution (and moves towards a z-distribution).

> The *Student t-distribution* is a family of probability distributions described by continuous, symmetrical, bell-shaped curves which are slightly flatter (more spread out) than the normal curve (z-distribution), but that approaches the normal curve as the sample size increases (gets closer to 30).

Because the work was considered to be a proprietary secret with the brewery, Gossett published his work in 1908 under the pen name "Student" which came to be associated with the name of the distribution. Like the normal distribution, the t-distribution is a family of distributions and, similarly to the standard normal distribution, the t-distribution is symmetrical about a mean of zero. The main parameter of the t-distribution is the degrees of freedom.

> *Degrees of freedom* (df) are directly related to the size of the random sample being used, and are a measure of the amount of useable information in the sample. For standard statistical problems, degrees of freedom is equal to n-1.

Each with a mean of zero

The student t-distribution is a family of distributions because there is a different distribution for each value of the degrees of freedom. The t-distribution, thus, describes a family of curves, each with a mean of zero. The standard deviation of the distribution depends on the degrees of freedom but is, in general, larger than 1.0 (which is the standard deviation of the standard normal distribution). Two such curves are illustrated in Figure 4-6 along with the standard normal distribution for comparison.

Figure 4-6   ***Normal Distribution and t-Distribution***

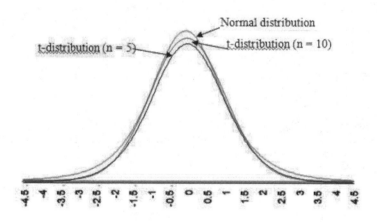

The Chi-Square (χ^2) Distribution

Another distribution closely related to the normal distribution is the chi-square distribution (χ^2). This distribution uses the Greek letter chi (pronounced "ky"). The chi-square distribution is different from the normal and t-distributions in that it is not symmetrical. In fact, the chi-square distribution is positively skewed (only considers values to the right of the mean). Like the t-distribution, the χ^2 distribution is a family of distributions with a degrees of freedom parameter and is also closely related to the normal distribution. To illustrate this connection with the normal distribution, suppose that you have a normally distributed variable with a mean of zero and a standard deviation of 1, as illustrated in Figure 4-7.

Figure 4-7 A Random Sample of 5 from a Standard Normal ($\mu = 0$, $\sigma = 1$) Distribution

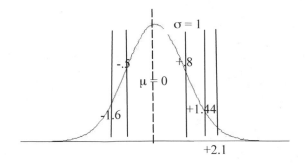

Now, draw a random sample of five values from that distribution—suppose you get values of -1.6, +0.8, +1.2, –0.5, and 2.1:

X-Value	$(X - \mu)^2$
-1.6	2.56
+0.8	0.64
+1.2	1.44
0.5	0.25
+2.1	4.41
Total	9.30

Because the mean of the distribution is already zero, these five values are deviations from the mean. If you square the deviations and add them together, the total (9.30) would be the sum of squared deviations (SSD) from a normal ($\mu = 0$, $\sigma = 1$) distribution for a particular sample of size $n = 5$. If you were to repeat this process thousands of times, you would get many different totals (e.g., 4.89, 2.18, 3.27, 1.54 …). Figure 4-8 shows the general shape of the distribution of values that would be obtained from samples of size $n = 5$. The SSD values for various sample sizes constitute elements of what we refer to as the *chi square distribution*:

> *Chi-square* (χ^2), is a probability distribution of the sum of squared deviations that result from sampling from a normal distribution (where $\mu = 0$, $\sigma = 1$). There is a different chi-square distribution for each sample size. The mean of each distribution is equal to its degrees of freedom (df), and the standard deviation is equal to $\sqrt{2df}$.

Figure 4-8 *Chi-square Distribution for 4 Degrees of Freedom (n = 5)*

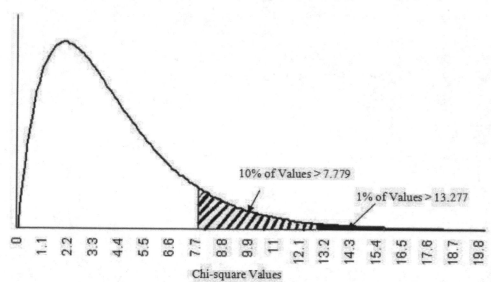

Chi-Square Curves

Being a sum of squared deviations, chi-square can take on any positive values from zero to infinity. As stated earlier, there is a different curve for each number of degrees of freedom. Thus, like the student t-distribution, the chi-square is a family of continuous distributions. They are skewed to the right for smaller degrees of freedom, but approach the normal curve as the degrees of freedom gets larger (i.e., as the sample size increases).

Since the chi-square distribution is derived from the sum of squared deviations about the mean from a normal distribution, you might wonder if there is a connection with variances that are also related to the sum of the squared deviations from a mean. Indeed, one of the uses of the χ^2 distribution is to describe the distribution of values for a sample variance. Since variances cannot be negative, the χ^2 distribution begins at zero.

F-distribution

The *F-distribution* is closely related to the χ^2 distribution and is also based on the normal distribution. Like the χ^2 distribution, the F-distribution is also related to variances and also begins at zero and is positively skewed. In fact, the F-distribution is a ratio of two χ^2 distributions each divided by their degrees of freedom. Since a variance has a chi-square distribution, we can look at the F distribution as the ratio of two variances. Since it is the ratio of two variances, the F-distribution has two degrees of freedom parameters, one for the numerator and one for the denominator (called df-numerator and df-denominator). Figure 4-9 illustrates several F-distributions. Notice that the distribution becomes less skewed (more symmetrical) as the degrees of freedom (and therefore sample size) increase.

We will not encounter the F-distribution again until Chapter 8, but it is important to introduce it now. In fact, although the normal distribution is very important to the theoretical and logical development of inferential statistics, most statistical inference involves one of these three special probability distributions, the t-distribution, χ^2 distribution or F-distribution.

Figure 4–9   *Example F-distributions*

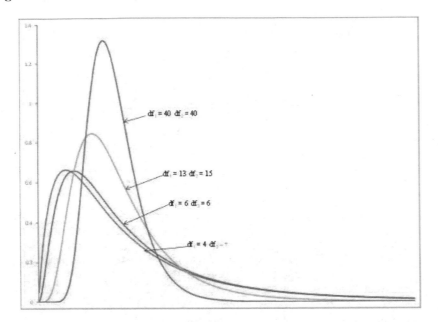

Finding Probabilities and Percentiles Using Excel and XLDataAnalyst

Although all probability problems can be solved with equations, it is easier and less error-prone to use the computer to solve such problems. Excel has built-in functions for all of the distributions we have described in this chapter and we have noted some of them previously. Unfortunately, versions of Excel before Office 2010 were not always consistent in the way in which they defined and used the functions. This made the use of these functions confusing and more difficult. If you are using an older version of Excel, we recommend that you use the probability calculator in XLDataAnalyst rather than the Excel functions.

Excel Probability Functions

The probability distributions in Excel 2010 have been improved to be more consistent with one another and therefore, easier to use. Most of the functions have two versions and some have three. One version is of the form NAME.DIST where NAME is replaced with the particular distribution name. For example, BINOM.DIST is the function for the binomial distribution. The DIST functions return a probability and the nature of the probability depends on the distribution and the arguments provided for the function. For continuous distributions, these functions always return the area to the left of the argument supplied to the function.

Another version of the function is in the form NAME.INV. These functions return a percentile value from the probability distribution. For example, NORM.INV returns a percentile from the normal probability distribution.

The final version of some of the continuous functions return the area to the right of the argument supplied to the function; however, this function does not exist for the normal distribution. Also, areas to the right of a given value can also be calculated using 1 minus the area to the left found using the DIST version of the function. Therefore, we will work only with the DIST and the INV versions of the functions.

The functions for the distributions described in this chapter along with their arguments are summarized in Table 4-3. Note that the Cumulative argument for all of the continuous distributions should always be set to TRUE. Setting this argument to FALSE returns the value of the density function, the height of the curve, rather than a probability.

Table 4-3   ***Common Excel Probability Functions***

Function	Arguments	Value Returned by Function
BINOM.DIST	X, n, prob_s, Cumulative	Exact probability of X in a binomial distribution with n trials and prob_s probability of success if Cumulative is FALSE, cumulative probability of X if TRUE.
BINOM.INV	n, prob_s, alpha	Approximate value for the alpha percentile of the binomial distribution with n trials and prob_s probability of success.
CHISQ.DIST	X, df, Cumulative	Area to the left of X in chi-square with df degrees of freedom
CHISQ.INV	alpha, df	Alpha percentile for the chi-square distribution with df degrees of freedom
F.DIST X	df1, df2, Cumulative	Area to the left in the F distribution with df1 and df2 degrees of freedom.
F.INV	alpha, df1, df2	Area to the left in the F distribution with df1 and df2 degrees of freedom.
NORM.DIST	X, xmean, std, Cumulative	Area to the left of X in a normal distribution with mean xmean and standard deviation std.
NORM.INV	alpha, xmean, std	Alpha percentile in the a normal distribution with mean xmean and standard deviation std
POISSON.DIST	X, xmean, Cumulative	Exact probability of X in a Poisson distribution with mean xmean if Cumulative is FALSE, cumulative probability of X if TRUE.
T.DIST	X, df, Cumulative	Area to the left of X in a t distribution with df degrees of freedom
T.INV	alpha, df	Alpha percentile in the t distribution with df degrees of freedom

Example 4-15

In Example 4-4, we explored the binomial distribution for a crystal manufacturer whose manufacturing process produced 10% defective wine glasses because of impurities in the acid bath. In a sample of four glasses, what is the probability that more than two glasses are defective?

Solution

We can solve this problem in two ways. We could find the probabilities of 3 or 4 glasses being defective and add the two probabilities; however, this method becomes unwieldy for problems with a larger number of alternatives. A better way to solve the problem is to find the cumulative probability of 2 or fewer glasses being defective and subtracting this probability from 1.0. Put the following formula into a cell in an Excel worksheet. The result should be .0037. You can verify this answer using the first approach.

$$=1-BINOM.DIST(2,4,0.1,TRUE)$$

Example 4-16

Find the area to the left of 7 in the chi-square distribution with 10 degrees of freedom.

Solution

Entering the following formula into Excel will result in a value of .274555

$$=CHISQ.DIST(7,10,TRUE)$$

Example 4-17

What is the 95th percentile of the t distribution with 19 degrees of freedom?

Solution

Entering the following formula into Excel will result in a value of .1729133

$$=T.INV(0.95, 19)$$

Example 4-18

In a normal distribution with a mean of 75 and a standard deviation of 13, what is the area to the right of 81?

Solution

Since this problem asks for the area to the right of the given value, we have to subtract the value returned by the NORM.DIST function from 1. Entering the following formula into Excel will result in a probability of .322206

$$=1-NORM.DIST(81,75,13,TRUE)$$

The Probability Calculator in XLDataAnalyst

XLDataAnalyst provides functions for all of the distributions that are discussed in this chapter that operate in a consistent fashion. If you are using an older version of Excel, you will find the probability calculator much easier to use than the Excel functions. The probability calculator is even more useful in the next chapter when solving problems from sampling distributions.

The Probability Calculator is located under the Utilities portion of the XLDataAnalyst ribbon. When this option is selected, the dialog shown in Figure 4-10 will appear. The combo box in the upper right corner of the dialog can be used to select a probability distribution to be used in the calculations.

Figure 4-10   *XLDataAnalyst Dialog for Probability Calculations*

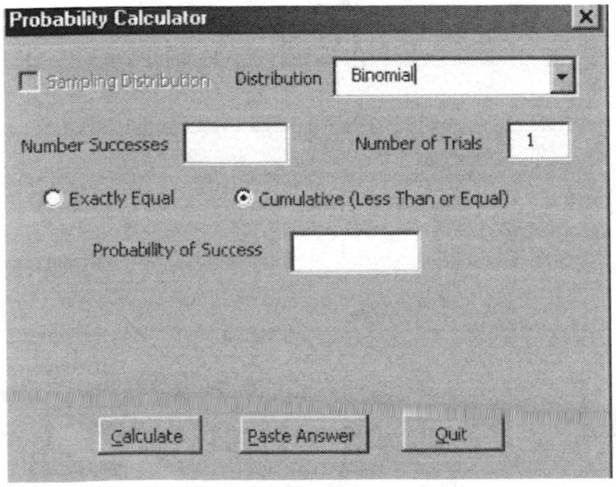

When you select different distributions, the input text boxes will change since different distributions have different parameters. After entering all of the required parameters, click the Calculate button to find the desired probability or percentile. The Paste Answer button can be used to paste the answer into the current active cell of a worksheet. The distribution options include the discrete Binomial and Poisson distributions as well as a variety of continuous distributions including the Normal, t, chi-square and F distributions. The specific functions are listed in Table 4-4.

Table 4-4   *Probability Functions in XLDataAnalyst*

Function Name	Inputs	Returns
Binomial-Percentile	Percentile, Num_Trials, Prob_Success	Approximate percentile from the binomial
Binomial-Probability	Num_Successes, Num_Trials, Prob_Success	Exact or Cumulative Probability
Chi-Square-Percentile	Percentile, df	Percentile from Chi-Square
Chi-Square-Probability	Value, df	Area to the left of a Value
Exponential-Probability	Value, Mean	Area to the left of a Value
F-Distribution-Percentile	Percentile, df_1, df_2	Percentile from the F
F-Distribution-Probability	Value, df_1, df_2	Area to the left of a Value
Normal-Percentile	Percentile, Pop_Mean, Pop_Std	Percentile from Normal
Normal-Probability	Value, Pop_Mean, Pop_Std	Area to the left of X
Poisson-Percentile	Percentile, Mean	Approximate Percentile from the Poisson
Poisson Probability	Value, Mean	Exact or Cumulative Probability
t-Distribution-Percentile	Percentile, df	Percentile from t
t-Distribution-Probability	Value, df	Area to the left of Value

Example 4-19

To illustrate the use of the probability calculator we will use the chi-square distribution that we discussed earlier. Recall that the example was based on a sample of 5 or a distribution with 4 degrees of freedom. Find the probability that the chi-square value will be less than 5.

Solution

Figure 4-11 illustrates the probability dialog for this problem along with the answer of .7127

Figure 4-11   *Probability Calculator Dialog for Example 4-19*

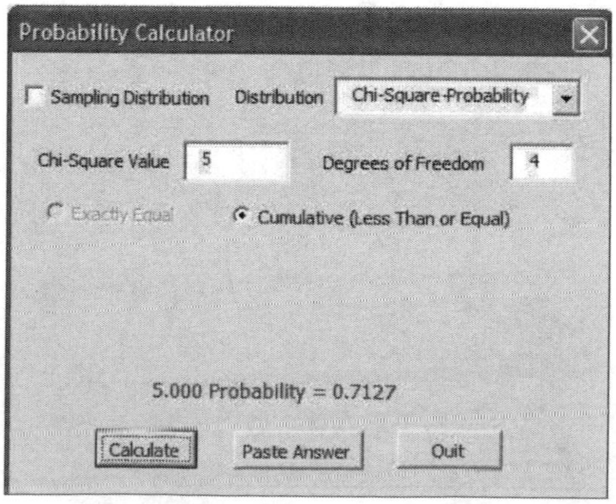

Example 4-20

For the same distribution, find the 90th percentile.

Solution

In this case, choose Chi-Square Percentile in the distribution box of the Probability Calculator. Figure 4-12 illustrates the probability dialog for this problem along with the solution of 7.7794. This value agrees with our earlier results in Figure 4-8.

Figure 4-12   ***Probability Calculator Dialog for Percentiles in Example 4-20***

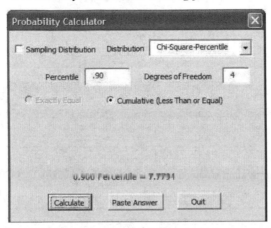

Example 4-21

In Example 4-10, we considered the situation of a normal distribution with a mean of 500 and a standard deviation of 30. What is the probability that an element selected at random from this population will have a value less than 475?

Solution

In this case, choose Normal Probability in the distribution box of the Probability Calculator. Figure 4-13 illustrates the probability dialog for this problem along with the solution of .2023.

Figure 4-13   ***Probability Calculator Dialog for Normal Probability in Example 4-21***

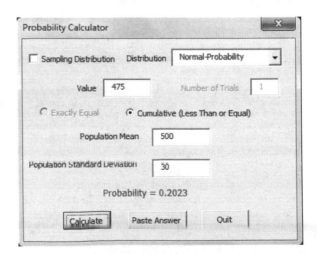

Exercises V

33. The PowerV engine plant operates 24 hours a day, 7 days a week. Since it is a very large facility, light bulbs burn out periodically and have to be replaced. Historical records indicate that on average about 6 bulbs burn out during a 24-hour day.

    (a) What is the probability that more than 7 bulbs will have to be replaced on a given day?

    (b) What is the probability that fewer than 3 bulbs will have to be replaced on a given day?

    (c) What is the probability that between 3 and 6 bulbs inclusively will burn out and have to be replaced on a given day?

34. Customers arrive at the Dugout Pharmacy at a rate of 10 per hour when the store is open.

    (a) What is the probability that fewer than 6 customers will arrive in an hour?

    (b) What is the probability that more than 13 will arrive during a given hour?

35. A survey of Seattle pharmacies found an average price of 100 tablets of Atenalol was 17.49 with a standard deviation of $.50.

    (a) What proportion of the stores charged more than $18 for Atenalol?

    (b) What proportion of the stores charged between $17 and $18 for Atenalol?

    (c) What is the value such that only 10% of the stores charge more than that price?

36. Historical monthly sales of the BEO Gadget Company have been normally distributed with a mean of $10 million and a standard deviation of $1 million.

    (a) What is the probability that the monthly sales next month will exceed $12 million?

    (b) What is the probability that monthly sales next month will be between $9 and $10 million?

    (c) What is the value such that monthly sales exceed that value only 3% of the time?

37. For a t-distribution with a sample size of 25:

    (a) What is the probability that the t-value will be less than -1.0?

    (b) What is the 5th percentile of the distribution?

    (c) What is the probability of a t-value between 1 and 2?

38. For a t-distribution with a sample size of 15:

    (a) What is the probability that the t-value will be greater than -1.5?

    (b) What is the 90th percentile of the distribution?

    (c) What is the probability of a t-value between -1.0 and 0?

39. For a chi-square distribution with a sample size of 16:

    (a) What is the probability that the chi-square value will be less than 13?

    (b) What is the 5th percentile of the distribution?

    (c) What is the probability of a chi-square value between 12 and 20?

40. For a chi-square distribution with a sample size of 10:

    (a) What is the probability that the chi-square value will be more than 12?

    (b) What is the 75th percentile of the distribution?

    (c) What is the probability that a chi-square value will be less than 7?

41.   According to the USDA, the annual per capita consumption of milk and cream in liquid form in 2011 was approximately 201 gallons (www.ers.usda.gov/datafiles/**Dairy**_Data/pcconsp_1_.xls). *Assuming that the standard deviation of consumption is 20 gallons and that the distribution follows a normal distribution,*

    (a) What is the probability that an individual adult from the population will consume more than 230 gallons of milk and cream per year?

    (b) Determine the probability that an individual selected at random from the population will consume less than 175 gallons of milk and cream annually.

    (c) What is the 95th percentile for the consumption of milk and cream?

42.   Sue Miller, Benefits Coordinator for Mega Bank, knows that historically the number of hours lost to employee illness has been normally distributed with an average 373 hours per week and a standard deviation of 29 hours.

    (a) What is the probability that during a given week, the number of employee hours lost due to illness is between 340 and 400 hours?

    (b) Sue wants to set an upper limit on how many hours are likely to be lost during a week. What is the value such that the number of hours lost will exceed this value only 1% of the time?

    (c) During the last week, Sue discovers that 335 hours were lost to employee illness. How likely is it for this to happen? Should Sue be concerned about this?

43.   George owns a restaurant and lounge called the Cozy Inn. George knows that sometimes customers leave without paying their bill. Sometimes this is just forgetfulness on the part of the customer and sometimes it is deliberate theft. George has tracked this behavior over the years and finds that the average rate of occurrence is about 6 per week.

    (a) What is the probability that during a given week 2 or fewer customers will leave without paying their tab?

    (b) George has hired some new employees and finds that during the past week 11 customers left without paying their bill. Does George have reason to be concerned?

44.   Extensive experience has taught the partners of the accounting firm Preston and Marshall that about 15% of stated accounts receivable have some errors in them. If this is true

    (a) What is the probability that the accounts receivables of a group of 10 clients will have zero errors?

    (b) What is the probability that a group of 15 clients will have 3 or more errors?

    (c) What is the expected number of errors in a group of 20 clients?

Opening Vignette Revisited

Before her meeting with Bob Moore, VP of Marketing Gail Tweedy is still uncertain how to best present the consumer panel results. She knows that 22 out of 30 of the panelists preferred the new fragrance to the competing brand, but doesn't know if that will convince Bob. She calls in Molly, her recently hired assistant and after listening to Gail's explanation of the situation, Molly immediately recognizes that this situation was like the Binomial problems she had studied in her Statistics class at school. After she explained the Binomial probability distribution to Gail, they agreed that it was clear that there were only 2 possible outcomes, making it a binomial situation, and that the consumer panel had produced 22 successes out of 30 trials. They also decided that, if there were only a 50-50 chance of a success (e.g., the panelists picked a fragrance at random) they should have observed only about 15 successes in the 30 trials. However, Gail knew that Bob Moore would not be satisfied that they did better than random guessing based on this information. After discussing the 60% market share principle with Molly, they both decided that the 60% figure might be the missing piece in the Binomial puzzle. They might be able to convince Bob if they could show that the chances of observing 22 or more successes in 30 trials with a probability of a success of .60 are quite small. This might show that the company was likely to capture 60% or more of the market share from the competing brand. Using Excel, Molly quickly calculated that the probability of observing 22 or more successes in this situation is .043524. Gail felt much more certain that she can use the panel information to convince Bob Moore that the new fragrance was worth marketing.

Summary

Probability distributions show the values that a random variable can assume, along with the probability of each value. Discrete distributions are based on counts of discrete events and continuous distributions on measurements (along an interval). The long-run expected value of a distribution is its mean, μ.

Binomial probabilities arise from experiments that have (1) only two outcomes, (2) a constant probability of success, and (3) independent trials. The binomial equation can be used for computation, but Excel can solve problems with even larger values of n. The binomial distribution has two parameters, its mean ($\mu = n\pi$), and standard deviation $[\sigma = \sqrt{n\pi(1-\pi)}]$

Poisson probabilities describe situations that have (1) many possible outcomes over a continuum of time or space, (2) low and constant probabilities of success, and (3) independent trials. The Poisson has only one parameter, its mean, λ, and describes "rare event" probabilities. It can, however, be used to approximate binomial distributions.

Normal probabilities arise from measurements on a continuous scale. The normal curve is continuous, symmetrical, bell-shaped and is defined by two parameters (μ and σ). Although there is a different normal curve for every μ and σ combination, any curve can be converted to standardized (z) form by expressing the X-scale in numbers of standard deviations. To do this, we find the difference between the mean and any other value ($X - \mu$), and divide it by the amount of one standard deviation. 68.3% of the area is within $\pm 1\sigma$, 95.5% of the area is within $\pm 2\sigma$, and 99.7% of the area is within $\pm 3\sigma$. In addition to being useful for describing natural measurements, the normal distribution is used to illustrate the logic of statistical inference. Three other continuous distributions related to the normal distribution, are: the student t-distribution, chi-square distribution and F-distribution which are also widely used in statistical inference.

Excel and XLDataAnalyst can easily compute binomial, Poisson, normal, t and chi-square probabilities, among others.

Chapter Glossary

Bernoulli Process	An experiment in which each trial has only two possible outcomes, the probability of a success is constant, and each trial is independent of the others.
Binomial Distribution	A probability distribution arising from a Bernoulli process with n trials.
Chi-square Distribution	A positively skewed probability distribution of the sum of squared deviations that result when sampling from a normal distribution.
Classical Probabilities	Probabilities based on equally likely outcomes that can be calculated prior to (i.e., *a priori*) an event on the basis of mathematical logic.
Continuous Probability Distributions	Probability distributions based on measurements of a continuous variable. The density function represents the height of the curve and probabilities are represented by areas.
Discrete Probability Distributions	Probability distributions based on counts that show the probability of each discrete event in the sample space.
Density Function	The mathematical function that defines the graph of a continuous probability distribution.
F-Distribution	A continuous distribution with two degrees of freedom parameters that can be defined as the ratio of two chi-square variables.
Normal Distribution	A continuous probability distribution that is described by a continuous, unimodal, symmetrical, bell-shaped curve.
Percentiles	A value such that a certain percentage of the probability distribution lies below that number.
Poisson Distribution	A discrete distribution used to describe the pattern of events over a continuous dimension of measurement, such as time or space.
Probability Distribution	A distribution that shows the values that a random variable can assume, along with the probability of each value.
Random Variable	A variable whose value is determined by chance.
Relative Frequency Probabilities	Probabilities based on historical frequencies or empirical evidence or experiments.
Standard Normal Distribution	A normal distribution with a mean of 0 and a standard deviation of 1.
Student t-Distribution	A family of probability distributions described by continuous, symmetrical, bell-shaped curves which are slightly flatter than the normal curve, but that approach the normal curve as the sample size increases.
Subjective Probabilities	Probabilities based on personal beliefs or judgment.
Uniform Distribution	A distribution where each value that the random variable can assume has the same probability as every other value.

Questions and Problems

45. A tour bus service in Philadelphia charges $5 per person and has experienced a uniform demand varying from 13 to 20 tourists, inclusive.

    (a) Construct a probability distribution where the random variable is the amount of revenue from tourists.

    (b) Compute the mean and standard deviation of the distribution.

46. A precision casting process produces missile parts that are 10% defective. A sample of 10 parts is selected at random from this process.

    (b) Compute the probability distribution of defectives in a sample of 10.

    (c) What is the probability there will be at least one defective part in the sample?

47. If a process produces parts that are 90% acceptable, (a) what is the probability that a sample of 20 will contain exactly 18 acceptable parts? (b) What is the probability that it will contain 18 or more acceptable parts?

48. The number of truck arrivals at a weighing station per hour follows a Poisson distribution, with a mean of 4.5 arrivals per hour. What is the probability that in an hour selected at random there will be (a) no arrivals; (b) exactly 5 arrivals; (c) 5 or more arrivals?

49. Assuming that the customer arrivals at the Fidelity Credit Union drive-through window with a mean of four per hour, find:

    (a) the probability that in a given hour more than eight customers will arrive at the drive-through window.

    (b) the probability that between three and six customers, inclusive, will arrive at the drive-through window in a given hour.

    (c) the probability that fewer than three customers will arrive at the window in a given 30-minute period.

50. Beer bottles (that average 5% defective) are packed in boxes of 50. What is the probability of 48 or more good bottles in a box selected at random?

51. Find the probability of the following:

    (a) Binomial: $P(X = 7 \mid n = 9, \pi = .35)$

    (b) Poisson: $P(X = 3 \mid \lambda = 5)$

    (c) Normal: $P(X \geq 60 \mid \mu = 52, \sigma = 6)$

    (d) Normal: $P(X = 6 \mid \mu = 5, \sigma = 2)$

52. Use the appropriate probability distribution to compute the following:

    (a) $P(X < 3 \mid n = 8, \pi = .50)$

    (b) $P(X \geq 19 \mid n = 20, \pi = .85)$

    (c) $P(X = 14 \mid n = 30, \pi = .50)$

    (d) $P(20.0 < X < 25.0 \mid \mu = 18, \sigma = 6)$

53. A brand of 60-watt light bulbs has a normally distributed lifetime with a mean of 1,000 hours and a standard deviation of 60 hours.

    (a) What percent of the bulbs wear out between 940 and 1060 hours?

    (b)   What percent of the bulbs last more than 1100 hours?

    (c)   98% of the bulbs last longer than how many hours?

    (d)   The middle 95.5% of the bulb life lies between what hours?

54.   According to the USDA, the annual per capita consumption of milk and cream in liquid form in 2011 was approximately 201 gallons (www.ers.usda.gov/datafiles/**Dairy**_Data/pcconsp_1_.xls). *Assuming that the standard deviation of consumption is 20 gallons and that the distribution follows a normal distribution,*

    (a)   What is the probability that an individual adult from the population will consume more than 230 gallons of milk and cream per year?

    (b)   Determine the probability that an individual selected at random from the population will consume less than 175 gallons of milk and cream annually.

    (c)   What is the 95th percentile for the consumption of milk and cream?

55.   Sue Miller, Benefits Coordinator for Mega Bank, knows that historically the number of hours lost to employee illness has been normally distributed with an average 373 hours per week and a standard deviation of 29 hours.

    (a)   What is the probability that during a given week, the number of employee hours lost due to illness is between 340 and 400 hours?

    (b)   Sue wants to set an upper limit on how many hours are likely to be lost during a week. What is the value such that the number of hours lost will exceed this value only 1% of the time?

    (c)   During the last week, Sue discovers that 335 hours were lost to employee illness. How likely is it for this to happen? Should Sue be concerned about this?

56.   George owns a restaurant and lounge called the Cozy Inn. George knows that sometimes customers leave without paying their bill. Sometimes this is just forgetfulness on the part of the customer and sometimes it is deliberate theft. George has tracked this behavior over the years and finds that the average rate of occurrence is about 6 per week.

    (a)   What is the probability that during a given week 2 or fewer customers will leave without paying their tab?

    (b)   George has hired some new employees and finds that during the past week 11 customers left without paying their bill. Does George have reason to be concerned?

57.   Extensive experience has taught the partners of the accounting firm Preston and Marshall that about 15% of stated accounts receivable have some errors in them. If this is true

    (a)   What is the probability that the accounts receivables of a group of 10 clients will have zero errors?

    (b)   What is the probability that a group of 15 clients will have 3 or more errors?

    (c)   What is the expected number of errors in a group of 20 clients?

Optional: The Normal and Poisson as Approximations to the Binomial

When tables were found in the back of books to find binomial probabilities, there was often a need to conserve space. Since binomial tables took up a good deal of room, it was advantageous to find useful approximations to replace these bulky tables with smaller ones that were already included in the text. This is one of the major reasons for devising the normal and Poisson approximations to the binomial distribution. In the computer era, these approximations are not really necessary and that is why they are included here only as optional material; however, there is one situation in inferential statistics where the normal approximation is useful. This situation occurs in deriving confidence intervals in Chapter 6. The reason is because of the need for percentiles. Percentiles are a problem in discrete probability distributions (like binomials) because a specific percentile may not exist in a given discrete distribution. For example, there may be no value such that 95% of the distribution lies below that value.

The binomial can often be approximated by either the Poisson or the normal distributions. If the proportion is very small (or very large), the Poisson approximation is best; otherwise, the normal may be best. Of course, the Poisson approximation will not solve the percentile problem of the binomial since it is also a discrete distribution. There is no set rule to follow, but following is a "rule of thumb" used by some statisticians.

Guidelines for Approximation to the Binomial

Use the *Poisson*:	When $\pi \leq .05$ or $\pi \geq .95$
Use the *Normal*:	When $.05 < \pi < .95$ and $n\pi > 5$

Figure 4-14 shows how the sample size and π values affect the shape of the binomial distribution as n increases from 5 to 25. Even for small samples, the binomial distribution approaches the normal distribution as π nears .50. This is because the binomial is symmetrical at $\pi = .50$. As the sample size gets larger, the approach to the normal distribution is very pronounced. But, if the combination of n and π is quite small (<5), the approximation may still not be satisfactory.

Figure 4-14   ***Binomial Approaches a Normal Distribution as n increases and π***

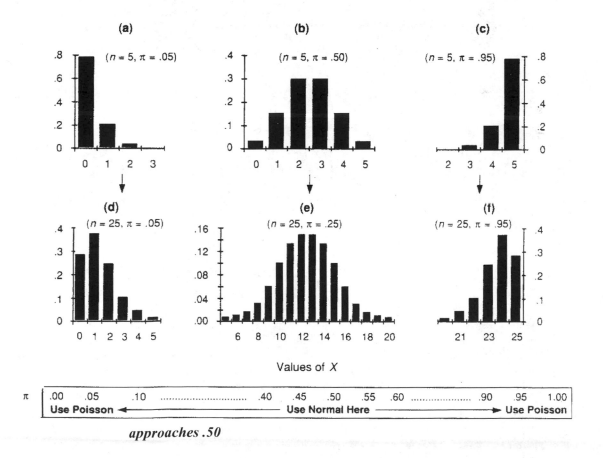

approaches .50

Mean and Standard Deviation

We have already illustrated the use of the Poisson to approximate the solution to binomial problems. Using the normal distribution is also quite straightforward. We let the mean and standard deviation of the normal distribution equal the corresponding statistics of the binomial:

$$\mu = n\pi \quad \sigma = \sqrt{n\pi(1 - \pi)} \qquad\qquad (4\text{-}17)$$

Continuity Correction

Insofar as the normal distribution is continuous, a continuity correction is sometimes needed when using the normal distribution to compute discrete probabilities. This is to account for the "gap" between discrete X-values. For example, suppose that you wished to use the normal distribution to compute the probability of a discrete value $X = 9$. This poses a problem because (1) the probability of any point (e.g., 9.0) on a continuous function is zero, and (2) for discrete data, there is a "gap" between 8 and 9 and between 9 and 10. We overcome this by letting our X-value include half the area in the gap on each side of X. Thus, to compute the probability of a single value of X, such as 9, we let X represent the area under the continuous function from 8.5 to 9.5.

Figure 4–15 illustrates the approximation by showing the rectangle on a continuous curve corresponding to the discrete value $X = 9$. Note that although the left side of the rectangle is slightly above the curve height at 8.5, there is a compensating error because the right side is slightly lower than the curve height at 9.5. As the sample size increases, this error (and compensating error) becomes smaller and smaller, so the (continuity) correction becomes less important.

Figure 4–15   *Normal Approximation with Continuity Correction*

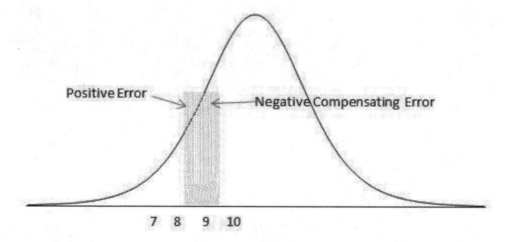

Example 4-22

Most of the employees at Green Meadow Dairy Cooperative favor a profit-sharing plan, but 30% of them oppose a current proposal. If a committee of 20 employees is selected at random, what is the probability that four or more of the committee members will oppose the proposal?

Solution

The binomial probability that four or more are opposed is:

$P(X \geq 4 \mid n = 20, \pi = .30) = 1.00 - \text{BINOM.DIST}(3, 20, .3, \text{TRUE}) = 1 - 0.107087 = 0.8929$

To use the normal approximation we first need to calculate the mean and standard deviation of the normal distribution:

$$\mu = n\pi = 20(.30) = 6 \qquad \text{and } \sigma = \sqrt{n\pi(1-\pi)} = \sqrt{(20)(.30)(.70)} = 2.05$$

After we make the correction for continuity (change 3 to 3.5) we can use NORM.DIST to find the probability:

$$1 - \text{NORM.DIST}(3.5, 6, 2.05, \text{TRUE}) = .8887$$

Both of the approximations are fairly close, partly because the continuity correction was made. This correction is unnecessary with large samples as the next example illustrates.

Example 4-23

Suppose that a population is guaranteed to be no more than 20% defective. A sample of 400 taken from a population has 102 defectives. If the true proportion is really .20, what is the probability that a random sample of 400 will contain 102 or more defective items?

Solution

We can calculate the exact probability using the BINOM.DIST function as:

$$1 - \text{BINOM.DIST}(101, 400, .20, \text{TRUE}) = 1 - 0.99559 = 0.00441$$

With the normal approximation:

$$\mu = n\pi = 400(.20) = 80 \qquad \text{and} \qquad \sigma = \sqrt{n\pi(1-\pi)} = \sqrt{(400)(.20)(.80)} = 8.0$$

The probability of 102 or more defective items is then the area to the right of 101:

$$=1 - \text{NORM.DIST}(101, 80, 8, \text{TRUE}) = 1 - 0.995668 = 0.004332$$

The correction for continuity would not get us any closer to the correct answer than this. In fact, it would make the approximation worse.

Exercises VI

58. A brokerage firm knows that occasionally a stockbroker will quote an incorrect price to a customer. Historically this has happens about 3% of the time. If the broker handles 60 calls on a given day, what is the probability that he will quote the wrong price three times? Use the Poisson approximation to answer the question. How close is the approximate answer to the correct answer using the binomial?

59. Hospital administrators know that about 2% of the population has a reaction of some kind to a chemical used in a particular surgery. If there are 20 surgeries scheduled for today what is the probability that there will be at least one reaction to the chemical using the Poisson approximation? How does this compare with the exact value using the binomial?

60. It is known that 32% of the population in a large city does not have health insurance. If there are 30 patients that come to the hospital emergency room on a given night, what is the probability that at least 5 will not have health insurance? Use the normal approximation to answer this question.

61. A telemarketing representative promoting the sale of storm doors considers a call "successful" if she can convince her phone respondents to accept a home visit from a company salesperson. Her historical success rate is 15%. Determine the probability that in the next 100 calls she will get (a) fewer than five successes; (b) 10 or more successes? Use the normal approximation to answer the questions. Compare your answers with the answers using the binomial in Exercise 10.

Chapter 5:

Sampling & Sampling Distributions

Chapter 5 Objectives

When you finish this chapter you should be able to:

1. Use random numbers to select a sample
2. Distinguish between judgment and probability sampling
3. Explain the meaning of a sampling distribution
4. Explain the concept of sampling error
5. Compute standard errors of means and proportions
6. Apply the finite population correction factor when necessary
7. Find probabilities and percentiles in sampling distributions of means, proportions and variances

Opening Vignette

Bill Montgomery founded M&M Custom Manufacturing 10 years ago. M&M started out as a small contract manufacturing company with 5 employees, but had grown to the point that there are now over 50 employees and the company does business internationally. Bill recently had lunch with one of M&M's most important customers and had been presented with a very attractive offer. M&M has been given the opportunity to be the exclusive supplier for a national chain of stores. The anticipated sales from this offer would increase M&M's overall sales by almost 500% and make them a major player in their industry. The "catch" in the contract is that M&M must absorb the loss on all defective units produced. The contract requires that M&M replace all defective units within 4 business days or face severe penalties. This is not of great concern to Bill if the proportion of defects is 1% or less. The current defect rate at M&M is quite low; however, Bill is not certain what effect the increase in production will have on defect rates. In addition, the new technologies that would have to be employed could also have an impact on defect rates. Whether or not this opportunity is financially attractive to M&M depends on the estimated defect rate and Bill knows that he must estimate that rate accurately or M&M could be in financial trouble.

Introduction

Marketing information can be crucial to a company's success. For example, Nike is currently the country's largest producer of athletic footwear, with annual sales of over $20.9 billion in fiscal 2011. The company accounts for nearly half of the global athletic shoe market. Several factors have helped propel Nike from a small manufacturer of running shoes in 1971 to the international giant they are today. Key among these factors has been the customer acceptance data they obtain from a sample of athletes and others who help with new designs and field tests of their existing products. Market information has truly been vital to the success of Nike!

Suppose that you are the unit manager for a chain of 15 retail stores marketing women's sweaters and sportswear in the Minnesota–Wisconsin area. You have a $500,000 budget to spend on next year's advertising and your manager is expecting you to increase sales by 20% or more. How do you decide which product features to emphasize in your sales promotion? Should you stress price, design, materials, or something else?

A good starting point for your advertising campaign would be to determine what features are important to your potential customers. Of course, you cannot survey all future customers to learn everyone's preferences—but you can make effective use of data taken from a sample of customers. Let's assume that you conduct a survey and your sample results reveal that the most important determinants of value among customers in your market area (by percent of respondents rating this feature highest) are:

Workmanship	13%	Fashion (style and colors)	31%
Convenience	24%	Materials	12%
Price	11%	Other	9%

These sample data suggest that you may want to focus your promotional message on the fashion and convenience aspects of your merchandise.

Sample information such as that illustrated above is also important to firms like Procter & Gamble and General Motors with each firm spending almost $4 billion on advertising alone in 2005[1]. With that amount of money at stake, companies like those must be confident that their sampling techniques are helping them make the best business-related decisions.

 This chapter is divided into two sections. In the first section, we will draw distinctions between types of samples and learn how to select a sample enabling us to make statistical inferences about a population. In the second section, we will learn about the concept of sampling distributions. The theory of sampling distributions is central to understanding statistics. Therefore, we will explore sampling distributions for the four parameters that we will discuss throughout the next four chapters: the mean, proportion, variance and median. This provides the foundation for inferential statistics that we will take up starting in Chapter 6.

Using Samples to Learn About Populations

Samples provide us with empirical data that can be analyzed statistically. In this section, we consider (1) reasons for sampling, (2) different types of sampling designs, and (3) potential errors with sampling.

Why Sample?

Managers frequently use sample data to make inferences about the characteristics of populations. Four possible reasons for using sample rather than population data include:

> 1. Testing an entire population may be impossible (or impractical).
>
> 2. The cost of surveying the population may be prohibitive.
>
> 3. The time requirements to complete a census may be prohibitive.
>
> 4. In some cases, sample results can be more accurate than performing a census.

Michelin would soon be out of business if they attempted to road test every tire they produced. It would be impractical for the Kellogg's to seek every potential consumer's opinion of a new breakfast cereal. In the same way, cost and time requirements often prompt companies to use sample data in statistical tests. In some cases, it may not be even possible to do a census. For example, a local building materials firm could not afford to do a compression (strength) test on each concrete block they produce because the testing process destroys the blocks; however, they may be able to test a few blocks out of each thousand, and use that information to draw an inference about the average compressive strength of the blocks produced during a given time period. Accuracy may seem like a dubious proposition at first; however, in some cases it is true. For example, in recent years, many experts have argued that the national census in the U.S. would be more accurate if it were based on a sample rather than a census of the entire population. The reason is due to nonsampling error or bias discussed in more detail later in this chapter. If the nonsampling error is larger than sampling error, then more accurate results can be expected from a sample than from a census.

Sampling Design

Information Required and Target Population

The first step in any statistical study is to state what information will be needed to answer the study's questions. This ensures that the data obtained are relevant and useful for decision-making. A corollary

---

[1] Advertising Age, June 27, 2005.

activity is the careful definition of the target population, or group of objects that will be studied. The population from which the sample is taken may or may not be the same as the target population. The most common instance of this is when animals are used instead of humans in medical studies. The research question may be how a particular product affects humans; however, since there are severe ethical difficulties in performing such experiments on humans, a company may use animals for testing instead[2]; yet, the target population should always be sampled if this can be done ethically and at a reasonable expense in time and money. If it is impossible to get an accurate list of the target population, some other group may be found and sampled that is sufficiently similar to the target population to provide reliable and valid conclusions. Another possibility would be to simulate the population characteristics on a computer, and "sample" from the simulated population distribution. If none of these is possible, the study may have to be redesigned.

Sample Frame

The collection of all members of a population to be studied is called a *sample frame*. Most frequently, the listing is a computer database, but it can be any well-defined group, such as a written file or even locations on a map. Each element of the frame need not be listed in a formal sense, but it must be a unique and identifiable entity that can be distinguished from other elements. But, if every element in the sample frame were observed we would have a census rather than a sample. As a consequence, we will be computing and using sample statistics to make inferences about the population parameters.

Types of Samples

Samples are frequently classified according to the manner in which the elements in the target population are selected. The two major categories are *nonprobability (or judgment) samples* and *probability samples*.

A *probability sample* is one in which each element of the population has a known nonzero chance of being included in the sample. Probability samples are determined by chance e.g., they are random. On the other hand, *nonprobability samples* usually have some elements with no chance of being included in the sample. With nonprobability samples, the elements in the sample are deliberately chosen, so the samples are nonrandom. There are advantages and disadvantages associated with each sample type as we will discuss shortly.

Errors in Sampling

Any data gathering activity (even a census) is subject to error. We are all aware of the possibilities of recording the wrong information or making mistakes while entering data into a computer. There is also the possibility of intentional errors which can be difficult to detect and combat. Two types of error, sampling and nonsampling errors, are of special concern in statistical analysis.

Nonsampling error is error due to flaws in the way the study is conducted. Some nonsampling errors are not systematic, such as errors in entering data into a computer. Other nonsampling errors can be systematic and introduce *bias* into a study. Bias is similar to having a bathroom scale that registers 5 pounds heavier than the actual weight or a speedometer that registers 10% slow. Mail surveys can be biased—especially when the respondents are self-selected. For example, a mail survey designed to gather people's opinions about gun control legislation is likely to be biased if the only people that respond are those that have strong feelings about gun control. Bias is a systematic (or nonrandom) error.

---

[2] Experimentation on animals brings with it a separate set of ethical issues as is often stressed by organizations such as PETA (People for the Ethical Treatment of Animals).

There are a wide variety of nonsampling errors. A 1978 publication from the Federal Committee on Statistical Methodology cited over 30 different types of nonsampling error[3]. Nonsampling errors are particularly problematic because:

- They are difficult, if not impossible, to measure

- They cannot be reduced, even if sample sizes are increased

The only way to minimize nonsampling error is to design a study very carefully. This includes the sampling frame and sampling procedures, testing all survey and interview methods, training interviewers and data recorders, and double checking all data entered into the system; however, even with a very thorough preparation and careful attention to details, nonsampling error can still occur. The most important task is to make sure that no bias exists in these nonsampling errors.

Sampling error is random error due to a sample not perfectly reflecting the characteristics of the population. Whenever there is variability in the population, the potential for sampling error exists. For example, suppose that a local chamber of commerce wished to use a sample of 50 households to estimate the median family income in their community. Income levels range from over $300,000 for families with dual income college graduates, down to around $18,000 for lower income and single-person households. An individual sample of 50 may not include a representative proportion of two-earner families, single men, minority families, single women, and so on. Therefore, the sample median income will most likely differ from the actual median income of the population.[4] This error in estimation is due to sampling error. It is an expected error and one you can learn to work with because it is predictable and we can measure and plan for it.

If good sampling procedures are followed, sampling error can usually be reduced by increasing the sample size (e.g., getting the size of the sample closer to the size of the population). Thus, in the previous example we might expect a sample of 1,000 households to yield a closer estimate of median family income than a sample of only 50; however, increasing the sample size will not correct for nonsampling error since this type of error would even be present in a census. Known bias usually requires an adjustment to the methodology or procedures used in the study.

Exercises I

1. Would you most likely use a sample, or a census, to do the following?

    (a) Learn what percentage of households in a three-block area use a local community center.

    (b) Assess public opinion on the use of military force to rescue hostages in a foreign country.

    (c) Determine whether individual stockholders wish to sell their stock to an investor who is attempting to take over control of the firm.

2. Explain why a sample, rather than a census, would be used to determine:

    (a) The types of toys preferred by preschoolers in Canada.

    (b) The "crash resistance" of a new automotive bumper.

    (c) The best diet to follow to avoid having a heart attack.

3. How does nonsampling error/bias differ from sampling error?

---

[3] Source: http://www.fcsm.gov/working-papers/sw4.html
[4] The U.S. Census Bureau estimates the real median family income in the United States in 2007 at $50,740.

Nonprobability and Probability Sampling

In this section we will describe the most widely used nonprobability and probability sampling procedures and discuss their advantages and disadvantages in more detail. Figure 5-1 lists some of the different types for each method:

Figure 5-1   ***Types of Probability and Nonprobability Samples***

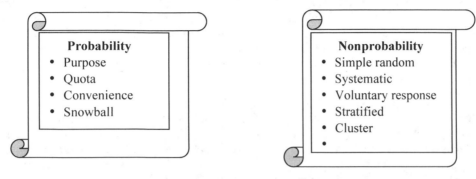

Probability
- Purpose
- Quota
- Convenience
- Snowball

Nonprobability
- Simple random
- Systematic
- Voluntary response
- Stratified
- Cluster
-

Nonprobability Sampling

Types of Nonprobability Samples

Three commonly used types of nonprobability samples are (1) purpose samples, (2) quota samples, and (3) convenience samples. A fourth method, (4) snowball sampling, is not as widely used, but is sometimes the only realistic way of generating a sample.

Purpose samples are selected to satisfy a specific purpose, like estimating a firm's product acceptance or measuring its productivity. The consumer price index (CPI) is one of the most widely used purpose samples in the United States, measuring the general level of prices in the economy. It is important because the wages of millions of workers and many government benefits are adjusted to this index annually. Note, however, that it does not include a random selection of items. Instead, it includes thousands of items that significantly impact the cost of living of most households, such as food, automobiles and rent costs. But, sometimes, purpose samples are deliberately chosen to misrepresent the total population. For example, a sample designed to explore the reaction of "gamers" to a new online offering may choose to recruit heavy online game users rather than trying to obtain a representative sample of the entire population of gamers.

Quota samples are samples taken from a population to ensure the sample exhibits certain characteristics. Usually, the person selecting elements for the sample will continue to sample a group until the quota is met. For example, an auto dealer trying to decide how many cars to carry in stock may ask a sample of 40 households about their intentions of purchasing a new car. The "quota" may include 30 households with two or more children, five apartment dwellers, and require that 60% of the respondents be female. Although the information from such samples may be useful, quota samples can contain selection bias because the subjects are chosen by the analyst and not randomly selected. Sometimes, however, having a certain quota may be more important than having a random sample. In our earlier example of a testing new online game, the opinions of the active "gaming" community may be more important than the opinions of a representative sample of the entire population.

Convenience samples are selected from subjects that are conveniently available such as mall intercept surveys, man-on-the-street TV interviews, and reader or viewer surveys. Like quota samples, convenience samples are open to selection bias. Some people may be more "approachable" than others, some might be too shy to appear on TV, or some people may never go to a particular mall and therefore could never participate in a mall intercept study. Especially susceptible to bias are surveys like Rate My Professors where the elements of the survey are self-selected. These surveys may be entertaining but they are not statistically relevant because we cannot attribute any statistical validity to them. In fact, evidence from convenience samples, such as mall intercept studies, has been ruled to be inadmissible as evidence in legal proceedings.

Snowball sampling is sometimes necessary where the desired characteristic is relatively rare in the population and therefore would not likely show up in a selected random sample. Snowball sampling begins by finding one individual, or a few individuals, with the desired characteristic to be in the sample and then ask them if they know other individuals with the desired characteristic to recruit to the group. By recruiting other participants, the sample "snowballs" in size. For example, suppose that your small travel agency in Billings, Montana developed some major contacts in the tourist industry in Turkey. You are interested in creating tour packages to that region, but would like to have some individuals who have been to Turkey in the past few years give you feedback on your initial plans so that they can be refined and improved. The chances of a random sample in Billings containing individuals who have traveled to Turkey in the last few years are relatively small. In this situation, a snowball sampling method would be perfectly appropriate.

Nonprobability or judgment samples involve some choice in deciding what elements will be included in the sample. For example, most exams by college instructors are "judgment samples" of the knowledge a student should have learned in the course. In some cases, judgment samples are the only practical way of obtaining information about a population—especially if it is very large or heterogeneous. In other cases, they are the most convenient or cost-effective method of sampling.

Limitations of Nonprobability Sampling

The limitations of nonprobability or judgment samples are quite severe and most statisticians are reluctant to use such samples. Nonprobability samples are subjective, and there is no satisfactory method of measuring their validity. Perhaps the greatest shortcoming is that they do not allow for an assessment of sampling error. Consequently, their analytical value is limited as we cannot reliably use them for making statistical inferences. In other words, our ability to make inferences based on the results from our sample to the population is severely impaired. Since the purpose of a statistical study is usually to make inferences about a population, this is a very serious limitation of nonprobability samples.

is not good

Probability Sampling

Probability samples are samples resulting from a random sampling process that gives each element of the population a measurable chance of being selected. Two key advantages of probability samples over nonprobability samples consist of:

- Incorporating a measure of the sampling error associated with the process.

- Allowing for the creation of statistical inferences about the population.

As suggested earlier, sampling error accounts for the fact that sample statistics vary from one sample to another and may deviate from the overall population value. Different samples may yield different results; however, the magnitude of the sampling error can be estimated (and to some extent controlled) in probability sampling. Given the knowledge of the sampling error, we can make valid statistical statements about the population being studied. This is, of course, the main purpose of most studies. That is why probability samples are more widely used in traditional statistical analysis.

Use this

There are four major mechanisms for probability samples:

1. Simple random sampling

2. Systematic sampling

3. Stratified sampling

4. Cluster sampling

Simple random sampling is the method of sample selection that gives each element in the population an **equal chance of being included in the sample**. The term "random" applies more to the sampling process than to the sample values obtained. In other words, taking a "random" sample does not guarantee that the results will appear to be random even if the process itself generates values randomly.

If the population values being sampled are discrete, random sampling means that the sampling process must give each element the same chance of being selected. If it is continuous, the probability of any range being included in the sample must be equal to the proportion of the population that lies in that interval. Using random numbers is one of the best ways of ensuring that a sample is random. In Example 5–1, we will use random numbers to ensure randomness in selecting a simple random sample.

Systematic samples are often an acceptable substitute for simple random sampling, especially when one is sampling from an ongoing process where all of the elements of the population cannot be listed because they have not been produced. For example, when sampling from a manufacturing process, the population includes all parts produced by the process, but some of these have not even been produced yet. With systematic sampling, a random starting point is first selected by using a random number generator. From there, additional elements are selected at fixed intervals of time. The first element in the sample is randomly selected and its position determines what other elements will be selected for the sample.

Example 5-1

A large retailer wishes to obtain a sample of $n = 30$ charge accounts from a listing of $N = 3,000$ accounts. How might this be done using a systematic sampling procedure?

Solution

1. To obtain the sample of 30 from 3,000, we must sample one account from each sequential listing of $N/n = 3,000/30 = 100$ accounts.

2. Use a random number in the range 1 to 100 to select the first account. Suppose that the number generated is 72. Then the first sample is account 72.

3. Sample every 100th account after that until $n = 30$ accounts are sampled. The second sample will then be account 172 (e.g., 72 + 100). Thus our selected accounts would be 72, 172, 272, 372, 472, ..., 2972.

Good description

Systematic sampling can be as representative as simple random sampling and usually requires less time and cost; however, one must consider the possibility of bias. Bias can occur if the sampling interval corresponds with some inherent patterns in the data. For example, a sample of wait times in a hospital emergency room may not be representative if the systematic interval (population value) was seven days and the sample selected results from Tuesday (which are lower because demand for emergency room services is higher on weekend days).

With *stratified sampling*, the population is partitioned into relatively homogeneous subgroups (or strata), based on some characteristics of the elements of the population. Random samples are then taken from each subgroup. Stratified sampling ensures that the sample will represent all levels of the given characteristic. For example, if we stratify by income, then the sample will contain representatives from all income levels across the population. A benefit of stratification is that the process of combining similar elements in strata may result in less variability within the groups and thus permit the use of smaller samples than might otherwise be required. Because (1) the chance of being selected in the sample depends on the subgroup the element is in and (2) each subgroup usually does not have the same number of elements, not all elements of the population have an equal chance of being included in the sample For example, using income level for stratification would mean that someone in the very upper income levels may well have a higher chance of being in the sample than someone in the lower income levels because there are fewer individuals in the first group and that group must be represented; however, if sampling is done proportionately, where the proportion of the sample in each group reflects their proportion in the population, then each element should have roughly the same chance of being in the sample (proportionate stratified sampling is the most common form).

As an example, suppose that a state economist wished to use sample data to estimate the average length of time employees have worked for their current employer. Suppose that some industries, such as the electrical utility industry, had relatively stable employment over the years, whereas others, such as high tech, experienced higher turnover. The economist may benefit from first grouping the firms by industry, randomly sampling from each industrial group, and then weighing the results in proportion to the percentage of employees each industry has of the total employees in the state. This would be a more accurate representation of the population as a whole.

The benefits of stratified sampling arise from the grouping of the population into strata that have similar characteristics (e.g., industry, geographical location, age, city size, etc.). If the individuals within groups are relatively homogeneous, a small sample may be sufficient to estimate the characteristic with the desired precision. If some groups have considerable variability, larger samples should be taken of those groups only. The results from each group can be given weights according to their importance. The primary benefit of a stratified sample can be a more accurate estimate of the population for a given sample size or a smaller sample size to obtain a given degree of precision.

Cluster sampling is the counterpart of stratified sampling where the population is arranged into heterogeneous subgroups (or clusters) often based on geographical location. The assumption is that each "cluster" contains a representative mix, comparable to what exists in the population itself. A random sample is selected from the subgroups or clusters. The primary purpose of cluster sampling is to save time and money in obtaining sample information.

As an example, suppose that a textbook publisher wished to estimate the amount of money a typical university student spends on textbooks each year. The sampling frame might include all several million students at the numerous universities scattered across the country. A random sample of 50 students, for example, might mean contacting (or visiting) 50 different universities; however, the sampling frame (university students) might first be "clustered" by university recognizing that the costs to business, engineering, liberal arts and other students are likely to be similar from one university to another. The publisher might randomly select just five universities as clusters. They could then conduct a second stage of the study by randomly selecting 100 students at each of those five universities to survey.

The advantage of cluster sampling is that the travel and sampling costs can be greatly reduced. Cluster sampling can sometimes provide a good basis for inference, and it can be done at a reasonable cost. It is especially advantageous in situations where simple random sampling is economically or physically impossible. For example, cluster sampling is widely used in door-to-door surveys in large cities where the clusters are based on geographical location to minimize travel times. In contrast to stratified sampling, the primary purpose of cluster sampling is to reduce costs.

Most survey research combines several of these techniques in selecting a sample, a process referred to as a *multistage* sampling. Each stage of the sampling process involves a probability sample, but different techniques may be used at different stages based on needs and available resources.

Probability or Nonprobability Samples?

There are advantages and disadvantages of each type of sampling method. But, in general, probability and nonprobability samples have certain strengths and weaknesses. Table 5-1 lists some of the most important differences between the two:

Table 5-1   *Comparison of Probability and Nonprobability Sampling Methods*

Factor	Probability	Nonprobability
Cost	Quite high	Usually low
Time	Longer	Shorter
Accuracy	Can be very high	Usually lower
Acceptance	Universally-accepted	Poor to reasonable acceptance
Ability to Generalize	Very good	Usually very poor

The primary benefits of nonprobability samples are in terms of time and cost; however, the price paid for this savings is the limited ability to generalize to the population at large and the lack of general acceptance for such methods. Thus, although nonprobability samples are sometimes necessary, and even occasionally preferred, they make it difficult, if not impossible, to generalize beyond the sample. Nonprobability samples introduce elements of human judgment that can bias statistical results in unpredictable ways. In order to make inferences about the population as a whole, one must utilize a probability sample. For these reasons, we will assume probability samples in the remainder of this text.

Exercises II

4. How does judgment sampling differ from probability sampling?

5. Which method of sampling involves:

   (a) Grouping the population into relatively homogeneous subgroups that contain less variability than within the total population?

   (b) Beginning at a random starting point and selecting additional elements at fixed intervals of time or sequential locations?

   (c) Arranging the population into heterogeneous subgroups that have compositions similar to each other?

6. Suppose that you were assigned the task of sampling 40 students in your college or university to find out how many terms it really takes students to obtain their degree. You wish to use your sample data to draw some inference about the average time required by all students. (a) Which type of sampling would you use?

7. Distinguish between simple random sampling and systematic sampling.

8. Distinguish between stratified sampling and cluster sampling.

9. A random telephone survey is to be made for a city parks department. Interviewers are instructed on how to use a random number to obtain a name from the first page of the phonebook. Then, they have to call the person listed in that same location on every fifth page in the book. (a) What type of sampling design is this? (b) Would this likely yield valid sample results (e.g., from both the sampling and bias error standpoints)?

Random Sampling Using Excel and XLDataAnalyst

Probability samples require that items be selected from the population by chance, or "at random." This ensures that there is no bias or control over which items are included in the sample. One common method is by using random numbers where different values of the numbers have equal chance of occurring. Prior to the widespread use of computers, random samples were commonly selected using random number tables; however, most modern spreadsheet packages, including Excel, have the capability of quickly generating random numbers that can be used to select samples.

Generating Random Numbers Using Excel

Excel can generate random numbers between 0 and 1 with the RAND() worksheet function. Simply putting the text "=RAND()" in a cell will produce a random number between zero and one[5]. You can then use these values as a basis for generating random numbers between any other values. For example, if you multiply the generated value by 100 and round the value off, you can generate random integers from 0 through 100; however, there is a RANDBETWEEN() function that will generate random integers between any two values. For example entering =RANDBETWEEN(1, 50) will generate a random integer between 1 and 50. If the data needs to be entered into the computer, use RANDBETWEEN(); if the data is already in an Excel file, use RAND(). More sophisticated random values can be generated using the Data Analysis Toolpak by selecting the Data Analysis option in the Analysis section of the Data ribbon tab. In the dialog box, select the Random Number Generation option. This allows you to generate values from specific distributions such as the normal distribution[6].

Example 5-2

A sales manager with 80 accounts would like to try a new promotional campaign on six accounts selected at random. Use the random number generator in Excel to select the numbers of the six accounts.

Solution

Assuming the customers are numbered from 01 through 80, we will need only two digit numbers between 1 and 80 to select our random sample. Put the following text in the first cell of a blank spreadsheet: =RANDBETWEEN(1,80). Then, copy this cell down to cells 2 through 10. Note that we only need 6 values for our sample but it is always a good idea to generate a few extra values in case we get duplicate numbers. Sample results are shown in Figure 5-2. (Note that your results will differ because each time the random number generator is used, different values will result). The first six unique numbers are: 68, 22, 37, 69, 59, and 15. Thus, the sample would include the 68th account, the 22nd account, and so on.

Figure 5-2   *Generated Random Numbers in Excel*

	A	B	C
1	68		
2	22		
3	37		
4	69		
5	59		
6	15		
7	60		
8	57		
9	26		
10	12		
11			

In many business situations, there are numbers such as account numbers or part numbers that are included in the organization's database. In these cases, the listing of such numbers in the database may constitute a satisfactory "sampling frame." If it is not possible to identify the elements of the population and assign numbers to them, a random sample might still be obtained if each element (and combination) has an equal chance of being selected; otherwise, some other type of sampling plan must be used.

---

[5] You must include the parentheses "()" after the function name. Simply typing "=RAND" will generate an error.
[6] There has been some debate about the adequacy of the random number generation process used in Excel in the RAND, RANDBETWEEN functions and in the Data Analysis Toolpak. The general consensus seems to be that the process has been improved in more recent versions such as Excel 2007 but that some problems remain; however, most experts also agree that the generation process is perfectly acceptable for generating small samples of numbers as we are doing here. Those doing more sophisticated simulations may want to find a suitable replacement for the Excel routines.

Random Sampling with Excel XLDataAnalyst

XLDataAnalyst will also generate a random sample from a set of data in an Excel spreadsheet. You can generate a simple random sample or a stratified random sample. The worksheet that contains the dataset that you wish to sample from should be the active worksheet when you choose this option. The option is selected by choosing the Random Sample option in the Utilities section of the XLDataAnalyst tab of the ribbon. When you select this option the dialog shown in Figure 5-3 will appear.

Figure 5-3   XLDataAnalyst Random Sampling Dialog

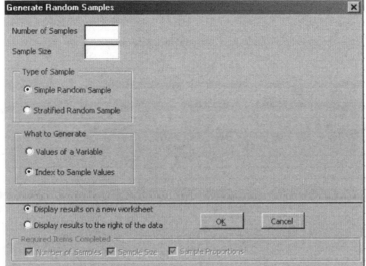

You first need to specify the number of samples that you wish to take and the desired sample size. The sample size entered must be no larger than the number of observations in the dataset. Since each sample is printed in a column of a worksheet, the limit on the number of samples is the limit on the number of columns in the version of Excel that you are using. Select the type of sample you wish to take, either simple random sample or stratified sample. If you elect to take a stratified sample, a list of discrete variables will be shown for you to select the variable that determines the strata or groups. This variable must be an existing variable with no more than 15 values.

There are two options that determine the type of values that are generated in the samples. In the default option, XLDataAnalyst generates an index to the list of observations in the dataset. For example, if there are 90 observations in the data set, XLDataAnalyst will generate random integers between 1 and 90 for the values in each sample. These index values can then be used to retrieve the original values using the LOOKUP function of Excel or by some other means. This option is especially useful if you want to sample entire records that have values for multiple variables. The other option is to include the actual values of a variable in the samples. When you select this option, a list of variables in the dataset will be shown so that you can select one variable to be sampled. Figure 5-4 shows the dialog when both the stratified sampling option and the Values of a Variable option are selected. In this example, the variable to be sampled is CurrentSal and the sample is to be stratified by Gender. For stratified sampling you must also specify the proportion to sample from each group.

Figure 5-4   Completed Dialog for Stratified Sampling With Variables

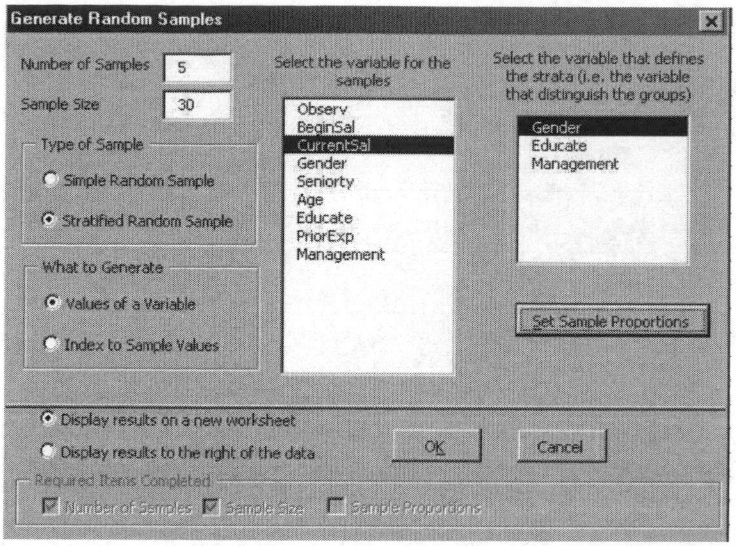

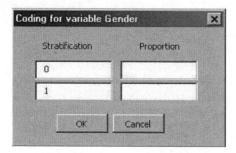

You set these proportions by clicking the Set Sample Proportions button below the list of stratification variables. When you click this button (or press the Alt-S keys), a dialog similar to Figure 5-5 will appear.

Figure 5-5   Dialog for Setting the Proportions In Each Strata

In this case, the stratification variable, Gender, has two possible values: 0 and 1. Enter the proportion for each group in the appropriate text box. For example if you enter .6 for the value 0 and .4 for the value 1 then 60% of each sample will be from the gender coded as 0 and 40% will be from the gender coded as 1. Note that all of the proportions must add up to 1.0. After you have finished specifying all of the options click the OK button to generate the samples.

Exercises III

10.   Using Excel, select a sample of 5 random numbers within the range 4,000 to 6,000.

11.   A stock brokerage firm maintains a list of 7,275 accounts and would like to draw a random sample of 15 accounts to test-market a new bond issue. Using Excel, identify the 15 accounts to be used in the study.

12.   The human resources manager of a firm with 200 employees would like to randomly sample 30 employees to assess their reaction to a recently implemented smoking policy. The list of employees is contained in the file Exercise 5-12.xlsx. (a) Select a simple random sample for the HR manager

using an index to the original values. b) Select a stratified sample where 30 % are in the Manufacturing area, 50% are in the Administrative area and 20% are in Sales.

13. An IRS computer has suggested that 20 income tax returns be randomly selected from a group of returns for audit. The social security numbers associated with the returns are provided in the file Exercise 5-13.xlsx. Select the 20 social security numbers to be included in the audit.

14. Helen Spence, the Vice-President of Human Resources at the Unified Bank, wants to sample the employees of the bank to determine their attitude toward a proposed change in the health care benefits package. She knows that it is important to sample a broad spectrum of employees from different areas of the organization. The file Exercise 5-14.xlsx contains a list of employees by employee number, and the department of the bank in which they work. Devise a sampling plan for Helen and take a random sample of 50 employees of the bank.

15. A pollster is planning of conducting a poll in the State of Idaho concerning whether or not the state should set up a government mandated health care exchange. He knows that the responses to the question could vary depending on a variety of factors. One of those is religious preference. The file Exercise 5-15.xlsx contains a list of eligible voters in one small town designated by a number, along with their stated religious preference. Create an appropriate random sample of 40 residents of this town.

Sampling Variation and Sampling Error

All four of the probability sampling methods use some type of random sampling. This is essential because it is the random nature of the sampling process (and the associated error) that enables us to make quantifiable inferences about the populations from which samples are drawn. Without knowing the degree of sampling error, there can be no statistical inference. Recall that in Chapter 1, we defined the concepts of common cause and special cause variabilities. We also stated that we had to know about the magnitude of common cause variability in order to interpret any deviation from the average or expected value. In the context of statistical inference, sampling error is common cause variation. In this section we define sampling error and describe how it is measured.

Sampling Error

Sampling error arises from inherent variation in the population, e.g., common cause variability. If individual values in a population differ, random samples taken from that population will also differ, depending on what elements happen to be included in the sample. To illustrate sampling variability, consider an example testing the ages of students in a classroom.

Example 5-3

An economics class contains 30 students. Two random samples of $n = 3$ students each are selected to estimate the mean age of the population of students in the class. The sample means are $\overline{X}_1 = 20.0$ and $\overline{X}_2 = 23.0$, as shown below. (Although the population parameter would not normally be known, for purposes of this example assume that data from the registrar's office reveal that the population mean age for this class is $\mu = 21.0$ years.) Identify the variability due to sampling error.

Ages of N = 30 Students (Population)

21	18	22	22	19	24	35	...	20
Samples				18 22 20			19 22 25	
Means of samples				$\overline{X}_1 = 20.0$			$\overline{X}_2 = 23.0$	

Population Mean μ $\hspace{5cm}$ $\mu = 21.0$

Solution

The sampling error of the sample means is:

$$\text{For } \bar{X}_1: \text{ variability} = \bar{X}_1 - \mu = 20.0 - 21.0 = -1.0 \text{ yr.}$$

$$\text{For } \bar{X}_2: \text{ variability} = \bar{X}_2: -\mu = 23.0 - 21.0 = 2.0 \text{ yr.}$$

The differences between sample means and the population mean μ are due to chance. Although $\bar{X}_1$ provides a closer estimate of μ than $\bar{X}_2$, both sample means will contain errors. Furthermore, if we didn't know the value of μ (which is common), we wouldn't know which estimate of sample means was closer to μ.

Insofar as our purpose with using sample statistics, like $\bar{X}$ is to estimate μ, we would like to be fairly confident that our sample statistic is close to the parameter value. Fortunately, we can control the amount of error by adjusting the size of the sample. This brings us to a consideration of sampling distributions and sample size. Although it is easiest to explain sampling distributions in terms of sample means, the same theory applies to sample proportions, sample variances, sample medians or any other sample statistic.

The Concept of a Sampling Distribution

Forming a Sampling Distribution

How many different samples of size $n = 3$ students could be drawn from a class (population) of 30 students? At first, it may seem like an unlikely high number, but 4,060 possible sample combinations exist[7]. Of course, it would not necessarily be the best use of time to identify all 4,060 different possibilities—much less calculate a mean for each one (and with such a small population, it would certainly make more sense to find the population mean by taking a census of the 30 students).

Nevertheless, let us suppose for a moment that we *did* take all 4,060 possible samples of $n = 3$ from the population of 30 students. We then calculate a mean for each sample, just as we calculated $\bar{X}_1: = 20.0$ and $\bar{X}_2: = 23.0$ in the previous example. After we calculated $\bar{X}_{4,060}$ we could form a frequency distribution of the sample means, just as we worked with the frequency distributions of individual values in Chapter 2. The difference here, of course, is that our distribution would be of sample means rather than of individual sample values. Figure 5–6 is an illustration of a histogram of the distribution, where the means are recorded to the nearest whole number.

---

[7] Combinations are the number of different ways of selecting n sample units from a population of N units if no duplications are permitted and the order of selection makes no difference. In this case there are 4,060 samples of size $n = 3$ that can be taken from a population of size 30.

Figure 5–6   *Frequency Distribution of Sample Means*

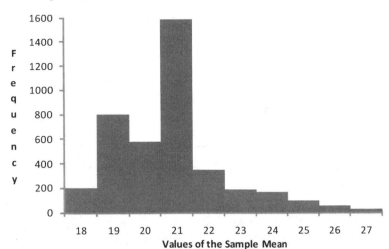

This distribution of sample means illustrates a sampling distribution. Using this distribution we could make statements about the likely values of the sample mean for samples of size three from this population. For example, we can see that the most likely values of the sample mean are from 19 to 22 years old and that it is highly unlikely to obtain a sample mean greater than 25 years.

Definition of a Sampling Distribution For the Sample Mean

If we expressed the frequencies with which various values of the sample means occurred as relative frequencies (or probabilities), we could refer to the probability distribution of the sample means as a sampling distribution of the means (taking samples repeatedly from the same population).

> A *sampling distribution* is a probability distribution of the sample means. It stipulates:
>
> 1. All possible values of $\bar{X}$ that can occur from samples of a given size, n.
>
> 2. The probabilities of each value of $\bar{X}$.

Table 5-2 illustrates the sampling distribution that would result from the sample means of Figure 5-6 where the probabilities are relative frequencies rather than actual frequencies.

Table 5-2   *Sampling Distribution of Ages of Students (from samples of n = 3)*

Mean Age $\bar{X}$	Probability $P(\bar{X})$
18	.05
19	.20
20	.14
21	.40
22	.10
23	.04
24	.03
25	.02
26	.01
27	.01
Total	1.00

Remember that a **sampling distribution applies to one sample size only** (in the case above, a sample of $n = 3$). Moreover, it is usually "theoretical" in that we would rarely (if ever) need to take all possible samples of a given size from a population, calculate their means, and compute the respective probabilities of the various means, as we have done here. But, the basic concept of a sampling distribution of the mean will be extremely useful to us later as it is critical to understanding statistical inference.

Mean and Standard Deviation of the Sampling Distribution

The statistics that will be most useful to us are, as before, the estimates of the central tendency and the variability of the distribution. For a distribution of sample means, the mean of all the $\bar{X}$s is simply the summation of all the possible sample means, divided by the number of sample means (4,060 in our illustration above). It is designated as $\mu_{\bar{X}}$. The standard deviation of the sampling distribution ($\sigma_{\bar{X}}$) is also designated with the subscript $\bar{X}$ to distinguish it from the standard deviation of the population, σ.

Mean of a sampling distribution of $\bar{X}$:	$\mu_{\bar{X}}$
Standard deviation of sampling distribution of $\bar{X}$:	$\sigma_{\bar{X}}$

The standard deviation of the sampling distribution of the means ($\bar{X}$s) is called the *standard error of the mean*. Mathematicians have proven two simple facts about the mean and the standard deviation of the sampling distribution:

1. The mean of the sampling distribution of $\bar{X}$ always equals the population mean, μ:
$$\mu_{\bar{X}} = \mu$$

2. The standard deviation of $\bar{X}$ always equals the population standard deviation divided by the square root of the sample size:

$$\sigma_{\bar{X}} = \sigma/\sqrt{n}$$

This means that the individual sample means will, on average, tend to equal the population mean μ. This is a consequence of the fact that a sample mean ($\bar{X}$), is an unbiased estimate of the population mean as we will see in the next chapter. It can be shown that the other two important sample statistics (the sample proportion p and the sample variance s^2) are also unbiased estimates of their respective population parameters (π and σ) so that the mean of their sampling distribution will also equal the appropriate population value.

These facts tell us that if we know the mean and the standard deviation of the population, we know the mean and standard deviation of the sampling distribution of the sample mean. But, what is the shape of this distribution? If the population follows a normal distribution, then it can be said that the sample means will also follow a normal distribution. If the population is not a normal distribution, then we have to rely on one of the most famous theorems in statistics: the Central Limit Theorem.

The Central Limit Theorem

As suggested in Figure 5-6, the sampling distribution for the small samples drawn from the class did not follow a symmetric pattern. Suppose that the sample size used to estimate their average age was increased from $n = 3$ to $n = 5$ or $n = 10$. The necessary sample size for an experiment depends on the nature of the target population. If the population is highly skewed, a larger sample is necessary. As the sample size increases, the shape of the sampling distribution reveals two effects. First, the extreme (high and low) values have less weight in the average, so that the sample $\bar{X}$s will be drawn closer to the population mean μ. This implies that if the sample size were increased to the same size as the population ($N = 30$), $\bar{X}$ would equal μ!

Second, depending on the shape of the population one is sampling from, as the sample size increases, the $\bar{X}$s tend to form a symmetrical distribution about their mean $\mu_{\bar{X}}$. For large samples, this approaches a normal distribution. Figure 5-7 illustrates this effect that is formalized in the expression of the central limit theorem.

Figure 5-7   ***Sampling Distributions Approach Normality as Sample Size Increases***

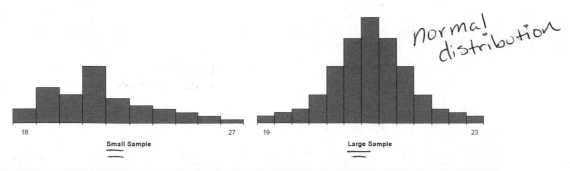

normal distribution

Central Limit Theorem:

As the sample size increases, the sampling distribution of $\bar{X}s$ becomes more and more like a normal distribution regardless of the distribution of the population.

Statisticians consider a **sample size of 30** to be "sufficiently large" that we can essentially view the sampling distribution to be a normal distribution. But, even for samples as small as 20, the sampling distribution approaches normality, especially if the population is not highly skewed. In addition, if the population itself is normally distributed, the sampling distribution will always be a normal distribution, even for very small sample sizes. *Large Sample → 30*

The central limit theorem is one of the most significant theorems in statistics. Most traditional inferential statistics is based on an assumption that the population of values follows a normal distribution; however, according to the central limit theorem, the nature of the population does not really matter if the sample size is large enough. For example, as depicted in Figure 5-8, large samples drawn from rectangular, triangular, skewed, or any other type of distribution, all yield sample means that tend to follow a normal distribution.

Figure 5-8   ***Sample Means Tend to be Normally Distributed for Any Population***

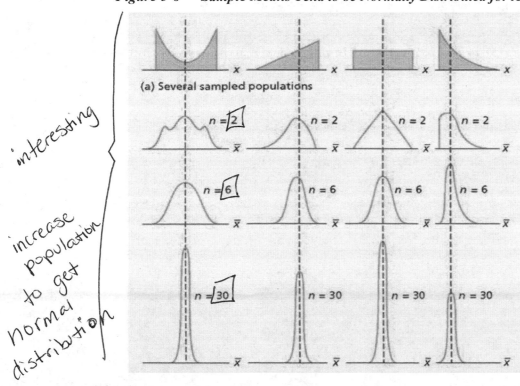

interesting

increase population to get normal distribution

Standard Error of the Sampling Distribution

The standard deviation of the distribution of sample means is similar to the population standard deviation with the exception that instead of individual X values, we are working with $\bar{X}$ values. This standard deviation of the $\bar{X}$s is called the *standard error of the mean*, and is designated $\sigma_{\bar{X}}$. It is, thus, a measure of the error, or the amount by which the sample means differ from the population mean μ. As Theorem 1 demonstrated, the standard error of the mean is a function of the population standard deviation and the sample size.

$$\sigma_{\bar{X}} = \frac{\sigma}{\sqrt{n}} \quad \text{don't use this equation} \tag{5-1}$$

The sampling distribution for other sample statistics will have standard deviations also referred to as standard errors. This leads to a general observation:

> The term standard error always refers to the standard deviation of a sampling distribution.

Therefore, we can talk about the standard error of the proportion, the standard error of the variance, or the standard error of any sample statistic.

Using the Standard Error

Once computed, we can use the standard error of the mean, $\sigma_{\bar{X}}$ to determine probabilities associated with sampling distributions in much the same manner that we have used the standard deviation when calculating probabilities associated with any other normal distribution. The difference is that we are working with a distribution of sample means ($\bar{X}$s) rather than a distribution of individual values. So we will use $\bar{X}$ and $\sigma_{\bar{X}}$ rather than X and σ as arguments in NORM.DIST or NORM.INV or in calculating a Z value of the standard normal distribution. Thus, for a known standard deviation, the Z-value for the sampling distribution is:

$$\text{Z-value for sampling distribution:} \qquad Z = \frac{\bar{X} - \mu}{\sigma_{\bar{X}}} \tag{5-2}$$

For samples of size 1 this equation is equivalent to the Z-values discussed in the last chapter. In the next example, we will need to calculate the standard error of the mean and then use that standard error to draw some conclusions about the sampling distribution of the means.

Example 5-4

Starbucks is considering opening a new retail store in the city of EagleCrest if the situation is right. One criterion is that the average household income is $50,000 or more. Starbucks is planning to use a random sample of $n = 40$ households to arrive at some estimate of the true mean household income. Suppose that a recent census of EagleCrest (N = 40,000 households), unknown to Starbucks, found an average household income of $51,000 with a standard deviation of $10,000.

    (a)   Can Starbucks be fairly sure that their sample mean will have the same value as the true average household income for the city?

    (b)   What is the probability that the sample mean will be (i) less than $52,000; (ii) less than $50,000?

    (c)   Explain the rationale behind using a sample of 40 records to help make this marketing decision.

Solution

(a) No, most of the sample means will have different values from the true mean. The standard deviation of the distribution of means (e.g., standard error of the mean) is fairly large.

$$\sigma_{\bar{X}} = \frac{\sigma}{\sqrt{n}} = \frac{10,000}{\sqrt{40}} \approx \$1,581$$

(b) The true mean is $\mu = \$51,000$, so we know that the mean of the sampling distribution is also $\$51,000$. We could also infer that approximately half of the sample means are above and below this amount. So, the probability of a sample mean being less than $\$51,000$ is .50. ?

We can use NORM.DIST to find the probability of $\$50,000$ or less as NORM.DIST(50000,51000,1581,TRUE) = .2635. That is about 26% of the sample means have values of less than $\$50,000$.

(c) The rationale is based on knowledge that the mean of the sampling distribution of $\bar{X}$ always equals the population mean and that the sampling distribution of $\bar{X}$ is approximately normal for samples as large as 40. This enables us to use the normal distribution to compute probabilities associated with the value of any particular sample mean.

Finite Population Correction Factor

In most business applications, a sample is only a small part of the population. Therefore, any sample is likely to be just as representative as another; however, when a sample encompasses a noticeably large part of the population, the chances that the sample mean will take on a value closer to the population mean are enhanced. This means that the standard error of the mean should be smaller in these situations than in situations where the sample constitutes an insignificant part of the population.

To illustrate, let us take an extreme case. Assume that a population of $N = 36$ credit accounts has a standard deviation of $\$48$ i.e., $\sigma = \$48$. If one took a sample of all 36 accounts, the sample mean would equal the population mean and the standard error of the mean should be zero. But, Equation 5-1 would give an incorrect result of:

$$\sigma_{\bar{X}} = \frac{\sigma}{\sqrt{n}} = \frac{48}{\sqrt{36}} = \$8$$

This means that equation 5-1 does not always give us a correct result because this equation is really an approximation that works well in most situations. It may not work properly when we take large samples from small populations. Equation 5-3 shows that the standard error of the mean has a correction factor that depends on the size of the sample relative to the population.

Corrected Standard Error: $\qquad \sigma_{\bar{X}} = \frac{\sigma}{\sqrt{n}} \sqrt{\frac{N-n}{N-1}}$ *Use this equation!* $\qquad (5\text{-}3)$

The *finite population correction factor*[8] is an adjustment for the sample size relative to the population. In our example, the sample size equals the population size so that N-n = 0. The correction factor gives a value of 0 and the standard error is correctly computed to be 0. As the sample size becomes small relative to the population size, the correction factor will approach 1.0. In fact, for sampling fractions (n/N) less than 5% the correction factor is so close to 1.0 that we can safely omit it in the computations; however, whenever the sampling fraction (n/N) is 5% or more of the population, the effect can be noticeable, and some correction is necessary. Fortunately, in most real world situations we are usually sampling less than 5% of the population and we can safely ignore the correction factor. *Can sometimes ignore*

---

[8] Actually, the term correction factor is not quite accurate. This seems to imply that the standard error must be corrected in certain situations. In actuality, the correction factor is technically always part of the equation. It is just that we can safely ignore it if we are sampling less than 5% of the population.

Example 5-5

To illustrate the use of the finite population correction factor, recall the problem presented in Example 5-4. In Example 5-4 we found that using a sample of 40 observations resulted in a probability of .2635 that the sample mean would have a value of less than $50,000. A sample mean less than $50,000 would cause Starbucks to decide against establishing a store in EagleCrest. Suppose that Starbucks wishes to consider using a larger sample (of $n = 400$) to arrive at an estimate of the true average household income in EagleCrest. Assume that other data are the same (e.g., the true—but unknown—μ is $51,000 and σ = $10,000).

(a) What is the probability that the mean of this larger size sample will be less than $50,000?

(b) Discuss the difference in the answer here versus the answer in Example 5–4.

Solution

(a) The mean of the probability distribution is still $51,000; however, insofar as the larger sample of $n = 400$ is 10% of the population of $N = 4,000$, we must apply the finite population correction factor when calculating the standard error. Using equation (5–4), we have

$$\sigma_{\bar{X}} = \frac{\sigma}{\sqrt{n}} \sqrt{\frac{N-n}{N-1}} = \frac{10,000}{\sqrt{400}} \sqrt{\frac{4,000-400}{4,000-1}} = (500)(.9487) = \$474.35$$

The sample means are still normally distributed about the population mean of $51,000, so the probability of a sample mean being less than $51,000 is still .50. To compute any other probabilities using the normal distribution, we use the standard error of the mean, as corrected by the finite population correction factor.

NORM.DIST(50000,51000,474.35,TRUE) = .0174

Thus $P(X < \$50,000) = .0174$. That is less than 17 out of a thousand of the sample means have values less than $50,000.

(b) Increasing the sample size from 40 to 400 improved the likelihood of getting a good estimate from the sample because it reduced the probability of obtaining a sample mean of less than $50,000 (from the sampling distribution with a true mean of $51,000). The major reason for this was because the increased sample size reduced the standard error to less than one-third of its original value (e.g., from $1,581 to $500); however, in this particular case the sample size was increased to over 5% of the population size—so the finite population correction factor also took effect. It resulted in a multiplier that further reduced the standard error to 94.87% of what is would have been if the sample were not large relative to the population size. These two effects reduced the chance of getting a misleadingly small sample mean value from about 26% to under 2%. The larger sample would thus improve the likelihood of getting a sample mean that would lead the firm to make the correct decision of opening a store in this city. On the other hand, taking a larger sample is more costly. Therefore before authorizing a larger sample, the responsible manager should consider whether the benefits of getting a closer estimate would, in fact, offset the additional costs.

Exercises IV

16. A random sample of 10 castings revealed an average weight of 37 lbs. although the population mean was later found to be 41 lbs. Explain how this could happen.

17. Suppose that a valid random sample of 49 records showed a family of four, in a given income class, paid an average tax of $5,972/year, whereas a survey of IRS records of all such taxpayers revealed the population value was actually $6,172, and σ = $1,400. (a) Explain how this difference might

happen. (b) What is the standard error of the mean? (c) Would you consider the sample a reasonably good estimate?

18. A population has a mean of $385 and standard deviation of $39. Find the standard error of the mean for samples of (a) $n = 9$; (b) $n = 100$. (c) How would your answer differ if $\mu = \$420$?

19. A grocery warehouse has 2,400 cartons with a mean weight of $\mu = 48.0$ lbs. and $\sigma = 16.0$ lbs. Compute the standard error of the mean (a) for samples of $n = 75$, and (b) $n = 800$.

20. Compute the standard error for the following (a) $n = 74$, $\mu = 650$, $\sigma = 8.6$; (b) $N = 400$, $n = 120$, $\sigma = 30$; (c) $N = 84,000$, $n = 225$, $\mu = \$35,760$, $\sigma = \$2,400$.

21. Rework part (a) of Example 5–5 assuming that $N = 40,000$ instead of $N = 4,000$. What effect does this have on the value of the standard error of the mean?

22. A market research firm conducts 5,000 library searches each year for customers who wish to find competitive information on anything from voice-activated computers to fried-chicken franchises. (Assume that actual billing information would reveal the firm's average charge/customer to be $860 with $\sigma = \$220$).

   (a) Suppose that a sample of $n = 50$ of the firm's searches is to be made to audit the charges. What standard error of the mean should be used for statistical inference?

   (b) Suppose that the sample is $n = 500$ instead of $n = 50$. Recompute $\sigma_{\bar{x}}$.

   (c) Explain any difference in your values in parts (a) and (b).

Sampling Distributions of Common Sample Statistics

In the previous section, we first derived the sampling distribution of the mean by calculating all possible sample means from a given population. In actual practice, of course, we almost never do this. For one thing, rarely do we have the entire population, as we did in the example. Without this information, we cannot derive the sampling distribution manually. In practice, we use standard probability distributions to represent the sampling distribution. We will now consider how other common sampling distributions can be represented by similar probability distributions.

Sampling Distribution of the Sample Mean When σ is Known

The previous discussion was concerned with sampling from a population with mean μ and standard deviation σ. In addition to identifying the standard deviation of the sampling distributions as $\sigma_{\bar{x}} = \sigma/\sqrt{n}$, the discussion brought out two important conclusions:

1. If the population is **normally distributed**, the distribution of sample means is normal for any size sample (both large and small).

2. If the population is **not normally distributed**, the central limit theorem tells us that the distribution of sample means is still approximately normal if the sample size is sufficiently large ($n \geq 30$).

If we know the population standard deviation, σ, we know that the sampling distribution of the sample means is a normal distribution with a mean equal to the population mean μ and a standard deviation (standard error) equal to the population standard deviation divided by the square root of n ($\sigma_{\bar{x}} = \sigma/\sqrt{n}$). We can then answer questions about the likelihood of observing different values of the sample mean when we take samples from that population.

Example 5-6

A French manufacturer of exotic perfumes is going to institute statistical process control (SPC) procedures in its manufacturing process. One point of emphasis is the point in the process after the bottles are filled with perfume. The amount of perfume in each bottle is supposed to be 6 oz., but the fills vary somewhat with a standard deviation of .10 ounces. If a sample of 25 bottles is taken, what is the probability that the average amount of perfume in the 25 bottles will be less than 5.95 ounces?

Solution

$$\mu_{\bar{x}} = 6 \qquad \sigma_{\bar{x}} = \frac{\sigma}{\sqrt{n}} = \frac{.1}{\sqrt{25}} = .02$$

We can use NORM.DIST to find the probability:

$$\text{NORM.DIST}(5.95,6,.02,\text{TRUE}) = .0062$$

That is about 6 chances in 1,000 that the average of the 25 bottles will be less than 5.95 ounces.

Exercises V

23. A population has $\mu = 28.0$ and $\sigma = 6.4$. If samples of $n = 64$ are used, what is the probability a sample mean will have a value of (a) less than 28.0; (b) greater than 30.0?

24. An agricultural extension service has randomly identified 60 individual acres of a certain area of Idaho farmland to measure the wheat production per acre. Assume that the true mean yield in this region is 95.0 bushels/acre, with a standard deviation of 24.0 bushels/acre.) (a) What form of probability distribution best describes all the possible sample means for samples of $n = 60$? Provide the mean and standard deviation of this distribution. What is the probability that the (one) sample mean to be taken by the extension service will have a value of (b) between 90.0 and 100.0 bushels/acre; (c) more than 100.0 bushes/acre; (d) less than 90 bushels/acre?

25. A random sample of 25 households is taken to determine the average household income in a certain area of the city. Suppose that the true average income in that area is $17,000 with a standard deviation of $2,000. (a) What probability distribution would best describe the sampling distribution of the sample means for samples of size 25 from this population? (b) What is the mean and standard deviation of this distribution? (c) What is the probability that a sample mean of 25 households will have sample mean between $16,800 and $17,400?

26. The Dillon Medical Service Bureau (MSB) manages several hospitals. As part of their billing procedure they have all patients assign a score of 0 to 100 to their hospital for the service they received in admissions, meals, tests and treatments, and so on. Based on reports from all 12,000 patients served last year, the service rating on "tests and treatments" had a mean of 81.0 and standard deviation of 12.0 points. A score of 80 points or better is considered passing.

     (a) Suppose that an auditing firm takes an independent random sample of 100 patient records to analyze the "tests and treatments" service. What is the probability their sample mean will represent a failing score.

     (b) Suppose that the audit sample is increased to 1,500. Recompute the value requested in part (a).

     (c) Explain any difference in your answers to parts (a) and (b).

Sampling Distribution of the Sample Mean when σ is Unknown

Although earlier discussions assumed that the population standard deviation was known, most business decisions are based on sample values where σ is not known, in which case s, the sample standard deviation, must be used to estimate σ. When s is used in place of σ, the standard deviation of the sampling distribution of $\bar{X}$ is calculated in the same way, but with the sample standard deviation substituted for the population standard deviation in Equation 5-1:

$$S_{\bar{X}} = \frac{S}{\sqrt{n}} \tag{5-4}$$

Suppose that you were to take repeated samples of size n from a normal (μ, σ^2) distribution, compute s and the associated standard error, and calculate a statistic similar to Z defined for the normal distribution.

$$t = \frac{\bar{X}-\mu}{S_{\bar{X}}} \quad \text{t-distribution} \tag{5-5}$$

This statistic would follow what is referred to as Student's t-distribution rather than a standard normal distribution. The t-distribution was discussed previously as a family of distributions which, like the standard normal distribution, have a mean of 0; however, the standard deviation of the t-distribution is larger than the standard deviation of the standard normal distribution.

Large Samples

As the sample size increases, the t-distribution becomes more and more like the standard normal distribution. In fact, for samples of 30 or more, t is virtually identical to the standard normal or Z-distribution. Many texts state that you should use the standard normal (Z) rather than the t-distribution for larger samples—even though the t is theoretically correct. For sample sizes of $n < 30$, the difference between the normal and the t-distribution is large enough to be noticeable and requires the use of the t. With readily available software for calculating values from the t distribution, we see no reason for this approximation and we will simply state:

> If the population standard deviation is unknown, the t-distribution is always the appropriate sampling distribution for the sample mean no matter what the sample size.

Use t - Distr. if unknown

The t-distribution is appropriate only if the population being sampled is normal. In practice, this Standard Distr. stipulation is more relevant for relatively small samples because the effect of a non-normal population lessens as the sample size increases and in most cases is not a problem for samples of 30 or more. If the population is severely skewed then the t-distribution should not be used.

Like most probability distributions, the t-distribution consists of a family of curves whose shapes depend on the parameters of the distribution. In the case of the student-t, the most important parameter is the **degrees of freedom** (df), parameter which is related to the sample size n.

In the case of the sample means, the degrees of freedom (df) are n – 1.

As with the normal distribution, Excel has a function for calculating probabilities in the t-distribution.

Example 5-7

A random sample of $n = 5$ customers of a large insurance company showed they carried an average of $15,000 in life insurance, with a standard deviation of $3,150. Assume that the insurance amounts are normally distributed.

(a)   Compute the estimated standard error of the mean, $S_{\bar{X}}$

(b)   Suppose that the true (population) mean insurance amount carried by policyholders of the company is $\mu = \$18,000$. What is the probability of getting a sample mean of $\bar{X} = \$15,000$ or less from a random sample of 5?

Solution

$$S_{\bar{X}} = \frac{S}{\sqrt{n}} = \frac{\$3,150}{\sqrt{5}} = \$1,409$$

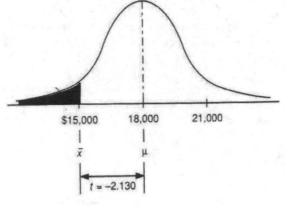

(a) t-value for sampling distribution:

$$t = \frac{\$15,00 - \$18,000}{\$1,409}$$

$$= -2.130$$

If you enter the following function in Excel, it will return a probability of .050104

=T.DIST(-2.130, 4, TRUE)

In a later section of this chapter, we will examine this function in more detail and also describe how to use XLDataAnalyst to find such probabilities.

Interpretation of the t-value

The t-value is interpreted much like the Z value for the standard normal distribution. In example 5-7 the calculated t-value of –2.130 can be interpreted as meaning that in a sampling distribution with a mean of $18,000 and an estimated standard error of $1,409, about 5% (precisely 5.01%) of the sample means would have a value of $15,000 or less. Insofar as the t-distribution is symmetrical, we could also conclude that about 5% (precisely 5.01%) of the sample means would have values greater than 2.130 standard errors above the mean. [This would correspond to the point $18,000 + (2.130 ($1,409), or about $21,000.] In other words, the t-distribution with 4 df tells us that for samples of size $n = 5$, about 10% of the area lies outside the limits of ± 2.130 standard errors of the mean.

Exercises VI

27. A tire manufacturer guarantees the life of a certain tire to be 40,000 miles. A random survey compares blowouts of these tires, and finds that a sample of seven tires has an average of 36,500 miles, with a standard deviation of 3,250 miles.

   (a) Find the estimated standard error of the mean.

   (b) What t-value would be used to determine the probability of getting an average of 40,000?

28. A small restaurant is comparing the past weeks sales. For the five-day week, the sales figures averaged $2,300 with a standard deviation of $400. Assuming sales are normally distributed, find the estimated standard error of the mean. Assuming the owner expected sales to be $2,500 a day, what t-value would be used to determine the probability of finding an average of $2,300? Explain what this t-value means.

29. A professor is wondering about class attendance. In general, he expects at least 90% of the class to attend in any given class. The current class that he is teaching has an enrollment of 60 students. At random, the teacher picks 6 days to do a head count and finds the average of those six days to be 53 students, with a standard deviation of 1.8. If attendance is normally distributed, find the estimated standard error of the mean. What t-value would be used to determine the probability of an average of 90% of the students being in attendance?

30. A random sample of yearly snowfall is taken for a particular city. Over a 75-year span, 5 years are selected at random and the average yearly snowfall of those years is 4.8 feet with a standard deviation of 1.1 feet. Assuming the average snowfall is normally distributed; find the estimated standard error of the mean. (a) Find the t-value (b) Find the probability of observing this value for the t.

Sampling Distributions of the Sample Proportion

For this and future discussions, we shall use the symbol π to designate a population proportion and p for the sample proportion. In Example 5-3, we considered the ages of 30 students in an Economics class. In that context, we discussed the process of taking samples of n = 3 from this "population" and deriving a sampling distribution of the mean using all 4,060 possible samples. Now, suppose that we used the samples to estimate the proportion of the population (π) that was 22 years old or more, instead of the mean of the population. The number of possible samples of size of $n = 3$ would be the same (e.g., 4,060). But, if we were to compute the proportion (p) of each sample that was 22 years old or more, only one of the three values in sample n_1 (of 18, 22, and 20) is 22 or more. So, the sample proportion from n_1 would be 1/3 or .333.[9]

Example 5-8

A computer chip manufacturing process has a known yield rate of 60% (e.g., 40% are defective). A random sample of 100 chips is collected for shipment to a customer overseas. Compute the standard error of proportion.

Solution

If we let π = the proportion defective, then $\pi = .40$.

$$\sigma_p = \sqrt{\frac{\pi(1-\pi)}{n}} = \sqrt{\frac{(.40)(.60)}{100}} = .049$$

If all sample proportions were calculated, we could form a sampling distribution of proportions, where the average, μ_p was the sum of all the sample p values divided by 4,060. The standard deviation of this sampling distribution of sample proportions is designated σ_p and could be calculated using the procedures from Chapter 3.

Mean of a sampling distribution of p:	μ_p
Standard deviation of sampling distribution of p:	σ_p

We can now apply the two theorems described earlier to sample proportions and observe that:

1. The mean of the distribution of sample proportions, μ_p, will always equal the population proportion, π. That is, $\mu_p = \pi$. The standard deviation of the sampling distribution is equal to the standard deviation in the population ($\sqrt{\pi(1-\pi)}$) divided by the square root of the sample size.

---

[9] Insofar as the samples here consist of only three students, and either zero, one, two, or all three of the students will be 22 years old or older, the only possible p values in this sampling distribution would be 0%, 33.3%, 66.7%, and 100%; however, if the sample size were increased to 10, the sampling distribution would have (11) possible values of 0%, 10%, 20%, and so on, up to 100%. The larger samples allow for the sample estimates to be closer to the true π value. This is one reason why small samples are seldom used to estimate population proportions.

> 2. The sampling distribution of sample proportions, p's, is the binomial distribution, but it can be approximated by the normal distribution if the sample size is fairly large and the proportion is not too close to either zero or 1.

Regarding (1), sample proportions are unbiased estimators of the population proportion, π; therefore the mean of all the sample proportions (of a given size) will always equal π. Regarding (2), we know that the true sampling distribution of the proportion is the binomial distribution. But, for larger samples, the normal approximation is usually satisfactory. The criteria we used earlier (Chapter 4) would suggest that the sampling distribution of proportions can be approximated by the normal distribution whenever $n(p) > 5$ and $n(1-p) > 5$; however, calculating the probabilities using BINOM.DIST in Excel or using XLDataAnalyst will give the exact probability rather than an approximate one. For this reason, we will stress the binomial sampling distribution in this text rather than the normal approximation.

Standard Error of the Proportion

The *standard error of the proportion* follows much the same logic as the standard error of the mean and is designated σ_p:

$$\sigma_p = \frac{\sqrt{\pi(1-\pi)}}{\sqrt{n}} = \sqrt{\frac{\pi(1-\pi)}{n}} \qquad (5\text{-}6)$$

The population proportion, π, can be expressed in either a decimal proportion or in a percentage and is frequently unknown; thus, we must work with sample statistics. In this situation, the sample value of p replaces the population parameter, π, in calculating the standard error of the proportion.

If we let s_p designate the estimated standard error of proportion as calculated from sample data, we have:

$$S_p = \sqrt{\frac{p(1-p)}{n}} \qquad (5\text{-}7)$$

Example 5-9

Confidential records of tests given at all high schools in a state show that 46% of all twelfth graders are able to pass a mathematics proficiency test containing simple algebra and geometry problems. Without access to this information, a national testing service gives a comparable mathematics test to a sample of 2,000 students and 880 pass the test.

(a) Use the sample data to estimate the standard error of proportion.
(b) Given that the true population is 46%, what is the probability the testing service sample would evidence a pass rate of 44% or less?
(c) What conclusion can you draw about the tests?

Solution

The sample proportion is $p = \frac{880}{2,000} = .440 = 44\%$

(a) $S_p = \sqrt{\frac{p(1-p)}{n}} = \sqrt{\frac{(.44)(.56)}{2,000}} = .0111$

(b) Since the sample is very large, we can use the normal approximation

NORM.DIST(.44,.46,.0111, TRUE) = .035788

(c) It is difficult to draw specific conclusions because we do not know how the tests were

administered, precisely how comparable they were, and so on; however, assuming they were exactly comparable, the probability of getting a sample pass rate of 44% or less from a population with a pass rate of 46% is only .0358. Hence, less than 4% of the sample proportions would be this low. This might cause administrators to question the validity of one (or both) of the tests or testing procedures.

Although the normal approximation usually gives us a probability close to the theoretically correct answer, we can use the binomial distribution to find the exact probability. In this case, a pass rate of 44% or less corresponds to 880 or fewer successes in 2000 trials with the probability of a success equal to .46. Then using the BINOMDIST function in Excel we would find

$$\text{BINOMDIST}(880, 2000, .46, \text{TRUE}) = .038063$$

Note that this is quite close to the value found using the normal approximation.

Exercises VII

31. A car manufacturer has a reject rate of 1% in a certain piston valve. If 100 valves are examined, compute the standard error of proportion. What is the probability that 2% or more of the valves will be defective?

32. The star basketball player has a three point shooting percentage of 44% (he misses 56% of his three point shots). If 50 of his shots are randomly selected, (a) what is the standard error of the proportion of shots made? (b) what is the probability that he will make 50% or more of the shots?

33. An insurance company is examining their policies, especially in a certain state where drivers seem to be causing more accidents. A report shows that, in this particular state, 8% of drivers have caused an accident in the past two years. Then, the company looks at the sample of drivers that they insure around the nation, and the results show that out of 300,000 customers, 27,000 have caused accidents during this period.

    (a) Use the sample data to estimate the standard error of the proportion.

    (b) What is the probability that the sample would show that 9% or more of drivers have caused accidents in the past two years when the true population proportion is 8%?

34. An accountant for a large clothing company needs to estimate the amount of material waste in the largest manufacturing plant. In a random sample of 645,000 yards of incoming cloth, 125,000 yards ends up as waste. (a) Use the sample data to estimate the standard error of the proportion of waste at the manufacturing plant, (b) find the probability that the sample proportion would be equal to the observed proportion or smaller if the true population proportion is 21%, and (c) explain your findings to the accountant.

35. An auto manufacturer conducts a survey of 200 new buyers of a particular car. The survey asks what the determining factor was in their decision to buy the car. Of the respondents, 29% noted reliability, 22% safety, 19% price, 17% performance, and 13% listed "other."

    (a) What is the mean number who gave each response?

    (b) Compute the standard deviation of the sampling distribution in terms of proportions and the numbers of those who answered "reliability" as their reason.

Sampling Distributions of the Sample Variance (Standard Deviation)

Although slightly more complicated, we can view the sampling distribution for sample variances (or standard deviations) in the same way as means or proportions. We will focus more on the sample variance than on the standard deviation in our discussions of sampling distributions. The meaning of the sampling distribution is the same as for means or proportions; it gives us all possible values for the sample variance along with their associated probabilities. In Example 5-3, we would calculate the sample variance for each of the 4,060 samples. The first sample n_1 (of 18, 22, and 20) would have a sample variance of $(18\text{-}20)^2 + (22\text{-}20)^2 + (20\text{-}20)^2/(3\text{-}1) = 4.0$. If we made a frequency distribution of all of the sample variances we could describe the sampling distribution of variances with its associated mean and standard deviation.

Just as we can use a theoretical probability distribution to describe the sampling distribution for the mean (normal or t-distribution, depending on our knowledge of the population standard deviation), and the proportion (binomial), we can also use another distribution to describe the sampling distribution of the sample variance. If we are sampling from a population that has a normal distribution, the sampling distribution for the sample variance is the **chi-square (χ^2) distribution**. To be more precise, the quantity $(n-1)s^2$ has a chi square distribution with n-1 degrees of freedom. As with the Z and the t-distributions, we can define the chi-square statistic with the following formula:

$$\chi^2 = \frac{(n-1)S^2}{\sigma^2} \qquad\qquad (5\text{-}8)$$

The mean of the sampling distribution for s^2 is the population variance (σ^2) and the variance is two times the population variance ($2\sigma^2$). Therefore, the standard deviation of the sampling distribution, the standard error of the variance, is $\sqrt{2\sigma^2} = \sqrt{2}\sigma$. We can calculate probabilities for the chi-square distribution using the CHISQ.DIST function in Excel or the probability generator in XLDataAnalyst.

You may at this point, expect a discussion of the sampling distribution for the sample standard deviation; however, there is a problem with standard deviations. There is no standard probability distribution that we can use for the sampling distribution of the standard deviation. For this reason, when we discuss inferential statistics, it will always be inferences about variances rather than standard deviations. This is really not a problem since the standard deviation has a simple relationship to the variance; **it is the square root of the variance**. Therefore, if we estimate the population variance to be $\sigma^2 = 25$ we would estimate the standard deviation to be $\sigma = \sqrt{25} = 5$. Consequently, when making inferences, if the question concerns standard deviations, we can simply turn it into a question about variances and then transform the results back to a standard deviation by taking the square root of the calculated value.

Example 5-10

In Example 5-7, we selected a random sample of $n = 5$ customers of a large insurance company. We found a sample standard deviation of $3,150 or a sample variance of $3,150^2 = 9,922,500$. What is the probability of finding a sample standard deviation of $3,150 or less if the true population standard deviation is actually $3,300. Assume that the insurance amounts are normally distributed.

Solution

Since sample variances follow a chi-square distribution we can use the CHIDIST function in Excel to find the desired probability. The CHIDIST function has two arguments, the value of the random variable (the chi-square value) and the degrees of freedom. As with the t-distribution, the degrees of freedom here are the sample size minus one (n-1); however, the CHIDIST function returns areas to the right of the given value which is the opposite of the NORM.DIST function that returns areas to the left. Therefore, we have to adjust by subtracting the returned value from 1.0 to get the desired area to the left. For our sample, we would calculate the chi-square value as:

$$\chi^2 = \frac{(5-1)(9,922,500)}{3,300^3} = 3.54428$$

Then, the probability can be found as:

$$\text{CHISQ.DIST}(3.644628,4,\text{TRUE})1 = .543769$$

The probability of finding a sample standard deviation of 3,150 or less if the population standard deviation is 3,300 is approximately .544.

Exercises VIII

36. Why do we use variances rather than standard deviations when discussing sampling distributions? Why is this not a problem?

37. The state patrol is surveying how fast people are driving on a particular stretch of highway. A random sample of 200 cars is clocked with radar and the variance of these speeds is 9.5. What is the probability of observing a variance this small or smaller if the true variance is actually 10?

38. The board of education is interested in how high school students are doing on their college placement exams. A sample of 500 exams is studied and the scores have a standard deviation of 29.4 points. What is the probability of observing a standard deviation this large or larger if the true standard deviation is 25 points?

39. The national weather service is conducting a study on the effects of global warming on specific temperatures. In the study, 100 cities worldwide cities are examined and their average temperatures are compared to those of 25 years ago. The 100-city study shows an increase in average temperatures, with the standard deviation of these increases being 6 degrees. What is the probability of observing a standard deviation this large or larger if the true standard deviation is only 5 degrees?

Other Sampling Distributions and Bootstrapping

There are other sample statistics that we will discuss in this text. We could also obtain sampling distributions for some of these statistics, but in many cases the sampling distributions are unknown, and are not as widely used as those of means, proportions and variances. There is a relatively new procedure for obtaining sampling distributions for these nonstandard situations called *bootstrapping*.

Bootstrapping and Sampling Distributions

Recall that we previously discussed the idea that a sampling distribution is a probability distribution of all possible values of a sample statistic. This sampling distribution would be the relative frequencies of the different values of the sample statistic if we took a large number of samples of a certain size from the population and calculated the value of the sample statistic each time. The idea of taking repeated samples from the population is the heart of bootstrapping.

Repeated sampling from a population is intuitively appealing, but not economically viable since taking thousands of samples from a population would be expensive; however, we could take many samples with replacement from this sample to represent repeated sampling from the population.

> **Bootstrapping**
>
> Since the sample represents the population from which it was drawn, assuming random sampling, repeated samples from the sample should represent what we would get if we were to take repeated samples from the population. Therefore, we can represent the sampling distribution for a sample statistic with the frequency distribution of the sample statistic when taking a large number of samples from the original sample. The standard deviation should be a reasonable estimate of the standard error of the sampling distribution.

Bootstrapping is now more widely adopted and we will see in some of the later chapters that the technique is utilized in XLDataAnalyst for certain sample statistics, especially the median.

Practice

Exploring Sampling Distributions Using Excel and XLDataAnalyst

Most standard texts illustrate the calculations involved with sampling distribution using standard tables for common probability distributions; however, many modern software packages have the capability of calculating such values more easily. We will first illustrate the use of the Excel functions in calculating these probabilities. Given some of the inherent limitations of some of the Excel functions, we will illustrate the use of the probability calculator in XLDataAnalyst to calculate those same probabilities.

Excel Functions

There are built-in functions in Excel for calculating probabilities in all of the sampling distributions discussed in this chapter. These are the same functions that we described in Chapter 4. For convenience, the functions are summarized in Table 5-3.

Table 5-3   *Excel Functions*

Excel Function & Arguments	Value Returned
BINOM.DIST(x, n, π, TRUE)	Cumulative Probability of x
NORM.DIST(x, μ, σ, TRUE)	Area to the left of x
T.DIST(x, df, TRUE)	Area to the left of x
CHISQ.DIST(x, df, TRUE)	Area to the left of x

Care needs to be taken to gather the appropriate values for x in the function. For the BINOM.DIST function, x must be the number of successes, even if the question is about proportions. For NORM.DIST, x will be either the value of the sample mean for sampling distributions of the mean, or a proportion for sampling distributions of a proportion. You must be careful with the NORM.DIST function to make sure that the standard deviation you use is the standard error of the mean or standard error of the proportion, not the standard deviation of the population. In other words, you must first calculate the standard error before using the NORM.DIST function.

The value of x in the T.DIST function must be the value of the t-statistic calculated using equation 5-5. For the CHISQ.DIST function, the value of x is the value of the chi-square statistic calculated using equation 5-12. Some examples will hopefully clarify these issues.

Example 5-11

A financial analyst at Sears wants to estimate the average account balance on Sears Cards used by Sears' customers. She takes a sample of 30 accounts and finds an average of $240.45 with a standard deviation of $20.13. If the true average account balance of all Sears Cards is actually $250, what is the probability of observing a sample mean this small or smaller?

Solution

Since we do not know the population standard deviation, but only the sample value, the student t is the appropriate sampling distribution.

$$S_{\bar{x}} = \frac{20.13}{\sqrt{30}} = 3.675218 \qquad t = \frac{240.45 - 250}{3.675128} = -2.59848$$

Using the appropriate Excel function we would find that T.DIST(2.59849, 29, TRUE) = .007283

It is extremely unlikely to observe a sample mean this small if the true population mean is $250. This may lead us to doubt that the true average balance is $250.

Example 5-12

In the previous example, we found a sample standard deviation of $20.13. What is the probability of observing a sample standard deviation this small or smaller if the true population standard deviation is actually $25?

Solution

Since the standard deviation does not have a sampling distribution, we must first translate this into a question about variances. The sample variance is $s^2 = 20.13^2 = 405.2169$ and the population variance is $\sigma^2 = 25^2 = 625$. The sampling distribution of the sample variance is the chi-square distribution.

$$\chi^2 = \frac{(n-1)S^2}{\sigma^2} = \frac{(30-1)(405.2169)}{625} = 18.80206$$

The probability we would like to know is CHISQ.DIST(18.80206, 29, TRUE) = .073742

Excel Templates

The Excel template for this chapter is the file called Sampling Distributions.xlsx. Figure 5-9 shows that there are 5 worksheets in this template. The first tab is named X-bar Sigma Known. This worksheet is to be used when we are interested in the sampling distribution of the sample mean and we know the population standard deviation.

Figure 5-9   Sampling Distributions Template

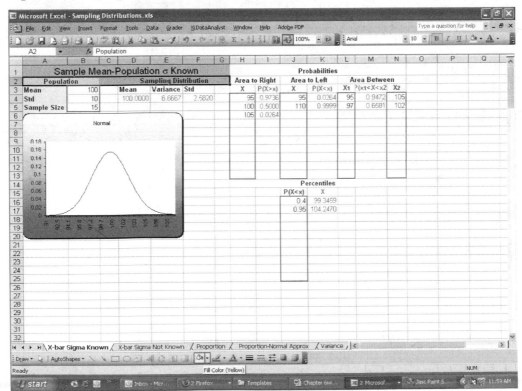

Therefore, the probability distribution used here is the normal distribution. The second tab, labeled X-bar Sigma Not Known, is for the t-distribution when the population standard deviation is unknown. The third and fourth tabs are for sample proportions. The third worksheet uses the binomial distribution that gives that exact probabilities, and the fourth worksheet uses the normal approximation which gives an approximate answer. The last worksheet uses the chi-square distribution to solve sampling distribution problems for the sample variance (or standard deviation).

Example 5-13

Solve the problem in Example 5-10 using the template.

Solution

The solution input and the resulting answer are shown in Figure 5-10 using the second worksheet of the template.

Figure 5-10   ***Solution to Example 5-13***

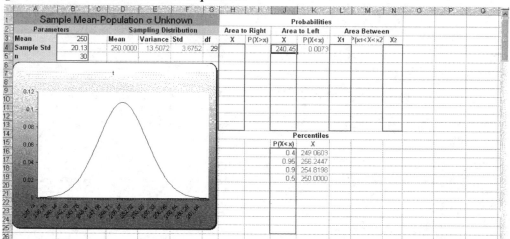

Example 5-14

Rework Example 5-11 using the appropriate template.

Solution

The solution using the Variance tab in the template is shown in Figure 5-11

Figure 5-11   ***Solution to Example 5-14***

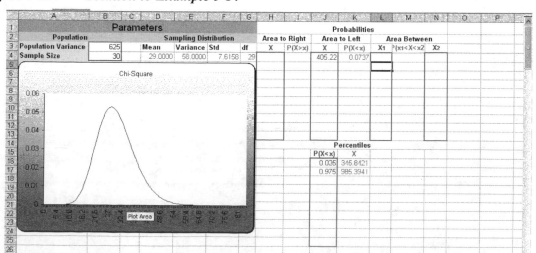

The Probability Calculator in XLDataAnalyst

XLDataAnalyst's probability calculator, located in the utility section of the tab, can be used to solve problems related to the sampling distribution of means, proportions or variances. The calculator can also be used for analyzing sampling distributions. The distributions most relevant to this chapter are shown in Table 5-4.

Table 5-4   *Sampling Distributions in XLDataAnalyst*

Function Name	Sampling Distribution	Returns
Binomial	Numbers or Proportions	Exact or Cumulative Probability
Chi-Square-Percentile	Sample Variances (Standard Deviations)	Percentile from Chi-Square
Chi-Square-Probability	Sample Variances (Standard Deviations)	Probability of a sample variance less than this value
Normal-Percentile	Sample Means (σ known) or Proportions (As Approximation)	Percentile from Normal
Normal-Probability	Sample Means (σ known) or Proportions (As Approximation)	Probability of a sample mean or proportion less than the given value
t-Distribution-Percentile	Sample Means (σ not known)	Percentile from t
t-Distribution-Probability	Sample Means (σ not known)	Probability of a sample mean or proportion less than the given value

The probability calculator is consistent and always returns *the area to the left for a cumulative probability*. If you need the area to the right of the given value, you must subtract from 1.0. Excel's probability calculator has a paste function to paste the answer into a cell on the spreadsheet.

The advantage of the probability calculator over the Excel functions is that it will automatically calculate the standard error. You do not need to perform this calculation before entering the data.

Example 5-15

Northwest Screw and Bolt produces high quality stainless steel bolts that are designed to be ½ in. in diameter. If it is known that the standard deviation of the bolt diameters is .1 inches, what is the probability that a sample of 50 bolts will have an average diameter greater than .54 inches?

Solution

We can use the Normal-Probability function to find the solution to this problem. The completed dialog is shown in Figure 5-12. Note that the Sampling Distribution box is checked since this is a question about the sampling distribution for the mean; however, this is not our final answer. Recall that these functions all return the area to the left of the given sample mean. Our problem, however, asked for the area to the right of .54. Therefore the correct answer is 1 - .9977 = .0023. We now see that it is very unlikely that we would see a sample mean of .54 or more in a sample of 50 from this population.

Figure 5-12   Completed Dialog for Example 5-15

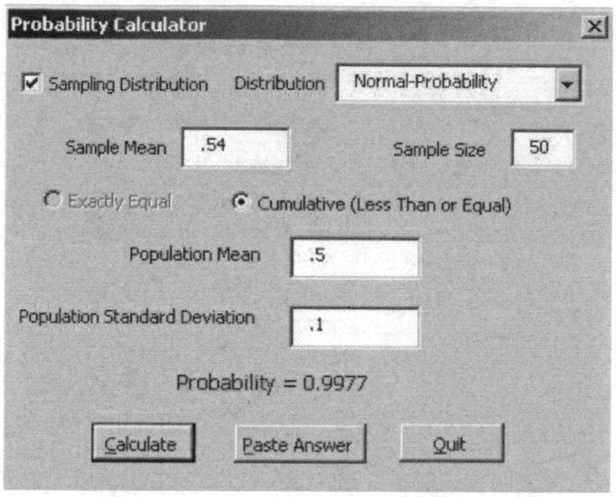

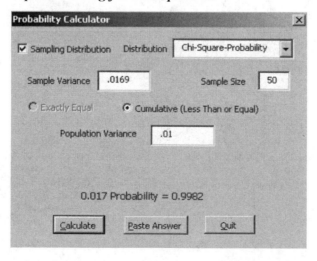

Example 5-16

In Example 5-15, we know that the population standard deviation is .10. What is the probability of finding a sample standard deviation of .13 or more in our sample of 50 from this population?

Solution

Figure 5-13 shows the complete information for Example 5-11. Note that our problem is in standard deviations, but the chi-square distribution requires variances; therefore, both the sample standard deviation of .13 and the population standard deviation of .10 have been squared to convert them into variances. Again, the function returns the area to the left and we want the area to the right; hence, our answer becomes 1 - .9982 = .0018.

Figure 5-13   Completed Dialog for Example 5-16

Example 5-17

A new bottle-filling machine recently purchased by Montana Microbrew is designed to fill each bottle with 12 ounces of beer. Although they know there will be some variability in the fill across bottles, management at Montana Microbrew is uncertain about what the standard deviation of the fills will be since this is a new machine and they have not yet had any experience with it. What is the probability that a sample of 30 bottles filled with the new machine will have an average fill of 11.95 ounces or less if the standard deviation of the 30 bottles is .20 ounces? The XLDataAnalyst dialog is shown in Figure 5-14. The chance of observing a sample average of 11.95 ounces or less is .0907.

Figure 5-14   Completed Dialog for Example 5-17

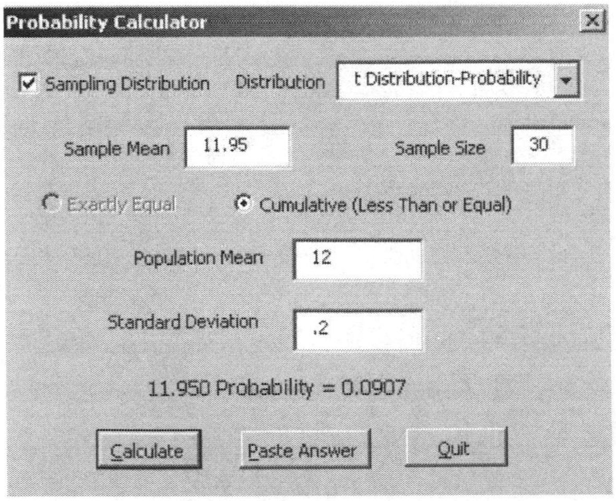

Sampling Distributions and Percentiles

We can use the probability calculator to find percentiles from the sampling distributions. Since the process is very similar to that of finding probabilities, we will only illustrate finding percentiles from the t-distribution for the mean. Percentiles for the other sampling distributions operate in the same fashion.

Example 5-18

The founder of A1 Realty wants to estimate the average selling price of new homes in EagleCrest. She decides to take a random sample of 25 new homes that have recently been placed on the market. Her calculations indicate that the average value in the sample is $140,125 with a sample standard deviation of $15,100. What is the 95th percentile of the sampling distribution for the mean selling price of samples of size 25 from this population if we assume that the population mean is actually $140,125? The completed probability calculator dialog is shown in Figure 5-15. Therefore, the 95th percentile of the sampling distribution is $145, 291.86.

Solution

Suppose that the founder of A1 Reality wanted to find the two percentiles that cut off the middle 95% of the sampling distribution. In other words, she wants to know the range where the sample mean is most likely (95% chance) to fall. Since we want the range to encompass 95% of the distribution, 5% will be outside this range. Since the distribution is symmetrical, 2.5% should be on each end of the distribution so that we want the .025 and .975 percentiles. Using the Probability Calculator would result in the values $133,892.03 and $146,357.97.

Figure 5-15   Completed Dialog for Percentiles of the t-distribution

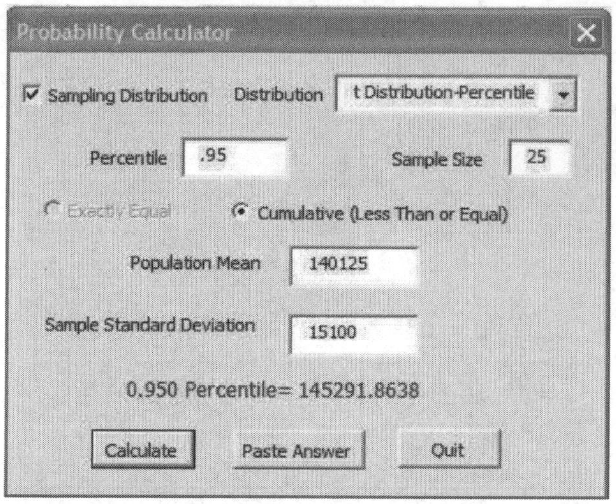

Exercises VII

40. For a sample of $n = 16$ drawn from a normal distribution having a mean of 150 and a standard deviation of $\sigma = 20$:

    (a) Find the mean $\mu_{\bar{X}}$ of the sampling distribution.

    (b) Find the standard deviation of the sampling distribution.

    (c) What proportion of the sample means will have values less than 150?

41. Determine the appropriate standard error for each of the following:

    (a) A population where $\mu = 180$, $\sigma = 28$, and $n = 100$

    (b) $n = 20$, $s = 3.4$, and $\bar{X} = 42.6$

    (c) A sampling distribution with mean $= 300$ and standard deviation $= 12$

42. Compute the standard error for the following: (a) $n = 25$, $\mu = 300$, $\sigma = 15$; (b) $n = 49$, $\pi = .58$; (c) $n = 16$, $\bar{X} = 90$, $s = 6$. (d) Given $\pi = .58$, $n = 100$, and $S_p = .05$, find the probability of obtaining a sample proportion of .60 or more.

43. A sample of 20 taxpayers with incomes in the range $40,000 to 50,000 showed they claim an average of $3,043 for medical care and $9,346 for total itemized deductions with standard deviations of $400 and $1,000, respectively.

    (a) Estimate the standard error for the medical care average.

    (b) Suppose that the true mean claim for medical care (of all taxpayers) was $2,903. What is the probability of observing a sample mean of $3,043 or more?

    (c) If the average itemized deductions for all taxpayers in this income range is $7,500, what is the probability of finding a sample mean of $9,346 or more? What is the standard error of the mean?

44. Records in a state agency show that the true average retirement income of married persons who have worked for 40 years is $30,000; however, these records are confidential; thus, the public does not have access to them. Suppose that a random sample of 25 persons conducted by a real estate firm reveals an average retirement income of $28,762 and a standard deviation of $3,000.

     (a)   Estimate the standard error of the mean for samples of 25 persons.

     (b)   If $30,000 is the correct population mean, what is the probability of obtaining a sample mean (of $28,762) or less?

     (c)   If the true population mean were $31,000 what is the probability of obtaining a sample mean this low or lower?

45.   A random sample of 30 billings is to be taken for a small medical clinic. Suppose that the average bill for the clinic is $235.50 and the standard deviation is $7.50.

     (a)   What is the correct sampling distribution for sample variance?

     (b)   What is the probability that a sample variance will be between 45 and 65 if a sample of 30 billings is taken?

     (c)   For a sample of 30 billings, what is the probability that the variance will be less than 40?

46.   A branch bank is planning on doing a study of wait times for tellers. They plan on randomly sampling 25 customers and timing their wait for a teller to become available. Suppose that the actual wait times at the bank have a normal distribution with a mean of 15 minutes and a standard deviation of 5 minutes.

     (a)   What is the correct sampling distribution for sample variance?

     (b)   What is the probability that a sample variance will be between 15 and 35, if a sample of 25 customers is taken?

     (c)   For a sample of 25 customers, what is the probability that the variance will be greater than 40?

47.   A random sample of 240 customers, taken by a city newspaper, showed that 180 of the 240 households clipped coupons from their papers at least once a week. (a) Estimate the standard error for the proportion of customers in this market area that clip coupons. (b) If the true proportion of customers who clipped coupons was $\pi = .70$, what is the probability of obtaining a sample proportion of .75 or higher?

48.   According to a census finding, the average income in a given city is $38,000 a year. A random survey of 10 people in that city finds the average to be $51,000 a year, with a standard deviation of $7,500 Assume a normal distribution. What is the probability that a 10-person sample would have an average income of $51,000 or more a year?

49.   A magazine targeted at "power computer users" plans on taking a survey of a random sample of 100 of its subscribers. One of the questions that will ask is whether or not the user plans on switching their operating system to Linux in the coming year.

     (a)   What is the sampling distribution for the proportion in the sample that will switch?

     (b)   If the true proportion of subscribers that plan to switch to Linux in the next year is .35, what is the probability that the sample proportion will be between 30% and 40%?

     (c)   What is the probability of the sample proportion being less than or equal to 25%, if the true proportion in the population is .35?

50.   A sample of 500 customers at a First National Bank branch (that has 4,000 accounts) revealed that 105 customers had some form of a loan. Estimate the standard error in terms of (a) the proportion of customers and (b) the number of customers who have loans in samples of 500 customers.

51.   Alice has kept detailed records for the Trail-rite Inn diner for the breakfast time slot. In the past individuals eating breakfast restaurant spend, on the average, $5.59 with a standard deviation of $0.35.

(a) What is the probability that a random sample of 15 people will spend an average of over $5.75 for breakfast combo meal? Assume a normal distribution of amounts spent.

(b) What is the probability that a random sample of 50 customers will spend between $5.40 and $5.80, on average?

Opening Vignette Revisited

Bill Montgomery has determined that most of the defects in the new process will likely arise in one key operation that involves some new untried technology. He decides to set up a prototype of this operation to obtain some samples to estimate the defect rate of the new process. A sample of 1,000 items produced by the prototype yields a defect rate of .008, which is less than the required 1%; however, Bill knows that this may just be the result of the sample obtained. To assess the risk involved, he decides to calculate the probability of obtaining a sample defect rate of .008, if the true defect rate is actually 2%. Using Excel and the BINOM.DIST function, he calculates that the probability of observing a defect rate of .8% or lower (8 or fewer failures in 1000 trials) if the true defect rate is 2% is only .001934. With this information, Bill is much more comfortable in believing that the true defect rate is likely 1% or less and decides to call the customer back and take them up on the original offer.

Summary

Managers use sample data for cost, time, and other practical reasons. But, samples can be subject to bias or nonsampling error and sampling error. Random selection helps reduce or eliminate bias. Sampling error is the difference between the sample statistic and the population parameter; it occurs because of the inherent variability in populations.

Judgment samples (e.g., purpose, quota, and convenience samples) involve choosing which elements are included in the sample. Probability samples result from a random selection and include a measure of sampling error, and permit statements of statistical inference. The four major subtypes of probability sampling are (a) simple random, (2) systematic, (3) stratified, and (4) cluster sampling.

A sampling distribution is a probability distribution of a sample statistic such as sample means ($\bar{X}$), proportions (p), or variances (S^2). It includes all possible values of the statistic, along with the probabilities of each. It can be proven that:

1. The mean of a sampling distribution (of $\bar{X}$, p or S^2s) always equals the population value (e.g., μ, π or σ^2).

2. The sampling distribution of the mean and proportion ($\bar{X}$, p) is approximately normal if the simple random sample size is sufficiently large.

The standard deviation of the sampling distribution is called the standard error. Standard errors are a function of the variability in the population, but usually are estimated from sample data:

Estimated standard error of mean: $\qquad S_{\bar{X}} = \dfrac{S}{\sqrt{n}}$

Estimated standard error of proportion: $\qquad S_p = \sqrt{\dfrac{p(1-p)}{n}}$

If sampling is done from a finite population, where the sample constitutes more than 5% of the population, the standard error should be multiplied by a finite population correction factor, to correct for a bias.

Theoretically, whenever σ is unknown, the sampling distribution follows a t-distribution, which is similar to a normal (Z) distribution but flatter. There is a different t-distribution for each degree of freedom (which we compute as n-1).

The sampling distribution for the variance is the chi-square distribution. As with the mean and the proportion, the mean of the sampling distribution is equal to the corresponding population parameter. The sampling distributions for our major sample statistics are summarized in the Table 5-5.

Table 5-5   Summary of Sampling Distributions

Sample Statistic	Sampling Distribution	Mean of Distribution	Std of Distribution
Mean ($\bar{X}$)	σ known—Normal	μ	$\dfrac{\sigma}{\sqrt{n}}$
	σ unknown—t		$\dfrac{S}{\sqrt{n}}$
Proportion	Binomial Normal approximation	π	$\sqrt{\dfrac{\pi(1-\pi)}{n}}$
Variance	Chi-Square	σ^2	$\sqrt{2\sigma^2}$

Chapter Glossary

Bias or Nonsampling Error	A "displacement" error due to a flaw or prejudice in the design, testing, or recording procedures.
Bootstrapping	A computer-based method for empirically generating a sampling distribution for a sample statistic
Central Limit Theorem	The sampling distribution of $\overline{X}$ is approximately normal if the simple random sample size is sufficiently large.
Cluster Sample	A sample where the population is divided into clusters (usually based on geography) with random samples taken and a census completed of each sampled cluster.
Convenience Sample	A sample where respondents are selected based on their convenience and availability.
Degrees of Freedom	A measure of the amount of useable information in the sample. Degrees of freedom are directly related to the size of the sample.
Finite Population Correction Factor	An adjustment to the standard error for the sample size relative to the population size.
Nonprobability or Judgment Samples	The elements in the sample deliberately chosen based on judgment or some other nonrandom basis.
Probability Samples	Samples that result from some form of random sampling process that gives elements a known chance of being selected.
Purpose Sample	The sample selected to satisfy a specific purpose.
Quota Sample	Sample taken to insure that a specified number of respondents in the sample have a given characteristic.
Sampling Distribution	A probability distribution of the values of a sample statistic.
Sampling Error	Random error due to the chance that a sample may not accurately reflect the characteristics of the population.
Sampling Frame	A compilation of all the members of the population to be studied.
Standard Error of the Mean	The standard deviation of the sampling distribution of the mean ($\overline{X}$s)
Standard Error of the Proportion	The standard deviation of the sampling distribution of the proportion.
Stratified Sample	A sample where the population is divided into strata based on some characteristic; then a random sample is taken within each strata.
Systematic Sample	A procedure where a random sample is taken by selecting a random number, then systematically selecting every value in the population that is a multiple of that number.

Questions and Problems

52. What are the most common reasons for sampling?

53. What is (a) a target population; (b) sampling frame; (c) bias; (d) sampling error?

54. A chemical company has 6,550 employees and needs to select five at random for a safety study. Using the RAND() function in Excel, generate the index numbers to take a random sample of 25 employees. (Assume that records contain employee numbers beginning at number 1.)

55. What type of sampling is (a) quota sampling; (b) stratified sampling; (c) random sampling? (d) Which of the three permit statistical inference?

56. A state forestry official proposes to obtain an estimate of the number of campers using a recreation site during the summer by randomly selecting a day, counting the campers, and then systematically counting the campers on that same day each week for the entire season. Discuss the validity of such a plan.

57. How does a sampling distribution of the means differ from a sampling distribution of the proportions?

58. Can sampling error be reduced by being more careful in taking the random sample? Explain.

59. A market research firm took a sample of 10 loan company customers to estimate the mean interest rate being paid on outstanding loans.

Customer No.	1	2	3	4	5	6	7	8	9	10
Interest rate (%)	23	13	17	19	20	21	16	18	17	20

   (a) Find the sample mean, $\bar{x}$.

   (b) Find the sample standard deviation.

   (c) Estimate the standard error of the mean.

60. Assume that the mean number of visitors during July at the state parks in Oregon is 240 per day, with a standard deviation of 80. If samples are randomly taken from 100 parks, what is the standard error of the mean?

61. State the *central limit theorem* and explain why it is so important for statistical reasoning.

62. The standard deviation of a statistic is frequently called the standard error of that statistic.

   (a) What is the standard error of the mean for samples of 100 drawn from a process that has a mean of 500 and a standard deviation of 40?

   (b) What is the effect on the standard error of the mean if the sample size is increased to 400?

   (c) What are the two factors that affect the size of the standard error of the mean?

63. Regarding the finite population correction factor:

   (a) When should it be used in computing the standard error of the mean?

   (b) Apply it in computing the standard error assuming that samples of 100 are selected from a population of 1,000 elements when $\sigma = 20.0$.

   (c) A sample of 100 oranges is selected from a large box to estimate the mean weight of the oranges. What additional information is required to make the estimate?

64. A random sample of 1,200 families revealed that 768 owned their own home. Compute the estimated standard error of proportion. If the true population proportion is actually .60 what is the probability of observing a value of the sample proportion this large or larger?

65. An accounting firm is planning for the next tax preparation season. From last year's returns, the firm collects a systematic random sample of 100 filings. The 100 filings showed an average preparation time of 90 minutes with a standard deviation of 140 minutes.

    (a) What is the standard error of the mean?

    (b) What is the probability that the mean completion time will be more than 120 minutes?

    (c) What is the probability that the mean completion time is between 1 and 2 hours, e.g., 60 and 120 minutes?

    (d) What is the 95th percentile of the sampling distribution for the mean?

66. In the situation described in problem 84, find the following probabilities.

    (a) What is the probability that the sample standard deviation will be greater than 160 minutes?

    (b) What is the probability that the sample standard deviation will be between 135 and 145 minutes?

    (c) What is the 99th percentile of the sampling distribution for the standard deviation?

67. A group of statistics students decided to conduct a survey at their university to find the mean average (mean) amount of time students spent studying per week. Based on a simple random sample, they surveyed 144 students. The statistics showed that students studied an average of 20 hours per week with a standard deviation of 10 hours.

    (a) What is the standard error of the mean?

    (b) What is the probability that a sample mean would exceed 20 hours per week?

    (c) What is the probability that average student study time is between 18 and 22 hours?

    (d) Between what two values do 98% of the sample means in this situation fall?

68. Intelligence Quotient (IQ) test scores are generally considered to be normally distributed with a mean of 100 and a standard deviation of 15. If we take a random sample of 25 individuals and administer the test:

    (a) What is the probability that the sample standard deviation will be greater than 20 points?

    (b) What is the probability that the sample standard deviation will be between 10 and 20 points?

    (c) Between what two values do 95% of the sample standard deviations for samples of this size fall?

69. In the situation described in problem 68:

    (a) What is the probability that the sample mean will be greater than 105?

    (b) What is the probability that the sample mean will be less than 90?

    (c) What is the 99th percentile of the sampling distribution for the mean?

70. A laundry detergent company packages its product into boxes labeled as containing 64 oz. Although some variation in the amount of detergent placed in each box is unavoidable, it is desirable for that variation to be kept as low as possible. If too much detergent is placed into the box it may spill over

and be wasted. If too little is placed into the box, customers may be unhappy and the company may face regulatory difficulties. Given the characteristics of the current filling technology, a standard deviation in the amount of fill in each box of 1.6 ounces is unavoidable. A higher standard deviation, however, indicates a problem with the process. In monitoring the process, the firm carefully measures the amount of detergent in a random sample of 50 boxes.

    (a). What is the probability that the measured sample standard deviation is 1.9 ounces or more?

    (b) If they observed a sample standard deviation of 1.9 ounces what should they conclude about the process? Is it working properly?

    (c) What is the 90th percentile of the sampling distribution?

71. The laundry detergent company in Exercise 70 is evaluating a new package-filling process developed by a group of its engineers. The new process promises to reduce the variability of the fill in the boxes. A random sample of 50 boxes filled by the new process is selected. The sample standard deviation in the fill of these boxes is 1.35 ounces. What are the implications of this?

72. A candy manufacturer wants to estimate the impact of an advertising campaign in a metropolitan area by measuring brand recognition for a new confection marketed for children. A random sample of 350 children from the area will be chosen and asked if then know about the brand.

    (a) If 35% of the children in the area have in fact actually heard of the brand, what is the probability that less than 28% of the children surveyed will know the brand?

    (b) If 35% of the children in the area have in fact actually heard of the brand, what is the value such that there is only a 5% chance of the proportion being less than that value?

73. An online furniture company has been receiving complaints from customers concerning delays in receipt of merchandise shipped to them. The furniture company suspects the fault lies with the trucking firm it employs to ship the furniture to its customers. The trucking firm assures the furniture company that the average time from shipment to deliver is 15 days with a standard deviation of 4 days. If the furniture company decides to check this with a random sample of 50 shipments

    (a) What is the probability that the average time between shipment and delivery will be between 14 and 16 days?

    (b) What are the values such that there is a 95% chance that the sample means will be between those two values?

74. A testing agency wishes to test the effectiveness of a new brake design in a particular automobile. The claim of the manufacturer is that the brakes will be able to stop an average driver traveling at 40 mph within 50 feet. If this is true

    (a) What is the probability that a random sample of 16 drivers will show an average stopping distance of 55 feet or more if the standard deviation of the sample is 6.36?

    (b) What is the 95th percentile of the distribution?

75. The cereal company that manufactures Chocolate Crunch cereals recently hired an advertising agency to run an ad campaign for the cereal. Now the company wants to determine whether or not the campaign increased sales of Chocolate Crunch. Prior to the campaign those who ate cold cereals consumed an average of 15.3 ounces of Chocolate Crunch with a standard deviation of 3.3 ounces. If the company takes a sample of 25 children chosen at random

    (a) What is the probability that their average consumption will be 16.1 ounces or more if the campaign has had no effect on consumption?

    (b) What are the 5th and 95th percentiles of the sampling distribution?

76. Burn-Bright Company manufactures wood and leaf fuel pellets for pellet stoves. The pellets come in 20, 40, and 50 pound bags. The quality supervisor in the packaging area has recently become concerned about the variation in the weights of the packaged 40 pound bags which are packaged on one of the older packaging machines in the plant. The standard deviation of the fill weights for the 40 pound bags is supposed to be 0.8 pounds according to the specifications. To test the fill weights the supervisor takes a sample of 20 bags and carefully weighs them.

   (a) What is the probability that the sample standard deviation will be 1 pound or more?

   (b) What are the values such that there is a 95% chance that the standard deviation will be between those two values?

77. Bob Farley, owner of the Bargain Barn Grocery store knows from past accounting records that sales at the store in the past have averaged $78. 27 with a standard deviation of $10.23. Bob is concerned that the recent recession may have had a negative impact on the average sales as people cut back on their spending. Bob proposes to take a random sample of 100 recent sales to investigate the current level of sales. Assuming that sales have remained at their historical levels:

   (a) What is the probability that the average sales in the sample will be between $77.00 and $79.00?

   (b) What is the 25th percentile of the sampling distribution?

   (c) What is the probability that the average sales in the sample will be less than $76.00?

78. Megabank operates a call center in Denver Colorado. Although call times vary considerably depending on the circumstances, it is Megabank's policy that its' call center associates spend an average of 5 minutes per call. A recent sample of sample of 25 calls took an average of 6.8 minutes with a standard deviation of 3 minutes. What is the probability of this happening if the policy is being met?

79. Marjie Smith sells hand painted Christmas tree ornaments on Etsy. It has been her experience that no matter how carefully she packs the items inevitably some will be damaged before reaching their destination. Based on past history about 12 percent of the items are damage upon arrival. Marjie usually sell to individual buyers but recently had a large order for 100 ornaments from a retailer in the Midwest. She has just heard from the retailer that 20% of the ornaments were damaged on arrival. What is the probability of 20% or more damaged items out of a shipment of 100?

Chapter 6:

Estimation and Confidence Intervals

Chapter 6 Objectives

When you finish this chapter you should be able to:

1. **Define point and interval estimates**
2. **Define a confidence interval**
3. **Estimate the value of a population mean**
4. **Estimate the value of a population proportion**
5. **Estimate the value of a population variance**
6. **Determine the appropriate sample size for a given degree of confidence**

Opening Vignette

Ray Burke is the head of purchasing for Piccadilly Grocery, a large grocery chain. Ray has become increasingly concerned about the costs associated with product distribution throughout the chain of retail stores. Of particular concern is the fleet of trucks Piccadilly uses to transport products to stores around the country. Ray recently received a visit from Bob, a representative of Roberson Tire Company, a ten-year old tire manufacturer that is looking to expand its business. Bob makes it clear to Ray that Roberson Tire really wants Piccadilly Grocery's tire business and will give them a special deal on their top-of-the line tires. Bob asks Ray what price it will take to get him to switch to Roberson tires. Ray quickly realizes that he cannot answer that question because he has no idea how well Roberson's tires will perform. After discussing the matter with Bob, Ray decides to purchase 50 tires from Roberson at a special discount and test the tires for wear after one month. At this point, Ray will be better able to estimate how long the tires will last, and what price he will be willing to pay.

Introduction

In this chapter, we begin our introduction to inferential statistics. Up to this point, the only inferential logic we have used was deductive logic to infer what we were likely to observe when taking a sample from a population with known parameters. We made these deductions based on our knowledge of sampling distributions. Now, we will discuss how we can estimate the unknown population parameters from a known sample. These inferences will also depend on our knowledge of sampling distributions.

Point and Interval Estimates

A *point estimate* is a single value of a sample statistic used to estimate a population parameter. For example, x-bar (sample mean) is the point estimate for mu (population mean). Thus far, we have worked primarily with the sample statistics $\bar{X}$, p, and s^2, which are point estimates of the parameters μ, π, and σ^2. We have used the sample standard deviation, s, as a point estimate of the population standard deviation σ and the sample median, M, as a point estimate of the population median η. Table 6.1 summarizes the population parameters and their corresponding sample statistics.

Table 6-1   **Population Parameters and their Sample Estimates**

 *important table*

	Population Parameter	Sample Statistic
Mean	μ	$\bar{X}$
Proportion	π	p
Variance	σ^2	s^2
Standard Deviation	σ	s
Median	η	M

Although any sample statistic can be used to provide a point estimate of a population parameter, some estimates are better than others. A good point estimate will have the following properties:

1. *Consistent*: The estimate gets closer to the population parameter (value being estimated) as the sample size increases

2. *Efficient:* The estimate will have a smaller standard error than other estimators of the same parameter

3. *Unbiased*: The estimate will, on average, equal the parameter value

All of the estimates in Table 6-1, except the sample standard deviation, have these properties. The sample standard deviation is a somewhat biased estimate of the population standard deviation.

Unfortunately, however, point estimates are rarely exactly on target. Worse yet, a point estimate does not tell us anything about how close the estimate is to the population value. Decision-makers really need to know (1) the limits within which the parameter is believed to lie and, (2) some measure of how likely those limits are to be correct.

To control for error, interval estimates are developed. A confidence *interval estimate* is a pair of values (computed from a sample statistic) that defines a range within which the population parameter is expected to lie. Moreover, confidence interval estimates also convey a measure of likelihood that the limits contain the unknown population parameter. Generally, a confidence interval depends on three elements:

1. The shape of the sampling distribution of the sample statistic involved.

2. The variability of the sampling distribution, usually measured as the standard error.

3. The desired degree of confidence that is desired or how confident we want to be that the interval contains the population value.

Interval estimates can apply to any population parameter. In this chapter, we will be primarily interested in population means, proportions, variances and medians. For example, confidence interval statements might read as follows:

Means: We are 95% confident that the true mean wage (μ) being paid by competitors in our state lies within the interval $14.60 to $16.30 per hour.

Proportions: We are 98% confident that the true proportion (π) of employees favoring the new medical plan lies within the interval 58.5% to 62.8%.

Variances: We are 99% confident that the true variance (σ^2) of wages in our industry lies between 42 and 55 dollars^2 (e.g., the population standard deviation (σ) lies between $6.48 and $7.42).

Medians: We are 97% confident that the true median wage for nurses in the state of Indiana lies between $15.52 and $22.31.

Assumptions and Conditions

The theory underlying confidence interval estimation is best understood by beginning with a population and a sample. Assume that we are estimating a population mean, μ, from a random sample of n observations, where the population standard deviation, σ, is known. Keep in mind a few points:

1. We are estimating the population mean—not the sample mean.

2. We are using sample data—an interval estimate is not needed if census data is available since we would then know the population mean.

3. Each estimate should state the limits within which the parameter is expected to lie, along with a measure of the amount of confidence in the estimate.

4. The width of the confidence limits depends on the amount of variability or dispersion in the sampling distribution of the means (i.e., standard error of the mean $\sigma_{\bar{x}}$).

Logic of Estimation

The sample statistic of each sample (of a given size), taken from a population, is a member of the sampling distribution of that statistic. Also, recall from the central limit theorem that the sampling distribution of sample means is approximately normal if the sample size is sufficiently large no matter the nature of the population.

Suppose that we let the normal curve shown in Figure 6-1 represent the true (but unknown) sampling distribution. Insofar as the sample means are normally distributed about the mean of the sample means, $\mu_{\bar{x}}$, which is equal to the population mean μ_x, we already know the proportion of sample means lie within one, two, or three standard errors of the true mean, as shown in Figure 6-1. For example, from Chapter 4 we know that 68.3% of all sample means ($\bar{X}$'s) will lie within $\pm 1\sigma_{\bar{x}}$ of the population mean, 95.5% are within $\pm 2\sigma_{\bar{x}}$, and 99.9% are within $\pm 3\sigma_{\bar{x}}$. This also means that 31.3% of all $\bar{X}$'s are outside $\pm 1\sigma_{\bar{x}}$, 4.5% are outside $\pm 2\sigma_{\bar{x}}$, and .03% are outside $\pm 3\sigma_{\bar{x}}$.

Assume we take only one sample, sample mean $\bar{X}_1$, which is one of many of $\bar{X}$'s that could be used. We would not know if the sample mean we selected is very close to μ or not. But, we do know that 95.5% of all the sample means would be within $\pm 2\sigma_{\bar{x}}$ of μ. The sample mean will be around the population mean only if the population mean is in that same interval (Figure 6-2).

If we established an interval of $\pm 2\sigma_{\bar{x}}$ about any individual sample mean and stated that the interval included μ, we would be correct 95.5% of the time. In a similar manner, if we established an interval of $\pm 3\sigma_{\bar{x}}$ we would be correct in claiming that the interval included the population mean 99.97% of the time.

Figure 6-1   Distribution of Sample Means

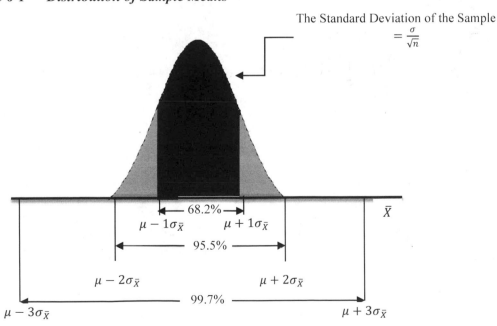

Figure 6-2   *Intervals Around the Population and Sample Mean*

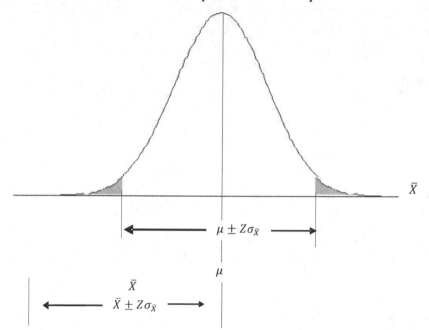

Following this logic we can express the confidence interval for samples from populations where σ is known as:

Confidence limits (σ known): $CL = \bar{X} \pm Z_{\alpha/2}\sigma_{\bar{X}}$ ⁣ *(6-1)*

In this equation, $Z_{\alpha/2}$ represents the "confidence coefficient," or the number of standard errors needed to represent a specified proportion of the area under the normal curve. The value α is one minus the degree of confidence and the division by 2 indicates that the area is split evenly between the two tails[1]. For example, with the normal distribution we know that 95% of the distribution is within plus or minus 1.96 standard deviations of the mean. The value 95% is the degree of confidence, α, representing the area outside this range, would be .05, and the value of $Z_{\alpha/2}$ would be 1.96. We divide the .05 evenly between the two tails of the distribution or .025 on each end. The lower and upper confidence limits are frequently designated as LCL and UCL respectively. The factor added and subtracted from the sample mean is often called the *margin of error*.

Confidence intervals are based on what we know about sampling distributions. Sampling distributions tell us that:

$$P(\mu - 2\sigma_{\bar{X}} \le \bar{X} \le \mu + 2\sigma_{\bar{X}}) = .955$$

But, we know that $\mu - 2\sigma_{\bar{X}} \le \bar{X} \le \mu + 2\sigma_{\bar{X}}$ only if $\bar{X} - 2\sigma_{\bar{X}} \le \mu \le \bar{X} + 2\sigma_{\bar{X}}$. In other words, the sample mean will be in the appropriate interval centered on the population mean if and only if the population mean lies in the same interval centered on the sample mean. The statement from the sampling distribution is a probability statement; however, the statement of the confidence interval is not a probability. **In other words, we cannot say that the probability the population mean is in the confidence interval is .955.** Classical statistics is based on a relative frequency view of probabilities. Therefore, we can only

---

[1] For symmetric distribution like the normal and t distributions the upper and lower tailed values are identical and we will drop the α/2 notation and just use the Z or t symbols for both; however, remember to divide the area equally between the two tails.

determine probabilities for repeatable events. But, in sampling tests, we have only gathered one sample and the need to see if the population mean is in its interval. That is why we refer to this as degree of confidence, rather than probability.

Degree of Confidence Explained

Confidence refers to the idea that the stated interval includes the true mean. This idea is **based on the procedure we follow** in making the interval estimate. For example, if we took repeated samplings from the population and followed the correct procedure of setting confidence limits at $\pm 2\sigma_{\bar{x}}$ from the sample mean, those limits would include the population parameter 95.5% of the time. The *degree of confidence* relates to finding the confidence interval; however, when we take one sample and create a confidence interval, we do not know whether it is one of the 95.5% of all confidence intervals that contains the population value or not. We have a unique event and we cannot define probabilities for it. In this sense, it is the interval itself that occurs by chance with a given probability. Therefore the confidence interval is the random variable, not the population mean.

Once a particular confidence interval is selected, it either *does* or *does not* include the population parameter μ. The true mean does not "fall" into some interval. From a relative frequency point of view, the population parameter, μ, **is not a random variable**. That is why statisticians refer to the chance that an interval includes the parameter as a level of confidence rather than a measure of probability. Probability refers to a random variable (e.g., the interval), but parameters (such as μ) are not random variables. In Bayesian statistics, where subjective probabilities are permitted, probabilistic statements can be made about a population parameter such as μ[2]; however, even in that case additional calculations are required and we cannot simply call the confidence interval a probability interval.

Confidence Interval Estimates of the Mean: σ Known

Our first example will illustrate the mostly theoretical situation where we are using a sample to estimate μ where the population standard deviation, σ, is known. Then, we will look at scenarios where σ is unknown.

If the population standard deviation is known, then we know that the sampling distribution of the sample mean is a normal distribution (if the population is normal) or is approximately normal (if the population is not normal but the sample size is ≥ 30). In this situation, the confidence interval for the population mean is:

$$CL = \bar{X} \pm Z\sigma_{\bar{x}} \qquad (6\text{-}2)$$

when σ is known!

Example 6-1 (σ known)

A California winery wishes to estimate the true weight of over 1,000 boxes of grapes that are being received from growers for processing. A sample of 49 boxes revealed a mean weight of 197.0 lb., and from past seasons, the population standard deviation is known to be $\sigma = 14.0$ lb. Compute a confidence interval estimate of the true mean weight per box (μ) that will give the winery 95% confidence of being correct.

---

[2] In Bayesian Statistics, they are called highest density regions rather than probability intervals but the meaning is the same.

Solution

(a) $CL = \bar{X} \pm Z\sigma_{\bar{X}}$ where Z-value is such that 95% of the area in the standard normal distribution is between $+$ and $-Z$, e.g., it is the .975 and .025 percentiles.

(b)

.025   .025

-1.96   1.96   *How do you get this?*

(c) $\sigma_{\bar{X}} = \frac{\sigma}{\sqrt{n}} = \frac{14}{\sqrt{49}} = 2.0$

(d) $LCL = \bar{X} - Z\sigma_{\bar{X}} = 197.0 - 1.96(2.0) = 193.1$ lbs.

$UCL = \bar{X} + Z\sigma_{\bar{X}} = 197.0 + 1.96(2.0) = 200.9$ lbs.

(e) Conclusion: The winery can be 95% confident that the true mean weight of the boxes of grapes lies within the interval 193.1 to 200.9 lbs. per box.

Confidence Interval Estimates of the Mean: σ Unknown

In Chapter 4 we stated that when σ is unknown, we use the sample standard deviation, s, as an estimator of σ. Also recall that the sampling distribution of sample means is described by the student's t-distribution that assumes that the samples are drawn from a normally distributed population. If the sample size is small (less than 30), there may be quite a difference between the t-distribution and the normal curve. But, even if the sample size is large, the t-distribution is still the proper distribution for the confidence interval. Thus we should use the t-distribution using n-1 degrees of freedom for setting confidence limits when σ is unknown:

$$CL = \bar{X} \pm tS_{\bar{X}}$$ *when σ is unknown!*   (6-3)

Example 6-2 (σ unknown)

Midwest Farm Cooperative has randomly sampled 25 farmers in a tri-state area to estimate the amount (lb./acre) of a certain chemical weed killer. The amounts follow a normal distribution. A sample is pulled with a sample mean of 120 lb. and sample standard deviation of 10 lb. Establish a 98% confidence interval estimate for the true population mean, μ.

Solution

We know that the relevant sampling distribution when σ is unknown is the student t-distribution. Therefore, the t-value we need is the value of t, which contains 98% distribution with degrees of freedom of n-1, or 25-1 = 24. In other words, we need the 1st and 99th percentiles. The confidence interval will then be:

$$CL = \bar{X} \pm tS_{\bar{X}}$$

(a) We can find the t-value using T.INV or the percentile t-distribution of the Probability Calculator in XLDataAnalyst. Either way we would find that the required value is 2.492159.

(b)

$$S_{\bar{X}} = \frac{S}{\sqrt{n}} = \frac{10}{\sqrt{25}} = 2 \text{ lb}$$

(c) Therefore,

CL = 120 ± (2.4922)(2)

LCL = 120 − 5 = 115 lbs/acre

UCL = 120 + 5 = 125 lbs/acre

(d) Conclusion

The Farm Cooperative can be 98% confident that the true mean amount of weed killer applied in the area is within the interval of 115 lbs./acre to 125 lbs./acre.

In Example 6-2, we do not know for certain whether the interval 115 to 125 lb. includes the true mean, μ. But, we have followed a procedure that will give us an interval that encompasses μ approximately 98% of the time.

In the next example, the sample is more than 5% of the population size, so we must apply the finite population correction factor for the calculation of the standard error.

Example 6-3 (σ unknown, n/N > 5%)

A stockbroker has taken a random sample of 400 of her company's 4,000 accounts to find the average number of mutual fund shares held by her firm's clients. The sample mean was $\bar{X}$ = 900 shares and s was 380 shares. What is the 95% confidence interval for μ?

Solution

$$CL = \bar{X} \pm tS_{\bar{X}}$$

(a) We can find the relevant t-value using T.INV or the Probability Calculator in XLDataAnalyst. Either way we get a t-value of 1.965927

N = total accounts
n = sample accounts

(b)

$$S_{\bar{X}} = \frac{s}{\sqrt{n}}\sqrt{\frac{N-n}{N-1}} = \frac{380}{\sqrt{400}}\sqrt{\frac{4,000-400}{4,000-1}} = 19.00(.95) = 18.03$$

(c)   CL = 900 ± (1.966)(18.03)

Therefore,

LCL = 900 − 35.45 = 865 shares (rounded)

UCL = 900 + 35.45 = 935 shares (rounded)

(d) Conclusion: The broker can be 95% confident that the true mean number of mutual fund shares held by her firm's clients lies within the interval 865 to 935 shares. Remember, the degree of confidence is not a probability. The 95% refers to the fact that we are 95% confident that the true mean is within the interval of 865 to 935 shares. In other words, if multiple intervals were established, we could expect to be correct about 95% of the time.

Exercises I

1.   Why are point estimates insufficient for many business decisions?

2.   What is an interval estimate?

3.   Distinguish among the terms consistent, efficient, and unbiased estimators.

4.   What is wrong with the following interval estimate statements:

   (a)   "I am quite sure the sample mean lies within the interval 54 to 60 hours."

   (b)   "There is a 95% probability the population value will fall within the range 345 to 365 pounds."

5.   Identify all the differences involved in computing a confidence interval for μ when σ is known versus when σ is not known?

6.   Peaches are shipped on a regular basis to a large distribution warehouse in Boise. A random sample of 81 boxes revealed a mean weight of 60.0 lbs. and a standard deviation of 3.6 lbs. For a 95% confidence interval, what is the value of (a) the estimated standard error, (b) the number of standard errors, t, and (c) the confidence limits. (d) Provide a conclusion based on your analysis.

7.   The materials handling manager at Buffalo Insulation Co. would like to make a 98% confidence interval estimate of the true mean weight of packaged containers of sawdust used in their manufacturing process. A random sample of 100 containers revealed a mean weight of 145.0 lbs. and a standard deviation of 6.0 lbs. Compute (a) the estimated standard error, (b) the confidence limits, and (c) state your conclusion.

8.   The accountant for a heating oil firm wishes to estimate the average number of days that delinquent accounts are overdue. The firm has 200 overdue accounts and the accountant's sample of 25 accounts shows an average overdue period of 65.5 days, with a standard deviation of 15 days. (a) What is the standard error that should be used to make an interval estimate? (b) What would be the 90% confidence interval estimate? (Assume that the population distribution is normal).

9.   Five dozen bags of chocolate candy are randomly selected from the output of a packaging machine to estimate the average package weight. The population standard deviation is known to be 15.0 grams. If the sample mean is 907.0 grams, compute a 98% confidence interval estimate of the population mean, μ.

10.   As an executive at SmartPhones Inc., you are about to introduce a new HD version of your best selling phone that will sell for $190. However, you decide to sample 100 users on how much they are willing to pay for the HD version of the phone. If the users in the sample on average are willing to pay $$210 with a standard deviation of $45, (a) what is the standard error of your sample? (b) What is the 95% confidence interval for the population mean? (c) What is the margin of error?

11.   Studies have shown that the average American consumes 22.2 teaspoons of added sugar every day, far exceeding the recommended limit of 5 teaspoons per day for women, 9 teaspoons a day for men, and 3 teaspoons for children. Assume Americans' sugar consumption of added sugars has a standard deviation of 5 teaspoons. What is the margin of error if a sample of 81 Americans is taken to determine the amount of added sugar in their diets?

12.   A toy manufacturer has produced 150 battery-operated transformers. A random test of 18 transformers revealed they ran (without recharge) an average of 14.60 hrs., with $s = 1.20$ hrs. Create a 95% confidence interval estimate of the mean number of hours the 150 transformers will function without recharge. (Assume that the population distribution of the number of hours is normal.)

Finding the Sample Size for Estimating the Mean

Up to this point we have assumed that the sample size in a statistical situation is given. But, in a realistic business situation, one of the first questions we will face is how large a sample do we need to take in order to be the most confident? If the population is fairly homogeneous, a small sample may suffice; however, for most business problems, larger samples are needed to give the desired precision. The downside to using a larger sample is that larger samples tend to increase the cost of the estimate. Therefore, the key to efficient estimation is to take a sample that is large enough to yield the desired precision, but not any larger so that we incur unnecessary cost.

Estimation Error

Estimate precision refers to the closeness of the sample estimate to the population parameter. On the other hand, *Estimation Error* is the difference between the value of the sample statistic and the value of the population parameter. Estimation error assumes that there is no non-sampling error. In any statistical study, we aim to increase the estimate precision and decrease the estimation error. In the distribution of sample means, estimation error is measured in the units of the standard error. Recalling that the standard error is $\sigma/\sqrt{n}$, we can see that as n increases the standard error decreases (while the precision increases).

Figure 6-3 uses the confidence interval logic to depict the estimation error. It shows the error interval around one sample mean (which, for convenience, we will assume is x-bar). The margin of error, e, is equal to one-half of the interval width. One-half the width is the product of the number of standard errors needed for the specified level of confidence, Z, times the amount of each standard error ($\sigma_{\bar{x}}$):

Margin of error: $e = Z \dfrac{\sigma}{\sqrt{n}}$ *(6-4)*

increase estimate precision

decrease estimate error

standard error $= \dfrac{\sigma}{\sqrt{n}}$

Figure 6-3   *Error in a Confidence Interval Estimate*

$\sigma_{\bar{x}} = \dfrac{\sigma}{\sqrt{n}}$

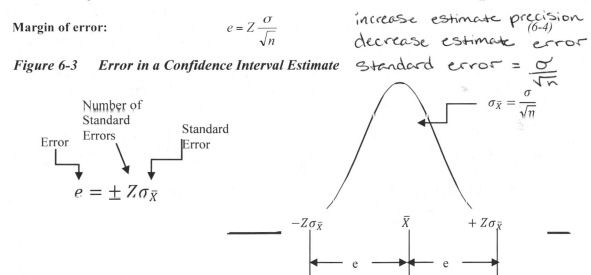

$$e = \pm Z\sigma_{\bar{X}}$$

Finding Sample Size: σ Known

The standard error in Figure 6-3 is dependent on the population standard deviation and the sample size. If we want to solve for n, we must use the specified level of confidence and the maximum error size:

Sample size (means: σ known): $n = \left(\dfrac{Z^2\sigma^2}{e^2}\right) = \left(\dfrac{Z\sigma}{e}\right)^2$ *(6-5)*

The values of n resulting from this calculation will often be a fractional value which needs to be rounded to an integer. The value should always be rounded up so that the resulting sample will provide a margin of error at least as small as that specified.

The sample size equation dictates the "spread" or the standard error of the sampling distribution. That is, if you specify the level of confidence (Z-value), along with a measure of the variability in the population (σ) and the maximum allowable error (e), the sampling distribution will be result in into a sample size that will satisfy all the specified conditions.

As might be expected, the more confident one wants to be, the larger the Z-value and the larger the sample must be. If the decision-maker is satisfied with being correct 95 out of 100 times, a Z-value of 1.96 will suffice. But, if a higher level of confidence is required, a 99.0% level ($Z = 2.58$) or 99.97% level ($Z = 3.00$) may be desirable.

[handwritten: You need Z-Value, σ, and e to find Sample Size →]

[handwritten: 95% = 1.96 z]
[handwritten: 99% = 2.58 z]
[handwritten: 99.97% = 3.00 z]

Example 6-4

An economist at Atlantic National Bank needs to develop a 95% confidence interval estimate of the mean annual family expenditure on housing in Maryland, within an accuracy of plus or minus $100. The population standard deviation is known to be $2,000. How large a sample should be taken?

Solution

$$n = (((1.96)(\$2,000))/\$100)^2 = 1,537$$

Finding Sample Size: σ Unknown

The "puzzling" aspect of computing a sample size is that equation (6-4) suggests that one must know σ *before* the sample is taken. In most situations, researchers have found that an estimate of σ is a satisfactory starting point. The best sources for such an estimate would be the standard deviation from a previous study, a pilot project, or a preliminary sample. A last resort that is not as accurate would be to have someone estimate the highest possible value for the variable of interest and the lowest possible value. Then, recalling from the empirical rule that almost all of the observations in a set of data are within $\pm 3 \sigma$ units of the mean, the range of values would be approximately 6 standard deviation units and we can then estimate the standard deviation as:

$$\text{Estimated } \sigma = \frac{\text{Max Value} - \text{Min Value}}{6} \qquad (6\text{-}6)$$

[handwritten: No way to know for sure]

Exercises II

13. (a) What is meant by the "margin of error" associated with a confidence interval? (b) In what units is the margin of error measured?

14. Compute the sample size required for the following: (a) 95% confidence that the interval is accurate within $\pm$ $40, $\sigma = \$280$; (b) 90% confidence, $e = 3$ min., $s = 18$ min.

15. A mining firm proposes to pay royalties on the basis of the average weight of ore removed from a random sample of several ore containers. Management wishes to have 95% confidence that the sample estimate is within 0.5 tons of the true value. If a preliminary sample yielded a mean weight of 18.0 tons and $s = 2.5$ tons, how large a sample is required?

16. A management analyst for a major airline needs to estimate (within ± 1.5 lbs.) the true mean weight of carry-on baggage for a certain transcontinental route. Previous data suggests that the standard deviation is very close to 8.0 lbs. How many passengers must be randomly selected to have their baggage weighed assuming the analyst wishes to be (a) 90% confident; (b) 99.97% confident?

17.   A fruit packing company manager wishes to take a sample to be 95.5% confident in estimating the true mean weight per box, with an accuracy of $\pm$ 0.15 lbs. Previous data reveal that the standard deviation of weights is 0.60 lbs. How large a sample should be taken?

18.   The medical director of Mercy Hospital has asked a staff analyst to develop a 98% confidence interval estimate of the time required for a certain type of heart surgery. She would like to be accurate within $\pm$ 6 min. Only 420 such operations have been performed nationwide. For the eight operations performed in the region of Mercy Hospital, $\overline{X}$ = 3.20 hr. and s = .30 hr. The analyst plans to take a random sample. How many surgeries should be included in the sample?

Confidence Interval Estimates of Proportion

Suppose that you wished to estimate the proportion of defective electronic chips that are being produced by an automated process. In this case: (1) there are only two outcomes—defective or nondefective, (2) the probabilities are constant from trial to trial, and (3) each trial is independent of the previous trial. Since this sampling distribution has just two possible outcomes, the binomial distribution would be used to establish the confidence interval estimate of the population proportion. But, the problem with using the binomial distribution is finding the appropriate percentile value. Especially, for small samples, the relevant value likely doesn't exist in the distribution. For example, with a sample of size five with π = .5, the following binomial distribution would result:

X	P(X)	Cumulative Probability
0	0.0313	0.0313
1	0.1563	0.1875
2	0.3125	0.5000
3	0.3125	0.8125
4	0.1563	0.9688
5	0.0313	1.0000

If we want a 95% confidence interval, we will need the .025 and .975 percentiles of the distribution; however, these values do not exist in the sampling distribution. The closest we could come is the .0313 and the .9668 percentiles for approximately a 94% confidence interval. It is often the case with the binomial distribution that the desired percentiles do not exist in the sampling distribution, especially with small sample sizes.

Estimates of the true value of π are usually not developed from small samples because proportions derived from small samples are not very precise. For example, in our sample of size 5 above, the outcomes are 0 through 5 defectives. Thus, the only values of sample proportion that could result are .00, .20, .40, .60, .80, or 1.00. This means that it may be impossible for our sample proportion to be close to the true population proportion. For example, if the true value of π were .31, the sample estimate could not be very close because the possible proportions from a sample of n = 5 are so limited.

Large samples are more common and there may be a close approximation to the desired percentiles in the binomial distribution. The Excel function BINOM.INV can be used to find these percentiles. Also, as we saw in Chapter 4 if the sample size is fairly large and the proportion is not too close to either zero or 1.0, we can use the normal distribution as an approximation to the binomial. The sampling distribution of proportions is well approximated by a normal distribution whenever $n\pi > 5$ and $n(1-\pi) > 5$.

The procedure for computing a confidence interval for the true proportion, π, is similar to what we used for constructing a confidence interval for the true mean. That is, the confidence limits are "established" around the sample statistic. In this case, the sample proportion is p, Z identifies the confidence level, and σ_p is the true value of the standard error of proportion:

$$\text{Confidence limits: } CL = p \pm Z\sigma_p \qquad (6\text{-}7)$$

If we use the binomial rather than the normal approximation, we can find the lower and upper limits (Bin_L and Bin_U) directly using BINOM.INV. This will return a percentile from the binomial distribution. Then, since the critical value of the binomial is in terms of the number of successes, we have to divide by the sample size to convert to a proportion. Our confidence interval then becomes:

$$LCL = \frac{Bin_L}{n} \quad UCL = \frac{Bin_U}{n} \qquad (6\text{-}8)$$

Both methods for estimating the confidence interval are approximations. The equation is based on the normal distribution as an approximation to the Binomial and equation 6-8 often requires approximate percentiles from the Binomial distribution.

However, a problem remains no matter which sampling distribution we use. Recall that the standard error of the proportion is calculated as:

$$\sigma_p = \sqrt{\frac{\pi(1-\pi)}{n}}$$

In addition, the BINOM.INV function requires a value for π. This means that in order to calculate the standard error (σ_p), or find the percentiles in the binomial, we must first know the value of π, the population parameter we are trying to estimate. As a result, we must use the sample proportion (p). Then, the equation for the normal approximation is calculated using the sample standard error, s_p:

$$\text{Confidence limits (proportions: } \pi \text{ unknown): } CL = p \pm Zs_p \qquad (6\text{-}9)$$

where,

$$S_p = \sqrt{\frac{p(1-p)}{n}}$$

Also, percentiles from the binomial can be used in place of the normal approximation with the sample proportion (p) used in place of π in the BINOM.INV function.

Example 6-5

A random sample of 250 employees from a large multinational firm shows that 50 were in favor of a proposed employee stock plan. Develop a 99% confidence interval estimate of the true proportion of employees that are in favor of the plan.

Solution

Good example problem

The sample proportion in favor is $p = 50/250 = .20$

$$CL = p \pm Zs_p \text{ where } Z = 2.58$$

$$S_p = \sqrt{\frac{p(1-p)}{n}} = \sqrt{\frac{(.2)(.8)}{250}} = .025$$

Therefore,

$$CL = .20 \pm (2.58)(.025)$$

$$LCL = .20 - .065 = .135$$

$$UCL = .20 + .065 = .265$$

Using the binomial we would get:

BINOM.INV(250, .2, .005) = 34   and   BINOM.INV(250, .2, .995) = 67 and

LCL = 26/250 = .136   UCL = 67/250 = .268

Conclusion: Using either method, the managers of the multinational firm can be 99% confident that the true percentage of employees of the firm who are in favor of the employee stock plan lies within the approximate interval 13.5% to 26.5%.

As you can see, the two methods yield very similar results. In truth, both methods are approximations. The normal distribution procedure is an approximation because the true sampling distribution is the binomial. The binomial method is usually an approximation because the exact percentile normally doesn't exist. For example, the cumulative probability for the lower value of 34 found above is actually the .005459 rather than .005. Similarly, the cumulative probability for the upper value of 67 is actually .996291 rather than .995.

As with sample means, when the sample constitutes 5% or more of the population, the finite population correction factor should be applied to correct the standard error when calculating confidence intervals.

Finding the Sample Size for Estimating a Population Proportion

The procedure for finding the sample size required to estimate a population proportion, π, is similar to that used for estimating a population mean. As with means, the maximum allowable error of a proportion, e, is half the width of the confidence interval; however, when working with proportions, the sample statistic, p, and allowable error, e, are stated as decimals (or percentages). Setting the maximum error (e) equal to the half width of the confidence interval we would have:

$$e = Z\sqrt{\frac{\pi(1-\pi)}{n}} = Z\frac{\sqrt{\pi(1-\pi)}}{\sqrt{n}}$$

If we, then, solve for "n" we would find:

$$n = \frac{Z^2\pi(1-\pi)}{e^2} \tag{6 10}$$

However, here we have a predicament. In order to find the required sample size we must know the value of π which is what we are trying to estimate. In practice, we would either use a conservative estimate for π, or take a preliminary sample to calculate a sample proportion, p, and use that value. When sample data is used, the sample size equation for estimating a population proportion (π) becomes:

$$n = \frac{Z^2 p(1-p)}{e^2} \tag{6-11}$$

Example 6-6

A random sample of county residents is to be taken to estimate the proportion in favor of a business and occupations (B&O) tax to raise funds for a new coliseum. The estimate must be accurate within ± 2 percentage points. How large a sample is needed to establish a 95% confidence interval? (Note: the county commissioners estimate that 70% of the residents favor the tax).

Solution

$Z^2 = (1.96)^2$

$P = .70 \quad e^2 = (.02)^2$

$$n = \frac{(1.96)^2(.70)(.30)}{(.02)^2} = 2,017 \text{ residents}$$

largest estimate
P = 50%
or .5

Finding Sample Size When No Preliminary Estimate Available

If the researcher has no idea of the true value of π and no estimate of π from a sample, he or she can ensure that the sample will be sufficiently large by using the most conservative value of p = .5. Obviously, the quantity p(1-p) is largest when p = .5. With a value of .5 p(1-p) = (.5)(.5) = .25, but if p = .4 then (.4) (.6) = .24, and for p = .3, (.3) (.7) = .21, and so on. By using .5 for p, the sample will be large enough to yield the desired precision in the worst-case scenario, and will yield more precision than needed if the proportion turns out to be something other than .5.

Exercises III

19. Why are small samples not recommended when estimating proportions?

20. Is a confidence interval estimate of a proportion likely to be as accurate as a confidence interval estimate of a mean? Explain.

21. A sample of 400 items was selected to create a 95% confidence interval estimate for the true proportion defect rate in the population. Of the total sample, 80 defective items were found. For a confidence interval calculation, find (a) the value of the sample proportion, *p*, and (b) the estimated standard error of proportion. (c) What are the confidence limits?

22. A survey of 800 potential customers revealed that 288 liked a proposed product enough to buy it. The marketing manager wishes to establish a 98% confidence interval estimate of the true proportion customers who like the product. (a) What is the estimated standard error of proportion? (b) Compute the 98% confidence limits. (c) Make a confidence interval statement conveying your result.

23. A local newspaper is trying to figure out the proportion of voters in favor of a certain referendum for the upcoming election. A random sample of 5,000 voters showed that 2,650 people favored the referendum. Compute a 95% confidence interval for the true proportion of voters in favor of the referendum.

24. For a sample of 100, construct a 95.5% confidence interval estimate if the sample proportion is (a) .10; (b) .40. (c) What conclusion can you draw about the precision of an estimate of π by comparing the width of the confidence intervals in parts (a) and (b)?

25. The personnel manager of a Houston defense contractor with 1,720 employees has taken a random sample of 125 employees to determine the political affiliations of the firm's employees. If 35 of those questioned claimed to be independents, what is the 90% confidence interval estimate for the proportion of independents in the firm?

26. The marketing manager of a major grocery chain store wants to obtain an estimate of the proportion of shoppers who shop at discount warehouses. He thinks the proportion is about 12%. How large a sample should be taken if he wishes to have 95.5% confidence that the results are accurate within two percentage points?

27. An informal survey by enthusiasts of bicycling suggests that 40% of all the new participants in the sport are over the age of 50. A bicycle manufacturer has asked you to take a random sample to make a more formal, 95% confidence interval estimate that is accurate to within ±2% of the correct value. How large a sample of new participants is required?

Confidence Interval Estimates of the Variance (Standard Deviation)

Confidence intervals for a population variance are more complex than intervals for means or proportions. Recall from Chapter 4 that the sampling distribution for a sample variance is the chi-square distribution. The following test statistic is used:

$$\chi^2 = \frac{(n-1)S^2}{\sigma^2} \qquad (6\text{-}12)$$

From this we can derive that:

$$\sigma^2 = \frac{(n-1)S^2}{\chi^2}$$

Just as we did with means and the proportions, we can use this formula to compute the upper and lower limits of the confidence interval. The appropriate values from the test statistic will be the percentiles $\chi^2_{\alpha/2}$ and $\chi^2_{1-\alpha/2}$ for a $(1-\alpha)\%$ confidence interval; however, there is an important factor that is unique to this situation. To find the lower limit of the confidence interval, we must divide the quantity $(n-1)s^2$ by the upper value from the chi-square distribution $(\chi^2_{1-\alpha/2})$ and for the upper limit we must divide by the lower value from the chi-square distribution $(\chi^2_{\alpha/2})$. This can be understood at an intuitive level by recalling that the chi-square distribution is not a symmetrical distribution, but rather a positively skewed distribution that begins at zero. This means that the values $\chi^2_{\alpha/2}$ and $\chi^2_{1-\alpha/2}$ will not be mirror images of each other. In fact, both will be positive values. You can also see that $\chi^2_{1-\alpha/2}$ will be larger than $\chi^2_{\alpha/2}$, e.g., $\chi^2_{.975}$ will be larger than $\chi^2_{.025}$. Since the lower limit of the confidence interval should be smaller than the upper limit, this means that we will need to divide the quantity $(n-1)s^2$ by the upper χ^2 value for the lower limit and by the lower χ^2 value to obtain the upper limit. Thus, our confidence limits become:

$$LCL = \frac{(n-1)S^2}{\chi^2_{1-\frac{\alpha}{2}}} \quad and$$

$$UCL = \frac{(n-1)S^2}{\chi^2_{\alpha/2}}$$

You can also see this algebraically by considering the following statement:

$$P(\chi^2 < \chi^2_{.975}) = .975 \ or \ P\left(\frac{(n-1)S^2}{\sigma^2} < \chi^2_{.975}\right) = .975 \ or \ P\left((n-1)S^2 < \sigma^2\chi^2_{.975}\right) = .975$$

But this means that:

$$P\left(\sigma^2 > \frac{(n-1)S^2}{\chi^2_{.975}}\right) = .975$$

Therefore the quantity $(n-1)s^2$ divided by the upper chi-square value is the lower limit of the confidence interval. A similar argument demonstrates that the upper limit is the same numerator divided by the lower tail χ^2 value.

Example 6-7

An accounting department wants to reduce the variability in their accounts payable process to reduce complaints about lengthy delays in payment. They first must need to know where they currently stand in this regard. To estimate the variability of accounts payable, they measure the payment delay for a sample of 30 accounts and find a sample standard deviation of 6.5 days and a sample variance of 42.25. They would like a 95% confidence interval for their estimate.

Solution

Using the CHIINV function or XLDataAnalyst we can find that $\chi^2_{.975} = 45.72228$ and $\chi^2_{.025} = 16.04705$ in a chi-square distribution with $(n-1) = 29$ degrees of freedom. Our confidence limits are:

$$LCL = \frac{(n-1)S^2}{\chi^2_{.975}} = \frac{(29)(42.25)}{45.72228} = 26.80$$

$$UCL = \frac{(n-1)S^2}{\chi^2_{.025}} = \frac{(29)(42.25)}{16.04705} = 76.35$$

Therefore we are 95% confident that the true population variance (σ^2) is between 26.80 and 76.35.

Interval Estimates for the Standard Deviation

Recall from Chapter 4 that the sample standard deviation does not have a specific sampling distribution. Rather, as an approximation to a confidence interval for the standard deviation we can find the confidence interval for the variance and take the square root of the upper and lower limits. Although this is not precisely a confidence interval for the standard deviation, it serves as a very close approximation, especially for larger samples. In Example 6-7, this would mean that the 95% confidence interval for the standard deviation of accounts payable delay is from $\sqrt{26.80} = 5.18$ to $\sqrt{76.35} = 8.74$ days.

Finding the Sample Size for Estimating the Variance (Standard Deviation)

We can also calculate the required sample size to estimate the variance with a given margin of error but the process is considerably more complex than for means and proportions. We will simply state that the required sample size can be calculated as follows:

$$n = 1.0 + .5\left(\frac{z_{\alpha/2}}{\log_e\left(1+\frac{e}{\sigma}\right)}\right)^2 \qquad (6\text{-}13)$$

Notice that this calculation requires an estimate of the population standard deviation. The same approach described previously for estimating the sample size when σ is unknown can be used here as well.

Example 6-8

In our accounts payable example (Example 6-9) we wanted to estimate the variance of the delays in payment. Suppose we wanted to derive a 95% confidence interval for this value and wanted the estimate to be accurate within ±1. Assume that we derived a preliminary estimate of the standard deviation of 3.5.

Solution

The required sample size would be:

$$n = 1.0 + .5\left(\frac{Z_{\alpha/2}}{\log_e\left(1+\frac{e}{\sigma}\right)}\right)^2 = n = 1.0 + .5\left(\frac{1.96}{\log_e\left(1+\frac{e}{3.5}\right)}\right)^2 \approx 32$$

Exercises IV

28. For a sample of 100, find the following confidence limits for the variance:

   (a) 95% limits when s = 30

   (b) 99.7% limits when s = 45

29. Peaches are shipped on a regular basis to a large distribution warehouse in Boise. A random sample of 81 boxes revealed a mean weight of 60.0 lb and a standard deviation of 3.6 lb. Find a 95% confidence interval for the standard deviation. Write out a statement expressing your conclusion (Assume that the population distribution is normal.).

30. The materials handling manager at Buffalo Insulation Co. would like to make a 98% confidence interval estimate of the true variance of the weight of packaged containers of sawdust used in their manufacturing process. A random sample of 100 containers revealed a mean weight of 145.0 lbs. and a standard deviation of 6.0 lbs. Compute the confidence limits for the population standard deviation and state your conclusion (Assume that the population distribution is normal.).

31. The accountant for a heating oil firm wishes to estimate the variance of the number of days that delinquent accounts are overdue. The accountant's sample of 25 accounts shows an average overdue period of 65.5 days, with a standard deviation of 15 days. What would be the 90% confidence interval estimate for the variance (Assume that the population distribution is normal)?

32. A management analyst for a major airline needs to estimate (to within ±1.5) the true variance of carry-on baggage for transcontinental flights. Previous data suggest that the standard deviation is very close to 8.0 lb. How many passengers must be randomly selected to have their baggage weighed assuming the analyst wishes to be (a) 90% confident; (b) 99.7% confident?

33. A fruit packing company manager wishes to take a sample of a packing line in order to be 95.5% confident in estimating the standard deviation of the weight per box, with an accuracy of plus or minus .40 lb. Previous data reveal that the standard deviation of weights is .60 lb. How large a sample should be taken?

Confidence Interval Estimates for the Median

As we discussed in Chapter 3, ordinal scale situations must use medians as the measure of "average" value since the mean does not have meaning for such a scale. For populations with skewed distributions, the median may also be preferred as a measure of central tendency. The confidence interval for the median is more difficult than the other measures discussed up to this point.

At the beginning of this chapter, we stated three factors that determine a confidence interval. The first factor was the shape of the sampling distribution of the sample statistic. In this instance, the sample statistic of interest is the sample median (M). Unfortunately, there is no sampling distribution for this statistic that holds across all situations. For large samples ("n" of 30 or more) the sampling distribution for the median can usually be approximated with the normal distribution, but the sampling distribution is unknown for smaller samples.

The second factor required for confidence intervals is a measure of the variability of the sampling distribution. Again, this is a problem for the sample median because there is no widely accepted measure of the standard error for the median. Therefore, even if we use the normal approximation to calculate the confidence interval we still have the problem of finding the standard error.

Confidence Intervals Using the Normal Approximation

There are two approaches to deriving a standard error: One uses the binomial distribution and the second uses the bootstrapping method discussed in Chapter 5.

Standard Error Using the Binomial

We can find an approximation to the standard error for any percentile, such as the median using the binomial distribution. For example, the definition of the median is that half of the values should be below the median and half above. Therefore, for any given observation the probability of it being less than the median is 0.50 and the probability of it being greater than the median is also 0.50. Thus, we can view this as a binomial problem with $\pi = .5$ and n being the sample size. Recall that for the binomial, the mean and standard deviation are $n\pi$ and $\sqrt{n\pi(1-\pi)}$ respectively. Thus, the position of the lower and upper limits of the confidence interval assuming a normal approximation and a 95% confidence level will be:

$$L = n\pi - 1.96\sqrt{n\pi(1-\pi)} = .5n - 1.96\sqrt{.25n}$$

$$U = n\pi + 1.96\sqrt{n\pi(1-\pi)} = .5n + 1.96\sqrt{.25n} \qquad (6\text{-}14)$$

Notice that these values provide the relative position of the upper and lower bounds in the dataset and should therefore be rounded off to the next higher integer. An alternative formulation finds the position of the lower bound as above and then finds the upper limit as:

$$U = (n+1) - L$$

This will generally give a somewhat more conservative (wider) confidence interval.

Example 6-9

Western Farm Cooperative has randomly sampled 100 farmers to estimate the yield (in bushels/acre) of this year's wheat crop. The data are contained in the file Example 6-9.xlsx. The sample median is 5.1 bushels. Establish a 95% confidence interval estimate for the true median, η.

Solution

Using .5 for π we can find the position of the limits as follows:

$$L = .5n - 1.96\sqrt{.25n} = (100)(.5) - 1.96\sqrt{.25(100)} = 50 - 9.8 = 40.2 \; or \; position \; 41$$

$$U = .5n + 1.96\sqrt{.25n} = (100)(.5) + 1.96\sqrt{.25(100)} = 50 + 9.8 = 59.8.2 \; or \; position \; 60$$

The value in the 41st position is 4.8 and the value in the 60th position is 5.2; thus the 95% confidence interval for the population median is from 4.8 to 5.2.

Conclusion: The Farm Cooperative can be 95% confident that the true median yield in this year's wheat crop is within the interval of 4.8 to 5.2 bushels/acre.

Standard Error Using Bootstrapping

Bootstrapping can be applied to find an approximation to the standard error for any sample statistic, not just the median. Bootstrapping involves generating a large number of "samples" from the population (usually 1,000 or more) by sampling with replacement. For each of these samples we can calculate the median. Recalling that our definition of the standard error is the standard deviation of the sampling distribution, and since these 1,000 values constitute an estimate of the sampling distribution, we can then estimate the standard error by calculating the standard deviation of these 1,000 medians. This estimated standard error can then be used, along with the normal distribution z-values, for large samples, to calculate the confidence interval as:

$$CL = M \pm Z_{\alpha/2} * \text{Standard Error}$$

We will not illustrate these two methods of computing the confidence interval for the median manually but return to this topic in the next section when we will use XLDataAnalyst. Also, as you might guess, there is no generally accepted method of calculating the required sample size for confidence intervals of the median.

Direct Estimation of the Confidence Interval Using Bootstrapping

A more direct way to use bootstrapping is to forgo the normal distribution assumption and directly use the appropriate percentiles from the bootstrapped medians. For example, with a 95% confidence interval we can find the 97.5^{th} and the 2.5^{th} percentiles from the generated medians and use these as our estimates of the upper and lower bounds of the confidence interval. For example, if we generate 1,000 medians, then the 25th value is the 2.5^{th} percentile and the 975th is the 97.5^{th} percentile. This is the approach normally taken in bootstrapping literature and is the method used in XLDataAnalyst.

Practice

Confidence Interval Estimates in Excel and XLDataAnalyst

Excel Functions

There are two functions in Excel function that can be used to calculate confidence intervals for the mean. The first function is CONFIDENCE.NORM which can be used when the population standard deviation, σ, is known. With a little more work, it can be used for confidence intervals for the proportion with the normal distribution. The syntax of the function is:

CONFIDENCE.NORM (alpha, standard_dev, size)

where alpha is 1 minus the desired degree of confidence. For a 95% confidence interval, alpha would be .05. Standard_dev is the assumed population standard. To use the function for the proportion you would have to calculate the standard deviation from the sample proportion as in Equation 6-7. The Size argument in the function is the sample size. The function returns the value that would need to be added to and subtracted from the sample mean (or proportion) to find the lower and upper limits of the confidence interval.

The second function (CONFIDENCE.T) can be used when the population standard deviation is not known and uses the student t distribution rather than the normal distribution. The arguments are the same but the standard deviation supplied to the function is the sample standard deviation, not a population value.

Example 6-10

Recall that in Example 6-1 a California winery wanted to estimate the true weight of boxes of grapes that were being received from growers for processing. A sample of 49 boxes revealed a mean weight of 197.0 lbs., and from past seasons, the population standard deviation was known to be $\sigma = 14.0$ lbs. Compute a confidence interval estimate of the true mean weight per box (μ) that will give the winery 95% confidence of being correct.

Solution

Entering the formula CONFIDENCE.NORM(.05, 14, 49) in Excel produces the result of 3.919928 or 3.9. Therefore, the lower confidence limit would be $197 - 3.9 = 193.1$ and the upper limit would be $197 + 3.9 = 200.9$ which are identical to the results found for Example 6-1 previously.

The Data Analysis Toolpak

The Data Analysis Toolpak in Excel can also be used to find confidence intervals for the mean. To find confidence intervals for the mean with the Data Analysis Toolpak, select Data Analysis in the Analysis section of the Data tab in the ribbon. The list of available routines as illustrated in Figure 6-4 will appear. Select the Descriptive Statistics option as you did in Chapter 3 to produce descriptive measures. Then, the dialogue shown in Figure 6-5 will appear on the screen. Indicate where the input data are on the worksheet and where you want to place the output. You can also use the mouse to highlight the range for the input data and the output range. If you have labels that you want to appear in the output make sure that they are included in the input range and check the box for Labels in First Row. **It is very important to make sure that you check the box labeled Summary Statistics or no output will be produced**. To produce confidence intervals for the mean (or proportion), check the box labeled Confidence Interval for the Mean and set the appropriate degree of confidence.

Figure 6-4   List of Routines in the Analysis Toolpak

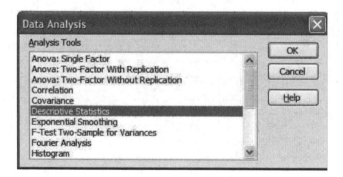

Example 6-11

In Example 6-10, we found a 95% confidence interval for the median number of bushels in this year's wheat crop. We can use that same data (in file Example 6-11.xlsx) to find the 95% confidence interval for the mean number of bushels using the Analysis Toolpak.

Solution

The resulting output from the Toolpak is shown in Figure 6-6. Notice that, like the CONFIDENCE.NORM function, the Toolpak does not give you the lower and upper bounds of the confidence interval, but only the amount to be added to and subtracted from the sample mean to find the confidence interval. You will still need to calculate the bounds of the interval yourself or enter equations in the output worksheet to calculate the bounds. In this case, the confidence interval is 4.959994 ± 0.20294 or from 4.76 to 5.16.

Figure 6-5   *Data Analysis Toolpak Descriptive Statistics Dialog Box*

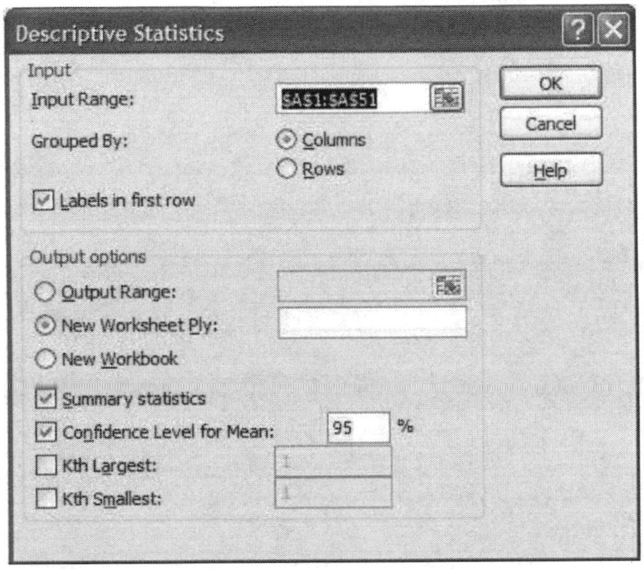

The Excel Template

The Excel template for confidence intervals is the file named Confidence Intervals.xlsx. As can be seen in Figure 6-7, there are five worksheets in this template. The first worksheet is used to calculate confidence intervals for the mean when the population standard deviation is known. This worksheet uses the normal distribution, hence the worksheet name (Means-Z). The next worksheets calculate confidence intervals for the mean when the population standard deviation is not known (Means-t), proportions (Proportions), and variances (Variances). In each of these worksheets, the confidence interval can be calculated from summarized data if the problem is given in that format or from the raw data by pasting the data into the appropriate range on the worksheet. The last worksheet in the template can be used to calculate the required sample size for the mean, proportion or variance.

Figure 6-6   Output from the Analysis Toolpak

	Bushels
Mean	4.959994
Standard Error	0.102277
Median	5.054652
Mode	#N/A
Standard Deviation	1.022769
Sample Variance	1.046056
Kurtosis	-0.02617
Skewness	-0.17847
Range	5.157632
Minimum	2.509023
Maximum	7.666656
Sum	495.9994
Count	100
Confidence Level(95.0%)	0.20294

Figure 6-7   The Confidence Intervals Template

	A	B	C	D	E	F	G	H	I
1	Confidence Intervals for Means					Data	n	Mean	Std
2	Population Standard Deviation Known					97	100	98.9400	10.2591
3	Population		Sample			90			
4	Std	4	Mean	24		108			
5	N		n	49		90			
6	Summarized Data					104			
7	Finite Population Correction		1.000000			90			
8	Deg of Confidence	Z Value	Lower Limit	Upper Limit		108			
9	99.00%	2.5758	22.5281	25.4719		96			
10	95.00%	1.9600	22.8800	25.1200		117			
11	90.00%	1.6449	23.0601	24.9399		102			
12	85.00%	1.4395	23.1774	24.8226		91			
13						103			
14						81			
15	Sample Data					95			
16	Finite Population Correction		1.000000			95			
17	Deg of Confidence	Z Value	Lower Limit	Upper Limit		122			
18	99.00%	2.5758	97.4681	100.4119		111			
19	95.00%	1.9600	97.8200	100.0600		99			
20	90.00%	1.6449	98.0001	99.8799		101			
21	85.00%	1.4395	98.1174	99.7626		98			
22						111			
23						96			
24						108			
25						109			
26						84			
27						99			
28						87			
29						110			
30						98			
31						94			
32						96			

Means-Z / Means-t / Proportions / Variances / Sample Size /

Example 6-12

We will utilize the same data as in Example 6-11 to illustrate the use of the templates. Since this is a sample and we do not know the population standard deviation, we need to use the second template for confidence intervals for the mean using the t-distribution.

Solution

The results are shown in Figure 6-8. Since we are dealing with raw data in this problem, we focus on the Sample Data section of the results. We obtain the same results as before: the 95% confidence interval runs from about 4.76 to 5.16. The advantage of the template is that we can get other confidence intervals very quickly by simply entering other confidence levels. For example, we can see that the 99% confidence interval runs from 4.69 to 5.23.

This sample template can also be used to solve the problems presented in earlier sections of this chapter where the data has already been summarized. Simply enter the appropriate information in the upper portions of the template and view the results in the Summarized Data section of the output. If a value is entered for the population size, the finite population correction factor will be calculated and used to adjust the confidence intervals. If this value is blank, the correction factor will be 1.0, as shown in Figure 6-8 and will not affect the interval.

Figure 6-8   Template Showing Solution to Example 6-12

Example 6-13

In Example 6-8, we considered the situation where a random sample of county residents was to be taken to estimate the proportion in favor of a business and occupations (B&O) tax to raise funds for a new coliseum. The estimate needed to be accurate within ± 2 percentage points. We want to know how large a sample will be needed for a 95% confidence interval if we believe that 70% of the residents favor the tax.

Solution

Using the last worksheet in the template produced the results shown in Figure 6-9 under Proportion. The required sample size is again calculated to be 2,017 people.

Figure 6-9   Solution for Example 6-13

	A	B	C	D	E	F	G	H
1			Sample Size Estimator					
2								
3	**Mean**		**Proportion**		**Variance**			
4	Degree of Confidence	0.9500	Degree of Confidence	0.9500	Degree of Confidence	0.9500		
5	Desired Error	5	Desired Error	0.02	Desired Error	1		
6	Estimated Std	20	Estimated Proportion	0.7	Estimated Std	3.5		
7								
8	Required Sample Size	62		2017		32		
9								
10								
11								
12								

Using XLDataAnalyst

Confidence intervals for means, proportions, medians, and standard deviations (variances) can be easily obtained in XLDataAnalyst when you have raw data. XLDataAnalyst will also calculate the required sample size to achieve a certain result for means, proportions and standard deviations (variances). There are two choices in the Tests for One Variable section of the XLDataAnalyst ribbon, as shown in Figure 6.10. The two options are "Tests and Intervals" and "Find Sample Size."

Figure 6-10   The XLDataAnalyst Ribbon

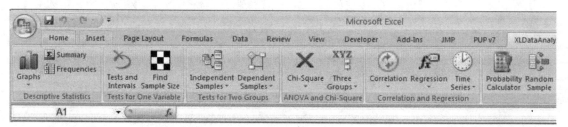

To estimate confidence intervals for a given set of data, choose the Tests and Intervals option. To calculate the required sample size, choose Find Sample Size. When you select the Tests and Intervals option, the dialogue shown in Figure 6-11 will be displayed. To derive a confidence interval, simply select the appropriate variable in the list of variables on the left and from the top panel select the box for a confidence interval for the mean (or proportion), for the median, or for the standard deviation (variance). You can also select any degree of confidence; the default is for a 95% confidence interval.

Figure 6-11   The Inference Dialog

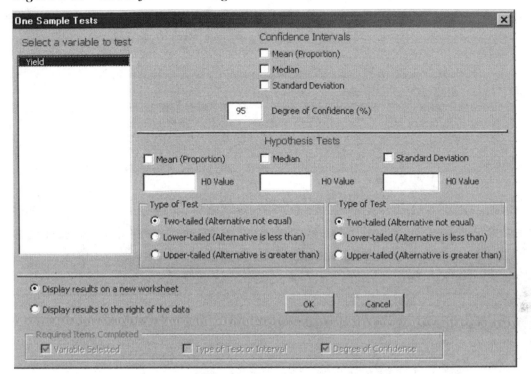

Example 6-14

The file Example 6-14.xlsx contains data from a sample of 90 employees for U.S. MegaBank. Find a 95% confidence interval for the following parameters: average current salary (CurrentSalary), proportion of females (Gender =1), median of the current salaries (CurrentSalary), and the standard deviation of current monthly salaries (CurrentSalalary).

Solution

The relevant XLDataAnalyst output for the variable CurrentSalary is shown in Figure 6-12. The average salary in the sample of 90 employees is $41,818.67 and we are 95% confident that the average salary of all bank employees is between $40,325.43 and $43,311.91. The median salary is $40,200 and the confidence interval using the binomial method is from $38,640 to $42,240. Using the Bootstrap method, the confidence interval is from $38,358 to $42,041. Notice that the Bootstrap method produces a narrower or more precise interval than the binomial method. This is usually, but not always, the case.

The sample standard deviation of salaries is $7,129.48 and we are 95% confident that the standard deviation of salaries for all employees is between $6,218.42 and $8,355.79.

Figure 6-12   *Output From XLDataAnalyst for Example 6-14*

One Sample Results For CurrentSal

Summary Measures

Sample Size	90.0000
Mean	41,818.6680
Median	40,200.0000
Variance	50,829,492.0000
Standard Deviation	7,129.4805

95.00% Confidence Interval for the Mean

Lower Limit	40,325.4258
Upper Limit	43,311.9102

95.00% Confidence Interval for the Standard Deviation

Lower Limit	6,218.4226
Upper Limit	8,355.7920

0.95% Confidence Interval for the Median
Binomial Method

Lower Limit	38,400.0000
Upper Limit	42,000.0000

Bootstrap Method

Lower Limit	38,643.0000
Upper Limit	42,120.0000

The results for the gender variable are shown in Figure 6-13. We can see that 64.4% of the employees in our sample are female. There are three different confidence intervals given for the population proportion. Normally, these different intervals will be very similar to one another. The first confidence interval uses the normal approximation to the binomial to calculate the interval. The second interval also uses the normal approximation but adjusts the interval using a method developed originally by Edwin B. Wilson[3] called the Wilson Score. Normal approximation can produce a lower bound less than 0 for very small proportions or an upper bound greater than 1.0 for very large proportions. Since a proportion cannot be negative or greater than 1.0, such bounds are meaningless. Of course, you can always round such bounds off to 0 or 1 but the Wilson Score is a more accurate method of calculating such intervals.

The final confidence interval is calculated using the binomial distribution. It is a matter of choice which method you use. The normal approximation method is the most common, but many have argued that the Wilson Score gives more accurate results. Normally, there will not be a great deal of difference between the three methods. Using the Wilson Score in our example, we can be 95% confident that the true proportion of female employees in the entire bank is between 54.15% and 73.56%.

---

[3] See R.G. Newcombe, 1998, Two-sided confidence intervals for the single proportion: Comparison of seven methods. *Statistics in Medicine*, 17, 857-872 for details.

Figure 6-13   *Results for Gender in Example 6-14*

One Sample Results For Gender

Summary Measures

Sample Size   90.0000
Proportion   0.6444

95.00% Confidence Interval for the Proportion

Lower Limit   0.5450
Upper Limit   0.7439

95.00% Confidence Interval for the Proportion using the Wilson Formulae

Lower Limit   0.5415
Upper Limit   0.7356

95.00% Confidence Interval for the Proportion using the Binomial

Lower Limit   0.5382
Upper Limit   0.7475

Exercises V

34.   The accountant for a local soft drink distributor wants to estimate the median number of days before accounts payable are paid. The accountant's sample of 45 accounts is contained in the file Exercise 6-34.xlsx. (a) What is the estimated median number of days before payment? (b) What is the 95% confidence interval for the population median?

35.   A game warden in Montana is looking to determine the number of hunters that visit a certain region on any given weekend. The sample number of hunters over 30-weekend periods is contained in the file Exercise 6-35.xlsx. (a) What is the estimated mean number of hunters for a weekend? (b) What is the 95% confidence interval for the mean? (c) What is the 95% confidence interval for the median number of hunters?

36.   Sam Coffe, the manager of a local club named The Scene, is trying to persuade a big named group to perform on a Saturday night. The group's manager will only book the band for clubs that have an average of 250 people in attendance. The data from the past 50 Saturdays at The Scene is contained in the file Exercise 6-36.xlsx. (a) What is the estimated mean attendance? (b) Compute the 95% confidence interval for the population mean. Can the manager make the claim that his club will have 250 people in it on a given Saturday night?

37.   A manager of a gym wants to know how many members desire assistance when they work out. A random sample of 200 members, 120 men and 80 women, is contained in the file Exercise 6-37.xlsx. (a) Estimate the percentage of men who want assistance using a 95% confidence interval. (b) Estimate the percentage of women who want assistance using a 90% confidence interval. (c) Estimate the percentage of all members who want assistance using a 99% confidence interval.

38.   A manufacturing manager has been asked to give an estimate of defective parts in a given shipment. A random sample of 100 parts is contained in the file Exercise 6-38.xlsx. Compute a 99% confidence interval for the true proportion of defective parts.

39.   A marketing researcher is trying to determine how many customers are satisfied with the company's new product. The researcher's task is to estimate a proportion, and she takes a random sample of 500 people who had recently purchased the product. The results are contained in the file Exercise 6-39.xlsx. Compute a 95% confidence interval for the true proportion of satisfied customers.

40. What sample size is required to estimate the weekly mean number of hours a household watches television, if the population is 10,000 households, within 1.5 hours, with a probability of .90? Previous studies indicate that the standard deviation is .8.

41. What sample size is required to estimate the mean amount of money in a population of 2,000 accounts within $1,500 with a 95% level of confidence, if a preliminary sample gives us s = 9.

42. Suppose you are thinking of opening a restaurant after you graduate in the spring. In trying to decide on the venture, a main concern is if you will be able to be profitable by the end of your first year. It would be far too complicated to try and account for all of the factors that would influence whether you would turn a profit the first year (competition, location, population density, etc.); however, you want to know the proportion of restaurants that realize a profit in their first year of operation. Assume you are going to estimate this proportion via sampling, and you would like your estimate to be within .05 of the true proportion with a confidence level of at least .95. How large must your random sample be?

43. A manager of a retail store is concerned with shoplifting and the losses that it is creating. An examination estimates that the percentage of customers who have shoplifted in the past week ranges from .3 to 10 percent. The upper management approves a "secret shopper" program and the manager wants to be very sure that the estimate will not differ from the actual number of shoplifters by more than .5 percent. How large should the sample be?

44. An automotive products company needs to estimate how long a new type of lubricating oil is effective in standard passenger cars. The company conducts a study using a random sample 50 cars in various road and weather conditions and records the mileage before an oil change is required. The results are contained in the file Exercise 6-44.xlsx. (a) Find a 95% confidence interval for the median number of miles before an oil change. (b) Find a 95% confidence interval for the variance of the number of miles before an oil change. (c) What is the point estimate of the standard deviation of miles before an oil change?

45. The El Burrito fast food chain in concerned about the time it takes to serve customers. In particular, they are concerned about some of the very long wait times. They sample 75 customers that arrive at one of their locations and record the time between when the customers enter the door when they have their order in hand. The data are contained in the file Exercise 6-45.xlsx. (a) Find the 95% confidence interval for the variance of the service times. (b) What is the 95% confidence interval for the population standard deviation?

Opening Vignette Revisited

Ray contacts the manager of the trucking fleet and explains the deal he has made with Bob. He asks for his help in installing the new tires on several trucks in their fleet. After a month of use, they plan to measure the amount of wear on the tires and estimate from those measurements how many miles the tires will last before they have to be replaced. The resulting data are contained in the file Chapter 6 Vignette.xlsx. Ray has his assistant Sally, a recently college grad, analyze the data to help him set a price. Sally reports back to Ray that the average estimated mileage of the 50 tires is about 44,670 miles. After Ray asks Sally how confident she is about that figure, Sally tells him that they should probably develop a confidence interval for the estimate of the mean tire life of all Roberson tires. A few hours later she returns to Ray's office and reports that the 95% confidence interval is from 43,221 miles to 46,119 miles. Ray tells Sally to be conservative and take the lower figure for further calculations. She should then use the historical information about their current tires and come up with a price estimate for Roberson Tire Company that would save Piccadilly some money on their tire purchases.

Summary

Point estimates (single values) of population parameters are useful, but they are typically inaccurate because of sampling error. Interval estimates (pairs of values) are more useful because they state a range within which the parameter is expected to lie. Confidence interval estimates also quantify the likelihood (level of confidence) that the parameter is contained within the stated interval. The degree of confidence lies in the procedure we follow. Following these procedures will result, for instance, in correct statements 95 percent of the time for a 95 percent confidence interval. Similar statements apply to other stated levels of confidence.

The confidence intervals for means and proportions consist of the sample statistic ($\bar{X}$ p) $\pm$ a specified number (Z) of standard errors ($\sigma_{\bar{x}}$ or σ_p). Because population values are unknown, we normally use sample standard errors to compute confidence intervals. The t-distribution is theoretically correct whenever σ is unknown; however, the t-distribution is not used for proportions, where the normal approximation can be used for large samples.

Therefore, the most widely-used expressions for confidence intervals are:

For means:
$$\text{CL} = \bar{X} \pm t \, s_{\bar{x}}$$

For proportions:
$$\text{CL} = p \pm Z \, s_p$$

If our sample is large, i.e., if the sample is more than 5% of the population, the standard error of the mean should be corrected by multiplying it by the finite population correction factor:

$$\sqrt{\frac{N - n}{N - 1}}$$

The confidence intervals for variances are computed using the chi-square distribution. The limits are calculated as:

$$\text{LCL} = \frac{(n-1)S^2}{\chi^2_{1-\frac{\alpha}{2}}} \quad \text{and}$$

$$\text{UCL} = \frac{(n-1)S^2}{\chi^2_{\alpha/2}}$$

To approximate the confidence interval for a standard deviation, simply compute the confidence interval for the variance and take the square root of the corresponding limits.

The confidence interval for the median is considerably more complex and is best left to statistical software such as XLDataAnalyst.

For typical situations (σ and π unknown), the sample sizes are computed as

For **Means**:
$$n = \left(\frac{Zs}{e}\right)^2$$

For **Proportions**:
$$n = \frac{Z^2 p(1-p)}{e^2}$$

Both equations require some prior estimate (either of s or of p), which may come from an estimate, historical data, or from a preliminary sample. Using $p = .50$ will, of course, result in a sufficiently large sample for any estimate of proportions.

The sample size calculations for variances (standard deviations) are somewhat more complex and also require a preliminary estimate of the standard deviation or variance. The required sample size is then calculated as:

$$n = 1.0 + .5 \left(\frac{z_{\alpha/2}}{\log_e\left(1+\frac{e}{\sigma}\right)} \right)^2$$

Unfortunately, there are no acceptable methods for calculating the required sample size for confidence interval estimates of the median.

Chapter Glossary

Bootstrapping	The process of deriving an estimate of the standard error by repeated sampling.
Consistency	A consistent estimator gets closer to the value being estimated as the sample size increases.
Degree of Confidence	The long-run relative frequency with which confidence intervals contain the population parameter.
Efficient	An efficient estimator will have a smaller standard error than other estimators of the same parameter.
Estimation Error	The difference between the value of the sample statistic and the value of the population parameter.
Interval Estimates	Pairs of values (computed from sample statistics) that define a range within which the population parameter is expected to lie.
Margin of Error	The half width of the confidence or the amount by which we expect the sample value to differ, either positively or negatively, from the population value.
Point Estimates	Single values of sample statistics used to estimate population parameters.
Unbiased	The estimator will, on average, equal the parameter value.

Questions and Problems

46. Explain the difference between a point estimate and an interval estimate of a population mean. Why don't we make interval estimates of the sample mean?

47. A mining firm in Nevada delivers ore to a concentrating plant in containers that are guaranteed to contain an average of 820 lbs. of ore:

 (a) If a sample of 400 containers revealed a mean of 808 lbs. and a standard deviation of $s = 32$ lbs., what is the 95% confidence interval for the true mean?

 (b) Because the true standard deviation is not known, both the sample mean and the sample standard deviation are random variables. Unless the population is normal, sample means are only approximately normally distributed. What distribution should be used to establish confidence intervals when σ is not known?

 (c) Establish a 95% confidence interval estimate for the true mean if a sample of 25 has an $\overline{X} = 808$ and $s = 32$.

 (d) Why is the interval for part (c) wider than that for part (a)?

48. A trainee in an advertising firm in Atlanta has been asked to find the average monthly expenditure by administrative assistants in a Salt Lake City for computer-related supplies:

 (a) What four factors would the trainee have to decide or determine before she can decide the sample size required?

 (b) Assume that the answers required in part (a) are: should be within $2 of the average monthly expenditure, the standard deviation based on a previous study is believed to be $20, and the desired confidence level (that the interval will really bracket the true mean) is to be .95. What sample size should be taken?

49. (c) A sample is to be taken for a 99% confidence interval estimate of the true mean of a process where the half-width of the confidence interval is to be within 1% of the mean—believed to be about 200:

 (a) How large should the sample be if the standard deviation is believed to be 12.0?

 (b) If the sample of the size indicated in part (a) is taken and the sample standard deviation is only 10.0, what is the effect on the confidence interval from the obtained solution?

 (c) What would be the result of overestimating the required sample size?

50. Sample proportions for a Bernoulli process are approximately normally distributed around the true proportion if the sample is large and neither π nor $(1 - \pi)$ is too small.

 (a) Compute the a point estimate of the true population proportion defective if a random sample of 400 from a production process contains 24 defective items.

 (b) Use the data given in part (a) to make a 95% confidence interval estimate of the true proportion defective.

 (c) Explain why the procedure used in part (b) is only an approximation.

51. Assume that a random sample of 400 items from a production process contains 24 defective items:

 (a) Make a point estimate of the number of defective items that will be found in lots of 400.

(b) Compute the standard error of the number of defectives in a sample of 400.

(c) Make a 95% confidence interval estimate of the number of defective units in lots of 400.

(d) Explain the difference between the answers found in Problems 80 and 81.

52. You are interested in determining what proportion of dentists actually recommend chewing a certain type of gum, whose ads claim it is recommended by 4 out of 5 dentists. In estimating the proportion, you take a random sample of 100 dentists and find that 74 recommend the gum. Given a 95% confidence interval, can the claims of the gum manufacturer be disputed?

53. A student working on a take-home test for marketing comes to you with a problem. He wants to determine how large a sample he should take to make a 95% confidence interval estimate of the true proportion of the population who use a particular product. The answer is to be within ±2 percentage points:

(a) What is the minimum sample size required?

(b) If a preliminary sample of 100 indicates that the true proportion is only about .20, revise the estimate of the sample size required.

(c) Why can you set a minimum sample size in this problem when you cannot set a minimum sample size for estimates of μ unless you have an estimate of σ?

54. Suppose that the retail firms listed in the Corporate Statistical Database (Appendix A) represent a preliminary sample taken for the purpose of preparing to estimate the proportion of retail firms (R) in the United States that have profit-sharing plans. If an accuracy of ±3% is desired, how many retail firms should be sampled? Assume that we wish to have 98% confidence in the results.

55. A professor of economics wants to estimate the variance of student grades by sampling her class. She wishes to be 93% confident with an accuracy of +/- 3 points. The standard deviation of grades is 5 points. How large does the sample have to be?

56. A management analyst is estimating the productivity of some 325 sewing machine operators in a clothing factory by sampling the time it takes workers to set up their (similar) machines. For five operators, the following times were obtained:

Times (min):   3.4   3.2   2.8   3.6   2.6

Construct a 98% confidence interval estimate for the setup time.

57. Quality control tests on a random sample of 36 electrode monitoring wires from an ongoing production process revealed the individual breaking strengths (pounds) recorded in the file Exercise 6-57.xlsx. Make a 95% confidence interval estimate of the true mean breaking strength and state your result.

58. As the purchasing manager for a computer manufacturer you are approached by a salesperson for a new startup company that manufacturers high-end lithium batteries for laptop computers and other electronic devices. The salesperson informs you that they have a new longer-lasting battery developed by a professor that will give your computers more time between recharges. You ask for a sample of 30 batteries that you can test in some prototype computers. When the batteries are delivered you place them in 30 of your computers and leave them on until the batteries go dead and the machine shuts down. The resulting times in hours are contained in the file Exercise 6-58.xlsx. (a) What is the median up-time for the new batteries? (b) Construct a 99% confidence interval for the median up time for all such batteries. (c) Construct a 99% confidence interval for the standard deviation of the up times in the population of batteries.

59. A research economist wants to estimate the average salary in the high-tech industries in the tri-state area. She collects data from a random sample of 50 workers on their annual salaries. The data is contained in the file Exercise 6-59.xlsx.

    (a) Derive a 90% confidence interval for the average salary for high-tech workers in this area.

    (b) What is the 90% confidence interval for the median salary? Is there any apparent skewness in the data?

60. As a young entrepreneur you have been approached by an old college buddy or yours that has an idea for a new business. Your friend has noticed that many residents in the rural western United States have problems with periodic power outages. However, since backup power generators are relatively expensive, these residents are reluctant to buy such devices for the occasional outages. Your friend's idea is to focus on certain areas and offer fuel cell backup devices for rent. Residents would sign up for a subscription to backup power plan and pay a nominal annual fee. In the event of a power outage they could contact the company which would deliver a backup power system within 12 hours. The customer would be charged an hourly fee which the system was in operation. You feel that the idea may have merit but want some hard data to work with. You commission a consulting company to do a survey of the residents in selected areas of Idaho, Washington, and Montana. The survey asks the respondent to estimate the average number of days that they are without power each year, and whether or not they would utilize a backup rental system as described in the survey. The results of the survey are contained in the file Exercise 6-60.xlsx.

    (a) Find a 95% confidence interval for the average number of days that people in these areas are without power each year. Find a 95% confidence interval for the median number of days spent without power. Does there appear to be any significant skewness in the data?

    (b) Find a 95% confidence interval for the standard deviation of the number of days spent without power. What would the empirical rule say would be the range of values that would cover 95% of the number of days without power?

    (c) Find a 95% confidence interval for the proportion of residents that would use this service if it were available.

61. The Lucky Strike Gold Mining Company has developed a new process designed to more efficiently extract gold from existing mines. If the new process is successful, it may make it economical to open up some mines that have been previously closed. The new process is used in a random sample of 40 locations and the yield (in pounds) per ton is recorded. The data are contained in the file Exercises 6-61.xlsx

    (a) Estimate the average yield of the new process. What is a 95% confidence interval for the population average yield?

    (b) What is the 95% confidence interval for the standard deviation of the yields?

62. Tailored for You is a high end clothing store in Illinois that is thinking of taking its clothing line to other states such as Indiana and Iowa. Jim Evans, the owner, has decided that he needs some more information before expanding. Some of the information that he needs relates to the mix of customers that frequent his store, the annual household income of these customers, the amount they spent the past year at his store, their gender, and whether or not it is important to them that they receive personalized attention when the they come to the store. He decides to hire a student from the local university to do a survey for him. The student selects a random sample of 50 customers and via a phone survey gathers the information contained in the file Exercises 6-62.xlsx. The information on the amount spent in the store is obtained from the internal account records at Tailor for You.

(a) Find a 95% confidence interval for the median household incomes for his customer base.

(b) Find a 95% confidence interval for the mean amount spent per year in his store. What is your best estimate of this value?

(c) Develop a 90% confidence interval for the standard deviation of the amounts spent per customer the past year. Using the point estimate for this value, between what two values should 95% of the amounts fall, if the distribution in the population is roughly like a normal distribution?

(d) Develop a 95% confidence interval for the proportion of customers that want personalized attentionwhen they come to the store. If you analyze the data separately for males and females is there any difference in their responses?

63. As an investigator for the FTC, you are in charge of investigating an advertising claim by a toothpaste manufacturer. The company has claimed that 4 out of 5 dentists recommend their product. You obtain a list of dentists from the American Dental Association and select a random sample of 50 dentists. You contact these 50 dentists and ask if they actually recommend this brand of toothpaste. The results are contained in the file Exercises 6-63.xlsx. Find the 95% confidence interval for the percentage of dentists that recommend this brand. Do the results support the manufacturer's claim?

Database Problems

Corporate Statistical Database

64. Using the Corporate Statistical Database, select 10 random samples of 36 firms and make a 90% confidence interval estimate of the current year earnings per share. Now calculate the average current year earnings per share across all 100 firms. What percentage of the time does this true "population" mean fall within your 10 confidence intervals?

65. Assume that the Corporate Statistical Database is a random sample of 100 firms listed on recognized stock exchanges. Use the data to make a 99% confidence interval estimate of the average dividend paid by firms listed on recognized stock exchanges and also the median dividend paid.

66. Again, assuming that the Corporate Statistical Database is a random of 100 firms listed on recognized stock exchanges, use the data to make a 95% confidence interval estimate of the standard deviation of the dividends paid by firms listed on recognized stock exchanges.

67. Assuming that the Corporate Statistical Database is a random sample of 100 firms, derive a 95% confidence interval for the percentage of companies that have a profit-sharing plan.

MegaCorp Employee Survey Database

68. Find a 99% confidence interval for the average value of the variables salary, years employed, and age.

69. Find a 95% confidence interval for the mean and median percentage that employees think they should pay for health insurance. What is the relationship between these two intervals and what do they tell you about employee perceptions?

70. Construct 95% confidence intervals for the percentage of employees that are married and also the percentage that are male.

71. Construct a 99% confidence interval for the average age and the variance of the ages. Based on this, what would you estimate about the population coefficient of variation (Hint, see Chapter 3 for the definition of this measure)?

Alaska Sport Fishing Survey

 72. Construct 95% and 99% confidence intervals for the following variables: (a) the number of fishing trips taken to Alaska (b) the amount spent on the last fishing trip to Alaska.

 73. Find a 95% confidence interval for the mean and median number of days spent on the last trip. What is the relationship between these two intervals and what do they tell you about the distribution of days spent?

 74. Construct 95% confidence intervals for the percentage of those responding that are married and also for the percentage that are male.

 75. Create a new variable in the data for age using the Year born variable. Construct a 99% confidence interval for the average age of the respondents.

Chapter 7:

Testing Hypotheses: One-Sample Tests

Opening Vignette
Concepts
Introduction
 Purpose of Hypothesis Testing
 Steps in the Testing Process
 Types of Hypothesis Tests
 The Logic of Hypothesis Testing
Null and Alternate Hypotheses
Types of Errors (Type I and Type II)
 How Errors Can Occur
 Bias In Favor of the Null Hypothesis
 The Concept of Power
Level of Significance and the p-value
 Level of significance
 p-values
Tests of Equivalence
Two-Tailed Versus One-Tailed Tests
The Hypothesis Testing Procedure
Testing the Population Mean: σ Known
Testing the Population Mean: σ Unknown
Testing the Population Proportion
Testing the Population Variance
Testing the Population Median
  Practice
Hypothesis Tests with Excel and XLDataAnalyst
 Excel Functions
 The Analysis Toolpak
 The Excel Template
 Using XLDataAnalyst
Opening Vignette Revisited
Summary
Chapter Glossary
CASE: International Printing and Publishing Company
Questions and Problems
Computing the Type II Error (Optional)
Power Curves and Operating Characteristic Curves (Optional)
 Power Curve
 Operating Characteristic Curve

Chapter 7 Objectives

When you finish this chapter you should be able to:

1. **Explain the logic of hypothesis testing**
2. **Formulate null and alternative hypotheses**
3. **Describe the standard hypothesis testing procedure**
4. **Define Type I and Type II Errors and Power**
5. **Distinguish between one-tailed and two-tailed tests**
6. **Test hypotheses about a population mean**
7. **Test hypotheses about a population proportion**
8. **Test hypotheses about a population variance**
9. **Test hypotheses about a population median**

Opening Vignette

Sally is a product engineer for Deltron, a manufacturer of automated meter-reading equipment. Deltron uses notebook computers in the field and many times, computers get bumped, dropped, and generally knocked around. Swell Computer Company claims that their new notebook can be dropped up to 12 feet without sustaining damage. If this claim is true, Swell's computers would be ideal for Deltron. Sally purchases a sample of 20 computers from Swell and she and her assistant, Bob, drop the computers at increasing heights until they fail. They found that the average height at failure in the sample of 20 computers was 11.4 feet, which is less than the 12-foot claim. Sally knows that this result could just be due to the particular sample of 20 computers that they received; however, she is not sure whether their results were because of sampling error or whether these results indicate a problem with the claim made by Swell.

Introduction

In this section, we will discuss the purpose and logic of hypothesis testing and the different types of tests. We will then explore the different hypotheses and types of errors that can occur when testing a hypothesis. Next, we will delineate the procedure for conducting a hypothesis test for one special situation and apply this procedure to different population parameters. When you finish the chapter, you should be able to formulate a hypothesis, select data from a population, test and analyze the data, and draw a conclusion about the statistical validity of the original hypothesis.

Purpose of Hypothesis Testing

A *hypothesis* is a statement, or claim, about a population parameter. For example, a manufacturer may advertise that its car batteries last an average of 60 months. Or a political candidate may state that he has a 54% approval rating. Hypothesis testing is a systematic technique of using random samples to test such claims.

> *Hypothesis testing* is a statistical procedure for using sample data to support or reject a hypothesis about a population parameter.

Hypothesis testing helps us decide whether the hypothesis should be rejected or not. It does not eliminate the possibility of error, but it does make use of proven statistical theory that enables the decision-maker to measure and control the chance of at least one type of error associated with the decision. In other words, hypothesis testing replaces what might otherwise be an intuitive decision-making process with an objective procedure that controls for the risk of making an incorrect decision.

Steps in the Testing Process

The procedure for testing a hypothesis is relatively standardized and consists of the following steps:

1. State the hypothesis and the criteria used for judgment.

2. Collect sample data and compare the sample results to our criteria.

3. Determine whether the sample results are statistically significant.

4. Draw a conclusion about the hypothesis (e.g., reject or do not reject it).

Types of Hypothesis Tests

important →

Mastering the subject of hypothesis testing can seem like an overwhelming task; however, we can simplify the task considerably by understanding what type of test is appropriate for a given situation.

First, we can categorize hypothesis tests into one-sample tests (which we discuss in this chapter), two-sample tests (discussed in Chapter 8), and tests for three or more samples (discussed in Chapter 9). Beyond that, we shall distinguish clearly between (1) tests of population means, μ, (2) tests of population proportions, π, (3) tests of population variances (σ^2), and (4) tests of population medians (η). Within each of these categories, we can also distinguish between one-tailed or two-tailed tests (but, we will get to that in due course.) The major types of hypothesis tests we will cover are:

Ch. 7 *One-Sample Tests (This Chapter)*	Does the sample evidence support the (hypothesized) population value?	• Tests using a single sample mean, $\bar{X}$ • Tests using as single sample proportion, p • Tests using a single sample variance, s^2 • Tests using a single sample median, M
Ch. 8 *Two-Sample (Group) Tests (Chapter 8)*	Do the two sample statistics reveal a significant difference between the (two hypothesized) population values?	• Tests using two sample means, $\bar{X}_1$ and $\bar{X}_2$ • Tests using two sample proportions, p_1 and p_2 • Tests using two sample variances, s_1^2 and s_2^2 • Tests using two sample medians, M_1 and M_2
Ch. 9 *Three-Sample (or more Group) Tests (Chapter 9)*	Do the three or more sample statistics reveal a significant difference between the three or more population values?	• Tests using three or more sample means, $\bar{X}_1, \bar{X}_2, ... \bar{X}_a$ (ANOVA) • Tests using three or more sample proportions. $P_1, P_2, ...P_a$ (Chi-Square) • Tests using three or more sample variances, $s_1^2, s_2^2, ... s_a^2$ • Tests using three or more sample medians, $M_1, M_2, ... M_a$

Chapter 10 will discuss tests of relationships between variables. Tests of hypotheses are indeed a major component of any study of statistics.

The Logic of Hypothesis Testing

The logic of hypothesis testing rests on the concept of sampling distributions that we discussed in Chapter 5. Let us summarize briefly the theoretical basis for hypothesis testing in terms of the various population parameters.

Means

Suppose that a CD manufacturer produces blank CDs that they claim can hold an average of 700 megabytes (MB) of data. The normal variability of the storage is 60 MB. The logical way to test that claim (hypothesized value) would be to take some blank CDs from their production output, measure their capacity (discounting defective portions of the disk), and compare the sample result (the sample mean, $\bar{X}$) with the claimed mean of 700 MB. This is exactly what takes place with a test of a hypothesis. But, we can go beyond a casual recognition of the sample result by taking advantage of our knowledge of the statistical distribution to which the sample statistic belongs, e.g. the sampling distribution.

Figure 7-1 shows how sampling distributions allow us to extract more information about the population parameter than might otherwise be expected. First, recall that random samples of a given size form a sampling distribution with mean μ, and standard deviation $\sigma_{\bar{X}}$. Figure 7-1 assumes a sample of 50 CDs and uses $\bar{X}s$ to depict the density function of the distribution. Recall that a sampling distribution of the means is a (theoretical) distribution of all the possible means from samples of a given size—**it is not a distribution of individual values**. The central limit theorem implies that those sample means will be approximately normally distributed about the population mean for reasonably large samples. The mean and standard deviation of that distribution of sample means will equal μ and $\sigma/\sqrt{n}$, respectively.

Figure 7-1   *Distribution of Sample Means for Hypothesis $\mu = 700$ MB*

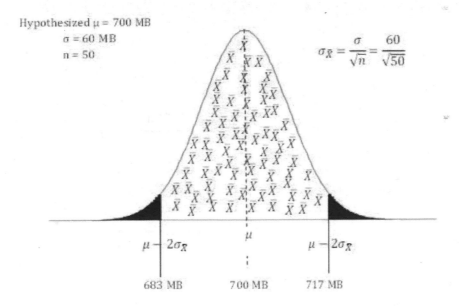

If the sample mean we get is close to the hypothesized value (e.g., $\bar{X} = 695\ MB$), it is reasonable to conclude that the small difference between the hypothesized mean (700 MB), and sample mean ($\bar{X} = 695$ MB), is probably due to chance e.g., sampling error; however, if $\bar{X}$ is a great distance from the hypothetical value (e.g., if it were 550 MB), we would feel more confident in concluding that the true mean of the population is not 700 MB. Our assurance rests on the knowledge that if the hypothesis is true, then 95.5% of the sample means will be within $\pm 2\sigma_{\bar{X}}$ and 99.97% within $\pm 3\sigma_{\bar{X}}$. Therefore, if $\sigma_{\bar{X}} = 8.5$ MB, as in Figure 7-1, we could expect 95.5% of all sample means to be within $\pm 2.00\sigma_{\bar{X}} = 17$, or within the range of 683 to 717 MB. A sample value of 550 MB would be highly unlikely.

Proportions

The same reasoning applies to tests of proportions, except that the random variable is discrete rather than continuous.

Suppose that a computer software firm wants to know what percent of personal computers in the health care industry are connected to a centralized database. Assume that management hypothesizes that 20% of the computers are connected to a central database, and they plan to sample 400 computers to see if the sample data do or do not support the hypothesis. The sampling distribution of proportions for samples of size n = 400 is approximately normal (like the distribution of means). As illustrated in Figure 7-2, for a hypothesized proportion of $\pi = .20$, the standard error of the proportion is .02. Thus, we would expect 95.5% of all sample proportions to be within ±2.00 σ_p or .04, of the hypothesized value of .20, if the hypothesis is true. Therefore, a sample proportion of p = .45, for example, would be highly unlikely and would suggest that the hypothesis was false.

Figure 7–2   Distribution of Sample Proportions for Hypothesis $\pi = .20$

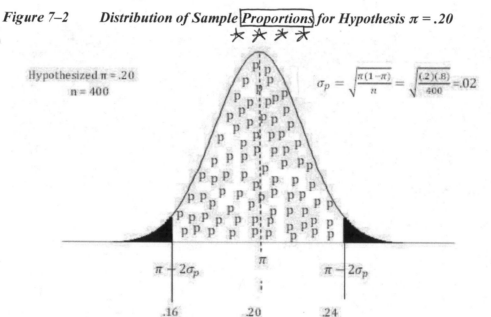

Hypothesized $\pi = .20$
$n = 400$

$$\sigma_p = \sqrt{\frac{\pi(1-\pi)}{n}} = \sqrt{\frac{(.2)(.8)}{400}} = .02$$

$\pi - 2\sigma_p \qquad \pi \qquad \pi - 2\sigma_p$

.16   .20   .24

Recall that the binomial distribution is the distribution for describing sample proportions; however, to have sufficient precision, most tests of hypotheses necessitate that large samples be used. Since large samples allow for the use of normal approximation, many authors have recommended using the normal distribution to test hypotheses about proportions; yet, the normal is only an approximation and the binomial is the appropriate distribution. Given that Excel can quickly calculate probabilities for the binomial there is no reason to use the normal approximation anymore. We utilized the normal approximation in the last chapter because it was sometimes difficult to find percentiles required for confidence intervals for the binomial. As we will notice, this does not present any problems for hypothesis testing.

Variances

The basic logic is the same in hypothesis tests for variances except the nature of the sampling distribution is different. Recall that the sampling distribution for the sample variance is the chi-square distribution.

As an example, suppose that a Human Resource Manager at a medical clinic in Chicago wants to know about the spread or dispersion of salaries paid to nurses in medical facilities in the city. She thinks that the standard deviation is about $2 per hour. Therefore, the hypothesized variance would be $\sigma^2 = (2)^2 = 4$. If a sample of 40 nurses is selected and their hourly salaries noted, then the sampling distribution for the sample variances should be a chi-square distribution with n-1 = 39 degrees of freedom (as the sample size is 40 and degrees of freedom is equal to n-1). In this distribution, 95% of the chi-square values should be between 23.653 and 58.12005 where the chi-square is calculated as:

$$\chi^2 = \frac{(n-1)S^2}{\sigma^2} \qquad (7\text{-}1)$$

Substituting the value of 4 for the population variance, 39 for (n-1) degrees of freedom and the appropriate values for χ^2 of 23.653 and 58.12005 provides limits for the sample variance of 2.43 and 5.96 as illustrated in Figure 7-3. Therefore, a sample variance near 4 in the sample would be expected, but a sample variance of e.g. 7.5 would be highly unlikely and suggest that the hypothesis is false.

Figure 7-3   *Chi-Square Distribution for a Sample of n = 40*

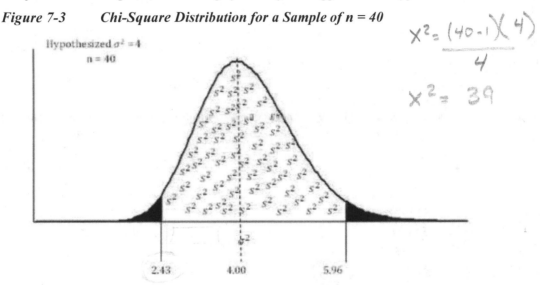

As we can see in Figure 7-3, the Chi-Square distribution is nearly symmetrical. As the degrees of freedom increase, the Chi-Square distribution becomes more symmetrical and more like a normal distribution.

Medians

A slight twist on the basic logic can be used when testing a hypothesis about a population median (η). The major problem with the median is that the sampling distribution for the sample median (M) depends greatly on the shape of the parent population distribution. Also, the median can be used for ordinal data where only the order of the numbers has meaning.

A test, called a sign test, has been devised that utilizes the basic definition of the median such that half of the observations are below and half are above that value. The test utilizes only the order information in the data. Starting with a hypothesized value of the population median (η), if the hypothesis is true, we would expect about half the values in the sample to be below that value and half above. We assign a negative sign (-) to sample values below the hypothesized mean and a plus sign (+) to those above. If the hypothesis is true, then the probability of the sign for a value being a plus or a minus should be .50. In other words, the proportion of plus signs (or minus signs) should be about .50, if the hypothesis is true. This is a binomial problem and we could apply the binomial distribution to analyze the hypothesis.

Consider the Human Resource Manager from the previous example. Knowing that the salaries are highly skewed, she wants to use the median as the measure of the average salary rather than the mean. She hypothesizes that the median hourly salary for nurses is $17. Therefore, in her sample of 40 nurses, she would expect that half of them (20 nurses) would have an hourly salary less than $17 and half would have a salary greater than $17. If the vast majority were less than $17 or greater than $17, then this would be evidence against the hypothesis.

A second test, called the signed rank test, uses the rankings of the data as well as the plus and minus signs. This test requires the additional assumption that the population has a symmetric distribution (an assumption not required for the sign test).

Summary of Hypothesis Testing Logic

With hypothesis testing, we first establish the hypothesis, or claim. Then, we collect sample data and compare the results to what might be expected based on the sampling distribution centered on the hypothesized value. This distribution is the criterion by which we judge the validity of the hypothesis. If the difference between the sample statistic and the parameter of the hypothesized distribution is small, we conclude that this difference is probably due to sampling error, and accept the hypothesis; however, if the difference is large, it is probably real and we reject the hypothesis.

We refer to a large difference as being *statistically significant*. This means that the difference is due to more than just sampling error, and that the sample is probably not from the hypothesized population. It does not mean, however, that the difference is significant in other respects. Even though a difference is statistically significant, it may be too small to be of any economic or social significance.

Null and Alternative Hypotheses

Tests of hypotheses begin with two statements. The first is expressed in a way that supports what is thought to be the existing condition, or claimed status. It is often a statement that an assumed condition exists—for example, that "the mean capacity of the CDs is 700 MB" or that "20% of computer owners are connected to a central database." The second statement describes the other (alternative) status in the event the original claim does not hold.

Null Hypothesis

The (first) statement is known as the null hypothesis, and designated H_0 (pronounced "H sub zero"). Null is frequently taken to mean no change in the status quo, being of no consequence, or equal to or amounting to nothing. It is a way of saying that conditions are normal or that established standards prevail. We hypothesize that things are as they have been in the past, or as they should be. Unless there is a substantial amount of evidence to the contrary, we will continue to assume that nothing has changed.

The null hypothesis is typically "set up" as a test that the population parameter is equal to one value (described by the hypothesized sampling distribution). It is formulated in a way that will take some solid evidence to discredit it based on the sampling data. **The null hypothesis is generally not what we want to demonstrate or prove**. The hypothesis test determines whether the sample data are sufficient to discredit or refute the null hypothesis. To possible null hypotheses for the four examples we described earlier could be:

Type of Test	Null Hypothesis	Meaning
Means	H_0: $\mu \geq 700$ MB	CD maker claims that average capacity of their CDs is 700 MB but it could be larger
Proportions	H_0: $\pi = .20$	Software manager thinks true proportion of PC users connected to a central database is $\pi = .20$
Variances	H_0: $\sigma^2 \leq 4$	HR manager thinks the variance of nurses' wages is 4 but may be less.
Medians	H_0: $\eta = 17$	HR manager thinks the median hourly nurses' wages are $17

Alternative Hypothesis

Every null hypothesis must be accompanied by an alternative hypothesis designated H_1 (pronounced "H sub one"). The two statements are complements, or opposites, of each other. Therefore, the alternative is a statement that conditions have changed or something is different and is expressed in the form of an inequality of $\neq$, $<$, or $>$. The alternative hypothesis should contain the statement that we are trying to demonstrate or show to be true. In many cases, the alternative identifies some new conditions a company would like to support, such as a lower error rate, a longer lasting light bulb, or a faster-acting medicine. In this sense, the alternative is the research or test hypothesis that is under study. It is often easier to begin with the alternative hypothesis that we are trying to demonstrate and then derive the null hypothesis from that alternative. Sample data may then either discredit the null hypothesis, and therefore support our alternative, or confirm the null and not provide evidence in favor of our alternative. Alternative hypotheses for the illustrations above would be:

Type of Test	Alternative Hypothesis	Meaning
Means	H_1: $\mu < 700$ MB	True mean capacity of the CDs is less than 700 MB
Proportions	H_1: $\pi \neq .20$	True proportion of PC users connected to a database is not .20
Variances	H_1: $\sigma^2 > 4$	The true variance of nurses' wages is greater than 4
Medians	H_1: $\eta \neq 17$	The true median hourly nurses' wages is not $17

Rejecting the Null

Rejecting the null hypothesis gives credibility to the alternative hypothesis and is equivalent to accepting the alternative; however, it does not prove that the alternative is true—proof comes only with a scientific investigation of all alternatives. Moreover, there is still some chance we may be making an error in rejecting the null (Type I Error). For operational purposes, managers will likely choose to act as though the alternative is correct, even though it is not proven to be true. In other words, in hypothesis testing our decision to reject the null will be the basis for taking action of some kind.

Not Rejecting (Accepting) the Null

If the null is not rejected, we conclude that the evidence is not sufficient to discredit it, so our conclusion is "do not reject." We still retain faith in the null hypothesis, or at least consider the null tenable and reserve judgment on it.

[handwritten: Some thing]

To say "Do not reject the null hypothesis" is not as strong as saying "Accept" the null outright (as confirmed), although many analysts do not distinguish between the two statements. The simple choices of accept and reject are sometimes more useful from a business decision-making standpoint. You may encounter both types of statements, although the intended meaning of "accept" is "do not reject." We limit our use of the term "accept" to when it is helpful to contrast acceptance and rejection. The understanding here is, of course, that acceptance of the null hypothesis does not constitute its proof; it simply indicates that we do not have sufficient evidence to disapprove it.

[handwritten: good example]

Testing hypotheses is sometimes likened to a trial. The defendant is charged (null hypothesis stated), but is presumed to be innocent until the evidence proves otherwise. If the data shows that the defendant is guilty beyond any reasonable doubt, the presumption of innocence (null hypothesis) is rejected and the defendant found guilty. Otherwise, the defendant is acquitted. But, being acquitted does not mean that we believe the defendant is innocent. It only means that there was not enough evidence (data) to prove the defendant guilty (reject the null hypothesis).

Types of Errors (Type I and Type II)

Statistical decisions, since they involve inductive inference, bring with them some risk of error. In this section, we define the two types of error to be aware of and show how they can occur. The errors associated with hypothesis testing are commonly designated as Type I and Type II error:

Error	Meaning	Probability of Error
Type I	Rejecting the null hypothesis when it is true	α
Type II	Not rejecting (accepting) the null hypothesis when it is false	β

Type I Error is making a mistake by rejecting the null hypothesis when it is really true. For example, rejecting the claim that the average capacity of the CDs is 700 MB when the population mean, μ, really does equal 700 MB. The risk of Type I Error is a probability designated by the Greek lowercase letter alpha (α).

Assume that the (unknown) population mean μ is really 700 MB, but when we take our sample of 100 CDs, we find a sample mean of $\bar{X} = 650$ MB. The low value of 650 would prompt us to reject the true hypothesis $H_0: \mu = 700$ MB, when it really should not be rejected. We would be committing a Type I Error: **We can only commit a Type I Error when H_0 is true.**

Type II Error is the mistake of failing to reject the null hypothesis when it should be rejected. For example, concluding that the average capacity of the CDs is 700 MB when it really is less than 700 would be a Type II Error. The risk of Type II Error is a probability designated by the Greek lowercase letter beta (β).

Suppose in the same situation that the population mean is really 690 MB. Suppose we obtain a sample mean of $\bar{X} = 695$ MB which is very close to the hypothesized value of 700. We would be tempted to accept the null hypothesis even though it should be rejected. We would be committing a Type II Error: **We can only commit a Type II Error when H_0 is false.**

In both cases, the errors were due to the sample data that was gathered. In the first case, we happened to get low values that caused us to reject a true hypothesis (Type I Error). In the second case, the values collected caused us to accept a false hypothesis (Type II Error). Both errors can happen and our hypothesis testing procedure should be designed to account for them. It can also help us "manage" them by assuring us that the chance of making one or the other of these errors is small.

Table 7-1   ***Possible Conclusions from a Hypothesis Test***

		Null Hypothesis is Either	
		True	False
Decision Is Either to	Not Reject	(Correct)	Type II Error β
	Reject	Type I Error α	(Correct) Power = $1-\beta$

Bias In Favor of the Null Hypothesis

Earlier we noted that the hypothesis testing process can be compared to the trial-by-jury process. Table 7-2 shows the parallels between the two situations. In the trial process, there is a built-in bias in favor of the defendant, where the defendant is considered to be innocent until proven guilty: ✗

Table 7-2   ***The Null Hypothesis as Defendant***

		Defendant (Null Hypothesis) is Either	
		Innocent (True)	Guilty (False)
Decision Is Either to	Acquit (Not Reject)	(Correct)	Type II Error β Guilty defendant goes free
	Convict (Reject)	Type I Error α Convict an innocent defendant	(Correct) Power = $1-\beta$

There is a recognized principle of jurisprudence that basically states that it is better to let a guilty person go free (not reject a false null hypothesis, or Type II Error) than to convict an innocent person (reject a true null hypothesis, or Type I Error). According to traditional statistical practice, we typically set the probability of a Type I Error to a small value. This means that, all things being equal, we will be more likely to make a Type II Error than a Type I Error. This is the main reason that we almost always place the argument we are trying to demonstrate in the alternative rather than the null hypothesis. If we can reject the null hypothesis, despite giving it the benefit of the doubt, then we have strong evidence for our claim. On the other hand, accepting the null hypothesis is not very impressive evidence, given the bias in favor of the null hypothesis.

The Concept of Power

There are two situations (depicted later in Table 7-3) where we will make a correct decision. The first is when the null hypothesis is true and we do not reject (we accept) the null hypothesis. Of greater interest, is the second case when the null hypothesis is false and we reject it. This is the opposite of a Type II Error and is also a correct decision. The probability of making this correct decision, called *power*, is designated as $1 - \beta$. Note that "power" is, in general, a good thing as it is a measure of our ability to correctly reject a false null hypothesis. As we will see, there is a close relationship between power and sample size.

Level of Significance and the p-value

Level of Significance

The control over the risk of Type I Error is embodied in the initial specifications of a hypothesis test. It is referred to as the level of significance of the test:

> The *level of significance* of a test is the risk that one is willing to take of rejecting a null hypothesis that is correct (e.g., the risk of Type I Error).

The level of significance is a complement to the confidence level and is typically specified before sample data are collected. Common levels of significance are 10%, 5%, 2%, and 1%.

Specifying the level of significance of a test defines the limits of how far a sample mean can be from the hypothesized mean μ and still be considered part of the sampling distribution around the hypothesized value of μ. If the sample statistic is "significantly" different from the hypothesized parameter, we should reject the null hypothesis. Statisticians sometimes refer to the region around the hypothesized parameter as the region of acceptance or non-rejection, and the region outside the specified limits as the region of rejection. Again, the word "acceptance" does not convey certitude about the hypothesis, but just that the evidence is not sufficient to reject it.

Figure 7-4 depicts the acceptance and rejection regions for the CD capacity example. Recall that we have hypothesized H_0: $\mu = 700$ MB. We know that if H_0 is true, samples will have $\bar{X}$s that are normally distributed around the hypothesized mean, μ. In Figure 7-4, the limits around μ are $\pm 1.96\sigma_{\bar{X}}$ away from μ, so 95% of all sample means will lie within those limits (if H_0 is true). This also means that 5% of the $\bar{X}$s will lie outside those limits (in the region of rejection) even if the null hypothesis is true:

Figure 7-4   ***Regions of Rejection and Non-Rejection***

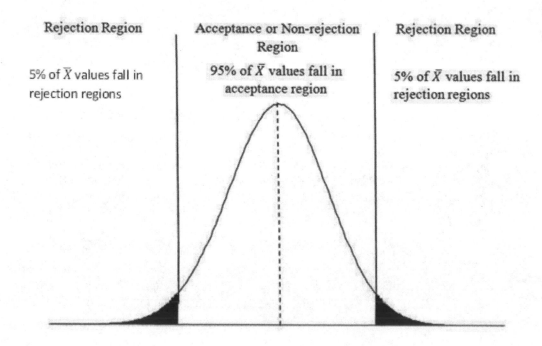

P-values

The p-value is similar to the level of significance and is the most common way to conduct a hypothesis test. In our discussions of sampling distributions in Chapter 5, we learned how to find the probability of observing different values of a sample statistic when sampling from a population with known parameters. This same logic leads to the p-value:

> A *p-value* is the probability of observing a sample statistic as extreme as or more extreme than the observed value of the sample statistic assuming the null hypothesis is true. The p-value can also be viewed as the smallest level of significance at which the null hypothesis can be rejected for a particular sample result when the null is true.

The logic of the p-value is that if the p-value is large, it is likely to observe this sample statistic if the null hypothesis is true and therefore, the null hypothesis should not be rejected. On the other hand, if the p-value is small (e.g. less than .05) then it is very unlikely to observe the value of the sample statistic if the null hypothesis is true and therefore, the null hypothesis should be rejected.

The p-value has several advantages and is the method that we will use the most throughout this text. For one thing, the interpretation of a p-value remains the same no matter what type of hypothesis test we are conducting or what population parameters we are interested in.

The decision process is:

> 1. Establish a level of significance (usually .01 or .05)
>
> 2. If the p-value is less than the level of significance, reject the null hypothesis. If the p-value is greater than or equal to the level of significance, then we cannot reject the null hypothesis.

Calculations of the p-values can be performed using the same methods in Excel as we discussed in Chapter 5. For normal and binomial problems, the Excel functions can be used and the Probability Calculator in XLDataAnalyst can be used for any problems. We will illustrate the calculations in the following sections.

Exercises I

1. Explain the purpose of hypothesis testing.

2. Is a test of a hypothesis a test of population parameters or a test of sample statistics? Explain.

3. What is the role of data in tests of hypotheses (i.e., how is data used in the testing procedure)?

4. Distinguish between (a) one-sample and two-sample tests; (b) tests of means and tests of proportions; (c) null and alternative hypotheses; (d) Type I and Type II Error.

5. Since statistics is such a precise science, why do we incur errors in the testing of hypotheses?

6. What type of error would be made in each of the following scenarios:

   (a) Accepting a shipment of computer chips that do not really meet specifications

   (b) Concluding that a production assembly time is still 2.5 minutes when it really has diminished to less than 2.5 minutes

   (c) Returning some raw materials, that should have been accepted, to a vendor

7. Does every business decision run the risk of either Type I or Type II Error? Explain.

8. Explain what is meant by the "significance of a test." How is the level of significance related to the concept of a Type I error? How is the level of significance related to the p-value?

9. Suppose that the null hypothesis H_0: $\mu = \$15,000$ is tested and rejected at the 5% level of significance. (a) What (exactly) would be meant by rejection at the 5% level? (b) Would the conclusion be "stronger" if it were rejected at the 10% level of significance?

Two-Tailed Tests Versus One-Tailed Tests

Tests of hypotheses are designated as *two-tailed* or *one-tailed tests*, depending on the location of the rejection region. As illustrated in Figure 7-5, two-tailed tests have the rejection area divided into equal portions on both sides of the mean in both tails of the distribution, whereas one-tailed tests have the rejection area concentrated in one end of the distribution only, on just one side of the mean.

Figure 7-5   *Rejection Regions for Two-tailed and One-tailed Tests*

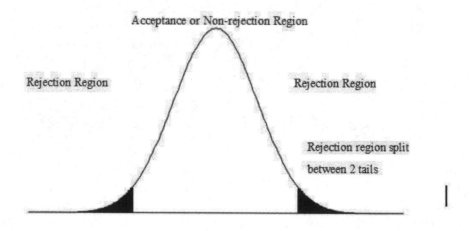

Two Tailed Test

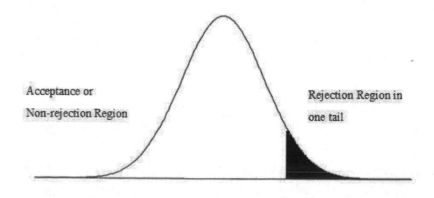

One-Tailed Test

Two-tailed Tests

Two-tailed tests are appropriate for situations where either a higher or lower value of the sample statistic should cause rejection of the null hypothesis. For example, recall the CD example where the capacity is supposed to be 700 MB. A capacity much less than 700 MB is unacceptable because consumers are depending on (and paying for) 700 MB of capacity. A capacity much greater than 700 MB is also unacceptable because material costs will be too high and standard CD players may have difficulties with the disks.

For a two-tailed test of the claimed capacity of the CDs, we have seen that the null and alternative hypotheses are:

$$H_0: \mu = 700 \text{ MB (null)}$$

$$H_1: \mu \neq 700 \text{ MB (alternative)}$$

The $\neq$ sign in the alternate hypothesis signifies that the null hypothesis can be rejected by sample values either significantly greater or less than 700 MB. There are two basic ways that we can conduct this hypothesis test. The first calculates the limits of the acceptance region (called the critical limits) as the criteria by which the acceptance or rejection of H_0 will be evaluated. They are designated C_1 and C_2 and can be stated either in terms of a test statistic such as the Z or t, or in actual units of the variable being tested (MB of storage). The second way is to calculate the p-value and use it in making the decision.

Example 7-1

A random sample of n = 100 CDs is taken to test the hypothesis $H_0: \mu = 700$ MB against the alternative $H_1: \mu \neq 700$ MB, at a $\alpha = 5\%$ level of significance. Assuming $\sigma = 40$ MB, determine the critical limits for the test of the hypothesis, and express them in terms of (a) the Z-value as a test statistic and (b) capacity in megabytes.

Solution

1. The limits are to be set at a distance that will include 100% – 5% = 95% of the area, with half on each side of the mean. We therefore need the Z-value for the .975 percentile, which we can find from NORMINV in Excel, or by using the probability calculator in XLDataAnalyst. The Z-value is 1.96. Therefore, the lower limit (C_1) is Z = –1.96 and the upper limit (C_2) is Z = +1.96 in terms of the Z test statistic. One approach is to use the critical values. We state the decision rule, and then after computing the z-statistic we make a decision.

2. The limits may be converted to units of MBs by multiplying Z by the standard error and subtracting that amount from the hypothesized mean stated in H_0 for C_1, and adding it for C_2. In this case, $\sigma_{\bar{x}} = \sigma/\sqrt{n} = 40/\sqrt{100} = 4.0 \, MB = 4.0$ MB. The limits are shown in the following table:

Limit in Z's	Conversion to Units	Limit in Megabytes
$C_1 = -1.96$	$C_1 = \mu - Z\sigma_{\bar{x}} = 700.0 - 1.96(4.0)$	= 692.2 MB
$C_2 = +1.96$	$C_2 = \mu + Z\sigma_{\bar{x}} = 700.0 + 1.96(4.0)$	= 707.8 MB

3. The critical limits are 692.2 MB and 707.8 MB. A sample mean outside these limits would cause one to reject the null hypothesis. (We are willing to do this because if the null hypothesis were true, only 5% of the sample means would lie outside these limits, and we are willing to be wrong 5% of the time).

4. The p-value approach depends on the sample value that is obtained. How we calculate the probability depends on whether the observed mean is greater than the hypothesized mean or smaller. If the sample mean is larger than the hypothesized mean, we would find the probability of observing a sample mean this large or larger (area to the right of the observed sample mean in the sampling distribution). Using NORM.DIST the appropriate formula for our CD manufacturer would be: 1 – NORM.DIST(sample mean, 700, 4,TRUE)

If the sample mean is smaller than the hypothesized value, we would find the probability of observing a sample mean this small or smaller (area to the left of the observed sample mean in the sampling distribution). Using NORM.DIST, the appropriate formula for our CD manufacturer would be: NORM.DIST(sample mean, 700, 4,TRUE)

One step remains in calculating our p-value. Since we are conducting a two-tailed test and are concerned with deviations in either direction, we should multiply the resulting value by 2. This will give us the final p-value for the observed sample mean which we can compare with the selected level of significance to accept or reject the null hypothesis.

One-tailed Tests

One-tailed tests are appropriate in situations where our goal is to demonstrate that the population value is less than (for lower or left-tailed test) or greater than (for upper or right-tailed test) the hypothesized value. The direction in the alternative hypothesis indicates whether the test is lower-tailed (<), or upper-tailed (>), as it points in the direction of the rejection region. Notice that the alternative hypothesis never contains an equality. The equal sign is always contained in the null hypothesis.

Example 7-2

Suppose that the CD manufacturer in Example 7-1 claims the capacity of their CDs is 700 <u>or more</u>. Using the same sample size (n = 100) and standard deviation σ = 40 MB, (a) state the null and alternative hypotheses. (b) Determine the critical limit for a 5% level test.

Solution

1. In this case, the null would be discredited by sample data that had a mean storage significantly lower than 700 MB, not if the storage is greater than 700. Therefore, the hypotheses are:

H_0: $\mu \geq 700$ MB

H_1: $\mu < 700$ MB

2. Because all 5% of the rejection region is in the lower tail of the distribution, the critical limit corresponds to the Z value that encompasses 5% of the area (the 5th percentile of the standard normal) or $Z = -1.645$. Using the same format as above, we have:

Limit in Z's	Conversion to Units	Limit in Pounds
$C_1 = -1.645$	$C_1 = \mu - Z\sigma_{\bar{x}} = 700.0 - 1.645(4.0)$	= 693.4 MB

Note that the presumption of credibility still rests with the null hypothesis. That is, in order to reject the H_0: $\mu \geq 700$, the sample mean must be 693.4 MB or less – which is unlikely if the true mean is in close proximity to 700 MB. The "burden of proof" rests heavily on the alternative hypothesis; otherwise, we retain faith in the null (status quo).

3. In this case, we would calculate the p-value as the probability of observing a value of the sample mean this small or smaller (area to the left of the observed sample mean in the sampling distribution). Using NORM.DIST, the appropriate formula for our CD manufacturer would be:

NORM.DIST(sample mean, 700, 4,TRUE)

Since the null hypothesis is true for values larger than the hypothesized value, there is no need to consider the upper tail of the distribution and therefore no reason to multiply the resulting value by 2. Thus, the value computed is the p-value.

Figure 7-6 summarizes the rejection limits for the three possible types of tests that could be made of the null hypothesis for our CD manufacturer. Two-tailed tests permit rejection of H_0 if the sample data vary from H_0 in either direction, whereas one-tailed tests permit rejection of H_0 if the sample data are significantly different in one direction only. Note that the alternative hypothesis clearly specifies the direction of the test, indicating whether the test is (1) lower-tailed, (2) two-tailed, or (3) upper-tailed.

Figure 7-6   *Rejection Limits and p-values for Two-tailed and One-tailed Tests*

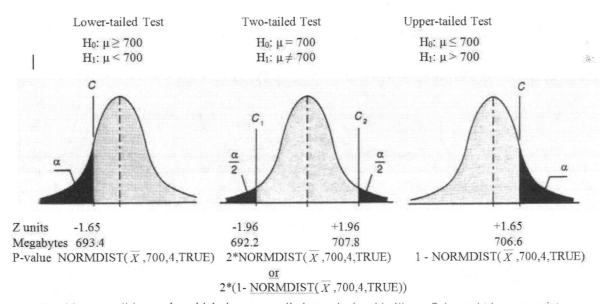

Consider a condition under which the upper-tailed test, depicted in Figure 7-6, might be appropriate. Suppose the CD manufacturer felt that a new production process gave their CDs an average capacity of more than 700 MB. The firm may wish to make that claim on the package label. To establish that the new process is producing a CD that is definitely capable of storing more than 700 MB would call for an upper-tailed test with the alternative hypothesis of H_1: $\mu > 700$ MB. In this case, the manufacturer would be looking to reject the null that $\mu \leq 700$ MB, which would imply acceptance of the alternative (that $\mu > 700$ MB). By using the alternative hypothesis as a research hypothesis, the manufacturer can gain evidence that the new CD storage is significantly greater than the hypothesized value. Moreover, the manufacturer would be making that claim with a well-defined risk of being wrong (e.g., 1%, 5%).

Tests of Equivalence

Because of the bias in favor of the null hypothesis, what we are trying to demonstrate is always in the alternative hypothesis. In the last section, the three alternative hypotheses were of the form:

$$H_1: \mu \neq 700 \qquad\qquad H_1: \mu < 700 \quad H_1: \mu > 700$$

But, what if we want to show that the mean is equal to 700, i.e.., what if we really want to show that the traditional null hypothesis is true? Such situations arise often in medical science, but are also common in a business environment. For example, engineers might devise a new process that promises to lower the variability of a process; yet, leave the average value the same. Demonstrating that the variance of the new process is less than that of the old process is straight-forward using traditional hypothesis tests. But, what about showing that the new process has the same mean as the old process? This would be proving the null hypothesis that is counter to traditional practice. The solution is *equivalence testing*. To illustrate the logic, let's go back to our CD example. Suppose that we wish to demonstrate that the average space on our CDs was 700 MB. In effect, what we would like to do is:

$$H_0: \mu \neq 700$$

$$H_1: \mu = 700$$

However, traditional hypothesis testing requires that the **equality appear in the null hypothesis**. A little reflection should convince you that what we really want to show is not that the mean is exactly 700.00, but that it is very close to 700 MB. In other words, that there is no practical difference between the mean and 700. If we can define the notion of practical difference numerically, then it is possible to demonstrate that the mean is, for all practical purposes, 700 MB. This requires that we be precise in what we mean by a practical difference in terms of a numerical value. We will call the small numerical value of the practical difference δ. Then, what we want to demonstrate is that the population mean μ is between 700 - δ and 700 + δ. We can do this with two hypothesis tests:

$$H_0: \mu \geq 700 + \delta$$

$$H_1: \mu < 700 + \delta$$

$$\text{and}$$

$$H_0: \mu \leq 700 - \delta$$

$$H_1: \mu > 700 - \delta$$

The first test, if we reject H_0, shows that the mean is < 700 + δ and the second, again if we reject H_0, shows that it is > 700 - δ which implies that it must be between the two values or[1]:

$$700 - \delta < \mu < 700 +$$

The first test, if we reject H_0, shows that the mean is < 700 + δ and the second, again if we reject H_0, shows that it is > 700 - δ which implies that it must be between the two values or

$$700 - \delta < \mu < 700 + \delta$$

Since this involves two one-sided hypothesis tests this procedure is often referred to as *Two One-Sided Tests* or TOST.

The Hypothesis Testing Procedure

Having discussed the theory underlying tests of hypotheses, let us now review a testing procedure that is widely followed in practice. We will explain and illustrate it with examples that follow in this chapter. In addition, you will find that this same procedure is applicable to numerous other tests in subsequent chapters.

---

[1] Since this involves two one-sided hypothesis tests this procedure is often referred to as *Two One-Sided Tests* or TOST.

important

> **Procedure for Testing Hypotheses**
>
> 1. Establish the null and alternative hypotheses (H_0 and H_1).
> 2. Identify he level of significance, α.
> 3. State the decision criteria for either the test statistic (e.g. -1.96, +1.96) or units of the data e.g., (692.2 MB and 707.8 MB) if not using p-values[2].
> 4. Calculate the test statistic (e.g., the Z value or t value) and the associated p-value[3]
> 5. State the conclusion (reject, or do not reject the H_0).

The test statistic is a measure from one of the standard sampling distributions. In this chapter it will be a normal distribution (Z), t-distribution (t), chi-square (χ), or binomial distribution. Note that if one uses the p-value the third step can be skipped since with the p-value, the decision criterion is established when we identify the significance level.

Example 7-3

Suppose that a test of the H_0: $\mu \leq 700$ MB revealed a sample mean of $\bar{X} = 707.4.0$ MB. Calculate the test statistic and p-value, if the standard error is $\sigma_{\bar{Y}} = 4.0$ MB.

Solution

In this case, we are working with a sampling distribution of sample $\bar{X}$'s, which is the normal distribution. Therefore, the normal distribution applies and the test statistic is measured in Z units:

$$Z = \frac{Sample\ Statistic - Population\ Parameter}{Standard\ Error} = \frac{\bar{X} - \mu}{\sigma_{\bar{X}}}$$

$$= \frac{707.4 - 700}{4} = 1.85$$

$Z = \dfrac{\bar{X} - U}{\sigma_{\bar{X}}}$

The p-value is the probability of observing a sample mean of 707.4 MB or more, if the population mean is only 700 MB. We can use NORMDIST to find this probability:

1 - NORMDIST(707.4,700,4,TRUE) = 1 - .967843 = .032157 *p-value*

The Z-value tells us that the sample mean is 1.85 standard errors (Z units) above the hypothesized mean. If the number of Z units exceeds the distance to the rejection region, we should reject the hypothesis. The p-value tells us that there are approximately 4 chances in 100 of observing a sample mean this large if the null hypothesis is true. If this p-value is less than our level of significance (α) we would reject the null hypothesis; otherwise, we cannot reject it. Therefore, if our level of significance was the traditional .05, we would reject the null hypothesis.

Example 7-3 used a one-tailed hypothesis test to compute the p-value. What happens if we have a two-tailed test? The p-value is calculated in exactly the same way as we did above; however, a two-tailed test

---

[2] Stating the decision criteria in terms of a test statistic or units of the data is not necessary if the p-value approach is used. Since most any statistical software will provide the p-value for the test we rarely specify the criteria in practice. We do so here to illustrate the logic of the process.
[3] If the p-value can be calculated without calculating the value of the test statistic, the computation of the test statistic is not necessary if you are using the p-value to make your decision about the null hypothesis.

indicates that the sample data can be either very large (to the right of the mean) or very small (to the left of the mean) to reject the null hypothesis. Since the p-value we calculated earlier is in only one tail of the distribution, we simply multiply the calculated p-value by two for a two-tailed test. Therefore, the p-value for this two-tailed test would be 2(.032157) = .064314. In this case we could not reject the null hypothesis as the computed p-value is greater than the significance level of .05.

This illustrates an important principle about one-tailed and two-tailed tests. There is always a greater chance of rejecting the null hypothesis with a one-tailed test than a two-tailed test because the p-value is cut in half (assuming that the sample mean is on the correct side). Another way of saying this is that a one-tailed test is always more powerful than a two-tailed test. Therefore, unless there is good reason to use a two-tailed test, a more conservative researcher will usually use a one-tailed test, if possible.

Exercises II

10. Explain (a) why you would use a two-tailed versus a one-tailed test of hypothesis, and (b) what is meant by a test statistic.

11. Regarding the critical limits for a test of hypothesis: (a) How many limits are used for a two-tailed test? (b) Which side of the mean is the limit for a lower-tailed test? (c) In what two ways can limits be stated?

12. Why are critical limits stated in terms of the number of standard errors (as opposed to the number of standard deviations)?

13. State the appropriate null and alternative hypotheses for the following:

    (a) A test is to be conducted for a health insurance firm. Past records suggest that the average hospital costs per patient per day are $860, but the insurance firm would like to show that costs are now significantly greater than $860.
    Quality control standards call for .50 in of tread depth on a certain grade of tire. Random samples are to be taken to test whether the tires are being manufactured according to specifications.

14. A production inspector has taken a sample of 80 electrical connectors to test the hypothesis that the resistance is 5.00 ohms (units) against the alternative that it is not 5.00 ohms at the 10% level of significance. Let $\sigma = .60$ ohm. State the critical limits for the test in terms of (a) Z values, and (b) units of the variable.

15. A tax consultant at an accounting firm has seen a publication that claims taxpayers, on average, list $1,000 in deductions to charitable organizations. The consultant feels that her firm's customers claim less than $1,000 and proposes to test the publication's claim of $1,000 at the 5% level of significance. She uses a random sample of twenty IRS tax returns from her firm's customers. Assuming the standard deviation is $75, what is the appropriate critical limit in terms of the (a) test statistic value, and (b) units of the variable? (Assume that the population distribution is normal).

Testing the Population Mean: σ Known

Now that we have established the logic of hypothesis testing, we can see how it applies to the tests of different population parameters. We will first discuss the tests about the population mean and will begin with the case where the population standard deviation is known. When σ is known, the sampling distribution of sample means is the normal distribution (a) for large samples ($n \geq 30$) from any population and (b) for all samples from a normally distributed population. Therefore, a Z-test statistic may be used here. But, Z is normally not appropriate for small samples (less than 30) from populations that are not normal.

We begin with a two-tailed test and use the example introduced earlier to illustrate the steps listed in the previous section of the procedure for testing hypotheses concerning population means.

Example 7-4

A CD manufacturer plans to advertise that their EQ700 CD disks have a mean capacity of 700 MB, and wants to know if the average capacity is different from this. A sample of n = 100 CDs revealed a mean of $\bar{X}$ = 690.0 MB, and σ is known to be 40 MB. Test the H_0 at the α = 5% level of significance.

Solution

1. The hypotheses are:

H_0: μ = 700

H_1: $\mu \neq$ 700

2. α = .05

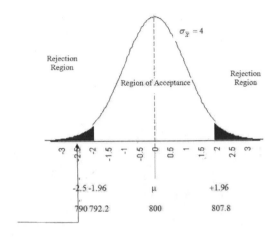

3. Use normal distribution:

Reject   if: Z < −1.96 or > +1.96

$$z = \frac{690 - 700}{4} = -2.5$$

4. The p-value can be calculated as

2*NORMDIST(690,700,4,TRUE) = 2*.00621 = 0.01249

5. Conclusion: Reject H_0: μ = 700 since −2.5 < −1.96 and the p-value is less than .05. Conclude that $\mu \neq$ 700 MB.

Computing the Z-test statistic and p-value is a straightforward way of completing the test; however, expressing the action limits in units of pounds may have some intuitive value at this point. Remember from this example that C_1 = 692.2 MB and C_2 = 707.8 MB. Using these action limits, it is perhaps more obvious that the sample mean of 690.0 MB falls outside this range of acceptance.

Inasmuch as the CD manufacturer's hypothesis that the average capacity is 700 MB is now rejected, a new estimate of the CD capacity should be made. This could easily be done by using the procedures for estimation discussed in Chapter 6. The manufacturer needs only to specify the confidence level desired. Then, knowing $\bar{X}$, σ, and n, the limits could readily be established using the standard form CL = $\bar{X} \pm Z\sigma_{\bar{X}}$.

One-tailed Test

One-tailed tests follow the same general format. Recall, however, that the sign in the alternative hypothesis points in the direction of the rejection region.

Example 7-5

The CD manufacturer of Example7-4 has another CD, GT 1200, made with a new technology developed at the local university that they believe will have a standard capacity of 1200 MB (or more). The manufacturer would be concerned if the CD capacity turned out to be significantly less than 1200 MB. A random sample of 36 CDs yielded a mean capacity of 1182 MB; σ is known to be 60 MB. Perform a one-tailed test of the H_0: $\mu \geq 1200$ using a 2% level of significance.

Solution

The claim being tested is that the CD capacity is 1200 MB or more, so we will reject it if the sample evidence shows an average capacity of significantly less than 1200 MB. This means that the rejection region will be in the lower tail of the distribution, and the alternative hypothesis will be pointing to less than 1200 MB.

1. The hypotheses are:

$$H_0: \mu \geq 1200$$
$$H_1: \mu < 1200$$

2. $\alpha = .02$.

3. Use normal distribution;

   reject if $Z < -2.05$.

   $$\sigma_{\bar{X}} = \frac{\sigma}{\sqrt{n}} = \frac{60}{\sqrt{36}} = 10$$

$$Z = \frac{1182 - 1200}{10}$$
$$= -1.80$$

4. The p-value can be calculated as NORMDIST(1182,1200,10,TRUE) = .03593

5. Conclusion: Do not reject H0: $\mu \geq 1200$ because $-1.80 > -2.05$ and the p-value is greater than .02. The data are not sufficient to conclude that mean capacity is < 1200 MB if the manufacturer is willing to incorrectly reject a true null hypothesis only 2% of the time.

If the action limit for Example 7-5 were expressed in megabytes, it would be:

$$C = \mu - Z\,\sigma_{\bar{X}} = 1,200.0 - 2.05(10.0) = 1,179.5 \text{ MB}$$

Therefore, the $\bar{X}$ value of 1,182 MB is not sufficient to reject the hypothesis that $\mu = 1,200$ or more. This illustrates how the "burden of proof" is on the alternative hypothesis. Even though the sample mean was less than 1,200 MB, it was not enough to completely discredit the null hypothesis. Recall, however, that the test does not "prove" the validity of the capacity claim of H_0. It simply states that the sample data are not sufficient to reject the claim, so the null is still tenable.

Testing the Population Mean: σ Unknown

Remember that for normally distributed populations with an unknown standard deviation, the sample means are distributed according to the **t-distribution**. For a sample of any size, the t-distribution is theoretically correct and can be used for setting confidence levels (as we have seen in Chapter 5 and for testing hypotheses (as we shall illustrate in this section).

With unknown σ, the test statistic shown in Equation 7-2 follows a t-distribution with n – 1 degrees of freedom. Therefore, the test statistic for tests where σ is unknown is:

$$t = \frac{\bar{X} - \mu}{s_{\bar{X}}} \qquad (7\text{-}2)$$

The t-value is then used to compute a p-value to compare with the level of significance.

Two-tailed Test

We will illustrate the t-distribution hypothesis testing procedure first with a two-tailed test that calls for the calculation of all values (including $\bar{X}$ and s). Then, we conclude this section on tests of population means with a one-tailed test of the same data, illustrating how the level of significance affects the conclusion.

Example 7-6

Powertech Chemical Co. has developed a replaceable fuel cell that converts stored chemicals and water directly into electrical current that can be used to power automobiles. They feel that the cells will power a car for an average of 60 hrs. before needing to be "recharged," and are now planning for the number of service centers that will be needed. A random test of eight cells resulted in the following operating times:

Cell No.	1	2	3	4	5	6	7	8
Hours of Service	64	57	65	59	66	58	68	67

Using a 5% level of significance, test the hypothesis that the true mean service life is 60 hrs.

Solution

1. The hypotheses are:

   $H_0: \mu = 60.0$ hrs
   $H_1: \mu \neq 60.0$ hrs

2. $\alpha = .05$

3. Use t-distribution for:

   $n - 1 = 8 - 1 = 7$ df;

   reject if $t < -2.3646$ or $t > +2.3646$.

4. First compute $\bar{X}$ and s:

   $\bar{X} = 63.0$ and $s = 4.34$

   Then $s_{\bar{X}} = \frac{4.34}{\sqrt{8}} = 1.534$

$s_{\bar{X}} = 1.534$

Rejection Region

Rejection Region

Region of Acceptance

$$t = \frac{\bar{X} - \mu}{s_{\bar{X}}} = \frac{63-60}{1.534} =\; 1.96$$

-2.3646

5. Using the Probability Calculator in XLDataAnalyst, the p-value is .0908

   Conclusion: Do not Reject $H_0: \mu = 60.0$ because $1.95 < 2.3646$ and the p-value is greater than .05. The sample evidence supports the claim of 60 hrs.

To make a claim that the mean operating time of the fuel cell is greater than 60 hrs. we should use a one-tailed test.

Example 7-7

Use the fuel cell data from Example 7-6:

$n = 8$ $\overline{X} = 63$ hrs $s = 4.34$ hrs $s_{\overline{X}} = 1.54$

(a)   Test the following H_0: $\mu \leq 60.0$ hr, H_1: $\mu > 60.0$ hr. Use $\alpha = .05$ level.

(b)   Suppose that the test in (a) were conducted at the .01 level. Discuss any differences in the results.

Solution

$$S_{\overline{X}} = 1.534$$

1. The hypotheses are:

   H_0: $\mu \leq 60.0$ hr
   H_1: $\mu > 60.0$ hr

2. $\alpha = .05$

3. Use the t-distribution for a one-tailed

test with $\alpha = .05$:

   $df = 8 - 1 = 7$

   Reject if t > + 1.895

$t = \dfrac{\overline{X} - \mu}{S_{\overline{X}}} =$

$\dfrac{63 - 60}{1.534} = 1.96$

Region of Acceptance

Rejection Region

4. Using XLDataAnalyst, p-value is .0457

5.   Conclusion: Reject H_0: $\mu \leq 60.0$ hr because 1.96> 1.895 and also because the p-value of .0457 is less than the significance level of .05

Conclusion: the mean operating time is greater than 60.0 hrs.

Notice that this result would not have been significant if we had used a .01 level of significance. For a .01 level test, the p-value would not allow us to reject the null hypothesis. In other words, we cannot conclude that the mean operating hours are greater than 60 hrs, if we are willing to be wrong only 1% of the time. The fact that we can reject the null hypothesis at the .05 level, but not the .01 level, is evident from the p-value of .0457. This is one of the advantages of the p-value approach. Anyone with a different risk level can immediately see whether or not they would reject the null hypothesis.

With the two-tailed test (Example 7–6), we were not able to reject the claim of 60 hrs. With the one-tailed test we could reject the claim. Thus, for the same data, the one-tailed test allowed us to make a "more powerful" statement than the two-tailed test; however, the data are not sufficiently strong to allow us to limit our risk of being wrong to 1%.

Testing the Population Proportion

Tests of proportions follow the same general format as tests of means. For example, suppose that a business consultant wished to test whether 30% of companies offer their sales representatives a salary plus commission. The three possible null and alternative hypotheses for the test could be:

Lower-Tailed Test	Two-Tailed Test	Upper-Tailed Test
$H_0: \pi \geq .30$	$H_0: \pi = .30$	$H_0: \pi \leq .30$
$H_1: \pi < .30$	$H_1: \pi \neq .30$	$H_1: \pi > .30$

There is an additional complication when testing hypotheses about proportions. Recall that the standard error of the proportion depends on the value of the population proportion;[4] however, when we are testing a hypothesis about π then we do not know it's value. This means we never know the true value of the standard error of proportion, σ_p – for if we did, we would also know π. But, we can use the hypothesized value of π to compute σ_p. This gives the benefit of the doubt to our hypothesized value, which is consistent with the philosophy of hypothesis testing. Notice that this differs from the computation of the standard error of proportion used for estimation problems. In estimation, we use the sample proportion, p, to compute the standard error of proportion s_p because we do not have a hypothesized value for π.

Recall that the sampling distribution for the proportion is the binomial. In calculating confidence intervals in Chapter 6, this posed a problem as the appropriate percentiles of the binomial distribution often do not exist. With large samples ($np > 5$ and $n(1-p) > 5$), however, the normal approximation to the binomial can be applied. We encounter a similar situation with hypothesis testing if we use a value of the test statistic or sampling distribution of the proportion as a critical value. In those cases, we would have to limit ourselves to large samples and use the test statistic.

$$Z = \frac{p - \pi}{\sigma_p} \tag{7-3}$$

Notice, however, that if we use p-values, we are not restricted to using the normal approximation, but can use the more appropriate binomial distribution. We will illustrate both methods in the following examples and compare the results of the two.

Example 7-8

The manager of a computer software firm feels that 20% of personal computer owners in its market area use database software. A random sample of 400 PC owners revealed that 68 used database software. Test the hypothesis at the $\alpha = .05$ level.

Solution

The problem statement does not specify a two-tailed test, but there is no evidence to suggest a claim of more or less than 20%; therefore a two-tailed test can be assumed. We will follow the same steps used for tests of means, with the major difference being in the computation of the standard error σ_p.

1. $H_0: \pi = .20$

     $H_1: \pi \neq .20$

2. $\alpha = .05$

3.   Use normal distribution; Reject H_0 if $Z < -1.96$ or $Z > +1.96$

$$p = \frac{68}{400} = .17 \qquad \sigma_p = \sqrt{\frac{(.2)(.8)}{400}} = .02$$

---

[4] Remember that the standard error of the proportion is $\sqrt{\frac{\pi(1-\pi)}{n}}$ which requires that we know π

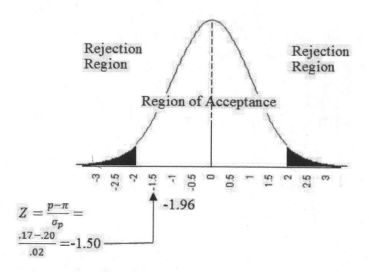

$$Z = \frac{p-\pi}{\sigma_p} =$$

$$\frac{.17-.20}{.02} = -1.50$$

4. We can calculate the p-value for the normal approximation using NORMDIST. We would find that NORM.DIST(.17,.2,.02,TRUE) = .066807. We would then have to multiply this by 2 (since it is a two-tailed test) to get our p-value of .133614.

    We can also calculate the p-value using the binomial and BINOM.DIST. We would first need to find the probability of finding 68 or fewer successes in 400 trials if the probability of a success is .20. We would calculate this as BINOM.DIST(68,400,.2,TRUE) = .073226 which when multiplied by 2 gives a p-value of .146452. Our decision is the same using both methods, but the p-values are somewhat different.

5. Conclusion: Do not reject H_0: $\pi = .20$ because $-1.5 > -1.96$ and because the p-value is greater than .05 in both cases. The sample data are not sufficient to conclude that the proportion of database users is something other than 20%.

As with means, the action limits could also be stated in the units of the problem (proportions) where we would have:

Limit in Z's	Conversion to Units	Limits in Percent
$C_1 = -1.96$	$C_1 = \pi - Z\sigma_p = .20 - 1.96(.02) = .161$	16%
$C_2 = +1.96$	$C_2 = \pi - Z\sigma_p = .20 + 1.96(.02) = .239$	24%

The sample proportion of .17 lies within these limits, so the null hypothesis retains its credibility.

Example 7-9

A cosmetics firm has developed a new sunscreen product that they feel will be a real winner, but they need the market share to be at least 30%. A sample of 900 prospective customers showed that 360 would potentially buy the firm's product. Can the firm be sufficiently certain that π is at least 30%?

Solution

The more traditional approach would be to trust the judgment of managers who already feel confident that the market will be at least 30%, and formulate an alternative hypothesis that will reject that assumption if the sample proportion is significantly less than 30% or .30. Following that track, we would have the rejection region on the lower tail of the distribution.

1. $H_0: \pi \geq .30$

   $H_1: \pi < .30$

2. α is unspecified, so let us assume a 05 level.

$$p = \frac{360}{900} = .40 \qquad \sigma_p = \sqrt{\frac{(.3)(.7)}{900}} = .0152$$

3. Use normal distribution; reject if $Z < -1.645$
4. Using the normal approximation, the

p-value is found by NORM.DIST(.40,.30, .0152, TRUE)

$= .99999999998$.

With the Binomial, we would

calculate BINOM.DIST(360, 900, .3, TRUE) =

.9999999999

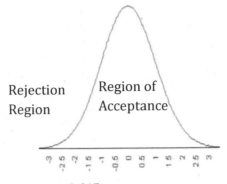

Rejection Region | Region of Acceptance

-1.645 π
.30

$$Z = \frac{p - \pi}{\sigma_p}$$

$$= \frac{.40 - .30}{.0152} = 6.58$$

Conclusion: Do not reject $H_0: \pi = .30$ because $6.58 > -1.645$ and the p-value is near 1.0. The results lend strong support to the H_0: that the proportion preferring the product is 30% or more.

Exercises III

16. State the null and alternative hypotheses for the following tests:

    (a) The average hourly pay of factory workers is $11.62 per hour.

    (b) Bestway Aluminum Siding will last 30 years or more.

    (c) Less than 65% of families in this country own their homes.

    (d) British citizens spend an average of 18 hrs/week watching television.

    (e) More than three-fourths of U.S workers are satisfied with their jobs.

17. Rework Example 7-4 assuming that the CD is EQ1000 with an assumed mean capacity of 1,000 MB and $\bar{X} = 990.0$ MB. Let $\sigma = 60$ MB and test at a 4% level of significance.

18. Could a hypothesis be accepted under a two-tailed test at a .10 level and rejected under a one-tailed test at the same level? Explain.

19. Administrators at Health Care Deluxe claim that, on average, patients are given attention within 14 minutes from the time they arrive. A state auditor, seeking to test this claim, sampled 400 customers and found their average time to obtain service was 15.0 minutes with a standard deviation of 10.0 min. (a) Use and $\alpha = .05$ level to test the claim. Show all (five) steps of the testing procedure, and state your conclusion. (b) State the reject limit(s) in units of minutes.

20. A social services agency is promoting the sale of light bulbs to raise funds for handicapped persons. They propose to guarantee that the bulbs will last 3,000 hrs or more. A test of 12 boxes of bulbs (with 12 in each box) revealed an average lifetime of 2,960 hrs, with a sample standard deviation of 360 hrs.

    (a) Using a test of hypotheses at the 2% level of significance, are the sample data sufficient to cause the agency to question the proposed guarantee?

    (b) If you were in charge of this project, would you hesitate offering the guarantee?

21. A major retailing firm is considering using daily newspapers to offer coupons to potential customers if newspapers are a sufficiently large source of the coupon market. A random sample of 185 customers revealed that 44 had clipped coupons from their daily newspapers. Use these data to test the hypothesis that at least 25% of potential customers use coupons from daily newspapers against the alternative that the proportion is less than 25%. Test at the $\alpha = 10\%$ level.

22. During a city council meeting, a council member said that 45% of her constituency was concerned about the amount of drug trafficking in the downtown city park.

    (a) State the null and alternative hypotheses of a two-tailed test to be conducted to validate the claim.

    (b) What would be the reject value if the council wished to make an 8% level test of this claim?

    (c) Assume that the council sampled 265 citizens and found that 146 were concerned about the drug traffic. Will this evidence invalidate the council member's claim?

23. A manufacturer of logging chains claims that their chains have a mean breaking strength of 120,000 lbs. A laboratory test of 20 chains shows only 117,000 lbs. with a standard deviation of 9,000 lbs. The laboratory wishes to test the manufacturer's claim at the .05 level against the alternative that the chain strength is less than 120,000 lbs.

    (a) State the null and alternative hypotheses.

    (b) State the test criteria.

    (c) Compute the test statistic and state your conclusion.

    (d) Would the decision have been the same if the laboratory test had revealed 115,000 lbs? Explain.

24. The following data shows the price/earnings (P/E) ratio of a random sample of 40 stocks (rounded to the nearest whole number). (a) Test the hypotheses that the mean P/E equals 11.0 at the .10 level of significance. (b) What is the highest level of significance (p value) at which the hypothesis could be rejected?

14	8	10	8	6	9	15	10	17	24
20	4	8	17	16	12	23	9	15	6
18	22	11	7	23	9	4	6	17	10
12	14	10	13	18	6	13	19	13	12

25. Production planners in a furniture factory want to know how much time is needed at each work center on a new assembly line. They feel that 4.6 minutes is enough for an upholstery operation and plan to allow that much time unless the sample time data are significantly less than that. Sample times on 14 pieces of furniture were as shown:

Item No	1	2	3	4	5	6	7	8	9	10	11	12	13	14
Min. req'd	4.2	4.5	4.6	3.9	4.5	4.4	4.5	4.2	4.6	4.7	4.3	3.8	4.5	4.4

Test the hypotheses that the mean time is 4.6 minutes at the 5% level. (a) Show all the steps of your procedure and state your conclusion. (b) Comment on the solution had you been asked to use the $\alpha = 1\%$ level.

Testing the Population Variance (Standard Deviation)

Recall from Chapter 5 that the sampling distribution for a sample variance was the chi-square distribution; or more accurately that the following test statistic has a chi-square distribution:

$$\chi^2 = \frac{(n-1)S^2}{\sigma^2} \tag{7-4}$$

We can use this test statistic in testing hypotheses about a population variance in exactly the same way we have used the z and the t statistics. For example, suppose that a process management consultant wants to test the hypothesis that the variance of waiting times at a bank is 9 minutes (with a standard deviation of 3 minutes).

The three possible hypotheses are:

Lower-Tailed Test	Two-Tailed Test	Upper-Tailed Test
H_0: $\sigma^2 \geq 9$	H_0: $\sigma^2 = 9$	H_0: $\sigma^2 \leq 9$
H_1: $\sigma^2 < 9$	H_1: $\sigma^2 \neq 9$	H_1: $\sigma^2 > 9$

Since this is a chi-square distribution scenario, we will need to calculate the value of the chi-square statistic using Equation 7-4 and then find the critical value from the chi-square distribution. We can use either the Probability Calculator in XLDataAnalyst to find the percentile or use the CHISQ.INV function in Excel with degrees of freedom of n-1.

Example 7-10

The Powertech Chemical Co. of Example 7-6 is also concerned about the variability of the times until recharge. The company believes that the variance of the times will not be greater than 15. The data on the 8 test cells is repeated below. At the .10 level of significance, do the data support the stated hypothesis?

Cell No.	1	2	3	4	5	6	7	8
Hours of Service	64	57	65	59	66	58	68	67

The calculated sample variance is 18.857.

Solution

Since the company believes that the variance can be no greater than 15, the null hypothesis will include the possibility that the variance is less than or equal to 15. Therefore, the alternative hypothesis would be that the variance is greater than 15, indicating an upper-tailed test.

1. H_0: $\sigma^2 \leq 15$

   H_1: $\sigma^2 > 15$

$$\chi^2 = \frac{(n-1)S^2}{\sigma^2}$$
$$= \frac{(8-1)(18.857)}{15}$$
$$= 8.799$$

2. $\alpha = .05$

$$\chi^2 = \frac{(n-1)S^2}{\sigma^2}$$
$$= \frac{(8-1)(18.857)}{15}$$
$$= 8.799$$

3.   Using Excel, we would find that

CHISQ.INV(.05,7) = 14.067 so that we will reject H_0

if the calculated value is greater than 14.067.

4.   The calculated value of the chi-square is: 8.799

5. We can also compute the p-value for the sample variance of 18.857. Using XLDataAnalyst, we would find a p-value of 1 - .7327 = .2673. Since this is greater than a = .05, we cannot reject the null hypothesis.

Conclusion: We cannot reject H_0 because 8.799 is less than 14.067 and because the p-value of .2673 is greater than .05. Therefore, we do not have enough evidence to conclude that the population variance is greater than 15 even though the sample variance is 18.857.

Exercises IV

26. If a sample contains 15 observations with a sample variance of 9.65 and we believe that the population variance is not larger than 8, what chi-squared value would we find to test the variance?

27. Suppose a sample of 20 observations has a sample variance of 14.999 and we believe that the population variance should not be larger than 15. What chi-squared value would we find to test the variance?

28. A sample contains 10 observations with a sample variance of 8.76. Can we conclude that the population variance is less than 7 at a 0.10 significance level?

29. A bank manager is examining a particular account's balance on the last day of every month. The data looks to the manager like the variance of the account is less than $100 at the end of every month. A sample over a six-month stretch has a variance of $110. At the .05 level of significance does the data support the manager's assumption?

30. A sample of 14 observations has a sample variance of 3.45. Can we conclude at the .05 significance level that the variance is less than 4?

31. A professor is looking at the variance of test scores for her class. She selected randomly 7 tests to examine and found that they contain the following scores: 91, 87, 85, 83, 88, 79, 81. Can she conclude that the variance is less than 15 at the .10 level of significance?

32. The braking distance of Type A brake pads is being tested by engineers. The engineers are looking for a variance of no more than 10. Using a .05 level of significance and the following distance data: (a) form hypothesis statements (b) define alpha (c) find the chi-squared limit (d) find the chi-squared value, and (e) state your conclusion.

Distance in feet: 17, 18, 21, 17, 16, 14, 19, and 18

Testing the Population Median

With ordinal data, the only meaningful measure of central tendency is the median. You may recall from prior chapters that there is no well-defined sampling distribution for the sample median; however, that does not mean that we cannot use statistical inference for medians. There are two tests for a single population median. The first test is very easy to understand, but is not very powerful. The second test is more powerful and is also used in other hypothesis testing situations

Sign Test

The simplest statistical test for a population median is called the sign test and the logic is quite straight-forward. Recall that the median is the value that divides the population data in half. This means that half of the population values are greater than the median and half are smaller. Therefore, if the null hypothesis is true, then about half of our sample values should be above the hypothesized median and half below.

In the sample data, code the observations as + or –, depending on whether they are greater than or less than the hypothesized median. Values exactly equal to the hypothesized median are omitted. If we call values above the median a "success" and values below the median a "failure", then the situation is like a binomial with $\pi = .5$. We can then use the binomial distribution to calculate the p-value for the sample observations.

Example 7-11

The head of the real estate association in Rock River believes that the median price of a house in the city is now higher than $90,000. The following data from a sample of 12 homes that have just recently sold in Rock River are as follows. Does the data support the hypothesis at the .05 level of significance?

House	1	2	3	4	5	6	7	8	9	10	11	12
Selling Price ($000)	89.0	95.0	101.0	85.5	74.0	110.0	90.5	93.4	98.8	91.0	105.4	99.0
Price – $90,000	-	+	+	-	-	+	+	+	+	+	+	+

Solution

Since the head of the real estate association believes that the median price is higher than $90,000, the sample data have to be strong enough to reject the hypothesis that the median price is $90,000 or less. Therefore, the appropriate test is an upper-tailed test.

1. $H_0: \eta \leq \$90,000$

   $H_1: \eta > \$90,000$

2. $\alpha = .05$

3. As shown in the table, there are 9 + signs out of 12 values. We can use the XLDataAnalyst probability calculator of the BINOMDIST function in Excel to find the probability of observing 9 or more successes out of 12 trials if the probability of a success is .5.

   1 - BINOMDIST(8, 12, .5, TRUE) = 1 - .927002 = .072998

4. Conclusion: Since the p-value of .073 is greater than .05, we cannot reject the null hypothesis. Therefore, there is not enough evidence to support the claim that the median price is higher than $90,000.

Wilcoxon Signed Rank Test

The Wilcoxon Signed Rank Test is the second way of testing a population median and will also be used for dependent samples test of medians. In this case, we will be using the W test statistic, calculated as follows:

1. Calculate the differences between each observation and the hypothesized value of the median.

2. Rank the absolute differences, ignoring the sign.

3. Place a + or a – on each rank, depending on the sign of the difference.

4. Calculate the sum of the ranks with a + sign and the sum with a - sign. For a two-tailed test, W is the minimum of these two values. For an upper tailed test, W is the sum of the + ranks. For a lower tailed test, W is the sum of the – ranks:

$$W = \sum R^{+(or-)} \qquad (7\text{-}5)$$

5. Compare this value with the critical value for the Wilcoxon Signed Ranks test or compute the p-value using an appropriate algorithm.

Under the null hypothesis, the sum of the positive and negative rank values should be about equal since the differences are equidistant around the hypothesized median. Calculation of the actual p-values is complex; however, for larger samples, we can use a normal approximation for the Signed Rank test. It can be shown that:

$$\mu_W = \frac{n(n+1)}{4} \qquad \sigma_W = \sqrt{\frac{n(n+1)(2n+1)}{24}} \qquad (7\text{-}6)$$

Then, we can calculate the Z as:

$$Z = \frac{W - \mu_W}{\sigma_W} \qquad (7\text{-}7)$$

Example 7-12

Returning to Example 7-11, we want to test the hypothesis that the median price of houses in Rock River is greater than $90,000.

Solution

X	Difference	Abs Difference	Ranking	R+	R-
89.0	-1.0	1.0	2.5		2.5
95.0	5.0	5.0	6	6	
101.0	11.0	11.0	9	9	
85.5	-4.5	4.5	5		5
74.0	-16.0	16.0	11		11
110.0	20.0	20.0	12	12	
90.5	0.5	0.5	1	1	
93.4	3.4	3.4	4	4	
98.8	8.8	8.8	7	7	
91.0	1.0	1.0	2.5	2.5	
105.4	15.4	15.4	10	10	
99.0	9.0	9.0	8	8	

The table above shows the calculation of the ranks with positive and negative rank values. The sum of the positive ranks (R^+) is 59.5 and the sum of the negative ranks (R^-) is 18.5. As we will see in the next section, the exact p-value is .046 so that we would reject the null hypothesis at the .05 level of significance. We could calculate a p-value using the normal approximation if the sample size was larger, but a sample of 12 is too small for the approximation.

Notice that we can reject the null hypothesis with the signed rank test where we could not with the sign test. This is an indication that the sign rank test is more powerful than the sign test. The reason for this should be clear: the sign test only considers whether or not a value is greater than the median or less than that value. It ignores the magnitude of the difference. By considering the rank order of these differences, the Wilcoxon Sign Rank test uses more information to produce a more powerful test of the null hypothesis.

Exercises V

*Note: For all problems, unless specified otherwise, use .05 as level of significance

33. A paramedic believes that the median number of calls that his team responds to in any given week is around 30 minutes. State the two hypothesis statements that you would use to test this claim.

34. A director of a company wants to examine the median income of the sales representatives in division. The director believes that the median income is over $40,000 a year and looks at a sample of 10 salespeople. Of the 10, 6 made more than $40,000 last year. Is the director correct in his assumption? Use a .05 level of significance.

35. As the head of programming at WBS, an independent television network, you have test-screened a new sitcom with 30 randomly selected consumers from your marketing panel group. The 30 consumers watch an episode of the proposed series and evaluate it on several scales from 1 to 100 (with 100 being the best rating). You require that the median evaluation in the population of viewers be more than 70 before you will move forward with a new show. The overall median rating for the sitcom in the sample was 75 with 20 of the evaluations being over 70 and 10 below. Should you move ahead with the proposed show?

36. The Ode Cologne fragrance company is considering a new line of cologne to replace a line that has been on the market for three years and is starting to lose market share. A random sample of 15 females consumers agree to test the new fragrance for 2 weeks. Each consumer is given a free bottle of the new fragrance and at the end of the two-week period each of the consumers rates the fragrance on a scale of 1 to 10. To be safe, the company wants to feel sure that the median rating of the fragrance in the population would be more than 7, on the 1 to 10 scale. The 15 ratings are given below. Can the company be confident that the median rating in the population would be more than 7?

> **Rating:** 9 4 8 6 9 8 10 8 10 5 8 8 9 7 8

Practice

Hypothesis Tests with Excel and XLDataAnalyst

Excel Functions

There is only one Excel function that can be used for one-sample hypothesis tests: the ZTEST function. The syntax of the function is:

$$\text{Z.TEST(range, } \mu_0, \text{ sigma)}$$

Range is a reference to a cell range that contains the observations; μ_o is the hypothesized value of the mean; sigma is the population standard deviation. The function returns the upper-tailed p-value of the Z-test. A lower-tailed test can be conducted by subtracting the returned value from 1.0 and a two-tailed test can be performed by multiplying the computed value by 2. You can use this function for the normal approximation to the binomial for proportions by calculating the population standard deviation from the hypothesized population proportion.

Example 7-13

Using the housing price data from Example 7-11, test the hypothesis that the mean selling price in the population is $90,000. Assume that the population standard deviation is $10,000. The data are as follows. Use a 5% level of significance.

Solution

1. H_0: $\mu = \$90,000$

    H_1: $\mu \neq \$90,000$

2. $\alpha = .05$

3. Arrange the data vertically in cells A2:A13 with a header in cell A1. Then, enter the following formula.

$$= Z.TEST(A2:A13,90,10)$$

The resulting p-value of 0.064453 must be multiplied by 2, giving a p-value of .129. Therefore, we would have to accept the null hypothesis.

The Analysis Toolpak

Unfortunately, the Analysis Toolpak does not have any tests for one-sample data. Therefore, we are quite restricted when using Excel for one-sample data. Fortunately, the tools that come with the text can help.

The Excel Template

The Excel templates can be used to perform all of the hypothesis tests that we discussed above. The relevant file is named One-Sample Hypothesis Tests.xls. As can be seen in Figure 7-7 below, there are five worksheets corresponding to the five tests discussed in this chapter.

When testing population means, the Z-test is used if the population standard deviation is known and the t-test is used if it is not known. Testing proportions uses both the exact binomial test and the normal approximation. Testing for a population median uses the sign test. In using the template, you may solve problems that contain raw data or problems that have the data already summarized, e.g., you are given values of the sample statistics without needing to calculate them. The raw data is entered in Column F, labeled Data, starting in row 2. Information about the summarized sample data as well as the information about the hypothesized population values are entered in the upper left side of the template.

Figure 7-7   *The Excel Template for One-Sample Hypothesis Tests*

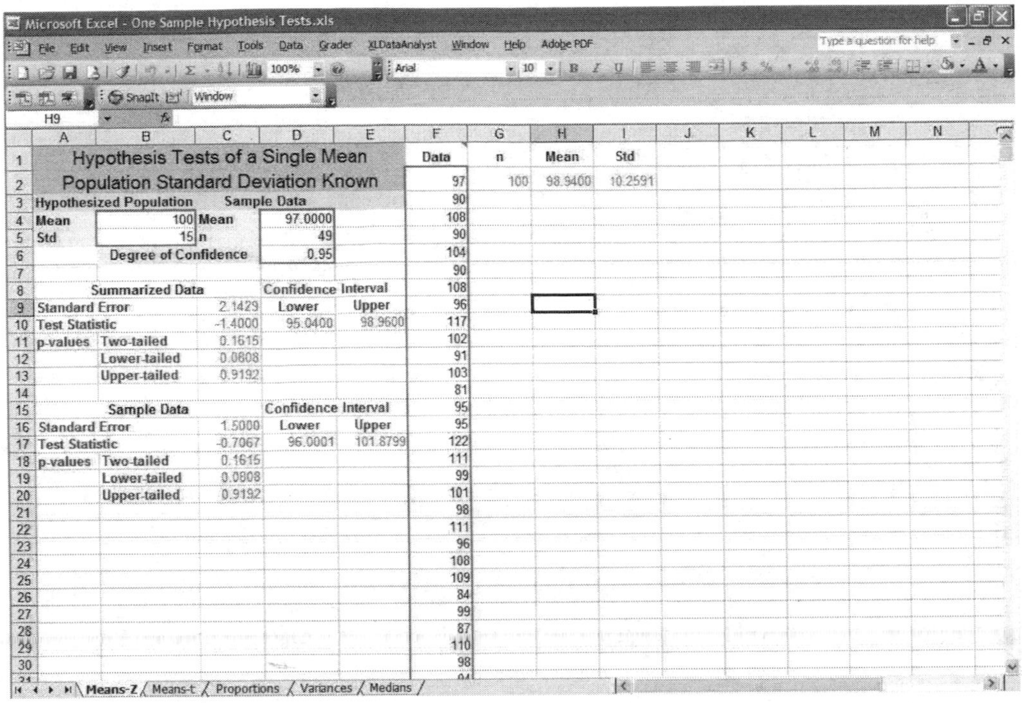

Example 7-14

In Example 7-6, we presented the PowerTech Chemical Company data on the hours of use for fuel cells (data repeated below). Test the hypothesis that the population mean is 60.

Cell No.	1	2	3	4	5	6	7	8
Hours of Service	64	57	65	59	66	58	68	67

Solution

1. The hypotheses are:

H_0: $\mu = 60.0$ hrs.

H_1: $\mu \neq 60.0$ hrs.

2. $\alpha = .10$

3.   The completed template is shown in Figure 7-8. For clarity, the summary information of the original template has been deleted. Also, the original data in the template has been deleted and replaced by the data above.

4.   The p-value for the two-tailed test of .0916 is very close to the value of .0908 that we calculated earlier. Using a significance level of .10 we can reject the null hypothesis and conclude that the mean number of hours is not 60.

Note that the .0916 value is an exact value while the .0908 value contains rounding error. This is another example that illustrates the fact that computer calculations will, in general, be more accurate than hand calculations.

Figure 7-8   Template Solution for Example 7-14

	A	B	C	D	E	F	G	H	I	J	K	L	M	N	O
						Data	n	Mean	Std						
1	Hypothesis Tests of a Single Mean														
2	Population Standard Deviation Unknown					64	8	63.0000	4.3425						
3	Hypothesized Population		Sample Data			57									
4	Mean	60	Mean			65									
5			Std			59									
6			n			66									
7		Degree of Confidence				58									
8						68									
9	Summarized Data			Confidence Interval		67									
10	Standard Error			Lower	Upper										
11	Test Statistic														
12	p-values	Two-tailed	FALSE												
13		Lower-tailed													
14		Upper-tailed													
15															
16	Sample Data			Confidence Interval											
17	Standard Error		1.5353	Lower	Upper										
18	Test Statistic		1.9540	61.9082											
19	p-values	Two-tailed	0.0916												
20		Lower-tailed	0.9542												
21		Upper-tailed	0.0458												

Means-Z \ **Means-t** / Proportions / Variances / Medians /

Example 7-15

To illustrate the use of summarized data, consider the situation of the HomeCloser Mortgage Company. The President of HomeCloser believes that the average price of homes has gone up in the past three months. Published data from three months ago placed the average selling price at $125,000. A sample of 30 recent closings shows a sample mean of $130,421 with a standard deviation of $8,324. Does the data support the President's claim?

Solution

1. The hypotheses are:

H_0: $\mu \le 125,000$

H_1: $\mu > 125,000$

2. $\alpha = .05$ since no value was given

3. The completed template is shown in Figure 7-9. For clarity, the sample data has been deleted so that only the summarized results are present in the template.

4. The template shows an upper-tailed p-value of .0006 that is highly significant.

5. We can reject the null hypothesis and conclude that the data strongly support the President's beliefs.

Figure 7-9   *Template Solution for Example 7-15*

	A	B	C	D	E	F	G	H	I	J	K	L
	N61	▼	fx									
1	Hypothesis Tests of a Single Mean					Data	n	Mean	Std			
2	Population Standard Deviation Unknown						0					
3	Hypothesized Population			Sample Data								
4	Mean		125000	Mean	130421.0000							
5				Std	8324							
6				n	30							
7		Degree of Confidence			0.95							
8												
9		Summarized Data		Confidence Interval								
10	Standard Error		1519.7475	Lower	Upper							
11	Test Statistic		3.5670	126828.5508	#######							
12	p-values	Two-tailed	0.0013									
13		Lower-tailed	0.9994									
14		Upper-tailed	0.0006									
15												
16		Sample Data		Confidence Interval								
17	Standard Error			Lower	Upper							
18	Test Statistic		#VALUE!		#VALUE!							
19	p-values	Two-tailed	#VALUE!									
20		Lower-tailed	#VALUE!									
21		Upper-tailed	#VALUE!									
22												
23												
24												
25												
26												
27												
28												
29												
30												

◄ ◄ ► ►◄ \ Means-Z \ **Means-t** / Proportions / Variances / Medians /

Using XLDataAnalyst

XLDataAnalyst makes conducting hypothesis tests easy and allows the analysis of more realistic datasets. The appropriate option is the Tests and Intervals option in the Tests for One Variable section of the XLDataAnalyst ribbon. The dialogue for this option is shown in Figure 7-10. To test a hypothesis, simply select the appropriate variable in the list of variables on the left. In the middle panel, check the box for a test of the mean (or proportion), the median, or the standard deviation (variance). You also need to specify the value in the null hypothesis and whether it is a two-tailed, lower-tail or upper-tail test.

Figure 7-10   *The Hypothesis Testing Dialog*

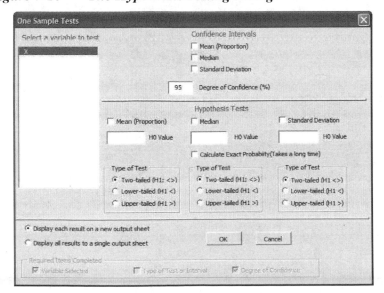

Example 7-16

Roberta Evans works as an Assistant VP of Operations at Municipal Hospital. One of her duties is to make sure that the admission and discharge processes are performed accurately and efficiently so as to not use unnecessary resources; however, it is also important to not inconvenience the patients or their families. To gain a better understanding of the processes and their current level of performance, she has had her assistant Bob, to gather data on several key measures over 50 days. This data, which we will utilize to illustrate the use of XLDataAnalyst, is contained in the file Example 7-16.xlsx included on the CD accompanying this text. The measures contained in the data are described in Table 7-4.

(a) Roberta Evans is concerned about the time patients spend waiting for the Financial Counselor. This wait is supposed to be 5 minutes or less, on average. Using the sample data, can we conclude that there is a problem in wait times, e.g., is the average wait longer than 5 minutes?

Solution

1. Our hypotheses are as follows:

   H_0: $\mu \leq 5$

   H_1: $\mu > 5$

2. To solve this problem, select Tests and Intervals in the ribbon. In the dialogue, select the Wait Finance variable and then check the box next to Mean (Proportion) in the Hypothesis Tests section, enter the value of 5 for the H_0 value and select upper-tailed test, then click OK. The output from XLDataAnalyst is shown in Figure 7-11.

Table 7-4   *Performance Measures Gathered at Municipal Hospital*

Variable	Description
Room Wait	Time patient spent waiting in room for discharge (in minutes)
Wait Finance	Time patient spent waiting for the Financial Counselor (in minutes)
Counseling Time	Time patient spent with the Financial Counselor (in minutes)
Counselor Idle	Percent of the day that the Financial Counselor was idle in fraction of a working day
Bills with Errors	Number of bills with errors that day
Complaint	Whether or not there was a patient complaint recorded that day

Figure 7-11   *XLDataAnalyst Output for Example 7-16 part (a)*

One Sample Results For Wait Finance

Summary Measures

Sample Size	50.0000
Mean	5.0200
Median	5.0000
Variance	5.4486
Standard Deviation	2.3342

Hypothesis test of Mean = 5 upper-tailed alternative

Degrees of Freedom	49.0000
t-test statistic	0.0606
p-value	0.4760

We can see from Figure 7-11 that the p-value is .476; hence, we cannot reject the null hypothesis. The average in the sample of 5.02 minutes supports the null hypothesis and does not indicate a problem with wait times for the financial counselor.

Example 7-17

Although the average counseling time appears to be safely within the guidelines of ½ hour, or 30 minutes, there is some concern about the variability of the times. Roberta feels that the standard deviation of the times should be no more than 5 minutes. If this is the case, then most of the counseling sessions will last 40 minutes or less. Do the data support Roberta's concerns? In other words, is there evidence that the standard deviation of the counseling times is more than 5 minutes?

Solution

1. Our hypotheses are as follows:

   H_0: $\sigma \le 5$

   H_1: $\sigma > 5$

2. To solve this problem, select Tests and Intervals from the ribbon. In the dialogue, select the Counseling Time and then check the box next to Standard Deviation in the Hypothesis Tests section, enter the value of 5 for the H_0 value and select upper-tailed test, then click OK. The output from XLDataAnalyst is shown in Figure 7-12.

Figure 7-12   *XLDataAnalyst Output for Example 7-16 part (b)*

One Sample Results For Counseling Time

Summary Measures

Sample Size	50.0000
Mean	29.3800
Median	29.5000
Variance	33.8731
Standard Deviation	5.8201

Hypothesis test of Standard Deviation = 5 upper-tailed alternative

Degrees of Freedom	49.0000
chi-square test statistic	66.3912
p-value	0.0496

The p-value is .0496. That means that we can reject the null hypothesis and conclude that the standard deviation of counseling times is indeed greater than 5 minutes. The sample standard deviation is 5.8201, indicating a standard deviation of almost 6 minutes. Roberta is right to be concerned.

Example 7-18

Historically, there has been a customer complaint on about 20% of the operating days at Municipal Hospital. There have been some indications that a recent quality improvement effort may be paying off. Is there evidence in the sample to indicate that the percent of days with a customer complaint has declined?

Solution

1. Our hypotheses are as follows:

    H_0: $\pi \geq .20$

    H_1: $\pi < .20$

To solve this problem, select Tests and Intervals from the ribbon. In the dialogue, select the Complaint variable and then check the box next to Mean (Proportion) in the Hypothesis Tests section. Enter the value of .2 for the H_0 value and select lower-tailed test, then click OK. The output from XLDataAnalyst is shown in Figure 7-13.

There are two p-values given for the test of proportions. The first is using the Z-statistic and the normal approximation to the binomial. The second p-value is using the exact probability from the binomial distribution. Since both p-values are greater than .05, we cannot reject the null hypothesis. The sample data do not provide sufficient evidence to indicate that the quality effort has reduced complaints. Notice also that the p-value for the normal approximation is lower than the exact value from the binomial. For samples less than 100 or so, the normal approximation often gives overly optimistic results compared to the exact results from the binomial. As with the t-test and the normal approximation, it is always best to use the exact results, if possible.

Figure 7-13   **XLDataAnalyst Output for Example 7-16 part (c)**

One Sample Results For Complaint

Summary Measures

Sample Size	50.0000
Proportion	0.1200

Hypothesis test of Proportion = 0.2 lower-tailed alternative

Z-test statistic	-1.4142
p-value using normal	0.0786
Exact p-value from Binomial	0.1034

Example 7-19

In Examples 7-11 and 7-12, we tested the null hypothesis that the median price of houses in Rock River was less than or equal to $90,000 versus the alternative that the median price was greater than $90,000. We previously tested the hypothesis manually, using the sign test and the Wilcoxon Rank Sum test. XLDataAnalyst will conduct these tests as well and also calculate exact p-values if the sample size is 30 or less. The results of running the median text on the data in the file Example 7-11 are shown below.

Notice once again, that the normal approximation gives slightly different results. In most cases, the two tests will be equal or close to equal, but as usual, the exact p-value is to be preferred, if it can be calculated.

Figure 7-14   **XLDataAnalyst Output for Example 7-16 part (c)**

One Sample Results For Selling Price ($000)

Summary Measures

Sample Size	12.0000
Mean	94.3833
Median	94.2000
Variance	91.0088
Standard Deviation	9.5399

Hypothesis test of Median = 90 upper-tailed alternative

Sign Test

Number of Minuses	3.0000
Number of Pluses	9.0000
p-value	0.0730

Wilcoxon Signed Ranks Test

Sum of Negative Ranks	18.5000
Sum of Positive Ranks	59.5000
Exact P-Value	0.0549

Normal Approximation

Z Value	1.6082
p-value	0.0539

Exercises VI

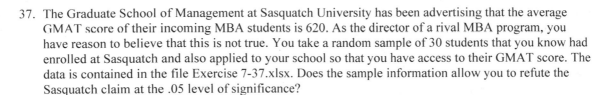

37. The Graduate School of Management at Sasquatch University has been advertising that the average GMAT score of their incoming MBA students is 620. As the director of a rival MBA program, you have reason to believe that this is not true. You take a random sample of 30 students that you know had enrolled at Sasquatch and also applied to your school so that you have access to their GMAT score. The data is contained in the file Exercise 7-37.xlsx. Does the sample information allow you to refute the Sasquatch claim at the .05 level of significance?

38. Catch the Beat Music Company, like most music companies, has been concerned about falling CD sales. They feel that the best way to recover and compete with the larger music companies is to start an online music download service, targeted at the preteen 10- to 12-year old group. They have commissioned a consulting company to survey the music-buying behavior of this age group. The consulting company has conducted a survey of 100 preteens in this age group in terms of the amount they spend per month on music, whether or not they have an Internet connection at home, and whether or not they would utilize such a service, if it were available. The results are contained in the file Exercise 7-38.xlsx.

    (a) The CFO of Catch the Beat has stated that the average monthly expenditures on music in the target market will have to be more than $5.00 per month to make the market attractive. Is there evidence at the .01 level of significance that this claim is true?

    (b) The CFO is also concerned about the variability of the monthly spending. She is afraid that if the standard deviation of the monthly spending is more than $1.00, the market may be too volatile. Is there evidence of this problem in the data at the .01 level of significance?

    (c) The VP of Marketing at Catch the Beat thinks that if the service is made available, they could capture more than 30% of the market. Does the sample data support this?

39. The Lucky Strike Gold Mining Company has developed a new process that is designed to more efficiently extract gold from existing mines. If the new process is successful, it may make it economical to open up some mines that have been previously closed. The old process was able to attain a yield of 11 pounds per ton. Lucky Strike has used the new process in a random sample of 40 locations and the yield (in pounds) per ton is recorded in the Exercise 7-39.xlsx. Based on the sample results, should Lucky Strike proceed with the new process? (Use a .05 level of significance).

40. Tailor to the Max is a small local clothing store in Kokomo, Indiana that is thinking of taking its clothing line statewide. Max, the owner, has decided that he needs some more information before considering expansion. Max's bank told him that he will need an upscale clientele in order to penetrate the markets in some of the larger cities. In particular, the average household income of his customer base should exceed $75,000. In addition, they would like a balanced clientele between male and female and in fact, they would like to have over 40% of the clients be female. A team from the local university has conducted a survey of a random sample of 40 customers and gathered the information contained in the file Exercises 7-40.xlsx.

    (a) Is there evidence in the sample to satisfy the bank in terms of the average household income in Tailor to the Max's customers, at the .01 level of significance?

    (b) Do the data support the desired mix requirement of having over 40% of the customers be female at the .05 level of significance?

41. The FTC has begun an investigation of the advertising claim made by a toothpaste manufacturer. The company has claimed that 4 out of 5 dentists recommend their product. The FTC has selected a random sample of 50 dentists who they contacted and asked if they actually recommend this brand of toothpaste. The results are contained in the file Exercises 7-41.xlsx. Does the FTC have sufficient evidence to charge the company with false advertising?

Opening Vignette Revisited

The data that Sally collected on the Swell Computer notebooks is contained in the file Chapter 7 Vignette.xls. To give Swell Computers the benefit of the doubt, Sally wants to accept their claim unless the data prove otherwise. She sets up her hypothesis test with Swell's claim as follows:

$H_0: \mu \geq 12$

$H_1: \mu < 12$

Using XLDataAnalyst, Sally obtained the results shown in Figure 7-15. The p-value of 0.0004 indicates strong evidence against Swell Computer's claim. Armed with this information, Sally is convinced that she needs to keep looking for the right notebook for Deltron.

Figure 7-15   XLDataAnalyst Output for the Deltron Problem

One Sample Results For Height

Summary Measures

Sample Size	20.0000
Mean	11.5000
Median	11.3600
Variance	0.3086
Standard Deviation	0.5555

Hypothesis test of Mean = 12 lower-tailed alternative

Degrees of Freedom	19.0000
t-test statistic	-4.0252
p-value	0.0004

Summary

A hypothesis is a claim about a population parameter. Hypothesis testing is a statistical procedure for using sample data to accept or reject that claim.

The null hypothesis (H_0) is a statement of "no change" from the expected, and the hypothesis testing process is set up to "favor" the null [that is, the calculated test statistic (Z, t, binomial, or χ^2) and the associated p-value must show that the sample statistic is significantly different from the hypothesized value in order to reject H_0]. Otherwise, we continue to assume that the null has credibility—even though we do not consider the acceptance of the null as any form of "proof." Rejecting the null hypothesis is a "stronger" conclusion than accepting the null hypothesis because the chance of making an error here is generally limited to the specified α risk (e.g., 1%, 5%). It implies acceptance of the alternative hypothesis. The null hypothesis always has the equal sign.

The alternative hypothesis (H_1) is frequently the research or test hypothesis that is under examination. In other words, it is what you are trying to demonstrate. The inequality sign in H_1 clearly indicates whether the test is a two-tailed ($\neq$), lower-tailed ($<$), or upper-tailed ($>$) test.

The hypothesis testing procedure involves either comparing the value of the sample statistic with the critical value from its sampling distribution, comparing the value of the test statistic with a percentile from its probability distribution, or comparing the p-value for the sample statistic with the level of significance (α).

Two types of errors, referred to as Type I and Type II, can occur in hypothesis testing. Type I Error is the error of rejecting a null hypothesis that is true. The risk of doing this is α, which is the specified level of significance of the test. Type II Error is the error of accepting the null hypothesis when it is false. This is the β risk. It corresponds to the area inside the action limits, but under the distribution centered on a specific value of the true parameter.

The appropriate test statistic for a hypothesis test depends on the sampling distribution for that sample statistic. When testing for the population mean, it will be either the Z or t-statistic, depending on whether or not you know the population standard deviation. For proportions, it is the binomial; although for large samples, the Z test can be used as an approximation. For variances, the appropriate test statistic is the chi square (χ^2). Lastly, for the median, which doesn't have a standard sampling distribution, we can use the sign test or the Wilcoxon Signed Ranks test.

Chapter Glossary

Alternative Hypothesis	Opposite of the Null Hypothesis and suggests that conditions have changed or that something is different.
Equivalence Testing	Hypothesis testing procedure that demonstrates that a population parameter is equal to a particular value, i.e., the traditional null hypothesis.
Hypothesis	A statement, or claim, about a population parameter.
Hypothesis Testing	A statistical procedure, using sample data, to support or reject a hypothesis about a population parameter.
Level of Significance	The risk that one is willing to take of rejecting a correct hypothesis (the risk of a Type I Error).
Null Hypothesis	The hypothesis tested in hypothesis testing. Usually, it represents the belief that conditions are normal, and established standards prevail.
One-tailed Tests	Appropriate where the null hypothesis should be rejected only if the sample statistic is significantly less (for lower-tailed test) or greater (upper-tailed test) than the hypothesized value.
P-Value	The probability of observing a sample statistic as extreme as, or more extreme than, the observed value of the sample statistic.
Sign Test	A test of medians based on the sign of the difference (positive or negative) between each of the values and the hypothesized value of the median.
Statistically-significant	A large difference, due to more than just sampling error. We can reject the null hypothesis.
Test Statistic	A measure from one of the standard sampling distributions.
Two-tailed Tests	Appropriate for situations where either a higher or lower value of the sample statistic should cause the rejection of the null hypothesis. The alternative hypothesis does not state a direction.
Type I Error	(α) Occurs when a null hypothesis is rejected when it is true.
Type II Error	(β) Occurs when not rejecting, or accepting, a false null hypothesis.

Questions and Problems

42. Which of the following statements about the tests of hypotheses are **false**?

    (a) The risk of committing a Type I Error is designated as β.

    (b) The value in the null hypothesis is assumed to equal the mean of a sampling distribution.

    (c) The major cause of Type I and II Errors is from mistakes made in recording data and in calculating results.

    (d) If a hypothesis is tested at the $\alpha = .05$ level and is not rejected, either the hypothesis is true or we are committing a Type II Error.

43. Both estimation (Chapter 6) and hypothesis testing (Chapter 7) involve the use of limits consisting of a number of standard errors. Distinguish between estimation and hypothesis testing in terms of (a) the value in the center of each interval and (b) the basic purpose of these two statistical procedures.

44. Assume that a null hypothesis for a two-tailed test is H_0: $\mu = 600$.

    (a) If the true value of the population mean is actually 600, give the two conclusions one might reach on the basis of the sample data. What type of error is made if H_0 is rejected?

    (b) If the true value of the population mean is actually 620, give the two conclusions one might reach on the basis of incomplete (sample) evidence. What type of error is made if H_0 is accepted when it is really false?

45. One year ago, the amount of third-class mail at Suffolk Station averaged 140 lbs./hr. The station can now apply for a budget increase if the rate exceeds 140 lbs./hr. State the null and alternative hypotheses that would be used by an analyst to test whether the weight of third-class mail processed per hour has increased over the last year.

46. In the last official ballot, 40% of high-income voters show a preference for a tax cut. A survey by a Republican pollster showed that 48% of the same voters favored a tax cut, whereas a survey by a Democratic pollster showed only 36%. State the null and alternative hypotheses for a test of whether the last official ballot figure of 40% is still accurate.

47. You are testing a hypothesis that a true mean is 400. You have found the standard error to be 2.0, and have established rejection limits at 394 and 406. If the true mean is actually 404, what is the probability of Type I Error?

48. You are conducting an upper-tailed test with a large sample and H_0: $\mu = 500$ and have calculated a standard error of 3.0. (a) What would be the action (reject) limit for $\alpha = .12$? (b) Suppose that $\overline{X} = 504.2$. Would H_0 be rejected? (c) What p-value corresponds to a sample test result of 504.2?

49. Suppose that a sample of 25 is drawn from a production process to perform a two-tailed test at the 5% level of significance to determine whether the mean production time of an item is 42.0 minutes. The results are $\overline{X} = 39.6$ and $s = 5$ minutes.

    (a) What sampling distribution would apply?

    (b) What reject values should be used?

    (c) Would a test at the .10 level of significance have wider acceptance limits?

    (d) Calculate the value of the test statistic and the p-value.

    (e) Should the null hypothesis be rejected?

50. Test the H_0: $\pi = .45$ against H_1: $\pi \neq .45$ at the 10% level, assuming that a sample of 300 resulted in p = .41.

51. Test the H_0: $\mu \geq 750$ hrs. against H_0: $\mu < 750$ at the $\alpha = 2.5\%$ level: (a) assuming a sample of n = 49 resulted in an $\bar{x} = 720$ hrs. and s = 70 hrs.; (b) assuming a sample of n = 9 resulted in an $\bar{X} = 720$ hrs. and s = 70 hrs. (c) Explain any differences in the conclusion from (a) and (b).

52. Set action or decision limits in each of the following cases, assuming that $\mu = 360.0$, $\sigma = 35.0$, and random samples are to be taken from an infinite population.

    (a) n = 100, probability of Type I Error specified at .05, both upper and lower limits

    (b) n = 100, probability of Type I Error specified at .01, with only an upper action limit

    (c) n = 400, probability of Type I Error specified at .05, and assuming that we are interested only in decreases in the true mean

    (d) n = 100, probability of Type II Error to be .05, if the true mean decreases to 352.0

53. Assume that a random sample was drawn from a population and the following data obtained: $\bar{X} = 224.2$, s = 28.0.

    (a) Make an estimate of the standard error of the mean if n = 400.

    (b) Test the null hypothesis H_0: $\mu = 225.0$ against the alternative H_1: $\mu \neq 225.0$ using the sample data and assuming a sample size of 400.

    (c) Make an estimate of the standard error of the mean for samples of 25.

    (d) Test the hypothesis of part (b), but assume the sample size was only 25.

    (e) Why did you use the t-distribution in part (d)?

    (f) Which line is used if n = 25?

    (g) Why can the standard normal distribution (area under the normal curve) be used when n is large?

54. A sample of 400 was drawn from a population with $\sigma = 16.0$. If the sample mean was 286, test the hypothesis H_0: $\mu = 290$; H_1: $\mu \neq 290$ (a) using the .01 level; (b) using the .05 level.

55. A manufacturer claims that his product never runs more than 10% below grade A. A random sample of 400, selected from a shipment of several hundred thousand, contained 52 units below grade A. Assume that we want to test the hypothesis H_0: $\pi \leq .10$ using the .05 level of significance.

    (a) What is a logical alternative hypothesis for an upper-tailed test?

    (b) What is σ_p?

    (c) Find:

    $$Z = \frac{p - \pi}{\sigma_p}$$

    (d) What is your conclusion?

    (e) Solve the problem assuming that there were only 2,000 in the total shipment.

56. A management analyst for a national health care firm is reviewing the time standard for their staff attendants to examine patients and prescribe some form of treatment. The firm has been allowing an average of 20 minutes. But, if the time required is significantly less than 20 minutes, there is too much

idle time; hence, the standard will be reduced. The data from a random sample of 53 patient times is contained in the file Exercise 7-56.xlsx.

(a) State the null and alternative hypotheses to test the claim that the mean time is less than 20 minutes.

(b) Would this sample data be sufficient to support the claim?

57. Chuck's Tea Company has been approached by a company that claims they have a more efficient machine to fill and seal his 1.05 oz. tea bags. They claim that the machine will reduce the variability of the fills while maintaining the average at 1.05 oz. The machine was brought in and used for two days in the production process. The fill weights of a random sample of 100 of the tea bags are contained in the file Exercise 7-57.xlsx. The standard deviation of the current equipment used to fill the bags is 0.08 oz. Do the sample results support the manufacturer's claims regarding the average and the variability of the fill weights? Test using a 0.05 significance level.

58. The Zendrophil Pharmaceutical Company has advertised a new pain reliever that claims to contain 50mg of Osakabitual as opposed to the 45mg contained in a competing brand. The CEO of the company that manufacturers the competing brand has complained to the FDA that the Zendrophil product does not contain 50mg as they claim. The FDA has taken a random sample of 150 pills from 150 different bottles sampled at random area drug stores. The amount of Osakabitual contained in each pill is contained in the file Exercise 7-58.xlsx. Should the FDA take action against Zendrophil for false advertising? Is there evidence in the sample that the Zendrophil contains any more of the active ingredient than the competing product?

59. According to the National Cattlemen's Beef Association (http://www.beefusa.org/beefindustrystatistics.aspx), the average consumption of beef in the United States in 2008 was 62.8 pounds per person per year and the annual consumption of chicken was 83.9 pounds. The Washington Fryer Commission has been conducting a Washington Grown Chicken campaign for several years. The Commission feels that this has led to an increase of chicken consumption in the state of Washington and a decrease in beef consumption. To test this, the Agricultural Economic group at a local university has conducted a survey of 30 Washington residents about their annual consumption of beef and chicken. The reported figures for beef and chicken consumption are provided in the file Exercise 7-59.xlsx.

(a) Do the data support the claim that beef consumption in Washington has declined since 2008? Test using a level of significance of .05.

(b) The standard deviation of annual beef consumption is thought to be about 10 pounds. Do the data support this?

(c) Do the survey data on chicken consumption support the belief that chicken consumption has increased since 2008?

60. A CEO in the hi-tech industry believes that the average salary in the industry is more than $55,000. Her assistant has gathered data from a random sample of 50 hi-tech employees in the area. The data are contained in the file Exercise 7-60.xlsx. Does the data support the CEO's claim?

Database Problems

Corporate Statistical Database

61. Test the following hypotheses at the .05 level of significance:

(a) The average price earnings ratio of all companies is $10.50 per share.

(b) The variance of the price earnings ratio of all companies is greater than 15.

62. The labor unions have claimed that corporations continue to downsize and outsource jobs overseas. They claim that the average number of employees has declined again this year. If the average number of employees was 15,000 last year, do the data support this claim?

63. An economist has claimed that the proportion of companies offering profit-sharing plans has gone down and is now less than 40%. Do the data support this claim at the .05 level of significance?

64. Assume that the banking and insurance firms listed in the Corporate Statistical Database of Appendix A constitute a random sample of the industry. Test the following hypotheses at the $\alpha = .05$ level:

    (a) The mean age of employees is 35 years old.

    (b) The average stock price in the industry is $37.00 or less.

    (c) Structure your test so that you can conclude that the annual dividend is more than $1.20 per share if you reject the null hypothesis

MegaCorp Employee Survey Database

65. The CEO of MegaCorp has been quoted in the local paper as saying that the average salary of nonmanagerial personnel at MegaCorp is $60,000. A journalist has called your office to see if you have data to back up this statement. From your sample, does the data indicate that the CEO's statement is not true?

66. The VP of HR is very concerned about the overall perception of employees about their benefits. From the data, can he be satisfied that the median perception of overall benefits is positive? (Hint: a rating of 4 is neutral).

67. Over lunch on Monday, you and the VP of HR had a discussion about the percentage of male and female employees at MegaCorp. He felt that there was about a 50-50 split while you felt that there was a slight majority of male employees. Do the sample data support your position at the .05 level of significance?

68. There has been some discussion in the senior ranks at MegaCorp about the "graying" of the workforce at MegaCorp. There is growing concern that the workforce at MegaCorp is getting older and that they need to start actively recruiting and retaining younger workers. The VP of Finance has asked to find out if the average age of the MegaCorp workers is over 40 years old. Is there evidence of this in the sample data?

Alaska Sport Fishing Survey

69. The Alaskan State Visitors Bureau is concerned that there are fewer people visiting Alaska on overnight fishing trips that there were 10 years ago. In a survey, the average number of overnight fishing trips that people had taken in the last five years was about 3.5. Do the data from the survey indicate that there may be a problem of fewer overnight visits to Alaska?

70. The State Tourist Business Association is concerned that the amount spent per trip has been declining even if the number of visitors has not. In the last survey conducted 10 years ago, it was found that the average amount spent on the last trip to Alaska was about $2,000. Do the data from the latest survey indicate that the Association should be concerned?

71. Historically, visitors for fishing trips to Alaska have been overwhelmingly male. In fact, in the last survey, the percentage of female respondents was only 5%. Is there any evidence in this survey that this percentage has changed?

72. The President of the State Visitors Bureau believes that there has been a trend toward more diverse groups coming to Alaska on fishing trips. In particular, she feels that although the average number of people per group may be the same, the variability in that number may have increased. The last survey indicated that the standard deviation of the number of people per group was about 6. Do the sample data substantiate the President's hunch?

Computing Type II Error and Power (Optional)

Thus far, we have concerned ourselves only with the α risk, or risk of Type I Error—which is the risk of rejecting the null hypothesis when it is true. For a two-tailed test, the hypothesis is true only when μ lies at the center of the sampling distribution. But for a one-tailed test, the hypothesis is also true for points below (for an upper-tailed test) or above (for a lower-tailed test) the mean.

Type II Error

We noted earlier that a Type II Error is accepting a null hypothesis when it is false. We quantify that risk as the probability or area of the sampling distribution that lies within the acceptance limits when the null hypothesis is false; however, to compute the Type II Error, one must first specify what the (true) value of the population parameter is. That is, each Type II Error calculation pertains to only one possible value of the true mean, proportion, variance, or median.

Let us illustrate this with an example (refer to Example 7-10) concerning the mean weight of luggage taken on an airline. Luggage weight is a critical variable for air carriers because it affects both the load on the aircraft engines and the amount of fuel needed to transport that load. For this example, suppose that we are interested in the chance of accepting a hypothesis that the mean weight of passenger luggage is 34 lbs. when it is actually some value heavier than that, say 35 lbs.

In Example 7-20, the probability of a Type II Error is quite high and therefore the power is fairly low. Recalling that the power of a test is $1 - \beta$, the power in this case is .252. In other words, there is a relatively low probability of rejecting the null hypothesis if the true mean weight is 35 lbs. But, there are also many other possible values of the true mean. It might be 25 lbs., 35 lbs., or perhaps even 65 lbs. Therefore, there are many possible values of Type II Error, as well. Each is a response to a "what if . . ." question, such as "What if the true mean is really X lbs.? Then, what is the probability of still accepting the hypothesis that it is 34 lbs.?" Hopefully, it is intuitively clear that the chance of a Type II Error would increase, the closer the true mean is to the hypothesized value of 34 lbs. Conversely, the closer the true mean is the hypothesized value, the lower the power of the test to correctly reject the null hypothesis.

Example 7-20

An airline baggage manager is testing the hypothesis that the true mean weight of baggage per passenger is 34.0 lbs., and has established rejection limits at $C_1 = 32.5$ lbs. and $C_2 = 35.5$ lbs. (The standard error was found to be .75 lbs.). What is the probability of Type II Error if the true (but unknown) mean is actually 35.0 lbs.?

Solution

A Type II Error can be committed because the true mean weight is really $\mu = 35.0$ lbs. instead of the hypothesized value of 34.0 lbs. The probability of Type II Error is equal to the area under the sampling distribution centered upon 35.0 lbs. that lies within the acceptance region from 32.5 lbs. to 35.5 lbs.

H_0: $\mu = 34.0$ lbs.

H_1: $\mu \neq 34.0$ lbs.

Computation of Type II Error   (If True $\mu = 35.0$ lbs.)

We can use the probability calculator in XLDataAnalyst or the NORMDIST function in Excel to calculate this probability. We need the area between 32.5 and 35.5 in a normal distribution with a mean of 35 lbs. and a standard error of .75.

$$\beta = \text{NORMDIST}(35.5, 35, .75, \text{TRUE} - \text{NORMDIST}(32.5, 35, .75, \text{TRUE}) =$$

$$.748 - .000 = .748$$

Example 7-21 carries forward with the calculation of several values of Type II Error:

Example 7-21

To illustrate the relationship between the true value of the population mean and the probability of a Type II error and power, calculate the probability of a Type II error for true mean values of 34.5 and 35.5.

Solution

$\mu = 34.5$

$$\beta = \text{NORMDIST}(35.5, 34.5, .75, \text{TRUE}) - \text{NORMDIST}(32.5, 34.5, .75, \text{TRUE})$$

$$= .909 - .004 = .905$$

$\mu = 35.5$

$$\beta = \text{NORMDIST}(35.5, 35.5, .75, \text{TRUE}) - \text{NORMDIST}(32.5, 35.5, .75, \text{TRUE})$$

$$= .500 - .000 = .500$$

From these two examples we can see that the probability of a Type II Error goes up (from .748 to .905) as the true value of the population mean gets closer to the hypothesized value and the probability of a Type II Error goes down (from .748 to .500) as the true value of the population mean moves away from the hypothesized value . Obviously, there are an infinite number of values for the probability of a Type II Error (and therefore of power) since there are an infinite number of possible values for the true population parameter. Since we are most interested in rejecting the null hypothesis, the focus is usually on the power rather than the probability of an error. Statisticians sometimes calculate enough of these values so that they can plot a curve of the probabilities of rejecting the null hypothesis as a function of the true values of the population parameter. Such a graph is called a power curve.

> A power curve is a graph showing a probability (or power) of rejecting a null hypothesis for different values of the true population parameter. Its probabilities are computed as $1 - \beta$.

Exercises

73. You are testing a hypothesis that a true mean is 400, have found the standard error to be 2.0, and have established rejection limits at 394 and 406. If the true mean is actually 407, what is the probability of Type II Error?

74. The accounting activity in a Savings and Loan is being studied and the analyst wishes to test the H_0: $\mu = 10.0$ minutes against H_1: $\mu < 10.0$ minutes at the $\alpha = .05$ level. The analyst uses a sample of 64 observations and finds that $s = 2.4$ minutes. If the true mean is actually 9.0 minutes, what is (a) the probability of Type II Error, and (b) the power of the test to reject a false null hypothesis?

Chapter 8:

Testing Hypotheses: Two-Sample Tests

Chapter 8 Objectives

When you finish this chapter you should be able to:

1. **Explain the difference between dependent and independent samples**
2. **Test the difference between:**
   - **Two independent means**
   - **Two independent proportions**
   - **Two independent variances**
   - **Two independent medians**
   - **Two dependent means**
   - **Two dependent proportions**
   - **Two dependent medians**
3. **Develop confidence interval estimates of the differences**

Opening Vignette

Ray Bezel is plant manager for Xorsky, a company that manufactures mechanical products used in the landing gear of airplanes. Ray is concerned about defects produced on the plant floor and the overall level of efficiency within the plant. One particular bottleneck in the facility is a machine that produces parts with high defect rates. A lot of time and energy is spent searching these parts for defects.

At a recent corporate meeting, a manager from another division suggested that Ray might want to look into a new piece of equipment that he had seen at a recent technology show. This machine is supposed to dramatically reduce defects and operate at a higher volume than their current machine. While the machine is expensive, it would be worth it to Xorsky to reduce delays on the floor. The next day, Ray contacts the manufacturer of the new machine and arranges to have one of the machines brought in for testing.

After the machine is set up and operating, the foreman started up the machine that Xorsky is currently using and produced 100 parts side-by-side using both machines. The parts produced by the old machine have 18 defective parts out of the one hundred produced. In contrast, the new machine only has 10 defects out of one hundred parts. Should this evidence convince Ray that the newer machine will produce fewer defective parts over the whole population?

The Logic of Two-Sample Tests[1]

The central theme of this chapter is the analysis of the differences between two groups. One of the most common questions in statistics entails: Is there a statistically-significant difference between the means (proportions, variances, or medians) of two groups? We generally begin with a null hypothesis of no difference, which is another way of stating that the two samples are both from a population having the same mean, μ (proportion, π, variance, σ^2, or median, η). Then, we let the data speak for itself, at a specified level of significance. This allows us to draw statistically-valid conclusions that take the risks of error into account.

In this introductory section, we review the theory underlying the test of differences of two-samples. Recall that in Chapter 7, we learned how to complete tests with one sample group. In the next section, we will introduce the distinction between independent and dependent samples. We will then discuss tests for

---

[1] The phrase "two samples" is used generically. It means there are two different groups that may or may not be from different samples. For example, if we divide a sample into males and females, it would be a two-sample (group) test even though they come from one original sample.

the differences between two independent samples for the four parameters (means, proportions, variances and medians). Next, we will introduce tests for differences between dependent samples for means, proportions and medians. Lastly, we will discuss how to use Excel and XLDataAnalyst to conduct these tests. After completing this chapter, (in addition to Chapter 7 on one-group tests), you should have a comprehensive understanding of both the theory and the practice of hypothesis tests.

> Sample statistics, be it mean, proportion, variance or median, from two different samples, are almost never equal, even if taken from exactly the same population. Therefore, how do we tell if the difference between two sample statistics is simply due to sampling error or if there is a real difference in the populations from which the samples are drawn? Intuitively, we know that if there is a very large difference between, for example, two sample means, then the means of the two groups in the population (μ_1 and μ_2) are probably not equal. Conversely, if the two sample means are very nearly equal, there is probably no real difference between the means of the two populations.

The logic for two-sample tests is very similar to that used for one-sample tests in Chapter 7. Recall that for one-sample tests, we determined the likelihood of observing a sample statistic, if the null hypothesis is true (the p-value). If the observed sample statistic is too different from the hypothesized population value, based on the sampling distribution of the test statistic, then we concluded that the sample statistic did not come from the hypothesized population and we rejected the null hypothesis. Here, we examine the likelihood of the difference between two sample statistics and if the difference is too great (level of significance is high) to be attributed to chance, we conclude that it is probably due to a real difference between the groups in the population. That difference would be considered *statistically significant.*

The theory underlying the tests of differences is similar to that used for one-sample tests based on our knowledge of the sampling distribution of means ($\bar{X}$), medians (M), proportions (p) and variances (s^2). Now, instead of the sampling distribution for one sample statistic we will be interested in the sampling distribution for the differences between two sample means ($\bar{X}_1 - \bar{X}_2$), the difference between two sample medians ($M_1 - M_2$), the difference in two proportions ($p_1 - p_2$) or the ratio of two sample variances (s_1^2/s_2^2). We will use test statistics from standard probability distributions for the sampling distributions.

Independent versus Dependent Samples

When testing for the differences between two groups, we need to specify whether the samples are from totally unrelated groups, e.g., *independent samples*, or whether the two samples are related in some way, e.g., *dependent samples*. Dependent samples can arise when we measure the same elements at two different points in time. For example, we may wish to evaluate the change in performance of employees attending a communications seminar. To accomplish this, we obtain performance data on each employee before and after the seminar to see if there is a difference. Dependent samples can also arise when the elements in the two groups are paired or matched on the basis of some characteristic. For example, to test two different point-of-sale displays we might want to put each display in several different stores and look at average sales for the two displays. Since we know that the overall volume of sales in the stores would impact sales of the products that we are displaying, we might want to match the stores in the two groups on the basis of store volume.

What does pairing accomplish? It enables us to eliminate (or minimize) the extraneous differences and focus specifically upon the differences of interest. By controlling for individual differences or environmental effects, the difference under study becomes less affected. Dependent samples offer more powerful tests than independent samples and are to be preferred when possible; however, independent samples (where samples are totally unrelated) are more common in statistics because of the difficulties with before & after designs and the lack of natural characteristics on which to match elements in most situations.

Figure 8-1   *Sampling Distributions of Differences*

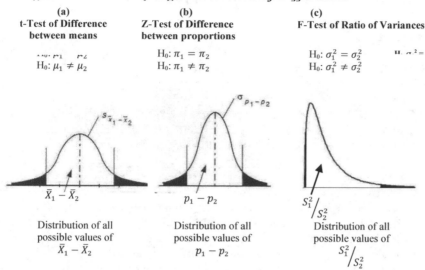

(a)	(b)	(c)
t-Test of Difference between means	**Z-Test of Difference between proportions**	**F-Test of Ratio of Variances**

$H_0: \mu_1 \neq \mu_2$ $H_0: \pi_1 = \pi_2$ $H_0: \sigma_1^2 = \sigma_2^2$

$H_0: \pi_1 \neq \pi_2$ $H_0: \sigma_1^2 \neq \sigma_2^2$

Distribution of all possible values of $\bar{X}_1 - \bar{X}_2$

Distribution of all possible values of $p_1 - p_2$

Distribution of all possible values of S_1^2 / S_2^2

Comparisons Using Two Independent Samples

Difference between Two Means

In comparing two means, we are assuming that the sample sizes, n_1, and n_2, are both taken randomly from populations that are normally distributed, and that the samples are independent. To compute the population standard error requires a knowledge of σ but, as we did in Chapter 7, we can use s as an estimator of σ and $s_{\bar{X}}$ as an estimator of $\sigma_{\bar{X}}$ when σ is unknown.

Test Statistic

The test statistic used for testing differences in means from two independent samples is similar in form to the one-sample statistic. In Chapter 7, the general form for the test for means was:

$$Test\ statistic = \frac{Sample\ Statistic - Population\ parameter}{Standard\ error}$$

where the test statistic was either a Z or a t, the sample statistic was the sample mean, and the population parameter was the population mean. Now, instead of $\bar{X}$ our sample statistic is $(\bar{X}_1 - \bar{X}_2)$ where the two sample means come from the individual means from our two groups of sample data. The population parameter is the hypothesized difference between the parameters in the population. The most typical situation is when the hypothesized difference is zero:

$$H_0: \mu_1 - \mu_2 = \text{no difference}$$

Stating the test statistic in terms of differences, we have:

$$Z\ or\ t = \frac{Observed\ sample\ difference - Hypothesized\ population\ difference}{Standard\ error\ of\ the\ difference} \qquad (8\text{-}1)$$

where the standard error of the difference is computed by combining the variances of the two samples. As before, the designation of $\sigma_{\bar{X}_1-\bar{X}_2}$ or $S_{\bar{X}_1-\bar{X}_2}$ depends on whether the population standard deviations are known or not.

Tests when σ Known

Analogous to the one-sample case, the test statistic, when σ is known is:

$$Z = \frac{(\bar{X}_1-\bar{X}_2)-(\mu_1-\mu_2)}{\sigma_{\bar{X}_1-\bar{X}_2}} \qquad (8\text{-}2)$$

where $\sigma_{\bar{X}_1-\bar{X}_2}$ is the standard error of the difference between means, calculated as:

$$\sigma_{\bar{X}_1-\bar{X}_2} = \sqrt{\frac{\sigma_1^2}{n_1} + \frac{\sigma_2^2}{n_2}} \qquad (8\text{-}3)$$

Since it is extremely rare that we would know the population variances of both groups, we will proceed to the more likely situation where the population standard deviations are not known.

Tests when σ Unknown

The hypotheses can be stated either as:

Form 1: H_0: $\mu_1 = \mu_2$ or H_0: $\mu_1 - \mu_2 = 0$

Form 2: H_1: $\mu_1 \neq \mu_2$ H_1: $\mu_1 - \mu_2 \neq 0$

Both statements are the same; however, tests can be conducted for differences of any specific numerical amount, such as 10 lbs. If a specific numerical difference other than zero is hypothesized, then the second form must be used.

For the more typical situation where σ is unknown, the t-distribution is the correct distribution to describe the differences in means:

$$t = \frac{(\bar{X}_1-\bar{X}_2)-(\mu_1-\mu_2)}{S_{\bar{X}_1-\bar{X}_2}} \qquad (8\text{-}4)$$

In the equation above, $S_{\bar{X}_1-\bar{X}_2}$ is the expression for the estimated standard error of the difference between the means, as calculated from the available sample data. There are two different t-tests, depending on the assumptions we make about the population variances. The first case assumes that the population variances are equal:

Assuming Equal Variances

Tests of the difference between means generally assume that both samples are from normally distributed populations, and that the populations have equal variances. In this case, the t-distribution is the appropriate test statistic; however, insofar as t-distribution values are affected by the sample size, and the samples from the two groups may be of different sizes, the standard error is calculated from a "pooled" or combined estimate of the sample variances, designated S_{Pooled}^2:

Pooled Variance Estimate: $S_{Pooled}^2 = \frac{(n_1-1)S_1^2+(n_2-1)S_2^2}{n_1+n_2-2}$ $\qquad (8\text{-}5)$

Note that the pooled variance is simply a weighted average of the two sample variances where the weights are the degrees of freedom in each sample[2]. Once the pooled estimate has been computed, the standard error of the difference between means is computed as:

Connects to last page →

$$s_{\bar{X}_1 - \bar{X}_2} = \sqrt{\frac{s^2_{Pooled}}{n_1} + \frac{s^2_{Pooled}}{n_2}}$$

(8-6)

The t-test statistic has a t-distribution with $(n_1 - 1) + (n_2 - 1) = n_1 + n_2 - 2$ degrees of freedom.

It may be helpful to illustrate the procedure by beginning with some original observations and carrying them through the testing procedure in a step-by-step fashion. Although we will prefer to let the computer perform the calculations, a manual calculation may help illustrate the connection with the previous chapters.

In the example that follows, we conduct a test to determine whether two population means are significantly different. First, we obtain a sample from each population and compute their means and standard deviations. Then, we follow the standard testing procedure. We (1) set up our null hypothesis concerning μ_1 and μ_2, (2) state our α level, (3) calculate the t-statistic using pooled sample variances and calculate the p-value. Finally, (4), we draw a conclusion.

Example 8-1

An automobile manufacturer in Italy is experiencing production delays because their engine supplier is unreliable. The firm can improve their delivery schedule and reduce their costs if they had a more reliable supplier. Top management has established that engineering can use an alternative supplier in Germany rather than the current supplier provided the gas mileage of both engines is the same. The problem is to demonstrate this similarity.

To help make the decision, engineering team acquires and installs the current supplier's engines in nine cars and the German engines in seven cars and collects data on the gas mileage under normal driving conditions. The data are shown in the following table, along with the deviations used to compute the variance of each sample. Test the hypothesis that the mileages are equal at the 5% level of significance.

	Current Supplier Motor Test				German Supplier Motor Test		
Motor no.	mpg x_1	$(x_1 - \bar{X}_1)$	$(x_1 - \bar{X}_1)^2$	Motor no.	mpg x_2	$(x_2 - \bar{X}_2)$	$(x_2 - \bar{X}_2)^2$
1	28	−3	9	1	25	−3	9
2	29	−2	4	2	27	−1	1
3	29	−2	4	3	27	−1	1
4	30	−1	1	4	28	0	0
5	31	0	0	5	28	0	0
6	32	1	1	6	30	2	4
7	33	2	4	7	31	3	9
8	33	2	4				
9	34	3	9				
Total	279		36	Total	196		24

Solution

$$\bar{X}_1 = \frac{279}{9} = 31.0 \quad \bar{X}_2 = \frac{196}{7} = 28.0$$

$$s_1^2 = \frac{\Sigma(X_{1_i} - \bar{X}_1)^2}{n_1 - 1} = \frac{36}{8} = 4.5 \quad s_2^2 = \frac{\Sigma(X_{2_i} - \bar{X}_2)^2}{n_2 - 1} = \frac{24}{6} = 4.0$$

1. H_0: $\mu_1 = \mu_2$

---

[2] Refer to Chapter 3 for a discussion on weighted averages.

H_1: $\mu_1 \neq \mu_2$

2.　　$\alpha = .05$

3. $S^2_{Pooled} = \dfrac{(n_1-1)s_1^2 + (n_2-1)s_2^2}{n_1+n_2-2} = \dfrac{(9-1)(4.5)+(7-1)(4.0)}{9+7-2} = 4.2857$

then

$$S_{\bar{X}_1-\bar{X}_2} = \sqrt{\dfrac{S^2_{Pooled}}{n_1} + \dfrac{S^2_{Pooled}}{n_2}} = \sqrt{\dfrac{4.2857}{9} + \dfrac{4.2857}{7}} = 1.04328$$

and

$$t = \dfrac{(\bar{X}_1 - \bar{X}_2) - (\mu_1 - \mu_2)}{S_{\bar{X}_1-\bar{X}_2}} = \dfrac{(31.0 - 28.0) - 0}{1.04328} = 2.8755$$

4. The p-value can be calculated using XLDataAnalyst recalling that the degrees of freedom in this case are $n_1 + n_2 - 2$. The p-value is $2(.0061) = .0122$.

5. Conclusion: Since the p-value of .0122 is less than .05, we can reject H_0: $\mu_1 = \mu_2$. The difference of 3.00 mpg would occur by chance less than 2% of the time if there were no real difference. Therefore, we conclude that the difference is not just due to sampling error, and that there is a statistically-significant difference in the gas mileages.

Good example where σ is not known (handwritten margin note)

Tests When the Variances Are Not Equal

When the variances, σ_1^2 and σ_2^2, cannot be assumed to be equal, the $(\bar{X}_1 - \bar{X}_2)$ difference still has a t-distribution and the t-statistic is calculated in the same way as in Equation 8-4; however, note that we calculate the standard error differently because we no longer assume that the variances are equal.

Not assuming equal variances:　　$S_{\bar{X}_1-\bar{X}_2} = \sqrt{\dfrac{s_1^2}{n_1} + \dfrac{s_2^2}{n_2}}$　　　　(8-7)

The degrees of freedom also require an adjustment and are a little more complicated in this situation; they are calculated as:

$$df = \dfrac{\left(\dfrac{s_1^2}{n_1} + \dfrac{s_2^2}{n_2}\right)^2}{\dfrac{\left(\dfrac{s_1^2}{n_1}\right)^2}{(n_1-1)} + \dfrac{\left(\dfrac{s_2^2}{n_2}\right)^2}{(n_2-1)}} \qquad (8-8)$$

With these adjustments, the test proceeds exactly as before.

Example 8-2

To illustrate the calculations, let's return to the situation in Example 8-1 but this time we will not assume that the population variances are equal.

Solution

Our previous calculations showed the following:

1.　　$\bar{X}_1 = \dfrac{279}{9} = 31.0$　　$\bar{X}_2 = \dfrac{196}{7} = 28.0$

　　　$s_1^2 = \dfrac{\Sigma(X_1 - \bar{X}_1)^2}{n_1 - 1} = \dfrac{36}{8} = 4.5$　　$s_2^2 = \dfrac{\Sigma(X_2 - \bar{X}_2)^2}{n_2 - 1} = \dfrac{6}{1} = 4.0$... (displayed as $= 6 = 4.0$)

2.　　H_0: $\mu_1 = \mu_2$

　　　H_1: $\mu_1 \neq \mu_2$

3.　　$\alpha = .05$

4. $$s_{\bar{X}_1 - \bar{X}_2} = \sqrt{\frac{s_1^2}{n_1} + \frac{s_2^2}{n_2}} = \sqrt{\frac{4.5}{9} + \frac{4.0}{7}} = 1.035$$

The degrees of freedom are calculated as:

$$df = \frac{\left(\frac{s_1^2}{n_1} + \frac{s_2^2}{n_2}\right)^2}{\frac{\left(\frac{s_1^2}{n_1}\right)^2}{(n_1 - 1)} + \frac{\left(\frac{s_2^2}{n_2}\right)^2}{(n_2 - 1)}} = \frac{\left(\frac{4.5}{9} + \frac{4.0}{7}\right)^2}{\frac{\left(\frac{4.5}{9}\right)^2}{(9 - 1)} + \frac{\left(\frac{4.5}{7}\right)^2}{(7 - 1)}} = 13.3995 \approx 13$$

Use t-distribution with 13 df:

$$t = \frac{(\bar{X}_1 - \bar{X}_2) - (\mu_1 - \mu_2)}{s_{\bar{X}_1 - \bar{X}_2}} = \frac{(31.0 - 28.0) - 0}{1.035} = 2.898$$

5. The p-value can be calculated using XLDataAnalyst. The p-value is 2(.0062) = .0125.

6. Conclusion: Since the p-value of .0125 is less than .05, we can reject H_0: $\mu_1 = \mu_2$. The difference of 3.00 mpg would occur by chance less than 2% of the time if there were no real difference in the population. Therefore, we conclude that the difference is not just due to sampling error, and that there is a statistically-significant difference in the average gas mileage of engines supplied by the current supplier and the German supplier.

Notice that the t-statistics are very similar in the two situations and the p-values are also very close. This is generally the case. Rarely does it make a difference in our conclusions whether or not we assume that the variances are equal; however, in certain cases (where the variances and the sample sizes of the two groups are very different) we can arrive at different conclusions with the two tests. For this reason, most statistical software, including XLDataAnalyst, will perform both tests. As we will see later, there is also a standard test to see if the two variances are in fact equal. XLDataAnalyst and most statistical software will also automatically perform that test as part of the test for the two means.

Confidence Interval Estimate for the Difference Between Two Means

When a hypothesis is rejected (and we conclude the population means are different), we may wish to establish a confidence interval estimate for the true difference between the two population means. The procedure is similar to setting a confidence interval for one sample mean, but in this case we establish an interval about the *difference* in means and we use the standard error to help set the width of this interval:

CL for $(\mu_1 - \mu_2)$ $\qquad\qquad$ $(\bar{X}_1 - \bar{X}_2) \pm t_{\alpha/2, df} s_{\bar{X}_1 - \bar{X}_2}$ $\qquad\qquad$ (8-9)

When calculating confidence intervals for small samples (generally smaller than 25 or 30) the standard error using the pooled variance should be used since the sample sizes are not large enough to provide adequate estimates of the separate variances.

Example 8-3

Establish a 95% confidence interval estimate for the true mean difference in gas mileage from Example 8-1, where $(\bar{X}_1 - \bar{X}_2)$ = 3.0 mpg, and $s_{\bar{X}_1 - \bar{X}_2}$ = 1.04328.

Solution

$$(\bar{X}_1 - \bar{X}_2) \pm t_{\frac{\alpha}{2}, df} S_{\bar{X}_1 - \bar{X}_2} = 3.0 \pm 2.144787 \ (1.04328)$$

$$= .762 \text{ to } 5.238 \text{ mpg}$$

We can be 95% confident that the true difference in gas mileage consumption in the two companies lies within the interval from 0.76 to 5.2 mpg. The fact that the 95% confidence interval for the difference between the two means does not include zero adds to the validity of our earlier test that the difference is significant.

Exercises I

1. Suppose that you wanted to test whether there was a difference in the planned increase in employment over the next six months in the electronics industry versus the auto industry. What null and alternative hypotheses would be appropriate?

2. In what way is the theory applied to tests of differences similar to the theory used for one-sample tests?

3. A restaurant franchiser considering two locations for a new restaurant has obtained the following data from random samples of two metropolitan areas:

	Location A	Location B
No firms sampled	150	95
Average hourly pay	$8.60	$9.10
Standard deviation	1.00	2.40

    Test whether there is a statistically-significant difference in the hourly pay at the two locations. Let $\alpha = .10$.

4. Compute the appropriate standard error for a test of differences given the following data: (i) $s_1 = 8$, $n_1 = 80$, $s_2 = 12$, $n_2 = 120$; (ii) $s_1 = 40$, $n_1 = 15$, $s_2 = 50$, $n_2 = 25$.

5. Office Products Co. is planning a nationwide marketing campaign and would like to determine whether the investment in computing and data transmission equipment by West Coast small businesses differs from Southeast small businesses. A survey of 35 western firms revealed they had an average of $12,820 invested in PCs, printers, answering machines, and computer modems (with $s = \$8,400$). The comparable survey of 40 southeastern firms yielded an average of $16,060, with $s = \$6,200$.

    (a) Without doing any computations, do the true mean investments appear to be different?

    (b) Test at the $\alpha = .01$ level to determine if the mean investments in the two regions are significantly different.

    (c) Would your conclusion be different if the $\alpha = .05$ level were used?

    (d) Explain any differences in your answer to (a) and your results from (b) and (c). What effect have the standard deviations of the data sets had on your conclusion?

    (e) What is the p-value for this test?

6. Crescent Machine Shop, experimenting with two methods of welding, found that it took 245 minutes to complete 75 parts using method 1, and 135 minutes to complete 45 parts using method 2. The standard deviations were $s_1 = .2$ minutes/part and $s_2 = .4$ minutes/part. (a) Test whether there is a real difference in the mean time to weld a part at the $\alpha = .01$ level. (b) If your difference in part (a) is significant, establish a 95% confidence interval for the amount of difference in the two methods.

7. A purchasing agent has tested (and rejected) a hypothesis that the prices for selected building materials are the same in Denver and Atlanta. If the difference between mean prices per unit at the two locations is $3.65 per ton and the standard error of difference is $0.42 per ton, construct a 96% confidence interval of the difference.

8. Statistics students at two state universities in Michigan were randomly selected and given similar exams. At university 1, where 50 students were tested, the average score was 82 with a standard deviation of 8, whereas at university 2, where 40 students were tested, the average score was 88 with a standard deviation of 6. Test whether the difference in performance between students in the two universities is significant at the 2% level.

Difference between Two Proportions

To test for a difference between two proportions, we must decide whether the difference observed in two independent sample proportions is large enough to stem from a real difference between the populations. There are two different tests for the difference between two proportions. The first is similar to Chapter 7 where we assume that the sample size is large and that we can use the normal approximation to the binomial. The second test does not use the normal approximation, but utilizes the chi-square distribution in a very different way.

Tests for Independent Samples Using Z

In this section, we are assuming that the sample sizes are relatively large so that the normal approximation can be used. Small-sample procedures are not commonly used here because a precise estimate of a proportion requires a reasonably large sample, usually of 100 or more. The hypothesis being tested is that the two population proportions are equal:

$$H_0: \pi_1 = \pi_2 \qquad \text{or} \qquad H_0: \pi_1 - \pi_2 = 0$$

$$H_1: \pi_1 \neq \pi_2 \qquad \qquad H_1: \pi_1 - \pi_2 \neq 0$$

The statistic for testing the difference in proportions from large independent samples is:

$$Z = \frac{(p_1 - p_2) - (\pi_1 - \pi_2)}{S_{p_1 - p_2}} \qquad\qquad (8\text{-}10)$$

In this equation, $(\pi_1 - \pi_2)$ is typically hypothesized to be zero, and $S_{p_1 - p_2}$ is the estimated standard error of the difference between the two proportions.

Finding the Standard Error

Recall that for the tests of two independent means we had two different tests: one that assumed that the population variances were equal and one that did not. For proportions, the variance is a function of the proportion and is equal to $\pi(1-\pi)$. In this case, the variance depends on the proportion. Since we are using sample data, we have only the sample values of p_1 and p_2 rather than the population proportions. The question is whether to use the two proportions separately to calculate the standard error (analogous to the unequal variances t-test) or to pool them in a common estimate and use the pooled value to calculate the standard error (analogous to the equal variance t-test). This leads to two different calculations of the standard error.

Pooled Estimate: With the pooled estimate, we combine the data from the two samples for a single estimate of the true value of the population proportion rather than the individual sample estimates. The combined estimate (in the forms for both proportions and for raw counts) is:

$$\text{Using Proportions:} \qquad \bar{p} = \frac{n_1(p_1) + n_2(p_2)}{n_1 + n_2}$$

Using Counts:

$$\bar{p} = \frac{x_1 + x_2}{n_1 + n_2}$$

where x_1 and x_2 are the number of successes in samples 1 and 2, respectively. Given this weighted estimate $\bar{p}$, we can then combine the samples in the calculation of the estimated standard error of the difference:

$$S_{p_1-p_2} = \sqrt{\frac{\bar{p}(1-\bar{p})}{n_1} + \frac{\bar{p}(1-\bar{p})}{n_2}} \quad \text{proportions are equal} \quad (8\text{-}11)$$

This pooled estimate of the standard error makes sense when testing the null hypothesis that the two population proportions are equal, e.g., that their difference is zero; however, suppose we want to test the hypothesis that the difference between the population proportions is something other than zero or that we want a confidence interval estimate of the difference between the population proportions. In this case, the pooled estimate does not work as we are not assuming that the population proportions are equal; thus, we should use the separate sample proportions to calculate the standard error:

$$S_{p_1-p_2} = \sqrt{\frac{p_1(1-p_1)}{n_1} + \frac{p_2(1-p_2)}{n_2}} \quad \text{difference other than zero} \quad (8\text{-}12)$$

The standard error that we use will depend on the situation. If we are testing a hypothesis that the population proportions are equal, use Equation 8-11 to calculate the standard error of the difference. If we are calculating a confidence interval or testing for a difference other than zero, use Equation 8-12.

Example 8-4

A manufacturer of computers has two suppliers for a keyboard component. Supplier A has a very compact unit and a lower price, whereas supplier B is in a better location and can respond faster to changing delivery requirements. A test for defects in random samples of 400 units from each supplier revealed the following:

	Supplier A	Supplier B
No. of units	$n_1 = 400$	$n_2 = 400$
No. of defectives	$x_1 = 82$	$x_2 = 94$
Percent defective	$p_1 = 82/400 = .205$	$p_2 = 94/400 = .235$

The difference in defects is rather small (3%), and the manufacturer wishes to test whether the proportion defective from each supplier is equal, or (alternatively) whether the difference is statistically significant at the 5% level.

Solution

1. $H_0: \pi_1 = \pi_2$

    $H_1: \pi_1 = \pi_2$

2. $\alpha = .05$

3. Use normal distribution, where $(p_1 - p_2) = .205 - .235 = -.03 \quad (\pi_1 \quad \pi_2) = 0$

4. Since the hypothesis assumes a zero difference, pool the sample proportions to calculate the standard error.

$$\bar{p} = \frac{x_1 + x_2}{n_1 + n_2} = \frac{82 + 94}{800} = .220$$

and

$$S_{p_1-p_2} = \sqrt{\frac{\bar{p}(1-\bar{p})}{n_1} + \frac{\bar{p}(1-\bar{p})}{n_2}} = \sqrt{\frac{(.22)(.78)}{400} + \frac{(.22)(.78)}{400}} = .0293$$

$$Z = \frac{(-.03)- 0}{.0293} = -1.024$$

5. The p-value can be calculated with NORMDIST(-1.024,0,1,TRUE) which would give a result of .3058.

6. Conclusion: Do not reject the hypothesis of equal proportions because the p-value is .3058, which is greater than .05. We cannot conclude that there is a statistically significant difference in the proportion of defective keyboard components from the two suppliers.

Confidence Interval for the Difference between Two Proportions

A confidence interval for the difference between two proportions can be established by following the standard confidence interval procedure:

$$CL \text{ for } (\pi_1 - \pi_2) \qquad\qquad (p_1 - p_2) \pm Zs_{p_1-p_2} \qquad\qquad (8\text{-}13)$$

Since we are not assuming that the population proportions are equal, there is no reason to combine the data to get a weighted estimate of π. The standard error of the difference is estimated directly from Equation 8-12.

Example 8-5

Construct a 95% confidence interval for the data from Example 8-4.

Solution

Recall that in a sample of 400 units, supplier A had 82 defects ($p_1 = .205$) and supplier B had 94 defects ($p_2 = .235$). Therefore:

$$S_{p_1-p_2} = \sqrt{\frac{(.205)(1 - .205)}{400} + \frac{(.235)(1 - .235)}{400}} = .02927$$

$$(p_1 - p_2) \pm Zs_{p_1-p_2}$$
$$= (.205 - .235) \pm 1.96(.02927)$$
$$= -.057 \text{ to } .027$$

Notice that the confidence interval includes zero which agrees with our hypothesis test where we were not able to reject the null hypothesis that there is no difference between the two proportions.

The Chi-Square Test for Proportions

There is another way of testing the hypothesis that two population proportions are equal. Although both methods provide equivalent results, there are advantages and disadvantages to each. The second method for testing hypotheses about proportions utilizes the chi-square distribution; however, this is entirely different from the way in which we have used the chi-square distribution up to this point. This utilizes what are called contingency tables. We previously introduced contingency tables in Chapter 2 when we discussed the relationship between two qualitative variables. Recall that contingency tables are tables of frequencies where the frequencies are classified by two other nominal scale variables. Such tables have many other uses as we will see later. Table 8-1 gives the contingency table for Example 8-4.

Table 8-1   ***Table of Actual Frequencies from Example 8-4***

Supplier	Defective	Not Defective	Total
A	82	318	400
B	94	306	400
Total	176	624	800

The chi-square test for contingency tables involves comparing observed frequencies to what we would expect under the null hypothesis. Recall that we calculated the pooled proportion of defectives as:

$$\bar{p} = \frac{x_1 + x_2}{n_1 + n_2} = \frac{82 + 94}{800} = .220$$

If the null hypothesis is true, $H_0: \pi_1 = \pi_2$, then we would expect the sample proportions for both suppliers to be about 0.22. In terms of frequencies, we would expect about 400(.220) = 88 defectives from both suppliers. Using this logic, Table 8-2 gives the expected frequencies based on the null hypothesis. In general terms, the expected frequencies can be calculated as the row total multiplied by the column total divided by the overall sample size.

If we let R_i be the row total and C_j be the column total, and n be the overall sample size, then the expected frequency (denoted f_e) is computed as:

Expected Frequency: $\qquad\qquad\qquad f_e = \frac{R_i C_j}{n}$ $\qquad\qquad$ *(8-14)*

Table 8-2   ***Table of Expected Frequencies from Example 8-4***

Supplier	Defective	Not Defective	Total
A	88	312	400
B	88	312	400
Total	176	624	800

The closer the actual frequencies are to the expected frequencies, the more likely it is that the null hypothesis is true. If the null hypothesis is false ($\pi_1 \neq \pi_2$), then the actual frequencies should differ from the expected frequencies. The chi-square statistic is based on this logic and is calculated as:

Chi-Square Statistic: $\qquad\qquad\qquad \chi^2 = \sum \frac{(f_o - f_e)^2}{f_e}$ $\qquad\qquad$ *(8-15)*

where f_e is the expected frequency in each cell and f_o is the observed frequency. For our example, the calculations are:

$$\chi^2 = \frac{(82-88)^2}{88} + \frac{(318-312)^2}{312} + \frac{(94-88)^2}{88} + \frac{(306-312)^2}{312} = 1.048951$$

But, how do we determine whether this is evidence in favor of or against the null hypothesis? For this we need to know the p-value. If you recall from the last two chapters, the chi-square test statistic has a degrees of freedom parameter. For the chi-square applied to contingency tables, the degrees of freedom consist of the number of rows minus one (r-1) multiplied by the number of columns minus one (c-1); therefore, degrees of freedom is: (r-1)(c-1). For tables such as this with two rows and two columns, the degrees of freedom are always (2-1)(2-1) = 1. We can use the CHIDIST function in Excel or the Probability Calculator in XLDataAnalyst and find the p-value. Using XLDataAnalyst, we would find that

(new function)

the p-value is $(1-.694251) = .3058$ which is well above .05 or any reasonable significance level[3]. Therefore, we cannot reject the null hypothesis.

There is a close relationship between the Z-test for the equality of two proportions, and the chi-square test. The p-values are identical (.3058 in each case) and if you square the z-value you will get the chi-square value. In Example 8-4, the z-value was (-1.024), and $(-1.024)^2 = 1.0486$ which is the same as the chi-square value, except for rounding error. As we will see, XLDataAnalyst prints out both results and without rounding error the results are identical. Why, then do we have two different tests? Are the tests redundant? Although the tests provide identical results here, there are two important differences.

Since the chi-square test is inherently two-tailed, it cannot be used for a one-tailed test. In other words, if our null hypothesis is H_0: $\pi_1 \leq \pi_2$ or H_0: $\pi_1 \geq \pi_2$, we have to use the Z-test since the chi-square is not capable of testing such a hypothesis. On the other hand, the Z-test cannot be used for tests of three or more proportions. As we will see in Chapter 9, the chi-square test can be extended to any number of groups. Thus, although the two tests can provide equivalent results in some cases, they are not interchangeable.

Exercises II

9. Random samples were taken from two regions of the country to learn what proportion of bankers thought interest rates would rise over the next quarter. Results were:

$$n_1 = 300, p_1 = .50 \quad n_2 = 270, p_2 = .30$$

(a) Compute S_{Pooled}. (b) Compute $S_{p_1-p_2}$. (c) Which value of standard error should be used for (i) testing that the difference between the two population proportions is zero, and for (ii) estimating the difference between the two population proportions.

10. Given the following data, test H_0: $\pi_1 = \pi_2$ against H_1: $\pi_1 \neq \pi_2$ at $\alpha = .05$

Sample 1	Sample 2
$n_1 = 50$, $p_1 = .22$	$n_2 = 100$, $p_2 = .18$

11. A market research firm must determine whether the proportion of households with Blu-Ray players is the same in two regions. Sample data are:

	Region 1 (Northeast)	Region 2 (Southeast)
No. households	150	200
Household with a DVD player	57	90

Test the hypothesis that the proportion of households with Blu-Ray players in two regions is equal at the 2% level of significance.

12. A government agency wishes to determine whether the nation's wealth is becoming more concentrated. The group used for the study is a sample from the top half of 1% of households. A study before an extended economic expansion suggested these households controlled 25% of the nation's wealth ($p_1 = .25$), whereas a later study suggested a value of 35% ($p_2 = .35$). If the standard error of the difference

---

[3] Note that the chi-square test here is inherently a two-tailed test so we do not have to multiply the resulting p-value by 2.

$s_{p_1-p_2}$, has been computed to be .022, test whether the apparent increase is statistically-significant at the 1% level. (*Hint*: use H_0: $\pi_2 \leq \pi_1$ and H_1: $\pi_2 > \pi_1$)

13. A major automobile manufacturer plans to evaluate the effectiveness of an expensive advertising campaign by analyzing consumer acceptance of the firm's image before and after the campaign. Samples of prospective customers revealed 205 in favor of the firm's image before the advertising campaign and 500 in favor after the campaign.

Before Advertising	After Advertising
$n_1 = 500$	$n_2 = 1,000$
Percent favoring = 205/500 = 41%	Percent favoring = 500/1,000 = 50%

Determine whether there has been a real change in consumer acceptance of the firm. Use a significance level of 1%.

14. Use the data from Problem 13 to compute the 95% confidence interval estimate for the true difference between the two proportions of 41% and 50%.

15. A multinational firm has hired a consultant to determine if workers in their domestic plants are as satisfied with their jobs as employees in their foreign plants. Results of the study are as follows:

	Domestic Plants	Foreign Plants
No. workers sampled	350	225
No. satisfied with job	245	189

(a) Test whether the proportions satisfied in the two locations are equal at the $\alpha = .05$ level.

(b) Establish a 90% confidence interval estimate of the difference between the two proportions.

(c) Did you use the same standard error of difference in both calculations? Explain.

Difference Between Variances

The test for two population variances is similar to our previous tests, but uses a different distribution. Although we introduced the F-distribution in Chapter 4, we have not had the need to apply it prior to now. As with the test for two independent means, we assume that the samples, n_1, and n_2, are both taken randomly from populations that are normally distributed and that the samples are independent[4]. We will now take a look at the two sample variances, S_1^2 and S_2^2 as evidence of the equality of the two population variances. As usual, our null hypothesis is that the two population variances are equal:

$$H_0: \sigma_1^2 = \sigma_2^2$$

$$H_1: \sigma_1^2 \neq \sigma_2^2$$

For means and proportions, we looked at the differences between the two sample means (or proportions) as evidence about the truth of the null hypothesis; however, with variances, the process is a little different. If you recall, the sampling distribution for a sample variance is the chi-square distribution. We used that distribution to construct confidence intervals for a single population variance and to conduct hypothesis tests of a population variance. In Chapter 5, we described the F-distribution as the ratio of two chi-square distributions. Rather than looking at the arithmetic difference between the two sample variances, we will look at the ratio of the two variances that has an F-distribution:

new distribution

---

[4] Note that this test assumes that both populations follow a normal distribution. If the populations do not have a normal distribution then the modified Levene (Browne-Forsyth) test described in Chapter 9 should be used instead.

$$F = \frac{S_1^2}{S_2^2} \qquad\qquad (8\text{-}16)$$

If the null hypothesis is true, we would expect that the two sample variances should be close to being equal and that this ratio would have a value of about 1.0. If the null hypothesis is false, the ratio may be much larger (if the first population variance is larger than the second), or much smaller (if the first population variance is smaller than the second). The remainder of the logic remains the same, however. We will still compute a p-value for the sample test statistic and compare it to the level of significance, to make our decision. The final information we need to test the hypothesis pertain to the degrees of freedom. Recall that the F-distribution has two degrees of freedom parameters, one for the numerator and one for the denominator. As with the chi-square distribution, the degrees of freedom for each sample are (n-1) so that the degrees of freedom are $(n_1 - 1)$ for the numerator and $(n_2 - 1)$ for the denominator.

Example 8-6 *important*

In Example 8-1 we tested the hypothesis that the engines from the two manufacturers had the same mileage. In that example, we calculated the sample variances of the two manufacturers' engines as well as the means. Use that data to test the hypothesis that the two population variances are equal.

Solution

From Example 8-1 we have:

$$S_1^2 = 4.5 \qquad S_2^2 = 4.0$$

1. $H_0: \sigma_1^2 = \sigma_2^2$

    $H_1: \sigma_1^2 \neq \sigma_2^2$

2. $\alpha = .05$

3. Use F distribution; degrees of freedom are $(9 - 1) = 8$ for the numerator and $(7 - 1) = 6$ for the denominator

4. $F = \frac{S_1^2}{S_2^2} = 1.125$ Using XLDataAnalyst the p-value is .5443

5. Conclusion: We cannot reject the null hypothesis since the p-value is greater than .05. The data is consistent with equal variance. We conclude that the population variances are equal. Recall that the equality of the variances is one of the assumptions of the t-test for means that assumes equal variances. We now have a method for testing that assumption. As we will see later, this type of test is commonly part of the output of statistical software so that we can determine which t-test is the most appropriate in a given situation.

Confidence Interval for the Ratio of Two Variances

Just as we have done for the other tests for two parameters, we can form a confidence interval for the variances. However, here rather than being a confidence interval for the difference between the two population values, it is an interval for the ratio of the two variances. As was the case for the confidence interval for a single variance in Chapter 6, the upper limit of the confidence interval uses the percentile from the lower tail of the distribution and the lower limit of the confidence interval uses the percentile from the upper tail of the distribution. The confidence limits are computed as

$$CL \; for \; \sigma_1^2 \Big/ \sigma_2^2 \qquad\qquad LCL = \frac{\frac{S_1^2}{S_2^2}}{F_{1-\alpha/2}} \; and \; UCL = \frac{\frac{S_1^2}{S_2^2}}{F_{\alpha/2}} \qquad\qquad (8\text{-}17)$$

Example 8-7

Using the data from Example 8-6 we can form a 95% confidence interval for the ratio of the two population variances.

1. Using the F distribution with 8 and 6 degrees of freedom we can use the probability calculator or the F.INV function to find the percentiles which are $F_{.975,\, 8,\, 6} = 5.5996$ and $F_{.025,\, 8,\, 6} = 0.2150.$

    Could use Calculator

2. Our confidence interval then becomes

$$LCL = \frac{\frac{4.5}{4}}{5.5996} = \frac{1.125}{5.5996} = .2009 \quad \text{and} \quad UCL = \frac{\frac{4.5}{4}}{0.2150} = \frac{1.125}{0.2150} = 5.2326$$

Remember that these confidence limits are for the ratio of the two variances which should be 1.0 if the variances are equal in the population. Since 1.0 is clearly within the confidence interval we can conclude that there is no reason to believe that the variances are different; the same conclusion reached in the hypothesis test.

Exercises III

16. If two variances are compared and the F-value is equal to 1, what does that tell us? What if the F-value is much larger than 1?

17. A track coach is comparing split times of two runners. The first runner has a variance of .8 seconds over 6 split times and the second has a variance of 1.1 seconds over 4 times. Find the F-value and state whether the difference in the variances is significant. Use a level of significance of .05.

18. A production manager is comparing the amount of time it takes two machines to produce the same product. The data is shown below:

M 1	4 min	7 min	5 min	6.5 min	4 min	8 min	5.5 min	6 min	4.5 min
M 2	6 min	3 min	3 min	5 min	7.8 min	6 min	9 min	5 min	6 min

    Find the variance for each machine and test to determine if the difference in the variances is significant.

19. Explain why an F-value close to 0 would imply a difference in variances. What about an F-value of 5?

20. An airline is looking at the variances of empty seats on two different flights over a 10-day span. The first flight departs in the morning and has a variance of 2.1 empty seats. The second flight is a nighttime flight that has a variance of 4.3 empty seats. Test to determine if the difference in variances is significant. Use a level of significance of .01.

21. An instructor is comparing test scores for his current class with those from the previous semester. The variance of test scores from the prior class was 63 in a class of 29 students. The current class has a variance of test scores of 79 in a class of 13 students. Is the difference between the variances significant?

22. Over the last week, temperatures in Seattle (in Fahrenheit) have been 44, 46, 51, 54, 49, 50, and 55. In Phoenix, the average temperatures were 79, 88, 83, 85, 88, 88, and 89. Find the variance for each city's temperatures and determine if the variances are significantly different. Use a level of significance of .05.

23. The department of transportation is reviewing roads that are heavily used and will need repairs soon. Two highway stretches are selected and the amount of traffic is compared over 30 days. When the data is collected, both stretches have nearly identical average cars per day; however, the first stretch has a variance of 80 cars per day and the second has a variance of 60 cars per day. Are these variances significantly different? Describe the practicality of knowing the difference in variances in situations similar to this.

Difference Between Medians

As with the other parameters we have discussed, the null hypothesis usually states that the two population medians are equal:

$$H_0: \eta_1 = \eta_2$$

$$H_1: \eta_1 \neq \eta_2$$

You might assume that to test this hypothesis we would look at the difference between the two sample medians ($M_1 - M_2$) as we did with means and proportions; however, the traditional tests for median proceeds somewhat differently from the tests we have described to this point.

The test for the equality of two independent medians was developed independently by Mann and Whitney and by Wilcoxon, respectively in the mid 1940's. The two tests, although formulated somewhat differently, can be shown to be equivalent. Thus, the test we will describe is sometimes called the Mann-Whitney U test and sometimes the Wilcoxon Rank Sum Test. We will refer to the test as the Mann-Whitney-Wilcoxon (MWW) test. The assumptions of the MWW test consist of:

- The values come from two independent random samples

- The measurement scale in the two samples is at least ordinal in nature.

If no further assumptions are made about the two groups, then the Mann-Whitney test is a test of whether or not the two population distributions differ in any way (shape, variability or location). If we also make the following assumption, then the test can be regarded as a test of locations, either means for interval or ratio data, or medians for ordinal data.

- The data have the same shape and variability in the two populations.

The calculation of the U statistic is fairly straight-forward. The data are first rank-ordered without regard to which group they came from. Next, the ranks are regrouped and the sum of the ranks in each group is calculated. Let's call these sums T_1 and T_2, respectively. The maximum sums for these ranks depend only on the sample size and can be calculated as shown in Equation 8-17:

Maximum Sums of Ranks $Max_1 = n_1 n_2 + \frac{n_1(n_1+1)}{2}$ $Max_2 = n_1 n_2 + \frac{n_2(n_2+1)}{2}$ *(8-18)*

The hypothesis test is in terms of the U statistic, calculated as indicated below:

Mann-Whitney U $U_1 = Max_1 - T_1$ $U_2 = Max_2 - T_2$ *(8-19)*

The procedure is easier to illustrate within the context of an example.

Example 8-8

As an advertising executive, you have been trying to capture a particular account for some time. Your client has recently approached you about a new advertising campaign in which they want to emphasize their product in humorous situations. You develop two potential ideas for ad campaigns and film a test ad for each approach. To test these ideas before showing them to the client, you preview the ads for a small randomly-selected group of people from your consumer panel. Eleven panelists view the first ad (Ad A) and 10 view the second (Ad B). Each panelist rates the ad that they viewed on a humor scale from 1 to 100. The ratings are shown in the table below and are contained in the file Example 8-7.xls. The medians are $M_1 = 85$ and $M_2 = 77.5$, respectively. Following is the data gathered from these studies:

Ad A	Ad B
83	75
72	64
77	77
91	70
88	65
85	81
78	80
93	78
89	79
84	82
92	

Solution

To calculate the MWW test, we first combine the ratings in order from smallest to largest while keeping track of which ad they came from. The results are listed in the table below:

Ad	Rating	Rank	A Ranks	B Ranks
B	64	1		1
B	65	2		2
B	70	3		3
A	72	4	4	
B	75	5		5
A	77	6.5	6.5	
B	77	6.5		6.5
A	78	8.5	8.5	
B	78	8.5		8.5
B	79	10		10
B	80	11		11
B	81	12		12
B	82	13		13
A	83	14	14	
A	84	15	15	
A	85	16	16	
A	88	17	17	
A	89	18	18	
A	91	19	19	
A	92	20	20	
A	93	21	21	
Sum			159	72

The items are ranked with tied rankings being assigned the average of the tied ranks. In the table above, the two ratings of 77 are tied for the 6th and 7th positions; therefore, both are assigned the average of those ranks or 6.5. The same is true for the two ratings of 78. The rank of the highest item should be equal to the total number of items (21 in this case) unless the highest values are a tie. After the items are ranked, the sum of the ranks is computed for each group. For Ad A, the sum of the ranks is $T_1 = 159$ and for Ad B the sum is $T_2 = 72$.

We can also calculate the maximum possible sum of ranks for the two ads. Since Ad A was rated by 11 people, the largest possible value for the sum of the ranks would be if all 11 of the rankings for this ad were the top 11 overall ratings. In other words, it would achieve a maximum value if the sum of the 11 rankings were $11 + 12 + 13 + 14 + 15 + 16 + 17 + 18 + 19 + 20 + 21 = 176$. A similar argument would hold for Ad B where the maximum would be $12 + 13 + 14 + 15 + 16 + 17 + 18 + 19 + 20 + 21 = 165$. These maximum values can also be directly computed from the sample sizes as follows:

$$Max_1 = n_1 n_2 + \frac{n_1(n_1 + 1)}{2} = (10)(11) + \frac{(11)(12)}{2} = 176$$

$$Max_2 = n_1 n_2 + \frac{n_2(n_2 + 1)}{2} = (10)(11) + \frac{(10)(11)}{2} = 165$$

where n_1 and n_2 are the respective sample sizes. The Mann-Whitney U statistic is then computed for each group by taking the maximum possible ranking for the group and subtracting the actual sum of the rankings for that group. If we represent the sum of the rankings for a group by T_i, then the U statistics are:

$$U_1 = Max_1 - T_1 = 176 - 159 = 17$$

$$U_2 = Max_2 - T_2 = 165 - 72 = 93$$

Notice that the values of U_1 and U_2 have to add up to the product of the two sample sizes. In our example, $U_1 + U_2 = 17 + 93 = 110 = (11)(10) = n_1 n_2$. This is always the case with these kinds of problems. That means that it doesn't matter if we work with U_1 or with U_2 since if we know one we can figure out the other.

The hypotheses for this test are:

$$H_0: \eta_1 = \eta_2$$

$$H_1: \eta_1 \neq \eta_2$$

This means that the sum of the ranks, and therefore the U values, should be equal in the two groups. Since the sum of the U values should be equal to the product of the two sample sizes, the U values for the two groups should both be $n_1 n_2 / 2$. In our example, both U values should be equal to $110/2 = 55$.

The question remains, however, how do we find the p-value for this test since we have no available sampling distribution? The logic is straightforward. We can calculate the number of possible ways that the $n_1 + n_2$ ranks could be combined into two groups with n_1 and n_2 values and then calculate the proportion of these combinations that would have a value as large or larger than the maximum of U_1 or U_2 (or alternative as small or smaller than the minimum of U_1 and U_2). This would give an exact p-value. The number of such combinations is given by:

$$\text{p-value} \rightarrow \frac{(n_1 + n_2)!}{n_1! n_2!}$$

This number gets quite large very quickly and would be difficult (if not impossible) to calculate by hand. Many statistics books contain tabled critical values for the U statistic for smaller sample sizes. XLDataAnalyst has a built-in routine for calculating the p-values for smaller samples, as we will see later. For larger sample sizes, the normal distribution can be used as an approximation. To use the normal distribution, we need to know the mean and standard deviation of the distribution of U values. Without worrying about the derivation, we will simply state that the following equations hold:

$$\mu_U = \frac{n_1 n_2}{2}$$

$$\sigma_U = \sqrt{\frac{n_1 n_2 (n_1 + n_2 + 1)}{12}} \qquad\qquad (8\text{-}20)$$

Next, we can use NORMDIST in Excel or the probability calculator in XLDataAnalyst to find the p-value. If we use the normal approximation in our sample problem, we would get the following results:

$$\mu_U = \frac{(11)(10)}{2} = 55$$

$$\sigma_U = \sqrt{\frac{(11)(10)(10+11+1)}{12}} = 14.2094$$

$$z = \frac{U_1 - \mu_U}{\sigma_U} = \frac{17 - 55}{14.20094} = -2.67588$$

Using NORMDIST, the p-value for this example is 2*(.0000244) = .0000488. Therefore, we can reject the null hypothesis and conclude that the two distributions are not identical. Since Ad A had the largest median (85 versus 77.5) we can conclude that the median rating of Ad A is larger than the median rating of Ad B.

Confidence Intervals for the Different Between Two Medians

As with the other tests in this chapter, we can also form confidence intervals for the difference between two medians. The first issue is estimating the difference between the two medians. One answer to this question is that the estimated difference is the difference between the two medians of the separate groups. A second estimate, called the Hodges-Lehmann estimate, looks at all of the paired differences between values in the two groups and takes the median of these differences as the estimate of the difference between the medians.

The question still remains, how to form a confidence interval around the estimated difference. Unfortunately, this question does not have an easy answer. This can be done in terms of the distribution for the U statistic which is too complex to go into here. Another alternative is to use the bootstrapping approach that we used for a single median in the last chapter. Both approaches are incorporated into XLDataAnalyst.

Testing Means When the Normality Assumption Does Not Hold

The MWW test can also be used as a hypothesis test for means. Recall that one of the assumptions of the t-test for independent means is that the samples are taken from populations with a normal distribution. Since the MWW test makes no assumptions about the population distributions, it can be used to test for the difference between means when the normality assumption is doubtful. In fact, the MWW test is more powerful in these circumstances and is the preferred test when the populations may not follow a normal distribution.

Exercises IV

24. What is the test used to determine the equality of medians? What are some of the assumptions of this test?

25. Why is the Mann-Whitney Wilcoxon test described in this section more appropriate for comparing two groups measured on an ordinal scale than the two-sample t-test described before?

26. Suppose that two college football conferences are examining the median attendance at each school in their conference. Suppose, after gathering the data, Conference A's teams ranked: 2, 4, 7, 8, 11, 13, 16, 17, 21, and 22. Conference B's teams ranked: 1, 3, 5, 6, 9, 10, 12, 14, 15, 18, 19, and 20. Are the median rankings the same? Two cities on the East Coast are comparing average daily temperatures to determine if their medians are the same. New York's average temperatures (in Fahrenheit) over a week are 61, 65, 62, 59, 69, 71, and 63. Boston's average temperatures during the same period are 58, 64, 59, 63, 67, 68, and 74. Do the median temperatures differ between the two cities?

27. Two competing proposals for new products were presented to two different consumer panels with 10 members each. Each member of the panels rated the new product that they were presented on a scale from 1 to 10. The ratings for the first proposed new product (Product A) were 8, 5, 6, 7, 4, 9, 9, 7, 8, and 3. The ratings for the second proposal (Product B) were 6, 5, 4, 3, 7, 4, 5, 7, 4, and 3. Is there a significant difference in the median ratings for the two product proposals? Which product should the firm market? Justify your answer. Two separate sections of the same course have completed the course evaluations for Professor Schmidt on a scale of 1 to 9. The 14 students in the first section gave Professor Schmidt overall ratings of 7, 6, 5, 5, 6, 7, 4, 1, 6, 4, 5, 6, 6, and 7 while the 12 students in the second section gave him ratings of 5, 3, 3, 6, 1, 3, 5, 4, 6, 5, 4, and 4. Professor Schmidt knows that course evaluations are likely not an interval scale so he wished to test whether or not the median ratings are the same in the two classes. Using a level of significance of .05, what conclusion should Professor Schmidt reach?

Comparisons Using Two Dependent Samples

The tests up to this point have all assumed that the samples were drawn independently for the two groups. As we discussed earlier in this chapter, sometimes the two groups may be from dependent or related samples. Such samples can arise in two ways:

- The observations in the two groups are matched on the bases of some characteristic. In general, this characteristic is called a blocking variable that we will discuss in Chapter 10.

- The observations in the two groups are based on the same identical respondents. These are often called repeated measures, or in the case of two groups, before-after comparisons. Typically, the measures are taken after a major event or treatment has occurred.

In either situation, the measures in the two groups are not independent of each other, but are correlated in that they come from respondents with similar characteristics or the same respondents. One obvious implication of these designs is that the sample sizes in the two groups must be equal since they are matched or paired in some way.

As noted earlier, such designs have advantages over tests for independent groups. With independent groups, there are many differences between groups that arise from the differences of the experimental units or respondents in each group. These differences are not related to the differences in the population parameters (means, proportions, medians or variances) and therefore are reflected in the standard error of the test. Since these differences inflate the standard error, they reduce the size of the test statistic and therefore make the test less powerful. Thus, pairing enables us to eliminate (or at least minimize) these extraneous differences and focus specifically upon the variable of interest. By controlling for individual differences or environmental effects, the difference under study becomes less contaminated by those effects and the tests become more powerful.

As with independent samples, we will discuss the tests for differences in the various parameters. The only issue that changes is that we will not discuss a test for differences between the variances for dependent samples since such a test has not yet been devised. Therefore, our discussion will only relate to means, proportions, and medians.

Difference Between Means: Dependent Samples

Hypothesis Tests

The null hypothesis for dependent means is identical to that for independent means:

$$H_0:\ \mu_1 = \mu_2 \qquad \text{or} \qquad H_0:\ \mu_1 - \mu_2 = 0$$

$$H_1:\ \mu_1 \neq \mu_2 \qquad\qquad\qquad\quad H_1:\ \mu_1 - \mu_2 \neq 0$$

However, the computations for paired samples are quite different from those for independent samples and are, in fact, even simpler. First, both samples **must be the same size**. Instead of using the original values, we perform all of the calculations with the difference scores obtained by subtracting one set of values from the corresponding matched observations. Next, we calculate the average and standard deviation of the difference scores. Instead of the standard error of the difference in means $s_{\bar{x}_1 - \bar{x}_2}$ that we used for independent groups, we use the standard error of the mean differences, $S_{\bar{d}}$, which is equal to the standard deviation of sample differences, S_d divided by $\sqrt{n}$:

$$S_{\bar{d}} = \frac{S_d}{\sqrt{n}} \qquad \text{Use this instead of} \qquad (8\text{-}21)$$

The value of S_d is computed in the same way as the standard deviation of any set of data—except that the values used are *difference scores* instead of the original values:

$$S_d = \sqrt{\frac{\Sigma(d - \bar{d})^2}{n-1}} \qquad (8\text{-}22)$$

The average difference scores are distributed following a t-distribution in the familiar form of the test statistic we first encountered in one-sample tests. As in the one-sample case, the test statistic is calculated as the sample statistic minus the hypothesized parameter, divided by the standard error of difference:

$$t = \frac{\bar{d} - \mu_d}{s_{\bar{d}}} \qquad (8\text{-}23)$$

The p-value is then calculated using the degrees of freedom, where df = number of pairs - 1. (This is derived from the fact that the mean differences of paired samples are distributed following the t-distribution, as stated earlier).

Although the new equations may seem different at first, an example will show that this procedure is equivalent to performing a one-sample t-test on the difference scores.

Example 8-9

Ten bank tellers are asked to help test whether a corrective training drill significantly improves the speed and accuracy with which they enter customer transactions into the bank's new software. They are first given a 5-minute "before treatment" test, then the drill, and finally, an "after treatment" test. The statistical analysis is intended to test the hypothesis that the drill has not significantly affected their speed and accuracy scores:

$$H_0:\ \mu_{\text{before}} = \mu_{\text{after}} \quad \text{or} \qquad H_0:\ \mu_{\text{before}} - \mu_{\text{after}} = 0$$

$$H_1: \mu_{\text{before}} \neq \mu_{\text{after}} \qquad\qquad H_1: \mu_{\text{before}} - \mu_{\text{after}} \neq 0$$

The data below show the before and after scores, along with the different scores needed to calculate the standard deviation of the differences, s_d. (*Remember* that these are not random samples from two independent populations. The scores on the second test are related to the scores on the first test because they were received by the same individuals. This enables the analyst to negate any variations that exist from one teller to the next, and focus on the real effects of the corrective drill):

Teller No.	Before Drill Score	After Drill Score	Difference d	Deviation $(d - \bar{d})$	Deviation Squared $(d - \bar{d})^2$
A	45	49	4	1	1
B	52	56	4	1	1
C	34	31	−3	−6	36
D	38	46	8	5	25
E	47	54	7	4	16
F	42	39	−3	−6	36
G	61	68	7	4	16
H	53	55	2	−1	1
I	52	50	−2	−5	25
J	49	55	6	3	9
Total			30		166

Solution

The mean difference value: $\bar{d} == \dfrac{S_d}{\sqrt{n}} = \dfrac{30}{10} = 3$

Standard deviation of differences: $S_d = \sqrt{\dfrac{\Sigma(d - \bar{d})^2}{n-1}} = \sqrt{\dfrac{166}{10-1}} = 4.295$

Standard error of the mean difference: $S_{\bar{d}} = \dfrac{S_d}{\sqrt{n}} = \dfrac{4.295}{\sqrt{10}} = 1.358$

Our hypothesized difference is zero, and we can follow the standard steps for testing a hypothesis:

1.　　$H_0: \mu_1 - \mu_2 = 0$ (or $H_0: \mu_d = 0$)

　　　$H_1: \mu_1 - \mu_2 \neq 0$

2.　　$\alpha = .05$
3.　　Use t-distribution with $n - 1 = 10 - 1 = 9$ df

In Example 8-8, we were asked to test for "any difference;" however, insofar as the drill was expected to have a positive effect on the speed and accuracy scores, it may be more logical to use a (more powerful) one-tailed test for this situation.

4.　　$t = \dfrac{3-0}{1.358} = 2.21$
5.　　Using XLDataAnalyst, we can determine the p-value for a t-statistic of 2.21 with 9 degrees of freedom is $2*(1-.972777) = .054445$ which is not quite significant at the .05 level.
6.　　Conclusion: Do not reject the hypothesis of no difference because the difference is not significant at the 5% level for this two-tailed test.

Example 8-10

Using the data of Example 8-9, test the hypothesis that the drill scores after the training are higher.

Solution

1. H_0: $\mu_1 \leq \mu_2$

   H_1: $\mu_1 > \mu_2$

2. $\alpha = .05$

3. Use t-distribution with $n - 1 = 10 - 1 = 9$ df

4. $t = 2.21$ (from Example 8-8)

5. Using XLDataAnalyst we find the p-value is $(1-.972777) = .027223$ which is significant at the .05 level.

6. Conclusion: Reject hypothesis of equal means because the p-value is less than .05. Conclude that there is an improvement in the speed and accuracy score.

We can reject the null hypothesis of no difference in scores with a one-tailed test because all the error probability (α) is in the upper tail of the distribution. As noted in Chapter 7, the one-tailed test always has more power (to reject a false null hypothesis) than a two-tailed test.

Confidence Interval for the Difference Between Means

When a test for the equality of differences is rejected, one may wish to establish a confidence interval for the true difference between the means of the paired samples. Insofar as the samples are dependent, we do not need to assume equal variances—as it was required for the confidence interval for the difference between means of two independent samples. The equation for constructing the confidence interval is similar to that used before, but now we use the symbols for paired or dependent samples, instead:

$$CL \text{ for } \mu_1 - \mu_2 \qquad \bar{d} \pm t_{\frac{\alpha}{2}, n-1} S_d \qquad (8\text{-}24)$$

Example 8-11

16 telemarketing representatives were tested on their ability to hold customers on the phone before and after a sales training session. If $\bar{d}$ is 10 min and $s_d = 5$, what is the 95% confidence interval for the true difference?

Solution

$$t_{.05/2, 15df} = 2.131 \qquad S_{\bar{d}} = \frac{S_d}{\sqrt{n}} = \frac{5}{\sqrt{16}} = 1.25$$

$$CL = 10 \pm 2.131 \,(1.25)$$

$$= 7.34 \text{ to } 12.66 \text{ min}$$

Exercises V

28. What advantage does the use of paired dependent samples hold over the use of independent samples?

29. Twenty managers were selected for a test to determine whether exposure to ethics training changed managerial decision results. At the beginning of the day, the managers were presented with a case and

scored on the basis of their answers to some ethical questions. Following a day of training, they were presented with a similar situation and given a second score based on their responses. Use the data below for a difference between means of paired samples test of H_0: $\mu_1 - \mu_2 = 0$:

$$n = 20 \quad \Sigma d = 96 \quad \Sigma(d - \bar{d})^2 = 560$$

Find (a) d, (b) s_d, (c) $S_{\bar{d}}$ and (d) t (e) Did the training result in a significant change in the managers' decision-making? (f) Do you feel the sample is large enough to draw a statistically-valid conclusion? Why or why not?

30. A production supervisor in a clothing factory is attempting to determine whether background music affects the productivity of her employees. While nine employees were working on a large order of the same items, she recorded the output during one week with no music and one week with music. Results are shown below:

Employee Name	Units Produced: No Music	Units Produced: With Music
Louise	92	99
Kathleen	87	83
Bridget	104	101
Meredith	76	83
Steven	88	91
Catherine	94	85
Jo	79	66
Bryant	96	83
Evelyn	94	92

(a) State H_0 and H_1.

(b) Does background music affect the productivity of the employees? Test using a 5% level of significance.

31. Sixty marketing representatives for a cosmetics company were rated (on a 1 to 10 scale) on their sales ability before and after a sales training seminar in Dallas. The results were: $\Sigma d = 78$ and $\Sigma(d - \bar{d})^2 = 408$. (a) Assuming that the seminar was expected to improve one's sales ability, perform a one-tailed test of H_1: $\mu_2 > \mu_1$. Use a 10% level of significance. (b) What assumptions must be made about the shape of the distribution of differences in order to perform the test in part (a)?

32. Ten pairs of students are selected for an experiment to determine if there is a difference in an in-class method of teaching statistics versus an online method. Each pair is carefully matched in terms of GPA, total course load, quantitative aptitude, and other variables. Then, one student from each pair is assigned to each method. The final exam scores are as follows:

Pair No.	1	2	3	4	5	6	7	8	9	10
In-class	78	85	69	92	87	88	75	91	83	84
Online	72	86	64	88	78	82	78	90	80	74

Compare the two different methods of instruction by testing the mean difference in the paired samples at the 2% level of significance.

33. (*One-tailed test of specified difference*) The manufacturer of a gasoline additive has, in the past, shown that adding a 6-oz bottle of their product *Mileage-Maker* to the gasoline tank will increase one's mileage. They have asked a research organization to test the claim that mileage is improved by 3 mpg. The research organization has agreed to test the alternative hypothesis that the difference in means is

less than 3 mpg at the $\alpha = .05$ level. Next, they carefully measured the mileage obtained from a tank of gasoline on six different makes of cars both before and after adding the chemical:

Auto No.	1	2	3	4	5	6
MPG before	28.6	35.4	32.2	41.8	27.2	39.4
MPG after	29.8	38.2	37.4	44.3	31.7	42.4

Use the data provided to conduct the test and state your conclusion.

34. In a test of the difference between two instructional techniques, using 10 pairs of equally qualified students, the students using method B scored an average of 4 points better than those using method A. If the standard error of the mean difference is 1.31 points, what is the 95% confidence interval for the true difference?

35. Given the following data from a test of the difference between means of two paired samples:

$$n = 20 \text{ pairs} \quad \sum d = 62 \quad \sum (d - \bar{d})^2 = 220$$

(a) Test H_0: $\mu_1 - \mu_2 = 0$ against H_1: $\mu_1 - \mu_2 \neq 0$ at the $\alpha = .10$ level.
(b) Establish a 90% confidence interval for the difference.
(c) Are the results from part a and b consistent?

Difference Between Two Dependent Proportions

Hypothesis Tests

The test for the difference between two proportions for dependent or correlated samples was developed in 1947 by Q. McNemar and is often called the McNemar test.[5] Like the chi-square test for two independent proportions, the McNemar test is based on a 2 by 2 contingency table. The rows of the table represent the two responses in the first group and the columns of the table represent the same two responses in the second group. As in the previous section on dependent means, we assume that the two groups are matched in some way or that they represent the same respondents at two different points in time. We will assume the same respondents at two different points in time. If we represent the two responses as + and –, then the table will appear as:

In the table, f_{11} represents the frequency with which the respondents responded + at both time 1 and time 2, f_{12} represents a + response at time 1 and a – response at time 2 and so on. The hypotheses are:

$$H_0: \pi_1 = \pi_2$$

$$H_1: \pi_1 \neq \pi_2$$

The logic of the test is fairly straightforward and involves the analysis of the frequencies of those who switch from one response to the other between the two times. For example, an individual responded + at time 1 and – at time 2 or – at time 1 and + at time 2. These two frequencies are f_{12} and f_{21}. If the null

---

[5] Although commonly used in the medical and social sciences, this simple test is rarely mentioned in business statistics books as noted by Berenson and Koppel (2005).

hypothesis is true, then these two frequencies should be equal. In other words, if there is no real change between time 1 and time 2, then the switching should be random. There should be just as many who switch from + to − as those who switch from − to + and the probability of each should be .5. Thus, the hypothesis can be tested using the binomial distribution with $\pi = .5$. For a one-tailed test, the p-value can be calculated as:

McNemar p-value one-tailed $\qquad P(X \leq min(f_{12}, f_{21}), f_{12} + f_{21}, .5)$ $\qquad\qquad$ (8-25)

For a two-tailed test, calculate the p-value in the same way and multiply it by two. This p-value can be found by using the BINOMDIST function in Excel. For larger sample sizes, the normal or chi-square can be used as an approximation. The normal approximation is:

$$Z = \frac{f_{12} - f_{21}}{\sqrt{f_{12} + f_{21}}}$$ $\qquad\qquad$ (8-26)

If you recall from our discussion of the tests for two independent proportions, the chi-square is simply the square of the Z. The chi-square statistic can be calculated as:

$$\chi^2 = \frac{(f_{12} - f_{21})^2}{f_{12} + f_{21}}$$ $\qquad\qquad$ (8-27)

Example 8-12

A scientist at the Holesnapple Soft Drink Company has come up with a new formula to sweeten the drink and the company managers think that the new formulation will induce people to switch from archrival Yorkapple to Holesnapple. A consumer panel of 200 consumers tastes both of the original drinks and expresses a preference for either Holesnapple or Yorkapple. A week later, the same consumer panel is reconvened and asked to taste the reformulated Holesnapple and Yorkapple and again express a preference between the two. The results are shown below:

		Time 2		
		Holesnapple	Yorkapple	Totals
Time 1	Holesnapple	80	6	86
	Yorkapple	22	92	114
	Totals	102	98	n = 200

Solution

The results indicate that 86 out of the 200 panelists preferred Holesnapple before the formula change, but after the change 102 out of the 200 preferred Holesnapple. Twenty-two of the panelists switched from Yorkapple at time 1 to Holesnapple at time 2, while only 6 switched the other way around. Is there evidence, at the .05 level of significance, that a higher proportion of people will now prefer the reformulated Holesnapple to Yorkapple?

1. $H_0: \pi_1 \geq \pi_2$

   $H_1: \pi_1 < \pi_2$

   Note: the 1 and 2 refer to Time 1 and Time 2

2. $\alpha = .05$

3. $f_{12} = 6 \quad f_{21} = 22$

4. p-value = BINOMDIST(6, 22, .5,TRUE) = .00186

5. Conclusion: Since the p-value is less than .05 we can reject the null hypothesis and conclude that the proportion of people who prefer Holesnapple has increased with the new formula.

We can also solve the problem using the normal distribution as an approximation. Using the normal distribution we would calculate:

$$Z = \frac{6-22}{\sqrt{6+22}} = \frac{-16}{5.291503} = -3.0237 \quad \text{p-value} = .001248$$

We would arrive at the same conclusion with the normal approximation as we did with the exact binomial value; however, we should also note that the p-value using the normal approximation is smaller than the exact value from the binomial. This means that the normal approximation is more likely to yield a Type I Error than the stated level of significance (.05). Thus, the exact binomial is to be preferred when possible.

Confidence Interval for the Difference Between Two Dependent Proportions

We can formulate the confidence interval for two dependent proportions, but we have to assume that the sample sizes are large enough for the normal approximation. The confidence interval is given as:

$$(p_1 - p_2) \pm Z_{1+-\frac{\alpha}{2}} \sqrt{\frac{p_1(1-p_1)}{n} + \frac{p_2(1-p_2)}{n} - \frac{2\left(\frac{f_{11}}{n}-p_1p_2\right)}{n}} \qquad (8\text{-}28)$$

This is similar to the confidence interval for independent proportions except that the equation for the standard error takes into account the correlations between the two sets of proportions by subtracting a term to account for this correlation.

Example 8 13

For the data in Example 8-11 we would have:

Solution

1. For a 95% confidence interval, the Z-value is 1.96

2. The standard error is computed as:

$$S_{p_1-p_2} = \sqrt{\frac{p_1(1-p_1)}{n} + \frac{p_2(1-p_2)}{n} - \frac{2\left(\frac{f_{11}}{n} - p_1p_2\right)}{n}}$$

$$= \sqrt{\frac{.43(1-.43)}{200} + \frac{.51(1-.51)}{200} - \frac{2\left(\frac{80}{200} - (.43)(.51)\right)}{200}} = .025846$$

The confidence interval is then:

$$(.43 - .51) \pm 1.96(.025846) = (-0.131 \text{ to } -0.029)$$

Exercises VI

36. A survey of local taxpayers asked voters if they would be in favor of an increased property tax. The results of 200 respondents showed that 17 would be in favor, with 183 not in favor. An information packet was sent out, detailing the distribution of the collected money, and the same 200 people were polled again. The second poll showed 53 more people joining the 17 in favor of the new tax making the new total in favor 70. Is there evidence at the .01 level of significance that more people now prefer the tax?

37. An environmental company surveyed people asking their opinion on whether or not the government had strict enough environmental laws. On first response, 88 out of 111 people stated that they felt the government had strict enough laws. After the first response, the respondents presented a series of facts on pollution and they were again asked the same question. After the facts had been presented, only 71 out of the 111 felt that the government had strict enough environmental laws. Is there evidence, at the .05 level of significance, that more people changed their minds?

38. At the start of their baseball season, a team lobbied the state government for a new stadium to be built with taxpayer money. The government surveyed 100,000 citizens and only 21% supported the new stadium; however, as the season progressed, the team experienced great success on the field and the owner of the team threatened to move the team to another city. As the playoffs started, the government decided to re-survey the community, and asked the same 100,000 people if they supported a new stadium. This time 34% said that they would be in favor of a new stadium being built. Is there evidence, at the .01 level of significance, that the public changed their mind?

39. A professor preparing for a final exam asked students if they preferred the test be given in the morning or evening. Six weeks before the final, 41 out of the 55 students voted for an evening final; however, the only option the professor had was to give the final at 6:00 on a Friday night. After hearing the time of the exam, the class asked to vote again and this time only 26 preferred the evening exam. Did the class change their minds, at a .05 level of significance?

Difference Between Two Dependent Medians

The test for dependent sample medians is the Wilcoxon Signed Ranks test. Like most of the tests for ordinal data, the Wilcoxon Signed Ranks test depends on rank orderings. In fact, this test is conducted in exactly the same way as the Signed Ranks test for a single median. In this case, however, it is the rank orderings of the differences between the two groups. The process for conducting this test is as follows:

---

1. Calculate the differences between the paired observations in the two groups.

2. Rank-order the absolute differences, ignoring the sign.

3. Place a + or a − on each rank, depending on the sign of the difference score.

4. Calculate the sum of the ranks with a + sign and the sum with a - sign. Select either the minimum of these two sums for a two-tailed test, the sum of the - ranks for an upper-tailed test (alternative is that group 1 is greater than group 2) or the sum of the + ranks for a lower-tailed test (alternative is that group 1 is less than group 2). This sum is the W statistic.

Wilcoxon Statistic:
$$W = \sum R^{+ \ (or-)}$$
(8-29)

Example 8-14

A statistics professor decided to try an experiment in one of her sections of introductory statistics. She presented the chapter on estimation using her traditional lecture approach and then asked her students to rate their satisfaction with the presentation using a scale from 1 to 20 with 1 being very poor to 20 being very good. She then repeated the material using interactive graphics and online applets and asked the students to rate the presentation again. The 25 ratings of each method are presented below:

Rating 1	Rating 2	Difference	Abs Diff	Ranking	R+	R-
11	16	-5	5	15		15
8	19	-11	11	24		24
13	16	-3	3	5.5		6.5
16	12	4	4	11	11	
16	9	7	7	18.5	18.5	
17	12	5	5	15	15	
5	14	-9	9	21.5		21.5
11	15	-4	4	11		11
15	11	4	4	11	11	
9	12	-3	3	5.5		6.5
10	8	2	2	3	3	
7	17	-10	10	23		23
6	9	-3	3	5.5		5.5
9	13	-4	4	11		11
10	17	-7	7	18.5		18.5
6	15	-9	9	21.5		21.5
10	18	-8	8	20		20
11	15	-4	4	11		11
12	12	0	0			
11	17	-6	6	17		17
11	13	-2	2	3		3
11	16	-5	5	15		15
16	18	-2	2	3		3
12	11	1	1	1	1	
11	8	3	3	5.5	6.5	

Is there evidence that the second presentation method was more popular than the traditional presentation?

Solution

$H_0: \eta_1 \geq \eta_2$

$H_1: \eta_1 < \eta_2$

The differences, absolute ranks and the signed ranks are shown in the table above. The sum of R^+ is 66 and the sum of R^- is 236. Since we have a lower-tailed test, we would expect R^+ to be less than R^- so we would use R^+ of 66 as the test statistic. A table of the critical values for the Wilcoxon test would show that a sum less than 69 would be significant at the .01 level. We can therefore reject the null hypothesis and conclude that the new method was indeed more popular with the students than the traditional approach.

As we had previously noted, the Wilcoxon Signed Ranks test is difficult for hand calculations and computing exact p-values can be difficult even with computers. For that reason, we will not provide any exercises with this section, but will provide exercises after the next section using XLDataAnalyst.

Practice

Comparing Two Samples Using Excel and XLDataAnalyst

As it was evident from many of the examples in this chapter, the calculations involved in two-sample tests are considerably more complex than those we encountered in Chapter 7 (dealing with one-sample tests). Therefore, it is even more valuable to have computer software to perform the calculations for us.

Excel Functions

The Excel function TTEST can be used to perform the three t-tests for means that we discussed in this chapter. The function will return the p-value, associated with the test. The syntax of the function is:

TTEST(range 1,range 2,tails,type)

The first two arguments are references to the range of cells in the worksheet that contain the data for the two groups. The tails argument has a value of 1 (for a one-tailed test) or 2 (for a two-tailed test). The final argument (type) specifies the type of test. A value of 1 indicates that the paired or dependent samples test is to be performed. A value of 2 indicates that this is an independent samples test that assumes equal variances. A value of 3 indicates an independent samples test that does not assume equal variances.

The Analysis Toolpak

The Data Analysis Toolpak in Excel can also be used to perform two-sample hypothesis tests. As before, to use the Toolpak, select Data Analysis in the Analysis section of the Data tab of the Excel ribbon. The list of available routines, illustrated in Figure 8-2, will appear.

Figure 8-2   ***Example List of Routines in the Data Analysis Toolpak***

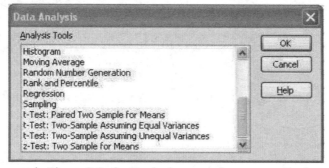

As you can see in Figure 8-2, the Toolpak can perform t-tests for dependent or paired samples, t-tests for independent samples either with equal or unequal variances and the Z-test for independent samples when the population standard deviations are known. In addition, the Toolpak also contains an F-test for two variances that does not appear in this figure. The required input is virtually the same for all of these tests. The primary information that you need to provide is the range of cells that contain the data for the two groups. Figure 8-3 illustrates the dialog for the independent samples t-test that assumes equal variances, using the data from the file Example 8-1.xls.

Figure 8-3   ***Sample Dialog from the Data Analysis Toolpak***

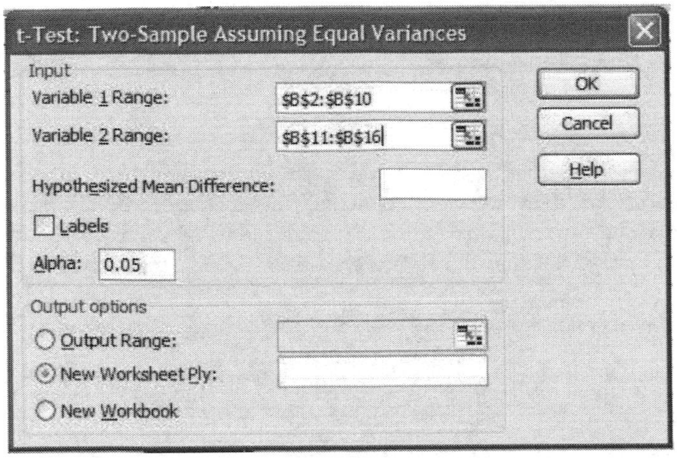

If the null hypothesis states a value of the difference between the population means different from zero, you must enter that value in the Hypothesized Mean Difference box. For the usual case of no difference, you may leave the box blank. If you want a significance level other than .05, change the value in the box labeled Alpha. Figure 8-4 illustrates the sample output using the data from Example 8-1. If you compare the results here with those calculated by hand earlier, you will see that the results agree within rounding error.

Figure 8-4   ***Sample Output from the Data Analysis Toolpak***

	Variable 1	Variable 2
Mean	31	28
Variance	4.5	4
Observations	9	7
Pooled Variance	4.285714	
Hypothesized Mean Difference	0	
Df	14	
T Stat	2.875543	
P(T<=t) one-tail	0.006109	
T Critical one-tail	1.76131	
P(T<=t) two-tail	0.012218	
t Critical two-tail	2.144787	

The Excel Templates

There are two templates included with the text for two-sample tests. One of them (Two Independent Samples Hypothesis Tests.xls) is for independent samples tests and the other (Two Dependent Samples Hypothesis Tests.xls) is for dependent samples. Both templates will be illustrated with one of the examples from this chapter.

Example 8-15

In Example 8-6 we used the F-test to check for the equality of the variances using the Example 8-1 data. We can perform the same analysis using the independent samples template.

Solution

Figure 8-5 illustrates the results using the Excel template. In this figure, both the Summarized Data and the Sample Data results pertain to the same example. As you can see, we obtain the same results as found in Example 8-6:

Example 8-16

In Example 8-11, we performed a test for two dependent sample proportions for the Holesnapple Soft Drink Company. The raw data are contained in the file Example 8-10.xls and the summarized frequencies are repeated in the table below. Use the Excel Template to solve this problem.

		Time 2		
		Holesnapple	Yorkapple	Totals
Time 1	Holesnapple	80	6	86
	Yorkapple	22	92	114
	Totals	102	98	n = 200

Solution

The solution, using both the summarized and raw data, is shown in Figure 8-6. Once again, we receive the same results as the hand calculations.

Figure 8-5 Illustration of the Two Independent Samples Template

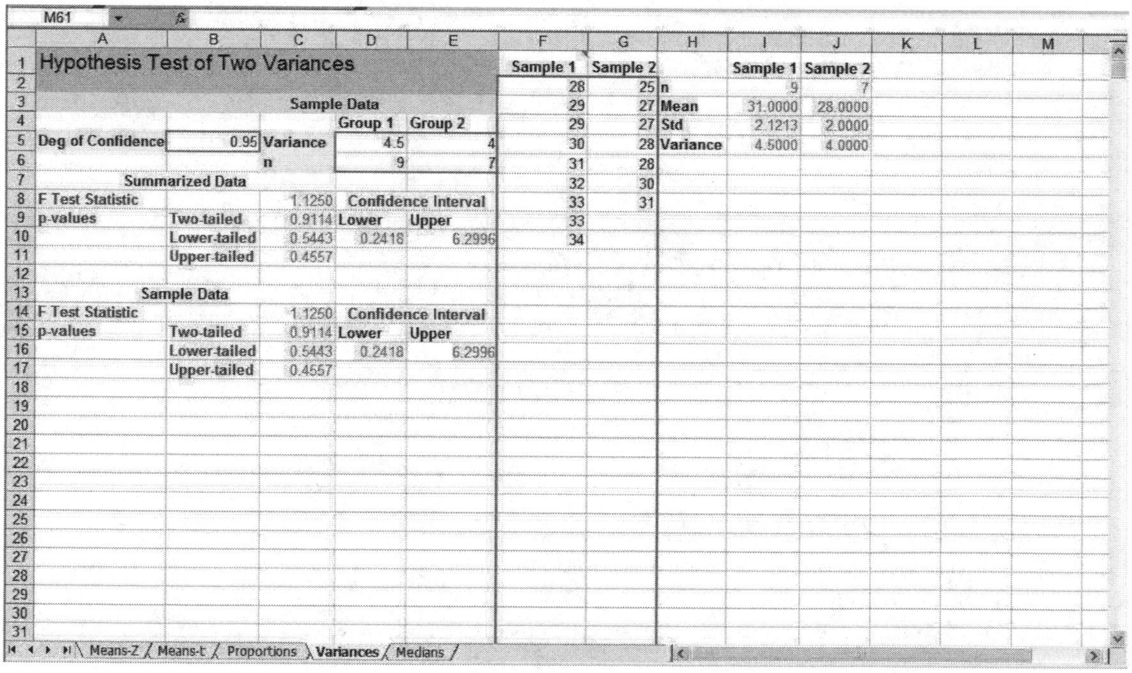

	A	B	C	D	E	F	G	H	I	J
1	Hypothesis Test of Two Variances					Sample 1	Sample 2		Sample 1	Sample 2
2						28	25	n	9	7
3			Sample Data			29	27	Mean	31.0000	28.0000
4				Group 1	Group 2	29	27	Std	2.1213	2.0000
5	Deg of Confidence	0.95	Variance	4.5	4	30	28	Variance	4.5000	4.0000
6			n	9	7	31	28			
7	Summarized Data					32	30			
8	F Test Statistic		1.1250	Confidence Interval		33	31			
9	p-values	Two-tailed	0.9114	Lower	Upper	33				
10		Lower-tailed	0.5443	0.2418	6.2996	34				
11		Upper-tailed	0.4557							
12										
13	Sample Data									
14	F Test Statistic		1.1250	Confidence Interval						
15	p-values	Two-tailed	0.9114	Lower	Upper					
16		Lower-tailed	0.5443	0.2418	6.2996					
17		Upper-tailed	0.4557							

Figure 8-6   ***Illustration of the Two Dependent Samples Template***

	A	B	C	D	E	F	G	H	I	J	K	L	M
1	Hypothesis Tests of Two Dependent Proportions					Sample 1	Sample 2		Sample 1	Sample 2			
2						1	1	Proportion	0.4300	0.5100			
3	Hypothesized Population			Sample Data		1	1	n	200	200			
4	Mean Difference			Success	Failure	1	1						
5	Deg of Confidence	0.95	Success	80	6	1	1						
6			Failure	22	92	1	1						
7	Summarized Data					1	1						
8	Successs-Failure	6	Proportion 1	0.4300	Difference	1	1						
9	Failure-Success	22	Proportion 2	0.5100	-0.0800	1	1						
10	McNemar Test					1	1						
11	p-values	Two-tailed	0.0037			1	1						
12		Lower-tailed	0.0019			1	1						
13		Upper-tailed	0.9995			1	1						
14	Normal Approximation			Confidence Interval		1	1						
15	Z Test Statistic		-3.0237	Lower	Upper	1	1						
16	p-values	Two-tailed	0.0025	-0.1307	-0.0293	1	1						
17		Lower-tailed	0.0012			1	1						
18		Upper-tailed	0.9988			1	1						
19						1	1						
20	Sample Data					1	1						
21	Successs-Failure	6.0000	Proportion 1	0.4300	Difference	1	1						
22	Failure-Success	22.0000	Proportion 2	0.5100	-0.0800	1	1						
23	McNemar Test					1	1						
24	p-values	Two-tailed	0.0037			1	1						
25		Lower-tailed	0.0019			1	1						
26		Upper-tailed	0.9995			1	1						
27	Normal Approximation			Confidence Interval		1	1						
28	Z Test Statistic		-3.0237	Lower	Upper	1	1						
29	p-values	Two-tailed	0.0025	-0.1516	-0.0084	1	1						
30		Lower-tailed	0.0012			1	1						

Means-t \ **Proportions** / Medians /

Using XLDataAnalyst

Two-sample tests can be easily performed using XLDataAnalyst. Figure 8-7 shows the portion of the XLDataAnalyst ribbon that performs test for two groups with the Two Independent Samples option selected.

Figure 8-7   ***Available Two Groups Tests in XLDataAnalyst***

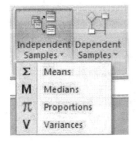

As you can see, you can select either Two Independent Samples or Two Dependent Samples. Figure 8-7 shows that XLDataAnalyst can perform all of the independent samples tests discussed in this chapter. These same options appear for the Dependent Samples option, except there is no selection for two dependent variances since that test does not exist.

The crucial factor in using XLDataAnalyst for two-sample tests is setting up the data in the appropriate format. The format for independent samples is to have a separate nominal scale variable that divides the data into two groups. This variable, the grouping variable, can have only two possible values. The other variable, the dependent variable, is the variable of interest in the hypothesis. An example of this type of data layout is shown in Figure 8-8 where Gender is the grouping variable and Salary is the dependent variable. This is the normal data layout or large-scale datasets, such as those in this text's appendix. For dependent samples, however, the data are arranged differently. XLDataAnalyst assumes that the data for dependent samples has already been separated into groups and the data should have two different variables, one for each group. This type of data layout is illustrated in Figure 8-8 that shows the data for Example 8-13.

Figure 8-8   Data Layouts for Independent and Dependent Samples

	A	B	C	D
1	Gender	Salary		
2	0	$40,775.00		
3	0	$47,315.00		
4	0	$35,749.00		
5	0	$42,689.00		
6	0	$47,920.00		
7	0	$41,729.00		
8	0	$43,074.00		
9	0	$48,786.00		
10	0	$44,301.00		
11	0	$51,693.00		
12	1	$47,257.00		
13	1	$47,246.00		
14	1	$55,096.00		
15	1	$38,930.00		
16	1	$40,687.00		
17	1	$38,733.00		
18	1	$45,973.00		
19	1	$35,362.00		
20	1	$39,577.00		
21	1	$48,185.00		
22				
23				
24				

	A	B	C
1	Rating 1	Rating 2	
2	11	16	
3	8	19	
4	13	16	
5	16	12	
6	16	9	
7	17	12	
8	5	14	
9	11	15	
10	15	11	
11	9	12	
12	10	8	
13	7	17	
14	6	9	
15	9	13	
16	10	17	
17	6	15	
18	10	18	
19	11	15	
20	12	12	
21	11	17	
22	11	13	
23	11	16	
24	16	18	

Once you have selected the type of test you want, a standard dialog, such as that shown in Figure 8-9 will appear. This dialogue box is very similar to that for the one-sample tests in Chapter 7. In this particular figure, the dialogue box illustrates the selection of the appropriate variables for Example 8-8 and specifies a 95% confidence interval and a two-tailed hypothesis test to show that the two population means are equal. After making your selections, click OK and the results will be presented. The output for Example 8-8 is presented in Figure 8-10.

Figure 8-9   Two-Sample Dialog Using Example 8-8

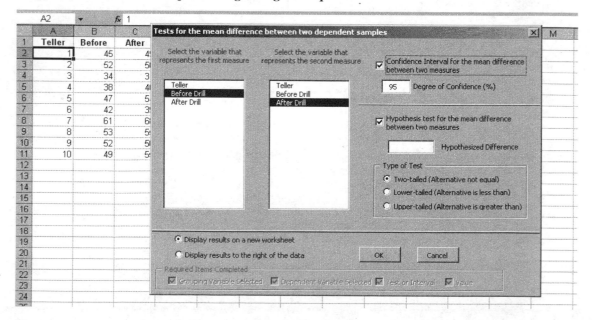

Figure 8-10   *XLDataAnalyst Output for Example 8-8*

Test For Differences Between Before Drill and After Drill

Summary Measures

Sample Size	10.0000
Mean Difference	-3.0000
Variance of Differences	18.4444
Standard Deviation of Differences	4.2947

0.95% Confidence Interval for the difference

Lower Limit	-6.0722
Upper Limit	0.0722

Hypothesis test of Mean Difference = 0 two-tailed alternative

Degrees of Freedom	9.0000
t-test statistic	-2.2090
p-value	0.0545

Exercises VII

40. Itron manufacturers meter-reading equipment for the utility industry. A new device has been developed that is designed to read the meters on houses from a truck traveling at 25 miles per hour down the street. To test the new equipment, Itron utilizes the device to read the meters from a random sample of 20 houses. At the same time the device is reading the meter, a human meter reader independently reads the meter. The 20 paired observations are contained in the file Exercises 8-40.xlsx. Test the hypothesis that the new device gives the same average readings as the human reader at the .05 level of significance.

41. The Opening Act Theatre Company is a nonprofit theatrical group. The survival of the group depends on several funding sources, but the most important are individual donors. In order to increase revenues from individual donors, Opening Act approached two marketing companies that specialize in nonprofit organizations for ideas. Each marketing company developed an appeal letter designed to increase individual giving. Opening Act sends out the two appeal letters to two separate random samples of 100 donors. The results of the letters are contained in the file Exercises 8-41.xlsx. Do the letters result in different response rates? What about the amount donated? What would you conclude from these data? Use a level of significance of .05.

42. Yogi's Sub Shop has been printing coupons in two local newspapers, the Nickel Nick and the Penny Wise, that are distributed free of charge in local shops. Yogi would like to know if there is a difference in the response to the two ads. Through a numbering system, he is able to track the coupons redeemed at the shop and has recorded whether or not a coupon was returned, as well as the amount of the purchase, if the coupon was redeemed. The data are contained in the file Exercise 8-42.xlsx. Is there a difference in the proportion of coupons redeemed from the two newspapers at the 5% level of significance?

43. Using the data in Exercise 8-42.xlsx, is there a difference in the average sales from the two ads? Is there a difference in the median sales?

44. The Marketing Director for Black Castle Hamburgers has devised a new point-of-sale display that she thinks will boost in-store sales at the restaurants. To test the effectiveness of the new ads, she places the new displays in 20 selected sites and retains the old displays in 20 other sites that are closely matched in

terms of location, overall sales and other selected factors. The resulting first week sales in dollars are in the file Exercise 8-44.xlsx. Is the new display effective? What is the level of significance of the results?

45. The regional manager of a retail chain is comparing monthly sales at two of her stores. The two stores have approximately the same average monthly sales; however, the manager wants to determine if there is a difference in the variability between the two stores. The manager collects 50 monthly statements from each store; the data are contained in the file Exercise 8-45.xlsx. At the .1 level of significance, determine if one store has a greater variability than the other. If the results are significant, which store has the greater variability?

Opening Vignette Revisited

Ray has gathered data from both the new and old machines. The data is contained in the file Chapter 8 Vignette.xls. The old machine had 18 defects while the new machine had only 10 defects; however, Ray knew that the difference between the two machines could be due to sampling error and there still may be no difference between the two machines. To determine if this was the case, Ray decided to test the hypothesis that the two machines were identical in terms of the proportion of defects produced. The results of the independent proportions test are shown in Figure 8-11.

Figure 8-11   ***Results of the Two Machine Comparison***

Two Sample Results For Defective

Summary Measures

	Old Machine	New Machine
Sample Size	100.000	100.000
Proportions	0.180	0.100
Standard Deviation	0.384	0.300
Sample Difference	-0.080	
Pooled Standard Deviation	0.347	
Standard Error of the Difference	0.049	

0.95% Confidence interval for the proportion difference Old Machine - New Machine

Lower Limit	-0.016
Upper Limit	0.176

Hypothesis test of the difference between Old Machine - New Machine = 0 two-tailed alternative

Z-test statistic	1.630
p-value	0.103
Chi-square statistic	2.658
p-value	0.103

Ray could see that, although there was a difference in the sample defect rates, this difference could be attributed to sampling error since the p-value was only .103. Therefore, Ray remained unconvinced that the new machine was in fact better than the old machine and decided not to purchase the new equipment.

Summary

This chapter extends the logic of hypothesis testing to tests for the difference between two groups. The null hypothesis typically states that the two groups are equal in terms of a population parameter such as the mean, proportion, median, or variance. The one-tail equivalent is that one group is larger than the other. If the difference between the corresponding sample statistics is larger than what might be expected from sampling error in the sampling distribution of the differences, we conclude that there is a statistically-significant difference.

A key factor in testing the two groups is whether the observations come from dependent samples or independent samples. Dependent samples require different testing procedures, but produce more powerful tests for the differences between the two population parameters than independent samples.

Independent sample tests for means and proportions are in many ways extensions of the tests for one-group tests presented in Chapter 7. When testing for means, an important distinction is whether or not we know the population variances or standard deviations. If we do, then the hypothesis test and corresponding confidence interval are based on the normal distribution; otherwise, they are based on the t-distribution. For the t-test, there are two types of tests: one assumes that the population variances are equal and the other does not make this assumption. Tests for two proportions can be conducted with an extension of the normal test for a single proportion or with a test based on the chi-square distribution. In the two-group case, these tests are entirely equivalent for a two-tailed hypothesis test; however, the test utilizing the normal distribution can be used for one-tailed tests while the chi-square test cannot. On the other hand, the chi-square test can be extended to three or more groups, as we will do in the next chapter. Tests for the equality of two population variances involve a new distribution previously introduced in Chapter 4: the F-distribution. The F-test looks at the ratio of the two-sample variances rather than the differences between the two values to test for the equality of the population variances. Under the null hypothesis, the expected ratio of the sample variances is 1.0. Tests of two population medians involve the notion of signed ranks first introduced with tests of a single median in Chapter 7. This notion of rank orderings is appropriate for ordinal scale data and utilizes the tests for medians.

For dependent samples, the tests are somewhat different. To test for means, the sample statistic is based on differences between values rather than the original values. The hypothesis test is then basically a one-sample t-test of the difference scores where the null hypothesis states that the average difference is equal to zero. The McNemar test is used for two dependent proportions. This test is a variation on the chi-square test used for two independent proportions.

Moreover, the test for two dependent medians (the Wilcoxon Signed Ranks test) like the dependent sample test for two means, is based on difference scores; however, since we are often dealing with ordinal data, the test utilizes only the ranks of the difference scores rather than the actual values. Variances or standard deviations cannot be tested for dependent samples since there is no statistical test for such a situation.

Since the hypothesis tests in this chapter are often difficult computationally, the use of computer software is even more of an advantage than it has been before. XLDataAnalyst can be used to perform all of the tests in this chapter quickly and efficiently. The Excel template accompanying this chapter can also solve most of the tests, with the exception of the Wilcoxon Signed Ranks test.

Chapter Glossary

Dependent Samples   Groups that are related or correlated in some way, either by matching individuals in the two groups on some characteristic or by having the same individuals in both groups (e.g., before and after).

Independent Samples   Groups that are independent or unrelated to each other. Typically, individuals are assigned to groups at random.

Statistically-Significant   The difference is too great to be attributed to chance. We conclude that it is probably due to a real difference between the groups in the population.

Questions and Problems

46. For testing the difference between means, what sampling distribution is theoretically correct when (a) σ is known? (b) σ is unknown?

47. Suppose that you're testing the difference between means from two small independent samples. What two assumptions apply?

48. An insurance company is planning to offer a new insurance/investment product to retired persons. They have sampled some retirees in two major markets to see if there is a difference in their retirement incomes (from pension and social security), with the following results:

	Region 1	Region 2
No. persons sampled	300	225
Mean retirement income/yr	$23,000	$27,500
Standard deviation	$3,000	$6,000

Is there a significant difference at the 5% level?

49. Two samples of $n = 16$ are drawn to test for the equality of means, and the difference turns out to be $\bar{X}_1 - \bar{X}_2 = 4.2$, with $s_1 = 4.0$ and $s_2 = 2.0$. What would be the t-value for the test?

50. Data were collected to test whether there was a difference in the salaries of secretaries who lived in the core area versus the suburban area of a major city. In a sample of 10 core residents, the mean salary was $24,450 with a standard deviation of $860. Suburban residents were classified as these who lived at least 8 miles from the core. Seventeen suburban residents were sampled. Both the mean salary ($26,900) and the standard deviation ($1,240) were higher than those from the core resident sample. Show all steps to test the alternative hypothesis that the mean salaries for suburban residents are higher than the mean salaries for residents living in the core area at the .01 level of significance.

51. A soft drink producer in California is evaluating an advertising campaign to promote the sale of its diet drink. To determine the effectiveness of the program, random samples of 2,000 persons were questioned before and after the advertisements ran. The following results were obtained:

Before: $n_1 = 2,000$ Number favoring company's product = 600

After: $n_2 = 2,000$ Number favoring company's product = 800

   (a) Is there a significant difference in preferences between the two time periods that would indicate that the campaign was successful (alpha is .05)?

52. The following data were collected in a survey to determine whether a new detergent (A) was really superior to a proven detergent (B). The ratings on a 500-point scale were as below:

Detergent A	Detergent B
$\bar{X}_1 = 426.0$	$\bar{X}_2 = 415.0$
$s_1 = 30.0$	$s_2 = 31.0$

   (a) Suppose that one were to test the hypothesis $H_0: \mu_1 \leq \mu_2$ against the alternative $H_1: \mu_1 > \mu_2$ using a sample of 100. Could the H_0 be rejected at the .05 level?

   (b) Assume that only 16 boxes of detergent were sampled from each brand. Could the H_0 be rejected at the .05 level?

   (c) Summarize your results from parts (a) and (b).

   (d) Why were you less likely to reject H_0 in part (b)?

(e)   Why did you have to use the *t*-distribution to solve part (b)?

53. Sixteen students were tested on their ability to remember information presented to them prior to and following a month-long period when they were given memory-enhancing medication, Lecithin, every day. The mean difference in their memory score was $\bar{d} = +10$ (improvement), and the standard error of the mean difference was 1.25 points. Compute the 95% confidence interval for the true difference.

54. In an attempt to determine whether there was a difference in performance between employees receiving their training on the job versus at a training school, 15 employees were carefully matched in terms of ability, age, and other factors. Then, one person from each pair was randomly assigned to each group. Scores reflecting their subsequent performance are given below and in the file Exercise 8-54.xlsx. The firm wishes to determine whether the difference in scores is large enough to reasonably conclude that one training procedure is superior to the other. Test the hypothesis that the means are equal at the .02 level of significance:

Pair No.	1	2	3	4	5	6	7	8	9	10	11	12	13	14	15
On-job score	76	80	94	88	90	82	76	81	83	86	78	76	79	84	80
School score	82	81	87	79	95	85	68	78	91	87	83	79	85	87	84

55. A research group is comparing the effectiveness of two different pain-killing drugs. Both drugs take the same average amount of time to take effect; however the group wants to study the variability of time until pain relief occurs. Drug A is given to 24 people and Drug B to 30. The data from the study are contained in the file Exercise 8-55.xlsx. At the .05 level of significance, can researchers conclude a significant difference in the variability of the drugs?

56. An automobile company is doing a preliminary study to determine which of two assembly plants, one in California and one in Ohio, they should phase out over the next three years. One of their criteria is to choose a plant with older workers, and therefore closer to retirement, so that the impact of layoffs will be minimized. Each plant employs several thousand workers so they have decided to take a sample of 50 employees from each plant. The ages of the 100 sampled workers are given in the file Exercise 8-56.xlsx.

(a)   Is there a significant difference in the average age of the workers at the two plants? Use a .05 level of significance.

(b)   Using a .05 level of significance, is there a significant difference in the variability of the workers' ages at the two plants?

(c)   Is there a significance difference in the median workers' ages at the two plants? Use a .05 level of significance.

57. Wandermere Realty wants to determine if the proportion of U.S. individuals in their region who own their own homes is any different in the 40 - 50 age group versus the 50 - 60 age group. They take a random sample of 200 households with the principal owner being in one of these two age groups. The data are contained in the file Exercise 8-57.xlsx. Is there a statistically-significant difference in the percentage of homeowners in the two groups (at the .05 level)?

58. The Olin Manufacturing Company has recently instituted statistical process control (SPC) in several of their plants. The VP of Manufacturing asked for data showing that the use of SPC has reduced the amount of rework at the plants. The file Exercise 8-58.xlsx contains the amount of rework in the month before the implementation of SPC and the month after for a randomly selected set of 40 products manufactured at the different plants. Is there evidence that SPC has reduced the average amount of rework (alpha is .05)?

59. A large Midwestern city has suspected that some manufacturing plants are discharging large amounts of industrial waste at one time rather than spacing them out in smaller amounts. This leads to a highly

erratic influx of effluents that are difficult to deal with. Although the Water Commissioner had asked the plants in the area discharge waste at a steady rate no greater than 100 lbs. per hour, there is one particular plant that was suspected of continuing the old practice. Effluents were measured at 60 random time intervals at other plants and at 60 random times at the suspected facility and the data are contained in the file Exercise 8-59.xlsx. Is there any evidence that the variability in effluents is greater at the suspected plant than at the others (alpha is .05)?

60. A marketing expert believes that the gender gap that was initially present in online shopping (more males than females) has been eliminated. To test this, the expert conducts a phone survey with a random sample of 300 individuals, records their gender and asks whether or not they have ever purchased anything online. The responses are contained in the file Exercise 8-60.xlsx. Is there a significant difference between males and females in terms of the proportion who purchase online (alpha is .05)?

Database Problems

Corporate Statistical Database

61. Assume the firms listed in the Corporate Statistical Database constitute random samples from normally distributed populations. Test the hypothesis that the price/earnings ratio of the retail firms equals that of the banking and insurance firms. Use a significance level of 10%. Does the assumption of equal variances hold in this situation?

62. Using the Corporate Statistical Database, test the hypothesis that the advertising expenditures are equal in the banking and insurance versus the transportation firms. Let $\alpha = .05$, and assume that the data constitute random samples of the industry drawn from normally distributed populations.

63. Using the Corporate Statistical Database, test the hypothesis that the variances of the advertising expenditures are equal in the banking and insurance versus the transportation firms. Let $\alpha = .05$, and assume that the data constitute random samples of the industry drawn from normally distributed populations.

64. A management analyst doing a plant location study has narrowed the choice of site down to a western location (in Washington, Oregon, or California), or an eastern one (in Massachusetts, New York, or New Jersey). Now the analyst wishes to compare income and salary levels in the two locations. Use the data from the Corporate Statistical Database.

(a) Is the mean state per capita income different in the two locations? [*Note*: The per capita income figures are from census data].

(b) Assuming that the salary data for the firms listed are representative of all salaries in the areas, use the HQ data to test whether there is a difference in the average annual salary of employees in the two locations. [*Note*: You may wish to sort the data according to state first].

MegaCorp Employee Survey Database

65. There have been grumblings among the Riteway employees that they are paid less in general than the Entron employees. Is there evidence to support this claim in the sample data? Test the hypothesis that the median overall satisfaction rating is the same in the Snackrite and CoreSteel groups. The VP of Human Resources is concerned that, although the average salaries may be similar, there may be more variability in salaries in the CoreSteel group compared to the other subsidiaries. Do the data provide evidence to support this claim? The President of the Entron group wants to know if his group is similar to employees at Snackrite. Compare the two groups in terms of the proportion of management personnel, proportion of salaried employees, gender, and average age. In what respects are the two groups significantly different?

Alaska Sport Fishing Survey

66. The head of the Alaska Tourism Council feels that those who travel in groups tend to stay longer than those who travel alone. Is there evidence of this in the data? (Hint: Create a variable that distinguishes between the responses where the People variable is 1 versus when it is greater than 1). In order to better market the state for tourism, the Tourism Council develops a survey to determine if there are significant differences between men and women as to the importance of the different characteristics of a sports fishing destination. Test whether or not the median responses are the same for the males and females with the 11 survey items.

67. Someone has suggested that the male visitors are more likely to be single than female visitors. Is there evidence of this in the sample? (Hint: Create a variable distinguishing between married and non-married individuals).

68. Some members in the Council have speculated that there are some key differences, especially in the frequency of visits, between those who stay with friends or relatives and those who stay in lodges or resorts. (1) Are there significant differences in the average number of trips in these two groups? (2) Are there significant differences in the variability of the number of trips?

Chapter 9:

Tests of Three or More Groups
ANOVA and Chi-Square

Opening Vignette
Introduction
Data Collection
Tests of Means: One-Way Analysis of Variance
- The Logic of ANOVA
- Modeling Effects in ANOVA and the ANOVA Table
- Computer Solution to One-Way ANOVA
- Post-Hoc Tests

Tests for Three or More Proportions
- Post-Hoc Tests
- Computer Solution for Tests of Three or More Proportions

Tests of Three or More Variances
Tests of Three or More Medians
Practice
Three Group Tests and ANOVA with Excel and XLDataAnalyst
- Excel Functions
- The Analysis Toolpak
- The Excel Template
- Using XLDataAnalyst

Opening Vignette Revisited
Summary
Chapter Glossary
Questions and Problems
Tests of Goodness of Fit (Optional)
- Fit of Data to a Uniform Distribution
- Fit of Data to a Normal Distribution

Two-Way Analysis of Variance (Optional)
Some Special ANOVA Designs (Optional)
- Randomized Block Design
- Repeated Measures Design

Chapter 9 Objectives

When you finish this chapter you should be able to:

1. **Understand the logic behind Analysis of Variance (ANOVA)**
2. **Use ANOVA to test for the difference among means of three or more groups**
3. **Use chi-square test to test for the differences between three or more proportions**
4. **Use the Levine test to test for three or more variances**
5. **Use the Kruskal-Wallace test to test for the difference between three or more medians**

Opening Vignette

Ray Popovich is the recently hired plant manager for AccuFab, a small manufacturing firm. Ray has been given specific instructions to reduce overhead costs by any possible means. During a recent staff meeting, a manufacturing foreman talked about a synthetic lubricant that can be used on the machines. This product is more expensive than what is currently used, but lasts much longer than other market offerings. Since your plant contains a lot of heavy machinery, lubricant is a very significant cost to your company. Ray is not sure if the longer life of the new product would be worth the additional cost, so he decides to compare three different brands of lubricant, including the new synthetic. In the trial, Ray instructed that the three brands be used on a random sample of 5 machines for one month. Based on the results, Ray calculated the average life per dollar and the data from the test are shown below. Ray needs a method of analyzing the results of his tests so that he can draw conclusions about which product is the most economical for the company.

Brand A	Brand B	Synthetic
10	13	21
12	15	20
15	18	22
8	11	27
19	22	25

Introduction

In the last chapter, we explored tests for the equality of means, variance, proportions and medians in two groups. In this chapter, we will extend those tests to three or more groups. Unlike two-sample tests, there is no test for three or more means when the population standard deviations are known. Therefore, in this chapter, we will no longer consider situations where the population standard deviation is known; however, we will extend the t-test for two means when the population standard deviations are unknown to three or more means by using Analysis of Variance (ANOVA). ANOVA is a set of techniques used to test hypotheses about three or more means using the F-test.

In this chapter, we will also extend the chi-square test to three or more proportions. Like ANOVA, this use of the chi-square distribution can be viewed more generally as a test of "goodness of fit." We will also extend the notion of rank tests for medians to three or more groups and introduce a new test for three or more variances, which is an extension of the F-test for two variances we looked at in the last chapter.

Data Collection

In the last chapter we explored the distinction between independent and dependent samples. That distinction is still relevant in this chapter as well. Most of our discussion in this chapter assumes independent samples. Dependent samples require more complex treatment and techniques; therefore, dependent sample means are discussed in the optional material at the end of this chapter.

Data from independent samples can be gathered in two different ways:

(handwritten note: how things are independent)

1. For nonexperimental data, the samples can be random samples from different population groups that are independent of one another. This type of data often arises naturally when samples are taken from a population and demographic data such as gender, location, organizational position, and other characteristics are recorded.

2. For data from an experiment, respondents are assigned to groups by the analyst conducting the study. For experiments, it is necessary that subjects be assigned randomly to groups. This does not guarantee that the groups will be independent, but it makes it more likely that they will be truly independent.

Although some of the techniques discussed in this chapter, such as analysis of variance, are often closely associated with the experimental method, data can arise from either experimental or nonexperimental studies. In either case, it is necessary that the groups be independent.

Tests of Means: One-Way Analysis of Variance

The simple one-way analysis of variance is used to test for the difference between three or more means. The general form of the hypotheses is:

$$H_0: \mu_1 = \mu_2 = \mu_3 = \ldots = \mu_a$$
$$H_1: \text{not } (\mu_1 = \mu_2 = \mu_3 = \ldots = \mu_a)$$

The alternative hypothesis states that the means are not all equal. There will almost always be some differences in the sample means—even if they come from the same population. But, if the difference among any of the group sample means is more than can be expected from normal sampling variation, we would reject the hypothesis that all the means are equal, and conclude that the population means are not equal.

Care must be taken in interpreting the meaning of the alternative hypothesis if the test rejects the null hypothesis. Following a rejection of the null hypothesis, it is tempting to infer that all of the means are different; however, the alternative hypothesis does not state that all of the means are different; only that they are not all the same. In other words, it states that at least two of the means are different. For example, if we have three groups, the null hypothesis would be:

$$H_0: \mu_1 = \mu_2 = \mu_3$$

If this hypothesis is rejected, there are several possibilities. First, it is possible that all three of the means are different, e.g. $\mu_1 \neq \mu_2 \neq \mu_3$; however, there are also three other possibilities, namely $\mu_1 = \mu_2 \neq \mu_3$, $\mu_1 \neq \mu_2 = \mu_3$ and $\mu_1 = \mu_2 \neq \mu_3$. Rejecting the null hypothesis does not tell us which of these three possibilities is true. We must perform additional tests, described later, to determine which means are different. For now, all we can say, if the null hypothesis is rejected is that at least two (and possibly more) of the means are different.

In addition to the null and alternative hypotheses, we also need to make three assumptions before proceeding:

- *Normality*: The populations of all groups follow a normal distribution

- *Homogeneity of Variances*: The population variances are the same in each group

- *Independence*: The groups are from independent samples[1].

Notice the similarity of these assumptions to those we made in the last chapter for the test of two independent means.

The Logic of ANOVA

At first glance, the name of the technique for testing of three or more means may seem like a misnomer. How do we test a hypothesis about means by analyzing variances? Hopefully, an examination of the logic underlying the analysis of variance will clarify the reasoning.

Example 9-1

MegaHen Investment Company recently purchased a large turkey farm for production of turkeys for overseas markets. A consultant engaged by MegaHen has advised them that there are three feeds commonly used to ensure quality breeders and produce rapid weight gains. She suggests conducting a statistical experiment to determine which feed produces the greatest weight gains. Each type of feed is fed to a randomly selected group of 5 turkeys and their weight gains are measured over a period of three months. The resulting weight gains in grams are shown in Table 9-1.

Table 9-1   *Weight Gains in Turkeys*

	Topnotch	Growbig	Max
	42	112	70
	96	96	17
	81	88	49
	95	135	24
	76	119	40
$\bar{X}_j$	78	110	40
S_j^2	480.5	347.5	441.5
Grand Mean $\bar{\bar{X}}$			76

Note that in Table 9-1 the mean and variance of each group has been calculated along with the overall grand mean (the mean of all 15 values irrespective of feed type). Recall from our assumptions that the three groups have a normal distribution in the population and that the variances in the population are the same in the three groups ($\sigma_1^2 = \sigma_2^2 = \sigma_3^2$). Putting these assumptions together with the null hypothesis that the means are equal would yield three totally overlapping distributions for the three groups depicted in Figure 9-1.

---

[1] In an experiment, this means that experimental units are assigned randomly to each group so that the groups are independent.

Figure 9-1   ***Three Normal Populations with $H_0: \mu_1 = \mu_2 = \mu_3$ True and $\sigma_1^2 = \sigma_2^2 = \sigma_3^2 = \sigma^2$***

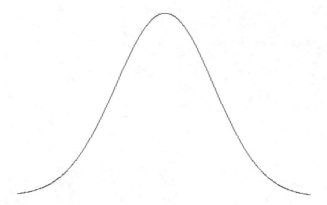

We basically have three independent samples from the same population so that the three sample variances (S_j^2 called *variability within groups*) are all estimates of the common population variance σ^2 and the three sample means are simply a sample of size three from the sampling distribution of the mean, as discussed in Chapter 5. This means that the variance of these three sample means (called *variability between groups*) is an estimate of the variance of the sampling distribution $\sigma_{\bar{X}}^2 = \sigma^2/n$. With a little algebra we would have $n\sigma_{\bar{X}}^2 = \sigma^2$. Therefore, n times the between groups variance will also be an estimate of the same common population variance. Therefore, under the null hypothesis, the variability between the groups should be equal to the variability within the groups.

Now suppose that our assumptions about the populations (normality and homogeneity of variances) hold, but that the null hypothesis is false. Further, assume that in fact, all three means are different from each other. We would then have a situation, as depicted in Figure 9-2.

Figure 9-2   ***Three Normal Populations with $H_0: \mu_1 = \mu_2 = \mu_3$ Not True***

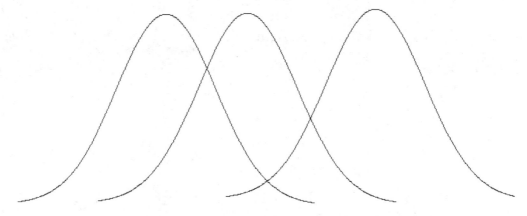

In this situation, we would expect the variability of the means to be much larger. In other words, the variability between the groups should be larger than the variability within the groups. The F-distribution can be used to test whether or not two variances are equal:

$$F = \frac{variance\ between\ groups}{variance\ within\ groups}$$

F - Test

We can illustrate these concepts in terms of our data from Example 9-1. As with the pooled variance, we can average the three sample variances to generate a pooled estimate of the population variance (within group variability). The calculations are as follows[2]:

$$Within\ Group\ Variability = (480.5 + 347.5 + 441.5)/3 = 423.17$$

Our estimate of the **within group** variability is 423.17. But, if we calculate the variance of the three sample means we would find that:

$$Between\ Group\ Variability = ((78\text{-}76)^2 + (110\text{-}76)^2 + (40\text{-}76)^2)/(3\text{-}1)) = 1,228$$

which if we multiply by 5 (our "n") would give us 6,140 which is our **between groups** variability. The ratio of these two variances is our F-value:

$$F = \frac{6,140}{423.17} = 14.51$$

We can use the FDIST function in Excel or the probability calculator in XLDataAnalyst to calculate the p-value for this value of F which would give us a p-value of .001. We should, therefore, reject the null hypothesis that the means are equal and conclude that at least two of the means are different.

Modeling Effects in ANOVA and the ANOVA Table

Although the preceding calculations illustrated the logic of the analysis of variance, the actual calculations of ANOVA are not performed this way and the results are presented in a different manner as well. The calculations are based on the idea of breaking the total variability of the data into component parts. This is based on a model of the influences on the individual observations in the data. Let μ equal the average of the three population means:

$$\mu = \frac{\Sigma \mu_j}{3}$$

We can then write the following equation for an individual observation (X) in the data pool:

$$X_{ij} = \mu + \mu_j - \mu + X_{ij} - \mu_j \qquad (9\text{-}1)$$

At one level, this is a trivial equation since the +μ and -μ terms and the +μ_j and -μ_j cancel out and we are left with the identity:

$$X_{ij} = X_{ij}$$

However, if we group the terms appropriately we have the following equation:

$$X_{ij} = \mu + (\mu_j - \mu) + (X_{ij} - \mu_j) \qquad (9\text{-}2)$$

Therefore, an individual observation is a function of the average weight gain, irrespective of the type of feed, plus the effect of the particular type of feed that this turkey received (the between groups or treatment effect), plus the normal error variability within a particular feed type (the within groups variability).

If we move the "μ" term in the above equation to the left side of the equation, we get:

$$X_{ij} - \mu = (\mu_j - \mu) + (X_{ij} - \mu_j) \qquad (9\text{-}3)$$

---

[2] We can use the simple average of the variances because the sample sizes are equal in all three groups. If the sample sizes are unequal we have to calculate a weighted average.

The portion on the left side of the equation is the deviation of the individual observations from the overall mean. The deviation about the overall mean can be broken into two parts: (1) the first is because the average weight gain for this type of feed differs from the overall average weight gain (the treatment effect), and (2) the second is the variability within this feed type or sampling error. If you take any value in the data set, you should be able to convince yourself that this identity holds. For example, the second turkey fed Growbig had a weight gain of 96 grams. Therefore:

$$(96 - 76) = (96 - 110) + (110 - 76)$$

$$20 = -14 + 34$$

Usually, we are interested in the squared deviations rather than the actual deviations. If we assume for the moment that the 5 values in each group are the entire population we are interested in, it can be shown that:

$$\sum_{j=1}^{a} \sum_{i=1}^{n} (X_{ij} - \mu)^2 = n \sum_{j=1}^{a} (\mu_j - \mu)^2 + \sum_{j=1}^{a} \sum_{i=1}^{n} (X_{ij} - \mu_j)^2 \qquad (9\text{-}4)$$

where i = 1 to n represents the observations within each group and j = 1 to a represents the groups.

The total variability of the values (the sum of the squared deviations) can be broken down into two components: the variability between groups and the variability within groups; however, equation 9-4 deals with population values. We can follow the same process with the sample values where the total variability is calculated as the sum of the squared deviations around the overall mean and is denoted as SST for *Sum of Squares Total:*

$$\text{Sum-of-Squares Total} \qquad SST = \sum_{j=1}^{a} \sum_{i=1}^{n} (X_{ij} - \bar{\bar{X}})^2$$

where $\bar{\bar{X}}$ (pronounced X bar bar) represents the overall or grand mean. In our example from above we would have:

$$SST = (42 - 76)^2 + (96 - 76)^2 + \ldots\ldots (24 - 76)^2 + (40 - 76)^2 = 17,358$$

SST can be broken down into two parts: the first part represents the variability within the groups and is denoted SSE for *Sum of Squares Error,* while the second part represents the between groups variability and is called *Sum of Squares Treatment,* denoted as SSA.

$$\text{Sum-of-Squares Error} \qquad SSE = \sum_{j=1}^{a} \left(\sum_{i=1}^{n} X_{ij} - \bar{X_j}^2 \right)$$

For the MegaHen example, we would calculate:

$$SSE = (42 - 78)^2 + (96 - 78)^2 + \ldots\ldots\ldots + (24 - 40)^2 + (40 - 40)^2 = 5,078 \qquad (9\text{-}5)$$

The other component represents the between groups variability and is called *sum of squares treatment* and denoted as SSA.

$$SSA = \sum_{j=1}^{a} n(\bar{X_j} - \bar{\bar{X}})^2$$

For our example the results would be:

$$SSA = 5*((78 - 76)^2 + (110 - 76)^2 + (40 - 76)^2) = 12,280$$

We can then see that the two components add up to the total variability:

$$\textbf{SST = SSA + SSE}$$

important ↗

$$\text{or } 17,358 = 5,078 + 12,280$$

The components of the total variability are illustrated in Figure 9-3:

Figure 9-3   ***Total Variability Broken Into Two Components for One-Way ANOVA***

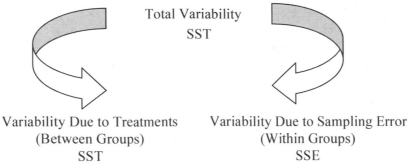

Total Variability
SST

Variability Due to Treatments
(Between Groups)
SST

Variability Due to Sampling Error
(Within Groups)
SSE

Sums of squares are rather like the numerator of a variance (e.g., the sum of squared deviations). If we divide these sums of squares by their corresponding degrees of freedom, we get what are called *mean squares (MS)*. This indicates the average of the squared values or the average squared deviation and is the basic concept of a variance. We normally calculate a mean square for treatments[3] (MSA) and a mean square error (MSE). Since there are three groups that we are studying, the degrees of freedom for treatments are treatments (k) – 1, or for our example 3 -1 = 2 and:

$$\text{MSA} = 12,280/2 = 6,140$$

degrees of freedom

For MSE, there are 5 observations in each group or 5 – 1 = 4 degrees of freedom. Since there are three groups, there are 3*4 = 12 degrees of freedom for the within group variability. Then:

$$\text{MSE} = 5,078/12 = 423.17$$

You might recognize these mean square values from our prior calculations of the variances in the last section. In fact, mean square is another term for a variance. The ratio of the mean squares for treatments to the mean square error is the F-value that we calculated before:

$$F = \text{MSA}/\text{MSE} = 6,140/423.17 = 14.51$$

The calculations of the analysis of variance are usually presented in table form and the result is called an *ANOVA Table*. The general form of the ANOVA table for a one-way ANOVA is illustrated in Table 9-2 and the results from our MegaHen example follow in Table 9-3:

Table 9-2   ***General ANOVA Table***

Source	SS	Df	MS	F
Treatments	SSA	a-1	MSA=SSA/(a-1)	MSA/MSE
Error	SSE	a(n-1)	MSE=SSE/a(n-1)	
Total	SST	an - 1		

---

[3] The term treatment comes from the experimental literature where the qualitative independent variable is often a "treatment" of some kind.

Table 9-3   *The ANOVA Table for Example 9-1*

Source	SS	df	MS	F	p-value
Treatments	12,280	2	6,140	14.51	.001
Error	5,078	12	423.17		
Total	17,358	14			

Notice two things about the ANOVA table in Table 9-3: (1) the sum of squares are additive in the sense that SST = SSA + SSE and the degrees of freedom are also additive. In other words, the degrees of freedom for treatments plus the degrees of freedom for error equal the total degrees of freedom. This is always true in ANOVA tables.

Post-Hoc Tests

Since the p-value in Table 9-3 is less than .05 (our given level of significance), we can reject the null hypothesis and conclude that the means are not all equal. Once we have rejected the null hypothesis we may be interested in knowing which means are in fact significantly different. Recall that rejecting the null hypothesis implies that at least two of the means are different; it does not necessarily mean that all of them are different. In our MegaHen example, since we have rejected the null hypothesis, at least one of the following three hypotheses can be rejected; but, which one(s):

$$H_0: \mu_1 = \mu_2$$
$$\text{or}$$
$$H_0: \mu_1 = \mu_3$$
$$\text{or}$$
$$H_0: \mu_2 = \mu_3$$

At first glance, it might seem that if we are interested in testing the mean difference for two groups in each case, we could just perform three different t-tests for independent samples as we did in Chapter 8 to find out which differences are statistically significant. However, there is a problem with that. If you recall from our discussions in Chapter 7 about the level significance (α) and the probability of a Type I error, if we set the level of significance at the traditional level of .05 then there is a 5% chance that we will make a Type I error. However, when we are performing more than one significance test, then the overall Type I error rate will become larger. To see this, suppose that we perform two independent t tests following a significant F tests in an ANOVA with each test performed at a .05 level of significance. Then; each test has only a 5% chance of a Type I error; yet, in performing two such tests, both tests have to not have a Type I error in order to avoid a Type I error for the two tests together. Since each test has a $(1-\alpha) = .95$ chance of not making a Type I error, the probability that both will not contain a Type I error is $(.95)(.95) = .9025$. Therefore, the chance of at least one of them containing a Type I error is $1 - .9025 = .0975$. The probability of at least one Type I error on the two tests is .0975 instead of the .05 level of significance. In general, for k tests the overall family-wise probability[4] of making at least one Type I error is:

Family-Wise Alpha $\alpha_{FW} = 1 - (1 - \alpha_{IT})^k$ (9-6)

where α_{IT} is the level of significance of each individual test. If we want the overall chance of a Type I error to be some small value, such as .05, we need to adjust the level of significance for each of the individual tests to make this happen. One approach, called the *Bonferroni method*, is to simply spread the error rate equally between the individual tests by setting the individual level of significance to:

---

[4] This is sometimes also called the experiment-wise error rate.

$$\alpha_{IT} = \frac{\alpha_{FW}}{k}$$

For example, if you were performing two tests and wanted a .05 level of significance over both tests, then you would perform both tests at the .05/2 = .025 level of significance. If you were going to perform three tests, then the level of significance for each tests would be .05/3 = .0167.

The problem with the Bonferroni approach is that it is very conservative. In other words, it can lead to an increase chance of a Type II error. There are a wide variety of statistical tests that control the family-wise error rate that are more powerful than the Bonferroni approach. All of these tests can be formulated in terms of a confidence interval test for the difference between two means:

$$\bar{X}_i - \bar{X}_j \pm Distribution\ Percentile * Standard\ Error$$

Post-hoc tests for analysis of variance use some form of the MSE for the standard error, but differ in terms of the test statistic used. The most widely used test in statistical software is the *Tukey test* sometimes also called the Tukey-Kramer test when the sample sizes are different in each group.

The Tukey confidence interval is:

$$\bar{X}_i - \bar{X}_j \pm \frac{q_\alpha}{\sqrt{2}} \sqrt{\frac{MSE}{n_i} + \frac{MSE}{n_j}} \qquad (9\text{-}7)$$

where q_α is the appropriate percentile from the studentized range distribution[5] with k treatment groups and degrees of freedom from the MSE for the ANOVA. You should be able to see the similarity of the standard error here to that of using the pooled variance, where the MSE acts as the pooled variance. The main difference is the use of the studentized range distribution which allows for control of the overall family-wise error rate.

The confidence interval can be used to test the null hypothesis that the means are equal. If the confidence interval contains 0 (if one limit is positive and the other negative), then we cannot reject the null hypothesis and must conclude that the means are indeed equal; however, if both limits are positive or both negative, then we can reject the null hypothesis and be 95% confident[6] that the true mean difference in the population is not zero.

Example 9-2

Calculate the Tukey tests results for Example 9-1.

Solution

MSE = 423.167

$q_{.05,3,12} = 3.77$

$$\frac{q_{.\alpha,k,df\,error}}{\sqrt{2}} \sqrt{\frac{MSE}{n_i} + \frac{MSE}{n_j}} = \frac{3.77}{\sqrt{2}} \sqrt{\frac{423.167}{5} + \frac{423.167}{5}} = 34.703$$

---

[5] The studentized range distribution is a difficult one to work with mathematically and we will not provide details for it here. XLDataAnalyst will perform the Tukey tests whenever an ANOVA is performed.

[6] 95% confidence is the standard confidence interval

Groups	Mean Difference	Lower Bound	Upper Bound
Topnotch – Growbig	-32.00	-66.703	2.703
Topnotch – Max	38.00	3.297	72.703
Growbig – Max	70.00	35.297	104.703

From these results, we can conclude that Topnotch produces significantly higher weight gains than does Max and that Growbig also produces significantly higher weight gains than does Max; however, we do not have sufficient evidence to conclude that there is a difference in the weight gains produced by Topnotch and Growbig. The difference between the two is fairly large and the upper bound is only slightly positive while the lower bound is a large negative value. If we wanted to investigate this difference further we would need to take a larger sample so see if the difference between Topnotch and Growbig is significant.

Exercises I

1. A consumer testing agency is comparing batteries from three different manufacturers in terms of time to failure. The resulting ANOVA table is shown below.

Source	SS	DF	MS	F
Batteries	195.8462	2	97.9231	10.6904
Error	247.3168	27	9.1599	
Total	443.1630	29		

    (a) Using the F.Dist function in Excel or the Probability Calculator in XLDataAnalyst, are there significant differences between the brands in terms of time to failure.

    (b) Assuming the mean time until failure of the three brands are as shown below and that the relevant percentile from the studentized range distribution is $q = 3.53$, which batteries show significantly different mean time until failure?

Battery A	Battery B	Battery C
13.44	15.51	9.36

2. The FDA is testing the effectiveness of four different brands of pain reliever. During the test volunteers with chronic pain resulting from different medical conditions, are given one of the medications and asked to report when the pain begins to diminish. The dependent variable is the time between taking the medication and when the pain begins to go away. The resulting ANOVA table is shown below.

Source	SS	DF	MS	F
Drug	508.5234	3	169.5078	11.4956
Error	530.8351	36	14.7454	
Total	1,039.3585	39		

    (a) Using the F.Dist function in Excel or the Probability Calculator in XLDataAnalyst, are there significant differences between the brands in terms of response times.

(b) Assuming the mean times of the four brands of pain reliever are as shown below and that the relevant percentile from the studentized range distribution is q = 3.53, which batteries show significantly different mean time until failure?

Pain Reliever A	Pain Reliever B	Pain Reliever C	Pain Reliever D
16.9400	22.6800	23.1300	26.9200

3. Tests were conducted using $n = 7$ random samples of six competitive brands (A, B, ..., F) of fast drying paint under controlled conditions. The resultant drying times (min) are shown below. Totals and summation values are also given, where $n_i = 7$ and $\bar{x}_i$ = the mean of column i. Using the data provided, test whether the drying times are equal for all six brands of paint. Let $\alpha = .01$, and report your results in the ANOVA table format.

	A	B	C	D	E	F	
	22	23	28	21	27	29	
	26	20	25	22	29	22	
	24	18	24	17	28	25	
	20	22	26	20	32	24	
	28	23	25	18	28	27	
	29	22	28	21	31	18	
	19	19	26	14	28	30	
Total	168	147	182	133	203	175	*Grand Mean*
Col. Mean $\bar{X}_j$	24	21	26	19	29	25	$\bar{\bar{X}} = 24$
$n_j(\bar{X}_j - 24)^2$	0	63	28	175	175	7.	*Total = 448*
$\sum (X - \bar{X}_j)^2$	90.	24.	14.	48.	20.	104.	*Total = 300*

4. The following ANOVA table represents part of the results from a study of the wait times from four different arrangements of waiting lines for services of tellers at a local savings and loan. Unfortunately, the other information from the table has been lost. Complete the missing elements of the table and test whether or not there are significant differences in the wait times of the four different arrangements.

Source	SS	DF	MS	F
Arrangements		3	20	
Error				
Total	100	19		

5. The following ANOVA table represents part of the results from a study on shelf location of items (top, middle, or bottom) and the sales of items in a local grocery store. Unfortunately, the other information from the table has been lost. Complete the missing elements of the table and test to see whether or not there are significant differences in sales for the three different locations.

Source	SS	DF	MS	F
Locations	200			
Error				
Total	500	29		

Tests for Three or More Proportions

In first section of this chapter we extended the idea of a t-test for the difference between two means to a test of three or more means with analysis of variance. Similarly, we now want to extend the tests for the difference between two population proportions to **three or more proportions**.

Analogous to the one-way ANOVA our hypotheses would be:

$$H_0: \pi_1 = \pi_2 = \pi_3 = \ ..... = \pi_a$$

$$H_1: \text{not } (\pi_1 = \pi_2 = \pi_3 = \ ..... = \pi_a)$$

As before, it would not be correct to state the alternative hypothesis as $H_1: \pi_1 \neq \pi_2 \neq \pi_3 \neq ... \neq \pi_a$. The alternative hypothesis is simply that at least two of the proportions are different. Fortunately, we do not need any new techniques to test this hypothesis. The chi-square test for two population proportions can be extended directly to three or more proportions.

Example 9-3

A large razor blade company has developed a new razor blade made out of a special alloy and their marketing department wants to test their new blade code, named Sazor, against their old blade along with two other blades from competitors. The department decides to test the four different blades (each disguised to not reveal the brand name) on four different groups of men. The men tried the blade given to them for one week and responded either positively or negatively as to whether or not they would buy the blade in the future. The marketing group wants to know if there are any differences in the proportion of men who responded positively to the four different types of blades. The results are presented in Table 9-4.

Table 9-4   Example 9-3 Data

	Sazor	Old Blade	Competitor 1	Competitor 2
Would Buy	18	11	19	20
Would Not Buy	2	9	6	15

The numbers in the table are frequencies, e.g., the number of respondents who responded in that manner. If the null hypothesis is true, we would expect the same proportion of men in each group to respond positively to the blades. For example, since 68% of the respondents overall respond positively (68 out of 100), we would expect 68% of the sample of 20 for Sazor to respond positively; or $20(.68) = 13.6$ would be the frequency we would expect in the first cell of the table. Similarly, we could compute the rest of the expected frequencies in the other cells. If the null hypothesis is true, we would expect the actual frequencies to be equal to the expected frequencies. However, since we are dealing with sample information, we would not expect the frequencies to be exactly equal. The basic question is "Are the differences between the expected and actual frequencies large enough to lead us to conclude that the null hypothesis is false?" To test this, we calculate a Chi-square value.

$$\chi^2 = \sum \frac{(f_o - f_e)^2}{f_e} \tag{9-8}$$

where f_o denotes the observed frequencies and f_e denotes the expected, or theoretical, frequencies. As in the last chapter, the expected frequencies are calculated as:

$$f_e = \frac{R_i C_j}{n} \tag{9-9}$$

where R_i and C_j are the row and column totals respectively.

Figure 9-4   *Example 9-3 Computed Chi-square*

		Sazor	Old Blade	Competitor 1	Competitor 2
Would	Observed	18	11	19	20
	Expected	13.60	13.60	17.00	23.80
	Cell Chi-square	1.42	0.50	0.24	0.61
Would Not	Observed	2	9	6	15
	Expected	6.40	6.4	8.0	11.20
	Cell Chi-square	3.03	1.06	0.50	1.29

$$\chi^2 = 8.633 \qquad df = 3 \qquad \text{p-value} = 0.0346$$

In this example, we would reject the null hypothesis and conclude that the proportion of men who would buy the blade is not the same in the four groups.

A word of caution is in order regarding chi-square tests in general. These tests do require reasonably large sample sizes. In particular, the significance tests are not appropriate if any of the expected frequencies are less than 5[7]. Any significance tests should be interpreted very cautiously if this is the case. In some cases, groups can be collapsed to form fewer groups which have expected frequencies greater than 5.

Post-Hoc Tests

In Example 9-3, we rejected the null hypothesis and concluded that the proportion of men who would buy the blade is not the same in the four groups. When we reject the null hypothesis, the question remains: Which groups are different? In other words, we need an appropriate post-hoc test for the difference between the pairs of groups. The techniques for post-hoc analysis with the chi-square are not as well developed as they are for analysis of variance. One commonly used post-hoc test is the *Mariscuilo test* which is part of XLDataAnalyst. We will discuss this test more in a later section when we discuss computer applications.

Exercises II

6. O'Haney's Inc owns three hotels in Seattle. The CEO of O'Haney's is concerned about no-shows, especially on the weekends. The table below shows the frequencies of "shows" and "no-shows" on Friday and Saturday nights over the past two months at the three hotels. Is there a significant difference in the proportion of no shows at the three hotels?

	Blue Lion	Pikes Inn	Capital Inn
Shows	120	100	95
No-Shows	18	27	10

7. Fragrance International had 100 males sample one of four brands of cologne and indicate whether or not they would be willing to purchase that cologne in the future. The data are contained in the table below. Is there a significant difference between the four brands in terms of the proportion that would purchase the cologne at the .01 level of significance?

---

[7] Some authors state that the analysis is compromised only if more than 20% of the cells have expected frequencies less than 5.

	Edge	Brazen	Stetson	Whistler
Would Buy	71	60	82	93
Would Not Buy	29	40	18	7

8. Big Mountain Airlines recently introduced daily flights between Seattle and the cities of Portland, Denver, and Salt Lake City. Some of the flights are full and others are only partially filled when they leave Seattle. Below are the data from the past three months on flights to the three destinations and whether they were full or not. Is there a significant difference between the three destinations in the proportion of full flights?

	Portland	Denver	Salt Lake City
Full	72	68	54
Partially Full	18	22	36

9. Personalize This is a designer of men's knit shirts which can be personalized by the customers with their name and a logo of their choosing. Sue Merk, the director of Marketing at the company, conducts an experiment to determine which of three magazines, Golf Magazine, Sports Illustrated, or ESPN the Magazine, would get the most attention from their ad. Sue placed an advertisement in all three magazines and a few weeks after the ad appeared e-mailed a random sample of 300 subscribers of each magazine a short questionnaire. One of the questions was whether or not they recalled the ad that appeared in the magazine that they subscribed to. The results appear in the table below. Is there a significant difference in the proportion of recall of the ads between the three magazines?

	Golf Magazine	Sports Illustrated	ESPN the Magazine
Recall	180	215	160
Do not Recall	120	85	140

Tests of Three or More Variances

The F-test for two variances that we illustrated in other chapters can also be extended to three or more variances. There are several tests for doing this. The test that we will discuss is called the *Modified Levene test*[8] and it is one of the options in XLDataAnalyst. Analogous to the tests for means and proportions, the null and alternative hypotheses are:

$$H_0: \sigma_1 = \sigma_2^2 = \sigma_3 = \ldots = \sigma_a^2$$

$$H_1: \text{ not } (\sigma_1 = \sigma_2^2 = \sigma_3 = \ldots = \sigma_a^2)$$

As with means and proportions, rejecting the null hypothesis does not mean that all of the variances are different; only that at least two of them are. The Levene test is equivalent to performing a one-way ANOVA test on the absolute deviations of the observations around the group mean or the group median. The most robust test utilizes the group medians to calculate the absolute deviations. This is also sometimes called the Brown-Forsyth version of the Levene test. To perform this test, we first convert the observations to absolute deviations around the median using Equation 9-10:

AbsoluteDeviations: $$|X_{ij} - M_j| \tag{9-10}$$

---

[8] This test is also sometimes called the Browne-Forsyth test.

Performing an analysis of variance on these absolute deviations will yield an F-value that can be treated as any other F-value in testing for significance in an F distribution with a-1 and a(n-1) degrees of freedom.

Example 9-4

To illustrate the data conversion process, we will return to Example 9-1 with the turkey feed example. The data on weight gains are repeated below. We want to prepare the data for the Levene test

Topnotch	Growbig	Max
42	112	70
96	96	17
81	88	49
95	135	24
76	119	40

Solution

To convert the data for the Levene test, we first need to calculate the medians for the three groups. Using the MEDIAN function in Excel we find that the median value for the three groups are 81, 112, and 40 respectively. Using Equation 9-10 we can then convert each observation to obtain the table below.

Topnotch	Growbig	Max
39	0	30
15	16	23
0	24	9
14	23	16
5	7	0

The above data would then be subjected to a one-way ANOVA to test the hypothesis about the equality of the variances. Because these calculations are relatively complex and have already been performed for the regular ANOVA, we will not perform them here, but will show the results in a later section when we discuss the computer solutions to the problem.

Testing for Homogeneity of Variances

Recall that one of the assumptions of the analysis of variance is the homogeneity of variances. This is precisely what we were testing with the Levene test, and indeed, this is one of the major uses of the Levene test and other similar tests for the equality of variances. Just as with the F-test of two variances, the Levene test can be used as a stand-alone hypothesis test or as a test of the assumptions underlying another test.

Tests of Three or More Medians

Kruskal-Wallis Test

The Kruskal-Wallis Test is the ordinal scale version of the one-way ANOVA. It is also a generalization of the Mann-Whitney-Wilcoxon Test for two independent samples. Recall that in the Mann-Whitney-Wilcoxon Test, we rank ordered all of the observations regardless of which group they were in and then calculated the sum of the ranks for the two groups, separately. The Kruskal-Wallis Test follows a similar procedure. Here, we have 1, 2, 3, ….. k independent samples, instead of just two. We first rank order the observations without regard to groups and then find the sum of the ranks for each group (R_i). The Kruskal-Wallis Test statistic is calculated as:

$$KW = \frac{12}{n(n+1)} \sum \frac{R_i^2}{n_i} - 3(n+1) \qquad (9\text{-}11)$$

This statistic has a chi-square distribution with (k − 1) degrees of freedom. Once again, we will not calculate these test statistics by hand, but will depend on the computer for accurate calculations.

Example 9-5

Batteries+ has developed a new lithium-based battery for use in iPods and mp3 players. They feel that their batteries will have a longer playtime or runtime (the on-time before a battery has to be recharged). They compare a sample of 5 of their batteries with those of three of their main competitors. Since battery lives have a positively skewed (not symmetric distribution), they are interested in differences between the median battery lives. The data are shown in Table 9-5 and are also contained in the file Example 9-5.xlsx.

Batteries+	Brand A	Brand B	Brand C
28	5	10	45
41	16	8	30
34	20	18	49
52	24	14	32
25	15	26	36

Solution

As with the Mann-Whitney Wilcoxon test from Chapter 8, the values are all ranked without regard to the group that they are in. The resulting ranks are shown in the table below:

1 = Batteries+		2 = Brand A		3 = Brand B		4 = Brand C	
Value	Rank	Value	Rank	Value	Rank	Value	Rank
28	9	5	20	10	18	45	3
41	4	16	15	8	19	30	8
34	6	20	13	18	14	49	2
52	1	24	12	14	17	32	7
25	11	15	16	26	10	36	5
Sum of Ranks	31		76		78		25

The Kruskal-Wallis test than then be calculated as

this describes it well [handwritten annotation]

$$KW = \frac{12}{n(n+1)} \sum \frac{R_i^2}{n_i} - 3(n+1)$$

$$= \frac{12}{20(20+1)} \left(\frac{31^2}{5} + \frac{76^2}{5} + \frac{78^2}{5} + \frac{25^2}{5} \right) - 3(20+1) = 13.8343$$

The degrees of freedom for this chi-square are 4-1 or 3. Using the CHISQ.DIST function or the probability calculator in XLDataAnalyst we would find a p-value of .00314. Therefore, there is a significant difference between the four medians. The four medians are shown below:

Battery Type	Batteries+	Brand A	Brand B	Brand C
Median	34	16	14	36

As you can see from the table, clearly Batteries + and Brand C have longer median battery lives than Brand A and Brand B in this sample. Further, the chi-square test indicates that at least one of these differences is statistically significant. The post-hoc tests in this area are less well developed than they are for means and proportions, but XLDataAnalyst will calculate a post-hoc test for the Kruskal-Wallis analysis.

Exercises III

10. Susan Olson, horticulturist for Santa's Christmas Tree Farm, is concerned that the trees currently being produced are not tall enough to be appealing to many people. In addition, she would like to shorten the growing season by producing trees that grew quicker. Through experimenting and with the help of the local university, she has developed three different fertilizers to help trees grow faster. She decides to conduct an experiment to see if there are any differences between the three fertilizers in terms of growth rate. She assigns 6 different trees to each of the three fertilizers and after three weeks measures the growth of the trees in inches. The results are shown below. Are there any differences in the median growth among the three different fertilizers?

Fertilizer 1	Fertilizer 2	Fertilizer 3
13	12	5
11	7	8
8	9	11
12	7	6
9	10	9
14	11	6

11. Chef Sally Randall is considering opening her own restaurant and has been scouting out possible locations for the business. Since her restaurant will be upscale with higher prices, she needs to locate in an area where people have sufficient income to patronize such an establishment. Sally has located three possible locations which would be suitable, one on the north hill, one in the valley, and one downtown, but is not sure about the incomes in the area. She hired a market research firm to do some random surveys about household incomes in the three areas. The results of the surveys in thousands of dollars are shown in the table below. Is there evidence that the three areas differ in terms of the medium household incomes? Which should Sally choose as the location for her restaurant?

North Hill	Valley	Downtown
97.7	66.7	114.7
108.1	87.0	111.6
102.4	75.6	104.3
107.2	90.3	113.1
79.7	72.8	116.1
91.5	90.4	116.2

12. The Arno Advertising agency is designing a new humorous ad for one of its largest clients. The design group currently has proposed three separate designs for consideration. Since this is a very important client, Bill Wilson, who is in charge of the project, decides to show the three different ads to three focus groups of 8 members each. Each member of the group will estimate how funny the ad was on a scale of 1 to 10. The ratings are shown below. Is there any evidence that the median ratings of the three ads are significantly different? Which ad would you choose if you were Bill Wilson?

Ad 1	Ad 2	Ad 3
6	6	6
5	8	8
5	7	1
6	6	4
3	7	3
5	9	5
9	9	3
7	10	5

13. A sleep researcher believes that workers who work odd hours get less sleep than people who work "normal" hours because of circadian rhythms. The researcher enlists 10 subjects who work the normal day shift (8:00AM to 4:00PM), the swing shift (4:00PM to midnight) and the graveyard shift (midnight to 8:00 AM). Each worker is asked to keep a sleep journal each night for five nights. The total amount of sleep for each worker is shown below. Is there any evidence that the median number of hours of sleep is less for the swing and graveyard shifts than for the day shift?

Day	Swing	Graveyard
37	34	34
47	28	24
28	36	37
38	28	29
34	32	21
46	38	27
50	34	37
46	36	39
42	36	33
41	34	29

Practice

Tests of Three or More Group Tests with Excel and XLDataAnalyst

Because of the complexity of the calculations in ANOVA and the other tests described in this chapter, it is easier to use the computer to perform the calculations.

Excel Functions

Although we can use Excel to perform the calculations of this chapter, there are no built-in functions to perform ANOVA or chi-square tests. We must either use the Analysis Toolpak, the Excel Templates or XLDataAnalyst.

The Analysis Toolpak

The Analysis Toolpak can be used to perform one-way ANOVA. The dialog for the Analysis Toolpak is shown in Figure 9-5. In this dialog, we want to select the option Anova: Single Factor. When you select this option you will see the dialog shown in Figure 9-6. This figure also shows the layout of the data necessary for the Analysis Toolpak ANOVA routine. Notice that this layout is different from the usual data layout in XLDataAnalyst and most statistical software packages. For the Analysis Toolpak, each group of data should be a separate column in the data. The data in Figure 9-6 are the data from Example 9-1.

Figure 9-5   *Data Analysis Toolpak Dialog*

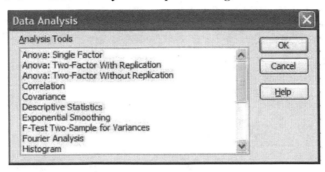

Select the Labels in First Row checkbox if your columns have a header row. The results for our sample data are shown in Figure 9-7. These results agree with our earlier calculations if you round the p-value off to three decimal places.

Figure 9-6   *The Single Factor ANOVA Dialog Box*

	A	B	C	D
1	Topnotch	Growbig	Max	
2	42.00	112.00	70.00	
3	96.00	96.00	17.00	
4	81.00	88.00	49.00	
5	95.00	135.00	24.00	
6	76.00	119.00	40.00	

Figure 9-7   *Results from the Analysis Toolpak for Example 9-1*

Anova: Single Factor

SUMMARY

Groups	Count	Sum	Average	Variance
Topnotch	5	390	78	480.5
Growbig	5	550	110	347.5
Max	5	200	40	441.5

ANOVA

Source of Variation	SS	df	MS	F	P-value	F crit
Between Groups	12280	2	6140	14.50965	0.000627	3.885294
Within Groups	5078	12	423.1667			
Total	17358	14				

The Excel Template

There are two excel templates that are relevant to this chapter. Most of the relevant tests are in the file ANOVA.xls. This template performs one-way and two-way ANOVAs, the Levene test for variances, and the Kruskal-Wallis test for medians. Since the chi-square test is used for a variety of purposes, these tests are contained in a separate template, called Chi-square.xls.

Figure 9-8 shows the general layout of the ANOVA.xls file. The types of tests that can be solved in this template are shown in the tabs of the worksheets at the bottom of the screen. The first worksheet for the one-way ANOVA is shown in the figure. Unlike many of the other templates that accompany the text, none of these worksheets can solve summary problems where the data is already summarized in some way. All of these tests assume that you have the raw data available. To use the template, simply enter the data into the area marked with the red rectangle in Columns G through L. You are restricted in this template to six groups and no more than 50 observations in a group. The data shown in Figure 9-8 is for Example 9-1. The results shown here are identical to those described previously for this example. The results of the Tukey tests are shown as confidence intervals and also graphically. The graph shows the confidence intervals for the Tukey tests centered on the hypothesized difference of zero.

The Levene Test

The worksheet labeled "Levene" can be used to perform the Levene test. The data entry is the same as for the one-way ANOVA. Figure 9-9 shows the input and results from the tests for equality of variances for the data from Example 9-1. The results indicate that there is not a significant difference between the variances (or standard deviations) of the three types of feed. The p-value is .9794 which indicates that the data are quite likely under the null hypothesis (we fail to reject the null hypothesis.)

Figure 9-8   The ANOVA Excel Template

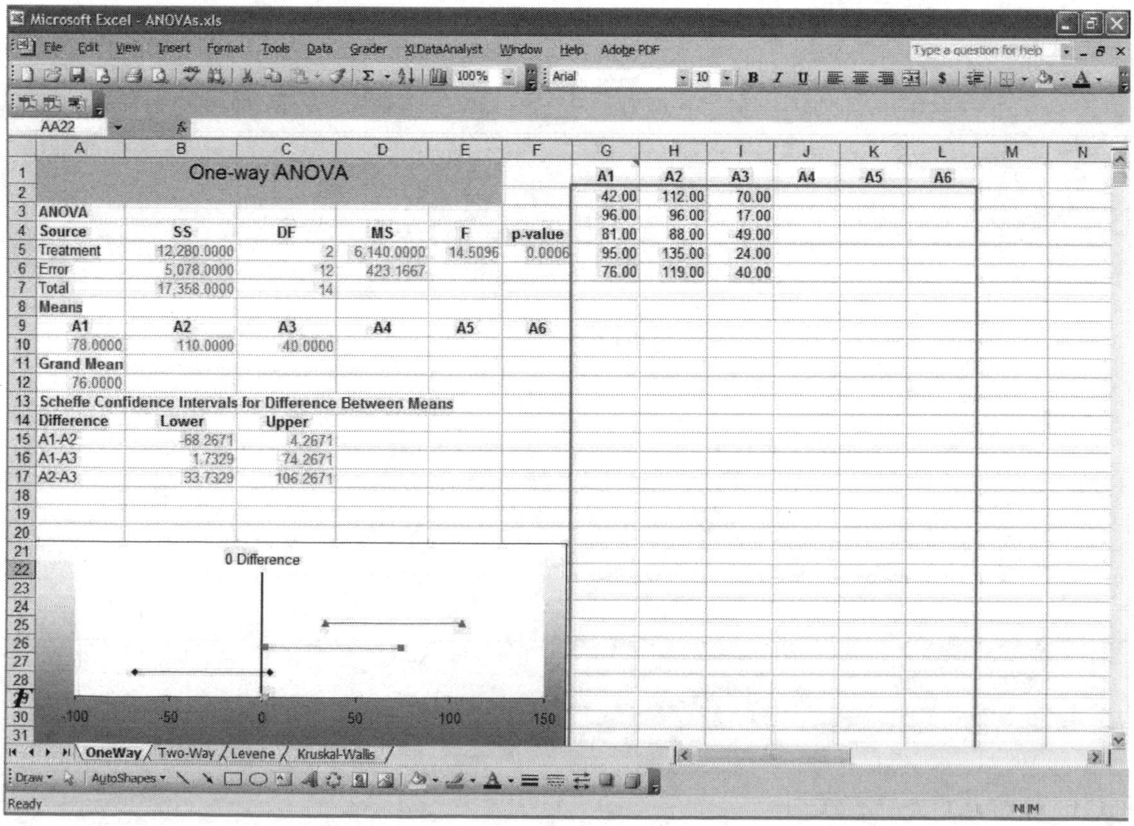

Figure 9-9 Template Input and Results for the Levene Test

	A	B	C	D	E	F	G	H	I	J	K	L	M
1	Levene Test						A1	A2	A3	A4	A5	A6	
2							42	112	70				
3	ANOVA						96	96	17				
4	Source	SS	DF	MS	F	p-value	81	88	49				
5	Treatment	6.5333	2	3.2667	0.0208	0.9794	95	135	24				
6	Error	1880.4000	12	156.7000			76	119	40				
7	Total	1886.9333	14										
8	Standard Deviations												
9	A1	A2	A3	A4	A5	A6							
10	21.9203	18.6414	21.0119										
11													
12													

Chi-Square Tests for Proportions

The chi-square tests for three or more proportions can be performed using the Chi-square.xls template. This template is shown in Figure 9-10. There are two worksheets in this template. The first, labeled "Chisquare," is used for problems in this chapter and those in Chapter 10. The worksheet labeled "Goodness-of-fit" is for goodness-of-fit tests which are covered in the optional material at the end of this chapter. The data from Example 9-3 are shown as the input to the Chisquare worksheet along with the results. Notice that the results agree with those found earlier. The template for chi-square problems can use either tabulated (frequencies already put in a table) or raw data. You should also note that the chi-square template cannot perform the Mariscuilo post-hoc tests. To perform these tests you must use XLDataAnalyst.

Figure 9-10 Template Input and Results for the Chi-square Test

Microsoft Excel - Chi-square.xls

	A	B	C	D	E	F	G	H	I	J	K	L	M	N
1	Chi-Square Tests												Row	Column
2													1	1
3	Observed Frequencies			1	2	3	4	5	6	7	8		1	1
4	Tabulated Data		1	18	11	19	20						1	1
5			2	2	9	6	15						1	1
6			3										1	1
7			4										1	1
8			5										1	1
9			6										1	1
10			7										1	1
11			8										1	1
12	Expected Frequencies			1	2	3	4	5	6	7	8		1	1
13			1	13.60	13.60	17.00	23.80						1	1
14	Summarized Data		2	6.40	6.40	6.00	11.20						1	1
15	Chi-square	8.6331	3										1	1
16	Deg of Fredom	3	4										1	1
17	p-value	0.0346	5										1	1
18			6										1	1
19			7										1	1
20			8										1	1
21													1	1
22	Observed Frequencies			1	2	3	4	5	6	7	8		1	1
23	Raw Data		1	22	4	34	5						1	1
24			2	39	10	42	68						1	2
25			3	77	3	96	80						1	2
26			4										1	2
27			5										1	2
28			6										1	3
29			7										1	3
30			8										1	3
31	Expected Frequencies			1	2	3	4	5	6	7	8		1	3
32			1	18.69	2.71	3.39	20.72						1	3
33	Sample Data		2	45.71	6.63	8.28	50.68						1	3
34	Chi-square	954.1265	3	73.60	10.67	13.33	81.60						1	3

ChiSquare / Goodness-of-Fit

Ready

Kruskal-Wallis Test

The Kruskal-Wallis test can also be performed using the ANOVA.xls template. To see how this template works we will consider an example of a four-group test of medians. To illustrate the template we will again use the data from Example 9-5.

Solution

The input data and the results for Example 9-5 are shown in Figure 9-11. Again, we see that the median battery playtimes are different and that the chi-square test is highly significant. It appears that the median playtime of the Batteries+ battery and those of Brand C are significantly higher than those of Brand A and Brand B. Unfortunately, post-hoc tests for Kruskal-Wallis are not well developed and such tests are not included in the template. However, XLDataAnalyst will calculate post-hoc for medians.

Figure 9-11 Data Inputs and Results for Example 9-5

AA29 fx =IF(L29<>"",RANK(L29,$G$2:$L$51,1),"")

	A	B	C	D	E	F	G	H	I	J	K
1	Kruskal-Wallis Test						Batteries+	Brand A	Brand B	Brand C	
2							28	5	10	45	
3	KW	13.8343					41	16	8	30	
4	P-value	0.0031					34	20	18	49	
5							52	24	14	32	
6	Medians						25	15	26	36	
7	Batteries+	Brand A	Brand B	Brand C							
8	34	16	14	36							
9											
10											
11											

Using XLDataAnalyst

Analysis of Variance

XLDataAnalyst includes procedures for performing one-way and two-way ANOVA tests along with the Levene test for variances and the Kruskal-Wallis test for medians. As with the templates, the chi-square tests for proportions are handled through a separate set of routines. The section of the ribbon that performs both chi-square tests and tests of three or more groups is shown in Figure 9-12. The data for Example 9-1 will be used to illustrate the use of XLDataAnalyst for analysis of variance. With the dataset loaded into Excel, click on the Three Groups drop-down button in the ribbon and select One-Way ANOVA from the menu. The dialog box shown in Figure 9-13 should appear. The list box on the left of the dialog will contain discrete variables in the dataset that might be an independent variable in ANOVA. In this case, there is only one listed variable, the Feed variable, which should be selected as the independent variable. The list on the right side of the dialog box lists all variables with more than two values that might be dependent variables in ANOVA. Select the Gain variable that contains the weight gain data. Click the OK button and the results illustrated in Figure 9-14 will appear on a new worksheet. As you can see, the computer results are identical to the results calculated above, except for being carried out to three decimal places.

Figure 9-12 The Three Group Section of the Ribbon

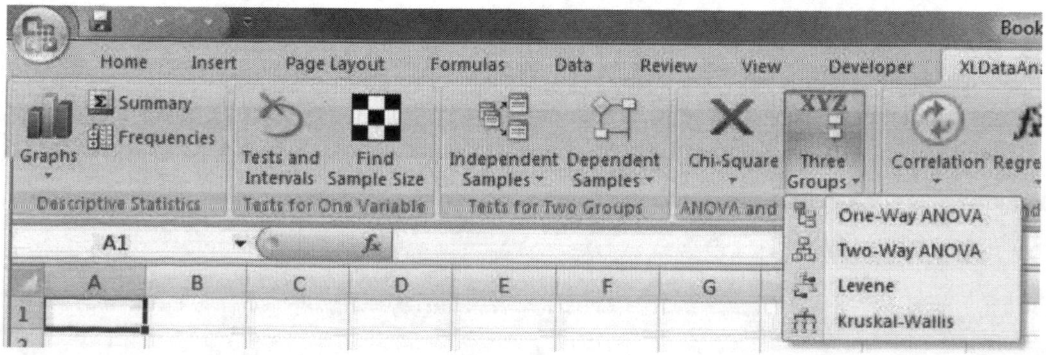

Figure 9-13   XLDataAnalyst Dialog for the One-Way ANOVA

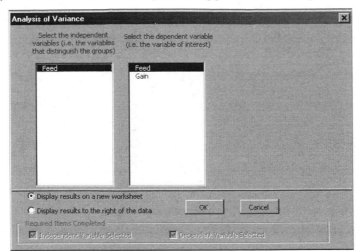

Figure 9-14   One-Way ANOVA Results for Example 9-1

ANOVA Results For Gain

ANOVA Table

Effect	Sum of Squares	DF	Mean Square	F	P-value
Feed	12,280.0000	2	6,140.0000	14.5097	0.0006
Error	5,078.0000	12	423.1667		
Total	17,358.0000	14			

Observed Means

Means for Feed

	Topnotch	Growbig	Max
	78.0000	110.0000	40.0000

Scheffe tests for Feed

	Mean Diff	Lower	Upper	Significant
Topnotch - Growbig	-32.0000	-68.2671	4.2671	
Topnotch - Max	38.0000	1.7329	74.2671	Yes
Growbig - Max	70.0000	33.7329	106.2671	Yes

Chi-square Tests

The Chi-square section of the ribbon for XLDataAnalyst is shown in Figure 9-15. There are two submenu options for chi-square tests. The first option is for situations where the data has already been tabulated and put into a frequency table. The second option is to be used when we have raw data. We will use the data from Example 9-3 here (in the form of the raw data) so you should use the second option. The dialog that results from this menu selection is shown in Figure 9-16. For this test, make sure that you check the box for the Mariscuilo test, as shown in Figure 9-16. The resulting output is shown in Figure 9-17.

Figure 9-15   The Chi-Square Section of the XLDataAnalyst Ribbon

Figure 9-16   XLDataAnalyst Dialog for Chi-square Tests

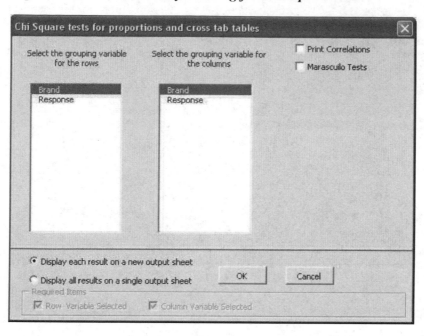

Figure 9-17   XLDataAnalyst Results for Example 9-3

Chi Square Results For Brand and Response

Observed Frequencies

		Response Would Buy	Would Not Buy	Row Totals	Percents
Brand	Sazor	18	2	20	0.2000
	Old Blade	11	9	20	0.2000
	Competitor 1	19	6	25	0.2500
	Competitor 2	20	15	35	0.3500
	Column Totals	68	32	100	
	Percents	0.6800	0.3200		

Results

Chi Square Value	8.6331
Degrees of Freedom	1
P-Value	0.0346

Proportions for Brand	Sazor	Old Blade	Competitor 1	Competitor 2
Warning: Some cell frequencies	0.1000	0.4500	0.2400	0.4286

Marascuilo tests for the proportion of Response = Would Not Buy

	Difference	P-value
Sazor - Old Blade	-0.3500	0.0071
Sazor - Competitor 1	-0.1400	0.1974
Sazor - Competitor 2	-0.3286	0.0022
Old Blade - Competitor 1	0.2100	0.1343
Old Blade - Competitor 2	0.0214	0.8776
Competitor 1 - Competitor 2	-0.1886	0.1147

The results for the chi-square tests are the same as those shown before for Example 9-3. After the summary of the chi-square test and the resulting p-value, the sample proportions for the four groups are displayed. Following these values is a warning printed out by XLDataAnalyst, indicating that some of the cell frequencies are very small (e.g., less than 5). The chi-square distribution is only a good approximation for contingency tables when the expected frequencies are fairly large. When some of the expected frequencies are less than 5, the value of the chi-square may be inflated which may produce more Type I errors than expected.

The results for the Mariscuilo tests for the differences between pairs of proportions are printed next with a p-value for each difference. These results show that the differences between Sazor and Old Blade and between Sazor and Competitor 2 are significant. This indicates that users responded more positively to the new brand (Sazor) than they did to the old brand or the blade of Competitor 2. The other differences have p-values greater than .05. We therefore, cannot say, for example, that there is a significant difference in proportions between Sazor and the blade of Competitor 1

The Levene Test

The Levene Test is accessed through the ANOVA menu, as illustrated previously in Figure 9-12. In Example 9-1, we assumed that the variances of the three groups were equal. We can now test that hypothesis, using the Levene Test. Figure 9-18 shows the output for the data in Example 9-1. The results show that the assumption of equal variances is very tenable for these data. We should note here that there are no post-hoc tests for the Levene Test. Therefore, even if we find a significant difference between the groups, we do not have a test to determine exactly where those differences lie.

Figure 9-18   Results of the Levene Test for Example 9-5

Levene Equality of Variances Test For Gain

Summary Measures

	Topnotch	Growbig	Max
Standard Deviation	21.9203	18.6414	21.0119
Sample Size	5	5	5

Levene's test

F Value	P-value
0.0208	0.9794

Kruskal-Wallis Test in XLDataAnalyst

The Kruskal-Wallis test in XLDataAnalyst requires the same type of input as the ANOVA and Levene tests. It is also selected from the ANOVA menu. The results for the Example 9-5 data are shown in Figure 9-19. As with the Template, we see that there are significant differences between the group medians. The post-hoc tests show that all the differences are statistically significant, except the difference between Batteries+ and Brand C and the difference between Brand A and Brand B.

Figure 9-19   *Results of the Kruskal-Wallis Test for Example 9-5*

Kruskal-Wallis Results For Battery

Kruskal-Wallis Test

Kruskal-Wallis H statistic	13.83428478
p-value	0.0031

Observed Medians and Average Ranks

	Batteries+	Brand A	Brand B	Brand C
Medians	34.0000	16.0000	14.0000	36.0000
Mean Ranks	14.8000	5.8000	5.4000	16.0000

Multiple Comparison Test for Average Ranks

	Diff Mean Ranks	Lower	Upper	Significant
Batteries+ - Brand A	9.0000	1.2761	16.7239	Yes
Batteries+ - Brand B	9.4000	1.6761	17.1239	Yes
Batteries+ - Brand C	-1.2000	-8.9239	6.5239	
Brand A - Brand B	0.4000	-7.3239	8.1239	
Brand A - Brand C	-10.2000	-17.9239	-2.4761	Yes
Brand B - Brand C	-10.6000	-18.3239	-2.8761	Yes

Exercises IV

14. A consumer group has conducted extensive testing of four new model cars. As part of this testing process they test drove 5 autos of each model. Part of the data gathered during the test drives was the fuel mileage in miles per gallon. This data is contained in the file Exercise 9-14.xlsx. Do the four models get the same mean gas mileage? If not, which ones are significantly different?

15. An airline that operates shuttle services between several cities is concerned about complaints of customers that planes have to wait for takeoff because of the slowness of baggage handling operations in getting baggage loaded on the planes. The chief operating officer orders a study of baggage loading times at the airports in Boston, New York, and Washington D.C. The loading times in minutes for 8 randomly selected flights at each airport are contained in the file Exercise 9-15.xlsx. Is there any evidence of differences in loading times for the three airports? Which airports should they be concerned about?

16. A pharmaceutical company has developed five types of treatments for a new hormone designed to enhance growth in livestock. The five types were tested on 25 animals, and the weight gains contained in the file Exercise 9-16.xlsx were reported (lb./week).

    (a) Test whether the mean gain is equal across all treatments, using a .01 level of significance.

    (b) Test the assumption of equal variance of the five treatments. Is the assumption tenable in this case?

17. Bob, the VP of Operations at Intermountain Telephone knows that a consistent response time to repair problems is very important to customers. Bob has gathered data on response times to problems from four different repair locations. The data are contained in File Exercise 9-17.xlsx. Is there evidence that the variability of response times is different at the four different repair locations, at the .05 level of significance?

18. Benzoil has developed a new synthetic oil that promises to increase gas mileage in most vehicles. The engineers have tested the new synthetic against two competing brands of motor oil. Each type of

oil was put into 10 cars and their gas mileage tested on a dynamometer. The results are contained in the file Exercise 9-18.xlsx. Do the results indicate that the new synthetic oil provides better gas mileage than the two competing brands?

19. Bubba's Fast Foods emphasizes the speed of service at their drive-through windows in their advertising. To gather data to support their advertising they sent 10 mystery shoppers with stop watches through their facility and those of three competing stores. The times between a customer placing their order and their departure are contained in the file Exercise 9-19.xlsx. Does the data support their advertising?

20. The council of a Native American tribe in the State of Washington operates casinos at three different locations. To test customer satisfaction at the three sites they randomly sample customers leaving each site and ask them if they would return to that casino in the future. The results are contained in the file Exercise 9-20.xlsx. Are there any differences in customer satisfaction between the three locations? Should the council be concerned about particular locations? If so, which ones.

21. The J. J. Wentworth Company is considering a change to their health care benefits where the employee would have a higher deductible but have a lower monthly payment for health insurance. Before implementing the plan the executive committee has decided to survey a sample of the employees to see if they would be in favor or opposed to the change. The data from a sample of 400 employees are contained in the file 9-21.xlsx where a 0 for the response indicates that the employee opposes the change and a 1 indicates that they favor the change. The data are divided up by department: IT, Marketing and Sales, Finance and Accounting, Operations, and Human Resources. Is the proportion of employees favoring the plan equal across the five departments? If not, which departments are different and how can management interpret these results?

22. Stetson Interstate Bank is concerned about the wait time of customers waiting to see a loan advisor at their various branches. Steve Wilson, Chief Operating Officer, has advised the Executive Committee that the average customer wait time at the various branches is approximately 5 minutes. However, the Executive Committee is concerned that this figure may mask some real problems if the variability of wait times is high. Therefore, they ask Steve to measure randomly selected customer wait times at four different banks and see if the variability of the wait times is the same across the four branches. The resulting data are contained in the file Exercises 9-22.xlsx. What can you tell the Executive Committee about the variability of wait times at the four branches?

23. The Rock Point Association of Realtors are interested in the relative prices of houses being sold in four different areas of town, the South Hill, the North Side, the East Valley, and the West Plains. They take a random sample of homes recently sold in the four areas. The data are contained in the file Exercise 9-23.xlsx. Are there any differences in the median selling prices between the four areas of the city? Are there any differences in the variability of the selling prices across these four areas?

24. Jim Alverez is a financial planner who specializes in clients that are nearing retirement age. A new client wants to invest a major portion of his savings in mutual funds but is unsure which one to invest in. The client obviously wants to get high returns on his money, but is also concerned about the risks involved. Through his research, Jim has narrowed the choices down to four funds: Unigaard, Blumberg, Garbergs, and Wagners. Jim compiles the average annual returns from the four funds from the ten most recent years in the file Exercise 9-24.xlsx. Is there evidence that one fund has a higher median return than other funds? Which fund appears to be the best? Are there any differences in the variability of returns for the four different funds?

Opening Vignette Revisited

The data that Ray gathered from his experiment are contained in the file Chapter 9 Vignette.xls. Ray first calculated the average life for the three types of machine oil. Brand A had an average life of 12.8, Brand B an average of 15.8, while the Synthetic oil had an average of 23.0. Therefore, it appears that the Synthetic does have a longer average machine life, but Ray is concerned that these differences may just be due to sampling error because of the particular machines chosen. He performs an ANOVA test to see if these differences are statistically significant. The results are shown below. These results indicate significant differences between the oils and that the Synthetic is significantly better than either Brand A or Brand B. There is no apparent significant difference between Brands A and B.

ANOVA Results For Avg Life

ANOVA Table

Effect	Sum of Squares	DF	Mean Square	F	P-value
Brand	274.7998	2	137.3999	8.9804	0.0041
Error	183.6001	12	15.3000		
Total	458.3999	14			

Observed Means

Means for Brand

	1	2	3
	12.8000	15.8000	23.0000

Scheffe tests for Brand

	Mean Diff	Lower	Upper	Significant
1 - 2	-3.0000	-9.8961	3.8961	
1 - 3	-10.2000	-17.0961	-3.3039	Yes
2 - 3	-7.2000	-14.0961	-0.3039	Yes

The results are encouraging, but Ray knows that the ANOVA results depend on the assumption of equal variances between the three groups. Ray decides to use the Levene Test whose results are shown below in the ANOVA table. These results indicate that the Synthetic brand does have a smaller standard deviation than Brands A and B, but that these differences are not statistically significant. Therefore, Ray decides that the assumptions of the ANOVA were satisfied, further convincing him that the Synthetic oil may be the best choice for the future.

Levene Equality of Variances Test For Avg Life

Summary Measures

	1	2	3
Standard Deviation	4.3243	4.3243	2.9155
Sample Size	5	5	5

Levene's test

F Value	P-value
0.2924	0.7516

Summary

This chapter extends the two-sample test to three or more samples. The null hypothesis still states that all of the means (proportion, variances, or medians) are equal and the alternative hypothesis states that they are not all equal, e.g., at least two of them are different. The extension of the two independent sample t-test to three or more groups is the one-way ANOVA (Analysis of Variance). Post-hoc tests must be used to determine which of the group means are significantly different. XLDataAnalyst includes one of these, the Scheffe Test. The test for three or more proportions is a direct extension of the chi-square test for two sample proportions. The Mariscuilo post hoc Test is used to determine which groups are significantly different. The test for three or more variances is the Levene Test, or more properly, the Brown-Forsyth version of the Levene Test. No post-hoc tests have been developed for the Levene Test, at this time. The Kruskal-Wallis Test is an extension of the Mann-Whitney-Wilcoxon Test to three or more groups.

Chapter Glossary

Analysis of Variance (ANOVA)	A method of testing the equality of two or more means by using variances and the F-distribution.
Homogeneity of Variances	The assumption that the population variances for all groups are equal.
Interaction	The effects of one treatment vary depending on the level of another treatment.
Kruskal-Wallis Test	A rank test of three or more independent medians.
Levene Test	A test of three or more independent variances.
Mariscuilo Test	A post-hoc test to see which groups are different following a significant chi-square test of three or more proportions.
Mean Squares	A sum of squares value divided by its corresponding degrees of freedom. Conceptually the same as a variance.
Post-Hoc Tests	Tests used after the rejection of a null hypothesis to see which specific groups are significantly different.
Scheffe Test	A post-hoc test to see which groups are different following a significant analysis of variance test.
Sum of Squares Error (SSE)	The sum of the squared deviations within the groups which is a measure of sampling error.
Sum of Squares Treatment (SSA)	The sum of the squared deviations of the group means around the overall mean.
Sum of Squares Total (SST)	The sum of the squared deviations of all of the observations around the overall mean.
Variability Between Groups	The variability between the means in the analysis of variance. An estimate of the treatment effects.
Variability Within Groups	The variability within the groups in the analysis of variance. An estimate of the inherent variability in the population, e.g., sampling error.

Questions and Problems

25. For the following, indicate (1) the type (name), of the statistical test to use, and (2) the type of the statistical distribution used in the test:

    (a) A test to determine whether five sample proportions come from populations that have equal proportions

    (b) A test to compare three population means to learn if they are equal

    (c) A test to find out whether four groups have the same median

    (d) A test to learn whether three sample variances came from populations with equal variances

26. The operations manager of a large airport wishes to determine if the air traffic is being allocated equally among four airport concourses (A, B, C, and D). Taking a random sample of 10 days she calculates the total number of incoming and outgoing passengers in each concourse from the flight records of the airlines utilizing the airport. The data are contained in the file Exercise 9-26.xlsx. Do the concourses receive equal use or are there differences between the concourses. If there are differences, which concourse(s) receive more use?

27. The Wall Street Journal periodically sponsors an Investment Dart Board contest pitting readers against experts from the Journal and stocks picked randomly by throwing darts at stock pages. The last contest was held in July of 2012 (http://online.wsj.com/article/SB10001424052702303962304577509072421196832.html). Assume that the data in file Exercise 9-27.xlsx represent the change in stock price for a group of stocks picked by readers, the experts and darts. Is there any evidence that the experts or the readers do better than the darts? Look at both mean and median changes in stock prices.

28. General Cereal Inc. is concerned that there may be too much variability in pricing of its products in certain cities. Such variability is viewed with suspicion by local consumers and may ultimately reflect poorly on General Cereal. Although they cannot dictate prices to local stores, they can try to use incentives to try and keep prices within a certain range. Using their leading product, Chocolate Delight, they randomly sample 10 stores in South Bend, Indianapolis, and Fr. Wayne Indiana. The price per box of the cereal in each store is contained in the file Exercise 9-28.xlsx. Is there evidence of more price variability in some cities than in others?

29. Eating habits vary widely from one country to another. A recent study in the BRIC countries (Brazil, Russia, India and China) examined eating habits in these four countries. One of the questions related to how often the respondent ate out rather than cooking at home http://www.interfaceasia.com/i news/news_38.html. The file Exercise 9-29.xlsx contains hypothetical data based on this study for the number of respondents who ate out at least once a week assuming100 respondents from each country. Are there significant differences in the proportion of people who eat out at least once a week in the four countries? Which countries are significantly different?

30. In the BRIC study of problem 29, the survey also asked respondents which of several food types they eat frequently. The file Exercise 9-30.xlsx contains hypothetical data on the respondents in each country who frequently ate chicken based on 100 respondents from each country. Are there any significant differences in the proportion of people who frequently eat chicken in the four countries? Which countries are significantly different?

31. Sarah and her husband are moving to Sleepy Hollow Indiana following their graduation from their MBA program. They have been told by friends that used to live there that the best neighborhoods are Willow Estates, Barclay Manor, and Bozarth Acres. Sarah wants to narrow the search down to one area of town as they won't have much time to house hunt between graduation and the start of their new jobs. She decides to select an area based on the median selling price of houses in that area. To

estimate whether there is a difference in the median price of houses in the three areas, she selects a random sample of houses in each area and records the asking price of those house. The data are contained in the file Exercise 9-31.xlsx. Is there a difference in the median price of houses in three areas? Which area should Sarah pick?

32. Stratomat, a manufacturer of high end golf balls, knows that the PGA pros and the low handicappers that buy their products require consistent performance from their golf balls. In testing their top line golf balls for the new golf season, Stratomat product designers have come up with three different design alternatives that should have about the same distance and spin performance. Management has decided that they will go with the design that produces the most consistent distance performance. The designers use Iron Mike, an automated machine that hits golf balls with a perfectly consistent stroke, to hit 10 balls of each design and carefully measure the distance traveled. The data are contained in the file Exercise 9-32.xlsx. Are there any significant differences in the variances of the distances of the three designs? Which design do you think Stratomat should use?

33. The benefits manager of a health maintenance organization (HMO) in St. Louis must decide whether her firm should provide different amounts of coverage for the same medical procedure in different cities. If the costs are "really higher" in some cities, she would like to propose different rates. But, with the varying charges of individual doctors, it is difficult to tell. She has obtained sample costs of the procedure in St. Louis, Kansas City, Indianapolis, and Chicago. The data are contained in the file Exercise 9-33.xlsx. Using a .05 level of significance, test whether there are real differences in average costs among the cities.

34. Consumer Reports tests the strength of kitchen garbage bags by adding weight to see how much weight the bag can sustain before breaking. Suppose the data in the file Exercise 9-34.xlsx represent five different tests of three different brands of garbage bag. The data represents pounds of weight before the bag breaks.

    (a) Is the mean breaking point the same for the three different brands? Is there a brand that you would prefer or that you would avoid given these results?

    (b) It is also desirable that bags be consistent in their strength. Is there evidence that the three brands differ in terms of the variability of the breaking points of the bags?

35. A government auditor is investigating the lending practices of three local banks. One question the auditor wishes to answer is whether or not the banks differ in terms of their rejection rates for loans. In other words, are some banks more difficult to obtain a loan from than others? The auditor randomly samples 300 loan applications submitted to each bank and notes whether they were accepted (coded 0) or rejected (coded 1). The responses for the three banks (Citizens United coded 1, National Bank coded 2, and InterState Bank coded 3) are contained in the file Chapter 9-35.xlsx. What do the data say about the auditor's question?

36. During parts of 2012 gas prices in parts of the Northwest appeared to be higher than in other parts of the country. There were even calls for a Department of Justice investigation into the differences. The file Exercise 9-36.xlsx contains hypothetical prices from randomly selected locations in Washington, Colorado, Kansas and Iowa during this time period. Does the data show significant differences in the median prices between the states? Is there evidence that prices are significantly higher in Washington than in the rest of the country? Is there a significant difference in the variability of gas prices over the four states sampled?

Database Problems

Corporate Statistical Database

(Note: Use .05 for alpha for all of the following problems)

37. Test the hypothesis that the price/earnings ratios of the following industries are equal: Utilities, Retail and Electronics. If they are not equal, which ones are different? Does the assumption of equal variances hold in this situation?

38. Are the percentages of firms that have profit sharing the same in the Utilities, Retail and Electronics industries? If not, which groups are different?

39. Are the median annual dividends the same in the Retail, Chemical and Drug, as well as Electronics firms?

40. Are the average salaries the same for the firms in the East (Massachusetts, New York, or New Jersey), the Midwest (Illinois, Indiana, Michigan and Ohio) and the West (Washington, Oregon, or California)? Are the variances the same in the three regions? Explain your findings.

MegaCorp Employee Survey Database

41. Are the average salaries the same in the four subsidiaries in the database? Is the assumption of equal variances plausible for this data?

42. Test the hypothesis that the median overall satisfaction rating is the same in the four subsidiaries.

43. The VP of Human Resources is concerned that some of the subsidiaries may not be hiring as many females and minorities as they should. Is there any evidence in the sample data that the percentage of females differ across the four subsidiaries? If so, where are the problem areas?

44. The CEO of MegaCorp wants to know if there are any differences between the four subsidiaries in terms of average salary, average number of years with the organization, or median overall satisfaction with benefits. Advise the CEO about any differences that may exist.

Alaska Sport Fishing Survey

45. The head of the Alaska Tourism Council feels that the amount spent while in the state depends on the annual household incomes. Are there any differences in the average or median amounts spent on their last trip between those that made less than $30,000, those who made $30,000 to $74,999, those who made $75,000 to $104,999, and those who made $105,000 or more? (Hint: Create a new variable that distinguishes between the different income groups).

46. The head of the Tourism Council also feels the state should market most heavily to those with higher incomes because they are more likely to return in the future. Is the proportion of those indicating that they plan to return in the next three years the same in the four income groups created in the previous problem?

47. Someone has suggested that the average number of overnight fishing trips may depend on whether the respondent is single/widowed, married, or divorced. Is there evidence of this in the sample? (Hint: Create a new variable combining widowed with single).

48. Some in the Council have speculated that there are some key differences, especially in frequency of visits, between those who indicate that they stay in lodges/resorts, those who stay with friends/relatives and those who indicate that they stay in other places. Are there significant differences in the average number of trips in these groups or in the variability of the number of trips?

Tests of Goodness of Fit (Optional)

Goodness of Fit tests determine if observed frequencies could have been derived from a known theoretical pattern, usually a probability distribution. The test uses the chi-square for contingency tables where the expected frequencies come not from a null hypothesis of equal proportions, but from a known distribution of values. The logic of comparing actual and expected frequencies in the chi-square test proceeds as usual. For example, chi-square tests can be used to determine whether empirical data actually conform to a statistical distribution such as the uniform, Poisson, normal, or binomial. We illustrate the procedure with examples using the uniform and normal distributions. Other procedures follow the same general idea.

Fit of Data to a Uniform Distribution

The simplest use of chi-square is to test the fit to a uniform distribution. Since each category has the same probability of occurrence, this test is equivalent to the equal proportion hypothesis test for three or more groups, discussed earlier in this chapter.

Example 9-6

The HR manager at a chemical plant wonders that workers are more prone to accidents on certain days or if all five workdays are the same with regard to the likelihood of an accident. A review of safety records shows that a plant had 50 accidents in the past two years. The days on which they occurred are shown in the table below. Test the hypothesis that the accident data are uniformly distributed at the $\alpha = .05$ level of significance.

Day	Accidents
Monday	8
Tuesday	10
Wednesday	12
Thursday	14
Friday	6
Total	50

Solution

Given our hypothesis that the distribution is uniform, there should be an equal number of accidents on each day of the week. The total number of accidents, 50, divided by the number of working days per week, 5, gives us the expected number of accidents per working day of 10. We can use the Chi-square.xls Template to solve this problem. The inputs and results are shown in Figure 9-20. As can be seen, there is no evidence that the null hypothesis is false; therefore, it appears that accidents are uniformly distributed throughout the week. Note that the input for the number of estimated parameters is set to zero here. That is because we do not have to calculate any sample statistics to use the goodness of fit test for the uniform distribution. As we will see shortly, for other distributions we may have to calculate some sample statistics in order to determine the expected frequencies. In these cases, the input for this cell will not be zero.

Figure 9-20   ***Inputs and Results for Example 9-6***

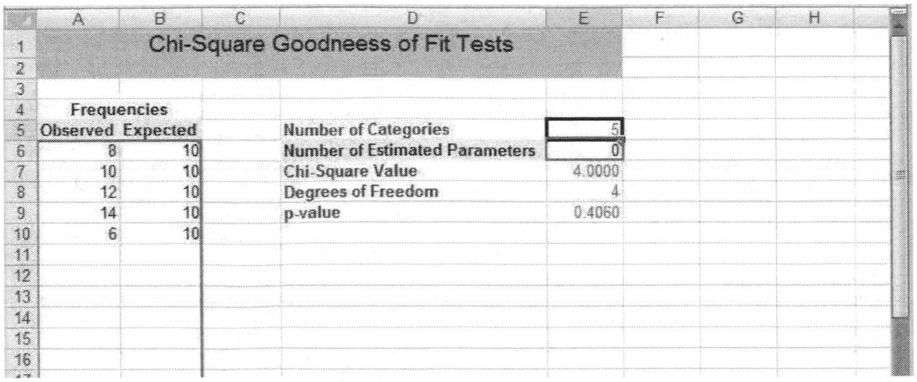

Fit of Data to a Normal Distribution

As we have seen, many statistical tests assume a normal distribution. It may not surprise you then, to find out that a common use of the chi-square goodness of fit test is to challenge the assumption that the data came from a normal distribution. Since the normal distribution is continuous, we normally deal with quantitative variables for this chi-square test. This test assumes that the data have already been grouped into a frequency table. Then, we must calculate the mean and the standard deviation of the sample data (to find two estimated parameters). Next, we must calculate the areas under the normal curve within each class interval using the estimated mean and standard deviation. The expected frequency for the interval is this area/ percentage multiplied by the sample size (n). An example, as the one below, may clarify the calculations.

Example 9-7

A drug company has measured the reaction time (min) for a new antibiotic to have an effect in the bloodstream of 200 randomly selected subjects. The mean of the 200 observations is calculated to be 45 with a standard deviation of 15. The values have been grouped into a frequency distribution as shown below. Can the reaction times be considered to follow a normal distribution?

Interval	Frequency
10 – 19.5	10
20 – 29.5	24
30 – 39.5	38
40 – 49.5	56
50 – 59.5	36
60 – 69.5	24
80 – 79.5	12

Solution

We first need to calculate the expected frequencies in each class under the normal distribution. We already know that the mean is 45 and the standard deviation is 15. We can use these facts and our knowledge of the normal distribution to calculate the expected frequencies. We will use the NORMDIST function in Excel to calculate the percentages for the table below using the sample mean and standard deviation as input parameters. For the first interval, the area will be the percentage of the normal distribution that is less than 19.5; therefore, we would enter the following input in Excel:

$$=NORMDIST(19.5, 45, 15, TRUE)$$

We would get an answer of .0446. For the next interval, we want the area between 19.5 and 29.5 so we would have to find the area to the left of 29.5 and then subtract out the area to the left of 19.5 to find the area of .1062. Subsequent intervals would proceed in the same fashion. The area for the last class interval would be the area to the right of the upper limit in the next to the last class interval (in this case to the right of 59.5). As a check, the areas should add up to 1.0. The expected frequencies are computed as the areas multiplied by the sample size (200 in this case); the sum of the expected frequencies should be equal to the sample size within rounding error. In the table below, the expected frequencies add up to 200.02 which is within acceptable rounding error.

Interval	Frequency	Area	Expected Frequencies
10 – 19.5	10	.0446	8.92
20 – 29.5	24	.1062	21.24
30 – 39.5	38	.2062	41.24
40 – 49.5	56	.2610	52.20
50 – 59.5	36	.2152	43.04
60 – 69.5	24	.1157	23.14
80 – 79.5	12	.0512	10.24

These expected frequencies can be used in the Chi-square.xls Template to solve the problem. The resulting inputs and results for Example 9-7 are shown in Figure 9-21. The data support the null hypothesis that the values are from a normal distribution since the p-value is .6435. Note that the estimated parameters value is set to 2 because we had to calculate a mean and a standard deviation in order to calculate the expected frequencies.

Figure 9-21 Inputs and Results for Example 9-7

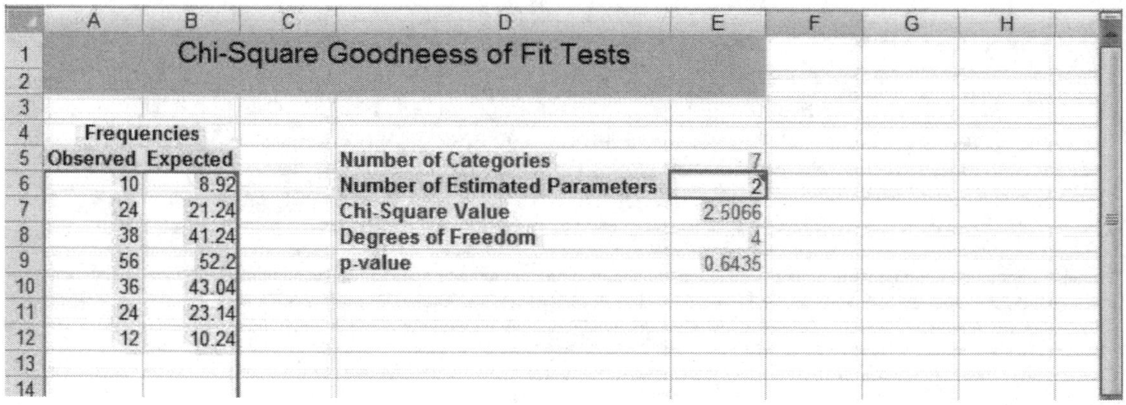

Chi-Square Goodneess of Fit Tests

Frequencies				
Observed	Expected			
10	8.92		Number of Categories	7
24	21.24		Number of Estimated Parameters	2
38	41.24		Chi-Square Value	2.5066
56	52.2		Degrees of Freedom	4
36	43.04		p-value	0.6435
24	23.14			
12	10.24			

Exercises V

49. Random samples of some stockroom items were counted to see if the actual (observed) counts agreed with the inventory records (expected). Compute the chi-square and p-values to determine if the observed and expected counts are in significant agreement. Use a .05 level of significance.

Item No.	**1**	**2**	**3**	**4**	**5**	**6**	**7**	**8**	**9**	**10**	**Total**
Observed f_o	15	18	65	80	80	55	20	35	18	74	460
Expected f_e	14	20	65	76	92	50	22	33	20	68	460

50. A new study is made of accident occurrences in an industrial plant to determine if accidents are equally likely on any day of the week. Given the results shown below, test whether the data are uniformly distributed.

Day	No. Accidents
Monday	15
Tuesday	20
Wednesday	25
Thursday	28
Friday	12
Total	100

51. A state lottery official claims that the winning digits are randomly selected and occur with an equal likelihood; however, the frequency of the last digit in the winning numbers has had the pattern shown below. Are the data sufficient to question the randomness of the winning numbers? Use a chi-square goodness-of-fit test at the .10 level of significance.

Winning digit	0	1	2	3	4	5	6	7	8	9	Total
No. occurrences	4	8	12	9	17	8	12	6	14	10	100

52. Given the sample data shown below and the $\alpha = .10$ level, test whether the data could have been taken from a normal distribution.

Class Boundaries	Observed Frequency	Expected Frequency
50.0 to under 60.0	4	7.9
60.0 to under 70.0	21	29.1
70.0 to under 80.0	50	46.0
80.0 to under 90.0	32	29.1
90.0 to under 100.0	13	7.9
Total	120	120.0

53. A random sample of 100 pieces of electronics was taken for a quality control test of electrical conductivity. The items were classified into seven classes with conductivity values as shown.

Conductivity Value Class Interval	Number of Items (f)
10 – 19	6
20 – 29	12
30 – 39	18
40 – 49	25
50 – 59	19
60 – 69	12
70 – 79	8
Total	100

(a) Compute the mean and standard deviation of the distribution.
(b) Compute the expected frequency of each class interval assuming that the conductivity measurements are normally distributed.
(c) Show the results of your test of the hypothesis that the characteristic is normally distributed using the .05 level of significance.

Two-Way Analysis of Variance (Optional)

In this chapter, we only considered a single treatment being applied to the experimental units. In some cases, we might be interested in two treatments and their joint effects. In the two-way analysis of variance we can break the total variability into separate effects for each treatment to see if they impact the dependent variable. In addition, we can also look at the joint effects of the two treatments called an *interaction*. The basic layout of the Two-Way ANOVA is illustrated in Figure 9-22.

Figure 9-22   *Basic Layout of Two-Way ANOVA*

	A_1	A_2	A_3	......	A_a
B_1	X_{111}	X_{121}	X_{131}		X_{1a1}
	X_{112}	X_{122}	X_{132}		X_{1a2}
	.	.	.		.
	X_{11n}	X_{12n}	X_{13n}		X_{1an}
B_2	X_{211}	X_{221}	X_{231}		X_{2a1}
	.	.	.		.
	X_{21n}	X_{22n}	X_{23n}		$X_{2an.}$
	.	.	.		.
B_b	X_{b11}	X_{b21}	X_{b31}		X_{ba1}
	.	.	.	.	.
	X_{b1n}	X_{b2n}	X_{b3n}		X_{ban}

In this case, we have two grouping or treatment variables (A and B). There are (a) levels of treatment A and (b) levels of treatment B. This is called a complete factorial design because there are observations under each possible combination of the two treatments. In this case, there are multiple hypotheses that can be tested. There is a null hypothesis that states there is no effect for treatment A (e.g., the means of the A groups are all equal) and a hypothesis that states there is no effect for treatment B (e.g., the means of the B groups are all equal). These effects are called *main effects*. In addition, we can ask whether or not the effects of treatment A depend on the level of treatment B (and vice versa) which is called an interaction effect. The third null hypothesis states that there is no interaction effect.

The notion of interactions is explored in greater detail below:

$$H_0: \mu_{A1} = \mu_{A2} = \mu_{A3} = \ldots \ldots = \mu_{Aa}$$

$$H_0: \mu_{B1} = \mu_{B2} = \mu_{B3} = \ldots \ldots = \mu_{Bb}$$

H_0: There is no interaction between A and B

As in the one-way ANOVA, we can break down the total sum of squares (SST) into components. In the two-way ANOVA, we have the effect due to treatment A (SSA), the effect due to treatment B (SSB) and the interaction effect (if there are multiple observations in each treatment combination) denoted by SSAB, and the error (SSE) Thus, SST can be broken down to be:

$$SST = SSA + SSB + SSAB + SSE$$

This decomposition of the total variability is depicted graphically in Figure 9-23. As usual in the analysis of variance, the results are presented in an ANOVA table as shown in Table 9-5.

Figure 9-23   **Total Variability Broken Into Four Components for Two-Way ANOVA**

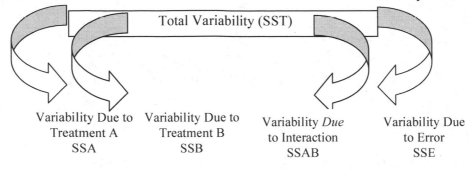

Table 9-5   **Two-Way ANOVA Table[9]**

Source	DF	SS	MS	F
Treatment(A)	a-1	SSA	MSA=SSA/(a-1)	MSA/MSE
Treatment(B)	b-1	SSB	MSB=SSB/(b-1)	MSB/MSE
Interaction(AB)	(a-1)(b-1)	SSAB	MSAB=SSAB/(a-1)(b-1)	MSAB/MSE
Error	ab(n-1)	SSE	MSE=SSE/ab(n-1)	
Total	abn-1	SST		

Note that the degrees of freedom and sums-of-squares are again additive as they were in the one-way ANOVA.

Example 9-8

Aroma Essence is a perfume company that wants to investigate the effects of advertising strategy and package design on sales of its primary product. Their advertising agency comes up with three different advertising strategies (labeled sophisticated, athletic or popular) and their marketing department prepares three different package designs (dubbed Sunset, Holidays and Fitness). Each combination of advertising strategy and package design is used in a different regional market for two weeks. The sales (in thousands of dollars) are recorded as the dependent variable. The results are listed in Table 9-6.

---

[9] The letter "a" represents the number of levels of the A treatment and the letter "b" represents the number of levels of the B treatment.

Table 9-6   ***Data for the Two-Way ANOVA***

	Sophisticated	Athletic	Popular
Sunset	2.80	2.04	1.39
	2.73	1.63	1.58
	2.65	1.72	1.41
Holidays	3.02	1.57	1.72
	3.29	1.50	1.40
	2.68	1.79	1.82
Fitness	2.47	2.73	1.42
	2.54	2.45	1.92
	2.32	2.61	1.33

We will not perform the manual calculations for the two-way ANOVA, but will instead focus on the use of XLDataAnalyst to perform the calculations. The dataset Example 9-8.xls contains the data for this example.

Before we look at the two-way ANOVA, notice that we could analyze this data as a one-way ANOVA to test the differences in sales between advertising strategies as well as perform a separate one-way ANOVA to test the differences between package designs. The results of the XLDataAnalyst analysis for the two one-way analyses are presented in Figures 9-24 and 9-25. The one-way analysis for package design (Figure 9-24) indicates the package design treatment had no effect on sales. We would have to conclude that the average sales are the same for all three package designs, e.g., that the package design did not have an effect. The one-way analysis for advertising strategy (Figure 9-25), however, indicates that this treatment did have a significant effect on sales and that all three means are significantly different from one another. The Sophisticated strategy produced the largest sales followed by the Athletic strategy and the Popular strategy produced the lowest sales.

Figure 9-24   One-Way ANOVA for Package Design

ANOVA Results For Sales

ANOVA Table

Effect	Sum of Squares	DF	Mean Square	F	P-value
Package	0.1686	2	0.0943	0.2538	0.7779
Error	8.9141	24	0.3714		
Total	9.1026	26			

Observed Means

Means for Package

	1	2	3
	1.9944	2.0878	2.1989

Scheffe tests for Package

	Mean Diff	Lower	Upper	Significant
1 - 2	-0.0933	-0.8428	0.6561	
1 - 3	-0.2044	-0.9539	0.5450	
2 - 3	-0.1111	-0.8606	0.6384	

Figure 9-25   *One-Way ANOVA for Advertising Strategy*

ANOVA Results For Sales

ANOVA Table

Effect	Sum of Squares	DF	Mean Square	F	P-value
AdStrat	6.2442	2	3.1221	26.2141	0.0000
Error	2.8584	24	0.1191		
Total	9.1026	26			

Observed Means

Means for AdStrat

	1	2	3
	2.7222	2.0044	1.5544

Scheffe tests for AdStrat

	Mean Diff	Lower	Upper	Significant
1 - 2	0.7178	0.2934	1.1422	Yes
1 - 3	1.1678	0.7434	1.5922	Yes
2 - 3	0.4500	0.0256	0.8744	Yes

Although the data can be analyzed as two one-way ANOVAs, there are significant advantages for analyzing the effects simultaneously as a two-way ANOVA. With the same data, select the two-way ANOVA option in the ANOVA and Chi-square group of the ribbon. The resulting dialog is shown in Figure 9-26. For the two-way ANOVA, select two independent variables from the list on the left (in this case select both Package and AdStrat) and select a single dependent variable from the list on the right (in this case Sales). The only difference between this dialog and the one for the one-way ANOVA is the addition of a checkbox to plot the two-way interactions. By default, this is checked which will produce the charts of the interactions. If you do not want to produce the charts, click this checkbox to uncheck it. The results of the two-way ANOVA are provided in Figure 9-27.

Figure 9-26   *Example XLDataAnalyst Dialog for the Two-Way ANOVA*

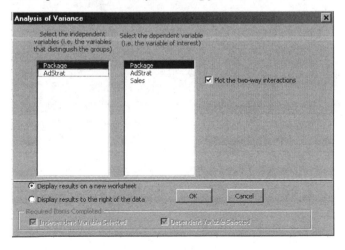

Figure 9-27   Two-Way ANOVA for Example 9-8

ANOVA Results For Sales

ANOVA Table

Effect	Sum of Squares	DF	Mean Square	F	P-value
Package	0.1886	2	0.0943	2.3516	0.1238
AdStrat	6.2442	2	3.1221	77.8723	0.0000
Package by AdStrat	1.9482	4	0.4870	12.1479	0.0001
Error	0.7217	18	0.0401		
Total	9.1026	26			

Observed Means

Means for Package

1	2	3
1.9944	2.0878	2.1989

Means for AdStrat

1	2	3
2.7222	2.0044	1.5544

Means for the interaction of Package(Rows) by AdStrat(Columns)

	1	2	3
1	2.7267	1.7967	1.4600
2	2.9967	1.6200	1.6467
3	2.4433	2.5967	1.5567

Scheffe tests for Package

	Mean Diff	Lower	Upper	Significant
1 - 2	-0.0933	-0.3450	0.1583	

Scheffe tests for AdStrat

	Mean Diff	Lower	Upper	Significant
1 - 2	0.7178	0.4661	0.9694	Yes
1 - 3	1.1678	0.9161	1.4194	Yes
2 - 3	0.4500	0.1983	0.7017	Yes

Note that the advertising strategy main effect is significant (p-value = 0.0000) and the package design main effect is not (p-value = 0.1238); however, that does not mean that the package design does not affect sales. An examination of the F for the interaction indicates that there is a significant interaction between the two treatments. This means that there is significant interaction between the variables and so the package design does have an effect on sales.

Interactions

An *interaction* means that the effects of one treatment on the dependent variable vary depending on the level of another treatment. In our example, that means that the effects of the advertising strategy on sales depend in some way on the package design used and vice versa. It is easiest to see what an interaction effect means by graphing the interaction. A graph of the means involves graphing the average values separately for each level of one treatment on the Y-axis with the levels of the second treatment on the X-axis. If there is no interaction between the two treatments, then the lines, when graphed, should be parallel to each other. Figure 9-28 (a) illustrates a situation where there is no interaction effect between the treatments. If the lines are not parallel, the effects of the plotted treatment vary depending on the level of the variable on the X-axis. Figure 9-28 (b) illustrates a situation where there is an interaction effect. In both figures, the treatment on the X-axis has three levels while the other treatment, plotted on the Y-axis, has two levels (there is a curve for each level.). You can see in part (a) of the figure that the difference between the two curves is constant (10 units) no matter what the level of the other treatment. In essence, the two treatments operate independently of one another in their effects on the dependent variable. Notice that we could also graph the interactions with the other treatment on the X axis and curves plotted for the other treatment. The same situation is plotted in this manner in Figure 9-29. Again, you can see that in the graphs with no interaction the lines are parallel while they are not when an interaction is present.

Figure 9-28   *Graphic Illustrations of an Interaction*

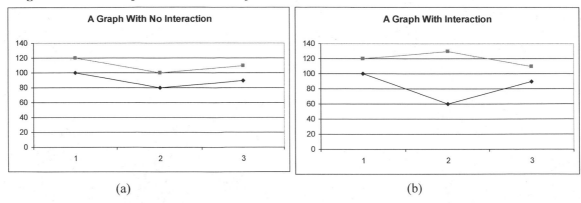

(a)   (b)

Figure 9-29   *The Same Interactions With the Axes Reversed*

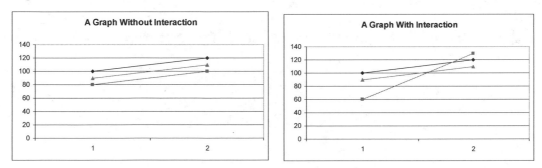

We can now return to Example 9-8 and look at the graphs of the interactions to better understand the effects of advertising strategy and package design on sales. Figures 9-30 and 9-31 show the two graphs. The lines are not parallel in either graph. Figure 9-30 shows that the three different package designs produce roughly the same sales for the Sophisticated and Popular advertising strategies, but not for the Athletic strategy. Here, the sales clearly increase with the Fitness package design as opposed to one of the other. There is an interaction in the sense that the Fitness package enhances the Athletic advertising strategy. The graph in Figure 9-31 shows that the Sophisticated advertising strategy leads to larger sales except when the Fitness package design is used. The Athletic advertising strategy produces sales at least as high as the Sophisticated strategy.

Figure 9-30 **Interaction Graph Plotting Package Design**

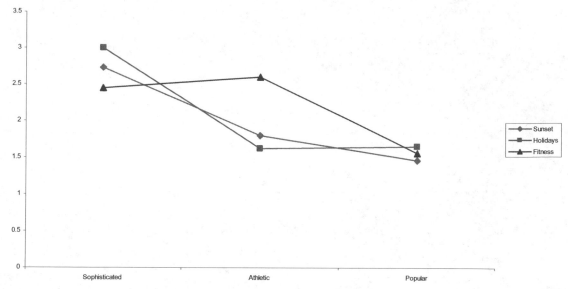

Figure 9-31 **Interaction Graph Plotting Advertising Strategy**

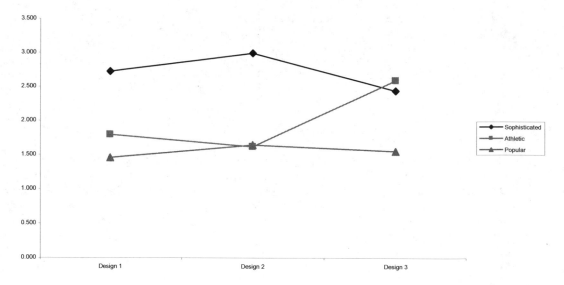

Exercises VI

54. Distinguish between one-way and two-way ANOVA tests. How do the null hypotheses differ for one-way and for two-way tests?

55. Resource Recycling Co. has conducted a demonstration study in five sections of the country to help evaluate the feasibility of establishing major waste reprocessing centers. The study entailed having six randomly selected households (in each of five cities) save their recyclable waste over a specific period. Analyze the data in the table below (and in file Exercise 9-55.xlsx) and state your conclusions at the $\alpha = .05$ level.

(a) Is there a significant difference in the amount of recyclable waste from one location to another?

(b) Is there a significant difference in weight among the types of waste products that could be collected?

(c) Is there any interactive effect between the city and the type of waste?

Pounds of Recyclable Materials Collected by Randomly Selected Households

	Location of Demonstration City									
	Northwest		Southwest		Central		Northeast		Southeast	
Aluminum	9	13	5	9	12	13	8	10	14	13
	11	10	8	12	11	15	6	7	11	19
	12	11	16	12	12	9	9	11	10	15
Glass	8	10	14	16	15	17	14	16	15	16
	6	5	18	15	14	15	16	18	16	19
	11	8	17	16	17	16	15	17	13	17
Plastic	10	8	6	9	5	8	7	9	14	16
	5	7	7	8	11	10	8	8	17	16
	10	8	10	8	8	6	9	6	15	15
Tin/steel	7	5	6	9	17	22	10	12	8	10
	6	9	8	8	16	19	12	14	9	7
	12	8	7	10	23	20	9	11	11	12

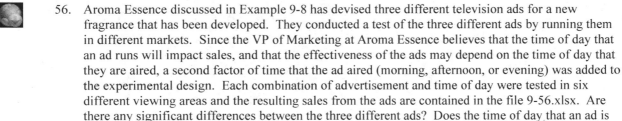

56. Aroma Essence discussed in Example 9-8 has devised three different television ads for a new fragrance that has been developed. They conducted a test of the three different ads by running them in different markets. Since the VP of Marketing at Aroma Essence believes that the time of day that an ad runs will impact sales, and that the effectiveness of the ads may depend on the time of day that they are aired, a second factor of time that the ad aired (morning, afternoon, or evening) was added to the experimental design. Each combination of advertisement and time of day were tested in six different viewing areas and the resulting sales from the ads are contained in the file 9-56.xlsx. Are there any significant differences between the three different ads? Does the time of day that an ad is run affect the sales resulting from the ad? Explain any interaction effects if the interaction is statistically significant.

57. The top Marketing Team at Higgly-Piggly Grocers Inc. is exploring the feasibility of charging differential rates for companies based on the shelf location of their products. As part of the feasibility study they conducted an experiment in several of their stores in which they manipulated the shelf location of a fixed set of products both in terms of height of the location (bottom, middle and top) and the location in the store (Front, Middle, Back). The results of the experiment in terms of units sold are contained in the file Exercises 9-57.xlsx. Interpret the results for the marketing team.

Special ANOVA Designs (Optional)

We will now discuss two special experimental designs. Although these special designs are analyzed exactly like a two-way ANOVA, they have a different purpose from the traditional factorial design of the two-way ANOVA. These two types of designs are often confused in introductory statistics texts.

Randomized Block Designs

In an experimental situation there are additional factors that impact the variable of interest besides the treatment effects being tested. Often these "nuisance" variables are not of primary interest to the analyst; however, if these variables are not explicitly accounted for in the analysis, the effects on the variable of interest are incorporated into the error term in the analysis of variance and inflate the mean square error which reduces the power of the test for the effects of the treatment of interest. If these factors can be identified and incorporated into the analysis it makes for a more powerful test of the treatments.

In statistical terminology, blocking is the arrangement of experimental units into groups of similar items based on some characteristic of the experimental unit. This characteristic is called a blocking variable. An experiment with one treatment variable and a blocking variable is called a randomized block design. Randomized block designs are analyzed in exactly the same way as any two-way ANOVA. We will first consider the simplest such design which is usually called the randomized block design in most introductory statistics books, but it is really a special case of the general randomized block design. We will, therefore, call this type a simple randomized block design or SRBD. The more general case addressed after this will be called the generalized randomized block design or GRBD.

Simple Randomized Block Designs (SRBD)

In the simple randomized block design only one observation of each block is included in the experiment. An example may help illustrate the analysis.

Example 9-9

Burke Inc. is a local distributor of snack food products. Their drivers travel to the various grocery, drug, and convenience stores in the area and restock the shelves to replenish items that are sold. The drivers also manage the in-store displays that are sometimes used for special promotions. Burke is interested in studying the effectiveness of four different point-of-sale displays. They plan an experiment in which they will place the four displays in different stores and then measure their effectiveness through the average sales generated. Burke's Director of Marketing knows that the type of store affects sales and want to make sure that this is taken into account; therefore, she insists that each display type be used in grocery stores, drug stores and convenience stores. Since the store type is a characteristic of the experimental units, it is a blocking variable treatment. The resulting data with average sales, measured in thousands, as the dependent variable are shown in Table 9-7 and are contained in the Excel file Example 9-9.xlsx.

To see why blocking is important, let's first analyze this data as a one-way ANOVA with display type as the only independent variable. The results are given in Figure 9-32 where we can see that the overall F-test of ANOVA indicates that the effect of display type is not statistically significant with a p-value of .6019.

Table 9-7   ***Data for Example 9-9***

	Display			
	A	**B**	**C**	**D**
Grocery	19	22	31	19
Drug	27	33	28	27
Convenience	22	25	20	21

Figure 9-32   XLDataAnalyst Results for Example 9-9 Without Blocking Effect

ANOVA Results For Sales

ANOVA Table

Effect	Sum of Squares	DF	Mean Square	F	P-value
Display	48.3335	3	16.1112	0.6554	0.6019
Error	196.6665	8	24.5833		
Total	245.0000	11			

Means for Display

	1	2	3	4
	22.6667	26.6667	26.3333	22.3333

Scheffe tests for Display

	Mean Diff	Lower	Upper	Significant
1 - 2	-4.0000	-18.1393	10.1393	
1 - 3	-3.6667	-17.8060	10.4727	
1 - 4	0.3333	-13.8060	14.4727	
2 - 3	0.3333	-13.8060	14.4727	
2 - 4	4.3333	-9.8060	18.4727	
3 - 4	4.0000	-10.1393	18.1393	

If we now analyze this data as two-way ANOVA taking into account the blocking variable, we would observe the results in Figure 9-33. The store type effect is not quite statistically significant with a p-value of .0871. Display type is still not statistically significant with a p-value of .4161; however, it is closer to statistical significance then when analyzed as a one-way ANOVA. What made the difference in the results? To see the reason, look at the sum of squares total (SST) and sum of squares error (SSE) values in the two analyses. The sum of squares total is the same for both results. This makes sense; the total variability is the total variability no matter how we divide it up. But, now look at the SSE values. The SSE for the one-way analysis was 196.665 while for the two-way analysis the SSE was 87.1667. What caused the reduction? The variability due to store type was removed from the error term resulting in a large drop in SSE. Even though there is a small drop in the degrees of freedom for error, the MSE is reduced even more and therefore provides a more powerful test. If you add the sums-of-squares for store type and error in the two-way analysis you will get the SSE from the one-way results (109.5 + 87.1667 = 196.6667) except for rounding error. The conclusion from this is that if the blocking variable has an effect on the dependent variable then including it in the analysis will reduce the error variability and produce a more powerful test of the other independent variable. Of course, if the blocking variable has no effect on the dependent variable, then including it in the analysis will not significantly affect the results.

Figure 9-33   XLDataAnalyst Results for Example 9-9 Using Blocking Variable

ANOVA Results For Sales

ANOVA Table

Effect	Sum of Squares	DF	Mean Square	F	P-value
Store Type	109.5000	2	54.7500	3.7686	0.0871
Display	48.3333	3	16.1111	1.1090	0.4161
Error	87.1667	6	14.5278		
Total	245.0000	11			

Means for Store Type

1	2	3
22.7500	28.7500	22.0000

Means for Display

1	2	3	4
22.6667	26.6667	26.3333	22.3333

Scheffe tests for Store Type

	Mean Diff	Lower	Upper	Significant
1 - 2	-6.0000	-14.6441	2.6441	
1 - 3	0.7500	-7.8941	9.3941	
2 - 3	6.7500	-1.8941	15.3941	

Scheffe tests for Display

	Mean Diff	Lower	Upper	Significant
1 - 2	-4.0000	-15.7567	7.7567	
1 - 3	-3.6667	-15.4233	8.0900	
1 - 4	0.3333	-11.4233	12.0900	
2 - 3	0.3333	-11.4233	12.0900	
2 - 4	4.3333	-7.4233	16.0900	
3 - 4	4.0000	-7.7567	15.7567	

You may notice that, although this is a two-way ANOVA there is no interaction effect in the ANOVA table. That is because there is only one observation for each combination of display and store type. In effect, the interaction of store type and display is the error term in the two-way ANOVA.

There is one additional problem with this analysis. There is very little power because there is only one observation for each combination of display type and store type. There is no reason that multiple observations cannot be included in each combination. Such a design is sometimes called a generalized randomized block design (GRBD).

Generalized Randomized Block Design

The generalized randomized block design expands the randomized block design by having 2 or more replications in each cell. The use of replications has two benefits:

1. It provides a more powerful test for the main treatment effects and also for the blocking variable.
2. It allows the assessment of the interaction of the treatment variable with the blocking variable.

In the situation facing Burke Inc., a significant interaction would indicate that the relative effectiveness of the displays well depend on the type of store they are used in.

Example 9-10

The Director of Marketing at Burke Inc. is concerned about the low power of the test and decides to collect more data. She feels that having three replications in each cell of the design will provide a more powerful test and yield a better picture of the effectiveness of the four different displays. She installs the four different displays in three grocery stores, three drug stores, and three convenience stores. The resulting average sales in thousands of dollars are shown in Table 9-8.

Table 9-8   *Data for Example 9-10*

	Display			
	A	**B**	**C**	**D**
Grocery	22	22	34	22
	19	24	34	19
	20	25	31	23
Drug	24	31	26	24
	25	33	28	27
	27	29	25	26
Convenience	21	25	22	21
	22	23	23	24
	22	26	20	22

Notice that this data layout is very similar to that for the two-way ANOVA in Example 9-8. The only difference is that the second variable is a blocking variable rather than a treatment effect. The analysis of the data is performed in exactly the same way. The results of the two-way ANOVA for these data are shown in Figure 9-34. We can see that there is now a significant main effect for display type, but there is also a significant main effect for store type, and more importantly, a significant interaction effect between store type and display type. The main effects of store type are clear; sales are highest in the drug stores followed by the grocery stores and lowest in the convenience stores. The results for display type are a little more complicated and are clearer if we look at the interaction effects. The charts of the interactions are given in Figure 9-35 and 9-36. The second chart clearly shows that higher than expected sales occur in grocery stores with Display C. This is what causes the significant interaction.

The use of replications has obviously increased the power of the test and revealed a much clearer picture of the effectiveness of the different displays. It also reveals that the effectiveness depends on the type of store in which the display is used. In general, it just makes sense to utilize replications in a randomized block design unless the cost of replications is too high. The replications allow a more powerful test of the main treatment effect, and equally important, allow the analyst to explore any interactions that my result between the treatment and blocking factors.

Figure 9-34 Analysis of the Randomized Block Design with Replications

ANOVA Results For Sales

ANOVA Table

Effect	Sum of Squares	DF	Mean Square	F	P-value
Store Type	122.0000	2	61.0000	24.1319	0.0000
Display	143.4167	3	47.8056	18.9121	0.0000
Store Type by Display	238.6667	6	39.7778	15.7363	0.0000
Error	60.6667	24	2.5278		
Total	564.7500	35			

Observed Means

Means for Store Type

1	2	3
24.5833	27.0833	22.5833

Means for Display

1	2	3	4
22.4444	26.4444	27.0000	23.1111

Means for the interaction of Store Type(Rows) by Display(Columns)

	1	2	3	4
1	20.3333	23.6667	33.0000	21.3333
2	25.3333	31.0000	26.3333	25.6667
3	21.6667	24.6667	21.6667	22.3333

Scheffe tests for Store Type

	Mean Diff	Lower	Upper	Significant
1 - 2	-2.5000	-4.1933	-0.8067	Yes
1 - 3	2.0000	0.3067	3.6933	Yes
2 - 3	4.5000	2.8067	6.1933	Yes

Scheffe tests for Display

	Mean Diff	Lower	Upper	Significant
1 - 2	-4.0000	-6.2517	-1.7483	Yes
1 - 3	-4.5556	-6.8073	-2.3038	Yes
1 - 4	-0.6667	-2.9184	1.5851	
2 - 3	-0.5556	-2.8073	1.6962	
2 - 4	3.3333	1.0816	5.5851	Yes
3 - 4	3.8889	1.6371	6.1406	Yes

Figure 9-35 Interaction Graph Plotting Display Type

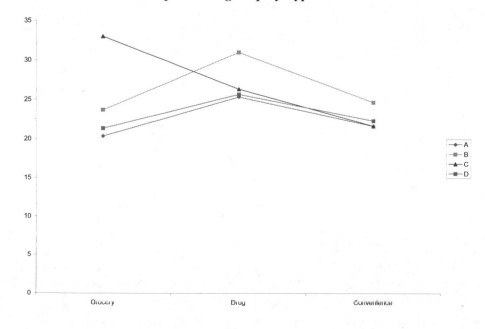

Figure 9-36   Interaction Graph Plotting Store Type

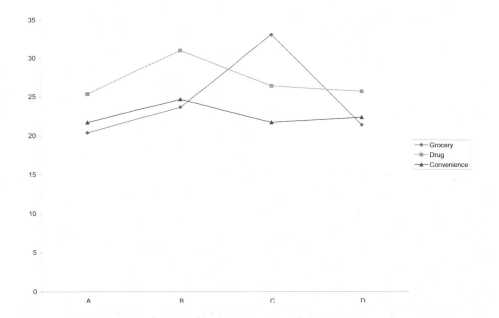

Repeated Measures Design

The repeated measures design is like a one-way ANOVA where each experimental unit receives each of the treatment levels rather than just one of them. In effect, the experimental units become the second independent variable.

Example 9-11

Swanson Research, a marketing research firm, has been asked by Dolly's Restaurant to conduct a test evaluating the perceived quality of their food as compared with three competitors (Durango's, Luiggi's Italian, and Cinibar's). To conduct the research Swanson brought in six outside "food experts" who were not familiar with any of the restaurants. Each of the experts (raters) was to eat in each restaurant in a random order and evaluate the quality of the food on a 100-point scale. Each expert evaluates all of the restaurants or treatment levels. We can analyze this as .a two-way ANOVA without replications where the people are the second treatment. The results of the ratings are given in Table 9-9.

Table 9-9   Data for Example 9-11

	Dolly's	Durango's	Luiggi's Italian	Cinibar's
Rater 1	70	61	82	74
Rater 2	77	75	88	76
Rater 3	76	67	90	80
Rater 4	80	63	96	76
Rater 5	84	66	92	84
Rater 6	78	68	98	86

Notice that this data arrangement looks much like that of the simple randomized block design considered earlier. In fact, some introductory texts confuse this with the SRBD when in fact, they are quite different. In the repeated measures design, it is the same experimental unit that appears under each treatment effect. Therefore, it does not make sense to have more than one observation in each cell because that would involve having the same experimental units undergo the same treatment more than once. On the other hand, in the simple randomized block design, it is a different experimental unit under each treatment so it does make sense to have replications.

The results of this analysis are presented in Figure 9-37. We can see from the results that Durango's is the highest rated and it is rated significantly higher than the other restaurants. Cinibars and Luiggi's are the second highest rated restaurants and both are rated significantly higher than Dolly's but we cannot distinguish between Cinibars and Luiggis. Notice that although this is a two-way ANOVA there is no interaction effect. That is because there is only one observation per cell and therefore no interaction. In effect, the interaction between raters and restaurants is the error term in this analysis.

Figure 9-37   *Analysis of Repeated Measures Data in Example 9-11*

ANOVA Results For Score

ANOVA Table

Effect	Sum of Squares	DF	Mean Square	F	P-value
Rater	283.3750	5	56.6750	3.7818	0.0205
Restaurant	1,787.4584	3	595.8195	39.7581	0.0000
Error	224.7916	15	14.9861		
Total	2,295.6250	23			

Observed Means

Means for Rater

1	2	3	4	5	6
71.7500	79.0000	78.2500	78.7500	81.5000	82.5000

Means for Restaurant

Cinibars	Dolly's	Durango's	Luiggi's
77.5000	66.6667	91.0000	79.3333

Scheffe tests for Restaurant

	Mean Diff	Lower	Upper	Significant
Cinibars - Dolly's	10.8333	3.8144	17.8522	Yes
Cinibars - Durango's	-13.5000	-20.5189	-6.4811	Yes
Cinibars - Luiggi's	-1.8333	-8.8522	5.1856	
Dolly's - Durango's	-24.3333	-31.3522	-17.3144	Yes
Dolly's - Luiggi's	-12.6667	-19.6856	-5.6478	Yes
Durango's - Luiggi's	11.6667	4.6478	18.6856	Yes

The more astute reader may have noticed that the data gathered in Example 9-11could have been analyzed as a simple one-way ANOVA if the analyst were not aware of the distinctive nature of the repeated measures design. This would be similar to analyzing dependent sample data as independent samples in Chapter 8. To see the effect of this, Figure 9-38 shows the same data analyzed as a one-way ANOVA. In this case, the one-way analysis shows the same significant differences as the repeated measures analysis using the two-way ANOVA. This, however, is not always true. To see the difference between the two, notice that the sum-of-squares, degrees of freedom and mean-square for the treatment are the same in both analyses. However, the corresponding values for error are not the same. This is because in the one-way ANOVA the individual differences that are represented by the raters are lumped into the error term. If you add the sum-of-squares due to raters with the error sum-of-squares in Figure 9-37, you will get the sum-of-squares error in Figure 9-38. However, the degrees of freedom also change so that the mean-square for error, although slightly larger, does not significantly alter the results. The main reason for this is that the raters rated the restaurants in very similar fashion. If the individual raters had rated the restaurants very differently the results of the two analyses might well be different. The point is that it is a dangerous practice to not use the appropriate analysis for the data that you have. Like blocking, the repeated measures analysis will often give you a more powerful test.

Figure 9-38   The One-Way Analysis of Example 9-11

ANOVA Results For Score

ANOVA Table

Effect	Sum of Squares	DF	Mean Square	F	P-value
Restaurant	1,787.4688	3	595.8229	23.4504	0.0000
Error	508.1563	20	25.4078		
Total	2,295.6250	23			

Means for Restaurant

	Dolly's	Durango's	Luiggi's	Cinibars
	77.5000	66.6667	91.0000	79.3333

Tukey multiple comparison tests for Restaurant

	Mean Diff	Lower	Upper	Significant
Dolly's - Durango's	10.8333	2.6885	18.9782	Yes
Dolly's - Luiggi's	-13.5000	-21.6449	-5.3551	Yes
Dolly's - Cinibars	-1.8333	-9.9782	6.3115	
Durango's - Luiggi's	-24.3333	-32.4782	-16.1885	Yes
Durango's - Cinibars	-12.6667	-20.8115	-4.5218	Yes
Luiggi's - Cinibars	11.6667	3.5218	19.8115	Yes

Exercises V

58. How do the repeated measures and randomized block designs discussed here relate to the independent versus dependent sample distinction from Chapter 8?

59. A national consumer group has decided to test the three major tax preparation software packages (Tax Booster, Taxes R Us, and J.S. Dock) to see if there are any differences between them in terms of the final tax bill for the returns calculated by the packages. Since the final tax bill will depend greatly on the specifics of the information provided for the individual returns, it is decided that the same returns will be analyzed by each of the packages. The data are contained in the file Exercise 9-59.xlsx. Analyze the data as a repeated measures design. Are there any significant differences between the three software packages? Analyze the data as a one-way ANOVA. Would your results change? Explain the differences, if any

60. Alice Walker is the proud owner of the "Just Like Mom's" cookie shop. Alice has noticed that customer requests for gluten free products has been increasing of late and decides to expand her selections to include gluten free products. She has developed four different versions of gluten free chocolate chip cookies that use different types of gluten free flour and decides to test them on customers. She bakes up batches using the four different recipes and when a customer comes in she asks them if they would like to try the gluten free cookies and rate them on their flavor and on the their texture on a scale from 1 to 20. She is aware that individual differences will influence the results so she asks each customer to sample all four cookies and evaluate each one. The results from 11 customers that sampled all four recipes are contained in the file Exercise 9-60.xlsx. Are there any significant differences between the four recipes in terms of the flavor ratings? Are there any significant differences in the texture ratings? Which recipe would you recommend for Alice and why?

61. Jim Hardin is the VP of Marketing for We Got Game, a developer of different types of games for the computer and for game consoles. Jim is interested in determining whether differences between the four deliver sources that We Got Game utilizes (online download from a web site, phone, by mail ordered from a catalog, or in one of their retail stores) in terms of the dollar amount spent. Since the

different categories of games (sports, action/adventure, and strategy) have different pricing structures, it is important to take this into account in the analysis. Jim selects a random sample of orders from the four sources where the entire order consists of games that are solely in one of the three categories. The data are contained in the file Exercise 9-61.xlsx. Are there any significant differences between the four sources of sales in terms of the average amount purchased? Are there any significant differences between the three game categories? Is there a significant interaction present? If so, explain the interaction effect.

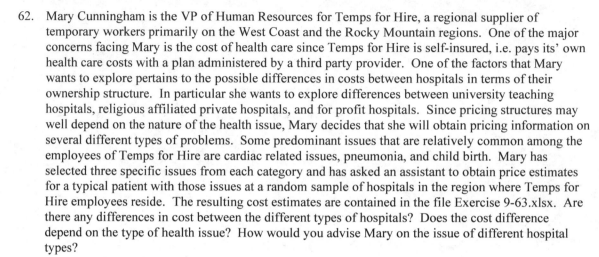

62. Mary Cunningham is the VP of Human Resources for Temps for Hire, a regional supplier of temporary workers primarily on the West Coast and the Rocky Mountain regions. One of the major concerns facing Mary is the cost of health care since Temps for Hire is self-insured, i.e. pays its' own health care costs with a plan administered by a third party provider. One of the factors that Mary wants to explore pertains to the possible differences in costs between hospitals in terms of their ownership structure. In particular she wants to explore differences between university teaching hospitals, religious affiliated private hospitals, and for profit hospitals. Since pricing structures may well depend on the nature of the health issue, Mary decides that she will obtain pricing information on several different types of problems. Some predominant issues that are relatively common among the employees of Temps for Hire are cardiac related issues, pneumonia, and child birth. Mary has selected three specific issues from each category and has asked an assistant to obtain price estimates for a typical patient with those issues at a random sample of hospitals in the region where Temps for Hire employees reside. The resulting cost estimates are contained in the file Exercise 9-63.xlsx. Are there any differences in cost between the different types of hospitals? Does the cost difference depend on the type of health issue? How would you advise Mary on the issue of different hospital types?

Chapter 10:

Regression and Correlation Analysis

Opening Vignette
Introduction: What is Regression and Correlation?
- Univariate and Bivariate Data
- Correlation versus Regression

Correlation Analysis
- The Correlation Coefficient
- Inferences about the Correlation Coefficient
- Caveats Concerning Correlation

Association for Nominal Scale Variables
- The Association of Two Nominal Scale Variables (Chi-Square)

Association for Ordinal Scale Variables
- Testing the Spearman Correlation Coefficient

Other Correlations
Simple Linear Regression
- Overview of Simple Linear Regression
- Calculating the Linear Regression Equation
- Using the Normal Equations
- Relationship of the Slope and the Correlation Coefficient
- Making a Point Estimate

Using the Regression Model for Inference
- Assumptions Underlying Regression
- The Standard Deviation of Regression
- Approximate Prediction Interval for Individual Values
- More Accurate Prediction Interval for Individual Values
- Confidence Interval for Mean Values
- Sources of Variability and The Coefficient of Determination
- Inferences about Regression
- Regression Diagnostics
    - *Practice*

Computer Solutions for Correlations
- Excel Functions
- The Data Analysis Toolpak
- The Excel Template
- Correlations Using XLDataAnalyst

Chapter 10 Objectives

When you finish this chapter you should be able to:

1. **Define the terms regression and correlation**
2. **Compute and interpret the correlation coefficient**
3. **Derive a regression equation from two sets of data**
4. **Use a regression equation to make inferences**
5. **Use chi-square to test the independence of two nominal scale variables**
6. **Use the Spearman rank correlation to measure relationships between two ordinal scale variables**

Opening Vignette

Sitting at her desk in the Market Research Department at the Milton Hotel chain, Susan is surprised to see her boss, Mary, who excitedly tells her that the company is considering opening a new hotel in Miami. She goes on to inform Susan that a committee will be awaiting Susan's suggestion about the marketing possibilities in this area within two weeks. Immediately, Susan realizes that she needs more information and that there must be other variables related to hotel visits that she can use to make accurate predictions. One variable that occurs to her is that the number of incoming airline flights per day may be related to the number of hotel guests for any given night. Susan and her assistant start to gather information and prepare scatter diagrams from two different data sources to show the relationship between the two variables. In comparing the scatter diagrams, both show a connection between the two variables, but it is difficult to tell whether they are the same or not and Susan realizes that she has no way to tell if the two sets of data show the same relationship or not. Susan decides that she needs to find a more exact way to determine the relationship between incoming flights and hotel guests.

Introduction: What is Regression and Correlation?

Univariate and Bivariate Data

Suppose you wanted to learn how long it takes cars to stop on a freeway. If you went out on a freeway with a stop sign and collected such information, you would no doubt find quite a difference in the stopping distances, as depicted in Figure 10-1 (a). If you had to predict the distance required to stop a car selected at random (Y), your best (point) estimate would probably be about 100 ft., the sample mean. This is because you would be working with *univariate* data (one variable), where the best estimator is the sample mean. We have been working primarily with univariate data until now.

Figure 10-1   Stopping Distance for Cars on Freeway

(a) Univariate Data

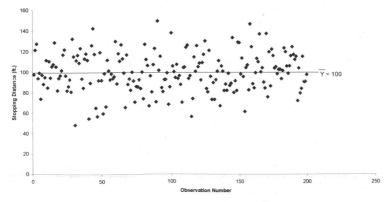

(b) Bivariate Data

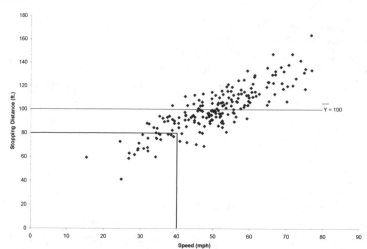

But, everyone knows that stopping distance is a function of many variables, especially speed. You might do a better job predicting the stopping distance by recognizing that it was dependent upon the speed of the car, X. If you collected data on both the speed and stopping distance, you would be working with *bivariate* (two variable) data. Then, as illustrated in Figure 10-1 (b), you might predict a stopping distance of 80 ft., if the car's speed is 40 mph; but, a distance of 160 ft., if the car is going 80 mph. Moreover, the closer the sample points lie to a single line drawn through all of the points, the better your estimate is likely to be.

Correlation versus Regression

In the bivariate case, the variable of interest, Y, is referred to as the *dependent variable* and the variable used as a predictor, X, is called the *independent variable*. One variable is the one we are interested in predicting, called the dependent variable, designated as Y. The other variable X, called the independent variable, is the one we use to predict the value of Y using the relationship between the two variables.

Using these terms, we can gain an intuitive meaning of the terms regression and correlation:

> *Regression Analysis* is the process of estimating the value of a dependent variable, Y, from one or more independent variables, X(s).
>
> *Correlation Analysis* is the process of determining the degree to which two or more variables, X and Y, are related.

The distinction between regression analysis and correlation analysis is subtle, but important. With correlation analysis, we are simply interested in the relationship between the two variables, X and Y. We do not distinguish between the two variables and the correlation between X and Y is the same as the correlation between Y and X. In regression analysis, however, we distinguish between the two variables. In regression, we assume that the X values are known and the Y variable is random. In correlation, we assume that both X and Y are random variables. In both correlation and regression we assume that the relationship between the two variables is linear in form and that all population distributions follow a normal distribution. Figure 10-2 illustrates the conceptual distinction between regression and correlation.

Figure 10-2   Distinction Between Regression and Correlation

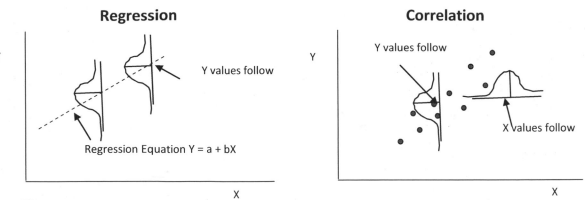

The distinction between regression and correlation analysis is very fuzzy and we will see that there is a very close relationship between the concepts and the computational procedures of the two.

Correlation Analysis

In correlation analysis, we are interested in the magnitude of the relationship between two variables, X and Y. We do not distinguish between them as independent or dependent variables, but we do assume that the relationship between the two variables is linear. A useful starting point for correlation analysis is a scatter plot or scatter diagram of the relationship.

> A *scatter diagram* is a plot of observed data points on X-Y coordinates to reveal a possible relationship between the variables.

Figure 10-3 shows a few sample scatter plots that illustrate different types and the strengths of relationships.

Figure 10-3   Scatter Diagram of X and Y Relationships

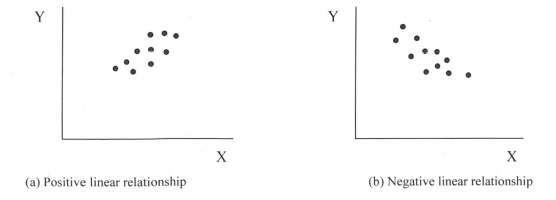

(a) Positive linear relationship   (b) Negative linear relationship

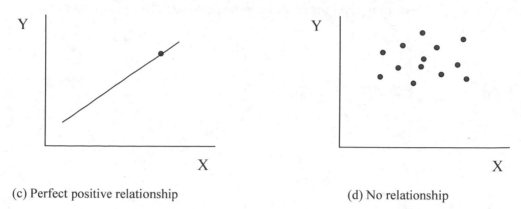

(c) Perfect positive relationship   (d) No relationship

Diagram (a) depicts a strong positive relationship and (b) a strong negative relationship. Diagram (c) depicts a perfect linear relationship between X and Y which means that we could perfectly predict the value of Y, if we knew the value of X and vice versa. Such perfect relationships are extremely rare in the real world. Diagram (d) indicates no apparent relationship between X and Y.

The Correlation Coefficient

Although scatter plots can indicate the general nature of the relationship between X and Y, it is often desirable to have a measure to summarize the relationship more compactly. The standard measure of relationship or association between two interval/ratio scaled variables is the coefficient of correlation (or correlation for short), designated as r:

> The *coefficient of correlation, r*, is a number between -1 and $+1$ that measures how closely two variables conform to a linear relationship, e.g., how closely they are related.

Correlations of -1 and +1 indicate a perfect negative or positive linear relationship, respectively, between two variables. Figure 10-3 (c) depicted a case where the correlation between X and Y would be +1.0. A correlation of 0 indicates that there is no relationship between X and Y; figure 10-3 (d) depicts such a situation. In most cases, the value of the correlation will be somewhere between 0 and 1.0 or between 0 and -1.0. The coefficient of correlation is calculated as:

covariance

$$\textbf{Coefficient of Correlation} \quad r = \frac{\Sigma(X-\bar{X})(Y-\bar{Y})}{\sqrt{\Sigma(X-\bar{X})^2 \, \Sigma(Y-\bar{Y})^2}} \quad\quad (10\text{-}1)$$

The numerator in the correlation coefficient equation if divided by (n-1) is the *covariance* which is a measure of how X and Y vary together or "co-vary." The covariance makes the correlation positive or negative. Figure 10-4 shows how the covariance will be either positive or negative, depending on the relationship between X and Y. In quadrant II both $(X - \bar{X})$ and $(Y - \bar{Y})$ are positive while in quadrant III both terms are negative so that their product $(\Sigma(X - \bar{X})(Y - \bar{Y}))$ is a positive value. In quadrant I the $(X - \bar{X})$ term is negative and the $(Y - \bar{Y})$ term is positive, yielding a negative product.

Finally, in quadrant IV the $(X - \bar{X})$ term is positive while the $(Y - \bar{Y})$ term is negative which again gives a negative product. In Figure 10-4 (a), most of the data points fall in quadrants II and III of the scatter diagram so that the covariance term is positive. In Figure 10-4 (b) on the other hand, most of the points fall in quadrants I and IV which are negative and will give a negative covariance.

Figure 10-4   ***Illustration of Covariance in Positive and Negative Relationships***

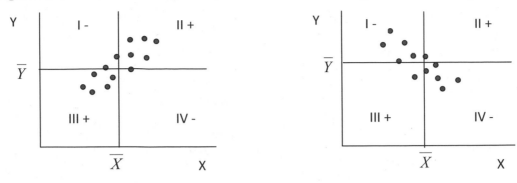

(a) Positive linear relationship   (b) Negative linear relationship

The denominator of the correlation coefficient is related to the variation of the two variables X and Y and is the product of the numerators of the standard deviation of X (S_X) and the standard deviation of Y (S_Y). The purpose of the denominator is to normalize the value to make sure that the absolute value of r is between 0 and 1.0.

Example 10-1

A city homebuilders association has collected the data shown in Table 10-1 in an attempt to relate the number of housing starts per month to the prevailing home loan interest rate at local banks.

Table 10-1 Data on Interest Rates and Number of Housing Starts

Interest Rate (X)	No. Housing Starts (Y)
18	4
12	10
8	20
7	18
14	12
9	15
16	6
20	3
16	4
10	8

Solution

Interest Rate (X)	No. Housing Starts (Y)	$(X - \bar{X})$	$(Y - \bar{Y})$	$(X - \bar{X})(Y - \bar{Y})$	$(X - \bar{X})^2$	$(Y - \bar{Y})^2$
18	4	5	-6	-30	25	36
12	10	-1	0	0	1	0
8	20	-5	10	-50	25	100
7	18	-6	8	-48	36	64
14	12	1	2	2	1	4
9	15	-4	5	-20	16	25

16	6	3	-4	-12	9	16
20	3	7	-7	-49	49	49
16	4	3	-6	-18	9	36
10	8	-3	-2	6	9	4
Sum 130	100			-219	180	334

$$\bar{X} = {}^{130}/_{10} = 13 \qquad \bar{Y} = {}^{100}/_{10} = 10$$

$$r = \frac{-219}{\sqrt{(180)(334)}} = \frac{-219}{245.1838} = -.89317$$

The correlation of -.89317 indicates a strong negative correlation between interest rates and the number of housing starts. In other words, as interest rates increase, there is a tendency for new housing starts to decrease.

Inferences about the Correlation Coefficient

As with other parameters we have talked about, like means, medians, proportions and variances, we will perform hypothesis tests for the correlation coefficient. As with the other parameters, we will designate the population correlation coefficient with a Greek letter, in this case, ρ (pronounced "rho"). We assume that both the X and Y variables have a normal distribution and that both are interval or ratio scaled. The hypothesis of interest is usually whether or not there is a relationship between X and Y in the population[1]:

$$H_0: \rho = 0$$

$$H_1: \rho \pm 0$$

The null hypothesis states that there is no relationship between X and Y in the population, and the alternative states that there is a relationship. The test statistic is the familiar t-distribution where the form, as before, is the sample statistic minus the hypothesized value (usually zero) divided by the standard error:

$$t = \frac{sample\ statistic - hypothesized\ value}{standar\ error}$$

$$t = \frac{r - \rho_0}{s_r} \qquad (10\text{-}2)$$

Where the standard error of the correlation (S_r) is calculated as,

$$s_r = \sqrt{\frac{1 - r^2}{n - 2}} \qquad (10\text{-}3)$$

The degrees of freedom for this test are n-2.

Example 10-2

Test for the significance of the correlation calculated in Example 10-1 where we calculated an r of -.89 from a sample of n = 10 paired of observations. Use a significance level of 2%.

---

[1] Although there is no logical reason why tests of correlation and other hypothesis tests in this chapter cannot be one tailed tests most analysts perform two tailed tests in practice and we will utilize two tailed tests throughout this chapter.

Solution

1. H_0: $\rho = 0$ (There is no correlation between the two variables)

    H_1: $\rho \pm 0$ (There is a nonzero correlation between the variables)

2. $\alpha = .02$

3. Use t with df $== 10-2 = 8$; reject if the p-value is less than .02

$$t = \frac{-.89317 - 0}{\sqrt{\frac{1-(-.80317)^2}{10-2}}} = \frac{-.89317}{.158999} = -5.61746$$

4. Using the probability calculator in XLDataAnalyst the p-value = 2(.00025) = .0005

5. Conclusion: Reject the null hypothesis and conclude that there is a nonzero correlation between the two variables in the population.

Caveats Concerning Correlation

Correlation coefficients are widely used, and often misinterpreted, so there are two cautions that you should keep in mind.

When you have a high correlation coefficient indicating a strong relationship between two variables, you may be tempted to conclude that the two variables have a cause-and-effect relationship. For example, we might want to jump to the conclusion that low interest rates cause increased housing purchases; however, that may not be the case and there may be alternative explanations for the relationship. For example, low interest rates might really draw funds out of the domestic market into better foreign investments. Maybe, the government has a policy of channeling federal funds into housing during recessionary periods when interest rates just happen to be low. Therefore, there might be a correlation between low interest rates and housing purchases. The point is that a significant correlation between two variables may be caused by other factors. Relationships that are caused by other outside factors are sometimes called *spurious relationships*. Therefore, we should not always infer causality when obtaining a significant correlation between two variables. Keep this in mind the next time you hear on the news that medical research has discovered a significant relationship (or correlation) between some lifestyle variable (such as bacon consumption) and obesity.

The second caution about correlations relates to the distinction between *practical* and *statistical significance*. If you examine the t-statistic in Equation 10-2 and its associated standard error in Equation 10-3, you will note that the value of the t-statistic (and therefore its associated p-value) depends only on the value of the correlation coefficient and the sample size. That means that any correlation, no matter how small, can be made statistically significant simply by obtaining a large enough sample size. For example, suppose that you conduct a study with 500 observations and you find a correlation of r = 0.10 between two variables. The t-value for the hypothesis test of zero correlation in the population is 22.37 (calculations will be shown later) and the resulting p-value is .0000, obviously highly statistically significant; however, the correlation is extremely small and of little practical significance.

We will discuss the coefficient of determination later in this chapter which is the percentage of variability that the relationship can predict. The coefficient of determination is calculated as the square of the correlation coefficient (r^2). In this case, the coefficient of determination is 0.01 which indicates that the relationship between the two variables accounts for only 1% of the variance, not much practical significance. It is always good to calculate the coefficient of determination whenever you have a correlation coefficient to determine whether or not the relationship is of practical as well as statistical significance.

Exercises I

1. What two items of information are conveyed by the correlation coefficient?

2. A study of the relationship between employment levels (Y in thousands) and freight car shipments (X) in a certain community yielded the following data:

$$n=100 \quad \sum X = 2,000 \quad \sum Y = 2,400 \quad \sum(X - \bar{X})(Y - \bar{Y}) = 894$$
$$\sum(X - \bar{X})^2 = 1,560 \quad \sum(Y - \bar{Y})^2 = 1,442$$

   (a) Compute the coefficient of correlation, and (b) Comment on the causal relationship between the two variables.

3. An agricultural economist has gathered data for a 30-year period on average rainfall in Kansas and the yield per acre of wheat in bushels. She has calculated the following values:

$$n=30 \quad \sum X = 91,618 \quad \sum Y = 184.95 \quad \sum(X - \bar{X})(Y - \bar{Y}) = 115.1482$$
$$\sum(X - \bar{X})^2 = 618.1146 \quad \sum(Y - \bar{Y})^2 = 86.09255$$

   (a) Compute the coefficient of correlation, and (b) Comment on the causal relationship between the two variables.

4. Pete has operated a small ice cream truck that travels through the residential neighborhoods in his hometown during his summer break from college for the past three years. He has data on the daily high temperature and his gross sales in dollars for 150 days over the three-year period. He has calculated the following values.

$$n=150 \quad \sum X = 12,630 \quad \sum Y = 15,000 \quad \sum(X - \bar{X})(Y - \bar{Y}) = 9831$$
$$\sum(X-\bar{X})^2 = 8,016 \quad \sum(Y-\bar{Y})^2 = 16,943$$

   (a) Compute the coefficient of correlation, and (b) Comment on the causal relationship between the two variables.

Association for Nominal Scale Variables

The Association of Two Nominal Scale Variables (Chi-Square)

In certain situations, we may be interested in the relationship between two nominal scale variables. For example, a union official might want to know whether or not there is a relationship between marital status and opinions toward unions (opposed, neutral, support) in a particular company. This uses the chi-square test for contingency tables and is commonly called the test of independence where the null hypothesis states that the two variables are independent of one another, e.g., that there is no relationship or association between them:

H_0: The two variables are independent

H_1: The two variables are related

The chi-square tests we looked at in previous chapters were limited to two rows (or columns) because we were dealing with proportions which involve binary (yes/no) variables. In the tests for independence or association there may be three or more rows or columns; however, the computations for the chi-square are the same as they were in the test for three or more proportions; it is only the interpretation that differs. Recall that the chi-square is calculated as:

$$\chi^2 = \sum \frac{(f_o - f_e)^2}{f_e} \qquad (10\text{-}4)$$

where the expected frequencies (f_e) are calculated as:

$$f_e = \frac{(RT)(CT)}{GT} \qquad (10\text{-}5)$$

where RT is the row total, CT is the column total, and GT is the grand total of all observations. The degrees of freedom for the test are (r-1)(c-1) where r is the number of rows and c is the number of columns. We can then conduct a hypothesis test using the usual chi-square distribution.

At this point, you may be wondering about the strength of the relationship. Is there a "correlation-like" measure that tells us how strong the relationship is? Unfortunately, the answer in the case of nominal scale variables is no. There is no single accepted measure of strength of relationship between nominal scale variables. When we discuss the use of computer software later in this chapter we will look at two measures of strength of association that are sometimes used.

Example 10-3

A subscription service states that preferences for different national magazines are independent of geographical location. A survey was taken in which 100 persons randomly chosen from three different geographical areas (East, Midwest, and South) were given a choice among three different magazines (UnWired, Music Today, and Popular Science). Each person expressed his/her preference for one of the magazines. The results are presented in Table 10-2 below. As we have stated before, this type of table is commonly called a contingency table.

Table 10-2   Data for Example 10-3

	UnWired	Music Today	Popular Science
East	75	50	175
Midwest	120	85	95
South	105	110	85

Using the .05 level of significance, is magazine preference independent of geographical region?

Solution

1. H_0: Magazine preference is independent of geographical region

    H_1: Magazine preference is dependent on geographical region

2. $\alpha = .05$

3. Use the chi-square distribution with df = (3-1)(3-1) = 4; reject if the p-value is less than .05

		UnWired	Music Today	Popular Science
East	Observed	75	50	175
	Expected	100.00	81.67	118.33
	Cell Chi Square	6.25	12.28	27.14
Midwest	Observed	120	85	95
	Expected	100.00	81.67	118.33
	Cell Chi Square	4.00	0.14	4.60
South	Observed	105	110	85
	Expected	100.00	81.67	118.33
	Cell Chi Square	0.25	9.83	9.39

4. $\chi^2 = 6.25 + 12.28 + \ldots 9.83 + 9.39 = 73.87$

    d.f. $= (3-1)(3-1) = 4$

    Using the Probability Calculator in XLDataAnalyst we find a p-value $= 0.0000$

5. Conclusion: Reject H_0 that they are independent because p-value is near 0. Magazine preference is dependent on the region of the country. From the observed frequencies, we can see that Popular Science tends to be the most popular magazine in the East while the Midwest leans somewhat toward UnWired and finally, that the South seems to prefer either UnWired or Music Today.

Exercises II

5. In an effort to forecast economic conditions for the upcoming year, a survey was conducted of representative academic, business, and government leaders, with the results as shown below and contained in the file Exercise 10-5.xlsx. Do the data suggest that one's forecast of the economy is independent of the source of his or her employment? Use the .01 level of significance.

	Frequencies				
	Depression	**Recession**	**Stability**	**Expansion**	**Total**
Academic Economists	24	28	17	11	80
Business Managers	15	21	43	21	100
Government Economists	11	11	20	28	70
Total	50	60	80	60	250

6. The data shown below, and in the file Exercise 10-6.xlsx, constitute a two-way classification of 5,000 insurance company clients grouped by age level and income level. Use the test of independence of principles of classification at the .05 level to determine whether the age of clients is independent of their income level.

	< 20 yr.	**20 < 50 yr.**	**≥ 50 yr.**	**Total**
High income	1,000	400	600	2,000
Medium income	900	600	300	1,800
Low income	800	300	100	1,200
Total	2,700	1,300	1,000	5,000

7. According to a recent Forbes article, so called millennials (Ages 25 to 34) have different perspectives on work, how to communicate, and career progress. Suppose that the data below and in the file Exercise 10-7 came from a survey of 1,000 workers in the United States. From this data can we conclude that preferences in communication are independent of age group?

	Face to Face	E-mail/Text	Phone
Millennial1	30	90	30
Generation Y	115	75	60
Generation X	140	60	50
Boomer	155	65	40

8. One theory of the behavior of stock markets is that the market follows a "random walk." One aspect of a random walk is that what happens on one day must be independent of what happened the previous day. The following table and the file Exercise 10-8 contains the frequencies with which a

stock goes up, goes down, or does not change for a day versus the previous days change. Test the hypothesis that changes over consecutive days are independent.

		Price Change Previous Day		
		Up	No Change	Down
Price Change Today	Up	155	39	81
	No Change	39	14	22
	Down	84	19	47

Association for Ordinal Scale Variables

When dealing with ordinal scale data, we cannot use the correlation coefficient as a measure of the relationship between variables. In these situations, we have to use a special rank correlation for ordinal variables:

> *Spearman's rank correlation coefficient* is a measure of the closeness of the relationship between the ranked values (as opposed to the numerical values) of two variables.

The Spearman rank correlation coefficient, r_s relies only on the squared difference in ranks, d, of each of the pairs of n observations. Therefore, the computation, or r_s, is as follows:

$$r_s = 1 - \frac{6 \sum d^2}{n(n^2 - 1)} \qquad (10\text{-}6)$$

As with the standard (Pearson) r, the rank correlation coefficient has the same range, -1.00 to +1.00, and the same general meaning. We will illustrate its computation in Example 10-4.

Example 10-4

A soft drink manufacturer is interested in determining whether or not there is a relationship between consumers' attitudes towards nutrition and their preferences for sweetness in soft drinks. A 25-point scale is developed to measure attitudes toward nutrition with a value of 1, indicating that good nutrition is nice, but not that important, to a value of 25 which indicates that nutrition is one of the most important goals in life. The scale is administered to a panel of 10 consumers who are then asked to evaluate a new super sweet drink being developed by the company on a scale from 1 to 20 with 20 being the highest evaluation. The results are presented in the table below:

Panelist	1	2	3	4	5	6	7	8	9	10
Nutrition Scale	13	9	11	8	22	14	6	12	17	20
Drink Evaluation	9	19	5	22	2	14	25	10	6	1

Solution

For r_s we need ranked data only, so we shall assign ranks from 1 (lowest) to 10 (highest) for each of the two variables. Thus the rankings for panelist 4 will be first with respect to nutrition and ninth with respect to the drink evaluation. If there are any ties in the rankings (there are not in this case), then they would be handled by the same averaging procedure used in other tests for ordinal data. The computations are shown in Table 10-3.

Table 10-3   ***Rank Correlation Computation***

Panelist	(1) Nutrition Rank X	(2) Drink Rank (Y)	(3) Difference $(1) - (2)$	(4) (Difference)^2 $[(1) - (2)]^2$
1	5	6	-1	1
2	8	3	5	25
3	7	8	-1	1
4	9	2	7	49
5	1	9	-8	64
6	4	4	0	0
7	10	1	9	81
8	6	5	1	1
9	3	7	-4	16
10	2	10	-8	64
				$\sum d^2 = 302$

$$r_s = 1 - \frac{6 \sum d^2}{n(n^2 - 1)} = 1 - \frac{6(302)}{10(100 - 1)} = -0.8303$$

The negative value suggests that the more important nutrition is, the lower the tendency for evaluation for the sweet drink and vice versa.

We should note two facts about the Spearman Rank Correlation. First, the Spearman value can also be obtained by simply applying the formula for the Pearson correlation coefficient described earlier in this chapter to the rank orders of the two variables. Second, the simplified formula given in Equation 10-6 applies only when there are no ties in the data. If there are ties in the data then the Spearman correlation must be calculated using the Pearson correlation equations in Equation 10-1 to obtain an accurate result. If there are only a few ties, however, the simplified formula will produce a good approximate value. Still, you need to be aware that the answer you get from the simplified formula will likely differ slightly from the results produced by statistical packages such as XLDataAnalyst, if there are ties in the ranks.

Testing the Spearman Correlation Coefficient

The r_s calculated from sample data can test a hypothesis of no correlation between the two populations in much the same manner as was done with the sample correlation coefficient, r. Special tables are available in reference texts for small numbers of paired observations; however, if 10 or more pairs of observations are available, a statistic for testing the H_0: $\rho_r = 0$ can be computed with the equation:

Test statistic for r$_s$: $$t = \frac{r_s - 0}{\sqrt{(1 - r_s^2)/(n - 2)}}$$ *(10-7)*

This statistic has a *t*-distribution with $n - 2$ degrees of freedom. You may recognize that this is the same calculation as used in equations 10-2 and 10-3 for testing H_0: $\rho = 0$, except that in equation 10-7, r_s is substituted for r.

Example 10-5

Test the hypothesis of no correlation in the ranked data of Example 10-4 at the .02 level.

Solution

1. H_0: $\rho_s = 0$

   H_1: $\rho_s \neq 0$

2. $\alpha = .02$.

3. $t = \dfrac{r_s - 0}{\sqrt{(1 - r_s^2)/(n-2)}} = \dfrac{-.8303 - 0}{\sqrt{(1 - -.8303^2)/(10-2)}} = -4.21389$

The p-value for this test statistic can be found using XLDataAnalyst and the value is .0015.

4. Conclusion: Reject hypothesis of no correlation in the ranked data. The ranked data provide strong evidence or a correlation between nutrition attitudes and evaluation of the soft drink.

Rejecting the hypothesis of no correlation leads us to conclude that there is a close relationship between nutrition attitudes and the evaluation of the sweet soft drink. Moreover, insofar as the sample correlation coefficient is negative, the two variables move in opposite directions. That is, attitudes of low importance of nutrition are associated with higher evaluations of the sweet drink and attitudes of higher importance of nutrition with lower evaluations of the sweet drink.

Exercises III

9. How does the Spearman rank correlation coefficient r_s differ from the standard (Pearson) coefficient of correlation, r?

10. The following data show the rank of 15 job candidates on two employment test criteria. Compute the rank correlation coefficient, r_s.

Candidate no.	1	2	3	4	5	6	7	8	9	10	11	12	13	14	15
Dexterity	12	5	15	2	4	9	13	10	3	11	7	14	1	6	8
Math ability	2	8	7	13	10	4	1	6	15	9	5	3	12	14	11

11. NASA wants to reduce the number of suppliers from a dozen down to half that many. She has asked one of her buyers to rate the 12 suppliers on the basis of quality of their components, and another to rate them on the basis of promptness in meeting delivery requirements. Using the results shown below, compute the rank correlation coefficient and test it at the .01 level of significance.

Supplier No.	1	2	3	4	5	6	7	8	9	10	11	12
Rank on quality	4	2	7	9	10	3	8	12	11	6	1	5
Rank on delivery	2	5	9	8	9	4	10	9	12	11	3	6

12. The product development department of a dairy products company has engaged two panels to help select which of ten new frozen dessert products to market. One panel consists of company personnel and the other of typical consumers. Each panel is asked to evaluate the market potential of the product on a score of 1 to 100. Results are as shown below.

	Score (1–100) of Dessert from Panel of:	
New Product	**Company Personnel**	**Typical Consumers**
A	68	74
B	92	75
C	77	58
D	45	52
E	75	48
F	83	63
G	90	68
H	86	68
I	72	30
J	95	82

(a) Calculate the rank correlation coefficient and comment on its meaning.

(b) Conduct a two-tailed test of the hypothesis that there is no correlation in the ranks assigned by the two panels at the .10 level of significance.

Other Correlations

Up to this point we have looked only at the relationship between two variables which were of the same type. For example, a ratio scaled variable with another ratio scaled variable, or an ordinal variable with another ordinal variable. You may be wondering about situations where it is desired to examine the relationship between two variables that have different scale types, for example a nominal scale variable and an interval or ratio scale variable. There are other types of correlation that are not often used in business but are used in other fields of study such as Education and Psychology. For example, a measure called a point biserial correlation can be computed between a continuous variable and a dichotomous variable. If the dichotomous variable is coded as 0-1, then the point biserial correlation is equivalent to the Pearson correlation between the two variables. Similarly, a rank biserial correlation can be calculated between an ordinal variable and a continuous interval or ratio scaled variable. These specialized correlations are beyond the scope of this text and will not be discussed here in detail.

Simple Linear Regression

Overview of Simple Linear Regression

The most basic form of regression analysis is *simple linear regression.* In this section, we will define this term more fully and see how a regression model is formulated.

Simple and Multiple Regression

Simple regression analysis uses only one independent variable, X, to estimate the value of the dependent variable, Y. In the introduction for this chapter, we discussed the relationship between speed and stopping distance when driving a car. If we were to perform a regression analysis to predict stopping distance from speed values, is would be a simple linear regression analysis. If, in addition to speed, we used data on road conditions, tire wear, and other variables to help predict stopping distance, we would be performing a multiple regression analysis. *Multiple regression* uses two or more independent variables, X(s), to better predict the (one) dependent variable, Y. This chapter will be limited to simple regression and correlation models and we will consider multiple regression in the next chapter.

Linear and Nonlinear Regression

The first step in a regression analysis is to correctly identify the nature of the relationship between the independent and dependent variables which can be described by constructing a scatter diagram. Figure 10-1(b) displayed a scatter diagram of the bivariate data relating speed to stopping distance. It happened to be a positive relationship (e.g., as X increased, Y generally increased), and appeared to be fairly linear (e.g., the points circulated around a diagonal, straight line).

Figure 10-5 shows some scatter diagram relationships that might be obtained from different data. Lines summarizing the relationship have been added to help describe the pattern of points. Note that (a) represents a "stronger" relationship than (b) because the data points lie closer to the line that typifies the relationship between X and Y. Also note that in (c), the relationship is curvilinear rather than linear. It cannot be adequately described by a straight line; therefore, a more complex regression model is needed. The variables in (d) form a "cloud" and do not appear to be related in a useful manner. For situations like this, X values are of no help in predicting Y, and further analysis is not usually justified.

Figure 10-5   Scatter Diagram of X and Y Relationships

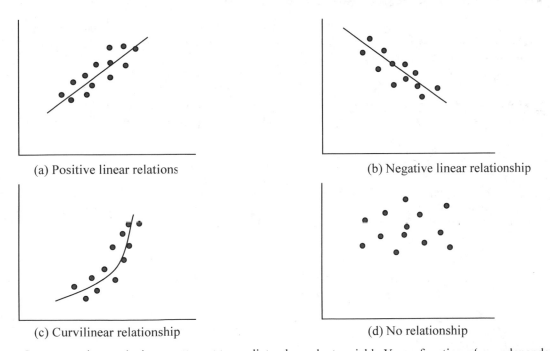

(a) Positive linear relations

(b) Negative linear relationship

(c) Curvilinear relationship

(d) No relationship

In a regression analysis, we attempt to predict a dependent variable Y as a function of an independent variable X, by fitting a functional relationship, represented by a curve or line; however, as illustrated in Figure 10-5, rarely will the points fall exactly on that curve. In other words, there will always be some error in predicting Y from X. This is true whether we are talking about a population or a sample. If we let the Greek letter epsilon, ε, depict the error of an estimate, then the value of the dependent variable, Y, is a function f, of the independent variable, X, and the amount of error, ε. So the generalized form of a regression model is:

$$Y = f(X) + \varepsilon$$

Different types of regression analysis used different functional form, f, to represent the relationship between X and Y. The simplest form is the linear relationship such as patterns (a) and (b). Analysis of data with nonlinear patterns will be discussed in a later chapter.

Simple Linear Regression Model

When the data points fall roughly in a straight-line pattern (either positive or negative), then a linear equation can be used to describe the relationship; however, we know that even in the population, the points will not fall exactly on the line. As with the stopping distance example, there is usually some difference (or error) in making an estimate. If we let α represent the population Y-intercept, β represent the population slope of the line, and ε represent, the error then the linear equation for the population can be written:

Population Regression Line: $\quad Y = \alpha + \beta X + \varepsilon$ *(10-8)*

The Y-intercept (α) is the point at which the line crosses the Y-axis; in other words, it is the average value of Y when X = 0. The slope (β) represents how much the average value of the dependent variable changes for each unit change in the independent variable. The important aspect of this equation is that even if we include the entire population, we still cannot perfectly predict Y from knowing X. There is still error in the relationship even in the population; however, we do assume that for any fixed point X, the mean of all the Y values lies on the line and can be predicted perfectly in the population.

Therefore, at any fixed "X" point on the line, we will assume that the mean of all the Y values lies on the line so that in the population we can predict the average value of Y for a given value of X (designated $\mu_{Y.X}$). Using our notation above then the linear equation for means in the population can be written as:

$$\mu_{Y.X} = \alpha + \beta X$$

Population values are rarely (if ever) known; therefore, our regression equation will normally be computed from sample data. Letting $\hat{Y}$ represent the calculated or predicted value of the dependent variable Y, we can express the sample linear regression model as:

Sample Regression Line: $\quad \hat{Y} = a + bX$ *(10-9)*

The y-intercept "a" and slope "b" are sample estimates of the population values (α and β) that we derive from the X and Y sample data points. The sample intercept (a) is the point at which the sample line crosses the Y-axis and is an estimate of α in the population. The sample slope (b) is the change in Y for one unit change in X in the sample and is an estimate of the population slope β.

Once the sample regression equation is derived, it can be used to predict values of the dependent variable (Y). These predicted values will be points that lie on the regression line, given a specific value of X. To calculate these values, we simply substitute the given value of X into the regression equation to calculate Y.

Steps in Regression

We can summarize the steps in determining and using the linear regression of Y on X as follows:

1. Collect observations (data) of the independent and dependent variables.

2. Determine the linear nature of the relationship (using a scatter diagram).

3. Compute the parameters (slope and intercept) and associated error of the regression model.

4. Use the regression model to predict values of the dependent variable.

5. Make any additional predictions and conduct hypothesis tests as desired.

Calculating the Linear Regression Equation

Assuming that data have been collected and a scatter diagram has confirmed the linear nature of the relationship, let us proceed with step 3, the computation of the regression line. In regression, we seek to derive a line that best fits the data we have collected, e.g., that comes as close as possible to the data points. In statistics, we often try to minimize the squared deviations or squared errors. This is called the *principle of least squares*. It can be shown that the least squares line of best fit is given by the line that satisfies the following three properties, as illustrated in Figure 10-6.

1. It passes through both $\bar{X}$ and $\bar{Y}$.

2. The sum of the deviations about the line (error) is zero ($\sum(Y - Y') = 0$).

3. The sum of the squared deviations about the line is a minimum (least squares), $\sum(Y - Y;)^2$ *is a minimum.*

Figure 10-6   Least Squares Line of Fit

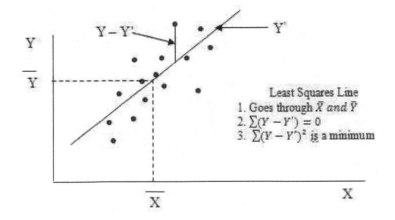

Although the equations for the parameters of this best fitting line can be derived from a set of equations, called the normal equations, we will simply state them here without proof:

Slope
$$b = \frac{\sum(X - \bar{X})(Y - \bar{Y})}{\sum(X - \bar{X})^2}$$
covariance

(10-10)

Y-intercept
$$a = \bar{Y} - b\bar{X}$$

(10-11)

Notice that the numerator of the intercept is the same numerator as that of the correlation r. That means that there is a relationship between the slope of the regression line and the correlation coefficient. We will explore this relationship in more detail shortly.

Example 10-6

Barron and Associates, a market research firm, want to see if there is a relationship between monthly client advertising expenditures and resulting sales the following month. If such a relationship can be developed it could be used in making advertising decisions and in predicting upcoming sales. Tom Barron has gathered historical data from a sample of ten different client firms. The values in the table are in hundreds of thousands of dollars.

Table 10-4   *Advertising Expenditures and Monthly Sales*

Firm Number	1	2	3	4	5	6	7	8	9	10
Advertising	7	9	5	8	6	9	7	4	8	7
Sales	10	12	6	9	8	11	10	5	10	9

Solution

First plot the observations of advertising and sales in a scatter diagram to verify the relationship is linear as shown in Figure 10-7.

Figure 10-7   Scatter Diagram of Advertising(X) and Sales(Y)

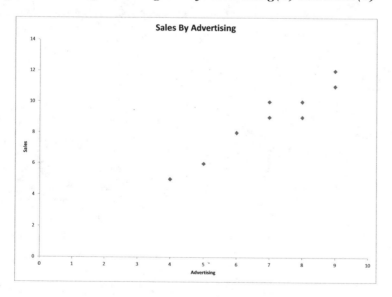

Note that the relationship appears to be linear, and it is positive; sales tend to increase as advertising increases; however, it is not a perfect relationship because all the points do not fall on a single diagonal straight line. Next, we must compute the slope and the intercept for the best fitting regression line.

Firm Number	Advertising X	Sales Y	$(X - \bar{X})$	$(Y - \bar{Y})$	$(X - \bar{X})(Y - \bar{Y})$	$(X - \bar{X})^2$
1	7	10	0	1	0	0
2	9	12	2	3	6	4
3	5	6	-2	-3	6	4
4	8	9	1	0	0	1
5	6	8	-1	-1	1	1
6	9	11	2	2	4	4
7	7	10	0	1	0	0
8	4	5	-3	-4	12	9
9	8	10	1	1	1	1
10	7	9	0	0	0	0
Totals	70	90	0	0	30	24

The sample means for the X and Y variables as:

$$\bar{X} = \frac{79}{10} = 7 \qquad \bar{Y} = \frac{90}{10} = 9$$

Using equations 10-3 and 10-4, we can then compute the slope and the intercept for our regression line:

Slope $\qquad b = \frac{\Sigma(X-\bar{X})(Y-\bar{Y})}{\Sigma(X-\bar{X})^2} = \frac{30}{24} = 1.25$

Intercept $a = \bar{Y} - b\bar{X} = 9 - (1.25)(7) = .25$

The regression equation is thus: $\hat{Y} = .25 + 1.25X$

The regression equation describes a line of best fit through the data points, as shown in Figure 10-8. Note that the line does pass through the point represented by the means of the X and Y values as our properties required. The intercept is at .25 units on the Y (strength) axis. The slope, b, tells us that the average strength increases 1.25 units for each unit increase in hardness.

Relationship of the Slope and the Correlation Coefficient

We have previously mentioned that there is a relationship between the correlation and the slope through the covariance. The two equations are shown together below so that we can more clearly see the relationship between the two values:

$$r = \frac{\Sigma(X-\bar{X})(Y-\bar{Y})}{\sqrt{\Sigma(X-\bar{X})^2 \, \Sigma(Y-\bar{Y})^2}} \qquad\qquad b = \frac{\Sigma(X-\bar{X})(Y-\bar{Y})}{\Sigma(X-\bar{X})^2}$$

Note that the covariance of X and Y is the numerator in both equations. Since the numerator is the only value in either equation that can be negative as well as positive, the slope and the correlation must have the same sign, either positive or negative; however, the value of the slope and the correlation will not be the same because they have different denominators[2]. The denominator of the correlation depends on the

---

[2] However, it can be shown that if both X and Y are standardized (i.e. turned into Z scores) then the slope of the regression line will equal the correlation.

variability of both X and Y and this is what keeps the absolute value of the correlation between 0 and 1. The denominator of the slope depends only on the variability of the X values.

Figure 10-8   *Regression Line for Advertising and Sales Data*

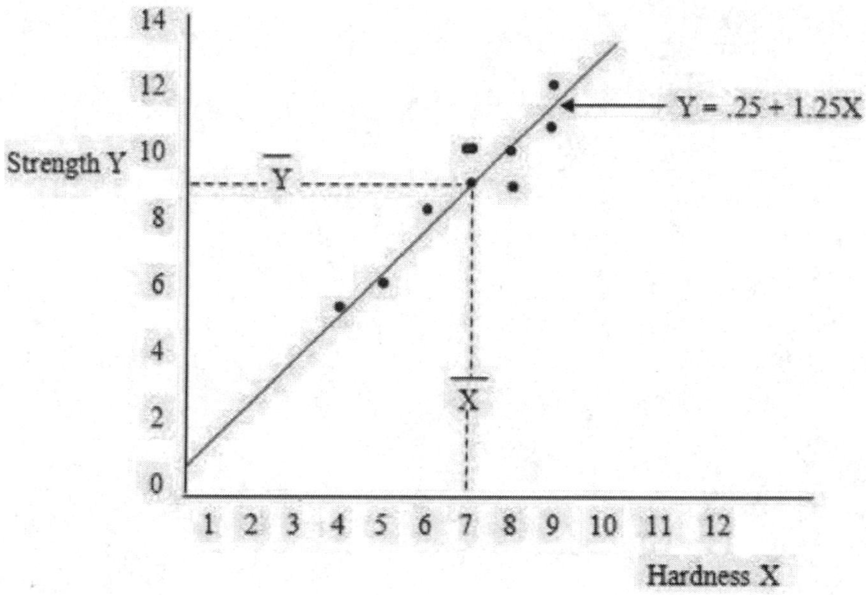

Determining a Point Estimate

Once the regression equation is developed, it can be used for estimating the value of Y, for a given value of X. If a point estimate is desired, simply substitute a value for X (the independent variable) into the equation, and solve for $\hat{Y}$ (the dependent variable). Any estimates should be limited to the approximate range within which the observed data lie, because the same relationship may not hold outside of this range. In other words, it is risky to make predictions outside the range of the X values that you have actually observed. That is one reason why we are seldom interested in the Y intercept term since rarely is there an observation in the data where X is equal to 0.

Example 10-7

Using the regression equation $\hat{Y} = .25 + 1.25X$, determine a point estimate of the sales when advertising expenditures are: (a) 10 and (b) 5. (c) Suppose the advertising expenditures for a given firm are 20. . Estimate the strength.

Solution

By substituting the value of X into the regression equation we have:

    (a) $\hat{Y} = .25 + 1.25X = .25 + 1.25(10) = 12.75$ hundred thousand dollars

    (b) $\hat{Y} = .25 + 1.25X = .25 + 1.25(5) = 6.50$ hundred thousand dollars

    (c) The X value of 20 lies too far outside the range to make a valid estimate.

These point estimates do, of course, suffer from the same weaknesses as the univariate data point estimates for the mean, proportion, median or variance that we worked with in earlier chapters, in that they are most likely incorrect. The slope, b, tells us that the estimated average sales increase 1.25 hundred thousand dollars for each one hundred thousand dollar increase in advertising expenditures. To enhance the value of our predictions, therefore, we must obtain a measure of the expected error of the estimate. In addition, we should be aware of the assumptions that underlie our estimates.

Exercises IV

13. How does regression differ from correlation?

14. Identify the independent variable in the following:

    (a) Highway funds are allocated to counties on the basis of population.

    (b) Purchase orders are counted to estimate storage space needs.

    (c) A survey of buyer intentions suggests strong Christmas sales of toys.

15. How does the general form of the regression model differ from the form we use for simple linear regression? Why is there a difference?

16. The following data were collected to measure the success of a training program for word processing employees.

Hours of training X	6	10	12	2	4	10	3	9	2	8	5	7
Number of errors/job	14	6	6	16	20	4	18	10	18	6	10	10

    (a)   Develop a scatter plot of the data.

    (b)   Do they appear to have a linear relationship?

    (c)   Is the slope positive or negative?

17. A retail sales manager would like to determine whether the number of coupons in their newspaper advertisements can be used to help predict sales of small appliances in the following week. Data from past weeks are:

	No. Coupons X	Sales ($000) Y
	4	5
	6	7
	9	8
	3	4
	2	5
	6	7
Total	30	36

    (a) Graph the data to confirm that a linear relationship exists.

    (b) Compute the least squares line of best fit.

    (c) Make a point estimate of sales when seven coupons are included in the advertisement in the previous week.

18. Suppose a line of best fit relating expenditures of selected international companies on research and development (R & D) to their export sales (both in $ millions) is $\hat{Y} = -.60 + 30.40 \, X$. Estimate the export sales for companies spending

    (a) $1.5 million on R & D

    (b) $80,000 on R & D

19. For the following data, compute the least squares line of best fit:

    $$n = 10 \quad \Sigma X = 6 \quad \Sigma Y = 15 \quad \Sigma(X - \bar{X})^2 = 36 \quad \Sigma Y - \bar{Y})^2 = 106 \quad \Sigma(X - \bar{X})(Y - \bar{Y}) = 54$$

20. Export Enterprises is a supplier of oil well drilling equipment and is attempting to forecast demand for one of their product lines (in units) on the basis of a foreign currency exchange rate. An analysis of 10 observations resulted in the following data:

    $$n = 10 \quad \Sigma X = 100 \quad \Sigma Y = 200 \quad \Sigma(X - \bar{X})^2 = 50 \quad \Sigma Y - \bar{Y})^2 = 94 \; = 36$$

    (a) Determine the resulting linear regression equation.

    (b) Use your equation to develop a point estimate of demand (Y) when the currency exchange rate is 1.40.

Using the Regression Model for Inference

So far, we have stated the general procedure for obtaining a regression equation in a descriptive manner. We want to extend our inquiry to how regression is used for making statistical inferences. In making statistical inferences, we need a measure of sample error; thus we will begin by recognizing the assumptions underlying regression and calculating the error associated with a regression.

Assumptions Underlying Regression

The least squares procedure we used to find the best fitting line is simply a deterministic mathematical procedure. There is no uncertainty associated with it, and it will work for any two variables; they do not need to have an independent/dependent relationship.

Regression uses the least squares procedure, but it goes beyond this deterministic relationship because the regression model assumes that the dependent (Y) variable is distributed according to a normal probability distribution. That is, for every given value of X, there are many possible values of Y. These individual Y values form a series of probability distributions around the regression line. Figure 10-9 illustrates three such distributions, which are referred to as conditional probability distributions of Y given X, or (Y.X). The regression line goes through the means ($\mu_{Y.X}$) of this set of distributions.

Figure 10-9   Conditional Distributions of Y Given X

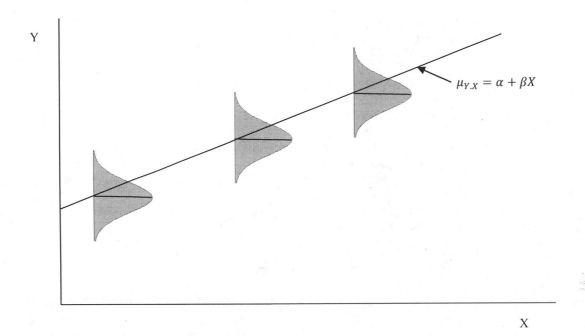

The assumptions of regression modeling relate to the error terms (ε) that appear in the population regression equation.

$$Y = \alpha + \beta X + \varepsilon$$

There is an error term for each value of X. The four assumptions about the error terms are:

1. The mean of the error terms is zero for all X

2. The error terms follow a normal distribution for each value of X

3. The variances of the error terms for all X are equal (homogeneity of variances)

4. The error terms are all independent of one another.

It is the normal assumption about the distribution of values that allows us to make inferential statements when working with regression models. Insofar as we assume that the Y values form a normal distribution about the regression line in the population, we can use the areas under the normal curve (or more correctly, under the student t-distribution) to establish prediction intervals within which we can predict Y values (given a value of X). This requires that we know the standard deviation of the sampling distribution—which is the topic we will discuss next.

The Standard Error of the Estimate

The third assumption above states that the variances, and therefore the standard deviations, of the Y values around the regression line for the different values of X are all equal. This means that there is a single population standard deviation $\sigma_{Y.X}$ that represents the variability of the Y values about the regression line in the population. This is the standard deviation we need to make inferential statements about the regression model. Since we will never know this population standard deviation, we need to estimate this value using sample data.

To estimate the population variability around the regression line we need the corresponding value in the sample. We can measure error in the sample as the difference between the actual value of Y and the calculated or predicted value of Y (or Y - $\hat{Y}$). We call this term a *residual*. Since each observation in the data will have a residual value, a useful measure of variability around the regression line might be the average residual; however, as we noted earlier when discussing the principle of least squares, the sum of the residuals is zero. This is similar to the situation with the sample mean where the sum of the deviations was zero. Here, we will look at the squared residuals for our measure of error. To estimate the population standard deviation about the regression line, we can use the sample standard deviation about the regression line. Remember that a sample standard deviation is the square root of the sum of the squared deviations of the values around the mean divided by the degrees of freedom (n-1). In this case, the mean is the regression line, designated by $\hat{Y}$, and the deviations are the sum of the squared differences between the points on the Y-axis and the regression line $\sum(Y - \hat{Y})^2$, e.g., the sum of the squared residuals. In this case, the degrees of freedom equals n-2 because we lose two degrees of freedom in estimating the two constants of the regression line (a and b) instead of just one in estimating a mean. The resulting equation for the standard deviation of the Y values about the regression line, $s_{y.x}$, is:

$$S_{y.x} = \sqrt{\frac{\sum(Y-\hat{Y})^2}{n-2}}$$ *(10-12)*

$S_{y.x}$ is a measure of distances in the Y direction, and not perpendicular to the regression line. The standard deviation of the regression line is also sometimes designated $S_{y.x}$ and is commonly referred to as the *standard error of the estimate*. This name is not the clearest verbiage because $s_{y.x}$ is really a standard deviation of points around the regression line. Nevertheless, this term is so widely used that we will use it here as well. Be aware that is it not a standard error in the sense that we have used it before; however, as we will see, the traditional standard error terms that we will use in regression are all derived from this value.

Example 10-8

Compute the standard error of the estimate for the data in Example 10-6.

Solution

The X and Y data points from Example 10-6 are repeated in the table below, along with the computation of each $\hat{Y}$ value, the deviations, the square of the deviations, and the sum of the squared deviations. These deviations or residuals represent the unexplained or random variation of the Y values about the regression line.

Table 10-5   ***Computation of the Sum of Squared Deviations About the Regression Line***

Firm Number	Advertising X	Sales Y	Point Estimate $\hat{Y}=.25+1.25X$	Deviation $(Y-\hat{Y})$	Squared Deviation $(Y-\hat{Y})^2$
1	7	10	9.00	1.00	1.0000
2	9	12	11.50	.50	.2500
3	5	6	6.50	-.50	.2500
4	8	9	10.25	-1.25	1.5625
5	6	8	7.75	.25	.0625
6	9	11	11.50	-.50	.2500
7	7	10	9.00	1.00	1.0000

8	4	5	5.25	-.25	.0625
9	8	10	10.25	-.25	.0625
10	7	9	9.00	.00	.0000
Totals	70	90		0.00	4.5000

$$S_{y.x} = \sqrt{\frac{\Sigma(Y - \hat{Y})^2}{n - 2}} = \sqrt{\frac{4.5}{10 - 2}} = .75$$

Once we have computed the standard error of the estimate, $S_{y.x}$, it can be used to help test the validity of the regression equation. It can also be used to make inferential statements in a manner similar to what we have done before when using other normal distributions. For example, if the points about the regression line are normally distributed, we can expect 68.26% of the observations to lie within $\pm 1 S_{y.x}$, 95.54% of them to lie within $\pm 2\, S_{y.x}$ and 99.97% of them to lie within $\pm 3 S_{y.x}$. Note, however, that we are referring to the location of individual Y values, not to the mean of a sample of Y values. For this reason, we do not refer to these estimates associated with regression as "confidence intervals" (of means). Instead, we refer to them as *prediction intervals* (of individual values).

Approximate Prediction Interval for Individual Values

We have already seen that we can make a point estimate of the mean of the regression line, or an individual value, by a value of X into the regression equation $\hat{Y} = a + bX$. We do not know the population standard deviation around the regression line but we are assuming that the distribution around the line in the population is a normal distribution. Therefore, the t-distribution should be used for establishing the prediction limits. Similar to our discussion of means in Chapter 6, we can calculate prediction limits for individual values of Y (designated as Y_{PL}) as:

Prediction Limits $\qquad\qquad Y_{PL} = \hat{Y} \pm t s_{y.x}$

As before, the t value has (n-2) degrees of freedom.

Example 10-9

Use the t-distribution to establish 95% prediction limits using the data from Example 10-6. Recall that there were 10 data points, that the derived regression equation was $\hat{Y} = .25 + 1.25X$, and that $s_{y.x}$ was calculated to be .75. Make an approximate interval prediction for strength, Y, when the surface hardness measurement is X = 8.5.

Solution

$$\hat{Y} = .25 + 1.25(8.5) = 10.88$$

$$t = t_{\alpha/2, n-2} = t_{.025,8} = 2.306$$

$$Y_{PLL} = 10.88 - 2.306(.75) = 9.15$$

$$Y_{PLU} = 10.88 + 2.306(.75) = 12.61$$

Thus we would predict that sales following a month where advertising expenditures were 8.5 hundred thousand dollars would be approximately within the range of 9.15 to 12.61 hundred thousand dollars. If the actual data conform to the underlying assumptions this should be a reasonably good approximate interval estimate for an individual item.

More Accurate Prediction Intervals for Individual Values

As you may have noticed, the discussion about prediction intervals, has to this point, been qualified by referring to the intervals as "approximate". This was with good reason. The true (population) regression line is $\mu_{Y.X} = \alpha + \beta X$. But we are estimating the population values of the Y-intercept (α) and the slope (β) with the point estimates a and b. We know point estimates are usually wrong, and we have no way of knowing whether our estimates agree with the true values or not. So we should allow for this uncertainty in our prediction interval—especially if our sample size is small.

There are two major sources of error—the possibility of an error in estimating the intercept and a possibility of an error in estimating the slope. Also, each regression line from a sample passes through its' own $\bar{X}$ and $\bar{Y}$ values. But these $\bar{X}$ and $\bar{Y}$ values are not necessarily equal to the true population means μ_X and μ_Y. As we said, the values of a and b are estimates and are subject to error so that these values will vary from one sample to the next.

The estimated $\hat{Y}$ value is least dependent on the true values of α and the slope β, i.e. the least susceptible to error in the estimates, when the X value is equal to the mean of the X values, μ_X. As we move away from this mean, we are less and less certain of the $\hat{Y}$ value because the error due to estimating α and β is magnified.

Error Adjustment

Fortunately, statisticians have derived a correction factor to adjust the standard error of the estimate for the additional uncertainties about the intercept and slope. The corrected standard error of the estimate for individual predictions is designated as S_{IND}:

$$S_{IND} = S_{y.x}\sqrt{1 + \frac{1}{n} + \frac{(X-\bar{X})^2}{\Sigma(X-\bar{X})^2}} \qquad (10\text{-}12)$$

where X is the particular value of the independent variable being used to produce the estimate.

The corrected form of s_{IND} includes an allowance for the distance between the value of X and the mean, the error in estimating the intercept, and the error in estimating the slope. The $(X - \bar{X})^2$ in the numerator squares the distance that a value, X, is from the sample mean $\bar{X}$. The $\Sigma(X - \bar{X})^2$ in the denominator is the total variation of the X values. Thus, the third factor under the square root reflects the fact that our uncertainty increases the more the value we are making the prediction for deviates from the mean. The effect of this is to give the prediction limits a flared effect as illustrated in Figure 10-10.

Figure 10-10   Prediction limits for 95% prediction intervals

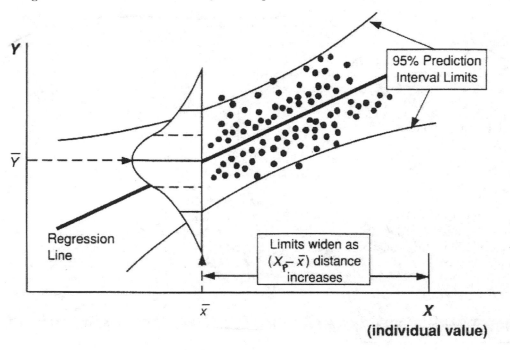

Example 10-10

Repeat the calculation of the 95% prediction limits requested in the previous example, except use the adjusted form of the standard error of the estimate from Equation 10-12. For this example, $\bar{X} = 7$ and $\sum(X - \bar{X})^2 = 24$.

Solution

$$\hat{Y} = .25 + 1.25(8.5) = 10.88$$

$$t = t_{./2, n-2} = t_{.025, 8} = 2.306$$

We now need to calculate the true standard error $s_{IND,}$

$$S_{IND} = S_{y.x}\sqrt{1 + \frac{1}{n} + \frac{(X - \bar{X})^2}{\sum(X - \bar{X})^2}} = (.75)\sqrt{1 + \frac{1}{10} + \frac{(8.5) - 7.0)^2}{24}} = (.75)(1.0926) = .82$$

The corrected prediction limits are thus:

$$Y_{PLL} = 10.88 - 2.306(.82) = 8.99 \quad \text{(Uncorrected limit was 9.15)}$$

$$Y_{PLU} = 10.88 + 2.306(.82) = 12.77 \quad \text{(Uncorrected limit was 12.61)}$$

Our corrected prediction of an individual months sales is within the range of 8.99 to 12.77 units. Note that these limits are not substantially different from the earlier limits, even though the sample size is quite small. For values of X further away from the mean the limits would change somewhat but normally there will not be a large difference between the approximate and corrected values.

Confidence Interval for Mean Values

Thus far we have assumed that the regression model would be used to predict an individual value of the dependent variable. We may also want to predict the average or mean value of the dependent variable. The point estimate $\hat{Y}$ is of course the same for both the mean and an individual value. But the distribution of sample means will tend to be much closer to the regression line than the distribution of individual values which means that the standard error will be less.

Estimation of the mean value of Y for a given value of X is analogous to the prediction interval estimation for an individual value except that the correction factor is different.

$$\text{Confidence Interval} \qquad \hat{Y}_L = \hat{Y} \pm tS_{CI}$$

$$S_{CI} = S_{y.x}\sqrt{\frac{1}{n} + \frac{(X-\bar{X})^2}{\Sigma(X-\bar{X})^2}} \qquad\qquad (10\text{-}13)$$

The correction factor is identical to the prediction interval correction except for the absence of the 1 under the radical (compare Equation 10-13 with 10-12). This means that the correction factor will be smaller for the mean than for the prediction interval and that the confidence interval will be narrower than the prediction interval.

Example 10-11

Calculate the confidence interval for Example 10-9.

Solution

$$\bar{X} = 7 \text{ and } \Sigma(X-\bar{X})^2 = 24$$

$$\hat{Y} = .25 + 1.25(8.5) = 10.88$$

$$t = t_{/2,n-2} = t_{.025,8} = 2.306$$

$$S_{CI} = S_{y.x}\sqrt{\frac{1}{n} + \frac{(X-\bar{X})^2}{\Sigma(X-\bar{X})^2}} = (.75)\sqrt{\frac{1}{10} + \frac{(8.5-7.0)^2}{24}} = (.75)(.44) = .33$$

The confidence interval for the mean is therefore:

$$\hat{Y}_{CLL} = 10.88 - 2.306(.33) = 10.12$$

$$\hat{Y}_{CLU} = 10.88 + 2.306(.33) = 11.64$$

Compare the limits of the confidence interval in Example 10-11 with those of the prediction interval in Example 10-10. As you can see, the confidence interval [10.12 to 11.64] is narrower than the prediction interval [8.99 to 12.77]. This will always be the case because there is more uncertainty in predicting an individual value than in predicting a mean and this is reflected in the standard error terms and therefore, in the width of the interval.

Sources of Variability and the Coefficient of Determination

When discussing analysis of variance we broke down the total variability of the dependent variable about its mean (sums-of-squares) into two parts, one due to treatments and one due to error. We can do a similar analysis for regression. Figure 10-11 illustrates the basic concept.

Figure 10-11 Explained and Unexplained Variation

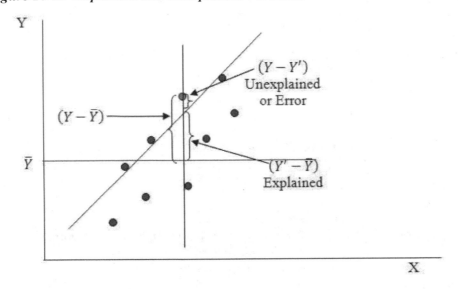

The logic of this breakdown is not difficult to follow. If we take an individual point Y, such as the one illustrated in Figure 10-11 (the red dot), we can look at the deviation of this point from its mean, $(Y - \bar{Y})$. The point illustrated in the figure is above the mean $\bar{Y}$; however, our regression equation predicts ($\hat{Y}$ that this value should be above the mean and predicts the difference $(\hat{Y} - \bar{Y})$; however, it does not predict that the point should be as far above the mean as it is. The part that is not predicted is the difference between the point and the regression line $(Y - \hat{Y})$ which we have called a residual. Thus, we can state that:

$$(Y - \bar{Y}) = (\hat{Y} - \bar{Y}) + (Y - \hat{Y})$$

We could use a similar logic with every point in the sample data. It can be shown, that the same relationships hold when we square all of the values and add them up over all values in the sample. Letting SST represent the total variability (sum of squared deviations about the mean) of the dependent variable Y, we can represent this decomposition in equation form as:

$$SST \quad = \quad SSR \quad + \quad SSE$$

or,

$$\sum(Y - \bar{Y})^2 = \sum(\hat{Y} - \bar{Y})^2 + \sum(Y - \hat{Y})^2 \qquad (10\text{-}14)$$

As Figure 10-11 and Equation 10-14 indicate, we can divide the total variability of the dependent variable Y into two parts: the part that our regression predicts (SSR) and that which it does not predict (SSE). The ratio of the predictable variability to the total variability is called the *coefficient of determination* (denoted r^2):

$$r^2 = \frac{SSR}{SST} \qquad (10\text{-}15)$$

R^2 is the percentage of variability in the dependent variable that our relationship predicts. Obviously, 1 minus this value is the percentage of the variability that our relationship does not predict and is equal to:

$$\frac{SSE}{SST}$$

Remember that the coefficient of determination is equal to the square of the coefficient of correlation. As we discussed at that time, r^2 is in many ways a better measure of the strength of the relationship between two variables than the coefficient of correlation because of its interpretation as the percentage of variability accounted for by the relationship.

The sum-of-squares error (SSE) is related to another concept introduced earlier. The standard error of the estimate was defined in Equation 10-12 as:

$$S_{Y.X} = \sqrt{\frac{\Sigma(Y - \hat{Y})^2}{n - 2}}$$

As indicated earlier, the numerator of this term is the sum-of-squares error or SSE so that,

$$S_{Y.X} = \sqrt{\frac{SSE}{n-2}} \qquad (10\text{-}16)$$

Example 10-12

Calculate SST, SSR, SSE and the coefficient of determination for Example 10-6. Table 10-6 contains the necessary calculations for SST and SSR. [Note: We have already calculated SSE = $\Sigma(Y-\hat{Y})^2$ = 4.50 when we calculated $s_{y.x}$ in Example 10-8. Also, in Example 10-6 we calculated $\Sigma Y = 90$ so that the mean of the Y values is 90/10 = 9.

Table 10-6   Calculations of SST and SSR

Firm Number	Advertising X	Sales Y	$\hat{Y}$ =.25 + 1.25X	$(Y - \bar{Y})^2$	$(\hat{Y} - \bar{Y})^2$
1	7	10	9.00	1	0
2	9	12	11.50	9	6.25
3	5	6	6.50	9	6.25
4	8	9	10.25	0	1.5625
5	6	8	7.75	1	1.5625
6	9	11	11.50	4	6.25
7	7	10	9.00	1	0
8	4	5	5.25	16	14.0625
9	8	10	10.25	1	1.5625
10	7	9	9.00	0	0
Totals				SST = 42	SSR = 37.5

Solution

SST = 42 SSR = 37.5   SSE = 4.5
r^2 = SST/SSR = 37.5/42 = .893

Therefore, we can state that the relationship between hardness and strength allows us to predict almost 90% of the sample variation in Y. This indicates a very strong relationship between strength and hardness Notice that the sums of squares in our example do add up as they should:

$$SST = SSR + SSE$$
$$42 = 37.5 + 4.5$$

Inferences about Regression

In linear regression we estimate two parameters for our regression line: the Y-intercept, a, and the slope, b. We know that these values are estimates of the population values α and β. We may want to test hypotheses about these population values or derive confidence intervals for their estimates. Although the Y-intercept is sometimes of interest in economic models, rarely are we interested in the population intercept in a decision-making situation; therefore, we will focus our discussion on the inference about the population slope, β.

Tests of the Population Slope

The more popular question is usually whether or not the regression line has any significant slope at all. If the X and Y variables are not related (as in Figure 10-5 (d)), the slope of the true (population) line would be zero, indicating that X would be of no help in predicting Y. The slope of the sample regression equation (b) will never be exactly zero but will be some nonzero value. The question becomes is the population slope zero and the reason that the sample slope does not equal zero is due to sampling error? Or is the nonzero sample slope an indication that the population slope is actually not zero (meaning there is a relationship between the two variables)? Thus, our hypotheses become:

$$H_0: \beta = 0$$

$$H_1: \beta \neq 0$$

If we can reject the null hypothesis, there is strong evidence to suggest that there is a relationship between X and Y in the population. Note that we could specify a value other than zero in the null hypothesis if we had reason to believe that the slope was equal to some specific nonzero value.

The test of a regression slope (or regression coefficient) follows the same general format that we have used for other tests. We specify the level of significance and then calculate the p-value from the appropriate distribution. In the case of the regression slope, the appropriate distribution is again the t-distribution. The test statistic is computed by dividing the difference between the sample value (b) and the hypothesized value (β) by the appropriate standard error term, S_b:

Test statistic for the slope: $\qquad t = \dfrac{b - \beta}{S_b} = \dfrac{b}{S_b}$

Here, S_b is the estimated standard error of the slope. As you might guess, the standard error of the slope is related to the standard error of the estimate and is computed using the equation:

$$S_b = \frac{S_{Y.X}}{\sqrt{\Sigma(X - \bar{X})^2}} \qquad\qquad (10\text{-}17)$$

Example 10-13

Test whether there is a valid relationship between advertising and sales in Example 10-6. Use a .05 level of significance. [Note: From previous examples we have calculated $\hat{Y} = .25 + 1.25X$, $S_{y.x} = .75$, and $\Sigma(X - \bar{X})^2 = 24$.]

Solution

1. $H_0: \beta = 0$ (There is no linear relationship between X and Y in the population).

       $H_1: \beta \pm 0$ (The population variables X and Y are linearly related)

2. $\alpha = .05$

3. $S_b = \dfrac{S_{Y.X}}{\sqrt{\Sigma(X-\bar{X})^2}} = \dfrac{.75}{\sqrt{24}} = .153$

       $t = \dfrac{b-0}{S_b} = \dfrac{1.25}{.153} = 8.17$

           Using XLDataAnalyst the p-value = 0.0000

4.   Conclusions: Reject $H_0: \beta = 0$ because the p-value is basically 0.0. There does appear to be a positive linear relationship between advertising and sales; on average, the more spent on advertising the larger sales are the following month over the range of values we have observed with these data.

Confidence Interval Estimate of the Population Slope

Once the hypothesis of zero slope is rejected, one might well ask, "If it isn't zero, what is it?" We do have a point estimate of the true slope (b = 1.25), but we may wish to have an interval estimate with a specified level of confidence. The computation of confidence limits for the true slope is similar in form to other confidence intervals we have worked with:

      CL for β $b \pm t_{\alpha/2, n-2} S_b$ *(10-18)*

Example 10-14

Provide a 95% conference interval estimate for the true slope of the regression line developed in Example 10-6. [Note: From previous examples we have calculated $\hat{Y} = .25 + 1.25X$, $s_b = .153$.]

Solution

$CL = b \pm t_{\alpha/2, n02} s_b$ where : $b = 1.25$, $t_{.025, 10-2} = 2.306$

$= 1.25 \pm 2.306(.153)$

$= 1.25 \pm .35$

$= .90$ to 1.60 in thousands of dollars

This confidence interval is relatively wide because the small sample size has yielded a b value that is not very precise. As the sample size is small, the estimate would not be very precise. With a larger sample size, s_b would be smaller and the estimate would be more precise.

Tests of the Population Coefficient of Determination

Another way of stating that there is no relationship between two variables X and Y is to say that the coefficient of determination is equal to zero. If the coefficient of determination is zero, knowing the relationship between X and Y tells us nothing about the variability of the Y values. Letting ρ^2 represent the population coefficient of determination, the hypotheses can be represented as:

$$H_0: \rho' = 0$$

$$H_1: \rho' \neq 0$$

When we defined the sample coefficient of determination, r^2, we discussed the process of dividing the total variability of the Y values, SST, into two components: SSR and SSE. As you might suspect, if we divide the sums-of-squares by their respective degrees of freedom (as we did in the analysis of variance) we would get mean squares; furthermore, we divide the mean squares and get an F-test of the null hypothesis. In fact, the hypothesis test of the coefficient of determination is typically presented in an ANOVA table, like 10-7.

Table 10-7   The General ANOVA Table for Testing the Coefficient of Determination

Source	SS	df	MS	F
Regression	SSR	1	MSR=SSR/1	MSR/MSE
Error	SSE	n-2	MSE=SSE/(n-2)	
Total	SST	n - 1		

***n = number of paired observations**

Example 10-15

Test the hypothesis that the population coefficient of determination is equal to zero for our strength hardness data in Example 10-6. Use a 1% level of significance. [Note: From previous calculations we already know SST = 42, SSR = 37.5, SSE = 4.5 and n = 10.

Solution

1. $H_0: \rho' = 0$ (There is no linear relationship between X and Y in the population).

    $H_1: \rho' \neq$ (The population variables X and Y are linearly related)

2. $\alpha = .01$

The ANOVA table for the example is provided below. Conclusions: Reject the null hypothesis because the p-value is near 0. There is a strong positive linear relationship between hardness and strength.

Source	SS	df	MS	F	p-value
Regression	37.5	1	37.5	66.67	0.0000
Error	4.5	8	.5625		
Total	42	9			

Comparison of Tests for Correlation, Slope and Coefficient of Determination

As you may have deduced by now, the three tests for the correlation coefficient, slope of the regression line, and the coefficient of determination are all testing the same basic hypothesis: "Is there a linear relationship between variables X and Y?" In fact, all three tests are equivalent. Recall that in Example 10-13 we calculated the t-value for the slope as:

$$t = \frac{b - 0}{S_b} = \frac{1.25}{.153} = 8.17$$

Since $r^2 = .893$, the correlation, r, must be the square root of this or .945. Using Equations 10-4 and 10-2, we can calculate the t-value for the hypothesis test for the correlation as:

$$S_r = \sqrt{\frac{(1 - r^2)}{n - 2}} = \sqrt{\frac{1 - .893}{8}} = .11565$$

$$t = \frac{r - 0}{S_r} = \frac{.945}{.11565} = 8.17$$

Notice that the t-values are identical. We found that the F-value for the test of the coefficient of determination was 66.67. If we take the square root of 66.67 we get 8.17 which is the value of the t-test for the slope and correlation. As we will see in the next section, all three tests produce equivalent p-values.. Therefore, in simple linear regression, the hypothesis tests of the population correlation, population slope, and the population coefficient of determination are entirely equivalent. We will see in Chapter 11, however, that this does not hold when we have multiple independent variables.

Exercises V

21. For the data in Exercise 17 complete the ANOVA table for the regression analysis.

    (a) Test the null hypothesis that the population coefficient of determination is equal to 0. Is the relationship between X and Y statistically significant?

    (b) Test the hypothesis that the population slope is equal to 0. How do these results compare with those in part (a)?

    (c) Develop a confidence interval for the average value of Y when X is equal to 5.

22. For the data in Exercise 19 complete the ANOVA table for the regression analysis. The summary data is reprinted below.

    $n = 10$ $\sum X = 6$ $\sum Y = 15$ $\sum (X - \bar{X})^2 = 36$ $\sum Y - \bar{Y})^2 = 106$ $\sum (X - \bar{X})(Y - \bar{Y}) = 54$

    (a) Test the null hypothesis that the population coefficient of determination is equal to 0. Is the relationship between X and Y statistically significant?

    (b) Test the hypothesis that the population slope is equal to 0. How do these results compare with those in part (a)?

23. For the Export Enterprises data in Exercise 20 complete the ANOVA table for the regression analysis. The summary data is reprinted below.

    $n = 10$ $\sum X = 100$ $\sum Y = 200$ $\sum (X - \bar{X})^2 = 50$ $\sum Y - \bar{Y})^2 = 94 = 36$

    (a) Test the null hypothesis that the population coefficient of determination is equal to 0. Is the relationship between X and Y statistically significant?

    (b) Test the hypothesis that the population slope is equal to 0. How do these results compare with those in part (a)?

    (c) Develop a prediction interval for the average value of Y when X is equal to 12.

Practice

Computer Solutions for Correlations

Excel Functions

There are Excel functions to calculate correlations and covariances and there are two functions to calculate the standard Pearson correlation. They have much the same syntax and return identical results. The two functions are:

CORREL(array1, array2)

PEARSON(array1, array2)

In both functions, array1 and array2 are normally references to a range of cells that contain the values for the two variables being correlated. If you want to calculate just the covariance term rather than the correlation, the following function should be used:

COVAR(array1, array2)

There is no direct function in Excel to calculate a Spearman rank correlation, but it can be calculated without too much effort. Since the Spearman rank correlation can be calculated as the normal Pearson correlation coefficient applied to the rank orders of the two variables, the RANK function can be used to obtain the rank orders and then the CORREL or PEARSON functions can be used to calculate the Spearman correlation.

Example 10-16

In Example 10-1, we calculated the Pearson coefficient of correlation using the data in the file, Example 10-1.xlsx; in Example 10-4 we calculated the Spearman correlation, using the same data. We now want to calculate the correlations using the functions of Excel.

Solution

Open the file Example 10-1.xlsx and enter either of the following equations in any blank cell of the worksheet:

=CORREL(A2:A11,B2:B11)   or   =PEARSON(A2:A11,B2:B11)

Both functions will return the value -0.90029.

The resulting solution for the Spearman correlation is shown in Figure 10-12 with the data in the file Example 10-4.xlsx. The formulae in columns C and D of the worksheet calculate the rank orders of the data in columns A and B. For example, the formula in Cell C2 reads

=RANK(A2,$A$2:$A$11)

Similar formulas complete the ranks for the other values. Cell F2 then contains the formula to calculate the correlation from those ranks

=CORREL(C2:C11, D2:D11)

The result of -.8303 is the same value we calculated in Example 10-4.

Figure 10-12   Results for Example 10-16

	F2		f_x	=CORREL(C2:C11, D2:D11)					
	A	B	C	D	E	F	G	H	I
1	Nutrition	Evaluation	Rank X	Rank Y		Spearman			
2	13	9	5	6		-0.8303			
3	9	19	8	3					
4	11	5	7	8					
5	8	22	9	2					
6	22	2	1	9					
7	14	14	4	4					
8	6	25	10	1					
9	12	10	6	5					
10	17	6	3	7					
11	20	1	2	10					
12									

There is an Excel function (CHISQ.TEST) to calculate the chi-square test of association, but it requires that you first calculate the expected frequencies before using the function; therefore, it is more difficult to use.

The Data Analysis Toolpak

Most software has an option to calculate correlations between any number of variables. The output is in the form of a *correlation matrix* that shows the correlation coefficients between all pairs of variables and possibly the p-value for the t-test that the population coefficient of correlation is equal to 0. The Data Analysis Toolpak can be used to calculate correlations between multiple variables. To calculate correlations, select Tools--Data Analysis from the Excel menu. The list of available routines, as illustrated in Figure 10-13, will appear. Select the option labeled Correlation as illustrated. The dialog, shown in Figure 10-14, will appear on the screen. Indicate the location of the input data on the worksheet and where you want to place the output. You can also use the mouse to highlight a range of cells for the input data and the output range. If you have labels that you want to appear in the output, make sure that they are included in the input range and check the box for Labels in First Row.

Figure 10-13   Routines of the Data Analysis Toolpak: Correlation

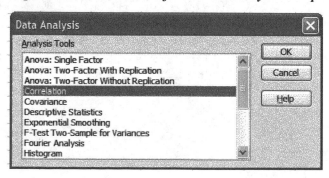

Figure 10-14   Dialog Box for Correlations in the Data Analysis Toolpak

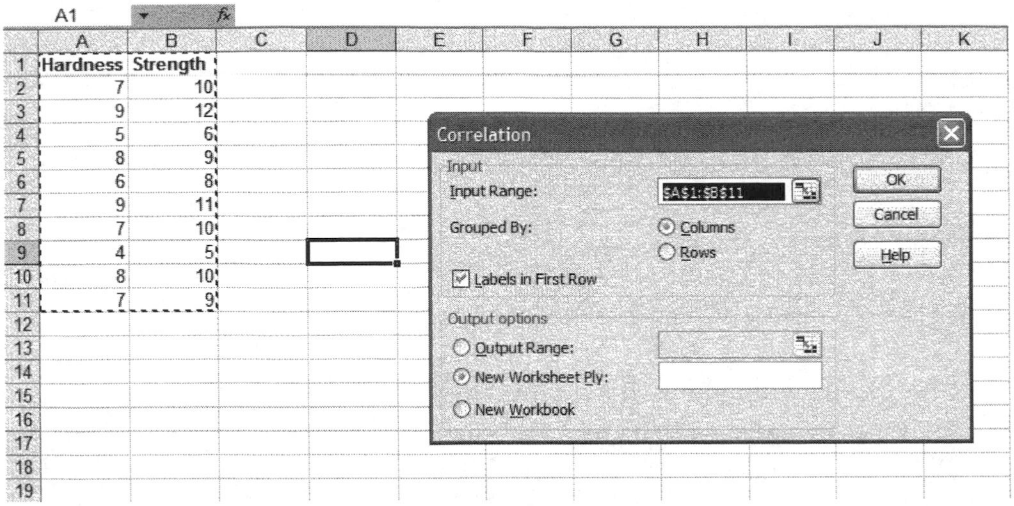

The results for the data in Example 10-1 are shown in Figure 10-15.

Figure 10-15   Correlation Output for Example 10-1 From the Data Analysis Toolpak

	Interest Rate	Housing Starts
Interest Rate	1	
Housing Starts	-0.90029	1

Correlations between a variable and itself are always 1.0 so that the diagonals of the correlation matrix are always 1.0. Although the Data Analysis Toolpak will calculate the correlation, note that it does not provide the output for the t-value or the p-value for the hypothesis test. To perform the hypothesis test, you must calculate the value of t and then use the TDIST function or XLDataAnalyst to find the p-value.

The Excel Template

The template for calculating correlations can be found in the file "Simple Regression & Correlation.xlsx." This Excel file contains the templates for both correlation analysis and simple regression analysis. The first worksheet is the Correlation template, as depicted in Figure 10-16. This worksheet provides the correlations for up to 5 variables. If you have more than 5 variables, you must use the Data Analysis Toolpak or XLDataAnalyst. To use the template, simply paste your data into the section marked with the red borders. If you have fewer than five variables, your data must start in the first column, Column G.

Figure 10-16   Correlation Template

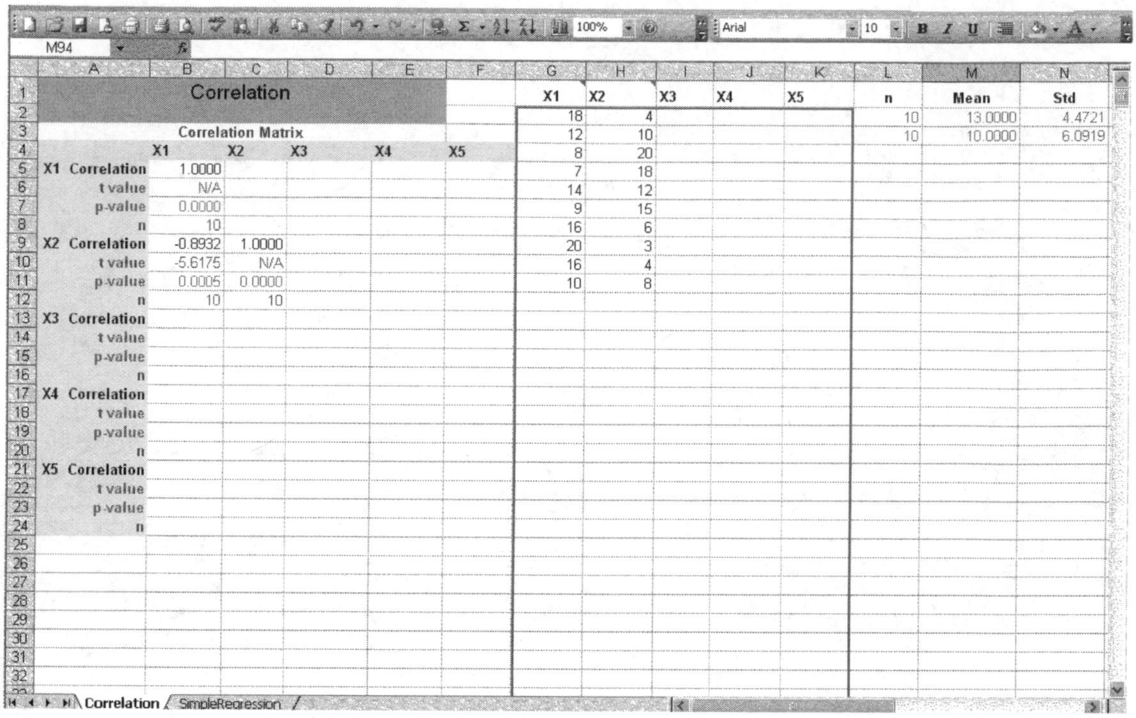

Example 10-17

Analyze the data in Example 10-1 using the Excel Template.

Solution

The solution to Example 10-1 is shown in Figure 10-16. We again find a coefficient of correlation of -.8932. The p-value of .0005 tells us this correlation is highly significant. In other words, we can reject the null hypothesis that the population correlation is equal to 0 (H_0: $\rho = 0$).

Correlations Using XLDataAnalyst

XLDataAnalyst can also be used to calculate correlations between multiple variables. Select the Correlations menu option and the Correlations submenu. The Spearman Correlations submenu produces a matrix of Spearman rank correlations. After selecting the appropriate menu options, the dialog box, illustrated in Figure 10-17, will appear. This same dialog applies to all three submenu options, Correlations, Covariances or Spearman Rank Correlations. Figure 10-17 illustrates the situation with the sample data file, Example 10-1.xlsx. From the list box on the left hand side of the dialog, select all of the variables that you want to include in the correlation matrix. In this case, select both Interest Rates and Housing Starts. The option buttons on the right hand side of the dialog box contain options dealing with missing data in a dataset.

Figure 10-17 *Sample Dialog Box for the Correlation or Covariance Options in XLDataAnalyst*

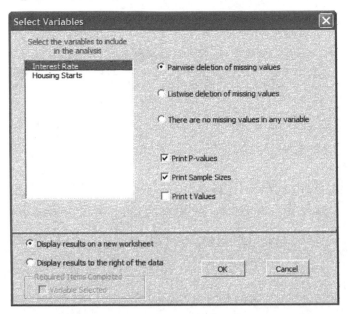

The first, and default option, is to perform a pairwise deletion of missing values. With this option, the correlation between two variables will be computed for all observations that have values for both variables. That means that different correlations could be based on a different number of observations, depending on the pattern of missing values. The second option will cause a listwise deletion of missing values. With this option, only observations that have values on all of the selected variables will be used in the calculation of the correlations. With this option, all correlations will be based on the same number of observations. The last option simply indicates that there are no missing values in the data; this option will speed, to some extent, the computations because XLDataAnalyst will not have to search the data for missing values.

The three check boxes in the dialog box (refer to Figure 10-17) are to print the p-values for the t-test for the correlation, to print the sample sizes for each correlation, and to print the t-values for each test. Both of the first two boxes are checked by default but if you click the appropriate check box you can omit either one or both of these options from the results or you can add the t-values by checking that box.

The final results for the data in Example 10-1 are given in Figure 10-18. The first line of each cell in the correlation matrix gives the correlation coefficient for the two variables. The correlation between interest rates and housing starts is -0.9003, as we computed earlier. The second line of output for each cell gives the t-value, if that option is selected. In this case, the t-value is -5.85. The next line of output gives the p-value of the t-test for the null hypothesis that the population correlation is equal to 0. For interest rates and housing starts the p-value is .0004, as we indicated before; therefore, we would reject the null hypothesis of zero correlation using any reasonable significance level. The third line of output for each cell contains the number of observations used in calculating the coefficient of correlation of that option. In this case, all 10 values are used because there is no missing data.

Figure 10-18   Output from XLDataAnalyst for the Data in Example 10-1

Correlation Matrix

	Interest Rate	Housing Starts
Interest Rate	1.0000	
	N/A	
	0.0000	
	10	
	-	
Housing Starts	0.8932	1.0000
	-	
	5.6175	N/A
	0.0005	1.0000
	10	10

Computer Solutions for Regression

Excel Functions

There are several functions in Excel that are related to linear regression. The first two functions, described here, separately calculate the intercept or constant term (a) and the slope of the line (b).

INTERCEPT(y values, x values)

SLOPE(y values, x values)

Example 10-18

Analyze the data in Example 10-6 using the INTERCEPT and SLOPE functions.

Solution

Open the file Example 10-6.xlsx and enter the text "Intercept" and "Slope" without the quote marks in cells in cell D3 and D4, respectively. Then, enter the following two formulas into cells E3 and E4:

=INTERCEPT(B2:B11, A2:A11)

=SLOPE(B2:B11, A2:A11)

Cell E3 should then contain the result .25 and cell E4 should contain the value 1.25 which are the same values for the intercept and slope that we calculated in Example 10-6.

There is another function that can also be used to calculate the values of the intercept and the slope of the best fitting regression line. This function, however, also returns other regression statistics of interest. This function is a little more complicated because the formula entered for the function is what is known as an array formula in Excel.

LINEST(y values, x values, constant, statistics)

Again, the y values and x values arguments are references to the range of cells that contain the values of the dependent and independent variables, respectively. The constant and statistics arguments are logical arguments. If constant is TRUE or omitted, then the y-intercept or constant term is calculated as usual. If the argument is false, then the constant is set to a value of 0. Statistics is a logical argument that, if set to true, results in an array of statistics from the best fitting line. If this argument is set to FALSE or omitted, then the function only returns the value of the intercept and slope. The other statistics that can be returned are the standard errors of the slope and intercept, the value of the coefficient of determination (r^2), the value of the F statistic, the degrees of freedom for the F-test and the Sum-of-Squares Regression (SSR) and the Sum-of-Squares Residual (SSE). To enter an array formula, you first need to highlight a set of blank cells in the worksheet, large enough to hold all of the output. After typing in the formula, hold down the Shift and Ctrl keys and simultaneously press the Enter key. You can tell an array formula by the curly brackets ({}) that Excel places around the formula.

Example 10-19

Analyze the data in Example 10-6 using the LINEST function.

Solution

Open the file Example 10-6.xlsx and highlight the range from D3 to E7. Then, enter the following formula and press Shift-Ctrl-Enter to enter the formula. The resulting worksheet should look like the worksheet shown in Figure 10-19.

Figure 10-19 Worksheet Illustrating the LINEST Function

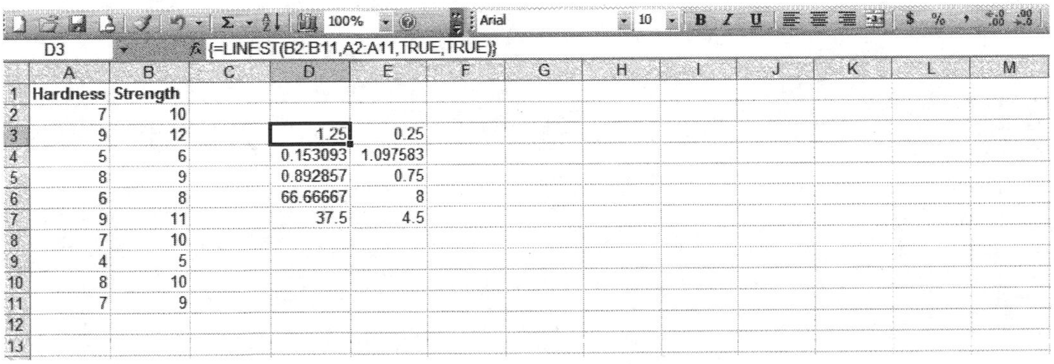

D3 {=LINEST(B2:B11,A2:A11,TRUE,TRUE)}

	A	B	C	D	E
1	Hardness	Strength			
2	7	10			
3	9	12		1.25	0.25
4	5	6		0.153093	1.097583
5	8	9		0.892857	0.75
6	6	8		66.66667	8
7	9	11		37.5	4.5
8	7	10			
9	4	5			
10	8	10			
11	7	9			
12					
13					

The top two values in the output array are 1.25 and .25 which are the slope (b) and the intercept (a) that we previously calculated in Example 10-6. The second row contains the standard errors for these two statistics. The .153 value is the same as the standard error of the slope (b) that we calculated in Example 10-13 when we performed the t-test for the population slope. The next line contains the value of r^2 and the standard error of the estimate. The value for r^2 is .89257 which agrees with the value of .893 that we calculated in Example 10-12 earlier. The standard error of the estimate is .75 which also agrees with the value we calculated in Example 10-8. The next row of the array contains the value for the F-statistic and the degrees of freedom for error in the ANOVA table for the F-test. These respective values of 66.666667 and 8 also agree with the values we calculated in Example 10-15. Finally, the last row of the array contains the sums-of-squares for regression and error. These respective values of 37.5 and 4.5 also agree with those we calculated in Example 10-15. It may help you to understand what these values represent if you come back to this figure after reading the sections on the output from the Data Analysis Toolpak and XLDataAnalyst and compare these values with that output.

The Data Analysis Toolpak

To perform a simple regression analysis, select Tools--Data Analysis from the Excel menu. The list of available routines, as illustrated in Figure 10-20, will appear.

Figure 10-20   Routines of the Data Analysis Toolpak: Regression

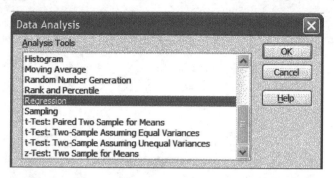

Select the option labeled Regression. The dialog box, shown in Figure 10-21, will appear. Indicate the location of the input data on the worksheet and where you want to place the output. You can also use the mouse to highlight range for the input data and the output range. If you have labels that you want to appear in the output, make sure that they are included in the input range and check the box for Labels in First Row.

Figure 10-21   Dialog Box for Regression in the Data Analysis Toolpak

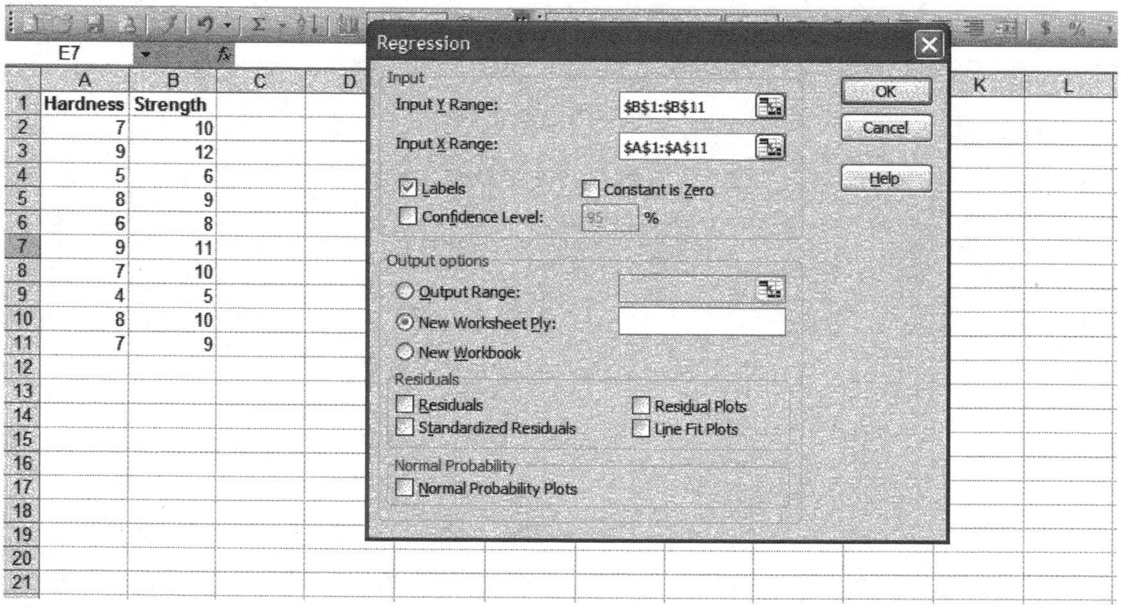

Many of the other options provided by check boxes in the dialog box will be discussed in the next chapter when we present regression diagnostics.

Example 10-20

Analyze the data from Example 10-6 with the Data Analysis Toolpak.

Solution

The settings for this problem are as shown in Figure 10-21. The resulting output is shown in Figure 10-22.

Figure 10-22   Output from the Data Analysis Toolpak for Example 10-20

SUMMARY OUTPUT

Regression Statistics	
Multiple R	0.944911
R Square	0.892857
Adjusted R Square	0.879464
Standard Error	0.75
Observations	10

ANOVA

	Df	SS	MS	F	Significance F
Regression	1	37.5	37.5	66.66667	3.77E-05
Residual	8	4.5	0.5625		
Total	9	42			

	Coefficients	Standard Error	t Stat	P-value	Lower 95%	Upper 95%
Intercept	0.25	1.097583	0.227773	0.825536	-2.28103	2.78103
Hardness	1.25	0.153093	8.164966	3.77E-05	0.896967	1.603033

Most of the output given in Figure 10-22 is standard for statistical software. As we will see, the output from XLDataAnalyst is in much the same format. The top part of the output gives summary measures. The first summary measure here is labeled Multiple R, but in simple regression this is really just the correlation coefficient, r. It is labeled as Multiple R since the meaning of the correlation changes when we talk about multiple regression in Chapter 11. Since most regression software is oriented toward multiple regression, the labeling of the output can be somewhat confusing at first for simple regression. The second value in the output is for the coefficient of determination, r^2. You can see that the R-Square value (.893) is the same value that we calculated in Example 10-12. The next value, the Adjusted R Square will be discussed in more detail in Chapter 11. The next value given in the output, the Standard Error, is the standard error of the estimate and it has a value of .75, the same value we calculated in Example 10-8. The final summary measure simply gives the number of observations in the data. Below the summary statistics, an ANOVA table is given for the test of the hypothesis that the population coefficient of determination is equal to zero. The ANOVA table shown in Figure 10-22 is basically the same as that calculated in Example 10-15 and produces the same value for the F statistic (The term Residual is used here instead of Error).

The final portion of the output provides the information for the regression parameters: the intercept and the slope. As we calculated before in Example 10-6, the intercept is 0.25 and the slope, identified here by the variable name Hardness, is 1.25. The standard error for the intercept and the slope are given next. The third column contains the t statistics to test the hypotheses that the intercept and slope are equal to zero in the population. The next column contains the p-values for these two tests. As we can see, the test for the intercept is not statistically significant, but the test for the slope is. Thus, we can reject the null hypothesis that the population slope is equal to zero and conclude that the slope is positive in the population, in other words, that there is a positive relationship between hardness and strength. The next two columns contain the 95% confidence intervals for the intercept and the slope.

The values calculated here by the Data Analysis Toolpak confirm the values that we calculated by hand earlier. Our conclusions about the relationship between hardness and strength remain the same.

The Excel Template

The template for simple regression is contained in the file Simple Regression & Correlation.xlsx. Figure 10-23 shows the resulting output using the data from Example 10-6 that we have been using for the other calculations.

Figure 10-23   Excel Template for Simple Regression With the Data from Example 10-16

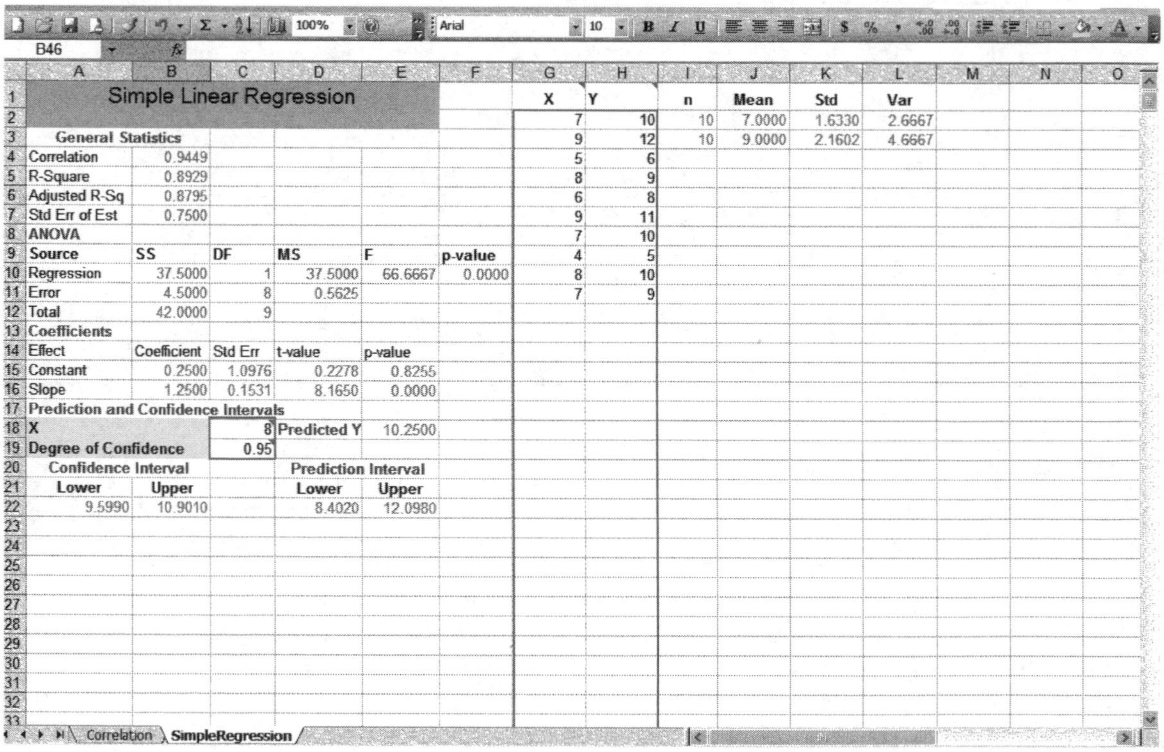

If you compare Figure 10-23 to Figure 10-22 you can see that most of the output is similar between the two methods with a few exceptions. First, the intercept term is labeled Constant rather than Intercept. Some statistical packages use the term Constant and some use the term Intercept. The term Intercept is used here to agree with the terminology in XLDataAnalyst. Second, the template does not produce confidence intervals for the intercept and slope. It does, however, perform the hypothesis test for both parameters. Lastly, the template has the capability of producing confidence and prediction intervals for a given value of the independent variable. You simply need to enter a value for X and the desired degree of confidence in the cells marked with the red outline. The values shown are for a hardness of 8. To get prediction and confidence intervals for other values of harness, simply change the value in cell C18 of the template.

Simple Regression Using XLDataAnalyst

We can use XLDataAnalyst to perform simple regression by selecting the Regression menu item and then selecting the Regression submenu. This will produce the dialog box, shown in Figure 10-24 for the data used in Example 10-6.

Use the list box on the left to select the independent variable (in this case Hardness) and the one to the right to select the dependent variable (Strength). Using the data in the file Example 10-6.xlsx the results in Figure 10-25 will be calculated by XLDataAnalyst. The output from XLDataAnalyst is very similar to that produced by both the Data Analysis Toolpak and by the Excel template.

Figure 10-24   XLDataAnalyst Dialog Box for Regression Analysis

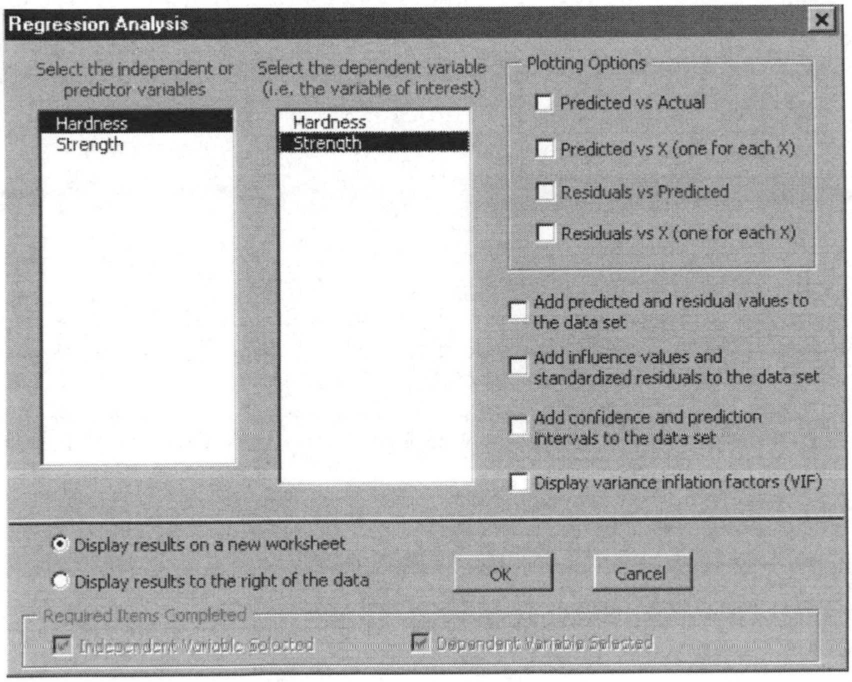

Figure 10-25   XLDataAnalyst Output for the Example 10-6 Data

Regression Analysis for Strength

Summary Measures

Multiple R	0.945
R-Square	0.893
Adj R-Square	0.879
Std Error of Est.	0.750

ANOVA Table

Effect	SS	DF	MS	F	P-value
Regression	37.500	1	37.500	66.667	0.000
Residual	4.500	8	0.563		
Total	42.000	9	4.667		

Regression Coefficients

Effect	Coefficient	Beta	Std Error	t-value	p-value
Constant	0.250		1.098	0.228	0.826
Hardness	1.250	0.945	0.153	8.165	0.000

The Hypothesis Tests for ρ, ρ^2, and β

There have been three hypothesis tests performed in correlation and simple regression. These three tests are entirely equivalent and all test whether or not there is a linear relationship between the two variables. It is easy to see this equivalence in terms of the computerized output. Let's go back and analyze Example 10-1 using simple regression as well as correlation. Figure 10-26 gives the results of the regression analysis using the template and Housing Starts as the independent variable while Interest Rates as the dependent variable. The figure also reproduces part of the correlation template from Figure 10-18.

Figure 10-26   A Comparison of Regression and Correlation for Example 10-1

Simple Linear Regression						Correlation	
General Statistics						**Correlation Matrix**	
Correlation	-0.8932						X1
R-Square	0.8105					X2 Correlation	-0.8932
Adjusted R-Sq	0.7868					t value	-5.6175
Std Err of Est	2.8746					p-value	0.0005
ANOVA						n	10
Source	SS	DF	MS	F	p-value		
Regression	282.7930	1	282.7930	34.2225	0.0004		
Error	66.1070	8	8.2634				
Total	348.9000	9					
Coefficients							
Effect	Coefficient	Std Err	t-value	p-value			
Constant	26.0139	2.9006	8.9683	0.0000			
Slope	-1.2301	0.2103	-5.8500	0.0004			

Note that there are four p-values in Figure 10-26. The ones we want to focus on here are the F-test in the ANOVA table, the t-test for the slope, and the t-test for the correlation coefficient. Notice that the p-values are the same for all four tests, 0.0004. Also note that the t-value for the slope test is exactly the same as the t-value for the correlation. We can also note that the F-value in the ANOVA table is exactly the square of the t-values for the correlation and slope. In other words, all three of these tests are entirely equivalent in this situation and test whether or not there is a linear relationship between the two variables.

Computer Solution for Chi-Square

In this chapter, the Chi-square distribution is used to test for association between nominal scale variables. We will usually want to use software to conduct such analyses but, as we will see, the options are a little more limited here than with most other tests.

Excel Functions

There is a function to calculate the chi-square test of association although you have to do some preliminary work first. The function requires that you first calculate the observed and expected frequencies somewhere on the worksheet. The following function will then return the p-value for the chi-square test of independence:

$$CHITEST(actual\_range, expected\_range)$$

In this function, the actual range and expected range are references to the range of cells with the observed and expected frequencies, respectively. Normally, the observed frequencies will be available or can be calculated using a pivot table[3].

The Data Analysis Toolpak

In our other tests, we have usually had a procedure available in the Data Analysis Toolpak to perform the analysis. For some reason, the Data Analysis Toolpak does not include a chi-square test of contingency tables. Thus, the Data Analysis Toolpak is of no help for these tests.

The Excel Template

The file Chi-Square.xlsx contains the template that performs general chi-square analysis. Figure 10-27 shows the template with the data from Exercise 10-13. As with most templates, you can either enter the summarized information, in this case the contingency table, or the raw data. The completed template shown in Figure 10-29 provides the summarized input for Example 10-3 with other data shown in the raw data. Comparing the results in Figure 10-27 to our original calculations in Exercise 10-3 shows the same results.

---

[3] See Chapter 2 for a more detailed discussion of using the pivot table wizard to compute a contingency table from raw data.

Figure 10-27   Chi-Square Template for Example 10-3

	A	B	C	D	E	F	G	H	I	J	K	L	M	N	O
	A1	▾		*fx* Chi-Square Tests									Row	Column	
1		Chi-Square Tests											1	1	
2													1	1	
3	Observed Frequencies			1	2	3	4	5	6	7	8		1	1	
4	Tabulated Data		1	75	50	175							1	1	
5			2	120	85	95							1	1	
6			3	105	110	85							1	1	
7			4										1	1	
8			5										1	1	
9			6										1	1	
10			7										1	1	
11			8										1	1	
12	Expected Frequencies			1	2	3	4	5	6	7	8		1	1	
13			1	100.00	81.67	118.33							1	1	
14	Summarized Data		2	100.00	81.67	118.33							1	1	
15	Chi-square	73.8717	3	100.00	81.67	118.33							1	1	
16	Deg of Fredom	4	4										1	1	
17	p-value	0.0000	5										1	1	
18			6										1	1	
19			7										1	1	
20			8										1	1	
21													1	1	
22	Observed Frequencies			1	2	3	4	5	6	7	8		1	1	
23	Raw Data		1	22	4	34	5						1	1	
24			2	39	10	42	68						1	2	
25			3	77	3	96	80						1	2	
26			4										1	2	
27			5										1	2	
28			6										1	3	

Chi-Square in XLDataAnalyst

To perform a chi-square analysis using XLDataAnalyst, select Chi-Square from the ribbon. You will note that there are two submenus, one labeled Non-Tabulated, the other Tabulated. In this case, these are not different computational procedures, but different options for the format of the data that is available to you. Sometimes you may have the raw non-tabulated data. In that case you would select the Non-Tabulated option. In other situations, you may have the raw data but only have the data already tabulated into a contingency table. In that case you would select the Tabulated option. Figure 10-28 shows the data from the file Example 10-3 which has already been tabulated into frequencies. Using the Tabulated submenu leads to the dialog shown in Figure 10-29.

Figure 10-28   Data Layout for Tabulated Data in the File Example 10-3

	A	B	C
1	Region	Magazine	Frequency
2	1	1	75
3	1	2	50
4	1	3	175
5	2	1	120
6	2	2	85
7	2	3	95
8	3	1	105
9	3	2	110
10	3	3	85
11			

Figure 10-29   XLDataAnalyst Dialog Box for the Chi-square Test with Tabulated Data

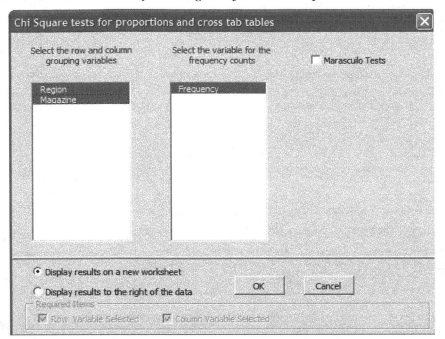

For tabulated data, select the nominal scale variables that define the rows and columns of the table in the first list box and the variable that contains the frequencies or counts in the second list. In this case, there are the only variables present in the data. Figure 10-30 shows the XLDataAnalyst output for Example 10-3.

Figure 10-30   XLDataAnalyst Output for Example 10-3

Chi Square Results For Region and Magazine

Observed Frequencies

		Frequency				
		UnWired	Music Today	Popular Science	**Row Totals**	**Percents**
Region	East	75	50	175	**300**	0.3333
	Midwest	120	85	95	**300**	0.3333
	South	105	110	85	**300**	0.3333
	Column Totals	**300**	**245**	**355**	**900**	
	Percents	**0.3333**	**0.2722**	**0.3944**		

Results

Chi Square Value	73.8717
Degrees of Freedom	2
P-Value	0.0000
Cramer's V	0.2026
Contingency Coefficient	0.2754

The results of the chi-square tests are identical to the results calculated previously in Example 10-3.in that the Chi-square value is the same and the p-value is also the same as well.

Earlier in this chapter, we noted that there is no single commonly accepted measure for the strength of relationship between nominal scale variables. There are two widely used measures of association that are symmetric like a correlation, e.g., the association between X and Y is the same as the association between Y and X. These two correlation-like measures are part of the XLDataAnalyst output.

The Cramer's V and the Contingency Coefficient are correlation like measures for nominal scale variables. Like any correlation, these measures are between 0 and 1 but unlike the Pearson or Spearman correlations, cannot be negative. This is because nominal scales do not imply ordering; hence, a negative relationship would not make sense. Since none of these measures are totally accepted as the best correlation measure for nominal scale variables, both measures are calculated by XLDataAnalyst. One problem with the contingency coefficient is that the maximum value depends on the number of rows and columns in the contingency table and is never 1.0. Cramer's V does not have this problem.

Exercises VI

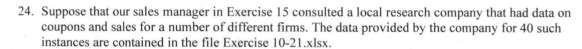 24. Suppose that our sales manager in Exercise 15 consulted a local research company that had data on coupons and sales for a number of different firms. The data provided by the company for 40 such instances are contained in the file Exercise 10-21.xlsx.

   (a) Create a scatter plot of the data. Does there appear to be a linear relationship between the two variables?

   (b) Derive an equation for predicting sales from the number of coupons inserted in the newspaper.

   (c) Interpret the slope of the regression line.

   (d) What would you predict if a firm included 9 coupons in the newspaper?

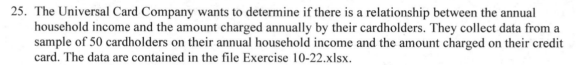 25. The Universal Card Company wants to determine if there is a relationship between the annual household income and the amount charged annually by their cardholders. They collect data from a sample of 50 cardholders on their annual household income and the amount charged on their credit card. The data are contained in the file Exercise 10-22.xlsx.

   (a) Create a scatter plot of the data. Does there appear to be a linear relationship between the two variables?

   (b) Derive an equation for predicting annual charges from household income.

   (c) Interpret the slope of the regression line.

   (d) What would you predict the annual charges would be in a household with $60,000 in annual income?

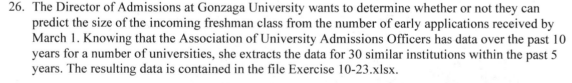 26. The Director of Admissions at Gonzaga University wants to determine whether or not they can predict the size of the incoming freshman class from the number of early applications received by March 1. Knowing that the Association of University Admissions Officers has data over the past 10 years for a number of universities, she extracts the data for 30 similar institutions within the past 5 years. The resulting data is contained in the file Exercise 10-23.xlsx.

   (a) Create a scatter plot of the data. Does there appear to be a linear relationship between the two variables?

   (b) Derive an equation predicting freshman class size from early applications.

   (c) Interpret the slope of the regression line.

   (d) What would you predict for the size of the incoming freshman class if early applications for next year were 9,000?

27. An organization for the promotion of the Human Resource function in organizations has conducted a small study on what characteristics of newly graduated college students are important to employers and how student perceptions match those of employers. A sample of 257 HR managers in a variety of industries were asked to rank order a set of characteristics based on the importance of those characteristics in hiring new employees for their firm. A sample of 250 college seniors were asked to rank the same characteristics according to how important they thought the characteristics were to employers. The average rankings of the characteristics by the two groups are contained in the file Exercise 10-27.

    (a) How well do the rankings of the students agree with the rankings of the managers?

    (b) Is the relationship between the two rankings statistically significant?

28. The More Value Furniture chain sends all of their new sales people through their standard training program. At the conclusion of the program, the directors of the training program rank order all of the trainees. More Value is interested in knowing how well these rankings predict future success in sales. For one group of 30 trainees, the company gathers performance evaluation data on the group 1 year after their training. These performance scores along with the rankings of the training directors are contained in the file Exercise 10-27. Is there a significant relationship between the rankings and the resulting performance evaluations?

29. Professor Anderson is examining the effect that attending class has on final grades. Throughout the semester Anderson keeps track of attendance in twenty classes, and then compares that with the final grades of each student. The data are contained in the file Exercise 10-22.xlsx.

    (a) Create a scatter plot of the data. Does attending class appear to influence final grades?

    (b) Derive an equation predicting final grades based on class attendance.

    (c) Interpret the slope of the regression line.

    (d) Based on your equation, what would be the final grade of a student who attends 40 classes? What is the predicted value for 45 classes?

30. Using the data from Exercise 10-23.

    (a) Is the relationship between coupons and sales statistically significant? Explain.

    (b) What percentage of the variability in sales does the relationship predict?

    (c) What is the standard error of the estimate for this regression?

31. Use the data on the Universal Card Company from Exercise 10-20 . The company wants to determine if there is a relationship between annual household income and the amount charged annually by their cardholders.

    (a) Test the hypothesis that the population coefficient of determination is equal to zero. What can you conclude based on the p-value?

    (b) What percentage of the variability in the amounts charged can this relationship explain? Is this a strong relationship?

    (c) Develop a 95% confidence interval for the average charges of a household with annual income of $60,000.

    (d) The company has received an application from a household with annual income of $60,000. What is a 95% confidence interval for the annual charges of this household? Is this interval wider or narrower than the interval developed in part (c) above?

32. An owner of a restaurant wants to determine what impact weather has on customers dining in the restaurant. Over a 60-day period, the owner observes how many customers come to the restaurant, as well as the average temperature during the evening hours. The data are contained in the file Exercise 10-28. (a) Create a scatter plot of the data. Does temperature appear to impact customers dining in the restaurant at .05 level of significance? (b) Derive an equation predicting customers from temperature. (c) How many customers would you expect when the temperature is 80 degrees? 50 degrees? 10 degrees?

33. A Silicon Valley-based technology company is looking to determine if the skill of their programmers deteriorates with age. Job performance was evaluated for each of the 25 programmers on a scale of 1 to 10, 10 being the highest. Use the age and performance data in the file Exercise 10-27.xlsx to (a) Create a scatter plot, (b) derive an equation predicting the relationship between age and performance, and (c) estimate the score a 40-year-old programmer would receive.

34. Billy Bob runs an auction house that sells livestock in Texas. Billy Bob wants to determine the relationship between the weight of a cow and the price it will sell at. Over several weeks, Billy Bob records the weight and selling price of 20 cows sold at the auction. The data are contained in the file Exercise 10-28.xlsx (a) Create a scatter plot of the data. How influential does weight appear to be on sales price at .05 level of significance? (b) Form an equation predicting sales price based on weight. (c) How heavy would a cow have to be to sell for $1,000?

35. After receiving your degree in Human Resource Management from the local university, you have been hired by a high tech company to recruit college graduates for sales positions. You know that you need to develop some diagnostic measures to help in predicting which potential applicants are likely to do well in a sales position. You decide to focus on some easily measured variables that would be relevant to recent college graduates. The measures you select are college GPA, percentage of college expenses paid for by the student, the number of nontechnical courses taken in college, and a widely used personality test of outgoingness. To see if your measures are in fact related to sales success, you select a sample of 50 sales employees in the company and gather information on your variables, along with their latest performance evaluation score on a scale from 0 to 100. The data are contained in the file Exercise 10-29.xlsx.

    (a) Derive a correlation matrix of the 5 variables.

    (b) Which correlations are statistically significant at the .05 level?

    (c) Which variable has the highest correlation with the performance evaluation scores?

    (d) Which variables look promising for predicting success in sales?

36. Rufus Porter owns several gas stations in Oregon. Mr. Porter believes that he can predict what type of gas (regular, premium, or super premium) an individual will by based on the type of vehicle they drive (compacts, sedans, SUVs, or pickups). His theory is that different types of people choose to buy a particular type of gas and also tend to buy similar types of vehicles. To test this theory that type of vehicle is related to type of gas purchased, you have stationed college students at randomly selected gas stations in Oregon where they record the type of vehicle and the type of gas purchased. The results are contained in the file Exercise 10-36. It the type of gas purchased independent of the type of vehicle? What do you think of Rufus's theory?

37. The Barton Manufacturing Group has manufacturing facilities in several different states. So far, Barton has been able to operate as a nonunion shop in all of their plants but knows that several unions have active plans to try and establish unions in Barton's facilities. The management of Barton wants to determine the attitudes of their employees to unionization and whether or not those attitudes depend on the plant. They survey a sample of employees at four of their largest plants (Plant A, Plant B, Plant C, and Plant D) on their attitude toward belonging to a union (For, Against,

No Opinion). The data are contained in the file Exercise 10-37. Are the attitudes toward union membership independent of the plant in which the employee works?

Opening Vignette Revisited

Recall that Susan had graphed a scatter diagram of the two sets of data (The data are contained in the two files Vignette10a.xlsx and Vignette10b.xlsx). The two scatter diagrams are shown in Figure 10-31.

Figure 10-31   Scatter Diagrams of the Two Sets of Data[4]

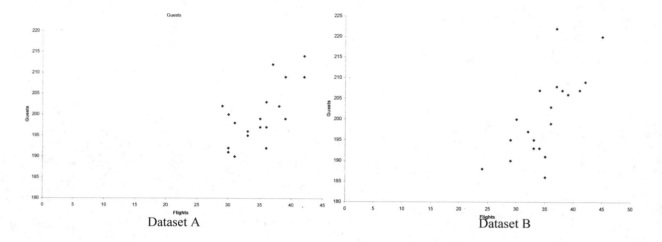

Dataset A   Dataset B

A casual glance at the two graphs shows that both exhibit a positive relationship between incoming flights and the number of guests at the hotel. Susan, however, needed a more exact way to express the relationship between the variables. Her assistant told Susan that they could add a trend line to the charts that displayed an equation describing the relationship between the two variables. The assistant selected the Chart menu followed by the Add Trendline submenu. In the resulting dialog box, she selected Linear as the type and then clicked the Options tab and checked the two boxes for Display equation on chart and Display R-square value on chart. This caused the formula for the equation to appear on the chart and calculated the coefficient of determination. The resulting charts for Susan's data are shown in Figure 10-32. The two equations and the r^2 values are repeated below:

Dataset A	$\hat{Y} = 158.16 + 1.1988X$	$r^2 = 0.4745$
Dataset B	$\hat{Y} = 149.72 + 1.4614X$	$r^2 = 0.5171$

Susan could see that the two equations were quite similar, but she didn't know how to compare them or what the r^2 value meant. She decided that she needed more help; therefore, she called Bob in the Operations area because she knew that he was familiar with statistics and could help her interpret the data. Bob asked her to send him the data and he would get back to her.

On Friday, Bob met with Susan to discuss the data. Bob told Sharon that the two sets of data seemed to be very similar and his analysis indicated that the two sets of numbers could be combined and then analyzed using regression analysis. He then showed Sharon the results of that analysis presented in Figure 10-33.

---

[4] Both charts have been formatted to have a minimum value of 180 on the Y-axis to make them comparable to each other.

Figure 10-32   Scatter Diagrams With the Equations and r^2 Displayed

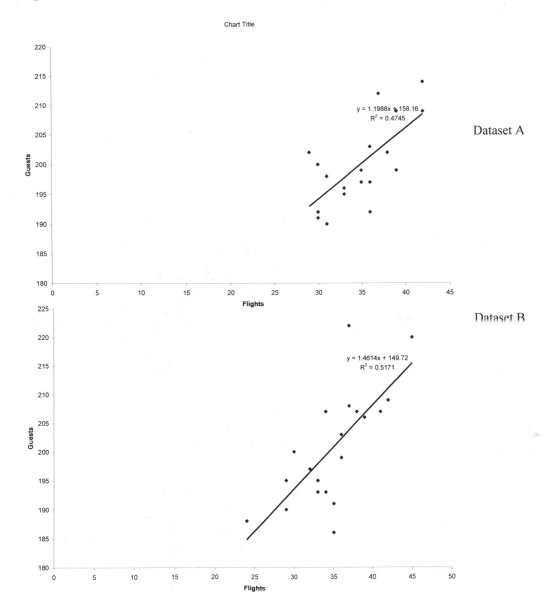

Bob told Susan that the relationship between the two variables was highly significant and accounted for about 50% of the variability in the number of guests. That means that about 50% of the variability was unaccounted for and related to other factors. He said that Susan should be able to improve her forecasting capabilities using the resulting equation and that this should help her greatly in determining staffing needs.

Figure 10-33   Regression Analysis for Combined Data

Regression Analysis for Guests

Summary Measures

Multiple R	0.706
R-Square	0.498
Adj R-Square	0.485
Std Error of Est.	6.076

ANOVA Table

Effect	SS	DF	MS	F	P-value
Regression	1,392.514	1	1,392.514	37.714	0.000
Residual	1,403.086	38	36.923		
Total	2,795.600	39	71.682		

Regression Coefficients

Effect	Coefficient	Beta	Std Error	t-value	p-value
Constant	152.962		7.784	19.650	0.000
Fllights	1.358	0.706	0.221	6.141	0.000

Summary

Simple linear regression and correlation are statistical techniques we use for analyzing bivariate (two-variable) data. The first step is to make a scatter diagram of the observed data points to confirm that the relationship is indeed linear.

The Pearson correlation coefficient, r, is a number between -1 and + 1 that tells how closely two variables conform to a linear relationship. A more understandable measure is the coefficient of determination, r^2, which expresses the explained variation as a percent of the total variation; however, the correlation coefficient is widely used. In addition, a relatively simple t-test is available to determine if the population correlation coefficient $\rho = 0$. We are cautioned that even a high correlation does not prove a cause-and-effect relationship exists. That is a matter for more controlled study and managerial judgment.

We can also assess the relationship between ordinal scale variables using the Spearman rank correlation. A simple t-test, similar to that of the Pearson correlation, can be used to test for statistical significance.

Relationships between nominal scale variables are examined in contingency tables. Hypotheses are tested using the chi-square tests of association. Cramers V and the Contingency Coefficient are two correlation like measures for nominal scales.

For regression, the X variable is independent and the Y variable (the one being predicted) is dependent. We can solve for the sample slope (b) and intercept (a) of the line of best fit through the sample points. The sample regression equation, $\hat{Y} = a + bX$, goes through $\bar{X}$ and $\bar{Y}$ and minimizes the variation (or residuals) of the observed points about the regression line. The slope (b) is related to the correlation (r) in that both have the same numerator, the covariance of X and Y. Therefore, the slope and the correlation must have the same sign and if the correlation is zero, the slope of the best fitting regression line will also be zero.

For every X value, the population regression model $Y = \alpha + \beta X + \epsilon$ assumes there is a normal distribution of Y values whose mean lies on the regression line. A regression line describes the relationship between any given value of X and the mean of the corresponding conditional probability distribution of Y ($\mu_{Y.X}$). We use this mean value of the sample regression line $\hat{Y}$ as a point estimate of Y for any given value of X. Any deviation of actual Y values from the regression line value is referred to as error. The most common measure of this error is the standard deviation of regression, which is called the standard error of estimate, $S_{Y.X}$.

Given the assumption that Y values are normally distributed about the regression line, we can establish prediction limits (for individual Y values) and confidence limits (for mean values of Y). The expression $Y_{PL} = \hat{Y} \pm ts_{y.x}$ is an approximate prediction interval for predicting Y from X. For more accurate predictions, the formula should be modified to take into account the slope and the intercept error resulting from the use of sample data, even though the correction is often quite small. The effect of this is to widen the prediction limits more as the X values deviate farther from the mean, $\bar{X}$, that the regression line passes through.

As in ANOVA, the total variability of the dependent variable Y (SST) can be broken down into two parts: sum-of-squares regression (SSR) and sum-of-squares error (SSE). The coefficient of determination (r^2) can also be defined as the ratio of SSR to SST, e.g., as the percentage of the total variability attributable to the relationship defined by the regression equation. The sum-of-squares error (SSE) is the sum of the squared residuals around the regression line and is related to the standard error of the estimate.

Hypotheses about the population slope (β) can be conducted as a t-test and confidence intervals can be established using the appropriate percentiles from the Student's t distribution. Tests of the coefficient of determination (r^2) are conducted using an F-test as part of an analysis of variance table derived from dividing the total variability of the dependent variable into parts. In simple regression, the hypothesis tests for the slope, the coefficient of determination, and the correlation coefficient are entirely equivalent.

There are functions in Excel that will calculate the covariances and Pearson's correlations. Combined with the RANK function in Excel, they can also calculate the Spearman correlation. There is also a function for the chi-square test, but it requires that considerable computation be performed prior to using the function.

The DataAnalysis Toolpak can be used to calculate correlation matrices for multiple variables using the Correlation procedure; however, the Toolpak does not perform the t-test for the significance of the correlations and is therefore of limited use for hypothesis testing.

The Correlation Template and XLDataAnalyst can both quickly and easily calculate correlations between multiple variables and perform the t-tests of significance. The template is limited to five variables, but there is no limit to the number of variables that can be used with XLDataAnalyst. XLDataAnalyst can also calculate Spearman correlations and can provide the output of a covariance matrix, as well.

Chapter Glossary

Bivariate Data	Analysis pertaining to two variables of interest.
Coefficient of Correlation	A number between –1 and +1, inclusive that is a measure of the strength of association between two variables.
Coefficient of Determination (r^2)	The ratio of the predictable variability to the total variability; the percentage of the total variability in the dependent variable that can be predicted by our regression equation.
Correlation Analysis	Process of determining the degree to which two or more variables are related.
Correlation Matrix	A matrix displaying the correlations among a group of variables.
Covariance	A measure of how much two variables vary together (co-vary). It is also the numerator of the correlation coefficient.
Dependent Variable	Variable of interest in a regression analysis; variable that is being predicted
Independent Variable	Predictor variable used to predict the dependent variable in a regression analysis.
Multiple Regression Analysis	Uses two or more independent variables, X(s), to better predict the (one) dependent variable, Y.
Practical Significance	The correlation, difference or effect is of practical importance; independent of statistical significance.
Principle of Least Squares	The statistical principle that tries to minimize the sum of the squared deviations of the actual values from the estimated or predicted values.
Prediction Intervals	Similar to a confidence interval, except that the value being estimated is not a summary measure like the mean, but an individual observation.
Regression Analysis	Process of estimating the value of the dependent variable (Y) from one or more independent variables (Xs).
Residual	Difference between the predicted value and the actual value in a regression analysis; also called error in regression analysis.
Scatter Diagram	A plot of observed data points on X-Y coordinates for the purpose of revealing a possible relationship between the variables.
Simple Regression Analysis	Uses only one independent variable, X, to estimate the value of the dependent variable, Y.
Spearman's Rank Correlation Coefficient	A special correlation coefficient for rank order or ordinal data.
Statistical Significance	The null hypothesis that the population correlation is zero can be rejected.

Standard Error of the Estimate

The standard deviation of the data points around the sample regression equation. Not a standard error in the usual sense of the standard deviation of a sample statistic, but it is used in deriving such standard error terms.

Univariate Data

Datasets where we are only interested in one variable at a time.

Questions and Problems

38. Compare and contrast the following terms:

   (a) dependent variable and independent variable.

   (b) positive relationship and negative relationship.

   (c) correlation and causation.

   (d) the standard deviations S_X, S_Y, and S_e.

39. Comment on the following:

   (a) Why should a scatter diagram be prepared as the first step in regression analysis?

   (b) Is it possible to mistakenly fit a straight line to data which are curvilinearly related?

   (c) What is the danger in making estimates of Y from X values that are outside the domain of the observed X values?

40. A stock market analyst is interested in whether she can predict a firm's profitability from the assets of the firm. She collects data from 20 different firms and the data are given in the file Exercise 10-34.xlsx. Develop a regression equation for predicting profitability from assets. Explain the results. What would be the predicted profitability for a firm with assets of 50 million dollars?

41. In the 1960's, data were collected for 21 countries on deaths from coronary heart disease per 100,000 persons age 35 to 64 and annual per capita cigarette consumption. The data are contained in the file Exercise 10-35.xlsx. What is the relationship between annual per capita consumption of cigarettes and deaths per 100,000 people? If a countries annual per capita consumption of cigarettes is 1700, what is the predicted number of deaths from coronary heart disease per 100,000?

42. The file Exercise 10-42.xlsx contains data from 1960 to 1985, in five year increments, on the annual production of beer, in millions of barrels, and the number of married people, in millions. What is the correlation between the two variables? Is the correlation statistically significant at the 05 level of significance? What can we conclude from this data? Does drinking beer lead to marriage or does marriage lead to beer drinking?

43. A consumer organization has gathered information for a sample of 50 recent model cars. For each vehicle, they recorded its horsepower, it weight and its estimated gasoline mileage. The results are contained in the file Exercise 10-43.xlsx. Develop a correlation matrix of the variables MPG, Horsepower and Weight. Which correlations are significant at .the 05 level of significance?

44. Randall Young conducts investigations of industrial accidents for a group of insurance companies. Accidents are often classified according the leading cause of the accident (Mechanical, Environmental, or Human). Randall thinks that people working odd shifts are more susceptible to accidents due to human causes than those working normal hours. Randall gathers data on a random sample of industrial accidents classified as due to Mechanical, Environmental, or Human causes and by the shift on which the accident occurs: Normal (8 to 4), Swing (4 to midnight) and Graveyard (midnight to 8). The data can be found in the file Exercise 10-44.xlsx. Is the cause of the accident independent of the type of the shift or is there a relationship between the two as Randall believes?

45. A friend of yours has a theory that there are gender preferences when it comes to the type of credit or charge card most often used. In particular, she thinks that men prefer American Express while women prefer the Discover card. The file Exercise 10-45.xlsx contains the results of a random sample of purchases at an online store and the type of card used (American Express, Discover, Visa, or Mastercard). Is there evidence that the type of card used is not independent of gender?

46. Professor Anderson is examining the effect that attending class has on final grades. Throughout the semester Dr. Anderson keeps track of attendance in twenty classes, and then compares that with the final grades of each student. The data are contained in the file Exercise 10-46.xlsx.

    (a) Plot a scatter plot of the data. Does attending class appear to influence final grades?

    (b) Derive an equation predicting final grades based on class attendance.

    (c) Interpret the slope of the regression line?

    (d) Based on your equation, what would be the final grade of a student who attends 40 classes? What would be the final grade of a student who attended 45 classes?

Database Problems

Corporate Statistical Database

47. Develop a correlation matrix between the following variables: years of operation, annual sales, earnings per share, and advertising and public relations expenses.

    (a) Which relationships are statistically significant?

    (b) Which pair of variables has the strongest relationship?

    (c) How strong is this relationship? Explain!

48. Use the electrical and electronic firms in the Corporate Database in the Appendix.

    (a) Let the current year earnings per share be the independent variable, X, and develop a regression equation to predict the annual dividend, Y.

    (b) Make a point estimate of the dividend for an individual firm that has $5.00 earnings per share.

49. Use the electrical and electronic firms in the Corporate Database.

    (a) What is the correlation between the current year earnings per share and the previous year's earnings per share? Is this correlation significant?

    (b) Using the same data, is there a significant correlation between the annual salary of employees and the state's per capita income?

50. Use all of the firms in the Corporate Database and let X = number of employees (or number in hundreds) and Y = annual sales ($m).

    (a) Determine the regression equation relating the number of employees to annual sales. Include a scatter diagram.

    (b) Using the equation, predict the annual sales for a firm that has 15,000 employees

    (c) What is the value of the standard error of the estimate?

    (d) Is the slope of the equation significant?

    (e) To what extent are the total annual sales explained by the number of employees?

51. Is the industrial classification of a firm independent of whether or not they have a profit sharing plan? If the relationship is statistically significant, how strong is the relationship?

MegaCorp Employee Survey Database

 52. The VP of Human Resources would like to know what variables are related to the four satisfaction measures for benefits. Correlate the following measures with the four satisfaction measures and report to the VP about which variables are related to satisfaction (age, years with MegaCorp, and current salary) at .05 level of significance.

 53. Select the most highly correlated variable from the previous problem and develop a regression equation.

    (a) What is the regression equation relating this variable to satisfaction?

    (b) Is the relationship statistically significant at .05 level of significance?

    (c) What percentage of the variability in satisfaction can we explain with this relationship?

 54. The Union that represents most of the hourly labor for MegaCorp has accused the company of attempting to undermine the principle of seniority in determining raises and other aspects of the company compensation system. The VP of Human Resources would like to know if there is a relationship between the years at the company and the current salary. Using only nonmanagement personnel, answer the following questions at .05 level of significance:

    (a) Is there a significant relationship between seniority and salary?

    (b) What percentage of the variability in salary can be explained by seniority?

    (c) What salary would be predicted for a worker with 10 years of seniority?

    (d) On average, how much is each additional year of seniority worth in terms of salary?

 55. Combining widow with the single category, is marital status independent of the subsidiary where the worker is employed?

 56. Calculate the Spearman rank correlations between the three satisfaction measures (health plan, cost of health plan, and retirement plan) with the overall satisfaction measures. Which correlations are significant?

Alaska Sport Fishing Survey

 57. Variables Imp1 through Imp11 in Columns J through T are significantly correlated with the amount of money that the visitors spent on their last trip to Alaska. The Chamber has argued that these are the variables that Alaska should be paying attention to. What can you tell them about this?

 58. Develop a regression equation at .05 level of significance to predict the amount of money spent on a trip from the number of people traveling in the party.

    (a) Interpret the slope and the intercept of the equation. Do these values make sense?

    (b) How much of the variability in money spent can this equation account for?

    (c) Is the relationship statistically significant?

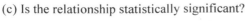 59. Is marital status independent of where people stayed on their last visit? Interpret the results.

60. Calculate the Spearman correlation coefficient between Education and the importance ratings of the visitors and test its significance at .05 level of significance. Which relationships are statistically significant?

61. A representative from the governor's office has called and asked if there is a relationship between the length of time spent planning a trip and the amount of money spent. Is there a significant relationship? Could you use this relationship to predict amount spent if you knew how much time a party spent planning their trip?

Chapter 11:

Multiple Regression

Chapter 11 Learning Objectives

When you finish this chapter you should be able to:

1. **Understand multiple linear regression models**
2. **Develop multiple linear regression equations**
3. **Learn how to make inferences in multiple regression**
4. **Evaluate diagnostics in regression**
5. **Utilize computer solutions for multiple regression**

Opening Vignette

Bill operates a franchise of the Sunshine Ice Cream Company. As the franchisee, Bill has an ice cream truck and buys his supplies from the Sunshine Company. Bill has been thinking about his purchases from the company and how difficult it is to predict how many supplies he needs. He has limited storage in a purchased freezer so he doesn't want to over-order supplies. On the other hand, if he runs out of supplies, he can lose potential sales. Bill knows that there are a variety of factors that affect ice cream sales with temperature being one such variable. Bill is also aware that his sales are very much a function of the number of hours he puts in driving his truck around the town. Bill has also developed limited radio and newspaper advertising which he thinks may also influence sales. Bill feels that if he can develop a model that takes these factors into account, he can better predict sales numbers; that would help him in ordering appropriate supply amounts.

Introduction

The purpose of this chapter is to gain an understanding of multiple regression and correlation. Inasmuch as this analysis can be complex and hand calculations very tedious, our approach will explain the underlying theory so you understand the reasons for, and the logic of, the procedures. Beyond that, we will rely heavily on Excel and XLDataAnalyst for the computations.

Multiple regression is a fairly straightforward extension of simple regression procedures. With simple regression we could depict the relationship on a two-dimensional (x, y) plane. But, when several independent variables are involved, the relationships cannot be so easily visualized for they extend into third and higher level dimensions, called *hyperplanes* Fortunately, the mechanics of finding the necessary constants and coefficients are well documented and computer software can easily perform the calculations.

Multiple Independent Variables

Recall the example from Chapter 10 about a state highway department wanting an accurate regression model of how long it will take cars to stop on a freeway. Obviously, speed of the vehicle is one factor that would determine stopping distance; however, data from one variable, such as speed, would not be sufficient to accurately predict stopping distance. If a car's brakes or tires were badly worn, the car would take longer to stop. If the highway was wet or the driver had been drinking, the stopping distance would likely be longer. Figure 11-1 presents the individual XY relationships of several independent variables, assuming that the effects of the other variables can be disregarded or held constant. Recall from simple regression models that we used one independent variable and lumped the effects of any other variables into what we conveniently called "unexplained error." With multiple regression, we use more independent variables in hopes they will explain some of that unexplained variability and therefore, reduce the unexplained error; thereby, developing a better predictive model.

Figure 11-1   *Dependent/Independent Variable Relationships*

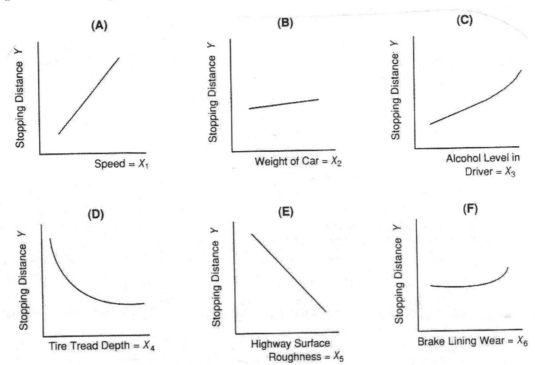

Numerous possible relationships exist, some of which are positive (a, b, c, and f in Figure 11-1) and others negative (d and e). Furthermore, some are linear (a, b, and e), whereas others may be nonlinear (c, d, and f). We want to identify those relationships that are statistically-significant and incorporate them into our model.

The Multiple Linear Regression Model

In multiple regression, we attempt to identify two or more independent variables (Xs) that share a linear relationship with the dependent variable, Y. But, the entire relationship of the variables need not be linear. If the relationship with a variable is linear or approximately linear over the range of interest, that variable may be useful in the model.

The generalized form of a multiple regression model is $Y = f(X_1, X_2, \ldots X_k, \varepsilon)$ where $X_1, X_2, \ldots, X_k$ represent the k independent variables and ε again represents the unaccounted-for error. In the stopping distance model, ε might include a driver's age, reaction times, or other variables that have not been explicitly factored into the model.

Using the above model as a guide, we can formulate an expression for the multiple linear regression of a population, similar to that performed for simple linear regression. For this, we let α represent a constant (comparable to the intercept of a simple regression model), and β represent the influence of each independent variable (i.e., the slope effect). The population model then becomes:

Population Regression Equation $Y = \alpha + \beta_1 X_1 + \beta_2 X_2 + \ldots \ldots \beta_n X_k + \varepsilon$ *(11-1)*

Since we usually work with sample data, we will be most concerned with the sample regression equation used to estimate the population values:

Sample Regression Equation $\qquad \hat{Y} = a + b_1X_1 + b_2X_2 + \ldots\ldots + b_nX_k$ $\qquad\qquad$ *(11-2)*

The mean of the Y values given each combination of X values, is then $\mu_{Y.X_1,X_2,X_3,...X_k}$, which we can condense to $\mu_{y..}$ The population model for describing the mean value of Y may be expressed as:

Population Mean Equation $\qquad \mu_{y..} = \alpha + \beta_1X_1 + \beta_2X_2 + \ldots\ldots \beta_nX_k$ $\qquad\qquad$ *(11-3)*

Regression Coefficients

It is important to have a clear understanding of the meaning of the *a* and *b* coefficients at this point as they signify values derived from sample data. The *a* value (the intercept) is a constant that represents the expected value of Y when all the X values equal zero. It constitutes a basis, or starting point, for the model. The *b* values are sample estimators of the true (population) regression coefficients, the β's. Note that each *b* value carries a subscript to indicate the independent variable to which it applies. Thus b_1 is the estimator of β_1 and b_2 is the estimator of β_2. We refer to b_1 and b_2 as the *sample regression coefficients.*[1]

The regression coefficients *(b* values) are typically of more interest than the constant *(a* value), as they describe the amount of change in the expected value of Y for each unit change in X (holding the other independent variables constant). That is, each regression coefficient describes the change that might be expected in Y if all the other X variables were held constant and that one independent variable is increased by one unit. The key part of this statement is that the other variables are held constant. If more than one variable changes at the same time, we cannot know what the change in Y will be.

Let us illustrate the interpretation of the regression coefficients. Suppose that an expression for stopping distance, Y, based upon speed, X_1, weight of car X_2, and alcohol level X_3, was:

$$\begin{array}{cccc} \hat{Y} = 0 + & 10X_1 + & .05X_2 + & 2.5X_3 \\ \text{(ft.)} & \text{(mph)} & \text{(lbs.)} & \text{(units)} \end{array}$$

A b_1 estimate of 10 would suggest that for an increase of 1 unit of X_1 we could expect Y to increase by 10 units. In other words, going one mile per hour faster (say from 55 to 56 mph) could be expected to increase the stopping distance by 10 feet in this sample. This assumes that the weight of the car (X_2) and alcohol level of the driver (X_3) are held constant. The other regression coefficients have a similar interpretation. Thus, if the car weight is increased by 100 lbs., the stopping distance might be expected to increase by $(100)(.05) = 5$ feet, assuming speed and alcohol levels remain unchanged.

Often, we want to make a statement about the relative importance of the independent variables in predicting the dependent variable. In our stopping distance example, which of the variables is the most important in predicting stopping distance? We cannot assume that it is speed because it has the largest regression coefficient. The magnitude of this value depends on the magnitude of the values of the independent variable. For example, it would change if we measured speed in kilometers per hour instead of miles per hour. *The standardized regression coefficients* are more useful in looking at the relative importance of different independent variables. The standardized coefficients are all measured on the same scale and represent the relative influence of the independent variables, provided that the independent variables are relatively uncorrelated. If the independent variables are highly correlated, then this is not true. We will discuss this issue when we introduce the concept of multicollinearity.

Standardized coefficients result from performing regression when all variables were standardized, e.g., standard scores. They can also be interpreted as the change in the dependent variable, if the corresponding independent variable changes by one standard deviation unit. Mostly, the standardized coefficients are useful for interpreting the relative importance of the variables. In our stopping distance problem, our standardized coefficients might be as follows:

$$Y = 0.65X_1 + .15X_2 + 0.42X_3$$

In this sample, speed would be the most important predictor followed by alcohol level and finally weight of the car. Standardized coefficients are somewhat controversial and should be interpreted with caution.

Once the multiple regression equation is formulated, the dependent variable, Y, can be estimated from the intercept (*a*) and the series of regression coefficients (*b* values) in a manner similar to simple regression. But, before proceeding with an example, let us identify some additional counterparts to simple regression that appear in multiple regression models.

Summary Measures

As with simple regression, we need measures that express how well our model fits the data. For example, we will find it useful to compute a standard error of the estimate for multiple regression (S_e) comparable to the $S_{Y.X}$ of simple regression. In multiple regression, this is a combined measure of the dispersion of actual values from the multiple regression hyperplane. Although it is more difficult to visualize this measure, it serves the same conceptual purpose as the corresponding measure in simple regression.

We will also need to compute a measure comparable to the simple coefficient of determination, r^2. With multivariate data, the *coefficient of multiple determination* is designated as R^2. The interpretation is much the same; the percentage of variability in the dependent variable explained by the model. Let us first see how the multiple regression equation is developed.

Finding the Multiple Linear Regression Equation

Model Assumptions

Multiple regression models are based upon similar assumptions to simple regression models, except more variables come into play. We begin with linear relationships between the dependent variable and each independent variable. Then, instead of developing a line of best fit through the data, our multiple regression equation presents an n-dimensional hyperplane of best fit. We assume that the errors about the hyperplane are random and normally distributed, with an expected value of zero. Moreover, they have a constant variance for all combined values of the independent variables. Our assumptions in multiple linear regression are:

---

1. There is a linear relationship between X_i and Y:
   $$Y = \alpha + \beta_1X_1 + \beta_2X_2 + \beta_3X_3 + \dots + \beta_kX_k + \varepsilon$$
2. The mean of the errors, ε, is 0 so that:
   $$\mu_{Y|X} = \beta_0 + \beta_1X_1 + \beta_2X_2 + \beta_3X_3 + \dots + \beta_kX_k$$
3. The variance of the errors, ε, is constant for all values of the independent variables (homogeneity of variances)
4. The distribution of the errors, ε, is a normal distribution for all values of the independent variables
5. The errors, ε, are independent of each other

Using XLDataAnalyst to Find the Multiple Regression Equation

Since the computations are complex, we will rely on Excel and XLDataAnalyst for all calculations. Other special purpose statistical packages will have comparable procedures for multiple regression. In the Concepts section of this chapter, we will illustrate the interpretation with the output. The actual use of XLDataAnalyst will be covered later in the Practice section.

Example 11-1

Automart Products Company supplies car care items such as antifreeze, stereos, and seat covers to retailers in 10 sales districts. In an effort to better predict their sales, a market analyst has collected the following data on Automart sales and two associated variables: (1) spendable income in the area and (2) automobile registrations in the market area. In Table 11-1 sales are in thousands of dollars, income is in millions of dollars, and automobile registrations are in thousands. This data is also contained in the file Example 11-1.xls.

Table 11-1   *Sales, Spendable Income and Automobile Registrations*

District	Sales of Automart Y	Spendable Income X_1	Automobile Registrations X_2
A	15	9	11
B	16	13	8
C	17	14	9
D	18	15	9
E	20	16	12
F	20	16	13
G	22	17	14
H	24	19	15
I	23	20	13
J	25	21	16

Confirm that the relationships between spendable income and sales (X_1 and Y), and between automobile registrations and sales (X_2 and Y) are linear using scatter plots and derive the multiple regression equation.

Solution

Figure 11-2 shows the scatter plots of the dependent variable (Sales) as a function of both independent variables (Income and Registrations). The relationships appear to be linear in both cases, as they should be.

For now we will concentrate on the portion of the output titled Regression Coefficients. As the output shows, the calculated constant term is equal to 3.460 and the regression coefficients for Income and Registrations are .639 and .527 respectively. Thus the regression equation is

$$\hat{Y} = 3.46 + .639X_1 + .527X_2$$

To interpret these values further, we must be cognizant of the units in which they are reported (i.e., sales in $ thousands, income in $ millions, and automobile registrations in thousands.) Thus the b_1 value of .639 means that an increase of $1,000,000 in income (1 unit) will produce an increase in $639 in sales (.639 thousands) if the number of registrations is held constant. Similarly, the b_2 value of .527 means that an increase of 1,000 registrations (1 unit) will produce a sales increase of $527 (.527 thousands) if the income remains constant.

We can also use this equation to make predictions. For example, if spendable income were $18,500,000 and automobile registrations were 12,380 the model would yield a point estimate of sales of:

$$\widehat{Y} = 3.46 + .639X_1 + .527X_2$$

$$\widehat{Y} = 3.46 + .639(18.50) + .527(12.38) = 21.81$$

Figure 11-2   **Scatter Plots for Example 11-1**

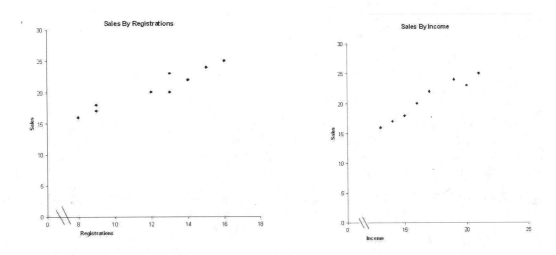

Figure 11-3   **XLDataAnalyst Output for Example 11-1**

Regression Analysis for Sales

Summary Measures

Multiple R	0.9963
R-Square	0.9927
Adj R-Square	0.9906
Std Error of Est.	0.3363

ANOVA Table

Effect	SS	DF	MS	F	P-value
Regression	107.2084	2	53.6042	474.0373	0.0000
Residual	0.7916	7	0.1131		
Total	108.0000	9	12.0000		

Regression Coefficients

Effect	Coefficient	Beta	Std Error	t-value	p-value
Constant	3.4599		0.5490	6.3022	0.0004
Spendable Income	0.6388	0.6563	0.0458	13.9422	0.0000
Auto Registrations	0.5266	0.4116	0.0602	8.7446	0.0001

Other Summary Measures for Multiple Regression

The top portion of the output in Figure 11-3 shows the summary measures for the regression. The R^2 value is the multiple coefficient of determination and equals 0.9927 in this case. This means that our regression equation predicts over 99% of the variability in sales for the sample data. This is a very strong relationship between the two independent variables, spendable income and automobile registration, with sales. The Multiple R shown in the output is the *multiple correlation* (R) and is the square root of the coefficient of determination. Unlike in simple regression, the multiple correlation is always positive, even if some of the regression coefficients are negative. Hence, the sign of R is not indicative of the direction of the relationship. Although multiple correlation is produced by most statistical packages, we will focus more on the coefficient of determination as a measure of fit since it has a more understandable interpretation.

Below the coefficient of determination is a value called Adj. R-Square which is the coefficient of determination (R^2) adjusted for sample size and the number of independent variables in the equation. The coefficient of determination is influenced by the strength of relationship between the independent and dependent variables, but also by the sample size, particularly if it is small, and by the number of independent variables. Let's consider each of these effects, in turn.

If the sample size is small relative to the number of independent variables, the relationship between the variables tends to be overstated. For example, if there were only two variables (one independent and one dependent) and two observations, both observations would fall exactly on the regression line regardless of the values in the two points and $R^2_{y..}$ would equal 1.0. Similarly, for a situation with three variables, a plane can conform to exactly the first three observations regardless of the values of Y, X_1, and X_2. This means that if there are only three observations for three variables, we would again expect $R^2_{y..}$ to be 1.0 regardless of the values for the variables. Of course, we would virtually always have more than one observation for each variable; therefore while this case is extreme, it illustrates the problem with small samples.

The coefficient of determination also depends on the number of independent variables used in the equation. If another independent variable is added, the value of R^2 will automatically increase whether or not that variable has any real relation to the dependent variable. The conceptual reason for this is because there will always be a small nonzero correlation between the added variable and the dependent variable even if the correlation between the two is zero. This will increase the value of R^2 by a small amount. To see if the new added variable really increases our ability to predict the dependent variable, we can look at the adjusted coefficient of determination (R^2_A). If it increases with the addition of the new variable, we can be more confident that the new variable does help us make predictions. The adjusted coefficient of determination is calculated as:

Adjusted R^2 $$R^2_A = 1 - \frac{\frac{SSE}{n-k-1}}{\frac{SST}{n-1}} = 1 - \frac{MSE}{MST} \qquad\qquad (11\text{-}4)$$

As Equation 11-4 shows, R^2_A adjusts the value of R^2 based on sample size and the number of independent variables, k. In Example 11-1, the adjustment to R^2 is minor, from .9927 to .9906. The logic of the adjusted R^2 is that the addition of a new independent variable will automatically reduce the sum-of-square error (SSE); however, adding a new variable will also decrease the degrees of freedom, the n-k-1 term, so that the MSE may actually decrease if the added variable does not reduce the SSE by more than it reduces the degrees of freedom.

Exercises I

1. Dream Home Real Estate Company is trying to develop a regression model to help them better predict selling prices for homes. They have randomly sampled 50 recently sold homes and have gathered data on selling price, square footage of the home, number of bedrooms, age of home in years, and whether or not it was a corner lot (coded 0 and 1). They first explore a model that predicts selling price from square footage and age. The XLDataAnalyst output is shown below.

Regression Analysis for Price

Summary Measures

Multiple R	0.7260
R-Square	0.5271
Adj R-Square	0.5174
Std Error of Est.	14,279.3623

ANOVA Table

Effect	SS	DF	MS	F	P-value
Regression	22,045,988,654.0676	2	11,022,994,327.0338	54.0607	0.0000
Residual	19,778,318,343.7224	97	203,900,189.1105		
Total	41,824,306,997.7900	99	422,467,747.4524		

Regression Coefficients

Effect	Coefficient	Beta	Std Error	t-value	p-value
Constant	25,492.2015		17,739.0840	1.4371	0.1539
Sq Feet	64.2626	0.7026	7.0675	9.0927	0.0000
Age	-115.3017	-0.0513	173.7908	-0.6635	0.5086

   (a) Write out the best fitting regression equation for the selling price of a house.

   (b) What would be the predicted selling price of a 3 bedroom 1300 square foot house on a corner lot that is 10 years old?

   (c) How much would an additional 100 square feet increase the average selling price of a house?

   (d) What percentage of the variability in selling price can be explained by the regression equation?

2. Sarah Barnhart, the VP of Human Resources at Ardmore Inc., recently read an article in her alumni magazine about predicting MBA student grade point average based on factors such as their undergraduate GPA and their GMAT score. Sarah recalls that she had some data that she had been meaning to use in attempting to predict the performance of newly hired MBA graduates that had information on their undergraduate and MBA grade point averages along with their GMAT scores. Finding the data she performs a regression analysis predicting MBA grade point average from their undergraduate GPA and their GMAT scores. The results are shown below.

Regression Analysis for MBA-GPA

Summary Measures

Multiple R	0.7518
R-Square	0.5652
Adj R-Square	0.5614
Std Error of Est.	0.2010

ANOVA Table

Effect	SS	DF	MS	F	P-value
Regression	12.1879	2	6.0939	150.7681	0.0000
Residual	9.3773	232	0.0404		
Total	21.5652	234	0.0922		

Regression Coefficients

Effect	Coefficient	Beta	Std Error	t-value	p-value
Constant	1.3107		0.1163	11.2672	0.0000
U-GPA	0.2393	0.3195	0.0378	6.3256	0.0000
GMAT	0.0022	0.5356	0.0002	10.6034	0.0000

(a) Write out the best fitting regression equation for the GPA in the MBA program.

(b) What would be the predicted MBA GPA for a student with an undergraduate GPA of 3.4 and a GMAT score of 610?

(c) What percentage of the variability in GPA can be explained by the regression equation?

(d) Which appears to be a more important predictor of the MBA GPA, undergraduate grade point average or GMAT score?

(e) Interpret the adjusted R-square for this model.

3. Ann Thompson, the Director of Admissions for a private university, wants to develop a tool for predicting how well students will perform at the university level based on data before they enter the university. In particular, she want to know how well she can predict their GPA at the end of the first two years at the university from their high school GPA and their SAT scores. She gathers data on a random sample of 76 students. The results of the regression analysis are shown below.

Regression Analysis for College GPA

Summary Measures

Multiple R	0.5520
R-Square	0.3047
Adj R-Square	0.2856
Std Error of Est.	0.2876

ANOVA Table

Effect	SS	DF	MS	F	P-value
Regression	2.6462	2	1.3231	15.9932	0.0000
Residual	6.0392	73	0.0827		
Total	8.6854	75	0.1158		

Regression Coefficients

Effect	Coefficient	Beta	Std Error	t-value	p-value
Constant	0.2897		0.5531	0.5238	0.6020
HS GPA	0.5465	0.4439	0.1261	4.3351	0.0000
SAT	0.0006	0.2201	0.0003	2.1490	0.0350

   (a)   Write out the best fitting regression equation for college GPA.

   (b)   What would be the predicted GPA for a student with a high school GPA of 3.2 and a SAT score of 1700?

   (c)   How would an additional 100 points on the SAT change the predicted university GPA?

   (d)   What percentage of the variability in the university GPA's can be explained by the regression equation?

4.   Steve Edwards is the VP of Marketing at Henry S. Jones a large auto company with dealerships in California, Oregon and Washington. Steve has decided to try and develop a model that would allow him to predict expected sales at each dealership but first he needs to find out what factors are involved in driving sales. Two obvious candidates are advertising and the number of salespeople at the dealership. To begin developing his model he gathers data on monthly sales, minutes of advertising (either TV or radio) and number of salespeople from the dealerships in the network. He has 75 monthly observations on which he performs a regression analysis. The results are shown below.

Regression Analysis for Cars Sold

Summary Measures

Multiple R	0.6325
R-Square	0.4000
Adj R-Square	0.3833
Std Error of Est.	20.4539

ANOVA Table

Effect	SS	DF	MS	F	P-value
Regression	20,081.0326	2	10,040.5163	23.9995	0.0000
Residual	30,122.1141	72	418.3627		
Total	50,203.1467	74	678.4209		

Regression Coefficients

Effect	Coefficient	Beta	Std Error	t-value	p-value
Constant	31.7597		12.7386	2.4932	0.0150
Advertising	1.9876	0.3965	0.4582	4.3377	0.0000
Salespeople	4.2874	0.4722	0.8300	5.1656	0.0000

   (a)   Write out the best fitting regression equation for car sales.

   (b)   Steve needs to forecast car sales next month at a dealership that plans on 25 minutes of advertising and employees 11 salespeople. What should his forecast be?

   (c)   How would an additional 1 minute of advertising change the predicted number of cars sold. How would an additional sales person impact the number of cars sold? Which is the more important predictor and why?

   (d)   What percentage of the variability in car sales can be explained by the regression equation?

Inferences in Multiple Regression

In the previous section we used sample data to find the multiple regression equation relating sales (Y) to spendable income (X_1) and automobile registrations (X_2). In this section, we will learn how to measure error associated with the multiple regression equation and how to conduct inferences about the population based on our sample regression equation.

The Standard Error of the Estimate

The most common measure of dispersion in multiple regression is the standard deviation of the actual points about the hyperplane defined by the regression equation[1]. This measure is referred to as the standard error of the estimate, but is designated as S_e; however the degrees of freedom are now the number of observations in the sample, n, minus the number of independent variables, k, minus 1 for the single dependent variable:

$$S_e = \sqrt{\frac{\Sigma(Y-Y')^2}{n-k-1}} \tag{11-5}$$

In simple regression, k was equal to 1 so that the denominator reduced to n-1-1 or n − 2. Although we will always let the computer calculate the actual value of the standard error term, an intuitive expression of S_e illustrates how the variation is accounted for:

$$S_e = \sqrt{\frac{Unexplained\ or\ residual\ variation\ in\ Y}{n-k-1}}$$

$$= \sqrt{\frac{Total\ variation\ in\ Y-(Variation\ in\ Y\ explained\ by\ the\ model)}{n-k-1}}$$

Calculating this value is tedious and best left to the computer. In Example 11-1, the calculated value of the standard error of the estimate, is 0.336 as was shown in Figure 11-3.

Prediction and Confidence Intervals for *Y*

Once the value of S_e has been computed, it can be used to establish predictions or confidence intervals for the dependent variable. We can illustrate the underlying concept by using the uncorrected standard error.

Example 11-2

Using the multiple regression equation and the standard error of the estimate derived in Example 11-1, make a 95% uncorrected individual prediction interval estimate of the Automart Sales in one district (Y), when spendable income (X_1) = 18 and car registrations (X_2) = 10.

Solution

From Example 11-1: $\hat{Y} = 3.460 + .639X_1 + .527X_2$

$S_e = .336$

---

[1] A hyperplane is an extension of fitting a straight line in two dimensions with simple regression to the multidimensional solution space with multiple independent variables.

We use the t-distribution for $n = 10$ and $k = 2$ independent variables

$Y_{PL} = \hat{Y} \pm {}_{t\alpha/2}S_e$ where: $\hat{Y} = 3.460 + .639(18) + .527(10) = 20.232$

$t = t_{.025, 10\text{-}2\text{-}1} = 2.365$

$Y_{PL} = 20.232 \pm 2.365(.336) = 20.232 \pm .795$
    $= 19.437$ to 21.027

The interval of 19.437 to 21.027 is a 95% (uncorrected) individual prediction limits estimate based on both X_1 and X_2. It is uncorrected, however, because it does not take into account the fact that both X-values used in the prediction $X_1 = 18$ and $X_2 = 10$) deviate from their means (16 and 12, respectively). Recall from simple regression in Chapter 10 that the standard error had to be corrected for a more accurate prediction interval estimate. The same is true in multiple regression, but the corrections are much more complex in this case. The full prediction and confidence intervals for multiple regression are:

Prediction Interval $Y_{PL} = \hat{Y}_{\alpha/2}S_e\sqrt{1 + distance}$ measure   (11-6)

Confidence Interval $Y_{CL} = \hat{Y}_{\alpha/2}S_e\sqrt{distance}$ measure   (11-7)

The "distance measure" is the correction for the distance of each of the X values from their mean. This can be calculated by most statistical software. The corrected interval will tend to be slightly larger since the interval becomes wider as the values of the independent variables deviate from their means.

Evaluating the Overall Regression Model

Thus far, we have developed the multiple regression model and used it to predict the value of the dependent variable. But, how do we know that it is a valid prediction? Does our model portray a significant relationship between the dependent and independent variables, or might the relationships be due simply to chance? This is one of the first questions to arise after developing a multiple regression model.

We can test the overall significance of the regression model using the ANOVA table in XLDataAnalyst. Recall that this analysis tests the hypothesis that the coefficient of determination equals zero:

H_0: $\rho^2 = 0$ (There is <u>no</u> relationship between the dependent variable and any independent variables).
H_1: $\rho^2 \neq 0$ (There is a relationship between the dependent variable and at least one of the independent variables).

The only way that the null hypothesis can be true ($\rho^2 = 0$) is if all of the regression coefficients in the population equal zero. If any regression coefficient in the population is not equal to zero, then that variable would predict at least some of the variability in the dependent variable. Therefore, another way to formulate the hypothesis would be:

H_0: $\beta_1 = \beta_2 = \beta_3 = \ldots = \beta_k = 0$
H_1: not ($\beta_1 = \beta_2 = \beta_3 = \ldots = \beta_k = 0$) or at least one of the β_i is not equal to 0

The general form of the ANOVA table for multiple regression is shown in Table 11-2 where the value k refers to the number of independent variables in the regression model.

Table 11-2   ***General ANOVA Table for Testing the Coefficient of Determination***

Source	SS	df	MS	F
Regression	SSR	k	MSR=SSR/k	MSR/MSE
Error	SSE	n-k-1	MSE=SSE/(n-k-1)	
Total	SST	n - 1		

Example 11-3

Using the ANOVA table for the XLDataAnalyst output of Figure 11-3 test the hypothesis that the population coefficient of determination is zero.

$$H_0: \rho^2 = 0$$
$$H_1: \rho^2 \neq 0$$

Solution

The ANOVA table from Figure 11-3 is shown in Figure 11-4.

Figure 11-4   ANOVA Table from Figure 11-3

ANOVA Table

Effect	SS	DF	MS	F	P-value
Regression	107.2084	2	53.6042	474.0373	0.0000
Residual	0.7916	7	0.1131		
Total	108.0000	9	12.0000		

The p-value of 0.0000 tells us that the sample coefficient of determination of .993 was not due to chance and that we can reject the null hypothesis and conclude that the population coefficient of determination is not zero; furthermore, it can be concluded that the overall regression model is statistically significant.

In simple regression, concluding that the overall regression model was significant was the same as concluding that the regression coefficient was nonzero; however, in multiple regression the significance of the overall regression model is slightly different and the F-test and the t-tests for coefficients are no longer equivalent. In multiple regression, concluding that the overall regression model is significant means that at least one of the regression coefficients is nonzero. In other words, at least one of the independent variables helps explain the variability in the dependent variable. Knowing this, we can proceed with further testing and using the model to see which variables are significant. A failure to reject the null hypothesis for the overall regression model would mean that none of the individual regression coefficients are different from zero and there would be no further need for testing the model.

Testing and Estimating the Regression Coefficients

Testing the Coefficients

If the overall model is significant, then at least one of the independent variables is related to the dependent variable and we need further testing to determine which independent variable(s) have significant regression coefficients. The null hypothesis in each case is:

H_0: $\beta_i = 0$ (The slope is zero; there is no linear relationship between Y and X_i)
H_1: $\beta_i \neq 0$ (The slope is not zero; there is a linear relationship between Y and X_i)

The tests indicate whether each independent variable is a statistically-significant explanatory variable for Y. The test uses the familiar t-distribution with $(n - k - 1)$ degrees of freedom. The format of the test statistic is as follows:

$$t = \frac{b_i - \beta_i}{s_{b_i}}$$
(11-8)

In this equation, b_i is the sample regression slope coefficient, β_i is the hypothesized value of the population regression coefficient (usually zero), and S_{b_i} is the standard error of the regression coefficient i. As with the t-test for the slope in simple regression, the standard error of the regression coefficient in multiple regression is related to the standard error of the estimate, s_e, but also takes into account the variability of the independent variable.

Example 11-4

Using the output for Example 11-1 in Figure 11-3 test whether or not the two regression coefficients are significantly different from zero. Use a .01 level of significance.

Solution

The output from Figure 11-3 related to the regression coefficients is shown again in Figure 11-5.

Figure 11-5   Regression Coefficients for Example 11-1

Regression Coefficients

Effect	Coefficient	Beta	Std Error	t-value	p-value
Constant	3.4599		0.5490	6.3022	0.0004
Spendable Income	0.6388	0.6563	0.0458	13.9422	0.0000
Auto Registrations	0.5266	0.4116	0.0602	8.7446	0.0001

(a) For X_1 (Income)

$\quad$ H_0: $\beta_1 = 0$
$\quad$ H_1: $\beta_1 \neq 0$

$\quad$ $\alpha = .01$

$t = \frac{.6388 - 0}{.0458} = 13.9422$ $\qquad$ p-value $= 0.0000$

Conclusion: Holding registrations constant reject H_0 because .0000 < .01 and conclude that the population regression coefficient is not zero. Income contributes significantly to predicting the dependent variable Sales.

(b) For X_2 (Registrations)

$\quad$ H_0: $\beta_2 = 0$
$\quad$ H_1: $\beta_2 \neq 0$
$\alpha = .01$

$$t = \frac{.5266 - 0}{.0602} = 8.7446 \qquad \text{p-value} = 0.0001$$

Conclusion: Holding income constant, reject H_0 because $.0001 < .01$ and conclude that the population regression coefficient is not zero. Automobile Registrations contribute significantly to predicting the dependent variable Sales.

Standardized Coefficients

In the example above, we concluded that both Income and Registrations significantly impacted sales; but we may wonder which had the larger effect, Income or Registrations. We can see that the regression coefficient for Income (.6388) is larger than that for Registrations (.5266); yet, as discussed earlier, these independent variables are not measured on the same scale and the computed regression coefficients reflect these scales. Therefore, we cannot directly compare the calculated regression coefficients. Most software, including XLDataAnalyst, will print out *standardized*, or *beta, coefficients* to compare regression coefficients. In other words, the standardized coefficients are on a common scale and are equivalent to performing the regression analysis when all of the variables, both dependent and independent, have been converted to standard scores. Thus, these coefficients measure the number of standard deviations that $\hat{Y}$ changes as a result of a change of 1 standard deviation of X_i. From the output we can see that the standardized coefficient (Beta) for Income is .6563 while the standardized coefficient for Registrations is .4116. Thus, a 1 standard deviation change in Income will increase the dependent variable, Y, by .6563 standard deviations, while a 1 standard deviation change in Registrations will only change Y by .4116 standard deviations. This indicates that Income has a larger impact on Y than Registrations.

Confidence Intervals for β_i

If the slope of a regression coefficient is significantly different from zero, we may wish to make a confidence interval estimate of the true population slope, β_i. Unfortunately, XLDataAnalyst, and most software packages, does not directly produce such estimates, but they are easily calculated from the output. We can construct the confidence interval estimates for any regression coefficients by following the same general procedure:

$$CL \; for \; \beta_i = b_i \pm t_{\frac{\alpha}{2}, n-k-1} S_{b_i} \tag{11-9}$$

Example 11-5

For the regression equation derived in Example 11-1, both regression coefficients were found to be statistically significant. Develop a 95% confidence interval estimate of the true slopes for both coefficients.

Solution

Using the probability calculator in XLDataAnalyst we can find that the t-value is $t_{.025, 10-2-1} = 2.365$

(a)   For the independent variable, Income, the confidence limit is

$$CL \; for \; \beta_1 = b_1 \pm t_{\frac{\alpha}{2}, n-k-1} S_{b_1}$$
$$= .6388 \pm 2.365(.0458)$$
$$= [.530 \; to \; .748]$$

We can be 95% confident that the true population regression coefficient for Income (β_1) lies within the range .530 to .748. (That is, intervals derived in this way will include the true value 95% of the time.)

(b)   For the independent variable, Registrations, the confidence limit is

$$CL \; for \; \beta_2 = b_2 \pm t_{\frac{\alpha}{2}, n-k-1} S_{b_2}$$
$$= .5266 \pm 2.365(.0602)$$
$$= [.385 \; to \; .669]$$

We can be 95% confident that the true population regression coefficient for Registrations (β_2) lies within the range .385 to .669.

Exercises II

5.   In Exercise 1 we developed a model for the Dream Home Real Estate Company to predict the selling price of houses. The output of this regression analysis is reproduced below. Use this output to answer the questions below.

Regression Analysis for Price

Summary Measures

Multiple R	0.7260
R-Square	0.5271
Adj R-Square	0.5174
Std Error of Est.	14,279.3623

ANOVA Table

Effect	SS	DF	MS	F	P-value
Regression	22,045,988,654.0676	2	11,022,994,327.0338	54.0607	0.0000
Residual	19,778,318,343.7224	97	203,900,189.1105		
Total	41,824,306,997.7900	99	422,467,747.4524		

Regression Coefficients

Effect	Coefficient	Beta	Std Error	t-value	p-value
Constant	25,492.2015		17,739.0840	1.4371	0.1539
Sq Feet	64.2626	0.7026	7.0675	9.0927	0.0000
Age	-115.3017	-0.0513	173.7908	-0.6635	0.5086

(a)   Is the overall model statistically significant?

(b)   If the overall model is significant, which of the regression coefficients is significantly different from zero?

(c)   What is the standard error of the estimate? Develop a 95% confidence interval for the regression coefficient for Age. Does this interval include zero? What are the implications of this?

6.   In Exercise 2 we developed a model for Sarah Barnhart the VP of Human Resources at Admore Inc. The model could be used to predict MBA GPA from undergraduate GPA and the students GMAT score. The XLDataAnalyst output is is reproduced below. Use this output to answer the questions below.

Regression Analysis for MBA-GPA

Summary Measures

Multiple R	0.7518
R-Square	0.5652
Adj R-Square	0.5614
Std Error of Est.	0.2010

ANOVA Table

Effect	SS	DF	MS	F	P-value
Regression	12.1879	2	6.0939	150.7681	0.0000
Residual	9.3773	232	0.0404		
Total	21.5652	234	0.0922		

Regression Coefficients

Effect	Coefficient	Beta	Std Error	t-value	p-value
Constant	1.3107		0.1163	11.2672	0.0000
U-GPA	0.2393	0.3195	0.0378	6.3256	0.0000
GMAT	0.0022	0.5356	0.0002	10.6034	0.0000

(a) Is the overall model statistically significant?

(b) If the overall model is statistically significant, which of the individual regression coefficients are significantly different from zero?

(c) Calculate a 95% confidence interval for the GMAT regression coefficient. Does this interval include zero? What are the implications of this.

(d) Which of the independent variables, undergraduate grade point average or GMAT score, is most important in predicting MBA GPA and why??

7. In Exercise 3 Ann Thompson developed a regression model to predict a student's GPA at the university level based on their high school GPA and their SAT score. The output of this regression analysis is reproduced below. Use this output to answer the questions below.

Regression Analysis for College GPA

Summary Measures

Multiple R	0.5520
R-Square	0.3047
Adj R-Square	0.2856
Std Error of Est.	0.2876

ANOVA Table

Effect	SS	DF	MS	F	P-value
Regression	2.6462	2	1.3231	15.9932	0.0000
Residual	6.0392	73	0.0827		
Total	8.6854	75	0.1158		

Regression Coefficients

Effect	Coefficient	Beta	Std Error	t-value	p-value
Constant	0.2897		0.5531	0.5238	0.6020
HS GPA	0.5465	0.4439	0.1261	4.3351	0.0000
SAT	0.0006	0.2201	0.0003	2.1490	0.0350

(a) Is the overall model statistically significant? Is each of the individual regression coefficients statistically significant?

(b) Which independent variable is most important in predicting the number of cars sold?

(c) Develop a 95% confidence interval for the advertising regression coefficient.

8. In Exercise 4 Steve Edwards developed a model at Henry S. Jones to predict monthly car sales at a dealership based on advertising minutes aired during that month and the number of salespeople. The output of this regression analysis is reproduced below. Use this output to answer the questions below.

Regression Analysis for Cars Sold

Summary Measures

Multiple R	0.6325
R-Square	0.4000
Adj R-Square	0.3833
Std Error of Est.	20.4539

ANOVA Table

Effect	SS	DF	MS	F	P-value
Regression	20,081.0326	2	10,040.5163	23.9995	0.0000
Residual	30,122.1141	72	418.3627		
Total	50,203.1467	74	678.4209		

Regression Coefficients

Effect	Coefficient	Beta	Std Error	t-value	p-value
Constant	31.7597		12.7386	2.4932	0.0150
Advertising	1.9876	0.3965	0.4582	4.3377	0.0000
Salespeople	4.2874	0.4722	0.8300	5.1656	0.0000

(a) Is the overall model statistically significant? Is each of the individual regression coefficients statistically significant?

(b) Which factor, advertising or salespeople, seems to be the most important in predicting car sales?

(c) Develop a 95% confidence interval for both regression coefficients.

Diagnostics in Regression

There are a number of assumptions that we make when conducting regression analysis, either simple or multiple. To increase confidence in our regression model, we should test these assumptions to see if they are reasonable or not. We did check for the reasonableness of the linearity assumption by developing scatter plots of the dependent variable against all of the independent variables. To further test the assumptions, and to check for problems with the data, we must perform some analysis of the residuals from the regression calculations.

Analysis of Residuals

An analysis of the residuals from regression analysis can sometimes identify violations of the assumptions. The analysis of residuals normally takes place in *residual plots* where the residuals are plotted on the Y-axis of a plot and another variable is plotted on the X-axis. There are two main types of residual plots: a plot of residuals versus predicted values and a plot of residuals versus independent variables.

Residuals vs. Predicted

Since the errors are assumed to be randomly distributed around a mean of zero, the plots of the residuals versus the predicted values should have no distinct "pattern" to them. Figure 11-6 illustrates a residual versus predicted plot with no indication of problems.

Figure 11-6   A Residual Plot With a Random Pattern

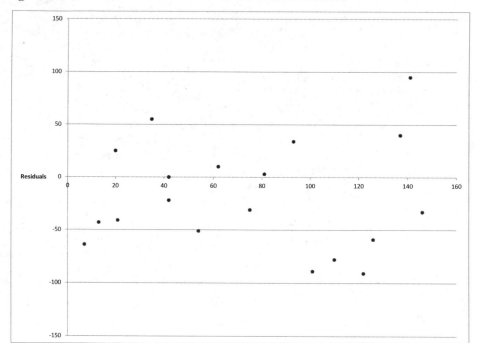

Two types of patterns can indicate a violation of the assumptions. One pattern is a V (or megaphone) pattern, typically opening to the right of the graph which can indicate a violation of the homogeneity of variances assumption. This assumption is violated when the variability of the values increases with the size of the values. The residuals will then increase for larger values giving a megaphone effect. Figure 11-7 illustrates such a pattern.

Figure 11-7   A Megaphone Pattern Indicating Unequal Variances

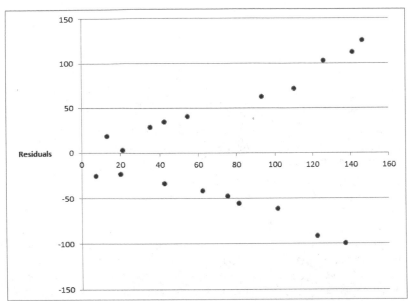

The second pattern that indicates a violation of one of the assumptions is curvilinear to the residuals. This often indicates a violation of the linearity assumption and perhaps a nonlinear relationship between the dependent and independent variables. Such a pattern is illustrated in Figure 11-8.

Figure 11-8   *A Curvilinear Pattern Indicating a Nonlinear Relationship*

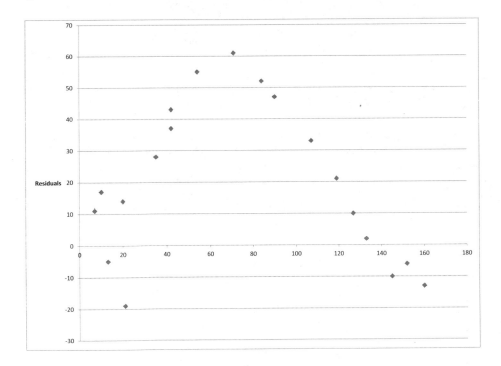

Residuals vs. Independent Variables

Residuals can be randomly distributed against each of the independent variables. Of particular concern in these plots is the linearity assumption. A curvilinear pattern, such as that of Figure 11-8, could indicate a nonlinear relationship between the dependent variable and that particular independent variable.

Sometimes other plots are produced in special circumstances. For example, a plot of "residuals versus time" for time-series data can uncover failures of the independence assumption. Time-series data sometimes exhibit *autocorrelation* such that the errors are correlated over time and the residuals are therefore not randomly distributed.

Checking for Outliers and Unusual Values

Another important diagnostic problem in regression analysis is checking for unusual data that might skew the overall results. Remember that *outliers* are observations that have an extreme value on the dependent variable. Such values can "pull" the regression equation away from other points in the dataset and produce a regression equation that does not fit the majority of the data. The cause of outliers should be investigated and the cause of the unusual value determined if possible. Sometimes, the outlier may be a result of a coding, obtaining or transcribing error that can be corrected. At other times, there may be no apparent reason for the unusual value. In such a case, it is up to the analyst to determine whether or not to remove the unusual value from the dataset. This is a subjective decision, but one with important consequences for the regression equation, derived from the data. Outliers can sometimes be spotted as extreme observations in a scatter plot or in one of the residual plots; however, it is not always easy to identify them in graphs. Another diagnostic tool for outliers is the use of *standardized residuals*.

Standardized Residuals

Standardized residuals are the ordinary residuals converted to standard scores. Since the mean of the residuals is always zero, standardized residuals are simply the residuals divided by the standard deviation of the residuals. XLDataAnalyst produces standardized residuals for each observation in the dataset. The standardized residuals are placed in the worksheet with the original observations. Standardized residuals greater than absolute 2.0 (greater than 2.0 or less than –2.0) indicate potential outliers. Standardized residuals greater than 3.0 in absolute value are almost certainly outliers. One test of the impact of outliers is to omit the relevant observations from the data and rerun the regression analysis. A comparison of the original solution and the revised solution will show how much impact the deleted values have had on the regression equation. It is then a matter of judgment which equation to use for further analysis or prediction.

Leverage Values

Other observations can influence the regression equation due to unusual values for the independent variables. These observations have more leverage in influencing the regression equation and measures of these observations are called *leverage values*. These observations cannot be identified easily from graphs and charts. XLDataAnalyst can produce leverage values as a diagnostic for this situation. In fact, the option that calculates standardized residuals for each observation will also produce a column of leverage values for each observation. The leverage value is a function of the number of independent variables and the sample size.

An observation may have too much influence on the regression equation if its leverage value exceeds the following value where "k", once again, is the number of independent variables:

Leverage Value Criterion $\dfrac{2(k+1)}{n}$ *(11-10)*

As with outliers, a test of the effects of observations with large leverage values is to recalculate the regression equation omitting those observations and comparing the two results.

Multicollinearity in Multiple Regression and its Diagnosis

There is a particular source of problems in multiple regression that you should be aware of as it can seriously distort the results of a multiple regression model.

> *Multicollinearity* occurs when some independent variables are highly correlated with each other. It seriously affects our ability to reliably estimate the individual regression coefficients.

For example, if we are predicting the selling price of houses we might consider independent variables such as location, number of rooms, and the number of square feet contained in the house. In this case, there may well be a moderate to high correlation between the number of square feet and the number of rooms in a house. When there is multicollinearity, the influence of one independent variable overlaps another, and it is difficult to determine what proportion of the effect is explained by any given independent variable.

The effects of multicollinearity may surface in a number of ways. When multicollinearity is present, the overall model may be significant, as indicated by the F-test; yet, none of the individual regression coefficients may be statistically significant. This is because the dependent variable, Y, is correlated with the weighted combination of the independent variables, some of which are accounted for the same overlapping variation. It is not clear which X variable is responsible for a given effect on Y. Therefore, the standard errors of the regression coefficients may be inflated and indicate that the individual coefficients are not significant. Another indication is that individual regression coefficients have the wrong sign in the calculated regression equation. For example, an independent variable may have a positive correlation with the dependent variable, but its regression coefficient is negative. Another indication of multicollinearity is that the coefficients of the independent variables change radically depending on whether other independent variables are present or absent from the equation. This is sometimes called the phenomenon of the "bouncing betas." This makes the interpretation of the regression coefficients virtually impossible because we don't know which is the "correct" value. To see the effect of this phenomenon we will look at an example of two datasets, one with multicollinearity, and the other without.

The first example is a situation where multicollinearity is not problematic. The correlation matrix for the dependent variable and the two independent variables is given in Table 11-3. An examination of this matrix reveals that the independent variables have virtually zero correlation (r = .009).

Table 11-3 Correlation Matrix with No Multicollinearity

	X_1	X_2	Y
X_1	1.000		
X_2	0.009	1.000	
Y	-0.870	-0.465	1.000

Performing a regression analysis first with both independent variables, and then with only one variable at a time, we would observe the regression coefficients shown in Table 11-4.

Table 11-4   Regression Coefficients with No Multicollinearity

	Both X_1 and X_2 included	Only X_1	Only X_2
X_1	-5.437	-5.462	
X_2	-21.012		-20.350

Notice that the values of the regression coefficients are nearly the same no matter if the other independent variable is included in the model or not.

Now consider another example where multicollinearity is a problem. In this case, there are three independent variables and one dependent variable. The correlation matrix for this example is shown in Table 11-5.

Table 11-5   Correlation Matrix with Multicollinearity

	X_1	X_2	X_3	Y
X_1	1.000			
X_2	-0.764	1.000		
X_3	0.793	-0.403	1.000	
Y	0.760	-0.286	.979	1.000

In this matrix, there is a large negative correlation between X_1 and X_2, and a large positive correlation between X_1 and X_3. Suppose we performed a regression analysis first on each variable by itself, then with all possible combinations of two independent variables, and finally with all three variables included in the model. The resulting regression coefficients are shown in Table 11-6

Table 11-6   Regression Coefficients with Multicollinearity

	All three variables	X_1 and X_2	X_1 and X_3	X_2 and X_3	Only X_1	Only X_2	Only X_3
X_1	0.027	0.115	-0.004		0.067		
X_2	0.097	0.235		0.043		-0.095	
X_3	0.525		0.623	0.634			0.602

Notice that the regression coefficients for a given independent variable vary widely, depending on which additional independent variables are included in the model, and change signs from positive to negative. For example, the calculated regression coefficients for X_2 range from -0.095 to 0.235. So, what is the "true" coefficient for this variable? Indeed, the correlation of X_2 with the dependent variable is negative; yet; its regression coefficient is positive when combined with either of the other two independent variables. That is the problem with multicollinearity—the regression coefficients are neither reliable nor interpretable. This does not mean that the equation cannot be used for prediction; only that we cannot interpret the regression coefficients or their significance tests. Multicollinearity does not affect the ability of the model to make predictions, but does make it difficult, if not impossible, to interpret the regression coefficients. Therefore, if we are interested in the values of the coefficients we should eliminate multicollinearity by deleting one or more of the variables.

Given that multicollinearity is a problem in regression, how do we identify it if it exists in our data? There are several indicators of potential problems:

- Significant and large correlations between pairs of independent variables

- A significant F-test for the overall model, but none of the t-tests for the individual regression coefficients is significant

- Estimated parameters with a sign opposite of that expected based on the correlations (see Tables 11-5 and 11-6 for an example).

A final indicator of possible multicollinearity pertains to *variance inflation factors* (VIF). XLDataAnalyst will produce these factors for each independent variable if the appropriate box in the Regression dialog box is checked. The output of the VIF values for our two sample illustrations in Table 11-4 and 11-6 are shown in Figure 11-9. Notice that when there is no multicollinearity, the VIF values are 1.0 or close to it; however, when multicollinearity is present, the values are much larger. Some sources state that VIF values of 10 or more are indicative of serious multicollinearity problems. Yet, we have seen that our second example exhibited multicollinearity and the largest VIF is 7.382. We would suggest that if the VIF is 5 or larger, one would be wise to investigate further for potential multicollinearity problems.

Figure 11-9   Variance Inflation Factors in the XLDataAnalyst Output

(a)   No Multicollinearity

Regression Coefficients

Effect	Coefficient	Beta	Std Error	t-value	p-value	VIF
Constant	562.151		21.093	26.651	0.000	
X_1	-5.437	-0.866	0.336	-16.170	0.000	1.000
X_2	-20.012	-0.457	2.343	-8.543	0.000	1.000

(b)   Multicollinearity Present

Regression Coefficients

Effect	Coefficient	Beta	Std Error	t-value	p-value	VIF
Constant	-10.170		3.473	-2.928	0.026	
Food	0.027	0.307	0.012	2.246	0.066	7.382
Non-Food	0.097	0.293	0.030	3.219	0.018	3.271
Size	0.525	0.854	0.059	8.869	0.000	3.670

Exercises III

9.   The following correlation matrix displays the relationship between the dependent variable (Y-life expectancy) and several independent variables, (

where:

Y- Life expectancy

X_1- Telephone mobile

X_2- TV per 000 population

X_3- Physician per 000 population

X_4- Nurses per 000 population

X_5- Per capita total expenditure on health at average exchange rate.

	X_1	X_2	X_3	X_4	X_5	Y
X_1	1.000					
X_2	0.274	1.000				
X_3	0.016	0.292	1.000			
X_4	0.028	0.358	0.947	1.00		
X_5	0.234	0.698	0.344	0.476	1.00	
Y	0.176	0.657	0.318	0.308	0.483	1.00

(a) Which of the variables has the highest correlation with the dependent variable?

(b) Which of the variables has the lowest correlation with the dependent variable?

(c) Do you see any potential issues with multicollinearity? Explain why. What would you recommend the next step should be?

10. The following estimated regression equation involves one dependent variable and two independent variables:

$$\hat{Y} = 58.90 + .036X_1 + .43X_2$$

Y- Life expectancy

X_1- TV per 000 population

X_2- Physician per 000 population

(a) Interpret the value of the y-intercept and the slope regression coefficients.

(b) Estimate the value of the life expectancy when the number of TVs per (000) is 500 and the Physician (per 000) is 4.0.

11. Refer to the information provided in Exercise 9. The number of observations is 170 (countries).

$$\hat{Y} = 58.90 + .036X_1 + .43X_2$$

From the multiple regression analysis, we found that:

SSTotal = 23,368   SSR = 10,488

a. Compute the value of the multiple coefficient of determination. At 0.05 level of significance, test the significance of the multiple coefficient of determination. State the null and the alternative hypotheses and the decision rule.

b. The following standard errors were computed for each of the regression slope coefficients:
$s_{b1} = 0.0035$ $s_{b2} = 0.1863$

Test whether or not the regression slope coefficients are significantly different from zero. Use a level of significance of 0.05. State the null and the alternative hypotheses.

12. As it is well known, many colleges and universities are offering courses and even entire programs online. The correlation matrix provided below displays the relationship between the dependent variable (Y): satisfaction with online courses and the following independent variables: age (X_1), the degree to which a student "likes" online courses (X_2), and the degree of the familiarity with the course(s) offered online. Do you see any potential issues with multicollinearity? Explain why.

	X_1	X_2	X_3	Y
X_1	1.000			
X_2	-0.079	1.000		
X_3	-0.069	0.475	1.000	
Y	0.418	0.242	0.146	1.00

13. Refer to the information provided in Exercise 4. After running the multiple regression equation, the following estimated regression equation and the respective standard errors (of each of the regression slope coefficients) were found:

$$\hat{Y} = -0.1738 + .0528X_1 + .2068X_2 + .06929X_3$$

$s_{b1} = 0.0068$ $s_{b2} = 0.0532$ $s_{b2} = 0.0691$

The number of observations (n) is assumed to be 240.

a. Develop a 95% confidence interval estimate of the true slopes for all the three coefficients.

b. Using a level of significance 0.05, test the significance of each of the independent variables. State the null and the alternative hypotheses. Would you consider removing any of the variables? Justify your answer.

14. The following is an ANOVA table from a multiple regression analysis:

ANOVA Table

Source	SS	df	MS	F	p-value
Regression	23.4354	2	11.7177	28.38	.0019
Residual	2.0646	5	0.4129		
Total	25.5000	7			

(a) At a 0.01 level of significance, test the significance of the regression model.

(b) What is the value of the explained variation? What is the value of the unexplained variation?

(c) Compute the standard error of estimate.

15. The following Excel Output pertains to a multiple regression analysis:

ANOVA
table

Source	SS	DF	MS	F	p-value
Regression	10.8094	2	5.4047	30.77	.0001
Residual	1.5806	9	0.1756		
Total	12.3900	11			

Regression output

Effect	Coefficient	std. error	t-value	p-value
Constant	4.3210	0.5904	7.319	.0000
X1	0.1305	0.0651	2.004	.0761
X2	-0.2583	0.0587	-4.397	.0017

(a) Provide the estimated regression equation.

(b) Test the significance of the model at 0.05 level of significance.

(c) Compute R^2 and interpret it.

(c) Test to determine if the regression slope coefficients are significantly different from zero. Use a level of significance of 0.05.

Nominal Scaled Variables in Regression

One of the assumptions of regression analysis is that all of the variables are measured on an interval or ratio scale. What happens if we have nominal scale variables in our data that we wish to use in predicting the dependent variable? It is possible to include nominal scale variables as independent variables in a regression analysis if they are coded properly. This often requires creating new "special" variables to represent the nominal scaled independent variables.

Dummy Coding

We can also include nominal scale variables in regression analysis through the use of *dummy variables*. Dummy variables are 0-1 variables that represent group membership. Consider the simplest case of a nominal scale with only two values, such as male and female. Let $X_1 = 1$, if female, $X_2 = 0$, if male. X_1 is then said to be a dummy coded variable. This variable can be used as an independent variable in regression analysis; however, the interpretation of the resulting regression coefficient is somewhat different from that of interval scaled variables. To understand the meaning of the regression coefficient, suppose we complete a regression analysis of a dependent variable with our dummy coded variable, as the only independent variable. Let μ_M be the population average of the dependent variable for males and μ_F be the population mean for females. We know that in the population, the mean of the dependent variable is a function of the population regression equation:

$$\mu_{Y|X} = \alpha + \beta X \qquad\qquad (11\text{-}11)$$

Now suppose that X_1 is 0, a male. Then equation 11-11 reduces to:

$$\mu_{Y|X} = \alpha$$

This means that $\mu_M = \alpha$

Now when X_1 is 1, a female, equation 11-11 reduces to:

$$\mu_{Y|X} = \mu_F = \alpha + \beta$$

But since $\alpha = \mu_M$

$$\mu_F = \alpha + \beta$$

$$\mu_F = \mu_M + \beta$$

or $\qquad \beta = \mu_F - \mu_M$

The Y-intercept represents the average value of the dependent variable for the group coded as 0 and the slope represents the difference between the average value for the group coded as 1 and the average value for the group coded as 0.

We can extend this to three values for the nominal scale independent variable. For example, suppose that we have three different groups in a computer training class (Beginner, Intermediate, and Advanced). We can code these three groups with two dummy variables X_1 and X_2 as follows:

Let X_1 = 1 if Beginner

= 0 otherwise

Let X_2 = 1 if Intermediate

= 0 otherwise

There are three possible combinations of values for the two dummy coded variables:

X_1 = 1 and X_2 = 0 Represents the Beginner

X_1 = 0 and X_2 = 1 Represents the Intermediate Group

X_1 = 0 and X_2 = 0 Represents the Advanced Group

In this way, the three original values are represented by only two dummy coded variables.

Then, let:

μ_B = population mean for the dependent variable for beginners

μ_I = population mean for the dependent variable for intermediate

μ_A = population mean for of the dependent variable for advanced

If we perform a regression analysis using these two dummy coded variables to predict a dependent variable, regression theory tells us that:

$$\mu_{Y|X} = \alpha + \beta_1 X_1 + \beta_2 X_2 \qquad\qquad (11\text{-}12)$$

Consider the case when both of the dummy coded variables have a value of zero, e.g., $X_1 = 0$ and $X_2 = 0$. This represents the advanced group and equation 11-12 reduces to:

$$\mu_{Y|X} = \mu_A = \alpha$$

Now consider the situation when $X_1 = 1$ and $X_2 = 0$. Equation 11-12 reduces to:

$$\mu_{Y|X} = \mu_B = \alpha + \beta_1$$

But since $\alpha = \mu_A$

$$\mu_B = \mu_A + \beta_1$$

$$\text{or} \qquad \beta_1 = \mu_B - \mu_A$$

Now consider, the final situation when $X_1 = 0$ and $X_2 = 1$. Equation 11-12 reduces to:

$$\mu_{Y|X} = \mu_I = \alpha + \beta_2$$

But since we already know that $\alpha = \mu_A$

$$\mu_I = \mu_A + \beta_2$$

$$\text{or} \qquad \beta_2 = \mu_I - \mu_A$$

The Y-intercept represents the average value of the dependent variable for the group represented when both dummy variables are coded as 0, the advanced users. The regression coefficient for the first dummy coded variable equals the difference between the population mean for the group coded as 1 (the beginners) and the group coded as zeros(the advanced users). The regression coefficient for the second dummy coded variable is equal to the difference between the population mean for the group coded as 1 on the second variable (the intermediate users) and the group coded as zero (the advanced users).

This can be extended to any number of levels in the independent variable by fixing one level as the reference group (0 on all dummy variables) and using a separate dummy variable to represent the other groups.

For K levels of a nominal scale variable (A, B, C, D, ... K)

Let group 1 be the reference group. Then,

Let $X_i = 1$ if member of group i+1
$\qquad = 0$ otherwise

Then,

$\alpha = \mu_A$

$\beta_2 = \mu_B - \mu_A$

$\beta_3 = \mu_C - \mu_A$

$$\beta_4 = \mu_D - \mu_A$$

...

....

....

$$\beta_K = \mu_K - \mu_A$$

Regression and ANOVA

If we can use nominal scale variables in regression, then we can theoretically perform tests such as analysis of variance using regression. This is indeed the case. To see how this is done we will return to Example 10-1, our initial example of a one-way ANOVA.

Example 11-6

Recall that Example 10-1 involved feeding three different types of feed (Topnotch, Growbig and Max) to young turkeys and then measuring their weight gain after a certain time period. The data are repeated in Table 11-7 along with the sample means for the three groups.

Table 11-7   Data for ANOVA

	Topnotch	Growbig	Max
	42	112	70
	96	96	17
	81	88	49
	95	135	24
	76	119	40
$\overline{X}_i$	78	110	40

The previous results of the one-way ANOVA are reproduced in Figure 11.10.

Solution

It is arbitrary which group serves as the reference group, so let's select the Max group to be the reference. We will then code two dummy variables as

Feed1 = 1 if Topnotch, 0 otherwise

Feed2 = 1 if Growbig, 0 otherwise

The data along with the two new dummy variables are shown in Figure 11-11. This data is also contained in the file Example 11-6.xls.

Using XLDataAnalyst we performed the regression analysis with the variable Gain as the dependent variable and the two variables Feed1 and Feed2 as the independent variables. The results are show in Figure 11-12. Notice that the results in the ANOVA table for regression are identical to those above with a one-way ANOVA. Also note that the regression coefficient for Feed1 is the mean for

Topnotch minus the mean for Max (78-40 = 38). The coefficient for Feed2 is the difference between the mean for Growbig and the mean for Max (110 – 40 = 70). Lastly, the constant or intercept is the mean for Max (40). The significance of the regression coefficient for Feed1 means that the difference between Topnotch and Max is statistically significant. A similar interpretation holds for the significance of the coefficient for Feed2.

Figure 11-10   ANOVA Results for Example 11-6

ANOVA Results For Gain

ANOVA Table

Effect	Sum of Squares	DF	Mean Square	F	P-value
Feed	12,280.000	2	6,140.000	14.510	0.001
Error	5,078.000	12	423.167		
Total	17,358.000	14			

Observed Means

Means for Feed

Topnotch	Growbig	Max
78.000	110.000	40.000

Figure 11-11   Example 11-6 Data with Dummy Variables

Feed	Gain	Feed1	Feed2
1	42.00	1	0
1	96.00	1	0
1	81.00	1	0
1	95.00	1	0
1	76.00	1	0
2	112.00	0	1
2	96.00	0	1
2	88.00	0	1
2	135.00	0	1
2	119.00	0	1
3	70.00	0	0
3	17.00	0	0
3	49.00	0	0
3	24.00	0	0
3	40.00	0	0

Figure 11-12   Regression Results for Example 11-6

Regression Analysis for Gain

Summary Measures

Multiple R	0.841
R-Square	0.707
Adj R-Square	0.659
Std Error of Est.	20.571

ANOVA Table

Effect	SS	DF	MS	F	P-value
Regression	12,280.000	2	6,140.000	14.510	0.001
Residual	5,078.000	12	423.167		
Total	17,358.000	14	1,239.857		

Regression Coefficients

Effect	Coeffient	Beta	Std Error	t-value	p-value
Constant	40.000		9.200	4.348	0.001
Dummy1	38.000	0.527	13.010	2.921	0.013
Dummy2	70.000	0.970	13.010	5.380	0.000

Exercises IV

The following exercises are repeated from Chapter 9. In these exercises, rather than using ANOVA, perform the calculations using dummy variables and regression analysis

 16. The council of a Native American tribe in the State of Washington operates casinos at three different locations. To test customer satisfaction at the three sites they randomly sample customers leaving each site and ask them if they would return to that casino in the future. The results are contained in the file Exercise 11-16.xlsx. Using dummy coded regression determine if there are any differences in customer satisfaction between the three locations? Should the council be concerned about particular locations? If so, which ones.

 17. Stetson Interstate Bank is concerned about the wait time of customers waiting to see a loan advisor at their various branches. Steve Wilson, Chief Operating Officer, has advised the Executive Committee that the average customer wait time at the various branches is approximately 5 minutes. To support his statement, Steve has measured randomly selected customer wait times at four different banks. The resulting data are contained in the file Exercises 11-17.xlsx. What can you tell the Executive Committee about the wait times at the four branches? Are they the same in the four branches?

 18. The Rock Point Association of Realtors are interested in the relative prices of houses being sold in four different areas of town, the South Hill, the North Side, the East Valley, and the West Plains. They take a random sample of homes recently sold in the four areas. The data are contained in the file Exercise 11-18.xlsx. Are there any differences in the average selling prices between the four areas of the city?

Finding the Best Predictor Variables

Stepwise Multiple Linear Regression

There are times when we have a large number of independent/predictor variables and we want to select the best set of variables to predict the dependent variable. There are several techniques for doing this, including Best Subsets Regression. The first set of techniques determines a "best" set of predictor variables by continuing to add or delete predictor variables as long as the fit can be improved. There are three different procedures for doing this:

- Forward Selection
- Backward Selection
- Stepwise Regression

Forward Selection

Forward selection begins by fitting all possible one-variable models and testing the H_O: $\beta_1 = 0$. The variable with the largest significant t-value (smallest p-value) is selected as X_1. Then, the remaining (k-1) variables are tried in combination with X_1 and testing for the hypothesis H_O: $\beta_2 = 0$. If there are significant variables, the one with the largest t-value (smallest p-value) becomes X_2. This process continues until no more significant variables can be found.

Backward Selection

Backward selection begins by fitting the model with all "k" independent variables. All possible one-variable models test the hypothesis $H_O: \beta_i = 0$ for each variable. The variable with the smallest nonsignificant t-value (largest p-value) is removed from the model. This process is repeated with the remaining k-1 variables. If there are nonsignificant variables, the least significant of them is dropped from the model. This process continues until all remaining independent variables are statistically significant.

Stepwise Regression

As in the forward selection process, stepwise begins by fitting all possible one-variable models and testing the $H_O: \beta_1 = 0$. The variable with the largest significant t-value (smallest p-value) is selected as X_1. Then the remaining (k-1) variables are tried in combination with X_1 and tested for the hypothesis $H_O: \beta_2 = 0$. If there are significant variables found, then the one with the largest t-value (smallest p-value) becomes X_2. In stepwise, if at this point variable X_1 becomes nonsignificant, it is removed from the model. This process continues until no more significant variables can be found. The only difference between stepwise and forward selection is the fact that in stepwise regression, variables are removed from the model if they are no longer significant.

Best Subsets Regression

Best subsets regression is the process of ordering possible combinations of predictor variables in terms of some fit measure, usually R^2. Depending on the software used, the best 1 predictor model, 2 predictor model, 3 predictor model and so on may be printed. Alternatively, the software may produce the fit measure for all combinations of predictors. This is the approach taken by XLDataAnalyst as we will see in the practice section. Some experts have cautioned about obtaining inflated estimates of R^2 using this approach. The basic argument is that the approach capitalizes on chance and that in a validation sample an entirely different model may yield the best fit. It is probably best to use this "shotgun" approach with caution.

Practice

Computer Solutions for Multiple Regression

Most of the regression procedures for multiple regression are the same as for simple regression. Here we will recap those procedures and then focus on those features, most relevant to multiple regression as opposed to simple regression.

Excel Functions

There are no Excel functions that can perform multiple regression, only simple regression. To run multiple regression you need to use either the DataAnalysis Toolpak or XLDataAnalyst.

The Data Analysis Toolpak

To perform a multiple regression analysis, select Tools--Data Analysis from the Excel menu. The list of available routines as illustrated in Figure 11-13 will appear.

Figure 11-13   Routines of the Data Analysis Toolpak: Regression

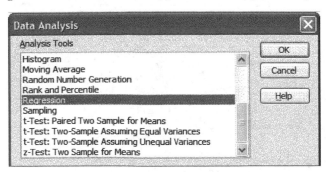

Select the option labeled "Regression" as illustrated. Then, the dialog shown in Figure 11-14 will appear on the screen. Indicate the location of the input data, including the dependent and all independent variables, on the worksheet and where you want to place the output. You can also use the mouse to highlight range for the input data and the output range. If you have labels that you want to appear in the output, make sure that they are included in the input range and check the box for Labels in First Row.

Figure 11-14   Dialog Box for Regression in the Data Analysis Toolpak

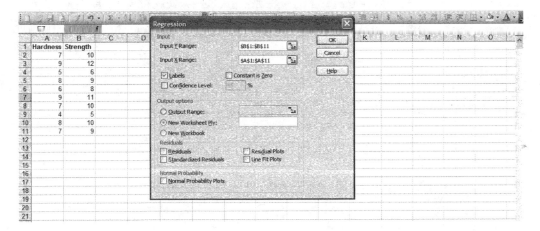

Many of the other options provided by check boxes in the dialog box are for regression diagnostics. Recall that many of the diagnostic tests in regression involve the use of residuals. The DataAnalysis Toolpak can produce many of these diagnostic tools.

Example 11-7

To illustrate the use of the DataAnalysis Toolpak let's go back to the data used in Example 11-1. Figure 11-15 illustrates the output from the DataAnalysis Toolpak for this data.

Solution

The output is similar in many ways to the output from XLDataAnalyst as we will see below. One statistic that the DataAnalysis Toolpak produces that is not standard with other statistical packages is the confidence intervals for the regression coefficients.

Figure 11-15   Example 11-1 Analyzed with the DataAnalysis Toolpak

SUMMARY OUTPUT

Regression Statistics	
Multiple R	0.996329
R Square	0.992671
Adjusted R	0.990577
Standard E	0.336274
Observatio	10

ANOVA

	df	SS	MS	F	ignificance F
Regressior	2	107.2084	53.60422	474.0373	3.37E-08
Residual	7	0.791561	0.11308		
Total	9	108			

	Coefficients	andard Err	t Stat	P-value	Lower 95%	Upper 95%	ower 95.0%	lpper 95.0%
Intercept	3.459916	0.549003	6.302183	0.000403	2.16173	4.758101	2.16173	4.758101
Income	0.638819	0.045819	13.94223	2.31E-06	0.530474	0.747163	0.530474	0.747163
Registratio	0.526582	0.060218	8.744609	5.14E-05	0.384189	0.668975	0.384189	0.668975

In addition to the standard output, the DataAnalysis Toolpak can also provide the analysis of residuals. Figure 11-16 shows the resulting residual output and plots for Example 11-7.

Figure 11-16   *Residuals Output from DataAnalysis Toolpak for Example 11-11*

RESIDUAL OUTPUT

Observatio	redicted Sal	Residuals	dard Residuals
1	15.00169	-0.00169	-0.00569
2	15.97722	0.022785	0.076829
3	17.14262	-0.14262	-0.48089
4	17.78143	0.218565	0.736988
5	20	0	0
6	20.52658	-0.52658	-1.7756
7	21.69198	0.308017	1.038612
8	23.4962	0.503797	1.698772
9	23.08186	-0.08186	-0.27601
10	25.30042	-0.30042	-1.013

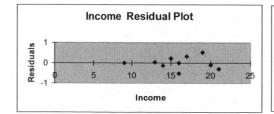

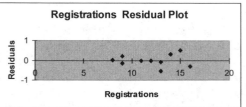

In addition to the residuals and residual plots, the DataAnalysis Toolpak can also produce line fit plots showing predicted and actual values as a function of the independent variables. This can be useful in detecting curvilinear relationships where the predicted and actual might diverge at the ends of the plots.

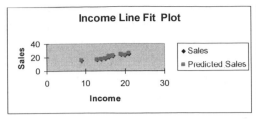
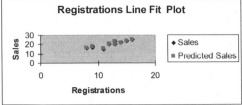

The last type of plot produced by the DataAnalysis Toolpak is the normal probability plot.

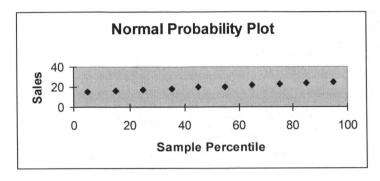

Multiple Regression Using XLDataAnalyst

XLDataAnalyst can perform most of the tasks involved in multiple regression. We have often demonstrated the value of using scatter plots as a pre-analysis tool in regression to make sure that the relationship between the dependent and independent variables are linear. XLDataAnalyst readily produces scatter plots. Although scatter plots were discussed in Chapter 2, a brief discussion is repeated here for completeness. To produce a scatter plot in XLDataAnalyst, select the Graphs menu in the Descriptive Statistics section of the ribbon and then select Scatter Plots. The resulting dialog box is shown in Figure 11-17. For the data in Example 11-1, we would select Income for the X-axis of the scatter plot and Sales for the Y-axis for the first graph, shown earlier in Figure 11-2. Follow a similar procedure for the second graph, but select Registrations for the X-axis.

Figure 11-17   Dialog Box for the Scatter Plots

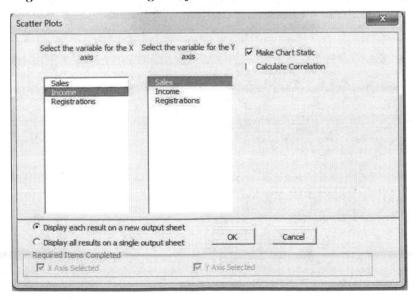

The standard dialog for multiple regression in XLDataAnalyst, as with simple regression, is accessed in the Correlation and Regression section of the ribbon by selecting the Regression option. There are three submenu options under Regression as shown in Figure 11-18. For multiple linear regression select the General Regression option.

Figure 11-18 Submenus of the Regression Option

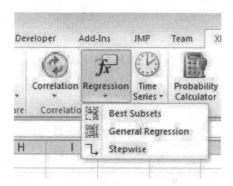

The standard regression dialog that results from the selection of this option is shown in Figure 11-19.

Figure 11-19   XLDataAnalyst Dialog Box for Multiple Regression Analysis

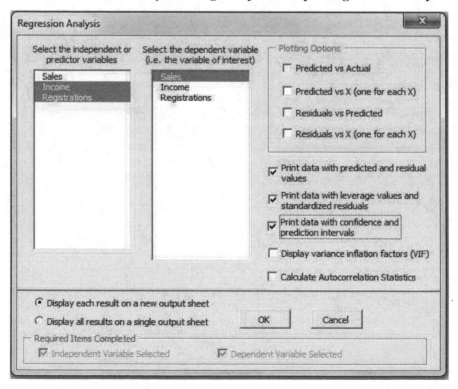

As with the DataAnalysis Toolpak, there are various options associated with the regression dialog box. The options in the upper right hand corner of the dialog box are used to generate plots of predicted values and residuals. These plots help diagnose problems with regression assumptions as discussed previously. Check each box for the desired plots.

The remaining options relate to providing the data with optional diagnostic information, such as influence values, residuals, prediction or confidence intervals. Moreover they are used in calculating additional diagnostic information, such as variance inflation factors, to diagnose multicollinearity, or the Durbin-Watson statistic for time series data. Figure 11-20 shows the standard output of the XLDataAnalyst regression procedure for Example 11-1 along with a sampling of some of the optional output.

Figure 11-20   Sample Output from the XLDataAnalyst Regression Procedure

Regression Analysis for Sales

Summary Measures

Multiple R	0.9963
R-Square	0.9927
Adj R-Square	0.9906
Std Error of Est.	0.3363

ANOVA Table

Effect	SS	DF	MS	F	P-value
Regression	107.2084	2	53.6042	474.0373	0.0000
Residual	0.7916	7	0.1131		
Total	108.0000	9	12.0000		

Regression Coefficients

Effect	Coefficient	Beta	Std Error	t-value	p-value
Constant	3.4599		0.5490	6.3022	0.0004
Income	0.6388	0.6563	0.0458	13.9422	0.0000
Registrations	0.5266	0.4116	0.0602	8.7446	0.0001

Observation	Predicted	Residuals	Influence	Std.Residuals	LowerConf	UpperConf	LowerPred	UpperPred
1	15.0017	-0.0017	0.7937	-0.0110	14.2933	15.7101	13.9367	16.0666
2	15.9772	0.0228	0.3549	0.0844	15.5035	16.4509	15.0517	16.9028
3	17.1426	-0.1426	0.2502	-0.4898	16.7449	17.5404	16.2535	18.0317
4	17.7814	0.2186	0.3008	0.7773	17.3453	18.2176	16.8745	18.6884
5	20.0000	0.0000	0.1000	0.0000	19.7485	20.2515	19.1660	20.8340
6	20.5266	-0.5266	0.1321	-1.6809	20.2376	20.8156	19.6805	21.3726
7	21.6920	0.3080	0.1759	1.0090	21.3584	22.0255	20.8297	22.5543
8	23.4962	0.5038	0.2367	1.7148	23.1093	23.8831	22.6119	24.3805
9	23.0819	-0.0819	0.2873	-0.2883	22.6556	23.5081	22.1797	23.9841
10	25.3004	-0.3004	0.3684	-1.1241	24.8178	25.7830	24.3703	26.2306

T
he upper section of Figure 11-20 shows the standard regression output, while the lower portion shows the optional output of the predicted values, residuals, influence values and confidence and prediction intervals.   Figure 11-21 shows some of the optional graphical output from XLDataAnalyst:

Figure 11-21   Sample Graphs from the XLDataAnalyst Regression Procedure

Predicted vs Actual

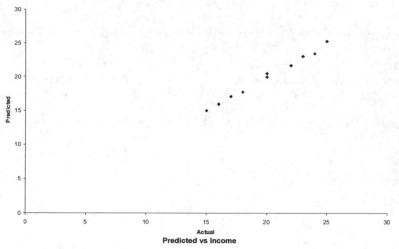

Predicted vs Income

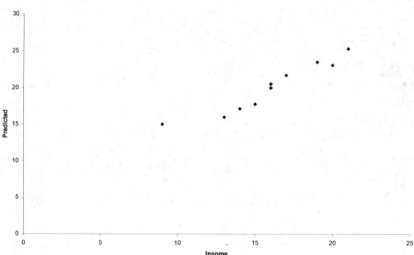

Residuals vs Predicted

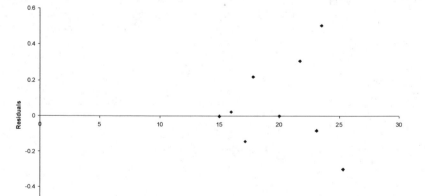

As mentioned before, XLDataAnalyst can also run stepwise and best subsets regression. To perform these tests, select the appropriate submenu item from the Regression Analysis option that was shown in Figure 11-18. When you select the Stepwise option, a new dialog box will be presented, as shown in Figure 11-22.

Figure 11-22   XLDataAnalyst Dialog for Stepwise Regression

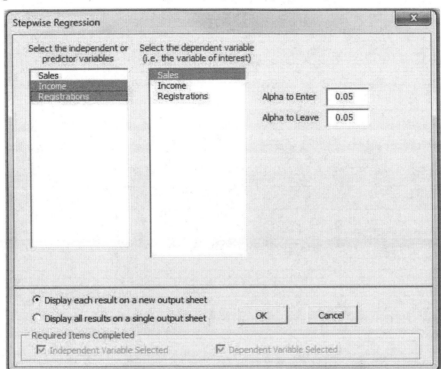

In the dialog box, select the independent or predictor variables in the left list box, in this case, Income and Registrations, and the dependent variable in the right list box, in this case, Sales. You have the option of changing the parameters used to select variables to enter or leave the model. The Alpha to Enter value is the criterion by which the decision will be made as to whether or not a predictor variable will be allowed to enter the model; the default value is .05. This means that on any step of the process, a variable must have a p-value of less than .05 to enter the model. If multiple predictors have p-values less than .05, then the predictor with the smallest p-value will be entered. Similarly, the Alpha to Leave value determines when a variable is removed from the model. The default value is .05, which means that if the p-value of an independent variable, currently in the model, is above .05 on any step, then that predictor will be removed from the model. You can modify either or both of these parameters to make it more or less difficult to enter or leave the model. The output for Example 11-1, using the default parameters is shown in Figure 11-23.

Figure 11-23   Stepwise Output for Example 11-1

Stepwise Procedure for Dependent Variable Sales

Step 1 Variable Income Entered   R-Square = 0.7891

Variable	Coefficient	Std Error	F-value	p-value
Constant	5.1228	1.6636	9.4829	0.0151
Income	0.9298	0.1017	83.5390	0.0000

Step 2 Variable Registrations Entered   R-Square = 0.9927

Variable	Coefficient	Std Error	F-value	p-value
Constant	3.4599	0.5490	39.7175	0.0004
Income	0.6388	0.0458	194.3857	0.0000
Registratio	0.5266	0.0602	76.4682	0.0001

The stepwise process took two steps with Income entered on the first step and Registrations entered on the second step. Since all of the variables are then included in the model, the process stops.

The dialog box for the Best Subset Regression procedure is simple, as can be seen in Figure 11-24. Simply select the independent variables and the dependent variable.

Figure 11-24   XLDataAnalyst Dialog for Best Subset Regression

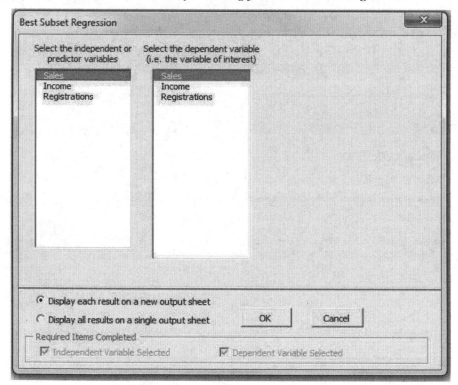

The output for the best subset regression is shown in Figure 11-25. In this case, the output is very short since there are only three possible models that can be developed with two predictors. With more independent variables, the output quickly becomes more detailed.

In this problem, the best model in terms of the highest R^2 is the one with both Income and Registrations as independent variables. In this case, the best subsets and stepwise procedures agree on the best model. That is not always the case.

Figure 11-25   XLDataAnalyst Best Subset Regression for Example 11-1

Best Subsets Regression for Dependent Variable Sales

Model No.	C(p)	R-square	Adj R-square	MSE	Variables in Model
1	3.0000	0.9927	0.9906	0.1131	Income, Registrations
2	77.4682	0.9126	0.9017	1.1798	Income
3	195.3857	0.7891	0.7628	2.8466	Registrations

Exercises V

The following exercises relate to a study of student satisfaction with online course delivery at a private university. Data was gathered on gender (0 = female, 1 = male), academic status (0 = graduate, 1=undergraduate), major (1 = Business Administration, 2 = Accounting, 3 = Undeclared, 4 = Other), marital status (0 = married, 1 = single) and distance from campus (0 = less than 1 mile, 1 = more than 1 mile), age in years, number of business courses taken online, number of blended courses taken, and five rating scale items related to satisfaction.

1. I like online courses
2. I think online courses are an appropriate way of learning in universities
3. I would take a course if I was, to some extent, familiar with the course material

The above questions were measured on a 5-point rating scale ranging from 1 (strongly disagree) to 5 (strongly agree

4. How satisfied were you with the courses offered online?
5. How satisfied were you with the blended courses?

These items were rated on a 5-point rating scale ranging from 1 (very dissatisfied) to 5 (very satisfied). The data are contained in the file Online Course Delivery.xlsx

19. Assume that the researcher is investigating the factors that impact students' satisfaction with online courses.

    (a) Consider the following variables as independent variables: gender (coded as 0=female, 1=male), age, academic status (0–graduate, 1=undergraduate), and appropriateness of offering the course online. Satisfaction with online courses is the dependent variable. Run a multiple regression analysis and provide the estimated regression equation(s). Test the significance of the model at a 0.05 level of significance.

    (b) Would you consider dropping any of the variables from the model? Justify your answer.

    (c) After dropping the variable(s) that are not significant, re-run the regression analysis. Present the regression equation(s) and interpret the regression slope coefficients.

20. The researcher is also interested in finding the best predictors of the students' satisfaction with online courses. Consider the following variables as predictors: gender, age, academic status, and appropriateness of offering the course online. Satisfaction with online courses is the dependent variable.

    (a) Perform a multiple regression analysis using a forward selection model.

    (b) Perform a multiple regression analysis using a backward selection model.

    (c)   Perform a multiple regression analysis using a stepwise selection model.

    (d)   Do you get the same results using the three methods?

21.   Consider the following variables as independent variables: marital status, the degree to which the student likes online courses, distance from campus, the familiarity with the course, and the number of courses taken online. Satisfaction with online courses is the dependent variable. Run a multiple regression analysis and provide the estimated regression equation(s). Test the significance of the model and the significance of each of the independent variables at a 0.05 level of significance.

22.   Consider the following variables as independent variables: marital status, the degree to which the student likes online courses, distance from campus, the familiarity with the course, and the number of courses taken online. Satisfaction with online courses is the dependent variable.

    (a)   Perform a multiple regression a using a forward selection model.

    (b)   Perform a multiple regression analysis using a backward selection model.

    (c)   Perform a multiple regression analysis using a stepwise selection model

The following exercises refer to a study conducted by Bob Young, a financial analyst with a large metropolitan bank. The study was conducted to investigate what factors relate to income, household debt levels, and the total value of deposits with the bank. A random sample 150 bank customers were interviewed to gather the appropriate data. Besides information on income and debt, the customers were asked to provide information on their age, years of education, years with current employer, and years at their current address. The data are contained in the file Household Finances.xlsx

23.   For the household finances data

    (a)   Develop a correlation matrix. Do you see any multicollinearity issues? Explain!

    (b)   Bob is interested to investigate the potential factors impacting income. Consider income as the dependent variable and Age, Education, and the Years at the current job as the independent variables. Run the proper regression analysis and provide the estimated regression model.

    (c)   Test the significance of the model and the significance of each of the independent variables at the 0.05 level of significance.

24.   Bob is also interested in examining the potential factors impacting deposits with the bank.

    (a)   Consider deposits as the dependent variable and Age, Education, and Income as the independent variables. Run the proper regression analysis and provide the estimated regression model.

    (b)   Test the significance of the model at the 0.05 level of significance.

    (c)   Develop a 95% confidence interval for the coefficients of age and education.

The following exercises are repeated from Chapter 9. In these exercises, rather than using ANOVA perform the calculations using dummy variables and regression analysis.

25.   Finally, Bob would like to develop and equation predicting debt levels based on age, education, number of years with the current employer, and income.

    (a)   Develop the regression equation for Bob and interpret the regression coefficients.

(b)   Which of the independent variables are statistically significant? Drop all nonsignificant predictor variables and reanalyze the data using the new model. How do the regression coefficients change?

The following exercises are repeated from Chapter 9. In these exercises, rather than using ANOVA, perform the calculations using dummy variables and regression analysis

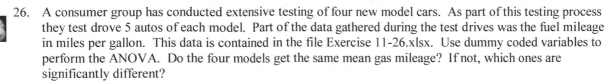

26.   A consumer group has conducted extensive testing of four new model cars. As part of this testing process they test drove 5 autos of each model. Part of the data gathered during the test drives was the fuel mileage in miles per gallon. This data is contained in the file Exercise 11-26.xlsx. Use dummy coded variables to perform the ANOVA. Do the four models get the same mean gas mileage? If not, which ones are significantly different?

27.   An airline that operates shuttle services between several cities is concerned about complaints of customers that planes have to wait for takeoff because of the slowness of baggage handling operations in getting baggage loaded on the planes. The chief operating officer orders a study of baggage loading times at the airports in Boston, New York, and Washington D.C. The loading times in minutes for 8 randomly selected flights at each airport are contained in the file Exercise 11-27.xlsx. Use dummy coded variables to conduct the analysis. Is there any evidence of differences in loading times for the three airports? Which airports should they be concerned about?

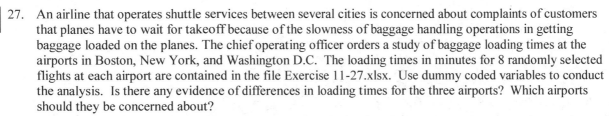

28.   A pharmaceutical company has developed five types of treatments for a new hormone designed to enhance growth in livestock. The five types were tested on 25 animals, and the weight gains contained in the file Exercise 11-28.xlsx were reported (lb./week). Using dummy coded variables and multiple regression test whether the mean gain is equal across all treatments, using a .01 level of significance.

Opening Vignette Revisited

Since Bill believes that his sales are primarily determined by the three factors of temperature, advertising and time spent on the street, he decides to gather data to test this. He has gone back through his records for the pasts two years and found sales data for the day after he placed either radio or newspaper ads. He noted the amount spent for advertising and using online data from the local newspaper he was able to find the high temperature for those days.. Since he always kept meticulous records of his time spent on the job, he was also able to determine the amount of time he spent out on the streets during those days. The data are contained in the file Vignette 11.xlsx. Bill first runs a regression analysis to see how much of the variability in sales can be predicted from the amount of advertising the day before, the daily high temperature and the amount of time he spends out driving his truck around town. The basic results are shown in Figure 11-26. Bill sees that the overall model is statistically significant and predicts almost 75% of the variability in sales. From the results of the regression coefficients, he observes that all three predictor variables are statistically significant with p-values well below .05. The standardized regression coefficients indicate that Hours worked is the most important predictor of sales. In this case, this interpretation makes sense, but requires caution since it depends on the predictor variables being uncorrelated.

Bill is somewhat concerned about how well the assumptions of regression analysis were satisfied in his data; therefore, he examined all of the plots of predicted and residuals versus the three independent variables. The plots did not show any patterns that indicated problems with the assumptions. The residual plot versus Hours, as shown in Figure 11-27, is typical of the pattern. Bill checks the variance inflation factors, presented in Figure 11-26, and concludes that multicollinearity is not an issue for this data since all of the values are very close to 1.

Figure 11-26   *Multiple Regression Results for Sales*

Regression Analysis for Sales

Summary Measures

Multiple R	0.8902
R-Square	0.7924
Adj R-Square	0.7654
Std Error of Est.	10.1223

ANOVA Table

Effect	SS	DF	MS	F	P-value
Regression	8,997.0849	3	2,999.0283	29.2698	0.0000
Residual	2,356.6115	23	102.4614		
Total	11,353.6964	26	436.6806		

Regression Coefficients

Effect	Coefficient	Beta	Std Error	t-value	p-value	VIF
Constant	-22.6947		53.2166	-0.4265	0.6737	
Temp	2.1099	0.3282	0.7674	2.7493	0.0114	1.5788
Hours	8.0098	0.7335	1.0545	7.5961	0.0000	1.0333
$Ads	0.3833	0.3944	0.1169	3.2797	0.0033	1.6020

Figure 11-27   *Plot of Residuals Versus Hours*

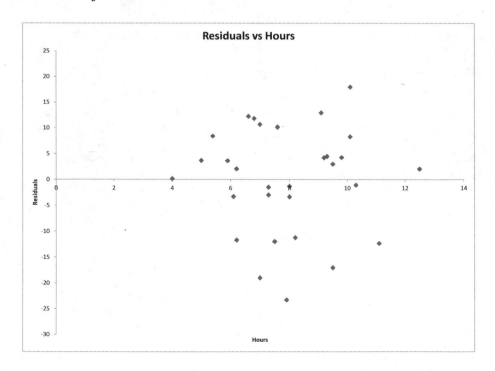

As one final check, Bill examines standardized residuals and the influence factors to check for outliers and unusual values in the data. These values are shown in Figure 11-28 for the 30 observations. Bill first calculates the influence value criteria using Equation 11-10:

$$\frac{2(k+1)}{n} = \frac{2(3+1)}{30} = .2667$$

Bill then examines the influence values in Figure 11-28 and finds that the fourth and twenty-third observations have influence values greater than the criterion (.2667). He also notes that the third observation has a standardized residual slightly less than -2. Just to be safe, Bill performs the regression analysis again with these three observations omitted. The results shown in Figure 11-29 are similar to the original results; consequently, Bill is confident that those three observations did not skew the results.

Figure 11-28   Residuals and Influence Values

Observation	Predicted	Residuals	Influence	Std.Residuals
1	221.1284	2.0716	0.2345	0.2196
2	242.6084	4.4616	0.1215	0.4415
3	262.3735	-23.2735	0.1049	-2.2815
4	245.3123	3.6677	0.3031	0.4075
5	227.5390	-3.2990	0.0774	-0.3186
6	235.5748	-1.3148	0.0916	-0.1279
7	262.4749	-2.9749	0.1329	-0.2963
8	245.7710	11.8290	0.0792	1.1433
9	232.5427	-1.4827	0.0689	-0.1425
10	256.2389	3.0011	0.0746	0.2893
11	252.9225	-3.3325	0.0531	-0.3176
12	226.4402	-11.7002	0.0840	-1.1339
13	266.1388	-16.9988	0.0808	-1.6445
14	248.2892	-1.0792	0.1545	-0.1089
15	249.8962	4.2638	0.1073	0.4185
16	285.0364	2.0336	0.2471	0.2174
17	224.6324	-11.9924	0.1599	-1.2135
18	233.7758	10.6642	0.0836	1.0332
19	270.2332	17.9668	0.1044	1.7608
20	253.3098	12.9502	0.0468	1.2302
21	251.6011	4.2189	0.0571	0.4030
22	210.8902	0.1498	0.2624	0.0162
23	221.1410	3.6190	0.4220	0.4415
24	259.6170	8.2830	0.0758	0.7991
25	251.7179	-12.3279	0.1797	-1.2624
26	226.0253	8.4047	0.0992	0.8213
27	252.6191	10.1609	0.0509	0.9673
28	253.0653	-18.9753	0.0766	-1.8315
29	266.2167	12.2533	0.2338	1.2983
30	265.5578	-11.2478	0.1323	-1.1199

Figure 11-29   Regression Analysis with Three Observations Omitted

Regression Analysis for Sales

Summary Measures

Multiple R	0.890189099
R-Square	0.792436631
Adj R-Square	0.765363149
Std Error of Est.	10.12232031

ANOVA Table

Effect	SS	DF	MS	F	P-value
Regression	8,997.0849	3.0000	2,999.0283	29.2698	0.0000
Residual	2,356.6115	23.0000	102.4614		
Total	11,353.6964	26.0000	436.6806		

Regression Coefficients

Effect	Coefficient	Beta	Std Error	t-value	p-value
Constant	-22.6947		53.2166	-0.4265	0.6737
Temp	2.1099	0.3282	0.7674	2.7493	0.0114
Hours	8.0098	0.7335	1.0545	7.5961	0.0000
$Ads	0.3833	0.3944	0.1169	3.2797	0.0033

Summary

The concepts of linear regression are extended to include multiple independent variables in the regression equation. Using multiple independent variables can improve predictions about the dependent variable by explaining some of the variation from using only one independent variable. The population regression equation is represented as $Y = \alpha + \beta_1 X_1 + \beta_2 X_2 + . \beta_n X_n + \varepsilon$. The sample regression equation, $\hat{Y} = a + b_1 X_1 + b_2 X_2 + …….. + b_n X_k$ is derived by fitting a hyperplane to the set of sample data points.

Similar to simple linear regression, the regression coefficients can be interpreted as the change in the dependent variable Y for a unit change in the independent variable, but with the additional stipulation that the other independent variables remain constant. With multiple independent variables we can examine the relative importance of the different independent variables using the standardized regression coefficients provided that the independent variables are not highly correlated.

Multiple regression has summary measures of model fit similar to simple linear regression. The standard error of the estimate and the coefficient of multiple determination are interpreted in much the same way as simple regression, but take into account the multidimensional model space of multiple regression.

The assumptions of multiple regression closely parallel those of simple regression. Since the solution process is more complex than simple regression, computers can perform all calculations of multiple regression. In addition to calculating the multiple coefficient of determination (R^2) XLDataAnalyst and the Data Analysis Toolpak also calculate a multiple correlation (R) which is the square root of the multiple coefficient of determination and is always positive even if some of the regression coefficients are negative. An adjusted R^2 is also calculated which adjusts the multiple coefficient of determination for sample size and the number of independent variables.

The standard error of the estimate can calculate approximate confidence and prediction intervals. Calculation of the corrected intervals is quite complex and best left to statistical software.

The statistical significance of the overall fit of model can be tested using the F-test of the ANOVA table produced by XLDataAnalyst. The standard error of the estimate along with the multiple correlation (R) , coefficient of multiple determination (R^2) and the Adjusted R^2 are calculated automatically. The null hypothesis that the population coefficient of determination (ρ^2) is equal to zero is tested with an F-test in an ANOVA table. This is also a test that all of the population regression coefficients (β_i) equal zero. Rejecting the null hypothesis indicates that at least one of the population regression coefficients is significantly different from zero. XLDataAnalysst also conducts t-tests for the individual regression coefficients. The sample regression coefficients (along with their standard errors) also provided by XLDataAnalyst can be used to compute confidence intervals for the population regression coefficients.

Diagnostics are necessary to test the reasonableness of the assumptions underlying the regression analysis. Much of the diagnostics tests revolve around the regression residuals, the difference between the actual values and the predicted values of the dependent variable; $(Y-\hat{Y})$. Plots of the residuals versus the predicted values, and plots of residuals versus the separate independent variables can ensure that the assumptions are met. In addition, standardized residuals and influence values can detect outliers or unusual values in the data that might have an undue influence on the results.

Multicollinearity is a problem for multiple regression and exists when some of the independent variables are highly correlated. Multicollinearity impacts the magnitude of the regression coefficients and makes their highly unreliable although it does not affect the ability to use the regression equation to make predictions. Besides examining the correlation matrix for the independent variables, variance inflation factors can diagnose multicollinearity.

Nominal variables can be used in multiple regression through the proper coding of the variables. Dummy coding involves creating dummy variables, coded as 0 or 1 to indicate group membership. One group forms a reference or base for comparison and the regression coefficients represent the difference between the mean of the relevant group and the mean of the base or reference group. In this way, analysis of variance (ANOVA) can be conducted using multiple regression techniques.

In many situations, an analyst may have a number of independent variables that may be related to a particular dependent variable. The goal is to pick the set of independent or predictor variables that best predict the value of the dependent variable. This can be done using either stepwise regression techniques or best subsets regression. Stepwise regression involves systematically adding or removing one independent variable at a time to the model until no further improvement in the fit of the model is possible. Best subsets regression considers all possible combinations of independent variables in terms of a particular measure of fit, usually R^2. The combination with the best fit is picked as the "best" model. There is debate among statisticians about the use of either approach to model development.

Although multiple regression is too advanced for Excel functions, the Data Analysis Toolpak can be used to perform the analysis. XLDataAnalyst can be used to perform the analysis and incorporates the fundamental diagnostic procedures as well.

Chapter Glossary

Hyperplanes	A plane in three or more dimensions used to fit a regression model for multiple independent variables.
Sample Regression Coefficients	Regression coefficients derived from sample data.
Unstandardized Regression Coefficients	Regression coefficients in the original units of the independent variable.
Standardized Regression Coefficients	Regression coefficients that have been converted to standard scores.

Coefficient of Multiple Determination	Percentage of variability in the dependent variable that can be explained by the model.
Multicollinearity	When some independent variables in a regression model are highly correlated with each other. Causes problems in interpreting the regression coefficients.
Variance Inflation Factors	Indicators used to detect multicollinearity problems.

Questions and Problems

29. Discuss the effect of the dummy variable in a regression equation.

30. Distinguish between forward, backward, and stepwise selection procedures in determining the best predictor variables.

31. The American Dream reality company wants to develop a regression equation that they can use to predict the market value of a house. They have gathered data from a random sample of 151 homes that have recently been on the market. The data contains the value of the house (as determined by its' selling price at the time of sale), lot size, square footage, the number of bedrooms and the age of the house. The data are contained in the file Exercise 11-31.xlsx.

   a. Develop a correlation matrix, including all the variables. Do you see any multicollinearity issues with this data set? Is such an issue to be expected in this case? Justify your answer.
   b. Run a multiple regression analysis using the value of the house as the dependent variable and all the remaining variables as the independent variables.
   c. Report the R^2 and interpret it. Test the significance of the multiple coefficient of determination at 0.01 level of significance. State the null and the alternative hypotheses.
   d. Provide the estimated regression equation. Interpret the partial regression coefficients.
   e. Test the significance of each of the independent variables at a 0.01 level of significance. Would you consider deleting any of the variables? Why?
   f. Delete any variable(s) as suggested in part e and re-run the multiple regression. Report the R^2 and interpret it. Test the significance of the multiple coefficient of determination at 0.01 level of significance
   g. Comment on any differences in R^2 computed in part c and f.
   h. Provide the "new" estimated regression equation.
   i. Construct of 99% confidence interval for the regression coefficient for "square footage."

The following questions use the data contained in the file World Wellbeing.xlsx. Gallup has developed metrics of "wellbeing" of the world's population (http://www.gallup.com/poll/126965/gallup-global-wellbeing.aspx). Based on a survey of residents in all countries of the world, they estimate the percentage of residents of a country that are "thriving," "struggling," and "suffering." The Thriving, Struggling, and Suffering indexes measure respondents' perceptions of life satisfaction both now and in the future. Respondents are asked to rate their present and future lives on a "ladder" scale with steps numbered from 0 to 10, where "0" indicates the worst possible life and "10" the best possible life. Individuals who rate their current lives a "7" or higher and their future an "8" or higher are considered thriving. Individuals are suffering if they report their current and future lives as a "4" or lower. All other individuals are considered struggling. Gallup also calculates and index of daily wellbeing using items measuring daily experiences (feeling well-rested, being treated with respect, smiling/laughter, learning/interest, enjoyment, physical pain, worry, sadness, stress, and anger). From these measures Gallup computes a daily wellbeing index. The percentage of residents in each category (thriving, struggling, and suffering) along with the daily wellbeing index for a sample of 154 countries are contained in the file World Wellbeing.xlsx. The file also contains information from the CIA World Factbook (https://www.cia.gov/library/publications/the-world-factbook/geos/ag.html) on several measures for those same countries. The additional data is on per capita DP, an index on sanitary conditions (0 to 100), percent of the population living in poverty, population literacy rate, percent of population living in urban areas, per capita health expenditures, and the inflation rate.

32. Develop a correlation matrix for the following variables: Percent of population suffering (Suffering), per capita GDP (GDP), Sanitary index (Sanitary), the percent of the population living in poverty (Poverty), the percent living in urban areas (Urban), and the inflation rate (Inflation).

   (a) Which correlations are statistically significant?

   (b) Develop a regression equation predicting Suffering using the other variables as predictors. Is there any evidence of multicollinearity?

   (c) Drop variables that you feel should be dropped from the equation and develop a final model predicting suffering. Justify your decisions to drop the variables and interpret the final regression coefficients.

33. Develop an equation predicting the daily wellbeing index (Daily) using the other variables. Justify your decisions regarding which variables to include in the model.

34. Using best subsets regression, develop a mode to predict Suffering and another to predict Thriving. How are the two models similar and how are they different?

35. Develop dummy coded variables for region of the world (Asia, Africa, Europe or Americas). Using these dummy coded variables does "suffering" differ among the different regions of the world? Which differences are statistically significant?

36. The file Exercise 11-36 contains data from undergraduate students enrolled in a business s class at a private university. The file contains information on gender, height, weight, number of siblings, whether the student attended a private or public high school, their high school GPA, their SAT score, and their college GPA at this point in time. Develop a regression equation predicting college GPA from gender, high school GPA, and SAT score. Which variables are statistically significant? Interpret the regression coefficient for gender.

The following exercises are repeated from Chapter 9. In these exercises, rather than using ANOVA, perform the calculations using dummy variables and regression analysis

37. Jim Alverez is a financial planner who specializes in clients that are nearing retirement age. A new client wants to invest a major portion of his savings in mutual funds but is unsure which one to invest in. The client obviously wants to get high returns on his money, but is also concerned about the risks involved. Through his research, Jim has narrowed the choices down to four funds: Unigaard, Blumberg, Garbergs, and Wagners. Jim compiles the average annual returns from the four funds from the ten most recent years in the file Exercise 11-37xlsx. Is there evidence that one fund has a higher median return than other funds? Which fund appears to be the best? Are there any differences in the variability of returns for the four different funds?

38. Bob, the VP of Operations at Intermountain Telephone knows that a consistent response time to repair problems is very important to customers. Bob has gathered data on response times to problems from four different repair locations. The data are contained in File Exercise 11-38xlsx. Is there evidence that the variability of response times is different at the four different repair locations, at the .05 level of significance?

Database Problems

Corporate Statistical Database

39. Develop a correlation matrix of sales (Sales), exports as a percent of sales (Exports), price per share ($PerShare), and number of employees (NumEmp). Which correlations are statistically significant? Are the significant relationships positive or negative?

40. Develop a regression equation predicting price per share ($PerShare) from years of operation (Years), annual sales (Sales), and number of employees (NumEmp).

    (a) Interpret all regression coefficients.

    (b) Which variables are significant predictors of price per share?

    (c) Predict the price per share for a company that has been in business for 25 years, has sales of $800 million, and has 4,000 employees.

41. Develop a regression equation predicting annual sales (Sales) using exports as a percent of sales (Exp), average annual salaries of employees (AvgSalary), and number of employees (NumEmp)

    (a) Interpret all regression coefficients.

    (b) Which variables are significant predictors of annual sales?

    (c) Predict the annual sales for a company that exports 20% (Exp), has 5,000 employees with an average salary of $30,000.

42. Use dummy coding, conduct an analysis of variance of annual dividends (Div$) by industry code. Which industries are significantly different? Interpret the regression coefficients for the significant differences.

MegaCorp Employee Survey Database

43. Develop a correlation matrix using the following variables: salary, age, years at the company, marital **status, gender, and education. Do you see any potential problems with multicollinearity? Would you** expect such issues to arise in this case?

44. The Union that represents most of the hourly labor for MegaCorp has accused the company of discrimination with regards to seniority, gender, and marital status. The VP of Human Resources would like to know if there is a relationship between the years at the company, age, gender, marital status and the current salary. Combining widow with the single category, run a multiple regression analysis, using the current salary as the dependent variable and the years at the company, age, gender, and marital status as the independent variables.

    (a) Report R^2 and interpret it. Test the significance of the relationship at a 0.01 level of significance.

    (b) Provide the estimated regression equation(s).

    (c) What salary would be predicted for a worker with 10 years of seniority, male, married, and 40 years old?

    (d) On average, how much is each additional year of seniority worth in terms of salary? Is it statistically significant?

    (e) On average, how much more do male employees make compared to female employees in terms of salary? Is the difference statistically significant?

(f)   Illustrate graphically the impact of the dummy variable, gender, on the dependent variable, salary.

(g)   Construct a 99% confidence interval for the coefficient of "age" variable and interpret it.

45.   For the situation in problem 39

(a)   Perform a backward regression analysis to determine the best predictor variables.

(b)   Perform a forward regression analysis to determine the best predictor variables.

46.   Perform a regression analysis predicting overall satisfaction with benefits using age, number of years employed at MegaCorp, gender, and current salary.

(a)   How much of the variability in satisfaction can we predict using this model?

(b)   Which regression coefficients are statistically significant?

(c)   Do there appear to be any problems with multicollinearity?

Alaska Sport Fishing Survey

47.   Develop a correlation matrix between the variables number of trips in the last five years (Trips), amount of money spent (Money), age (hint: use year born to calculate age), gender (Gender), and household income (Income).

(a)   Which correlations are statistically significant?

(b)   Would you anticipate multicollinearity problems using these variables as independent variables in a regression analysis?

48.   Develop a regression equation predicting the amount of money spent (Money) from age (hint: use year born to calculate age), and gender.

(a)   Interpret the regression coefficients. What is the implication of the coefficient for gender?

(b)   What is the predicted amount that would be spent by a 45 year female?

49.   Develop a correlation matrix of all of the variables in the data.

(a)   Is there another variable that might help predict the amount of money spent in Exercise 48?

(b)   Enter the variable that you selected in to the regression analysis. Does it increase the predictability of the model? Is it worth keeping in the model?

Chapter 12

Analysis and Forecasting of Time Series Data

Opening Vignette Revisited
Summary
Questions and Problems

Chapter 12 Learning Objectives

When you finish this chapter you should be able to:

1. **Describe the classical components of a time series.**
2. **Compute average, trend and seasonal values.**
3. **Develop forecasts from time-related data.**
4. **Compute simple and composite index numbers.**

Opening Vignette

Jim Belmore is the owner of a local frozen yogurt franchise of the Frozen Delight chain. One of the concerns that keeps Jim awake at night (there are many) is trying to predict how various flavors will sell in his store so that he can keep the proper amounts of each in stock to avoid disappointing any of his customers, or worse, losing them to his competitor, Almost Gelato, down the street. Jim has been keeping records of monthly sales of each of his top-selling flavors for the past three years but is not sure what to do with the data.

Concepts

Introduction

This chapter deals with a common problem in business: extracting information from time series data. This information is often used to forecast future events; but, it is also used for planning purposes in a variety of areas. By *time series* data, we mean simply data that has been gathered at equally spaced intervals over a period of time. The data gathering intervals can be hourly, daily, weekly, monthly or any other common period of time. In this chapter, we will look at techniques to extract information from such data that will enable us to make better forecasts of the future and consequently make better decisions.

In addition, we will discuss the use of index numbers. Index numbers track changes in a value relative to a fixed base period. The changes are typically recorded over time, relative to a base point in time; however, index numbers can also be derived in other situations where time is not involved. For example, a purchasing power parity index compares the amount of money required to purchase a common basket of goods and services in different countries to calculate an implicit exchange rate; however, we will focus on time-based index numbers. Index numbers are commonly used in finance and economics and some of them, such as the Dow Jones Industrial Average or the Consumer Price Index, are widely quoted in the popular press and most people in the U.S. have at least a rudimentary knowledge of these indices.

Exploring Time Series Data

Time series data measures a variable over equally spaced time periods. The data depicts the changes in that variable over time. The primary purpose of analyzing time series data is to be able to predict or forecast the value of the variable in future time periods. An example will help illustrate the basics of time series data.

Example 12-1

J&G Distributors sells various beverages over a three county area in northern Indiana. Bud Gillis, the VP of Finance, feels that sales and revenues have been increasing over the years, but he does not have a firm idea of how to forecast future revenues for intermediate and long range planning. Bud has collected revenue data by quarter over the past six years. This data is contained in the file Example 12-1.xlsx. Figure 12-1 shows a graph, created in Excel, of the revenue data.

Figure 12-1   ***Revenue by Quarter Over the Past Six Years***

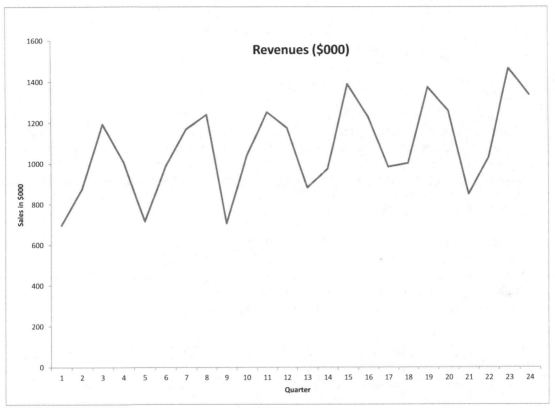

As can be seen in Figure 12-1, there can be considerable variability in time series data. The key to analyzing such data is to try and isolate the systematic portion of the variability from the random variability. We can then use these systematic components to predict what will happen in the future. The basic premise of forecasting using time series data is that what happened in the past will continue into the future. Discussion of these systematic components and how to estimate them comprises the bulk of this chapter.

Components of Time Series Data

There are common components present in time series data. Some components are always present in time series data and others may or may not be present in a given set of data. Isolating the values of these components is central to understanding the data and being able to forecast future values for the series.

Average

Every time series has an underlying average value which may change over time. Therefore, reference to the *average* value is time specific, e.g., the average at this particular time. This component is present in any time series data.

Trend

Trend is often described as the long-term growth or decline of a time series over time. In other words, it is a change in the average value for the time series. Trend can be positive, indicating that data is moving in an upward direction, or negative, indicating that data is moving in a downward direction. The data in Figure 12-1 display a slight positive trend. Trend may or may not be present in any given time series.

Seasonal

Seasonal effects are systematic recurring patterns that repeat after a certain number of time periods. The number of periods before the pattern repeats itself is called the *seasonal cycle*. The seasonal cycle is always one year or less. Sometimes the seasonal cycle can be one week or even one day. Common seasonal cycles are 12 or 4 for annual cycles or 5, 6, or 7 for weekly cycles. Seasonal effects can even be part of a daily cycle, as in the restaurant industry. Not all time series data contain seasonal effects. The data in Figure 12-1 exhibit very pronounced seasonal effects with the low point occurring in the first period of the cycle and the high point occurring in the third period.

Cyclical

Economists often talk about business cycles when describing the variation of economic data over time. This long-term wave like pattern of economic data takes place over several years and is used to describe economic phenomena such as inflation and recession along with other changes in the monetary and financial sectors. Cyclical variation differs from seasonal fluctuations in that:

- Cyclical variation occurs in cycles much longer than one year while seasonal variations always have a duration of one year or less.
- Seasonal effects are of the same magnitude from one cycle to the next while cyclical variation generally differs in amplitude from one cycle to the next.
- Seasonal effects are systematic and predictable while cyclical variations are seldom predictable in advance, but can only be discerned after the fact.

Since cyclical variability is seldom predictable in advance, it is of little value in forecasting and will not be discussed further in this chapter.

Irregular (Error)

Irregular or error variability is the result of many small causes that are unpredictable. Such variability is random in nature. Every set of time series data has irregular (or error) variability.

Isolating the systematic (average, trend, and seasonal) effects of a time series from the irregular or error variability is important because it allows us to better understand the forces at work in creating variability in the data and because it allows us to make more systematic forecasts of future events using the estimates of these systematic drivers of the data. The components can be combined additively,

$$Y_t = A_t + T_t + S_t + I_t \qquad\qquad (12\text{-}1)$$

or multiplicatively,

$$Y_t = A_t \cdot T_t \cdot S_t \cdot I_t \qquad\qquad (12\text{-}2)$$

where Y_t is the predicted or forecast value of the time series at time t, A_t is the underlying average level at time period t, T_t is the trend at time period t, S_t is the appropriate seasonal effect for time period t, and I_t represents irregular or random error at time period t.

Logically, a model could also be a mixture of additive and multiplicative components. For example, a perfectly appropriate model might be:

$$Y_t = [(A_t + T_t) \cdot S_t] + I_t$$

Specifying a model for a given set of time series data involves identifying which components are present in the data, in particular trend and seasonal effects, along with specifying how they should be combined to produce the overall pattern of data over time.

Examining Autocorrelations

Sometimes, an examination of autocorrelations in the data can give an indication of whether trend or seasonal effects might be present in the data. *Autocorrelations* are the correlations between values of a time series at different points in time[1]. For example, a one period autocorrelation would be the correlation of each of the values in the time series with the values one time period later in the time series. An *autocorrelation plot* or *correlogram* is a graph of the autocorrelations at different time lags usually including a 95% confidence interval centered on a correlation of zero. Recall that a trend is the period-by-period increase in the average value. Therefore, if there is a trend in the data, we should expect a correlation between successive elements of the time series. In other words, we would expect a significant one period autocorrelation. If there are seasonal effects, the seasonal cycle should be reflected in the autocorrelations. For example, if the data are quarterly and if there is a seasonal effect, then values four periods apart should be positively correlated. A correlogram for Example 12-1 produced by XLDataAnalyst is shown in Figure 12-2. The autocorrelations are represented as dark lines emanating from the straight line at a correlation of zero. Six time lags are used in the calculations here. Figure 12-2 shows that two of the autocorrelations (lags of 2 and 4) exceed the limits of the 95% confidence interval for a correlation of zero. The t-statistics for the autocorrelations are shown in Figure 12-3. The p-values for the autocorrelations of lags 2 and 4 are less than the .05 level of significance. The autocorrelations for other time lags are not statistically significant.

---

[1] We will not make a distinction between the terms autocorrelation and serial correlation. Serial correlation is most often used in the context of regression analysis and is where we will use the term in this text.

Figure 12-2   *Correlogram for the Data from Example 12-1*

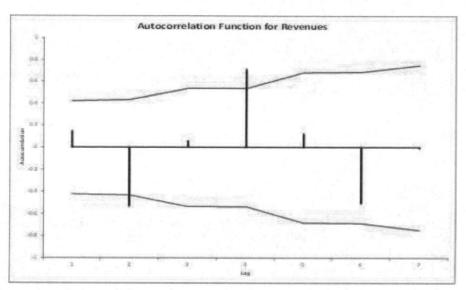

Figure 12-3   *Autocorrelations and Significance Values for Example 12-1*

Autocorrelation Function for Revenues

Lag	Autocorrelation	t	p-value	Q	p-value
1	0.1464	0.7172	0.4802	0.5814	0.4458
2	-0.5303	-2.5441	0.0178	8.5586	0.0139
3	0.0566	0.2189	0.8286	8.6538	0.0343
4	0.7082	2.7329	0.0116	24.3025	0.0001
5	0.1214	0.3678	0.7162	24.7866	0.0002
6	-0.5032	-1.5159	0.1426	33.5644	0.0000

Since we noted seasonal effect in Figure 12-1, the significant positive autocorrelation for a lag of 4 periods is to be expected; however, we also noted a slight trend to the data which should show up as a significant 1 period autocorrelation. We can see from Figures 12-2 and 12-3 that this does not happen. The reason for this is that the seasonal effects "swamp" the trend effects in the autocorrelation pattern. If the seasonal effects are very pronounced, then they can easily mask the trend effects in the correlogram. We will return to the discussion of autocorrelation later in this chapter and we will see that autocorrelations can be quite useful in developing forecasting models based on time series data.

Forecast Errors and Model Fit

When we fit a model to time series data or use the model to predict future events, there will always be discrepancies between the predictions of the model and what actually occurs. These *forecast errors* need to be taken into account when determining how well a given model fits the data and should be monitored when implementing a forecasting system to make sure that it is working properly.

Measures of Error

At the simplest level, forecast error at any time period t is computed as:

Error
$$e_t = Y_t - F_t \qquad\qquad (12\text{-}3)$$

where Y_t is the actual value observed at time period t and F_t is the forecast or predicted value at time period t. Another term sometimes used for errors is *residuals*. As in regression analysis, the residual is the difference between what is actually observed and what has been predicted. These forecast errors or residuals can be summarized in different ways to produce a measure of model fit and allow monitoring of the forecasting system. There are several common measures of forecast error. One such measure is the *average error*. The average error is simply:

Average Error
$$\bar{e} = \frac{\sum_{t=1}^{n}(Y_t - F_t)}{n} \qquad\qquad (12\text{-}4)$$

Average error is most useful in monitoring an existing forecasting system rather than as a measure of how well a model fits the data. One reason it is less useful for model fitting is that the average error is by definition equal to zero for some models. For example, with regression-based methods discussed later, the forecast errors are the residuals in regression terminology and the sum of the residuals is always zero in a regression model. However, as a monitor of an ongoing forecasting system, the average error can be used to detect if the forecast has a systematic bias, e.g., if the errors are consistently negative or positive. If there is no bias, the positive and negative errors should balance out and the average error should be close to zero; however, if the forecast has a bias, the average error will increase in a negative or positive direction since the positive and negative deviations will not balance each other out.

One way to avoid the problem of the average error being forced to zero in some models is to look at the average of the absolute forecast errors. This measure is called the *mean absolute deviation* or MAD and is defined as:

Mean Absolute Deviation
$$\text{MAD} = \frac{\sum_{t=1}^{n}|Y_t - F_t|}{n} \qquad\qquad (12\text{-}5)$$

Since we sum the absolute value of the errors, the MAD will always be a positive value and will only be zero in the unlikely event that all of the forecasts are perfectly accurate.

Another way of avoiding the zero average error problem is to square the errors before averaging them. Since the squaring process also eliminates negative values, this always results in a positive value. This measure is called the *mean square error* or MSE and is defined as:

Mean Square Error
$$\text{MSE} = \frac{\sum_{t=1}^{n}(Y_t - F_t)^2}{n} \qquad\qquad (12\text{-}6)$$

The concept of a mean square error which was introduced in the analysis of variance (ANOVA) and revisited in regression analysis is really just the variance of the forecast errors. The mean square error also has more desirable mathematical properties and is a better statistical measure than the mean absolute deviation. However, the squaring process means that the mean square error will be quite large and will always be larger than the mean absolute deviation except when all of the errors are zero. In particular, the mean square error severely penalizes large errors. Therefore, as a practical matter, the choice of MAD or MSE as a measure of error comes down to the consequences of forecast error. If large errors can have disastrous consequences we will want a model that minimizes the mean square error. On the other hand, if a few large forecast errors do not have terribly serious consequences, we may want a model that minimizes the mean absolute deviation.

Since the mean square error is simply a variance, another natural measure of error would be to take the square root of the variance to obtain the standard deviation, σ:

Standard Deviation $\qquad$ $\sigma = \sqrt{MSE} = \sqrt{\dfrac{\sum_{t=1}^{n}(Y_t - F_t)^2}{n}}$ $\qquad$ (12-7)

An advantage of the standard deviation is, like the MAD, it is in the same units of the original data unlike the MSE which is in squared units.

A popular measure of forecast error which takes into account the magnitude of the error relative to the values being predicted is the *mean absolute percentage error* or MAPE. The MAPE is defined as:

Mean Absolute Percentage Error $\qquad$ $\text{MAPE} = \dfrac{\sum_{t=1}^{n}\left|\dfrac{Y_t - F_t}{Y_t}\right|}{n}$ $\qquad$ (12-8)

The MAPE is an especially popular measure of error when comparing different models. It is especially important when comparing models for different time series where the magnitude of the numbers is quite different.

Example 12-2

Bob Jones is the owner and manager of the Heavenly Bean Espresso stand. Bob orders coffee beans once a week and has to predict what gross sales will be in units to estimate the amount of coffee he will need. Up to now Bob has been basing his forecasts on the previous week's sales and his "gut feeling" about how good next week's sales will be. He has kept track of his forecasts and the actual sales over the past 12 weeks and that information is contained in Table 12-1. Bob uses the data to calculate the various error measures as shown in Table 12-1.

Table 12-1 Calculations of Error Measures for Example 12-2

Week	Unit Sales	Forecast	Error	Absolute Error	Square Error	Absolute Percent Error
1	852	800	52	52	2,704	.061
2	962	850	112	112	12,544	.116
3	978	1,000	-22	22	484	.022
4	832	850	-18	18	324	.022
5	835	850	-15	15	225	.018
6	1,079	850	229	229	52,441	.212
7	871	1,000	-129	129	16,641	.148
8	1,116	900	216	216	46,656	.194
9	770	950	-180	180	32,400	.234
10	1,101	850	251	251	63,001	.228
11	923	1,000	-77	77	5,929	.083
12	951	1,000	-49	49	2,401	.052
Averages	$\bar{Y} = 939.167$	$\bar{F} = 908.333$	$\bar{e} = 30.833$	MAD = 112.50	MSE=19,645.83	MAPE = 0.116

The standard deviation of the forecast errors is the square root of the MSE or 140.16.

Model Fit

There is no absolute standard against which one can assess the quality of a model or forecasting system. Rather, one normally has to compare different models in terms of their error measures. The assumption is that a model that fits the available current data the best will be the most useful in forecasting future events; however, there is no guarantee that this will be the case. There are two procedures that can be used independently of other models to assess the quality of fit.

Using a Validation Sample

Sometimes models provide a good fit to the data used to develop the model but perform poorly in predicting future observations. This is called *overfitting* which means the model conforms too closely to the idiosyncrasies of the data used to fit the model. One way to get a better idea of how well a model will perform with future data is to hold out part of the data from the model fitting process and then see how well the fitted model performs in predicting the values in the hold out sample. The hold out sample is called a *validation sample*. We will have more to say about validation samples later in the chapter.

Examining Autocorrelations

If the model that has been fit to the data includes all of the components present in the time series and provides adequate estimates of their values, the only component that should remain in the time series should be the irregular or random component. Another way of stating this is that the residuals, the value left after subtracting out the model predictions, should be random in nature and there should be no systematic components in these residuals. One way of determining whether or not the residuals are random in nature is by looking at the autocorrelations. If the only variability left in the residuals is random, then all of the autocorrelations for different time lags should be zero statistically.

Tracking Forecast Errors

The prudent forecaster will closely monitor the forecasting system once implemented to ensure that the system is working properly and that nothing has changed in the environment which will cause changes in the time series data. Most formal monitoring systems make use of some measure of forecast error in combination with a measure of forecast variability. For example, a simple monitoring system might just use the forecast error each time period along with a measure of forecast error to set limits on the forecast error. As long as the forecast error is within these limits, the process is deemed to be operating correctly without problems. A forecast error outside these limits would be an automatic signal that there may be a problem with the system. If we assume that the forecast errors are random and normally distributed when the system is operating properly, we could use two standard deviations as the limits since we know from a normal distribution that 95% of the observations should be within plus or minus two standard deviations. Taking the square root of the mean square error gives us the standard deviation of the forecast errors so that the monitoring limits would be:

$$\pm 2\sqrt{MSE}$$

In Example 12-2, the limits would be ± 2(140.16) or ±280.32. As long as forecast errors are between -280.32 and +280.32, the system would be considered to be operating properly. If we observe an error outside these limits we may need to revise our forecasting model by incorporating additional components such as trend or at the very least recalibrate our model in some way.

Exercises I

1. Describe the components of a time series. Describe how each component can be identified in a graph of the time series data.

2. What is an autocorrelation? How are the components of the time series reflected in the autocorrelations for the data?

3. What is meant by time series data? What is the key to using time series data to predict future values?

4. The following table shows the marriage and divorce rates (number per 100,000 in population) in the United States from 1980 to 2009. The data are also contained in the file Exercise 12-4.xlsx. Using Excel, graph the two time series. What can you conclude about any trends in the data?

Year	Marriage Rate	Divorce Rate	Year	Marriage Rate	Divorce Rate
1980	10.60	5.20	1995	8.90	4.40
1981	10.60	5.30	1996	8.80	4.30
1982	10.80	5.10	1997	8.90	4.30
1983	10.50	5.00	1998	8.40	4.20
1984	10.50	4.90	1999	8.60	4.10
1985	10.20	5.00	2000	8.50	4.20
1986	10.00	4.80	2001	8.40	4.00
1987	9.90	4.80	2002	7.80	4.00
1988	9.70	4.80	2003	7.50	3.80
1989	9.70	4.70	2004	7.80	3.70
1990	9.80	4.70	2005	7.50	3.60
1991	9.40	4.70	2006	7.60	3.60
1992	9.20	4.80	2007	7.40	3.70
1993	9.00	4.60	2008	7.30	3.60
1994	9.10	4.60	2009	6.80	3.53

Source: U.S. Dept. of Health and Human Services, National Center for Health Statistics. Web: www.cdc.gov/nchs/.

5. The table below shows the annual vehicle production (both cars and commercial) for the top five countries over the past 10 years. The data are also contained in the file Exercise 12-5.xlsx. Graph the data using Excel. What can you conclude about world automobile production over this time span? Are there any "unusual" data points?

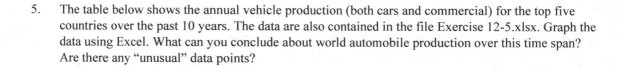
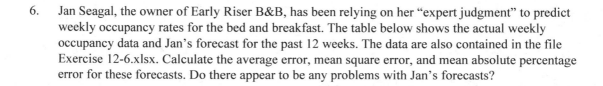

Country	2002	2003	2004	2005	2006	2007	2008	2009	2010	2011
China	3,286,804	4,443,686	5,234,496	5,708,421	7,188,708	8,882,456	9,299,180	13,790,994	18,264,761	18,264,667
United States	12,279,582	12,114,971	11,989,387	11,946,653	11,263,986	10,780,729	8,693,541	5,731,397	7,762,544	8,653,560
Japan	10,257,315	10,286,218	10,511,518	10,799,659	11,484,233	11,596,327	11,575,644	7,934,057	9,628,920	8,398,654
Germany	5,469,309	5,506,629	5,569,954	5,757,710	5,819,614	6,213,460	6,045,730	5,209,857	5,905,985	6,311,318
South Korea	3,147,584	3,177,870	3,469,464	3,699,350	3,840,102	4,086,308	3,826,682	3,512,926	4,271,741	4,657,094

Source: International Organization of Motor Vehicle Manufacturers (OICA). Web: http://oica.net/

6. Jan Seagal, the owner of Early Riser B&B, has been relying on her "expert judgment" to predict weekly occupancy rates for the bed and breakfast. The table below shows the actual weekly occupancy data and Jan's forecast for the past 12 weeks. The data are also contained in the file Exercise 12-6.xlsx. Calculate the average error, mean square error, and mean absolute percentage error for these forecasts. Do there appear to be any problems with Jan's forecasts?

Occupancy	Forecast
16	14
17	18
17	16
11	12
20	17
18	16
9	11
16	15
15	12
15	14
12	12
20	18

7. Matt Riley operates a small retail shop that sells sports cards and memorabilia. In the past, Matt has tried to predict the next week's sales by assuming that they would be the same as the previous week's sales. Sales in dollars for the past 20 weeks are shown in the table below. The data are also contained in the file Exercise 12-7.xlsx. Implement Matt's forecasting scheme in an Excel spreadsheet and calculate average error, mean square error, and mean absolute percentage error for this forecasting method. Comment on the quality of Matt's forecasting method.

Week	Sales
1	1146.63
2	1268.60
3	1377.92
4	1379.34
5	1317.39
6	933.37
7	1397.36
8	1652.69
9	1488.44
10	1357.74
11	1434.37
12	1015.41
13	1356.62
14	1323.43
15	1390.14
16	1515.19
17	1674.94
18	1492.51
19	1659.23
20	1171.62

8. Quarterly earnings per share for the Molson Coors Brewing Company over approximately 5 years are shown in the table below. The data are also contained in the file Exercise 12-8.xlsx. The correlogram and the autocorrelations are also shown. Based on these results, comment on the evidence for possible trend and seasonal effects in this time series data.

Year	Quarter	EPS
2007	4	0.92
2008	1	0.19
	2	0.42
	3	0.92
	4	0.51
2009	1	0.41
	2	1.01
	3	1.26
	4	1.19
2010	1	0.56
	2	1.27
	3	1.37
	4	0.58
2011	1	0.44
	2	1.18
	3	1.06
	4	0.95
2012	1	0.44
	2	0.57

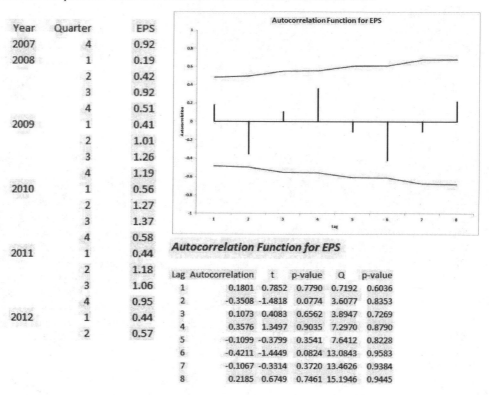

Autocorrelation Function for EPS

Lag	Autocorrelation	t	p-value	Q	p-value
1	0.1801	0.7852	0.7790	0.7192	0.6036
2	-0.3508	-1.4818	0.0774	3.6077	0.8353
3	0.1073	0.4083	0.6562	3.8947	0.7269
4	0.3576	1.3497	0.9035	7.2970	0.8790
5	-0.1099	-0.3799	0.3541	7.6412	0.8228
6	-0.4211	-1.4449	0.0824	13.0843	0.9583
7	-0.1067	-0.3314	0.3720	13.4626	0.9384
8	0.2185	0.6749	0.7461	15.1946	0.9445

Estimating an Average Value: Smoothing Random Variation

The most basic systematic component of any time series is the underlying average value. If this is the only component of the time series, the only task is to filter out the random error from the time series to isolate the underlying average value. This can be done either using a moving average approach or via exponential smoothing.

Moving Average

A *moving average* is an average value that changes over time to incorporate the latest information available. Each moving average value includes a fixed number of observations (k) in the calculations of the average. In other words, the moving average at any time period t is the average of the k most recent observations in the time series, or:

Moving Average
$$A_t = \frac{\sum_{i=t-k+1}^{t} Y_i}{n}$$
(12-9)

For a four period moving average, for example, the estimate of the average value would be the average of the four most recent observations.

Example 12-3

To illustrate the calculations, we will use the first three years (12 quarters) of revenue data from Example 12-1. This data, as shown in Table 12-2, will be used to calculate a four period moving average. Since we need four values to calculate an average, the moving average cannot be calculated until after period 4 when we have four observations. The first average is the average of the values (697, 876, 1193, and 1008) which is 943.5. The moving average for period 5 is the average of the four most recent periods or the average of (876, 1193, 1008, and 718) or 948.75. The other values in the moving average column are calculated similarly as shown in Table 12-2.

Table 12-2   Calculations of the Moving Average for Example 12-3

Quarter	Revenue	Moving Average	Forecast	Error	Abs Error	Squared Error	Percent Error
1	697						
2	876						
3	1193						
4	1008	943.5					
5	718	948.75	943.5	-225.5	225.5	50850.25	0.314
6	991	977.5	948.75	42.5	42.5	1785.063	0.043
7	1170	971.75	977.5	192.5	192.5	37056.25	0.166
8	1241	1030.33	971.75	269.25	269.25	72495.56	0.217
9	707	1027.25	1030.33	-323	323	104329	0.457
10	1041	1039.75	1027.25	13.75	13.75	189.0625	0.013
11	1253	1060.5	1039.75	213.25	213.25	45475.56	0.170
12	1176	1044.25	1060.5	115.5	115.5	13340.25	0.098
Averages				$\bar{e} = 37.25$	MAD = 174.38	MSE = 40690.13	MAPE = 0.185

Since the only component of our time series at this point is the average value, our forecast for the next time period will be equal to the current estimate of the average or:

$$F_{t+1} = A_t \qquad (12\text{-}10)$$

The column labeled Forecast contains the forecast value for each time period. The following columns calculate the forecast error or residual, the absolute error and the squared error from which we can calculate the average error (e), the mean absolute deviation (MAD), the mean square error (MSE), and the mean absolute percentage error (MAPE).

Exponential Smoothing

Exponential smoothing is a very popular approach to estimating components of time series data in businesses. The logic of the approach is based on a common sense notion that the most recent data in a time series is more indicative of what is likely to happen in the future than older data. Therefore, the most recent data should have greater weight in calculating the estimates and that the weight of the data items should decrease with age. The equation for estimating the average in a time series is:

Smoothed Average $\qquad A_t = A_{t-1} + \alpha(Y_t - A_{t-1}) \qquad (12\text{-}11)$

Alpha (α) is called the *smoothing coefficient* and is a value between zero and one, i.e. a percentage. One way of understanding Equation 12-11 is that the updated estimate of the average (A_t) is the old estimate of the average (A_{t-1}) plus a percentage of the difference between the actual value at time period t (Y_t) and the old estimate (A_{t-1}). The relationship can be expressed as:

$$\text{New estimate} = \text{Old Estimate} + \%(\text{Actual value} - \text{Old Estimate})$$ (12-12)

We will call the relationship in Equation 12-12 the fundamental equation for exponential smoothing. As we will see later, exponential smoothing uses the same approach to revising estimates for any component of the time series.

As with the moving average, since the only component assumed here is the average component, the forecast for the next time period is the updated estimate of the average, as in Equation 12-10. Therefore, another way of understanding Equation 12-11 is that A_{t-1} is the forecast for time period t and the term $(Y_t - A_{t-1})$ in the equation is really the forecast error or residual for time period t Therefore, the new average, and consequently the forecast for the next time period, is the old forecast adjusted by a percentage of the forecast error. If our previous forecast was too low (the forecast error is positive), the new forecast will be adjusted upward. If the previous forecast was too high (the forecast error is negative), the new forecast will be revised downward.

In order to begin using Equation 12-11 we need two values: a value for the smoothing coefficient α and a value for the average at time period zero (A_o), to use in revising the average in the first period of the time series. Normally, A_0 is simply set to the value in the first period so that there is no forecast error in the first period and the revision begins with the second period data. The choice of a smoothing coefficient is more complex and will be examined in more detail shortly. For now, to keep the arithmetic easier, we will set the smoothing coefficient to 0.10. The calculations for the first three years data of Example 12-3 are shown in Table 12-3. As with the moving average, the forecast for each time period is the previous period's estimate of the average (Equation 12-10).

Table 12-3   *Calculations of Exponential Smoothing for Example 12-3*

Quarter	Revenue	Average	Forecast	Error	Abs Error	Squared Error	Percent Error
1	697	697					
2	876	714.9	697	179	179	32041	0.204
3	1193	762.71	714.9	478.1	478.1	228579.61	0.401
4	1008	787.24	762.71	245.29	245.29	60167.18	0.243
5	718	780.32	787.24	-69.24	69.24	4794.04	0.096
6	991	801.38	780.32	210.68	210.68	44388.13	0.213
7	1170	838.25	801.38	368.62	368.62	135878.06	0.315
8	1241	878.52	838.25	402.75	402.75	162211.4	0.325
9	707	861.37	878.52	-171.52	171.52	29419.35	0.243
10	1041	879.33	861.37	179.63	179.63	32267.43	0.173
11	1253	916.7	879.33	373.67	373.67	139627.94	0.298
12	1176	942.63	916.7	259.3	259.3	67237.22	0.220
Averages				$\bar{e} = 223.3$	MAD = 267.07	MSE = 76977.95	MAPE = 0.235

Equation 12-11 illustrates very well the principles of exponential smoothing, but it does not give us insight into the weighting aspects of the model. As stated earlier, exponential smoothing is based on weighing the most recent data the heaviest with the weight of the data decreasing as the data gets older. Another version of the equation helps illustrate this aspect of the model. Equation 12-11 can also be written as:

$$A_t = \alpha Y_t + (1 - \alpha)A_{t-1}$$ (12-13)

However, the term A_{t-1} can also be written using Equation 12-13; therefore, we can expand this to:

$$A_t = \alpha Y_t + (1 - \alpha)[\alpha Y_{t-1} + (1 - \alpha)A_{t-2}]$$

$$A_t = \alpha Y_t + \alpha(1 - \alpha)Y_{t-1} + (1 - \alpha)^2 A_{t-2}$$

But, then A_{t-2} can also be written in the form of Equation 12-13, so we can continue to expand this to:

$$A_t = \alpha Y_t + \alpha(1-\alpha)Y_{t-1} + \alpha(1-\alpha)^2 Y_{t-2} + \alpha(1-\alpha)^3 Y_{t-3} \dots\dots$$

The title exponential smoothing refers to the exponent for $(1-\alpha)$ which increases as the data gets older. However, since α is a percentage, this means that the weight decreases, as the data gets older. The relative weighting of the recent versus past data depends on the value for the smoothing coefficient, α. The smaller the value of α, the more "smoothing" is applied to the fluctuations in the time series and the less the estimate responds to these fluctuations. In other words, for small values of α, the past data is weighed more heavily relative to the new data. On the other hand, for large values of α, the recent data is weighed very heavily and less weight is given to older data. This means that the revised estimate will respond more quickly to fluctuations or changes in the time series pattern. This tradeoff is illustrated in Table 12-4 for smoothing coefficients of 0.1 and 0.8.

Table 12-4   ***Illustration of Weighting in Exponential Smoothing***

Period	Weight	$\alpha = .1$	$\alpha = .8$
t	α	.1000	.8000
t-1	$\alpha(1-\alpha)$	.0900	.1600
t-2	$\alpha(1-\alpha)^2$	.0810	.0320
t-3	$\alpha(1-\alpha)^3$	.0729	.0064
t-4	$\alpha(1-\alpha)^4$	.0656	.0013
t-5	$\alpha(1-\alpha)^5$	.0590	.0003
t-6	$\alpha(1-\alpha)^6$	.0531	.0001
t-7	$\alpha(1-\alpha)^7$	.0478	.0000
t-8	$\alpha(1-\alpha)^8$	.0430	.0000
t-9	$\alpha(1-\alpha)^9$	.0387	.0000

For both smoothing coefficients, the weight decreases as the data gets older; however the weight decreases much faster for the .8 coefficient than it does for a coefficient of .1. There is a fundamental tradeoff involved with selecting a value for the smoothing coefficient. The smaller the smoothing coefficient, the more the forecasts will smooth out fluctuations in the data. If these fluctuations are just random fluctuations, then this is a good thing. The converse of this is that the system will also be slow to respond when things change in the environment. For example, if an upward trend develops in the time series, a small smoothing coefficient would make the system slow to respond to this change. A large smoothing coefficient, on the other hand will respond quickly to changes in the environment, but it will also respond more to random fluctuations which increases the MAD and MSE. There is no right or wrong answer to this dilemma; however, by tradition, most practitioners choose to use small smoothing coefficients in normal circumstances while utilizing monitoring systems to detect changes in the environment.

Exercises II

9. Explain how increasing or decreasing the smoothing coefficient α impacts the forecasts of the exponential smoothing model.

10. A friend has discovered that you are learning about time series forecasting models and asks you to explain to him how exponential smoothing models work in general. How do you respond?

11. For the data in Exercise 6, use Excel to model a three-period moving average forecast. Calculate the average error, mean square error, and mean absolute percentage error for the resulting forecasts. How do these values compare with the results of Jan's subjective forecasts in Exercise 6?

12. For the data in Exercise 7, use Excel to calculate an exponential smoothing model with a smoothing coefficient of 0.1. Calculate the average error, mean square error, and mean absolute percentage error for the resulting forecasts. How do these values compare with the results of Matt's forecasting technique in Exercise 7?

13. Sarah Kennedy, the Executive Director of the Almira County Counseling Center, has been having difficulty scheduling adequate staff for the growing demand for the Center's services. She has gone back through the records of the past 20 weeks and recorded the number of clients served each week. The results are shown in the table below and are also contained in the file Exercise 12-13.xlsx. Develop a system for Sarah that will track the average weekly demand and allow forecasts for the upcoming week. Justify your use of the particular method you have chosen.

Week	Clients
1	67
2	76
3	55
4	72
5	81
6	85
7	63
8	44
9	50
10	65
11	57
12	81
13	39
14	76
15	88
16	46
17	76
18	65
19	60
20	68

Estimating Trend

In our discussion of the components of time series data, we described trend as the long-term growth or decline of a time series over time. More technically, trend is a real change in the average value of the time series over time. In this sense, trend is a systematic part of the time series and does not reflect mere random fluctuations. If a trend exists in the time series, we will want to derive an estimate of that trend and include it in our forecasting system to reduce forecast error. There are two primary ways of estimating trend in time series data. One is an extension of the exponential smoothing models discussed in the last section. A second method is using the familiar regression techniques of Chapter 10 on time series data.

Exponential Smoothing Methods

Trend can also be estimated using the smoothing principle expressed in Equation 12-12 that the new estimate is the old estimate plus a percentage of the difference between the actual value and the old estimate. Expressed as an equation:

Smoothed Trend $$T_t = T_{t-1} + \beta[(A_t - A_{t-1}) - T_{t-1}]$$ *(12-14)*

where T represents the trend estimate and β is a smoothing coefficient for the trend just like α which is used for the average. Recall that trend is the change in the average value so that $A_t - A_{t-1}$ represent the actual trend and Equation 12-14 follows the basic logic of exponential smoothing. Notice that estimating trend in this way requires that we also estimate the average. However, the equation for the average requires some revision to reflect that we also have a trend component. The equation for the average is:

Smoothed Average $$A_t = A_{t-1} + T_{t-1} + \alpha[Y_t - (A_{t-1} + T_{t-1})]$$ *(12-15)*

If you compare Equation 12-15 with Equation 12-11, you will notice that the only difference is that the old average used in the forecast now includes the trend since our model now predicts that the average will increase from one time period to the next by an amount equal to the trend (T). Equations 12-14 and 12-15 taken together are known as the *Holt Model* in the forecasting literature. Since our model now includes a trend as well as an average, our equation used to forecast into the future is:

Forecast with Trend $$F_{t+k} = A_t + kT_t$$ *(12-16)*

where k is the number of periods into the future we are forecasting. For one period into the future the forecast would be simply the average plus the trend: $A_t + T_t$.

Although the computations are becoming a little more complex, we can still easily perform them using Excel. To perform the calculations with trend we first need to specify a beginning value of trend (T_0) and a value for the smoothing coefficient β. Normally, the beginning Trend is set to 0, indicating no trend at first. The tradeoffs in setting β are the same as those involved with setting α and the usual practice is to use a small value for β as well. Here to simplify the calculations we will use .10 for both α and β. The calculations for Example 12-3 are illustrated in Table 12-5.

Table 12-5   ***Calculations of Exponential Smoothing with Trend for Example 12-3***

	Revenue	Average	Trend	Forecast	Error	Abs Error	Squared Error	Percent Error
1	697	697	0					
2	876	714.9	1.79	697	179	179	32041	0.204
3	1193	764.32	6.55	716.69	476.31	476.31	226871.22	0.399
4	1008	794.59	8.92	770.87	237.13	237.13	56,228.6900	0.235
5	718	794.96	8.07	803.51	-85.51	85.51	7,312.1400	0.119
6	991	821.83	9.95	803.03	187.97	187.97	35,333.02	0.190
7	1170	865.60	13.33	831.78	338.22	338.22	114,396.00	0.289
8	1241	915.148	16.95	878.93	362.07	362.07	131,095.47	0.292
9	707	909.58	14.70	932.09	-225.09	225.09	50,664.58	0.318
10	1041	935.95	15.87	924.28	116.72	116.72	13,623.52	0.112
11	1253	981.94	18.88	951.82	301.18	301.18	90,709.16	0.240
12	1176	1,018.34	20.63	1,000.82	175.18	175.18	30,688.60	0.149
Averages					$\bar{e} = 171.93$	MAD = 223.70	MSE = 65746.95	MAPE = 0.212

Our final estimate of the average revenue is 1,018.34 and the final estimate of the trend is 20.63. We can use these values to predict future revenues. The forecast revenues for the next time period would be

1,018.34 + 20.63 or 1,038.97. We would predict that two periods from now the revenues should be 1,018.34 + (2)20.63 or 1,059.60.

If you compare these results with those of the model that only included the average value, you will see that the error measures are improved when the trend is included. To reduce the errors further we will have to include a third component for seasonal effects which we will do in a later section of this chapter.

Regression Based Methods

As an alternative to exponential smoothing we can use regression techniques to fit a curve to the set of points in the time series data. The simplest curve that can be fit to time series data is a straight line. This type of curve assumes that the trend is a constant number of units over time. However, not all trends consist of a constant number of units. For example, interest on financial instruments is typically calculated as a constant percentage over time. This means that the amount of the trend in units may change over time. Such trends are called nonlinear trends. We will focus mostly on linear trends in this chapter but will also briefly discuss how to estimate nonlinear trends.

Linear Trends

Fitting a linear trend to time series data involves the same basic principles of simple regression discussed in Chapter 10 using the time periods as the independent or predictor variable. The trend is then represented by the slope of the regression line. Analogous to the equation for a straight line in Chapter 10, we can write the time series regression as:

Forecast for Linear Trend $F_t = a + bt$ *(12-17)*

The predicted value of the time series at any particular time (F_t) is equal to the Y-intercept (a) plus the time period (t) multiplied by the slope (b). The Y-intercept is the value of the time series at time period zero and is analogous to the beginning average value (A_0) in the exponential smoothing models. The slope is the trend of the time series, i.e., the change in the average value per time period.

The easiest way to derive a linear trend equation for a set of time series data is to use the charting capabilities in Excel which are covered later in this chapter. Figure 12-4 was produced using the data from Example 12-3 and the Scatter Plot option. The Trendline option in the Analysis section of the chart Layout tab was used to insert a linear trend line into the chart and the additional trendline options were used to put the equation into the figure. As you can see from the figure, there is a slight upward trend to the data with a slope of 27.41. If you compare this value to the final estimate of the trend using exponential smoothing, you will see that the trend here is nearly twice as large as the estimate using exponential smoothing. This is partly because of the small smoothing coefficient used for the trend in that example.

Figure 12-4　　　　*Linear Trend Line for Example 12-3*

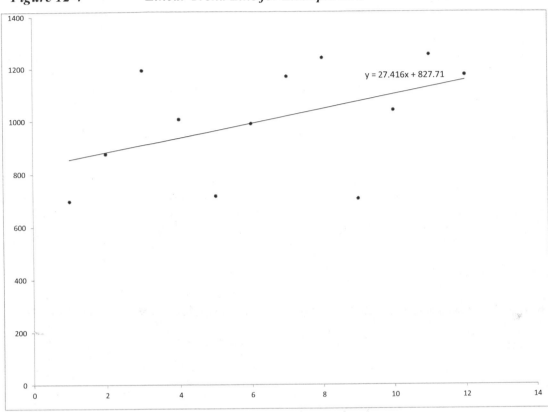

We can use the equation for our trend line to calculate the forecast values and errors as we did with the other models. The results are shown in Table 12-6.

Table 12-6　　　　*Error Calculations Using the Linear Trend Model for Example 12-3*

Quarter	Revenue	Forecast	Error	Abs Error	Squared Error	Percent Error
1	697	855.12	-158.12	158.12	25001.93	0.227
2	876	882.53	-6.53	6.53	42.64	0.007
3	1193	909.94	283.06	283.06	80122.96	0.237
4	1008	937.35	70.65	70.65	4991.42	0.070
5	718	964.76	-246.76	246.76	60890.50	0.344
6	991	992.17	-1.17	1.17	1.37	0.001
7	1170	1019.58	150.42	150.42	22626.18	0.129
8	1241	1046.99	194.01	194.01	37639.88	0.156
9	707	1074.40	-367.40	367.40	134982.80	0.520
10	1041	1101.81	-60.81	60.81	3697.86	0.058
11	1253	1129.22	123.78	123.78	15321.49	0.099
12	1176	1156.63	19.37	19.37	375.2	0.020
Averages			$\bar{e} = 0.04$	MAD = 140.17	MSE = 32141.18	MAPE = 0.156

If you compare these results with the results of using the exponential smoothing approach in Table 12-6, you will see that the regression approach results in smaller errors than the smoothing approach. This is partly the result of using arbitrary values for the beginning average and the beginning trend in the smoothing models. If we had used more realistic estimates for these values, we would have found smaller errors for the smoothing approach. In fact, some analysts will perform a regression analysis to get the intercept to use for the starting average value in the smoothing model and the slope to estimate the beginning trend. This can significantly improve the results of the smoothing models.

You may also note that the average error in Table 12-6 is very small and near zero. This is not by accident. Linear regression uses the principle of least squares which minimizes the sum of squared residuals or errors as we discussed in Chapter 10. This approach implies that the sum of the residuals will always be zero. The slight nonzero value for the average error in Table 12-6 is because we have rounded off the true values of the intercept and slope. If we had used the actual values, the average error would have been exactly zero. This implies that an average error of zero using the regression approach is not always an indicator of a great fit for the model. It is simply a byproduct of the principle of least squares.

Examining the actual errors in Table 12-6 reveals an interesting pattern. Since these are quarterly data, the annual cycle would be four periods (there are four quarters in a year). Looking at the first year data (Quarters 1 through 4) in Table 12-6, we see that the error is negative in the first two quarters and positive in the last two quarters. We can also see in the table that this pattern is repeated in each of the other two years. This systematic recurring pattern is indicative of seasonal effect in the data. We will discuss this final component of a time series in a later section.

Nonlinear Trend

A linear trend model assumes that the trend represents an increase (decrease) of a constant number of units per time period. However, many time series in business and economics do not increase (or decrease) at a constant rate. We will discuss two types of nonlinear trend.

Exponential Trend

Many values in business and economics, particularly financial data, increase by a constant percentage change rather than a constant number of units. An interest paying savings account is a common example of this. Assuming that you do not withdraw the interest earned on the account, the amount by which the account increases each year changes from year to year, but the percentage change (the interest rate) remains constant. Such a set of data exhibits an exponential trend rather than a linear trend. The exponential trend model can be written as:

Exponential Trend $$Y_t = ae^{bt}$$ (12-18)

As with the linear trend model, the constant (a) represents the value of Y at time period 0, i.e. the Y intercept. The constant (e) is the base of the natural logarithms, and t is the time period. The value (b) represents the percentage change in Y per time period. If b is positive, then the trend is positive and b is the growth rate. If b is negative, then the trend is negative and b represents the rate of decline. An example of an exponential growth trend is shown in Figure 12-5.

Figure 12-5   ***Example of Exponential Trend***

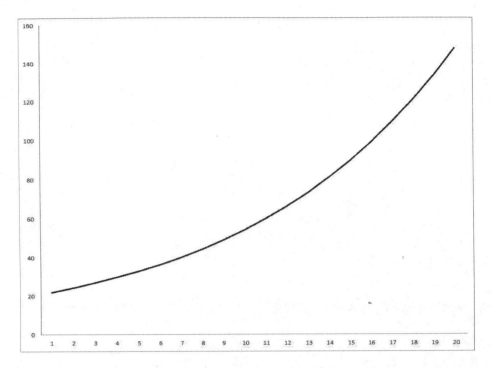

An exponential model can be fit to a set of data by using the Trendline options in the Layout section after creating a scatter plot just as we did for the linear model. Figure 12-6 shows the scatter plot and best fitting exponential model for the Example 12-3 data. You can see in Figure 12-6 that the best fitting exponential curve is nearly linear. The resulting equation shows a constant (a) of 819.27 and a growth rate (b) of .0282 or about 3%. The error calculations for this trend equation are shown in Table 12-7. A comparison of Table 12-7 with Table 12-6 shows very similar results for both linear and nonlinear trend models indicating little evidence of a nonlinear trend, as indicated by the best fitting curve in Figure 12-6.

Figure 12-6   *Scatter Plot and Trend Line for the Exponential Model in Example 12-3*

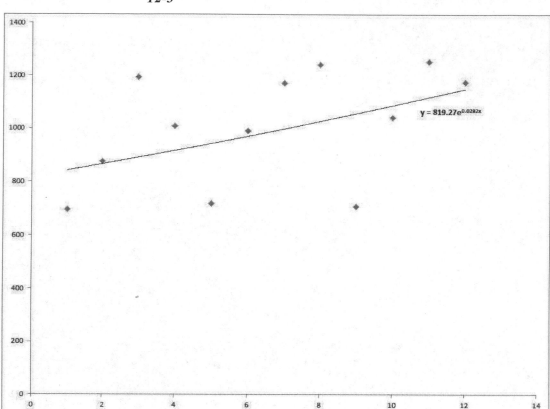

Table 12-7   *Error Calculations Using the Exponential Trend Model for Example 12-3*

Quarter	Revenue	Forecast	Error	Abs Error	Squared Error	Percent Error
1	697	842.70	-145.70	145.70	21228.49	0.209
2	876	866.80	9.20	9.20	84.64	0.011
3	1193	891.60	301.40	301.40	90841.96	0.253
4	1008	917.10	90.92	90.92	8262.81	0.090
5	718	943.33	-225.33	225.33	50773.61	0.314
6	991	970.31	20.69	20.69	428.08	0.021
7	1170	998.06	171.94	171.94	29563.36	0.147
8	1241	1026.61	214.39	214.39	45963.07	0.173
9	707	1055.97	-348.97	348.97	121780.10	0.494
10	1041	1086.17	-45.17	45.17	2040.33	0.043
11	1253	1117.24	135.76	135.76	18430.78	0.108
12	1176	1149.19	26.81	26.81	718.78	0.023
Averages			$\bar{e}$ = 17.16	MAD = 144.69	MSE = 32509.66	MAPE = 0.160

Estimating the parameters a and b for Equation 12-18 can also be done using the linear model on transformed data. Taking the logarithms of both sides of the equation yields:

Logarithmic Version $Log(Y_t) = Log(a) + bLog(t)$ *(12-19)*

This version is in the form of the linear equation $Y = a + bt$ and can be estimated using the same method as for linear trend.

Polynomial Models and Quadratic Trend

Polynomial models are a general class of models with successive terms in the model raised to an increasing power. The general form of the polynomial model is:

Polynomial Model $\qquad Y_t = a + b_1 t + b_2 t^2 + b_3 t^3 + \cdots \ldots b_k t^k$ $\qquad\qquad$ *(12-20)*

A two order polynomial model, sometimes called a quadratic model, can be useful in representing situations where the trend changes over time. The quadratic trend model is written as:

Quadratic Trend $\qquad\qquad\qquad Y_t = a + b_1 t + b_2 t^2$ $\qquad\qquad\qquad$ *(12-21)*

The general trend is either upward or downward depending on the sign of the coefficient b_1. The change in the trend is represented by the coefficient b_2. If b_2 is positive, the trend increases at an increasing rate and the curve looks somewhat like the exponential model. A curve where the trend is increasing but at a decreasing rate, is shown in Figure 12-7.

Figure 12-7 $\qquad\qquad$ **Quadratic Trend with an Increasing Trend at a Decreasing Rate**

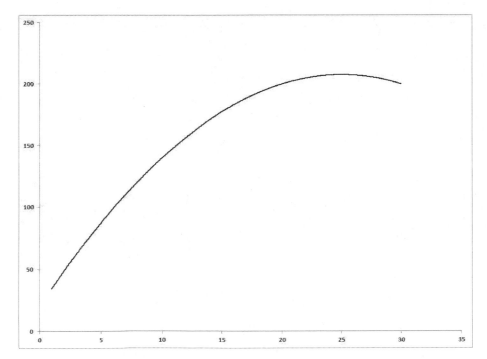

One characteristic of a polynomial model is that it will always have at least one inflection point. An *inflection point* is a point where the curve changes from an upward (downward) direction to a downward (upward) direction. A quadratic or second order polynomial will have exactly 1 inflection point. A third order polynomial will have two inflection points, and so on. In Figure 12-7 the inflection point occurs at time period 25. Up to that point the curve is increasing. After period 25, the curve is a decreasing function of time.

Quadratic and higher order polynomial models can be fit using the Trendline options in a scatter plot in Excel similar to the process used for linear and exponential trends.

Exercises III

14. Discuss the difference between exponential smoothing estimates of trend and regression methods. How do the underlying assumptions about trend differ?

15. Describe how the nature of the trend differs between linear regression, the exponential model and the quadratic model.

16. The table below and the file Exercise 12-16.xlsx contain the annual print advertising expenditures in U.S. Newspapers from 1997 through 2011. Use an exponential smoothing model to estimate the annual trend in newspaper print advertising over this time period. Comment on the implications for the newspaper industry.

Year	Ad Dollars
1997	$41,330.00
1998	$43,925.00
1999	$46,289.00
2000	$48,670.00
2001	$44,305.00
2002	$44,102.00
2003	$44,939.00
2004	$46,703.00
2005	$47,408.00
2006	$46,611.34
2007	$42,209.00
2008	$34,739.52
2009	$24,821.00
2010	$22,795.24
2011	$20,691.80

Source: Newspaper Association of America: http://www.naa.org/Trends-and-Numbers/Advertising-Expenditures/

17. For the data in problem 16, estimate a linear trend and an exponential trend. Which is more appropriate for this data and why?

18. The quarterly Industrial Production Index published by the Federal Reserve Board for the years 2004 through 2008 is shown below and contained in the file Exercise 12-18.xlsx. Fit a quadratic equation to the data. What are the economic implications of these data?

Year	Quarter	IPI
2004	1	91.5899
	2	91.9801
	3	92.4875
	4	93.7987
2005	1	95.1540
	2	95.5847

	3	95.2083
	4	95.9640
2006	1	96.9167
	2	97.5267
	3	97.8902
	4	98.0260
2007	1	99.0075
	2	100.1219
	3	100.3639
	4	100.5067
2008	1	100.2161
	2	98.7166
	3	95.4649
	4	91.4240

Estimating Seasonal Effects

Recall from our discussion of time series components that seasonal effects are systematic recurring patterns that repeat after a certain number of time periods. The number of periods before the pattern repeats itself is called the seasonal cycle. Therefore, the first task is to specify the seasonal cycle, which in most cases is obvious. Seasonal cycles are normally either on an annual, weekly, or daily basis. If it is an annual cycle, then the number of periods in the cycle is based on the given data. If you have monthly data, the cycle is 12 periods; and if you have quarterly data, it is four periods. If the cycle is a weekly cycle, the number of periods in the cycle is usually the number of days worked during the week, either 5, 6, or 7. Daily cycles exist in many service environments especially those based on food or beverages. For example, a restaurant will have daily seasonal patterns based on the three principal eating times, breakfast, lunch, and dinner.

Once the number of periods in the seasonal cycle is determined, we know how many seasonal values we need to estimate since there should be a seasonal estimate for each period of the cycle. We then need to determine how the seasonal component interacts with the other components of the time series, either additively or multiplicatively. An additive seasonal effect is one where the time series value is a constant number of units above or below average. For example, January demand for a product may be 110 units above average. The seasonal effect is the same no matter what the average demand happens to be. A value of 0 would indicate no seasonal effect for a given time period. Most commonly, seasonal effects are assumed to be multiplicative such that the seasonal effect is a percentage of the average demand. For example, January demand is 10% above average. The magnitude of the seasonal effect will then depend on the average level of demand and a value of 1 indicates no seasonal effect for a given time period. We will examine methods to estimate both additive and multiplicative seasonal effects.

There are basically three principal approaches to estimating seasonal effects, although there are variations around each of these methods.

Exponential Smoothing Methods

The exponential smoothing estimates of seasonal effects use the same basic principle set forth in Equation 12-12. However, because of the seasonal cycle and the requirements for a separate seasonal estimate for each period of the cycle, the calculations become difficult even using Excel. We will examine the basic equations to see the logic of the approach, but leave the calculations to the computer.

The process begins by updating an old estimate of the effect. Assuming multiplicative seasonal effects, the equation for the seasonal component is:

$$S_t = S_{t-c} + \gamma(\frac{Y_t}{A_t} - S_{t-c}) \qquad (12\text{-}22)$$

At first glance, this equation may look nothing like the previous equations for exponential smoothing, but on close inspection, it does follow the same basic pattern. To understand this equation, it is necessary to note that seasonal effects are calculated for the part of the seasonal cycle the current time period is in. Therefore, the old estimate of the seasonal effect is not the seasonal effect from the previous time period, but the seasonal effect calculated one cycle ago, or t-c. For example, if the current time period is 13, the seasonal effect to be updated is the one that was updated one year ago (period 1). The smoothing coefficient γ is also a value between 0 and 1 and functions just like the smoothing coefficients α and β for the average and trend. The value (Y_t/A_t) is the actual seasonal effect for this time period since it represents the percentage difference between the actual effect and the currently updated average. This obviously requires that the estimate of the average already be updated for this period. The updated estimate of the average will be calculated using variants of either Equation 12-11 or 12-15 depending on whether or not a trend component is included in the model. Equation 12-23 is used for a model without trend and Equation 12-24 is used for a model that includes trend:

$$A_t = A_{t-1} + \alpha(\frac{Y_t}{S_{t-c}} - A_{t-1}) \qquad (12\text{-}23)$$

$$A_t = A_{t-1} + \alpha[\frac{Y_t}{S_{t-c}} - (A_{t-1} + T_{t-1})] \qquad (12\text{-}24)$$

The only change from the previous equations for updating the average is that the actual value in time period t (Y_t) is first deseasonalized before calculating the updated average. According to our model, the actual value in a time period is the predicted value multiplied by the seasonal estimate. Since multiplication includes the seasonal effect, to remove the seasonal effect (*deseasonalize* the data) we divide the actual value by the seasonal effect.

Using seasonal effects in the exponential smoothing model requires that we specify a value for the smoothing coefficient γ as well as initial values for each of the seasonal effects in the seasonal cycle. If no estimates are available for the seasonal effects we simply follow the practice established for the trend and specify no seasonal effects which implies that each seasonal effect is initially set to 1.0.

The forecast value for the future depends on whether or not a trend effect is included with the seasonal effect. If trend is included along with the seasonal effects, the resulting model is called the *Winters Model*. The resulting forecast for future time period (t+k) would be:

$$F_{t+k} = (A_t + kT_t)S_{t+k-c} \qquad (12\text{-}25)$$

If no trend is included, the forecast for any future time period would be:

$$F_{t+k} = A_t S_{t+k-c} \qquad (12\text{-}26)$$

Note that in each case, the appropriate value for that period in the seasonal cycle must be used for the seasonal value.

Since seasonal values are updated only once in each seasonal cycle, estimating seasonal effects requires more data than other models. As a rule of thumb, we should have at least three values to estimate a seasonal effect which means that we should have at least three cycles worth of data. For data on an annual cycle, that means we should have at least three years of data before estimating seasonal effects. Obviously the more data we have the better the estimates will be.

Although unusual, additive seasonal effects can also be estimated using exponential smoothing. The only modification is to replace division by subtraction. For example, Equation 12-22 would become:

$$S_t = S_{t-c} + \gamma[(Y_t - A_t) - S_{t-c}]$$

Equations 12-23 and 12-24 would be adjusted accordingly. Then, the forecasts would be:

$$F_{t+k} = A_t + kT_t + S_{t+k-c}$$

Regression Based Methods

Seasonal effects can also be estimated using regression analysis using dummy variables as described in Chapter 11. Recall that dummy variables are used to represent groups or qualitative characteristics. In the present context, the groups are the different periods of the seasonal cycle. It takes $k-1$ dummy variables to represent k groups. Therefore, quarterly data would require 3 dummy variables to represent the four quarters and monthly data would take 11 dummy variables to represent the 12 months.

Since multiple regression procedures are extremely difficult to perform by hand, we will reserve illustrations of this procedure until the Practice section of this chapter. One item we do need to note here is that linear regression procedures assume that the seasonal effects are additive in nature. Therefore, they cannot be used directly to estimate multiplicative effects; however, a simple revision of the procedure can be used to estimate multiplicative seasonal effects. Multiplicative models can be estimated with linear regression by transforming the dependent variable by taking logarithms of the values. We will also illustrate this process later in the chapter.

Decomposition Methods

Decomposition methods have a long history in time series analysis and vary from relatively simple procedures to the more complex methods, such as the X-12-ARIMA model used by the Census Bureau[2]. Decomposition methods generally assume a multiplicative model as we will do here. The general logic of the approach is relatively straightforward. In general notation, the multiplicative model assumes that the time series value at time t is:

$$Y_t = T_t S_t I_t \qquad (12\text{-}27)$$

where T_t is the trend, S_t is the appropriate seasonal effect and I_t is the irregular or random component. If we divide the time series values by the trend component we are left with the seasonal and irregular components:

$$\frac{Y_t}{T_t} = \frac{T_t S_t I_t}{T_t} = S_t I_t \qquad (12\text{-}28)$$

If the random or irregular effects can be removed, then only the seasonal component remains. The basic approach is to use some method to smooth out the random variability and then use the ratios of the time series values to the trend to estimate the seasonal effects. The method we will use is relatively straightforward and is called the *ratio to moving average* method. The method begins with a moving

---

[2] A free version of the software is available from the Census Bureau web site for PC's, Macs and Linux.

average of the number of periods in the seasonal cycle. Unlike the moving averages we calculated previously, these averages are then centered in the middle time period of the average rather than at the end of the period. The corresponding time series values in that period are then divided by the moving average, as in Equation 12-28, to estimate the seasonal effect for that period. The values for each period of the seasonal cycle are averaged to produce the estimates of the seasonal effect for that period. An example will help illustrate the method.

Example 12-4

Now that Bob Jones is getting a handle on his weekly forecasts for the Heavenly Bean Espresso stand (See Example 12-2) he realizes that he might be able to adjust staffing levels better if he can more accurately predict his daily sales. Because of an agreement with his wife and kids that he would take weekends off, Heavenly Bean is only open Monday through Friday. It seems to Bob that daily sales fluctuate in a somewhat systematic fashion with Monday, Wednesday and Friday being his best days. He decides to start by seeing if there are indeed systematic seasonal components to his daily sales that he can use to adjust schedules to insure adequate staff for the peak days. Going back to his daily receipts, Bob breaks down the weekly sales figures for the first three weeks into daily sales. The results are shown in Table 12-8.

Since the seasonal cycle is 5 days, Bob starts by calculating the 5-day moving averages beginning with the first week. The first average is the average of the first week's daily sales which is 170.4. He centers this average on the middle of the data which is Wednesday of the first week, as shown in the table. He then calculates the other moving averages for which he has enough data. Note that the last moving average that can be centered is the Wednesday of the last week because any moving average after that would have to extend into next week. After calculating these ratios, he is ready to calculate the seasonal effects by averaging the ratios for each day of the week. The seasonal effect for Monday is the average of the two Monday ratios (1.3115 and 1.1284) to get 1.2199. In other words, Monday sales are about 22% above average. All of the resulting seasonal values are shown in Table 12-9. From this table, we can see that sales are above average on Monday and Wednesday, about average on Friday and slightly below average on Tuesday and Thursday.

Table 12-8   *Daily Sales at Heavenly Beans*

Week	Day	Unit Sales	Moving Average	Ratio to Moving Average
1	M	205		
	T	150		
	W	190	170.4	1.115
	R	142	177.4	0.8005
	F	165	180.4	0.9146
2	M	240	183.0	1.3115
	T	165	187.0	0.8824
	W	203	195.6	1.0378
	R	162	192.6	0.8411
	F	208	196.0	1.0612
3	M	225	199.4	1.1284
	T	182	196.0	0.9256
	W	220	195.6	1.1247
	R	145		
	F	206		

Table 12-9   ***Final Seasonal Effect Estimates[3]***

Day	Seasonal Estimate
M	1.2199
T	0.9055
W	1.0925
R	0.8208
F	0.9879

Exercises IV

19. Compare and contrast the exponential smoothing, regression, and decomposition approaches to estimating seasonal effects. What factors would lead you to pick one approach over the others?

20. Given the following values and their associated moving average estimates, estimate the seasonal effects assuming quarterly effects and an annual cycle. The data are also contained in the file Exercise 12-20.xlsx.

Quarter	Value	Moving Average
1	78	95.13
2	89	96.50
3	121	98.88
4	104	102.13
5	85	104.50
6	108	100.25
7	121	94.88
8	70	93.25
9	76	92.25
10	104	94.63
11	117	99.25
12	93	101.88
13	90	104.13
14	111	103.13
15	128	102.13
16	74	104.50

21. The table below contains the daily sales of a hobby shop open 5 days a week. The table also shows the moving average estimate for each period. The data in this table can also be found in the file Exercise 12-21.xlsx. For this data calculate the estimated seasonal effects for the five days in the seasonal cycle.

Sales	Moving Average
$108.80	102.04
88.29	102.99
70.32	102.62

---

[3] Technically, these estimates need one further adjustment to make sure that they add up to 5. That adjustment is skipped here for simplicity.

104.89	100.44
140.80	96.10
97.89	93.21
66.60	95.35
55.88	95.90
115.56	99.82
143.59	105.76
117.49	107.50
96.26	104.68
64.61	103.07
101.46	99.91
135.55	98.19
101.68	100.85
87.63	99.30
77.93	101.15
93.71	102.55
144.78	95.09

Autocorrelation and Time Series Data

We briefly introduced autocorrelations earlier in this chapter when discussing model fit. Autocorrelation can be used to discern whether certain components are present in a particular time series. Namely, autocorrelation analysis can be used to determine whether or not trend or seasonal effects should be included in a model for a set of data. Autocorrelations are useful for answering three questions about a set of time series data:

- Do the data vary randomly over time?
- Is there a trend in the data?
- Are there seasonal patterns in the data?

Autocorrelation Patterns in Time Series Data

If there is only an average value and random or irregular variation in the time series data, there should not be any systematic pattern to the data. This implies that there should not be any significant autocorrelations in the correlogram. Figure 12-8 shows a correlogram for a set of data that varies randomly around a constant average value[4]. As can be seen in Figure 12-8, the correlations are all rather small and there is no systematic pattern to the correlations.

---

[4] The data for Figure 12-8 is contained in the file Data with only Random Variability.xlsx.

Figure 12-8   ***Correlogram with Only Random Variation***

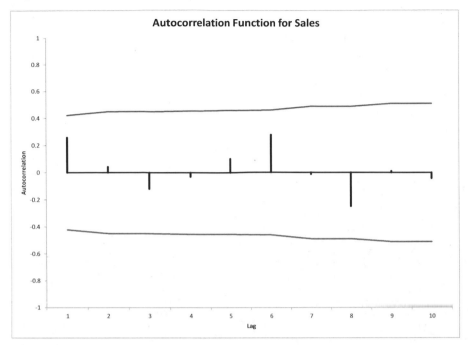

If there is a trend in the data, but no seasonal effects, there should be a strong and statistically significant autocorrelation for a lag of 1 period. There may also be a strong correlation with a lag of two periods, but the magnitude of the correlation should decrease over time. The correlogram shown in Figure 12-9 illustrates the autocorrelations where there is a strong trend in the data, but no seasonal effects[5]. As you can see, the largest correlation is for a lag of 1 period with the correlations decreasing over time. This is a typical pattern where there is a trend in the data.

Figure 12-9   ***Correlogram for Data with Trend but no Seasonal Effects***

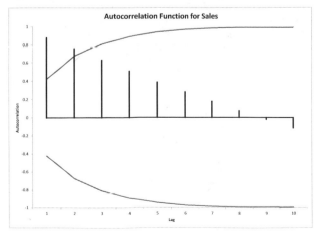

[5] The data for Figure 12-9 is contained in the file Data with Trend Only.xlsx.

The presence of seasonal effects tends to mask the presence of trend in the autocorrelation pattern but does reveal the presence of the seasonal component. To illustrate this, we will go back to Example 12-1 where the revenues revealed a strong seasonal component as well as a trend. The correlogram for this example is shown in Figure 12-10. For seasonal data, one would expect strong positive correlations for lags equal to the seasonal cycle or multiples of it. Since this data is quarterly, we would expect strong positive correlations for lags of 4, 8, 12, etc. As you can see in Figure 12-10, there are indeed strong positive correlations for lags of 4 and 8.

Figure 12-10   **Correlogram for the Example 12-1 Data**

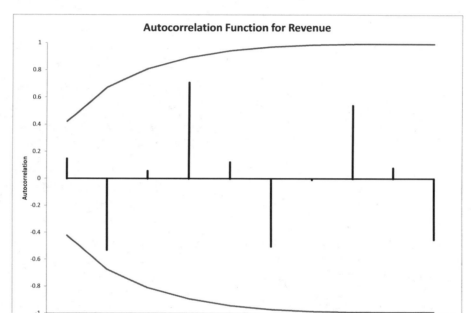

A close examination of Figure 12-1 reveals that there is a lag of two quarters between the peaks or high points and the valleys or low points in the time series because of the seasonal effects. Therefore, we would expect a large negative correlation for lags of 2, 6, and 10 in our data which we indeed see in Figure 12-10.

As noted before, the swings in the correlogram produced by seasonal effects often mask the patterns produced by trend. In Figure 12-8, the trend present in the data does not show in the correlogram because of the peaks and valleys produced by the seasonal effects. Therefore, if seasonal effects are present in a given time series, the time series should be deseasonalized before examining the correlogram for evidence of trend. Deseasonalizing the data means to remove the seasonal effect from the data. If the seasonal component is additive then the seasonal estimate is added or subtracted from the data as appropriate. If the seasonal effect is multiplicative, then the data are deseasonalized by dividing the data values by the appropriate seasonal estimate.

Autocorrelation and Regression Analysis

Chapters 10 and 11 discussed regression models involving a dependent variable Y and one or more independent variables X. One of the formal assumptions of linear regression is particularly problematic when both Y and X are time series data. Standard regression analysis assumes that the prediction errors for any value of Y are independent of the errors for all other values of Y. If there is autocorrelation in the data, this assumption will be violated when predicting Y from X.

Detecting Autocorrelation

A common form of autocorrelation in time series data is called *first-order serial correlation* and is one in which the error term for a time period is correlated with the error term of the previous time period. Usually, this correlation will be positive. This means that if the regression equation tends to under predict the value in one time period (the residual $Y - \hat{Y}$ is positive), it will tend to under predict in the next time period, as well. Conversely, if the equation over predicts in one time period (the residual $Y - \hat{Y}$ is negative), then it will also tend to over predict in the next time period. This type of correlation can lead to spurious correlations between two time series variables and incorrect inferences about the relationships between two variables X and Y. In particular, the correlation between the two variables can be artificially inflated and the standard error terms for the regression coefficients can be seriously underestimated.

A widely used test for first-order serial correlation is the *Durbin-Watson Test (DW Test)*. Since serial correlation relates to the error terms in the regression equation, the Durbin-Watson Test examines the residuals of the regression analysis. Letting e_t represent the residual or error at time period t ($Y_t - \hat{Y}_t$), the Durbin-Watson statistic can be written as:

$$DW = \frac{\sum(e_t - e_{t-1})^2}{\sum e_t^2}$$

(12-29)

The null hypothesis of the DW Test is that the first-order serial autocorrelation (ρ) is equal to zero. Since autocorrelation in time series data is generally positive, this is usually conducted as a one-tailed upper-tailed test.

The DW statistic ranges from 0 to 4. Under the null hypothesis, the statistic should have a value of around 2. If there is significant autocorrelation the value will be closer to 0 (significant negative autocorrelation will produce values closer to 4). A rule of thumb common in the literature is that DW values between 1.5 and 2.5 indicate no significant autocorrelation. The statistical test of this hypothesis is complicated for several reasons. The calculation of the p-value for this test statistic is very complex and does not always converge on a value. Tables have been provided for the test statistic but they show not only rejection and acceptance regions but also zones of indecision. Often the calculated statistic falls in the zone of indecision leaving the analyst in limbo with no p-value to provide guidance.

Although the Durbin-Watson statistic has been the most popular method of examining serial autocorrelation, it has been criticized on a number of fronts besides the difficulties in calculating p-values. The statistic as presented here is not valid if a lagged term is present as an independent variable in the regression equation. There have been modifications of the statistic to fit some of these situations. The statistic is also not appropriate for serial correlations with lags greater than 1 period and assumes that there are no missing values in the data.

An alternative to the DW statistic is the *Breusch-Godfrey Test* (BG), also called the Lagrange Multiplier Test. Like the Durbin-Watson Test, BG focuses on the residuals. However, unlike the DW Test, it has a clear and easily calculated p-value. The basic idea of the test is to use the residuals from the original analysis as the dependent variable in a regression analysis. The independent variables include all of the original independent variables plus as many lags of residuals (p) as considered appropriate. If the sample size is large, then the statistic $(n-p)R^2$ has a chi-square distribution which can be used to calculate p-values. The main drawback is that there is no method for determining the number of lags (p) in advance. Also, the calculation of the p-values requires large samples. Both the DW and BG test statistics can be calculated by XLDataAnalyst and will be discussed in more detail in the Practice section of this chapter.

In addition, the residuals from the regression model can be saved and analyzed using autocorrelation analysis. If the independence assumption is satisfied, then the residuals should not show any significant autocorrelations. A correlogram and the associated test statistics can be used to assess the assumption.

Correcting for Autocorrelation

The question remains, what can be done if significant autocorrelation is present in the data? The answer to this question depends on what causes the autocorrelation. Some common causes of autocorrelation and their correlations are:

1. Relevant independent variables omitted from model. Sometimes, especially with economic data, autocorrelation can occur because a relevant explanatory variable has not been included as an independent variable in the model. Inclusion of that variable may eliminate the autocorrelation.

2. Misspecification of the mathematical form of the model. Specifying a linear model when a nonlinear form is appropriate can introduce autocorrelation in the error terms. Specifying the appropriate form such as exponential or polynomial can solve the problem.

3. Omitting seasonal or other systematic effects from the model. Seasonal effects, if not taken into account in the model, will almost always result in autocorrelation of error terms. Simply adding seasonal effects to the model should eliminate the problem in this case.

4. Errors are truly not random. This might be called true autocorrelation in that external factors such as business cycles, drought, changes in fashion or other factors may introduce correlated errors. In this case, a technique called *differencing* can be used to remove the autocorrelation. Another solution is to use *lag variables* in the regression equation.

Differencing involves transforming variables by taking the difference between the value at time t and the value at another time period. Most often the distance is one period or first order differencing so that each observation is transformed as the value in that period minus the value in the previous time period, $Y_t^* = Y_t - Y_{t-1}$. This creates an obvious problem in the first period observation since generally there is no data from the previous period. If no estimate exists of the previous value, then the first period data must be dropped from the analysis. For a simple regression of time series data where the independent variable is the time period, only the dependent variable needs to be transformed since the differences between the time values are constant. For regression where at least one of the independent variables is something other than time, then both the dependent and independent variables need to be transformed. The revised regression equation then becomes:

$$Y_t^* = a + bX_t^*$$

where $Y_t^* = Y_t - Y_{t-1}$ and $X_t^* = X_t - X_{t-1}$. In plain terms, both the independent and dependent variables are transformed by differencing and then the regression is performed on the transformed variables. The autocorrelations should be examined after this analysis to make sure that the autocorrelation has been removed. Differencing is included as an option in XLDataAnalyst as described later in this chapter.

A second option for removing autocorrelation is to use lagged values for the dependent or independent variables. A lag variable is the simply the original variable offset by one time period. In other words, a lagged independent variable would be calculated as:

$$X_t^* = X_{t-1}.$$

Lagging can be applied to the independent variables, the dependent variable, or both. Some theoretical basis should exist for lagging the chosen variables.

Exercises V

22. Explain the advantage of the Breusch-Godfrey Test over the Durbin-Watson Test.

23. The correlogram below represents the autocorrelations for quarterly sales data. Interpret the correlogram. What components appear to be present in the time series?

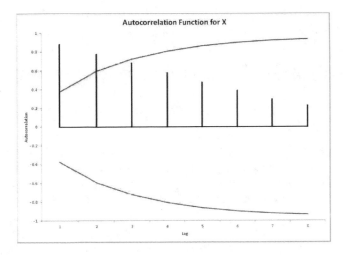

24. The correlogram below represents the autocorrelations for quarterly sales data. Interpret the correlogram. What components appear to be present in the time series?

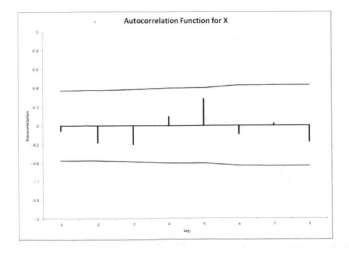

25. The correlogram below represents the autocorrelations for quarterly sales data. Interpret the correlogram. What components appear to be present in the time series?

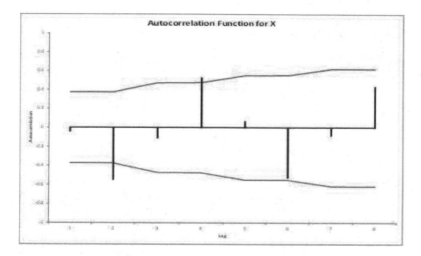

Putting it all Together in a Forecast

In theory, one can calculate the average, trend, and seasonal effects using any of the methods described previously in this chapter and combine them into a forecast. In practice, however, if an analyst uses exponential smoothing for one of the components such as the average, they usually use exponential smoothing for all components. Therefore, if they included a trend model, they would typically use the Holt's model, and when trend and seasonal effects are included, they would use the Winters' Model; however, this is not a logical requirement of any of the models. For example, if an analyst believed that the seasonal effect is an additive one, there is no reason they could not combine an exponential smoothing model such as the Holt's model with additive seasonal effects calculated using regression analysis. More common is the combination of the additive trend computed using linear regression with multiplicative seasonal effects calculated using decomposition methods. The point is that the most important part of forecasting is including all of the relevant components present in the time series, and only those components, and not how the components are estimated. In this section, we will explore some practical matters in deriving a forecasting model from time series data.

Fitting the Model

Fitting the model involves three fundamental issues:

- What components (average, trend, seasonal) are to be included in the model?
- How should we combine the components (additive or multiplicative)?
- How should we estimate these components (exponential smoothing or regression)?

The process of answering these questions involves trial and error using the different methods on the data. How well the model "fits" the data is assessed using the forecasts errors (average error, MAD, MSE and standard deviation, and MAPE) described in an earlier section. There is some redundancy in the measures in that the MAD, MSE and standard deviation are closely related to each other. The average error is useful for assessing the bias of the forecasts. The average error should be about zero. A large positive (negative) value indicates that the model is systematically underestimating (overestimating) the actual value. In the forecasting literature, the MAPE has been the most popular overall error measure to determine how well the model fits the data.

Determining the Components

The average and random or irregular components are implicitly part of any model; however, the trend and seasonal components are optional. At first, it might seem to make sense to include all of the components in a model "just-in-case." In other words, include both trend and seasonal effects just in case they are present in the time series being modeled; however, this is not always a wise strategy. There are consequences of including components in the model that are not present in the data. The consequence is an increased variability in the forecast errors. This is because even though the component may be nonexistent in the population that generates the data, the estimate of that component from the data will not be exactly zero for additive trend or seasonal effects, or one for multiplicative trend or seasonal effects. The model fit to the current data may better predict the current data but will add more variability to the error in forecasting the future. To see this, consider the situation of only an average component and random error in the time series. The projected future values can then be defined by:

$$Y_{t+k} = A_t + \varepsilon$$

where ε represents the random error component and k is the number of periods into the future. If we add a trend component to the model, then the projected future values would become:

$$Y_{t+k} = A_t + T_t + \varepsilon$$

Although we have already stated that there is no trend, it is highly unlikely that the trend estimate (T_t) will be exactly zero. It will likely have some small nonzero value which reflects random error. The effect then will be to add additional error to the future forecasts. Therefore, care should be taken when including components in the model to make sure that they are actually present in the data. Regression analysis, with its accompanying significance tests, can be used to help ensure that there is a real presence of the components in the data.

Additive or Multiplicative Effects

The question of additive versus multiplicative effects has no easy answer. In the forecasting literature, additive trend and multiplicative seasonal effects are the most common assumptions. Sometimes a scatter plot and regression analysis can be used to determine whether the linear assumption of additive trend is appropriate or if a nonlinear model is more appropriate. The R^2 statistic from the regression analysis is a natural measure to assess which type of trend is most appropriate for the current data. Alternatively, different models that use additive or multiplicative effects can be fit to the data and the traditional error measures such as MAD, MSE and MAPE can be used to determine which type of model best fits the data. Ultimately, however, judgment will be called for in determining whether or not the trend is by a constant amount (additive) or by at a constant rate (multiplicative).

Multiplicative seasonal effects are by far the most common assumption; however, the fit of competing models such as the Winters Model which assumes multiplicative seasonal effects and the regression model with dummy variables for additive seasonal effects can be compared to see which fits the data best; however, caution must be exercised when comparing regression model with other types of models such as exponential smoothing. One consequence of the principle of least squares used in fitting a regression model is that the sum of the residuals is always equal to zero. This means that the average error for a regression model will always be equal to zero. Therefore, the average error is not a good measure to use when comparing regression based models with other models. Measures such as the MAD, MSE, standard deviation and MAPE are more appropriate.

Estimating the Components

The principal ways of estimating the average, trend, and seasonal effects discussed in this chapter are moving averages, exponential smoothing and regression for averages and trend, and exponential smoothing, ratio to moving average, and regression analysis for seasonal effects. The choices for seasonal effects can be further narrowed if the question of additive or multiplicative effects has already been answered. If the choice has been made to utilize additive seasonal effects, then regression analysis should be used to estimate those effects. If the choice is to use multiplicative seasonal effects, then the choice comes down to exponential smoothing or the decomposition approach using the ratio to moving averages method.

For trend, the choice is typically between an exponential smoothing or a regression based approach. One consideration is whether or not the trend is believed to be static or not. A static trend would be one that does not change over time. For example, a static additive trend would be for a certain number of units per time period which would not change. Since regression analysis assumes that the trend remains the same throughout the time period of the data, it should only be used in situations where the trend is static. On the other hand, exponential smoothing does not assume a constant trend and is therefore much more suitable for situations where the trend is dynamic or changing in nature.

There is no logical reason why you cannot combine components estimated by different methods into a hybrid model. For example, you could combine seasonal effects estimated using the decomposition approach with a trend model estimated with regression. Or you could use the intercept and slope parameters of a regression analysis as the starting values for the average and trend in a Holt type exponential smoothing model.

Overfitting the Model

Overfitting is said to occur when a model fits the sample data used to fit the model very well but does a poor job of predicting future data. The cause of overfitting is the model adapting to the idiosyncrasies of the sample data rather than to general tendencies. The danger of overfitting goes up as the sample size gets smaller or the number of parameters in the model becomes larger. The usual way of avoiding overfitting is to divide the data into two parts. The first set of data is variously called the warm-up sample, training sample, or fitting sample and is used to estimate the parameters of the model. The second set of data, usually called the validation data, is then used to see how well the fitted model will predict new data using the usual error measures described earlier in this chapter. If the error results in the validation sample are much worse than those in the warm-up or training sample, then we have evidence of overfitting. If overfitting exists, then we may want to go back and revise our model or gather new data.

This use of a warm-up and a validation sample can be used to select the type of model. We have previously suggested using the error measures to select what type of components to use in a model. We can also extend this to what type of model to use, for example, exponential smoothing or regression analysis. But it is still a good idea to use both a warm-up sample and a validation sample because, all things being equal, we should select the method that produces the best results on the validation data rather than the one that best fits the warm-up data since our primary purpose is to predict future data. We will illustrate this use of the validation data in the Practice section when we discuss using XLDataAnalyst on time series data.

Exercises VI

26. The XLDataAnalyst time series analysis section allows the user to specify warm-up and validation periods for the model. Discuss why this is important.

27. A simple exponential smoothing model and a Holt exponential smoothing model including trend are both fit to a set of time series data. The following error measures are obtained. Which model would be the best of the two for this situation? Explain your reasoning.

	Average Error	Standard Deviation	MAPE
Simple Smoothing	48.5533	226.0042	0.1276
Holt Model	0.2063	224.9319	0.1233

28. An analyst is fitting a model to data that clearly have seasonal effects but she is uncertain if the effects are additive or multiplicative. To test this she estimates both a Winters exponential smoothing model that includes multiplicative seasonal effects and a regression model that includes additive seasonal effects. The following results are obtained. Which model would you recommend for the analyst and why?

	R^2	Average Error	Standard Deviation	MAPE
Regression	.9329	0.0	56.1975	-0.0031
Winters		26.6506	159.4249	.1142

29. A friend has argued that when it comes to time series analysis, you should always include all components such as trend or seasonal effects in the model just in case they are present. How do you respond to this?

Index Numbers

Index numbers provide a mechanism for comparing different quantities by measuring them relative to a comparison or base point. For example, it is common to compare different currencies by measuring their value relative to the U.S. dollar. In fact, we have already looked at index numbers when we discussed the concept of seasonal effects. The estimates of seasonal effects are essentially a comparison of the values of the time series relative to an average value.

Since our emphasis in this chapter is on time series data, we will focus on index numbers calculated relative to a base period in time. Thus, index numbers are useful in describing the change in values over time in time series data. Index numbers can be classified as being simple or aggregate (sometimes called composite). A *simple index* number measures the change in a single value. An *aggregate index* measures the change in a group of items over time. Aggregate indexes can be further classified into unweighted or weighted aggregates. An unweighted index is one in which the individual values are simply summed to arrive at an overall value. For a weighted index, the individual values are multiplied by a weight before summing the values. We will look at both types of aggregate indices in a moment. First, we will to look at simple index numbers.

Simple Index Numbers

Index numbers are really just another way of looking at trends or changes over time. Index numbers are ratios of the values relative to a *base period* usually expressed as a multiple of 100. Letting Y_t represent the value at time t and Y_b represent the same value in the base period, the index is calculated as:

Index
$$I_t = \left(\frac{Y_t}{Y_b}\right) 100$$
(12-30)

Example 12-5

To illustrate the calculations we will return to Example 12-1, but this time we will look at annual revenues at J&G Distributors rather than quarterly revenues. The annual revenues are shown in the table below.

Year	2006	2007	2008	2009	2010	2011
Revenue	3774	4120	4177	4479	4621	4683

Letting the base year be 2006, we can calculate the revenues in 2012 relative to the revenues in 2006 as:

$$I_{2012} = \left(\frac{4683}{3774}\right) 100 = 124$$

In other words, revenues in 2012 were approximately 24% higher than they were in 2006. Table 12-10 shows the index numbers for all years in the example.

Table 12-10   ***Index Numbers for Revenues in Example 12-3 Relative to the Year 2006***

Year	2006	2007	2008	2009	2010	2011
Index	100	109	111	119	122	124

Notice that the index of the base year is 100. A little reflection should convince you that this always has to be true. Also, notice that using index numbers makes it easier to examine the year-to-year changes. For example, there were large jumps in revenue from 2006 to 2007 and from 2008 to 2009 with smaller increases in the other years.

Most indices are either based on price, quantities, or value. Value is calculated as the product of a price times a quantity. For example, annual revenues in Example 12-3 are computed by multiplying the number of items sold by their price. Increased revenues could be the result of increased prices, or increased number of units sold, or a combination of the two. Whether we look at price, quantity, or value depends largely on our interests. If our interests are on matters of inflation or changes in monetary values over time we are most likely to look at indexes related to price. If we are more interested in phenomena such as productivity or output, we are more likely to look at a quantity index. Most common indexes are similar to the one examined in this example, a value index, which is a combination of both changes in monetary value and changes in quantity.

Aggregate (Composite) Index Numbers

Most familiar indexes are aggregate or composite measures rather than simple index numbers. An aggregate or composite index measures changes for a group of related items over time rather than a single item. Such composite indexes are very common in economics and are among the more widely reported government statistical measures. For example, the well-known consumer price index is a widely used measure of inflation in the U.S. We will look at this particular index in more detail in the next section.

Example 12-6

J&G Distributors hosts an annual party in early June for their employees and their families. Bud Gilles, the VP of Finance, has been concerned about the rising costs of the party and has gathered data on the costs over the past 6 years. The prices of the various items purchased for the party over the past 6 years are shown in Table 12-11.

Table 12-11   ***Costs of Party Items for Past Six Years***

Year	2007	2008	2009	2010	2011	2012
Beer/bottle	$0.69	$0.74	$0.78	$0.85	$0.87	$0.95
Wine/bottle	$4.65	$4.68	$4.72	$4.87	$4.96	$5.05
Soda/can	$0.18	$0.19	$0.21	$0.21	$0.25	$0.27
Food/person	$7.23	$7.55	$7.63	$7.72	$7.95	$8.36
Entertainment	$1,846	$1,987	$2,007	$2,146	$2,275	$2,350

We can calculate a simple price index for the party by adding up the prices in the given year and those in the base year.

Simple Price Index $$I = \left(\frac{\sum P_t}{\sum P_b}\right)$$ (12-31)

Using 2007 as the base year, we find the price totals and index values shown in Table 12-12.

Table 12-12   ***Price Totals and Price Index Values with 2007 as the Base Year***

Year	2007	2008	2009	2010	2011	2012
Totals	$1,858.75	$2,000.16	$2,020.34	$2,159.65	$2,289.03	$2,364.63
Index	100	108	109	116	123	127

These index values indicate that prices jumped quite rapidly in 2010 and 2011 with smaller increases in the other years; however, in looking at these figures, Bud Gilles realizes that there is a problem with this simple index as it treats all of the items the same in calculating the total even though the purchased quantities are quite different. For example, entertainment is a onetime cost while food is a per-person cost and soda, beer, and wine are a per-unit cost. This is what is called an unweighted aggregate index. A better index can be arrived at by considering the quantities purchased and use these as weights in calculating what is really a value index rather than a simple price index.

Weighted Aggregate Price Index $\qquad I = \left(\dfrac{\sum P_t Q}{\sum P_b Q}\right)$ $\qquad$ *(12-32)*

Bud Gilles estimates that they usually purchase about 100 bottles of beer, 15 bottles of wine, and 200 cans of soda. Normally there are about 100 people in attendance at the event.

Year		2007		2008		2009		2010		2011		2012	
	Quantity	Price	$	Price	$	Price	$	Price	$	Price	$	Price	$
Beer	100	$0.69	$69	$0.74	$74	$0.78	$78	$0.85	$80	$0.87	$87	$0.95	$95
Wine	15	$4.65	$69.75	$4.68	$70.20	$4.72	$70.80	$4.87	$73.05	$4.96	$74.40	$5.05	$75.75
Soda	200	$0.18	$36	$0.19	$38	$0.21	$42	$0.21	$42	$0.25	$50	$0.27	$54
Food	100	$7.23	$723	$7.55	$755	$7.63	$763	$7.72	$772	$7.95	$795	$8.36	$836
Entertainment	1	$1,846	$1,846	$1,987	$1,987	$2,007	$2,007	$2,146	$2,146	$2,275	$2,275	$2,350	$2,350

Table 12-12 $\qquad$ ***Price Totals and Price Index Values with 2007 as the Base Year***

Year	2007	2008	2009	2010	2011	2012
Totals	$2,743.75	$2.924.20	$2,960.80	$3,118.05	$3,281.40	$3,410.75
Index	100	107	108	114	120	124

As you can see, the price indexes change somewhat when we use the weighted aggregate index. Sometimes this change can be quite dramatic depending on the differences in quantities used.

The weighted index that we calculated makes an important assumption, namely that the quantity used for each item remains constant over the time period being analyzed. When prices vary over time, quantities used also usually vary over time as well. If the amount of variability in the quantities is small, the use of an average or typical value as we did in the example above may not appreciably distort the results. However, the variability in quantity increases the risk of misrepresentation using an average quantity also increases. There are two approaches to the situation where quantities as well as prices vary over time. The first is to use the quantities for the base period for the weights in calculating the index values for all time periods. This is called the *Laspeyres Index* and it is calculated as:

Laspeyres Index $\qquad I = \left(\dfrac{\sum P_t Q_b}{\sum P_b Q_b}\right)$ $\qquad$ *(12-33)*

Alternatively, we could use the quantity in the reference period (time t) for the calculations. This is called the *Paasche Index* and is calculated as:

Paasche Index $\qquad I = \left(\dfrac{\sum P_t Q_t}{\sum P_b Q_t}\right)$ $\qquad$ *(12-34)*

The Laspeyres Index is the more popular of the two. For one reason, it is easier to use and update each time period since the quantity used stays the same. It is also a more "pure" price index since only the price varies from one period to another; however, the Laspeyres Index does have a significant shortcoming. It gives great weight to items that have significant price shifts from one period to the next. As anyone who has studied economics at even the most basic level knows, when prices change significantly, often the quantity sold (demand) also changes significantly; however the quantity does not change in the Laspeyres Index which means that the results may not be totally realistic.

Since neither the Laspeyres nor Paasche Indexes are without problems, other index numbers have been proposed that are averages of these two index values. Full coverage of these indexes are beyond the scope of this text.

You may have noticed that the aggregate indexes discussed here were indexes of price with quantities as the weights. We could just as easily focus on quantity with price as the weight. Although most popular aggregate measures used in economics focus on price, you should be aware that we could just as easily focus on the quantity aspects of overall value.

Using Index Numbers

Index numbers are widely used in business and economics to measure changes in a variable over time or to compare economic indicators from different countries with different currencies. The most widely reported index numbers are aggregate indexes. In this section, we will look at some well-known index numbers and at how index numbers can be used to deflate time series data.

Common Economic Index Numbers

Consumer Price Index

The *Consumer Price Index* (CPI) has become the best-known indicator of inflation in the U.S and other countries. The CPI has been published by the U.S. Department of Labor since 1913 and changes in the CPI are widely reported as changes in the inflation rate by the popular press. The CPI measures the aggregate total price of a market basket of goods and services purchased by a typical family relative to a base period (currently 1982 – 1984). Both the items in the market basket and the base period are changed periodically to update the index and keep it relevant. There are actually two CPI values: the Consumer Price Index for Urban Workers (CPI-U) is the index most often reported by the media as a measure of inflation and the Consumer Price Index for Urban Wage Earners and Clerical Workers (CPI-W) is the index typically used as the official inflation value in labor contracts. Both CPI indexes are Laspeyres Indexes.

Producer Price Index

The U.S. Department of Labor also publishes *the Producer Price Index* (PPI) which measures the aggregate price of a set of goods sold by wholesalers. The base year for the PPI is 1982. This measure is a Laspeyres Index like the CPI and is used as a leading indicator of future changes in the CPI.

Import and Export Price Indexes

The *Import Price Index* (IPI) measures prices paid for goods imported into a country. Changes in the IPI are watched as indicators of the trade balance of a country, the difference between the total value of imports and the total value of exports. The trade balance impacts the value of the currency of a country. Since the U.S. is currently a net importer, major changes in the IPI can indicate a significant change in the inflation rate. The IPI is also used to determine if a change in the value of imports indicates a change in the volume of imports or a change in prices charged.

The *Export Price Index* (EPI) is a similar measure of the prices paid for goods exported from a country. Like the IPI, the EPI is used to determine whether or not changes in the value of exports are due to a change in the volume of exports or simply reflects price inflation.

Deflating a Time Series

A common use of index numbers is to deflate or remove inflation from a set of time series data. Deflating time series data provides a way of determining *real* changes in the time series that does not reflect the impact of general inflation. For example if your wages increase by 5% over a certain time period, but inflation has actually increased by 6%, then your *real* wages have actually decreased over that time. Deflating a time series consists of dividing the values in the series by an index number, called a *deflator*, that represents inflation.

$$Deflated\ Value \qquad\qquad Y_{t_{Adj}} = \frac{Y_t}{Index_t}(100) \qquad\qquad (12\text{-}35)$$

where Index is the value of the index being used to deflate the time series at time period t.

Example 12-7

In Example 12-5 we examined the annual revenues for J&G Distributors. These values are reproduced in Table 12-13. The values in the revenue column indicate steadily increasing revenues from 2006 through 2011; however, these values do not take into account any inflation during that period. The column labeled PPI contains the values from the U.S. PPI index for the Finished Consumer Food category as of December for that year. We can use this index as a measure of inflation for J&G and calculated their deflated revenues which are shown in the column labeled Adjusted Revenues. These values show a much different picture. Rather than steadily increasing revenues seen in the raw data, we now see steady revenues except for the years 2008 and 2009.

Table 12-13   ***Revenues at J&G Distributors Adjusted by the PPI***

Year	Revenue	PPI	Adjusted Revenues
2006	3,774	160.4	2,352.9
2007	4,120	172	2,395.3
2008	4,177	178.5	2,340.1
2009	4,479	179.7	2,492.5
2010	4,621	186.1	2,483.1
2011	4,683	197.3	2,373.5

Index Numbers and Market Segments

Marketing professionals sometimes use index numbers to understand buying behavior and market potential in different market segments. Most often this takes the form of a market index for the different market segments. The market index is derived by dividing the percentage of users in a market segment by the percentage of the population in the same segment multiplied by 100.

Market Index
$$MI = \frac{P_{Users}}{P_{Population}}(100)$$
(12-36)

It is easiest to understand this use of index numbers through an example.

Example 12-8

Bob Jones, the owner and manager of the Heavenly Bean Espresso stand, attended a recent Chamber of Commerce meeting where they described a recent survey of area residents on their buying habits along with various demographic characteristics. One of the questions asked was whether or not the respondent frequently purchased specialty coffee drinks at area locations. Bob is primarily interested in the different age segments as they relate to those that responded positively to this question. Since individuals younger than 18 and those over age 75 are much less likely to buy coffee-flavored drinks, Bob focuses on age groups 18 and above and age 75 or below and divides them into groups as shown in Table 12-14. The population values in each age group come from the most recent census of the area while the number of users in each age group is taken from the results of the survey.

Table 12-14   **Market Index Calculations for Coffee Drink Consumption**

Age	Population	Percent	Users	Percent	Index
18-25	12218	17.1%	247	24.7%	144
26-35	13935	19.5%	203	20.3%	104
36-45	16498	23.1%	169	16.9%	73
46-55	14257	20.0%	162	16.2%	81
56-65	8218	11.5%	138	13.8%	120
66-75	6198	8.7%	81	8.1%	93
Total	71324		1000		

Market index values over 100 indicate segments with good potential target markets because they have high population density and/or heavy usage. In the case of consumption of specialty coffee drinks, the best segments are 18-25 and 56-65.

Exercises VII

30. The annual costs of ingredients used by Donuts on Parade for the past 6 years are shown below. Compute the annual cost index values using 2006 as the base year. Comment on the changes in costs for Donuts on Parade.

Year	2006	2007	2008	2009	2010	2011
Costs (thousands of dollars)	130.32	133.43	142.15	143.26	144.27	145.91

31. The Rent-a-Ride car rental service has maintained records on gasoline usage over the past seven years. The annual usage in thousands of gallons is shown below. Calculate the index values for gasoline usage using 2008 as the base year. What do the index values tell you about gasoline usage at Rent-a-Ride?

Year	2005	2006	2007	2008	2009	2010	2011
Gasoline usage (thousands of gallons)	136.44	148.67	155.01	130.51	129.19	144.87	154.17

32. The tables below show the average prices and annual per capita consumptions for milk in the United States for the years 2000 through 2006.

   (a) Using 2000 as the base year, construct a Laspeyres index of milk prices from 2000 to 2006.

   (b) Construct a Paasche Index of the milk prices from 2000 to 2006.

Prices

Year	2000	2001	2002	2003	2004	2005	2006
Whole Milk	$3.59	3.68	3.54	3.59	4.01	4.07	4.16
Low Fat Milk	$3.11	3.24	3.13	3.13	3.45	3.46	3.5

Per Capita Consumption (Gallons)

Year	2000	2001	2002	2003	2004	2005	2006
Whole Milk	8.1	7.8	7.7	7.6	7.3	7.0	6.7
Low Fat Milk	14.4	14.2	14.2	14.0	14.0	14.1	14.2

Data adapted from the United States Department of Agriculture: http://www.ers.usda.gov/data-products/food-expenditures.aspx

33. The tables below show the annual production of gold and silver in the United States between the years 2000 and 2010.

    (a) Using 2000 as the base year, construct a Laspeyres Index of the aggregate value of gold and silver produced in the United States from 2000 to 2006.

    (b) Construct a Paasche Index of the total value of gold and silver mined in the United States from 2000 to 2006.

	Production in Metric Tons										
	2000	2001	2002	2003	2004	2005	2006	2007	2008	2009	2010
Gold	353	335	298	277	258	256	252	238	233	223	231
Silver	1,980	1,740	1,350	1,240	1,250	1,230	1,160	1,280	1,250	1,250	1,270

	Value in Thousands of Dollars/ton										
	2000	2001	2002	2003	2004	2005	2006	2007	2008	2009	2010
Gold	9,010	8,750	10,000	11,700	13,200	14,300	19,500	22,400	28,000	31,300	39,500
Silver	161	140	148	157	207	236	373	432	483	472	643

Data from the U.S. Geological Survey: http://minerals.usgs.gov/ds/2005/140/index.html

34. Annual retail and food sales in trillions of dollars from 2000 through 2011 are shown in the table below. Also displayed in the table are the annual consumer price index (CPI) values for the same years. Deflate the retail sales figures using the CPI. What conclusions can you draw from this information?

	Retail Sales in Trillions of Dollars and CPI											
	2000	2001	2002	2003	2004	2005	2006	2007	2008	2009	2010	2011
Sales	3.29	3.38	3.46	3.61	3.85	4.09	4.30	4.44	4.40	4.08	4.31	4.65
CPI	172.2	177.1	179.9	184.0	188.9	195.3	201.6	207.3	215.3	214.5	218.1	224.9

Data on retail sales from http://www.census.gov/retail/. CPI data from http://www.usinflationcalculator.com/inflation/consumer-price-index-and-annual-percent-changes-from-1913-to-2008/

35. Average retail inventories in trillions of dollars from 2000 through 2011 are shown in the table below. Also displayed in the table are the annual consumer price index (CPI) values for the same years. Deflate the inventory figures using the CPI. What conclusions can you draw from this information?

	Average Retail Inventories in Trillions of Dollars and CPI											
	2000	2001	2002	2003	2004	2005	2006	2007	2008	2009	2010	2011
Inventories	0.395	0.402	0.404	0.424	0.450	0.463	0.483	0.495	0.495	0.441	0.443	0.463
CPI	172.2	177.1	179.9	184.0	188.9	195.3	201.6	207.3	215.3	214.5	218.1	224.9

Data on retail sales from http://www.census.gov/retail/. CPI data from
http://www.usinflationcalculator.com/inflation/consumer-price-index-and-annual-percent-changes-from-1913-to-2008/

Practice

Computer Solutions for Time Series Data

Setting up the Data

To use any of the tools discussed in this section, you must first set up your data appropriately. You need the time series data values but you also need to set up a variable that represents time. Normally, this variable will simply consist of a sequence of integers from 1 to n where n is the number of time periods. The revenue data from Table 12-2 for Example 12-3 is shown in Figure 12-11. Since there are 12 quarters of data the column headed "Quarters" contains the sequential integers from 1 to 12. This type of setup is needed to use most of the tools described in this section.

Figure 12-11   *Excel Worksheet for Example 12-3 Data*

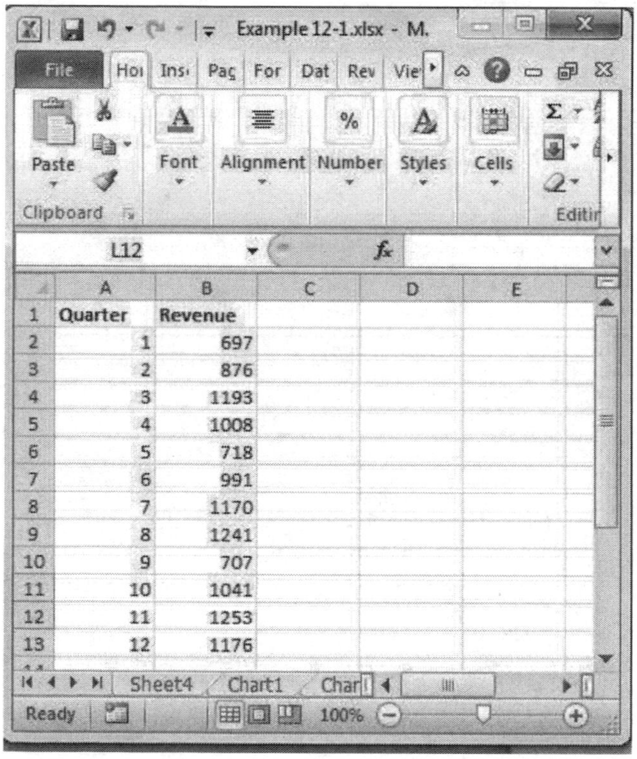

Using the Charting Features in Excel

The charting capabilities incorporated into Excel can be used to estimate the parameters of linear and nonlinear regression models to time series data. To chart the data and estimate the equations, first select the time period data along with the time series values, as shown in Figure 12-12. On the Insert tab of

Excel, select Scatter in the Charts section and select the first option for a scatter plot with no lines as shown in Figure 12-12. This action will produce a scatter plot on the worksheet.

Figure 12-12   *Creating a Scatter Plot in Excel*

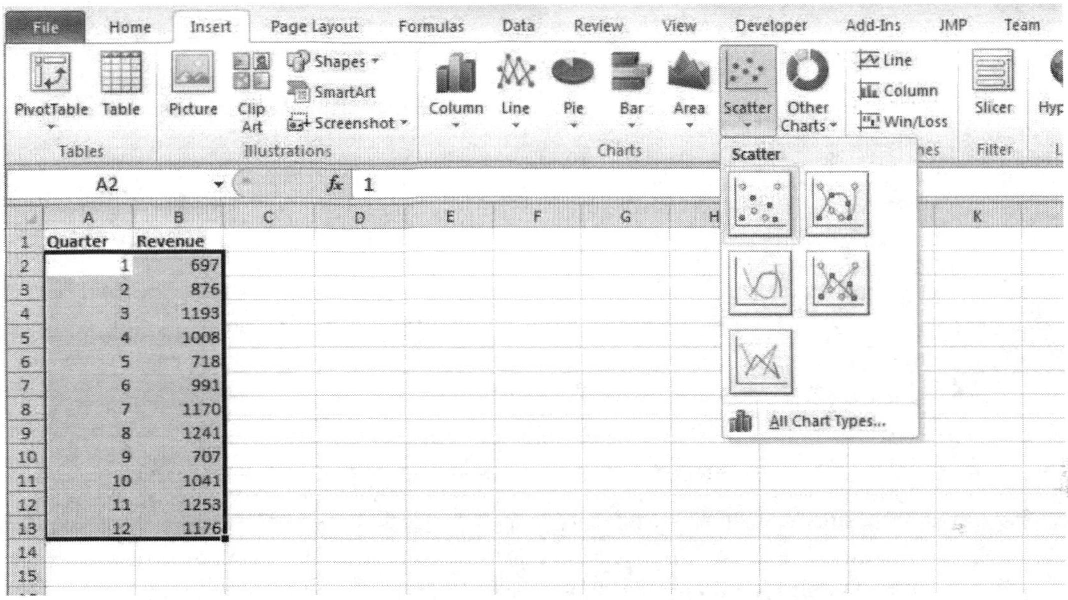

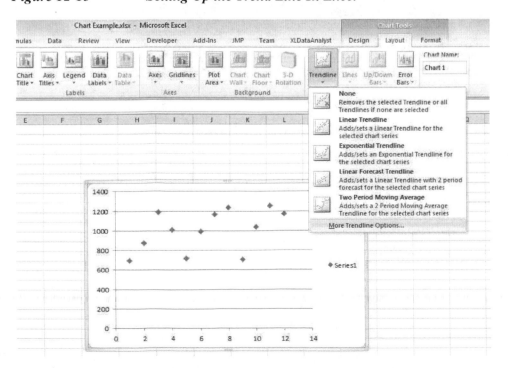

To solve for the linear equation, highlight the chart and from the Chart Tools section under Layout select Trendline and More Trendline Options, as shown in Figure 12-13. This will result in the dialog box shown in Figure 12-14. Note that you can select the type of trend line directly without going to More Trendline Options. However, doing so will not display the equation in the graph and you will still have to go to the More Options dialog to do that. By going directly to these options you will have more flexibility in how the trend line is calculated and displayed.

Figure 12-13   *Setting Up the Trend Line In Excel*

Figure 12-14   ***Trendline Options Dialog***

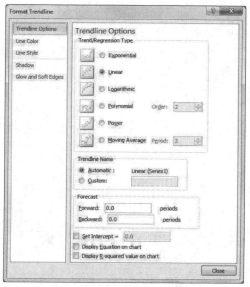

You can now set the options that you want. Make sure that you check the box that reads Display Equation on Chart so that the equation will be visible. You can also display the coefficient of determination by checking the Display R-squared Value on Chart option and you can select the type of trend line you want to calculate. The default is for a Linear equation, i.e., linear regression. You can also perform nonlinear regressions by selecting the Exponential, Logarithmic, Polynomial, or Power options. There is even an option to display a Moving Average model. You can also use some of the other charting options to change the style color of the line, if you wish. The resulting chart is shown in Figure 12-15. You may have to move the text box in the graph so that it does not overlay the chart to make it more visible.

Figure 12-15   ***Completed Chart with the Linear Trend Line***

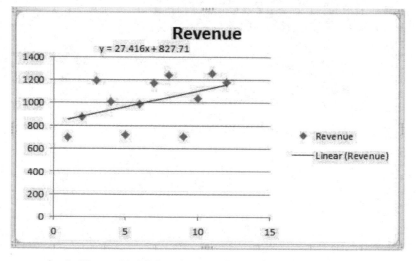

You may notice in Figure 12-15 that the equation, as displayed, is somewhat different from the normal presentation of the equation. The format of the equation in the scatter plot is of the form:

$$Y = bX + a$$

In Figure 12-15, the constant term has a value of 827.71 and the slope is 27.416.

After creating the trend line you can change it to a different type by selecting the trend line first and then going to the Trendline options. If you do not select the trend line first, selecting different types of curves will produce a new trend line each time rather than changing the existing curve.

Excel Functions

The same functions used in Chapter 10, namely INTEPT, SLOPE, and LINEST, can be used for time series data as well. We will focus here on LINEST and a closely related version of this function called LOGEST. Both functions are array functions and therefore require a different approach than the simple functions. Array functions return more than one value and must be entered using the Ctrl-Shift-Enter key combination. The LINEST function is described in more detail in Chapter 10. The LINEST function syntax is:

LINEST(y values, x values, constant, statistics)

The y-values and x-values are both ranges for the dependent and independent variables, respectively. The constant argument is either true or false. If the value is true, the constant (y-intercept) term is estimated; if false, it is set to zero. The statistics value is also true or false. If true, all of the summary statistics are returned; if false, only the parameter estimates for a and b are returned. To use the function, highlight a blank section of the spreadsheet which contains the data with 5 rows and 2 columns. Enter the function with the equals sign and enter, then press the Ctrl-Shift-Enter key combination.

The LOGEST function has the same syntax as the LINEST function. However the model fit is the exponential function rather than the linear function (see Equation 12-20 for the exponential function). To illustrate the functions we will use the data from Example 12-3. Figure 12-16 shows the results of both the LINEST and LOGEST functions for this example.

Figure 12-16   *Results for the LINEST Function*

	A	B	C	D	E	F
1	Period	Revenue		LINEST Results		
2	1	697		27.41608	827.7121	
3	2	876		16.42304	120.8703	
4	3	1193		0.217943	196.391	
5	4	1008		2.786787	10	
6	5	718		107484.8	385694.2	
7	6	991		LOGEST Results		
8	7	1170		1.028567	819.2655	
9	8	1241		0.017591	0.129465	
10	9	707		0.204061	0.210356	
11	10	1041		2.563779	10	
12	11	1253		0.113446	0.442496	
13	12	1176				
14						

To interpret the results, understand the order of the output from the two functions. Table 12-14 shows the format of the output for the functions. We can see that the r-squared for the linear function is .2179 and for the exponential function it is .2041. Therefore, the simpler linear function fits this data better than the nonlinear exponential function.

Table 12-14   ***Output Format for the LINEST and LOGEST Functions***

Row 1	b-slope	a-constant
Row 2	S_b-standard error of b	S_a-standard error of a
Row 3	R^2coefficient of determination	S_e-standard error of the estimate
Row 4	F-F value from ANOVA	df-degrees of freedom numerator
Row 5	SSR-sum-of-squares regression	SSE-sum-of-squares error

Data Analysis Toolpak

The Data Analysis Toolpak can perform some of the analyses we have discussed in this chapter but not all of them. Of course, the Toolpak can perform simple regression analysis as described in Chapter 10. Since it can also perform multiple regression as described in Chapter 11, it can be used to estimate additive seasonal effects as well. We will not repeat the discussion of how to use the Toolpak to perform regression here. Refer to Chapters 10 and 11 for a complete description of how to do that. Here we will focus on the additional time series methods that the Toolpak can perform.

The Data Analysis Toolpak has options for performing simple exponential smoothing and moving averages. It does not have procedures for the analysis of trend or seasonal effects. It does have capabilities for Fourier analysis which is sometimes used in analyzing time series data but we will not discuss these techniques here. Figure 12-17 shows the Data Analysis Toolpak dialog with the two methods that we will discuss here. The two options are Exponential Smoothing and Moving Average.

Figure 12-17   ***Data Analysis Toolpak Dialog***

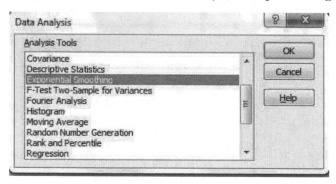

Moving Average

To illustrate the moving average option in the Toolpak we will return to the data used in Example 12-3. When the moving average option is selected in the Toolpak menu, the dialog box shown in Figure 12-18 will be displayed. The dialog box requires you to specify the input range for the data and the output range for the results. The required model parameter labeled Interval is the number of periods in the moving average. In Example 12-3 we used a four-period moving average and will do so again here. You can check the box for Chart Output if you would like the Toolpak to produce a chart of the data and the results. Entering a value of 4 for the Interval and cell C2 for the start of the output range, the Toolpak calculates the results shown in Figure 12-19. The #N/A error messages at the beginning of the output are normal and simply indicate that the moving average cannot be calculated until we have 4 data points. The remainder of the C column contain the estimates of the average value for that period. If you compare these values with those in Table 12-2 you will find that the results here are identical to those calculated by hand earlier.

Figure 12-18   *Moving Average Dialog in the Data Analysis Toolpak*

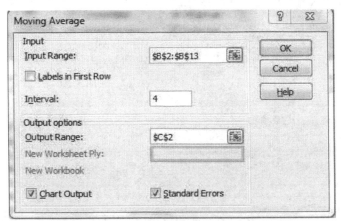

Figure 12-19   *Data Analysis Toolpak Moving Average Results for Example 12-3*

	A	B	C
1	Period	Revenue	
2	1	697	#N/A
3	2	876	#N/A
4	3	1193	#N/A
5	4	1008	943.5
6	5	718	948.75
7	6	991	977.5
8	7	1170	971.75
9	8	1241	1030
10	9	707	1027.25
11	10	1041	1039.75
12	11	1253	1060.5
13	12	1176	1044.25
14			

Exponential Smoothing

When the Exponential Smoothing option shown in Figure 12-17 is selected, the dialog shown in Figure 12-20 will be displayed. As with the Moving Average option, you will be required to specify the input range for the data and the output range for the results. Although you might think that the parameter requested would represent the smoothing coefficient to use in the model, the parameter input requested is labeled Damping Factor. This is actually one minus the smoothing coefficient. Or,

$$\text{Damping Factor} = 1 - \alpha$$

For example, if you want a smoothing coefficient of .10, you would enter .90 for the Damping Factor in the dialog box. Since we used a smoothing coefficient of .10 in our original analysis of this data we entered a value of .90 for the damping factor and obtained the results shown in Figure 12-21. These results also agree with the values calculated by hand and presented in Table 12-3.

Figure 12-20   *Exponential Smoothing Dialog Box in the Data Analysis Toolpak*

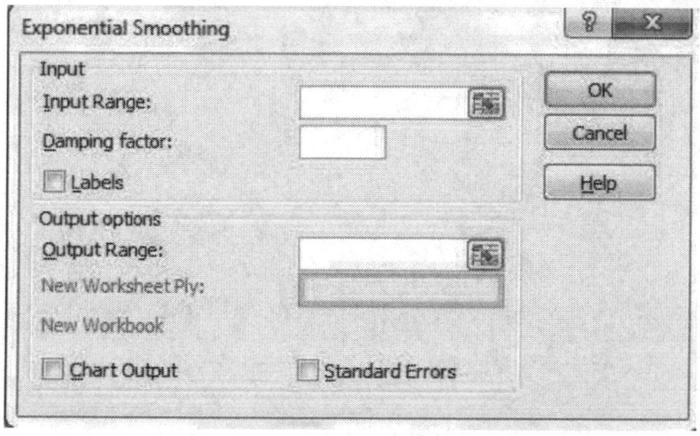

Figure 12-21   *Data Analysis Toolpak Exponential Smoothing Results for Example 12-3*

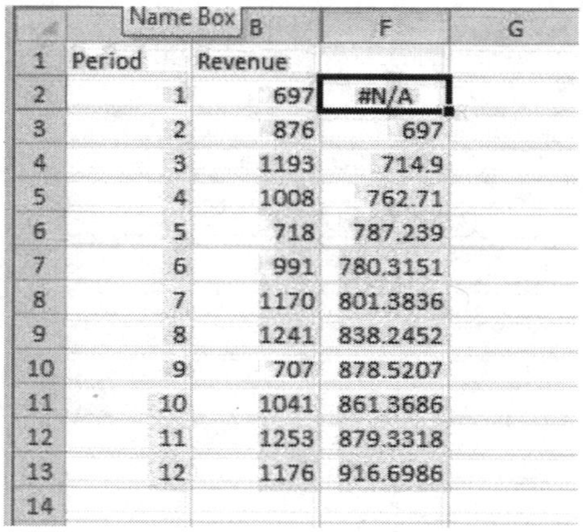

	Period	Revenue (B)	F	G
1	Period	Revenue		
2	1	697	#N/A	
3	2	876	697	
4	3	1193	714.9	
5	4	1008	762.71	
6	5	718	787.239	
7	6	991	780.3151	
8	7	1170	801.3836	
9	8	1241	838.2452	
10	9	707	878.5207	
11	10	1041	861.3686	
12	11	1253	879.3318	
13	12	1176	916.6986	
14				

Time Series Analysis Using XLDataAnalyst

We discussed the use of XLDataAnalyst to perform regression analysis in Chapters 10 and 11. Therefore, XLDataAnalyst can be used to perform time series regression and to estimate additive seasonal effects using dummy variables; however, there are additional tools built into XLDataAnalyst for time series analysis. Figure 12-22 shows the relevant section of the XLDataAnalyst ribbon. In addition to the routines for correlation and regression, there is an additional menu for Time Series analysis which contains options for autocorrelation, differencing, and time series forecasting that we will discuss in more detail in this section.

Figure 12-22   ***XLDataAnalyst Ribbon Section for Time Series Analysis***

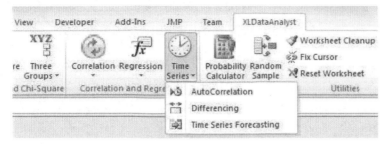

Autocorrelation

The AutoCorrelation option is used to produce a correlogram of a set of time series data. When you select the autocorrelation option, the dialog box shown in Figure 12-23 will be shown. To plot the correlogram you need to select a variable from the data, the number of lags for which you wish to calculate autocorrelations, the number of parameters in the original model, and the degree of confidence. The default number of lags is 10 (which is fairly high) but for large data sets will work fine. The number of lags that you specify should be based on what you are interested in. Previously we discussed the use of autocorrelation with trend and seasonal effects. We noted that the existence of trend in the data should produce a significant positive first order autocorrelation in the data so that lags of 2 to 4 should be sufficient to detect the existence of trend in the data. For seasonal effects, a significant positive correlation should correspond to the seasonal cycle. For quarterly data that would be four; therefore, 4 or 5 lags would be sufficient; however, for monthly data we would need lags of at least 12. If there is not sufficient data to calculate the number of lags that you specify, XLDataAnalyst will warn you that there is not sufficient data to calculate all of the lags.

Figure 12-23   ***Autocorrelation Dialog***

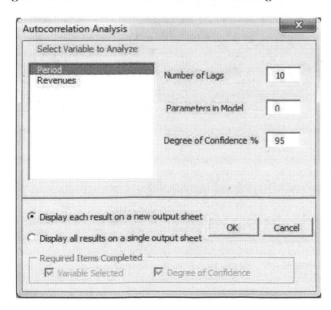

The item labeled "Parameters in Model" is used in the Ljung-Box tests discussed below. The default value is zero. If you are examining autocorrelations of original data, this is the appropriate setting;

however, if you are examining the residuals from a regression or other model you should enter the number of parameters estimated in that model in this box. For a simple regression, for example, the correct value would be 2. For multiple regression, the value would be the number of independent variables plus the constant term.

The degree of confidence setting is used for the correlogram plots. The default is for 95% confidence intervals but you can enter any value that you wish.

We have previously illustrated the output of the autocorrelation routines in XLDataAnalyst. The output consists of two parts. The first part is a worksheet with the correlation values and tests of significance which are shown in Figure 12-24 for Example 12-1 with the number of lags set to five. The second part of the output is the autocorrelation plot or correlogram. This graph is shown in Figure 12-25.

Figure 12-24   *Autocorrelation Output for Example 12-1*

Autocorrelation Function for Revenues

Lag	Autocorrelation	t	p-value	Q	p-value
1	0.1464	0.7172	0.4802	0.5814	0.4458
2	-0.5303	-2.5441	0.0178	8.5586	0.0139
3	0.0566	0.2189	0.8286	8.6538	0.0343
4	0.7082	2.7329	0.0116	24.3025	0.0001
5	0.1214	0.3678	0.7162	24.7866	0.0002

Figure 12-25   *Correlogram for Example 12-1*

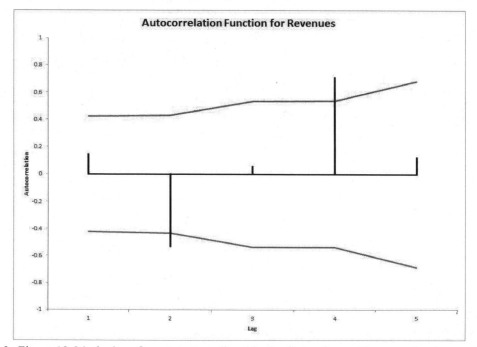

In Figure 12-24, the lags from 1 to 5 are listed in the first column. The second column gives the autocorrelation for that lag. The third column contains the t-statistic for that autocorrelation. The fourth column shows the p-value for that t-statistic. We can see that there is a significant negative autocorrelation for a lag of 2 periods and a significant positive autocorrelation for a lag of 4 periods with p-values less than .05. The last two columns require a little more explanation.

The t-tests performed in the third and fourth columns test for each of the individual autocorrelations. Each of these has a certain level of significance, for example .05; however, the overall probability of making a Type I error in the entire set of tests is unknown. This is similar to the situation of performing separate t-tests in analysis of variance from Chapter 9. In that case we explored post-hoc tests as a response to the problem. There are similar tests designed for autocorrelations in the analysis of time series data. One widely used such test is the Ljung-Box Q statistic[6]. The Q-statistic, which is displayed in the fifth column of the output, has a chi-square distribution from which the p-values in the last column are obtained. The degrees of freedom for a given test are equal to $h - m$ where h is the number of lags being tested and m is the number of parameters in the model that was estimated. In this situation, no model has been estimated so that m has a value of zero. If the autocorrelations were for residuals derived from a regression model, then m would be the number of parameters estimated in the original regression equation. The null hypothesis for a given Q-test is that all of the correlations from lag 1 to that point are equal to zero. The alternative is that at least one of them is not equal to zero. For example, for a lag of 4 periods, the hypotheses are:

$$H_0: \rho_1 = \rho_2 = \rho_3 = \rho_4 = 0$$

$$H_1: not(\rho_1 = \rho_2 = \rho_3 = \rho_4 = 0)$$

Note the similarity here to the hypotheses in Chapter 9. For the output in Figure 12-24 the Q-value is 24.3025 and the p-value is .0001. We can safely reject the null hypothesis and state that at least one of the first four autocorrelations is significantly different from zero.

Differencing

We previously noted that autocorrelation violates one of the assumptions of linear regression and that one approach to removing autocorrelation from time series data is a method called differencing. Differencing involves creating a new variable where the observations in the new variable are the original values minus the value m periods prior to that time in the sequence. In other words, each value in the new variable Y^* is:

$$Y_t^* = Y_t - Y_m$$

In most cases, m is equal to 1 but can be set at any value depending on the lag of the autocorrelation that is to be removed. To remove first order autocorrelation, set m to 1. To remove the autocorrelation for a lag of 4 you would set m to 4. To perform differencing in XLDataAnalyst, select the Differencing option from the XLDataAnalyst ribbon shown in Figure 12-22 and the dialog box shown in Figure 12-26 will appear. Select a variable from the list to be transformed, enter the lag value m, and the letter of the column where you want to place the new values. The default lag is 1 period and the default column is the column immediately to the right of the last column of data in your dataset.

---

[6] This statistic is also sometimes called the Box-Pierce statistic. The statistic implemented in XLDataAnalyst is the later improvement on the original Box-Pierce statistic published by Ljung and Box.

Figure 12-26 **Differencing Dialog Box from XLDataAnalyst**

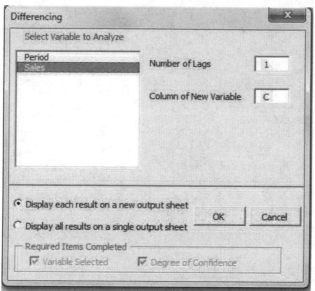

In producing the correlogram in Figure 12-7 we used a set of data that contained a trend but no seasonal effects. Figure 12-7 demonstrated the typical pattern of trend data with no seasonal effects. The autocorrelation for a 1-period lag is positive and statistically significant. Often, the 2-period lag autocorrelation is also significant but somewhat less than the 1-period lag. The correlations remain positive but diminish in value as the lag increases. We will use the same data here to illustrate the effects of differencing. Figure 12-27 shows the results of differencing the sales data from this data. Notice that data is lost in the differencing process. In general, the first m data values are lost where m is the number of lags selected. In this case the lag is 1, so that only one data value is lost.

Since we have used first order differencing the large and statistically significant 1-lag autocorrelation should be removed from the new variables. Figure 12-28 shows the resulting correlogram for the new variable. Note that the 1-lag autocorrelation is no longer positive, but rather it is now negative. All of the other positive autocorrelations have been reduced as well.

Figure 12-27   *Results of Differencing Sales Data with Trend Only*

	A	B	C	D
1	Period	Sales	Differences	
2	1	1013		
3	2	1036	23	
4	3	1052	16	
5	4	1076	24	
6	5	1090	14	
7	6	1122	32	
8	7	1140	18	
9	8	1154	14	
10	9	1189	35	
11	10	1190	1	
12	11	1228	38	
13	12	1247	19	
14	13	1253	6	
15	14	1279	26	
16	15	1307	28	
17	16	1330	23	
18	17	1341	11	
19	18	1357	16	
20	19	1372	15	
21	20	1403	31	
22	21	1416	13	
23	22	1444	28	
24	23	1460	16	
25	24	1467	7	
26				

Figure 12-28   *Correlogram of the Variable Created by Differencing*

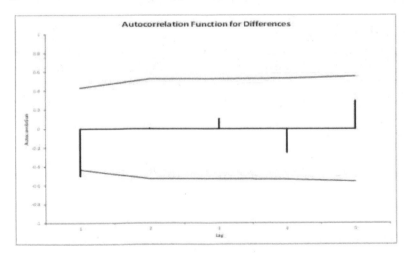

Time Series Forecasting

The third and final option in the Time Series section of the XLDataAnalyst ribbon is the Time Series Forecasting option. This is the most complex procedure and is capable of performing all of the methods discussed in this chapter from simple moving averages to smoothing models that include trend and seasonal effects. The dialog box that is displayed when this option is selected is shown in Figure 12-29.

Figure 12-29   ***Time Series Forecasting Dialog Box***

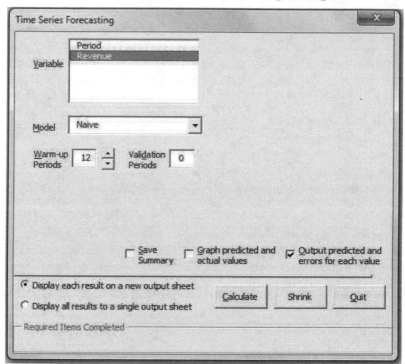

This dialog is similar to the Probability Calculator in XLDataAnalyst in that it remains on the screen even after you perform the calculations. You must explicitly close the dialog box by clicking the Quit button. To use the routines, select a variable to analyze in the list box at the top. You will need to select a model to use in analyzing the data. You can vary the warm-up and validation periods by changing the value in the warm-up period box or by using the spinner next to the box. The default is to use all of the data as warm-up. If you decrease the number of periods in the warm-up, XLDataAnalyst will automatically add those to the validation periods.

There are three check boxes in the dialog. The first is to save the summary of the results which creates a worksheet containing the model used, the parameters of the model, the errors both during the warm-up and validation periods, and the final parameter estimates. This is useful if you want to directly compare the results from different models on the same data. The second check box is to graph the predicted and actual values. If you wish to view the graph, check this box. The third check box, which is checked by default, provides the outputs of the predicted values and errors for each value in the data to a new worksheet.

The dialog box contains three command buttons. The first button, labeled Calculate, uses the current model and input parameters to fit the model to the data when clicked. The second button, labeled Shrink, shrinks the dialog down to a smaller size as shown in Figure 12-30 enabling you to have more screen space to review the results. To restore the dialog to its original size, simply click inside the rectangular box as shown in Figure 12-30. The final button closes the time series button when clicked.

Figure 12-30   ***Shrunken Dialog Box with Restoration Click Area***

The combo box labeled <u>M</u>odel is used to select the model to apply to the data. The complete list of options for model type is shown in Figure 12-31.

Figure 12-31   ***List of Available Model Options***

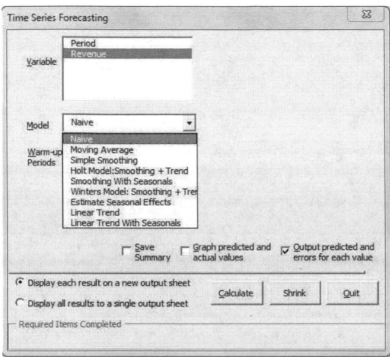

The Naïve model is essentially a baseline model, which is really not a model at all. The Naïve model forecasts that the value for the next period will be the same as the last period's value. No parameters are required for this model. As you change the model in the combo box, additional options will appear that require you to specify the appropriate parameters for the model currently chosen. For example, selecting the Moving Average option changes the dialog to appear like Figure 12-32. In Example 12-3, we calculated a 4-period moving average; thus, a 4 has been entered here to replicate those results. The results of the analysis are presented in Figure 12-33. If you compare the forecasts in Figure 12-33 with those previously calculated in Table 2-2 you can see that the major results and errors are the same within rounding differences. Figure 12-34 shows the Chart for this example produced by checking the appropriate box in the dialog.

Figure 12-32   *Dialog Box for the Moving Average Model*

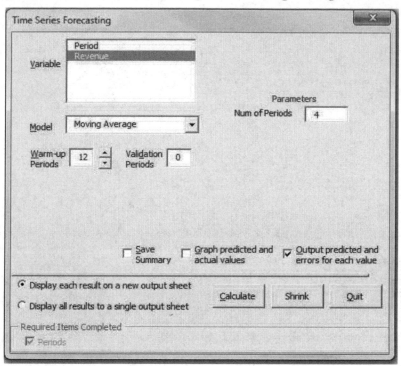

Figure 12-33   *Results for the Four-Period Moving Average Model*

Moving Average Model for Revenues

Period	Demand	Forecast	Error
1	697.0000		
2	876.0000		
3	1,193.0000		
4	1,008.0000		
5	718.0000	943.5000	-225.5000
6	991.0000	948.7500	42.2500
7	1,170.0000	977.5000	192.5000
8	1,241.0000	971.7500	269.2500
9	707.0000	1,030.0000	-323.0000
10	1,041.0000	1,027.2500	13.7500
11	1,253.0000	1,039.7500	213.2500
12	1,176.0000	1,060.5000	115.5000

Warm-up Periods

Average Error	MAD	MSE	Std	MAPE
37.2500	174.3750	40,690.1250	201.7179	0.1846

Final Parameter Estimates

Average	1,060.5000

Figure 12-34   *Chart for the Four Period Moving Average Model*

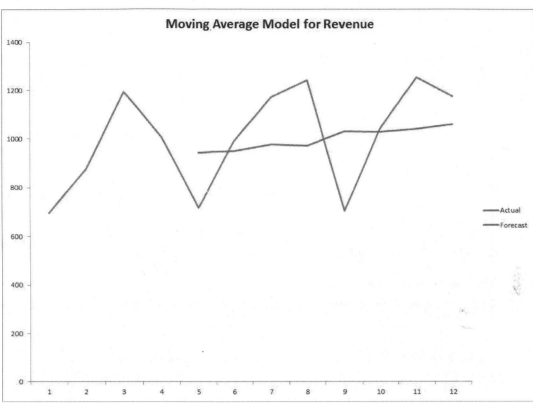

Regression Based Models

The regression methods discussed in Chapters 10 and 11 can, of course, be used for time series data as well; however, the simple linear regression methods are also contained within the Time Series Forecasting option. The last two models in the model options shown in Figure 12-31 are Linear Trend and Linear Trend with Seasonals. As the names imply, these two models both apply linear regression to the time series data. The second of these (Linear Trend with Seasonals) also estimates seasonal effects and deseasonalizes the data before deriving the regression equation. We will illustrate this method using the Example 12-4 daily sales data.

When this model is selected, the dialog box changes to look like the one shown in Figure 12-35. Since we are using seasonal effect, you must specify the length in periods of the seasonal cycle. Since we are dealing with daily data with 5 days a week, a value of 5 is entered for the seasonal cycle. Although XLDataAnalyst will calculate the seasonal effects using the ratio to moving average approach, you can also set the values for the seasonal effects and force XLDataAnalyst to use those values. Simply enter the values into the appropriate boxes and check the box that is labeled Use Given Seasonal Estimates. If this box is not checked or values are not entered for the seasonal effects they will be automatically calculated by XLDataAnalyst. The results obtained using this method and having XLDataAnalyst estimate the seasonal effects are shown in Figure 12-36.

Figure 12-35   *Dialog Box for Linear Trend with Seasonals Model*

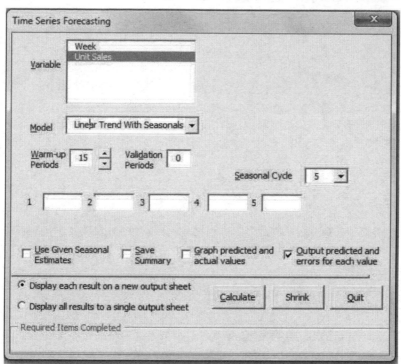

Figure 12-36   *Results for Linear Trend with Seasonals Model*

Trend Projection With Seasonals for Unit Sales

Period	Demand	Forecast	Error
1	205.0000	215.0259	-10.0259
2	150.0000	160.8842	-10.8842
3	190.0000	195.6758	-5.6758
4	142.0000	148.1715	-6.1715
5	165.0000	179.7486	-14.7486
6	240.0000	223.6935	16.3065
7	165.0000	167.3175	-2.3175
8	203.0000	203.4383	-0.4383
9	162.0000	154.0032	7.9968
10	208.0000	186.7679	21.2321
11	225.0000	232.3611	-7.3611
12	182.0000	173.7508	8.2492
13	220.0000	211.2007	8.7993
14	145.0000	159.8348	-14.8348
15	206.0000	193.7871	12.2129

Warm-up Periods

Average Error	MAD	MSE	Std	MAPE
0.1559	9.8170	124.1277	11.1413	0.0523

Final Parameter Estimates

Intercept	175.7714
Slope	1.4286

Seasonal Effects

1	1.2135
2	0.9007
3	1.0867
4	0.8164
5	0.9827

If you compare the seasonal estimates with those calculated earlier in Table 12-9 you will notice that they are all slightly smaller. That is because XLDataAnalyst has performed the additional test to make sure that the estimates add up to 5, which is the value of the seasonal cycle.

You may also notice that the sales values in Figure 12.24 are not the original values in the data that we started with. This is because XLDataAnalyst deseasonalizes the data before fitting the regression equation. The values shown in Figure 12-36 are the deseasonalized sales. The final regression equation is:

$$\hat{Y} = 175.7714 + 1.4286t$$

Sales are increasing by about 1.5 units per day or about 7.5 units per week.

Although XLDataAnalyst does not include a model for nonlinear trend, you can easily perform a nonlinear analysis on the logarithms of the data as described earlier in this chapter.

Exponential Smoothing Models

XLDataAnalyst can fit four different exponential smoothing models. The most basic is the Simple Smoothing Model, shown in Figure 12-37 which includes only an average value and no trend or seasonal effects. The Holt Model: Smoothing + Trend option adds a trend component to the simple smoothing model. The Smoothing with Seasonals option adds the seasonal component, but no trend. Finally, the Winters Model: Smoothing + Trend + Seasonals includes both trend and seasonal effects.

To illustrate, we will fit the Holt Model to the Example 12-3 data. Selecting the Holt model from the XLDataAnalyst menu shown in Figure 12-31 results in the dialog box shown in Figure 12-37.

Figure 12-37   *Dialog Box for the Holt Smoothing Plus Trend Model*

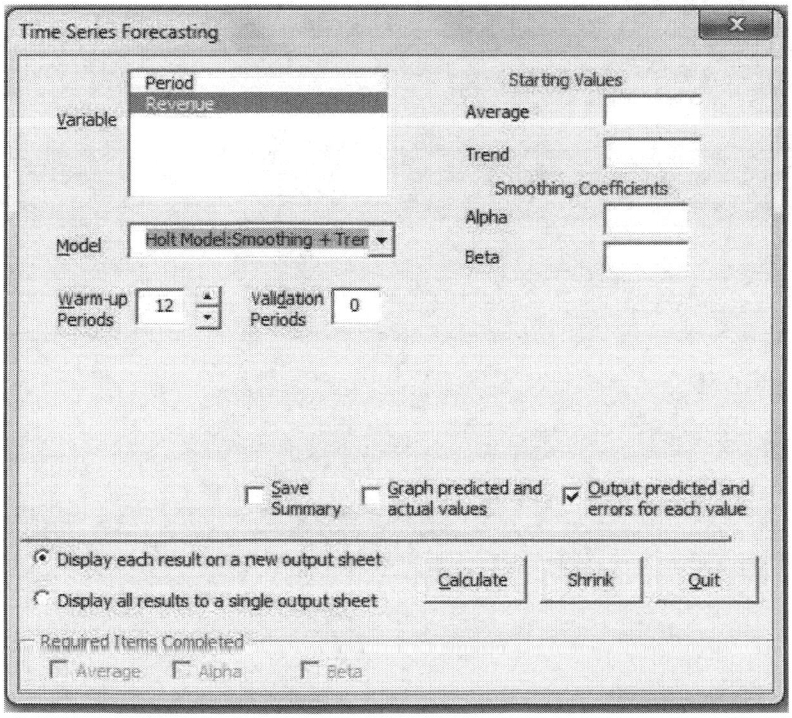

The Holt Model requires four input values. The starting values for the average and the trend need to be specified. Either an estimate of the average at the beginning of the series can be used or if none is available simply use the first value in the data. There will then be zero error for the first period and the model will be revised in the second period. If there is an estimate available for the trend it can be used here or if none if available simply enter a value of zero for the trend or leave it blank. If the trend is left blank it is assumed to be zero.

Values also need to be entered for the smoothing coefficients alpha (α) and beta (β). These should be decimal values between 0 and 1. The tradeoff between smoothing out random fluctuations (low values of the coefficients) versus detecting changes in the time series (high values of the coefficients) was discussed earlier in this chapter. Lower values of the smoothing coefficients (commonly 0.10 to 0.30) are commonly used in practice.

In Table 2-5 we used the first revenue value of 697 for the beginning average, zero for the beginning trend, and 0.10 for both smoothing coefficients. Using the same values, XLDataAnalyst produces the results shown in Figure 12-38. If you compare the values here with those in Table 12-5 you can see that the forecasts and error measures are the same as those calculated there.

Figure 12-38   ***Results of the Holt Model on the Example 12-3 Data***

Holt Model: Smoothing Plus Trend for Revenues

Period	Demand	Forecast	Error
1	697.0000	697.0000	0.0000
2	876.0000	697.0000	179.0000
3	1,193.0000	716.6900	476.3100
4	1,008.0000	770.8741	237.1259
5	718.0000	803.5110	-85.5110
6	991.0000	803.0292	187.9708
7	1,170.0000	831.7753	338.2247
8	1,241.0000	878.9289	362.0711
9	707.0000	932.0879	-225.0879
10	1,041.0000	924.2802	116.7198
11	1,253.0000	951.8204	301.1796
12	1,176.0000	1,000.8184	175.1816

Warm-up Periods

Average Error	MAD	MSE	Std	MAPE
171.9321	223.6985	65,746.9453	256.4117	0.2124

Final Parameter Estimates

Average	1,018.3365
Trend	20.6318

Autocorrelation In Regression

Earlier, we discussed the problem of autocorrelation with regression analysis. When autocorrelation is present, which is common in time series data, the independence of errors assumption of regression is violated. We previously discussed that the Durbin-Watson statistic is often used to detect the presence of autocorrelation. Because of difficulties with the Durbin-Watson statistic, the Breusch-Godfrey Test was suggested as an alternative. XLDataAnalyst will perform both types of tests. When performing any regression analysis that involves data that has been gathered at different points in time, you should always calculate these statistics to see if autocorrelation is a problem. To illustrate this consider the following example.

Example 12-9

In the 1950's, a study was performed attempting to predict per capita ice cream sales using the variables price, per capita income, and average daily temperature. The data were collected over 30 four-week periods. A portion of the data is shown below and the full dataset is contained in the file Example 12-9.xlsx.

Period	Consumption	Price	Income	Temperature
1	0.386	0.27	78	41
2	0.374	0.282	79	56
3	0.393	0.277	81	63
4	0.425	0.28	80	68
5	0.406	0.272	76	69
6	0.344	0.262	78	65
7	0.327	0.275	82	61
8	0.288	0.267	79	47
9	0.269	0.265	76	32
10	0.256	0.277	79	24
11	0.286	0.282	82	28
12	0.298	0.27	85	26
13	0.329	0.272	86	32
14	0.318	0.287	83	40

Consumption represents the number of pints consumed per resident during that time period, price is the average price of a pint of ice cream during that period, weekly family income in dollars, and temperature is the average temperature in degrees Fahrenheit during that time period[7]. Figure 12-39 shows the regression dialog box with the option to calculate autocorrelation statistics selected. When this option is selected the dialog box shown in Figure 12-40 will appear. In this dialog box, you need to specify the number of lag periods to use in the Breusch-Godfrey tests. The default of 4 periods is usually fine for this. The results for Example 12-9 are shown in Figure 12-41.

---

[7] This data set was modified from a data set in the Data and Story Library website at http://lib.stat.cmu.edu/DASL/Stories/IceCreamConsumption.html.

Figure 12-39   *Completed Regression Dialog Box for Example 12-9*

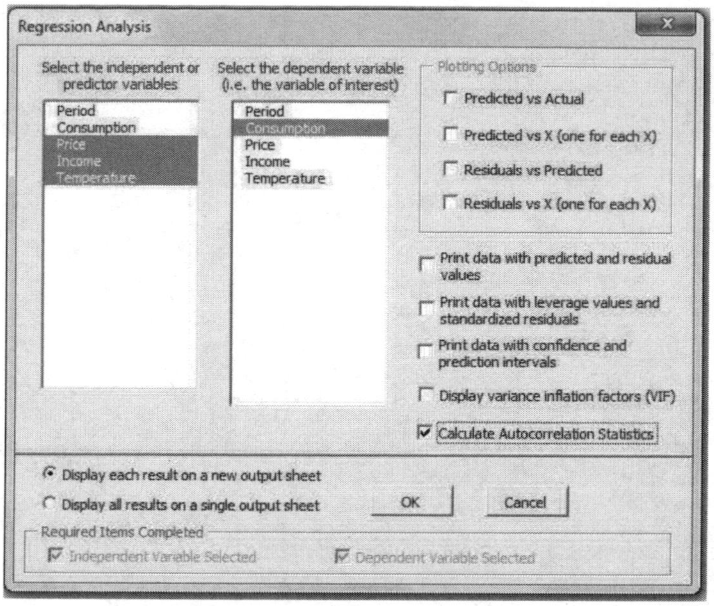

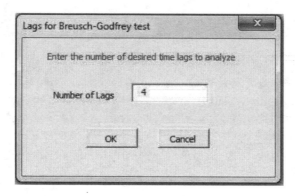

Figure 12-40   *Dialog Box for Breusch-Godfrey Lags*

Figure 12-41   *XLDataAnalyst Results for Example 12-9*

Regression Analysis for Consumption

Summary Measures

Multiple R	0.8479
R-Square	0.7190
Adj R-Square	0.6866
Std Error of Est.	0.0368

ANOVA Table

Effect	SS	DF	MS	F	P-value
Regression	0.0903	3	0.0301	22.1749	0.0000
Residual	0.0353	26	0.0014		
Total	0.1255	29	0.0043		

Regression Coefficients

Effect	Coefficient	Beta	Std Error	t-value	p-value
Constant	0.1973		0.2702	0.7302	0.4718
Price	-1.0444	-0.1324	0.8344	-1.2518	0.2218
Income	0.0033	0.3140	0.0012	2.8237	0.0090
Temperature	0.0035	0.8633	0.0004	7.7622	0.0000

Autocorrelation Results

Durbin-Watson   1.021169711

Breusch-Godfrey Analysis

Lag	R-Square	P-Value
1	0.1622	0.0331
2	0.1825	0.0932
3	0.1871	0.2131
4	0.2184	0.3079

Figure 12-41 shows that the overall model is highly significant and predicts approximately 72% of the variability in ice cream consumption. Both Income and Temperature show significant regression coefficients; however, Figure 12-41 also shows a Durbin-Watson statistic of .656 which is considerably below the guidelines for the statistic when there is no autocorrelation. Moreover, the Breusch-Godfrey tests show that there is a significant 1-period autocorrelation. This indicates that autocorrelation may be a significant problem for this analysis. When autocorrelation is present, standard error terms in the regression may be underestimated and spurious significant results can occur. To test for this, differencing was applied to all of the independent and dependent variables using the Differencing option in XLDataAnalyst. The regression analysis was then recalculated using the differenced variables. The results are shown in Figure 12-42.

Figure 12-42   **Results for Example 12-9 After Differencing the Variables**

Regression Analysis for Diff Consumption

Summary Measures

Multiple R	0.6375
R-Square	0.4064
Adj R-Square	0.3351
Std Error of Est.	0.0336

ANOVA Table

Effect	SS	DF	MS	F	P-value
Regression	0.0193	3	0.0064	5.7045	0.0041
Residual	0.0282	25	0.0011		
Total	0.0475	28	0.0017		

Regression Coefficients

Effect	Coefficient	Beta	Std Error	t-value	p-value
Constant	0.0034		0.0064	0.5343	0.5978
Diff Price	−0.9292	−0.1982	0.7282	−1.2760	0.2137
Diff Income	−0.0022	−0.1555	0.0022	−0.9878	0.3327
Diff Temperature	0.0027	0.5622	0.0007	3.5953	0.0014

Autocorrelation Results

Durbin-Watson   2.027325433

Breusch-Godfrey Analysis

Lag	R-Square	P-Value
1	0.0510	0.2405
2	0.0695	0.4194
3	0.0979	0.5219
4	0.1279	0.6117

The results in Figure 12-42 clearly show that differencing has succeeded in eliminating the autocorrelation in the data. The results also show that when the autocorrelation is eliminated, Income is no longer statistically significant; however, Temperature still has a statistically significant regression coefficient. This indicates that the relationship between income and ice cream consumption in the original analysis was likely a spurious relationship resulting from the autocorrelation present in the data. The results also reinforce our conclusions about the effect of temperature on ice cream sales since this relationship persists even when the autocorrelation is removed from the data.

Exercises VIII

36. The file Exercise 12-36.xlsx contains the closing price of Sears's (SHLD) stock at the beginning of the month for a 3-year period from March from 3/1/2010 to 2/1/2013. Fit both a linear and an exponential trend line to the data. Which model would you choose for this data? Explain why.

37. The file Exercise 12-37.xlsx contains the closing price of Arctic Cat's (ACAT) stock at the beginning of the month for a 3-year period from March from 3/1/2010 to 2/1/2013. Fit both a linear

and an exponential trend line to the data. Which model would you choose for this data? Explain why.

38. Melissa works in the Marketing Department at AloTech Inc. One of her responsibilities is forecasting demand for the new AcerZ2 product which has been on the market for 12 months now. The past 12 months demand for the AcerZ2 in thousands of units is contained in the file Exercise 12-38.xlsx.

    (a) Graph the data. Does there appear to be a trend in the data.

    (b) Is the trend linear or nonlinear? Support your answer with data from the appropriate analyses.

    (c) Develop a model for Melissa to use and provide a forecast for the coming month.

39. Sam's Sporting Goods store tracks sales by item to better manage their inventory and improve their forecasting system. The data in the file Exercise 12-39.xlsx represents monthly sales of 3-pack sleeves of Top-Flite XLDataAnalyst Tour Trajectory golf balls.

    (a) Fit a Holt trend smoothing model to the data. What coefficients seem to work best?

    (b) Fit a Winters Smoothing Model with trend and seasonal effects to the data. Does this model fit the data better than the Holt Model? Explain.

40. The file Exercise 12-40.xlsx contains the annual print advertising expenditures in U.S. Newspapers from 1997 through 2011. Use an exponential smoothing model to estimate the annual trend in newspaper print advertising over this time period. Comment on the implications for the newspaper industry.

41. The Frosty Delight soda company tracks sales of its flagship product Rusty Pirate Root Beer quarterly. The data are contained in the file Exercise 12-41.xlsx.

    (a) Fit a multiplicative seasonal model using linear trend to the data. How well does the model fit?

    (b) Fit an additive seasonal model to the data using linear trend. Which model would you recommend for Frosty Delight and why?

    (c) Using the model you recommended in part (b), forecast Rusty Pirate Root Beer sales for the next four quarters.

Opening Vignette Revisited

Jim Belmore decides to start by analyzing the data for one flavor, Tooty-Fruity. He starts by graphing the data over time to see if he can detect any patterns. The graph is shown in Figure 12-43.

Figure 12-43   ***Graph of Tooty-Fruity Sales***

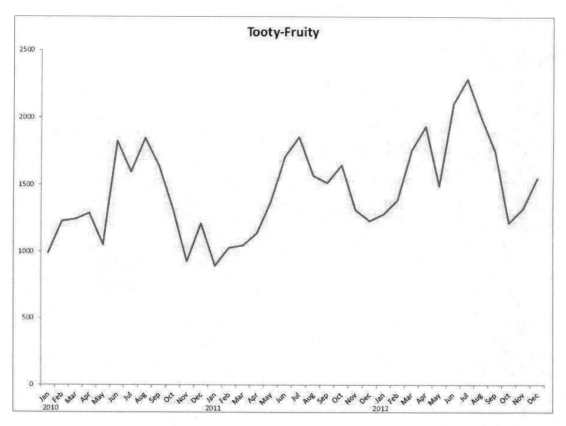

After looking at the graph, Jim is relatively certain that there are seasonal patterns in the data. In particular, it appears that sales are highest in the months of June, July, and August which makes sense as these are the months with the highest temperatures. Since he believes that the seasonal effects are multiplicative rather than additive, Jim decides to estimate the seasonal effects using the ratio to moving average approach. Selecting Time Series Analysis in the XLDataAnalyst ribbon he completes the dialog box to estimate seasonal effects as shown in Figure 12-44. The results of the analysis are shown in Figure 12-45 where the period number refers to the period in the seasonal cycle. January is period 1 and December is period 12.

Figure 12-44   **Completed Dialog to Estimate Seasonal Effects for Tooty-Fruity**

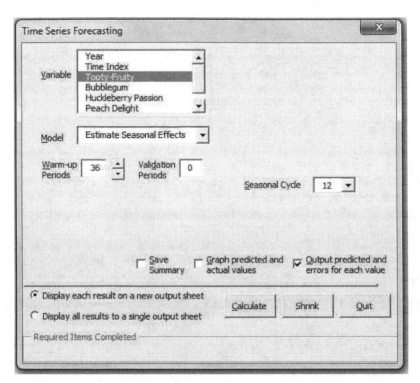

Figure 12-45   **Seasonal Effect Estimates for Tooty-Fruity**

Seasonal Estimates for Tooty-Fruity

Period	Seasonal Effect
1	0.7320
2	0.8067
3	0.9224
4	1.0092
5	0.9590
6	1.2565
7	1.2628
8	1.2454
9	1.1391
10	1.0472
11	0.7735
12	0.8464

As Jim anticipated, June, July, and August (periods 6, 7, and 8) have the largest seasonal effects. The 1.2565 estimate for June indicates that June sales are almost 26% above average. On the other hand, the January index of .7320 indicates that January sales are almost 27% below average.

Having estimated the seasonal effects, Jim now turns his attention to the trend. Figure 12-43 indicates a slight upward movement in Tooty-Fruity sales over the past 3 years. Jim does not believe that the trend in sales for this product changes much over time and feels comfortable using a static approach such as regression analysis to estimate the trend; however, just to be safe, he also plans to use exponential smoothing to estimate the trend. Jim knows that if he uses the Holt Model to estimate the trend he will have to first deseasonalize the data since there are clearly seasonal effects in the time series. Alternatively, he could use the Winters Model which also includes trend and uses the seasonal estimates from Figure 12-45 as the starting values for the seasonal effects in the Winters Model as well as a small smoothing coefficient for seasonal effects in the model. Jim decides to use the later approach. After again selecting Time Series Analysis in the XLDataAnalyst ribbon, Jim completes the time series dialog box as shown in Figure 12-46. Because he does not want to have the model respond to random fluctuations, he selects a small coefficient (Alpha of .1) as the smoothing coefficient for the average value. Since he already has reliable estimates of the seasonal effects, he also sets the smoothing coefficient for the seasonal effects to a small value (Gamma of .1). The smoothing coefficient for trend he sets to a slightly higher value so that the trend estimate will adjust more quickly (Beta of .3). He sets the beginning average equal to the first period data value (990) and the initial trend to 0 since he does not have an estimate for that value. The starting values for the seasonal effects are set to the values from Figure 12-45. The results of this analysis are shown in Figure 12-47.

Figure 12-46   Completed Dialog Box for the Winters Model for Tooty-Fruity

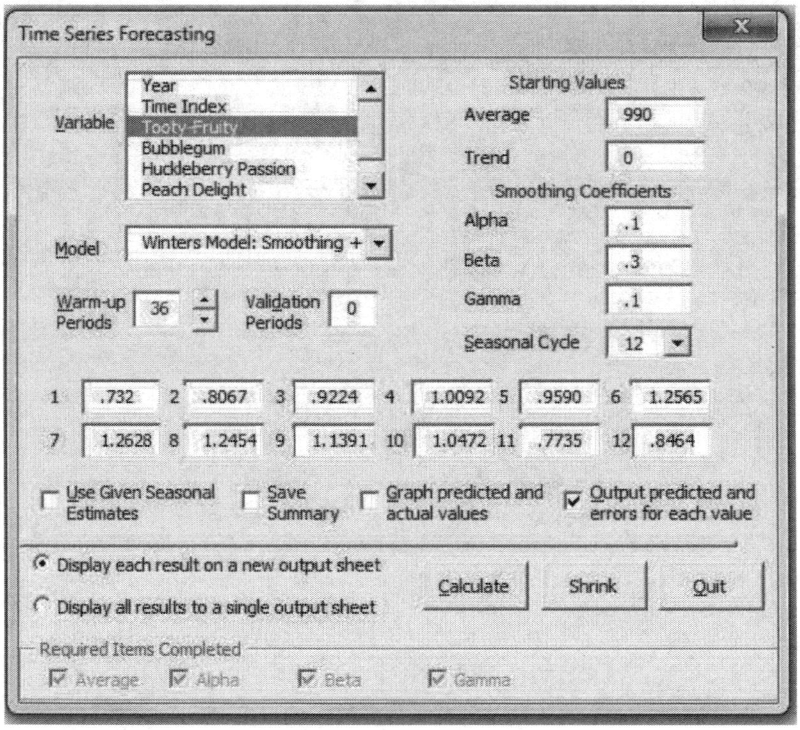

Figure 12-47   ***Results of the Winters Model for Tooty-Fruity***

Warm-up Periods

Average Error	MAD	MSE	Std	MAPE
0.8757	190.9894	55,013.4727	234.5495	0.1428

Final Parameter Estimates

Average	1,765.2856
Trend	9.8945

Seasonal Effects

1	0.7546
2	0.8360
3	0.9396
4	1.0158
5	0.9475
6	1.2680
7	1.2715
8	1.2347
9	1.1239
10	1.0163
11	0.7758
12	0.8500

From Figure 12-47, Jim estimates that there is a trend of about 10 (trend estimate of 9.8945) units per month over this three-year period. The standard deviation of the errors (234.5495) indicates that the error component of the time series is approximately 235 units.

Jim next wants to estimate the trend using regression analysis; however, since there are clearly seasonal effects in the data, he must first deseasonalize the data before performing the analysis. Using the seasonal estimates from Figure 12-45, he divides the sales value for each period by its corresponding seasonal estimate. For example, the 990 for January demand is divided by the January seasonal estimate of .7456 to obtain a value of 1352.433. He uses a similar process to deseasonalize the rest of the data. To perform the analysis, Jim has a choice of using regular regression analysis using the Regression option of the XLDataAnalyst ribbon or the Time Series option.

Summary

A time series is a set of observations at fixed time intervals over a period of time. Time series data is primarily used in business to predict future values in the series. Models can be fit to the data to try and estimate the systematic components of the series, an average value, trend, and seasonal effects, so that the estimates can be used to make predictions. Autocorrelations can sometimes be used to detect the presence of trend or seasonal effects.

No model is able to perfectly predict events in a time series so it is important to take into account the errors in prediction and track such errors when making forecasts. Summary measures of error include average error, the mean absolute deviation (MAD), the mean square error (MSE), standard deviation (σ), and the mean absolute percentage error (MAPE). The fit of a model is gauged by one or more of these error measures. It is important to also track and monitor errors when using a model to forecast future events.

Estimating an average value can be done using moving averages or exponential smoothing. Exponential smoothing uses more of the data than a moving average and weighs more recent data most heavily. Trend can be estimated using exponential smoothing methods (Holt Model) or with regression procedures. Regression techniques can fit either linear or nonlinear trend.

Seasonal effects can be either additive or multiplicative and are estimated using exponential smoothing, regression methods, or a decomposition approach. An exponential Smoothing Model which includes trend and seasonal effects is called the Winters Model. Seasonal effects in the Winters Model are typically treated as multiplicative effects. Regression analysis can be used to estimate additive seasonal effects while the decomposition approach estimates multiplicative seasonal effects typically using the ratio to moving average method.

Autocorrelations or serial correlations are correlations between values measured at different points in time. Patterns in the autocorrelations at different lags can be utilized to determine if trend or seasonal effects are present in a time series; however, autocorrelations between errors or residuals in regressions analysis, often called serial correlation, indicates a violation of the assumptions of regression. If serial correlation is detected using the Durbin-Watson or the Breusch-Godfrey Test, then steps should be taken to remove the autocorrelation. This may involve modifying the model to include additional variables or changing the functional form of the model. Sometimes differencing can be used to remove autocorrelation caused by business cycles or other outside influences.

Developing a method of forecasting involves determining which components to include in the model, how the components are combined (additive or multiplicative) and how to estimate the components. Regardless of how the model is derived, care must be taken to protect against overfitting the model to the existing data.

Index numbers are used to compare quantities by measuring them relative to a base point. Simple indexes measure change in a single value. An aggregate index measures the change in a group of items over time. Aggregate indexes can be further classified as weighted or unweighted. Most commonly reported economic index numbers such as the Consumer Price Index (CPI), the Producer Price Index, and the Import and Export Price Index are weighted aggregate indexes. A Laspeyres Index is a weighted aggregate index where the weight is the quantity in the base period of the index. A Paasche Index uses the quantity in the reference period for the weight rather than the base period.

Scatter plots with trend lines can be used in Excel to explore trend patterns in time series data and the LINEST and LOGEST functions can be used to estimate the parameters of linear and nonlinear models. The DataAnalysis Toolpak can be used to perform simple exponential smoothing and linear regression. XLDataAnalyst can perform regression analysis as demonstrated in Chapters 10 and 11. In addition, the Time Series components of XLDataAnalyst can be used to perform virtually all of the time series procedures described in this chapter.

Chapter Glossary

Aggregate Index	An index that measures the changes in multiple variables over time.
Autocorrelation	A correlation between values measured at different points in time. Sometimes called serial correlation.
Autocorrelation Plot	A graph of the correlations at different time lags often with 95% confidence limits. Also called a correlogram.
Average	Represents the average value of a time series which may vary over time.
Average Error	The simple average of the forecast errors.
Base Period	The denominator of an index number. All index values are relative to this base period.
Breusch-Godfrey Test	An alternative to the Durbin-Watson Test for first-order serial correlation. Also called the Lagrange Multiplier Test.
Consumer Price Index	An aggregate index of a basket of consumer goods widely used as a measure of inflation in the United States.
Correlogram	A graph of the correlations at different time lags often with 95% confidence limits. Also called an autocorrelation plot.
Deflator	An index number used to adjust time series data for inflation.
Deseasonalize	Removing seasonal effects by dividing (or subtracting) the appropriate seasonal estimate.
Differencing	A method of reducing autocorrelation in time series data by taking the difference between the value at time t and the value at another time period.
Durbin-Watson Test	A commonly used statistic to test for first-order serial correlation in time series data.
First-Order Serial Correlation	Usually means the same as autocorrelation. Some authors restrict the use of this term when the correlation is between two different variables lagged by one period.
Exponential Smoothing	A class of time series forecasting models where all values in the time series receive a weight but more recent data are weighted more heavily.
Export Price Index	An index that measures prices paid for goods exported from a country.
Forecast Error	The difference between a model prediction and the actual value. Also called a residual.

Holt Model	An exponential smoothing model which includes trend as well as an average value.
Import Price Index	An index that measures prices paid for goods imported into a country.
Inflection Point	A point in a quadratic model where the curve changes direction.
Lagged Variable	A transformed time series variable where the new value of the variable at time *t* is the value of the variable at time *t-1*.
Laspeyres Index	A weighted aggregate index where the quantities for the base period are used as the weights in calculating the index values for all time periods.
Mean Absolute Deviation	The average of the absolute errors.
Mean Absolute Percentage Error	The average of the ratio of the absolute errors divided by the actual values, expressed in %
Mean Square Error	The average of the squared errors.
Moving Average	An estimate of the average in time series data which uses a fixed number of values in calculating the average each time period.
Overfitting	A situation where the model conforms too closely to the idiosyncrasies of the data used to fit the model and therefore does a poor job of predicting new data.
Paasche Index	A weighted aggregate index where the quantities for the reference period rather than the base period are used as the weights in calculating the index values in each time period.
Producer Price Index	An aggregate price index of a set of goods sold by wholesalers.
Ratio to Moving Average	A method of estimating seasonal effects which looks at the ratio of the observed values to a moving average.
Residual	A difference between the value predicted by a model and the actual value. Another term for error commonly used in regression analysis.
Seasonal Cycle	The number of time periods before a seasonal pattern repeats itself.
Seasonal Effects	Systematic fluctuations around an average value that are repeated in predictable cycles.
Simple Index	An index that measures the changes in only one variable over time.
Smoothing Coefficient	A value between 0 and 1 that is used to smooth out random fluctuations in time series data in an exponential smoothing model.
Time Series Data	Data gathered at equally spaced intervals over a period of time.
Trend	An upward or downward change in the average value of a time series.

Validation Sample	A portion of the sample that is withheld and not used in fitting the model, but it is rather used to assess the validity of the resulting fitted model.
Winters Model	An exponential smoothing model that includes average, trend, and seasonal components.

Questions and Problems

42. The following tables show the production in thousands of tons and the price per thousand tons of two minerals, palladium and platinum, mined in the State of Montana. The data are also contained in the file Exercise 12-42.xlsx.

	Quantity									
	1999	2000	2001	2002	2003	2004	2005	2006	2007	2008
Palladium	9800	10300	12100	14800	14000	13700	13300	14400	12800	11900
Platinum	2920	3110	3610	4390	4170	4040	3920	4290	3860	3580

	Price									
Palladium	$11.63	22.14	19.59	10.95	6.53	7.45	6.55	10.42	11.56	11.43
Platinum	$12.19	17.65	17.15	17.43	22.33	27.23	28.83	36.83	41.97	50.84

Source: U.S. Bureau of Mines: http://minerals.usgs.gov/minerals/pubs/state/mt.html#myb

(a) Calculate quantity and price indexes for both minerals using 2000 as the base year. What are the trends in these variables over this 10 year period?

(b) Calculate the Laspeyres value index for the value of the two minerals using 2000 as the base year.

(c) Calculate the Paasche value index for the value of the two minerals. How does this index compare with the Laspeyres index from part b?

43. The Heltron Manufacturing Company is considering relocating a manufacturing facility to the Spokane Washington area. A key concern in this decision is the cost of labor in the Spokane area. Heltron needs semi-skilled and administrative workers for the new plant. The data shown below and also contained in the file Exercise 12-43.xlsx contains information on the hourly wage rates and the average number of workers in each category for the past 10 years.

Year	2003	2004	2005	2006	2007	2008	2009	2010	2011	2012
Semi Skilled Wages	12.54	12.67	12.76	12.87	13.01	12.98	12.79	13.07	13.16	13.27
Semi-Skilled Number	6,707	6,676	6,631	6,608	6,627	6,568	6,382	6,370	6,544	6,635
Administrative Wages	17.29	17.36	17.44	17.51	17.59	17.68	17.61	17.72	17.79	17.86
Administrative Number	12,177	12,021	11,914	11,959	11,972	11,859	11,134	11,829	11,998	12,058

(d) Calculate quantity and price indexes for both types of labor using 2005 as the base year. What are the trends in these variables over this 10-year period?

(e) Calculate the Laspeyres value index for the value of the two types of labor using 2005 as the base year.

(f) Calculate the Paasche value index for the value of the two types of labor. How does this index compare with the Laspeyres index from part b?

44. The file Exercise 12-44.xlsx contains monthly values of the Misery Index from October 2005 through October 2012. The Misery Index, first proposed by economist Arthur Okun, is the sum of the unemployment rate and the inflation rate.

(a) Use regression analysis to predict the misery index using the period number as an independent variable. Make sure to run autocorrelation statistics. Does there appear to be a trend? Is autocorrelation a problem for this analysis?

(b) Use differencing on the misery index and rerun the analysis from part a using the differenced misery index as the dependent variable. Is there still a significant trend?

45. Nuevo Energia is a growing company in the fuel cell industry. The number of employees each year over the past 10 years is contained in the file Exercise 12-45.xlsx. The Human Resources Department at Nuevo Energia needs to develop a system to forecast future employee growth for planning purposes. Using the data provided, develop a model that Human Resources can use to forecast the number of employees for the next 3 years. Support your choice of model with concrete data on model performance.

46. The Bayside Resort operates along the coast of Oregon near a scenic golf course. Bayside has data on monthly room occupancy over the past five years. The data are contained in the file Exercise 12-46.xlsx. Develop a model Bayside can use to forecast future monthly occupancy rates. Justify your inclusion of model components based on data for model performance. What would be your forecasts for the next 12 months assuming that it is now the end of December?

47. The Value Discount store has applied to the United Consumer Bank for a loan to expand their store by buying the shop next to their current store in the strip mall and combining the two spaces. The bank officer in charge of their loan application asks for a monthly forecast of sales for the coming year beginning in January 2014. Max Klinger, the owner of Value Discount has monthly sales data for the past four years. This data is contained in the file Exercise 12-47.xlsx.

(a) Graph the data and comment on what components appear to be present in the time series.

(b) Estimate the current average sales level and the trend in sales. Discuss whether or not the model to predict next year's sales should include a trend or not.

(c) Estimate seasonal effects from the data. Justify the method that you use to estimate the seasonal effects.

(d) Forecast next year's sales for Value Discount using all of the appropriate components.

impact to the self results in a loss of integrative complexity and function. Figure 6.2 illustrates the progression and pathways of self-alterations caused by trauma.

The loss of structural cohesion precipitates defenses against anxiety and vulnerability to ego-adaptive processes in terms of need gratification and maintenance of selfhood. Regression can occur as the component parts of the self undergo dissolution, disunity, and fragmentation.

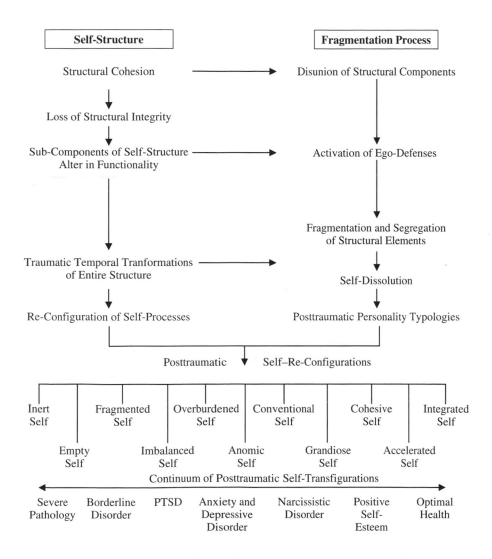

Fig. 6.2 Trauma and the Pathway of Self-Fragmentation (Source: Wilson, 2003)

The intricate structural cohesion breaks apart, unraveling and thus requiring more and more energy from defenses to guard the painful sense of annihilation, disintegration, and ineffectiveness in coping with external demands. It is as if the "organ" of the self shrinks or diminishes, filling up with the affect engendered by trauma, which now occupies and encroaches on more conscious and unconscious ego space. Henry Krystal (1988a) has reached a similar understanding:

> I came to the conclusion that the final common path of traumatization was the development of overwhelming affects ... the physical immobilization observable in the catanoid state is accompanied by a massive blocking of virtually all mental activity — not just affects, but all initiative, judgment, and other activity — to the point that "walking death" may ensue. This may serve as a model of an adult traumatic state. (pp. 142, 145)

Clearly, then, the dissolution of the self can result in profound changes in psychological functioning, which cross-cuts all of the dimensions of the self: coherency, connection, continuity, energy, autonomy, and organismic vitality. The personality reconfigures into clinically describable typologies. Such posttraumatic states can become pathological and constitute forms of complex PTSD (Courtois, 2002; Herman, 1992; Wilson et al., 2001) or severe mental illness. As Lifton observed (1967, 1993), survivors nevertheless universally face the task of "protean" transformation and the rebuilding of the fragmented self. This reconstruction of the traumatized self is a process of gradual integration of the trauma experience; the reintegration of the "old" self into a new configuration (Wilson, 1980, 1982, 1989).

Core Dimensions of the Self Injured by Trauma

> Our mind remembers, our brain remembers, our body remembers and our spirit/soul remembers. When a powerful [traumatic] memory is recalled, our entire system remembers.

> Father N.D. Sinclair, 1993

It is possible to further understand the dynamics of posttraumatic self typologies described earlier by examining how each of the core dimensions of the self is injured by traumatic experiences. *The core dimensions of the self, in their healthy developmental forms, reflect optimal levels of each dimension; all the parts of the architecture of the self are functionally integrated in the service of psychological health and efficacy in adaptive behavior.* Further, it is clinically and scientifically important to specify the strength and weakness of each posttraumatic typology. For each of the six dimensions of the self structure, we can utilize a 6-point rating scale of degrees of optimal function: pathological (– – –), very weak (– –), or weak (–); strong (+ + +), moderate (+ +), or low (+). This simple rating scale enables comparisons and contrasts of each dimension between the posttraumatic typologies.

Assessing Posttraumatic Self-Reconfigurations

Figure 6.3 illustrates how each dimension of the self structure is damaged by severe trauma or as deviated from optimal states of functioning. It also indicates the relative weakness or strength of the dimension of the self following trauma and the degree of change from optimal functioning. For example, the inert-self typology is pathologically weak in all dimensions, reflecting massive decentering and fragmentation of the self described by Krystal (1988a) as catanoid surrender. Psychic numbing is

Optimal Self-Functioning (+++)

Post-Trauma Self-Typologies (Self-Dimensions)	Coherency	Connection	Continuity	Energy	Autonomy	Vitality
Inert ("Dead") Self (Surrender)	- - -	- - -	- - -	- - -	- - -	- - -
Empty Self (Depressed)	-	- -	- -	- -	- -	- - -
Fragmented Self (Diffusion)	- - -	- -	- -	+	-	- -
Imbalanced Self (Instability)	- -	-	- -	+	- - -	-
Overburdened Self (Fixated)	-	+	+	+	+	-
Anomic Self (Normlessness)	- -	- -	-	+	+	- -
Conventional Self (Adjusted)	+	++	++	+	-	+
Grandiose Self (Exhibitionistic)	+	+	+++	+++	++	++
Cohesive/Vital Self (Resilient)	+++	+++	+++	++	++	++
Accelerated Self (Post-Conventional)	+++	++	+	+++	+++	+++
Integrated-Transcendent Self (Actualized)	+++	+++	+++	+++	+++	+++

Key: Optimal Degrees of Strength in Dimensions of Self

Weakness: (- - -) Pathological   **Strength:** (+) Low
(- -) Very Weak   (++) Moderate
(-) Weak   (+++) Strong

Fig. 6.3 Core Dimensions of Self Injured by Trauma (Source: Wilson, 2002)

perfused throughout the ego. Despair and emptiness prevail. We can speak meaningfully of a "broken spirit." The empty self is also weak, helpless, and overwhelmed by depressive affects. Vitality is missing and victims/survivors are insecure, safety-seeking, and profoundly mistrustful, lacking in autonomy and initiative. The anomic self is weak, alienated from social norms, but has some degree of continuity and the minimal capacity to mobilize energy for restorative purposes. The anomic self is rootless and adrift, seeking a source of attachment to provide grounding. The fragmented self has a profound loss of coherence, disrupted continuity, and identity diffusion. Such persons are prone to dissociation, anxiety, and have unstable self-object relations. The overburdened self is "trapped in the trauma" (Wilson, 1980, 1989) and fixated to trauma's impact to the self. However, there is more strength available in the form of energy, autonomy, connection (usually to fellow survivors) to form a sense of "survivor identity." The overburdened self often adapts by obsessive-compulsive behavioral defenses, compensatory action, and rigidified patterns of living. Similarly, the imbalanced self is emotionally labile and unstable, manifesting splitting and self-object deficits characteristic of borderline personality disorder. The components of the self structure are nonarticulated. Such persons seek reassurance, nurturance, love, and security. They are anxious, agitated, and volatile. The conventional self is, in contrast, relatively adjusted to social norms and the capacity to carry out activation of daily living, albeit with compromises to their sense of vitality and well-being, experienced as free-floating or general anxiety disorders. Such persons are conforming, group-oriented, and approval-seeking.

The cohesive self, accelerated self, and integrated self represent different forms of integration and ego synthesis for mastering experience, including resolution of trauma. The integrated transcendent self is transformative in nature and capable of utilizing (i.e., transforming) the negative energy (affect) from trauma to build a new, healthy identity hallmarked by individuation and actualization. In contrast, the psychosocially accelerated self (Wilson, 1980) manifests alienation from norms, resistance to acculturation, and autonomy from social norms. In a descriptive sense, they are iconoclastic "outsiders," "time-warped," accelerated in epigenetic development, and able to forge new identities congruent with strong drives toward self-reliance in a prosocial, humanitarian, and postconventional orientation (Wilson, 1980).

The continuum of self-alterations is a way of analyzing the spectrum of self-disintegration, the loss of structural coherence, and the subsequent manner in which restorative efforts reconfigure into healthier modalities of integration complexity. Ernest Wolfe (1990) has written that

> The person whose self-regresses from a state of cohesion to one of partial or total loss of structure experiences this as a loss of self-esteem, or a feeling of emptiness, depression, worthlessness, or anxiety. This change in the structured state of the self has been termed fragmentation. Fragmentation occurs in varying degrees and does not imply com-

plete dissolution of the self ... fragmentation is sometimes experienced as the terrifying certainty of imminent death, which signals a process of apparently irreversible dissolution of the self. The experience of a crumbling self is so unpleasant that people will do almost anything to escape the perception brought about by fragmentation ... fragmentation means regression toward lessened cohesion, more permeable boundaries, diminished energy and vitality and disturbed harmonious balance. (p. 39)

We can see that, the "disturbed harmonious balance" is psychic disequilibrium in the component dimensions of the self, produced by the allostatic load of trauma. As we have noted, allostasis is the psychobiological process of reestablishing stability following the destructuring of the self (Wilson et al., 2001). The reversal of disturbed balance, affective dysregulation in posttraumatic ego-states, is a goal of treatment to facilitate the processes of self-reconstruction. Stated simply, the survivor has to reinvent him- or herself in order to resume life with a sense of vitality, connection, and autonomy, but, perhaps, without a sense of continuity to the past. In reinventing the posttraumatic self, the "old self" gets shed, like an exoskeleton, and is replaced with a more vital and functional one.

THE LOSS OF STRUCTURAL COHERENCE: PSYCHOLOGICAL INVERSION EXPERIENCES IN TRAUMA

Our knowledge of the enormous complexities of the trauma experience and its impact to the organism is in its infancy. Understanding traumatic impact to the self and spirit is like understanding a gigantic asteroid's impact to the planet. There are diverse impacts to "terra firma," some superficial and others that permeate the core magma, disturbing its organization and massive molten liquidity and leaving huge craters on the surface. In an analogous way, it is possible to understand the loss of structural coherence as a form of psychological inversion experience that is present in certain forms of trauma. The inversion experience is a new term that I am introducing here for further classification of how self-processes can be affected by extreme stress experiences.

Psychological *inversion experiences* are the reversal of normal, consensual reality caused by the trauma experience and impact of excessive stress to the self. Inversion experiences are associated with altered states of awareness, perception, cognition, and motivation in which the understanding of reality inverts its order, function, and structural integrity. Inversion experiences are not dissociative episodes, but can involve dissociative features as reactions to threat and changes to existence and adaptive capacities. The individual's understanding of reality inverts its order; "shape shifting," "inside out," "upside down," in transformative permutations, like looking at a kaleidoscope of changing patterns. The inversion experience is a palindromal psychological phenomenon. Each twist of trauma's kaleidoscope produces a new perceptual pattern, often overwhelming to the ego's capacity for processing its unusual stimulus field.

There are different types of psychological inversion experiences: moral, political, social, interpersonal, and self, which are summarized in Figure 6.4. Further, there can be several forms of inversion present at the same time, depending on the nature of the trauma experience. Torture, for example, involves moral and political inversion (e.g., suffering equals justice). Inversion experiences can be transparent when experience shifts focus, meaning, and grounding, changing the experiential planes of existence, which results in psychic functioning in the vortex of trauma — a form of oscillatory immersion into overwhelming unnatural order, an "odd ecology" with strange dimensions not previously experienced.

In the inversion experience, there is often a rapid and radical shift in time-space perspective. The continuity and flow of life alters, as if entering the "twilight zone" of an alien land at the first light of dawn. There is a sense of strangeness to individual perception. Moreover, unusual amodal perceptions of reality have been studied in infant developmental processes. For example, Daniel Stern (1985) notes

> infants thus appear to have an innate general capacity, which can be called *amodal perceptions* — to take information received in one sensory modality and somehow translate it into another sensory modality — the information is probably not experienced as belonging to any one sensory mode. More likely, it transcends mode or channel and exists in some unknown supra-modal form. It is not, then, a simple issue of direct translation across modalities. Rather, it involves an encoding into still mysterious amodal representations, which can be recognized in any of the sensory modes. (p. 51, emphasis added)

The concept of *amodal perception* is intrinsic to the trauma-induced inversion experience; a transmodal sensory-perceptual and cognitive experience. In this way, it is possible to see that traumatic experiences can cause a psychological recapitulation of infantile amodal perception — a return to earlier, less-organized forms of environmental encounters. Trauma induced disequilibrium likely leads the brain to search its memory for prior patterns of amodal or transmodal perception, which it finds in the archives of infantile modalities of perceptual experience. The inversion experience occurs because the trauma event cannot be matched readily in cognitive encoding to expectancies, that is, there are no current cognitive schema to assimilate the "oddness" of the experience nor is there a "ready-match" in existing cognitive schema. The absence of all but primitive infantile memories of amodal perceptions thus creates lacunae in preexisting cognitive schematic structures of information processing.

What is the nature of the trauma environment associated with the inversion experience? In this ecologically odd psychological environment, there is a confusion of rules, order, procedures, and expectancies.

Psychological Inversion Reversal of Normal Reality Caused by the Experience of Traumatic Stress

Definition: An alteration or change in awareness, perception, cognition, and motivation in which the understanding of reality inverts its order, function, and structural integrity.

Types of Inversion

Moral inversion: Inversion of normative moral order (e.g., good is bad; evil is good, etc.)
Political inversion: Inversion of the political order of power
Social inversion: Rapid shift in normal sociocultural order
Interpersonal inversion: Inversion in attachments and self-object relationships
Self-inversion: Inversion of the structural coherence of the self

Dimensions of Inversion Experience

Amodal and transmodal sensory, perceptual, and cognitive processes
Radical shift in time-space perspective and sudden shift of the normal order
Sense of "unreality"; disorientation (i.e., abnormal vs. normal, bad vs. good, slavery vs. freedom, abuse vs. affection, etc.)
Confusion of rules, order, procedures, laws, justice, fairness, etc.
Uncertainty as to appropriate action, initiative, coping
Fears of self-dissolution, self-annihilation, or decompensation into mental illness
Absence of organizing framework: perception, cognitive encoding, classification, experienced cognitive disequilibrium
Loss of sense of grounding/centering to the self
Challenge to core beliefs, loss of meaning, and the encounter of "ecological oddness" (i.e., a strange, alien world)
Appraisals of threat imposed by changes induced by inversion experience
Reversal of normal-expectable baseline with abnormal baseline expectations
Changed sense of self-in-world; existence, and meaning of life
A subjective sense of free falling into the abyss of nothingness, a vortex of the unknown or "psychological worm-hole" phenomenon
Loss of symbolic integrity and meaning (i.e., nonfunctionality of value and meaning systems).
A temporary or prolonged decentering of the planes or subparadigms of self-experience

Fig. 6.4 Psychological Inversion Experiences

This is especially characteristic of torture experiences (Ortiz, 2001). A radical shift in perspective occurs quickly and can persist for prolonged periods of time as a feeling or sense of unreality and uncertainty as to what actions and initiatives to take. The various psychic compasses for orientation and direction are nonfunctional or of limited usefulness. There is an Alice in Wonderland–like construal of events; an absence of functional organizing cognitive frameworks for coping and self-directed action. This amodal perception of "ecological oddness," the experience of *ineffable unreality* (i.e., loss of the natural order), diminishes emotional grounding, one's anchor point of being-in-the-world. The sense of the world itself becomes strange. Reality is supplanted with unreality; abnormality transposes reality. The surreal becomes real. Figure and ground perceptual processes reverse, flip-flopping like a tachistoscopic presentation of images in the mind's eye. As Stern (1985) described for early infantile perception, the transmodal perception seeks a way of assimilating the perceptions into schema. In our terms, this would include the adult transduction of the trauma experience in transmodal forms. Hence, the proprioception of the inversion experience as a cognitive-perception process; its experienced form is processed in a transmodal way.

Inversion Processes and Dissociation

Although the inversion experience has aspects of dissociation, it is not the same as a dissociative disorder or dissociation per se in the face of threat. The inversion experience cannot necessarily disrupt the normally integrative functions of conscious memory, identity, or capacity for self-reference. In the inversion experience, there is typically no manifestation of amnesia, fugue, de-personalization, or dissociative identity disorder. Rather, psychological inversion is the subjective sense of self-separation, the loss of self-centering in experience without orienting mile-markers or distinct points of reference. Individual knowledge of time, space, and orientation seems nonexistent, inapparent, or suspended. It is as if they have experienced an astronomical "worm hole," a psychological tunnel to another dimension in which time and space take on new meaning. This is perhaps why Stern (1985) refers to this phenomenon in infants as supramodal perception; it is beyond separate clear-channeled modes of perceptual experience. After extreme trauma, the individual feels as if they are looking at reality, as they knew it, upside down and free-falling into the abyss of the unknown accompanied by the terror of their spiritual essence evaporating into nothingness. Like an astronaut suddenly and unexpectedly untethered from the secure ties to the space shuttle, he or she drifts aimlessly into the vastness of the trauma universe. (This chapter was written prior to the explosion of the space shuttle *Columbia* on February 1, 2003. The seven astronauts appeared to have lived for several minutes before descending to Earth. We can only wonder as to the terror of their experience in a helpless abyss of unforeseen disaster.)

In mythology, the inversion experience, as well as the abyss experience, has been referred to as the demonic encounter with unknown forces of darkness and power (Campbell, 1949; Kalsched, 1996). It is precisely at such moments, in the dread of nothingness, that the spirit emerges to confront death or begin a new journey of uncertainty. Thought of somewhat differently, amodal and transmodal perceptions give birth to the possibility of new modalities of self-configuration as a result of transduced and assimilated experiences that emerge out of the traumatic event. As noted by Wilson (1980), the traumatic confrontation with the specter of death can cause a rapid disequilibrium in cognitive schemas, including concepts of the meaning of life, values, beliefs, and perspectives of one's ontological existence.

THE ABYSS EXPERIENCE: THE "BLACK HOLE" OF PSYCHOLOGICAL PHENOMENA

Trauma's Vast Chasm of Dark Empty Space

Wilson

The inversion experience and the abyss experience are related phenomena. These forms of experience do not characterize every trauma or individuals' reaction to them. They are primordial, archetypal, human experiences of being and the soul, the inner-most core of existence that transcends the outward appearance of the body and the "persona" (mask) of self-presentation. Carl Jung (1950) referred to such experiences as transformative, which lead to significant changes in self functioning and the organization of the self-structure. Traumatic experiences get beneath the mask (persona) of the self.

The abyss experience is not a new psychological phenomenon. Mythology and literature are replete with epics and narratives (e.g., *Odyssey*; *Iliad*; King Arthur; Beowulf; Siddartha, Baghava Gita) that describe the experiences of the abyss encounters with the demonic, the "underworld," or the dark, shadowy side of life.

The Abyss Experience in Philosophic Writing

In philosophy, Hegel (1807) spoke of the abyss experience in his work, which anticipated psychoanalysis and Freud's and Janet's explication of unconscious phenomena and dissociation. In his book *The Unconscious Abyss*, Mill (2002) notes that for Hegel the abyss "is the primary source of our suffering, at once containing both the monstrous and sublime" (p. 61). He cites Hegel's 1807 book, *The Philosophy of the Spirit*, in which Hegel believed that "life of feeling is primordially associated with the domain of the abyss in all its archaic shapes. In its beginning, spirit originally manifests itself as the unconscious" (as cited in Mill, 2002, p. 15).

In reference to the idea of self-dissolution, Mill (2002) states that insanity is a regressive withdrawal back into the abyss; rational conscious reverted to the life of feeling as a therapeutic effort to ameliorate the 'wounds of the spirit' (p. 14, emphasis added). In summarizing Hegel's position, Mill asks

> Does the abyss resist being integrated into spirit? ... Is the urge for unity or the drive toward the absolute simultaneously in opposition to a competing urge to withdraw in the face of nostalgia within the abyss of spirits unconscious beginning? ... Spirit can never rid itself of its desire for the recovery of lost unity, the yearning to return to its primitive existence, its original condition. (p. 202)

In both philosophical and psychological thinking, a century before the advances made by Janet (1907), Freud (1917), and Jung (1907) in understanding the role of dissociation, we can see that Hegel and his predecessors proposed that severe mental disturbances were associated with the "unconscious abyss" and "wounding of the spirit" (p. 34).

Dimensions of the Abyss Experience

What is it that constitutes the abyss experience? In the most fundamental analysis, there are five primary dimensions to the abyss experience: (a) the confrontation with evil and death (i.e., powerful negative forces); (b) the experience of soul death and nonbeing; (c) the sense of abandonment by humanity; (d) the sense of ultimate aloneness and despairing; and (e) the cosmic challenge of meaning. Extreme or catastrophic trauma involves the individual subjective experience of these dimensions of profoundly disturbing and life-altering encounters. In his book, *Hero With a Thousand Faces*, Joseph Campbell (1949) describes in rich detail how these themes appear in all cultures as transpersonal episodes of a journey self-individuation:

> This first stage of the mythological journey — which we have designated the call to adventure — signifies destiny has summoned the hero and transferred his spiritual center of gravity from within the pale of his society to a zone of danger. ... [W]ith the personification of his destiny to guide and aid him, the hero goes forward in his adventure until he comes to the threshold guardian at the entrance to the zone of magnified power. Such custodians bound the world in the four directions — also up and down — standby for the limits of the hero's present sphere, or life horizon. *Beyond them is darkness, the unknown, and danger.* (pp. 58, 77, emphasis added)

Mythology informs us that in the trauma encounter, each individual confronts, willingly or not, the darkness of the unknown and a personal journey of uncertainty that portends changes to the self as yet unrealized in their potential for growth or destruction.

The dimensions of the abyss experience involve qualities of psychological phenomena that correspond to each component of the trauma experience and its impact to the self. Table 6.3 summarizes these intrapsychic experiences as related to: (a) identity/self, (b) the loss of connection (i.e., self, others, culture), (c) extreme aloneness: detached separation and isolation, and (d) spirituality: higher power and the numinous experience.

As Campbell's (1949) classic and illuminating work suggests, the abyss experience is among the most human of psychic struggles. It encompasses polarities in the self of the diabolic versus transcendent configurations of experience. These bipolar dimensions of the abyss of trauma reflect internal conflict within the self; universal human struggles with overcoming fear, anxiety, and uncertainty in the face of foreboding and dark powers. The bipolar dimensions are poles of tension and energy, sparking like electrical surges within the self and spirit. Table 6.4 summarizes these elements, which typify the demonic versus the transcendent. In the abyss of trauma, the diabolic is characterized as: demonic, unholy, cursed, damned, sinister, depraved, evil, and Mephistophelean in nature; the darkness of being. The transcendent polarity is unity, virtuous, godly, numinous, seraphic, holy, a peak experience, and the lightness of being (Wilson, 2002a).

The inversion experience, in relation to the abyss experience, can also be thought of as the oscillatory immersion in the vast chasm of trauma's abyss — the vortex of fear and trembling — as the self attempts to maintain coherence, continuity, and vitality in reaction to the perceived attacks to its existence. The polarities of the abyss experience in oscillatory states of resonance are whirling, confusing, dizzying, vertiginous, and momentous. Oscillatory Immersion in the abyss experience represents "figure" and "ground" perceptual reversals, the "in and out" of a safe grounding place. They can be overwhelming, leading to a sense of imminent death of oneself in the face of demonic powers. At such moments, for example in torture, starvation, total displacement from home without material resources or possessions, repeated childhood abuse, prolonged political internment, catastrophic destruction of

TABLE 6.3 Abyss Experience: The "Black Hole" of Psychological Phenomena —A Vast Chasm of Dark Empty Space

Dimensions of Trauma Abyss	Psychological Phenomena
Confrontation with evil and death	Trauma experience
Experience of soul death and nonbeing	Self/identity
Abandonment by humanity	Loss of connection
Ultimate aloneness and despairing	Separation and isolation
Cosmic challenge of meaning	Spirituality/higher power (numinous)

Source: Wilson, 2002.

TABLE 6.4 Diabolic Versus Transcendent Forms of Abyss Experience

Abyss Experience: Polarities in Self-Experience		
Diabolic	vs	Transcendent
Darkness of being, despair		Lightness of being, euphoric
Demonic, mephistophelean		Virtuous, seraphic
Hell		Numinous
Excrucable		Morally iconic
Unholy		Peak experience
Cursed		Blessed, godly
Damned		Righteous, holy
Isolated separateness		Oneness, unity, higher connections
Sinister, evil, depraved		Goodness, virtuous, ineffable

Source: Wilson, 2002.

civilization, and so forth, the person might wish to die and cry out to God or one's mother for salvation. As a personal clinical observation, I have found that in the face of imminent death or life-threatening injury, the person requests the help of God or mother figure. In thousands of clinical cases, I have never heard a description where the person confronting near death or abject terror during the abyss experience requested someone other than God or his or her mother. No one cries out for his or her uncle, favorite teacher, or sibling. It is rescue and salvation from God or the nurturing, loving mother that we request in the face of potential death. We seek relief at such moments from the Highest Power with unlimited authority and the capacity to comfort. *The abyss and inversion experiences unhinge the interconnections of the self, altering meaning and purpose to existence.* In their wake, nothing less than God or the Eternal Mother will seem strong enough to save someone from total annihilation.

The overcoming of the abyss experience is transcendence, the re-creation and reconfiguration of the self. Mythologically, this has been described as rebirth and transfiguration. It is the psychological task of reinventing the bases of meaning, the pattern of attachments and relationships, and the attributes of hope, faith, and caring. Transcendence of the abyss experience transforms and evolves into healthy integration and the capacity for peak experiences and a personalized sense of the numinous. Transcendence of the abyss of profoundly traumatic experiences is self-metamorphosis as individuation of the self and the bases for self-actualization. Transformation of profoundly traumatic life experiences is spiritual embodiment of the ineffable essence of one's soul as alive and connected to the numinous. Jung (1950) similarly noted that such transfiguration is "that of the change, transmutation, or transformation of one's being" (CW9, par. 202).

IDENTITY AND SELF-CONTINUITY FOLLOWING TRAUMA: RECONFIGURATION IN EGO PROCESSES

> The outer trauma ends and its effects may be largely "forgotten" but the psychological sequelae of the trauma continue to haunt the inner world.
>
> Kalsched, 1996, p. 13

> Identity formation, thus, can be said to have a self aspect and ego aspect.
>
> Erikson, 1968, p. 211

It is impossible to understand the deleterious impact to the self without insight into the structure of identity. There is no psychological existence without a sense of personal identity. In semantic (psychological) connotation, the word identity is closest in meaning to "soul." Erik Erikson (1968), who wrote insightfully about identity in the life-course, spoke of identity as a sense of sameness and continuity to the ego's "synthesizing methods" in time and space (p. 50). Further, Erikson's (1968) work with traumatized World War II veterans led him to understand self-dissolution and to use the term identity-diffusion to characterize the loss in identity as a central agency of the self structure.

It is useful and important to incorporate Erikson's seminal work into our analysis of the dissolution of the self. Using the concepts of continuity–discontinuity and identity integration–identity diffusion, we can construct two conceptual axes that reveal four modalities of identity: (1) amorphous self, (2) transitional self, (3) integrated self, and (4) unintegrated self. These relationships are illustrated in Figure 6.5 with the larger, outer figure representing the self and the smaller, center figure the style and form of ego processes.

As derived from the conceptual axes, there are four dimensions of the self structure and four qualities of ego processes. The product of crossing *identity diffusion* and *self continuity* represents the *unintegrated self* in which ego processes are vulnerable, fragile, and unstable. The combination of *identity diffusion* and *self discontinuity* illustrates the amorphous, disorganized self structure and fragmented ego processes. The *amorphous self* embraces the typologies described earlier as inert, empty, and fragmented; the most severely disturbed and nonfunctional structure of the self components. On the other hand, the conceptual axes of *identity integration* and *self discontinuity* characterize the *transitional self* and discernible qualities of ego-coherency. Further, the quality of integrated identity in the *transitional self* provides stability but *without* a sense of continuity. The trauma survivor experiences changes in the planes of the self and a "broken connection" to the past. However, stability in identity integration enables ego coherence in the transition of further differentiating the dimension of the self. We can see that the *integrated self* reflects both self-continuity and identity integration. The stability of the self structure is associated with strong functional

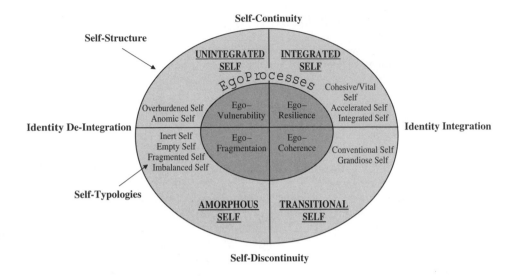

Fig. 6.5 Identity and Continuity in Self-Processes Following Trauma (Source: Wilson, 2002)

qualities to the dimensions of the self (i.e., continuity, vitality, energy, autonomy, coherence, affectivity), which, in turn, are associated with *ego resiliency*, the capacity to maintain flexible and adaptive ego processes.

In summary, these eight modalities of self-functioning are useful conceptual and clinical paradigms to understand the continuum of self-dissolution. Understanding identity structures and ego-space configurations is critical to all posttraumatic therapies since trauma "lives" inside these "chambers" of the psyche. These clinical phenomena are empirically verifiable by psychological testing and the understanding of how trauma gets embedded in organismic processes (Wilson, 2003). The impact of trauma to the self results in injuries to psychic structures governing the structural integrity of the self and functional efficacy of ego processes. Insight into these configurational entities as to processing trauma is especially advantageous in treatment. Stated simply, it allows a portal of entry into the ego space of the client's self-presentation (i.e., self-object) at any point in the course of treatment (Watkins & Watkins, 1997; Wilson et al., 2001).

EGO PROCESSES, SELF-COHERENCE, AND IDENTITY FOLLOWING TRAUMA

> I knew who I was before I went to Vietnam at age 18. I don't know
> who I am now, 35 years later — it all seems like one big blur.

> Vietnam Veteran patient, as stated to John P. Wilson

In a classificatory schema, we can now combine the frameworks of understanding to achieve more predictive, analytic power in clinical work.
Table 6.5 summarizes these relationships, which are useful to clinical
work. The classificatory schema represents a way of understanding the
relative degrees of structural coherence to the self following trauma. Self-
dissolution is not an "all or none" phenomenon. It represents degrees of
disunion to the bases and functions of the self. Traumatic impact varies in
terms of which dimensions of the structure are weakened, disjointed, or
no longer functional. In massive trauma, the entire structure can collapse
and crumble into fragments of what once existed. The amorphous self,
for example, literally means incomplete, formless, unstructured, and
inchoate. The opposite polarity, the integrated self, is complete, formed,
structured, efficacious, and differentiated. Between the anchor points of
the continuum of self-dissolution–integration are the *unintegrated self* and
the *transitional self.* Although these forms of self-configuration reflect
traumatic injuries to components of self-functioning, they also represent
interim points in the direction of healthier, integrated self-structure. As
the self reconfigures, the trauma survivor experiences greater degrees of
vitality, energy, connectedness to self and others, wholeness, well-being, a
new continuity, sameness, and a sense of unity.

The Self and the Archetype of Trauma

> My findings in regard to complexes corroborate this somewhat disqui-
> eting picture of the possibilities of psychic disintegration, for funda-
> mentally there is no difference in principle between a fragmenting
> personality and the complex.

> Jung, 1954, CW8, pars. 200 203

Our discussion of trauma's impact to the individual has focused primarily on three interrelated facets of personality: the self-structure, personal identity, and ego processes. It is equally important to recognize the
clinical significance of the trauma archetype and the trauma complex in
relation to the self (Wilson, 2002, 2003).

Jung (1929, 1963, 1971) developed the concept of the archetype in
which he stated "archetypes are identical psychic structures common to
all" which comprise the "archaic heritage of humanity" (CW, V, pars.
224, 259). According to Monte and Sollod (2002), archetypes are
"dominant image forms, cumulative affects of perceptually repeated
experience on the nervous system" (p.135). In that regard the trauma

TABLE 6.5 Ego Processes, Self-Coherence, and Identity Following Trauma

Posttraumatic Self-Typology	Characteristic Ego Processes	Clinical Descriptions
I. *Amorphous self clusters:*	*Ego fragmentation*	
1. Inert/dead self		Surrender, catanoid, regressed
2. Empty self	Identity diffusion	Depression, vacuum state, passive
3. Fragmented self	Self-discontinuity	Diffusion, disintegrated, mistrustful
4. Imbalance self		Borderline, unstable, nonarticulated
II. *Unintegrated self clusters:*	Ego vulnerability	
5. Overburdened self	Identity diffusion	Fixated, rigid, overcontrolled
6. Anomic self	Self-continuity	Normless, alienated, nonattached
III. *Transitional self clusters:*	Ego cohesion	
7. Conventional self	Identity integration	Adjusted, conforming, approval-seeking
8. Grandiose self	Self-discontinuity	Exhibitionistic, narcissistic, insolent
IV. *Integrated self clusters:*	Ego resilience	
9. Cohesive/vital self		Resilience, hardiness, flexible
10. Psychosocial/accelerated self	Identity Integration	Spiritual, individuation, existential
11. Reintegrated self	Self-continuity	Transcendent, self-actualizing, unity

Source: Wilson, 2003.

archetype is a transpersonal species-specific modality of experience, common to all cultures with variations in mythology (Campbell, 1949). In the Jungian perspective, archetypes are epiphenomenal experiences of unconscious energies, a sort of psychological magnetic field that acts to influence patterns of behavior. The trauma archetype is part of the collective unconscious, but its content depends on personal, conscious experience (Wilson, 2002).

The *trauma archetype*, as I am proposing the concept, represents universal forms of traumatic experiences embedded within the organism. It is universal because it exists in all cultures throughout recorded history. The *trauma experience* is found in all human communities and produces generic, injurious effects to the organism. Individual trauma, however, determines the nature of the consequences of trauma to the psyche. The properties of the trauma archetype are listed in Figure 6.6, which is one of many archetypes that interact dynamically with one another. The trauma archetype embraces the nature of psychic encounters with the stressors that define trauma (Wilson & Lindy, 1994). There is the threat to psychological and physical well-being, the confrontation with death imagery, and the specter of self and soul death, which Lifton (1967) termed the death encounter. The trauma archetype involves subjective conscious and unconscious alteration in psychic states, allostatic changes in organismic functioning, disequilibration in states of meaning and belief, impacts to the structure of the self, ego processes, and cognitive processes. The dialetic of the trauma archetype as polarities in the unconscious also involves the moral task of formulating pro-social dispositions versus the struggle with abject despair and meaninglessness. As noted earlier, the trauma archetype, located in the core of the self, comprises a psychological function of spiritual transformation in a journey of self-discovery — that is, the "myth of the hero," as described by Campbell (1949), in which there is the confrontation with trauma (i.e., "encounter with darkness"); the return from the trauma encounter and the processes of self-reconstruction, transformation, and healing.

We can understand the *trauma complex* as a personal assimilation and configuration of the trauma experience as an individual variation on the universality of such experiences. *The trauma complex and the archetype do not stand alone; they are yoked phenomena.* The trauma archetype articulates dynamically with all other archetypal relations, activating them and primordial images of their collective energies as condensations of personal experience. For example, as a consequence of self-dissolution and ego fragmentation (e.g., the amorphous self), the individual can have a strong need for nurturance, protection, care, and safety. Such a need for security, safety, and nurturance can activate other archetypal images — the Great Mother, the Wise Old Man, the Trickster, or the Child. Based on the history of the person, their unconscious is a reservoir of memories of such life-experiences imagoes (Storr, 1999). The fragility of their psychic condition after trauma can activate archetypal images of the caring, warm comforting of a mother; the solid, mature

Dimensions:
1. The trauma archetype is present in all human cultures, universal in its effects, and manifest in overt behavioral patterns and internal intrapsychic processes, especially the trauma complex.
2. The trauma archetype evokes altered psychological states, which include changes in consciousness, memory, orientation to time, space, and person, and appear in the trauma complex.
3. The trauma archetype evokes allostatic changes in the organism (posttraumatic impacts, such as personality change, PTSD, allostatic dysregulation), which are expressed in common neurobiological pathways.
4. The trauma archetype contains the experience of threat to psychological and physical well-being.
5. The trauma archetype involves confrontation with the fear of death.
6. The trauma archetype evokes the specter of self-deintegration, dissolution, and soul (psychic) death (i.e., loss of identity), and is expressed in the trauma complex.
7. The trauma archetype is a manifestation of overwhelmingly stressful experience to the organization of self, identity, and belief systems and appears as part of the structure of the trauma complex.
8. The trauma archetype stimulates cognitive attributions of meaning and causality for injury, suffering, loss, death (i.e., altered core beliefs), which appear in the trauma complex.
9. The trauma archetype energizes posttraumatic tasks of defense, recovery, healing, and growth, which include the development of PTSD as a trauma complex.
10. The trauma archetype activates polarities of meaning attribution; the formulation of prosocial-humanitarian morality versus abject despair and meaninglessness paradigm.
11. The trauma archetype can evoke spiritual transformation: individual journey/"encounter with darkness" return/transformation/reemergence, healing (Campbell, 1949). The evocation of a "spirit" transformation is manifest in the trauma complex.

Fig. 6.6 Trauma Archetype (Universal Forms of Traumatic Experience) (Source: Wilson, 2002.)

strength of a wise old man who promises a future without fears; or the image of a heroic rescuer to pull them out of their state of despair, help-lessness, or self-absorption. Such archetypal icons, images, fantasies, or mental representations are activated in the service of staving-off the progressive forces of self-dissolution, a regressive pull into the deep chasm of the abyss's dark empty space. The images are epiphenomenal manifestations of conflicting psychic energies. In other words, they capture, in a more general way, the gestalt form of the identity and humanity of the person. Trauma archetypal relations and the specific contents of the trauma complex are shown in Figure 6.7. For example,

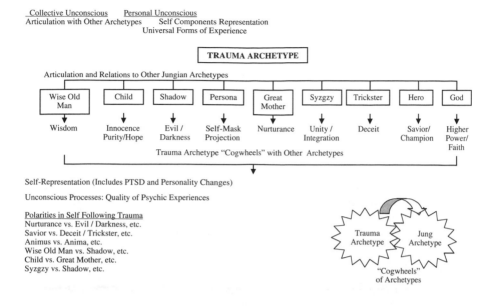

Fig. 6.7 Trauma Archetypal Relations

nurturance versus evil and deceit; the child versus the trickster; the shadow versus the hero; the persona versus the trauma archetype.

Moreover, it is clinically relevant to note that in psychotherapy, the contents of the patients' dreams, transference projections, trauma-specific reactions, and construal of the therapist's person (e.g., role enactments assumed by the therapist in archetypal symbols and forms) are all possibilities associated with the dynamics of the trauma archetype (Wilson, 2002; Wilson & Lindy, 1994). Like a character in a dramatic play, the therapist can be "type-cast" into a particular role by the patient (e.g., perpetrator, father-mother figure, saint, fellow survivor, judge, executioner, etc.).

CONSTELLATION OF PSYCHIC COMPLEXES AND THE TRAUMA COMPLEX

Jung (1934) presented a review of the nature and composition of the various types of psychic complexes. This analysis identified the psychodynamics of complexes and their constellation within the personal unconscious of the individual and how, in turn, they articulate with archetypes in the unconscious. He specified eight dimensions of constellated complexes, which are quoted verbatim here:

(1) a disturbed state of consciousness; (2) unity of consciousness disrupted; (3) intentions of the will impeded or impaired; (4) memory noticeably affected; (5) energy [of complex] sometimes exceeds conscious intention; (6) active complex momentarily creates a state of duress; (7) compulsive thinking and acting; and (8) diminished judicial responsibility. (1934, pars. 200–203)

These universal dimensions of constellated complexes are important to identifying the central dimensions of the trauma complex as an unconscious dynamic, which includes PTSD and dissociation, as well as articulating with other archetypal forms of experience. The trauma complex is a dynamic intrapsychic mechanism resulting from traumatization that has the power to articulate and has a "cogwheeling" effect with other complexes and archetypes (Wilson, 2002a, 2002b, 2003). The trauma complex is more than an aggregate of symptoms that define PTSD, anxiety, depressive, and dissociative disorders; it is a depth of intrapsychic experience organized primarily at unconscious levels around the trauma experience, which becomes a central motivational force within the self-structure of the person. Once constellated, the trauma complex has the capacity to influence psychic functioning in terms of affect regulation, thinking, memory, fantasy, interpersonal relationships, and current perceptions of reality. To quote Jung (1960/1969)

> this image [complex] has a powerful inner coherence, it has its own wholeness and, in addition, relatively *high degree of autonomy*, so that it is subject to the control of the conscious mind to only a limited extent, and therefore behaves like an *animated foreign body* in the sphere of consciousness. (par. 201, emphasis added)

This passage illustrates that once constellated, a psychic complex takes on an "animated" force that is nested within the personal unconscious, containing energy (i.e., affects, cognitions, perceptual processes), which has structural coherence and a "high degree of autonomy" to influence behavior. Jung (1934, CW8, par. 253) asserts: "complexes are psychic fragments which have split off owing to traumatic influence."

In my view, the trauma complex does not exist in an isolated state; it interacts dynamically with other aspects of the self, including other constellated complexes and unconscious material contained in the vault of the unconscious. In terms of being a determinant of action, the trauma complex not only has its own power and energy as a result of its formation after a traumatic event, but it can also combine and fuse with other, preexisting complexes to set in motion a vast array of intrapsychic processes. The trauma complex consumes psychic energy and will, of necessity, activate and influence other aspects of the personal unconscious in attempts to process the traumatic experience (van der Kolk, van der Hart, & Marmar, 1996).

The Archetypal World of the Traumatized

What is the nature of this inner archetypal world of the traumatized? (See Figure 6.8) Trauma is injury inflicted to the organism at many interrelated levels of functioning. Traumatic psychological injury can pierce through layers of psychic inner space like a high-explosive bullet with an armor-piercing tip that can rip through a massive foot of reinforced steel plates. Moreover, as Rangell (1976) observed so poignantly:

> In spite of the vastness of the unconscious psychic space is limited. There is room and time in any individual for only limited amount of cognitive ideation and a finite number of memories, fantasies and accompanying affects ... traumatic memories of any kind encroach on this psychic timespace and reduce its available quantity; this is why psychic traumata age people. (p. 13)

The analysis of unconscious expression of trauma in archetypal and individual modalities of self-dissolution allows presentation of the dimension of the trauma complex in Figure 6.9. The trauma complex is defined by two conceptual axes: *universal idiosyncratic* and *archetypal historically bound*.

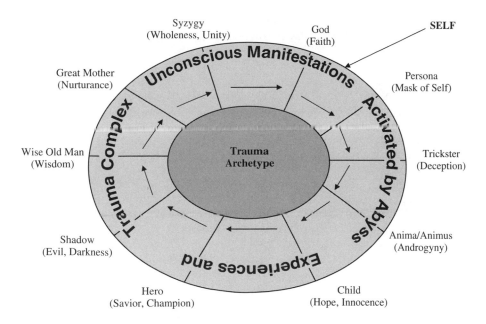

Fig. 6.8 Trauma Archetype and Its Relation to Jungian Archetypes (Source: Wilson, 2002)

1. The trauma complex is a feeling-toned complex that develops in accordance with the trauma archetype.
2. The trauma complex is comprised of effects, images, perceptions, and cognitions associated with the trauma experience.
3. The trauma complex is mythological in nature and takes form in accordance with culture and symbolic, mythological representations of reality.
4. The trauma complex contains the affective responses of the abyss experience: fear, terror, horror, helplessness, dissociation.
5. The trauma complex articulates with other psychological complexes and innate archetypes in a "cogwheeling," interactive manner.
6. The trauma complex can become central in the self-structure and reflect alterations in identity, ego processes, the self-structure and systems of personal meaning.
7. The trauma complex contains motivational power.
8. The trauma complex is expressed in personality processes (e.g., traits, motives, attributes).
9. The trauma complex is primarily unconscious.
10. The trauma complex contains the polarities of the abyss experience: diabolic versus transcendent, which are universal variants in the search for meaning in the trauma experience.

Fig. 6.9 The Trauma Complex (Source: Wilson, 2002a, 2002b)

Based on Jung's (1961) work and the literature on traumatic damage to the self, it is possible to derive 10 dimensions or distinct criteria from the trauma complex: (1) contains universal and idiosyncratic content; (2) is comprised of affects, images, perceptions, and cognitions associated with the experiences; (3) is mythological in nature; (4) contains affective experiences of the abyss and inversion experiences; (5) articulates with other complexes and archetypes; (6) is central in the self-structure (e.g., PTSD); (7) contains motivational power; (8) is expressed in personality processes; (9) is primarily unconscious; and (10) contains polarities of the diabolic versus transcendent in posttraumatic processing. The trauma complex and archetype are broader conceptualizations of posttraumatic injuries than PTSD. As a specific type of trauma, it is a *constellated complex* with dual dimensions, like two sides of a coin — the demonic and transcendent. It includes psychiatric symptoms of PTSD, depression, anxiety, and narcissism, but its magnitude within the self is much larger in size and psychodynamic impact. The trauma complex is to PTSD as a dam is to a river. Both phenomena contain potential power, energy, and flow as natural psychic forces. The trauma archetype is to the trauma complex as the generic is to the idiosyncratic. The trauma complex, like all psychological complexes, is a unified, individualized constellation of affectively toned images, emotions, perceptions, cognitions, and so forth.

What activates the trauma complex? As with any complex associated with an archetype, trauma-specific cues, memories of prior trauma, or activation of the negative polarities of other archetypes and dynamically unconscious material can activate the trauma complex. Once activated, the trauma complex has its own energy manifested in disregulated affect — anger, rage, anxiety, depression, dysphoria, grief, malaise, apprehension, and uncertainty. The disregulated affects can connect directly to PTSD reactions, or more generally, to reintegration of old memories and negative affect associated with prior life episodes of vulnerability, fear, abuse, trauma, or loss of protection.

THE COGWHEELING MECHANISMS OF TRAUMA COMPLEXES AND ARCHETYPES

The Jungian analyst Donald Kalsched (1996) notes that dissociation is the central mechanism in the trauma complex to manage intolerable affects. Dissociation in its various forms (e.g., amnesia, depersonalization) is a type of self-alteration in experiential dimensions. The trauma complex "cogwheels" with the psychic material stored in the unconscious. The greater the magnitude of trauma, the more "tooth and spoke" cogwheeling occurs among the elements of cognitive information storage in memory. The experience of trauma can cause many "file drawers" to open in the unconscious storage cabinet. In extreme trauma, the file drawers open, revealing many folders of recorded personal history in each drawer, in rows and rows of files, stored in level after level, in the large warehouse of the mind designed for long-term storage of important and valued information. And, like the ancient pyramids, the files are kept in many places, some elegant burial tombs, sacred chambers, and secret passages to even more hidden rooms. The unsealing of the portals of entry into the pyramid casts light into a dark space. Traversing the passageways to the interior rooms of the pyramid can be dangerous if obstacles are not carefully negotiated. However, with a good guide and proper lighting, the discovery of the inner sanctums of the self can illuminate rich treasures, which, seen in their entirety, comprised the art, architecture, and fabrics that make up the constellation of artifacts. The trauma complex is a constellation of residues or "psychic artifacts" of the trauma experience constellated with other complexes of the psyche. Metaphorically, the trauma complex is, in essence, one facet of a mirrored surface on a globe of archetypes rotating in the stream of time, space, and the continuity of existence.

CONCLUSION

In this chapter, I have presented different ways of understanding trauma's impact to the self. In severe cases of trauma, its impact to the self results in alterations including deintegration, fragmentation, dissolution, dissociation, splintering, or obliterative annihilation. The broken spirit is a metaphor for "soul injury" and the diminution of humanness that can be relatively short lived or a permanent state of psychic existence, which has been given different psychiatric labels of limited usefulness.

Traumatization is the resultant state of psychic injury inflicted from outside forces. Traumatization is ultimately an organismic condition; it is injury to the whole of being. All parts of consciousness — executive function, memory, cognitive processing, and somatic expression of its impact — are synergistically affected in discernible ways. Traumatic experiences do not stand alone in the mind. Nor is PTSD a unidimensional self-contained syndrome. Trauma and PTSD are twin processes nested in much larger components of organismic functioning. Nevertheless, our focus on trauma's impact to personality processes, the self, ego processes, and identity has allowed discovery of forms of self-alteration (i.e., amorphous self, unintegrated self, transitional self, and integrated self) and reintegration following resolution and the healing of traumatic injuries. The forms of self-dissolution have specific typologies associated with ego processes (i.e., ego fragmentation, ego vulnerability, ego coherence, and ego resilience). The analysis of the forms of self-deintegration, their categories and typologies, has enabled us to construct a meaningful continuum from fragmentation to integration; from broken spirit to self-individuation in self-actualizing modes of being. The interrelationship of these processes of coping with trauma is summarized in Figure 6.10 as processes of self-transfiguration.

The dissolutions and alterations in the self are part of a larger matrix of psychological changes wrought by trauma. The trauma archetype and the trauma complex each have a defining set of interrelated characteristics as well as twin processes with a nidus in the self. They include the abyss and inversion experience. The trauma archetype is a universal, transpersonal set of experiences, common to all cultures, and human communities that represent one form of archetypal experience. Due to the threat to existence contained in extreme stress experiences, the trauma complex can be a more powerful motivational phenomenon than any other form of experience. The trauma complex is an individually constellated set of memories, experiences, images, and effects that are associated with the archetype of trauma. The trauma complex is a construct that is superordinate to PTSD, but that includes the dynamics of the syndrome. It contains the psychobiological impact of trauma, damage to the self, PTSD, and residues of the abyss and inversion experiences. The trauma complex is a prototypical and mythological representation of reality, interweaving the images of the demonic versus the transcendent. Trauma experiences and their residues can become central in life-course trajectory. The trauma complex acts like a cogwheel with other complexes, archetypes, and facets of PTSD, a fact that defines the complexity of trauma in terms of mind, body, and spirit. These phe-

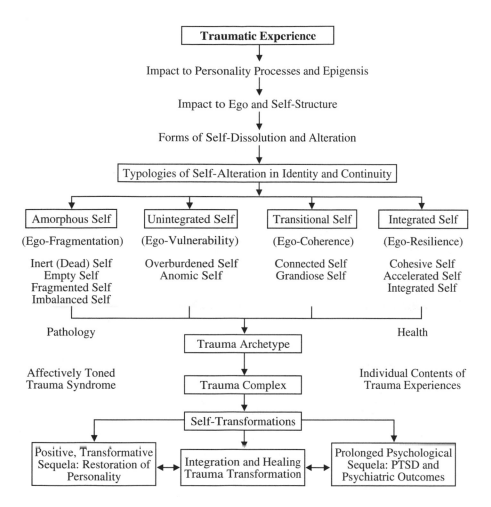

Fig. 6.10 Trauma and the Self-Transfigurations

nomena are summarized in Figure 6.11 quite simply with a "mandala" of the self with the dialectic polarities of the demonic versus transcendent, the ego versus the spiritual, mediated by the self as the psychic force of organismic integrity. Jung (1934) stated that mandalas

> usually appear in situations of *psychic confusion and disorientation.* The archetype thereby is constellated representing a pattern of order which, like a psychological view finder marked with a cross or circle divided into four, is superimposed on the *psychic chaos* so that each content falls into place and the *weltering confusion* is held together by a protective circle ... at the same time they are yanhas, instruments with whose help the order is brought into being. (par. 803, emphasis added)

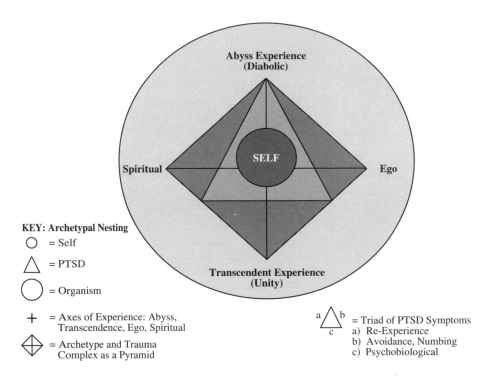

Fig. 6.11 Trauma Archetype Mandala

The trauma mandala represents PTSD as embedded in the self within the trauma archetype and complex, which, in turn, is nested within the organism. In understanding the broken spirit, we seek to understand transformation in personality, of which there are many variations caused by trauma and other difficult experiences in life. In speaking of the vicissitudes of self-transformation, Jung (1950) remarked

> Nature herself demands a death and rebirth. These processes develop considerable psychic effects, which would be sufficient in themselves to make any thoughtful person ask himself what really happened to him. ... Mandalas are birth places, vessels of birth in the most literal sense, lotus flowers in which a Buddha comes to life. Sitting in a lotus seat, the yogi sees himself transfigured into an immortal. (p. 64, par. 234)

The mandala of the trauma archetype is a symbol of the self, like the lotus flower, which awaits transfiguration by those who possess it.

REFERENCES

Agger, I., & Jensen, S. (1993). *The psychosocial trauma of torture*. In J. P. Wilson and B. Raphael (Eds.), *International handbook of traumatic stress syndromes* (pp. 703–715). New York: Plenum Press.

Breslau, N. (1998). Epidemiology of trauma and posttraumatic stress disorder. In R. Yehuda (Ed.), *Psychological trauma* (pp. 1–27). Washington, DC: American Psychiatric Press.

Campbell, J. (1949). *Hero with a thousand faces*. New York: Penguin Books.

Chu, J. A. (1998). *Rebuilding shattered lives: The responsible treatment of complex posttraumatic and dissociative disorders*. New York: Wiley.

Courtois, C. (1999). *Recollections of sexual abuse*. New York: W. W. Norton.

Erikson, E. (1950). *Childhood and society*. New York: W. W. Norton.

Erikson, E. H. (1968). *Identity, youth & crisis*. New York: W. W. Norton.

Frankl, V. (1984). *The will to meaning: Foundations and applications of logotherapy*. New York: Plume Books.

Frankl, V. E. (1988). *The will to meaning: Foundations and applications of logotherapy*. New York: Meridian Books.

Frankl, V. (1994). *Man's search for ultimate meaning*. Massachusetts: Perseus Publishing.

Freud, S. (1896). *Aeitology of the neuroses*. Standard Edition. London: Hogarth Press.

Freud, S. (1911). *On narcissism*. New York: W. W. Norton.

Freud, S. (1916). *The introductory lectures on psychoanalysis*. Part III. Standard Edition. London: Hogarth Press.

Freud, S. (1917a). *Introductory lecture on psychoanalysis*. New York: W. W. Norton.

Freud, S. (1917b). *New introductory lectures on psychoanalysis*. New York: W. W. Norton.

Freud, S. (1920a). *Beyond the pleasure principle*. New York: W. W. Norton.

Freud, S. (1920b). *Introduction to psychoanalysis and the war neuroses*. Standard Edition (Vol. 27, pp. 207–210). London: Hogarth Press.

Friedman, M. J. (2000a). *Posttraumatic & acute stress disorders*. Kansas City: Compact Clinicals.

Friedman, M. J. (2000b). *Post-traumatic stress disorder: The latest assessment and treatment strategies*. Kansas City: Compact Clinicals.

Froddy, M., and Kashima, Y. (2002). Self and identity: What is the conception of the persons assumed in the current literature? In Y. Kashima, M. Froddy, & M. Platow (Eds.), *Self and identity* (pp. 3–27). Mahmah, NJ: Lawrence Erlbaum.

Gerrity, E., Keane, T. M., & Tuma, F. (2001). *The mental health consequence of torture*. New York: Kluwer/Plenum Press.

Goodwin, J. (1999). The body finds its voice. Part IV. In J. Goodwin & R. Attias (Eds.), *Splintered reflections* (pp. 281–283). New York: Basic Books.

Goodwin, J., & Attias, R. (Eds.). (1999). *Splintered reflections*. New York: Basic Books.

Goodwin, J. M. (1993). *Re-discovering childhood trauma*. Washington, DC: American Psychiatric Press.

Hegel, J. (1807). *The philosophy of the spirit*. London: Routledge.

Herman, J. (1992). *Trauma and recovery*. New York: Basic Books.

Horowitz, M. (1986). *Stress response syndromes*. Northvale, NJ: Jason Aronson.

Horowitz, M. J. (1999). *Essential papers on post-traumatic stress disorder.* New York: New York University Press.

Horowitz, M. J., Wilner, N. R., & Alvarez, W. (1979). Impact of event scale: A measure of subject stress. *Psychosomatic Medicine, 41,* 209–218.

Janet, P. (1900). *L'automatisure* psychologiqene. Paris: Balliere.

Janet, P. (1907). *The major symptoms of hysteria.* London: Macmillan.

Jaranson, J., & Popkin, M. (1998). *Caring for victims of torture.* Washington, DC: APA Press.

Jung, C. G. (1907). The Collectd Works (Bollingen Series XX, 20 vols.). Trans. R. F. C. Hull. In H. Read, M. Fordham, & G. Alder (Eds). Princeton, NJ: Princeton University Press.

Jung, C. G. (1929). The Collected Works (Bollingen Series XX, 20 vols.). Trans. R. F. C. Hull. In H. Read, M. Fordham, & G. Alder (Eds.). *The therapeutic value of abreaction* (CW 16). Princeton, NJ: Princeton University Press.

Jung, C. G. (1934). The Collected Works (Bollingen Series XX, 20 vols.). Trans. R. F. C. Hull. In H. Read, M. Fordham, & G. Alder (Eds.). *A review of psychological complexes* (CW 8). Princeton, NJ: Princeton University Press.

Jung, C. G. (1950). The Collected Works (Bollingen Series XX, 20 vols.). Trans. R. F. C. Hull. In H. Read, M. Fordham, & G. Alder (Eds.). *Four archetypes* (CW 4). Princeton, NJ: Princeton University Press.

Jung, C. G. (1960). The Collected Works (Bollingen Series XX, 20 vols.). Trans. R. F. C. Hull. In H. Read, M. Fordham, & G. Alder (Eds.). *The psychogenesis of mental disease* (CW 3). Princeton, NJ: Princeton University Press.

Jung, C. G. (1960/1969). The Collected Works (Bollingen Series XX, 20 vols.). Trans. R. F. C. Hull. In H. Read, M. Fordham, & G. Alder (Eds.). *The structure and dynamics of the psyche* (CW 8). Princeton, NJ: Princeton University Press.

Jung, C. G. (1961). The Collected Works (Bollingen Series XX, 20 vols.). Trans. R. F. C. Hull. In H. Read, M. Fordham, & G. Alder (Eds.). Princeton, NJ: Princeton University Press.

Jung, C. G. (1963). The Collected Works (Bollingen Series XX, 20 vols.). Trans. R. F. C. Hull. In H. Read, M. Fordham, & G. Alder (Eds.). Civilian in transition (CW 10). Princeton, NJ: Princeton University Press.

Kahana, B., Harel, Z., & Kahana, E. (1988). Predictors of psychological well being among survivors of the Holocaust. In J. P. Wilson, Z. Harel, & B. Kahana (Eds.), *Human adaptation: From the Holocaust to Vietnam* (pp. 171–192). New York: Plenum Press.

Kalsched, D. (1996). *The inner world of trauma: Archetypal defenses of the personal spirit.* London: Routledge.

Kluft, R. P. (1991). The hospital treatment of multiple personality disorders. *Psychiatric Clinic of North America, 14,* 695–719.

Kluft, R. (1996). MDD: A legacy of trauma. In C. R. Pfeffer (Ed.), *Severe stress and mental disturbances in children* (pp. 411–488), Washington, DC: American Psychiatric Association Press.

Kohut, H. (1971). *The analysis of the self.* New York: International University Press.

Kohut, H. (1977). *The restoration of the self.* New York: International University Press.

Krystal, H. (1968). *Massive psychic trauma.* New York: International University Press.

Krystal, H. (1988a). *Integration and healing.* Hillsdale, NJ: Analytic Press.

Krystal, H. (1988b). *Massive psychic trauma.* New York: International University Press.

Leary, M. P., & Tangney, J. P. (Eds.). (2003). *Handbook of self and identity.* New York: Guilford Publications.

Lifton, R .J. (1967). *Death in life: The survivors of Hiroshima.* New York: Simon & Schuster.

Lifton, R. J. (1976). *The life of the self.* New York: Simon & Schuster.

Lifton, R. J. (1979). *The broken connection: On death and the continuity of life.* New York: Basic Books.

Lifton, R. J. (1993). From Hiroshima to the nazi doctors: The evolution of psychoformative approaches to understanding traumatic stress syndromes. In J. P. Wilson, & B. Raphael (Eds.), *International handbook of traumatic stress syndromes* (pp. 11–25). New York: Plenum Press.

Lindy, J. D., & Lifton, R. J. (2001). *Beyond invisible walls.* New York: Brunner-Routledge.

Lindy, J. D., & Wilson, J. P. (1994). Empathic strain and therapist defense: Type I and type II CTR's. In J. P. Wilson, & J. D. Lindy (Eds.), *Countertransference in the treatment of PTSD* (pp. 31–61). New York: Guilford Publications.

Lindy, J. D., & Wilson, J. P. (2001). An allostatic approach to the psychodynamic understanding of PTSD. In J. P. Wilson, M. J. Friedman, & J. D. Lindy (Eds.), *Treating psychological trauma and PTSD* (pp. 125–139). New York: Guilford Publications.

Marmar, C., Weiss, D., & Metzler, T. .J. (1997). The peritraumatic dissociative experiences scale. In J. P. Wilson, & T. M. Keane (Eds.), *Assessing psychological trauma and PTSD* (pp. 412–429). New York: Guilford Publications.

McEwen, B. (1998). Protective and damaging effects of stress mediators. *Seminars of the Beth Israel Deaconess Medical Center, 338* (3), 171–179.

Mill, J. (2002). *The unconscious abyss.* New York: Wiley.

Mischel, W., & Morf, C. (2003). The self as a psychosocial dynamic processing system: A meta-psychological perspective. In M. P. Leary, & J. P. Tangney (Eds.), *Handbook of self and identity.* New York: Guilford Publications.

Monte, C., & Sollod, R. (2002). *Beneath the mask: Theories of personality* (7th ed.). New York: Wiley.

Nader, K. (1997). Assessing traumatic experiences in children. In J. P. Wilson & T. M. Keane (Eds.). *Assessing psychological trauma and PTSD* (pp. 291–349). New York: Guilford Publications.

Nader, K. (2004). Assessing traumatic experiences in children. In J. P. Wilson, & T. M. Keane (Eds.), *Assessing psychological trauma and PTSD* (2nd ed.). (in press). New York: Guilford Publications.

Niederland, W. (1968). Clinical observations of the survivor syndrome. *International Journal of Psycho-Analysis, 49,* 313–315.

Niederland, W. G. (1964). Psychiatric disorders among persecution victims — A contribution to the understanding of concentration camp pathology and its aftermath. *Journal of Nervous and Mental Disorders, 139,* 458–474.

Nijenhuis, E. R. S., & van der Hart, O. (1999a). Forgetting and re-experiencing trauma: From anesthesia to pain. In J. M. Goodwin, & R. Attias (Eds.), *Splintered reflections* (pp. 9–39). New York: Basic Books.

Nijenhuis, E. R. S., & van der Hart, O. (1999b). Somatoform dissociative phenomena: A Janetian perspective. In J. M. Goodwin, & R. Attias (Eds.), *Splintered reflections* (pp. 89–129). New York: Basic Books.

Ortiz, D. (2001). The survivor perspective: Voices from the center. In E. Gerrity, T. M. Keane, & F. Tuma (Eds.), *Mental health consequences of torture* (pp. 3–13). New York: Kluwer/Plenum Press.

Parsons, E. (1988a). Post-traumatic self-disorders. In J. P. Wilson, Z. Harel, & B. Kahana (Eds.), *Human adaptation to extreme stress: From the Holocaust to Vietnam* (pp. 245–279). New York: Plenum Press.

Parsons, E. (1988b). Theoretical and practical considerations in psychotherapy of Vietnam war veterans. In J. P. Wilson, Z. Harel, & B. Kahana (Eds.), *Human adaptation to extreme stress* (pp. 245–261). New York: Plenum Press.

Putnam, F. (1989). *Diagonsis and treatmnet of multiple personality disorders*. New York: Guilford Publications.

Putnam, F. (1997). *Dissociation in children and adolescents*. New York: Guilford Publications.

Pynoos, R., & Nader, K. (1993). Issues in the treatment of posttraumatic stress in children. In J. P. Wilson & B. Raphael (Eds.), *International handbook of traumatic stress syndromes* (pp. 527–535). New York: Plenum Press.

Rangell, L. (1976). Discussion of the Buffalo Creek disaster: The course of psychic trauma. *American Journal of Psychiatry, 133,* 313–316.

Rogers, C. (1951). *Client centered therapy*. New York: Houghton-Mifflin.

Shapiro, D. (1981). *Autonomy and rigid character*. New York: Basic Books.

Simpson, M. (1993). Traumatic stress and the bruising of the soul: The effects of torture and coercive interrogation. In J. P. Wilson, & B. Raphael (Eds.). *International handbook of traumatic stress syndromes* (pp. 667–685). New York: Plenum Press.

Sinclair, N. D. (Fr.). (1993). *Horrific traumata*. New York: Haworth Press.

Stern, D. (1985). *The interpersonal world of the infant*. New York: Basic Books.

Storr, A. (1999). *The essential Jung*. Princeton, NJ: Princeton University Press.

Ulman, R. B., & Brothers, D. (1988). *The shattered self*. Hillsdale, NJ: Analytic Press.

van der Kolk, B., van der Hart, O., & Marmar, C. (1996). Dissociation and information processing in PTSD. In B. van der Kolk, A. C. McFarlane, & L. Weisaeth (Eds.), *Traumatic stress* (pp. 303–331). New York: Guilford Publications.

van der Kolk, B., McFarlane, A. C., & Weisaeth, L. (1997). *Traumatic stress*. New York: Guilford Publications.

Volkan, Vamık. (2002). *The third reich in the unconscious*. New York: Brunner-Routledge.

Watkins, J. G., & Watkins, H. H. (1997). *Ego-states*. New York: W. W. Norton.

Williams, M. B., & Somers, J. (2002). *Simple and complex PTSD*. New York: Haworth Press.

Wilson, J. P. (1980). Conflict, stress and growth: The effects of war on psychosocial development among Vietnam veterans. In C. R. Figley & K. S. Leventam (Eds.), *Strangers at home: Vietnam veterans since the war* (pp. 123–165). New York: Praeger Press.

Wilson, J. P., Harel, Z., & Kahana, B. (1988). *Human adaption to extreme stress: From Holocaust to Vietnam*. New York & London: Plenum Press.

Wilson, J. P. (1989a). *Trauma, transformation and healing*. New York: Brunner-Mazel.

Wilson, J. P. (1989b). *Trauma, transformation and healing: An integration approval to theory, research and posttraumatic theory*. New York: Brunner/Mazel, Inc.

Wilson, J. P., & Lindy, J. (1994). *Counter-transference in the treatment of PTSD.* New York: Guilford Publications.

Wilson, J. P., & Moran, T. (1997). Psychological trauma: PTSD and spirituality. *Journal of Psychology and Theology, 26*(2), 168–178.

Wilson, J. P., Friedman, M. J., & Lindy, J. D. (2001). *Treating psychological trauma and PTSD.* New York: Guilford Publications.

Wilson, J. P. (2002a, October 12). The abyss experience and the trauma complex: Mental health response to weapons of mass destruction: Terrorist attacks. Presentation at St. Joseph's University, Philadelphia, PA.

Wilson, J. P. (2002b, November 10). An organismic, holistic model of complex PTSD. Presentation at the International Society for Traumatic Stress Studies' 18th annual meeting, Baltimore, MD.

Wilson. J. P. (2003, February 16). Target goals & interventions for PTSD: From trauma to the abyss experience. Presentation at the International Critical Incident Stress Foundation's 7th World Congress on Stress, Trauma and Coping. Baltimore, MD.

Wolfe, E. (1990). *Treating the self.* New York: Guilford Publications.

Public Mental Health and Culture: Disasters as a Challenge to Western Mental Health Care Models, the Self, and PTSD

JOOP DE JONG

Western psychosocial experts such as psychologists, social workers, or psychiatrists are trained to assess a person presenting with stress-related complaints, followed by a diagnosis, treatment plan, and therapy. They mostly provide psychotherapy or pharmacotherapy within the culture of an existing mental health care system that has already been built up and that they will rarely question. This reality is quite different from the "crisis zones" in the world. Complex humanitarian emergencies, natural or human-made disasters, affect large and often displaced civilian populations. Complex emergencies involve a combination of factors such as interstate or intrastate violence, terrorism, recurring food shortages, or co-occurring natural disasters. These factors result in high levels of physical and mental morbidity or mortality. This chapter examines the consequences of complex humanitarian emergencies as a challenge to the mental health profession. The chapter will also examine one of the major challenges for mental health practitioners — understanding the role of culture in disasters. Culture permeates the whole process of traumatization and recovery from traumatic stress. The context of crisis zones interacts with culturally mediated systems of meaning such as religion or causative attribution, and with practices such as cults, rituals, and social support systems. I will illustrate the importance of cultural factors by focusing on local variations in the construction of the self, in the interpretation of traumatic stressors, the ways the events are appraised, in variations in coping strategies, and in the expression of people's plight in terms of idioms of distress or psychopathology.

COMPLEX HUMANITARIAN EMERGENCIES AS A CHALLENGE TO THE MENTAL HEALTH PROFESSION

Complex humanitarian emergencies are a challenge to our profession for a variety of reasons (de Jong & Komproe, 2002; de Jong, Komproe, & van Ommeren, 2003). First, there is a huge discrepancy between the availability of mental health (para)professionals and the numbers of people estimated to have mental health problems. The bulk of the 35 million refugees and internally displaced worldwide reside in countries that on average have less than one psychiatrist, psychologist, or psychiatric nurse per 100,000 people (WHO, 2001). These figures are even too optimistic for some of the conflict zones of the past decade. African countries such as Angola, Burundi, Congo, Eritrea, Ethiopia, Mozambique, Rwanda, or South-Sudan have 1 psychiatrist per 4 to 10 million inhabitants. Asian countries such as Burma, Cambodia, Indonesia, or Iraq these figures vary from 1 psychiatrist per 200,000 to 1 to 2 million inhabitants. In a country like Algeria many psychologists and psychiatrists have escaped the fundamentalist violence in the country, and in Iraq only about 20 of the 130 psychiatrists were still present when the army surrendered. Even before the beginning of the armed conflict most war-torn countries faced great difficulties to cover a substantial part of their population with mental health services, which in general were hospital rather then community based. After the hostilities broke out, the remaining mental health professionals were confronted with huge groups of people suffering from psychosocial problems, which in itself would pose a problem to almost any existing mental health care system. For example, even the 500,000 people estimated to need some form of psychological support after the 9/11 attacks in United States overextend the existing service capacity, despite the fact that New York has the highest density of mental health professionals worldwide (Herman & Susser, 2003).

A second challenge to the mental health profession is related to the accessibility of services and to equity in service provision (which in this context means that individuals with the same condition should have equal access to mental health services). The majority of refugees and internally displaced persons (IDPs) reside in peripheral and often barren areas that even in peacetime are underserviced by allopathic (mental) health providers. Survivors are often too poor to pay for (the travel to) the service or too afraid to leave their home area. Therefore, nongovernment offices (NGOs), governments, and the United Nations can only achieve equity by balancing the needs of the local indigenous population with the needs of newcomers and by preventing rivalry between both groups.

A third challenge is related to culture, a recurrent theme in this chapter. Survivors often belong to a different subcultural and socioeconomic group than those who seek to offer help. Sophisticated or eloquent helpers from urban areas are often regarded with distrust. Moreover, survivors might express their plight in a specific discourse or in a local *idiom of distress* and use different explanatory models. Modern service delivery systems, even if they are community oriented, tend to exclude specific groups. Exclusion exists for several reasons. The mental health professionals might not be adequately trained to deal with certain problems or have limited treatment possibilities for certain complex problems (e.g., dissociative behavioral patterns or complex PTSD). Or mental health professionals might feel unable to transcend their countertransference or group countertransference. For example, they might have differing political convictions or feel unable to work with Muslim or Buddhist militants; or they might have to work with representatives of ethnic groups who are collectively accused of being perpetrators, such as the Hutu in Rwanda; or they might be confronted with perpetrators of violence such as ex-rebels, ex-combatants, or former child soldiers. Another reason to exclude specific groups from services is that survivors could be stigmatized (e.g., rape survivors or people with a physical and/or a mental handicap being perceived as the product of magic-religious forces). Survivors could also exclude themselves from services because they do not trust or understand the rationale of modern psychosocial or mental health support. For example, in many countries, people from lower socioeconomic strata are less likely to seek help from modern allopathic services, even if these services are free.

Local traditional service systems can offer a fourth challenge. In view of the aforementioned scarcity of allopathic service providers, healers can be regarded as natural allies for a number of reasons. Healers are omnipresent, varying from about 1 healer per 25 to 500 inhabitants in a range of low-income countries (de Jong, 2001a). Although almost half of the population in high-income countries regularly use some form of alternative medicine, there is considerable use of traditional healers in low-income countries, ranging from 40% in China to 80% in African countries (WHO, 2002). Healers are socially and culturally accepted since they work part time as a healer while continuing their work in their communities. They enjoy ascribed authority because their capacity to heal is often transmitted over generations along patrilinear or matrilinear lines. Although their expertise is not condensed in academic writing, healers have impressed researchers by the wide variety of psychotherapeutic interventions they use. Cultures develop resiliency and coping strategies in the form of mourning, healing, purification, reconciliation, and commemoration rituals to heal the wounds of the past (de Jong, 2002a, 2002b). Healers play an important role by performing these types of rituals. For example, in Mozambique and Sierra Leone healers have been performing cleansing rituals that allow ex-child soldiers to be reintegrated in society. In Uganda rituals were one of the interventions used to assist rebels who had been looting and plundering for years to make the transition from a combat mode to a civil mode, thus facilitating their reintegration into society (de Jong, 2000). In Uganda and Sudan healers perform rituals that allow female rape survivors to continue their lives without the social stigma of being blamed for the rape or without canceling previous marriage arrangements. In Nepal healers perform purification rituals when adolescents show symptoms of medically unexplained illnesses caused by possession by spirits that were thought to be disturbed by the filth in a refugee camp (van Ommeren, Sharma et al., 2001). Healers perform mourning rituals that can be complicated due to armed conflict. For example, the rebel movement Renamo in Mozambique, set up by Rhodesian and maintained by South African intelligence services, as well as the Lord Resistance Army in north Uganda, required recruits to perform their duties far from their families with a view to decrease social control that might hamper their dedication to the struggle against the Frelimo regime. When in Mozambique these recruits were declared missing after the war, the healers' associations allowed families to do their mourning rituals by substituting for the culturally required corpse any belonging of the dead person. In Sri Lanka healers are involved in ceremonies such as Shraddhanjali, which is a mass grieving ceremony that promotes unity and collective action within the grief-stricken community (Somasundaram & Jamunanantha, 2002). In Cambodia some healers and monks are renowned for treating children's diseases or illnesses brought on by human interference such as sorcery; many are experts in pharmacological treatment, gathering plants outside their houses, which they sometimes prepare in elaborate pharmacies. Each sort of traditional healer offers a particular target intervention: the monks tend to focus on advice and calming people's anxieties; the *kruu*, the trained healers, provided medication and magical rituals to help rid people of invading spells and spirits and, through the public ritual, to reintegrate the person into the local community; the mediums, mostly women, offered an intercession with the ancestors and in this way act as remoralizing counselors for women who cannot face their futures; the traditional birth attendants help families through difficulties around childbirth and the puerperium (van de Put & Eisenbruch, 2002). Unfortunately only a few studies exist that evaluate the treatment effects of healers, while more than a thousand quantitative studies on the outcome of psychotherapy have been carried out (de Jong, 2001a). Moreover, almost all outcome studies on healers show methodological shortcomings. To conclude, collaboration with the healing complex is a large and yet mostly unexplored challenge; healers often are the carriers of accumulated wisdom and can play an important role in recovery of a disrupted postconflict society. They possess qualities that make them ideal primary psychosocial health care workers, that is, they are omnipresent, well informed about psychosocial stressors, and they are part and parcel of the local culture. However, as applies to most Western-oriented intervention programs as well, additional information is required to assess to what extent they are effective. Moreover, since the success of an allopathic treatment is often attributed to a healer, many local or expatriate helpers with advanced education perceive healers as a competition to their academic status or as people who encroach on their turf.

A fifth challenge to mental health professionals is that most conflicts are the result of political, economic, and sociocultural processes. Hence, sequelae of such conflicts can likely only be resolved by multilevel, multisectoral public health approaches informed by social sciences (especially medical anthropology), behavioral sciences, and epidemiology. Protracted conflicts that are related to competition for power and resources result in predatory social formations; they affect large, displaced, and mostly poor populations, and they are often accompanied by cycles of violence (Hamburg, George, & Ballentine, 1999). Conflicts that are protracted in duration are an additional challenge and require flexible but sustainable solutions, both functionally and geographically. For example, the conflicts in Afghanistan, Indonesia, and the African Great Lake region require that paraprofessionals from among the survivors move to other areas together with the displaced persons when the armed conflict dictates a continuation of their journeys.

CULTURE AND THE SELF

Western psychologists and psychiatrists often assume that people in low-income countries have similar concepts about phenomena such as consciousness, attention, perception, will, the self, or personality (Kim, Triandis, Kagitcibasi, Sang-Chin Choi, & Yoon, 1994; Lewis-Fernandes & Kleinman, 1994). In relation to traumatic stress, Ulman and Brothers (1988, p. 7) state

> It is because the self is the process, center of mental activity for organizing the meaning of experience in that a serious disturbance or

interference in its ability to function constitutes a trauma. The person's sense of self or experience of the self is critical to its organizing activity. Thus, any occurrence taking an unconscious meaning that seriously challenges or undermines this sense may be experienced as a traumatic shattering of the self ... A person ceases to secure selfhood without some center for organizing experience into meaning structures. (as cited in Chapter 6)

These words follow the writing of Kierkegaard, James, Hobbes, Locke, and Descartes. They characterize the Western concept of the self and the personhood as an autonomous, individualized, volitional, and independent entity having control over one's existence and environment through rational means. Non-Western cultures often conceptualize the self in relation to its environment and emphasize the interdependence of the self. Parellel to the ego, the super ego, and the id, ethnoanalysts have postulated the existence of a group ego, a group super ego, and a group id (Parin, Morgenthaler, & Parin-Mattèy, 1963). Hsu (1971) described the social construction of personhood or Jen in Chinese and Japanese culture as a number of concentric layers involving the unconscious, the interpersonal, the intimate, and wider society. The Lohorung in Nepal perceive the self as an interaction of an ancestral substance (*saya*) with a live-bringing concept (*lawa*) (Hardman, 2000). In West Africa (Horton, 1993; Kwasi, 1980) and in the African-Surinamese-Caribbean tradition, many people have similar conceptions about the self. For Creole Surinamese a human being consists of a biological part of body and blood, and a spiritual part that consists of the triade *djodjo*, *kra*, and *jorka*. Every human being has one male and one female djodjo that offer protection and prosperity (which in West Africa is often represented as descending along patrilinear or matrilinear lines). The djodjo transmit the pure soul, the kra, from the Supreme Being to the human being. The djodjo and the kra are present at conception. In the course of life the jorka is added to this dyad. The jorka consists of life experience, breath, memory, and personality. Upon death the jorka remains among the ancestors to guard the living. Both djodjo and jorka are anthropomorphic. Their human traits can manifest themselves in good or bad qualities that can complement or compete with each other. These different notions of the self across cultures have important implications for the comprehension of people's reactions to traumatic stress. Wilson (Chapter 6 in this volume) distinguishes 11 typologies of self-reconfiguration following extreme trauma and key descriptions of ego processes, personality, and psychopathology associated with each form of structural reorganization. He distinguishes, for example, the inert self (or soul death), resulting in catatonic or paranoid states, brief psychosis, or PTSD; the empty self, leading to depression and PTSD; and the fragmented self, resulting in dissociation, PTSD, or borderline personality. Although these typologies can be clinically useful for a psychodynamic culture, they do not have universal value in cultures where the self is conceptualized as composite and where the self might include supernatural elements with anthropomorphic traits or states. These cultural differences in the perception of the self have far-reaching consequences for the process of psychodiagnosis in general and for the barely explored cultural field of traumatic stress in particular. A dream or a nightmare can have another meaning when it is attributed to (a part of) someone's soul leaving the body or a soul of someone else visiting the dreamer. For example, a nightmare (*sramay*) has a different meaning for traumatized Cambodians, because the dreamer could be visited by a deceased family member during the night. An autoscopic or out-of-body experience related to extreme peritraumatic dissociation can be fully comprehensible for someone who attributes this experience to part of his or her soul watching the body. Words like shattering, splintering, or fragmentation of the self can be redundant for people who express their plight in the idiom of distress of spirit possession that fits well with their concept of a soul consisting of multiple parts. Antisocial or substance abuse behavior can be better understood when it is attributed to some ancestral substance that is part of the self (which obviously can hamper treatment if adverse social behavior is externally attributed to some anthropomorphic part of the soul). Dependent personality disorder can appear to be a Western cultural diagnostic construct that does not fit the interdependency that is prevalent in non-Western cultures. When disorders of extreme stress (DES) in different cultures were studied, problems with conceptual, content, semantic, or technical equivalence were found (de Jong & van Ommeren, 2002; Flaherty, Gaviria, Pathak, Mitchell, Wintrob, Richman, et al., 1988). For example, the average prevalence of the domain of suicidal ideation in respondents with DES in our study is almost nine times lower than in the DSM field trial. This might be a result of a problem of technical equivalence (i.e., a socially desirable answer) since suicide is considered taboo in both the Islamic and Coptic religions, while in Buddhism it might result in numerous reincarnations as an inferior being like an animal. In many African and Asian cultures part of the soul of someone who commits suicide can become a capricious wandering spirit attacking family members or others, resulting in all kinds of predicaments. When we studied the dissociative dimension of DES we came across similar difficulties.

The structured interview for disorders of extreme stress (SIDES) question about "spacing out when you feel frightened or under stress" creates a problem with semantic equivalence, because this dissociative experience is very hard to translate (even in most Western European languages). Moreover, anything close to "spacing out" is often related to a spirit taking possession of the person in non-Western cultures, as opposed to the association between spacing out and illegal drug use in the West. Similarly, another aspect of dissociation, for example by asking if "you sometimes feel like there are two people living inside you who control how you behave at different times," creates a problem of conceptual equivalence (i.e., is the same theoretical construct measured in each culture). Even in the West one might wonder if someone who truly dissociates per definition is able to perceive two forces within him- or herself since there mostly is partial or total amnesia between subpersonalities. If so, it requires a high level of cognitive introspection (which also seemed to be absent in the West, for example, in the Salpêtrière at the end of the 18th and beginning of the 19th centuries when these concepts were developed). In non-Western cultures the same is true today. Even healers and shamans who go into trance many times a day would not mention that it "feels like there are two people living inside them who control their behavior." Even more so for an average respondent who handles an external attribution for the dissociative experience by attributing it to an ancestor, a deity, a ghost, or a part of his or her soul (de Jong, van der Kolk, Komproe, Spinazzola, & van Ommeren, 2004).

To conclude, a conception of the self that is more congruent with non-Western cultures results in a different perspective on a range of normal and psychopathological phenomena. It is noteworthy that these non-Western concepts of the self show amazing similarities with modern concepts and their neurobiological substrate distinguishing the apparent normal personality and emotional personalities (Nijenhuijs, van der Hart, & Steele, 2002).

CULTURE AND TRAUMATIC STRESS, MODERATORS, AND OUTCOMES

The remainder of this chapter will describe how culture molds the relationship between traumatic and other events, moderators, and outcomes. I will provide illustrations of the pervasive effect of cultural factors on current models of stress in psychology and psychiatry.

Obeyesekere (1985) wrote that "the work of culture is the process whereby painful motives and affects are transformed into publicly accepted sets of meaning and symbols." Each refugee, internally displaced person (IDP), or immigrant has to relate to a process of acculturative stress and find an identity within the new environment. In the words of Tseng and Strelzer (1977): "as a result of enculturation, every individual learns a language, a religion, or other meaning system, specifying how the forces of nature operate in the world, as well as norms of behavior, and patterns of experiencing the environment." Examples of the importance of culture will be given by following common stress models with a cultural lens. These stress models most often distinguish a traumatic stressor resulting in psychological and psychiatric problems mediated by a range of protective and vulnerability factors.

Traumatic Stressors and Their Appraisal

We do not know how culture influences recall of traumatic events, nor do we know how culture influences the measurement of traumatic events. Green (1993) has suggested eight generic dimensions of trauma: (1) threat to life and limb; (2) severe physical harm or injury; (3) receipt of intentional injury/harm; (4) exposure to the grotesque; (5) violent/sudden loss of a loved one; (6) witnessing or learning of violence to a loved one; (7) learning of exposure to a noxious agent; and (8) causing death or severe harm to another. Although most of these dimensions seem to have a universal character, they can be perceived differently in specific cultures or minority groups.

Regarding the first dimension, threat to life and limb, we found, for example, that group rape of abducted women in Uganda can be dealt with by a collective purification ritual under the aegis of the elderly; whereas in Algeria, Cambodia, or Namibia the shame caused by rape can lead to suicide or marginalization of the victim. Surprisingly, even in the latter cultures it was found that most women were willing to talk about rape in an interview situation, and it appeared that the reluctance of the interviewers to discuss rape was sometimes greater than the reluctance of the survivors to discuss it.

With the second dimension, severe physical harm or injury, it has been argued that violence in the family is a universal stressor that is often aggravated by continuous traumatic stress in many cultures. However, in some cultures — for example in Latin America and Southeast Asia — attitudes tend to be lenient toward wife-battering, whereas in other cultures it is found to be unacceptable (Finkler, 1997).

In Buddhist and African cultures, which believe in reincarnation, the loss of a family member (dimensions 5 and 6 according to Green) can have a different impact. The loss of an older loved person who has children and some accumulated wealth can be acceptable in African animistic cultures, since it is believed that the person will travel to the reign of the ancestors and occupy an intermediary position between the living and the dead (Bagilishya, 2000; de Jong & Van Schaik, 1994). Yet the death of a child in the same culture is a disaster, even though some people seem to think that parents suffer less in cultures with high exposure to child mortality.

We also know little about the ways people appraise personal loss versus property loss in different cultural settings. One can imagine that detachment, which is as an ultimate goal in Buddhism, decreases the impact of property loss. However, one might question whether detachment is the focus of concern of poor Tibetans or Cambodians struggling with survival. From our clinical experience it seems that relatively rich people who lose everything have more difficulty coping than those whose losses are smaller.

Similarly, political conviction can be an important factor in grief or mourning as has been described in Gaza (Qouta, 2000; Qouta &

El-Sarraj, 2002). Albanian Kosovar families who lost a family member in the war in 1999 regard their deceased family members as martyrs. This view can on the one hand alleviate their loss, while on the other hand complicate the mourning process. A child soldier who is a perpetrator (dimension 8) can be regarded as a hero in certain countries. Even exposure to the grotesque can be mediated by religious convictions, such as the role of karma in Buddhism in Asia or divine persecution during the Holocaust (Abramson, 2000; van de Put, & Eisenbruch, 2002).

The assessment of the severity of traumatic exposure and its appraisal in a specific cultural setting is a complex issue that will require future collaboration with cultural informants and social scientists.

Resources

Cultural factors mediate the person's ability to utilize resources when trying to cope with a disaster. As stated previously, autonomy and individualization are important Western values, which in other cultures can be perceived as selfishness. The value of autonomy among many Westerners is different from the dependency and interdependency in many low-income countries. This interdependency can be threatened by the disruption of the social network with a subsequent weakening of people's individual or collective identity. Interdependency and mutual support systems can be challenged, for example, when a culture prescribes costly rites of passage that family members no longer can afford. Some cultures allow for creative solutions, but others require saving their meager resources until the ritual can be performed properly. Ancestral spirits and deities providing protection and consolation are a resource in a variety of cultures. However, people may fear that the ghosts of the deceased can seek revenge if the mourning rituals have not been carried out in the proper way. Like other anxieties, this fear can lead to experiences of possession or epidemics of medically unexplained illnesses. The individual or group possession can manifest itself in the spirit idiom of a specific culture, allowing people to reexperience and abreact their anxieties and fears. Among the Masai, traditional healers gave this stress response a label and incorporated it within the traditional healing rituals (de Vries, 1996). Collective possession can also be interpreted as a "popular mode of stress resolution," like the Jangue Jangue movement in Guinea Bissau or the "cults of violence and counter-violence" in Mozambique (de Jong, 1987, 2004). If resources are minimal and dowries cannot be paid, premarital sex, teenage pregnancies, and prostitution tend to become more common. Refugees often have to compete with local populations for resources like land and food, which were scarce even before the conflict started.

A social network can function as a resourceful protective factor when a family is of average size. But if many adults die due to war or AIDS, a large extended family can turn into a vulnerability factor. When I worked as a psychiatrist in West Africa, male clients were often struggling with where to draw the boundaries of their responsibilities. If they chose to care for their nuclear family, the extended family would be angry and could seek revenge through gossip, witchcraft, or sorcery. If they chose to care for their extended family, their house would be inundated with family members requesting food or fees for education. As a result, their wives regarded themselves as the slaves of their husbands' extended families. Despite these possible controversies, families are often the main source of social capital and the main provider of mental health care for refugees and poor rural populations. Murthy (1998) mentions that the family is often seen as a substitute for professional care, rather than as an essential component of mental support. Efforts have been made to understand the needs of families, to provide them with support and training skills, to help organize family groups, and to help families in networking. To prevent families from putting away their ill relatives, these needs must be addressed in a planned manner. It is quite obvious that public mental health programs need to incorporate the extended family in its interventions and keep children within their family context. Moreover, interventions should preferably take place in the vicinity of the recipients' homes.

Coping Behavior

From prehistoric times onward cultures have developed coping strategies to deal with traumatic stress or mental illness. Both problem-focused and emotion-focused coping are influenced by culture. Once indigenous coping strategies and resources are identified and understood, they can be fostered and encouraged as a form of prevention or intervention. There exists growing consensus that intervention programs should emphasize processes of salutogenesis (i.e., looking at resiliency, health promoting factors, and useful coping styles to maintain people's health).

Grief provides a good example of the influence of culture on coping. Coping with grief is one of the essential tasks of survivors in (post)disaster and (post)conflict situations. There are several dimensions distinguishing cultures regarding grief and bereavement. In contrast to low-income countries, high-income countries use concepts such as counseling during the process of dying, grief, or terminal care. In low-income countries, people's attention is especially focused on various supernatural beliefs that vary across cultures and include (a) that the dead communicate with the living, (b) that other people's supernatural abilities (e.g., witchcraft or sorcery) can cause death, (c) that the ghost of the deceased will take revenge if one does not complete proper rituals for the deceased, (d) that verbalizing the name of the deceased is dangerous, (e) that a newborn is a reincarnation of a deceased person, (f) that hearing or seeing the deceased person is normal, and (g) that tie-breaking customs are useful to cope with loss (de Jong & van Schaik

1994; Goody, 1962; Irish, Lundquist, & Nelsen, 1993; Parkes, Laungani & Young, 1997; Rosenblatt, Walsh, & Jackson, 1976; Thomas, 1982). Thus, in these cultures problems are expressed less in a psychological way and more as an interaction between the supernatural, including the ancestors and the living. Anger toward the deceased is another important difference in grief between African and Euro-American cultures. The common Christian habit is to encourage saying nothing but good about the dead and this can hinder the expression of negative feelings toward the person who somehow left the living behind. As Wortmann and Silver (1989) have argued that in the West the bereaved person's social network frequently employs strategies to get the bereaved to inhibit displays of distress. This inhibition in Western culture includes discouraging the display of feelings ("Tears won't bring him back."); minimizing the loss ("You had many good years together."); encouraging the bereaved person to recover more quickly ("You should get out and do more."); portraying their own past experiences as being similar to that the bereaved has experienced ("I know how you feel. I lost my second cousin."); and offering advice ("You should consider getting a dog. They're wonderful companions.").

In African cultures the expression of emotions such as anger is often permitted in a ritual context. For example, on several occasions I witnessed funeral rites allowing the family to ridicule the dead in a kind of *comedia del arte*, expressing avarice, laziness, or stuttering. Another example is the wife of a deceased Afro-Caribbean head of a upper-class family in the Netherlands asking her children "to put four mud cunts in his coffin" so that he could enjoy adultery in afterlife as he sometimes did alive.

Among mental health professionals, verbal expressions of distress are questioned as a universal coping strategy. According to several authors the disclosure of the "conspiracy of silence" only took place in the 1970s (Flanzbaum, 1999). Western experts sometimes project, in my view, a stereotypical opinion by stating that non-Westerners do not want to discuss the past, and that the supposed willingness or "working through" of Westerners is a typical product of our Judaic-Christian tradition of confession and catharsis (Summerfield, 2000; Tricket, 1995). This stereotype is often supported by another stereotype, that non-Westerners somatize rather than psychologize their distress, even though there is a substantial body of evidence supporting the view that somatizing is the rule rather than the exception around the globe (e.g., Üstün & Sartorius, 1995). A more useful approach is to look at cultural differences in the way people somatize. In this case cultural consistency, rather than cultural differences, leads to misunderstanding. The above two stereotypes have added to a third one: the notion that it is impossible to do anything substantial or meaningful regarding massive traumatic stress. This erroneous view has resulted in an avoidance of the issue of psychological suffering and its consequences, which in turn has contributed to a "conspiracy of silence." Despite these stereotypes, there seems to exist some universal ambivalence around the expression of distress: "it is good to forget the past" and "time heals wounds" can be described as coping strategies in many areas around the world. Refugees and survivors of disasters might say that they never want to talk about their pasts and that their lives are directed toward the future. Yet, they often discuss their pasts with their fellow human beings. In our experience, it is a universal phenomenon that people feel relieved after verbally expressing their distress of the past when interventions are culturally congruent. Obviously, there are differences across cultures. For example, discussions with Africans from various socioeconomic backgrounds show clearly that the issues of individual and collective grief and bereavement are perceived as much more important — both in terms of personal and economic consequences — in Africa than in the West. These differences are related to factors such as religion, the belief in (proper) reincarnation, and the belief in or the fear of ancestors or spirits, even after the advent of Christianity, Islam, or Buddhism. Buddhist Asians can attribute their plight to kharma, but simultaneously approach the ancestors and pre-Buddhist spirits to improve their fate (Somasundaram & Jamunanantha, 2002; van de Put & Eisenbruch, 2002).

In addition to narration, the body mediates in perceiving and expressing grief and suffering. Time and again we realize the extent to which culture-specific notions of anatomy and physiology interact with etiologic factors causing misfortune or illness. For example, when our Cambodian Transcultural Psychosocial Organization (TPO) team had to arrange a blood transfusion, it found that nobody including the family was willing to give blood. It appeared that the belief in Khmer culture was that everybody is gifted from birth onward with a fixed amount of blood that is located in the upper part of the skull. Tapping blood means that the level of blood in the head decreases, but the blood that is given to another cannot be substituted later in life. From a phenomenological perspective, Merlau Ponty describes the relation between body and culture as follows: "the body is the medium through which people experience their cultural world; bodily experience reflects the culture in which it occurs" (as cited in Becker, Beyene, & Ken, 2000). Kleinman (1988) adds an interactional component when he says that suffering is experienced within "the nested context of embodiment: collective, intersubjective, individual. Embodiment means that the body is seen as the threshold through which the subject's lived experience of the world is incorporated and realized." Translating these words to the reality of psychosocial and mental health care implies that psychosocial and mental work is imbued with physical aspects. It ranges from diagnosing tropical and other disorders, synthesizing divergent explanatory models, clarifying the interaction between magic and supernatural causative factors and the body, and using the body as an important vehicle for healing, both for the people asking and providing support.

To conclude, it seems that we are only at the initial stage of understanding differences and similarities across cultures. Apparently there exists a universal ambiguity in dealing with a traumatic past. People are also ambivalent about what they bring forward in their daily discourse and what they actually do or appreciate when it comes to coping with traumatic stress. People might feel they do not want to embarrass their fellow survivors by asking about their haunting pasts, and yet survivors can find enormous relief when they share their memories with others, whether through a self-help group, an individual or family session, or a ritual. Getting beyond the surface will enable us to determine what are appropriate coping strategies to satisfy universal human necessities while also taking into account the specific sociocultural context.

Consequences

The last part of the model explains the importance of culture in understanding the social, environmental, physical, and mental health consequences to trauma. The lack of understanding of the sociocultural context has been criticized both by clinicians and by culturally informed epidemiologists. Some aspects of this criticism are summarized in this section.

1. The category fallacy: Western psychodiagnostic categories, as defined in DSM-IV or ICD-10, often are not appropriate in non-Western cultures. They can reify a Western culturally constructed concept and use it in cross-cultural research procedures, a procedure called the category fallacy (Kleinman, 1977; Kleinman & Good, 1985). That is, one first defines the Western category, then starts looking for that category in a non-Western culture, and subsequently finds what was defined earlier, leading to a *quod erat demonstrandum* ("that what had to be proven"). However, if one would carefully listen to people's phenomenological stories (also known as narrative, psychobiography, or thick description), the reported complaints might not match the Western category. For example, in most studies on PTSD, including that of Shrestha et al. (1998), investigators first define PTSD along DSM-IV criteria and then search for that "disorder." Even though most scholars find PTSD around the globe, the conclusion that PTSD is similar in all cultures is false, since the studies did not look for differences that might have yielded so-far-unknown (sub)types or variations of the disorder. For that reason, we cannot rule out the possibility that PTSD is an a priori, culture-bound construct. We therefore prefer the term (post)traumatic stress syndrome [(P)TSS]. A similar reasoning can be applied to most psychiatric disorders (cf. Young, 2002).

2. Beyond classification systems: Even if one agrees that most of the Western categories do apply in low-income countries, there can still be considerable differences in the way people perceive or express their plight or illnesses. For example, stress and depression are often described as "thinking too much" in low-income countries. Globally it might be more appropriate to perceive depression as a loss of vital substance or of a part of the soul than as a "sinking of mood." The expression of feelings of guilt and shame can vary from one culture to another. A person can have a number of physical sensations, such as heat, cold, prickling sensations in some parts of the body, pulsating experiences, moving heaviness through the abdomen, discomfort of the heart, creeping sensations under the skin or the skull, or bubbling sensations in the head (de Jong, 2002b). Or alternatively, the distress can be expressed in a variety of dissociative patterns, which even the local culture might find difficult to assess as normal or deviant (for example when people display a so-called hysterical state or a possession trance). These behaviors can be seen as typical templates that the culture gives to its members to express their plight.

The same holds for the way people express complaints or emotions in their language. The local language or *lingua franca* can use a number of expressions, metaphors, proverbs, or emotion words to express a complaint or an emotion that are quite different from western jargon. Therefore, one has to carefully make an inventory of the expression of distress in other cultures (the "idioms of distress") before one can conclude that the way people perceive their problem is the same as the DSM/ICD categories. If these diagnostic challenges are not met, various diagnostic errors can occur. Either a clinician can miss the PTSD diagnosis because associated features are most prominent, or the associated features can be overlooked because of the presence of PTSD.

3. *The diversity of trauma reactions*: Blank (1994) has written a useful guide for the clinician evaluating posttraumatic responses, in which he repeatedly emphasizes the variety of reactions to trauma. He says that when assessing the plight of a refugee, one has to take into account that the reactions to trauma are often intertwined with the cultural transitions they are confronted with, along with acculturative stress, culture shock, and cultural bereavement (Eisenbruch, 1984a, 1984b). This elicits questions regarding etiology and whether one is dealing with traumatic stress, the effects of daily hassles, or a combination of coping style and acculturation. One might hypothesize that a comorbid disorder such as depression improves when life circumstances become stable and people are less confronted with adverse life events, but that the stronger neurobiological component of PTSD can persist longer. For example, preliminary analysis of the data of our MIM-study (multisite impact of human-made disaster) shows that coping style and social support improve people's quality of life and decrease the disability caused by PTSD. However, in contrast to depressive and anxiety disorder, coping and social support do not affect the PTSD as such. A similar pattern was observed in a diagnostic study among Bhutanese refugees in Nepal (van Ommeren, de Jong et al., 2001).

4. *Adapting instruments across cultures*: A diagnostic or research instrument developed in one culture has to be tested before being applied in another culture. This helps to bring understanding of the concepts

underlying the items of the instrument, testing them for their content, semantic, conceptual, and technical validity. This will show if a concept that is relevant in one culture has significance in another. How to properly adapt instruments has been described elsewhere (de Jong & van Ommeren, 2002; van Ommeren et al., 1999).

5. *Cultural flaws of psychiatric epidemilogical instruments*: The current epidemiological approach might not reveal that Western diagnostic constructs are culture-bound. This might be because the algorithms and the exclusionary and skip rules of the major diagnostic instruments such as the diagnostic interview schedule (DIS) and the composite international diagnostic interview (CIDI) are such that dimensional analyses are impossible. In other words, Western classificatory systems are limited because their decision rules to produce diagnoses are bound by the aforementioned category fallacy. In addition, current epidemiological techniques will not help us solve the problem of comorbidity, which to a large extent is caused by the poor validity of Western diagnostic categories.

6. *Amplifying the PTSD paradigm*: Research in postconflict situations has gravitated toward the epidemiology and treatment of PTSD. Yet, the study of this Western diagnostic category in non-Western contexts can lead to its reification without evidence that this category is the most relevant of possible descriptions of local survivors' mental health problems (Marsella, Friedman, Gerrity, & Scurfield, 1996; Shrestha et al., 1998). This has resulted in selective attention to PTSD in many intervention programs at the expense of other types of mental health problems that are elevated as well. In our MIM-study we found that PTSD is not only associated with an experience of conflict violence, but also with a range of other stressors such as the quality of the camps or daily difficulties (de Jong et al., 2001). We also found that rates of disorder tend to be significantly higher in people who had experienced armed conflict–associated violence. The largest risk ratios were for PTSD, ranging from 10.03 in Palestine to 3.14 in Algeria. Interestingly, for mood disorder, risk ratios were 6.06 in Ethiopia and 4.53 in Palestine. For other anxiety disorders, risk ratios ranged from 2.10 to 3.16 in Ethiopia, Algeria, and Palestine (de Jong, Komproe, & van Ommeren, 2003a). Moreover, we found that disability was more associated with mood disorder and anxiety disorder than with PTSD. This calls for a paradigm shift among professionals who focus more or less solely on PTSD within trauma rehabilitation programs. Postconflict programs should get beyond a narrow PTSD focus and address a wide range of problems and disorders.

CONCLUSION

One of the challenges of the next decades is a worldwide inventory of traumatic stress reactions by using a phenomenological approach employing a combination of qualitative and quantitative research methods (de Jong & van Ommeren, 2002). It is expected that this will yield a neurobiological and universal core at the biological end of a continuum with a large variety of culturally induced phenomena at the sociopsychological end of the continuum. This requires intensive collaboration between mental health professionals and social science, especially anthropology. As this chapter has shown, this is one of the many future challenges that culture poses to our profession.

REFERENCES

Abramson, H. (2000). The esh kodesh of rabbi Kalonimus Kalmish Shapiro: A Hasidic treatise on communal trauma from the Holocaust. *Transcultural Psychiatry, 37*(3), 321–335.

Bagilishya, D. (2000). Mourning and recovery from trauma: In Rwanda, tears flow within. *Transcultural Psychiatry, 37*(3), 337–353.

Becker, G., Beyene, Y., & Ken, P. (2000). Health, welfare reform, and narratives of uncertainty among Cambodian refugees. *Culture, Medicine and Psychiatry, 2,* 139–163.

Blank, A. S. (1994). Clinical detection, diagnosis and differential diagnosis of PTSD. *Psychiatric Clinics of North America, 8,* 351–384.

de Jong, J. (2000). Traumatic stress among ex-combatants. In N. Pauwels (Ed.), *War force to work force. Global perspectives on demobilization and reintegration.* Baden-Baden: Nomos Verlag.

de Jong, J. T. V. M. (1987). *A descent into African psychiatry.* Amsterdam: Royal Tropical Institute.

de Jong, J. T. V. M. (2001a). Remnants of the colonial past: The difference in outcome of mental disorders in high- and low-income countries. In D. Bhugra & R. Littlewood (Eds.), *Colonialism and mental health.* New Delhi: Oxford University Press.

de Jong, J. T. V. M. (Ed.). (2002a). *Trauma, war and violence: Public mental health in socio-cultural context.* New York: Plenum/Kluwer.

de Jong, J. T. V. M. (2002b). Public mental health, traumatic stress and human rights violations in low-income countries: A culturally appropriate model in times of conflict, disaster and peace. In J. de Joop T. V. M. (Ed.), *Trauma, war and violence: Public mental health in socio-cultural context* (pp. 1–91). New York: Plenum/Kluwer.

de Jong, J. T. V. M. (2004). Mass dissociation and possession in (post-)war conditions as "popular modes of stress resolution." In preparation.

de Jong J. T. V. M., & Komproe, I. H. (2002). Closing the gap between psychiatric epidemiology and mental health in post-conflict situations. *Lancet, 359,* 1793–1794.

de Jong, J. T. V. M., Komproe, I., & van Ommeren, M. (2003a). Common mental disorders in postconflict settings. *Lancet, 361*(6), 2128–2130.

de Jong, J. T. V. M., Komproe, I., & van Ommeren, M. (2003b). Terrorism, human-made and natural disasters as a professional and ethical challenge to psychiatry. *International Psychiatry, 1*(1), 8–9.

de Jong, J. T. V. M., Komproe, I. H., van Ommeren, M., El-Masri, M., Mesfin, A., Khaled, N. et al. (2001b). Lifetime events and post-traumatic stress disorder in four post-conflict settings. *JAMA, 286*(5), 555–562.

de Jong, J. T. V. M., van der Kolk, B., Komproe, I., Spinazzola, J., & van Ommeren, M. (2004). *Disorders of extreme stress (DESNOS) and comorbidity in four post-conflict countries.* Manuscript sumitted for publication.

de Jong, J. T. V. M., & van Ommeren, M. H. (2002c). Toward a culture informed epidemiology: Combining qualitative and quantitative research in trans-cultural contexts. *Transcultural Psychiatry, 39*(4), 422–433.

de Jong, J. T. V. M., & van Schaik, M. M. (1994). Culturele en religieuze aspecten van traumaverwerking naar aanleiding van de Bijlmerramp [Cultural and religious aspects of coping with trauma after the Bijlmer disaster]. *Tijdschrift voor Psychiatrie, 36*(4), 291–304.

de Vries, M. W. (1996). Trauma in cultural perspective. In B. van der Kolk, A. C. McFarlane, & L. Weisaeth (Eds.), *Traumatic stress: The effects of overwhelming experience on mind, body and society* (pp. 398–417). New York: Guilford.

Eisenbruch, M. (1984a). Cross-cultural aspects of bereavement: I, A conceptual framework for comparative analysis. *Culture, Medicine and Psychiatry, 8*(3), 283–309.

Eisenbruch, M. (1984b). Cross-cultural aspects of bereavement: II, Ethnic and cultural variations in the development of bereavement practices. *Culture, Medicine and Psychiatry, 8*(4), 315–347.

Finkler, K. (1997). Gender, domestic violence and sickness in Mexico. *Social Science and Medicine, 45*(8), 1147–1160.

Flaherty, J. A., Moises Gaviria, F., Pathak, D., Mitchell, T., Wintrob, R., Richman, J. A., & Birz, S. (1988). Developing instruments for cross-cultural research. *Journal of Nervous and Mental Disease, 176*(5), 257–263.

Flanzbaum, H. (Ed.). (1999). *The Americanization of the Holocaust.* Baltimore: Johns Hopkins University Press.

Goody, J. (1962). *Death, property and the ancestors: A study of the mortuary customs of the Lodagaa of West Africa.* Stanford, CA: Stanford University Press.

Green, A. (1992). *Introduction to health planning in developing countries.* Oxford, England: Oxford University Press.

Green, B. L. (1993). Identifying survivors at risk: trauma and stressors at cross events. In J. P. Wilson & B. Raphael (Eds.), *International handbook of traumatic stress syndromes* (pp. 135–144). New York: Plenum Press.

Hamburg, D. A., George, A., & Ballentine, K. (1999). Preventing deadly conflict: The critical role of leadership. *Archive of General Psychiatry, 56*(11), 971–976.

Hardman, C. E. (2000). Other worlds: Notions of self and emotions among the Lohorung Rai. Berg, 320.

Herman, D. B., & Susser, E. S. (2003). The World Trade Center attack: mental health and treatment implications. *International psychiatry, 1*(1), 2–4.

Hiegel, J. P. (1996). Traditional medicine and traditional healers. In J. T. V. M. de Jong & L. Clark (Eds.), *Mental health of refugees* (pp. 89–101). Geneva: WHO and UNHCR.

Horton, R. (1993). *Patterns of thought in Africa and the west.* Cambridge: Cambridge University Press.

Hsu, F. L. (1971). Psychosocial homeostasis and Jen: Conceptual tools for advancing psychological anthropology. *American Anthropologist, 73*, 23–44.

Irish, D. P., Lundquist, K. F., & Nelsen, V. J. (Eds.). (1993). *Ethnic variation in dying, death and grief: Diversity in universality.* Washington, DC: Taylor & Francis.

Kim, U., Triandis, H. C., Kagitcibasi, C., Sang-Chin Choi, Y., & Yoon, G. (1994). *Individualism and collectivism. Theory, method, application.* London: Sage.

Kleinman, A. (1977). Depression, somatization and the new cross-cultural psychiatry. *Social Science and Medicine, 11*, 3–10.

Kleinman, A. (1988). *The illness narratives: Suffering, healing and the human condition.* New York: Basic Books.

Kleinman A., & Good, B. (Eds.). (1985). *Culture and depression.* Berkeley, CA: University of California Press.

Kwasi, W. (1980). *Philosophy and an African culture.* Cambridge: Cambridge University Press.

Lewis-Fernandez, R., & Kleinman, A. (1994). Culture, personality and psychopathology. *Journal of Abnormal Psychology, 103*(1), 67–71.

Marsella, A. J., Friedman, M. J., Gerrity, E. T., Scurfield, R. M. (Eds.). (1996). Ethnocultural aspects of posttraumatic stress disorder: Issues, research, and clinical applications. Washington DC: American Psychological Association Press.

Murthy, R. S. (1998). Rural psychiatry in developing counties. *Psychiatric Services, 49*(7), 967–969.

Nijenhuis, E. R. S., van der Hart, O., & Steele, K. (2002). The emerging psychobiology of trauma-related dissociation and dissociative disorders. In H. D'Haenen, J. A. Den Boer, H. Westenberg, & P. Willner (Eds.), *Textbook of biological psychiatry* (pp. 1079–1098). London: Wiley.

Obeseyesekere, G. (1985). Depression, Bhuddism and the work of culture. In A. Kleinman & B. Good (Eds.), *Culture and depression* (pp. 134–152). Berkeley, CA: University of California Press.

Parin, P., Morgenthaler, F., & Parin-Mattèy, G. (1963). *Die Weissen denken zuviel.* Zürich: Atlantis.

Parkes, C. M., Laungani, P., & Young, B. (Eds.). (1997). *Death and bereavement across cultures.* London: Routledge.

Rosenblatt, P. C., Walsh, R. P., & Jackson, D. A. (1976). *Grief and mourning in cross-cultural perspective.* New Haven, CT: HRAF Press.

Qouta, S. (2000). *Trauma, violence and mental health: The Palestinian experience.* Published doctoral dissertation, Vrije Universiteit, Amsterdam.

Qouta, S., & El-Sarraj, E. (2002). Community mental health as practiced by the Gaza community mental health programme. In J. de Joop T. V. M. (Ed.), *Trauma, war and violence: Public mental health in socio-cultural context* (pp. 317–337). New York: Plenum/Kluwer.

Shrestha, N. M., Sharma, B., van Ommeren, M., Regmi, S., Makaju, R., Komproe, I., et al. (1998). Impact of torture on refugees displaced within the developing world: symptomatology among Bhutanese refug refugees in Nepal. *JAMA, 280*, 443–448.

Somasundaram, D., & Jamunanantha, C. S. (2002). Psychosocial consequences of war. In J. de Jong T. V. M. (Ed.), *Trauma, war and violence: Public mental health in socio-cultural context* (pp. 205–295). New York: Plenum/Kluwer.

Summerfield, D. (2000). Childhood, war, refugeedom and "trauma": Three core questions for mental health professionals. *Transcultural Psychiatry, 37*(3), 417–435.

Thomas, L. (1982). *La mort Africaine: Idéologie funéraire en Afrique noire* [African death: Funeral ideology in black Africa]. Paris: Payot.

Tricket, E. J. (1995). The community context of disaster and traumatic stress: An ecological perspective from community psychology. In S. E. Hobfoll & M. W. De Vries (Eds.), *Extreme stress and communities: impact and intervention* (pp. 11–25). Boston: Kluwer.

Tseng, W.-S., & Strelzer, J. (Eds.). (1997). *Culture and psychopathology: A guide to clinical assessment.* New York: Brunner/Mazel.

Ulman, R. B., & Brothers, D. (1988). *The shattered self.* Hillsdale, NJ: Analytic Press.

Üstün, T. B., & Sartorius, N. (Eds.). (1995). *Mental illness in general health care.* Chichester, England: Wiley.

van de Put, W. A. C. M., & Eisenbruch, M. (2002) The Cambodian experience. In J. de Jong T. V. M. (Ed.), *Trauma, war and violence: Public mental health in socio-cultural context* (pp. 93–157). New York: Plenum/Kluwer.

van Ommeren, M., de Jong, J. T. V. M., Sharma, B., Komproe, I., Thapa, S., & Cardea, E. (2001). Prevalence of psychiatric disorders among tortured Bhutanese refugees in Nepal. *Archives of General Psychiatry, 58,* 475–482.

van Ommeren, M., Sharma, B., Komproe, I., Poudyal, B., Sharma G. K., Cardeña, E. et al. (2001). Trauma and loss as determinants of medically unexplained epidemic illness in a Bhutanese refugee camp. *Psychological Medicine, 31,* 7, 1259–1267.

van Ommeren, M., Sharma, B., Thapa, S., Makaju, R., Prasain, D., Bhattarai, R. et al. (1999). Preparing instruments for transcultural research: Use of the translation monitoring form with Nepali-speaking Bhutanese refugees. *Transcultural Psychiatry, 36*(3), 285–301.

World Health Organization (WHO). (2001). *Atlas of mental health resources in the world.* Geneva: Author.

World Health Organization (WHO). (2002, May). *Traditional medicine strategy 2002–2005.* Retrieved from http//:www.who.int/medicines/organization/trm/orgtrmmain.shtml.

Wortmann, C. B., & Silver, R. C. (1989). The myths of coping with loss. *Journal of Consulting and Clinical Psychology, 57,* 349–357.

Young, A. (2002, October 1–3). *Collective trauma, psychiatric morbidity and the epidemiology of dubious knowledge.* Lecture at the Health and Social Justice convention. Amman-Jordan.

Posttraumatic Treatments: Guidelines for Practitioners

Posttraumatic Treatments: Guidelines for Practitioners

Introduction

JOHN P. WILSON

Part III contains six chapters that provide guidelines for practitioners working with asylum seekers, refugees, and war and torture victims. Each contains a different focal point, and yet they are all interrelated in specific ways that range from the use of interpreters to the basic requirement of creating a safe therapeutic sanctuary in which to use different therapeutic treatment techniques, such as group therapy, cognitive behavioral therapy, and emotionally supportive interventions. Moreover, related to these phenomena are the needs for good clinical supervision and the understanding of countertransference processes, which inevitably crop up during the work.

In Chapter 8, Guus van der Veer and Adeline van Waning discuss the need to create a safe therapeutic sanctuary in the treatment setting. What is a safe sanctuary for clients suffering from trauma, PTSD, and the stress of asylum seeking? First, it is physical safety in the present living conditions. Psychological safety includes the freedom from fear, threat, chaos, and deprivation of essential needs. Second, it is a sense of trust and security in the therapeutic relationship, knowing that the therapist is an ally and advocate. Third, it is a sense of stability and continuity. A safe therapeutic sanctuary contains all three of these dimensions, which van der Veer and van Waning believe to be necessary for good treatment outcomes. They state: "the sense and safety of most traumatized refugees and asylum seekers has been shattered due to their traumatic experiences, the process of uprooting and their often unsafe position in the country of exile." They also make the important observation that when refugees are asked at the termination of treatment what was most helpful to them, "they remember a particular remark of the therapist that led to their looking at themselves or their surroundings in a completely new way." This remark is noteworthy because it underscores two fundamental principles in psychotherapy: (1) the patient's capacity to reframe his or her difficult personal experiences; and (2) having a strong sense of connection to a trusted therapist in a safe therapeutic environment.

Chapter 9 is by Silvana Turkovic, Johannes E. Hovens, and Rudolf Gregurek. Their central focal point is the consequence of the war in former Yugoslavia in which over 250,000 people died and thousands were wounded, interned in concentration camps, and tortured. The war produced large numbers of refugees in Croatia and Bosnia-Herzegovina who sought shelter and assistance both during the war years (1991–1995) and after the Dayton, Ohio, peace accords.

In the chapter, Turkovic, Hovens, and Gregurek describe three interrelated facets of the refugee experience: (1) displacement and dislocation; (2) the reception of refugees within host countries; and (3) community-based programs and individualized treatments for the war victims. In discussing displacement and refuge, the authors detail the range of common experiences encountered by ordinary citizens suddenly plunged into the abyss of war and ethnic cleansing. Whether by preparing to flee, forced migration, or escape from harms way, the situation is fraught with peril, danger, and the constant threat of injury, death, capture, torture, rape, or execution. However, if the displaced person is lucky enough, he or she will eventually reach a refugee camp or humanitarian assistance from UNHCR, which was commissioned by the United Nations in 1967 to deal with such situations. While refugee camps offer protection and meet minimum needs for survival, they are replete with the psychological stresses of uncertainty as to one's future and the welfare of loved ones who are missing, captured, interned in concentration camps, or have "disappeared." After survival in the refugee camp or other places of hospice, the refugees eventually reach a place where they can avail themselves of community-sponsored psychosocial treatment programs. The authors note: "a community approach is primarily supportive in nature, and should strive after strengthening the coping skills of the population." It should be noted that there are many pathways to strengthening psychological health in war victims and refugees, and the authors discuss these. The chapter ends with some cautionary remarks on the complexity of trauma presentations in persons who have endured so much trauma over a long period of time.

In Chapter 10, Boris Droždek and John P. Wilson present a very detailed set of guidelines for individual and group psychotherapy with asylum seekers and refugees. This chapter presents guidelines on methodology and the management of difficult clinical cases. To begin, the authors differentiate between "covering" and "uncovering" approaches to treatment. Uncovering treatments employ a range of therapeutic interventions, which include: group treatment, individual treatment, empowerment techniques, cognitive-behavioral treatment, and specific forms of after-care. In the treatment of refugees and asylum seekers in Holland, an integrated phase-oriented model is employed for a period of 1 to 2 years. Each phase has a specific set of goals and employs treatment techniques consonant with the objectives specified for any of the five phases of treatment: (1) establishing the therapeutic alliance; (2) life histories; (3) cognitive-behavioral treatments for PTSD; (4) current identity issues and adaptation to the host culture; and (5) termination and relapse prevention. Contained within each phase are specific procedures and goals, such as wiring an autobiography in phase 2 and psychoeducation about stressors, trauma, and PTSD in phase 1. Also, in phase 5, there are graduation rituals and preparations for leaving the security of the day treatment hospital.

Droždek and Wilson identify universal themes common to asylum seekers, which emerge after case presentations and discussions about the nature of their fleeing their countries of origin and coming to Holland. These themes include: (a) damage to core belief systems; (b) fear of loss of control over feeling of rage and anxiety; (c) shame over helplessness evoked by torture or war trauma; (d) rage and grief at the sudden loss of control of plan; (e) survivor guilt; and (f) grief, impacted grief, and traumatic bereavement. These core themes cross-cut the phases of treatment and often are expressed in transference reactions, acting-out behaviors, and testing of therapists' limits, especially in regard to boundary management and safety.

In Chapter 11, John P. Wilson presents a discussion of the role of empathy in the treatment of trauma and PTSD. Here the process of maintaining empathic attunement is defined in relationship to transference and countertransference processes during treatment. Wilson defines empathy as the psychobiological capacity to understand the phenomenal reality of the patient. He defines six modes of empathic attunement and four modes of empathic strain that operate dynamically during the course of treatment. Empathic attunement is conceptualized on a continuum, which ranges from separation and detachment to optimal connection and attachment to the client. This continuum of empathic modalities is conceived as a balance beam on which the therapist attempts to maintain balance between the inherent strains posed by listening to trauma narrations and in vivo work with PTSD clients, which tax the capacity to sustain empathic attunement.

Wilson suggests that there are various forms of trauma-specific transference in work with traumatized clients. He suggests that trauma transference is transmitted through seven different channels to the therapist: affects, defenses, somatic states, ego states, personality processes, unconscious memory, and cognitive-perceptual processes. In

Wilson's view, these seven channels of trauma transmission encode data about the nature of the patient's trauma experience and how it was processed by them. Likewise, he proposes that the therapist attempts to decode the data being transmitted in trauma transference. Thus, the patient encodes and transmits through trauma transference the subtle and overt features of their PTSD and states of traumatization. The therapist, in turn, attempts to decode these signals containing encoded information in the seven different channels of transmission. Thought of in dynamic terms, this process creates the matrix of transference — countertransference possibilities. Finally, Wilson delineates how countertransference processes can have a pathogenic consequence leading to any of six possible outcomes: (1) cessation or termination of the treatment process, (2) fixation within a phase of recovery, (3) regression in the service of ego and security, (4) intensification of transference, (5) acting out, and (6) dissociation as defense.

In Chapter 12, Johan Lansen and Ton Haans extend the ideas described in Chapter 11. Their chapter presents a detailed discussion of critical issues for the supervision process. Since work with asylum seekers and refugees is inherently stressful, therapists who treat them require good supervision to avoid going off track, pathogenic countertransference reactions, and problems with boundary management.

The authors report on data accumulated through the course of their work from the 1990s through 2002 in different centers in Holland, Scandinavia, and Germany. Their clinical work and supervision includes victims of war, including Holocaust survivors. The data that formed the basis for their work came from 100 supervised cases of individuals who were counseled between one to four times a week. Among the central reasons discussed for the need for supervision is to ensure the well-being of the care provider so he or she can maintain empathic attunement. They state: "The specific nature of treating victims of violence, persecution and torture brings along traumatic stress in the helping relationship, damaging assistants by a process of empathy, induction and enactment." To illustrate the problems of effective supervision, Lansen and Haans presented case examples that present the complexities inherent in therapy and the supervision process. These case illustrations then provide a transition to discuss the core factors that are essential in supervision: (a) therapeutic skills in the therapist, (b) case conceptualization, (c) professional roles and boundary management, (d) sustaining emotional sensitivity to the patient, and (e) honest self-evaluation by the therapist as to their limits of their competence. These five factors can be viewed as important areas for the therapist to discuss and critically evaluate in the treatment process. On the other side of the coin, the supervisor's role also involves five elements pertaining to: (1) monitoring and evaluating the therapist, (2) giving instruction and advice, (3) modeling necessary therapeutic interventions, (4) case consultation, and

(5) providing emotional support and the sharing of professional experience. This chapter also includes special considerations to supervising group therapy and treatment teams that must work together as, for example, described by Drožđek and Wilson in their chapter on integrated phase–oriented treatment of asylum seekers who utilize multiple modalities of treatment over an extended period of time.

Chapter 13 is by Hanneke Bot and Cecilia Wadensjo who discuss the role of interpreters and language differences during the treatment process. How do therapists working with asylum seekers and refugees who speak a foreign language know that they are correctly understanding the trauma narrations and other stories of their clients? In a similar manner, how do therapists know that the translations they receive from translators are correct in nuance, affective tone, and meaning?

The authors begin by raising questions as to the significance of the process of therapy when a third-party interpreter is present. Is it helpful or a hindrance? Does it change the dynamic quality of interaction between the client and therapist? Although the authors provide no definitive answer to these questions, they raise other important questions and affirm the need to have translators present to provide conceptual data for the therapeutic process. They note: "Our position is that an interpreter is basically present in a therapy to translate the words of patient and therapist — we are not talking about interpreters as co-therapists or cultural mediators ... nevertheless, the presence of an interpreter transforms the social encounter."

Bot and Wadensjo provide the reader with many important technical and psychological insights about using translators in the individual or group therapeutic context. A brief list includes: (a) the need for comprehensive knowledge of the patient's language and idiomatic expressions; (b) awareness of the possibility of vicarious traumatization in the translator from listening to trauma narratives, (c) the need to establish trust in the translators in the same way as the therapist; (d) the need to recognize the limits of the translator's role and to not "take over" the therapeutic process; and (e) the awareness of gender differences and how they might influence the nature of disclosure and transference by the patient.

8

Creating a Safe Therapeutic Sanctuary

GUUS VAN DER VEER AND ADELINE VAN WANING

Most experienced psychotherapists will agree with the assumption that psychotherapy is more likely to be successful if the client feels safe with the therapist, within what we will call the "safe therapeutic sanctuary." This chapter will examine the ingredients necessary for making a safe therapeutic sanctuary for asylum seekers and refugees. Working with this specific category of traumatized people, who have been uprooted from their familiar cultural environment, brings specific challenges. Because many of them live under unfavorable conditions and in a social environment that often is not exactly welcoming, there are added difficulties in creating an atmosphere of safety during the therapeutic sessions.

We will describe safety as the result of an interaction between psychotherapist and patient, in which, next to the psychotherapeutic strategies and techniques that the therapist is applying, his or her attitude of understanding, empathy, and compassion are important ingredients.

After a literature review on the need for safety, different aspects of the safe therapeutic sanctuary will be explored. First, we will discuss how safety can be created by explanation of the therapeutic procedure (safety through understanding), by enhancing one's abilities for being a safe therapist, by dealing with differences in cultural meaning and expression, and by establishing transcultural communication. We will then examine those challenges and pitfalls in creating a safe therapeutic sanctuary that are related to the emotional movements that inevitably occur during therapy with traumatized refugees and asylum seekers: love, rage, and not-knowing or doubt.

The chapter will conclude with a discussion of the most helpful ingredients of psychotherapy with traumatized refugees and asylum seekers, the essentials of the therapist in terms of knowledge and technical skills, and the attitude of the therapist.

LITERATURE REVIEW: THE NEED FOR SAFETY

In this literature overview we address four aspects of safety: safety and the traumatic past, safety in present living conditions, safety within the therapy relationship, and safety for the therapist.

Basic Safety and the Traumatic Past

During a traumatic experience a person's sense of safety is seriously threatened. According to Judith Herman (1992) the first task of recovery after traumatization is to establish the survivor's safety. This task takes precedence over all others, for no other therapeutic work can possibly succeed if safety has not been adequately secured. This safety includes protection from the maltreatment of others and care for basic needs, such as, safe living quarters, eating and sleeping properly, obtaining needed medical care, financial security, and a supportive social network. At the time that an asylum seeker or refugee requests assistance from a psychotherapist, this factual safety might not be completely reestablished.

Traumatic experiences can disrupt the psychological functioning of the survivor (Allen, 2001), for example, damaging experiences brought about by other people can eventually result in unbearable emotional states that the survivor might try to escape through deliberate self-harm.

Living through a traumatic incident or a sequence of traumatic experiences scatters a person's actual security. As a result, the inner sense of safety (or maybe we should say safety illusion) of the traumatized person is also undermined. Janoff-Bullman (1992) describes how victimizing life events challenge three basic assumptions or beliefs about oneself in the world: the belief in personal invulnerability; the view of oneself in a positive light, being worthy, good; and the belief in a meaningful, orderly world. This theme will resonate throughout the whole therapy and recovery process.

Safety and Present Living Conditions

The aftermath of traumatic experiences is not the only problem asylum seekers and refugees with posttraumatic stress disorder (PTSD) have to deal with. Many refugees are living under conditions that perpetuate the feeling that security is lacking, perhaps because their own legal status or the legal status of family members is unclear. The mere fact of living in a society with a different culture, of which one does not understand the customs and habits, can cause additional feelings of insecurity (van der Veer, 1998).

The stress connected with the circumstances after migration are important in causing or continuing subjective mental health problems. Steel et al. (1999) did research in this field and noted that 14% of PTSD symptoms were caused by postmigration factors, such as general health condition and daily hassles.

Safety Within the Therapy Relationship

In an overview of treatment approaches with traumatized persons, Allen (1995) stresses the importance of first establishing safety. Chu (1992) has proposed the acronym SAFER to represent five ingredients or focal points in the early stages of therapy that lay the foundation for remembering and exploring traumatic experience: *Self-care* entails refraining from self-destructive and suicidal behavior by finding better ways of soothing oneself and less destructive ways of coping with stress. *Acknowledgment* of trauma means accepting the role of traumatic experience in one's problems rather than seeing oneself as "crazy" or "bad." *Functioning* refers to the need to maintain normal functioning to the extent possible, whether by means of employment, volunteer jobs, going to school, or participating actively in treatment programs. *Expression* refers to the need to find some constructive outlet for expressing feelings that are hard to bear, such as art, music, physical activity, or writing. *Relationship* addresses the need for social supports, including a therapeutic relationship.

Van der Kolk (1996) emphasizes that a sense of relative safety and predictability is a precondition for any activity that involves effective planning and goal-directed action, including psychotherapy. Safety is viewed as the initial aim of therapy with traumatized patients; it is part of the process of helping the traumatized person to move from being haunted by the past and interpreting subsequent emotionally arousing stimuli as a return of the trauma, to being fully engaged in the present and becoming capable of responding to current exigencies.

Newman, Kaloupek, and Keane (1996) mention establishing safety as an integral part of the assessment process, because a thorough assessment of PTSD requires that an individual identify and describe traumatic memories, feelings, and symptoms, which are often accompanied by strong emotional reactions. Psychological safety is important, which includes trust in the clinician and the associated ability to communicate extreme feelings and reactions.

Safety for the Therapist

Likewise, in order to help a client, it is important that the therapist feels safe. The therapist, even if well experienced in working with traumatized clients, might feel less safe with a client from a cultural background he or she is not completely familiar with. The therapist needs a sense of safety in order to be able to provide a safe atmosphere for the client (McCann & Pearlman, 1990). As a first step, he or she needs to be aware of the matters that can cause feelings of insecurity. For example, the therapist has to face the fact he or she cannot be sure which way the specific cultural background of a refugee has influenced the patient's personality development. Also, the therapist cannot be sure how culturally determined differences in family life and child development could be reflected in specific ways of coping with stress, psychological problems, or forms of transference the therapist might not be familiar with.

Yet there is no reason to let oneself be intimidated by cultural differences in personality development as long as there are strong indications that above all cultural differences, the needs, feelings, and vulnerabilities we experience as people are the same the world over. The way people react to psychological trauma does not seem to be very dependent on cultural background (cf. Alexander, Klein, Workneh, & Miller, 1981; Somasundaran, 1993).

For the therapist to feel safe also includes having a minimum of knowledge of therapeutic approaches and interventions. Different approaches to safety are described in other chapters of this book. Normalizing responses and giving the client control are two ways a therapist can enhance a feeling of safety.

Normalizing Responses

Normalizing responses include all explicit and implicit communications to the client indicating that others have experienced similar reactions; such as anticipating or predicting reactions, and verbal interventions reflecting the experiences of the therapist with other clients who have been in comparable circumstances (Newman et al., 1996).

Giving the Client Control

Another safety-promoting intervention is to give the client choices and opportunities to feel in control of the therapeutic process. This can include scheduling sessions, answering questions, trying out relaxation exercises, and different ways of dealing with unpleasant mental states.

For traumatized clients with dissociative problems, techniques from hypnotherapy can be used to increase a feeling of safety (Turner, McFarlane, & van der Kolk, 1996). For example, the client might be asked to place his or her traumatic memories inside some imaginary "safe" or box; this often fosters the containment of such memories.

Asking the client to create an imaginary "safe place" can also serve as a base from which dissociated memories can be approached.

In conclusion, the sense of safety of most traumatized refugees and asylum seekers has been shattered due to their traumatic experiences, the process of uprooting, and their often unsafe position in the country of exile. It is important that they experience safety within the therapeutic relationship. For a safe therapeutic sanctuary to come into existence, the therapist also needs to feel safe. The therapist's sense of safety can be threatened for various reasons, including the cultural differences between the refugee and him- or herself.

WHAT IS SAFETY AND HOW CAN I CREATE IT?

A Safe Therapeutic "Holding"

Safety for the client means that he or she can have a feeling of being at ease, of not being afraid. When a client feels safe, he or she is not feeling threatened, intimidated, or humiliated. Moreover, if the client is experiencing trust in the strength of the therapist, he or she is not afraid of harming the therapist by saying what is on his or her mind.

Safety Through Understanding

The client's sense of safety is in part dependent of his or her understanding of the therapeutic procedure. It helps if the client has been explained the goals of the procedures used by the therapist for assessment and therapy. A sense of safety thus can be promoted by discussing the roles and responsibilities of therapist and client, and by explaining the "rules of the game" as to cancellations, attendance, and availability. Discussing confidentiality can be very reassuring for the client. For many refugees and asylum seekers the sometimes required correspondence with official institutions has a ring of threat and unsafety; clear explanation needs to be given to the client, which might include giving written documentation.

BEING A SAFE THERAPIST

In order to remain a safe helper for the client, the therapist must show the qualities of awareness, a capacity for containment, and a capacity for keeping optimal distance.

Awareness

The therapist is to be aware of the way that the stories told by his clients are affecting him or her. The therapist should be able to reflect on his or her own feelings, thoughts, and actions, to mindfully monitor and control him- or herself so as not to enact or act impulsively upon heartfelt feelings shared in the stories of the client. The therapist needs to develop a good sense for the real, and needs the ability to mourn his or her own "shattered assumptions" in a way that does not burden the refugee client.

This awareness includes an understanding of the transference roles the therapist is placed in by the refugee. Is the therapist made into a savior who needs to be able to solve everything, to repair everything? Does the therapist feel put in the position of passive on-looker, one who is only allowed to watch, to witness, and be made guilty because of that? Or is the therapist made into an offender, in what he or she does to the client, in what cannot be given, in where he or she fails; as a coinhabitant of the country that distances the client?

Capacity for Containment

The client's feeling of safety is strongly dependent on the therapist's attitude toward the client. In order to be a safe therapist, it is necessary for the therapist to "contain" and handle the emotions and possible disruptions in beliefs that are brought up in him or her; this is accomplished when the therapist becomes aware of the transference role he or she is placed in by the client and through listening to the story of the client. Can the client trust that the therapist "survives," not only his or her stories, but also the rage, desperateness, and possible aggression toward the therapist? That the therapist can tolerate being "tested"? Can the client trust that the therapist can tolerate the projections made toward him or her, and that he or she can "detoxify" projective identifications[1] and give them back to the client in such a way that they can be processed and accepted as his or her own (Lindy, 1996; van Waning, 2000)? Can the client trust that the therapist will be able to protect him- or herself and not become vicariously traumatized?

The stories told by traumatized refugees can undermine the therapist's beliefs and the "cognitive schemas" for the following themes (McCann & Pearlman, 1990):

1. *Trust*. Many refugees have been betrayed, deceived, or their trust has been violated. Therefore, their stories can make the therapist more cynical. The cynical therapist will not be of much help to the refugee

---

[1] By projection I mean the placing outward of one's own undesired aspects, toward another, to be rid of them. In projective identification, a less mature form of projection, these aspects are also controlled within the other, in a special complex coercive interaction.

in reestablishing some trust in other people and finding some hope for the future.

2. *Safety.* Stories of the clients that portray human vulnerability can bring an enhanced awareness of the fragility of life in the mind of the therapist. He or she can experience an increase in thoughts and images associated with personal vulnerability. The therapist could become preoccupied in thinking about precautions against possible violations, which could make him or her an inadequate listener.

3. *Powerlessness.* Powerlessness in the situation of oppression or imprisonment, as well as powerlessness within the social context of the new country, can lead to feelings of paralysis, helplessness, and depression for the refugee. The therapist might experience similar feelings of helplessness and powerlessness within the therapeutic contact, and that can bring up negative feelings (like irritation) toward the client.

In this way, the stories told by the client can evoke all kinds of emotional reactions — sometimes called countertransference reactions — in the therapist. These reactions can include rage, horror, guilt, shame, grief, and mourning (Danieli, 1984). Whether these reactions are harmful to the therapy process depends on the extent to which the therapist is able to engage in a parallel process to that of the client, the process of transforming and integrating these experiences of horror and violation. The therapist needs to handle his or her reactions in such a way that the client will not feel threatened or antagonized. The therapist needs to be able to contain these feelings and to discriminate, if his or her own emotions surface because of the projections of the client, when to discuss these projections in an empathic way.

Capacity for Keeping Optimal Distance

All strong emotional reactions in the therapist can be transformed into defenses. These defenses limit the therapist's ability to adequately perceive what is evolving in the therapeutic interaction. They interfere with his or her ability to be completely "with" the client. Some defenses are: numbing, denying, avoiding, taking distance, clasping to professional role and protocol, and reducing the counseling to the application of method and theory.

For example, when the client feels very powerless, the therapist might feel "sucked in" and not be able to offer anything, being completely with empty hands; on the other hand, the therapist might try defensively to escape these powerless feelings by turning passive into active with fantasies of great personal power and with promises and inadequate actions.

Wilson and Lindy (1994) describe two basic types of distance and proximity of a therapist with the client:

Type I: Great distance, with the following patterns: disavowal of parts of the clients story; minimizing of experiences and feelings of the client; distortion of the content; avoiding of too painful aspects of the story; indifference or reservedness to the client; keeping distance, withdrawal as therapist.

Type II: Reactions are characterized by a strong proximity: being dependent on the client, overinvolved or identified with the client; savior behavior, overactive; overemphasizing the role of trauma in the life of the refugee.

Optimal distance could mean taking the client's story seriously and keeping present with the client, with an emotional involvement that is embedded in awareness, self-monitoring, and self-reflection.

SAFETY, CULTURAL MEANING, AND EXPRESSION

Explanation and Reassurance

Everyone who seeks assistance for emotional problems wants to be treated by an expert whom he or she considers trustworthy (Pederson, 1981). But the criteria by which someone is considered an expert, safe, and trustworthy are not the same in all cultures. The same goes for specific therapeutic techniques; what is considered as useful and credible in one culture can be thought of as stupid or immoral in another culture. The therapist has to be attentive to these differences. For instance, when the therapist wants to use the discussion of dreams as a therapeutic technique, he or she has to be informed about the ways in which dreams are interpreted in the refugee's cultural background. This knowledge can help the therapist to convince the client that the therapist's own approach to work with dream is worth trying.

Due to differences in cultural background, helping refugees means also dealing with the condition of refugees having divergent ideas about mental problems and the way they should be treated. The kind of help a Western therapist can offer to a refugee does not always correspond to what a doctor or healer in his or her own culture would offer (Kinzie, 1978). For example, the refugee might expect to be cured quickly, in which case the concept of slowly working through issues in a long-lasting procedure is both strange and difficult to comprehend. The therapist will have to explain this matter.

In the eyes of the Western therapist the distinction between "madness" and "normality" can be much less strict than is generally believed in some African or Asian cultures (Kortmann, 1986). Some refugees come from cultures where visiting a psychiatrist is proof of madness. In such cases, the therapist has to explain his or her view on complaints and symptoms of the clients and offer reassurance as to the normality of them.

Sometimes this convincing and reassuring is unnecessary because the refugee has strong confidence in the helping professional exactly because the latter belongs to a different culture. For instance, the client might think his or her culture is backward and that the therapist, because he or she is White, is more objective, more trustworthy, or better educated.

Accepting Cultural Forms of Expression of Suffering and Offering Alternatives

Refugees from non-Western cultures might express their complaints in a manner unfamiliar to the Western therapist. Giel (1984) describes the moaning and sighing of patients in an Addis Abbeba outpatients department. Initially, he found this behavior theatrical, but his interpreter was impressed by their suffering. Further investigation revealed these patients were not just pretending but really were sick. The same apparently theatrical behavior can often be observed in refugees, especially those who have not been in exile a long time. In such cases, the therapist has to refrain from quick judgments about the sincerity of the clients in question. It can be helpful at some stage to give the clients feedback about how their, in some Western eyes "histrionic" behavior, could be misinterpreted.

Lack of understanding of cultural forms of expression of suffering can be an obstacle to diagnosis and by consequence make the relationship unsafe. A diagnostic mistake can easily be made in interpreting behavior that impresses the Western clinician as theatrical, manipulative, troublesome, or avoidant. Observations of such behavior can convince the practitioner to diagnose a refugee as suffering from a personality disorder.

It is therefore important to realize that the concept of psychiatric disturbance is not free from value judgments; no more than the concept of repression is (Kutchins & Kirk, 1997; Mezzich, Kleinman, Fabrega, & Parron, 1996; van Waning, 1999). It is important to realize our tendency to translate the "strange" into the familiar, to want to pin it down in our own familiar categories and technical terms. Much is unavoidably lost in this process of translation: through our selective perception, by the "kneading" and transforming of what is perceived, and by our inability to perceive what is unknown.

Discussing Norms and Values

The refugee can be accustomed to other norms relating to what counts as morally responsible or healthy behavior. In such cases it is useful to explore these norms in a respectful way (cf. Agger, 1988; Bala, 2001;

Brown, 1986), and to point out the differences with current norms in the country of exile.

Ahmed, a 25-year-old refugee from the Middle East, was very worried about his younger brother, who had gone into exile with him and for whom he felt responsible. He had caught his brother masturbating and was worried about the consequences of this for his health. The therapist asked Ahmed what he thought about the physical consequences of masturbation and how he viewed it morally. Also, he explained that research in the West had shown masturbation to be a common form of sexual behavior, that it was seen as a preparation for other forms of sexuality, and the majority of the population did not view masturbation as morally objectionable.

Norms can also differ with regard to behavior during the therapy. In some cultures it seems to be normal for the client to give the therapist gifts. Some refugees maintain this habit in their contacts with Western therapists. If the therapist is not in the habit of accepting gifts, he or she will have to make this clear in a tactful manner.

Corrective feedback from the therapist can help the refugee to understand what kinds of behavior are acceptable or unacceptable in particular situations (De Anda, 1984). This understanding will make the client feel safer, both inside and outside the therapist's consulting room. In some situations, however, it is desirable for the therapist to conform to the norms and values of the client.

Bashar, an Islamic refugee, always drank a cup of coffee during the weekly therapeutic sessions. During Ramadan the therapist offered him his usual cup of coffee, but he refused. The therapist asked him about the way in which he celebrated Ramadan. Once the therapist understood the ritualistic aspects of Ramadan, he no longer offered coffee during that month's sessions but also out of respect he did not drink coffee in Bashar's presence.

Also in this context, the therapist should consider how his or her clothing will be viewed by refugees from various cultural backgrounds (Vontress, 1981), or examine the magazine covers in the waiting room from the point of view of the clients.

Accepting and Exploring Cultural Ideas About Disease and Traumatic Experiences

There are also cultural differences in the causes people ascribe to illnesses. For instance, in the Cambodian culture, illness is thought to be the consequence of coming into contact with dangerous spirits, witchcraft, or sorcery (Eisenbruch & Handelman, 1989; van der Put, 1997). The same belief can be found in India (Srinivasa & Trivedi, 1982), in some Caribbean (Cancelmo, Millán, & Vasquez, 1990), and in African cultures. Occasionally this explanation for illness will be mentioned by refugees. The unexperienced therapist might view such convictions as bizarre or delusional and misinterpret them as signs of a psychotic disorder. In order to make the client feel safe, the therapist needs to take such explanations seriously and discuss them with respect. The client might then be able to accept the fact that the therapist personally has different ideas.

Cultural differences might also become apparent in the ideas people have about the cause of traumatic experiences. Mollica and Son (1988) report that Cambodian refugees who have been tortured relate this to the Buddhist concept of karma. Because of their karma, they feel in some way responsible for their own suffering. This is opposed by the Western conception that torture is something done to the individual for political reasons. More generally speaking, it is important for the therapist to understand the cultural framework within which certain symptoms are evaluated and the causal explanations implicit in any cultural framework (Lee & Lu, 1989).

SAFETY AND TRANSCULTURAL COMMUNICATION

Dealing With Communication Problems

Cultural difference can cause problems in nonverbal communication, and with that lessen the experienced safety for the client. Refugees from Indochinese cultures tend to mask their personal suffering by polite gestures and smiles (Denley, 1987). In general, Southeast Asian clients often seem to avoid expressing their emotions in a verbal or nonverbal way. They tend to express psychic distress through physical complaints. In the first contacts the therapist can mistakenly perceive them as passive; this passivity, however, should be seen as a cultural expression of respect for authority (Tsui & Schultz, 1985). Also, the therapist should be aware that people from particular cultures consider eye contact as threatening or disrespectful.

According to our observations, people from Middle Eastern countries begin talking about trivial matters, even a bit tediously, before they are ready to discuss what is really bothering them. Therefore, an inexperienced or impatient therapist might underestimate the seriousness of their problems.

A therapist should be careful to use a nondirective approach in his or her treatment techniques (Sundberg, 1981). Many refugees are unfamiliar with this approach, misinterpreting it as a sign of inadequacy or lack of interest. More generally, it is important for the therapist to take time to explain again and again how the treatment works, why he or she asks certain questions, and what he or she expects from the refugee.

A therapist cannot always recognize when a misunderstanding has arisen. As a result, the refugee might interrupt the treatment. Any time a refugee misses an appointment the therapist must ask him- or herself whether some communication problem might unknowingly exist. In such cases the misunderstanding might be cleared up if the therapist takes the effort to invite the refugee to come again by phoning or sending a personal letter.

Whatever the cultural background of the refugee, however, there is no need for the therapist to compromise his or her professional attitude. Genuine interest, respect, and tolerance for the anxiety in the client are basic conditions for counseling and therapy. Of course, the therapist has to make sure these features are also recognized by the refugee.

To overcome communication problems the therapist must become informed about cultural differences and develop cultural empathy (Dahl, 1989). The therapist also has to be aware that cultural sensitivity can shift into cultural stereotyping when the therapist underestimates the individual differences between people from the same culture.

The helping professional can become informed about the cultural background of refugees by studying anthropological and other relevant sources about the cultures in question, or by contacting local experts. Learning information such as the fact that Southeast Asian parents can become very anxious if one comments on the beauty or good health of their baby, for fear of attracting evil spirits (Olness, 1986) can be very helpful in counseling a client from Southeast Asia. Of course, the refugee can also be an important informant. Many refugees are aware that communication problems can develop and they are ready to offer explanations if the therapist shows some interest. The therapist can also prevent compounding the communication problems by explaining rules and standards common to Western society.

Language Problems and Misunderstanding

The ideal safe therapeutic situation seems to be one where both therapist and client speak the same language fluently. Unfortunately this is not always true; sometimes it is easier to discuss a private matter or a taboo in a second language, rather than in one's native tongue (Sundberg, 1981). Whatever the case might be, psychotherapy with refugees often means working with people who have grown up speaking a very different language from your own. Refugees with personal problems often have difficulty concentrating or cannot remember what they have been taught. This usually has a negative effect on their efforts to learn the language of the country in which they are in exile.

In the case of refugees who do speak the therapist's language it is necessary to realize that they might have only a limited vocabulary of common terms. They might not know or understand many of the terms they need to describe or express their emotions. This means they will be limited in their ability to articulate their problems. The therapist must be cautious to make sure what is said comes across in the intended manner. He or she must be alert for misunderstandings stemming from the use of an unfamiliar language. In such cases therapeutic sessions will be slower than usual and often cannot be limited to the usual 45 minutes.

It is worthwhile for a good and safe relationship for the therapist to learn a few words in the language of the client, such as words of greeting and saying goodbye. Even if the therapist cannot speak the refugee's native language, some knowledge of its syntax will help the therapist to understand the problems the refugee has and can help to reduce misunderstandings. The therapist can check whether the refugee has understood abstract concepts by asking him or her to give examples in return (Kortmann, 1986). The refugee can be taught concepts that facilitate communication in the same way.

Translated questionnaires, such as the Hopkins Symptom Checklist (Mollica, Wyshak, de Marneffe, Khuon, & Lavelle, 1987), which implements subtly articulated mental complaints and feelings, could help to facilitate communication by finding translations in European languages for feelings the refugee considers important.

Even if the therapist speaks the refugee's native language fluently, there can still be misunderstandings if the therapist is unaware of certain customs in the refugee's culture. Swartz (1987) describes the *hlonipa* tradition among the Xhosa speaking peoples of South Africa. In this tradition it is taboo for a woman to use certain words, including the names of her male relatives and that of her husband. Therapists who were unfamiliar with this tradition thought the Xhosa women who came to them for help had language problems, or even that they were mentally deranged.

Working With Interpreters

When the language barrier between therapist and client is so great that they cannot communicate adequately, then an interpreter can be used. This leads to an unusual situation: communication proceeds through a third person, usually not trained to give assistance, but who nonetheless makes a personal contribution to the course of the encounter. Adding a third person can make the situation less safe, in the sense that it will make it more difficult for the refugee to express thoughts he or she considers as childish, shameful, or evil. Yet the refugee at times will consider the interpreter to be a great help when trying to express him- or herself. Some withdrawn refugees actually cheer up when the interpreter arrives (Bot, 1996).

Cooperation Between Therapist and Interpreter

The therapist will have to build a working relationship with the interpreter. It can be helpful to take time to inform the interpreter about the basic principles of the therapist's approach, for example, that the therapist will assume the client has to make decisions for him- or herself, that the topics discussed during sessions will remain confidential, that silence during sessions can be meaningful, and so forth. Also, the counseler should instruct the interpreter to translate as literally as possible by speaking in the first person whenever the person speaking does so (Pentz-Moller, Hermansen, Bentsen, & Knudsen, 1988), by not trying to translate an incoherent sentence more coherently than it was originally spoken, and by translating short phrases one after another instead of translating a group of statements by giving a summary. It can also be very useful for the therapist to have a preparatory conversation with the interpreter before a session in which the objective of the session is discussed. It can be very enlightening to check whether certain questions (e.g., about sexual behavior) can be expressed at all by this interpreter in the client's language. An evaluation after the session can be aimed at discussing the interpreter's emotions and the difficulties he or she encountered with regard to the translation.

It would also be good for a therapist to work together with the same interpreters as much as possible. This would increase the therapist's understanding of other cultures. Changing the interpretor during an ongoing therapeutic contact could also be very useful because it could bring different aspects of the refugee to the fore and in that way contribute to the effectiveness of the therapeutic contact (Bot, 1996).

In spite of the language barrier, when speaking the therapist should maintain eye contact with the client, not turning to the interpreter when the interpreter speaks. This seems to facilitate the client's understanding of what is being said without the intervention of the interpreter. Keeping questions and remarks concise also helps to improve communication. Long questions mean the therapist has to direct more of his or her attention to the interpreter than to the client. It can at times be useful for the therapist to explain to the interpreter why he or she is saying, or asking, certain things.

Using an interpreter from the same area as the refugee has an advantage. Not only would they then share the same language but also the same cultural background. Sometimes it is tempting to use this expertise by asking the interpreter for his or her opinion on the client's emotions during the session. Such interventions break the conventional boundaries of the interpreter's role; he or she in a way becomes a bicul-tural cotherapist. Proper training is necessary to enable an interpreter to fulfill this role adequately and in a way that feels safe to the client. In the United States a lot of experience has been gained in the cooperation between American and Vietnamese or Cambodian cotherapists and in providing special training programs for the latter (i.e., Teter, Mauldin, Nhol, Conkin, & Sum, 1987).

In conclusion, the treatment of traumatized asylum seekers and refugees requires safety within the therapeutic sanctuary and under-standing of the therapeutic procedure by the client and a therapist who can radiate safety because he or she has enough awareness of his or her own mental processes, because he or she has a capacity for containment, and because he or she is able to keep optimal distance. For safety to develop, differences in cultural meaning and expression have to be dealt with and transcultural communication has to be established.

CHALLENGES AND PITFALLS

As it should now be clear, creating a safe therapeutic sanctuary is only possible if the therapist understands the variety of reasons why a traumatized refugee or asylum seeker feels unsafe. It requires understanding of the psychological consequences of traumatization and cultural uprooting and knowledge of the refugee's present living conditions; it also requires self-monitoring and the capacity for containment.

The greatest pitfall here is that the therapist thinks that being a neutral professional, using the aforementioned professional capacities, is sufficient. However, in order to be able to provide a safe therapeutic sanctuary, the therapist needs to have a certain attitude and take a moral stand. We will try to describe this position by describing three basic emotions, or perhaps emotional movements, that are relevant to the refugee and helper alike: love, rage, and not-knowing or doubt.

In what is to follow, we present a more experiential working through of the theme of creating a safe therapeutic sanctuary, more in a way of looking from the inside. With that approach we will elaborate on challenges and pitfalls. Discussion of the different aspects will be based on practical examples.

To recognize the three experiences — love, rage, and not-knowing — in oneself, to (learn to) tolerate them without losing compassion for oneself, to explore and get to know the experiences, and oneself for that matter, and to share them, are paramount in any therapy.

The terminology chosen has to do with entities that are not easily observable or measurable; they can only be perceived directly by means of contemplation and introspection. The terms love,[2] rage, and not-knowing and doubt can help therapists to reflect on the course of the contacts with refugees, on the role played by their own emotions, on the client's emotions, and on their mutual influence. Also for group discussions or supervisory interviews this experiential approach can be enlightening.

LOVE AND SAFETY

Love is an emotional phenomenon that, whenever it is encountered by a therapist in his or her professional capacity with a refugee, includes the following: an unconditionally positive attitude, unhampered empathy, a transcultural approach, a certain fascination with the client, and a

---

[2] The use of the word love is inspired by the biblical text of 1 Corinthians 13:2: "And though I have the gift of prophecy, and understand all mysteries, and all knowledge; and though I have all faith, so that I could remove mountains, and have not love, I am nothing" (Authorized King James Version).

feeling of personal involvement. This attitude strongly influences the degree in which the refugee client will feel safe in the therapy.

Fascination and Unconditionality

How can a therapist form any idea of what the refugee sitting opposite to him or her has lived through and endured? To begin with, the therapist has to be fascinated by the question of what it is like to live as an uprooted person in the new country, after many drastic, unpleasant experiences. The therapist must also have a basically positive attitude toward refugees. For parents who love their newborn baby, it is love at first sight; the baby doesn't need to prove that he or she is worthy of their love. In an analogous way, therapists dealing with refugees work on the premise that every individual refugee is an asset to society until proven otherwise (Rogers, 1961).

> Selda had been in psychotherapy for a year when her younger brother Kadir unexpectedly arrived in the Netherlands. Kadir had just turned 20. He had fled after an outburst of organized violence in the town where he lived. During the incident in question his friend Farudin, with whom he had a relationship, was killed before his very eyes. Kadir suffered from nightmares, from which he would wake up screaming. Selda noticed this when he stayed at her house on weekends; during the week Kadir lived in an Investigation Centre in the eastern Netherlands. Selda also told her therapist that Kadir suffered from a lot from headaches, and that he had once told her that what he really wanted was to join his friend. That had really upset her; she was afraid he would commit suicide. She said further that Kadir did want help, he had gone to the doctor at the Centre, but he would only give him some analgesics for his headaches.
>
> Selda's therapist then tried to get Kadir taken on by one of the therapy teams, by filling in the appropriate form. The application was discussed and the following comment was sent in return: "Not suitable for our team, as our foundation does not specialize in homosexual problems." Selda's therapist did not take this lying down and sent the form to another team. And so it ended up in the pigeonhole of one of the authors of this article, who read the information, felt touched, and invited Kadir for an interview.
>
> The help offered to Kadir produced results. Kadir has virtually no remaining symptoms and is actively involved with putting his life in the Netherlands in order. That is partly due to the cooperation of his psychotherapist with a colleague who managed to prescribe the right combination of drugs. A colleague from refugee aid services also played an important role; she found an enthusiastic volunteer who helps Kadir with his Dutch.
>
> Above all, the psychotherapist listened and allowed Kadir to say what was on his mind. Whenever the therapist himself began a discussion, it

was about love. Kadir, for example, emphasized how dreadful it was that he had lost his lover. The therapist underlined that, asked how he experienced that loss in everyday life, and added that Kadir appeared to have a great capacity to love another human being.

The therapist encouraged Kadir to give expression to what was going on inside of him by means of collages (Santini & Marsal Roig, 1999). That really helped. Now and then the therapist devoted a few minutes to discussing Kadir's symptoms. He asked what Kadir was doing about his symptoms; sometimes during the discussion they came up with alternatives. Knowledge of symptom-oriented therapeutic techniques (van der Veer, 1992, 1998) was very useful here.

Systematic, methodical work based on a theoretically worked out psychotherapeutic approach took place, therefore, but had no great priority within the treatment. The therapist mainly tried to make sure that Kadir felt he had contact and was at least slightly understood during their meetings. The therapist wanted to give Kadir the feeling that he was really trying to put himself in his place, that he wanted to know what it was like to be Kadir in sad and hopeless times; so that just for a moment Kadir would feel less lonely.

The therapist tried to be empathetic and offer safety and consolation — consolation in the sense of closeness within the contact. In other words, the therapist tried, within the boundaries of his professional role, to love Kadir. That turned out not to be so difficult, even though Kadir could be extremely annoying. Whenever he was, there was always an understandable reason.

Love and Empathy

As a therapist one also comes across clients for whom it is not easy to feel any love at all. That happens particularly when empathy is blocked for one reason or another; when the therapist has trouble in departing from his or her own position and imagining what it is like for someone in the position of the client. This, understandably, creates a less safe atmosphere for the client.

Mohammed had been referred by the doctor at the Asylum Seekers Centre where he was staying. He had gone to this doctor because he wanted a room of his own. The reason he gave was that he suffered from nightmares from which he woke up screaming. That's why he didn't want to share a room with others. He also suffered from flashbacks of war, corpses, and torture. He said that the desire for a room of his own was the only reason why he had approached the institution.

Mohammed had lived in the Netherlands for more than 2 years. An in-depth interview by an immigration officer had only taken place after 18 months. During that interview Mohammed had experienced the attitude of the contact official as very harsh, which had angered him.

Mohammed gave an agitated, depressed impression. He couldn't say what kept him going, but declared that he often fantasized about suicide. "Can't you understand that I need peace and quiet?" he said to his therapist. The therapist agreed and kept it to that, Mohammed flew into a rage and said that he didn't want to come anymore because the therapist wasn't doing anything to help him get a room. After two sessions both sides were frustrated and irritated — Mohammed, because the therapist had not acceded to his wish that he support him with a written declaration that Mohammed needed a room of his own; the therapist, because in his view Mohammed was not motivated, even though Mohammed had confided a considerable amount of personal information. This information was about traumatic experiences in his early youth and about his traumatic experiences in prison, including sexual abuse. There was no question of love after those two intake sessions, even though the colleague was a very caring person.

Perhaps it would have been a different story if the therapist had realized sooner that the desire and need for more privacy in a person with serious traumatic stress complaints were very realistic. It had gone against the grain that Mohammed had asked for a declaration right at the start. This made it difficult for him to put himself in Mohammed's position. There was a temporary lack of empathy in the therapist and of safety in the therapeutic relationship. That didn't last long. After two sessions the therapist wrote the requested declaration with full conviction. Then Mohammed felt at last that the urgent nature of his symptoms had been understood, that he had made contact with someone who understood him. Shortly afterward the therapist received the following letter from a woman friend of Mohammed:

I translated your declaration for Mohammed and he is very grateful to you. He is absolutely delighted that at last there is someone who takes him seriously, who values him as he deserves and who doesn't — thank God, I would like to add — dismiss everything as manipulative behavior. I know Mohammed very well and I'm glad that he has found someone at last who believes in him. That is what he needed and that is extremely important to him: to be taken seriously. He asked me to be sure to pass this on to you.

From that moment there was a much more positive understanding between Mohammed and the therapist. Empathy seems to be a precondition for feeling safe, for love, and for the possible development of a fruitful therapeutic relationship. And it seems that it can sometimes be necessary, in the early motivation phase of a course of therapy, to be present and to do something.

Obstacles to Empathy

On a basis of empathy, of immersion in the other, contact can be created. That contact forms the basis of any form of specialized therapy. Therapists are not always able to immerse themselves in another person. That is the case for example when the therapist believes that everybody should be treated exactly the same way, and that no one should be allowed privileges or extra protection. By so doing the therapist sets him- or herself up as guardian of the principle: one rule for all. Refugees, like everyone else, are not peas in a pod; they are impassioned people with their own personal expressions of the usual and universal needs, in the physiological sense (food, drink, sleep), of safety, security, love, self-respect, and self-realization (Maslow, 1970), needs that deserve understanding and respect.

It is just as difficult for empathy to exist when a therapist employs a particular line of interpretation regarding the complaints of the client and does not realize that the client has a different line of interpretation, or when he or she dismisses the client's way of interpreting problems as irrelevant. Empathy within the therapeutic contact is also difficult to establish when the therapist feels under pressure from third parties and cannot or will not oppose this. That happens, for example, when the therapist's colleagues believe that treatment should proceed according to a particular code, or when the institution considers a fully completed intake form more important than the question of whether the client feels safe and at ease.

Speaking more generally, it seems that empathetic contact is obstructed whenever the therapist has some rigid conviction about work and because of this conviction he or she has something else on the agenda than what the client finds important at that moment, which has priority. Enforcing one's own agenda is always at the cost of empathy and safety.

Involvement or Overinvolvement?

An important norm prevalent among many Western therapists is that a professional therapist treats disturbances in a professional way, that is to say, according to particular procedures over which there is a consensus. A therapist who admits that he or she sometimes departs from procedures to help unique people, rather than treat disturbances, breaches this code and can no longer rely on being taken as professional by his or her colleagues. In recent publications, the treatment of clients with posttraumatic stress syndrome nowadays often seems to be conceptualized as the implementation of therapeutic techniques, preferably techniques based on empirical evidence (Foa, Keane & Friedman, 2000). In this approach, psychotherapy could easily be reduced to the treatment of disorders according to protocols. Protocols, with their crystallized knowledge and experience, certainly have their strong sides as a starting point. But they are not enough.

Another implicit norm can, again with some exaggeration, be stated that professional contact with someone seeking help should not feel like meaningful personal contact. If the therapist experiences contact with a client as personal and meaningful for him- or herself, the therapist runs the risk of being considered as overinvolved and therefore unprofessional by his or her professional colleagues. Some people associate words such as liking and love with reference to clients or patients in the first instance with overinvolvement and the risk of overstepping boundaries. In that case, however, we are concerned with more or less crude outbursts of egocentric, nonempathetic behavior and needs on the part of therapists, and certainly not with love. We are referring here to forms of love that are acknowledging and nonpossessive, love which can encompass and let go (cf. Hoffman, 2000; Young-Eisendrath, 2001). As early as 1906 Freud wrote that it is essentially love that brings about healing (letter to Jung, June 6, 1906, see Freud & Jung, 1977); and in 1926 he described the role of the analyst as that of a "secular pastoral worker" (Freud, 1926/1959).

Aid to refugees demands safety and loving commitment. The question is what form this commitment should take. Some refugees derive much benefit from an explicitly affirmative remark or an actual pat on the back. With others one can feel in advance that this would only make them feel uncomfortable, that they are happier when the therapist outwardly adopts a more clinical attitude. Making boundaries can be a form of love, and also, in the therapy aiming at empowerment and enlarging self-sufficiency, the rounding up and letting go of the client. An inwardly loving approach on the therapist's part does not mean that he or she has to behave in a particular way, or that he or she ought or ought not to say certain things. The word love here refers to a process that can be seen and felt in widely different ways, and certainly not only to predictable forms of piety. Love, respect, and open acceptance can be seen as messages that are transmitted. Not everyone is on the same wavelength. It is up to the therapist to find the frequencies that lie within the range that can be received by the refugee without too much disturbance or interference. That's where the therapist needs his or her intuitive capacities.

In the above discussion the word love is used in connection with an empathetic attitude, with transcultural openness, and with personal commitment, within a safe "holding." Concepts such as love and compassion do not refer to a tangible object; love is not an entity one can put a finger on (Wilber, 1998). Love has to do with a positive basic position toward the refugee and with a firm resolution to track down one's own prejudices, automatic reactions, and transferences. From this position one regards each refugee as a unique individual, not as a specimen of a particular sort. In the attempt to make real personal contact, the therapist does not avoid a feeling of personal commitment.

Empathy, love, and compassion are components of all cultures, religions, and eras. They have their own terms and meanings: from the Bodhisattva's *karuna* in Buddhism to the *hesed* in the Judaic tradition, from *agape* as preached by Jesus to *Allah Ar-Rahman, Ar-Rahim* in Islam (Fastiggi, 2000).

RAGE AND SAFETY

When there is little empathy, this can lead to frustration and rage. Both parties in the therapeutic situation can experience that. The contact can be felt as more distant and cool, or in close, hot, and angry preoccupation; anyhow, safety is suffering.

The consciously and legitimately acknowledged rage of the therapist can serve as a signal and a source of energy (Lowen, 1967). But before it gets to that stage, rage can sometimes be extremely burdening.

Rage can be felt by the refugee, and rage can be felt by the therapist; often there will be reverberations. It is possible that the rage that is not acknowledged by the one is felt or acted out by the other.

Rage as Source of Energy

Kadir went into therapy with one of the authors after having been rejected as a client by colleagues elsewhere. However the initial rejection of Kadir as a client might be interpreted, the fact remains that the rejection of Kadir's cry for help made the psychotherapist angry. This anger, whether justified or not, possibly made the psychotherapist even more motivated to help Kadir, and perhaps even more inventive in looking for means of making contact with him. And of course, the awareness and self-monitoring of the therapist about possible conditions and influences from other sources to his rage than Kadir's situation were part of his professional stance.

Kadir was also full of rage, incidentally, and in this sense client and therapist were on the same wavelength from the very start. Kadir was furious about what had been done to him in his own country. He was furious with the people at the medical service in the Investigation Centre who, in Kadir's view, had not taken him seriously. The therapist gave him a lot of opportunities to express his rage, without ever throwing doubt on the reason for his anger or trying to put it into proportion; although he naturally had his own views on that.

The Cause of Rage

Someone who basically wants to associate with his fellow men in a loving way will almost choke with rage if he or she experiences oppression, is then placed in a dependent position, and is subsequently humiliated by temporarily or permanently hard-hearted people who are not interested in him or her as a person. Perhaps that was the cause of the rage of Mohammed, the client who asked for a declaration during his first session. However that might be, therapy for refugees means coping with powerlessness and rage, with "working through," digesting, and understanding rage for the therapist (and sometimes expertly filtering and temporarily camouflaging rage in its expression), and the sometimes compulsive rage of the client.

It is of importance to identify the cause of the anger as far as possible. With some refugees the cause of their rage lies in traumatic experiences. With many refugees the rage is partly understandable as a natural and essentially very respectable and understandable reaction to the rebuffs they often experience from the moment they ask for asylum. This unfriendly treatment occasionally arouses vicarious rage in therapists.

In the course of years we have been able to see how refugee policy has changed in many Western countries: from an initially generous policy, via a policy of restriction and discouragement, to a policy of deterrence. The effects of this are experienced practically by therapists. The policy of deterrence most of the time rests on two pillars: a system of juridical rules, which is designed to get refugees out of the country on arrival as far as is legally permissible, and a reception system, which, although doubtlessly introduced with the best intentions, works as a total institution (Goffman, 1961) in which refugees are made to a large degree dependent and powerless. Which person who has seen an Asylum Seekers Centre from the inside would want to live there him- or herself or could tolerate the idea of his or her children growing up in this unsafe environment?

Rage as Burden

Both systems, the legal system and the reception system, will unavoidably arouse rage and opposition in the individuals who, in their unsafe life situation, become entangled in them. This rage is dumped on the social services: on the supervisors in the centers, on the medical reception center, on the social workers exercising custody over single unaccompanied minors, and also on therapists in the mental health sector. Broadly speaking these therapists can react in two ways. First, by cutting themselves off from their clients' feelings, and by ascribing the clients' rage to, for example, trauma, or to an antisocial or manipulative personality structure. Second, by sharing their clients' feelings of powerless rage and thereby becoming personally touched and possibly burdened by it (for these attitudes see section, "A Safe Therapeutic 'Holding'"). If they go for the first option, they will keep personal contact with asylum seekers at a distance and treat them strictly according to the principle of one rule for all; whereby they will naturally provoke more aggressive or manipulative reactions. If they go for the second option and get involved, they run the risk of being dismissed by others as overinvolved. Sympathizing with the powerlessness of asylum seekers becomes a lot more bearable if one concentrates on the inventiveness some asylum seekers use to find ways to cope with the oppressive aspects of their reception, and in so doing manage to beat the system.

Dealing with Rage

Dealing with rage in a professional way demands an empathetic approach toward the rage and connected powerlessness felt by the client and one's own (substitute) rage. The rage can be directed against institutions and persons, including oneself and the refugee, as probably was the case in the example of Mohammed. It is important that the therapist, with awareness and self-monitoring, quickly recognizes the rage as a signal and develops an adequate coping repertoire with which he or she can transform rage into insight and positive energy (Rosenberg, 1999).

NOT-KNOWING, DOUBT, AND SAFETY

Therapist and refugee are in some respects partners in not-knowing and doubt. The knowledge and expertise of the therapist does not provide answers to all the questions that confront him or her and the refugee. How safe can one feel with not-knowing?

Not-Knowing and Doubt on the Part of the Therapist

In the refugee's everyday life much time is taken up by practical aspects of living such as residence permits, reuniting the family, the naturalization process, or the living situation. These often drag on for years. So in addition to a painful past, there is a present full of dependence on authorities and institutions, and future prospects that have been carefully blocked by government measures. There are thus many pathogenic factors in the government's treatment of asylum seekers. That is enough to make therapists wonder from time to time what purpose mental health care for refugees actually serves.

Existential Questions of Refugees

Questions on the part of the therapist about meaning, giving meaning, and meaningfulness are not based purely on rational analysis; they also have to do with the feelings that refugees express during therapeutic contacts. From time to time a therapist who treats refugees has to work with clients who desperately wonder whether there is any point in going on living. A former child soldier from Guinea who was terrified of being sent back said: "Sometimes I think: why did my mother give birth to me?" A lonely Somali boy of 20 who still didn't have a residence permit after 5 years, being unable to train for anything, wondered: "Why do I have to live, and why without any family at all?" When Kadir first went to his therapist he also had little desire to go on living. With existentially and essentially unsafe life conditions, questions about "the meaning of life" and the meaning we can give to it are perhaps implicitly the most important theme in therapy (cf. Frankl, 1963; Janoff-Bulman, 1992).

Not-Knowing, Doubt, Loss, and Consolation

There are three possible causes that lead a person to feeling that life is pointless (van Dantzig, 2000). The first is a biochemical disturbance, which can be treated with antidepressive or other drugs. The second cause is an emotional aridity resulting from an unfavorable upbringing or life history; psychotherapeutic treatment is then appropriate. The third cause is a recent painful loss, and this individual must be consoled. This means that someone, a therapist for example, does his or her best to create a safe environment and understand what that loss means and why it is so painful (van der Veer, 1999); this is only possible if the therapist accepts that he or she is just as powerless to undo the loss suffered as the person being counseled.

With refugees who are wondering about the meaning of life, all three causes can possibly play a role. The latter cause, a painful loss, is often the decisive one. And in that case, shared powerlessness and consolation are more appropriate than strict adherence to the protocol, which can come across as an underestimation of the intensity of the loss suffered by the refugee.

When a therapist offers consolation in the way described above, he or she is not "curing a sick person" but rather caring for a soul in pain. The therapeutic session acts as the balm that is necessary because the collective rituals of one's own culture or religion cannot be performed. It is necessary because the pastoral care from one's own culture or religion is not available; because the appropriate rituals[3] cannot be performed, even if religious leaders are present in the new country. This can be for practical reasons (for instance, a certain type of flower is not available in the new country), because it doesn't fit the local rules (one cannot just slaughter a goat), but it will mainly be because the local social life within which rituals take place is not present.

As we have said, consolation is about experiencing safety, understanding, and closeness when enduring sadness and powerlessness. In particular, the experience of powerlessness and knowing that one doesn't know (Batchelor, 1990; Bion, 1970) is a heavy burden for therapists. When one realizes that therapeutic techniques and theoretical knowledge, learned by the sweat of one's brow, have little success in the treatment of a particular refugee, one can easily begin to doubt the usefulness of therapy, even if it is clear that the client benefits from the contact.

It is not, although, a burdening task as such for the therapist to share sadness and powerlessness with a client. The following excerpt from a case study is an example.

---

[3] The Tamil culture, for example, has 20 or so traditional forms of healing that are important for collectively coming to terms with traumatic loss (Somasundaran, 2000).

> Reza was referred to me 13 years ago by a teacher at his school. This teacher had asked the class to write an essay entitled: what I believe in. Reza wrote one sentence only: I don't believe in anything.

> In one of our ten sessions Reza described in bloody detail how his brother had been murdered before his very eyes. He wept as he spoke, and my eyes also filled with tears. Which Reza didn't seem to notice, by the way. At the end of the session Reza said, in perfect Dutch, "it was very enjoyable." I wouldn't have put it like that, but it made sense, I'd felt that at the time. I felt very happy for a moment when Reza said that. Afterwards I looked back on the session as a sort of mystical experience. As it says in the Book of Revelations [*sic*]: silence in heaven, about the space of half an hour.[4] (Authorized King James Version)

> But Reza expressed it differently, he used the word enjoyable. And now I understand that in that way he summarised the session in its deepest essence. A good funeral also ends enjoyably.

Reza and the therapist shared an experience of existential truth. This truth includes and transcends possible agreeable or nonagreeable emotions and can be experienced as a deep sense of joy.

We have never been asked directly by a client what we consider to be the meaning of life. Why is that? In a case history discussion one of us (van der Veer) made the following comment on this question.

> I suspect that the reason is as follows: the moment I feel that a client is sharing his despair with me, and I feel with him instead of professing like an enlightened guru to understand something about life, the client experiences contact, consolation, the opposite of loneliness. My lack of rock-solid faith and my irresolution in the face of existential questions appear to have a calming and reassuring effect on my clients. The common experience of not understanding anything about life makes life once more worth living.

Paradoxically, the acknowledgment and sharing of true existential unsafeness, insecurity, and impermanence can empower one to an inner unshakable experience of "safety."

CONCLUSION

The sense of safety of most traumatized refugees and asylum seekers has been shattered due to their traumatic experiences, the process of uprooting, and their often unsafe position in the country of exile. It is important for them to experience safety within the therapeutic relationship.

---

[4] "And when He had opened the seventh seal, there was silence in heaven about the space of half an hour." Revelation 8:1.

For a safe therapeutic sanctuary to come into existence, the therapist needs to feel safe. His or her sense of safety can be threatened for various reasons, including the cultural differences between the refugee and him- or herself.

In the treatment of traumatized asylum seekers and refugees, safety within the therapeutic sanctuary requires understanding of the therapeutic procedure by the client and a therapist who can radiate safety because he or she has enough awareness of his or her own mental processes, because he or she has a capacity for containment, and because he or she is able to keep optimal distance. For safety to develop, differences in cultural meaning and expression have to be dealt with and transcultural communication has to be established.

Moreover, the development of safety within the therapeutic sanctuary is dependent on the therapist's ability to deal with the basic emotional movements that are inevitably part of therapy with refugees and asylum seekers: love, rage, and not-knowing or doubt.

From these conclusions, we can now see three themes: what helps in psychotherapy with refugees and asylum seekers, what the essential tools for the therapist are, and what attitude is required from the therapist.

What Helps?

If one asks refugees at the termination of a course of therapy what helped them most during the treatment, it often appears that they remember a particular remark of the therapist that led to their looking at themselves or their surroundings in a completely new way. Quite often the therapist can no longer bring the remark in question to mind. It is always something that was apparently said in passing; not a carefully planned intervention according to a protocol. But they are clearly interventions that stem from the integrated approach described in this chapter, in which technical knowledge is integrated into a moral attitude. We can therefore assume that this moral, but at the same time professional, position is the common denominator and therefore the core of the matter. It is about an attitude; one that is characterized by love and compassion, respect for the rage of refugees, and interest in their doubts and uncertainties in existential questions.

This moral attitude should be accompanied by a feeling of responsibility for the global community in which the conflicts occur from which refugees try to escape, and responsibility for the new community for the refugee, in which processes occur that sometimes make the lives of refugees even harder to bear.

What Are Essential Tools for the Therapist?

Safety is an interaction. What can a therapist do to facilitate the co-creation of a good-enough safe therapeutic sanctuary? The tools for the therapist include: love for people who have had dreadful experiences, who have been sorely tried, who possibly do not completely toe the line. It includes an open eye for the global situation, which can hardly fail to lead to unease and rage about inhumanity in the therapist's country and the rest of the world, rage as a signal that can lead to constructive action. The tools includes the acceptance of permanent irresolution with regard to the meaning of life, in the sense of tolerance of doubts and not-knowing, and being able to entrust, to accept. If one has contact with the refugee from this viewpoint and begins to understand what everyday life is like for him or her, the rest is usually self-evident, at least for a professional therapist. Technical knowledge covers only a fraction of what occurs during a therapeutic session, the application of particular therapeutic techniques is certainly not the most important part. A systematic approach, whether or not formalized in a protocol, can be a start, but in the end every treatment is a unique interpersonal endeavor. Knowledge and technique could just as well be seen as the "carrier wave" that makes it possible for a message of love and hope to be transmitted by the therapist and received by the client.

Change in Attitude

Well-trained and experienced therapists sometimes need time to free themselves from all sorts of, in their eyes, self-evident and therefore often unspoken norms and values about how therapy ought to be done; norms and values that do not function in the contact with marginalized victims of political violence. Sometimes therapists have to learn to go against the rules in a sense, to set aside protocols or to give teammates who do so the chance to share with them the doubts and uncertainties that then ensue. Well-trained therapists sometimes also have to be encouraged to trust their intuition[5] more and to use this intuition in a scientific way. Sometimes they need to experiment with pushing back traditional professional boundaries and to be prepared to answer for it. The common ground and motivation is creating a safe therapeutic sanctuary where the client can be as he or she really is. As one of us (van Waning) expressed in a group meeting

> My training in familiar western psychotherapeutic approaches offers me, among other things, means of diagnosis, frameworks and hypotheses which I can explore further. I know that they represent one way of looking at the world and dealing with the world, and that many other ways exist. They offer me something, but restrict me as well.

---

[5] Intuition here means an inner form of knowing. It has to do with a combination of thinking and feeling, which produces more information than separate thinking and feeling added together. Scientific use of intuition entails self-observation (introspection) by the therapist, reflection on his or her actions based on intuition, and the testing of the effects of these actions based on intuition (Wilber, 1998).

Fortunately my training has also helped me to think about myself in more subtle terms. I have learned to recognize my own feelings more quickly. I can do more with my intuition. I better recognize transference phenomena. Through that I can track down my prejudices and blind spots more quickly. Thanks to my training I can bear such feelings as uncertainty, powerlessness, ambivalence and not-knowing rather more easily. By trial and error. My training has made me more tolerant towards and more curious about what is alien in myself. But in practice what I learned during my training was not enough, and now and then I even find it a hindrance.

I continue to develop my own tools, and myself as a tool. I continue to learn, to unlearn and to "re-learn." And the last two are the most difficult. When a woman from Afghanistan talks about the children she had to leave behind when fleeing, I realize that I have no psychotherapeutic techniques which can provide her with inner peace. I realize further that that is not the point at that moment. What is the point is that I am present, that I am a witness. In order to be completely present and offer a safe therapeutic sanctuary it is more important that I empty myself than that I draw on the "fullness" of knowledge and skill which I acquired through my training. That sometimes makes me do and say things that I didn't learn during my training. The training certainly continues to resonate. What I do hopefully embraces, transcends and deepens what my training offered me.

A change in attitude is not brought about by the provision of still more standardized learning packages or training modules. It is the result of a personal process of development.

Working with refugees in essence is not different from working with other people with complex problems, and that applies as well for the attitude described. Still there are a number of caveats. Working with refugees requires that the therapist cooperate with seriously traumatized persons, who lost their trusted cultural context and who have to find a new balance in a society in which they are marginalized. Working with refugees therefore makes a personal appeal on the therapist. The helper will be a more truthful therapist when he or she is aware that there can be little imagination of that which cannot be imagined, what we people afflict on each other, and what we still have to give with the client. A more effective therapist can also allow him- or herself to be surprised by uncommon ways of coping, originating in a different culture. Therapy with refugees is not only about them, there and then, but certainly also about us, here and now, as we could have been them.

RECOMMENDATIONS FOR FUTURE RESEARCH

The research discussed in most of the professional literature on the treatment of traumatized people is focused on the effect of applying psychotherapeutic techniques according to fixed protocols. This research needs to be supplemented with research aimed at describing the subtle intersubjective interactional processes between therapists and clients, and the inner processes of therapists.

Recognizing this interaction between therapist and client as a legitimate source of scientific knowledge, we need to develop a well-articulated epistomology of practicing knowledge that illuminates the relationship among conceptual understanding, instrumental knowledge, and professional expertise. If we were to develop a better understanding of the knowledge processes of practice, we might be more able to include the experientally based body of knowledge that is tested in expert practice as part of its professional foundation (Hoshmand & Polkinghorne, 1992).

Research of clinical practice requires a specific methodology, one that focuses on qualitative research and uses methods such as *Verstehen*, registration, classification of information on the basis of common-sense categories, participatory observation, intersubjective testing, the selection of directive theoretical metaphors through study of literature, extrapolation and deduction, the scientific use of intuition, hermeneutic interpretation of patterns, conceptual encounter, and eidetic reduction (Chi, Glaser, & Farr, 1988; Fonagy, Gergely, Jurist, & Target, 2002; McLeod, 2001; van der Veer, 1993; Wilber, 1998, 2000). Psychotherapists, especially those who start to work with a new target group of clients, should be trained in using these methods of research.

REFERENCES

Agger, I. (1988). *Psychological aspects of torture with special emphasis on sexual torture: Sequels and treatment perspectives.* Copenhagen: Institute of Cultural Sociology.

Alexander, A. A., Klein, M. H., Workneh, F., & Miller, M. H. (1981). Psychotherapy and the foreign student. In P. B. Pederson, J. G. Draguns, W. J. Lonner, & J. E. Trimble (Eds.), *Counselling across cultures* (revised and expanded ed., pp. 226–243). Honolulu: University Press of Hawaii.

Allen, J. G. (1995). *Coping with trauma — A guide to self-understanding.* Washington, DC: American Psychiatric Press.

Allen, J. G. (2001). *Traumatic relationships and serious mental disorders.* Chichester: Wiley.

Bala, J. (2001). The interplay of stressful and protective processes in refugee families. In L. Van Willigen (Ed.), *Health hazards of organized violence in children. Coping and protective factors* (pp. 43–52). Utrecht: Pharos.

Batchelor, S. (1990). *The faith to doubt.* Berkeley, CA: Parallax.

Bion, W. (1970). *Attention and interpretation.* London: Tavistock.

Bot, H. (1996). *Working with interpretors in psychotherapy.* Paper presented at the first congress of the World Council for Psychotherapy, September. Wolfheze, The Netherlands, Psychiatric Hospital Wolfheze.

Brown, L. S. (1986). From alienation to connection: Feminist therapy with posttraumatic stress disorder. *Women Therapy, 5,* 101–106.

Cancelmo, J. A., Millán, F., & Vazquez, C. I. (1990). Culture and symptomatology — The role of personal meaning in diagnosis and treatment: A case study. *American Journal of Psychoanalysis, 50*, 137–149.

Chi, M. T. H., Glaser, R., & Farr, M. J. (1988). The nature of expertise. Hillsdale, NJ: Lawrence Erlbaum Associates.

Chu, J. A. (1992). The therapeutic roller coaster: Dilemmas in the treatment of childhood abuse survivors. *Journal of Psychotherapy Practice and Research, 1*, 351–370.

Dahl, C. (1989). Some problems of cross-cultural psychotherapy with refugees seeking treatment. *American Journal of Psychoanalysis, 49*, 19–32.

Danieli, Y. (1984). Psychotherapists' participation in the conspiracy of silence about the Holocaust. *Psychoanalytic Psychology, 1*, 23–42.

De Anda, D. (1984). Bicultural socialization: Factors affecting the minority experience. *Social Work, 29*, 101–107.

Denley, J. (1987). Personal communication as cited in J. Reid & T. Strong, *Torture and trauma* (p. 96). Sydney: Cumberland College of Health Services.

Eisenbruch, M., & Handelman, L. (1989). Development of an explanatory model of illness schedule for Cambodian refugee patients. *Journal of Refugee Studies, 2*, 243–256.

Fastiggi, R. L. (2000). Towards the dialogue of love. In J. Beversluis (Ed.), *Source book of the world's religions* (pp. 348–349). Novato, CA: New World Library.

Foa, E. B.., Keane, T. M., & Friedman, M. J. (Eds.) (2000). *Effective treatments for PTSD.* New York/London: Guilford Publications.

Fonagy, P., Gergely, G., Jurist, E. L., & Target, M. (Eds.). (2002). *Affect regulation, mentalization, and the development of the self.* New York: Other Press.

Frankl, V. E. (1963). *Man's search for meaning: An introduction to logotherapy.* New York: Washington Square Press.

Freud, S. (1926/1959). *The question of lay analysis.* Standard Edition (Vol. 20, pp. 179–258). London: Hogarth.

Freud, S., & Jung, C. G. (1977). *The Freud/Jung letters.* London: Hogarth.

Giel, R. (1984). *Vreemde zielen. Een sociaal-psychiatrische verkenning in andere culturen* [Foreign souls. A social-psychiatric exploration in other cultures]. Meppel, Boom.

Goffman, E. (1961). *Asylums — Essays on the social situation of mental patients and other inmates.* Garden City, NY: Anchor Books.

Herman, J. L. (1992). *Trauma and recovery.* New York: Basic Books.

Hoffman, I. Z. (2000). *Ritual and spontaneity in the psychoanalytic process — A dialectical-constructivist view.* Hillsdale, NJ and London: Analytic Press.

Hoshmand, L. T., & Polkinghorne, D. E. (1992). Redefining the science-practice relationship in professional training. *American Psychologist, 47*, 55–66.

Janoff-Bulman, R. (1992). *Shattered assumptions. Towards a new psychology of trauma.* New York: Free Press.

Kinzie, J. D. (1978). Lessons from cross-cultural psychotherapy. *American Journal of Psychotherapy, 32*, 110–120.

Kortmann, F. (1986). *Problemen in transculturele communicatie* [Problems in transcultural communication]. Assen: Van Gorcum.

Kutchins, H., & Kirk, S. A. (1999). *Making us crazy — DSM: The psychiatric bible and the creation of mental disorders.* London: Constable.

Lee, E., & Lu, F. (1989). Assessment and treatment of Asian-American survivors of mass violence. *Journal of Traumatic Stress, 2*, 93–120.

Lindy, J. D. (1996). Psychoanalytic psychotherapy of posttraumatic stress disorder — The nature of the therapeutic relationship. In B. van der Kolk, A. McFarlane, & L. Weisaeth (Eds.), *Traumatic stress — The effects of overwhelming experience on mind, body, and society* (pp. 525–536). New York: Guilford Publications.

Lowen, A. (1967). *The betrayal of the body.* New York: Macmillan.

Maslow, A. H. (1970). *Motivation and personality.* New York: Harper & Row.

McCann, L., & Pearlman, L. A. (1990). Vicarious traumatization: A framework for understanding the psychological effects of working with victims. *Journal of Traumatic Stress, 3,* 131–149.

McLeod, J. (2001). *Qualitative research in counselling and psychotherapy.* London: Sage.

Mezzich, J. E., Kleinman, A., Fabrega, H., & Parron, D. (Eds.). (1996). *Culture and psychiatric diagnosis, a DSM-IV perspective.* Washington DC: American Psychiatric Press.

Mollica, R. F., & Son, L. (1988). *Cultural dimensions in the evaluation and treatment of sexual trauma: an overview.* Unpublished study.

Mollica, R. F., Wyshak, G., De Marneffe, D., Khuon, F., & Lavelle, J. (1987). Indochinese versions of the Hopkins Symptom Checklist—25: A screening instrument for the psychiatric care of refugees. *American Journal of Psychiatry, 144,* 497–500.

Newman, E., Kaloupek, D. G., & Keane, T. M. (1996). Assessment of posttraumatic stress disorder in clinical and research settings. In B. Van der Kolk, A. C. McFarlane, & L. Weisaeth (Eds.), *Traumatic stress — The effects of overwhelming experience on mind, body, and society* (pp. 242–275). New York: Guilford Publications.

Olness, K. N. (1986). On "Reflections on caring for Indochinese children and youths." *Developmental and Behavioural Pediatrics, 7,* 129–130.

Pederson, P. B. (1981). The cultural inclusiveness of counselling. In P. B. Pederson, J. G. Draguns, W. J. Lonner, & J. E. Trimble (Eds.), *Counselling across cultures* (revised and expanded ed., pp. 22–58). Honolulu: University Press of Hawaii.

Pentz-Moller, V., Hermansen, A., Bentsen, E., & Knudsen, I. H. (1988). *Interpretation in the rehabilitation of torture victims at the RCT.* Copenhagen: International Research and Rehabilitation Centre for Torture Victims.

Rogers, C. R. (1961). *On becoming a person.* Boston: Houghton Mifflin.

Rosenberg, M. B. (1999). *Nonviolent communication. A language of compassion.* Del Mar, CA: Puddle Dancer Press.

Santini, I., & Marsal Roig, C. (1999). *De deur van de hoop. Integrale multidimensionele groepstherapie voor vluchtelingen* [The door of hope. Integrative multidimensional group therapy for refugees]. Utrecht: Pharos.

Somasundaran, D. J. (1993). Psychiatric morbidity due to war in northern Sri Lanka. In J. P. Wilson & B. Raphael (Eds.), *International handbook of traumatic stress syndromes* (pp. 333–348). New York: Plenum Press.

Somasundaran, D. (2000). *Psychosocial needs. A report for the framework for relief, reconciliation and rehabilitation 2000.* Jaffna: University of Jaffna, Department of Psychiatry.

Srinivasa, D. K., & Trivedi, S. (1982). Knowledge and attitude of mental diseases in a rural community of South India. *Social Science and Medicine, 16,* 1635–1639.

Steel, Z., Silove, D., Bird, K., McGorry, P., & Mohan, P. (1999). Pathways from war trauma to posttraumatic stress symptoms among Tamil asylum seekers, refugees, and immigrants. *Journal of Traumatic Stress, 12*, 421–435.

Sundberg, N. D. (1981). Research and research hypotheses about effectiveness in intercultural counselling. In P. B. Pederson, J. G. Draguns, W. J. Lonner, & J. E. Trimble (Eds.), *Counselling across cultures* (revised and expanded ed., pp. 304–342). Honolulu: University Press of Hawaii.

Swartz, L. (1987). Transcultural psychiatry in South Africa. Part II. Cross cultural issues in mental health practice. *Transcultural Psychiatric Research Review, 24*, 5–30.

Teter, H., Mauldin, D., Nhol, S., Conkin, D., & Sum, S. (1987). *Treatment through training: A Cambodian mental health workshop.* San Francisco: International Institute of San Francisco.

Tsui, P., & Schultz, G. L. (1985). Failure of rapport: Why psychotherapeutic engagement fails in the treatment of Asian clients. *American Journal of Orthopsychiatry, 55*, 561–569.

Turner, S. W., McFarlane, A. C., & van der Kolk, B. A. (1996). The therapeutic environment and new explorations in the treatment of posttramatic stress disorder. In B. A. van der Kolk, A. C. McFarlane, & L. Weisaeth (Eds.), *Traumatic stress — The effects of overwhelming experience on mind, body, and society* (pp. 537–558). New York: Guilford Publications.

van Dantzig, A. (2000). *Mensen onder elkaar. Essays over geestelijke gezondheidszorg* [People among themselves. Essays on mental health care]. Amsterdam: Boom.

van de Put, W. (1997). *Self, time and Buddhism in Cambodia: Some clinical implications.* Phnom Penh: IPSER Community Mental Health Program.

van der Kolk, B. A. (1996). A general approach to treatment of posttraumatic stress disorder. In B. A. van der Kolk, A. C. McFarlane, & L. Weisaeth (Eds.), *Traumatic stress — The effects of overwhelming experience on mind, body, and society* (pp. 417–440). New York: Guilford Publications

van der Veer, G. (1992). *Counselling and therapy with refugees. Psychological problems of victims of war, torture and repression.* Chichester: Wiley.

van der Veer, G. (1993). *Psychotherapy with refugees. An exploration.* Amsterdam: Stichting voor Culturele Studies.

van der Veer, G. (1998). Counselling and therapy with refugees and victims of trauma. Chichester: Wiley.

van der Veer, G. (1999). Psychotherapy with traumatised refugees and asylum seekers: Working through traumatic experiences or helping to cope with loneliness. *Torture, 9*(2), 49–53.

van Waning, A. (1999). Inleiding bij het thema multiculturele samenleving en psychoanalyse [Introduction to the theme: Multicultural society and psychoanalysis]. In A. Van Waning (Ed.), *Multiculturele samenleving en psychoanalyse* [Multicultural society and psychoanalysis] (pp. 1–13). Assen: van Gorcum.

van Waning, A. (2000). From splitting to mutuality, beyond heroism and tragedy: Remarks on peace, war, and psychoanalytic insights. *Mind and Human Interaction, 11*, 270–282.

Vontress, C. E. (1981). Racial and ethnic barriers in counselling. In P. B. Pederson, J. G. Draguns, W. J. Lonner, & J. E. Trimble (Eds.), *Counselling across cultures* (revised and expanded ed., pp. 87–107). Honolulu: University Press of Hawaii.

Wilber, K. (1998). *The marriage between sense and soul. Integrating science and religion.* New York: Broadway Books.

Wilber, K. (2000). *Integral psychology — Consciousness, spirit, psychology, therapy.* Boston and London: Shambala.

Wilson, J. P., & Lindy, J. D. (Eds.). (1994). *Countertransference in the treatment of PTSD.* New York: Guilford Publications.

Young-Eisendrath, P. (2001). When the fruit ripens: Alleviating suffering and increasing compassion as goals of clinical psychoanalysis. *Psychoanalytic Quarterly, 70,* 265–285.

9

Strengthening Psychological Health in War Victims and Refugees

SILVANA TURKOVIĆ, JOHANNES E. HOVENS, AND
RUDOLF GREGUREK

The town of Vukovar lies at the banks of the Danube, where the river Vuka flows into it. It is the most eastern part of Croatia, in Slavonia. In 1990 there were about 45,000 inhabitants of which 47% were Croatian and 32% Serbs. The town became known to the world when the war between Serbia and Croatia exploded. The beginning of the war started right after the 1990 elections in the former Yugoslavian republics. In Serbia the Communist Party under the new name of the Socialist Party remained in power and claimed that all Serbs should live in one state as they were supposedly in danger. Serbian extremists in Croatia were armed by the former Yugoslavian army. Road blocks around Knin in the Krajina region appeared. In the early summer of 1991, bombardments in the Vukovar region started. Early August most of the surrounding villages of Vukovar were occupied by the Serbs. On September 14 a fierce attack on Vukovar took place. Over 600 tanks surrounded the city. For each of the next 15 days about 60 to 80 severely wounded people were brought into the hospital. During the siege of 3 months more then 1,800 people, most of them civilians, were treated in the hospital. Lightly wounded stayed at home as going to the hospital was dangerous. On October 4 the Vukovar hospital was bombed. The people of Vukovar fled to shelters, housing up to 700 people. On November 18 the city fell (Silber & Little, 1995; Stengl, 2003). The city was no more. More than 500 people died during the siege. Two thirds of them were civilians, including eight children. Photos of Vukovar's destruction resemble the destruction of the city of Ieper during the battle of Passendale in the Great War.

The following days were chaotic. Buildings were still burning. Corpses littered the streets. The civilians who came out of their shelters were extremely shocked. Contact with the outside world was not possible and representatives of international organizations were not allowed to enter the city. The Serbian army took several hundred civilians and the wounded from the hospital and executed them, among them more then 400 patients from the hospital. Over 5,000 people were taken to prison camps in Serbia. Many of them never came back. Croats and other non-Serbs were driven out of the region. The Balkan wars, with all their cruelties of torture and ethnic cleansing, had started. In all, 31,732 people from the Vukovar district were scattered throughout Croatia and abroad (Stengl, 2003). In 1996 the first preparations were made for the refugees to return to Vukovar.

The first three months of intense combat in Croatia claimed over 12,000 lives. About 250,000 people from the occupied Croatian territories had to find refuge in other parts of the country. The first displaced persons arrived in the capital Zagreb in early September 1991. They were followed by waves of arrivals triggered by the military Serbian campaigns. According to Mesić (1992) 47% of the refugees were able to take only their personal belongings, but 43% did not even manage to do that.

The war spread rapidly to Bosnia-Herzegovina, where more than 200,000 people in 3 years were killed in combat, concentration camps, and by execution during ethnic cleansing. More than a million Bosnians, approximately a quarter of the population, fled from their country. Three hundred and fifty thousand sought refuge in Croatia, 650,000 to other European countries. At the peak of the refugee crisis in Croatia, there were over 700,000 refugees and displaced persons in the country, about 15% of the country's entire population.

Although this chapter will mainly focus on the problems of the refugees and displaced persons from Croatia and Bosnia-Herzegovina, those problems are exemplary for the world of displaced persons and refugees in general. It should be realized that the refugee problem is not a minor one. According to the World Refugee Survey (2002) in 57 countries there are numerous uprooted people, while 94 countries are hosting them. The number of refugees since 1992 fluctuates between 13.5 and 16 million people; the number of displaced persons fluctuates around 20 million. Yearly around 35 million persons are uprooted. As of December 2001, the top five countries with uprooted persons are Sudan, Afghanistan, Palestine, Colombia, and Congo-Kinshasa with over 2 million in every country. Each refugee or displaced person meets considerable stress. Each person has to cope with the strains of day-to-day life, whether it is in Africa, Asia, or Europe. A great number of them have suffered from traumatic stress and a considerable number of them suffer from posttraumatic stress disorder (PTSD). But then, even in severe circumstances, not everybody develops a clinical psychiatric disorder (de Jong et al., 2001).

This chapter describes the experience and consequences of displacement, the context in which it is happening, and the psychological sequelae. We describe the internal reception of displaced persons and reception of refugees and asylum seekers in Western countries. Pitfalls in the assistance will be outlined. Community-based programs and more individualized treatments will be considered. Diagnostics aspects and limitations of treatment will be discussed.

DISPLACEMENT AND REFUGE

Since mankind settled itself, there have always been periods that communities moved away from their grounds. In general, there were two reasons to do so: famine and war. In both cases this is understandable. With famine, people try to change their impending hunger death. At new grounds there are new opportunities to find food and shelter. With war, the possibility of the premature end of one's life is also at hand.

Nevertheless, the moment of flight differs for individuals and communities. Roughly, one can see three kinds of refuge:

Preparedness to flee. The community notices that the weather has been bad in the season and expects with almost certainty that the harvest will fail and decides to search for better grounds. The community or individuals have heard about the rumors of the approaching war. In neighboring regions and cities death and destruction have come to the population.

Escape. The community is taken by surprise, either by natural disaster or a sudden invasion of an army. The inhabitants try to find a safe way out, either in groups or as individuals.

Forced migration. This is a political situation in which, after the occupation of the territory, new powers decide to expel large parts of the old inhabitants.

For all three kinds of displacement and refuge, numerous examples can be found in history, literature, and recent developments in the world.

Preparedness to Flee

It may be that in certain rural areas, it is not uncommon that food shortages happen relatively frequently. Such communities live in hardship and are prepared to pack their belongings and start over at a different place. More often, however, such a decision is difficult to make. Life can be hard, but moving might seem impossible. The community can decide to stay and try to survive, because leaving has such severe consequences. The burial grounds of the ancestors must be left behind; the structure of the community might be disrupted, as other leadership skills are necessary on the road more so than at home. It is also impossible to predict whether one is welcome in a different area, and whether food is more available somewhere else. The personal belongings have to be taken for hundreds of miles. And if they do leave, there is always loss and related grief and frequently hardships on the way to a new location.

The Dinka people in southern Sudan, for example, originally a people who held livestock and raised cattle, were devastated by the famine and war in the 1970s of the 20th century. They fled through most of southern Sudan, only to find out that famine and war were everywhere. By the loss of their cattle and the struggle for life they lost their social structure. Instead of taking care of each other, it was each man for himself. Although they traveled for great distances, losing the cattle meant losing their means of survival. Many of them, now, live in refugee camps.

With an approaching war, whether it is an evacuation of the population by their own authorities or a decision by communities themselves or even individuals, a similar difficult decision has to be made. What is going to happen to us if we stay? Will there be food? What is the invading army going to do? Will we be welcome in a different place or country? Can we go to family? What can we take? What is going to happen to our house, with our bank savings? Such a decision does not only depend on the fact that war is coming to your area, but also on what the rumors are on the approaching army. Will there be looting? Will there be executions or atrocities? What happened in other places? Can we leave safely?

In recent years we have frequently seen photos of groups of refugees passing borders with only a few personals belongings, people leaving by trains with small suitcases. The photos are almost similar to those of the exodus of the 20th-century Jews from Germany in the 1930s. The resemblance with the more recent events in Croatia, Bosnia-Herzegovina, and Kosovo is striking. A great evil is coming. And although it is not a formal classic war between armies, the decision to leave is based on the perceived and expected danger. Fear plays a major role. It will be combined with grief about the losses.

Escape

What happens to people during an impact of a natural disaster has been described by Tyhurst (1951) in his classic paper. In an acute disaster, there are three phases: the period of impact, of recoil, and of post-trauma. The period of impact can last from a few minutes to some hours. It is the period of maximal stress. Reactions of individuals are mostly automatic. Tyhurst describes three reaction patterns. Some 12 to 25% act extremely rational. They are aware of what is happening, make plans of action, and carry that through. The majority, about 75%, are "stunned and bewildered." Their attention is narrowed; there is no awareness of subjective emotion, although physiological fear reactions are manifest. Reactions are automatic. A third group of about 10 to 25% are confused and have extreme anxiety, preventing them from acting. The phase of impact is also the period of direct deaths, whether from the disaster itself or from panic reactions.

In the phase of recoil people show quite individual reaction patterns. It is the period that they show overt emotional responses and are aware of them. Reactions vary from anxiety, fear, and anger. People are trying to find shelter and have a tendency to be with others and to talk to each other about what has happened. Recent debriefing techniques are most often initiated in this period, and it has been shown that people subjectively appreciate that they were contacted to discuss the event, and that they were dissatisfied when they were not contacted. The evidence on debriefing, however, shows that an approach based on eliciting emotional responses has an inverse effect. Supportive techniques appear to be more useful (see Hovens, 2002).

In the acute phase of war, like a bombardment, the situation is different from a natural disaster in the perspective of time. Although in the case of natural disasters the time perspective, in general, is limited, in the case of war this is more unpredictable. An attack can last for days without any interruption; interruptions can vary from a few hours to days. The initial responses of the people can be the same as in natural disasters. The period of recoil is more difficult to define. It is unclear when the battle is over so people can start to get themselves together. It can also be unclear what is going to happen next, thus prolonging the impact phase and the accompanying fears. In the Afghanistan war after September 11, 2002, for example, there was extensive bombing, fierce fighting in several places, and afterward a number of incidents, but life could take its regular course. In Bosnia-Herzegovina, on the other hand, war acts were followed by brutal ethnic cleansing, in combination with torture and executions. This is a completely different situation. And in the case of Bosnia-Herzegovina, life did not take its normal course. The continuity of unpredictability during the initial phases of war, which are much longer than in natural disasters, can be related to the higher percentages of PTSD cases. It can be hypothesized that the biological system will be more exhausted by continuous extreme anxiety levels, thus resulting in more psychopathology.

The final phase of posttrauma is lifelong. In this phase we see psychiatric reactions, which are currently mainly summarized in PTSD, but which also can include depressive states, brief psychotic states, and existential syndromes.

Although PTSD is not present in everyone who has had severe psychological trauma (Yehuda & McFarlane, 1995), it also has been shown that it can have a true lifelong impact for those it affects. Kessler, Sonnega, Bromet, Hughes, and Nelson (1995), for example, found that PTSD is not likely to remit in about half the cases, even if treated. In a community study among older Dutch survivors of World War II, Bramsen (1995) found that 50 years later 10% of the population was still frequently disturbed by distressing memories and that even 24% avoided situations that reminded them of the war. Thirty percent of the respondents said that the war was the worst thing they had ever experienced. Five percent of the population met the criteria for PTSD. Bramsen found that the number of war experiences was related to the PTSD diagnosis. Also, in other areas of research the severity of the trauma has been linked to this disorder. Kleber, Brom, and Defares (1986), for example, mention the number of dead and wounded, the number of deceased family members, the extent of loss of property. This list can be easily extended with different kinds of experiences, like torture, lack of food and water, imprisonment, and so forth, as they are mentioned, for example, in the Harvard Trauma Questionnaire (Mollica et al., 1996).

The escape from the disaster or war area is different in the three phases. During the impact escape it is primarily a matter of survival, which depends on luck and probably of coolness. Escape to a true safe area is an individual affair, which in general is not really planned. One finds oneself in a situation or place, which makes it possible to leave the unsafe area. In general, in such an escape a person has nothing to take along. The person will only survive if he or she manages to arrive at a safe place where food and shelter are available.

During the period of recoil, escape can be organized by the population or groups themselves, or by authorities from outside, in which case it will be called evacuation.

Forced Migration

After the initial phase of a disaster or war, three situations can arise. First, the situation can still be dangerous, or considered dangerous, and the authorities might decide to evacuate the region. Second, the area is considered an unsafe place, where a new violent event could happen anytime. The disaster or the consequences of the disaster make it impossible to take care of the population, for example, in the case of a large flood, or war activities that will soon start over again, such as with bombardments. With loss of property and with casualties the psychological impact with this exodus is different from the situation in which the community was prepared to leave. The people are in shock about what has happened to them, they have lost friends and family, most of their belongings, and have to leave without preparing themselves, psychologically and materially. Furthermore, most often the structure of the community is disrupted. In general, this is an extension of the impact phase.

Another possibility is that the community decides to leave as they consider the area unsafe. This resembles in greater part the evacuation situation, but if the community itself decides to leave, some of its sociological structure will have to be reorganized. The most important difference can be that there is opposition from the authorities to the self-organized evacuation.

In both cases authorities and the local community can be in conflict against each other. In the first case, the people themselves might consider the area as safe, yet they are forced by the government to leave; and in the second case they also have to manage with the opposition of the authorities.

The third situation occurs when the people are expelled by an invading army. This is a situation in which there is no control at all. The soldiers start looting, torturing, raping, and expelling individuals and groups. History shows that this has happened often since ancient times.

SOME CASES OF WAR AND FORCED MIGRATION

A model of how people react in the preliminary phase, the impact phase, and the following phases is theoretically interesting, and it might be helpful in a scientific way. But what happens to real people can only be illustrated by their stories, and even perpetrators are affected. We relate some of these first-person accounts in the sections that follow.

Prijedor, Bosnia-Herzegovina 1992: A Woman — A Case of War

We knew there was a war and we were sure it would not come to us. The war existed only on TV and the TV could be switched off. We continued with our daily activities, not fearing disaster. Some time ago, we saw people in other republics, as they had fled from horror. They looked like living corpses, having nothing but their clothes. The houses around them and their cornfields were in flames. But again it seemed a dream; it was our country and it could not happen to us. We had a good army to protect us: The Yugoslavian National Army (JNA). And then again we didn't do anything wrong.

Suddenly there they were: drunken soldiers, if you could name them soldiers. Then we knew. Three, four, or five days ago there was commotion. The tanks and the army came. We didn't worry. It was our army: the JNA; no reason for fear. All of a sudden they started to shoot. We didn't understand. Those of us who had one, fled to the shelter. Others fled with a whole group to the woods.

I stayed. I couldn't believe that this was really happening. Then they came. Drunk and stinking, with guns and knives in their hands. They took the men who pleaded for their lives, and shot them. The only reaction was a laugh of drunken soldiers having pleasure in killing. They went into the houses, looking for young women. The women tried to hide themselves by putting ugly clothes on. The mothers tried to protect the girls by putting a pile of blankets upon them. It didn't help.

They took us out and ordered us to take our clothes off. Before this moment we had never undressed in front of man. Not even our own men, not even in the darkness of the wedding room. Some of us shouted that we had a little baby, but nothing helped. The rapings started. Five, ten, twenty soldiers. There was no way to count them. They did all kind of sex with us. With a couple of men on one woman at the same time. Even with eleven and thirteen-year-old girls. We pleaded, cried, and begged. They laughed, and before they left, they threw grenades into houses where people were.

Srebrenica, Bosnia-Herzegovina 1992–1995: A Soldier — A Case of Forced Migration

We lived in a little place near Srebrenica. I had a young wife and we lived with my family together in one house. We had some husband-and-wife quarrels, but I can say we were happy. I worked in a city not far from our village. There I saw and heard people from other parts of the country telling horrible stories. But I had my family and I tried to do my work as good as possible. It was April or May (I don't remember anymore), when I heard that the soldiers had come into my house and had raped my wife. When I reached the house, my wife told me she had been raped. We decided to flee to Srebrenica, the city that was in the hands of our people. The passage was long and dangerous. On the way we stayed in the houses of relatives and friends during the day. At night we were hiding in the woods. Finally, we reached the city, which was a living hell. All people from surrounding areas came to Srebrenica. The city was full of refugees. There was not enough room and food for all of us. Those having no house begged for food, blankets. Many of them were starving to death on the street. I found a safe place for my family. I joined one of the four armies in Srebrenica, which gave me the opportunity to take care of my family. As a soldier, I was able to hear where and when food droppings took place. With other soldiers I attacked surrounding villages in order to find and steal some food. During these actions, we killed people, sometimes these were old people, but it was they or we.

The year 1993 was horrible. The humanitarian aid could not reach the city. Occasional food droppings took place. People followed desperately the planes. Once the food was dropped quarrels, fights, and even killings took place. Everybody wanted some food. I heard we could go to Zepa, another enclave where UN-soldiers sold salt, flour, and even shoes. It was a difficult journey, because it was wintertime and we were not equipped for such weather. Everywhere there were booby traps and hidden posts of the enemy. Many people lost their lives.

In 1995, we heard that we would be released from this hell. The world was coming to save us. The planes would come and bomb the enemy. We kept our frontlines and defended the city, waiting for help. One day we saw the promised planes and looked at them as if God arrived. We had hope. But nothing happened. From different sides and from the commander we heard that the city was bound to fall. The men had to move to the mountains, while the women had to go to the UN compound in Potocari. It was a total chaos and there was no time to say goodbye to our wives and children. I thought I'd never see my family again. I moved in a long row of men to the mountains. We headed to a free area. Then, real hell started. They shot at us, but we could not see them. We panicked and were drawn apart from each other. Afterwards, we looked for survivors and then, we tried to move on. Then, the following happened: they started to use poisoning gas. Some people lost their mind; they took their hand grenade and activated it. Not only they, but also all the other people around them were cut into pieces. I stopped and tried to think. I concluded: if they are attacking us, they must be following us. They move into the same direction as we are. If so, then they left Srebrenica, which means: there cannot be many of them left in the city. By sorting this out, I decided not to go forwards but backwards, back to Srebrenica. On my way back, I met another man. We decided to stay in the mountains, trying to find a place to hide. We found a cave where we were protected. Every day one of us went to look for food, while the other one protected the hiding place. We ate everything we found. The taste of the things was not bad, but we lost our teeth. This lasted for six months. Then we decided to move on. We didn't know which direction to go, but, by coincidence (or something else), we reached a safe area. After having identified ourselves we were provided with good food and medical care. There I heard that my wife and two children were safe and sound in Holland. After a couple of months, I joined them. Coming there, I was confused. I couldn't figure out whether my past and Srebrenica was a dream, or whether this country and this life now was a dream.

I know only one thing for sure: this country changed my wife. She told me that from now on she would become an emancipated woman. I didn't like that.

West Africa 1996: An African Girl — Another Case of War and Forced Migration

My whole life I was living in a village in Africa. I lived there with my family, and I never left my village. Sometimes a missionary came to our community. He was a White man, with the Bible in his hands. This was the first book I ever saw, and it was an important book. It spoke about God, and because of this book I learned to write and to read. Most fascinating were the pictures. All the people on the pictures were White, and I thought: this is how heaven must look like.

That day we did the usual things: taking care of the children, the fields, and animals. I was in my house with my parents and my husband when the rebels came. They started to shoot at my family and I saw three of them being killed in front of my eyes. There was no time for grief. The rebels decided that I was a young, good-looking girl and they took me to their camp. I cannot explain how it was there, because too much happened, and all bad things. There they called me "Big Mama," because I was a well-fed African girl. We, the young girls, had to take care of the rebels, cooking, cleaning, etc. Every night I was raped. There were lots of them. I couldn't count them.

One day when the rebels were busy with some action I decided to flee. I didn't know where I was going. I was afraid but everything was better than staying in the camp. I ran into the jungle, and I ran for two days and two nights. I tried not to stop. I tried to look at the sun because I was afraid of snakes. By the third day I couldn't run anymore. I was exhausted and decided to get out of the jungle. I reached the road and saw a truck. The driver stopped. By some miracle he didn't belong to the rebels. He drove me to the capital city and advised me to leave the country. He told me to go the harbor, find a ship, and hide myself there. I listened to him. I waited til the night came. Then I went to the harbor and found a ship where I hided myself. I was ill and had a fever. I had nothing to drink and nothing to eat. This must have lasted for several days. One day a man came downstairs and discovered me. He was very angry and told me that if I would have been a man he would have thrown me overboard. The following days he took care of me. He brought me food, medicine, and water. He told me that at the next stop he would throw me out. That next stop happened to be Rotterdam (I didn't know it by then) in the Netherlands. I left the ship and I found myself in a very, very cold place, full of White people. I thought about the pictures in the Bible and the White people on these pictures. I was sure that I was in heaven.

Skopje-Vukovar November 1991: A Perpetrator — A Case of Repentance?

I was living in Skopje, Macedonia, and had a good life, a nice job, a wife, and two children, who obeyed me. One night, the police came and ordered me to serve into the JNA. As I was a reservist, I was obliged to obey them. They put me in a car and drove away. I didn't know where we were heading for. After passing a couple of military posts, I heard that it was my task to liberate Vukovar. We went there. We were no regular army. The JNA with their artillery was behind us. My colleagues were drinking and singing songs. There at the time, things happened you cannot imagine. I can't talk about it.

One day, somewhere outside Vukovar we saw a young woman with two children. They were lost or something. We were with 25 to 30 men. Before I knew, it happened. We all ran to those three. We took the mother, ripped her clothes off and one by one we used her, did on her. All the time the two children were there, looking what was happening. I think they were about 8 and 10 years old. After we had done our jobs and emptied ourselves, we wanted to leave. The woman stood up, walked to a lamppost and started to bump with her head on it. After some time she fell on the ground; dead in her own blood. The children were all the time there.

We went on. Some of us laughing and singing. Since then I don't laugh anymore.

THE RECEPTION OF REFUGEES

In the convention and protocol relating to the status of refugees, 1951 respectively 1967, the United Nations stressed the humanitarian approach, which was human rights and people-oriented (UNHCR, 1996). Despite the fact that many countries accepted these documents, the influx of a large contingent of refugees is seldom easily accepted by receiving communities. The refugees might disrupt the older community, depend on food and shelter in the new region, and can form an undesired economic force. Apart from that refugees can also look different, have different manners, languages, religions, and wear different clothes. This can set them apart from the autochthonic population, and it can lead to tension in both the receiving community and in the group of refugees, especially when the economic situation in the area is bad.

Most often the refugees are taken to reception camps, in receiving countries often called reception centers, but refugees refer to them usually as "the camp." These camps provide shelter, food, and water. One can discuss what is most important in such a camp. Clearly, a refugee camp in Sudan or Sierra Leone has different properties than a camp in Croatia or in the Netherlands. The camps must be evaluated against the surrounding environment: a rat in the shower in Sierra Leone may be of less importance than a rat in a Dutch toilet. People do compare their living quarters with the quarters where the autochthonic population is living.

There is always a certain amount of stress in the camp. Space is limited. One has to live with nonfamily members and, in refugee camps in the West, even with people from completely different cultures. Frequently, the camp is perceived as a prison. The refugees are not allowed to work, they have to sit and be bored, and they become easily irritated. Bad memories can be strengthened by inactivity and depression, and regression can become prominent. It might be clear that a stay in a camp should be as short as possible, for the individual but also for the camp itself, because camps tend to become separate communities with a strong tendency to evolve into ghettos, and ghettos lead to more aggressive acts (Zimbardo, 1970).

RECEPTION IN CROATIA

In the course of the war, imposed on the Republic of Croatia in 1991, and later on in Bosnia-Herzegovina, the number of refugees and displaced persons had been growing constantly. At the height of the war 5,000 refugees a day arrived in Croatia.

The first refugees, mainly from Croatia itself, were housed in hotels at the Adriatic coast. When more and more refugees arrived, they had to stay in barracks. At first, in the early phase of the reception, there was no time to handle psychological problems, with providing food and shelter the primary goal. But Croatia quickly recognized that the refugees might need psychological help (Klain, 1992; Moro & Vidović, 1992). A systematic plan of providing accommodation and physical and psychological protection was worked out. Psychiatrists, psychologists, and social workers were given the task of doing group work with the refugees in the refugee centers.

Forced migration is indubitably one of the most difficult forms of psychosocial stress that can affect an individual or a larger group. Their existence, their psychophysical health, and their social position are threatened. During the exile, the end of which is not yet in sight, horrified by the nonsense of the war devastations, affected by disbelief and fright because of hate of their friends and fellow citizens, they are confronted with an identity crisis. Everything that was built into the foundation of their notion about themselves — job, friends, home, life targets, and values — is exposed to devastation and destruction.

During the war people experience the most difficult frustrations and psychic traumas, which compel them to search for the vicinity of other people. In such a way, numerous small, medium-sized, and large groups are formed, which after some time and in proportion to the distress, become very cohesive. A person searches for salvation in a group because one has to belong to someone and must depend on someone. Refugees and displaced persons, as a large group who has lived through numerous traumatic experiences, have something in common, something that separates them from the rest of the population, that being the traumatic experiences they have lived through.

What follows is our experience with several refugee groups in reception camps. In our opinion, this is not specific for the Bosnian refugees, and can be generalized for the greater part to the refugee population as a whole (Gregurek, 1999; Gregurek, Peršić-Brida, & Štalekar, 1994; Tocilj-Šimunkovi & Gruden, 1999).

The arrival of the refugees in the camp is accompanied by a first reaction of relief and gratitude because of getting out of the territory of direct war destruction. This "honeymoon" is of short duration. Life of a refugee is full of psychological and interpersonal processes and conflicts. Many of the refugees have suffered from psychological trauma.

Almost all of them have witnessed the destruction of their homes and communities. They still live in constant anxiety for the safety of family members whose whereabouts are unknown. They may have suffered torture and most of them saw the enemy carry off family members or friends. The traditional extended family with a strong patriarchal structure has been disrupted; either by the carrying off of the men or by losing them during the flight. Thus, support from the family is lost. People are thrown to their own resources amid a situation that does not resemble in any way their former lives. In short, there is an enormous loss; loss by separation, abandonment, or death; loss of persons, property, and even beliefs and values, often resulting in a loss of self-respect.

Refugees in this stage typically show a desperate and passive attitude. Their losses are a main topic. An almost standard reaction is: "We had everything; houses, and TV-sets, radios, fridges, and our children had fruit whenever they wished. They could go into a garden and pick up what they preferred to eat, and now we have to eat what's given to us. Only if you should know how our place was well kept in order, what the houses were like. We used to get together during the holidays with good food and in good company, but ... now." And, there is a complex of anger reactions: "You are not able to understand what we have experienced. You do not know what a war is. You have everything. You have not lost anything." At that moment, they start discussing how they have survived, telling stories about torture, dead corpses, and so forth, but without emotional involvement, as if to shock the caregiver.

In the beginning, refugees do need essentials of which they cannot take care of themselves. Refugee workers organize this for them, but at the same time this will reinforce helplessness. It is a matter of judgment, common sense, and timing to find a balance in organizing things for them and helping them to organize it themselves. If handled carelessly the refugees might act helplessly even in a situation that could be managed without difficulties. For example, a pregnant Bosnian refugee woman in labor was waiting for hours for the arrival of the refugee team to take her to the hospital. Her family was sitting and waiting with her, although they could have summoned an ambulance easily by themselves.

One can and probably should support recently arrived refugees for a short period of time with their initial helplessness, but one also has to help them to take life gradually into their own hands again by stimulating them to take care of their own basic needs. A way to do so might be organizing a committee to take over the distribution of humanitarian aid care for basic sanitary needs. This seems also helpful in restructuring the community's organization. After that, it was noticeable that the rooms in the barracks were given more attention, too; that they became more of apartments; and that even the environment became more decorative, with flowers growing.

What happens in the long run depends on many factors, which might not be under the control of the refugees. Is there the possibility of integration in a healthy way into the new country in a reasonable time span or are there problems with the asylum procedure, which is often the case in Western Europe these days, which prevents integration for many years?

RECEPTION IN THE NETHERLANDS

When Croatia was receiving a great influx of refugees and the war in Bosnia-Herzegovina was still going on, a huge stream of refugees was gradually moving toward Slovenia. From there they went to other (predominantly Western) countries. Most of those people did not have any idea of where they were going and what their destination would be. Many of them had never been to places other than their hometowns. What they wanted was a safe place far away from the war at home.

In the meantime, Western countries and the media were closely following what happened in former Yugoslavia. Although many in the West saw on television horrible war images and long rows of desperate people walking around with only a plastic bag in their hands, they did not expect that this disaster would come close to them and that it would become part of their own reality. The number of refugees overwhelmed the majority of the Western countries, not being prepared to shelter such numbers. They were willing to be of assistance, but they did not know how to handle the large groups entering their country.

In the Netherlands, occasionally, a train full of refugees would enter the country. It was crowded with the sick, the old, the wounded, and with mothers and their crying children. At this stage Dutch inhabitants were willing to accept refugees, and some even offered to house families in their own homes. But when a larger contingent of refugees entered, the Netherlands was taken by surprise. The Dutch Red Cross offered a solution for this on a much bigger scale. They opened three reception centers where refugees were provided with the most basic life necessities.

Three months after this initiative, the Dutch government started assisting these centers by offering material help. They provided them with medical care, social work, and activity centers. The Dutch government also opened its own centers, each taking in around 600 to 700 people. In these centers several families were frequently housed together in one big room. Not being familiar to one another, they did not perceive privacy anymore. Only an iron cupboard shielded their space.

Naturally there was tension and mistrust among the refugees, not only because of different families sharing the same living space, but because the war in their countries was still ravaging and one was not aware of the position of the other. Mistrust and feelings of (un)safety became stronger when they found out their ethnic backgrounds: Serbs, Croats, and Muslims were all together. In the reception camps questions were asked by the refugees why others had left, and what role they had had in the war. At the same time, most of them were missing family members and were trying to track them down. Day and night, they would watch television, continuously following the latest news about the war. This added to their mental weariness, and it increased their aggressiveness, which directed itself to their family and neighbors.

As time passed, they started trying to change their situation by getting a better room, nicer clothes, and so forth. These activities could take whole days of quarrelling and making deals. Regularly, there were quarrels because someone felt that one family was more privileged than another.

Quarrels with the staff of the center were even more frequent. There were complaints about the food, the water, the doctors, the medication, and so forth. Nothing was as good as at home. They missed their houses, their cars, and other property. Not only facing the loss and having to live in a new reality, they also idealized the old situation, as if only those memories had survived and they needed them to restore some dignity in an uncertain future.

In this period Mental Health Organizations felt obliged to take some initiative with two kinds of approaches at different centers. The first approach was psychological help based on transcultural psychology and psychiatry. Both professionals and volunteers aimed these interventions toward the understanding of the refugees' problems with a reference to the cultural background of the subjects. We are not aware of any publication about this work, but from our experiences in the field we understood that both professionals and refugees became disappointed. The refugees appeared not to understand what was expected from them. They felt that their problems were not resolved and were dissatisfied with the lack of information about what was happening in Bosnia-Herzegovina itself.

A second kind of program is aimed at activities to accomplish therapeutic goals. Learning the Dutch language was taken as a starting point and a means to assist refugees (Martič-Biočina, Visković-Amleh, & Špol-Jar-Vižlina, 1994). The importance of learning the language of the foreign country is of utmost importance to integrate into a new society. It can even be used as a measure for adjustment. Unfortunately, the results of the course were only limited. This was partly due to different levels of education in the refugee group, but also due to problems related to the situation in which the refugees found themselves and to their trauma-related symptoms, such as concentration problems. In another reception center (Drožđek, De Zan, & Turković, 1998), a different approach inspired by the experiences in Crotia was used and proven to be successful. Here a psychiatrist and psychologist with Croatian backgrounds served as team leaders. They contacted, as a starting point, leaders in the refugee community in order to gain their trust and support from the community. An inventory was made in collaboration with them about what kind of psychological help was needed. It was made clear that the refugee workers had to be active in contacting the refugees. Refugees were personally invited to take part in groups where practical advice was given on how to integrate into the Netherlands, but where it was also possible to discuss traumatic experiences and provide education on psychological damage following massive war trauma and forced migration.

COMMUNITY TREATMENT AND PITFALLS

It is not a matter of debate whether refugees were exposed to enormous stress or traumatic experiences. They did. It is also not a question whether humanitarian aid should be provided. It should. And psychological care is also necessary. But how and when interventions are needed is less clear.

In deciding what is the best, one first of all should realize that it is impossible to give everybody a personal treatment; even for therapy in groups there are not enough therapists. Second, it would be overkill as the majority of the people do not need specific treatment, as they will not develop PTSD or a related disorder. Third, we can assume that communities have ways of coping that are very well suited to them. For example, in some communities war is depicted and explained by way of drama. The community can be given the tools to set up such a play.

Summerfield (1995), a critic of the PTSD concept, is a realist when he describes that terrorization of whole populations is used as a means of social control (p. 27). He believes that trauma must be understood "in terms of the relationship between the individual and his society, with outcomes influenced by cultural, social, and political forces" (p. 28). And "the majority will cope with recovery as a collective activity, seeking assistance directed primarily at their social rather than their mental lives" (p. 28). Undoubtedly he is right. There are numerous examples of how communities incorporate their traumatic experiences in their histories, their theater plays, and how they reorganize their society. This means that the greatest effort should be put in reorganizing society, even in communities abroad.

That does not mean, however, that psychological support is not necessary. It always is. Giving comfort in an educated way is always helpful (Hovens, 2002), especially when reorganizing or restructuring the community. A step further is education. In Croatia and Bosnia-Herzegovina, for example, the people were educated by radio on traumatic stress with the intention to make them understand the psychological effects of psychological trauma. Educating them how to handle their responses has been proven to be appreciated, as about 60% of the population listened twice a month to the weekly broadcasts (K. de Jong, March 2003, Amsterdam, personal communication), based on MSF's house survey after the execution of the program in Sarajewo 1995.

In refugees in reception camps the situation is more complex. Their experiences, in general, surpass the traumatic experiences of the general populations, and their posttrauma reactions can be much more complex. As mentioned before, the community structure is disrupted, there are not only fear and avoidance reactions to traumatic experiences, but also grief and continuous worry about the future and family members left behind (Hondius & van Willigen, 1992), and on the individual level there is a disruption of values and beliefs. Nevertheless, a community approach is indicated in the first place, for the same reasons as mentioned above.

A community approach is primarily supportive in nature and should strive after strengthening the coping skills of the population. Such supportive psychological help has aspects of taking control over one's life again by decreasing uncertainty, which can be handled by establishing an effective information system about issues relevant to the population.

Another important aspect in control is encouraging the population to take part in normal daily activities, work, and sports, which are helpful in regaining self-respect and self-confidence. Psychological help also involves social activities. The group should be encouraged to establish and to engage in self-organizing and self-help. Supporting the opportunity to discuss the experiences can also be helpful, and finally education about the consequences of traumatic stress should be provided (Vižek-Vidović, 1992). These supportive measures do not need the highest level of professional help.

Timing in these interventions is of the greatest importance. It makes no sense to start educating without distinction. Neither is it useful to discuss traumatic experiences in an emotional way. Respectfully, one has to consider what is necessary at that moment, through dialogue with the refugees.

Probably the most important intervention one can make is in trying to restore social relationships and structure, with consideration of and respect for the culture of the population involved. In a hierarchical structure, such as the Bosnian population is, one can try to find the spokesmen in the camp and reinforce them. This will lead to more reinforcement of their status and they might be willing to help get other supportive interventions off the ground.

Apart from all the pitfalls that dominate every sort of intervention and treatment in working with refugees the major pitfall with mental health workers is the erroneous belief that everything they see is PTSD and needs professional mental health. Only a minority, although that minority can be substantial (de Jong et al., 2001), needs treatment for PTSD. One also should remember that the refugee population in a camp also has a proportion of people who already had psychiatric problems, which might not be trauma related. In the general population severe mental disorders with hallucinations have a prevalence of 1 to 2%. Another 10 to 15% has anxiety disorders or depression, not directly related to psychological trauma. In survivors the numbers can be less, as possibly only the strong survived, but they still will be there. In these people a professional diagnosis might be useful, and professional treatment for that specific disorder might be necessary.

Another major pitfall is the belief that traumatic experiences have to be discussed at length. That may be necessary for those that truly developed PTSD. Too much talk about horrifying things, while not stressing the importance of normal activities, will ultimately lead to passive and depressive reactions in the subjects instead of supporting them in active coping styles.

A final pitfall is taking over the daily activities from the refugees. This happens quite often and is most often the case in inexperienced refugee workers who are overwhelmed themselves by the experiences of the refugees. Although it is understandable that one feels pity for the refugee about what happened, it is not very helpful to remain in that mind-set. A respectful listening without trying to undo what has happened is most often enough.

AN EXAMPLE OF PITFALLS: A HOSPITAL IN THE NETHERLANDS

In the fall of 1994 a small hospital was initiated in the Netherlands to deal with trauma treatment for refugees and asylum seekers with PTSD or posttraumatic-related symptomatology in an inpatient unit (Hovens & Romme, 2001). Research showed that referrals were adequate as 82% suffered from PTSD (Klein, Hovens, Rodenburg, & Rijnders, 1998). The initial model for treatment was based on Herman's model (1992), in which powerlessness and disconnection or isolation are key words to the understanding of traumatization. The model presupposes that traumatization is a sufficient condition to develop PTSD. Thus, patients are expected to have had a normal psychological development prior to the traumatization.

It was expected that offering a safe environment, provided by the holding capacity and structure of the clinic, would be essential before starting treatment. Such an environment, it was hoped, would offer patients help whenever they felt desperate during the day or night. Activities to participate in and the opportunity to talk about the traumatic experiences were believed to form the most important ingredients of the program.

From day one, however, staff members were flooded with problems and were not always able to find suitable solutions. It was expected that patients would more or less follow their day program, but they didn't. Due to their sleeping problems, they refused to come out of bed, and at the same time also refused to go to sleep. During the daytime they frequently took naps. Of course, in the morning the staff woke everyone up. Often the patients did not respond or told the sociotherapist that they thought they were acting like prison guards. No therapy was performed punctually; staff members struggled to cope with this problem and frequently changed their program.

In the nonverbal experiential therapies (psychomotor therapy, creative and music therapy) some groups were started, but once again no one showed up. Nonverbal therapists believed it was not their duty to go and get the patients. They considered that to be a sociotherapist's task, while the sociotherapists thought it the responsibility of the patients. In the end the nonverbal therapists started doing individual therapies with those patients they considered to have sufficient motivation.

The sociotherapy groups did not work out very well either. Either patients obeyed staff members but did their duties in a meaningless fashion, or they became angry and told the staff that they did not accept forced labor.

During these first 6 months 32 patients were admitted. Nine left because of conflicts with the staff, 15 stayed for a period of more than 6 months, and 8 left in an ameliorated condition within 3 months.

In retrospect, it is easy to see what went wrong. Patients with PTSD were expected to be "normal" people who had suffered terribly from traumatic experiences, but it is truly a psychiatric disorder with a number of specific symptoms. Failing to consider it a psychiatric disorder and suggesting that PTSD is a normal reaction to extreme stress is a pitfall that leads to acceptance of psychopathology instead of aiming at a change to a more appropriate behavior. Among inpatients it was noticed that apart from the nightmares and intrusions of past events, severe hyperarousal along with distrust and depressive passivity were also present. The patients did not have "pure" PTSD, but a mixture of depressive and anxiety disorders in combination with PTSD.

The majority of the staff thought that keeping busy was crucial to recovery and so tried to bombard patients with activities and interventions that were aimed at active participation and the working through of trauma by way of exposure. On many occasions staff members tried to understand the behavior of patients in the light of their traumatic experiences, and from this perspective accepted any behavior. It was a matter of fact that the staff did not sufficiently take into account the psychiatric problems of patients.

Although the therapy program appeared to be structured, in fact there was no structure at all; and this was called flexibility. As a consequence patients learned to avoid treatment altogether by making false claims about having a meeting with one of the therapists. This allowed them to do as they wished.

The staff, above all, did not see what was at stake; being flexible led to staff competition about who was providing the therapy that successfully got the patients out of bed. As there were no negative consequences when patients did not follow specific therapies, a situation was created in which patients dictated the events at the clinic.

At the same time many staff interventions were aimed at working through the traumatic experiences. Psychotherapists believed, from a therapeutic point of view, that it was important for patients to talk about their traumatic pasts while experiencing the accompanying grief and pain. The nonverbal therapists thought that the patients should draw pictures of their traumas, as they were often unable to talk about those experiences. Even sociotherapists saw all behavior of patients in terms of trauma.

Unfortunately, the patients told us that they preferred not to think or speak about their traumatic pasts. Therapists countered this by assuring patients that talking was absolutely necessary. The result was daily reenactments in the clinic. Overall, too many interventions were made each week, and it was unclear who was to make what intervention, at what level, and no one knew which interventions were really needed or necessary.

These findings suggest that, although from a theoretical perspective talking about traumatic experiences can be very important in reducing anxiety about past events and contributing to their acceptance, at the same time it might also be a potential pitfall as the theoretical position does not take into account the current state of the patient, who may be too aroused to discuss the traumatic memories.

CONCLUSION

As it should now be clear, taking care of large groups of refugees is not easy. Refugee workers tend to be overwhelmed by the experiences told to them by the refugees. Although it is human to feel pity for the survivor and have the feeling to undo the horrible things done to them, it is not a professional attitude. In refugees, grief and anger prevail and refugee workers get confronted with those emotions, whether they are on the surface or hidden inside the individual, they are there. Probably the most prevalent reaction to these anger and grief reactions is to label them as PTSD. For the past 20 years, PTSD has been on the front page and it is strongly believed that discussing the traumatic experiences is helpful. That might be the case, but in general such intensive kinds of therapy are only indicated for patients with the true psychiatric disorder of PTSD.

In a larger group of refugees, people are more helped by an active approach, using the coping strategies and skills of the people. In a community approach, it is necessary to strengthen the natural tendency of people to seek help within themselves by restructuring and reorganizing their social interactions, in which traumatic experiences might be discussed. After that they should be helped to get active in daily activities, as this will reestablish their self-confidence and self-respect. Education should also be part of that process.

Similarly, techniques as discussed above can be helpful for individuals in psychotherapy settings. Even in individuals with severe PTSD, it might be important to first reestablish social bonds and strengthen their healthy capacities. However, it might also be the case that in these individuals the PTSD prevents the use of healthy coping strategies, in which case the PTSD should be treated first. What comes first is a matter of good clinical judgment.

REFERENCES

Bramsen, I. (1995). *The long-term psychological adjustmentof World War II survivors in the Netherlands.* Delft, The Netherlands: Eburon.

De Jong, J. T. V. M., Komproe, I. H., Van Ommeren, M., El-Masri, M., Araya, M., Khaled, N., et al. (2001). Lifetime events and posttraumatic stress disorder in 4 postconflict settings. *Journal of the American Medical Association, 286,* 555–562.

Drožđek, B., De Zan, D., & Turković, S. (1998). Short-term group psychotherapy of ex-concentration camp prisoners from Bosnia-Herzegovina. *Acta Medica Croatica, 52,* 119–125.

Gregurek, R. (1999). Countertransference problems in the treatment of a mixed group of war veterans and female partners of war veterans. *Croatian Medical Journal, 40,* 493–497.

Gregurek, R., Peršić-Brida, M., & Štalekar, V. (1994). Envy and gratitude in a large group of refugees. *Collegium Antropologicum, 18,* 231–241.

Gregurek, R., Tocilj-Šimunkovi, G., & Gruden, V. (1999). Trauma and reconstruction in a large group of refugees. *Collegium Antropologicum, 23,* 299–308.

Herman, J. L. (1992). *Trauma and recovery.* New York: Basic Books, HarperCollins.

Hondius, A. J. K., & van Willigen, L. H. M. (1992). *Vluchtelingen en gezondheid, deel II.* [Refugees and health, Volume II]. Amsterdam, The Netherlands: Swets & Zeitlinger.

Hovens, J. F. (2002). Les debriefing psychologies a-t-il un sens? [Psychological debriefing in discussion]. In E. De Soir & E. Vermeiren (Eds.), *Les debriefins psychologiques en question* (pp. 131–144). Antwerpen, België: Garant.

Hovens, J. E., & Romme, E. (2001). From chaos to structure: Development of treatment at *de Vonk.* In M. Verwey (Ed.), *Trauma and empowerment* (pp. 207–218). Berlin: VWB.

Kessler, R. C., Sonnega, A., Bromet, E., Hughes, M., & Nelson, C. B. (1995). Posttraumatic stress disorder in the national comorbidity survey. *Archives of General Psychiatry, 52,* 1048–1060.

Klain, E. (1992). Organization and functions of the mental health department of the M.C.H. In E. Klain (Ed.), *Psychology and psychiatry of a war* (pp. 279–288). Zagreb, Croatia: Faculty of Medicine, University of Zagreb.

Kleber, R. J., Brom, D., & Defares, P. B. (1986). *Traumatische ervaringen, gevolgen en verwerking.* [Traumatic experiences, consequences, and working through]. Lisse, The Netherlands: Swets & Zeitlinger.

Klein, W. C., Hovens, J. E. J. M., Rodenburg, J. J., & Rijnders, R. J. M. (1998). Psychiatrische symptomen bij vluchtelingen: een epidemiologische studie bij aangemelde patiënten. [Psychiatric symptoms in refugees: An epidemiological study in referred patients]. *Nederlands Tijdschrift voor Geneeskunde, 142,* 1724–1728.

Martič-Biočina, S., Visković-Amleh, I., & Špoljar-Vržina, M. (1994). Curative factors experienced in an activity oriented group with Bosnian refugees in the Zuidlarense camp (the Netherlands): Psychotherapeutic and cross-cultural aspects. *Coll. Antropol., 18*, 205–213.

Mesić, M. (1992). *Osjetljivi i ljuti ljudi, hrvatske izbjeglice i prognanici* [Sensitive and angry people, Croatian refugees and displaced persons]. Zagreb: Office for refugees and displaced persons of the Government of the Republic of Croatia, Institute for Migrations.

Mollica, R. F., Caspi-Yavin, Y., Lavelle, J., Tor, S., Yang, T., Chan, S., et al. (1996). Harvard Trauma Questionnaire (HTQ): Manual for Cambodian, Laotian, and Vietnamese versions. *Torture, 6*(Supp. 1), 19–33.

Moro, L., & Vidović, V. (1992). Organizations for assistance to displaced persons. In E. Klain (Ed.), *Psychology and psychiatry of a war* (pp. 182–184). Zagreb, Croatia: Faculty of Medicine, University of Zagreb.

Silber, L., & Little, A. (1995). *The death of Yugoslavia*. London: Penguin.

Stengl, V. *The city of Vukovar*. Retrieved February 20, 2003, from www.vukovar.hr.

Summerfield, D. (1995). Addressing human response to war and atrocity: Major challenges in research and practices and the limitations of western psychiatric methods. In R. J. Kleber, C. R. Figley, & B. P. R. Gersons (Eds.), *Beyond trauma: Cultural and societal dynamics* (pp. 17–29). New York: Plenum Press.

Tyhurst, J. S. (1951). Individual reactions to community disaster. *American Journal of Psychiatry, 107*, 764–769.

United Nations High Commissioner of Refugees(UNHCR). (1996). *Convention and protocol relating to the status of refugees* (original 1951 and 1967). Geneva: Author, Public Information Section.

Vižek-Vidović, V. (1992). Psychological aspects of displacement. In E. Klain (Ed.), *Psychology and psychiatry of a war* (pp. 279–288). Zagreb, Croatia: Faculty of Medicine, University of Zagreb.

World Refugee Survey 2002. (2002, June 13). *World refugee statistics*. Retrieved February 20, 2003, from www.refugees.org/statistics.

Yehuda, R., & McFarlane, A. C. (1995). Conflict between current knowledge about posttraumatic stress disorder and its original conceptual basis. *American Journal of Psychiatry, 152*, 1705–1713.

Zimbardo, P. G. (1970). The human choice: Individuation, reason, and order versus deindividuation, impulse, and chaos. In W. J. Arnold & D. Levine (Eds.), *1969 Nebraska symposium on motivation* (pp. 237–307). Lincoln, NE: University of Nebraska Press.

10

Uncovering: Trauma-Focused Treatment Techniques With Asylum Seekers

BORIS DROŽĐEK AND JOHN P. WILSON

Life is lived forward, but understood backward.
Soren Kierkegaard
(cf. Fine, 1999)
And, finally they left, not unlike children, into a sovereign place with hope. A journey of the soul, spirits mended, hearts once again renewed for the blessings of life's goodness.
John P. Wilson, 2003

TRAUMA, MIGRATION, AND CULTURAL DIFFERENCES: THE STRESS TRIAD

Traumatized asylum seekers, refugees, and torture victims are persons who suffer from complex and chronic forms of posttraumatic stress disorder (PTSD) (APA, 1994). Beyond trauma, they have experienced the spectrum of psychological, social, and economic stresses of forced migration. Many have broken spirits and have lost hope. Despair and helplessness are often paramount in a web of uncertainty.

In working with these victims, clinicians should recognize the uniqueness of their stressors in order to adequately provide good care and treatment. It is critical to be culturally sensitive when diagnosing and treating this vulnerable population. A culturally sensitive approach takes into account the therapist's own ethnocentricity and is open to alternative cultural perspectives of psychological problems.

Traumatized asylum seekers seek refuge in another country as a result of being persecuted or after being submitted to war, torture, terrorism, or political violence. They have suffered many losses: home, properties, possessions, homeland, occupation, customs, and social roles within and outside the family. In psychosocial ways, some have lost their sense of personal identity and experienced a loss of continuity and self-sameness. In resettling, they have been submitted to secondary stressors, which include threats and dangers due to illegal travel, compulsory prostitution, threat of discovery, and abandonment.

On arrival in another country, refugees submit a request for asylum. Until this request is granted they have minimal legal rights and are unable to participate in the host society. In some European countries, asylum-seeking procedures can take more than 7 years. In other countries, asylum seekers have only 48 hours to present evidence of being endangered in their countries of origin. In some countries, asylum seekers are imprisoned upon arrival because of not having proper travel documents, and they then await a residence permit in prisons and closed refugee camps. The bureaucratic processes of seeking asylum incur a high risk of retraumatization, including threatened repatriation, which is sufficient to cause an exacerbation of PTSD symptoms and depression (McCarrol, Fagan, Hermsen, & Ursano, 1997; Silove, McIntosh, & Becker, 1993).

Asylum seekers are confronted with new stressors due to poor living conditions, racism, issues of language barriers, changed family relationships, and different cultural traditions while waiting to be recognized as refugees. Asylum seekers are often ambivalent regarding their exile situations. On the one hand, they have relief at being alive and having an opportunity to start a "new life" in another country. On the other hand, there is sadness due to losses, trauma experienced, and anxiety caused by not knowing how to rebuild a new existence in an unknown surrounding. After several years, even when asylum seekers obtain refugee status, these sources of stress remain due to efforts to rehabilitate themselves. It is often the case that the horrors of political upheaval and war continue in their countries of origin, with family members and friends residing there, resulting in "uncertainty at distance."

Posttraumatic damage in asylum seekers and refugees extends beyond diagnostic criteria for PTSD (APA, 1994). Many victims suffer from core belief changes, developmental arrest, dissociative disorders, PTSD, depression, and substance abuse. Treating only PTSD symptoms and not providing care in the context of the person's current life is insufficient and could constitute a "conspiracy of silence" surrounding the issues of traumatization (Danieli, 1980).

DILEMMAS ABOUT TREATMENT: "TO TREAT OR NOT TO TREAT?" "NOW OR LATER?"

Different opinions exist with regards to therapeutic strategies in treatment of trauma victims. One crucial issue is the timing of treatment. Some clinicians argue for immediate treatment (Bremner, Douglas, Southwick, Darnell, & Charney, 1996; Solomon & Benbenishty, 1986). Other authors suggest that treatment of PTSD can start only after necessary feelings of basic safety are established (Herman, 1993).

In many Western countries, the policies toward asylum seekers have been conservative, that is, they wait to offer necessary help until refugees have official legal status. In these situations, treatment opportunities are made contingent on the victim's legal status and disposition as a refugee.

It is our experience that traumatized asylum seekers can be helped with their posttraumatic injuries independent of their legal standing (Droždek, 1997, 2001). Timely treatment helps restore basic trust and feelings of safety. The absence of trust makes adaptation to forced migration and asylum seeking even more stressful and can aggravate previous separations and earlier reactions to loss and trauma. The assumption that asylum seekers should "survive" migration and a long application procedure before treatment is potentially pathogenic. It seems that adequate psychological and social support during the *initial* phase of adaptation to migration is of the utmost importance to successful adaptation. Early psychosocial support is a decisive factor in the development and severity of PTSD symptoms (Engdahl, Dikel, Eberly, & Blank, 1997; Fontana & Rosenheck, 1994; Johnson, Lubin, Rosenheck, Fontana, Southwick, & Charney, 1997) and a crucial protective factor against the development of PTSD (Boscarino, 1995; Neria, Solomon, & Dekel, 1998; Wilson, Friedman, & Lindy, 2001). Lack of timely support closes off avenues for victims to ventilate their feelings and to assimilate the meaning of their experiences. Under these circumstances, acute stress reactions become salient. Victims will manifest dysfunctional adjustments in attempts to cope with their symptoms. Further, there is strong evidence that the longer PTSD symptoms persist, the less potential there is for remission (Kessler, Sonnega, Bromet, Hughes, & Nelson, 1995). General health concerns are also present since chronic PTSD is associated with poor health, frequent utilization of medical services, substance abuse, and higher cardiovascular morbidity (Droždek, Noor, Lutt, & Foy 2003; Ekblad & Roth, 1997; Friedman & Schnurr, 1995). An active approach with asylum seekers is preferable since most have no previous history of psychiatric illness. However, having psychological problems is stigmatizing in many countries, and interpretations of the meaning of psychological problems varies from culture to culture, which is one of the reasons why there is initial resistance to seeking help (Lee & Lu, 1988; Mollica, Wyshak, Lavelle, Truong, Tor, & Yang, 1990; Motta, 1993; Priebe & Esmaili, 1997). Nevertheless, by providing a secure therapeutic setting, basic trust and feelings of safety can be restored, especially since other sources of reassurance and care might be unavailable to asylum seekers.

COVERING AND UNCOVERING APPROACHES TO THE TREATMENT OF REFUGEES

The types of psychological treatment of traumatized asylum seekers and refugees differ in form and approach, depending on the needs and capacities of clients. Foy, Glynn, Schnurr, Jankowski, Wattenberg, Weiss, et al. (1992) distinguished two generic approaches: "covering" and "uncovering" treatment modalities. Asylum-seeking persons need support and structure in order to restore social patterns similar to what they had in their countries of origin. Empowerment techniques can help to reestablish a balance between psychological stress and coping resources. Where possible, traumatized asylum seekers and refugees can be treated successfully with "uncovering" treatment methods. Adequate clinical assistance can be combined with psychosocial interventions to effectively treat problems and avoid the traps of simply "medicating" overt psychological distress (Summerfield, 1997).

SUPPORTIVE AND TRAUMA-FOCUSED APPROACHES TO TREATMENT

The aim of supportive therapies is to mobilize the capacity for persons to cope with and resolve trauma-related problems. In an atmosphere of acceptance and emotional safety, treatments focus on correction of emotional experiences (Foy, Schnurr, Weiss, Wattenberg, Glynn, Marmar, et al., 2001). It is expected that trauma victims will generalize these salutary experiences to other areas of psychosocial functioning. Research evidence shows that cognitive behavioral therapies (CBTs) are effective in ameliorating PTSD symptoms (Wilson, Friedman, & Lindy, 2001). Thus, supportive therapies can offer a "corrective emotional context" in which to modify the effects of trauma, gradually readjusting the trauma-influenced worldviews and establishing more efficacious functioning.

"Uncovering" or trauma-focused therapies are traditionally divided into psychodynamic and cognitive-behavioral approaches. Psychodynamic approaches aim to provide trauma survivors understanding and insight about their experiences, and place emphasis on psychosocial defenses against vulnerability. The psychodynamic approach involves the exploration of conscious and unconscious ego processes as a result of trauma (Lindy & Wilson, 2001). It also promotes integration of unmetabolized traumatic material (Lindy & Wilson, 2001).

Cognitive-behavioral approaches aim at reducing PTSD symptoms by enhancing control of anxiety-based symptoms. CBT emphasizes application of systematic, prolonged exposure (PE) and cognitive restructuring of individual trauma experiences and relapse-prevention training. The latter approach enhances clients' coping skills and resources for maintaining control over specific PTSD and related symptoms (Foy, Ruzek, Glynn, Riney, & Gusman, 1997).

Cognitive interventions involve encouraging torture survivors, for example, to view behaviors under duress as normal responses necessary for survival in situations involving impossible choices (Basoglu, 1998). Cognitive-behavioral therapy (CBT) includes various anxiety-management strategies: stress management, relaxation training, cognitive restructuring, breathing techniques, social skills training, and distraction techniques. Research evidence shows that CBTs are effective in ameliorating PTSD symptoms (Wilson, Friedman, & Lindy, 2001). Research evidence also indicates that a combination of treatment techniques can be more effective than single-treatment modalities (Foa, Keane, & Friedman, 2000; Lindy, Wilson, & Friedman, 2001).

In selecting clinical modalities, there are more stringent requirements for "uncovering" techniques. Individuals need to be psychologically stable, have adequate impulse control, be able to tolerate strong affect, and be willing to reexperience their traumas. Supportive group therapy can be a better match for less-stable individuals or for those who do not accept the rationale for personal trauma processing (Foy, Glynn, Schnurr, Jankowski, Wattenberg, Weiss, et al., 1992).

Historically, different forms of "covering" and "uncovering" therapies have been developed. Wilson, Friedman, & Lindy (2001) review the various treatment approaches for PTSD. Regardless of the form of the therapy chosen, questions pertinent to the "uncovering" or "shoring up of defenses" approach remain paramount, and most treatments use aspects of both (Goodman & Weiss, 1998).

Short-term treatment strategies for different populations of trauma victims have been reported in literature (Nieves-Grafals, 2001). The approaches include short-term dynamic psychotherapy (Marmar, 1991), supportive work (Prout & Schwartz, 1991), thought control (Warda & Bryant, 1998), hypnosis (Cardena, Maldonado, Hart van der, & Spiegel, 2000), and eye movement desensitization reprocessing (EMDR) (Cahill, Carrigan, & Frueh, 1999; McNally, 1999; Poole, de Johng, & Spector, 1999; Shapiro, 1989). Clinicians have focused on interventions with families and couples because they provide a natural support network (Brende & Goldsmith, 1991; Craine, Hanks, & Stevens, 1992; Harkness & Zador, 2001; Miller, 1999; Rabin & Nardi, 1991). A combination of didactic and cognitive-behavioral strategies has been used successfully with war veterans and in groups (Lubin, Loris, Burt, & Johnson,

1998; Matsakis, 1992). Culture-specific techniques, such as the testimony method, have been developed (Aresti, 1988; Doerr-Zegers, Hartmann, Lira, & Weinstein, 1992; Kinzie, 2001). The testimony method relies on detailed written accounts of the trauma to assist in the catharsis and reintegration of the experience. Testimonies can further be used as a document of human rights violation in the struggle against torture and serve a role in the litigation process.

INDIVIDUAL AND GROUP TREATMENT APPROACHES FOR ASYLUM SEEKERS AND REFUGEES

Supportive and trauma-focused approaches are utilized in individual and group formats. Group psychotherapy is the treatment of choice for some PTSD patients (Herman, 1992; Koller, Marmar, & Kanas, 1992; Scurfield, 1993). Group treatment offers a supportive community and opportunities to identify with others who have shared a similar traumatic experience. In the treatment of asylum seekers and refugees, group therapy seems to be the treatment of choice. Asylum seekers and refugees suffer from isolation and social withdrawal, multiple traumatization, and forced migration. As a result of their experiences, they are suspicious and mistrustful of others (e.g., especially fellow countrymen) because of fear of retraumatization, betrayal, and so forth. They might suffer from high emotional arousal, fear of losing control over anger, aggressive impulses, or depression, which result in even greater isolation. Asylum seekers and refugees also live marginally in the host country. Those who migrate to a new culture without their families or persons of the same culture might not have the support of those who are in the same transitional position. A solid family group, when present and emotionally available, provides a "safe container" to manage and articulate the radical transition of forced migration (Le Roy, 1994). For many asylum seekers and refugees, a treatment group can have the same function. The group-treatment format offers opportunities to share common characteristics and to reattach emotionally to others.

Group therapy has emerged as a widely used treatment for PTSD, despite the preliminary nature of the evidence from research evaluating group techniques. Even with methodological limitations that constrain the scientific conclusions that can be drawn, positive treatment outcomes have been reported in most studies, lending general empirical support for the use of group therapy with trauma survivors. While three types (supportive, psychodynamic, and cognitive-behavioral) of group therapies are represented in the literature, treatment outcome findings do not presently favor a particular type. Indeed, it may well be that the three types are best used in sequence across recognizable phases of treatment for trauma survivors. At the present time, it is clear that much more research is warranted to identify techniques and procedures that produce superior outcomes (Foy, Schnurr, Weiss, Wattenberg, Glynn, Marmar, et al., 2001).

GROUP TREATMENTS ARE NOT FOR EVERYONE

Not all asylum seekers and refugees can be treated in a group format. The absence of positive motivational criteria is a counterindication for inclusion in group treatment. For example, torture victims who are unable to disclose personal concerns in a group might require individual treatment, especially for survivors of sexual torture. A more practical reason is not having enough clients who meet the positive motivational criteria for group treatment and who are not compatible by gender or language factors. In that case, a multilingual group can be formed. Due to the complexity of communication, such a group should be a supportive one (eventually combined with individual trauma-focused therapy) and contain no more than three interpreters. Using more than three translators in a group of 8 to 9 clients leads to difficult communication patterns and problems of group cohesion, without which there is a lack of permeability in communication, which makes group bonding difficult.

Asylum seekers are generally good candidates for group treatment modalities (see Figure 10.1). In comparison with other populations of trauma victims, indications for group treatment of asylum seekers and refugees surprisingly seem to be much less exclusive. Most asylum seekers have no prior experience with psychotherapy and mental health services and have not thought about sharing their psychological problems outside of their primary support network. Personal self-disclosure is predominantly a Western culture concept and alien to refugees. A "stable" living arrangement reflects life in a reception center with little privacy and restricted opportunities. The ability to connect with others and share similar traumatic experiences, as well as being of the same gender and speaking the same language as other group members, are the most important criteria. However, asylum seekers and refugees can be helped, even while being threatened with repatriation, having family members in danger in their country of origin, and not being able to participate in the host society. But, for sure, the therapeutic task is not an easy one.

PHASE-ORIENTED TREATMENT APPROACHES: AN INTEGRATIVE MODEL

The model for trauma-focused "uncovering" treatment of asylum seekers and refugees is one that has been developed and implemented during the past decade. In the Netherlands, we are working with groups of traumatized victims of political and war violence from all over the world who became asylum seekers and refugees in that country. This approach, known as the Den Bosch model (Droždek, 2001; Droždek,

- Higher functional levels of object relations (Ford, Fisher, & Larson, 1997), and presence of attachment capacities;
- Ability to establish interpersonal trust with other group members and leaders;
- Not being actively suicidal or homicidal;
- No current alcohol or drug abuse;
- Sharing similar traumatic experiences with other group members;
- Being compatible for gender and language (not necessary ethnicity) with other members;
- Willing to abide by rules of group confidentiality;
- Not being psychotic, severely paranoid, or sociopath;
- Not having severe cognitive deficits (among others as a consequence of head trauma during torture);
- Not being violent or out of control of impulses;
- Not being bullies, monopolizers, or scapegoat the group process;
- Being able to tolerate strong affects and high anxiety arousal;
- Strong enough motivation and willingness to share personal traumatic experiences in a group.

Fig. 10.1 Indication Criteria for Group Therapy of Asylum Seekers

van Dijk, & de Winter, 2002), is similar to phase-oriented trauma treatments and especially the five-phase model developed by Meichenbaum (1994). It incorporates some important adaptations, given the unique needs of asylum seekers and refugees. To date, there have been no empirical studies of this model.

The Den Bosch model can be applied in individual and group formats and combined with nonverbal therapies (see Chapters 14, 16, 17 in this volume). Originally, it was designed as a group-treatment program within an intensive, 3-day a week, multidisciplinary day-treatment setting. The model combines different approaches and interventions and focuses on traumatic events and issues caused by forced migration. It tries to enrich Western-oriented psychotherapy methods with a culturally sensitive attitude, which makes its use possible with ethnically different populations. Asylum seekers can participate in trauma-focused treatment while being confronted with existential uncertainty due to the risk of repatriation. To be sure, it is no easy task for them to undertake.

The Den Bosch model combines psychodynamic, cognitive-behavioral therapy (CBT), and supportive treatment approaches. It is designed to help members place their traumas in a life-span developmental perspective. The purpose of treatment is to help members clarify their reactions to traumatic events, including cognitions about the meaning of their experiences. Treatment gives each individual the opportunity to reconstruct the history of what happened to him or her and to integrate dissociated emotions and memories (Rozynko & Dondershine, 1991; Wilson, Friedman, & Lindy, 2001).

Another goal of the model is to reduce PTSD symptoms and to enhance victims' control of disregulated affects through prolonged exposure and cognitive restructuring techniques. There is also an autobiographical emphasis concerned with the trauma history.

Relapse prevention training is another goal. It provides coping skills and resources for maintaining control over specific PTSD symptoms

(Foy, Ruzek, Glynn, Riney, & Gusman, 1997). Recognizing that chronic PTSD frequently involves lifelong risk for symptom recurrence, treatment challenges members to set realistic goals while managing risks of symptom exacerbation. Intensive treatment is followed by an after-care program of unlimited duration, recognizing the ongoing needs of the chronically traumatized.

The goal of achieving a "corrective emotional experience" is also important and members get opportunities to reevaluate their damaged core beliefs (Janoff-Bulman, 1985). New methods of dealing with stress are learned, and clients establish bonds with therapists and other group members that will facilitate future therapy. The Den Bosch treatment model can be effectuated on three levels: by understanding and incorporating trauma experiences and their consequences into identity; by reducing intrusive PTSD symptoms, and by establishing corrective emotional experiences and repairing damaged core beliefs.

MAKING CONTACT WITH DIVERSE TRAUMA CLIENTELE

To establish the therapeutic alliance at least five factors are of critical significance to outcome. First, a mutually respectful relationship between therapist and client is needed. Second, the creation of trust and safety is essential and promoted by transparency, calmness, and predictability of action. The clinical program, with its different phases, goals, interventions, and expectations from clients is presented to clients before treatment begins. Third, program guidelines have to be respected and "secret agendas" are not permitted. Fourth, therapists exhibit tolerance and have the capacity to "decode messages" from their clients. These messages are sometimes "hidden" due to different cultural backgrounds. Fifth, a culturally sensitive attitude must be adopted by therapists. Therapists ask clients to guide them about issues rooted in their culture. Some practical tips help therapists to establish a better contact. A therapist is expected to be familiar with culturally appropriate greetings and styles of interaction. For example, signs of respect vary from culture to culture, from putting a hand on the chest after shaking hands in the Middle East or North Africa; kissing hands in Afghanistan; to kissing a shoulder in Iran. A two-handed handshake from an Ethiopian man signals respect, affection, and trust, while clients from Iran or Afghanistan will never enter a room before the therapist out of respect. These customs convey some understanding between client and therapist that goes beyond words. They help to develop the relationship and allay the anxiety inherent in talking to a stranger about personal concerns (Nieves-Grafals, 2001).

IMPORTANCE OF AUTHENTICITY IN THERAPISTS

Therapists are expected to be authentic. Awareness of one's own professional role is of crucial importance due to transference and countertransference issues in trauma treatment (see Chapter 11 of this volume). Therapists can develop a whole spectrum of countertransference roles from becoming the clients "rescuer" to withdrawing from the therapeutic relationship and terminating treatment prematurely (see Chapter 11 of this volume; Wilson & Lindy, 1994). Unlike many traditional psychotherapeutic settings, therapists are expected to advocate for their clients outside of the treatment setting. Contacts with lawyers, ministries, social services, and so forth are established as a part of a comprehensive and morally responsible treatment plan. Therapists, of course, need to be aware of their professional boundaries. They should not go "too far" in advocacy roles. Supervision is therefore always important, given this proactive clinical stance.

Therapists are passionate about their work and compassionate with their clients. Therapists make it clear that they are firmly against the use of violence in the context of political terror and human rights violations. Therapists have to adjust their therapeutic styles to fit their own personality because a key healing ingredient is the genuineness of the relationship (Stadter, 1996).

In a group format, the therapist is a professional leader who is active and concerned with the group members' well-being (Lystad, Rice, & Kaplan, 1996). Therapists adopt an active unstructured listening stance since such a demeanor is reassuring for refugees. A silent therapist can be perceived as cold and rejecting, raising the client's anxiety. It is very important for the therapist to have the "split-eye view" of group functioning throughout treatment with attention focused simultaneously on the structure of the treatment process and group dynamics. Refugee clients provide a sense of commonality, cohesion, and opportunity to restore a sense of usefulness through helping others. Group members will exhibit catharsis, commonality of experience, and guidance while participating in a group.

GROUP STRUCTURE AND INITIAL TREATMENT EXPECTATIONS

The membership of the group is optimally comprised of eight to nine persons. It is helpful if members are homogeneous in terms of ego functioning, interpersonal skills, and ability to confront defenses. Members should be of the same gender and speak the same language. However, positive results have been reported in mixed-gender groups of refugee and war victims (Tocilj-Simunkovic & Tata Arcel, 1998) and heterogeneous nonrefugee groups mixing trauma survivors and nontraumatized individuals (Nicholas & Forrester, 1999). In our experience, mixing male with female clients is not recommended when victims have experienced sexual violence. Fear of stigma due to sexual violation makes sharing of these experiences with the opposite sex difficult, if not impossible. Same interpreters should be used throughout treatment. Translation "in person" is preferred to that by phone. The group must be of a "closed" type.

There are usually two group facilitators in each group. A male and female therapist couple is preferable. This combination offers clients the experience that the "other gender can understand their trauma" without being adversely impacted by the trauma story. Candidates are screened by facilitators in order to determine their readiness for group treatment before joining the group. In cases where members have no prior treatment, personality assessments are made. Individuals with evident sociopathy, personality disorders, or motivation for secondary gain are disastrous to group cohesion and therapeutic goal attainment.

It is recommended to document the veracity of traumatic experiences. However, this is difficult since records for asylum seekers might not be available. Therapists may have to rely on collateral information and reports from clients that support authenticity of disclosures.

Questioning clients during intake about what their expectations are for treatment is based on the idea of clients' active participation in diagnosis and treatment. These questions can be sometimes very confusing for non-Western clients, who do not understand them, might feel misunderstood, and not taken seriously ("If I knew that, I would not come to consult you"). When working with clients from non-Western cultures, it is important to consider the role of "the doctor" in countries of origin. A friendly, nonegalitarian client-therapist relationship is preferable. Trauma clients need to feel protected by a therapist, who forms a "cocoon" around their tumultuous ego states and can be idealized as protector. The "cocoon of safety" is considered a prerequisite for experiencing distressive affect (Garfield & Leveroni, 2000). Later in treatment, deidealization of the therapist takes place with clients showing less regressive tendencies.

The time-limited group treatment model is designed to last for 1 year and consists of twice weekly group sessions lasting 1.5 hours. Due to the complexity of asylum seekers' and refugees' problems and use of interpreters, treatment takes both patience and time.

In comparison to individual forms of therapy for PTSD, group therapies tend to be more structured and place rigid requirements upon individual participation. There is less flexibility for accommodating clients' individual needs that can arise during the course of therapy. Group sessions are thematic, structured by therapists, and focus on traumatic events. Other foci, such as emergent personal relationships between group members or processes within a group, are avoided. Conflicts within a group have to be handled expeditiously with sensitivity for culturally rooted conflict management methods.

In a trauma-focused group, culturally sensitive interpretations are used as needed. As treatment progresses well, the therapist does not have to insist on searching for explanatory schema within clients' cultural backgrounds. A culturally sensitive approach is important in the pre- and postexposure phases of trauma treatment and includes illness models, problems definition, treatment expectations, adaptation to forced migration, or cultural differences between the original and host country.

AN OVERVIEW OF THE FIVE-PHASE TREATMENT MODEL

The treatment model consists of five phases. The introductory phase is devoted to building a therapeutic alliance, group cohesion, setting group norms, rules, defining the group members' individual problems, psychoeducation, and treatment of symptoms. The second phase involves case concepts and members' life stories. The third phase utilizes cognitive behavioral treatments. The fourth phase focuses on members' present and future, their current worries, and issues of identity, cultural differences, adaptation to the host society, danger of repatriation, and changes in core beliefs. In the fifth phase, issues of treatment termination, relapse prevention, and preparation of clients for joining a self-help group are processed. Completion of the treatment is marked by a ritualized farewell ceremony (see Figure 10.2).

After the intensive treatment, clients enroll in the after-care program where they can remain for an indefinite period of time. Long-term object constancy is of utmost importance for asylum seekers and refugees with chronic posttraumatic damage. The therapist and a peer group should remain available to the client in times of need, much like that of a small-town primary care physician. The therapist-client relationship extends beyond the termination of sessions and acts as an "invisible safety net" that will allow the client to seek therapy should the need arise again (Nieves-Grafals, 2001).

Phase 1: Establishing the Therapeutic Alliance

During the first phase, treatment is focused on establishment of the therapeutic alliance and assessment of clients' problems. This phase takes approximately 10 sessions and is didactic. In all phases of treatment therapists can use flip-chart visual aids as necessary to support their presentation in groups.

The first issues discussed are norms, rules, and values of group treatment. Clients are asked to be on time and to indicate when they cannot attend sessions. They cannot smoke or drink during sessions. They can leave the treatment room *only* if they feel that they are at imminent risk of explosive violence or if they cannot tolerate their anxiety. In case of medical problems, such as those associated with torture, clients can

Phase 1	Phase 2	Phase 3	Phase 4	Phase 5
Norms, values, and rules of group psychotherapy Therapeutic alliance Psychoeducation Assessment of problems Treatment goals/ expectation Treatment of symptoms	Presentation of biographies Other topics: Damaged core beliefs Fear of loss of control Guilt Shame Grief	Telling the trauma story Exposure and cognitive restructuring	Reconnecting the present with the past and the future Damaged core beliefs Roles and identity Coping strategies Current worries and future outlooks	Psychoeducation Relapse prevention Treatment evaluation Farewell ritual

After-Care Program
Topics: relapse, daily-life stress, marital, child-rearing or job/professional problems, medication control, procedure of seeking asylum, guiding, support, and advocacy

Fig. 10.2 The Phase-Oriented Trauma Treatment

stand up and stretch during the session. Aggressive behavior, use of drugs, alcohol, cellular phones, or possession of weapons are strictly forbidden and violations will result in expulsion from the group. Facilitators are harsh in sanctioning this rule because of members' pronounced anxiety and mistrust of one another due to their prior life experiences. Members cannot discuss group issues outside of sessions.

The use of translators requires agreements among members who are asked to wait their turn to say something in the group unless otherwise decided by facilitators. Although painstaking, translators make translations after individual contributions. This means, of course, that members are not supposed to talk with one another, allowing translation only at the end of discussion. This makes spontaneous conversation in the group difficult, but it enables facilitators to follow the process and intervene in a timely way. Members are taught that respect, safety, and trust are the key components of a group treatment. Clients often do not feel safe when surrounded with compatriots, fearing they might be spies. Gossip might be a part of their culture and life within a resettlement center where people "control" one another in an effort to create a secure environment. If the information about participants in group treatment spreads throughout the community, asylum seekers worry that others might think they are "crazy" and avoid them.

While defining norms and values of group treatment, therapists are warm, optimistic, and purposely authoritarian. Regulations are not submitted to discussion and members are required to accept them. However, clients can comment on group rules. They might want to "see how far they can go" in questioning the therapist's authority or escape from the anxiety-evoking anomie of a beginning group. In one group, a client stated that he knew about group treatment in the center, even before he started treatment. This meant, he said, that in previous groups, members were talking about issues with other nonparticipants, and that the confidentiality rule makes no sense.

Psychoeducation

The first phase of the model includes education. Facilitators teach members about topics including: PTSD symptoms, memory dysfunction following trauma, changes in brain function and other biological consequences of extreme traumatization, the process of forced migration, torture, and its consequences. Group members are made aware of the specific goals of torture. As pointed out by Somnier and Genefke (1986), there is evidence that torture is scientifically designed with the purpose of distorting normal psychological mechanisms and the personality of the victim. Education includes the description of the treatment protocol and themes that will be addressed. Therapists act analogously to good surgeons, presenting a "complete surgery procedure to their clients before they operate." Clear structure, basic rules about safety, and awareness of the therapeutic alliance are necessary to counter retraumatization of the client (Wilson & Lindy, 1994).

Education is important because it informs clients about the nature of their psychological disturbances and lowers anxiety over the fear of "going crazy." Some clients do not understand why they are suffering from PTSD symptoms when the immediate threat of danger has passed. Others doubt their self-esteem and ask themselves whether they have become "sick and weak."

The consequences of traumatization are presented and discussed. A biopsychosocial model is used to explain PTSD as a normal reaction to abnormal stress and life-threatening situations. Therapists indicate that part of the recovery process is to establish control over painful memories. Generally, the use of metaphors is helpful and well accepted. For example, "a victim has an old wound that is half open and soft on the inside. That is why this wound still hurts." In treatment therapists try to "reopen the wound, clean it out and let it heal" (Vesti, Somnier, & Kastrup, 1992). Therapists explain, while discussing treatment, that its goal is not to forget traumas from the past, but to help victims accept them, continue their lives, and gain control over intrusive symptoms.

Patients have different thoughts regarding their mental health status and treatment needs: "I am not crazy; so why should I be treated"; "I want to forget all"; "I do not want to forget anything"; "Nobody can help me, bad things happened and that's it."

Clients are warned that it is not uncommon to feel worse in the course of treatment because painful memories are being stimulated through discussion. It is explained that such states are temporary and the end result of the treatment is a superior level of functioning and feelings of well-being.

Potential Pitfalls in Phase 1 Treatment

Clients with different cultural backgrounds usually do not have problems understanding and accepting the clinical conceptualization of their problems. Suffering from PTSD is explained as a prolonged stress response and that there is no need to feel the stigma of being a psychiatric patient. Nevertheless, some groups of clients need additional education and explanations.

For example, patients from some African countries have problems accepting treatment and verbalizing their traumatic experiences because of beliefs that it is inappropriate to talk about "deceased ones." By doing so, the deceased spirits awaken because of a lack of respect. Other clients present their expectations for treatment: "If I get another child, I'll feel much better" (getting a child is a present from God, and a sign that God has forgiven me), or "I just want my children to find their way in the new country and have a better life. This will cure all my wounds." These clients require a longer process of negotiation prior to group treatment. Other clients have specific explanations for causality in suffering. In some African societies it is believed that one deserves "traumatic events" when they happened. One gets punished because of faults ancestors made in the past. In these societies, "a collective superego" dominates over the individual one (Peltzer, 1995). Yet clients can believe in the concept of karma and reincarnation. They believe that their present life circumstances are determined by their deeds in previous lives. This encourages a greater sense of fatalism and acceptance of suffering (Morris & Silove, 1992). Fatalism is also inherent in Islam, where one's faith is in the hands of God.

Idealization of Therapists as Rescuers

The didactic teaching approach helps victims idealize their therapists. To clients, therapists appear to have answers to the critical questions and understand what has happened and know the "secret of healing." Idealization is present because clients see their therapists as safe persons who will help them. This idealizing perspective creates an asymmetrical client-therapist relationship. One of the pitfalls for Western therapists is that they might try to replace this relationship with an egalitarian one and not be able to tolerate clients' submissive behavior and cultural-based expectations. A pitfall is the tendency to interpret the client's need for regression as a personality trait or disorder, a resistance, or as an attempt to achieve secondary gain. It is necessary to be aware that some clients overgeneralize their therapist's power. It is important for the therapist to limit unrealistic expectations and unambiguously define the professional role. The therapist needs to support clients in solving social and legal problems but to remain within the boundaries of a professional role.

Education enables clients to recognize their symptoms and place them within the PTSD stress paradigm. Therapists share information and identify similarities in member dispositions in order to promote communication and group cohesion. They give permission to talk about subjects of importance. Clients who want to explain excessive aspects of their traumatic experiences are asked by therapists not to do so. They will have this opportunity later on in treatment.

Transparency and predictability of the therapist promote safety in the group. Group leaders facilitate an atmosphere of "safety" and a sense of confidence in their competence. Active leadership is necessary early in group development. Whenever it seems appropriate, however, the leaders solicit input and commentary from the group members themselves (Foy, Schnurr, Weiss, Wattenberg, Glynn, Marmar, et al., 2001).

At the start of treatment, the "seductive clinical attitude" is therapeutically helpful. Therapists profile themselves as experienced professional authorities, knowledgeable about trauma and its consequences, who are able to contain clients' feelings and provide answers to questions. Clients find it reassuring that therapists recognize their pain and connect it to their traumatic experiences. Although therapists can present themselves as being equal or even submissive to clients, they show a clear intention to learn from their experiences by allowing clients to be "guides" to the treatment process. The art of alternating between these two roles (i.e., seductive oscillation) is the foundation of the "seductive therapeutic attitude." It is useful for the therapist to learn the client's language and use native words whenever possible to strengthen respect, attachment, and the therapeutic alliance.

Setting Initial Treatment Goals

Once problems have been defined through education, treatment goals have to be set. Clients are invited to define three personal goals to achieve within a year's time. These goals have to be as measurable and precisely formulated as possible. Clients set goals such as having fewer nightmares, being able to play with their children without getting irritable, or sleeping 5 hours per night without awakening. Unrealistic goals and expectations can be corrected. Later, these goals can be incorporated into treatment. Strategies necessary to achieve goals are discussed as well. Therapists make clear that clients share responsibility for treatment outcome and that progress occurs *only* when therapist and client are a team.

Treatment of PTSD symptoms and comorbidity is an important task within the first phase of treatment, but also continues into the second phase. Where necessary, medication is prescribed. The use of medication is not compulsory but is encouraged because of effectiveness in providing symptom relief (Friedman, 2001). Positive effects of medication promote clients' trust in treatment and make forthcoming confrontation with traumatic reexperiencing easier to tolerate.

Relaxation Techniques

Relaxation exercise techniques are used to relieve symptoms. Relaxation exercises are combined with listening to recorded material at home. The therapist makes an audio tape of the relaxation exercise and advises clients to listen to the tape as necessary. A tape with the therapist's voice can serve the function of a transitory transference object. Similar to guided imagery, "permissive hypnotherapy" exercise teaches clients to automatically switch to safe and pleasurable memories when they experience distressing memories. This exercise can also be recorded on a tape and given to clients. Some problems associated with this method range from clients not being able to close their eyes during exercise out of fear of losing control, to those of not being able to concentrate on good memories and getting overwhelmed by intrusive, distressing trauma-related imagery.

Emergent Group Structure and Role Conflict

In the 9th or the 10th session, conflicts between members often occur. Members blame others for breaking the rules, especially that of confidentiality. They fight for leadership. In a group of clients from Iran and Afghanistan, for example, facilitators were confronted with a tendency of the majority of members to generalize their experiences, ideas, and beliefs. The client would present something in the group not as a personal belief, but as the "ultimate and only possible truth." This attitude led to conflicts since members had differing points of view.

It is important to avoid the *improper validation* of personal tragedies such as who has suffered the most or who has lost more. Group treatment is focused on recovery and regaining control over one's life, not on the severity of an individual's tragedy. Resistance is typically expressed by anxiety and lack of trust through forms of tardiness, reluctance to participate in group sessions, and open questioning of the usefulness of the group therapy.

A Case Example: Tschechnya War and Torture Victims

In a group of male war and torture victims from Tschechnya, two members competed for attention and monopolized the group. As a result, other members did not have much "space" in which to participate. When one client shared something in the group, the other one immediately shared more material. These two clients were the most respected in the group. One was the eldest, and the other had most recently left Tschechnya and had spent the most time in the war zone. They were fighting for power and control in this early phase of the group and others did not react to them.

One of the clients told about the devaluation of morals in Tschechnya. As the war went on people stopped respecting each other. The elderly, for example, would be physically overpowered by the younger when trying to get sugar from humanitarian aid. Before the war, such behavior was unacceptable; the elderly were the most respected in society. During the war, one had to survive. "You never know whether and if more are going to arrive. I still feel like I'm in the war," said the younger client. The therapists interpreted the parallel between the fighting for humanitarian aid during the war and for the therapist's attention in the group. They reassured the group that their attention for clients' problems will be present throughout the treatment and not disappear like "a pack of sugar." The monopolizing for power, control, and attention stopped immediately following integrative feedback.

Issues of Cultural Norms in Treatment

Examples of the influence of culture on treatment are important to understand. In a group of Iranian male clients, for example, age is traditionally more valued than experience or education. Respect for the elderly and their viewpoints is an important norm. In one group, younger members, who were several years out of country and whose traditional identity had transformed into a more Westernized one, started to oppose traditional values and challenged the norm of respect. In another group, elderly clients who were traditionally expected to take leadership positions were not able to do so because of posttraumatic psychiatric damage. It took time before younger group members assumed the leadership role and overcame the fear of insulting elderly group members.

Survivors from republics of the former Soviet Union (Azerbaijan, Armenia, Tschechnya, Nagorno-Karabah) provide another example. This group needed authoritarian leadership because of the historically shaped background of former Soviet people. While living under the communist regime they had less freedom but more hierarchical social structure. When the Soviet Union dissolved, people were more open and did not have to rehearse their "cultural identity" in an "underground" way. At the same time, safety disappeared and old ethnic conflicts resumed. Being forced to migrate, these victims came to the Netherlands where they were told that they were free from political constraints. Now, the problem was how to be authentic when it had been forbidden or dangerous in the past. In this group, an authoritarian type of leadership made clients less anxious and facilitated their participation. In a treatment setting victims can separate from a group identity in a safe way and enjoy their own individual selfhood without being killed, damaged, or punished for political reasons.

Group psychotherapy, like the natural development of small groups, evolves through a series of phases. Social psychologists who study group dynamics have referred to three predictable phases as "forming, storming, norming and performing" (Aronoff & Wilson, 1985). Yalom (1995) had developed a technique to stimulate "storming" in group psychotherapy by asking members to comment on each other's "good" and "bad" characteristics as observed in the group. This task evokes a wide range of affect and information about the issues that confront individual members and the group as a whole. It also exposes therapists to their vulnerability, differences in cultural perceptions, and how criticisms are received among the group members. Indeed, as documented in research or group dynamics, a "storming exercise or phase" is usually followed by greater cohesion and "norm" establishment. In several groups of clients from the Middle East, this exercise had an almost disastrous impact on group cohesion. Group members only complimented each other, while small-scale animosities between them were obviously present in the group at the time. When facilitators insisted on truth in the group and confronted members with their behavior, members started to talk about each other's good and bad characteristics in order to please therapists, but very soon felt insulted and stopped talking at all. Later on, therapists learned that in some clients' culture, people do not criticize one another openly, and that they even do not know how to do that in a polite, constructive, and noninsulting way. At the same time they also seemed to be having problems with reception of criticism. Therapists learned that this exercise focuses too much on interpersonal dynamics within a group, while focuses other than trauma, in an uncovering, trauma-focused group of asylum seekers and refugees must be avoided. Clients themselves criticized the exercise, saying that it had a bad influence on group cohesion. They found it difficult to cause other group members to be sad through their criticism, they were afraid of their own reactions on criticism, and afraid of misuse of information shared in the group. Also, they were afraid of being authentic, because expressing meaning and opinions brought them into problems earlier in life.

Nonverbal Techniques of Trust Building

Coping with group tensions can be facilitated by nonverbal exercises. These exercises strengthen group cohesion, reestablish connection between mind and body (grounding), and foster communication between members on an experiential level. Members might be asked to massage each other (potentially dangerous in a group of victims of sexual violence) or clasp themselves over the body. A group can carry one member on their hands through the therapy room or carefully support one member while the rest of the group forms a circle around the person. Members can be asked to communicate with one another nonverbally or to copy one another's idiosyncrasies, breathing, or posture. In another exercise, members sit on the ground in pairs, leaning on another's back and supporting each other in order to be aware of their own strengths and that of other group members.

It is also possible to make use of dramatic techniques. For example, in the case of having a group member who was afraid of sharing, an empty chair is put in the middle of the group circle and a "virtual" group member with the same background and problems as the client sat on it. Members were asked to discuss their doubts about sharing in a group and developed hypotheses about why they had doubts, uncertainties, and apprehensions.

A few words need to be said about the communication in the group. While talking, facilitators try to establish eye contact with group members. However, when members talk, they usually look at the translator even when they are responding directly to facilitator's questions. This interferes with the facilitator's ability to positively affirm members' self-disclosures. We have found few, if any, alternatives to this process. At the end of the first phase facilitators help members make a list of the individual presentations that will take place in the second phase.

Phase 2: Focus on Trauma and Autobiography

Phase 2 is 20 weeks long in a small group of 8 or 9 members. In this phase clients present their life stories. Each presentation takes at least one session. Members are expected to talk about significant events in their life.

History and Life-Span Review

A presentation can start with the birth of a client, but if necessary, a complete family history. The therapist ensures that relevant themes, like background, lifestyle, cultural issues, or traditions, are raised for consideration. The aim is to give a balanced presentation with emphasis on both "good" and "bad" memories to counterbalance tendencies to present only with a victim identity. Therapists make clients aware of a continuum of their existence in time and try to reestablish links between past, present, and future (Grinberg & Grinberg, 1984). This perceived gap in time perspective is typically a consequence of forced migration and traumatization. It is explained that traumatic experiences leave people "mute" and unable to find words to describe what has happened to them. Finding words to describe one's experiences is conceptualized as an important step toward recovery and the processing of trauma.

During the client's presentation, group members ask questions and request clarifications. At the same time they are instructed not to make statements about value choices and to avoid discussions about politics and religion. The structured presentations provide the opportunity for group members to share in the leadership role from which they benefit by gaining increased self-esteem and motivation.

Universal Themes Common to Asylum Seekers

After case presentations, facilitators direct the group process and offer consideration of universal themes common to trauma survivors. These include: (a) damaged core beliefs of trust and safety; (b) fear of loss of control over feelings of rage and anxiety; (c) shame over the helplessness evoked by torture or war trauma; (d) rage and grief at the sudden loss of control over life plans; (e) guilt and shame over surviving and being unable to save others; and (f) grief over the loss of significant others through death and exile. Sessions begin with a didactic, educational phase, explaining the "roots" of the above mentioned themes. Education lowers anxiety and defines these experiences as universal. Facilitators stimulate group interaction around a chosen topic, stress its universality, promote mutual respect among group members, and discuss individual coping strategies. When a client gets retraumatized in treatment, core beliefs get altered more rapidly than PTSD symptoms.

Testing the Therapists' Limits to Maintain a Safe Holding Environment

Disclosure of painful feelings is frequently accompanied by testing the therapists' ability to understand the horrors of torture and war (Wilson & Lindy, 1994). Group members need to feel reassured that therapists know how to encourage self-disclosure, particularly when overwhelming affects are emerging. Clients try to avoid unpleasant feelings by attempts to steer the process into discussions of international political events, history, or problems they face in seeking asylum.

In a group of male torture victims from Iran and Afghanistan, for example, clients had different political backgrounds and were members of different political parties. Group discussion about politics and religion replicated the political conflict the clients had in their countries of origin and endangered the cohesion of the group. It was a form of individual and collective resistance to the treatment process.

At the end of the second phase, members are asked to prepare future discussions of trauma experiences. At this point, groups show minimal defenses against CBT exposure treatment. Drop-outs occur, however, when trauma themes are discussed and the group is prepared for exposure therapy.

In terms of conflict resolution, different strategies are used that originate in understanding the members' cultures. Therapists assume responsibility and actively intervene in conflict. The primary binding factors for conflict resolution are the shared traumatic experiences as a consequence of war, political violence, and losses due to forced migration. Working through their psychological consequences is a primary goal of group treatment. However, an in-depth exploration of personal conflict, at this point, is contraindicated. Such therapeutic activity is properly the province of individual treatment.

Phase 3: Telling the Trauma Story: Prolonged Exposure and Cognitive Restructuring

After 4 months, the group enters phase 3 of treatment. This phase takes about 12 to 15 sessions to complete. In phase 3, the "past" is the focus of treatment. *Telling the trauma story is the central task.* Here, the need for safety is balanced with the need to face what happened during the trauma. Facilitators and clients "travel" together symbolically to places where members' most traumatizing experiences occurred. Together, the group reexperiences the trauma of the other clients and attempts to find answers to such questions as: "Why did this happen to me? Am I responsible for the traumatic event?" "What am I going to do if the same thing happens again?"

Limited degrees of trauma exposure (i.e., reexperiencing) and cognitive restructuring are the techniques used in this phase according to specific protocol (Carroll & Foy, 2000). Little adaptation is needed in order to make them useful for asylum seekers and refugees. In each session a client presents his or her story. Exposure therapy is evaluated every fourth session. Doing exposure therapy sequentially with eight to nine persons is stressful, taxing, and potentially retraumatizing. The risk for burn-out, compassion fatigue, and countertransference is high (see Chapter 11 of this volume).

In phase 3, cohesion and solidarity in the group are at their highest level. Members take care of one another, and therapists facilitate the formation of a buddy system. Before starting exposure treatment, each member is assigned as a "buddy." The buddy's "task" is to support a peer and help him or her get through difficult times of the exposure phase. Members are informed that the risk of PTSD symptoms intensifies during exposure treatment.

Trauma Exposure and Reexperience as a Three-Act Play

The treatment procedure has an autobiographical emphasis that combines individual narrative construction and the group responsibility of bearing witness in a nonjudgmental way. By encouraging group members to repeatedly experience their personal traumas, as well as being exposed vicariously to those of other group members, the procedure automatically evokes trauma processing.

Therapists prepare clients *prior* to exposure sessions. Since reexperiencing past horrors causes significant suffering, the client's medical condition is assessed before treatment. Cardiovascular risk warrants exclusion from this type of trauma treatment. The therapist helps the client select a traumatic scene from his or her past. The traumatic event that client reexperiences, fears, or avoids the most is the one that is selected for exposure treatment. The scenes involve a tragic outcome with a fear of death being the dominant emotional reaction. Themes of perpetration or rage are avoided. Exposure lasts for about 45 minutes and is organized as a "three-act play metaphor."

Act 1 contains a description of events prior to a tragic moment. Act 2 is a vivid description of a traumatic incident. Here the therapist concentrates on affect, thoughts, details, sensory perceptions, and reactions during the event. Act 3 is a description of the aftermath of trauma. The client is asked about the meaning that the event has had in his or her life. The client is asked to tell his or her story in the first-person present tense, as if the event were occurring now, and to close his or her eyes during narration. Interestingly, most clients keep their eyes open out of fear of losing control. The exposure session can begin and end with a relaxation exercise for the whole group. The client sits next to the therapist who leads the exposure treatment. A tape recorder is used to record the session. The cotherapist sits on the other side of the group circle and monitors others during the session. Other group members are instructed to listen to exposure and, if possible, not to leave the room or make noise.

The therapist monitors the client and interrupts his or her narration if the client is in danger of losing control. The therapist states: "If I ask you to talk about something that is too *painful*, please tell me, and I will stop immediately. In order to help you I have to know as many details as possible about your story." In our experience, clients never ask the therapist to stop. However, the therapist informs the client that episodes of losing control are rare, but if the emotional intensity becomes too great, the client can briefly stop as necessary. After the exposure, group members have the opportunity to talk about the emotional impact of the session.

Dosing Treatment and Measuring Affective Distress

To prevent dissociation, it is important that clients' affective involvement be dosed. The therapist measures the client's heart rate and uses the subjective units of distress (SUDs) scale to determine discomfort levels. Monitoring sheets are used to record heart rate and SUDs. The procedure is repeated at the end of exposure. When an exposure session starts, the client tells his or her trauma "story" with as much imagery and detail as possible. The goal is to have the victim tell the "story" without omitting details or rushing to avoid painful memories and feelings. The therapist uses "sensory prompts" (e.g., "What are you seeing? hearing? smelling?"). It is helpful to use a metaphor of "stopping the movie camera" to improve the client's visual image clarity (e.g., "We can stop the movie now, and focus with the camera on this detail.").

Role of Translator During Exposure Treatment

The role of translator is very important during exposure. The client is taught to stop the narrative when feeling overloaded. A translation can be requested when the counselor thinks that the client might lose control. Pressing the "start" and "stop" buttons of a cassette tape recorder can serve to control exposure. When the client hears the click of the recorder he or she can distance him- or herself from traumatic memories or prepare to continue with the story. The therapist does not record the entire session, only the trauma narrative and the translation of his or her own questions. In this way, the recorded material is in the same language, which makes it easier to review. Therapists should be attuned to subtle but significant omissions or incongruities in narration since they identify dysfunctional thoughts, thinking, and distortions about the trauma. Once finished and the client's heart rate and SUDs have been measured, group discussion of the trauma story can begin.

Case Examples: Hossein From Iran and Soeren From Armenia

After the exposure treatment of Hossein, an Iranian war veteran, the group focused on his reactions. Hossein felt guilty. He was in a situation in which he was seriously wounded and left a wounded comrade at the frontline. Hossein could not carry him through the minefields as he himself was wounded and being chased by enemy soldiers. The comrade was alive, unconscious, and severely bleeding from the neck. Hossein believed that either they both would be killed or that only he could survive by taking care of himself.

Analyzing his feelings, Hossein told the group that he felt guilty because he "permitted" himself to be wounded earlier that day. Instead of waiting in the frontline trenches, he went to help others who were stuck in the minefields. He succeeded in bringing them back to the base camp but was wounded in the process. The therapist's task, at this point, was to reframe Hossein's traumatic experience into an act of strength and courage rather than reinforcing his feelings of powerlessness, shame, and guilt.

In another example, Soeren, an Armenian man from Azerbaijan, felt guilt and shame because of the torture and humiliation he endured. Also, he witnessed the rape of his wife and could not prevent it. Afterward, he was very angry with the perpetrators and continued his political activities in the country of asylum. It was suggested that when he felt guilty and ashamed, Soeren experienced what perpetrators want him to feel, namely, shame. Therefore, to fight back he had to overcome these feelings. Soeren expressed surprise and said that he had not thought about the situation in that way. Some months later, he echoed the therapist's words while trying to help another group member.

At the end of the exposure treatment, clients are asked to comfort others by hugging them or sharing an encouraging message: "I am glad that you have survived," "I am proud of you," "You are strong," "Your suffering was not in vain," or "You are not alone, I am with you."

Homework Assignment: Desensitization Through Repeated Exposures

In the course of the treatment clients have homework assignments. They are asked to listen to recorded exposure material and rate their distress before and after listening. The optimal number of homework trials ranges from 8 to 15. Homework sessions end when the client is bored and listening does not provoke distress. However, the frequency of listening to the tapes varies from individual to individual. Some clients want to go through the assignment as fast as possible. Others continuously postpone the assignment. We recommend listening to the tapes one or two times a week, especially before the group gathers, so that clients have an opportunity to get support during a session. Repeated exposure facilitates desensitization of distressing trauma-related memories.

Problems and Pitfalls in Phase 3 Treatment: A Need for Creativity

In a group of male asylum seekers from Tschechnya, the level of mistrust remained very high throughout the first two treatment phases. Clients were frightened of the exposure therapy and had difficulties accepting its rationale. After some time they stated in the session that they could not permit themselves to trust one another, since they still run a risk of being repatriated. In case of repatriation they will have to be alert again and mistrust others in order to survive. Also, they told that sharing the problems with one another, and especially showing emotions, were not culturally appropriate behaviors for men. At the same time they trusted the therapist and his positive experiences with exposure treatment. At that moment the pros and cons of exposure therapy in individual and group format were discussed in the group, and clients had to choose for themselves the format they preferred. They chose not to witness one another's exposure sessions, but to be present with the whole group after the individual exposure in order to be of support to the exposed client. The therapist agreed, worked temporarily in individual format, and continued group therapy again in phase 4.

Phase 4: Past, Present, and Future Orientations

In the fourth phase of treatment, connections have to be established between the client's past, present, and future. The focus moves from the traumatic past to forced migration and resettlement issues. Sessions are thematic and structured. It takes about 30 sessions to complete this phase. Cognitive restructuring of dysfunctional thoughts and modification of shattered basic assumptions are continued. The therapist reviews themes of clients' distorted beliefs. Treatment focuses on pre- and posttrauma changes in basic worldview assumptions. Shame, guilt, blame, powerlessness, controllability of one's life, relationship toward perpetrators, fate, fear of aggression, or safety are important issues discussed.

Case Example: Mohammad the Torture Victim

In one group, Mohammad, a man from the Middle East, told about his torture experiences, his flight from the country, and feelings of betrayal toward his party comrades whom he had left behind in danger. He explained that authorities had imprisoned his father because they could not capture Mohammad as their prisoner. Mohammad felt guilty and developed fantasies of returning to exchange his life for his father's freedom. The therapist suggested that perpetrators were still controlling his life at a distance by imprisoning his father and inducing guilt feelings in him, which might be taken as a sign that they still perceived him as a serious threat, a "dangerous enemy" to be destroyed. It was suggested that they saw Mohammad as a revolutionary figure even though he was thousands of miles away from home. Also, in this context Mohammad's forced migration after torture can be reframed as the ultimate victory over his perpetrators. Perpetrators designed torture in order to warn the society about consequences of being against the prevalent political regime. The torture victim was supposed to stay in the home country and be a symbol of this warning. When the victim migrated, it not only foiled the perpetrator's plans but proved his resistance.

Denial of Refugee Status and Fear of Repatriation

In phase 4, the nature and efficacy of coping strategies are discussed. In a group of torture survivors, for example, clients discussed strategies they used to survive imprisonment and torture. Active resistance was portrayed and others exaggerated their anxiety in front of perpetrators. Others explain how they dissociated and made their bodies painless while being tortured. Discussion about coping strategies is usually implemented whenever asylum seekers get rejected by immigration services and confront possible repatriation. When assessing damaged core beliefs, a Western therapist should be aware of his or her personal bias. Expecting clients with different backgrounds and war and torture experiences to share one's personal beliefs about the world and others is seen as a sign of disrespect and a lack of understanding and is potentially damaging to the therapeutic alliance.

A migrant and a victim of a former military regime from a South American country visited the country of origin for vacation for the first time after 8 years. In the meantime, democracy had returned to her country. One day she heard a noise in the garden. Her first thought was that someone was spying on her. She started to think about what she had said in her conversation with family members and worried. Later, she was surprised by her reaction. Residing outside the country for years, she had not thought about persecution and the need for vigilance.

In phase 4, identity issues and restoring clients' feeling of continuity of existence are important. In a situation of radical relocation, asylum seekers have no primary or secondary groups to support them. Structuring sessions around identity themes, such as: "Who was I?"; "Who am I?," and "Who do I want to be?" can help restore feelings of self-continuity. Clients are asked to focus on the question of past identity by making statements describing who they were in the past. These statements are written on a "flip chart" and kept for discussion. Typically, clients present themselves as strong individuals with positive characteristics. However, when they are asked to depict their present and future identities, they state that they are worthless asylum seekers, without a role or a place in culture, and report identity confusion. Therapists insist on clients defining their statements as precisely as possible and then use these statements to facilitate cognitive reframing and understanding in how identity is affected by radical transmission. During the process, members are asked to comment on three questions: "Why did it happen to me?," "What should I do if I find myself in the same situation again?" and "Would I change anything in my life if I could?"

The Use of Role Play Fantasy to Reconnect to Lost Homeland

In discussing homesickness, clients are asked to fantasize that they are invisible and visiting their home country without danger. They are asked to indicate the places they would visit and what they would take home as a souvenir. This exercise usually generates good memories and can empower positive feelings about their present lives.

My Culture, Their Culture: Cognitive Comparisons of "We and Them"

"We and them," a structured exercise, occurs in phase 4. Facilitators ask clients to summarize the positive and negative sides of their own and the host culture. For example, is it possible to adopt a new identity that is a combination of the best characteristics of the home and the host culture? Does one have to immerse oneself completely in the host culture in order to survive?

At the end of phase 4, other issues come into focus. Marital, child-rearing, asylum-seeking, or job problems can be addressed in the group. Members' daily structure is discussed in order to reconnect them with ordinary life. Daily activities can be examined and crisis moments identified. Recreational and self-care activities can be prescribed, and opportunities for work and hobbies are discussed. In a group of refugees, their professional and social rehabilitation is also discussed. Where necessary, additional interventions or visits take place (e.g., home, family, marital). Therapists regularly review recorded exposure tapes and motivate clients to complete this task, stressing that trauma treatment is about repetition of exposure to unpleasant memories of difficult experiences. They might use the "no pain, no gain" metaphor at this point. Where possible, facilitators discuss the fate of the tapes after completion. It is suggested that one might keep the tape, destroy it, bury it, or record his or her favorite music over it.

Problems and Pitfalls in Phase 4 Treatment

In an African male group the issues of clients' expectations from and perspectives in the future were discussed. The group showed much resistance and seemed not to understand why this topic was so important. The therapist did not have a clue of what was happening in the group since he always had good experiences in other non-African groups with discussing this topic. Finally, the clients told the therapist that they did not perceive the topic as relevant because they did not have much life left any more. The clients were predominantly in their late 30s and early 40s. "In our country many people die in their late 40s, and it does not make much sense to make plans for the future." From that moment on the therapist chose to focus on possible changes in life expectancy due to migration.

Phase 5: Termination, Relapse Prevention, and Future Orientation

In phase 5, the last seven sessions focus on termination, treatment follow-up sessions, and evaluation. Clients learn that they are vulnerable to future episodes of PTSD. Transition periods, such as relocation, divorce, death of loved ones, loss of job, children leaving home, the anniversary of trauma or migration, retirement, and return visits to the homeland, can trigger relapse. Predicting stress points for clients can help to prevent a recurrence of symptoms. It is strongly suggested that clients avoid loneliness and make efforts to stay attached to significant others. They have to search actively for activities and a structured daily life. Therapists try to instill hope by defining relapse as an opportunity to learn and not as a failure. The therapist's future availability is emphasized in case of a relapse.

The clients evaluate treatment effectiveness. It is emphasized that the staff wants to improve the program and values client comments. A torture survivor from Middle East, for example, used a metaphor during evaluation. He told the therapists that "he, just like a bird, needs two wings to fly. One wing is emotions, and the other is balance. Before treatment he had used only one wing, the one of the balance, flew in circles, and always fell on the ground. Now he can fly well, using both wings, and dares to feel again." One client summarized the effects of treatment: "At this point I still do not know whether I am going to be repatriated or forced to live a life of an illegal immigrant in the host country but I am not afraid any more. I can take care of myself again and fight for a future. I still have nightmares but not as much as before. Most important for me is that I know again who I am, what has happened to me, and how to continue my life." Energy and capacities that were previously bound to the traumatic past are released and can be used constructively in solving current problems.

The last two sessions focus on the termination of treatment. The topics include separation anxieties, experiences with earlier life losses, as well as planning a farewell ritual. Clients usually report feeling sad, fear relapse, and a loss of the daily life structure. Therapists encourage the group to continue meeting on a self-help basis. The "bus metaphor" is used to explain to clients the importance of the future meetings. "The clients were traveling in a bus from their home countries to the host country. When the bus arrived to the host country, after many months of travel and thousands of miles, it needed lots of repair. Therapists were there to repair the bus and make it possible for the bus to continue its journey. But once repaired, clients have to choose among themselves who is going to be their driver in the future."

Termination and Closing Rituals: Saying Good-Bye and Sharing a Collective Meal

In the final session, the team of therapists and clients individually address one another. They recollect the "nicest" and the "most difficult" moments experienced together. Therapists present a certificate of completion, together with a specially designed antiracism and antitorture pin upon graduation. Clients are asked to write down a positive message for other group members. The messages are placed in envelopes and given to clients as a source of strength in the future.

The last day of treatment ends with a festive meal prepared by clients with dancing and music. Clients take farewell photos of each other, the group, and the staff. They also photograph their chair and the wall in the group session room and building itself. It appears that they want to document their experiences and have reminders of the program and their recovery. In analyzing this phenomenon we discovered that there are clients with and without photos from the past. The latter ones took more photos and more passionately documented their experiences. It seems that treatment has counteracted the trauma and loss in their lives and helped them find their souls again.

AFTER-CARE PROGRAM

Upon cessation of the treatment, clients usually fall into a societal vacuum due to the lack of resources for rebuilding creative lives, marginalization, and enforced passivity in the host society. Their vulnerability due to chronic posttraumatic damage can remain active and they run the high risk for relapse. At the same time clients remain in need of object-constancy on a long-term basis and availability of safety and support resources.

Staff participation is very limited in the after-care program. Self-help groups have a contact person from the center to provide support, information, advocacy, or referral in case of relapse. The after-care programs are oriented toward social issues and not toward medical or psychological problems. In case of relapse and exacerbation of posttraumatic symptoms, clients are referred to the treatment center and, if possible, to the same therapist that treated them. For most of the clients, the idea that help is accessible enables them to continue life without intensive contact with mental health professionals. Having a contact case manager at the treatment facility is important for the development of clients' psychological well-being in the future.

REFERENCES

American Psychiatric Association (APA). (1994). *Diagnostic and statistical manual of mental disorders* (4th ed.). Washington, DC: Author.

Aresti, L. (1988). Political reality and psychological damage. In A. Aron (Ed.), *Flight, exile, and return: Mental health and the refugee* (pp. 23–42). San Francisco: Committee for Health Rights in Central America.

Aronoff, J., & Wilson, J. P. (1985). Personality in the social process. Hillsdale, NJ: Lawrence Erlbaum Associates.

Basoglu, M. (1998). Behavioral and cognitive treatment of survivors of torture. In J. M. Jaranson & M. K. Popkin (Eds.), *Caring for victims of torture* (pp. 131–148). Washington, DC: APA.

Boscarino, J. A. (1995). Post-traumatic stress and associated disorders among Vietnam veterans: The significance of combat exposure and social support. *Journal of Traumatic Stress, 8*, 317–336.

Bremner, D. J., Southwick, S. M., Darnell, A., & Charney, D. S. (1996). Chronic PTSD in Vietnam combat veterans: Course of illness and substance abuse. *American Journal of Psychiatry, 153*, 369–375.

Brende, J., & Goldsmith, R. (1991). Post-traumatic stress disorder in families. *Journal of Contemporary Psychotherapy, 21*, 115–125.

Cahill, S., Carrigan, M., & Frueh, B. C. (1999). Does EMDR work? And if so, why? *Journal of Anxiety Disorders, 13*, 5–33.

Cardena, E., Maldonado, J., Hart van der, O., & Spiegel, D. (2000). Guidelines for treatment of PTSD: Hypnosis. *Journal of Traumatic Stress, 13*(4), 580–584.

Carroll, E. M., & Foy, D. W. (2000). Assessment and treatment of combat-related post-traumatic stress disorder in a medical center setting. In E. B. Foa, T. M. Keane, & M. J. Friedman (Eds.), *Effective treatments for PTSD* (pp. 39–68). New York: Guilford.

Craine, M., Hanks, R., & Stevens, H. (1992). Mapping family stress: The application of family adaptation theory to post-traumatic stress disorder. *American Journal of Family Therapy, 20,* 195–203.

Danieli, Y. (1980). Countertransference in the treatment and study of Nazi Holocaust survivors and their children. *Victimology, 5,* 355–367.

Doerr-Zegers, O., Hartmann, L., Lina, E., Weinstein, E. (1992). Torture: Psychiatric sequelae and phenomenology. *Psychiatry, 55,* 177–184.

Droždek, B. (1997). The follow-up study of ex-concentration camp prisoners from Bosnia-Herzegovina: 3 years later. *Journal of Nervous and Mental Disease, 185*(11), 690–694.

Droždek, B. (2001). Can traumatized asylum seekers be treated ? In M. Verwey (Ed.), *Trauma and empowerment* (pp. 219–231). Berlin: VWB.

Droždek, B., van Dijk, M., & de Winter, B. (2002). Omdat ik niet meer weet wie ik ben: Over het gebruik van ervaringsgerichte therapieen in de behandeling van getraumatiseerde asielzoekers [Because I do not know who I am anymore: The use of experiential therapies in treatment of traumatizied asylum seekers]. In E. van Meekeren, A. Limburg-Okken, & R. May (Eds.), *Culturen binnen psychiatrie-muren: Geestelijke gezondheidszorg in een multiculturele samenleving* [Culture within psychiatry—walls: Mental health in a multicultural society] (pp. 179–187). Amsterdam: Boom.

Droždek, B. , Noor, A. K., Lutt, M., & Foy, D. W. (2003). Chronic PTSD and medical services utilization by asylum seekers. *Journal of Refugee Studies, 16*(2), 202–211.

Ekblad, S., & Roth, G. (1997). Diagnosing posttraumatic stress disorder in multicultural patients in a Stockholm psychiatric clinic. *Journal of Nervous and Mental Disorders, 185*(2), 102–107.

Engdahl B., Dikel, T. N., Eberly, R., & Blank, A. (1997). Posttraumatic stress disorder in a community group of former prisoners of war: A normative response to severe trauma. *American Journal of Psychiatry, 154*(11), 1576–1581.

Fine, G. A. (1999). Socially shared cognition, affect and behavior: A review and integration. *Personality and Social Psychology Review, 3* (4), 278–302.

Foa, E. B., Keene, T. M., & Friedman, M. J. (2000). Guidelines for treatment of PTSD. *Journal of Traumatic Stress, 13* (4), 539–555.

Fontana, A., & Rosenheck, R. (1994). Posttraumatic stress disorder among Vietnam theater veterans: A causal model of etiology in a community sample. *Journal of Nervous and Mental Disease, 182,* 677–684.

Ford, J. D., Fisher, P., & Larson, L. (1997). Object relations as a predictor of treatment outcome with chronic posttraumatic stress disorder. *Journal of Consulting and Clinical Psychology, 65*(4), 547–559.

Foy, D. W., Glynn, S. M., Schnurr, P. P., Jankowski, M. K., Wattenberg, M. S., Weiss, D. S., et al. (1992). Group therapy. In D. W. Foy (Ed.), *Treating PTSD: Cognitive-behavioral strategies* (pp. 155–175). New York: Guilford Publications.

Foy, D. W., Ruzek, J. I., Glynn, S. M., Riney, S. A., & Gusman, F. D. (1997). Trauma focus group therapy for combat-related PTSD. *Session: Psychotherapy in Practice, 3,* 59–73.

Foy, D. W., Schnurr, P. P., Weiss, D. S., Wattenberg, M. S., Glynn, S. M., Marmar, C. R., et al. (2001). Group psychotherapy for PTSD. In J. P. Wilson, M. J. Friedman, & J. D. Lindy (Eds.), *Treating psychological trauma & PTSD* (pp. 183–202). New York: Guilford Publications.

Friedman, M. J., Charney, D. S., & Deutch, A. Y. (Eds.) (2001). Allostatic versus empirical perspectives on pharmacotherapy of PTSD. In J. P. Wilson, M. J. Friedman, & J. D. Lindy (Eds.), *Treating psychological trauma & PTSD* (pp. 94–124). New York: Guilford.

Friedman, M. J., & Schnurr, P. P. (1995). The relationship between trauma, posttraumatic stress disorder, and physical health. In M. J. Friedman et al. (Eds.), *Neurological and clinical consequences of stress. From normal adaptation to post-traumatic stress disorder* (pp. 507–524). Philadelphia: Lippincott-Raven.

Garfield, D., & Leveroni, C. (2000). The use of self-psychological concepts in a veteran affairs PTSD clinic. *Bulletin of the Menninger Clinic, 64*(3), 344–364.

Gilbert, C. (1988). Sexual abuse and group therapy. *Journal of Psychosocial Nursing, 26,* 19–23.

Goodman, M., & Weiss, D. (1998). Double trauma: A group therapy approach for Vietnam veterans suffering from war and childhood trauma. *International Journal of Group Psychotherapy, 49*(1), 39–54.

Grinberg, L., & Grinberg, R. (1984). *Psychoanalytic perspectives on migration and exile.* New Haven, CT: Yale University Press.

Harkness, L., & Zador, N. (2001). Treatment of PTSD in families and couples. In J. P. Wilson, M. J. Friedman, & J. D. Lindy (Eds.), *Treating psychological trauma & PTSD* (pp. 335–353). New York: Guilford.

Herman, J. L. (1992). *Trauma and recovery.* New York: Basic Books.

Janoff-Bulman, R. (1985). The aftermath of victimisation: Rebuilding shattered assumptions. In C. R. Figley (Ed.), *Trauma and its wake (Vol. 1) The study and treatment of posttraumatic stress disorder* (pp. 15–35). New York: Brunner/Mazel.

Johnson, D. R., Lubin, H., Rosenheck, R., Fontana, A., Southwick, S., & Charney, D. (1997). The impact of the homecoming reception on the development of the post-traumatic stress disorder: The West Haven Homecoming Stress Scale (WHHSS). *Journal of Traumatic Stress, 10,* 259–277.

Kessler, R. C., Sonnega, A., Bromet, E., Hughes, M., & Nelson, C. B. (1995). Posttraumatic stress disorder in the National Comorbidity Survey. *Archives of General Psychiatry, 52,* 1048–1060.

Kinzie, D. J. (2001). Psychotherapy for massively traumatized refugees: The therapist variable. *American Journal of Psychotherapy, 55* (4), 475–490.

Koller, P. et al. (1992). Psychodynamic group treatment of posttraumatic stress disorder in Vietnam veterans. *International Journal of Group Psychotherapy, 42*(2), 225–246.

Lee, E., & Lu, F. (1988). Assessment and treatment of Asian-American survivors of mass violence. *Journal of Traumatic Stress, 2,* 93–120.

Le Roy, J. (1994). Group analysis and culture. In M. Pines (Ed.), *The psyche and the social world* (pp. 180–201). London: Routledge.

Lindy, J. D., & Wilson, J. P. (2001). An allostatic approach to the psychodynamic understanding of PTSD. In J. P. Wilson, M. J. Friedman, and J. D. Lindy (Eds.), *Treating psychological trauma and PTSD* (pp. 125–138). New York: Guilford Publications.

Lindy, J. D., Wilson, J. P., & Friedman, M. J. (2001). Case history analysis of the treatments for PTSD: Lessons learned. In J. P. Wilson, M. J. Friedman, and J. D. Lindy (Eds.), *Treating psychological trauma and PTSD* (385–408). New York: Guilford Publications.

Lubin, H., Loris, M., Burt, J., & Johnson, D. R. (1998). Efficacy of psychoeducational group therapy in reducing symptoms of posttraumatic stress disorder among multiply traumatized women. *American Journal of Psychiatry, 9*, 1172–1177.

Lystad, M., Rice, M., & Kaplan, S. (1996). Domestic violence. In S. Kaplan (Ed.), *Family violence: A clinical and legal guide* (pp. 139–180). Washington, DC: APA.

Marmar, C. (1991). Brief dynamic therapy of post-traumatic stress disorder. *Psychiatric Annals, 21*, 405–414.

Matsakis, A. (1992). *I can't get over it: A handbook for trauma survivors.* Oakland, CA: New Harbinger.

McCarrol, J. E., Fagan, J. G., Hermsen, J. M., & Ursano, R. J. (1997). Posttraumatic stress disorder in U.S. Army Vietnam veterans who served in the Persian Gulf War. *Journal of Nervous and Mental Disease, 185*(11), 682–685.

McNally, R. J. (1999). Research on eye movement desensitization and reprocessing (EMDR) as a treatment for PTSD. *PTSD Research Quarterly, 10*, 1–7.

Meichenbaum, D. (1994). *Treating post-traumatic stress disorder: A handbook and practice manual for therapy.* Chichester: Wiley.

Miller, L. (1999). Treating posttraumatic stress disorder in children and families: Basic principles and clinical applications. *American Journal of Family Therapy, 27*, 21–34.

Mollica, R. F., Wyshak, G., Lavelle, J., Truong, T., Tor, S., & Yang, T. (1990). Assessing symptom change in Southeast Asian refugee survivors of mass violence and torture. *American Journal of Psychiatry, 147*, 83–88.

Morris, P., & Silove, D. (1992). Cultural influences in psychotherapy with refugee survivors of torture and trauma. *Hospital and Community Psychiatry, 43*(8), 820–824.

Motta, R. W. (1993). Psychotherapy for Vietnam-related posttraumatic stress disorders. *Psychological Reports, 73*, 67–77.

Neria, Y., Solomon, Z., & Dekel, R. (1998). An eighteen-year follow-up study of Israeli prisoners of war and combat veterans. *Journal of Nervous and Mental Disease, 186*, 174–182.

Nicholas, M., & Forrester, A. (1999). Advantages of heterogeneous therapy groups in the psychotherapy of the traumatically abused: Treating the problem as well as the person. *International Journal of Group Psychotherapy, 49*(3), 323–342.

Nieves-Grafals, S. (2001). Brief therapy of civil war-related trauma: A case study. *Cultural Diversity and Ethnic Minority Psychology, 7*(4), 387–389.

Peltzer, K. (1995). *Psychology and health in African cultures: Examples of ethnopsychotherapeutic practice.* In K. Peltzer (Ed.),   (pp. 77–88). Frankfurt/Main: IKO.

Poole, A. D., de Johng, A., & Spector, J. (1999). Power therapies: Evidence versus emotion. *Behavioral and Cognitive Psychotherapy, 27*, 3–8.

Priebe, S., & Esmaili, S. (1997). Long-term mental sequelae of torture in Iran — who seeks treatment. *Journal of Nervous and Mental Disease, 185*(2), 74–77.

Prout, M., & Schwartz, R. (1991). Post-traumatic stress disorder: A brief integrated approach. *International Journal of Short-Term Psychotherapy, 6*, 113–124.

Rabin, C., & Nardi, C. (1991). Treating post-traumatic stress disorder couples: A psychoeducational program. *Community Mental Health Journal, 27,* 209–224.

Rozynko, V., & Dondershine, H. (1991). Trauma focus group therapy for Vietnam veterans with PTSD. *Psychotherapy, 28,* 157–161.

Scurfield, R. (1993). Treatment of posttraumatic stress disorder among Vietnam veterans. In J. P. Wilson & B. Raphael (Eds.), *International handbook of traumatic stress syndromes* (pp. 879–888). New York: Plenum.

Shapiro, F. (1989). Eye movement desensitization: A new treatment for post-traumatic stress disorder. *Journal of Behavior Therapy and Experimental Psychiatry, 20,* 211–217.

Silove, D., McIntosh, P., & Becker, R. (1993). Risk of retraumatization of asylum-seekers in Australia. *Australian and New Zealand Journal of Psychiatry, 27,* 606–612.

Solomon, Z., & Benbenishty, R. (1986). The role of proximity, immediacy, and expectancy in frontline treatment of combat stress reaction among Israelis in the Lebanon war. *American Journal of Psychiatry, 143,* 613–617.

Somnier, F. E., & Genefke, I. K. (1986). Psychotherapy for victims of torture. *British Journal of Psychiatry, 149,* 323–329.

Stadter, M. (1996). *Object relations brief therapy: The therapeutic relationship in short-term work.* Northvale, NJ: Jason Aronson.

Summerfield, D. (1997). Legacy of war: Beyond "trauma" to the social fabric. *Lancet, 349,* 1568.

Tocilj-Simunkovic, G., & Tata Arcel, L. (1998). Group psychotherapy with victims of torture. In L. Tata Arcel (Ed.), *War violence, trauma, and the coping process: Armed conflict in Europe and survivor responses* (pp. 143–154). Copenhagen: IRCT.

Vesti, P., Somnier, F., & Kastrup, M. (1992). Doing psychotherapy with torture survivors. In P. Vesti, F. Somnier, & M. Kastrup (Eds.), *Psychotherapy with torture survivors* (pp. 37–51). Copenhagen: IRCT.

Warda, G., & Bryant, R. A. (1998). Thought control strategies in acute stress disorder. *Behavior Research and Therapy, 36,* 1171–1175.

Wilson, J. P. & Lindy, J. D. (1994). Empathetic strain and countertransference. In J. P. Wilson & J. D. Lindy (Eds.), *Countertransference in the treatment of PTSD* (pp. 5–30). New York: Guilford Publications.

Wilson, J. P. et al. (1994). Empathic strain and therapist defense: Type I and II CTRS. In J. P. Wilson & J. D. Lindy (Eds.), *Countertransference in the treatment of PTSD* (pp. 31–61). New York: Guilford.

Wilson, J. P., Friedman, M. J., & Lindy, J. D. (Eds.) (2001). *Treating psychological trauma and PTSD.* New York: Guilford Publications.

Yalom, I. D. (1995). *The theory and practice of group psychotherapy.* New York: Basic Books.

11

Empathy, Trauma Transmission, and Countertransference in Posttraumatic Psychotherapy

JOHN P. WILSON

> Listen to the voices of trauma. Can you hear their cry? Their pain
> exudes emotional blood from psychic pores. Nights are broken by
> frightening intrusions from ghosts of the past. Bodies hold memories,
> secrets and scars locked into sinew, glands and neurons. Weary souls of
> the abyss seeking peace in their souls.
>
> Wilson

Trauma is part of the human condition and ever present in the lives of
ordinary people throughout the world. Traumatic events punctuate
recorded history in a manner parallel to momentous achievements that
advance civilization. Traumatic events are the product of human intentions, the randomness of nature, and acts of God. Traumatic experiences
are archetypal in nature and have their own psychological structure and
energy (Wilson, 2002). Traumatic experiences vary along many different "stressor" dimensions and have simple and complex effects on the

human psyche (Wilson & Lindy, 1994). Traumatic experiences are not only different qualitatively and quantitatively from each other, but are subjectively experienced in individual ways through the life history of the person, the filters of culture and language, and the nature of injury inflicted on the organism in all of its integrated wholeness. Trauma can strike at the surface or the deepest core of the self — the very "soul" and inner-most identity of the person. Traumatic experiences can lead to transformations of the personality, spirit, beliefs, and understanding of the meaning of life. In that same sense, traumatic experience can alter life-course trajectories and have multigenerational legacies (Danieli, 1998). In a broader perspective, massive or catastrophic trauma can permanently alter, eradicate, or damage entire societies, cultures, and nations (Lifton, 1967, 1993). Indeed, as an archetypal form, trauma can be a psychic force of enormous power in the individual and collective unconscious of the species. Unmetabolized trauma of a violent nature caused by wars, terrorism, torture, genocide, ethnic cleansing, and the purposeful abuse of others can unleash destructive forces within the fabric of civilization (Freud, 1917, 1928; Jung, 1929; Wilson, Friedman, & Lindy, 2001).

Trauma that is unhealed, unresolved, and unintegrated into a healthy balance within the self has the potential to be repeated, reenacted, acted-out, projected, or externalized in relationships and gives rise to destructive and self-destructive motivational forces. When we look at the "mandala" of trauma in archetypal forms, its presentation can be the vicissitudes of the demonic in its Mephistophelean forms, expressing the excrucable, depraved, unholy, sinister, vile, and evil elements of the darkness of being, which intrusively invade the sanctity of human experiences and seraphic essence of loving relationships.

Listening and observing carefully, the voices and faces of trauma are "snapshots" of the existential struggle to remain whole, vital, and to restore that part of the self damaged by trauma. The stories of the survivors are inevitably universal variants on the archetypal abyss of the trauma complex (Wilson, 2002). However, for the therapist, counselor, and others in the healing role, it is the encounter with the voices and faces of the trauma patient that is difficult and painful. Listening empathically to trauma stories is demanding and stressful. To remain sensitive and finely attuned to the internal experience of the individuals psychological injuries requires more than understanding that an event was traumatic — it requires skill and a capacity to use empathy to access the inner scars of the psyche and the organism. Effective posttraumatic therapy or treatment is more than the application of a clinical technique; it is the capacity to facilitate self-healing by helping the patient mobilize and transform the negative energies, memories, and emotions of posttraumatic stress disorder (PTSD) and associated conditions into a healthy self-synthesis, which evolves into a positive integration of the trauma experience. However, in the role of a professional therapist, counselor, and so forth, there is a significant and certain risk of empathic distress, compassion fatigue, burn-out, and more technically (or traditionally), countertransference processes.

EMPATHY, EMPATHIC ATTUNEMENT, AND EMPATHIC STRAINS IN TRAUMA WORK: THE VOICES AND FACES OF TRAUMA

Listen to the voices of trauma. They are like the top edge of a wave about to break over turbulent water, beneath which lies a potentially deadly rip curl ready to drag the person under the surface. What follows are trauma vignettes: images of the abyss experience.[1]

FDNY

"All I could make out was his FDNY badge — *the rest was indescribable — crushed, burnt remains of a firefighter.*" (Disaster Worker, World Trade Center, 2001, emphasis added)

Crushed

"My best friend was crushed underneath a building and asked me for help, so I tried desperately to help her, but my efforts meant nothing, so I ran away with another friend. *I hear her voice even now; I'll never be able to forget it.*" (Hiroshima, 1945, emphasis added)

Frozen in Agony

"There were charred dead bodies scattered all over a burned-out field that once was a residential area. *Bodies frozen in agony reaching up toward the sky.* Unidentified bodies left like that for days." (Hiroshima, 1945, emphasis added)

Japanese Sword of Damocles

"On the final day, we were taken out to the site of our trial. Twenty-four prisoners were squatting there with their hands tied behind their backs. They were blindfolded. A big hole had been dug — ten meters long, two meters wide, and more than three meters deep. The regimental commander, the battalion commanders, and the company commanders all took the seats arranged for them. Second Lieutenant Tanaka bowed to the regimental commander and reported, 'We shall now begin.' He ordered a soldier on fatigue duty to haul one of the prisoners

---

[1] Abyss experience is the confrontation with the archetype of trauma; the demonic, and darkness of being (Wilson, 2002).

to the edge of the pit; the prisoner was kicked when he resisted. The soldier finally dragged him over and forced him to his knees. Tanaka turned toward us and looked into each of our faces in turn. 'Heads should be cut off like this,' he said, unsheathing his army sword. He scooped water from a bucket with a dipper, then poured it over both sides of the blade. Swishing off the water, he raised his sword in a long arc. *Standing behind the prisoner, Tanaka steadied himself, legs spread apart, and cut off the man's head with a shout, 'Yo!' The head flew more than a meter away. Blood spurted up in two fountains from the body and sprayed into the hole.* The scene was so appalling that I felt I couldn't breathe. All the candidate officer stiffened. Second Lieutenant Tanaka designated the person on the right end of our line to go next. I was fourth. When my turn came, the only thought I had was 'Don't do anything unseemly!' I didn't want to disgrace myself. I bowed to the regimental commander and stepped forward. Contrary to my expectations, my feet firmly met the ground. One thin, worn-out prisoner was at the edge of the pit, blindfolded. I unsheathed my sword, a gift from my brother-in-law, wet it down as the lieutenant had demonstrated, and stood behind the man. The prisoner didn't move. He kept his head lowered. Perhaps he was resigned to his fate. I was tense, thinking I couldn't afford to fail. I took a deep breath and recovered my composure. *I steadied myself, holding the sword at a point above my right shoulder, and swung down with one breath. The head flew away and the body tumbled down, spouting blood. The air reeked from all that blood. I washed blood off the blade then wiped it with the paper provided. Fat stuck to it and wouldn't come off. I noticed, when I sheathed it, that my sword was slightly bent.* At that moment, I felt something change inside me. I don't know how to put it, but *I gained strength somewhere in my gut.* Some of the officer candidates slashed the head by mistake. One prisoner ran around crazily, his blindfold hanging down, his head gashed. 'Stab him!' Tanaka ordered. The candidate officer swung and missed again. 'You fool!' Tanaka scolded. This time Tanaka swung his sword. All of us did. *Everyone got covered with blood as we butchered him.*" (*Japan at War, An Oral History,* Cook, 1993, p. 121)

Innocent Brains

"Her [10-year-old] head was injured and *her brain stuck out of her fractured skull where she hit the hard concrete surface.* Her left eye popped out onto her cheekbone and blood was coming down her face. She was still alive but unconscious. I see that at night when I try to go to sleep." (Civil Disaster, Anonymous Patient, JPW 1989, emphasis added)

Skinned and Pinned

"We were on search and destroy patrol when we came across his body [American soldier]. *He had been captured, pinned to a tree and skinned alive.* His genitals were stuck in his mouth and his eyes were still wide open." (Vietnam Veteran, Bon Song, 1969, emphasis added)

Rape Your Children or We Will For You

"I was given another choice: I rape my daughter or the guard does. I tried to reason with them, telling them that she was an innocent child. I pleaded with them not to humiliate her, not to hurt her, but instead to *rape me,* to do with me what they wanted. They laughed and repeated the two choices. I looked at my daughter hoping that she would tell me what to do — our eyes met and I knew that I could not save her from those wretched men. I lowered my eyes in *shame* to keep from seeing my daughter abused. One guard held my face up, forcing me to watch this horrible scene. *I watched, motionless, as she was raped before me and her little brother. When they were through, they forced me to do what they had done to her.* My own daughter, my son forced to watch it all. How could anyone do that? What kind of men are they? What kind of father am I?" (Ortiz, 2001, p.18, emphasis added)

Death's Aroma

"I can still *smell those dead bodies in my nostrils even now."* (Buffalo Creek Dam Disaster, 1974, emphasis added)

Human Rain

"It was his last day in Vietnam. He insisted on walking 'point' [first] man. We were near Cambodia — the Black Virgin Mountain area of Tay Ninh. He never saw the command detonated landmine as he stepped on it. *Pieces and parts of his body rained on us — like a shower in blood and pieces of flesh. It smelled horrible. We found what was left of his head and put it in a body bag."* (Vietnam Veteran, Tay Ninh, 1970, emphasis added)

Footsteps

"I could tell by my stepfathers footsteps on the wooden hallway floor whether he was drunk when he came down the hallway to my room. When he started in on me [sexual abuse], *I left my body and went away* to a corner of the room, in the ceiling, with my teddy bear." (Sexual Abuse Victim, 1993, emphasis added)

No Flesh, and Lots of Bones

"I saw one woman — one corpse with the flesh removed from the bones ... then about 100 people, mostly women and children, none of them with

clothes on, lying on the asphalt pleading for help." (Hiroshima, 1945, emphasis added)

Eyes, Ears, Nose, and Mouth

"I went over and started taking pieces of wood from the woodpile, and I found a body. I picked up the back of her hair, what hair she had left. She didn't have no clothes on, and *I turned her over and the blood and mud and water came out of her eyes and nose and mouth and ears.* I had to go get clean." (Buffalo Creek Dam Disaster, 1974, emphasis added)

Top Gun in Thailand

"We were on duty in Thailand and received a call that an F-4 Phantom jet was on fire. It landed burning and we [paramedics] responded. We put out the fire and opened the cockpit. The smoke was still pouring out. *I took off the pilots' helmet and blood ran out of his eyes and mouth from his burnt, black face.* He was dead. It was his birthday and he was my best friend. We had planned to party that night." (Vietnam Veteran, Thailand, 1968, emphasis added)

Frankenstein or Freddy Kruger?

"When I woke up after surgery in the burn unit in Japan, they made me look at myself in the mirror. The nurse handed me a mirror and I threw-up [vomited] when I saw the black deformed image that used to be me. I cried for days — it was like looking at a disfigured Halloween mask of a monster." (Vietnam Veteran, 1970, Army Burn Unit Hospital, Japan)

Blood on the Tracks

"The Serb snipers were active 24 hours a day. My first hour in Sarajevo, I saw dead bodies on the tram line — women, children and old men — killed in the afternoon — blood on the railroad/tram tracks. What kind of war is this? That was just the beginning — everyday some innocent person was killed by a sniper. There were so many killings that they began burying people in the city parks. Bosnia was an evil genocide and the senseless killing has never left me. I still see the blood on the tracks and remember those innocent people." (John P. Wilson, 1994, Sarajevo, emphasis added)

Towering Inferno

"I still *hear the screams* and the sounds of the towers collapsing. *I wake up in a sweat, seeing the bodies falling from the tower* — it could have been me — I was on my way to work there [Tower I]. The next day, September

12, 2001, I couldn't feel much of anything. *I was just numb and completely overwhelmed.* New York seemed dead to me. I can still *smell* ground zero in my mind — *it won't ever go away.*" (World Trade Center, 2001, emphasis added)

P.O.W.'s Crucifixion

"We were forced to watch as he [American P.O.W.] was tortured. They staked him to a pole and broke his bones with a metal rod, starting with his shins. *They inserted a sharp barb-hooked hanger in his belly into his liver and tugged on it until he screamed as if dying.* They shot him slowly, starting with his legs and worked their way up his body, one bullet at a time until the last one killed him … a shot in the forehead. *He had a look of horror in his eyes.* We were forced to watch and warned not to try to escape the camp in Cambodia, where we got caught. He tried to escape and we were given a lesson." (Vietnam Veteran, 1970, emphasis added)

No Limits to Marquis de Sade

"During his first arrest 'L' tried to commit suicide, but he was shot in the leg and taken directly to a notorious prison. There he was immediately beaten brutally over his entire body, hooded, and subjected to falanga [beating the souls of the feet]. The torture continued and 'L' was forced to lick up blood from the floor. He was suspended on a cross, kicked over his entire body, and kept awake for days. Not broken by the physical torture, 'L' was subjected to psychological torture. He was placed in a room between a mother and a daughter. The mother was whipped and ordered not to make a sound or the daughter would be abused. He was subjected to mock execution several times; on one such occasion he was drenched with liters of petrol, and the torturers fumbled with matches in front of him. Threatened with homosexual rape and beaten to unconsciousness, he also received electrical torture around the ears. His nose was broken repeatedly, and he developed bleeding from the stomach and hemorrhagic vomiting. He was suspended both head up and feet up, and burned with cigarettes over his body. He could exhibit a multitude of scars from these burns. Subsequently, 'L' was isolated for about a year in a very small, completely barren cell. In this new prison he was also subjected to Russian roulette and deprivation of food. Later because of gangrene of the feet he was taken to a hospital outside the prison, and there he managed to escape." (Torture Victim, RCT, 1992)

Saigon Refugee and Asylum Seeker

"I was captured before the end of the war in Saigon in 1975. As an officer of the Vietnam Army, I was taken north with other P.O.W.'s who were officers. We were put in bamboo cages. … Everyday we were spread eagled on a flat table and tortured. They would ask questions and burn our skin, nipples, and face with cigarettes. ... I ran away one night and escaped. I came to the U.S. seeking asylum. I dream of these experiences even today." (Vietnam Refugee, 2002)

Hippocrates Incurable Vivisection

"Cannibalism and vivisection of allied flyers by the Japanese is quite well documented. Kyushu Imperial University officials, for example, have acknowledged vivisecting eight B-29 crewmen in experiments carried out on May 17, 23, 29 and June 3, 1945. In one experiment, Ishiyama extracted an American PoW's lungs and placed them in a surgical pan. He made an incision in the lung artery and allowed blood to flow into the chest cavity, killing the man. In another experiment, Ishiyama removed a prisoner's stomach, then cut five ribs and held a large artery near the heart to determine how long he could stop the blood flow before the victim died. In a third, another Japanese doctor made four openings in a prisoner's skull and inserted a knife into the brain to see what the reaction would be. The prisoner died." (Ienaga, 1968)

As we read these vignettes, they evoke our own associations, images, feelings, and attempts to frame a context and perspective of understanding. Each voice is unique, real, and a part of history, past, and present. These authentic vignettes are only excerpts of much more detailed trauma stories of some of my patients.

EMPATHY, EMPATHIC ATTUNEMENT, AND EMPATHIC STRAIN IN TRAUMA WORK

Trauma work challenges the therapist's or professional's capacity to be empathic and effective when working with clients who suffer from PTSD. Seeing the faces of trauma clients and listening to their voices, their individual stories, is a form of traumatic encounter in itself, which has been called secondary traumatization (Stamm, 1997), vicarious traumatization (Pearlman & Saativne, 1997), compassion fatigue (Figley, 1997), empathic strain (Wilson & Lindy, 1994), trauma-related affective reactions (ARs, Wilson & Lindy, 1994), and trauma-related countertransference processes (CTRs). Trauma work and the role of the therapist require immersion into the phenomenal reality and ego state of the person suffering from PTSD.

Empathic attunement is the capacity to resonate efficiently and accurately to another's state of being; to match self-other understanding; to have knowledge of the internal psychological ego states of another who has suffered a trauma. Empathic capacity is the ability for empathic attunement and varies greatly among therapists working with PTSD patients. Effective posttraumatic therapy rests on the cornerstone of empathic ability and the capacity to sustain empathic attunement.

Empathic capacity is a fundamental dimension of the psychobiology of empathy. In a sense, a good therapist or listener of a trauma victim has the ability to "decode" trauma stories and trauma-specific transference (TST) reactions (Wilson & Lindy, 1994). Empathic attunement is part of the process of decoding, a "signal detection" of information flowing from the patient (sender) to the therapist who, in some basic respects, serves as a "radio" or "satellite" receiver who "hones in" on a signal being transmitted and decodes its message. Indeed, it is entirely possible to speak of trauma-specific transference reactions, the disclosure of the trauma story, and the "flow" of affect, cognition, and behaviors (including especially nonverbal actions), as multileveled messages being "sent" from the patient to the therapist. If visualized, one would see patterns or images of energy in wave form emanating from the trauma client and manifesting themselves in various amplitudes and frequencies as they flow in patterns toward the receptor site of the therapist's mind and consciousness. However, to adequately receive and decode the message without "noise" or "interference," the therapist must have the capacity for decoding, interpreting, and responding with information to the client as part of the interactional communication sequence (Wilson & Lindy, 1994). Historically, Freud used a similar metaphor in one of his few writings on countertransference. In a paper written in 1912 to general medical practitioners, he stated

> To put it into a formula: [the therapist] must turn his own unconscious like a receptive organ toward the transmitting unconscious of the patient. He must adjust himself to the patient as a telephone receiver is adjusted to the transmitting microphone. Just as the receiver converts back into sound waves the electric oscillations ... so the doctors unconscious is able, from the derivation of the unconscious which are communicated to him, to reconstruct the unconscious, which has determined the patients free associations." (p. 110, emphasis added)

Thus, Freud understood that the interactional communication sequence in treatment was dynamic in nature and involved both the patient's and therapist's unconscious processes. However, he did not elaborate on the mechanisms of countertransference in detail. In his widely cited 1910 paper, Freud stated that it was critical for the analyst to

> recognize this counter-transference in himself and overcome it ... we have noticed that no psychoanalyst goes further than his own complexes and resistances permit, and we consequently require that he shall begin activity with a self-analysis and continually carry it deeper while he is making his own observations on his patients. Anyone who fails to produce results in a self-analysis of this kind may at once give up any idea of being able to treat patients by analysis. (pp. 141–142)

This passage illustrates that Freud believed that a therapist's self-knowledge of how his or her own unconscious thought processes were activated "by the transmitting unconscious of the patient" was central to successful treatment. We can view the role of empathy as central to posttraumatic therapy; it is a vehicle to portals of entry in the interior space of the psyche. Like ancient pyramids, the ego has secret passageways into inner sanctums, rooms, and chambers, which are rich in artifacts, valued objects, and elegant burial tombs.

Empathy is the psychological capacity to identify and understand another person's psychological state of being (Wilson & Lindy, 1994). Empathic attunement allows access to the passageway and portals of the ego's "pyramid." As defined fundamentally by Kohut (1959, 1977), empathy is a form of "knowing," information processing, and "data collection" about the patient. Rowe and MacIsaac (1991) state that "empathic immersion into the patient's experience focuses the analyst's attention upon what it is like to be the subject rather than the target of the patient's wishes and demands" (p. 18). In a similar manner they note that "the empathic process is employed solely as a scientific tool to enable the analyst eventually to make interpretations to the patient that are as accurate and complete as possible" (p. 64). Thus, we can view empathy as the primary tool by which to access the ego state of the patient suffering from PTSD. Slatker (1987), in a review of empathy in analytic theory, states

> empathy is based on counter-identification; indeed, it is counter-identi-
> fication that permits our empathy to be therapeutically useful ... the
> analysts negative counter-transferential reactions can cause his empa-
> thy to diminish or even vanish altogether. When this happens, he may
> become vulnerable to additional negative counter-transference
> reactions. (p. 203)

The patient's ego state, or ego-spatial configuration, includes the organization of experience into memory and function, which governs attempts at adaptation to self, others, and the world. It represents the fluctuating dimensions of self-reference, which includes cognitive functions, affect regulation, ego identity, and a sense of well-being (Wilson, Friedman, & Lindy, 2001). Moreover, there are at least five portals of entry into the ego state of the PTSD client (Wilson, Friedman, & Lindy, 2001), which are pathways created by PTSD symptoms organized into five clusters within the organism: for example, in the PTSD triad: (1) reexperiencing, (2) avoidance, (3) hyperarousal, and (4) ego identity/ self-processes, and (5) interpersonal attachment. These five portals of entry allow the therapist to understand the different symptom "channels" or manifestations that comprise the information transmission being generated in specific forms of transference during treatment. Empathy, as one method of connecting to the ego state and unconscious process of the trauma client, allows the therapist to creatively attune to *five* different channels of information transmission being generated by the patient.

INFORMATION TRANSMISSION OR "FLOW" IN THE TRANSFERENCE: COUNTERTRANSFERENCE MATRIX

When the patient and therapist are together in the safety of the clinician's office, an exchange of information occurs during the treatment. To an outside observer, not much appears to be happening except a verbal exchange for a brief period of time. Indeed, if videotaped and presented to viewers without sound content, it would appear that the two people talking could be anywhere — for example, at a restaurant, a residential living room, a hotel lobby, or a business office seated across a desk. Indeed, Freud (1917) made a similar comment about the process of psychoanalysis:

> Nothing takes place in a psychoanalytic treatment but an interchange of words between the patient and the analyst. The patient talks, tells of his past experiences and present impressions, complains, confesses to his wishes and his emotional impulses. The doctor listens, tries to direct the patients' processes of thoughts, exhorts, forces his attention in certain directions, gives him explanations and observes the reactions of understanding or rejection which he in this way provokes in him. (pp. 19–20)

Freud's observation about "an exchange" of words and the role of the analyst as one who gently guided conversation and the process of free association is useful because it points to the active role of the therapist as one who observes, gathers information, and probes inquiries into different areas of the patient's past history. It is clear from his work that Freud (1912) understood that the therapist must use his "unconscious" as a "receptive organ" to the "transmitting unconscious of the patient." The process of dynamic interchange between the patient and the analyst involves "unconscious" and "conscious" reception of information. In other words, *there are multiple channels of information being transmitted by the patient*: (a) words, (b) affect, (c) memories, (d) thoughts, (e) body posture, (f) voice modulations, (g) expression of their personality, and (h) "here and now" ego-state presentations or the saliency of their integrative consciousness during a period of time. These dimensions of the patient, in the *context* of a therapeutic relationship, can be meaningfully thought of as forms of information transmission about their individual dynamics. They are transference projections or transmissions of psychological functioning. The transmissions of "data" are different types of information flows emanating from the patient through encoded channels. The information is coded or encrypted through the transference. Figure 11.1 illustrates these mechanisms and reveals that the patient (sender) projects an information flow in a variety of forms, including transference dynamics. The analyst (receiver) is the object of the patient's information transmission who attempts clinically to "decode" the information encoded in the different channels.

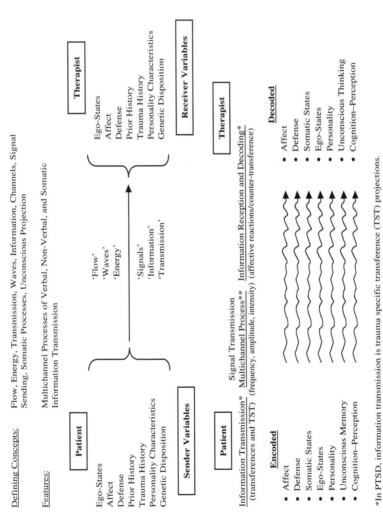

"The transmitting unconscious of the patient" (S. Freud, 1912)

Defining Concepts: Flow, Energy, Transmission, Waves, Information, Channels, Signal
                      Sending, Somatic Processes, Unconscious Projection

Features: Multichannel Processes of Verbal, Non-Verbal, and Somatic
                      Information Transmission

Therapist

Ego-States
Affect
Defense
Prior History
Trauma History
Personality Characteristics
Genetic Disposition

Receiver Variables

Therapist

Decoded

• Affect
• Defense
• Somatic States
• Ego-States
• Personality
• Unconscious Thinking
• Cognition–Perception

'Flow'
'Waves'
'Energy'

'Signals'
'Information'
'Transmission'

Information Reception and Decoding*
(affective reactions/counter-transference)

Patient

Ego-States
Affect
Defense
Prior History
Trauma History
Personality Characteristics
Genetic Disposition

Sender Variables

Patient

Information Transmission*   Signal Transmission
(transferences and TST)   Multichannel Process**
                             (frequency, amplitude, intensity)

Encoded

• Affect
• Defense
• Somatic States
• Ego-States
• Personality
• Unconscious Memory
• Cognition–Perception

*In PTSD, information transmission is trauma specific transference (TST) projections.

**Multichannel process varies in frequency, amplitude, intensity modulation in each channel (e.g., affect, defense, somatic complaints)

Fig. 11.1   Information Flow in Transference: Countertransference Matrix

When we think of posttraumatic therapy as an active process, it is possible to use words such as flow, wave, signal, energy, transmission, information gathering, and so forth to characterize the nature of the transmitting the unconscious of the patient. These defining concepts illustrate the features of a multichanneled process of verbal and nonverbal information transmissions, which we have previously referred to as *trauma-specific transference* (TST), and vary in their *intensity, frequency, amplitude*, and *modulation* in each channel of information transmission. In this regard, it is possible to conceptualize that at any given time there are seven separate channels transmitting to the therapist (affect, defense, somatic states, ego states, personality, unconscious memory, and cognitive processes). Further, these same seven channels exist as potential receptor sites in the therapist. In a manner similar to a neuron, information "flows" or is transmitted from one part of the nerve across a synapse to an awaiting receptor location that receives the transmission, decodes it, and activates another process. In essence then, encoded information is transmitted and decoded and capable of being processed for use in the treatment process. When construed in this way, we can see that empathic attunement is a vehicle for accurate reception of the information being generated by the patient. Therapeutic effectiveness requires accurate decoding of the channels, the ability and capacity to "hold" (i.e., store) the information without it overloading the capacities of the therapist channels (system overload). Transference and countertransference are old words used to describe the intricate and extraordinarily interesting process of human communication in the context of psychotherapy.

TRAUMA-SPECIFIC TRANSFERENCE TRANSMISSIONS (TSTT): ORGANISMIC PROJECTIONS OF EMBEDDED PSYCHIC TRAUMA

Figure 11.2 illustrates how PTSD symptoms get transmitted during the process of psychotherapy. It is especially important to understand TSTT since it is always present during the treatment prior to resolution and integration of the trauma experience and the manifestation of PTSD. It is my belief, and clinically demonstrable in training work, that TSTT consisted of a set of cues that are "leaked" out in subtle expressions in the seven channels shown in Figure 11.1. More specifically, there are at least 65 distinct symptoms of PTSD (Wilson, Friedman, & Lindy, 2001) as well as unconscious projections of the trauma experience across the five clusters of PTSD symptoms: (1) reexperiencing, (2) avoidance/denial, (3) psychological hyperreactivity, (4) ego states, and (5) interpersonal processes. In this regard, it is possible to speak of TSTT as omnipresent. It is as if the victim "speaks" out saying, "See what happened to me — look at what the trauma did to change the way I used to be." Thus, the TSTT is an unconscious ego-state projection of the entire

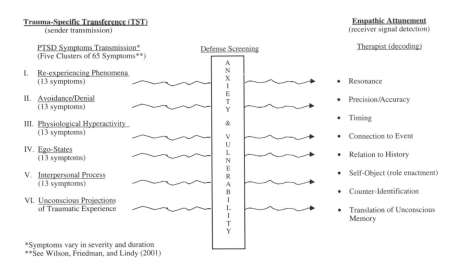

Fig. 11.2 Trauma Specific Transference Transmission (TST)

organism's response to traumatization and the changes induced at all levels of psychological functioning (i.e., allostatic changes; see Wilson, Friedman, & Lindy, 2001 for a discussion). Further, the unconscious is a kind of "diplomatic spokesperson" who conveys messages to the therapist in this information transmission through the seven channels. Unconscious projections require decoding and understanding; they are behavioral manifestations, sometimes symbolic, of that which the patient cannot express or recall by conscious effort.

Case Example: Mashed Brains at Dawn

A Vietnam War veteran patient used to pick at the soles of his boots with a pencil as he talked for years about his overwhelming combat experiences. He would repeatedly say, "You know, doc, there is something missing about that nightlong fire-fight," with a sad, tired, and forlorn expression on his prematurely aged face. As it turned out, the unconscious memory of his picking at his boots was a reenactment of using a stick to pick out from the cleats in his boots the mashed brains of one of his buddies who died in the nightlong fire-fight that killed all but three platoon members. This action of picking at his boots during treatment is a clear example of TSTT and repetition compulsion of the original postcombat reaction. It was as if his unconscious voice was transmitting the message: "Look here, doc, here is the clue to what I can't remember." Indeed, when his amnesia dissipated, the entire forgotten sequence of events returned to his memory about the night battle that changed his life forever as a 19-year-old soldier. The terror, fear of annihilation, and immersion into human carnage was devastating to his ego and capacity to master the experience. However, he always recalled sitting on a log picking at the gray brain matter in the morning at "first light" as the sun broke through clouds in the mountains of the central highlands of Vietnam in 1967. The image of a young soldier sitting alone, battle weary and totally exhausted, picking human brains from the sole of his battle worn combat boots, encapsulated his current reality of being alone, divorced, isolated, alienated from others, and depressed. For him, the memories of war were both his link to the past, buddies killed, and his search for meaning. The unintegrated memories were bittersweet companions; they tortured him and sustained him at the same time. His unconscious fear was that to let go of the most powerful experience of his life was to let go of himself and his identity. The question for him, of course, centered around the issue of, "What's left, doc?" Indeed, we could say that he was "picking" at the meaning of his life after Vietnam.

The magnitude of the complexity of TSTT cannot be underestimated in the treatment of PTSD. It is one of the critically important features that differentiates PTSD treatment from that of therapeutic approaches to other disorders, including anxiety disorders. The clinicians ability to decode TSTT will be strongly associated with therapeutic outcome. Viewed in this way, the central role of empathic attunement takes on a clearer focus since it is one of the primary clinical skills by which to enter one of the portals of entry into the PTSD patient's ego state. Conceptually, however, there is an advantage for this perspective, since knowledge of the fact that there are seven channels of information for five clusters of PTSD symptoms allows the therapist ways of "knowing" and approaching how to decode the TSTT and other transmissions. Further, recognizing the universality of unconscious projections of the traumatic experience in any of the seven channels of the PTSD symptoms, enables the therapist to formulate hypotheses and informed intuitions about the meaning and significance of any interactional sequence during treatment. In this regard, it is my belief that there is no randomness to the patterns of TSTT; they have meaning and significance at all times.

Moreover, as Figure 11.2 illustrates, ego defenses serve as "screens," "filters," or "blocks" and control mechanisms to TSTT transmissions. The various defenses are control mechanisms directly concerned with anxiety and states of vulnerability. The greater the experienced (conscious or unconscious) anxiety and inner vulnerability, the more the defenses will be utilized to stave-off threats (i.e., reexperienced traumatic memories) that were originally embedded in the trauma experience or that activate prior emotional trauma or conflicts from the patient's history. However, I wish to make it clear that what I am proposing is not the classic Freudian paradigm of trauma and ego defense (Freud, 1917, 1920). Rather, it is a paradigm in which allostatic transformations caused by trauma alter organismic functioning in a holistic, dynamic manner. These alterations produced by trauma impact all levels of psychological functioning. The organismic impacts are dynamically interrelated and express themselves in various channels of behavior. Traumatic encoding of experience is organismic; it is not an isolated subsystem of memory, affect, perception, or motivation. TSTT are direct manifestations of this set of organismic changes caused by trauma. Traumatic experiences, by definition, are forms of extreme stress with varying degrees of power to energize the organisms functioning and natural state of well-being. Traumatic experiences are not of the same type as normal development life experiences; they are beyond the line demarcating "unusual" and "normal" from "unusual" and "abnormal." Extreme trauma, especially catastrophic trauma involving the abyss experience (Wilson, 2002), can be thought of as "Big Bang" phenomena in a manner akin to the Big Bang theory of the universe. The Big Bang of profoundly catastrophic trauma rattles the organism to the core, rearranging its essential form but without destroying it completely. The result of the "shake up" to organismic functioning is allostatic transformations of energy, which now have a "program" and "life-force" of their own until treatment and healing restores organismic well-being, albeit in a new structural configuration than existed prior to the shattering caused by the trauma experience.

A MODEL OF EMPATHY IN TRAUMA WORK

By nature, the professional work with trauma patients presents many dilemmas to analysts, psychotherapists, counselors, medical personnel, and researchers. There is nothing ordinary or "normally" routine in attempting to understand the impact of trauma to an individual. Listening to and encountering the faces and voices of trauma patients is often stressful and difficult because traumatic experiences produce injuries to the spirit, body, and psyche, which makes it difficult to sustain empathy without losing concentration, attention to details of their trauma experiences, or feeling overwhelmed at the nature of a particular traumatic event. Traumatic events anchor the extreme point of the stressor continuum. Powerful affective reactions to trauma stories and the unfolding of the patient's history are normative and expectable (Wilson & Lindy, 1994). Similarly, it is empirically demonstrable that there are predictable patterns of psychological and physiological arousal when therapists, students, researchers, or others respond to the presentations of human distress, accounts of personal trauma, or the report of stressful life events (Ickes, 1997; Wilson & Lindy, 1994). There is a psychobiological capacity for empathy, and elsewhere we have argued that it is an important adaptive function in human social interaction, which potentially has profound consequences for the evolution of the species (Wilson & Lindy, 1994). Thus, understanding empathic processes in work with PTSD and victims of trauma in a variety of settings (e.g., medical triage, crisis intervention, emergency medicine, disaster responses, military defusings, critical incident debriefings, psychotherapy, etc.) is essential to successful treatment or intervention outcomes.

STRUCTURE AND DYNAMICS OF INTERPERSONAL PROCESSES IN TREATMENT

Figure 11.3 presents the overall conceptual framework for understanding the structure and dynamics of interpersonal processes in the treatment of trauma and PTSD. The figure illustrates the sequential flow of activities in a dynamic way during treatment.

In the way of a summary, it can be seen that the patient presents with PTSD and other symptoms, which are filtered through ego defenses (i.e., "screens"). The encoded trauma experience is organismically embedded in somatic states and traumatic memory. The registration of trauma in psychobiological forms is then transmitted during the course of treatment through seven separate channels: (1) affect, (2) defense, (3) somatic states, (4) cognition/perception, (5) personality, (6) ego states, and (7) unconscious manifestations. The translation of trauma-specific encoding is subsequently expressed in a variety of ways, especially trauma-specific transference (TST). Specifically, trauma-specific transference has four dimensions: (a) the content of the trauma of the trauma story, (b) the complexity and intensity of the traumatic experience, (c) the ambiguity — clarity of transference projections, and (d) the affect arousal potential (AAP) for the therapist; the degree to which an affect is stirred in the analyst. In treatment, the role of the therapist involves trauma reception, the registration and decoding of the information transmitted by the patient. In a sense, the analyst has to decode encrypted trauma material that is being transmitted by the patient. Trauma-specific transferences always contain information as to unmetabolized aspects of their particular traumatic experience. Further, depending on the severity of traumatization, TST contains the power to challenge the therapist's ability to sustain empathic attunement and sets up modalities of empathic attunement and empathic strain. The loss of attunement by the analyst will result in forms of empathic strain, countertransference, and compassion fatigue, which have the potential to disrupt the process of treatment. In contrast, the maintenance of qualities of empathic attunement (i.e., resonance, isochronicity, accuracy, etc.) enable good tracking of the TST and other dynamics of the trauma client. Finally, the therapist can be cast into one of many "role enactments" in their countertransferential reactions to the patient; a process described as dual unfolding by Racker (1968).

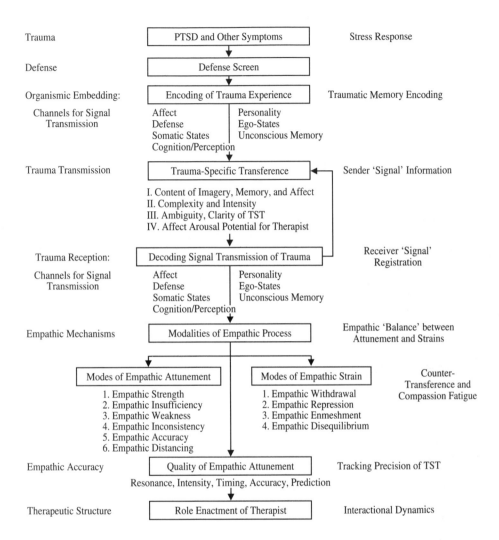

Fig. 11.3 Structure and Dynamics of Interpersonal Processes in Treatment of PTSD: Organismic Transmissions of the Patient

PSYCHOBIOLOGICAL SYNCHRONY: THE BASES OF EMPATHIC ATTUNEMENT, MATCHING PHENOMENA, AND RESPONSE CONGRUENCE

In the treatment of PTSD and its associated comorbidities (Wilson, Friedman, & Lindy, 2001), psychobiological synchrony simply means that the therapist is "in phase" with the client. However, to be "in phase" and synchronized with a patient can refer to various psychological and physiological phenomena. The study of psychological synchrony is not new, and experimental research (Levenson & Ruef, 1997) has examined the phenomenon of therapists' reactions to their patients and found evidence for response matching of autonomic nervous system functioning. Levenson and Ruef (1997) state

> With the exception of those times when the therapist was said to be distracted by other concerns, they found that heart rate changes during these episodes were generally similar for both patient and therapist ... the therapist's and patient's heart rate moved in similar directions as the levels of tension varied, but moved in opposite directions when the patient antagonism toward the therapist. (p. 48)

Consistent with my views of the role and significance of empathy to PTSD treatment, in particular, and trauma work more generally (i.e., emergency medicine, disaster response, acute intervention, critical incident debriefing), Levenson and Ruef (1997) suggest that *empathic accuracy* involves a *parallelism* between two individuals in a variety of contexts, including psychotherapy: "empathic accuracy — a state in which one person (the subject) can accurately tell what another person (the target) is feeling — will be marked by psychological parallelism between the subject and target" (p. 62). Thus, physiological parallelism can be thought of as part of the core mechanisms that govern empathic attunement, matching phenomena, and response congruence in the treatment of trauma patients. However, this is precisely where the potential difficulty lies because research evidence found that affective intensity (e.g., therapist exposure to the power of trauma stories and ultimate horror; hostility toward the therapist, etc.) was associated with "distraction" or a loss of empathic attunement. The receiver's capacity to sustain precise signal decoding was disrupted due to internal emotional states (e.g., fear, anxiety, uncertainty) and simultaneously activated dysynchronous defensive-security operations to quell the disrupted state of equilibrium or to reduce tension (empathic strain) created by the loss of synchrony. Levenson and Ruef (1997) suggest a similar formulation from experimental research and state: "that high physiological arousal on the part of the sender is associated with *low accuracy* in the receivers' ratings of the targets' affect" (p. 61, emphasis added). This finding has direct relevance and application to the treatment of PTSD because, by definition, traumatic events constitute the extreme end of the continuum of stressful life events and the patient's reports of life-threatening, horrific, dangerous, or catastrophic experiences, which contain the potential of *maximum affective arousal*. The voices and faces of trauma patients confront therapists on a regular basis with emotionally laden, disturbing, and often shameful accounts of human encounters with fragmenting effects of trauma (Wilson, 2002). Abyss experiences, in brief, present the therapists with reports of encounters with the darkest episodes of human existence and the specter of injury or death at the hands of fate or calculated, willful human malevolence. To sustain empathy effectively means that therapists must open themselves to the uncomfortable parallelism of patients' disregulated affect, pain, and struggle to overcome their injuries. Empathic strains, strong affective reactions, and countertransference reactions are indigenous to PTSD treatment. The question is how are they best managed in the service of maintaining empathic attunement to the inner reality of the patients' experiences?

DIMENSIONS OF EMPATHIC FUNCTIONING: A CONTINUUM OF ATTUNEMENT TO SEPARATION AND DETACHMENT

Empathic functioning exists on a continuum that ranges from minimal to optimal functioning in terms of empathic attunement. The continuum represents *qualities* of empathic functioning at any given time in the course of posttraumatic therapy. The specific quality or adequacy of empathic attunement spans the spectrum from none (absent or disengaged) to partial (moderate) to optimal (maximal) connection and active engagement with the patient. A conceptualization of a continuum of empathic attunement is dynamic in nature and mirrors the reality that many factors influence the *disposition* to empathic functioning (detachment versus attunement), ranging from clinical experience in trauma work, personal history, fatigue, and stress-related states, and the raw power of the trauma story of the patient to evoke strong affective reactions and countertransference processes in treatment (see Figure 11.4).

The continuum of empathic functioning is a useful way to think about the adequacy of active therapeutic engagement with the patient. Minimal empathic functioning is the absence or only partial achievement of empathic attunement. There is a failure to relate to the client in a manner that manifests therapeutic congruency. On the other hand, therapeutic empathic congruency means that the therapist understands by having knowledge of the internal ego state of the trauma client, even if the client cannot verbalize all of his or her inner thoughts, feelings, and memories. In this regard, the therapist "decodes" the flow of information emanating from the trauma client and receives it without distorting "noises," "signals," or defenses generated by his or her attempts to match understanding (i.e., congruent empathy) of the trauma experience of the client. The matching process of adequate signal detection and responsive communication includes both "here-and-now" processes and the traversing back in time into the patient's subjective reality of his or her trauma experience. In that regard, it is as if the therapist joins with the patient's memory and rides along like a fellow passenger on a journey of discovery in which the patient says — "Look at this; experience this event or situation with me, and see what happened here long ago."

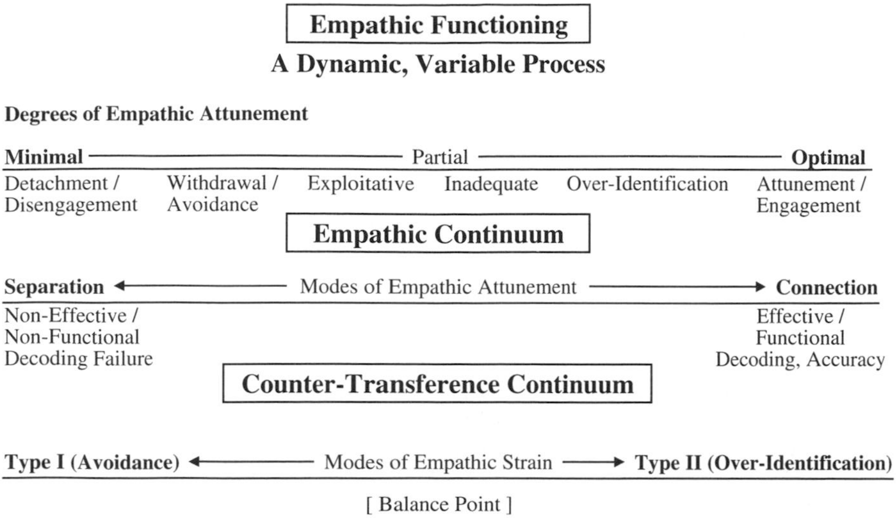

Empathic Functioning

A Dynamic, Variable Process

Degrees of Empathic Attunement

Minimal ───────────────	Partial	─────────────── Optimal
Detachment / Withdrawal /	Exploitative Inadequate Over-Identification	Attunement /
Disengagement Avoidance		Engagement

Empathic Continuum

Separation ◄────────	Modes of Empathic Attunement	────────► Connection
Non-Effective /		Effective /
Non-Functional		Functional
Decoding Failure		Decoding, Accuracy

Counter-Transference Continuum

Type I (Avoidance) ◄──────	Modes of Empathic Strain ──────►	Type II (Over-Identification)

[Balance Point]

Fig. 11.4 Continuum of Empathic Functioning: Detachment Versus Attunement

Together, much like two persons seated together in an adventure park journey (i.e., a "theme park"), they experience the memories and emotions in a common flow that reveals the nidus of the trauma experience. In sharing the reliving of the trauma together, the therapist exerts much energy and concentration to empathically attune to the client while at the same time maintaining a "third eye" observation and protector of interpersonal boundaries. Clearly, this is among the reasons that Kohut (1977) thought of empathy as a process of knowing or data collection. However, to be an accurate recorder or collector the trauma patient's data requires four interrelated dimensions of empathic functioning: (1) empathic capacity, (2) empathic tolerance and sensitivity, (3) empathic endurance, and (4) empathic resistance.

It is important to recognize that strains imposed on the process of attunement in posttraumatic therapy can cause empathic breaks or ruptures. A rupture, cessation, or sudden loss of empathic attunement reflects the inability to continuously track, understand, and accurately experience the ego states and frame of reference of another person (Wilson & Lindy, 1994). Thus, understanding the factors that lead to a disruption in empathic functioning is necessary for identification of the traps, pitfalls, and potential trouble areas imposed by compassion fatigue, burn-out, overwhelming affective responses, and the existence of disruptive countertransference (Figley, 2002; Wilson & Lindy, 1994).

MODES OF EMPATHIC STRAIN: THERAPISTS' REACTIVE STYLES

The experience of empathic strain occurs when empathic attunement gets challenged, overwhelmed, or rendered inadequate in the face of the patient's transference or self-presentation as part of the dyadic or group interactional sequence. Empathic strain can be experienced in a variety of ways that can result in complete countertransferential processes (see Figure 11.5. However, empathic strain is typically manifest as increased tension, anxiety, problems of focus in concentration or attention, or increased autonomic nervous system activity (heart rate, respiration, etc.). Empathic strain can also appear in somatic forms as muscle tension, sleepiness or drowsiness, gastric distress, headaches, fatigue, or more idiosyncratic reactions such as rubbing ones eyes, localized muscle spasms, or urinary urgency. Further, empathic strain can be conscious or unconscious in nature and potentially associated with rapid shifts in emotional states (e.g., anger, disdain, fear, horror) and cognitive processes (e.g., fantasies of escape, rescue, thoughts about nonclinical activity, etc.).

Empathic strain results from those interpersonal events in psychotherapy that weaken, injure, or force beyond reasonable limits a positive

I.   **EMPATHIC DISEQUILIBRIUM**
   a) *Defining Conceptual Axis*: Normative, objective affective reactions and disposition to Type II — countertransference (Normative — Overidentification) associated with reactions to trauma story.
   b) *Features*: Empathic strain, experienced disequilibrium of personal states; shifts in well-being, uncertainty, vulnerability, and security.
II. **EMPATHIC WITHDRAWAL**
   a) *Defining Conceptual Axis*: Normative, objective affective reaction and disposition to Type I — countertransference (Normative — Avoidance) associated with personal reactions to trauma story.
   b) *Features*: Withdrawal from empathic attunement, separation, avoidance and security operations (i.e., unconscious defense processes), feelings of uncertainty and inadequacy; reliance on blank facade, misperceptions of transference.
III. **EMPATHIC ENMESHMENT**
   a) *Defining Conceptual Axis*: Personalized — idiosyncratic reactions to trauma story and disposition to Type II (overidentification) countertransference.
   b) *Features*: Personalized affective reactions; activation of personal issues; tendency to cross boundaries; overinvolvement with patient; excessive amplification of attunement responses; reciprocal dependency.
IV. **EMPATHIC REPRESSION**
   a) *Defining Conceptual Axis*: Personalized — idiosyncratic reactions to trauma story and disposition to Type I (avoidance) countertransference.
   b) *Features*: Personal repression of memories, conflicts, and unresolved problems aroused by the interactional sequence with patient. Loss of attunement may be severe and damaging to therapeutic outcome. Withdrawal, denial, and distancing are all defensive operations.

Fig. 11.5 Modes of Empathic Strain

therapeutic response to the client. Countertransference processes are only one source of empathic strain, yet we believe that in the treatment of PTSD, CTRs are perhaps the primary causes of treatment failure.

Building on the seminal works of Cohen (1952), Wolstein (1988), Tansey and Burke (1989), Slatker (1987), Danieli (1988), Lindy (1988), Parson (1988), Wilson (1989), Maroda (1991), Scurfield (1993), Wilson and Lindy (1994), Dalenberg (2000), Lindy and Lifton (2001) it is possible to construct a schema for understanding modalities of empathic strain in the treatment of PTSD. Figure 11.6 illustrates these forms of empathic strain in a two-dimensional representation, based on Type I and Type II modes of CTRs crossed by the axis of objective and subjective countertransference processes.

TYPE I AND TYPE II COUNTERTRANSFERENCE

Objective CTRs are expectable affective and cognitive reactions experienced by the therapist in response to the personality, behavior, and trauma story of the client. Subjective CTRs are personal reactions that originate from the therapist's own personal conflicts, idiosyncracies, or unresolved issues from life-course development.

Type I and Type II modes of countertransference refer respectively to the primary tendencies of counterphobic avoidance, distancing, and detachment reactions as opposed to tendencies to overidentify and become enmeshed with the client. Type I CTRs typically include forms of denial, minimization, distortion, counterphobic reactions, avoidance,

TYPE OF REACTION

(Universal, Objective, Indigenous Reactions)

	Normative	

	I. Empathic Disequilibrium Uncertainty Vulnerability Unmodulated Affect	II. Empathic Withdrawal Blank Screen Facade Intellectualization Misperception of Dynamics	
Type II CTR (Over-Identification)	III. Empathic Enmeshment Loss of Boundaries Over-Involvement Reciprocal Dependency	IV. Empathic Repression Withdrawal Denial Distancing	Type I CTR (Avoidance)

	Personalized	

(Particular, Subjective, Idiosyncratic Reactions)

Fig. 11.6   Reactive Style of Therapist

detachment, and withdrawal from an empathic stance toward the client. Type II CTRs, in contrast, involve forms of overidentification, overidealization, enmeshment, and excessive advocacy for the client, as well as behaviors that elicit guilt reactions.

As Figure 11.6 illustrates, the combination of the two axes of countertransference processes produces four distinct modes or styles of empathic strain, which we have identified as: (1) empathic withdrawal, (2) empathic repression, (3) empathic enmeshment, and (4) empathic disequilibrium. Although a therapist can experience one style or reaction pattern more than another, it is possible to experience any or all of the modes of empathic strain during the course of treatment with a traumatized client (see Wilson & Lindy, 1994 for an extended discussion).

THE FOUR MODES OF EMPATHIC STRAIN IN COUNTERTRANSFERENCE

Empathic Withdrawal: ES Mode I

Empathic withdrawal is a mode of countertransference strain that occurs when the therapist experiences expected affective and cognitive reactions during treatment, and he or she is predisposed by defensive style and personality characteristics toward Type I avoidance and detachment responses. In this mode, a rupture occurs in the empathic stance toward the client. The result is often the loss of capacity for sustained empathic inquiry due to overreliance on the "blank-screen" or conventional, or recently delegated or taught (for new therapist) therapeutic techniques. These reactions block the painful task of integrating the trauma experience and can lead the therapist to misperceive or misinterpret the behavior and psychodynamics of the client on the basis of previous assumptions.

Empathic Repression: ES Mode II

A similar process occurs in *empathic repression*, in which the transference issues of the patient reactivate conflicts and unresolved personal concerns in the therapist's life. Thus, a personalized subjective reaction, combined with a disposition toward a Type I CTR, can be associated with repressive countermeasures by the therapist. His or her inward focus on areas of personal conflict is likely to be associated with an unwitting and unconscious withdrawal from the therapeutic role and denial of the full significance of the clinical issues being presented by the client.

Empathic Enmeshment: ES Mode III

The third mode of strain, *empathic enmeshment*, is the result of the therapist's tendency toward Type II CTRs coupled with subjective reactions during treatment. In this mode of empathic strain, the clinician leaves the therapeutic role by becoming overinvolved and overidentified with the client. The most common consequence is pathological enmeshment and a loss of role boundaries in the context of treatment. In the treatment of PTSD, therapists with a personal history of trauma and victimization are especially vulnerable to this mode of empathic strain and can unconsciously attempt to rescue traumatized clients as an indirect way of dealing with their own unintegrated personal conflicts (Wilson & Thomas, 2000). Perhaps the greatest danger that occurs within this mode of empathic strain is the potential for the therapist to unconsciously reenact personal problems through pathological enmeshment. When this occurs it not only causes an abandonment of the empathic stance toward the person seeking help but can lead to secondary victimization or the intensification of transference themes that the patient brought to treatment in the first place.

Empathic Disequilibrium: ES Mode IV

Empathic disequilibrium, as Figure 11.6 indicates, is characterized by a disposition to Type II CTRs and the experience of objective reactions during treatment, especially in work with patients suffering from PTSD and comorbid conditions. This mode of strain is characterized by somatic discomfort, feelings of insecurity and uncertainty as to how to deal with the client, and more. It occurs commonly in therapists who experience either Type I or Type II CTRs.

CASE HISTORY: THE SOCCER GAME

Teresa, a woman in her 20s, disclosed to her counselor the following trauma story regarding her internment in a South American prison for political dissenters. Her captors demeaned and abused her sexually, using rape in all its human forms. Next, they unleashed specially conditioned Alsatian dogs that intimidated, threatened, and bit her, drawing blood from her breasts. The dogs then had sexual intercourse with her. During these events the captors watched, laughed, and made humiliating and disparaging remarks. Next, her captors beheaded her two young children while forcing her to watch. They kicked her children's decapitated heads as "soccer balls." Finally they then placed her in an isolation cell and carried out a mock execution.

The counselor who was helping this client was badly shaken during the session when the trauma story was told and sought relief from the tension she experienced throughout the hour of treatment. Her reaction was such that she was overwhelmed by the content of the trauma story, which raised personal issues for her, as she was herself a woman in prime child-bearing years. In the case example, the therapist indicated that she felt overwhelmed, tense, vulnerable, uncertain of her own capacity to bind anxiety, and she experienced increased physiological arousal. She stated that she felt somewhat insecure in regard to her ability to adequately treat the torture victim, despite having worked quite successfully with other torture victims in the past. In particular, her objective CTR included vivid images of seeing the heads of the murdered children on the ground being sadistically abused by the victim's captors. These visual images and her natural identification with the woman as a mother and brutalized person were associated with an extreme state of autonomic nervous system arousal (e.g., heart palpitations, intense anxiety). Her concern following the session was that if she could not more effectively modulate her affect she would not be successful in her clinical efforts. An associated concern centered around her fear that the torture victim might become further isolated from sources of help or even worse, commit suicide.

This case illustration also indicates that empathic overarousal is associated with powerful affect reactions (e.g., anxiety, motor tension) and cognitive processes (e.g., images of sadistic torture) that extend beyond the therapy hour in distressing ways associated with self-doubt, feelings of vulnerability, and a need to discharge the therapist's hyperaroused state.

It is interesting to note that one consequence of empathy is that the therapist can experience degrees of hyperarousal that are proportional to the level of hyperarousal the patient manifests as part of his or her PTSD. Clearly, this is a type of dual unfolding in the dynamics of transference and countertransference. This is another example of psychophysiological parallelism in empathic congruence and matching phenomena.

Later in work of this nature, the client might begin to reexperience trauma-related feelings that he or she feels are activated in vivo during the therapy. Teresa, the torture survivor, for example, could feel that the therapist is failing to protect her from harsh, current political forces blocking immigration and thereby persecuting her anew. She might feel that the therapist is judging her for sacrificing her children to her political cause, irreverently dismissing her attachment to her dead children, or failing to hear her sadness and pain at now feeling inhibited sexually (thereby disrespecting her sexuality). As each of these elements in the trauma situation is partially reenacted and transferred onto the treatment, new trauma-based countertransferences can appear, impairing empathy by rupture, repression, enmeshment, or overarousal, until these processes are understood as part of the dual unfolding of the treatment.

Individual Variations in Modes of Empathic Strain

A two-dimensional model for a topology of countertransference has its limitations, and I am not suggesting that *all* relevant CTRs to PTSD fit into one of the four quadrants. For example, CTR reactions might also need to be categorized in terms of affect range and intensity, trauma role reenacted, defense cluster mobilized, symptom experienced by therapist, or segment of the treatment frame distorted. Neither do we wish to imply a static mode, one that confines CTR in a given treatment to one quadrant. Indeed, there is more likely a dynamic interplay among quadrants over time in a single case. Nevertheless, this model provides an important starting point, one that includes rather than excludes other dimensions and, for purposes of clinical use, establishes an important point of orientation. This dynamic model can be empirically demonstrated by critical analysis of videotaped role playing of PTSD cases to see in situ the modes of empathic strain and countertransference.

THE IMPACT OF EMPATHIC STRAIN AND COUNTERTRANSFERENCE ON THE PSYCHOTHERAPY OF TRAUMA SURVIVORS

The understanding of empathic stress permits analysis of the factors that determine CTRs and how CTRs, in turn, affect the phases of stress recovery and potentially cause pathological results to the client. What happens to the treatment process and the phases of recovery when there is a loss of empathic attunement?

Figure 11.7 shows in graphic form how the modes of empathic strain impact on the development of Type I and Type II countertransference processes. Elsewhere, Wilson and Lindy (1994) have presented a detailed discussion of these processes and dynamics in posttraumatic therapy. However, space restrictions enable only a condensed summary explanation here.

There are many determinants of CTRs in treatment. Figure 11.7 illustrates four major determinants of CTR in posttraumatic therapy, each of which singly or interactively can give birth to empathic strain. Empathic strain can result in one of many types of countertransference reactions and role enactments by the therapist (Wilson, Friedman, & Lindy, 2001). Moreover, a CTR can impact any phase of the recovery process, leading to a rupture of empathy and a loss of the therapeutic role function. When this occurs, as it inevitably does, a potentially pathological outcome can occur resulting in the following outcomes: (a) cessation or stasis in the recovery process; (b) fixation within a phase or stage in recovery; (c) regressive behaviors; (d) intensification of transference issue; (e) acting out behaviors; and (f) dissociation.

ANXIETY AND DEFENSIVENESS IN THE ANALYST DURING TREATMENT OF THE PATIENT

Defensive behavior by the therapist is typically counterproductive to the successful treatment of PTSD. Similarly, the experience of anxiety and defensiveness during posttraumatic therapy is expectable and universal, especially given the context of the treatment focus. The idea

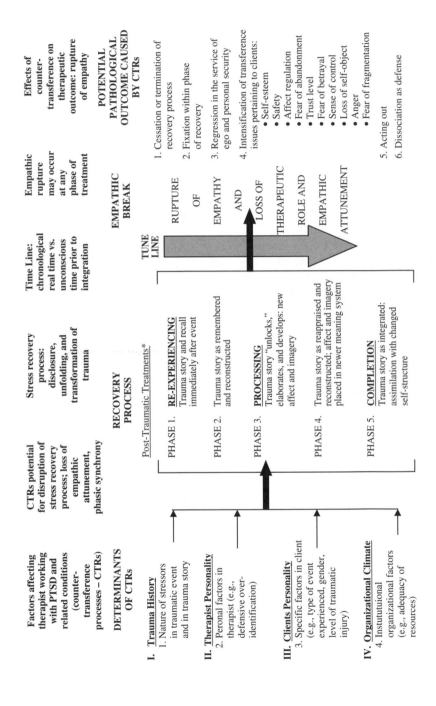

Fig. 11.7 Countertransference (CTR) Effects on Recovery From Trauma and Violence

that the analyst's level of anxiety and defensiveness is a potential problem in countertransference is not new and has been the subject of
extensive investigation (Wolstein, 1988). In 1952, Mabel Blake Cohen
wrote a remarkable and insightful paper titled "Countertransference and
Anxiety" in which she proposed five therapeutic situations likely to produce anxiety and countertransference.

> The main situations in the doctor-patient relationship that undermine
> the therapeutic role and therapy may result in anxiety in the therapist
> can be listed as follows: (1) when the doctor is *helpless* to affect the
> patients' memories; (2) when the doctor is treated continually as an
> *object of fear, hatred,* or *contempt*; (3) when the patient calls on the doc-
> tor for advice or reassurance as evidence of his professional compe-
> tence or interest in the patient; (4) when the patient attempts to
> establish a relationship of *romantic love* with the doctor; and (5) when
> the patient calls on the doctor for other intimacy. (cited in Wolstein,
> 1988, p. 73, emphasis added)

This passage is germane to our focus on empathy and countertransference because it highlights the situations likely to produce
anxiety, namely, when the patient expresses strong emotions of *fear,
hatred* (anger, rage), *contempt* (hostility, disdain, degradation), or
romantic love (sexualized feelings, or demands for succorance, etc.).
As applied to PTSD, many of the sequela of traumatic experiences
that involved those affects (fear, hatred, contempt, helplessness,
love) were prominent reactions to the stressors present in the event.
Thus, TSTT (trauma-specific transference transmission) involves
such strong affects, which the patient typically finds difficult to
modulate. The patient then "transmits" his or her anxiety, defensiveness, and fears to the therapist, often an unconscious transmission, as
a request for help because of the patient's feelings of insecurity,
uncertainty, and confusion brought about by the trauma. The therapist receives this anxiety-based transmission and attempts to
"decode" its meaning while sustaining empathy in the treatment process (see Figure 11.8).

Cohen (1952) lists 18 specific signs of anxiety and defensiveness in
the analyst during treatment. These findings are particularly interesting
for three basic reasons. First, the publication is 50 years old and still
very relevant today to PTSD treatment approaches, although that was
not her focus at the time. Second, it closely matches our description of
Type I and Type II countertransference reactions. Third, recent empirical research confirms the presence of all 18 signs of anxiety and defensiveness in posttraumatic therapy (Dalenberg, 2000; Danieli, 1988,
1994; Wilson & Thomas, in press). Moreover, Wilson and Lindy (1994)
in a previous study, listed four categories of information that constitute
potential manifestations of countertransference reactions. Figure 11.9
summarizes the factors, which parallel those found in other research

Signs of Anxiety and Defensiveness in Analyst*	Modes of Empathic Strain (A) and Type I or Type II (B)** Countertransference Reactions (1994)		
	Mode A	CTR B	
Unreasonable dislike for patient	III	I	(disdain, repression)
Failure to identify with patient	III	I	(detachment, withdrawal)
Nonresponsiveness to emotional distress of patient	II	I	(distance, avoidance)
Overwhelmed by patient's problems	I	II	(disequilibrium)
Excessive liking of patient	III	II	(enmeshment)
Dreads therapy session/uncomfortable during session	II	I	(fear, anxiety)
Preoccupation with patient outside office	III	II	(overinvolvement)
Inattention, problems of concentration, drowsiness, sleepy	II	I	(avoidance, denial, withdrawal)
Preoccupation with own (personal) affairs	II	I	(avoidance, withdrawal)
Analyst has problems with time management (late to session)	II	I	(avoidance, withdrawal)
Argumentative with patient	III	II	(overinvolvement, defensive)
Defensive with patient; feels vulnerable	III	II	(overidentification, defensive)
Countertransference distortion	II	I	(withdrawal, misperception of dynamics)
Analyst elicits affect; prods patient	III	II	(enmeshment)
Overconcerned with confidentiality	III	II	(enmeshment)
Oversympathetic due to mistreatment by authority of patient	III	II	(overidentification)
Urge to help in acting	I	II	(overidentification, prosocial, disequilibrium)
Patient appears in analyst's dreams	III	II	(overidentification)

*From Cohen, pp. 231–243.
**After Wilson & Lindy, 1994.

Fig. 11.8 Anxiety and Defensiveness in Analyst During Treatment of Patient

(Dalenberg, 2000; Danieli, 1988, 1994; Figley, 2002; Lindy & Lifton, 2001; Wilson & Thomas, in press).

Figure 11.9 summarizes four sets of indicators of CTRs in the psychotherapy of trauma survivors: (1) physiological and physical reactions, (2)

I. Physiological and Physical Reactions

Symptoms of increased ANS arousal (e.g., heart palpitations, muscle tension)
Somatic reactions to trauma story or therapy as a contextual process (e.g., stomach pain)
Sleep disturbances; nightmares of patient's trauma
Agitation, inability to relax, on edge, hypersensitivity
Inattention, drowsiness, avoidance reactions, yawning, rubbing eyes
Uncontrolled and unintended displays of emotion
Isochronicity: physiological parallelism to affective state, client

II. Emotional Reactions

Irritability, annoyance, disdain, or resentment toward client
Anxiety and fear
Depression and helpless
Anger, rage, hostility, passive aggression
Detachment, denial, avoidance, numbing, or desires for aloneness and isolation
Sadistic/masochistic feelings
Voyeuristic and sexualized feelings
Horror, disgust, dread, loathing, terror
Confusion, psychic overload, overwhelmed, foggy after session
Guilt, shame, and embarrassment
Sadness, grief, sorrow
Fatigue, exhaustion, feeling 'drained', 'spent', 'wasted', 'depleted'

III. Psychological Reactions

Detachment reactions based on defenses of intellectualization, rationalization, isolation, denial, minimization, fantasy
Overidentification based on defenses of projection, introjection, denial, altruism

IV. Signs and Behavioral Symptoms of CTRs That May Be Conscious or Unconscious

Preoccupation with patient's trauma history, dreams, or presentation during treatment
Rescue fantasies: problem fixer, hero, rescuer, "dragon slayer," "white knight," good parents, etc.
Forgetting, lapse of attention, parapraxes
Leave therapeutic role stance of empathy
Overhostility, anger toward client
Relief when client misses appointment or wish that client not show for session
Repeated scheduling problems by therapist
Denial of feelings and/or denial of need for supervision/consultation
Narcissistic belief in role of being specialist in PTSD
Excessive concern/identification with client (e.g., take trauma impact "home")
Psychic numbing or emotional constriction; desexualization
Self-medication as numbing (i.e., use of alcohol, etc. to reduce affect and preoccupation)
Loss of boundaries during therapy
Preoccupation with referring client or terminating treatment

Wilson & Lindy, 1994.

Fig. 11.9 Factors Indicative of CTRs in Therapist/Helper

affective reactions, (3) psychological reactions, and (4) behavioral symptoms. These four categories were derived by talking extensively with colleagues in the field who work with trauma survivors (i.e., members of the ISTSS — International Society for Traumatic Stress Studies). For example, nearly all stated that physical reactions were common (e.g., headaches, increased motor tension, flushing, sleeplessness, increased autonomic nervous system [ANS] arousal), and were a salient clue that countertransference was at work. Notice how closely the clusters match up to Cohen's (1952) formulation of anxiety and defense.

ORGANISMIC TUNING: THE POSITIVE THERAPEUTIC EFFECTS OF EMPATHIC ATTUNEMENT

Implicit in our analysis of the effects of empathic congruence in the treatment of psychological trauma and PTSD is the assumption that *phasic synchrony,* as a psychobiological phenomenon, is a process associated with natural healing. I am using the natural healing to describe positive allostatic readjustment following trauma; a recalibration of the organisms adaptation to stress and movement toward a resolution of the unmetabolized psychic elements of the trauma experience (Wilson, Friedman, & Lindy, 2002). Positive allostasis is restabilization following change; a reorganization of the organism following the fragmenting impact of trauma. The configuration of organismic restructuring as positive allostasis has many variations that range on a continuum from minimal to radical transformation of the self and manifestations in behavior. However, it must be recognized that at this time we have no classification system of the phases, forms, or patterns of personality transformations that occur as part of positive allostatic reorganization. Neither do we have a handbook of typologies of the forms of posttraumatic self-integration, which classify forms of healthy personality that emerge beyond the pathology of PTSD and its comorbidities. Considered in a broader perspective, we do not yet understand the positive organismic sources that are associated with resiliency, a sense of coherency, and transformative integration of ego space and the structure of the self (Wilson, Friedman, & Lindy, 2001; Wilson & Raphael, 1993). A dynamic theory of positive allostasis following trauma requires an understanding of the abyss experience of trauma and the trauma archetype and its complexes (Wilson, 2002).

The *trauma complex,* as part of the *trauma archetype,* conceptualizes posttraumatic impacts in a much broader perspective of PTSD than that of a stress-related anxiety disorder. Focusing clinical attention only on PTSD is like looking at a two-dimensional portrait of a person; it is missing a third dimension that embraces the totality of unconscious functioning of the trauma survivor. Stated in simple terms, PTSD is a surface manifestation of a much deeper human phenomenon involving the universal archetype of trauma and the many constellations of the trauma complex, which, in turn, articulate with all other archetypal experiences (Wilson, 2002). PTSD is only part of the organismic change produced by trauma; a more dynamic understanding involving unconscious trauma complexes and other processes of the self. And, while PTSD is an important part of clinical focus, it is not the only dimension of central psychotherapeutic significance.

A shift of focus allows us to now examine how it is that empathic accuracy, as a qualitative phenomenon, relates to the successful treatment of psychological trauma and PTSD. Figure 11.10 summarizes 15 points of understanding how empathic congruence, phasic synchrony, and so forth facilitate the dynamic mechanisms that occur in the therapeutic encounter, which are salutogenic.

---

1. Empathy and the quantity of information
2. Empathy and the quality of information
3. Trauma linkage: Coupling the elements together
4. The gestalt of trauma
5. Precision and accuracy of decoding trauma-specific information
6. The role of empathy in informational density and cognitive complexity
7. Empathy and portals of entry to ego-space configuration
8. Trauma disclosure and reduction of defensiveness
9. Clarity in understanding: Ego defenses built around traumatization
10. Positive allostasis: Restabilization following change caused by trauma
11. Threshold of TST (trauma-specific transference) recognition and utilization in treatment
12. Symbolization of trauma experience
13. Empathy and information storage: Future stockpiles
14. Individual therapist awareness of empathic strain, compassion fatigue, and countertransference processes
15. Isochronicity and organismic tuning: Holistic healing through positive allostatic restabilization

---

Fig. 11.10 Isochronicity and Organismic Tuning: The Positive Therapeutic Effects of Empathic Attunement

Isochronicity and Therapeutic Synergy

Empathy and the Quantity of Information

Empathic congruence leads to the disclosure of a sufficient quantity of information. Because of phasic synchrony and isochronicity, the establishment of empathic congruence facilitates the patient feeling understood, secure, and desirous of explaining how they have changed and been affected by the traumatic experience.

Empathy and the Quality of Information

By definition, phasic synchrony and empathic attunement with good resonance (precision) will generate accurate information "flow" from the patient.
The ability of the therapist to stay phasically synchronized enhances the
quality and detail of information about the trauma experience and its
impact to the existing personality dynamics and history of the patient.

Trauma Linkage: Coupling the Trauma Elements Together

Empathic attunement facilitates the therapist's ability to make the
necessary links in the reconstruction of the patient's trauma history.
Trauma linkage means that both the therapist and the patient can discover how the magnitude of trauma restructured the organism, altering
the configuration of ego space and the constellation of self-processes.
Establishing trauma links to the various elements of the allostatic
changes wrought by the trauma enables discovery of how the trauma
complex was formed (Wilson, Friedman, & Lindy, 2001). In this way,
both the patient and the therapist can "see" the entire picture of the
trauma's impact in a manner similar to looking together at an x-ray,
MRI, or PET scan of the body or brain. More specifically, once the
structure of the trauma complex is evident, the process of therapy
becomes analogous to having a functional MRI image in real time to
understand organismic functioning in a holistic manner. In other words,
the dynamics of the process become transparent.

The Gestalt of Trauma

The establishment of the linkages in the trauma complex facilitate
understanding the "gestalt of trauma" in the life of the patient. The
gestalt of trauma means the ability to fit all of the pieces of the puzzle
together; to see the whole constellation as well as the individual parts in
a manner not evident in their original state following the changes produced by traumatic impact.

Precision and Accuracy of Decoding Trauma-Specific Information

Empathic attunement is synonymous with precision and accuracy in
responding to the patient. Empathic congruence and phasic synchrony in
therapeutic orientation enables the decoding of TST and the unconscious
transmission of "leaked" information that the patient wishes to convey
but may not be able to verbalize. Unconscious transmissions, especially in
nonverbal body posture or somatic complaints, can represent condensed
symbolic material with multiple meanings that have been warded-off by
defenses or transformed into symbolized communications.

The Role of Empathy in Informational Density and Cognitive Complexity

The treatment of trauma and PTSD is a dynamic, dual, unfolding process (Wilson & Lindy, 1994). The patient and therapist have reciprocal effects on each other during the course of treatment. They are like fellow sojourners on a trip that encounters the unknown and, at times, frightened chasm of psychic uncertainty. However, the capacity for sustained empathic attunement yields changes in the cognitive processes of the therapist: (a) information density, and (b) cognitive complexity, which are related by-products of the encoding knowledge about the patient's psychodynamics (Aronoff & Wilson, 1985). Information density refers to the amount (density) of the elements configured in the ego space of the patient's trauma complex, and cognitive complexity refers to organizational differentiation of that material in the therapist. Thus, empathic accuracy facilitates greater cognitive complexity of information processing by the therapist.

Empathy and Portals of Entry to Ego-Space Configuration

Empathic attunement enables the therapist to more easily identify the various portals of entry into the patient's ego space and the nexus of the trauma complex. Wilson, Friedman, and Lindy (2001) have identified five portals of access to the interior sanctum of PTSD processes — the five clusters of PTSD symptom configurations. The creative therapist who is empathically attuned can quite readily enter these portals as avenues of gaining more information as to how the patient is processing the traumatic experience. Trauma alters the organisms in synergistic ways — some subtle and others in intricately complicated ways. Further, one implication of phasic synchrony is an ability to resonate with the organismic expressions of traumatic impacts, for example, to ego defenses and areas of emotional vulnerability and injury; physiological hyperreactivity, dreams, affective lability, resistances, and areas of avoidance, denial, disavowal, and numbing. Since PTSD symptoms are transduced into seven channels of symptom transmission, access to the portals of entry into the ego space of the patient is like walking down a dark passageway into the various chambers hidden by the facade of the patient's persona. Empathic congruence becomes a beacon of light that illuminates the pathways, focusing light in the necessary areas to properly traverse the hallway.

Trauma Disclosure and Reduction of Defensiveness

Entry into the ego space of the patient via empathic congruence and the mechanisms of phasic synchrony facilitates a more complete disclosure of the contents of the trauma narrative by the patient. Simultaneously, this process of disclosure will, over time, result in a reduction in the need for defensive guardedness. Genuine empathic attunement conveys the message from the therapist that he or she is the source of comfort and safety who will protect the patient from his or her fears and anxieties associated with organismic disequilibrium resulting from allostatic changes in the pretrauma baseline of functioning.

Clarity in Understanding Ego-Defenses Built Around Traumatization

As a corollary to increased trauma disclosure and a reduction of defensiveness in the patient, the therapist naturally develops understanding and clarity as to the role of ego defenses in protecting areas of vulnerability associated with traumatization. Authentic empathic attunement is one form of what Carl Rogers (1951) termed unconditional positive regard for the patient. The process of sustained authentic attunement results in the therapist having a broader vista of the operation of the patient's defenses, which, paradoxically, lessens the patient's need for utilization in the *context* of a therapeutic sanctuary and can be experienced by the patient as a place of rock-solid safety amid the inner turmoil of uncertainty and the search for meaning and purpose to the traumatic experience itself.

Positive Allostasis: Restabilization Following Change Caused by Trauma

Empathic attunement in its various permeations also serves to facilitate positive allostasis (Wilson, Friedman, & Lindy, 2001). As noted by McEwen (1998), allostasis refers to the body's effort to maintain stability through change when stress places demands on the organism's adaptive capacity. Positive allostasis refers to restabilization following change caused by trauma. However, it is not a return to the previous baseline of functioning. Rather, it is the creation of a new configuration of adaptation. As noted by Horowitz (1986), a process of accommodation occurs in processing the trauma experience — what was ego alien (trauma) is now assimilated into a new cognitive-affective structure in ego processes and the self. Although positive allostasis is not the same as health, it is a central mechanism in the process of healing. In this regard, transformation of the trauma experience into an integrative, efficacious self-modality without debilitating symptoms of anxiety, depression, substance abuse, PTSD, and so forth can be regarded as the core of healing and organismic resilience.

Threshold of TST (Trauma-Specific Transference) Recognition and Utilization in Treatment

The therapist's capacity to recognize and properly utilize TST varies greatly in the treatment of PTSD. Empathic congruence and phasic synchrony enable a faster threshold of recognition of TST — to recognize and use this form of transference in the treatment process. As stated earlier, TST is considered to be present throughout the course of treatment, and, therefore, empathic attunement enables recognition of its transmissions, dynamic significance, and critical importance as information "leakage" from the patient to the therapist.

Symbolization of Trauma Experience

The capacity of humans to symbolize experience has long been recognized in the psychodynamic literature (Freud, 1917; Jung, 1929; Lindy, 1993). Traumatic experiences, as archetypal phenomena, are also symbolized to express the intrapsychic processes of the patient (Early, 1993; Kalscheid, 1998). Empathic accuracy serves as a vehicle by which to understand the idiosyncratic manifestation of the trauma experience. The symbolization of trauma experience is yet another variation on "information transmission" from the patient — it is his or her way of saying, "Look at this symbol — it contains representations of how I was affected by trauma — it is a clue for you to understand that which I cannot fully verbalize." We can also think of symbols of trauma as encapsulated information that contains categories of data that link elements of the trauma experience in a unified manner. The symbols are generated by the unconscious architect of the patient who creates an object of expression. Interpretation of, or understanding its meaning, can be obscured to the patient's conscious awareness, but of course, unconsciously informative when accurately interpreted.

Empathy and Information Storage: Future Stockpiles

Empathic accuracy and congruence is associated with the capacity to receive, decode, and use information generated by the patient. In addition to the quantity and quality of information retrieved through the patient's multichanneled transmissions, such data can be stored by the therapist for future use in formulating the nature of psychodynamic functioning. Clearly, having more information about the patient is critically important in several ways: First, to formulate hypotheses about the operation of allostatic mechanisms in PTSD and associated comorbidities; second, to use the stored information as an additional tool of sustained empathic attunement, including, for example, hypothesis testing with the patient about his or her functioning; third, to increase prediction through empathic accuracy, for example, to anticipate patterns of behavior likely to be expressed by the patient in the course of "working through" the trauma (assimilation and accommodation of unmetabolized traumatic material).

Increased Therapist Awareness of Empathic Strain, Compassion, Fatigue, and Countertransference Processes

As a natural consequence of sustained empathic attunement, empathic congruence, matching phenomenon, and so forth, the therapist will develop greater self-awareness and insight into his or her own reactions to the work of treatment. Clearly, good empathic capacity implies not only awareness of the patient's internal psychological state, but of the therapist's internal affective and psychological processes. Thus, self-directed empathic introspection (i.e., self-monitoring) is a way in which the analyst identifies his or her own reactions indicative of empathic strains, compassion, fatigue, and countertransference processes. It must also be recognized that in the dual-unfolding processes of treatment, the analyst utilizes his or her own defensive "screens" in precisely the same dynamic manner as the patient. In other words, therapists have "blocks" to their own reception and transmission capacities.

Isochronicity and Organismic Tuning: Holistic Healing Through Positive Allostatic Restabilization

Organismic tuning refers to positive allostatic readjustment following a traumatic experience. Positive allostasis refers to restabilization in a holistic way that promotes growth, resilience, and efficacious functioning rather than stasis, fixation, fragmentation, and maladaptive psychopathology. *Organismic tuning*, or isochronicity, is a natural consequence of consistent, sustained, empathic inquiry. Organismic tuning also reflects holistic, synergistic, interactive effects in the psychobiology of human stress response (Friedman, 2000). Sustained, consistent, empathic congruence, which accurately decodes the transference and trauma-specific transmissions of the patient, facilitates positive allostatic restabilization, leading to organismic growth, health, optimal functioning, and movement toward the increased self-actualization of potentials (Wilson, Friedman, & Lindy, 2001).

In conclusion, we can see that empathy, trauma transmissions via transference projections, and countertransference are three parts of a therapeutic symphony. The musical score was written by the patient's life and trauma experience. Each part has its own themes, movements, and motifs, which comprise the symphonic work of treatment.

REFERENCES

Aronoff, J., & Wilson, J. P. (1985). *Personality in the social process.* Mahwah, NJ: Lawrence Erlbaum Associates.

Cohen, M. B. (1952). Countertransference and anxiety. *Psychiatry, 15,* 231–243.

Cook, H. T., & Cook, T. F. (1993). *Japan at war: An oral history.* New York: Free Press.

Dalenberg, C. (2000). *Countertransference and PTSD.* Washington, DC: APA Press.

Danieli, Y. (1988). Confronting the unimaginable: Psychotherapists' reactions to victims of the Nazi Holocaust. In J. P. Wilson, Z. Harel, & B. Kahana (Eds.), *Human adaptation to extreme stress* (pp. 219–237). New York: Plenum Press.

Early, E. (1993). *The raven's return: The influences of psychological trauma on individuals and culture.* Wilmette, IL: Chiron Publications.

Figley, C. (1997). *Compassion fatigue.* New York: Brunner-Mazel.

Figley, C. (2002). *Treating compassion fatigue.* New York: Brunner-Routledge.

Freud, S. (1910). *The future prospects of psychoanalytic therapy. Standard Edition,* Vol. 11 (pp. 141–142). London: Hogarth Press.

Freud, S. (1912). *Recommendations to physicians practicing psychoanalysis. Standard Edition,* Vol. 12 (pp. 111–120). London: Hogarth Press.

Freud, S. (1917). *Introductory lecture on psychoanalysis.* New York: W. W. Norton.

Freud, S. (1920). *Beyond the pleasure principle.* New York: W. W. Norton.

Friedman, M. J. (2000). *Posttraumatic & acute stress disorders.* Kansas City, MO: Compact Clinicals.

Gorkin, M. (1987). *The uses of countertransference.* Northvale, NJ: Jason Aronson.

Horowitz, M. (1986). *Stress response syndromes.* Northvale, NJ: Jason Aronson.

Ickes, W. (1997). *Empathic accuracy.* New York: Guilford Publications.

Jung, C. G. (1929). The Collected Works (Bollingen Series XX, 20 vols.). Trans. R. F. C. Hull. In H. Read, M. Fordham, & G. Adler (Eds.), *The therapeutic value of abreaction* (CW 16). Princeton, NJ: Princeton University Press.

Kalsched, D. (1996). *The inner world of trauma: Archetypal defenses of the personal spirit.* London: Routledge.

Kohut, H. (1959). Introspection, empathy and psychoanalysis. *Journal of American Psychoanalytic Association, 7,* 459–483.

Kohut, H. (1977). *Restoration of the self.* New York: International University Press.

Levenson, R. W., & Ruef, A. M. (1997). Psychological aspects of emotional knowledge. In W. Ickes (Ed.), *Emapathic accuracy* (pp. 44–73). New York: Guilford Publications.

Lifton, R. J. (1967). *Death in life: The survivors of Hiroshima.* New York: Simon & Schuster.

Lifton, R. J. (1993). From Hiroshima to the Nazi doctors: The evolution of psychoformative approaches to understanding traumatic stress syndromes. In J. P. Wilson & B. Raphael (Eds.), *International handbook of traumatic stress syndromes* (pp. 11–25). New York: Plenum Press.

Lindy, J. (1988). *Vietnam: A casebook.* New York: Brunner-Mazel.

Lindy, J. (1993). Focal psychoanalytic psychotherapy of PTSD. In J. P. Wilson & B. Raphael (Eds.), *The international handbook of traumatic stress syndromes* (pp. 803–811). New York: Plenum Press.

Lindy, J. D., & Lifton, R. J. (2001). *Beyond invisible walls.* New York: Brunner-Routledge.

Maroda, K. J. (1991). *The power of countertransference.* New York: John Wiley & Sons.

McEwen, B. (1998). Protective and damaging effects of stress mediators. *Seminars of the Beth Israel Deaconess Medical Center,* 338(3), 171–179.

Parsons, E. (1988). Posttraumatic self-disorder: Theoretical and practical considesrations for psychotherapy of victim war veterans. In J. P. Wilson, Z. Harel, & B. Kahana (Eds.), *Human adaptation to extreme stress* (pp. 245–279). New York: Plenum Press.

Pearlman, L., & Saatvikne, K. (1997). *Trauma and the therapist.* New York: Norton.

Racker, H. (1968). *Transference and countertransference.* New York: International University Press.

Rogers, C. (1951). *Client centered therapy.* New York: Houghton-Mifflin.

Rowe, T., & MacIsaac, J. (1991). *Empathic attunement.* Northvale, NJ: Jason Aronson Press.

Scurfield, R. M. (1993). Treatment of posttraumatic syndrome disorder among Vietnam veterans. In J. P. Wilson & B. Raphael (Eds.), *The international handbook of traumatic stress syndromes* (pp. 879–889). New York: Plenum Press.

Slatker, E. (1987). *Countertransference.* Northvale, NJ: Jason Aronson.

Stamm, B. H. (1997). *Secondary traumatic stress: Self-care for clinicians, researchers and educators.* Cutherville, MD: Sidran Press.

Tansey, M. J., & Burke, W. F. (1989). *Understanding countertransference.* Hillsdale, NJ: Lawrence Erlbaum Associates.

Wilson, J. P. (1989). *Trauma, transformation and healing. An integration approval to theory, research and posttraumatic theory.* New York: Brunner/Mazel.

Wilson, J. P. (2002, October 11). *The abyss experience and catastrophic stress.* Presented at St. Joseph's University Conference on Terrorism and Weapons of Mass Destruction, Philadelphia.

Wilson, J. P. (2002a, October 12). *The abyss experience and the trauma complex: Mental health response to weapons of mass destruction: Terrorist attacks.* Presentation at St. Joseph's University, Philadelphia.

Wilson, J. P. (2002b, November 10). *An organismic, holistic model of complex PTSD.* Presentation at the International Society for Traumatic Stress Studies' 18th annual meeting, Baltimore, MD.

Wilson, J. P., & Drožđek, B. (2004). *Broken Spirits: The treatment of PTSD in asylum seekers and refugees.* New York: Guilford Publications.

Wilson, J. P., & Lindy, J. (1994). *Counter-transference in the treatment of PTSD.* New York: Guilford Publications.

Wilson, J. P., & Raphael, B. (1992). *The international handbook of traumatic stress syndromes.* New York: Plenum Press.

Wilson, J. P., & Thomas, R. (in press). *Empathy in the treatment of trauma and PTSD.* New York: Brunner-Routledge.

Wilson, J. P., Friedman, M., & Lindy, J. (2001). *Treating psychological trauma and PTSD.* New York: Guilford Publications.

Wolstein, B. (1988). *Essential paper on countertransference.* New York: New York University Press.

12

Clinical Supervision for Trauma Therapists

JOHAN LANSEN AND TON HAANS

Supervision is gradually becoming a familiar kind of support for workers in the fields of mental health and social work — besides the regular supervision in training curricula of psychiatrists, psychotherapists, and social workers. Professionals do realize that even after many years of practice it can be very helpful to once again have some supervision on different aspects of their work. This need for supervision is especially clear for individual therapists as well as teams of professionals in institutions who assist traumatized refugees. To those who have worked as therapists in this field, this might be clear from the start. It may not be clear, however, to therapists and caregivers in other fields, as well as to administrators, sponsors, and others. Therefore, we want to emphasize the need for supervision in this particular area.

The main factors that lend support to arguments for supervision have shown up in the course of many years of personal experience in doing supervision. We have made an inventory from our own material, accumulated mainly by Johan Lansen, in the course of the 1990s until 2002 from our work as supervisors in different centers, in Holland as well as in Scandinavian countries and in Germany, and also in private practice. In these centers, taken together, a mixed population was treated, mainly senior survivors of nazi terror and refugees from countries all over the world who were traumatized by persecution and torture. This material consists of loose notes, serving as support for the value of memory and staying attentive during supervision sessions.

From the several hundred cases of supervision of treatments of traumatized refugees and other survivors of political violence we have selected those whose content we could precisely reconstruct through mere legibility and volume. Our intention was to make an attempt at charting these cases, in order to find out which problems during treatment motivated caregivers to ask for supervision. The selected material consisted of notes of 100 supervised cases, most of them presented 1 to 4 times in supervision sessions. We shall refrain from further description of a methodological sort, as this material, jotted down for no other purpose than being of immediate support during sessions for ourselves, does not serve for scientific purposes. Here we just consider the results of our investigation as a pragmatic illustration that could have heuristic value.

Those problems during treatment that led to a demand for supervision are to be distinguished from the manifest questions uttered by supervisees at the end of their exposition of the case and treatment, like:

> "I get stuck. Is it justified to go on further like this or ..."
> "Do we have to call in a psychiatrist to judge the danger of suicide?"
> "I am becoming more and more anxious with this patient and I wonder what is going on."
> "We have a wonderful contact, but I can't get around to trauma therapy."

In this chapter we first examine the reasons of providing supervision and provide some examples. Next, we give a definition of supervision as a shared reflexive activity. Finally, we describe supervision as a dyadic activity, as a group activity, and in a team.

SUPERVISION, WHY?

In an attempt at classifying the problems from our material we arrived at three group classifications: difficulties in building a good case concept, emotional impact of the work on therapists, and a group of not very frequent problems of a divergent nature.

The first group of problems concerns difficulties in understanding the case, using unproductive working models, lack of knowledge about trauma and culture, and as a result applying inappropriate therapeutic methods. We take them together under the heading *case concept*.

Many caregivers are inclined to think exclusively in clinical concepts, discounting in the process the social, economic, and political sequelea. Most of them are therapists who have a strong orientation toward the concept of PTSD, or classical behavior therapeutic helping methods that are to our knowledge insufficient to explain the complex sequelea of traumas like persecution, torture, flight, and asylum seeking in other countries.

Yet one does find quite a number of therapists with a psychodynamic orientation, whose working models are grounded in models of a disturbed personality development (like in neurotic or borderline pathology). Their concept of trauma and loss does not apply to a victim whose personality is fairly average in his own cultural context, but who becomes severely damaged after the personality has been largely completed (it is even more complicated when a child is subjected to such a trauma). There is a tendency in such therapists to consider problems in self-esteem, aggression toward partners and children, lack of confidence in others, splitting of caregivers in extremes of good and bad, manipulative behavior, and so forth in terms of existing models of pathology in citizens of their own people. They do not see these phenomena as possible consequences of destruction caused by extreme trauma, by difficult and inescapable circumstances in the life of a refugee, or as cultural differences. Sometimes therapists exhibit a mere lack of experience in doing therapy at all, which can lead to a lack of understanding. In some circumstances — particularly in countries where care and treatment are administered by the charity system — one can find idealistic but inexperienced family doctors and other professionals who run into complicated matters of therapy. And in specialized centers it is not uncommon to meet professionals who are doing excellent nonverbal therapy, but who might need lots of information and guidance when forced by a particular case to add a strong verbal component to their work (using supportive interventions, psychoeducation, etc.).

There is a special reason to acquire more insight in working with complex human tragedy and patients from other cultures. Although training courses about how to treat refugees have been provided to many therapists, this is not enough. Even experienced therapists, those who have been working successfully with a regular population of patients from their own country, can feel at a loss when confronted with traumatized refugees from other countries. While looking for symptoms of PTSD they might not recognize or understand the patient's demoralization or aggressiveness, they might come up with untimely treatments that will not be of any help, or they might fail to see why there are frequent relapses of symptoms. They might not understand why concepts of pathology or treatment, as learned in their ordinary work, cannot apply to this population. They can become inclined to consider this work as extremely difficult (which is not necessarily the case) or as culturally out of reach (which is mostly overestimated) (cf. van der Veer, 1998).

The second category of problems concerns problematic countertransference reactions and emerging problems of burn-out, heavy emotional impact, and even vicarious traumatization or secondary traumatic stress. It is mostly about the *personal impact* on therapists from their patients: their personality, their trauma history, and their behavior and expectations in and during therapy. Sometimes it is connected with negative attitudes in society about victims and refugees. Therapists might feel discounted in their work by friends and from reactions in society.

We find here fixations in countertransference positions as mentioned by Wilson, Lindy, & Raphael (1994): a fixation in a position of too much empathy and not enough inner distance, leading to enmeshment in therapies, confusion, lack of progress, feelings of helplessness and anger in therapists (empathic enmeshment), and a fixation in a position of too much distance, loss of empathy, often after a period of too much involvement, followed by disappointment, feelings of helplessness, and guilt (empathic repression). In most cases of problems in countertransference in our material, the first position (overidentification, overengagement with empathic enmeshment) was present. This connects to the phenomenon that many individual therapists and workers in teams are in danger of burn-out or worse: developing symptoms of so-called vicarious traumatization or of secondary traumatic stress. This applies to helpers in a rather broad sort of framework: psychotherapists of different disciplinary backgrounds, psychiatrists, social workers, physiotherapists, psychomotor therapists, art therapists, and also regular medical assistants. The many lay volunteers helping refugees are also among this category. They are often very enthusiast and empathic helpers without much knowledge of trauma, and not very experienced in reflecting upon what they are doing or upon the emotional impact of this work. Apart from guidance and education on trauma, they need supervision, individually or in groups, focusing on tasks and limits of their work. A supervisor has to pay special attention to their mental well-being.

The specific nature of treating victims of violence, persecution, and torture brings along traumatic stress in the helping relationship, damaging assistants by a process of empathy, induction, and enactment (Haans, 1998; Lansen, 1999). The result is that therapists and other assistants can sometimes suffer from burn-out or from typical PTSD symptoms, but are also at risk of undergoing some change of personality, becoming cynical, withdrawn, unhappy, and losing faith in their capacity for healing. This will have a strong impact within teams, as interpersonal relationships will suffer. We do not consider secondary traumatic stress and its effects as some intensification of countertransference (though sometimes the development follows this path). However, as with countertransference, we think that burn-out and other reactions are important phenomena, which belong under the heading of "What does this work do to me and my feelings as a therapist?"

Secondary traumatic stress in its more elaborate form was rather infrequently present in our material: roughly 5 to 10% of the therapists are affected, in our estimation. There were, however, many therapists with general symptoms of stress. Even whole teams have showed signs of stress. There are other problems that we will discuss as a group, such as the problems of *divergent categories*. Whereas the former two categories are highly represented among the cases, in this third group we find special situations, which although not highly exceptional, are numerically less important. Reasons for asking for supervision could be

- an actual case of handling aggression in a patient;
- ethical questions about perpetrators;
- conflicts with translators;
- cases with general psychiatric syndromes;
- the need for other therapies, not present in this particular center;
- role confusion, as patients have needs in other areas and for which help is not always available (social and legal problems, permission to stay, etc.);
- quick changes in target groups (after becoming used to a population, for instance, from the Balkan, all of a sudden a new wave of victims/survivors from Central Africa or an Asian country might arrive. Such a new group can have other expectations from care and treatment, other ideas about torture, in particular sexual torture, about roles of a doctor or therapist, and about what is appropriate to communicate);
- unstable work situations (depending on the country where one is working you can find very different situations. In a country like Holland you might be working in the regular mental health service. In a neighboring country like Germany, this work is considered as charity, so that workers are hardly sure of a paid job).

TWO CASE ILLUSTRATIONS

Here we present two examples to illustrate the two first categories of problems that can lead to a request for supervision. The first case presents a difficult *case concept*. The patient is a 40-year-old male refugee from Iran, married, and father of two children (6 and 9 years old). This man, a convinced communist, was for a long time imprisoned and heavily tortured under the shah regime. After an initial and rather long period of mental resistance he could no longer stand the psychological and physical torture; he gave in, mentally and physically broken, and betrayed other fighters. After having promised further cooperation with the regime, he was set free. Rather soon afterward he fled to the former Soviet Union, where he married a girl from his own country, who was studying there. After some years in the Soviet Union they had the opportunity to move to the former German Democratic Republic (GDR), where he got a job in the medical sector as a technician. The 1989 political changes in the GDR meant for him a resurgence of his anxieties. The "capitalist" West Germany was triumphant; he saw it as a great threat for his security, as he was afraid of being thrown out with his family and being extradited to the ayatollah regime (which he considered even worse than the shah regime from which he had suffered so much). On top of this anxiety he experienced the bitter reality of losing his job during a period of modernization of the hospital according to

Western standards. A chronic ailment of one of his children made the situation worse. His former nightmares came back, and he became more and more depressed.

He was invited by his brother who lived as a recognized legal refugee in Holland to come over with his family. He too managed to be recognized with his family as refugees in Holland. As he could not practice his job in the Netherlands, he accepted a job as taxi driver. He earned a sufficient amount of money but felt miserable in this job. He felt discriminated against by many passengers, but also by his fellow taxi drivers, who made jokes, he thought, at his expense (there might have been more than a kernel of truth in this). Gradually his nightmares increased, he felt physically weak, and he suffered from mental absences and disorientation in his work, which led to some dangerous and strange situations. His wife, who supported him very much, became desperate. Through the medical circuits, after a lot of doctor shopping and medical examinations, he was referred to a special unit for psychosocial care of refugees. A psychotherapist and a physiotherapist with some background knowledge of psychotherapy took him into treatment. In the first phase of treatment his confidence in both therapists was growing; but after some time there was a standstill. He seemed to be completely absorbed by his problems, finding no room within himself to look quietly to his problems. He understood the rationale of the therapy, he knew that it was important to reflect and become engaged in some practical therapeutic measures, but he just could not manage to do that. A psychiatric consultant started a treatment with antidepressant medication, but that did not bring any change. The physiotherapist, who treated his complaints of pain and tenderness in body parts where he had been tortured, did not make any progress either.

This case was brought up for supervision because both therapists got stuck. The overall impression of the psychotherapist was that this man was like someone living but dead. He was broken. The physiotherapist felt that this man liked to come for treatment, but had given up. She began to feel his hesitation to come; she thought that he would drop out soon. Nothing moved, he was like a deserted quarry. She had a heavy feeling herself after every session. The question of both supervisees, summarized, was: "What approach, what sort of assistance, does this man need?"

In the discussion all sorts of aspects came to the fore, but special aspects, such as his betrayal by his country and his heavy torture causing him to betray his friends, became the focus. He also felt betrayed by the political changes in Eastern Europe. His wife could no longer stand the situation and she felt near breakdown. Betrayal is a theme that came to the surface in the discussion, but it rapidly disappeared again. The therapists brought it up again with the feeling that they had to go on with him: stopping therapy now would be a new betrayal. They wanted to go on, they did not dislike this man, but they did not have a clear picture, they felt ungrounded themselves. Of course, the reactions and feelings of the therapists were important in this case.

The main point, however, is that they failed to appreciate the impact of this patient's existential frame of reference. These therapists, trained in a cognitive-directive approach with an activist "color," got stuck in the tragic aspect of this man, who had a type of posttraumatic reaction that is well known among many of the survivors of World War II. The survivor of persecution and concentration camp has been physically and mentally broken — not completely, otherwise there would have been no survival — and spontaneous recovery after liberation has only partially succeeded. Although on a social level there may seem to be a reasonably functioning person during many years, there can be a mental decline, an existence characterized by many medical complaints, lack of vitality, some symptoms from the PTSD categories like sleeplessness and nightmares, and often mistrust in other human beings. Inability to enjoy any feeling of pleasure (anhedonia) and to feel and express emotions in words (alexithymia) can be present (Krystal, 1988). It is as if these patients are back in a wordless state with a lack of basic capacities of positive feelings.

Although these clinical pictures are well known from Holocaust literature, we find time and again that young therapists are not familiar with them and that older therapists tend to "forget" them. This no doubt has to do with some sort of avoidance of confrontation with even the clinical description of the terrible effects of this sort of aggression. Supervision provides a climate to look together at these clinical aspects and to discover in quiet and reflective moments a clinical world, which speaks of the damage patients suffer from. Therapists must refrain from their desire to see a quick result in such cases. What seemed most important in this case is that therapists remained loyal and faithful toward this patient. They had to shift their thinking, becoming more supportive and being more available during several years of not so frequent contact. This way they created a therapeutic environment enabling this man, notwithstanding his chronic complaints of pains and nightmares, to feel himself a person of this world: he was alive again.

The next case example illustrates some problems of *countertransference*. This case presents a young woman without any formal education, 21 years old, who belonged to an ethnic minority in a country in the Middle East. For about 2 years she had been living in a Western European country. She, a farmer's daughter, had experienced since she was 10 years old how police and military forces regularly searched their village and her family's farm, shouting, crying, smashing the furniture, driving the village population together onto the square, then shooting over their heads.

When she was 14 years of age she had thrown herself as a protective shield in front of her father, when he was being beaten up on such an occasion. She was arrested, thrown into a cell, beaten, and tortured with electric shocks and forced to drink salt water during terrible heat.

On occasion of a later intimidating and terrorizing action against this village she was arrested again and sexually molested. When she was released, her father could help her to flee. Shortly after arrival as a refugee in this European country she married another refugee from her country. The marriage took place in a ceremony of her religion (no civil marriage). After some time she began having mental attacks where all of a sudden she felt subject to massive intrusive images from the time of her detention. Then she would scream, throw off her clothes, beat herself, and throw hot water or hot tea on her body. She would then have heavy headaches, rolling her head sideways, shaking, and have stomach aches. These attacks were labeled psychogenic. She got treatment at a center for traumatized refugees. She was seen by a psychotherapist and by a medical doctor, both females. There was a good contact with both caregivers. She related about the torture sessions. She described her marriage as a patriotic sort of endeavor. There was love, there was sex, but she did not enjoy it. As a sort of act of independence she did not want to marry before a civil servant (obliged in the asylum country): she intended to marry formally in her country, when there would have been installed a registration service of her own people. Again and again her emotions were boiling over after telephone conversations with her parents, or when she heard news about new acts of violence against her family, friends, and village. In the therapeutic sessions she idealized the time before the beginning of violence in her area: life was a fairytale, peaceful, living in harmony and prosperity. She also related her daily fantasies in her daydreams: she is back in her own country and she supplies the fighters in the field with food and weapons, but on returning home she is taken prisoner and tortured. These therapeutic sessions remained centered around her attacks and fantasies. There was no change. It was like a vicious circle, maintained by telephone calls with relatives and contact with other "patriots" who were refugees like her. The psychotherapist wanted to intervene with attempts at reflection, suggestions for other behavior, advice to stop calling home, in brief to interrupt this vicious circle. But then the patient's aggression arose. She wanted to decide for herself what was good and not good. She felt insulted by such so-called therapeutic suggestions; in turn she accused the therapist of having no idea about her (the patient's) inner world, as the therapist has never experienced what she had gone through.

The therapist found it difficult to bear the vehement aggression. She felt herself condemned to silence; she was heavily annoyed by not feeling able to interrupt the patient's unproductive attacks. Meanwhile, the other caregiver, the doctor, was being idealized. She had given some tranquilizers, which were taken faithfully. However, the doctor had to listen to the same enthusiastically told painful experiences and heroic fantasies. The doctor was rather anxious about the self-damage caused by throwing hot tea on her body. It is as if the patient continued the torture, being a torturer against herself. The doctor had feelings of inferiority ("I have not been tortured"), but at the same time she felt abused by this patient, because she too could not persuade the patient to make some changes in behavior. The doctor felt that both power and helplessness were present in the consulting room. Trauma work, such as both therapists were familiar with, did not occur at all. This sort of therapy was being interrupted with what they called "dramatic enactment of fairytales." Briefly, the question for supervision was: "We know what has to be done (trauma work) but we feel helpless. Tell us what to do."

On further discussion both therapists readily admit having lost their grip on the situation by their own feelings of countertransference. They felt fascinated by this young woman's vitality and energy, who as a girl had shown courage and saw her torture as a necessary sacrifice, as a contribution to the struggle of her people, not to be lamented. She was nothing, her people and its cause everything. On a certain level it brought some sort of sensation and vitality to the therapists. On another level they felt inferior. The enactment of this patient's suffering in heroic form dominated the patient as well as the caregivers, and as long as they too were under the spell, no change would occur. This powerful process interfered with the therapists' capacity to take a look at their own concept of trauma work, and that this might not be the most practical at this stage.

"Holding" (Winnicott, 1960) as well as "containing" (Bion, 1962, 1969) of this patient was here the primary aim, and maybe in the long term more important for the resolution of several aspects of traumatic damage in her life. This patient presented a very complicated mesh of psychological and intrapsychic problems: ties and obligations toward her father; dignity through chastity and/or through patriotism, in conflict with each other; being lost in a strange world; taking a step forward in case of danger. It was clear that the therapeutic technique should be calm and capable of containing this patient. In some cases this can be done in a clinical situation only, but here could not be accomplished. The most important question turned out to be which one of the two therapists would have the courage to engage in "battle" alone. In fact, working with two therapists had implied that the problems were too heavy for one! There was no need for two therapists. An interesting and a bit unusual and "rocky" therapy was successful in the end after the psychotherapist continued to work but the medical doctor left the case. The remaining therapist was able to take control in the case by serving for a time as a sort of older sister, while being supported by supervision.

In the examples presented one can discover important aspects of supervision. In the first example, the case of the 40-year-old man from Iran, there is a strong aspect of *education* (also called the *formative function* of supervision), an element of teaching about extreme psychotrauma and its possible aftermath on human personality. The therapist learned how to better understand the plight of this patient and the heavy road to sufficient recovery, with total recovery being an unattainable goal. In the second example the therapists suffered from a blind spot, caused by the emotional impact of the case. The supervisory process in this case had an element of *strong emotional support,* even with some elements of confrontation, while both therapists were affected by the patient's "heroic" sorrow. The supervision needed to give mental support to the supervisee through understanding these processes and emotional impact, and bringing them to light. How to deal effectively with such an emotional involvement, instead of reacting defensively, is an important point in supervision. Therapists learn to handle these and other cases, and in the process often other aspects are involved, like *maintaining boundaries* and *roles,* and even some ethical aspects. This means that there is an important element of *quality improvement* as a result of supervision. We think that in a supervisory relationship one of the main functions of the supervisory work is *supportive,* connected to the emotional aspect of the therapeutic relationship — even in many cases where the problem seems to be mainly a cognitive one. Furthermore, supervision ideally yields an *educational* gain — to know better "what," "how to," and "why." Finally, there is a limited aspect of a *managerial* sort in the sense of monitoring ethical standards and ensuring standards of quality care for patients, teams, and centers. We will come back to this more in detail later.

A BRIEF LOOK AT CULTURE

It is clear that psychiatrists and psychologists have to walk on two tracks: on the one hand they have to check what they see and hear with their own professional concepts; on the other hand they have to be empathic for the cultural universe of the patient. Professionals do not have to give up their own concepts; they must be able to relativize them and see things from the patient's perspective. This is what is called intercultural competence, and such an attitude requires much effort and a lot of concentration. Many refugees who are treated in this system need some form of assistance for pathological reactions after traumatic events. It is of utmost interest that treaters try to identify with their history and present difficulties, with their world of uprooting and loss, in order to get a picture of their complaints. It goes by itself that many patients do not show up with a complete picture of PTSD. Like the survivors of nazi terror, they might suffer from depression, often expressed in somatic symptoms, sleep disorders, outbursts of aggressive behavior, or total demoralization.

What is needed for a good understanding between therapists and patients can require a longer phase of psychoeducation than is usual for Western patients. But what stands out is that from our spectrum of psychiatric help and therapies certain aspects are more helpful. There is no reason to discard our Western concepts of diagnosis or treatment, provided we are able to translate the inner world and history of the patient into our concepts, and, in return, our concepts into their universe of thinking. Is this so different from what we usually do with our Western patients? No and yes. It is always necessary to offer a treatment that will fit the patient and to have good contact with a patient in order to get this patient involved in treatment. This means that there are always some cultural elements involved, even with patients from our own population. Yet this requires more energy on our part. It is like learning to speak a foreign language; it is said that Charlemagne compared learning a language with acquiring another soul. A supervisor should be sensitive to the lack of understanding between patients from another culture and a therapist, and he or she should encourage helping professionals in Western society to acquire a bit of a "new soul."

WHAT IS CLINICAL SUPERVISION?

In a complicated context of work, where factors such as those already mentioned and of course other factors can motivate a request for supervision, it would be too simple to stress the usefulness of supervision only. More is needed. Supervision should be considered in a context of a "package" of measures like special courses, team-building, selection of workers, good leadership, and a clear treatment philosophy. The culture in a team or treatment center should be a learning culture. However, for the purpose of this chapter we will focus on supervision only. In some countries supervision is seen as a mere *administrative* sort of activity: a supervisor is a senior person, higher in line. Often he or she is your direct boss. The supervisor is monitoring what you are doing and tells you how and what to do. *Clinical supervision* is something else. It is practiced, for example, in the field of psychotherapy. A supervisor is an experienced therapist whose task is to monitor future therapists and their first therapies as part of a training curriculum in this method. Often but not always the clinical supervisor has special training in how to do supervision. Supervision is here a mixed bag of tasks: monitoring, doing some clinical teaching, giving some instruction, giving encouragement and emotional support, helping to reflect on the case and the relationship, especially upon transference and countertransference, and teaching how to use this relationship in therapy. In our field of work supervision comes close to this form. However, there are a few other points to consider.

Briefly, we see supervision in this field not so much as a training in a specific treatment method, but rather as means to gain competence for treating a certain target group of patients: victims, or if you want, survivors, of organized violence who are suffering from complex trauma sequelea in often complicated situations. Therapists in this field are often experienced therapists, who have already acquired a degree of psychiatric or psychotherapeutic competence in the field of regular mental health. Supervision is a shared reflection of an expert in the field — the supervisor, together with such therapists, the supervisee(s) — focus on the supervisee's work in order to give the supervisee more cognitive knowledge, emotional depth, and methodical skills. It should lead to better treatments, and the patients should profit from this improvement of quality of therapists.

Supervision needs *structure*. A contract gives a basic structure. It can be a written or oral contract, with mutual agreement about conditions, ways of working during supervision (use of tapes or role play?), and about contents. So it is not only about time, place, number of sessions, frequency, and fees, when and how to evaluate, and so forth. It is also about the subject matter — the focus of reflection — during supervision: Should we work case-oriented, process-oriented, person-oriented in individual supervision? In group supervision and team supervision it is about the same matters; the focus might also be on group and team interactions. It is wise to be specific beforehand about these things, as many problems during supervision arise about disagreements of what supervision is about.

In this context we will add a few words about the settings of supervision. For practical reasons we restrict ourselves to those settings that are the ones most frequently met in the field of treatment of survivors of organized violence: individual supervision, group supervision, supervision of a team, supervision for team leaders, and supervision for supportive assistants.

Individual Supervision

The setting is one-to-one: one supervisor, one supervisee. This is mainly case-oriented supervision. A couple of therapists, working with the same patient (for instance a psychotherapist and an art therapist jointly treat the same patient), can be considered as an extension of this setting.

Group Supervision

Group supervision is best for therapists who are in a free relationship toward each other, mostly therapists who work independently. Here too it concerns mostly case supervision. The process of supervision has a lot in common with individual supervision; however, a group automatically creates such a unique setting that the supervisor's task is considerably different. We will discuss this later in this chapter.

Supervision of a Team

A team is also a sort of group, but members of the team are mostly far from being independent workers. The context in which the members are embedded determines aims and tasks, and there exist all sorts of rules about division of tasks, responsibility toward team leadership, and so forth.

Supervision for Team Leaders

A less-frequent organizational level is supervision for team leaders. Problems in a team, problems with other parts of an organization to which a team belongs, or problematic relations with the outside world can induce team leadership to ask for supervision.

Supervision for Supportive Assistants

Another less-frequent level of supervision is supervision for supportive assistants. This is used in settings where severely traumatized patients are treated: translators, secretarial and administrative personnel, also housekeeping workers might ask for supervision about behavior and role aspects, or about the emotional impact of their work. We might find many volunteer workers in this category.

Supervision: The Concept

In summary, we present a definition of supervision from the more traditional field. From the many definitions of supervision that exist we prefer the one given by Loganbill, Hardy, and Delworth (1982), which states: "Supervision is an intensive, interpersonally focused, one-to-one relationship in which one person is designated to facilitate the development of therapeutic competence in the other person" (p. 7).

This definition, of course, is not perfect; it lacks provisions for other settings like group or team supervision. The British Association of Counseling rightly adds the statement that the primary purpose of supervision is to protect the best interests of the client.

Supervision has flourished in the fields of social work and of psychotherapy. Other mental health workers, however, also have profited from the development of concepts and practice of supervision. There is even some sort of inflation of the concept. In many cases the term supervision is too easily applied. For instance, in our country (the Netherlands) there is confusion about supervision in the field of psychiatry. Even in 1993 Van der Post's study about supervision in the training of psychiatrists concluded that there is almost no supervision proper in the training of resident psychiatrists, except for the sector psychotherapy (in 2004 the situation has hardly changed). Other aspects of the training, like individual teaching, giving guidance for practice, being the line manager of the so-called supervisee, or for other aspects of the relationship between the head of the department and the trainee psychiatrist are inappropriately relegated to the concept of supervision. It is our opinion that the term supervision should only be used for a relationship where the supervisee has responsibility as therapist for his or her patients; whereas the supervisor has responsibility for the process of supervision. This type of relationship is found mainly in supervision of practitioners who are advanced in their training or who are qualified practitioners already. Sometimes this supervision proper is called consultancy supervision, a term which possibly brings confusion with the concept of "consultation." It is not our intention to focus on all of the differences between supervision and adjacent areas, like consultation, guidance in practice, tutorial training, or even forms of supportive therapy. The point we want to emphasize is that a good supervisor should not be the supervisee's trainer, line manager, or therapist.

Finally, from the discussion following the examples given it may be clear that we prefer the definition:

> Supervision is a contracted activity; it is a shared reflection between an external expert, the supervisor, and another professional, the supervisee (in groups or teams: other professionals, the supervisees), focused on the supervisee's work, in order to give the supervisee more cognitive, more emotional, and more methodical depth and skills. Supervision should lead to a more independent position of the supervisee, based on competence. It is expected that the supervisee's clients will profit from this increase in competence. (W. Lammers, pers. comm. — clinical psychologist and director of the Institut für Angewandte Sozialwissenschaften at Maienfeld, Switzerland. He uses this in his teaching courses of supervision.)

CASE SUPERVISION I

We might first have a look at case supervision by enumerating some facets we deal with in individual supervision. A lot has been written about case supervision from the angle of individual supervision for training purposes. Different facets are important for our purpose (see Figure 12.1).

The *patient* is the subject of the case discussion. The therapist in his or her role as supervisee brings up a summary of the patient's story: his or her normal life, previous to the traumatizing events. The trauma

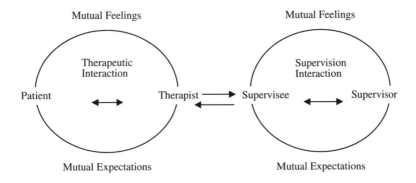

Fig. 12.1 Treatment and Supervision Interaction

history, his or her personal reactions during and after those events, and whether there been any assistance during these events or afterward are explored. The history of escape or liberation, of flight and life in Western countries, is examined. What are the patient's complaints? What are this person's resiliencies? Is he or she able to look at his or her own reactions connected with trauma and loss; is he or she aware of any personal possibility of assimilating the trauma? How is the patient responding to treatment?

It is important that this summary implicates a working model of the patient as a person, as a victim, and as a survivor, and also includes the present-day social context. This is what we mean by a *case concept*, the inner image of the patient as seen by the therapist.

The next facet in supervision is the *therapist*, who is seen as a supervisee in the supervisory relationship. The therapist is a qualified person, but not always trained in treating severely traumatized people from other cultures. But he or she is (ideally) supposed to be sufficiently trained in the profession for having self-discipline and not transgressing boundaries. This self-discipline also implies a personal style and personal methods, to which the therapist adheres. This also includes the capacity for establishing a relationship of confidence with the patient, and in principle also a capacity for engaging a patient as much as possible in his or her own treatment. The therapist also respects the patient's self-image (an important ethical point), giving the patient as much control in his or her therapy and destiny as possible.

The therapist, a human being of flesh and blood, has his or her own reactions toward all of what happens in therapy: feelings of happiness, honor, very positive feelings of self; or on the other hand uneasiness, distrust, anger, sorrow, feelings of impotence, feeling of being obliged to fulfill high expectations, and so on. The impact of a patient's sad story, the reaction toward events of persecution and genocide in general, the feelings when being sucked into a world of traumatic feelings can involve risks for the therapist (burn-out, vicarious traumatization, secondary traumatic stress). Of course, no therapist will always respond to this ideal picture; treatment of traumatized refugees makes even very experienced therapists insecure. But we use this picture as a sort of checklist in order to find out what might disturb a therapy, rather than as a goal to be perfectly met.

The *therapeutic interaction* is the third element we want to consider. This interaction can be directly visible and audible on video and tape, but we seldom use these resources. Most patients who have been persecuted harbor a lot of suspicion against the use of these techniques, as is quite understandable.

It is important in supervision to realize the meaning of the presence of an interpreter. A therapist can have problems with the interpreter's role, or fear the judgment of the interpreter about the quality of the therapist's work. Both therapist and interpreter might be anxious about having to pass some sort of "exam."

Where there is no tape recording, everything is based on the supervisee's report. The more a climate of trust is established in the supervision, the easier it will be for the supervisee: a shared, confidential reflection. This will make it easier for the therapist to bring up his or her feelings of insecurity about the patient and the interpreter's role.

Most important in the therapeutic interaction is the treatment concept, its theoretical and technical underpinnings, and the way this is made clear to the patient. Why does the therapist say and act in such a manner, and what is expected from the patient, and why? One can call this a sort of "*rationale*" that acts as a framework for treatment. It has, of course, a great deal to do with the case concept and with the therapeutic theories and methods that a therapist has learned to master. However, a therapy should not be a ready-made sort of thing. It should rather be some "good" made to measure (of course, the same applies to supervision). In therapies and supervision we have to monitor whether this "rationale" is really understood and accepted by the patient. Even if such a rationale is in principle correct, it is often introduced a bit prematurely: the patient is not yet "ready" for it. Important forms of introductory work have to be done, implicating psychoeducation. As this has to be done with supportive elements — for example, introducing elements of immediate help like relaxation methods or sleeping medication and so forth — this requires a careful attitude on the therapist's part. This introductory phase is a tricky one; in supervision one often meets problems caused by not having paid enough attention to this phase. Unclear or contradictory expectations about what treatment is, based on ignorance, naiveté, or experience with more traditional approaches in therapies for people of one's own country, can interfere with establishing a shared "rationale" of work.

The fourth and fifth factors to be considered are intimately intertwined. It is about *mutual feelings* and *expectations*. Even after having established a shared "rationale," therapist and patient can experience a world of feelings and expectations of a more personal character.

Regarding the patient, the therapist is viewed as someone who can be trusted, often a rare and precious phenomenon for a refugee. Or, as in classical transference, a therapist might resemble a patient's father, mother, teacher, or siblings. Fantasies, recollections, and wishes can come up. Often life previous to the traumatic events is idealized, and part of the idealization can be transferred to this newly trusted person. Other past or present events can concur to this idealistic picture. Circumstances can be very difficult, hope might disappear, revitalization (reactualization) of the trauma by recent events can occur. They can lead to very irrational high expectations of treatment and the therapist; in the patient's view he or she is or should act as a rescuing person, contrary to the "rationale" that has been agreed upon. Other expectations can lead to a blurring of role expectations: a therapist can be expected — as being on the side of a patient — to share his or her political ideas, connected with taking action of some sort. A therapist might also be expected to react positively for invitations for family happenings, religious festivals, and so forth. "Classical" feelings of countertransference, from the therapist's own life history, can also play a role. For reasons of simplicity one might call this world of expectations, fantasies, and wishes, both in the patient and therapist, transference and countertransference. However, one has to realize that the patients treated represent a special world of events and meanings, far exceeding our "regular" therapeutic work. This does not only apply to the traumatic events, but also to the culturally defined helping relationship. In supervision of these therapies, role expectation and its negative consequences for both parties involved are often in focus.

The other facets that play a role in the situation of the supervision are the supervisee, the supervisor, the actual interaction going on between them, and their mutual expectations and feelings. However, the length of this chapter does not permit a comprehensive description. We shall limit ourselves to a selection of just a few elements. The supervisory situation is a phenomenon that can contain all sorts of parallels from the therapeutic system to be supervised. It is, of course, not an exact copy. Processes and goals are essentially different. There is also a basic difference in position of the "client" in both situations: the patient has suffered and is suffering from real trauma and loss, the supervisee shares this story but is not the primary traumatized person (sometimes secondary traumatic stress in the therapist can become manifest for the first time in supervision). The motives for asking for therapy are essentially different from asking for supervision.

Nevertheless, as the story of trauma treatment comes to life, some elements will come up: the horrors from a patient's story, the emotions of the therapist (in positions that can vary from distancing to enmeshment), expectations, and counterexpectations. One might say that the dynamic qualities of the story of a patient's life and treatment, also of mutual expectations and feelings between patient and therapist, do exert a sort of induction, through the therapist (i.e., supervisee) into the supervision.

The supervisor listens to this, asks clarifying questions during the exposé of the case, and measures consciously and unconsciously what he or she hears with the body of knowledge and experience from his or her own work, both as a therapist and as a supervisor.

Both supervisee and supervisor have their own expectations. These expectations must have a realistic character, based mainly on the expectations of the roles as a supervisee and a supervisor. They might have to be clarified during the supervisory process, and sometimes parallel phenomena, originating in mutual expectations within the supervised therapy, can intrude. As much as therapy might influence — as a parallel phenomenon — the climate of supervision, so is in reverse the supervisor's attitude and his or her respect for the supervisee capable of influencing the climate of a supervised therapy.

The style of interaction and the emotional climate of supervision are essentials. Are they favorable to the process of reflection? That is, is there a shared reflection in which both parties are involved in an atmosphere of confidence, nonjudgment, and emotional support? Supervision should never be an examination!

In the definition of supervision we have portrayed the supervisor as an external expert. Expertise in doing therapies and expertise in the field of trauma as such is not sufficient. Supervision has become a separate branch in the helping professions; there are very good therapists who are bad supervisors. Nevertheless, a supervisor must have the required qualities for being a good therapist. Moreover, a supervisor should have had specific training in supervision, including theory, as well as a lot of supervised supervision. For practical reasons there are not many supervisors at present in this field of trauma therapy who have been able to become both a trauma expert and a trained supervisor.

CASE SUPERVISION II

The previous section highlighted a number of facets that are a part of the process of individual supervision. They are facets of both therapy and partly of the supervisory situation itself. They are important to have in mind as a supervisor as a background in order to see what is going on in therapy and supervision. In traditional supervision we are used to considering these factors as the primary elements to look at in the here and now of supervision. In the practical situation of supervision sessions, however, we often loose contact with the concrete situation of a supervisee and his or her actual interventions. We need more concrete monitoring categories in order to stay close to the actual ongoing therapy. In other words, we need to focus more attention on foci that enable us to follow more closely what a therapist was doing.

Although always keeping at the back of our minds those facets of supervision, we found some foci for monitoring when doing supervision in the work of the American professor of supervision Elizabeth L. Holloway (1995). According to her what we as supervisors monitor can be grouped into five broad areas. They are about the work assigned to or expected from therapists and other assistants. What a therapist does, his or her tasks, can be ordered into these five broad areas. When doing supervision these tasks are called *supervisory tasks* (see Figure 12.2). We have worked out a variation of her "tasks." Some of them, like case concept, professional role, and emotional sensitivity, come close to the problems that motivate therapists in asking for supervision, as we described above.

Task ▶ / Function ▼	Counseling skill	Case conceptualization	Professional role	Emotional awareness	Self-evaluation
Monitoring/evaluation					
Advising/instructing					
Modeling					
Consulting					
Supporting/sharing					

Fig. 12.2 Tasks and Functions (E. Holloway)

Counseling Skills

These basic counseling skills are a part of giving psychosocial assistance in general and psychotherapy in particular. For example, is a therapist capable of making contact? Does he or she use simple language, which is sufficient in order to carry over what he or she wants the patient to know and think of? Can the therapist make use of an interpreter in treatment and remain him- or herself in the process? Does the therapist master the treatment techniques he or she wants to use, like mirroring in counseling, or reinforcement techniques in behavior therapy? Is the therapist able to involve a patient in working together, even when minimal insight or resilience seems to be available to the patient? Is the therapist able to find a good "rationale" that is understandable and acceptable for this patient? Does the therapist have a feeling for timing? Is the therapist able to organize other sources of assistance for the patient, if needed? Does the therapist take good notes of the therapeutic process?

Case Conceptualization

We have mentioned previously the importance of a case concept. Here we summarize briefly: it is about the clinical picture a therapist has of a patient. What sort of person is the patient? What are important events in his or her life, what is the damage caused by traumatic events, by heavy loss, by actual circumstances? What is lacking in this history and picture, and is this owing to the patient or the therapist? What concepts does the therapist use, from psychopathology as usual in mental health disciplines, from developmental psychology, from psychotraumatology? Does the therapist have an eye for the patient's resiliencies?

The Professional Role and Its Boundaries

Has the therapist developed a personal style in his or her work? Can the therapist use theories and methods in a flexible way, so that they are helpful frames for working models in matters of case concept and treatment concept and are not dominating dogmatic systems? Is the therapist flexible without loosing boundaries of his or her role? Can the therapist be firm enough in his or her role versus all sorts of pushing and pulling by the patient or his or her relatives? How does the therapist handle questions and demands of patients, which are not usual in dealing with patients from the therapist's own country, like being invited to the patient's home? How does the therapist handle ethical aspects in his or her work and in matters of boundaries? Does the therapist consult with colleagues sufficiently, and how does he or she handle the role as a supervisee?

Emotional Sensitivity to the Patient and to Him- or Herself

Does the therapist easily recognize and take into account the patient's expectations? Does the therapist have an eye for culturally sensitive aspects, like shame and honor in patients from a shame culture? Does the therapist monitor his or her feelings closely in therapy? Is there a good equilibrium between empathy and distance? Does the therapist easily recognize the danger of slipping into overinvolvement or too much distance? Does the therapist show signs of burn-out or other signs of emotional impact?

Self-Evaluation

Self-evaluation is necessary for all therapists when doing therapy. The important thing for a therapist to learn is to recognize limits in his or her competence in what he or she can do according to his or her training and capacities, taking into account the patient and his or her situation. This is an important ethical responsibility for a therapist. To what degree is the supervisee dependent on judgments of the supervisor in this matter; to what extent is the therapist learning to do this by him- or herself? Does the therapist learn to see whether he or she really makes progress in a treatment, and how effective his or her efforts and interventions are? This is most important for a therapist's professional growth, but also for the process of supervision, as a supervisor is dependent upon the supervisee's report to see what needs to be worked on in supervision.

Besides the *supervisory tasks* Elizabeth Holloway also mentions the *functions* of a supervisor. She enumerates five primary functions a supervisor engages in while interacting with the supervisee. For reasons of clarity we prefer to refer in our teaching of supervision to tasks and functions as the "whats" (what is he monitoring) and the "hows" (how is he doing it). These "hows" are listed here.

Monitoring and Evaluating

A supervisor is almost always monitoring consciously and unconsciously what is going on in a therapy; it is a continual process. Monitoring is connected with evaluating. A supervisor generally does not evaluate in terms of a formal sort (using formal criteria), unless it is a supervision as part of a formal training. However, also within the clinical supervision that we are describing evaluation remains an important element of the "hows." A supervisor regularly communicates judgments and evaluation of the supervisee's behavior as it relates to the professional role. Here a one-sided element of the relationship comes in, the initiative to communicate and judge in this respect is largely unidirectional.

Instructing and Advising

A supervisor has to instruct and advise. He or she has more experience in the field than the supervisee, and the reason for asking for supervision is explicitly to learn more from a more knowledgeable and capable person. Instructing and advising are teacher-student functions.

Modeling

The supervisor acts as a model of professional behavior and practice: implicitly in the way he or she formulates (or in his or her attitude) having contact during the session, the way he or she is reflecting, the way he or she shows self-evaluation. It is also explicit in the way he or she demonstrates interventions. The communication here is largely bidirectional and the interpersonal distance is reduced in respect to previously mentioned "hows."

Consulting

Finding solutions for problems in clinical and professional situations is made easier by the supervisor by asking for information and opinions from the supervisee. They reflect together about a problem. Although the supervisor uses his or her expert power, communication is bidirectional and largely interactive. In the process the supervisor is encouraging the supervisee to evaluate his or her therapeutic behavior rather than making a judgment.

Supporting and Sharing

The supervisor supports the supervisee through empathic attention, encouragement, and constructive confrontation. Support often comes by sharing in an empathic way the therapist's own perception of the supervisee's interventions, emotions, and attitudes. This direct communication can also mean confrontation of a positive sort. An atmosphere of mutual respect and confidence is required. Communication is bidirectional and interactive. The participants are fully engaged in sharing feelings and opinions connected with the work.

In a pragmatic approach to the supervisory process one might say that the "whats" and the "hows" taken together determine largely the process of supervision. There are other aspects of the process of supervision, like contextual factors (e.g., the setting in which it occurs) and phases of the process that have to be considered. It is outside the scope of this chapter to consider these factors.

GROUP SUPERVISION

Case supervision in a group is in principle not different from individual case supervision. However, the practice of group supervision and the supervisor's tasks are rather different. Participants in group supervision can be therapists who work as independent therapists, having a practice of their own. They can also be workers employed by different centers or institutions. A group supervisor does not work in any of the work settings in which the supervisees are employed; he or she is an outside supervisor, not involved in any direct working relationship of another sort. For a really independent relationship, supervisees should ideally not be employed in the same organization. This is not so easy in the area of treating traumatized refugees. That is why we sometimes accept two members (no more) who belong to the same agency, provided they are not in a hierarchical relationship to each other. Thus, this kind of group supervision is basically different from team supervision in respect to formal relationships between members. Although a team by definition is also a small working group, team members are not really working independently from each other, but they are responsible to the same team leadership. This has far-reaching consequences for supervision, which will be dealt with later. The number of participants can vary; for group supervision we consider four to six members (supervisees) an ideal size; but three or seven members will also work.

A group supervisor does not work as if he or she would be doing individual supervision; if this were true, a supervisor might soon be exhausted, having to pay attention in the same concentrated way, as is the case in individual supervision, before an audience that is more passive and whose creativity is not much explored. Procter (2000) describes such a form of group supervision and the specific reasons for using it as "authoritative group supervision." Additionally, it would be unfortunate not to make use of the tremendous experience that is found in skilled therapists present as supervisees, certainly when they are actively exchanging partners. The result of a shared reflection in such a group, if properly stimulated and communicated, can yield much more than the sum of all individual reflections taken together. One may sum up advantages of group supervision as follows:

- There is a lot of mutual support from supervisees as a group of peers,
- There is less dependence on one supervisor,
- There is a larger variety in reactions, sometimes other nonconversational techniques are possible, like role-playing or mirroring.

These advantages will not always be automatically present. A climate has to be established in such a group that will favor mutual support and sharing, rather than competition and negative criticism. There are groups that have a tendency to be overcritical. Groups do have a potential for being destructive, if not properly monitored and checked. For instance, instead of offering an opportunity for sharing a variety of reactions toward the case that is being presented, a group as a whole can lie in wait for an innocent "victim" who has made some elementary "mistakes," and come down upon him or her in "condescending teaching." Or this poor colleague needs major support and is set in the center of conversation time and again. Senior supervisees can collide to form a lecturing subgroup as a defense against emotional material. We have seen this phenomenon many times. Our guess is that it has to do with some (unconscious) envy of a supervisor's position as an expert. It might also have to do with the sort of work that is being supervised; treatment of traumatized refugees is after all treatment of victims of aggression by perpetrators whose aggression, whether they are high or low in office, is considered by themselves as justified. Persecutors are superior and aggressive. In some ways this will influence their victims and through them undigested "material" of this sort will come up in therapies, affecting therapists. It will certainly be present in group and team supervision.

Sometimes these emotional experiences emerge, and within a framework of "emotional awareness" we can pay attention to them. By taking structuring measures in conducting sessions of group supervision we try to make a setting in which mutual support, sharing, constructive confrontation, and learning are possible. In this way we take the sting out of aggression, which mostly suffices to establish a good working climate. So group supervision should be structured and all participants have to stick to it — a matter of contract. All participants have to support the structure, but the group supervisor has the final responsibility in maintaining the rules of the game.

These points of departure connect very well to the classification Brigid Proctor provides in her book *Group Supervision* (2000, pp. 37–38). She distinguishes four types of supervision groups:

• Authoritative group supervision — supervision in a group;
• Participative group supervision — supervision with the group;
• Cooperative group supervision — supervision by the group;
• Peer group supervision.

The last type pertains less for our goal, since there is no supervisor. In the Netherlands we call this "intervision," a way of mutual support with very specific methodological consequences. The first type of group supervision is mainly individual supervision in the group. Group members are witnesses of the individual supervision and each group member gets a turn. In the participative type the supervisor is "responsible for supervising and managing the group; also for inducing and facilitating supervisees as co-supervisors" (p. 38). In the cooperative group the supervisor "is a group facilitator and supervision monitor; supervisees also contract to actively co-supervise" (p. 38).

Johan Lansen developed a supervision method that allows the supervisor to start a group as a participative type, which eventually can develop into a cooperative group. The reasons for this model stem from different sources. Because many of our supervisees in the group come from remote areas or have different working shifts it is nearly impossible to have all the group members always present. So a fixed procedure in each session gives all group members the possibility to connect if they have been absent.

There are several phases that stimulate group members to identify with other aspects than their own ingenuity and cultural backgrounds, and helps them to respond more differentiatedly when they approach the supervisor's position.

This is how we develop this identification model. In the first session for group supervision we present a lecture that proposes what we have described in previous paragraphs: explaining what the concept of supervision is, defining group supervision and the foci of attention (the "whats"). We expect participants to take an active part in the supervision, first of all by an active role in short identification exercises during supervision and also as sharing their feelings and opinions. Then we proceed to the actual supervisory session.

A case will be presented by one of the participants, just as in individual supervision. The participant finishes by formulating some questions. Afterward there is an opportunity for clarifying questions from the other participants, although not for venting advice or opinions. After the inner image of the supervisee is sufficiently shared with the other group members we give the following identification exercises.

First, we ask for identification with the *patient as a person*. Apart from the supervisee who has presented the case, all other participants are asked to identify with the patient, with his or her life and misfortune. In comparison to individual supervision, where there is only one person, the supervisor, who might identify as an outsider with the patient, group supervision produces a far richer context for divergent identifications with the same patient. A minute or two of silence may be needed in order to better concentrate on this position. After that, a round follows in which each of the participants is asked to tell what she or he feels from this patient's perspective. Often feelings of depression and helplessness are voiced, and expectations of treatment and the therapist are stated. This produces a number of important pictures, which frequently lead to a better understanding of the difficulties in treatment. The supervisee who brought the case in does not have to be silent during such a round. The group as a whole benefits more by a full commentary afterward from his or her perspective, telling what was gained in the process, when all have spoken and the conversation continues. Sometimes such a round of identification is sufficient to stimulate the combined reflection in such a way that the problem of the supervisee has come to a solution, or is reduced to a lesser proportion as the supervisee sees other aspects that are more relevant to the progress of treatment. It is often necessary to continue with a new exercise of identification.

The second exercise is identification with the *supervisee's position as the therapist* of this patient. We do not primarily ask for identification with this particular supervisee as an individual, but for identification with the position of the supervisee as therapist, for example, how would they feel if they were the therapist here, treating this patient. So all participants have to imagine for themselves the task and burden they might feel if they were involved in this case. This identification with the task of the therapist gives them an opportunity to reflect on the cognitive and emotional aspects of the case, as if it were a case of their own. Afterward a round of sharing follows again, in which is asked: "How do you feel in this position, having to treat this patient?" Not: "What would you do?" This prevents premature advice like "If I were you, I would ..." — that would be identification with the supervisor position. Hereafter the supervisee-therapist reactions to what his or her peers have brought up.

These exercises of identification offer an instructive experience to the supervisee. He or she recognizes much in what his or her peers have said, which is mostly very supportive, but also gains by hearing new aspects. It gives another, often new perspective on patient and treatment. Soon several suggestions come to the fore, often illustrated with experience from others' own cases, for changes in case concept, treatment, or attitude of the therapist. The supervisee's active participation in the conversation can bring new questions and ideas. Sometimes the supervisee has already gained so much that we can conclude the session. In other cases the session continues with further reflection on the case and treatment.

This can lead to the introduction of a third round of identification, namely, with the *position of the supervisor*. This gives supervisees the opportunity to give advice, of consulting, of instructing from their own knowledge and practice, of being a model, and so on. This is now, after the preceding identification rounds, more acceptable to the supervisee than would have been the case in a previous phase of the session. It is the supervisor's task to guide and stimulate this process. He or she should protect the supervisee against negative criticism. The supervisor can comment on reactions that come from participants. At the end of the session the supervisor must ask the supervisee what has been gained in this process. For all supervisees, the widening of the world of concepts and ideas is considerably greater than in individual supervision.

After having completed the case discussion the group supervisor can do an additional round of information seeking as to what has been gained by the "other" supervisees in following this process. This can lead to some short additional information by referring to other cases.

The course of a session can also be a bit different. It happens at times that it is handy to ask for identification with another person, for example, with the patient's partner or parents. Or at times a discussion brings up a question from someone to the supervisor: "What would you do if you were the therapist for this patient?" This can be a good occasion for consulting the group. Looking back at this model it will be clear that the supervisor's role is quite different from his role in individual supervision. In fact the supervisor has to act at two levels: at the level of guiding the group in exercises and reflection, and then ensuring that the "foci of attention" (the "whats") get proper attention. At the first level, the group supervisor's task is mainly to stimulate and monitor this process. With some knowledge of group work in general and group dynamics in particular, this is not a difficult task to complete. The supervisor has to keep a special eye on the supervisee and check his or her reactions, determining whether he or she recognizes something, can use some of it, and if not, why not. At the second level the supervisor has to monitor whether, through reactions of feelings after each exercise, or by a comment of the supervisee and further reflection and discussion, enough material is presented relevant to the different "whats": the skills, case conceptualization, professional role, emotional sensitivity, and self-evaluation. If needed, the supervisor has to point out one or two of these "whats."

There are great advantages in such structured group supervision. If properly guided, there is hardly any disadvantage. One might consider that parallel processes in group supervision are less clear, and that there is less time from the supervisor for each individual member. We do consider these disadvantages of comparatively minor importance. One risk of group supervision is practically excluded by structuring: the risk that some members might try to engage in dynamics of this group as "preoccupation." There is one additional advantage that has not yet been mentioned: those who have participated in such a group can have better ideas about tasks and functions of supervision in general. For some supervisees the next step is learning to be a supervisor themselves.

INTRODUCTION TO TEAM SUPERVISION

There are two main types of supervision in a team. One type is sometimes called team supervision proper, which has as its focus the *interaction* between team members, the way they work and communicate, and the tensions that arise in the team. Although its *focus* is not a case that is brought up for supervision, its *purpose* is not different from other forms of clinical supervision: it is a joint reflection on what belongs to the focus, with the aim of increasing the professional competence and autonomy of the team members.

The second type of supervision in a team is *case-oriented*, which in its form is not so different from case supervision in a group. What really does make a great difference between case supervision in a team compared to in a group is the nature of team relationship. This is so determinative that it overshadows by far all the superficial similarities between case supervision in a group or team.

A team as such has essential properties that influence both kinds of supervision. Team members are involved with each other in many ways. There are hierarchical relationships in a team of a different degree, and there is a shared common task. There are official and informal work-oriented relationships, and also human likes and dislikes, which in a group of independently working therapists can play a minor role. There is a world within the team and a world outside of it. The outside world expects a certain achievement from the team as a whole, and sometimes the team is subordinated to leadership from above, especially when the team is part of a larger organization (the Red Cross, a hospital, a welfare organization). All this makes a great difference for the way one experiences one's work and for the climate in which one performs. And it has consequences for supervision. A team supervisor — whatever the focus of supervision is — must be aware of this and recognize those influences on the behavior of members of the team or on team behavior as a whole. And this supervisor should be able to contain those effects in the supervision sessions.

Therefore, in both cases of supervision a team supervisor should have advanced knowledge of teams, characteristics of team leadership, and of collaboration between members. Such a supervisor should have knowledge of issues like team composition, development of teams, problems in a team, team culture, and destructive processes in teams. This knowledge should enable the supervisor to examine and diagnose the problems that are brought up for supervision in a team. Such knowledge gives a profound deepening to the supervisor's work, which will stimulate the joint reflection.

CASE ILLUSTRATION OF SUPERVISION IN A TEAM

Ibrahim is a dedicated social worker with extra training in pedagogics. He comes from the Near East and is a member of a team that treats tortured political refugees, in a country in Northern Europe. Ibrahim handles the case of Ahmed, a young academically educated client from the Middle East, a member of a splinter group of the Palestinian Liberty Organization. In the country where he was active he was invited one day to visit the secret police for interrogation. After several visits it dawned on him that they wanted him to spy on his fellow faction members. When he refused, a process of intimidation started, which had a certain pattern. He was invited to the local headquarters, but on every occasion for the very next day. On this next day they kept him waiting for many hours in which he heard the cries of people being tortured, and also shooting. Afterward it was his turn; he was beaten, insulted verbally, and threatened with execution. This procedure was repeated throughout 2 years, in which Ahmed was subjected many times to mock executions. Finally, they started to summon his wife, too; she was brutally beaten. Then they decided to flee to Europe. However, before their flight his torturers told him that they had raped his wife. After their flight he started complaining of headaches; medication did not help much. And the relationship with his wife deteriorated because of his suspicion that she had actually been raped, which in his culture casts a heavy strain on the relationship. In his therapeutic sessions with Ibrahim, Ahmed is very open, very sad, and mentions his thoughts of suicide.

Ibrahim assists Ahmed the way he successfully does with other Muslims. Ibrahim knows the Koran very well, but also the religious customs that have accumulated during the ages of Islamic culture. With tales and parables from this tradition he tries to give comfort and insight to Ahmed, not unlike wise, benevolent, traditional pastors in other religions do. He devotes his time and attention, guided by parental feelings. It is not psychotherapy proper, it is not like therapy for European intellectuals, but this pedagogical sort of therapy mostly works well for Ibrahim's clients. However, with Ahmed this seems no definite solution. He always leaves Ibrahim, after their conversation, in an optimistic mood, only to return one week later in the same sad mood as before, talking of his misery, his mistrust in his wife, and mentioning his suicidal thoughts.

Ibrahim rightly decides to bring up this case for supervision in the team. His questions are: "Is there a real danger of suicide? How do I handle this case further, as there seems to be no progress, only repetition?"

In the round of identification with the patient the European team members identified very much with the academic education of Ahmed and his disappointment with the therapy. They do not feel at ease with Ibrahim's so-called simple, infantilizing approach. Non-Western members identified very much with Ahmed's ambivalence toward the rape of his wife and the impossibility to make himself and his family a decent future.

In the round of identification with the position of Ibrahim some confusion arises. Most team members express the feeling of being stuck, some thought they should ask a psychiatrist for assessment of the danger of suicide. Other members express their insecurity and insufficiency of the educational therapeutic method. Some other psychotherapeutic team members suggest that Ahmed be transferred to them instead of being subjected to Ibrahim's pedagogic and pseudoreligious "treatment."

The third round was very complicated. Team members found it very difficult to identify with the supervisory role and fixed themselves very much on the positions they had taken in the preceding rounds. These were related to their ethnic background, their academic education, but also to the length they were working in the center. Ibrahim's case has brought several sources of tension in this team to light. There is rivalry in this team between disciplines; it has been present for a long time, but remained hidden behind a facade of idealistic team harmony. The team has a few other members from second and third world countries, bringing along their own methods. The Western European team members feel threatened in their superiority of methods and ideas; there is the shameful thought — so disturbing that it can hardly be brought up — that the team will do better without foreigners around. And finally, almost all of the team members, but especially the European members, have a strong defensive attitude toward what we call "tragedy." They very much relied on clinical, psychiatric interventions to "relieve" the suffering. Such a tragedy is visible in Ahmed, who suffers because of his plight, because of his mistrust, where medication, action, mental support, and other measures are good but insufficient. It will take time, maybe years, before this patient will have worked through his existential tragedy. And it will take much energy from Ibrahim to go on, finding new ways of being able to hear his client's discomforting stories. Ibrahim, but also the other team members, are stuck in a collusion of avoiding feelings of tragedy. At an unconscious level, they forbid these feelings in their patients and in themselves. And in this process they have been very quick to deny their own aggressive feelings of rivalry between different disciplines, of anxiety toward elements foreign to their own world of values, of anxiety for blows toward their own feelings of superiority.

This example shows us how case supervision is not merely case supervision, but also an important means of bringing to light the functioning of the team and its tensions: between disciplines, members of different cultures, or tensions related to the work itself, with its tragic aspects. Case supervision can highlight the latent problems in a team. These adjacent themes emerge during the sessions for case supervision, and as such they are not the primary focus of reflection. Yet some words should be said about it. For instance, a short reflection might take place about the further necessity of dealing with these team problems somewhere else, maybe in a special team session without the supervisor. The outcome might also be that the team is also in need of supervision focused on the team interaction. The case supervisor would be wise not to act automatically as the one who is available for this purpose. Supervision is an activity based on a contract, and if the contract is about case supervision, a supervisor has to be faithful to his or her role as agreed to in the contract. In case of emergency a case supervisor might agree, after discussion, to change the focus of supervision for one or two sessions to the interaction in the team: a change of contract for a short duration. Thereafter all should return to the previous situation of case supervision. But if regular continuous supervision for team interaction is required, it would be best to look for a new supervisor who could start examining the team and its situation, and to negotiate a new contract for supervision focused more on interaction of the team members.

Team Characteristics

The case supervisor is limited in the ways he or she can help the team members to maintain their "observing ego." The team members must remain able to reflect upon their ways of treatment, and there are some obstacles the case supervisor should take into account. These relate to the composition of a team, team culture, team structure, and the context of a team.

The *composition* of Ibrahim's team was a source of many divergences. People from different cultures and backgrounds want to work together, but they work in specific areas. It is not always clear where the boundaries of such a team are. Medical specialists — among whom might also be a psychiatrist — are often external consultants. Sometimes the team has only a few salaried members, but a wide circle of professional and lay volunteers support it. Do they belong to such a team or not? Does secretarial or other staff belong to the team, or are they clearly distinguished as "subteams"? Those are important matters to consider when a team is asking for supervision. Often professional therapists will ask for supervision, particularly when case supervision is demanded. It might be wise to consider the question whether other workers (interpreters, telephone operators, secretaries) might need separate supervision. They could be exposed to considerable stress as well, being also subjected to the emotional impact of the work.

Another complicating factor can be that members stem from other cultures, sometimes from countries where many refugees come from. It can be desirable, because of their knowledge of the language and culture, that a team includes such members. However, it is a mistake to think that their presence will bring only advantages. Sometimes their fellow countrymen do not trust them as therapist or interpreter. But there is also a more specific reason: a treatment team is also a sort of bridge toward society in the country of asylum and the context of treatment is partly determined by this society. Therapists are, therefore, also some sort of buffer, loaded with all sorts of ambivalence that belongs to this position. It is essential to have enough members in a team who represent the norms and cultural values of the country of asylum. Foreign members should at least be sufficiently knowledgeable of these norms and values. On the other hand, members of the team should be sufficiently open to them, so that the team is properly integrated.

In Ibrahim's team there was a *culture* of denial of the composition of the team. Strong animosities between cultures and educational disciplines were denied. But when the tragedies in the clients' lives were denied, there was a common standard to relieve the suffering as quick as possible. Ibrahim tried to do so with his religious educational interventions, psychiatrists with medication, and the psychotherapists with behavior therapy methods. This led to processes as described by Lansen (1999), in translation:

> by a process of projective identification dangerous and indigestible mental contents (from traumatic material) are being acted out in interpersonal relationships (team members towards each other). If this process goes on for a certain time, it acts as a slowly working poison. A team that is affected this way suffers from mutual tensions and conflicts of such intensity, that it seems a mutual persecution of some sort. There is a strong rigidity in mutual attitudes, there are many boundary transgressions by unjustified meddling in each other's roles, expectations of each other's roles and attitudes are irrational, and one plays the game that in German is called "ausgrenzen": exclusion and repulsion of each other. The intensity of this process is a hindrance for a sound, critical self-reflection. (p. 469)

It became clear in this case supervision that the culture obstructed shared reflection in supervision. Then the supervisor had to look at the structure of this team. At a surface level, at a task level, things seemed well arranged. At the more unconscious depth level the divergences between team members provoked jealousy and rivalry, which stood in the way of identifications with the position of the therapist and the supervisor (round 2 and 3). They could more easily identify with the patient, although here too the diverging backgrounds were noticeable. In the next sessions the case supervisor maintained the supervision structure and facilitated adequate identifications among colleagues and alternative modes of action. Gradually team members were more able to shift perspectives and to become more empathic toward one another.

In the preceding example the team context was not so relevant. A team can be a small independent center, working mostly outside of the regular health service in a country. Such a team is often dependent on gifts from private persons, from a church, or other charitable organizations. Sometimes such a team has a semiautonomous existence under the roof of a hospital or other institution. In a few countries teams are a regular part of the health system. These differences of context mean a lot for team culture. Work in a recognized institution gives quite another feeling to the workers than, for instance, working under pressure of a hostile government. This is the case in several centers in the second and third world countries where human rights are far from being respected. Even in countries in Northern Europe a negative sentiment toward foreigners in the population can influence the climate within a team.

When a team is part of a regular or university hospital within the health system of a "welfare state," the climate in such a team tends to become not very different from other teams within this system. There might be a danger that the needs of such a team (for instance extra money for interpreters, for longer lasting therapy hours, or for supervision) are not appreciated by their surroundings. Or a team leader is in a buffer position between team members and his or her superior, who is not used to the work and needs of this team. For each team the influence of this context has to be taken into account when doing supervision.

DOING TEAM SUPERVISION

In this section we focus on a number of issues concerning team supervision, each introduced by a question.

What sort of experience should a team supervisor have, apart from having learned how to do supervision and how to treat severely traumatised patients? We think a team supervisor should have worked him- or herself in a team, for a number of years, where one has worked closely with other team members in treating patients with severe disorders or personality problems. Of course it is preferred for this to have been a team working with traumatized patients. Having been a leader can be helpful. In this way a prospective team supervisor would have gathered the best experience about what it means to work in a team; a firm ground would have been laid in order to be able to recognize aspects of team functioning and the profound influence these aspects have on functioning of the individual team members.

Supervision in a team, where the focus is on interaction and collaboration in a team, is often asked for when a team is in a beginning phase, or in a phase of transition. Team interaction and team cooperation are important issues for team leadership. But in such phases team leadership might feel the necessity for asking for outside help. In form, supervision of this kind (focused on team interaction) resembles supervision in any closely working team in (mental) health or welfare organizations. Supervisors for this supervision activity might be easier to find, since experience with and knowledge about trauma therapy generally is less necessary here. Supervisors who have worked in related fields, who have experience with supervision in teams, who work for "difficult" clients (drug addicts, young schizophrenics, AIDS patients) can be quite competent for this purpose. Still we think that it is a requirement that those supervisors at least have experience with and knowledge about the emotional impact in teams treating traumatized patients. Without that, important elements can be missed in diagnosing what is going on in a team.

What about the practical form of supervising a team, is this different from doing supervision in a group of independently working therapists? In case-oriented team supervision the practical form is not very different from group supervision. The supervisor can do it in about the same way. There is one important modification, however; the team situation as such has to be taken into account, often by mentioning it explicitly. It is wise to ask in the beginning of a session about important events that may have happened in the team since the previous session. And in case supervision, important issues clarifying team characteristics can appear, which are also relevant to the context of the supervised therapy itself, as we have seen in our discussion on team composition above, in the case of Ibrahim's therapy with Ahmed. Therefore, it is a good habit to conclude a session of team supervision only after a round in which attention has been paid to the importance of this case for the team.

What does this session, this particular case, tell us about the climate in the team; how does it affect different members of the team; of what does it remind them with a view on their work and collaboration as a team? As in all supervision, such a round is not a rigid, compulsory sort of thing. Sometimes it is not necessary. In very defensive teams it might be counterproductive. Of course, it is also a matter of tact. But the point is that everyone should realize that such a round is an opportunity. Once the practice has been established, team members might feel it to be useful. Often such a reflection opens an opportunity for further discussion of a problem in additional team meetings.

If one is asked to do supervision in a team, what should one start with? The first step is orientation. One should not start supervision before having made a contract. One should not make a contract without negotiations. And one should not negotiate without having made a good orientation about the need of a team, what supervision is required, what expectations exist about the how, the what, and the effect of supervision, and about the freedom and obligations of the supervisor. Effective orientation and proper negotiations are essential. A good orientation needs to be done by reading documentation about the team and its tasks and by reading yearly reports and other publications of the team or about the team. More important still are conversations (one or two) with the entire team, with team leaders, and with authorities higher in line; the latter is the case if the team's autonomy (including the team leader) does not go so far that the team might decide in important matters for itself. Such conversations can reveal interesting information: a request for supervision can come from a team that is inexperienced in the field, such as a newly begun team. This team might expect the supervisor to give a lot of know-how about treatment, knowledge, and even instruction. Maybe such a team is not yet ready for supervision. Regular training in diagnostics and methods might be more appropriate. It might happen that the supervisor who has been asked is the only person who is available for such a purpose; he or she has to decide whether to take on this task for a certain time. At least it should be properly labeled as training, rather than as supervision. Supervision can also be requested rather late, for example, when a considerable number of members of the team have been hit by burn-out, vicarious traumatization, or secondary traumatic stress, or when conflicts in a team have made all members weary. It is important to find out whether supervision has any chance of succeeding in helping to restore this team. Regrettably, sometimes such chances are minimal. In that case a reorganization or even shutting down completely and starting a new team might be better.

Sometimes supervision is asked for in a team where leadership does not function well. Cooperation and communication in such a team suffer, the quality of work deteriorates; the expectation is that the supervisor as éminence grise by his or her contribution will interrupt the disadvantageous consequences of the situation. If that would be the case and nothing would change regarding poor team leadership, supervision could go on without end. Of course, this is not good supervision; supervision is an activity by which supervisees have to grow, which also means the whole team, including leadership, should develop within themselves. Supervision for the team leader would be a better answer for the time being, with the focus on leadership issues in a team like this.

Sometimes a team leader, or another authority who is outside the team but has a responsibility for the team in the hierarchy of the organization, makes a request for team supervision. The problems in the team are insurmountable with regular means, and now an outside supervisor is called on to help. Although this is a good motive, something else might be at stake: supervision could be asked for reasons of pacification or even domestication. Such a motive should be put on the table and taken to the team; almost certainly a further dialogue between team and such an authority will follow, of an intense nature maybe, but not necessarily negative. The prospective supervisor should remind both parties that his or her task is not to force a team to law and order, but to help a team in reflecting about its work and cooperation. Of course the outcome can be that people can adapt themselves better toward each other or their organization as an advantageous effect. Another fruit of reflection might be that team members realize that the problem is not in the team but in society. Changes in society regarding refugees, government rules, and changing norms in the organizations in which the team is situated create an atmosphere and rules of the game, which interfere with proper team work. One should not forget that each team has a unique history, including sometimes having had supervision. Inquiries after experience in a team with previous supervision can be very revealing!

After orientation and diagnosis of the situation, the next step is negotiating a contract. In fact there are frequently two levels of making a contract: the level of team managers or directors (formal leaders) and the level of the team. The first level, the leadership, might not be necessary if a team is autonomous or if full decision power rests with the team leader, and if the team leader is also a fellow worker in the team. If a manager who is not a fellow worker holds team leadership he or she will not or should not regularly participate in case supervision. Then negotiations and contracting have to be made on different levels. At times a manager might not have the power to decide, and the organizational level of negotiation and contracting is one or two steps higher up.

Negotiations at the managerial level always concern, apart from financial issues and secondary conditions, the degree of freedom for supervision. Supervision should be a free space; that is essential. Supervisees should feel as free as possible in bringing in problems about their work, and in saying what they think and feel about it. It is a reflection that requires all participants to be open. That openness should not be endangered by hierarchical sanctions from outside or inside the team. The supervisor has to be safeguarded against having to report about persons or situations in the team. His contact with formal leaders should be scarce and only contain statements of a general nature. He can for instance report about supervision as being in action, sometimes as going on or being in full swing, as being required for another 6 months and the like.

The supervisor should also claim freedom to reflect with the team upon the organizational context of the team. However, it is not the supervisor's duty to report (on behalf of the team) to those higher in rank about such issues. The team itself should bring issues of organizational context further. At the team level, negotiations are about time, place, frequency, and so on. More fundamental issues of negotiations are:

- What will be the focus for supervision: case supervision or supervision about team interaction?
- What will be the contribution of the members in terms of initiative, energy, and bringing in cases (preparation)?
- What commitment is there to reveal in principle what one is thinking and feeling about a case, a therapist/supervisee, the mutual relationship, about the supervisor?
- What about confidentiality?
- What about the freedom, not the obligation, for the supervisor, to add a bit of teaching if this should be required to his opinion?
- What will be the degree of freedom for the supervisor to make revealing remarks about attitudes and some psychological issues (not to do therapy!)?
- What other issues are pertinent to contents and involvement?
- Is there agreement about regular evaluations of supervision?

Obviously, negotiations will not always be successful with such conditions. A team might disagree with a prospective supervisor about the focus of supervision. Or negotiations might bring out that there is not enough desire to change, or not enough involvement. A team might not like a supervisor's personal style. A team might also desire more role play or other methods that a supervisor cannot give or that he or she considers inappropriate for this team. There is no reason for negotiations to be lengthy; if agreement seems hard to reach, it is better to agree about this disagreement and part company.

CONCLUSION

This chapter is written for future supervisors, supervisees, therapists, team leaders, and directors in centers and institutions where traumatized survivors of persecution, torture, and violence are treated. It is our conviction that clinical supervision of the kind described in this chapter will benefit a great deal of workers and their teams.

Of course, much more could be said; a book could be written about this subject. Many examples could be given about practice and other elements might have been added. Still we believe the material in this chapter (and within this volume) will give a reasonably good idea about the importance and special character of supervision in this field.

Supervision in itself, no matter how important it may be, is not sufficient; it should be part of a package of supporting measures, like training courses, good peer supervision, quality control, good selection of leaders and workers, and adequate attention given by organizations and society. Most of all, individual workers and teams should be eager to learn; nothing is more healthy than being a member of a learning culture!

We are happy if we have succeeded in giving some fruit for reflection from our practical experience of working with Holocaust survivors and traumatized refugees. Much of this material has been used and tried by us for basic and advanced teaching of supervision and peer group supervision in the Netherlands and abroad.

REFERENCES

Bion, W. R. (1962). *Learning from experience.* London: Heinemann.

Bion, W. R (1969). *Experiences in groups.* London: Tavistock.

Haans, A. H. M. (1998). *Het Labyrinth van Ares. Werkbelasting door Hulp aan Geweldsoverlevenden* [The Labyrinth of Ares. The burden of work in assisting survivors of violence]. Utrecht: Pharos.

Holloway, E. L.(1995). *Clinical supervision. A systems approach.* Thousand Oaks, CA: Sage.

Krystal, H. (1988). *Integration and self-healing. Affect, trauma and alexithymia.* Hillsdale, NJ: Analytic Press.

Lansen, J. (1999). Secundaire traumatisering bij de Individuele Hulpverlener en in het team [Secondary traumatization in individual assistants and in teams]. In P. G. H. Aarts & W. Visser (Eds.), *Trauma. Diagnostiek en Behandeling* [Trauma, diagnostics and treatment] (pp. 459–473). Utracht, ICODO; and Houten: Bohn Stafleu Van Loghum.

Loganbill, C., Hardy, E., & Delworth, E. (1982). Supervision, a conceptional model. *Counseling Psychologist, USA, 10*(1), 3–42.

Proctor, B. (2000). *Group supervision. A guide to creative practice.* London: Sage.

van der Post, L. (1993). Supervisie tijdens de Opleiding tot Psychiater [Supervision in the training of psychiatrists]. In H. M. Van Praag–Van Asperen & P. H. Van Praag (Eds.), *Handboek Supervisie en Intervisie in de Psychotherapie* [Manual of supervision and intervision in psychotherapy] (chapter XIV, pp. 225–240). Amersfoort: Academische Uitgeverij.

van der Veer, G. (1998). *Counseling and therapy with refugees and victims of trauma* (2nd ed.). Chichester: John Wiley & Sons.

Wilson, J. P., Lindy, J. D., & Raphael, B. (1994). Empathic strain and therapist defense: Type I and II CTRs. In J. P. Wilson & J. D. Lindy (Eds.), *Countertransference in the treatment of PTSD* (chapter 2, pp. 31–61). New York: Guilford Publications.

Winnicott, D. W. (1960). The theory of the parent-infant relationship. In *The maturational processes and the facilitating environment. Studies in the theory of emotional development* (pp. 37–55). London: Hogarth.

13

The Presence of a Third Party: A Dialogical View on Interpreter-Assisted Treatment

HANNEKE BOT AND CECILIA WADENSJÖ

When treating refugees and asylum seekers, the situation very often arises that there is no common language in which therapy can be carried out. In these cases it is necessary to introduce an interpreter. The obvious advantage of using an interpreter is that refugees who have only recently arrived in the host country can receive treatment quickly. In this chapter, less obvious advantages as well as possible difficulties with using interpreters during treatment will be highlighted.

There are two important characteristics of therapy. First, it is a "talking cure" in which words are weighed carefully. Second, it is built on an intimate and trustful relationship between two people — patient and therapist. These two aspects obviously change in certain ways when an interpreter is introduced. Is it at all possible to do therapy with patients who are unable or unwilling to speak the language of the therapist? Some authors argue against this. For instance, Yahyaoui (1988) claims that by using an interpreter, you end up treating the unconscious of the interpreter him- or herself, instead of that of the patient.

A second argument against interpreters in therapy is that information can be lost and meaning can become distorted. This fear, we argue, is partly due to an everyday understanding of words as carriers of speakers' intentions, which can be explained as a monological view of language and mind. A dialogical view of language radically modifies the whole idea of information being lost and meaning becoming distorted. Seen from a dialogical perspective, a single person cannot control the meaning of words, phrases, and utterances. In this view, people — speakers and listeners — are understood to make sense of words as they are contributed to interaction. The difference between these perspectives will be outlined below.

So, the question is what the presence of a third party with the mission to translate does to a therapy session and to therapy in general. In this chapter we will explain how treatment with interpreters is different from the usual situation. In our view, this kind of care has its own, specific potential that could be an added value. We do not in this chapter suggest solving all possible problems with interpreters at once. First, there are differences between individual interpreters as far as professional training is concerned, between individual therapists when it comes to their attitudes to interpreters, between various settings, and so forth. Second, what is more in focus here is that the nature of interpreter-mediated therapeutic interaction is too complex for simple solutions. What we offer is an approach and a set of analytical tools. These can be used to develop one's skill of interacting in interpreter-mediated treatment and one's proficiency in introducing patients to this specific mode of communication. It is our firm belief that therapists need an elaborate understanding of the nature of interpreter-mediated interaction and that interpreters in their turn need to be educated specifically for interpreting in face-to-face therapeutic interaction. This chapter is about interpreting and not about "cultural mediation." Our stance is that an interpreter is there to translate what therapist and patient say — at the same time we acknowledge that interpreters do communicate and that is what this chapter is about.

This chapter is also about *professional* interpreters, those who have some education and training to do the job and who are paid to do so. So it is not about children, relatives, or auxiliary workers who are brought in to translate. We think it is obvious that family members are not fit to interpret as their closeness to the patient makes it difficult to talk about intimate issues. Haffner (1992) has shown this clearly with her example of the 7-year-old child who was asked to translate to her mother that the ultrasound showed that her brother-to-be was dead. In general Takens (2001) has shown that some distance between people is needed to be able to talk about the issues therapy is about. Finally, this chapter will not discuss whether therapy with the assistance of interpreters is possible or not. It already happens, so it is worth exploring and explaining.

MONOLOGISM AND DIALOGISM: OPPOSITE AND COMPLEMENTARY PERSPECTIVES

Following the language philosophy of Bakhtin (1979, 1986) one can make an important distinction between a monological and a dialogical view of language and mind. Linell (1998) discusses at length this distinction and its analytical implications when used in studies of talk in social interaction. Wadensjö (1992, 1998) applies the distinction in her work on interpreter-mediated immigration hearings and medical encounters.

Monologism is quite dominant in the everyday understanding of language. It implies that words and expressions are understood to have fixed meanings that can also be used metaphorically. It entails that people speaking the same language are assumed to be attaching the same meaning to the same words. Monologism also implies that the decision of the speaker alone to use certain words defines the meaning of what is said. As was indicated above, the claim that information can be "lost" and meanings become "distorted" in the process of translation is based on a monological view of language and mind.

In contrast, when applying a dialogical view on language and mind, meanings of words and expressions are understood as being partly established between people in interaction. Meaning cannot be separated from the context in which the words are used and where sense is being made. Words and expressions can simultaneously make sense in various ways to different people as well as to the same individual at various times. Interlocutors understand talk in interaction partly drawing on their knowledge of the conventional use of the current language(s) and partly on their experience of the current specific situation and speech genre. In a dialogical view of language and mind, meanings of words are not glued to lexical items, but are created and re-created by sense-making subjects.

The theoretical distinction between monologism and dialogism is useful in understanding what is happening in the practice of interpreting. A monological understanding of language implies emphasizing the importance of everyday, taken-for-granted equivalent meanings of words (as if they were listed in a dictionary); while dialogism focuses more on the intersubjective creation of meaning within the specific and changing context of a particular social encounter. In theory, the distinction between monologism and dialogism can seem obvious; however, in practice, both views can apply simultaneously, to various degrees. While they are working, interpreters need to apply a monological understanding of language. Every now and then during the course of a conversation, they need to "take" a chunk of words out of context in order to translate it into another language. Obviously, interpreters (as well as therapists) also need to understand what they are doing in dialogical terms. In other words, they need to be aware of the mutual impact they (their communicative behavior generally and their talk specifically) have on common interaction.

ONE-, TWO-, AND THREE-PERSON PSYCHOLOGY

An important distinction in the theory and practice of modern psychotherapy is that between a one-person psychology and a two-person psychology. A one-person psychology stems from the classical psychoanalytical idea in which the analyst analyses the psyche of his or her patient without being part of the therapeutic process him- or herself. The analyst would follow the "rules of abstinence," meaning that he or she would refrain from expressing emotions and personal involvement and would treat any reaction of the patient on his or her person as stemming from the patient and the patient's history alone. This one-person psychological stance, described as a "paradigm" by Gill (1994), has been criticized from within the psychoanalytical movement on logical grounds. As Watzlawick and his colleagues (1967) phrased it: "one cannot not communicate" (p. 49). From outside psychoanalytical circles the idea of a one-person psychology has also been criticized. It was seen as inhuman, as logically impossible and as denying the social interaction that takes place when people communicate (Gill, 1994, pp. 36, 37). Based on this, the notion of a two-person psychology developed. Psychotherapy is then perceived as a cooperative effort of both patient and therapist. There is emphasis on the creation of a "working relationship," there is recognition of the fact that there has to be a "match" between therapist and patient, and the therapeutic process is seen as the intersubjective reconstruction of the patient's life narrative.

In a two-person psychology therapist and patient construct meaning in their interaction. This way of thinking comes very close to the ideas of dialogism as described above. Seen from a dialogical perspective, the words of therapist and patient get their specific meaning in the intersubjective therapeutic reality. The idea of a one-person psychology has now been refuted as a realistic possibility on logical grounds. However, it is still in use as a therapeutic technique in which the therapist will be as noninvolved as possible in order to get specific therapeutic results. Recent Dutch research shows that in psychoanalytical practice both one-person and two-person psychology are in use in treatment (Gomperts, 2001). Psychotherapies are usually oriented at a two-person psychology, but one-person psychological techniques can be used there, too.

So, what happens when an interpreter is introduced into the therapeutic process? One could keep thinking in two-person, or even one-person, psychological terms, thus implying that the interpreter is not a part of the therapeutic process. This position, however, can be argued against on the same ground as the one-person psychology. It would imply that it is possible for the interpreter to "not communicate," to be invisible as it were. In the same way as a one-person psychology can be used as a technique, however, it is also possible to use both one-person and two-person psychology in interpreter-mediated psychotherapy. Using both these techniques would indeed imply using the interpreter as a "translation machine." The techniques will work in different ways depending on whether the participants share the same view of the situation or not. Like therapists, interpreters, and patients also have their respective expectations concerning their own and other's involvement in the conversation. These expectations can, of course, clash or agree. Within a treatment, and within a session, there would therefore be episodes that are more like a one- or two-person psychology, in which the interpreter acts and is being treated as a "translation machine," and there will be instances in which the interpreter becomes included in conversation as a full-fledged participant. Understanding it as a technique one avoids denying that the interpreter de facto is interacting with the other participants in the encounter, even if their participation is different from that of the others. Whatever technique the therapist uses, the presence of an interpreter in a therapeutic exchange transforms the situation into what we would label a "three-person psychology."

Unlike therapists, not all interpreters working with traumatized refugees and asylum seekers are trained specifically in psychology or in therapeutic techniques. Arguably, any therapeutic technique presupposes not only the therapist's expertise, but also the interpreter's general understanding of what is going on. Therapists therefore need to be explicit about their expectations vis-à-vis the interpreter. The two of them need a shared, at some level, understanding of the rules of the "language game" — in Wittgenstein's (1958) sense — they play. When discussing interpreters' education, few people would argue against their need to have a basic knowledge of psychotherapeutic theory and practice. As Lindbom-Jacobson (1995) suggests, however, a certain antagonism and a tendency to mix up the two professional roles can occur in cases where the interpreter and the therapist share a very similar educational background.

THERAPEUTIC LANGUAGE

Our position is that an interpreter is basically present in a therapy session to translate the words of patient and therapist. We are not talking about interpreters as cotherapists or cultural mediators. Nevertheless, the presence of an interpreter transforms the social encounter. There are a number of specificities that belong to this "communicative pas de trios" (Wadensjö, 1998, p. 12) that we will be dealing with here. We will describe their potential impact on therapy and relate them to the theoretical framework explained above. The examples we use to illustrate the various phenomena are drawn from Bot's (forthcoming) research data, collected in Dutch institutions for mental health care.

LEXICON, GRAMMAR, AND STYLE

One of the basic tasks of interpreters is to translate the words spoken in one language into another language. This is not an easy task. Sometimes it is easy to think of a word in one language as having a clear and straightforward equivalent in another language, but often a range of possible corresponding words and expressions comes to mind. This range of words contains synonyms, words that can mean more or less the same but conventionally are used in different contexts and have different connotations. Languages also differ in their grammatical rules. Grammar forces speakers to say things in specific ways. When translating, interpreters have to transform what was said into another grammatical mold. So matters of lexicon and grammar force the interpreter to make (more or less conscious) choices. The way interpreters understand what was said, their proficiency in various lexicon (idiolects) and the grammatical idiosyncrasies of the source and target language will define the wording of the translation. It should be noted that these issues are evident and important from a monological point of view, but can have a different meaning from a dialogical perspective.

There is not only the content matter of what has been said but also the specific style of the speakers that may be difficult to incorporate in the instant interpretation. During a particular session between Bot and a patient, the interpreter addressed her, i.e., the therapist, directly and said: "He speaks very poetically and I'm sorry I cannot translate that well to you." This enabled Bot to say, "The interpreter says you speak very nicely; I'm so sorry I cannot understand you directly so I could appreciate it better." The interpreter then translated this comment and the patient was visibly very pleased by what he heard.

SPOKEN VERSUS WRITTEN LANGUAGE

To a professionally trained and experienced interpreter translation goes more or less automatically. It is worth pointing out, however, that the fluency of the translated version can hide a fragmented and stumbling original utterance. There is of course no fluency unless the interpreter is fluent in the two languages in question. An interpreter who lacks knowledge in a working language can make a stumbling second version also of a fluently spoken original. Interpreter's hesitations and search for words can also be due to their lacking confidence in the situation. At any rate, the impression a patient's narrative makes on the therapist is influenced by the style in which the interpreter performs it.

To be in perfect command of a language is not the same, however, as speaking "as a book," in a written language style. Spoken language is ordinarily very different from written language. Although speakers use grammatical rules (which one can see when people correct themselves), spontaneous spoken interaction is characterized by a nonwritten language-style grammar. For instance, speakers can start an utterance, stop after a few words, restart with a rephrasing of what they have just said, and then continue, without bothering to complete a full grammatical sentence as one would do in writing. Repetition is very common in spontaneous spoken language. Detailed transcriptions of spontaneous spoken interaction usually look like unintelligible gibberish to the untrained eye. These transcriptions often need to be read out loud in order to understand that it might have made perfect sense to the people talking. This fragmented characteristic of spoken language makes it very difficult to repeat word-by-word, let alone to reproduce a translation that follows the original in all its meanderings. Provided the interpreter is in perfect command of both working languages, the interpretation is usually more structured and more adapted to written language grammar than the original (cf. Wadensjö, 1998, p. 147).

From a monological point of view the more structured translation represents a problem; the character of the interpretation is different from that of the original. A dialogical perspective though, takes into account that people in interaction listen selectively precisely because spoken language is redundant. Moreover, in interpreter-mediated interaction people can, although they might not understand the words of their interlocutor directly, nevertheless hear if the speaker hesitates, halts, changes intonation, and so forth. Also, a translation that mimics a very fragmented and hesitant original can be perceived as exaggerated, as not just translating but also evaluating what has been said. It can easily give the impression of "parroting" (cf. Berg-Seligson, 1990, p. 193; Wadensjö, 1998, p. 273). It can furthermore lead the listener to the conclusion that this is a bad interpreter who does not speak the language fluently. Interpreters can avoid even trying to repeat the fragmented character of a preceding utterance in order to save the speaker's and/or their own face.

For instance, a young Russian man had an appointment for a medical checkup at a Swedish clinic and expressed a wish to be tested for venereal diseases. The nurse he talked to asked him about possible symptoms in a matter-of-fact manner. The patient started to talk, but came up with nothing more than embarrassed sighs and fragments of talk, which he repeated several times. To the interpreter, it was obvious that the man experienced difficulties in expressing what was on his mind. She didn't repeat the exact wording (and sighing) of the man, partly because incoherent talk is difficult to restate and partly because her efforts were directed toward supporting interaction and helping the patient overcome his embarrassment. She summarized what he had said so far with coherent expressions like "don't know how to say this." Eventually, the interpreter, waiting for a substantial chunk of talk to be translatable, provided feedback tokens like "uhm" and "okay." The interpreter in this way probably met the man's expectations, but not the nurse's. To her it was less obvious that the man was searching for words. The nurse got the impression that the interpreter was doing so; that she was "censoring" the patient and excluding herself, the nurse, from the exchange. (This case is described in detail in Wadensjö, 1998, pp. 166–179.)

We assume in trauma treatment similar things happen when people want to talk about hurtful and shameful experiences but find it also difficult to do so. Patients' search for words will not be translated as such by the interpreter, either the process will be translated (like above) or a summary of the utterance will be given. In our experience, a therapist who is sensitive to patients' difficulties in formulating what is on their minds during therapy can provide much of the support that the patient in the above vignette got from the interpreter. By offering full attention, eye contact, nodding, suggesting the patient to take his or her time, and so forth, a therapist can help establish a shared focus in their exchange and draw the patient's attention from the interpreter. In doing so the therapist helps the patient to see that it is the therapist who is in charge of the encounter.

FACE-WORK

"Face-work," as defined by Goffman (1967), is what people in interaction perform in order to counteract the risk of hurting another person's feelings by disrespectful behavior, which in turn can lead to loss in self-respect. In ordinary conversation speakers are not normally intending to abuse each other but are keeping up conventional forms of politeness. If not instructed specifically to ignore these, there is an evident risk — or chance, if you wish — that the person appointed to facilitate communication will "smooth" possible face-threats.

An obvious example of this smoothing is how interpreters handle the varying conventions in the use of second-person singular and second-person plural (the *tu* and *vous* forms) respectively. For instance in Dutch, as well as in Swedish the *tu* form is more widely used than in French, German, Spanish, Russian, and other languages to address strangers as well as friends. If not instructed specifically to refrain from this, interpreters might compensate for the difference in conventional use by translating for instance a Dutch *jij* or a Swedish *du* into a French *vous* or a Russian *vy*, in order to save face.

Another example comes from Bot's (forthcoming) survey. An Iranian interpreter said he would never translate the word "rape" literally, although an equivalent word exists in Persian. He said it would be "like slapping the patient in the face" and he did not think that that would be what the therapist intends when he uses the word. So he would translate it like "have you been treated like a beast."

What needs to be considered here is that psychotherapy is different from ordinary conversation. In therapy one is supposed to talk about shameful experiences, hurtful events, and so forth. Obscuring these subjects in order to save face by deliberately using euphemistic vocabulary where the therapist purposely used face-threatening words can, from a therapeutic point of view, be counterproductive. The conclusion to be drawn here primarily concerns reliance, insofar that if an interpreter trusts the therapist to be aware of what he or she is demanding from the patient and to take full responsibility for the therapeutic consequences of his or her ways with words, the interpreter can feel confident that he or she is doing the right thing even if the interpreter feels that he or she (on the therapist's behalf) is hurting the patient's feelings. In the second part of this chapter, which deals more specifically with relationships, we will come back to the issue of trust.

TRAUMA STORIES

Treating refugees and asylum seekers often means that at a certain point in time memories of very traumatic events have to be dealt with. These people enter treatment because they have not yet managed to incorporate certain experiences in their life histories. If they had, it would be relatively easy to talk about them, but it is exactly these "traumatized memories" — as opposed to "memories of trauma" — that have to be worked with. Nijenhuis (2001) describes some characteristics of traumatized memories and memories of trauma. We will here stress some of them. Traumatized memories usually follow a fixed format, a standardized version of what happened. Whatever audience the story is told to, the speaker tends to repeat the same lines, to use the same words. Also, once a person starts talking about these events, the story tends to come out as an uninterrupted stream of words. Therapists usually prefer not to interrupt, afraid that the patient will clam up and keep his or her misery within, out of reach for treatment. This can lead to a difficult dilemma in interpreter-mediated therapy.

If "getting a complete translation" is emphasized, the stream of words would have to be interrupted to enable the interpreter to translate every word and expression uttered. But this carries the risk of discouraging the patient to continue his or her story. Another possibility is to allow the patient to continue, knowing that this will necessarily lead to a summarized translation, probably giving only a broad idea of what the experience was like. Memories of trauma are different from these traumatic memories. Memories of trauma have become embedded in the person's life story. It is a narrative that is adapted to those a person is telling his or her story to; the story can be shortened, different emphasis can be made, or it can be told in more symbolic terms (Nijenhuis, 2001). Important for working with an interpreter is that the narrator can adapt to his or her audience when speaking about memories of a traumatic event — this also means the narrator can take the needs of the interpreter into account, for example, by stopping every few sentences to let the interpreter do his or her job. Here we also see how the presence of an interpreter can help by highlighting certain behavior of the patient. A patient who is able to accommodate and cooperate with the interpreter shows important healthy behavior. The therapist can use this diagnostically and as a supportive intervention.

From a monological perspective, summarized translations would be considered problematic. By applying a dialogical point of view though, one can choose to emphasize the importance of other aspects, for example, that the patient gets to tell a story and is actively listened to, even though it has not been fully understood by the therapist. Also, one would take into account that patients' stories will have to be told, repeated, and retold in different words over and over again during the course of a treatment. The content matter of a patient's story will reach the therapist eventually — after many sketchy and incomplete original and translated versions have reached him or her during the course of time. When interpreters are fixed on a monological perspective, they can feel unhappy and insufficient with this procedure. On the other hand, when they have learned about the nature of traumatized memories and of some of the intricacies of treatment, they can feel secure that the therapist will see to it that the patient gets to tell his or her story again and again, as many times as the treatment demands. Moreover, interpreters who know that the retelling of "the same" stories has a specific significance in therapy can also understand that the therapist is asking many times "the same" question not because he or she fails to understand (the interpreter's translations of) the patient's words, but because this repetition is what therapy is all about.

The therapist has to balance the needs of all three participants: the needs of the patient to tell his or her story, the need of the interpreter to give an adequate interpretation and his or her own need to "be with" the patient in interaction. Experience will teach therapists how to handle this in practice, when to interrupt, and when to let patients go on talking, even if it is unclear what they are aiming at.

FOCUS ON MENTAL PROCESSES

In general, therapeutic talk is very much about what is going on in people's minds. The focus is on how people have been and are experiencing certain events. Therapists will word their interventions in such a way as to point to mental processes in order to encourage the patient to start thinking about these events in terms of what they meant to them personally. The following is an example of how the therapist's reference to mental processes is understood to mean something more concrete by the interpreter.

Segment 1

Therapist: Kan je voorstellen dat jouw dochter hetzelfde gevoel kan hebben?
Gloss: Can you imagine that your daughter can have the same feeling?
Interpreter: Motewajjeh mîshawîd keh dochtaretân ham hamîn ehsâs râ dârad?[1]
Gloss: Do (you) notice that your daughter also has the same feeling?

Did the interpreter hear all the words that were spoken and fill in what he expected could have been there? Could it be that he was not aware of the therapist's special interest in mental processes and the importance of the specific wording of this intervention and thus brushed over the details? Or did the interpreter simply try to meet the expectations of the patient whom he assumed not to be aware of Western therapeutic techniques? Or did the interpreter find the suggested topic — the daughter's feelings — face threatening? In the following example the patient has just been telling the therapist that he can become angry very easily for no apparent reason. He continues to say that he becomes so angry that he fails to notice what he is doing. The therapist attempts to make the patient relate these feelings to his traumatic memories. The following sequence then occurs:

Segment 2

Therapist: Wanneer weet u dan waar u wel bent? [...] het is alsof je eigenlijk even weg bent, ofzo?
Gloss: When do you know where you are, [...] It's like you actually are away for a while, or something?
Interpreter: Mîgûyand keh mîdânîd dar ân lahzeh kojâ'îd? mîgûyand shâyad înjûrî bâshad keh yek lahzeh dar wâqe' nemîdânîd kojâ hastîd?
Gloss: He says you know at that moment where you are. He says maybe it is like at that moment in fact you do not know where you are?
Patient: Moshakhkhas yanî keh makânam cheh jâ'î hast?
Gloss: Exactly you mean where is my place?
Interpreter: Nemîdânîd keh kojâ'îd?
Gloss: You don't know where you are?
Patient: Nah, nemîdânam, aslan mîgûyam keh hîch hâlat-e khodam râ nemîfahmam.
Gloss: No, I don't know, in general I do not understand my situation.
Interpreter: Ik weet inderdaad niet waar ik op dat moment ben. Ik ben mezelf niet.
Gloss: I do not know indeed where I am at that moment. I'm not myself.

---

[1]The examples are drawn from the transcription of video-recordings of naturally occurring sessions. The Persian in all examples is transliterated from the Persian script following the English convention.

The therapist in a postinterview revealed that he at this point had intended to suggest to the patient that his thoughts were somewhere else, not in the situation that he got angry at, but with some memories of far more terrible things that had happened to him in the past. The patient, however, is apparently unsure about how to understand the question and asks back after some hesitation "Exactly you mean where is my place?" as if it could have concerned the physical circumstances when this happened. The interpreter does not translate this question, but repeats the last part of his latest translation. The patient than reacts with the somewhat vague "I don't know, in general I do not understand my situation." Interesting is that this is being translated by the interpreter as "I do not know indeed where I am at that moment. I'm not myself." The translated version of the answer thus partly repeats the question at the same time as it is focused specifically on the mental processes just mentioned. Thus, it is answering quite well to the therapists' expectations without revealing what the patient's initial confusion was all about. The patient soon continues on a track that is considered valuable by the therapist, although it was not the line of thought he had intended to find. Although the therapist could have noticed the patient's confusion, he remains unaware of its content.

We imagine that when interpreters are trained in the basic ideas of psychotherapy, including the role of communication itself, they will understand more easily what the therapist is aiming at and translate accordingly. They will also feel secure enough to let the primary parties sort out their misunderstandings, without being afraid of losing their trust in them as interpreters, as professionals in their own trade. Moreover, we want to emphasize that occasional confusions and misunderstandings are not necessarily due to the interpreter's shortcomings and do not inevitably lead to communicative breakdown. On the contrary, the therapist can sometimes consider a "misunderstanding" to be fruitful because it provokes more talk on a certain topic and can therefore help the patient to clarify his or her thoughts on it.

PARTICIPATION FRAMEWORK

The above example involves a sequence that can serve to illustrate another specific feature of the "communicative pas de trois." In one of his utterances, the interpreter specifies the current participation framework (Goffman, 1981; Wadensjö, 1998, pp. 86–94). Twice he mentions explicitly that he is speaking for someone else: "He says you know at that moment where you are. He says ..." In countries like Sweden and the Netherlands, professionally trained interpreters are instructed to translate using the "I form." Nevertheless, interpreters occasionally can feel the need to distinguish between the meaning self and the talking self, to meet what they understand as the expectation of the current listener, for instance to protect their own and the listener's face when they are uttering something they might experience to be face threatening. One interpreter in Bot's data was observed using the I form when translating the words of the patient and using the he-says form when translating the words of the therapist. His rationale for this behavior was that he felt the patient might misunderstand who is talking when he translated, while he assumed that the therapist would understand the procedure.

Referring to the person who spoke the words originally might be meant to clarify the "meaning self," but it could give rise to other problems, as in the following example, where the therapist starts by repeating something the patient just said.

Segment 3

Therapist:	Mmm, eh, u kunt u niet controleren, zegt u, maar heeft u zelf het gevoel dat u op dat moment niet weet wat u doet?
Gloss:	Mmm, eh, you cannot control yourself, you say, but do you have the feeling yourself that at that moment you do not know what you are doing?
Interpreter:	Mîgûyand keh shomâ khodetân râ nemîtawânîd kontorol bekonîd, montehâ mîgûyand âyâ khodetân ân ehsâs râ dârîd keh dar ân lahzeh nemîdânîd keh cheh kâr dârîd mîkonîd?
Gloss:	He says that you cannot control yourself, but he says, you yourself have the feeling at that moment that you do not know what you are doing?

In the interpreter's version it is no longer clear that the therapist here made a reference to the patient's words (the therapeutic technique of "mirroring"). Words that originally were spoken by the patient ("I cannot control myself") now seem to come from the therapist. Following his habit of specifying the source of the utterance when speaking for the therapist, using a "he says" formulation, the interpreter in this sequence might have tried to avoid what would have become a rather complicated phrase: "He says, that you said that you cannot control yourself …" Whatever was the interpreter's intention — something we can know little of — in the cited sequence, the therapist's mirroring technique was evidently put out of play. Bot is working on a systematic investigation of interpreters' use of direct address ("I") and "he says" formulations respectively, in her material. The findings can be correlated, for instance, to the topics being discussed (for example, whether face-threatening or not) and to the interpreters' training and proficiency (in languages, dialogue interpreting, therapy, and so forth).

As a conclusion so far, we feel it is safe to say that interpreters' specification of the participation framework by using formulations such as "he says" instead of direct address does not automatically make it easier for the parties to understand one another. We think awareness of the aforementioned tendencies in interpreters' discourse can make therapists (and interpreters) better prepared for three-party therapeutic talk.

THERAPEUTIC RELATIONSHIP

So far we have been concentrating on what people say and hear in interpreter-mediated therapy. We will now continue with what people see and experience without words, what can be called relational aspects.

Therapist as an Active Listener

Active listening is an important ingredient of therapeutic technique. Active listening includes providing feedback. By back channeling a listener normally encourages the current speaker to go on talking. The therapist's back-channeling behavior is normally part of the technique that will encourage patients to tell their stories. In interpreter-mediated sessions, the therapist's and the patient's feedback is delayed, coming only after the interpreter's version of the preceding speaker's utterance. There are two points to be made here. First, a number of studies of interpreter-mediated interaction (e.g., Englund Dimitrova, 1997; Linell, Wadensjö, & Jönsson, 1992) have shown that feedback parts of utterances tend not to be translated. An "uhm" intended to encourage someone to go on talking, indicating that the listener is "with you" is dependent on its immediate context. Interpreter's back-channeling behavior tends to be less frequent compared to that of "ordinary" listeners. This can partly be explained by the fact that they are not contributing to interaction on their own behalf, but listening in order to be able to provide a second version of what just has been said. Partly, at least in conflicting situations, it can be explained as a result of the interpreter's striving to appear nonpartial. An "uhm" or a nod in the speaker's direction could be interpreted by the other party as an agreement.

Therapists might occasionally find it useful to utilize the time during which the interpreter is talking to formulate the next intervention. The prolonged listening time might also, however, be used to observe what is happening nonverbally, which is sometimes felt to be even more important. In order to build more direct rapport with the patient, therapists can react to nonverbal communication; for instance, if a patient suddenly looks astonished, they can choose to react directly on the observation.

Bot's data give an example of this. The patient has been talking about his feelings of guilt that give him a lot of discomfort. At those moments he grabs his head with both his hands. The therapist asks: "What happens, is there something with your head?" which is translated by the interpreter. The patient reacts "I feel my head is becoming very heavy."

Here the therapist shows that he is attentive to the patient by focusing on what happens "here and now." In conversation without an interpreter it is usually the listener who gazes at the speaker while the speaker does not look at the listener (Goodwin, 1981). Goodwin even asserts "gazing at a hearer is inappropriate" (p. 45) — this applies to multiparty conversation where all participants are supposed to direct themselves to the speaker and not to watch other listeners. Primary speakers in interpreter-mediated talk are usually instructed specifically to look at each other and not at the interpreter. This instruction, which often is communicated explicitly to therapists and sometimes also to patients, goes against the observations of Goodwin of "ordinary" behavior. The instruction implies gazing at a listener while the interpreter speaks, it implies showing "disengagement behavior" toward the interpreter (not looking at him while he is the speaker), it implies to the interpreter to continue talking while he is lacking the usual "attention indicators" from the listeners. If this instruction is carried out, the way "gaze" is used in interpreter-mediated talk is different from monolingual conversation. It also implies that "gaze" can be used specifically, for example, to show attention, to indicate that one wants to take a turn in speaking, and so forth. Our experience is that patients usually follow the "ordinary" gaze behavior — they look at the interpreter while he or she is talking probably because it feels "rude" to not do so. The therapist can use the interpreter's turn to watch the patient and observe his or her reactions, but has to make sure this is not intrusive, as it goes against the grain of ordinary polite behavior in conversation. Also here therapists have to learn through experience to use their ordinary communication skills in a different way.

Interpreter-mediated talk is per definition a transcultural event. Goodwin mentions (in a footnote) that "ethnographic literature provides some striking exceptions" (1981, p. 57) to what he says about gaze in this book. He mentions examples from India. In the Netherlands it is accepted as "folk knowledge" that people from non-Western cultures are different in their gaze behavior. Gazing at a speaker would be seen as impolite and indecent behavior. Men and women are not supposed to look each other in the eye; subordinates do not look at their superiors. Although we doubt whether these differences between cultures are as marked as the folk knowledge wants us to believe, cultural issues can also influence the way gaze is used in interpreter-mediated dialogue.

Transference and Countertransference

Transference and countertransference are complicated therapeutic concepts originating from psychoanalytical theory and practice. Over the years the significance attached to these concepts and the meaning they have been given have changed considerably. It has been noted that in interpreter-mediated psychotherapy it "becomes 200% more complex and involves the patient's transference to both clinician and interpreter, countertransference among both of the latter toward the patient" (Westermeijer, 1990, p. 747) and the relationship between the therapist and the interpreter. One could just as well say that the processes are not simply doubled but tripled. The problem in this discussion is that there is no documented evidence of what happens to (counter)transference feelings and their expression in interpreter-mediated therapy. We take (counter)transference here as the experience of feelings that are evoked during the session, but which have their origin in relationships of the persons concerned with important others in the past.

Transference feelings (of patient toward the therapist) can only be known if they are brought out into the open. They must be expressed before they can be discussed together with other material that has appeared in the session. Likewise countertransference feelings can only be understood because the therapist is supposed to know his or her own input in the relationship and can thus distinguish between what comes from him- or herself and what can be attributed to the patient and the particular therapeutic situation. In order to talk about (counter)transference with regard to the interpreter one would thus have to know what and how the patient feels vis-à-vis the interpreter, and one would have to have insight into what realistically stems from the interpreter and what does not. As far as we know, there has been no research into these questions and we also have the strong impression that these issues have never been dealt with in a rigorous way in practice. The issue has been discussed in Scandinavian therapeutic literature in a case study by Lindbom-Jacobson (1992, 1995). In her experience the therapeutic situation with an interpreter implies that the regressive aspects of a patient's personality come forth more intensively and faster than in the dyadic encounter. Provided the occurrence of a fast regression, the situation also invites the patient to place positive feelings on one and negative on the other person present; to make a childish divide between "the good" and "the bad." In order to handle this situation, Lindbom-Jacobson argues, it is important to support the interpreter's integrity and neutrality; to make clear that the interpreter is part of the therapeutic frame, established and kept throughout the therapy. In an interview study among therapists Lidberg (2001) notes that, according to her informants, a split of transference between interpreter and therapist seems more likely to occur with patients suffering from borderline problems compared to other cases. The advantage of working with an interpreter would thus be that certain aspects of a patients' behavior are put under a magnifying glass, as it were, and are easier to observe by the vigilant therapist. In Bot's data there is another interesting incident. The patient talks about his anger toward his son. He says that he "treats his son in a punishing way," whereupon the interpreter asks "You mean you beat him?" The interpreter later said to Bot that this was "a question for clarification, to make sure what the patient meant." The interpreter could, however, have just translated what the patient said and he could have left the initiative for a clarifying question with the therapist. It is possible that the question was a "countertransference question," that is, deriving from the interpreter's own life experiences or from his experience as interpreter of trauma stories. But this is mere speculation as long as there has not been an in-depth analysis of the interpreter's motivations. We think this might be interesting for research purposes, but it is definitely not something that belongs to the job description of an interpreter. Observations about the social relationships between the participants of interpreter-mediated dialogue and their effects on feelings of being in or excluded, facilitating or inhibiting talk, are often described under the heading of (counter)transference.

THERAPIST/INTERPRETER RELATIONSHIP

One thing is certain: compared to monolingual therapy, interpreter-mediated psychotherapy introduces one more person who, at least occasionally, needs attention and who constantly gives attention, at least to what is being said. From the point of view of the therapist this means a big change: from being the master-cook in his own kitchen there is suddenly someone observing his trade. And this person is not just an innocent and uninformed bystander but someone who has had the opportunity of looking into many similar kitchens and who can compare, favorably or unfavorably, what he sees and hears with other therapists. Bot (forthcoming) has found that therapists, especially when they are still inexperienced, often worry about the interpreters' judgment of their work. They sometimes feel they have to apologize to the interpreter because "there is actually so little they could do for these people" (meaning asylum seekers and refugees) or they feel the urge to explain their behavior and the underlying therapeutic justification to the interpreter. In her work as therapist, Bot has heard interpreters expressing opinions about what they see happening during therapy. For instance, one interpreter said that he felt therapists should give more hope to their patients. According to him they should say things like "it will become alright, I'm sure." And he added "I've heard therapists are not even allowed to say such things." And as we all know, this is indeed true: therapists are not supposed to give false hope.

To judge from interviews with therapists, interpreters' attention can also give rise to positive feelings. For instance, one therapist in Bot's material said that he liked working with interpreters as it made him feel less lonely. Specifically when listening to cruel and sad stories from refugees and asylum seekers it gave him some comfort and support when he knew the interpreter was listening as well — even though they did not discuss these stories together.

PROFESSIONAL RELATIONSHIP

Therapists have to deal with the fact that interpreter and patient pay attention to each other — in whatever form — and this can be seen as positive or negative. For a therapist this may feel like a narcissistic blow (Bot, 1998) as he or she has to share the patient's attention with the interpreter, but it can also be seen as supportive for the treatment. In Bot's earlier mentioned survey it became very clear that the interpreters usually had more contact with the patients than they were supposed to according to their instructions. These instructions basically mean that the interpreter should behave as a "neutral person," "just translating what is said." "Neutrality" is a key word when describing the attitude of a professional interpreter. In practice, however, neutrality is a very difficult concept. Behavior intended to be neutral can be experienced as disinterested or distant (cf. Wadensjö, 1998, pp. 283–284).

Interpreters working for interpreter agencies are sometimes also specifically instructed not to engage in personal relationships with patients. This rule of thumb is similar to the rules applying to therapists' relationships with their patients.

In practice, contact between interpreter and patient in Bot's material ranged from some small talk when sitting together in the waiting room to having coffee together after the session "to talk things over" and the exchange of private telephone numbers. Interpreters are instructed not to have these contacts, but most therapists in Bot's survey were remarkably lenient about such behavior as long as they were informed of what was going on and felt it could be open to discussion if it was in danger of becoming countertherapeutic. In Swedish mental health care settings, the general and official rule, stressed in various educations, is that any kind of private contact between interpreter and patient is seen as nonprofessional from the point of view of therapists and interpreters alike.

The rule is established in view of certain negative psychological effects of working with traumatized refugees and asylum seekers that has been noted among interpreters. In the professional training of trauma therapists a well-known concept is, for instance, vicarious traumatization (e.g., McCann & Pearlman, 1990). Baistow's study (2000) of interpreters in several European countries revealed a high need for and low availability of emotional and psychological support. They reported that their "invisibility" and relative "powerlessness" in the sessions made this need even higher than they felt it must be for the involved therapists. Therapists' need for supervision is dealt with in a separate chapter of this book. The interpreters' need for professional counseling and advice seems to be less acknowledged. The existing organizational and economical conditions seldom allow for providing interpreters with proper supervision. Some therapists in the Swedish context (Lindbom-Jacobson, 1995) practice a routine that is meant to compensate somewhat for the interpreters' lack of supervision. They offer them to stay behind for 10 or 15 minutes after each session to talk about personal feelings and thoughts with the therapist, not as a duty, but as a right.

If we look on interpreter-mediated therapy as a three-person psychology, the discussion about the professional attitude of the therapist can also be applied to the professional behavior of the interpreter. In the psychotherapeutic profession there is a distinction between "boundary transgressions" — behavior that goes beyond what is described as professional behavior, but is not harmful to the patient and the treatment — and "boundary violations" — boundary crossings that are harmful (Gutheil & Gabbard, 1993). In line with this distinction psychotherapists have developed and are developing their ideas of professional behavior: from a "blank screen" Freudian analyst to a modern psychotherapist who sees him or herself as an instrument in an intersubjective exchange. They have established ideas about what behavior is appropriate with which patients and in what situations. Although social relationships will not be approved of, empathic, friendly, concerned behavior is allowed or even recommended. Subsequently, therapists can also think of the professional behavior of interpreters in a flexible way. This does not mean that the same rules have to apply to interpreters and therapists alike.

Trust and (In)dependency

Trust is an important aspect of a therapeutic relationship. Traumatized patients suffering from a posttraumatic stress disorder have, one could say by definition, problems with trusting their fellow human beings. In general it might be wise to see trust as an envisaged result of therapy and not as a prerequisite. An example of this is the following.

One of the patients in Bot's study, who had done his therapy with the help of an interpreter but was now sufficiently fluent in Dutch to talk to the interviewer, said

> I really needed treatment but I did not speak the language [Dutch] at all at that time. So I really needed this interpreter. I found it very difficult, in my country nobody trusts each other so how could I speak while this interpreter had to translate my words? But I really needed this treatment so I told myself I should go along. Now, this interpreter has become a sort of friend of mine! I find this very important, that I have learned that I can even trust my fellow countrymen if I only take the time to get to know them.

We also want to emphasize here again though that the matter of trust concerns all three participants in the exchange and not just the patient. In the Netherlands, 90% of the interpreters working for the agencies serving the health sector are of foreign extraction. A qualified guess would be that the situation is similar in Sweden, as well as in many other countries receiving immigrants and refugees. So very often the interpreter comes from the same region as the patient. This can lead to mistrust, as in the example cited above. Also in some instances patients have expressed their disappointment with interpreters as they felt their behavior was inappropriate. For example, they were laughing when the patient felt there was nothing to laugh about or they reported that the interpreter and the therapist were cracking jokes together and the patient felt excluded. There is a delicate balance to be kept. The patient might feel excluded if the therapist and the interpreter demonstrate an alliance between themselves too overtly. This can result in difficulties in building up a working relationship involving all three of them. Often, however, it is comforting for patients to be assisted by a fellow country-man or woman, and it is usually a relief for them to be able to express what is on their minds in their own language. Also it is our experience that patients see it as a sign that they are being taken seriously by the therapist when an interpreter is hired to help.

In our experience, particularly in the beginning of a therapy, the patient can be occupied with the interpreter's reactions to what he or she has to say, fearing that his or her story will be wrongly understood or incorrectly retold, or hesitating to burden someone, whose professional status he or she might be unsure of, with his or her private troubles. Some therapists try to counteract a possible, unwanted shared attention between patient and interpreter by placing the interpreter out of the patient's sight, for instance behind him, or far away in the room. Such an arrangement might also be motivated by a wish to protect the interpreter from getting too involved or negatively affected. To our knowledge, how the progression of a session is influenced by the way the three people are positioned in the room is just beginning to become an issue in the scientific literature. A recent case study (Wadensjö, 2001) exploring and comparing two interpreter-assisted therapeutic encounters suggests that the position of the interpreter potentially can facilitate as well as obstruct the participant's talk, which in turn can have an impact on all three participants' experience of "being with" one another, and hence on the refugee-patient's willingness and ability to retell traumatic memories.

In the particular therapy in question, other characteristics of the situations may have also had an impact on the development of each of the two encounters. For instance, the patient — a young man — might have felt more protective in relation to his first interpreter, and therefore unwilling to share his most horrifying memories in her presence. The patient started to talk about these when another interpreter was called for, a month later. The first mentioned was a beautiful young woman, the second a middle-aged man. The two interpreters originated from different parts of former Yugoslavia. The woman had lived in the same part as the patient; the man hadn't.

It is impossible to predict exactly how a shared (between interpreter and client and/or therapist) membership in one or the other social and cultural group influences an ongoing therapy. It is evident, however, that comembership in all kinds of groups (ethnic, gender, age, language, etc.) can be used as a communicative resource and therefore can indeed have an impact on the development of interaction. Psychotherapy with the assistance of an interpreter can be very demanding for all parties involved. It always put high demands on the therapist's imagination and inventiveness as they should take all these factors and possibilities into account. At the same time they may themselves feel excluded and insecure, knowing that the interpreter and the patient share the same cultural and/or ethnic background. In particular, therapists can feel excluded when the interpreter asks the patient a clarifying question and this results in a discussion in their native language.

Linked to this matter of trust is the issue of intimacy. Therapy commonly deals with intimate matters that are not easy to discuss: with demeaning and humiliating events, with shameful behavior, with feelings of guilt, with aggressive and sexual abuse, and so on. It can be difficult enough to talk about these matters with one person, let alone when a third person is present. We have also heard patients say, however, that they liked the fact that two people heard their stories. The more people know about these terrible things, the better.

Not speaking the *lingua franca* of the country one lives in can make people feel very insecure and dependent on the good intentions of others to try to understand them and not to abuse their ignorance. Being dependent on the services of an interpreter can be very difficult for some people. Bot interviewed patients who told her that they felt this dependency was difficult to bear. They wanted to tell their own story themselves without an intermediary. This encouraged these interviewees to put a lot of effort into learning the Dutch language — something that can be seen as "healthy behavior." It should not be overlooked, however, that this difficulty to accept this (realistic) dependency can be a psychological problem that needs therapeutic attention. The same applies also to the afore-mentioned issue of trust: a lack of trust can be understandable in the light of someone's personal history and realistic in the light of the political situation in the world, but it can also be a therapeutic problem that needs attention in the treatment. Trust and (in)dependency are always issues that come up in psychotherapy. When working with an interpreter, these issues are brought into the session directly and appear in a magnified way. This can be used to the advantage of the treatment.

CONCLUSION

At the end of this chapter we want to emphasize a few matters. First of all we want to repeat Watzlawick's famous adage that it is impossible "not to communicate." In interpreter-mediated individual psychotherapy there are three persons present and they all communicate. Although interpreters can try to behave like translation-machines and therapists can try to treat them like that and instruct their patients to do the same, they never are.

Second, throughout this chapter, we have made the theoretical distinction between "the words" and "the relationship." In practice these two aspects are closely interrelated.

Third, therapists learn to become sensitive to whatever happens during a session with a patient. The same holds true when the therapy involves an interpreter. Is the patient able to engage in a constructive working relationship with the therapist and the interpreter? Are certain topics systematically skirted, and is this due to the presence of the interpreter? Can these issues be discussed in the session, maybe even with the interpreter? There are some guidelines to be given, but our conviction is that these should not be allowed to become restrictive, as the meaning of words, expressions, and behavior in practice is always tied to the specific situation, to the current context. One can develop experience and refine techniques of the three-person psychology, but the work will never become routine.

In this chapter we have described several aspects of interpreter-mediated therapy — we are aware that so many other aspects have gone unmentioned. For instance, we did not examine the fear of many therapists that they somehow lose control of the session when an interpreter is engaged. In view of a three-person psychology this fear might get redefined: control could be seen as a joint responsibility. Bot's forthcoming study devotes serious attention to this issue.

Moreover, we did not examine gender, although we suppose it has an influence on how interpreted therapeutic conversation proceeds, just as it has on talk in general and on noninterpreted psychotherapy. Also, we did not dwell upon the differences between various psychotherapies, which can also exert an influence. Behavioral therapy, eye movement desensitization and restructuring (EMDR), cognitive restructuring, and specific therapeutic interventions (analytical interpretations can pose difficult philosophical questions in interpreter-mediated psychotherapy), were not focused upon. We have limited ourselves to those aspects that have been the subject of systematic research, but it is clear that a lot of work remains to be done in order to get further insight into these subjects.

ACKNOWLEDGMENT

We wish to thank Marianne Holme and Tom Koole for valuable comments on an earlier draft of the present text and Jan Morgan for critical proofreading. This research was supported by a grant from the Swedish Council for Social Research (93-2002: 14).

REFERENCES

Baistow, K. (2000). *Dealing with other people's tragedies the psychological and emotional impact of community interpreting.* Brunel University/Babelea.

Bakhtin, M. M. (1979). *Estetika Slovesnogo Tvorchestva* [The aesthetics of verbal art]. Moscow: Isskusstvo.

Bakhtin, M. M. (1986). Speech genres and other late essays (V. W. McGee, Trans.). In C. Emerson & M. Holquist (Eds.), Austin: University of Texas Press.

Berg-Seligson, S. (1990). *The bilingual courtroom.* Chicago: University of Chicago Press.

Bot, J. (1998). Werken met Tolken in Psychotherapie [Working with interpreters in psychotherapy]. *Journal for Psychotherapy 24*(5), 311–327.

Bot, J. (forthcoming). Ph.D. dissertation. Within the framework of her Ph.D. project Bot has interviewed a group of 20 therapists, interpreters and patients with ample experience in interpreter-mediated psychotherapeutic treatment and video-recorded six interpreted-mediated psychotherapy sessions in three institutions for ambulatory mental health care in the Netherlands.

Englund-Dimitrova, B. (1997). Degree of interpreter responsibility in the interaction process in community interpeting. In S. E. Carr, R. Roberts, A. Dufour, & D. Steyn (Eds.), *The critical link: Interpreters in the community* (pp. 147–164). Amsterdam and Philadelphia: Benjamins.

Gill, M. M. (1994). *Psychoanalysis in transition, a personal view.* Hillsdale, NJ and London: Analytic Press.

Goffman, E. (1967). On face-work: An analysis of ritual elements in social interaction. In *Interactional ritual, essays on face-to-face behaviour* (pp. 5–45). New York: Pantheon Books. (Reprinted from *Psychiatry: Journal for the Study of Interpersonal Processes, 18*(3), 1955, 213–231.)

Goffman, E. (1981). *Forms of talk.* Philadelphia: University of Pennsylvania Press.

Gomperts, W. J. (2001). Een terugblik. In A. R. Boerwinkel & W. J.Gomperts (Eds.), *Alleen en met z'n tweeën, One- en two-persons psychologie in de psychoanalyse* [Alone and together one and two person psychology in psychoanalysis] (pp. 45–65). Assen: Koninklijke Van Gorcum.

Goodwin, C. (1981). *Conversational organisation, interaction between speakers and hearers.* New York: Academic Press.

Gutheil, T. G., & Gabbard, G. O. (1993). The concept of boundaries in clinical practice: Theoretical and risk-management dimensions. *American Journal of Psychiatry, 150*(2), 188–196.

Haffner, L. (1992). Translation is not enough, interpreting in a medical setting, cross cultural medicine — A decade later. *Western Journal of Medicine, 157*(2), 255–259.

Lidberg, C. (2001). *Tolk i psykoterapi — en studie ur terapeutperspektiv* [Intrepreter in psychotherapy — a study from the perspective of therapists]. Linköping: Centre for Medical Treatment of Refugees (Report no. 24).

Lindbom-Jacobson, M. (1992). Överförings- och motöverföringsaspekter i psykoterapi med tolk (Den terapeutiska "triaden") [Aspects of transference and counter-transference in psychotherapy with the assistance of interpreters] in *Lines,* journal published by the Psychosocial Center for Refugees, Oslo, Norway, No. 1/1992.

Lindbom-Jacobson, M. (1995). Psykoterapi med tolk [Psychotherapy with the assistance of an interpreter]. In A. Hjern (Ed.), *Diagnostik och behandling av traumatiserade flyktingar* [Diagnostics and treatment of traumatized refugees] (pp. 159–166). Lund: Studentlitteratur.

Linell, P. (1998). *Approaching dialogue — Talk, interaction and contexts in dialogical perspectives.* Amsterdam/Philadelphia: John Benjamins.

Linell, P., Wadensjö, C., & Jönsson, L. (1992). Establishing communicative contact through a dialogue interpreter. In A. Grindsted & J. Wagner (Eds.), *Communication for specific purposes — Fachsprachliche Kommunikation* (pp. 125–142). Tübingen: Gunter Narr.

McCann, L., & Pearlman, L. A. (1990). Vicarious traumatization: A framework for understanding the psychological effects of working with victims. *Journal of Traumatic Stress, 3*(1), 1.

Nijenhuis, E. R. S. (2001, December 12). *Traumatische herinneringen: lichamelijk, emotioneel, gedissocieeerd, presentatie op de studiedag Gedeelde Eenheid.* Lichaam en Geest, Amsterdam.

Takens, R. J. (2001). *Een vreemde nabij: enkele aspecten van de psychotherapeutische relatie onderzocht* [A stranger close by, some aspects of the psychotherapeutic relationship investigated]. Lisse: Swets & Zeitlinger

Wadensjö, C. (1992). *Interpreting as interaction — On dialogue interpreting in immigration hearings and medical encounters.* Linköping Studies in Arts and Science No. 83, Linköping: Department of Communication Studies.

Wadensjö, C. (1998). *Interpreting as interaction.* Language in Social Life Series. London and New York: Longman.

Wadensjö, C. (2001). Interpreting in crisis — The interpreter's position in therapeutic encounters. In I. Mason (Ed.), *Triadic exchanges — Studies in dialogue interpreting* (pp. 71–85). Manchester: St. Jerome Publishing.

Watzlawick, P., Helmick Beavin, J., & Jackson, D. D. (1967). *Pragmatics of human communication — A study of interactional patterns, pathologies and paradoxes.* New York: Norton.

Westermeijer, J. (1990). Working with an interpreter in psychiatric assessment and treatment. *Journal of Nervous and Mental Disease, 178*(120), 745–749.

Wittgenstein, L. (1958). *Philosophical investigations.* London: Basil Blackwell.

Yahyaoui, A. (1988). *Consultation familiale ethnopsychanalitique: le cadre interculturel, troubles du language et de la filiation* [Ethnopsychoanalytic family consultation: the intercultural framework, difficulties in language and relationship]. Grenoble: Editions La Pensée Sauvage.

Nonverbal and Experiential Therapies

Nonverbal and Experiential Therapies

Introduction

JOHN P. WILSON

Part IV of the book focuses on nontraditional approaches to clinical-therapeutic work with asylum seekers and refugees. There are four chapters in this section, each focusing on different nonverbal and experiential forms of therapy.

In Chapter 14, Bram de Winter and Boris Drožđek discuss psycho-motor therapy. This chapter focuses on how active involvement in sports, gymnastic-like exercises demanding team cooperation, and other types of psychomotor activity can have a strong therapeutic effect as well as serve as an adjunct to other modalities of treatment. They note: "it is an eclectic treatment method that uses body experiences and movement as the portal of entrance and vehicle for psychotherapy." They quote the aphorism, "let me see you play and I'll tell you who you are," and indicate that it contains truth and diagnostic significance. By carefully observing the emotions, movements, intensity of activity, and energy level of the client, much can be learned about the personality dynamics.

In their psychomotor activities, the authors describe a five-phase model that parallels a model described by Drožđek and Wilson for psychotherapy of asylum seekers in the day hospital program in Holland. Each of the five phases has a goal. For example, in phase 1, observations are made of behavioral patterns; in phase 2 there is a confrontation and discussion about psychomotor behavior patterns that suggest defensiveness, withdrawal, or noncooperative and mistrustful attitudes; and skipping to phase 5, there is emphasis on cooperative, integrative work with others. Finally, the authors discuss specific psychomotor techniques (e.g., walking blindfolded; the balance beam; mattress surfing; the survival track in gymnasium; the flying bench, etc.) that are most interesting to study since they show how psychomotor play is actually an epiphenomenal expression of intrapsychic dynamics.

Chapter 15, by Sylvia Karcher, is based on work done at the Berlin, Germany, Center for Torture Victims. The author notes that since the creation of the center in 1992, body psychotherapy has been an integral part of the treatment program.

To begin, it is useful to place this work in perspective. We know from various studies that the body encodes and stores the memory of trauma. Traumatic memories and emotions are interrelated and expressed in somatic forms. Hence, body psychotherapy can unlock repressed emotions and traumatic memories by helping the patient reestablish a healthy connection to their bodies and emotional states, especially since torture inflicts horrific damage and injuries to the body, mind, and spirit.

She describes several treatments including concentrative movement therapy (CMT). Karcher indicates that CMT has four basic dimensions: (1) the body dialogue needed to establish an interrelationship with oneself; (2) the bodily experience in treatment that consists of "signals" of information about trauma; (3) body therapy that reveals information concerning social competence; and (4) the nonverbal bodily experiences that activate verbal experiences connected to traumatized states. These basic dimensions are especially relevant to body psychotherapy with torture victims who suffer from pain, tissue damage, and PTSD. Simply touching the body of a torture victim is sufficient to rekindle flashbacks, dissociative states, and traumatic memories. Therefore, bodily psychotherapies proceed slowly and gently in uncovering areas of physical and psychological pain, using different physical techniques to help restore in a gradual way the capacity to feel. In a sense, body psychotherapy, through sensitive procedures and techniques, attempts to restore what was taken away by the torture experience; to facilitate organismic self-healing to the fullest extent possible at all levels of integration.

Chapter 16, by Truus Wertheim-Cahen, Marion van Dijk, Karin Schouten, Inge Roozen, and Boris Drožđek, specifically focuses on the use of art therapy in the treatment of asylum seekers and refugees. Art therapy is a means to allow the traumatized patient to express what he or she is feeling and has experienced through various forms of artistic expression: painting, sculpture, pottery making, and so forth. In essence, the basic therapeutic idea is to help the patient externalize what is "inside" by making representations of it on the "outside" in paintings and artwork. The chapter contains three illustrative examples: a 42-year-old Armenian refugee who drew a weeping willow tree with a frightening, monstrous devil emerging from the tree's trunk and extending into the branches and two other drawings depicting a phoenix rising from its ashes and the construction of a new house. In each case, the drawings represent or symbolize the traumatic and unmetabolized experiences of the person. And, since most refugees do not speak the language of the host country, art therapy provides a window on the psyche that makes talking about the experience much easier.

In Chapter 17, Jaap Orth, Letty Doorschodt, Jack Verburgt, and Boris Drožđek discuss another nonverbal experiential form of treatment: music therapy. The authors have titled their chapter in an indirect reference to the musical and popular motion picture *The Sound of Music.*

Music therapy basically shares the same objectives of the other experiential therapies to assist the patient in expressing what he or she is feeling and remembering about the exodus from his or her homeland and the stresses that accompanied the journey. The authors noted that especially in terms of PTSD symptoms, "music therapists mainly focus on reducing the emotional stress and anxiety level, as to channel/redirect emotions via healthy outlets and develop relaxation and diversion." How is this done? The authors list many different forms of musical therapy, which include: (a) singing; (b) learning to play an instrument; (c) group collaborative "jam sessions" on musical instruments or to previously recorded music; (d) guided imagery to music; (e) relaxation and desensitization procedures to music; (f) live recordings of the patient's own music as expressions of psychological states; and (g) activating trauma-related affects through specially selected musical compositions. These techniques are used in conjunction with psychotherapy and are a part of the phasic sequence of treatment described in Part III by Drožđek and Wilson (see chapter 10).

14

Psychomotor Therapy: Healing by Action

BRAM DE WINTER AND BORIS DROŽĐEK

A BALL IS IRRESISTIBLE

When a group of clients goes to the gym for the first time, the therapist makes sure that there are some balls and badminton equipment lying around. Then, the therapist observes what happens, and what clients do spontaneously in the first couple of minutes of the session. After having observed the initial behavior and reactions, the therapist decides what to do in this first session. In the first meeting it is not likely that clients are going to use the badminton set at all. Two players are needed for that game, and the group of patients has no group qualities yet. Generally, some members of a beginners' group would dare to play with a ball of their own choice, alone. The majority of the group would just sit and wait in silence for therapist's instructions. After a brief welcome address the therapist decides which ball game is to be played. In psychomotor therapy, in order to prevent cognitive processes from interfering with the intuitive act of playing, one plays first and talks later. That is the moment when the therapy process starts.

Is playing soccer or basketball a form of trauma therapy? Can running with a ball, and trying to score, have a therapeutic value and help overcome experiences of overwhelming existential fear and distress? The answer is yes. Playing soccer or basketball is not the solution, but it is the beginning of a process of trauma treatment through action instead of talking. In this chapter we will illustrate this with words. However, it would be better to do this in action in the gym, with some balls lying around — a ball is irresistible for most of us.

PSYCHOMOTOR THERAPY: SOME BACKGROUND INFORMATION

Psychomotor therapy, as a method of psychosocial care, was developed in the Netherlands after World War II. It is an eclectic treatment method that uses body experiences and movement as the portal of entrance and the vehicle for psychotherapy. In the Netherlands, it is a well-accepted discipline that is elaborated and implemented in most psychiatric clinics. Specialized educational programs for psychomotor therapists exist on every level of education. The methods originate in various treatments and schools. Physical education, sports, massage, and dance contribute significantly to the therapy's activities, as well as body-work, relaxation techniques, sensory awareness, bioenergetics, and Pesso-System/psychomotor therapy (Pesso & Crandell, 1991). However, there is still a need to develop new arrangements and methods for the specific needs of new populations such as traumatized asylum seekers and refugees.

"Let me see you play and I'll tell you who you are" is an intriguing statement illustrating the possibilities of psychomotor therapy. This is not literally true, but it is indicative of a line of thinking and working. For instance, when playing soccer we can see the players' conduct restrained by norms of common decency and rules of the game. If we define the latter loosely, we see a fairly natural picture of the possible patterns of conduct a person uses in his or her everyday life. The psychomotor therapist develops and offers motor arrangements to clients with the purpose of observing their conduct. Analysis of their conduct can help clarify client's problems and encourage finding new behavioral patterns in problem situations. Then, the therapist can create another arrangement to train the new behavior.

In psychomotor therapy with asylum seekers and refugees, the therapist searches for appropriate metaphors for the important life events of his or her clients. The therapist incorporates them into motor arrangements and, finally, tries to give them a more desirable ending. In doing so, the clients are provided with a new set of corrective bodily experiences that might work as an antidote for their traumatic experiences. They form an alternative set of new memories clients can refer to.

Community Soccer

A soccer ball attracted a group of African refugees that entered the gym for the first time, and the therapist suggested that a special kind of soccer should be played. He called it "community soccer." It is an individual game. Every player has two pins, placed about 3 feet apart from each other, forming a kind of a goal. The player is supposed to defend those pins and not let others shoot them down. One can get more pins by shooting down a pin that belongs to another player. When a player loses both pins, he or she is supposed to join another player, and help that player defend his or her pins. The organization of this game gives every player a chance to choose how to play the game — out in the field, trying to shoot down other players' pins, getting new pins, or defending his or her own. One can take risks or try to be invisible. One can run or barely move.

When both pins are lost, the player experiences an intriguing kind of distress. Many players feel displaced when there is nothing left that belongs to them. Some tend to leave the game and sit and watch, as if they have no right to play the game any longer. Others remain in the area where their pins once stood, while there is no objective reason to do so any more. In a way it feels like home. Although the reason for the behavioral pattern has disappeared, the pattern remains. This arrangement is a good metaphor for the dilemma that the homeless and displaced persons confront, whether to leave or stay, attack, defend, or disappear and stop fighting for life completely.

After a while, the therapist instructs every player who lost both pins to seek someone with pins to form a team and play together. For the homeless, this new rule creates a new place, a new home, and a new sense of belonging in this game. It gives them a partner and an asylum!

Based on experiences with group treatment of Western psychiatric patients, the therapist would expect that clients are looking for a partner to form couples and after that, perhaps, larger groups. At the end of a session, he or she might expect a game between two large teams to take place. That did not happen in this group of traumatized African refugees. The first player who lost both pins went on to be the best soccer player in the group, the one with the most pins, and asked others if he could become their mate. He was accepted. Astonishingly, the next player did the same. Instead of looking for another relatively "wealthy" loner, he joined the group of two and a group of three was formed. This pattern repeated itself several times. The group around the best soccer player continued to grow in numbers, strength, and wealth while confronting a decreasing number of relatively weak individuals. Every "asylum-seeking" player in this game joined the big group instead of associating with another individual. The big group gained in power with every new member over the remaining unorganized individuals.

The particular way in which the group members played the game showed the therapist the patterns of survival they currently use in their everyday lives. Feeling safe within a large and powerful group seemed to be more important than taking risks, or forming new individual relationships with a potentially higher level of vulnerability. All clients seemed to be looking for the safety of the big family.

Finally, when interpreting the observed behavioral pattern, the therapist was confronted with a dilemma. Does the observed behavior have its roots in the clients' cultural background of a predominantly collectivist society or is it caused mainly by traumatic experiences? Is choosing the safety of a large group by African clients a cultural feature or a fear-bound symptom of their posttraumatic damage, or both? It is important for the therapist to examine the observed behavior from different viewpoints all the time.

STRUCTURE OF THE TREATMENT IN A MULTIDISCIPLINARY TEAM

Psychomotor therapy, as it will be described in this chapter, was designed as one of the treatment approaches implemented within a multidisciplinary trauma treatment program. Within this program, psychomotor therapy is combined with art and music therapy, as well as with group psychotherapy and medication (Chapters 10, 17, and 16 in this volume describe other approaches used in this treatment program).

From the beginning of the development of this program, the five-phase model of trauma treatment (Meichenbaum, 1994) was adopted. Although the model offered the necessary clinical structure, it was not primarily designed for nonverbal, experiential therapies. Necessary adaptations were made because of the special characteristics of problems presented by the asylum seekers and refugees. These adaptations are described elsewhere in this book (Chapter 10).

At the beginning, all verbal and nonverbal therapies in this program, including psychomotor therapy, followed simultaneously the same path. In other words, according to the five-phase model, when exposure had to be done and the client's traumatic past was the focus of treatment, clients were overexposed and overloaded with a whole spectrum of confronting tasks in both verbal and nonverbal therapies. Soon the team realized that this was not a productive strategy. Then, the team started developing new strategies and completing the mosaic of a multidisciplinary treatment program. It turned out that every therapy within the program has to follow its own path and pace.

Therapies are compatible but they do not necessarily have to follow the same structure and focus on the same topics in different phases of the five-phase treatment model. For example, when the pressure was high in the confronting exposure sessions of the psychotherapy group, it was wise to offer sports-oriented activities within psychomotor therapy. They offered opportunities to clients to blow off steam, to forget about the past for a moment, and, at least temporarily, to relax. Another example was that of the art therapy, where clients get used to confronting their traumatic memories through their artworks, long before they are expected to find words to describe them in group psychotherapy. In art therapy, the fear of talking about the unbearable and the unspeakable was elaborated, at first, by creating a visual representation of traumatic memories and adding just a few words to it (see Chapter 16 in this volume).

Creating good teamwork is very complex. However, when every team member has a notion of the path ahead, a good view of the group dynamics, and feels free to follow his or her intuition, the complexity of the work becomes more a source of intriguing pleasure than a problem.

In this process a new model emerged, where psychomotor therapy aims at psychoeducating through experience. This model seeks to strengthen the cohesion of the group before the exposure phase, offers relaxation during the exposure period, and works on reducing posttraumatic damage after exposure (see Table 14.1).

TABLE 14.1 Five-Phase Trauma Treatment Model: Overview of the Goals in Group Psychotherapy and Psychomotor Therapy, Including Five Typical Psychomotor Arrangements

Phase 1	Phase 2	Phase 3	Phase 4	Phase 5
Goals and Themes in Group Psychotherapy				
Psychoeducation	Biography	Reconstruction	Focus on	Relapse
Norms and values	presentation	of traumatic	present and	prevention
	Stabilization	memory	future	After care
Treatment goals	of symptoms	Exposure	Identity issues	Farewell ritual
			Support	
			Core beliefs	
			Changes	
Goals in Psychomotor Therapy and Typical Arrangements				
Observation	Confronting	Relaxation	Individual	The final
of the	existing	by pleasure	goals	exam
behavioral	behavioral	in playing	Training new	Integration by
patterns/state	patterns		behavior in	adding
of life	Exploring new		the group	personal
	patterns		Fear	assets to the
	Cohesion		management	group
	forming			performance
	within a			
	group			
Community	Survival track	Generalized	Flying bench	Over the net
soccer	Mattress	play		
	surfing			

PHASES OF TREATMENT

Phase 1: Orientation, the State of Life/Behavioral Patterns

In phase 1 the clients and the therapist must get acquainted with one another, and a working alliance with its rules, norms, and values is established. Another important task for the therapist is to observe the level of disturbance in the conduct of the clients. How lonely and isolated are they? And how do they react to the presence of others?

Traumatized asylum seekers and refugees often behave like lonely wolves. Their loneliness shows even when they are in the company of others. Silent distress and their second nature of staying out of sight resembles a wolf that has lost its pack, vulnerable, being on its own, hiding, crying at the moon, or not even doing that. The most profound existential experiences causing their suffering are those of complete helplessness and desolation. Nevertheless, they are also born survivors. They are capable of changing their lives in such a way that they can overcome the death threats and survive.

The technique clients use in order to survive is often a form of detachment, and the cost they have to pay for using it is very high, for example, emotionally they can cut themselves off from others or suffer from a violated self-perception: "No one can help me or understand my suffering, because I am the only one with experiences like these." Psychomotor therapy helps create a treatment group out of 8 to 10 individuals who are detached from one another, a bunch of scared lonely wolves. Psychomotor therapy, with its specific motor arrangements, can help these people create a group with therapeutic qualities, a group with mutual understanding, social stratification, and personal involvement, a group to belong to.

In this phase psychomotor therapy offers activities that can be done alone or in small subgroups. The client can choose the way and level of his or her own involvement. One can participate alone or form alliances with other group members. Here, the therapist observes the behavioral patterns and tendencies of clients. The above-described "community soccer" is an arrangement used in this phase. Individual structured warming-up instructions and games without previously formed teams are of great value, too.

Phase 2: Confronting Lifestyles and Group Cohesion Building

In phase 2 psychomotor therapy tackles clients' tendency to avoid deeper contact with others and it seeks their acknowledgment of the importance of working together on their healing process in the group. The offered activities are designed to show the adverse effects of working alone, and the advantages, opportunities, and better results when working together with others.

The standard motor arrangement used is called the survival track. It holds a metaphor for the clients' flight histories. It triggers the authentic flight behavior and offers opportunities to experiment with new solutions, with a new behavior.

The Survival Track

The survival track consists of a series of gym obstacles placed in a row. They form a track that seems to be very difficult to walk through. It poses a serious risk to the clients if they want to run through it. When standing on a bench at the beginning of the track, the client has to make a dive to a rope and swing to an almost 4-foot high vaulting buck. Then he or she must dive to a pair of rings, 10 feet high and swing to another buck, descend over a pole, dive for a large rope ladder, and swing in it to reach the last gym buck, where he or she reaches the end of the track. This way of mastering it is risky and for many clients is impossible to do. However, the track is designed in such a way that there are several hidden alternative ways of mastering it.

The group as a whole has the task to reach the other side of the track without touching the ground. Additionally, some luggage must be carried to the other side, also without touching the ground. The luggage consists of all sorts of light material, like ropes, rings, or balls in a large bucket. This material can be considered a burden, but it can also be useful in finding alternative solutions for mastering the track. The task is defined as a group task, and if one group member touches the ground, the whole group has to return to the start position and start all over again. This is an essential part of the intervention. The therapist needs to be strict in monitoring and sanctioning violations of this rule.

When clients start with this exercise, a typical behavioral pattern can be observed. Good athletes within the group are able to master the track in the most difficult way, and with a lot of risks. They make the dive to the rope, reach for the rings, jump to the buck, and get to the other side. They are relieved when they have accomplished the task. They are safe. Then, they suddenly realize that other members of the group are not able to follow them and that their efforts up to then were of almost no value. In a very physical way, they realize that the path they have to follow in the therapy must be shared with the whole group. They have to respect others and take their capacities into account, and to lean and depend on their help: "We can't do it on our own anymore, as each of us did it for a long time." The athletes must start all over again. They learn to listen to the ones with minor physical abilities, who must speak up instead of hiding their lesser abilities. They learn by trial and error as they find as a group alternative ways to cope with the situation and master the survival track. Isolation and detachment, a consequence of traumatic experiences and forced migration, are demonstrated and tackled with this arrangement.

Psychomotor therapy proceeds in this phase with many other activities designed to develop and strengthen group cohesion, first, in small subgroups, and, later, in the whole group. These arrangements often appear impossible to solve, but they can usually be mastered with the combined efforts of the whole group. The amount of fear evoked in these exercises is relatively low. There is always an existential challenge built in the arrangements that requires the engagement of the individual to function in the group.

Other arrangements might include the group bringing heavy luggage to an island without touching the ground (e.g., a mattress, placed in the middle of the gym) or piling up together on a vaulting buck where there is little space. Members might also be requested to climb a ladder that is only supported by other group members or fall from a height onto the arms of the group members.

Mattress Surfing

A fine piece of work can be done with an old, abandoned landing mattress. It is a piece of foam, 6.5 by 5 feet, 15.5 inches thick, in plastic and with an antislip layer on one side. Although it cannot be used anymore as a safety device for jump landing, it is a great surfing carpet. When turned upside down with the smooth surface to the ground, one can dive and surf for considerable distance through the gym. It is great fun!

Also, it is a beautiful motor arrangement when one tries to surf together with someone else. The dive must be simultaneous or one of the partners hits the ground instead of surfing on the mattress. Lack of timing to each other will be obvious. In a beginners group, this exercise offers a good opportunity for clients to learn to work together while confronting a mild existential challenge in a complex way.

At the end of this phase the group is usually able to work as a collective. The individuals have already acquired the feeling of belonging and the knowledge that they are together with others in the therapy process. The group is able to enter the next phase of treatment.

Phase 3: Focus on the Past, Exposure, and Play

Since phase 3 is dominated by the emotionally exhausting and intense work in group psychotherapy, where the clients' traumatic past is being addressed, psychomotor therapy must not add to the stress. The task is to bring some relief by offering mind-distracting activities. The group's favorite sport, like soccer or volleyball, is played or interesting new activities, like inline-skating, can be learned. Catharsis-evoking activities, like throwing hard, beating ferociously, pushing and pulling hard might be beneficial to blow off steam and express physically the feelings evoked in exposure sessions.

Phase 4: Individual Goals, Managing Fear

By phase 4 the group has acquired some beneficial internal qualities. Thus, it is possible to work on individual topics in a holding environment. Working on shattered core beliefs is important, but the crucial topic and focus of this phase is the management of fear.

Our clients survived by using an extreme and effective method of coping with the unbearable fear: dissociation. At the beginning, this strategy seems to be the only solution to escape from the life-threatening circumstances. However, it soon becomes addicting and burdens everyday life. It is important to rediscover and empower other possibilities of coping with fear and diminish the immediate occurrence of the dissociation reflex in situations of danger.

The main clinical problem here is that the time span available to intervene is extremely short. On one hand, when there is no experience of fear, it is not possible to work on new coping strategies. On the other hand, when there is fear, the dissociation reflex rapidly blocks other alternative behaviors.

Psychomotor arrangements need to create a fearful situation and enlarge the time span to intervene before dissociation occurs. The motor arrangement called the flying bench is an adequate vehicle to tackle this problem.

The Flying Bench

The group members are invited to move back and forth over a gym bench. The bench is hanging with rope ladders from the ceiling, about a foot and a half above the ground. The bench moves freely, but uncertainty is not evolving into fear because the client can easily jump off at this height. Later on, the bench is gradually hung higher and higher, even up to 10 to 12 feet above the ground, so that every group member can reach the point where he or she experiences fear. There is no device placed under the bench to catch a falling person. There is no suggestion of rescuing the client when he or she is on the flying bench. Clients can walk, run, crawl, sit down, shuffle, or move whatever way they like. They can ask other group member for help in any form they want since that is a good strategy of fear management. Nevertheless, clients are basically on their own in this situation.

Throughout this exercise the therapist comments on clients' different styles of coping with the danger of falling off the bench, labeling them as personal styles in trying to do the impossible: to put away the fear. The therapist suggests that under the actual circumstances, the ultimate form of courage is respecting one's personal boundaries. The therapist and the group applaud the decisions clients make while standing on the flying bench and become aware of the bodily signals of fear, especially the decision to say "No, I don't dare to walk the bench, I have reached my limits." When the client sits down on the bench and slides to the other side, he or she is effectively managing fear without dissociating. When the client has reached that stage, the therapist asks him or her to climb on the bench once again at the next higher level, stay there, not moving, and feel again the fear for a moment before coming down for the last time. At that point, clients have a quiet moment of experiencing physical symptoms of fear, in the certainty that they can easily end the pressure themselves by coming down.

It is not surprising to them that while up there on the bench, their knees start to tremble and their bodies sweat. Clients can anticipate this moment and have a chance to think about possible solutions. So, when they sit down on the bench and move in whatever way they choose, while being supported by the applause of the group, they are in fact managing their fear in an alternative way. This time, dissociation is not necessary. The reflex is neutralized.

This arrangement is also demanding for the spectators. While sitting and watching, they try to be of help to the individual on the bench. However, they are instructed to wait for the bench walker to ask for help and not to do more than they are asked for. That is a difficult task.

At first, having the group members talk to the person up high on the bench did not please the therapist. The therapist was afraid that the client would lose concentration. But that was not the case. The danger of falling evokes a maximum of concentration, and when conversation is possible the therapist knows that the client is in contact with the surroundings, and not dissociating.

Another arrangement that can be used in this phase evaluates the trust that clients have in one another. In this assignment the client is asked to walk blindfolded through the gym, while other group members protect him or her from bumping into obstacles.

Phase 5: Farewell, Integration, and the Final Exam

At the conclusion of treatment the group has changed. It became able to master complex and risky tasks, with a suitable equilibrium between risks and challenge. It can combine individual assets with good teamwork in order to optimize the group performance. In phase 5 the therapist asks the clients to perform tasks that require a high level of functioning, calling these tasks the "final exams."

Over the Net

The task of this arrangement is that the whole group crosses over a volleyball net (about 8 feet high) without touching it, while one group member is not allowed to touch any material at all, except the ground. Clients can use any gymnastic materials they can find in the gym and build constructions in order to achieve the task. This task requires a high quality of group dynamics. This task can only be achieved when there is good communication, an atmosphere that allows creative thinking, and a good team spirit. Relevant special abilities of individual clients need to be used while respecting personal boundaries and limitations.

Generally, the group chooses the smallest and lightest client to cross over the net without touching any materials at all. Would that client be capable of withstanding the pressure of the group and decide on his or her own what risks he or she is willing to take? Is he or she going to respect the personal boundaries? Would there be enough flexibility in the group to alter plans that are too dangerous or evoke too much fear? Can the group offer sufficient support to those who need it? Can the individual ask for help without feeling as a second-class member or appearing too demanding? Does it take in account the individual's assets with regards to the goal of the group? It is indeed the final exam!

The group of Iranian and Afghani refugees, who had to master this complex task, consisted of very creative and athletic people. After building a construction they decided that the best athlete, a world-class karate master, would make a dive over the net in order to get to the other side without touching the construction. He climbed on the shoulders of two men, who got a firm grip with their hands under his feet, and after counting to three he was launched and pushed off for an elegant dive over the net. With a roll he landed on a thick mattress made for jump landings. It was a beautiful example of using one's personal abilities for the benefit of the group. However, the group had to find another solution since touching the landing device was not allowed. They succeeded when they chose to lift with great care the smallest group member over the net in the arms of a strong man, who had already reached the other side of the net.

In the concluding phase of the treatment a farewell ritual takes place. The group is invited to evoke the golden moments that were experienced during the therapy. This ritual highlights the progress every group member made in an anecdotal way that is recognizable to all the participants. It is a part of a larger farewell party, mainly organized by the clients. This party has a lot of evaluations, food, dance, singing, crying, speeches, hugs, and laughter.

WORKING WITH OPEN GROUPS

The treatment strategies described above are inappropriate for use in open groups, where new members can be admitted at any time and at any level of the group process. In such a group different phases can be present simultaneously depending on each client's level. The therapist must bear in mind that the abilities of the members differ greatly and limit the choice of the motor arrangements. What is appropriate for one client is perhaps too difficult, too dangerous, or even incomprehensible for another. Often the therapist must choose less confronting, safer motor arrangements in order to avoid casualties. Also, since open groups are generally of a supportive type, not all the above-described arrangements are appropriate for that context. Existential challenge is an important precondition for healing of trauma due to torture or war experiences. The lack of this particular challenge can delay or block the healing process. Arrangements like "the flying bench" or "over the net" are often too dangerous for such a heterogeneous group.

Thus, the structure of the phase-oriented treatment model needs to be abandoned and replaced by a process-oriented line of working. Now, it is very important to have a moment-to-moment assessment of the situation in the group. It is the opportunity that counts in this group, not the systematic logic. The therapist has to adapt quickly to the opportunities that arise in the group and choose a suitable work form. The goals and vehicles of the treatment are the same; the structure is far less clear and appears rather chaotic at times. Nevertheless, the systematic model is useful as a reminder that every group member must go through the described phases individually in order to reach the therapeutic goals. The therapist needs to have a "helicopter" view and a creative mind to link all individual therapeutic needs into one psychomotor arrangement. The solution is to offer activities that bear different learning possibilities to allow every group member to choose the ones he or she is capable of and ready to do. Reaching an "island" (mentioned earlier) is an arrangement that provides an excellent opportunity to learn leadership skills by listening carefully to the others, allowing new group members to gain trust in perhaps only one group member, and encouraging creative group solutions to the assigned arrangement. Motor arrangements must be solvable in several ways, so that no one is forced to disregard his or her physical and psychological boundaries and limitations. The therapist must have a good grasp of the psychological pressure to perform that is inflicted on the newcomers to the group. He or she needs to be ready to intervene when necessary.

The positive side of working with open groups is that the group culture and positive experience with psychomotor therapy as a treatment technique is transferred from the old group members to the newcomer very rapidly. Clients come and leave, but a stable therapy setting remains. The therapist does not have to explain repeatedly that psychomotor therapy, as a treatment method, is a valuable tool for healing.

WORKING WITH MULTILANGUAGE GROUPS

Three aspects are important when applying psychomotor therapy in multilanguage groups. First, the pace and the style of work are affected. Second, the possibility to use risky motor arrangements must be critically evaluated. Lastly, the diversity of cultures mingled into one group influences the therapeutic process.

Pace and Style of Working

When communication between group members takes place, with the mediation of several interpreters, the working process is slowed down severely. Under these circumstances, "Let the arrangement talk for itself" is an important credo. The therapist limits his or her verbal interactions with clients. He or she just comments on the performances of the group and does not engage in discussions, which is very time consuming and complex. The therapist limits him- or herself to interpretations of clients' bodily conduct and stimulates creation of adequate alternatives.

Risky Motor Arrangements in Multilanguage Groups

Risky motor group arrangements under time pressure must be avoided because of the increased danger due to slow communication. If one client yells a warning in Russian and two interpreters have to translate it before the Arab-speaking client understands the message, the damage is usually already done.

Cultural Diversity in Multilanguage Groups

Diversity in culture can influence the therapeutic possibilities and performance of a group. Experience teaches us that some combinations of cultures work quite well, while others do not. Some combinations result in trouble caused by racial prejudices, which are enhanced by total unfamiliarity of the cultural subgroups. Cultural differences can also exist within a group of people speaking the same language. Sometimes, differences between people from the city and the countryside of the same country are much bigger than differences between people from different continents.

Contact Through Teasing

In a group of male clients coming from three different countries, two of the three Arabic-speaking men were very disturbing for the rest of the group. When coming into the gym clients throw balls at the basket before the session starts. They prepare themselves individually for the coming session. It is an important moment because one can practice his or her skills, show off a little, challenge others, or stay invisible.

The two Arabic-speaking clients greatly frustrated this play. One stood under the basket with a ball and bounced away from the basket every approaching ball. He was very good at it and nobody had a chance to score. At first it was funny but it soon became irritating to the group. The client seemed not willing to give up this behavior, even when the therapists instructed him to do so. He enjoyed it very much and did not grasp the irritation he caused to the group.

The other Arabic-speaking client had much fun throwing basketballs from a long distance over the group, circling around the basket, not to score but to scare the rest of the members. He laughed with great pleasure when he frightened somebody. It was a dangerous practice and the therapist had to forbid it. He had to do that every session. The client did not seem to understand how dangerous his behavior was. The therapist tried to interpret this behavior as a consequence of traumatization, but he did not find a satisfactory explanation.

Later on, the therapist shared his experiences with the Arabic interpreter. He was told that the Arabs from that region are well known as people who can play with language, are fond of humor and wit in their communications, and prefer a teasing contact among men. Then the therapist realized that his two clients were only acting like they did at home when they had fun, making the world a predictable place. Of course, they could not really understand the therapist's problems with their behavior.

This anecdote illustrates the kind of problems one is confronted with when working with several cultures in a multilanguage group. One has to learn by trial and error what combinations are most appropriate. The fact is that it is not possible to generalize the findings.

WORKING WITH FEMALE GROUPS

In female groups, the common problem of sexual torture is not openly discussed. It is too dangerous, shameful, and confrontational for most group members. When they do, clients usually address this topic in an indirect manner. They speak about someone they know well who has experienced dreadful things. The direct danger for the women is that, according to religious and cultural rules, the husband of a sexually abused woman has to repudiate his wife when he hears about it. No wonder that this topic is taboo. Even in a one-to-one conversation with a female therapist the presence of an interpreter can be risky. Established techniques for working through sexual trauma are of no value in this situation.

It is very complicated for a male therapist to work with a group of female sexual torture victims. Clients might identify the therapist with a male perpetrator or the therapist might expect this to happen. In reaction, he can easily adopt a very protective attitude and develop rescue fantasies. In psychomotor therapy we face some special difficulties due to the physical proximity and contact in the course of treatment. In play, attack and defense are always felt in a bodily way. These factors evoke the automatic defense reflexes developed by the sexually traumatized women. We do not want to trigger a disassociation effect when playing catch with our clients. In a way we are "walking on eggs." Under these circumstances, trust in the therapist is crucial.

Group Culture Transfer in Open Female Groups

At the start of our open female group, Bram de Winter was the only male staff member working with the group. It was tricky. Most women had been sexually tortured and here they were supposed to deal with a man where physical contact was possible. For 3 months, the therapist tried to be reliable, predictable, safe, friendly, and not too demanding while encouraging women to use the emerging opportunities in psychomotor therapy. There was a high rate of headache complaints present, preventing women from participating in treatment, and much unwillingness to go along with the therapist's suggestions about what to do in sessions. Then in despair, the therapist changed his attitude, laid back, and started being more passive. He continued with sessions where the group "just talked" about anything. In one session he told them more about himself. This self-disclosure turned out to be very important. The only man in the group, with a lot of potentially triggering and frightening attributes, became a man with a heart. Accepting this man to work with the female group became a part of the group's culture.

From that moment on the therapist never had much trouble working in this open group. The older members explicitly or implicitly informed every new member that the male therapist was considered reliable and all right. After a relatively short period of mild testing, new clients fitted smoothly into the group and followed the treatment.

Most of the women were frustrated with the cultural expectation that their husbands must protect them and were often experiencing an overwhelming vulnerability in life. Given the fact that they had fewer possibilities to engage in sports and physical education earlier in life, they were at the beginning somewhat reluctant to try to master the challenges of the psychomotor arrangements. However, after some successful tries and being challenged by the ways that the male groups master the task, the feelings of helplessness and vulnerability were neutralized. The women began to take pride in their performances. They often had to find solutions other than those used by the males, who could rely more on their physical strength. They enjoyed very much outsmarting them.

Creativity in Achieving the Impossible

A group of Russian-speaking women from different ex-Soviet Union republics mastered the survival track with great skill, despite the fact that a 65-year-old lady had to lean on a cane while walking with utmost difficulty due to severe somatic dysfunction.

When the therapist explained the arrangement that woman decided silently not to participate in it. She tried to make herself invisible as she used to do so often in her life. She sat silently in the darkest corner of the gym without any sign of involvement. Her strategy succeeded. The group was busy making plans how to master the track and came up with some good solutions. They found ways to avoid the risky dives to the ropes and rings while reaching the other side of the track. They were proud and cheerful until the therapist reminded them that the task was to bring the whole group to the other side. The "invisible" lady declared that she would skip this assignment, but the therapist made it clear that it was the group's responsibility to motivate her and escort her to the other side of the track.

Then a creative process of great beauty developed. The group adjusted and arranged the track in such a way that even the disabled lady could walk it. Basically, they split all the materials and formed a path, without touching the ground themselves. When she saw the opportunity to participate in the arrangement, an intriguing scene evolved. In an instant, the "invisible," uninvolved, and sad person without any energy completely transformed. Her eyes started to twinkle. She almost jumped up. She went to the starting point and waited for the group members to escort her to the other side. She was able to instruct the women how to help her and decided to leave her walking cane behind. When parts of the new-formed track were too dangerous for her, her body reacted accordingly. She and her mates were able to listen to those bodily signs and alter the track and their support appropriately. The excitement and satisfaction afterward in the group were noticeable. Addressing the deeply rooted feelings of helplessness, by providing bodily correctional experiences, is the main task of psychomotor therapy here. The group is the medium and the vehicle to make this happen.

Therapeutic gain mostly comes from the activation of the autonomy and growing self-reliance and self-respect. Playing and having fun is far more popular in female groups than in male groups. Among males, sports are performed seriously and with great drive. The offered motor arrangements in female groups are not different from those for men. However, every arrangement must be evaluated in the light of the goals that have to be achieved and the possibilities of the group members. The role of a male therapist in such a group is modest but important. By offering corrective experiences the male therapist creates an opportunity for his female clients to restore some trust in a man, and hopefully in men in general.

Although the initial group consisted of women coming from three different continents, with different religious backgrounds, and speaking as many as four different languages, the participants experienced the therapy as beneficial. This was despite the fact that an open discussion about traumatic experiences never took place. The women seemed to absorb the beneficial contents of the therapy. They were helped by covert expression of trauma-related emotions.

LOYALTY AND TRUST, PITFALLS IN HOMOGENEOUS GROUPS

Homogeneous groups seem to have great advantages over mixed groups. There are no language problems, no vast cultural differences, and no racism. With a homogeneous group the work is not disturbed by a diversity of side effects. However, other complicated dynamics exist.

One of our groups consisted of male refugees, all coming from the same town of Srebrenica in Bosnia-Herzegovina. They had been in group and individual psychotherapy treatment for 6 months when psychomotor therapy was added to their program.

In arrangements designed to observe and stimulate group cohesion, like the survival track, the group performed very well. "Piece of cake, we had far more difficult situations to overcome," the clients commented. In other arrangements they also acted in a homogeneous way, like a very effective unit.

While playing soccer, one member played rough and in an irresponsible way, frightening the therapist and perhaps other group members. Since inflicting fear is forbidden in psychomotor therapy, the therapist intervened. The group immediately stopped playing in a dangerous way and there was no further discussion about this incident in the group.

Walking Blindfolded

A couple of sessions later, the therapist decided to test the group members' ability to trust their fellow men. He invited one member to walk blindfolded through the gym while the others were instructed to prevent him from hitting obstacles and hurting himself. The result was amazing. The blindfolded member seemed to have no confidence at all in other group members. He immediately created a strategy to be safe without help of other group members. He started his journey in the middle of the gym and went around in small safe circles. All the members were asked to take their turns. While walking blindfolded every group member chose a different strategy that enabled him to be fully independent of the help of the others. One walked slowly, with both hands in front of him, protecting his face, leaning backward and carefully tapping with one foot before him before advancing. Another one memorized the layout of the gym, started walking from the middle, and knew that he could walk six steps to the left, then four steps to the right, and so on, without bumping into obstacles. He did not need anyone to rely on. Astonishingly in this exercise, a highly cohesive, well-functioning group seemed to be formed out of members that barely had confidence in each other.

The pitfall in working with this group lies in the confusion of interpretations of trust and loyalty. When the therapist asks a homogeneous group of refugees, such as this, to perform a group task, loyalty is a strong motivation. The group acts as a harmonious unity, defending itself against the aggressive outside force — the therapist, with his high demands and peculiar motor arrangements. However, when the therapist asks one person from this group to perform solo, this client feels and acts as if he is alone in the world and is very vulnerable. His movements express this, too. Even though he was able to accomplish a complicated group task adequately, he finds being at the mercy of other group members unbearable.

Trust in fellow men is severely jeopardized by trauma. When one tries to bring some cohesion in a group of strangers brought together for group therapy, cohesive behavior does not imply mutual trust. Trust is a core belief that is shattered by trauma and needs time and care to be reestablished.

The findings from the above-described psychomotor therapy session led to a very important breakthrough in the group psychotherapy session later that week. Trust became the subject of the psychotherapy session. The group members disclosed for the first time that they were burdened with extensive knowledge they have about one another's war past. They knew each other in excess. There were too many secret animosities in the group related to their participation in different and competing military and paramilitary units during the war. That disabled a fruitful therapy. At the same time, the War Tribunal for the crimes committed during the war in ex-Yugoslavia was actively persecuting some Srebrenica warlords. This brought complicated political actualities into the group and triggered old animosities. In this group the issue of trust became discussable only after the members had the bodily experience of a mistrust reflex and saw one another struggling with accepting the help of the others. In this case, psychomotor therapy, as an experiential, nonverbal treatment technique, facilitated further developments within the group psychotherapy. The bodily conduct is unmistakably open. It cannot be denied or masked. It is accessible for discussion.

All this illustrates again that the interplay of verbal and experiential techniques in treatment of traumatized asylum seekers and refugees can be very fruitful. The combination of different mediums in treatment opens more portals of entrance in the emotional experiences due to trauma. It facilitates stronger and more effective possibilities for treatment. Psychomotor therapy adds unmasked bodily functioning to the therapy process. And all we need to start with is a ball, because a ball is irresistible to most of us.

REFERENCES

Meichenbaum, D. (1994). Treating post-traumatic stress disorder: A handbook and practice manual for therapy. Chichester: Wiley.

Pesso, A., & Crandell, J. (1991). Moving psychotherapy: Theory and applications of the Pesso system/psychomotor therapy. New York: Brookline.

15

Body Psychotherapy With Survivors of Torture

SYLVIA KARCHER

This chapter is based on experiences gained in the Berlin Center for the Treatment of Torture Victims (BZFO). Since the establishment of the center in 1992, body psychotherapeutic treatment with the method of concentrative movement therapy (CMT) has been an integral part of therapeutic offers. After interdisciplinary diagnostics by medical doctors, social workers, and psychologists, the therapeutic team discusses which form of therapy is indicated.

An indication for body-oriented psychotherapy is psychosomatic, usually chronic pain resulting from the particular experience of violence of torture survivors. The pain manifests itself as disorders in bodily experience, body perception, and relationships.

CONCENTRATIVE MOVEMENT THERAPY

CMT originated with Elsa Gindler, a teacher of gymnastics in Berlin during the 1920s. Her core message is that if the body is given attention, bodily experience changes. In the United States, a further development of this method by Gindler's student Charlotte Selver led to the method of "sensory awareness." In Germany, the further development was based on the theoretical background of clinical psychotherapy and psychosomatics.

A common characteristic is the integration of perception and movement into the psychotherapeutic process. Today it is practiced in special psychosomatic hospitals both in individual and group therapies.

CMT traces one's own history as recorded in the body and the present situation in life. CMT makes it possible to bring positive, suppressed forces into play once more and to remember repressed experiences. The basis of CMT is direct work with one's own body at rest and in movement.

CMT facilitates resource-oriented work, activation of problems, and development of coping strategies. It is embedded in the framework of experiences with space, time, objects, and other human beings.

The following *effective factors* make CMT especially suitable for working with traumatized patients:

- the therapeutic process as interrelationship experience and bodily dialogue,
- bodily experience of the patient as a basis of the therapeutic process,
- expansion of social competence through testing one's actions in the therapeutic setting,
- active nonverbal components dealing with bodily perception and interaction alternate with verbal components. That which has been experienced is named, its meaning is reflected upon and deepened through associations (Pokorny, Hochgerner, & Cserny, 1996).

THERAPEUTIC GOALS IN THE WORK WITH TORTURE SURVIVORS

The goal of therapy is the conscious internalization and integration of the reality of the trauma into the self-concept of the person affected. This can succeed if the traumatic events are expressed and communicated on different levels. Associated feelings that had to be repressed can be given space. Recognizing one's experiences as things that have really happened is an important step toward integration.

The following therapeutic goals of CMT are helpful for the integration of the trauma:

- pain reduction and understanding the pain;
- improved body feeling and differentiated perception of body;
- holistic bodily experience and integration of split-off body parts;
- getting access to painful, inanimate, and unloved body parts;
- experiencing body boundaries, perceiving spatial boundaries, and observing limitations on time;
- sensing the liveliness of the body via breath, voice, movement, strength, and creativity;
- stabilization and anchoring of bodily resources;
- testing and expansion of scopes of action and movement;
- regaining self-esteem and self-confidence.

From the therapeutic goals, the following *indications for trauma therapy* with CMT can be deduced:

1. psychosomatic problems, especially pain states;
2. early disorders: narcissistic and borderline disorders, especially disorders of the body schema;
3. disorders of body perception, feelings of fragmentation in body experience;
4. disorders of relationship experience.

Dissociative disorders and psychotic states require a different setting: stronger structure and stronger verbal accompanying as well as shorter sequences. Here the focus is on individual work, in the here and now. Contraindications include severe hysteric neuroses and depersonalization-derealization syndrome.

BODY IMAGES OF TRAUMATIZED PATIENTS

Patients with complex posttraumatic stress disorder (PTSD) (Hermann, 1992) often have difficulty verbalizing their boundary-transgressing body experiences, especially since they were thrown back to a level of speechlessness during their traumatic experiences. A body picture can help to express this speechlessness and bring an immediate experience onto a different level. In body pictures, the bodily experience and the emotional relationship with one's own body are expressed, as well as one's handling of the body. Experiences and conflicts that have led to an impairment of bodily experience become visible.

Two examples of this are given as a way of explanation. Mr. O. is a Kurd from Turkey. During 12 years in prison and 9 years of severe torture, he participated in hunger strikes and death fasts. He has been living in Germany for 5 years and is not allowed to work, as he is still in the asylum process. He does not know whether he will be granted asylum and stay in Germany or whether he will be deported one day.

He calls his body picture (see Figure 15.1), which he draws with black chalk, "hortlak" (Kurdish for "ghost") and describes his feeling with the following words: "like a living being — but dead, like a statue." He notices that the pupils and eyelashes are missing and adds that you are blind without pupils. This is how he feels. He describes ear noises. He only draws himself down to the chest and remarks that he is unable to feel the rest of his body. He feels as if his head carried his feet and therefore asks himself whether he is still normal. The picture does not show his extremities. He explains that he cannot use his hands and feet because he is not allowed to work; therefore, he cannot feel them.

Mrs. X. is a Palestinian from Syria, 48 years of age, who experienced 2 years of imprisonment with massive torture. She describes her body

Fig. 15.1   Body Picture of Traumatized Male Patient

picture (see Figure 15.2) as follows: "When I was in prison they cut off my hair and tore my hair out during the interrogations. I lost my honor. I am always sad and cry a lot and have severe headaches. My heart is very heavy and black. They led me away in handcuffs, everybody saw me."

The body pictures of people who have been tortured show similarities: usually dark colors are chosen. Pain is often marked in red. Hands and arms, feet and legs are frequently missing. The body posture is often stooped. Sometimes the body contours are barely visible, drawn with uneven strokes and broken lines. When sexual torture was experienced, the pelvic area is usually not represented.

The patient's remarks to his or her own picture provide important clues for further treatment and diagnostics. The body psychotherapy plan that follows is guided by the patient's subjective descriptions, ideas, and experience regarding his or her picture. In the case of Mr. O., the focus of the work was initially on the perception of his hands and feet. In the case of Mrs. X., the main emphasis was placed on grieving over the loss of her home, family, and friends as well as the humiliation and shame she experienced. Body pictures are like snapshots. They change during the course of body therapy, usually in the direction of wholeness.

FUNDAMENTALS OF TREATMENT

The BZFO treats people who have become victims of political persecution and torture as well as civil war refugees. CMT treatment of these two groups does not differ significantly, since we are working with the symptoms of the persons affected. In both cases, the most salient common characteristics are chronic pain and experiences of sexual violence, which both women and

Fig. 15.2 Body Picture of Traumatized Female Patient

men have experienced and which are usually tabooed and associated with shame. However, the factors that increase the pain are different. Refugees traumatized by war differ from torture survivors in that their pains, anxieties, nightmares, and flashbacks are triggered by ongoing war in their native country or by televised pictures of wars in other countries.

Gender-specific considerations play an important role in our therapies. Thus, the preference of female and male therapists and interpreters is discussed with the patients, and their wishes are taken into account. Furthermore, there are gender-specific group offers (for additional details, see Wenk-Ansohn, 2002). The posttraumatic symptomatology is influenced by experiences of migration and exile, especially those of insecure residence status. The fear and powerlessness caused by ongoing stresses of exile are existential topics and often determine the treatment (Birck & Weber, 2003). They are an additional traumatic factor and frequently reinforce mental disorders (Birck, 2002).

In therapy, culture-specific resources and traditional healing methods are included in the treatment if possible. The concepts of health and disease of the respective culture are explored and integrated into a holistic treatment approach in which the consciously experienced body is seen as a unity (Karcher, 2001).

THERAPEUTIC PROCESS

Introduction of the Patient

Mrs. A. is a small, delicate 32-year-old Roma woman from former Yugoslavia. She sits on the edge of her chair, with downcast eyes, her shoulders are rolled inward and raised. She clutches her handbag and does not establish eye contact with me or with the interpreter. She looks frozen and remains emotionally indifferent, answers only briefly or not at all, and stares absent-mindedly.

The medical doctor who treats her has told me about the history of her persecution: During the war, she spent 3 weeks in a cellar where she was incarcerated under terrible conditions, together with her 4-month-old son and some of her relatives. There she was brutally beaten and raped by soldiers. Her baby was torn from her breast and severely abused, so that she thought it was dead. Her relatives were killed before her eyes. She finally managed to escape to a forest, thus saving her own and her child's life.

Since then, her son, who is now 10 years old, has been suffering from behavioral disorders; he is currently treated by our child psychotherapists. She has two other children, 2 and 7 years of age. She is now divorced.

Mrs. A. gradually reveals that she is suffering from sleep disorders and nightmares in which she constantly reexperiences scenes from the cellar and her flight. She complains about severe headaches, tension in her shoulders, arms, and legs, back pains, abdominal ailments, as well as pain and feelings of tightness in the chest. She does not feel any connection to her hands and her feet. She describes herself with the feeling of "being without skin."

Furthermore, she describes her fear of losing her children, whom she requests to always have near her. At night, when she awakes from nightmares, her 7-year-old daughter has to shake her before she regains consciousness. Her expectations from treatment are

- She would like to forget what happened.
- She would like to be the person she used to be before the war.
- She would like to get rid of her constant pain and the stiffness in her body and to be able to sleep again.

Reflection

With frightening clarity, Mrs. A.'s stooped posture, lack of visual contact, quiet voice, and manifold symptoms illustrated how violence and torture committed by human hands had led to a breakdown of interhuman relations and communication. Her body's boundaries were no longer respected, the perpetrators had invaded her innermost part, and had destroyed the unity of her mind and body. At a later stage, she expressed this in the following words: "They have erased my soul." She had lost her primal trust.

DISORDERS IN EXPERIENCING RELATIONSHIPS AND BODILY EXPERIENCES

Traumatic injuries can be so terrible that they cannot be verbalized: they are unspeakable. The place of attack where psyche and identity are damaged is the body. The traumatic reactions find their expression in a disturbed body experience. They can manifest themselves in complete rigidity. The ego was systematically destroyed.

Patients frequently react with a high level of arousal and outbursts of rage. Often they do not understand their behavior and are ashamed of it. Other patients can only feel or sense themselves through vagabond pains. They reject their bodies as a carrier of symptoms storing memories of torture and no longer feel at home in it. They are restless; they suffer from increased heart beat, pressure, and feelings of tightness in the chest; they describe themselves in the following terms: "My soul is sick, my head is crazy. I feel as if I am locked within myself." Their body experience is fragmented; interrelationship between head, trunk, and limbs is no longer perceived.

Women who have been exposed to sexualized violence often report that they experience their body's boundaries as if they were permeable and that they feel defenseless. Here their memories manifest themselves as anxiety, depression, and somatoform pain states, such as headache and back pain, abdominal ailments, bladder disorders, indigestion, menstrual disorders, feelings of disgust, and eating disorders. They describe their bodies as not belonging to them, as alien, stained, and depreciated (see Fischer & Riedesser, 1998). Severe dissociative disorders, which can be interpreted as a protection against shame, are conspicuously frequent.

PAIN IN TORTURE SURVIVORS: A PSYCHODYNAMIC PERSPECTIVE

In psychodynamic concepts seeking to explain constant pains, the pain is understood as an expression of some underlying intrapsychic conflict:

- as embodied traumatic memory;
- as an expression of feelings and emotions such as anger, shame, anxiety, guilt, or grief which have to be repressed because they are too threatening or painful;
- as a result of tension states, especially in the jaw, head, shoulders, back, and abdomen, which had to be built up in order to keep helpless rage "inside";
- as a tension that had to be built up during the actual traumatization and maintained afterward as a necessary "protective cover," for example, against beatings and electrical shocks;
- as a tension of a generalized anxiety disorder;
- as psychic defense of a depression, in the sense of "holding against" (*Gegenhalten*) (Wenk-Ansohn, 1998);
- as a relief from feelings of guilt: solidarity suffering with one's own people while one is in safety.

FIRST THERAPY SESSION: SETTING, ESTABLISHMENT OF A RELATIONSHIP, SYMBOLIC REPRESENTATION OF PAIN

During the initial therapy sessions, the interpreter was an important connection between the language and culture of the patient and the therapist. Whenever Mrs. A. established eye contact at all, she looked at the interpreter. When I enquired about her ailments, she touched her neck, her right shoulder, her upper arms, and elbows, and said: "As heavy as stones." Then she pointed at all the other joints, all the way down to the feet. She complained that her whole body was hurting.

I asked her to get up and to select one object out of many different objects distributed across the room that could express her pain so that I could imagine what it felt like. I accompanied her while she was searching the room. In a basket filled with stones, she did not seem to find anything suitable. Finally, she chose the largest of different colorful sandbags, took it with both hands, moaned, and said: "This is how they are." After she had carried it on her hands through the room for a while, I offered to relieve her of the weight. When she gave it to me, I asked: "This heavy?" She nodded and remarked that all her pain was contained in this red sandbag. She quickly took it from me again and put it on her shoulders. However, she did not react to my inquiring interpretation whether all the heaviness she had experienced was in the sandbag. I explained to her that our body remembers everything that happened to it and often expressed it in the form of pain, but that it is also capable of remembering positive experiences. I asked her whether she knew what was helpful for her whenever she suffered from pain. She embraced her shoulders with both her hands and remembered a massage her 7-year-old daughter had given her. I showed her how she could stroke her arms with her hands, starting with her shoulders, all the way down to her fingertips. She imitated my movement, but in a rather indifferent manner. Furthermore, she was unable to feel a connection between her shoulders and her fingers. She explained to me that she did not like her body, because it felt like a stone.

When we sat across the table from each other, I explained to her the cause of her pain and that it was a perfectly normal reaction of her body to totally absurd and inhuman experiences.

Reflection

Establishment of Relationship From a Therapeutic Perspective

I can offer Mrs. A. a reliable outer framework with clear arrangements as well as a therapeutic room that guarantees her security, where she feels that she is in good hands, appreciated, and protected. It is a place where the injustice done to her can be named and gains recognized, where I become visible and perceptible as an ally in our relationship.

During the interaction with the therapist, Mrs. A. experienced for a moment that the burden was lifted. However, she drew a clear line when I suggested that pain might be caused by embodied memories. She did not want to initiate any memory work at such an early stage.

WORKING WITH SYMBOLS

The interior of the room in which CMT takes place is conducive to regression and to test new possibilities for action. It is furnished with a round table and chairs, large pillows on the floor, and all sorts of different objects. Among other things, the creative material includes balls, ropes, stones, little sandbags, shells, wooden sticks, and blankets. Due to their material, size, color, form, and weight, they facilitate concrete sensory experiences. Their symbolic content is determined by subjective experience. This can initiate memory work by wakening experiences and associations. At the same time, they can be used as transitional objects. Making one's own choices and decisions is an important step in the process of regaining autonomy and self-responsibility.

PSYCHOEDUCATION

Many torture survivors are disturbed about their manifold complaints, which they are unable to understand or categorize. Some of them imagine that they are crazy or going mad. In order to counteract this in a stabilizing way, information about the causes of the symptoms and the processes in the body is necessary. Thus, the symptoms become less frightening and lose their terrifying aspects (Jordi, 2001, p. 87).

SUMMARY OF THE SESSIONS THAT FOLLOWED

Mrs. A. attended all therapy sessions regularly and with overpunctuality. At the beginning, her pain and tension in the shoulder girdle and the arms were almost always in the foreground. Together we tried to find out what might be good for her. She rejected warmth for fear of losing consciousness, but did not object to a treatment of her shoulders while sitting. Using resting material, we tried to find a pain-reducing, relaxed position for her head and arms; I covered her hurting shoulders and back with a blanket. She commented: "This is how my mother covered me when I was a child." It was a positive memory. She appeared to need the warm protection of the blanket and requested it time after time. When I inquired about other therapeutic wishes, she just said: "You must know what is good for me, you are the therapist." Just like all other steps, I announced each movement of the hand before I made it and asked whether it was okay. She was remarkably good at telling me exactly what was good and what was not good for her. Thus, she initially felt that the contact with my hands between her shoulder blades was too close, despite the blanket in between. However, a ball between my hands and the blanket felt good. She was asked to choose between a rubber ball and a rough-surface ball and opted for the rough-surface ball because she was able to feel it more clearly. Slowly I rolled across her entire shoulder girdle and her back while applying slight pressure. In the further course of therapy, she requested this rolling with the rough-surface ball time and again. Later, when she felt more secure, I was able to establish contact with her body with my hands even without a blanket. During treatment, she always kept her normal clothes on. With firm, clear movements of the hand, I showed her the contours of her body, so that she was able to sense her bodily boundaries and to allow a feeling of wholeness to grow.

Toward the end of our sessions, a ritual developed. It arose from her desire to be able to feel herself more clearly during her states of absent-mindedness. We sat on stools facing each other, and each of us ran over her own body contours with a rough-surface ball, from head to toe. She watched closely how I did it. I gave her a rough-surface ball to take home. To this day, she carries it in her handbag "so that the kids don't play with it and so that I think of you." Sometimes she remembers the ball during her states of absence, rolls it over her body, and manages to reemerge from her states of absence without the help of her daughter.

Reflection

"This is how my mother covered me when I was a child" — we refer to these early positive body memories and try to use them as a resource. Survivors of torture have experienced body contact as an injury, "memory pains" are the result: "Here, exactly where it hurts, they kicked me with their boots." Research conducted by van der Kolk (1998, p. 77) shows that "traumatic experiences are immediately stored as sensations or emotional states without being compared to early experiences and without being rewritten into a personal history" and that "traumatic memories appear as sensory and emotional contents of the imagination and as somatic sensations which can be transformed into communicable language only to a limited extent." These memories that "got stuck" in the body can be named through direct body contact; pain can be connected with the original feelings of unlived rage, grief, shame, or fear and thus become accessible to processing.

Touch

Touch is the establishment of a relationship at the body's boundaries. It can form a bridge to other human beings, especially when language fails. As soon as we consciously touch another person with our hands, we enter into a body dialogue. The question arises to the right moment, duration, and quality of the touch. It can be supportive, warming, protective, demonstrative, tender, firm, restrictive, or confrontational. Touch always requires the patient's consent. The number of necessary protective layers between the patient's body and the therapist's hands must be determined verbally. Sometimes more pressure applied by the therapist's hands provides more security, sometimes a slight touch suffices. A dialogical body contact can arise between the patient's breath and the therapist's responding hands or through the occurrence of tension and relaxation. Despite the patient's permission to touch him or her, body surface and musculature can clearly signal defense via heightened tension. When trust has been established, the patient is often able to "let go" and to free him- or herself from the tension and rigidity. Through careful, respectful and affirmative contact at the body's boundaries, early childhood experiences of protection, warmth, being held, and wholeness can be relived. When the patient learns that he or she is worthy of being touched, this acceptance of his or her person can lead to a new attitude toward his or her own body and can have a healing effect.

In the case of Mrs. A., the therapeutic goal was to enable her to gain access to her body without the massages of her daughter in order to develop positive body feelings again, and to pave the way for pain reduction via attentive care.

To envelop her hurting shoulders and entire body with a blanket served to protect her and to clarify her body contours, as well as rolling a rough ball over them. Experience shows that contact via material induces less fear than direct bodily contact with hands. Only at a much later stage, when we had become more familiar with each other, did she want to be touched by my hands. Thus, as a repetition of the early mother-child dialogue taking place on an entirely preverbal level, I was able to provide her with emotional availability, security, protection, and support. I intended to enable her to feel orientation, security, and familiarity in her body. To this end, I named the firm and the soft parts, the muscles and bones that I touched, and hence I always stayed in touch with her, also through my voice.

Apart from providing an emotional link to the positive experiences of the therapy, the rough-surface ball that I gave her was supposed to help her to acquire a holistic body experience and to counteract her feeling of fragmentation and dissociation. During the first sessions, Mrs. A. was able to experience that she was protected and appreciated and that her boundaries were respected. This facilitated the development of trust and a workable relationship that could carry the therapeutic process further.

MAIN ASPECTS OF CONTINUED THERAPY

Initially, basic body work was the focus of subsequent treatment. The point of departure was her own place, which I asked her to choose in the therapy room. Mrs. A. chose a wooden stool. At first she sat at the edge again. Her feet were intertwined and barely touched the floor. She had sat down with her back to the wall, facing the window and the door. For the subsequent hours, this became her preferred seat. She found it difficult to sit down on the whole surface of the stool. Analogous situations from her current everyday life came to her mind: situations in which she did not dare to "take up her space." In a rather playful manner, I let her try to use the wall as a firm support for her back, to lean against it, to press against it, to release herself, and sit freely. At the same time I asked her to find out what was good for her *today*. We worked on the perception of her feet in contact with the firm ground via the pressure and strength of her legs and pelvis. Through my structuring offers, she was able to "grasp" her bones and muscles with her own hands and to feel them as an inner framework.

By testing her mobility, she was able to experience her joints and the connections they established in her body. Here the spinal column with its supportive function and mobility was given special attention. She discovered more and more stability in her body with which she felt more secure.

Time and again, menacing memories came to the surface and threatened to submerge her. These memories were accompanied by intense feelings, such as anger and grief, which intensified her pain. Therefore, the stabilizing body work I repeated with her and the reliability of our relationship were all the more important. She also drew the experience that she was capable of distancing herself from the trauma after approaching it through the perception of reality in the here and now, for instance by describing the therapy room.

She often had a feeling of tightness in her chest and throat. The memory of a rifle someone had pointed at her throat emerged. For the first time, she was able to talk about her fear and to recognize a connection between that which she had experienced and the physical symptoms. Breathing exercises helped her to change the feelings of constriction and to feel the inner spaces of her body more clearly.

Sitting on a big ball allowed her to perform playful movements, which reminded her of belly dancing and relieved her tension and pain. With this ball she could also test her strength. Holding the ball between our hands, we pushed each other through the room. For the first time I saw her smiling. Over many months, I repeated these supportive, stabilizing body suggestions with her, using different initial positions: while sitting, standing, walking, and later while lying, which she was most afraid of.

After a couple of weeks she dared to widen her scope of activity. She entered into a relationship with me in an active manner by deliberately rolling a ball toward me. Later we continued the contact with colorful marbles. On a different occasion, we used long colored ropes to tie a connection and to test closeness and distance between us. Strength and support were tested with a strong rope tied in a circle.

Reflection

In the first phase of therapy, Mrs. A. had been provided with a motherly room in which the soft and cozy aspects, the stabilization of body boundaries, and the reduction of pain (also involving physiotherapeutic measures) had taken precedence. This was followed by suggestions how to develop her personal autonomy. Now the relationship with one's own body, with space, with objects, and with the therapist was given priority. This strengthened the ego and resuscitated resources. Bodily resources had to be regained, physically anchored, and used. Experiencing support, flexibility, strength, and orientation gave her security and formed the basis for approaching the traumatic images that now increasingly came to the surface. Body work also included the choice of a place of her own as a good emotional space providing safety. In the arrangement of one's own place in the room, the current life situation is often represented symbolically, but it is also a possibility for establishing contact with the environment. Truly settling down in a place, not at the front edge or in the farthest corner, but filling it and "taking up space," was another step on the way to self-confidence. From here, the connection between the feet and the firm, supporting ground could be sensed and tested in order to rediscover one's own basis. This "earthing" or "grounding" contact of the feet could be used to stand up and straighten oneself. Our work on the topic of "support and being supported" could be experienced physically and did not have to take place in the imagination alone. The demonstration of her own spine enabled Mrs. A. to experience and grasp her own structures, stability, and strength. The experience of flexible connections and the grasping of the entire body with the hands aimed for a sensitization and stabilization of the body's boundaries and were conducive to a holistic body feeling. Through experiences with breathing rhythm, another structuring element, the body's inner spaces, and hence one's own liveliness could be felt again. In the course of the body therapy it became apparent that it was only through the relationship with and the appreciation by the therapist that the negatively experienced body becomes a pleasant experience.

FINDING AN EXPRESSION FOR THE UNSPEAKABLE

After a while, Mrs. A. suffered from increased pain symptoms again. A flashback, caused by a car that had stopped in front of her home with squealing tires when she stepped out of the house, had triggered memories of her traumatic experiences. She did not manage to get rid of the images and came to the therapy session with severe headaches, which dominated and almost paralyzed her. She could not find words for it, but she was capable of symbolically representing her problem with an object. To this end, she chose a black lizard that she pointed at from a distance with visible feelings of disgust. She was afraid of this animal and remarked that whenever she thought of bad things, she had a feeling as if animals, especially cats, crawled into her belly. I suggested that she wrap the animal up and deposit it in a place of her choosing. Since she did not want to touch the lizard, she asked me to fetch it from the shelf and to put it on a blanket she had unfolded. Moaning and clearly disgusted, she wrapped it up in this woolen blanket, then she tied it up with a long cord with great effort accompanied by angry outbursts. She produced an oblong package that she carried out of the therapy room and put down in the backmost corner of the corridor where she weighted it down with a pillow. After this effort, both of us went to the open window and breathed deeply. At first she seemed relieved, but then she flew into a rage again. She cursed loudly. I encouraged her to stamp her foot, so that she could physically express her anger with her whole body. It was amazing how much strength this fragile woman developed. But suddenly she was overcome with pain, threw herself on the floor, and burst into heartrending sobs. In between, she kept shouting angry words from which I concluded that someone had covered her mouth in order to prevent her from screaming. Here she was allowed to scream, and all the feelings that had got stuck inside her could get outside. Totally exhausted, she dozed off on the floor. I accompanied this sequence with my hands between her shoulder blades.

Reflection

Pain is updated by traumatic memory fragments that come to the surface. Patients either reach states of high agitation, which are barely controllable, or they become rigid. Methodologically, CMT starts off with the process of symbolization. If the word is not available as a symbol of the memory, an object can express and revive the traumatic situation. Due to the invitation to wrap the traumatic material and to lock it away, the trauma can be handled. The therapist is no longer the direct container for the trauma. The symbolization produces a triangulation; an intermediary space comes into existence: the trauma can be deposited.

FINAL STAGE OF THERAPY

After wrapping up the lizard as a symbol of her trauma, she became calmer. However, there were still phases when she suffered from severe pain, especially when she had problems with her children or her divorced husband. Now I no longer treated her on the regressive level; instead, I increasingly tried to establish a connection between her complaints and her current problems. Sometimes this succeeded. Now she was better able to recognize interconnections and no longer sank into such great despair, since she had experienced possibilities for helping herself better and for using her resources.

We increasingly worked while standing, concentrating on her stability and the first conscious steps. On the whole, during the course of the two years of therapy, her symptoms had clearly decreased.

EFFECTS OF TRAUMA WORK ON THE CMT THERAPISTS AND PITFALLS

In CMT, the body dialogue is very important for the therapeutic relationship. In the therapeutic process, CMT therapists are facing their clients as a direct physical presence. Special attention is given to careful bodily contact, the right moment, and the quality of touch. Bodily contact is always a tightrope walk between necessary closeness and necessary distance. Violations can be caused by too little or too much contact.

In body psychotherapy, attention must be devoted especially to one's own bodily countertransference. This includes symptoms that can be felt in the body during the treatment, such as tensions, headaches, stomach trouble, and tiredness. They are used as an important instrument in body psychotherapy (Karcher, 2000, p. 36; Wenk-Ansohn, 2002, p. 70).

The pitfalls of the treatment can include:

- ignorance of one's own bodily countertransference phenomenon,
- too much closeness and too much distance,
- premature preoccupation with traumatic contents without inner or outer stabilization,
- leaving the patient's resources out of consideration.

REFERENCES

Birck, A. (2002). Psychotherapie mit traumatisierten Flüchtlingen. Gesellschaftliche Bedingungen und therapeutische Konsequenzen [Psychotherapy with traumatized refugees: Social situation and therapeutic consequences]. *Psychotraumatologie, 3*(42). Retrieved from www.thieme.de/psychotrauma (12 Nov 2002).

Birck, A., & Weber, R. (2003). Behandlungszentrum für Folteropfer Berlin [Berlin Center for the Treatment of Torture Victims]. In J. Radice von Wogau, H. Eimmermacher, & A. Lanfranchi (Eds.), *Interkulturelle Therapie und Beratung* [Intercultural therapy and conseling] (pp. 148–160). Beltz: Weinheim

Fischer, G., & Riedesser, P. (1998). *Lehrbuch der Psychotraumatologie* [Textbook of psychotraumatology]. Munich: München: Reinhardt.

Hermann, J. (1992). Complex PTSD: Syndrome in survivors of prolonged and repeated trauma. *Journal of Traumatic Stress, 5,* 377–391.

Jordi, A. (2001). Körpertherapie mit gefolterten Menschen. Vom Schmerz zur Beziehung [Body therapy with people who have been tortured. From pain to relationship]. In C. Moser, D. Nyfeler, & V. Verwey (Eds.), *Traumatisierungen von Flüchtlingen und Asyl Suchenden* [Traumatization of refugees and asylum seekers] (pp. 85–96). Zürich: Seismo Verlag.

Karcher, S. (2000, January). Körpererleben und Beziehungserleben — Konzentrative Bewegungstherapie mit Überlebenden von Folter [Body experience and experience of relationships — concentrative movement therapy with torture survivors]. *Psychotherapy in Dialogue, March*, 28–37.

Karcher, S. (2001). In my fingertips I don't have a soul anymore. In S. Graessner, N. Gurris, & C. Pross (Eds.), *At the side of torture survivors* (pp. 70–94). Baltimore: Johns Hopkins University Press.

van der Kolk, B. A. (1998). Die Psychobiologie traumatischer Erinnerungen [The psychobiology of traumatic memories]. In A. Streeck-Fischer (Ed.), *Adoleszenz und trauma* [Adolescents and trauma] (p. 77). Göttingen: Vandenhoeck & Ruprecht.

van der Kolk, B. A., McFarlane, A. C., & Weisaeth, L. (Eds.). (1996). *Traumatic stress*, Fundamentals and treatment approaches. Junfermann, Paderborn: Studia Universitätsverlag, Innsbruck.

Pokorny, V., Hochgerner, M., & Cserny, S. (Eds.). (1996). *Konzentrative Bewegungstherapie. Von der körperorientierten Methode zum psychotherapeutischen Verfahren* [Concentrative movement therapy. From body-oriented method to psychotherapeutic procedure]. Wien: Facultas.

Wenk-Ansohn, M. (2002). Folgen sexualisierter Folter [Sequelae of sexualized torture]. In A. Birck, C. Pross, & J. Lanssen, (Eds.), *Das Unsagbare. Die Arbeit mit Traumatisierten im Behandlungszentrum für Folteropfer Berlin* [The unspeakable working with traumatized persons in the Center for the Treatment of Torture Victims Berlin] (pp. 57–77). Berlin: Springer.

16

About a Weeping Willow, a Phoenix Rising From Its Ashes, and Building a House ... Art Therapy With Refugees: Three Different Perspectives

TRUUS WERTHEIM-CAHEN, MARION VAN DIJK, KARIN SCHOUTEN, INGE ROOZEN, AND BORIS DROŽĐEK

My drawings represent a life of pain and sorrow. They are my broken dreams. Once I was a beautiful girl. My parents were warm and loving people. I loved to dance, I was an excellent student, and had little to worry about. So I do know what being happy means. But it all seems so long ago. I am no longer able to recall that feeling. I have lost my parents and my husband. I have been raped and tortured and fled from my native country. My head is so heavy that I can hardly carry it. My head and body have become separated. I paint a large tree, and while I paint, I watch it turn into a weeping willow, strong and proud with fluttering leaves, my face is within it. For weeks I continue working at it. Then slowly my face changes into the face of the devil. Satan with long sharp nails is crushing my heart.

My paintings are the containers of my tears. While painting and drawing I always weep, still at the same time it gives me space to breathe. As I express my pain on paper, others can see it. It enables me to narrate the story of my life. I had no words for my sorrows, but now I can share some moments of it with you. Maybe I could tell my story before, but I was unable to feel anything but hurt. I had to relearn how to feel. That was painful, but somehow my burden became easier to carry. Now I do know what I feel and why I feel what I feel. There are moments, in which I even try to think about the future. My words may evaporate, but my paintings will remain. (Figure 16.1)

This retrospective of an art therapy experience comes from Fanya, a 42-year-old refugee from Armenia. It briefly illustrates how psychological trauma is foremost a destruction of meaning and a fragmentation of one's sense of identity. On a small scale Fanya's story demonstrates how through art therapy she became able to reconnect her past with the present, and how art-making contributed to a restoration of her sense of identity.

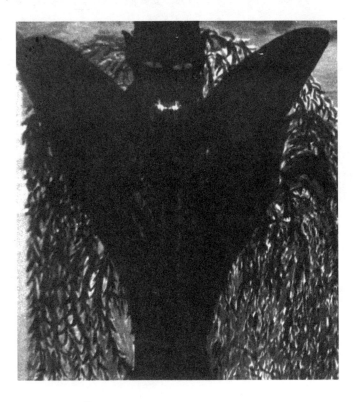

Fig. 16.1 Weeping Willow

In art therapy the person's creativity is activated by means of art-making for the purpose of fostering and/or maintaining mental health. In Dutch mental health care, like in most Western countries, the use of art-making as a therapeutic means has a longstanding history (Wertheim-Cahen, 2003). In this chapter we describe how creativity and art-making are used for treatment and psychosocial support of traumatized asylum seekers and refugees.

Depending on the setting in which art therapy takes place, the focus can be merely on the images that evolve from the art-making process or on the healing qualities of the art-making process itself. In art therapy these two different approaches often intertwine in practice and are labeled as art-in-therapy and art-as-therapy (Kramer, 2000). In the art-in-therapy approach art-making is often goal-oriented, for example, trauma treatment, and subservient to a stricter medical-psychological structure. The main focus lies on articulation of the meaning of the image in order to help its creator gain better insight into his or her situation. In this approach, sharing one's images and commenting on them in a group adds extra meaning and significance.

In the art-as-therapy approach the emphasis is on the very activities of painting or working with clay, which can be soothing, comforting, cathartic, or challenging. Experimenting with materials and the use of certain colors will easily evoke all kinds of feelings (Wertheim-Cahen, 2003). The resulting images can elicit emotions, too. Their meaning does not necessary have to be articulated, and it frequently remains implicit. In this approach it is relevant that art-making is related to playing. Like in child's play, painting or drawing easily becomes a process in which one's inner world becomes linked to the outside reality, and significant life events can be reenacted on a symbolic level (Winicott, 1982).

The objectives and the method of art therapy interventions usually depend on three aspects: the particular problems of the population to be treated, the setting in which art therapy is conducted, and the therapy format. The problems of refugees arise in the first place from their having been threatened in their very existence. Asylum seekers hold an outcast position in the host society and are forced into passivity. Many find themselves alone with painful memories and fear for the future (Wertheim-Cahen, 2000a, 2000b). Recent experiences of war, torture, humiliation, flight, and their present living conditions have caused many to mistrust their fellow human beings.

The general objective of art therapy for refugees and asylum seekers is to activate those feelings and by means of art expression to reduce stress, rebuild trust, and lessen their sense of isolation. Sometimes art therapy merely offers asylum seekers a temporary distraction from their hopeless position and helps them to endure their present state. For others art therapy interventions are instrumental in helping patients regaining control over intrusive and traumatic memories.

Within each setting the art therapist explores how the patient's creativity and his or her capability to visually express him- or herself can be engaged in addressing his or her particular problems (Wertheim-Cahen, 1999). Depending on a patient's ego strength the approach will focus on confronting his or her traumatic experiences in order to integrate them or merely offering support. The format is important because it makes a difference to work individually, in a closed group, or in an open group. Also the duration and frequency of the interventions influence the effect of art therapy. In this chapter we examine art therapy with refugees in three different settings — a day treatment facility, a residential clinical setting, and a school for the physically handicapped. Each setting represents a different art therapeutic approach. In the first setting the accent is on art-in-therapy, in the second more on art-as-therapy, and in the third both approaches are equally mixed.

DAY TREATMENT SETTING: TRAUMA-FOCUSED TREATMENT

Art therapy in the day treatment center was part of a multidisciplinary group treatment program for traumatized asylum seekers. Psychotherapy (see Chapter 10 of this volume), sociotherapy, music therapy (see Chapter 17 of this volume), and psychomotor therapy (see Chapter 14 of this volume) complemented each other and were conducted in all-female or all-male groups. Patients came from different countries and cultures. Participation in the program did not require a permanent residence permit, usually a first demand to gain admission to trauma treatment. The overall objective was to help patients to regain their self-respect as human beings and to reclaim control over their emotional lives. Therefore, the program offered a confronting approach directly focusing on the traumatic experiences of its participants.

In order to participate patients needed a certain amount of resilience and emotional strength. During one year they followed a program divided into five phases (see Chapter 10 of this volume). In the first phase the focus was on orientation, in the second phase on stabilization, in the third phase on the past, in the fourth phase on the present and the future, and in the fifth phase on parting. Art therapy sessions took place once a week, with each session lasting 75 minutes. By means of specific assignments patients were stimulated to review their lives step by step and to also focus on the positive experiences, which under the weight of the traumatic events often seem to disappear from their memories. Contrary to psychomotor therapy within this phased treatment program, art therapy follows the same path as group psychotherapy. The same topics, at the same time, within a particular phase are in the focus. However, the pace of art therapy might be somewhat faster than that of group psychotherapy. This means that before talking about certain topics within group psychotherapy, patients have had a chance to address them without words in art therapy.

The first step in art therapy is establishing a feeling of safety in the group, as well as in the room where art therapy takes place. In order to get to know each other, the studio, and get acquainted with different art materials, participants are asked to make a personal folder for storing their future drawings. The making of a folder signifies the confidentiality of what they are about to disclose. At the same time by giving it a certain design or painting it in a particular color, this enables the maker to bestow a personal touch. Although in art therapy drawings and clay figures are indeed seen as the first means of expression, verbalizing traumatic memories within art therapy is seen as necessary for integration. Therefore, interpreters take part in all sessions. The fact that translators are available, however, does not mean that participants are obliged to talk about what they depict. Participants do have some choice in when and how they will share their experiences. Sometimes their images send a clear enough message. Apart from that cultural differences are to be taken into account, too. For example in some cultures it is imperative to follow or obey the oldest member in the group. For some this can pose a barrier for sharing certain memories or expressing one's true feelings (Drožđek, van Dijk, & de Winter, 2002).

To give the reader an impression of art therapy in this setting a brief illustration of each phase will be given.

Orientation

In the orientation phase, patients are asked to introduce themselves to one another on paper. Ahmad, a 40-year-old lawyer from Iran, made a drawing with oil crayons. In the center of the picture he put himself on some kind of bench encircled by sketchy images of torture. He commented: "In my life I have been tortured many times, sometimes physically, other times in a psychological way. I have been capable to endure hunger and pain. But never have I showed my tears to my torturers," and Ahmed spoke while looking at his drawing and cried.

Stabilization

At some time in the stabilization phase, participants are asked to picture their lives in eight images, from birth until their present state (see Figure 16.2). Each participant gets a big piece of paper folded in eight even-sized sections, allowing space for eight images. Khalid, a 30-year-old male refugee from Iran and a veteran from the Iran-Iraq war, drew episodes of "his childhood," "family," "his school," "his military service," "the war front," and "saying farewell to his family and friends." Before his last image he stopped drawing and started writing instead: "1996 arrest," "torture," and next "flight out of my country." For him some events were clearly easier to picture, while others were easier to write

Fig. 16.2 An Example of Eight Episodes of the Life of a Refugee

down. In following art therapy sessions, each time drawing became more difficult and Khalid started writing. Initially he did not want his writings to be translated, but eventually he did. Most refugees find this assignment, which usually takes up several sessions, very demanding. For some it evokes episodes of their lives they find too confronting to depict. Others will be able to picture them, but are unable to comment. Some may not draw at all, or after they have pictured some episode, cover it up. Later on some may, or may not, decide to uncover that image. Sharing takes place in different ways: by merely looking together at the images, by writing, or by talking about them. Writing often seems to be an intermediary form between image-making and talking.

The Past

In focusing on the past, the third phase, patients are asked to further explore and reconstruct their life story. One of the assignments is to "make a trip through your home country choosing your own starting point and final destination."

With colored pencils Rahdi made a very simple childlike drawing without perspective. He started drawing a line curling over the surface of the paper, representing a road. On the line he drew a small car. Later as he showed his drawing to the group, keeping his eyes fixed on the paper, he explained: "I was blindfolded …", then closing his eyes he continued and took the therapist and the group with him on the journey, which then again seemed to take place in his head, describing every detail. "There were bumps on the road, one turn to the right, another one to the left, the heat, children's voices." While talking he perspired severely. His hands became fists. Then he reopened his eyes and observed his drawing. "I see that I even drew trees, it may seem strange but this road, is the one I drew in my imagination, that very day, when I was heading towards prison. They had me blindfolded, but I try to remember."

The Present and Future

The purpose of focusing on the present and the future in the fourth phase is to encourage patients to become aware of their personal force and resilience and to gather courage to look forward. In this phase the group is asked to work with clay, a highly expressive material. Alya, a refugee from Somalia, had lost both her parents and participated in a female group. She made a female figure and she commented: "I did make this statuette to reintroduce myself to this group. I made a body that is able to support my head. A statue that has arms and legs. I can stand up again, walk exist" (see Figure 16.3). Her words illustrate that indeed the objective had been reached.

Parting

In the fifth and last phase participants are asked to think about what to do with their work, as the program's end is approaching.

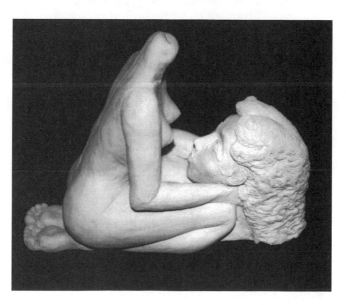

Fig. 16.3 Statue With Arms and Legs

Rahman, a 29-year-old political refugee from Iran, was struggling with his decision about what to do with his drawings. "Everything is important," he claimed, "but there are drawings I don't want to take with me. On one hand my drawings are like new photographs. I cherish the images I have made of the people I love, of the time I was a student at the university in my country. But at the same time they confuse me. To look at my friends causes so much grief and pain that it makes me want to throw them away. I feel that I should not hate, not harbor revenge. That would make me as evil as my perpetrators. Allah represents justice, he will judge."

For some refugees the fact that everything takes place in the group can be an obstacle. The emotional elasticity of each individual does not necessary match that of the group as a whole. For some, the group can signify containment and support. For others the exposure in the group can form an obstruction. In that case additional individual contact with the therapist can be helpful.

This happened in the case of Anwar, a political refugee and a former high functionary from Sudan who suffered from panic attacks, nightmares, and sleeplessness. When he started therapy he had already been in Holland for 2 years. He took part in a group of eight men mostly from Iraq and Iran, and often failed to show up for art therapy. In the orientation phase, he made his folder black. Later on, when asked to make eight images of different episodes in his life, he only partly followed the instructions. He painted everything black, even the sun. At a certain moment he indicated that he was unable to function in the group. He asked if he could see the art therapist alone (presumably because she was a woman and an outsider to his culture). In the meeting that followed, Anwar talked to the therapist without an interpreter, in broken English, about his 1-year incarceration in prison. He told about the terrible atrocities engraved in his memory. How as a prisoner he was forced to roam through, as he expresses it, "a phantom house." To illustrate his story he made a sketch. Taking his drawing as a lead Anwar described being guided through numerous small rooms with low ceilings: "I saw people hanging upside down, other prisoners being crucified, men raping other men." All the time he pointed at his drawing. Overcome with deep shame about what had happened to him, he struggled to find words, and hesitantly he revealed: "I have been one of them, I have never told this to anyone, nor have I shared this secret with my wife, my lawyer (procedures to get a residence permit are in process), a counselor, or anyone else. I am the head of my family. I am a man and a Muslim." Talking about this period in his life with other participants in the group had been impossible so far. But after a few individual sessions, Anwar took his drawing to the group and showed it to the others. Sharing his image with his peers, his eyes were silently searching for acknowledgment from other participants, and he visibly sensed their recognition.

The example of Anwar shows how, if a particular assignment turns out to be too confronting, the therapy program allows its participants to deviate from it. Operating within the frame of this treatment program demands from the art therapist, on one hand to follow each particular phase but at the same time to allow each participant his or her own pace.

A CLINICAL WARD SETTING

A rather different art therapy approach is followed in a residential clinical setting. This clinic named Phoenix specializes in treatment of refugees and is part of a large mental hospital. Patients admitted to Phoenix suffer from different psychiatric disorders, usually as a consequence of their traumatic experiences. The treatment focuses on the complex intertwining of culture, trauma, and psychiatric disturbances. Here, like in the day treatment setting described earlier, most patients find themselves confronted with the danger of repatriation, as procedures of getting asylum are still in process. Patients are treated with medication and different forms of psychotherapy. According to personal preference and affinity they are indicated for music therapy, art therapy, or both.

Art therapy sessions take place in an open group in which the art therapist tries to find a personal approach for every patient. Consequently, they benefit from art therapy on different levels. The idea of working individually but together in one room makes the patient feel connected and less alone. Each session takes 1.5 hours once a week. The focus is on art-as-therapy, which means that the process of art-making itself is considered the most important healing force. When patients first arrive the art therapist explains that art-making might offer them a form of recreation, but that it can also offer possibilities to depict one's thoughts, dreams, or experiences. The art therapist assists patients in their choice for certain materials, teaches the use of them, and generally helps them with the art-making process. Since for some patients drawing spontaneously is very unusual, they can start by looking at art reproductions, or at photos, sometimes related to their cultures. From all the pictures they can pick one they like and use it as a source of inspiration, or even copy it. It is up to the patient if he or she wants to discuss or talk about the meaning of his or her work (Betensky, 1995). No interpreters take part in the art therapy sessions.

The concept of art therapy is rather strange to non-Western patients. Because of this it is sometimes difficult to motivate them to attend. Apart from that there are several other reasons why patients might fail to show up. In the case of the clinic described, art therapy sessions are conducted in a separate building situated in the woods. This location is about a half mile distance from the patients' residence building. Some, because they still see threat and danger everywhere, fear the distance they have to cover when walking from the ward to the studio. Others feel uncomfortable because they miss compatriots in their group.

Sometimes patients claim that their physical condition makes their attendance impossible. Some need to get acquainted with the therapist before joining the treatment. For some it seems impossible to attend therapy without a formal and extensive introduction, like for example drinking tea together with the therapist. Therefore, the art therapist often goes to the ward to introduce herself and invite the newcomer personally. Before patients arrive, the art therapist takes out their work and displays it on the table, always on the same spot, to emphasize that each patient has a place of his or her own. Patients' complaints vary from hearing voices, to headaches, sleeplessness, and nightmares.

In close-up we will follow the art therapy process of Sahar, a 34-year-old patient from former Yugoslavia. Sahar attended art therapy together with four fellow patients — three men, respectively from Armenia, Bosnia, and Iran, and one woman from Ossetia. These four patients formed the background for Sahar's art therapeutic process, which will be very briefly portrayed first.

Irina

To Irina from Ossetia art therapy has been foremost important because of her contact with the art therapist. The informality of being engaged in art activities facilitated that contact. Irina was 55 years old and had fled from her homeland, together with her sick husband and two sons. Although she has lived in Holland for 9 years, she still holds no residence permit. Irina complained a lot about physical pains. She liked to come to the studio, made a friendly and intelligent impression, but never talked about her problems. Irina had chosen to copy an image of quiet scenery with trees. While working on it in soft colors she first made the landscape look deserted, and the trees narrow and bending. Working on it for months she slowly changed her trees into firmer ones. Sometimes she spent a whole session just sitting and looking at what she had made before, without changing a thing. Gradually she turned the landscape into the village of her birth. In it she drew a road, which ended in a spot of light. It represented her wish to go to Jesus. Making this particular image helped her to convey her religious feelings, which were a part of her identity (Wertheim-Cahen, 2003).

Mahmoud

To Mahmoud from Iran, art therapy seemed to offer a possibility to mourn his many losses. He looked sad and much older than his 44 years. The first time he came he drew two houses, one for himself and the other one for his 5-year-old son whom he had to leave behind in Iran. In magazines he looked for pictures that he cut out to stick into the houses. In his son's house he put a photo of a boy. Every time he came to art therapy he first looked at this picture and caressed the photo of the boy. He seemed very sad about all the friends and family he had lost and is haunted by memories of torture and imprisonment. When he told how he sometimes hears his dead friends call out his name, the art therapist suggested that he dedicate a drawing to his friends. Mahmoud consented and drew their graves, writing their names on them. Mahmoud attended treatment more or less regularly, but he stopped when a fellow Iranian patient left the group.

Youseph

Youseph from Azerbaijan knew that at the moment he finished his treatment, he would be deported back to his country. To this somber-looking 39-year-old man art therapy offered mainly a distraction from his worries about the future. It also increased his feeling of self-esteem. Only for art therapy was he willing to leave the ward. One of the images he chose to copy was a chained little bird in a cage. In art therapy he gradually became more active and took more initiative. He developed his painting skills and also liked to frame his pictures. These activities seemed to give him some grip and at the same time working independently increased his self-confidence. During art therapy was the only time he was reported to be seen smiling. As his day of departure approached his condition deteriorated and he was moved to a closed unit.

Sergei

To Sergei, a tall 40-year-old man from Armenia, art therapy also was a place where he seemed able to unwind. He did not come very often, but when he did he tried to communicate his thoughts on paper in a limited way. At one point he drew a big tank. He carefully started coloring it green. On the tank he wrote: "no more war." He took back this personal statement to the ward where he proudly showed it. A week later, after a severe anxiety attack, he died of heart failure.

Sahar

The death of a fellow patient, the threat of immediate deportation for another, missing fellow compatriots, and also different customs — languages and social backgrounds of the group members have to be taken into account in Sahar's art therapy process. The first time he did not show up for art therapy, the art therapist went out to get him from the ward. Together they covered the distance from the ward to the art studio. As a plane suddenly flew over the hospital's compound, Sahar shrank and covered his ears in fear. From that first session on, however, he never failed to show up. During long periods, he forcefully worked on small pieces of paper. He drew endless tunnels, black holes, and bottomless pits, commenting: "I am looking for a way out, but cannot find it." Other images from his hand were a round room with many doors, a room with no light, a coffin, trees without leaves, closed doors. It seemed like an endless repetition of the same desolate and suffocating theme. At some point the art therapist cautiously tried to get Sahar to change this pattern. She suggested that he draw with a gray crayon instead of the black one he always used. He complied, but his images did not really change, nor their meaning (see Figures 16.4 and 16.5).

At some point again she suggested that he draw something more positive and more spacious, like a spot he would like to imagine himself to be in. "Impossible," he says, "I cannot make anything else, but I will try." Then he drew a man in a small boat floating on an immense sea. When asked if land might be nearby, he replied, "I don't know, it may be here," pointing in the distance far away from the paper. Although he had indeed created a different image, it was just as desolate as the ones before. The impact remained the same. His work expressed his loneliness and a feeling of being locked in. Nevertheless, Sahar kept coming to the art therapy sessions. He said: "here at least I can express what I feel inside." When, due to holidays, there was no art-therapy, he was disappointed. Although Sahar was still imprisoned by his images, he was also looking for a way out.

To get Sahar to change his subject became a slow and cautious process. Being stuck in the repetition of painful images that he kept depicting seemed to provide him with a sense of control. Apparently it was necessary to follow his pace and stay with him until he felt safe enough to make the shift from stereotypical images to something new. Too much pressure from the art therapist could easily have made him feel

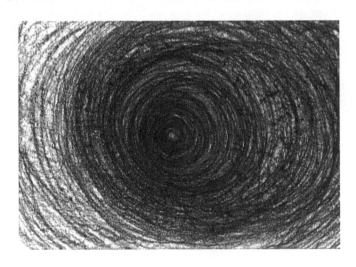

Fig. 16.4 Tunnel

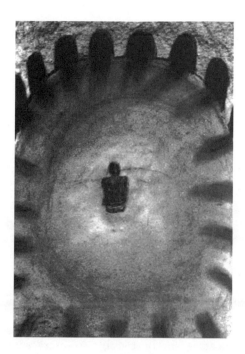

Fig. 16.5 Round Room

victimized once again. Slowly a change in his work became noticeable. While drawing he now took more space for himself and used more force. His movements become broader and wider. On a paper, larger than he usually chose to work on, he painted a black background on which he put dabs of paint in bright colors. After having finished he climbed on a chair to look at it from a distance (see Figure 16.6).

Then a period followed in which Sahar was tense, restless, and full of repressed anger. During art therapy sessions he paced up and down as if searching for something. One time he suddenly sat down next to the pottery wheel, took some clay, and tried to give it a shape. But the result did not satisfy him. In order to make him use his physical force, the art therapist suggested to try and make a really big piece. Together they pinned a large piece of paper on the wall. For a while he worked intensely. A male figure appeared. Instead of giving it a head he drew a huge spiral full of explosions. Looking at it from a distance, Sahar commented: "a bad image. I don't want to look at it." With the help of the therapist he took down the drawing. A dense layer of pulverized crayons on the floor displayed the amount of power he had put into his efforts. Next time he again came in looking agonized. Suddenly he said, "I would like to make a Phoenix." After discussing with the art therapist how his Phoenix should look, he took a piece of clay and started modeling a bird arising from its ashes. Although he did not elaborate on the

Fig. 16.6 Colors

fact that the ward where he resided bore the same name, or on the symbolical significance of his "Phoenix," he started changing. While formerly keeping very much to himself he now appeared to be more trustful, communicative, and better able to interact with others. Sometimes he even participated in discussions about religion or politics.

Next, Sahar made a rectangular shape of clay. When the clay was dry he worked like a sculptor cutting and grating it as if it were a piece of stone. It seemed an outlet for his anger. It is springtime and outside factors began to influence him. To him spring brought back memories of the war in the Balkans, which also started in spring. The Serbian president had just been murdered and the war in Iraq was approaching. All these events upset him greatly. In art therapy he nevertheless kept working very concentrated and unlike before he now managed to walk and cycle alone over the compound of the hospital. One day, while grating a block of clay, a particle broke off. He jumped aside and was very upset, wanting to leave the session. But the therapist persuaded him to stay and act out his frustration and anger on a big piece of paper, which he did. From this incident on Sahar seemed to be more aware of how his impulsive reactions were connected to his painful memories and how the broken piece of clay triggered his dormant feelings of rage and grief. Next time he brought a tape with quiet and sad music. Listening to this music he worked with clay, making a bent human figure. He paid much attention to the face, giving it a grief-stricken look. The therapist told him that she noticed the sadness of this statuette. He nodded in agreement.

Summarizing, during his 1-year stay in the clinic Sahar had succeeded to liberate himself from his haunting stereotype images, and now allowed himself to express his feelings at the appropriate moment. First, he became capable of expressing his anger and later also his grief and sorrow about all that had been broken and destroyed in his life (Laub & Podell, 1995).

Although the fact remains that the problems the refugees face are enormous, art therapy administers a meaningful contribution. It offers patients, who on top of their traumatic past are isolated by their illness and their position as exiles and strangers in an unfamiliar language and culture, a means to express themselves and to make themselves "visible."

CHILDREN OF REFUGEES

Although children of refugees and asylum seekers tend to adapt much faster to their new surroundings and living conditions than their parents do, they too are affected by their experiences of war and flight (Wertheim-Cahen & de Jong, 1995). Even more so if they have been left maimed physically as a result of them.

In the Netherlands a few of those children, a very small minority, attend a special school for the physically handicapped. Most children in this school suffer from physical disabilities due to congenital causes, progressive muscle diseases, and brain injuries. Apart from regular education the school offers occupational and physical therapy. Psychosocial problems are discussed in small counseling groups, and art therapy has been recently added to the program. The setting in the school differs from the previous ones in the sense that the school is also equipped with toys and playing materials. Playing, like art-making, is a self-healing activity. It helps children to digest painful and distressing matters. The results of these activities often bear a symbolic significance, but also the mere activity itself can make it easier for a child to talk about topics not easily spoken about (Hellendoorn, 1985).

The art therapy room in the school contains a large variety of art and handicraft materials but also some toys and games. Art therapy sessions are conducted on an individual base once a week on the school's premises.

Hasib

We will follow the art therapy process of Hasib, a 13-year-old boy from Afghanistan. At age 6, as a result of a rocket attack in his country, he lost both legs. At the same time his little sister was killed. After the family's flight to Holland, yet another sibling died, leaving Hasib with only one younger brother. Hasib usually moved around in a wheelchair. The school psychologist referred him to art therapy because he seemed very troubled after his brother's death. In the class he had become restless and preoccupied.

By the time of his first encounter with the art therapist he had been in Holland for 5 years and spoke Dutch adequately. Hasib was active in several sports for the handicapped. As he talked about his daily life he seemed open and showed a good sense of humor. Soon a trusting relationship between him and the art therapist was established.

In his first session Hasib paints a very small snake in vast woods. He talks about how in Afghanistan he often used to find dead snakes, driven over by cars. Another time he makes an embossment of an angry bear showing his sharp, big claws. "They have taken the meat from the bear," he commented, "but this will not happen again." Fascinated by toy building bricks, which he finds in the art therapy room, he starts to build a house. He gives it small windows but no door. While building he talks about his grief over the recent death of his little brother. The GP failed to properly assess the sick boy's situation. Hasib, speaking Dutch better than his parents, had to beg on the telephone for an ambulance, which arrived too late. Having first used toy bricks to build a house, the next time he wants to fabricate bricks himself to build what he refers to as a "real house." While making preparations he talks about how drug trafficking makes the neighborhood where he lives unsafe. Recently an asylum seeker there had been murdered.

Two days after September 11, 2001, Hasib is waiting outside the therapy room for the therapist to arrive. Appalled by what has happened he immediately starts talking about how glad he is that his acquaintances who worked in the Twin Towers are okay. While building, he talks about children who are afraid of a third world war. When asked whether he is afraid too, he responds: "To me it has always been war." Then he starts talking about Afghan soldiers who are capable of killing people in a gamble over a cigarette. He imagines a father who goes shopping for his children and then gets killed as a result of such a gamble. At the end of the session he covers the walls of his house with glue. The following sessions he expresses his worry about the coming attack on his country, and he continues working on his house. He tells how big and beautiful the house he once lived in had been, and how he used to play in the huge garden with an aviary inside.

At some moments when he feels better, Hasib experiments with colors and tries out different ways of fabricating bricks for building. At other moments, when concern about his relatives back in Afghanistan overwhelms him, he built slipshod and in a high tempo. His way of constructing becomes mechanical and the results unstable. On the roof of his building he plans to erect a tower, comparing his building to the World Trade Center. He believes that in Afghanistan, like in the United States, there should be big buildings like the Twin Towers.

In a following session he talks about all the destroyed houses in Afghanistan that he would like to rebuild. He also speaks about the attack on his home in which he lost his legs and his sister was deadly wounded. Talking about these events he seems to accept them as inevitable facts in his life. In the house, which until then had no windows, he then makes a very big arch-shaped window (see Figure 16.7). Leaving this session he almost looks relieved.

Fig. 16.7 House

The bombardments of Afghanistan started and again Hasib seemed very depressed. Building seemed to have become an act to keep up his spirits. Instead of two he erects four towers on the roof of his house.

Then his younger brother gets seriously ill. Very much afraid of also losing him, he covers the walls of his house with a fat layer of plaster that he has fabricated from powder. "It should be as solid and sound as possible." He plans to give his house to his brother.

As his brother's condition deteriorates, Hasib told about voices in his head that continuously "talk." He hopes it all to be a bad dream, from which he would wake up soon. Having finished his house he does not know what he wants anymore. The therapist suggests to him to design a get-well card for his brother. His head hurts so much that he does not even know anymore how to write his brother's name.

The next session his brother appears to be doing somewhat better. Hasib tells how he sees images from the war. Asked if he would like to draw them, he says: "Why draw soldiers? I prefer drawing peace." He starts making what he calls a statue of peace: a sitting figure with his head leaning on his arms looking with big eyes to what is happening around him. He comments that this man is sad about what he sees. Then he cuts off a leg, saying: "He has lost his leg in the war" (see Figure 16.8).

His brother's condition keeps improving, and Hasib again wants to talk about what is happening in the world. Meanwhile, he attempts to make a socle for his statue, but the construction sags and he knocks it down. He emphasizes that the man who had lost his leg is contemplating the world. Another difficult period follows. Gradually it becomes clear that his brother will have permanent brain damage. Hasib starts fabricating a wooden house, again for his brother. This new enterprise proves to be too demanding as he lacks concentration. He is often very sad and looks tired. He sees the sorrow of his parents and therefore does not want to burden them with his own grief. He finds it difficult to cry and indicates that he hopes his hands will do that for him. In this period he draws for the first time a landscape of Afghanistan and then tells about the unrelenting shooting and about living in continual fear of being attacked.

A new phase in therapy starts. Hasib has taken up the plan to make a real painting on canvas. First he starts studying how to draw people, which he finds very difficult. Especially drawing his own body is a confrontation because of his amputated legs. All the same he finally succeeds in drawing himself without legs, sitting on a bench with a friend.

Fig. 16.8 A Man Who Is Sad About What He Sees

As the end of therapy comes in sight, his brother is getting much better. Hasib starts a new painting, a big, crying eye in a red sky, which he entitles: "terrified eye" (see Figure 16.9). It represents his grief about the war and its consequences.

Proud of his accomplishment and at the same time aware of its significance he comments: "It is not just a nice picture." During the last sessions Hasib looks back at everything he has made. He wants the therapist to keep his work and "maybe show it to other kids." The art therapist makes photographs of his work and he takes them home, together with his paintings.

Looking back Hasib feels how art therapy had supported him during a very demanding period in his life. The art therapy room provided a place where attention could be totally focused on him, where talking about his worries and preoccupations was encouraged, and became possible. The art therapist helped him to express his feelings. While building and painting Hasib allowed himself to be vulnerable. Art-making made talking about hardship, grief, and loss easier. With his big hands, using the tiny bricks for building became an act in which he could contain the traumatic events at a sensory and tactile level (Malchiodi, 1998; Steele, 2003). At the same time they offered him a symbolic outlet for his feelings, as well as a structure that safeguarded him from getting totally overwhelmed by those feelings. A house is a place where you belong and which provides shelter. To Hasib it may have symbolized his ruined house in his homeland as well as his own body. Building houses

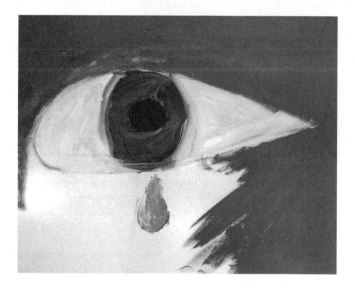

Fig. 16.9 Terrified Eye

became an act in which, against all odds, he could keep himself upright. At the end of the therapy period he seemed to realize this. Art therapy encouraged Hasib to use his creativity and has made him more flexible. For children at risk, knowing how to use their creativity and being flexible will hopefully prevent future undesirable or pathological developments (Melzak, 1992).

CONCLUSION

In this chapter an illustration has been given of how art therapy complements verbal counseling and/or other experiential therapies. In Western countries refugees and asylum seekers and their children are newcomers to the national mental health care system. Art therapists are, in a sense, pioneers adjusting their skills to this "new" population and adapting them to the particular setting they are working in (Wertheim-Cahen, 1995a, 1995b; Zwart & Nieuwenhuis, 2000). In the case of a day treatment center, the art therapist integrated her approach into the five-phase model, carefully balancing between offering structure and freedom. In the clinical setting the art therapist found a way for every patient to, on his or her own level and within his or her own cultural realm, benefit from art-making.

The school for the physically handicapped recently acknowledged that their group counseling program did not sufficiently meet the needs of the refugee children in their care. Hasib was the first child to be able to attend art therapy in the setting of the school. As pioneers the authors of this chapter, in different ways, are conveying their knowledge and experiences to several psychosocial programs in postwar zones. For example Wertheim-Cahen is an advisor to the development of creative arts therapies programs for children, for nongovernmental organizations, like Warchild Netherlands and Mala Serena; Van Dijk is giving art therapy training for M.S.F. (Médecins sans Frontières), all in postwar zones. In the Netherlands Schouten is currently developing ambulant art therapy programs for refugee women, and Roozen is pioneering as an art therapist for the war-traumatized refugee children in the school for physically handicapped.

Art therapy is based on several assumptions. First, that the mobilization of a person's creativity is an activating force to help change one's outlook on the world. Second, it is based on the idea that art expression is complementary to language in the sense that words alone seldom suffice to allow a person to fully express his or her emotional world. And also to really reach and touch one's emotional world words alone seldom are sufficient (Wertheim-Cahen, 2003). Third, there is the advantage that for most people, because they are unaccustomed to express themselves that way, art expression makes it easier for them to drop their defenses and let themselves go (Wadeson, 1980).

Notwithstanding the different settings and methods described in this chapter, several common art therapeutic aspects are beneficial to refugees and asylum seekers and also complementary to other forms of support and treatment. They are summarized in the sections that follow.

Therapy in an Art Studio

The ambience in the art studio is informal. For many patients this diminishes the sense of hierarchy inherent to other therapeutic settings. The informality facilitates the development of a certain intimacy required to address emotions like grief, shame, guilt, and loss of face. For many non-Western refugees, expressing emotions outside the family is more or less taboo. The fact that during art therapy therapist and patient focus not only on emotional problems but also move around and discuss materials and technical matters helps in a way to bring into balance the uneven relationship between helper and patient. This is an asymmetry for which refugees, being in a constant state of dependency, have become very sensitive.

Art-making as an activity provides, even if temporarily, an escape from the refugee's state of forced passivity and powerlessness. Mobilization of creativity helps traumatized refugees to disentangle from the captivity of their traumatic memories. It can encourage them, even if only for the duration of the art therapy session, to widen their horizons. In the shielded environment of the art studio, art expression has the potential to relax and console, as well as to let off steam. It is inherent to the structure of art and art-making that the creator can alternate between recreation and confrontation. For a traumatized patient this means that he or she can draw away from traumatic memories, as well as address them.

Images

Sometimes the images evolving from the art-making process are a result of an intentional assignment. At other times they take shape by chance, as the result from a free art-making process. Even one image can represent a complete narrative. As stated earlier in this chapter, many refugees live with their memories of torture, imprisonment, and flight, and they live in exile. Lack of communication about those experiences makes them lonely and isolated. Merely talking about those events for different reasons can be complex and difficult. However, communication through image-making offers a starting point for lifting their loneliness and isolation.

Narrative

Many refugees don't speak the language of their helpers. In counseling and psychotherapy, with or without interpreters, this remains a complicating factor. For most asylum seekers telling their story has become an ordeal, as many have had to retell their painful history over and over again to nonemphatic immigration officials. They then have to be extremely careful with their words, as their future might depend on it. Sometimes experiences have been so humiliating that sharing them is just too shameful. In traumatic memories images precede language and serve as a bridge to finding words. Therapeutic relevance of art-making for traumatized refugees lies in the fact that by painting and drawing, (traumatic) experiences for which there are (yet) no words, can be expressed and shared (Wertheim-Cahen, 1990, 1991, 1994). Images represent stories that cannot be put into words. They can be a first vessel to break through the isolation and loneliness of a traumatized refugee and help him or her to testify about his or her experiences. Severe traumatic experiences often leave victims literally speechless. For many refugees, talking about their pasts is just too painful, and with uncertainty and instability dominating their daily lives, they just cannot afford to feel that pain. Traumatic memories often tend not to be stored in language, but in body and senses (Wertheim-Cahen, 1991). Art as well as music and movement directly appeal to body and senses where these memories are stored. Art is also a means by which people can allow themselves to be touched.

Sometimes being engaged in activities like playing, drawing, or painting makes talking easier. We saw several examples where drawings and paintings enabled refugees to testify about what they had experienced (Wertheim-Cahen, 2003). The art therapist witnesses how the images grow and become an empathic "audience." So do the group members as they act as each other's "audience," even by just looking and not talking.

Most important of all, art-making, in the sense of fabricating something that bears a personal mark and can be seen by others, restores the refugees' self-respect. Be it a weeping willow, a phoenix rising from its ashes, or a house.

REFERENCES

Betensky, M. G. (1995). *What do you see? Phenomenology of therapeutic art expression*. London and Bristol: Jessica Kingsley Publishers.

Droždek B., van Dijk, M., & de Winter, B. (2002). Omdat ik niet meer weet wie ik ben [Because I don't know who I am]. In E. van Meekeren, A. Limburg-Okken, & R. May, R. (Eds.), *Culturen binnen Psychiatrie — Muren (pp. 179–187)*. Amsterdam: Boom.

Hellendoorn, J. R. (Ed.). (1985). *Therapie kind en spel. Bijdragen tot de beeldcommunicatie* [Child and play: contributions to communication through images]. Deventer: van Loghum Slaterus.

Kramer, E. (2000). *Art as therapy, collected papers*. L. A. Garety (Ed.). London and Philadelphia: Jessica Kingsley Publishers.

Laub, L., & Podell, D. (1995). Art and trauma. *International Journal of Psycho-Analysis, 76*, 991, 1005.

Malchiodi, C. (1998). *Understanding children's drawings.* London: Jessica Kingsley Publishers.

Melzak, S. (1992). Secrecy, privacy, survival, repressive regimes, and growing up. *Bulletin of the Anna Freud Center, 15,* 205–224.

Steele, W. (2003). Using drawings in short-time trauma resolution. In C. Machiode (Ed.), *Handbook of art therapy* (pp. 139–151). New York: Guilford.

van Dijk, M., de Winter, B., & Droždek, B. (1998). *Art therapy with traumatised asylum seekers and refugees.* Paper presented at the European Conference on Psychotrauma, Asylum seekers, Refugees: Pitfalls in treatment, political and judicial context. Vught, the Netherlands.

Wadeson, H. (1980). *Art psychotherapy.* New York. John Wiley & Sons.

Wertheim-Cahen, T. (1986). Beeldende therapie als psychotherapeutische methode bij de behandeling van oorlogsgetroffenen [Drawn by experience] (book). *Icodo-info 3/4,* 7–18.

Wertheim-Cahen, T. (1990). *Getekend bestaan* [Drawn by experience] (video). Utrecht: Video STUG Arnhem.

Wertheim-Cahen, T. (1991). *Getekend Bestaan , creatieve therapie met oorlogsgetroffenen .* Utrecht: ICODO.

Wertheim-Cahen T. (1994). De klei heeft mij mondig gemaakt. In *Kind in Indie, oorlogservaringen en hun gevolgen, in Maandblad voor de geestelijke volksgezondheid* (vol. 4, pp. 414–425). Utrecht: Pharos.

Wertheim-Cahen, T. (1995a). Art therapy with asylum seekers: Humanitarian relief. In D. Dokter (Ed.), *Arts therapists, refugees and migrants, reaching across borders* (pp. 41–61). London Philadelphia: Jessica Kingsley.

Wertheim-Cahen, T. (1995b). Het leven getekend, creatieve therapie met vluchtelingen [Life in images, art therapy with refugees]. *Phaxx, 3,* 11–13.

Wertheim-Cahen, T. (1999). De rol van vaktherapieën bij de behandeling van psychotrauma [Experimental therapies in psychotrauma]. In P. Aarts & W. Visser (Eds.), *Trauma, diagnostiek en behandeling* (pp. 339–355). Bohn: Stafleu en van Loghum Houten.

Wertheim-Cahen, T. (Ed.). (2000a). *Huizen van Karton creatieve therapie met asielzoekers: mogelijkheden en onmogelijkhede* [Carton houses, creative arts therapies with asylum seekers]. Utrecht: Pharos.

Wertheim-Cahen, T. (2000b). In D. Dokter (Ed.), *Exile: Refugees and the arts therapies.* University of Hertfordshire.

Wertheim-Cahen, T. (2003). Van intuitie naar cognitie, 40 jaar beeldende therapie [From intuition to cognition, 40 years of art therapy]. *Maandblad voor de geestelijke volksgezondheid, 7/8,* 666–683.

Wertheim-Cahen, T. (2004). Art therapy a different setting, a different approach. In B. Lloyd & D. Kalmanovitz (Eds.), *Art therapy and political violence,* New York: Brunner Routledge.

Wertheim-Cahen, T., & de Jong, G. (1995). Vluchtelingenzorg en Beeldend Creatieve Therapie creatieve therapie en vluchtelingen [Refugee care and art therapy]. *Icodo info, 3/4,* 98–107.

Winicott, D. (1982). Playing and reality. New York: Routledge Tavistock.

Zwart, M., & Nieuwenhuis, L. (2000). Mourning rituals in non-verbal therapy with traumatised refugees. In D. Dokter (Ed.), *Exile: Refugees and the arts therapies* (pp. 62–80). University of Hertfordshire.

17

Sounds of Trauma: An Introduction to Methodology in Music Therapy With Traumatized Refugees in Clinical and Outpatient Settings

JAAP ORTH, LETTY DOORSCHODT, JACK
VERBURGT, AND BORIS DROŽĐEK

In the past 20 years music therapy has been used extensively for trauma treatment. In relevant literature on this subject, goals, causality, experiences, and personal approaches have already been described. However, a clear methodical account of music therapy in the treatment of traumatized refugees seems to be lacking. Methods of music therapy in trauma treatment, which have been described else-where, have mainly dealt with war veterans, victims of maltreatment or sexual abuse, and victims of disasters. Because in the treatment of traumatized refugees, cultural differences and stress factors caused by their present circumstances play a major role, the previously mentioned methods are not or hardly useful. The music therapists of War Child, a group that works with children in war zones or in postwar environments, often have to deal with cultural differences and stress-inducing factors. They described their experiences mainly by way of exploration and with clinical examples and major themes emerging from the ways in which the clients experience their music therapy (Lang & McInerney, 2002). Because music therapists now deal more often with traumatized refugees, and the demand for documentation, research, and a methodical description has grown, we would like to make a contribution with this chapter to the development of a methodology. We describe the method of music therapy from two points of view: music therapy with traumatized refugees within a clinical setting and within an outpatient setting.

MUSIC THERAPY AND TRAUMA TREATMENT

Some of the intense effects of traumas on the person's body, mind, and spirit can be observed in the way that the traumatized often alternate between a state of "overwhelm and intense re-experiencing of the trauma, and a state of emotional constriction and numbing which can include avoidance of people, places and events that might trigger traumatic associations and bring on intolerable anxiety or panic" (Austin in Sutton, 2002, p. 232). When these posttraumatic reactions continue for a long time it is known as posttramatic stress disorder (PTSD). PTSD comprises three main groups of problems, which can be categorized under the headings of intrusive, avoidance, and arousal symptoms.

The purpose of using music therapy for the treatment of posttraumatic complaints is to help the clients (1) get in contact with and give space to actual emotions that are not dominated by trauma, (2) start the process of making existential choices, and (3) regain control over their own lives.

When dealing with intrusive and arousal symptoms, music therapists mainly focus on reducing the emotional stress and anxiety level, to channel/redirect emotions via healthy outlets, and develop relaxation or diversion. In order to accomplish this, sleep-inducing tapes, relaxation through music, or other means are used to provide a way for a person to express his or her feelings in a safe way. Instrumental and singing improvisations are often used for this purpose.

Austin (2002) applies "vocal holding techniques" in her trauma treatment of adult clients, who suffer from the symptoms of childhood abuse, emotional deprivation, and inadequate parenting. This is a vocal improvisation method that she developed using two chords intentionally combined with her own voice. She does this to create a consistent and stable musical environment that facilitates improvised singing within the client-therapist relationship. This is also a way to develop social interaction and communicative skills to seek assistance and distraction through others as well as facilitating integration.

Music therapists, when dealing with avoidance symptoms, stimulate an increased awareness of self, validating one's feelings and identifying emotions. For this purpose forms of improvisation are offered, including forms with singing and discussions and/or music paired with associations to trigger memories.

Zharinova-Sanderson (2002) uses in her music therapy with traumatized refugees (folk) songs her clients know from their cultural heritage to share memories and thoughts from their native countries. A tradition that is still much very alive in other cultures helps her clients to express themselves enthusiastically and authentically; furthermore, it strengthens the tie with their own identity. With the client teaching, singing, and performing his or her traditional songs, an easy link is created with his or her own cultural identity and with memories and situations associated with this music. Zharinova-Sanderson explains that it assists the change of the client's dependent role to a role of an expert.

On the whole strategies are offered to improve one's image, self-esteem, self-confidence, and self-acceptance and to increase trust in oneself and others (Sears, 2002). Some music therapists use mainly instrumental or vocal improvisation routines originated in the analytically oriented music therapy (Austin, 2002; Priestley, 1975).

DIFFERENT MUSIC THERAPY METHODS

Here we will look at music therapy methods already in use. These methods are mainly used while treating Vietnam veterans, children who are victim of maltreatment or sexual abuse, and children in postwar environments and victims of disasters. After an introduction on improvisation within music therapy vocal holding techniques, singing and discussions, and guided imagery will be described.

Improvisational Music Therapy

Music therapy can involve the client and therapist in a broad range of musical experiences. The main ones are improvising, performing, composing, notating, verbalizing, and listening to music. Methods that employ improvising as a primary therapeutic experience are referred to as improvisational music therapy. Bruscia (1987) describes the term improvise in different situations as a creative activity that commonly occurs in everyday life, in the performing arts (music, dance, and drama), and in the respective arts therapies. He says improvising in everyday language means to make something up as one goes along, and that in certain situations, it can also mean to create or fabricate something from whatever sources are available. In music improvising is defined as "the art of spontaneously creating music (ex tempore) while playing, rather than performing a composition already written" (Bruscia, 1987, p. 5). In a music therapy context Bruscia thinks that improvising encompasses elements of all these definitions and calls it inventive, spontaneous, extemporaneous, and resourceful, and it involves creating and playing simultaneously. According to Smeijsters (1995) the musical behavior during improvisation, which takes place some distance way from the present-day reality, is really the same as behavior in daily life when sudden changes take place, when you have to let go of the old ways and the new situation must be addressed. Similar adaptations can be observed by people who, in order to enhance their own secure environment, are locked in rigid patterns and are unable to cope with any changes (van den Hurk & Smeijsters, 1991).

The basic philosophy of improvisational music therapy is that these techniques elicit client's responses from every level. It develops contact with the client within the context of the musical experience. The role of a music therapist in this model often works supportively, creating a musical emotional environment that accepts and enhances the client's responses. This method provides experiences for socialization, communication, and expression of feelings and emotions among group participants. The instruments most commonly used for instrumental improvisation in music therapy are rhythm instruments and Orff instruments, such as xylophones and metallophones.

Vocal Holding Techniques

The music therapist can also integrate movement, speech, and drama in this model. One of the models that integrates speech in improvisation is vocal holding techniques, a method that Austin (1999) developed. This method has proven effective in creating an opportunity for a safe, therapeutic regression in which dissociated and/or unconscious feelings, memories, and situations can gradually be accessed, experienced, understood, and integrated. In vocal holding techniques an improvisational structure is usually limited to two chords in combination with the therapist's voice in order to establish a predictable, secure musical and psychological container that facilitates improvised singing. She found the combination of improvised singing and verbal processing to be one of the most effective ways of working with the unresolved traumas of childhood. The method proved to be especially useful in working through developmental injuries and arrests due to traumatic ruptures in the mother-child relationship and/or empathic failures at crucial developmental junctures. The inner world of the traumatized clients contains split off, dissociated parts of the self, which are often externalized in the client-therapist relationship and can be worked with in the transference-countertransference situation (Davies & Frawley, 1994). In this method, the relationship field is enlarged to include transference and countertransference to and in the music. Austin (2002) stated:

> Vocal holding initially tends to promote a positive transference, that of the longed for good mother of early infancy and childhood. This highly empathic musical environment is fertile soil in which trust can grow and feelings can be brought to light. If the therapeutic relationship feels trustworthy enough, the traumatised client will begin to differentiate feelings such as grief, terror and rage. At those moments, the therapist and the music have to be experienced by the client as strong and resilient enough to withstand these intense affects. The therapist might alter the music somewhat to reflect the client's changing emotional intensity. (p. 240)

Singing and Discussions

In treatment of trauma, singing can be restorative for a variety of reasons. Austin (2002) names three: on a physiological level, singing facilitates deep breathing; deep breathing slows the heart rate and calms the nervous system, stilling the mind and the body; and relaxation is the result. Singing is also a neuromuscular activity, and muscular patterns are closely linked to psychological patterns and emotional response (Newham, 1998). When we sing, internally resonating vibrations break up and release blockages of energy, which is particularly relevant to the traumatized who have frozen, numbed off areas in the body that hold traumatic experiences. Austin quotes according to Levine (1997): "this residue of unresolved, undischarged energy gets trapped in the nervous system and creates the debilitating symptoms associated with trauma. Singing can enable the traumatized client to reconnect with his or her essential nature by providing access to, and an outlet for, intense feelings" (Austin, 2002, p. 235).

> The act of singing is empowering: sensing the life force flowing through the body; feeling one's strength in the ability to produce strong and prolonged tones; experiencing one's creativity in the process of making something beautiful; having the ability to move oneself and others; and hearing one's own voice mirroring back the undeniable confirmation of existence. Owning one's voice is owning one's authority and ending a cycle of victimisation. (Austin, 2002, p. 236)

Austin's (2002) purpose of using singing in trauma treatment as stated here is especially interesting because she views it as bridging the division between mental and physical problems. In other cultures this division does not seem as obvious. Therapeutic treatment in Europe and the United States is directed toward the integration of traumatic experiences in the psyche of the person requesting help. Criticism of present-day care provision focuses in particular on its strong verbal and individualistic bias and on its segmented and highly regulated structure (van Dijk, 2001).

Singing and discussions, a method described on the War Child Web site, is used mainly by music therapists working with children in postwar environments. In this method the music stimulates clients' responses to the lyric parts. Sometimes the music itself encourages the expression of thoughts and feelings associated with the songs. Typical procedures of this method might go as follows: The therapist usually opens the session by singing songs familiar to the clients. After singing several songs, the therapist leads a discussion related to the themes of the songs. Once each client has expressed and discussed his or her own thoughts, feelings, and ideas, the therapist improvises a song with the words from the clients. This can be a very positive conclusion of the session (in fact, the therapist makes a song to be positive) so that each client might carry over his or her feelings and emotions in productive ways (Mostar Music Centre).

Guided Imagery and Music

Guided imagery music (GIM) is a method developed by Helen Bonny (1986). The method is based on the basic assumption that it is indeed possible to select the most appropriate music depending on the problems of the client. GIM is often used to help treat severe posttraumatic stress, where, through imagery, a client is able to identify his or her fears and the realities of the past. GIM refers to the use of music to stimulate a state of self-hypnosis, which is achieved through ones imagination. The act of listening to (classical) music is combined with a relaxed state of mind and body in order to evoke imagery for the purpose of self-actualization. The emotions stimulated by appropriate music guide a patient through his or her own thoughts. The imagery a client creates is often representative of problems or difficulties in the client's life. The client can then take what he or she discovers and solve unresolved issues, thus helping heal the mind and spirit. GIM does not intend to cure or treat symptoms; rather it is in search of a client's inner awareness to focus on and identify problems. There is a belief that everyone can understand his or her problems and has the ability to overcome the problem within the self. Because GIM deals with a form of self-hypnosis and is deeply rooted to emotional problems and the subconscience, it is most often associated with music therapy in connection to psychology. Professionals who practice GIM in full clinical form have been intensively trained how to select music for a client's particular needs and how to help guide the client to imagery interpretations. GIM is often used in the treatment of traumatized war veterans.

In the treatment of traumatized refugees GIM does not always seem practical, because in dealing with refugees from other cultures, it is often hard to find existing music that corresponds to the emotional state and needs of the client. Our experience is that there can be great differences between the perception and interpretation of music in the various cultures. Furthermore, refugees often find themselves in a situation they experience as unsafe and stressful, so they cannot fully concentrate on the music and fully open up to it.

MUSIC THERAPY IN ACTION: A CLINICAL PERSPECTIVE

The Clinical Setting

Jaap Orth is a music therapist in the Phoenix-centre, part of the mental health organization De Gelderse Roos in the Netherlands. This cross-cultural center is a highly specialized inpatient treatment facility for refugees and asylum seekers. It serves as a "last resort" for treatment-resistant disorders, with special attention to social and cultural aspects in assessment and treatment. Refugees and asylum seekers with all kinds of psychiatric disorders (including culture-bound syndromes) are admitted, specifically those cases in which inpatient treatment in general mental health facilities fail to adequately diagnose or treat them.

Historical Overview

Since Jaap Orth started in 1982 with music therapy dealing with severely traumatized refugees, he has used many different methods. Some of the methods that were used by other music therapists in trauma treatment, which were described in the previous paragraph, he used partly or he adapted them for traumatized refugees. He also experimented with new methods. This was necessary because when dealing with traumatized refugees, various aspects like differences in culture, language, and stress-inducing aspects caused by their present situation play a major role and have consequences for the treatment. After some time the obstacles, but also the advantages, of a music therapeutic approach became clear.

With cultural differences, it is important to have sufficient knowledge of other cultures; not only about the different norms, but also the different opinions about "being ill" and how they deal with the sickness. The interpretation of "unhealthiness" can differ greatly between cultures. Limburg-Okken (1989) and Kirmayer (2002) give examples of the somatizing of complaints. Three quarters of the world population experience complaints in a physical way. But in the Western world complaints often manifests themselves into a mental complaint.

The different music cultures also make use of music therapy different when dealing with clients in the West. In comparison with our Western culture, there are often major differences in perception and interpretation of music and the way people express their perceptions. This enforces the use of non-Western musical instruments, but the music therapist often has inadequate knowledge about the effect the selected music will have on the client (Orth, 1992).

Orth developed and built musical instruments, which made it possible to improvise in a pentatonic way and play quarter tones.

Using the music the clients themselves bring is an easy way to tune into their music culture and overcome the differences between our music culture and theirs. The therapist must submerge and be open to the other music; this is made easier with the availability of the Internet with access to examples of all types of music. Many traumatized refugees can clearly indicate what music they themselves would select to relax by.

Stress-inducing factors that traumatized refugees have to deal with play a prominent part in the music therapy. Often clients cannot start from a safe "home base" to digest the intensive reactions, which are a result of the therapy. Anxiety about family back home or still in the asylum-seekers center, about their status, or about housing and discrimination make it hard to concentrate on the treatment and on their own development. Music therapy also alleviates paralyzing and dominating thoughts and other worries. Another aspect that hampers the use of music was that many clients found it difficult to cope with loud sounds, which were associated with the war violence they had experienced at close hand. Loud sounds were also associated with executions and bombardments. Sometimes music was used while they were tortured and then music became part of the trauma (de Koning, 1996). This fact was revealed when in one of our group sessions a woman had a flashback of the execution of her father when one of her fellow group members played a roll on a marching drum. Her father's execution, which she witnessed, was accompanied by the rolls of a drum. Because in this group therapy certain music could easily evoke intrusive memories, it was necessary to surround these sessions with plenty of safety.

In music therapy, not knowing the client's language is not always a hindrance. When using their mother tongue to express thoughts and memories doing musical improvisations, the clients seem to create a more fluid flow of words, as the therapist could not understand them. And in the evaluation of the improvisations afterward, they could choose to be quiet or explain in a different way certain phrases they expressed in the improvisation. So the language gap was advantageous to them and offered extra safety. It is often not necessary to understand one another when making music together and playing instrumental improvisations. The language gap, however, makes working together more complicated and causes limitations to the way the clients can make themselves verbally understood.

The author's impression is that because the shocking incidents that caused the trauma took place very recently, certain musical activities seem to increase resistance and tension, and also because music was sometimes part of the traumatic experience or because the clients could not cope with loud sounds. Then music can evoke such intense feelings, memories, and associations that it should be avidly avoided. Above all it is hard to control feelings that are related to a trauma. Besides a secure safe working environment, the methods used should be inviting as well as deemed safe by the clients. These approaches must include all possibilities to explore resulting feelings, to shape or reduce them, while at the same time producing a great desire to express and sometimes literally shout out these feelings. I (Orth) often have to work in the music therapy between these two forces; on one side the extreme need to control feelings and on the other side the extreme need to express what is felt.

Developing a Set of Methods

Initially I (Orth) worked with a relatively homogenous group of Vietnamese refugees. I focused on enhancing their own identities by concentrating on their own culture. I studied Vietnamese music and the social meaning and various means of expression this music could offer these clients. After 1995 it was no longer possible to work with these groups of homogenous Vietnamese refugees because refugees from many other countries started to arrive. The groups became heterogeneous and there was a need to concentrate more on integration and look for common cultural elements. Pop music seemed especially relevant to the younger clients in the target groups as music they could all relate to from their own cultural background. Some groups could be made up from as many as 10 different cultures: refugees from Somalia, Azerbaijan, Cambodia, and Chile all together in one group. For me as the therapist and for the participants also, it was often an extraordinary experience that in such a short time, sometimes as quick as 15 minutes, it was possible to play, sing, and dance together with such a diverse mixture of people who could hardly understand one another. Besides, in changing from working within a single culture-based homogeneous group to a heterogeneous cross-cultural approach, we find that in music therapy we focus more and more on individual treatment. Furthermore, we are developing a methodological foundation of such treatment.

From experience we have learned that direct attention to the sustained traumas could cause anxiety, resistance, and avoidance. In music therapy we focus on dealing with the client's own situation, handling his or her own problems and nonverbal expression of feelings. It is noticeable that traumatized refugees often are able to sing about their misery, but find it much harder to talk about it. The instrumental music accompanying verbal improvisation, when closely related to the moods and needs of the client, seems to form a safe and inviting platform to express their feelings. Because there is the accompanying music, silences in singing become less tense, and intense emotional outbursts seem to be part of the music. The client feels supported by the music, which supports the mood he or she is in, and new phrases seem to flow free and automatically.

Music therapy often takes place in an individual format. A group of people sharing the same problems, however, offers various opportunities such as mutual recognition and support. Aspects of treatment with respect to these problems are often similar; for example, exerting influence on, and dealing with, feelings and experiencing the actual reality (Orth, 2001).

Since music therapy has been part of the treatment program of Phoenix, expertise has been acquired in the fields of

- Providing people with the means of emotional expression of feelings like homesickness, loneliness, despair, and so forth;
- Keeping and developing people's cultural identity and their orientation according to the culture of their native country. Listening to and playing the music of their own country stimulates the experience of their culture. Especially in a process of adaptation, it is important for them to remain in touch with their own cultures. One could say that culture shows the limits of what is or is not allowed or possible; culture gives people something to hold on to. Music, a means of expression giving shape to culture in a manifold way, which is appealing to the senses, provides the patient with a certain cultural security;
- Offering musical structure as safe limits within which a client can express him- or herself and experiment;
- Stimulating social interaction. Because most clients are still dealing with their own problems, it is not yet possible to mean a great deal to somebody else. Music therapy is a way to improve mutual contact, communication, and group sense (bonding);
- Doing things together "constructively," having positive experiences, and enjoying things together;
- Developing positive aspects of present psychic functioning, including ego-strengthening activities aimed to stimulate initiative, to stimulate people to use their own talents, to make people influence their own (musical) environment, and to actually make the clients experience their own lives.

FIVE APPROACHES TO MUSIC THERAPY

In the paragraphs that follow we will look at five fully worked out approaches to methods of music therapy that Orth often used in the past 20 years and that proved to be most suitable and successful in the treatment of seriously traumatized refugees (Orth, 2002). The main idea behind these methods is to strengthen self-determination, the ability to manage one's own affairs, and development. This method should also offer possibilities to intensively express thoughts and feelings regarding past experiences within a safe environment and then tentatively be confronted with the memories of those experiences. (There's a sixth method Orth sometimes uses but has not yet fully crystallized and described: the focusing technique of Gendlin combined with music (Smeijsters, 2000). The methods include

1. Select and record your own tape/CD of music to relax by.
2. Live recording of your own performed music to relax by.
3. Learn how to play an instrument and play together.
4. Making your own musical product. (This form will not be described in depth because it is an obvious method.)
5. Controlled expression of thoughts and feelings through improvisation. (The description of this method is in the form of an extensive process description followed by a case account, where a combination of these methods was applied.)

Select and Record Your Own Tape/CD

> Y., a refugee from Iraq, was in his home country supervisor of the irrigation water pumps on a large estate. Because one of the pumps overheated, broke down, and caused a fire, he was heavily punished and tortured. After this incident he managed to escape and flee to the Netherlands. Here he now suffers from severe insomnia. Together we make a tape with the sounds of running water. If he can listen to this tape before going to bed, he relaxes and gets to sleep. Clients often say that certain music evokes pleasant memories, that they can dream and that the music comforts them when they feel lonely.

The client can take the tape/CD with the selected music pieces home and play the music when he or she feels tense or cannot get to sleep and it has a positive influence on his or her mood. The self-control of the client is enhanced when he or she can modify his or her own thoughts and moods.

Another possibility is to record "live" music played by the clients or the group of clients with the available instruments. I will describe this option in the next paragraph. The first possibility — select and record your own tape/CD of personally relaxing music, mostly using music the client provides. First listen to the different fragments of music together. Then record the parts the client finds most relaxing which he or she could play when tension rises or he or she worries too much. The most suitable music is standard instrumental, predictable, of slow pace, and with an even rhythm. The selected music parts are often existing pieces, familiar to the client, pleasant to his or her ear, and evoking positive associations. Therefore, the client has to pinpoint what he or she is looking for. There is plenty of ethnic music available on the Internet for this selection.

The process of selecting this music by the client must focus on his or her actual situation and enhance the feeling that he or she is in control of his or her own destiny, mood, and well-being. It is desirable for the client be asked to provide, as much as possible, his or her own music or selection, because it is hard to judge from one cultural background how other cultures appreciate and experience certain music. Feelings of sadness, happiness, and other associations that music might produce can vary greatly in different cultures (Orth, 1992).

Another advantage in bringing your own music is that by talking about this music one can make connections with the client's background and home country. Memories and feelings are often coupled to a certain music piece and will give it a special meaning. Some refugees might have packed their favorite CD or tape before leaving. This music will be very important as a link to certain situations or people back home. Sometimes clients have to be reminded that they have got this music. This music is often not suitable for relaxation, but can be used as an association to talk about memories of home.

As a variation on the above, the therapist or the client can record a personal story, memories, or a fantasy. It is advantageous to first make a list of the client's pleasant situations, like walking along the beach, in the woods, the sounds of birds, or the surf, and so forth. Tapes of 25 minutes that can be played continuously are best. The music has to be renewed regularly during treatment, when the needs of the client change.

Live Recording of Your Own Performed Music

Creating your own relaxation music by means of improvisation offers an attractive and pleasant therapy. This method can be used for individuals as well as for groups and will be introduced by a warm-up to get rid of dominating thoughts and to get closer to your own feelings. For warming up in a session we usually play a set score with a closed structure and set rhythm. Slowly we try to diverge from the score and the set rhythm and experiment with songs with more feelings.

After the warm-up the clients choose sounds and instruments that give pleasant feelings or evoke relaxing associations. We use various (acoustic) instruments, like xylophones and harps, which are tuned in pentatonic scales. (The pentatonic scale is comparable to the diatonic scale [C-D-E-F-G-A-B] of which the fourth and the seventh tone are left out. The pentatonic major scale [C-D-E-G-A] in fact comprises the same tones as the minor scale [A-C-D-E-G]. In the former the central tone is C; in the latter it is A. If an accompaniment with the major chords C, F, and G is called for, then C is the keynote. If the minor chords are needed [Am, Dm, and E], the keynote is A.) Rainmakers, ocean drum, and small rhythm instruments, like rhythm-eggs, are very useful. (A rainmaker is a closed wooden tube filled with seeds or small gravel that imitates the sound of falling rain or water. An ocean drum is a small drum with small metal balls in it that imitates the breakers of the sea when you move it.)

One of the members of the group is the director/composer who decides who plays what instrument. The director also determines the tempo and the dynamics. Once the improvisation has started, the therapist accompanies the group by playing recurring chord schemes on the piano or the guitar. The accompaniment functions only as a supporting structure to simplify the improvisation and to stress certain atmospheres by playing minor or major keys and different rhythms. The director conducts.

It is a special sensation to witness how people from different countries, having trouble to verbally communicate and often being self-centered, all start playing together in a few minutes time. People are watching one another; they are focused on playing together. Language is no longer a barrier.

The experience of being able to influence one's own mood by making one's own relaxation music, often recorded for use in the ward, is a valuable contribution to the cure of the traumatized clients in general. It is of even more value to the director, who becomes aware of the influence he or she has on fellow group members. It is the momentary relief of the hustle and bustle of thoughts, getting the chance to be involved with the things happening around you, that leads to relaxation and creates the circumstances needed to be able to deal with trauma. This will strengthen the clients and provide them with the means to focus on the future.

Apart from these ego strengthening activities and group experience, this program provides ways for emotional expression and experiencing one's own cultural identity.

Learn How to Play an Instrument and Play Together

Many clients expect to learn how to play an instrument during music therapy. However, this is normally not the intention, but it can happen when it offers a possibility to get out of a state of anxiety and a mode for expression, structured by playing music together. Often we use drumming for this purpose. Because many clients, especially in the beginning of therapy, find it hard to cope with loud sounds, we sometimes use ear protectors. Drumming is both a difficult technical and physical effort with hands and feet acting independently and it requires some ability to keep a rhythm. It demands concentration and targeted exertion, and this combination hardly leaves room for other thoughts or engagements, which results in a better control over tension. Music involves reality orientations in many forms and on such levels as the situation requires. The various stimuli include aural (both musical and verbal), the feel of the instrument itself, visual (musical notation and conductor cues), and the individual's own body. The individual's responses can be judged for appropriateness to real stimuli, built on the time ordered necessities of a given musical situation (Sears, 2002). The traumatized clients seem to accept and express their feelings through the music better after they get rid of their dominating thoughts and anxiety. Especially this acceptance and expression of their own feelings is something many traumatized clients find difficult. To play music together and so to communicate intuitively with others is essential.

> A. is an 18-year-old ex-child soldier from Sierra Leone with PTSD. A. suffers from reliving experiences, nightmares, chaos in his head, anxiety and panic disorders, and he fears loss of control and tension. He isolates himself from the other clients and worries a lot. Assisted by music therapy I try to break through his social isolation and offer him a means to express himself in a controlled and safe way. Due to his interest for pop music, I taught him to drum a basic pop rhythm. In two sessions A. managed to play this rhythm. Concentrating for 15 to 20 minutes on the drums seemed to give a relaxing feeling and he indicated that he did not feel any anxiety when playing. But he played rather like a robot and not always at the same pace. This changed when I accompanied him on my electric guitar with chords in his rhythm and found the connection. When I played more dominatingly, A. changed from playing as an individual to playing more as a unit. He managed to drum with more fluidity and rhythm. Afterward we did experiments with changes of pace and change of the dynamics when I played faster, slower, harder, or softer. A. adjusted easily to changes of pace and dynamics I created in our play. In order to adjust to changes of pace and dynamics he had to diverge from his fixed pattern and trust his own feeling for rhythm. A. obviously enjoyed this experience and his drumming became even more meaningful when we started to practice solos and included improvisations. In five sessions I could challenge A. to follow me in play and then drum faster, louder, and more briskly, but also adjust when I played slower or pianissimo.

Being able to drum the basic pop rhythm and my stabilizing influence as guitar player on his performance, formed for A. a safe foundation to fully surrendering to the music and to experimenting safely with the expressions of his feelings. He beat his frustrations out on the drum set. With me playing the guitar, cajoling, challenging, and supporting A., he seemed to find this an agreeable controlled way to release pressure and to cope with feelings of inability and frustrations.

In drumming, his behavior is a reflection of his self-expressive needs. The adaptability of music provides many avenues for self-expression in performance and listening; they run from simple and random to complex and highly organized. Such a wide range also offers many socially acceptable ways of expressing negative feelings, energetic behavior, or closeness, any of which can reduce the need for expression in more overt, unacceptable forms. The movement from random expression to organized, meaningful expression is the goal. In this case musical activity provides a range of emotional expression. Expressions not otherwise permitted were acceptable in music.

Making Your Own Musical Product

To record your own story on tape or CD can be an inviting way to tell and deal with your story. It is a personal product a client can let other people listen to, can hide away, or keep for him- or herself only.

Near the end of the treatment this is a suitable method. Sometimes we compile a tape of the previously made tapes. Sometimes we play "live" music or use music that is essential to the story of the client, and the client then tells, raps, or sings to it.

Before the recording, the client writes down his or her story (e.g., about the client's escape or the treatment process). The client sings or tells this story and the therapist frames it with suitable music chosen by the client. This music can be performed by the therapist or together with the client or it can be prerecorded music. As music often evokes certain feelings, or because music expresses exactly someone's feelings, the client, especially now, should select matching music.

In this method there is little or no improvisation; the story and the order of the story are mainly predetermined as well as the practical means to express the story. Many clients utilize symbolic images for their stories.

> M. tells in the "song" about a beautiful singing bird, which is threatened in her environment, is maltreated, and then has to escape from the area. The bird cannot fly any longer because of the maltreatment and has to recover in a safe place, there it licks its wounds and becomes stronger again so as to be able to return. Between the lines M. tells us about her setbacks in the process of her own recovery and thanks the people who have helped her.

Making a tape or CD such as this one can be a way to evaluate and support the final stages and completion of the treatment.

Controlled Expression of Thoughts and Feelings Through Improvisation

In musical improvisation someone can express him- or herself directly. Norms and perfectionism can be relaxed or ignored and a "mistake" does not impede the self-awareness, but can be used as a spontaneous occurrence and offer new possibilities. We use the effect that music has to enhance verbal and nonverbal social interaction and communication. It is easier to talk with music in the background, and gaps in the talking or singing are no longer threatening. Clients can express through music feelings otherwise not expressible. The therapist's playing and his or her constant presence create a safe foundation where the client can experiment and improvise and be continually involved with his or her actual surroundings. An awareness of others and the relation to them are constantly required in the process of achieving a musical expression and interpretation.

In the method, through "controlled expression of thoughts and feelings through improvisation," the therapist, together with the client, looks for "live" music that in regard to mood, pace, and atmosphere is similar to the mood of the client at that moment. This can easily be achieved by using a keyboard or guitar as base instrument. I usually first experiment with the pace, then with the key, and finally with the musical styles and chord pattern. It is advisable to keep searching and asking for the clients' preference, until it is pleasing enough and he or she is able to represent and express his or her thoughts. Of fering choices and working collaboratively in searching for the fitting chords empowers the client and helps to create a safe therapeutic environment (Austin, 2002).

When the desired chord pattern, pace, and style have been found, the "live music" can be used as a foundation for the vocal improvisation. The chords pattern in a fitting key is played continuously. If there is an amplifying system, the client could use a microphone and by using the sound effects on the sound system, change the mood of the voice to his or her needs. It is also easy to make a sound recording. The client will be asked to speak or sing texts or thoughts that come to mind. We have experienced that this is reasonably easily done and that there is hardly any hesitance. Striking here is that when the client sings, it is seldom out of tune or in a wrong rhythm. This does happen more often when the client sings existing music. The continuous repetition of the chords pattern creates a safe structure in which the client can express his or her thoughts and where he or she feels at ease and understood, in this set-ting it feels logical when pauses or silences appear in the story or text. In this routine the client looks for the appropriate music him- or herself that converges with his or her mood and also decides whether to talk or to sing.

Dealing with singing in this context Smeijsters (1989) says that although singing has a strong connection with a language, the text in singing is less important than in language. Speaking and writing have a function to express a thought coherently. As words themselves are symbols of certain objects, subjects, and actions, they are sufficient to communicate that statement. The text in a song is not considered suffi-cient in itself, but must be completed with musical information. This musical information is in many cases more important than the text. It is understandable that a text can get more meaning through the music. Smeijsters also says

> For small children who do not have the power of language, sounds indeed are the only way to communicate. At the beginning these sounds are hardly distinguishable, nothing more than a shout at the moment the child wants to be fed or cleaned. Afterwards the child starts to play with this sound and so the rudiments of its future musical expressions, based on his own culture, are founded. The function of the shout is mainly instrumental. The child wants to be satisfied and shouts in order to exert power over its surroundings. In the first

instance adults also shout, when they cannot cope with the situation in another way. The shout is the last means to try to control a situation. In other words, the shout is an expression of mental discord and frustration and at the same time a signal to the outside world. This shout can be cultivated with musical assistance, but it can express the same feelings. Mainly because shouting is not an accepted way of expression, people seek a sublimated expression, an expression that is acceptable. (Smeijsters, 1989, p. 92)

Musical singing makes it possible to express the mental frustration, but even if the music does not serve as a power source in the communication, expressing themselves in this way allows people the feeling that they regain the power over their own existence.

The language in which to talk or to sing in improvisations is decided by the client. Singing or talking in his or her own mother tongue is often easier and offers more safety because the therapist cannot understand it. On the other hand, it can also be more difficult, because it is closer to the client and more direct. Most of the time the clients start off in English or French and later on they continue in their own language. Then you can, most of the time, see and hear more emotions. After the improvisation I normally ask the client what they talked or sang about and what they felt. Also we discuss how to continue; are we changing the style, are we going to do instrumental improvisation or just listening?

What is important is that the client, after the improvisation, can handle what he or she released or what (maybe against his or her prior intention) has been expressed. For this reason we have to agree beforehand how to deal with these fierce emotional feelings or whether is it essential to have a good ending to the session, where the music therapist could offer a relaxing routine.

VARIATIONS

As a subject for an improvisation, reoccurring thoughts from dreams or in sleeplessness could also be used. The client can be asked to note these thoughts when he or she cannot sleep or when jolted awake after a dream. This approach is used regularly, so it helps the client to sleep at night and to deal with thoughts and problems during the day.

Certain themes for the improvisation return regularly. For the variation only the music will be altered, while the key words or the theme stays almost the same. So the perspective changes, from where the client looks at his or her own thoughts (e.g., blues text is used as a base, but the music is changed into a rock and roll or rap style). Using this variation a heavy theme could still sound optimistic. On the other hand, it is also possible to stay with a trusted style of music and just change the text.

An Example[1]

As an example I will give an account of the music therapy with M., in which a combination of different strategies was used (Drogendijk, 2000):

> M., a young man from an African country, has, after many traumatic events, escaped to the Netherlands. In his home country he was a child soldier. The military kidnapped him when he was 12 years old. His mother was killed before his eyes, when she attempted to keep him safe from the claws of the army. The rest of the family has probably also been murdered. As a child soldier he was forced to do many activities, including sexual. In the war he had to fight and he killed people sometimes under the influence of drugs. He had to kill his "blood brother" when he got mutually wounded during a fight and he did not want him captured by the opponents. During the fighting he himself was also wounded. Two years before his admission he escaped to the Netherlands. He has befriended a Dutch woman and has a daughter with this woman. The day before they intended to get married, the authorities canceled the marriage. At the moment of his admission he still had not received his definite residence permit.

At the beginning of his treatment M. could not cope with his tension. He expressed this tension by hitting the trees outside with sticks. He also was suffering from insomnia because he was tortured by nightmares of such magnitude that he was afraid to go to sleep. And further M. (maybe under pressure from his lady friend) was pushing himself to get better as soon as possible. He was often negative about the future and said that he was worthless and could not do anything. This resulted in his determination to follow and succeed in his therapy.

In the treatment of M. the music therapy had at the beginning the following functions and goals:

- trying to control the tensions;
- being able to handle the traumatic memories and the emotions they produced;
- developing a feeling that he could manage his own life;
- gaining confidence by learning different forms of music.

During the first sessions he was asked what he wanted to do in music therapy. He said he wanted to learn how to make music. M. proves to be a very motivated client. He finished his tasks with great accuracy. And furthermore he was eager to learn and was a perfectionist. When he did not succeed in some task he got angry. He measured himself not

---

[1] For the text of this example I used the account of Mrs. Drogendijck who, as a student of psychology, participated in this therapy.

to sick people, but concluded that he could not do anything; he did not take his special situation into account.

Control the Tensions

At certain moments the tensions were rising during the therapy. M. sat himself at the piano and hit the keys in arrhythmic fashion, without melody or theme. I went to the drum set and started to play the drums. First I played as fast as he played, but then I started to play slower and controlled. M. was forced to adjust and also play slower.

Because I offered him a structure, I could influence the way M. responded. The musical structure formed a safe foundation on which the client could let go. M. also took drumming lessons, an additional opportunity to indulge in a very structured way.

Handling the Traumatic Memories and the Emotions They Produce

I asked M. to write down everything that worried and/or kept him awake at night. M. made two texts, the first concerning his situation in the Netherlands and a second where he narrated in short the history of his country. In this text he also briefly described his own experiences.

In the beginning M. did not want to sing in the African music style he used to improvise on usually; probably because the frightening memories were rising faster through sensorial perception. We therefore decided to start singing to western pop music.

Once when he was singing the text about his home country in a minor key, he suddenly left the room, because the tension had risen too high. Screaming, he returned to the ward. He found it difficult to sing because he believed he could not sing properly. In the following weeks we altered the texts and he then practiced the singing itself.

Making song texts is an effective way to structure the thoughts of traumatic experiences (Orth & Verburgt, 1998). Rewriting older texts and making new texts result in less tension than before. After three months, twice weekly music therapy, we reached a break through. Together with a psychology student who did work experience in the clinic and followed the music therapy sessions with M., we prepared ourselves as usual and tuned the instruments and got the installation ready. With just the two of us playing African-sounding music, M. walked in. He took a place behind the microphone and improvised on the music. It seems that the words fell into place and the melody came naturally. He talked about the things that happened in his life as a young soldier and about the death of his family. At that moment he fully surrendered, probably too far because the tension this session produced had risen too high and he walked out. During the following sessions, I had the feeling that he wanted to see how far he could go with the recollection of his memories.

In order to give more structure to his improvisations, he started to write song texts again. At the end he eventually sang these texts accompanied by African music, and he could handle the tension better when talking about his experiences.

Developing a Feeling That You Can Manage Your Own Life

M. was allowed to indicate what he wants to do in the therapy session. He also indicated how far he wanted to go. Also in making songs he was in charge. After a difficult session he chose to leave or talk about his feelings. Sometimes, when he requested this, we listened to nice music. Having the client decide for him- or herself can reduce feelings of inability.

Gaining Confidence by Learning Different Forms of Music

Most of the time we recorded the music. M. was proud to let fellow participants and nurses hear these recorded music fragments in the living room. His ability to drum gave him a lot of confidence.

Because M., besides telling his story through the music, could also express the feelings linked to it, it aided him in coping with the traumatic experiences. Making a recording and listening to it also made it possible to deal with it in a more distant manner. M. could express himself easier, because the music invited him to do so and gave him a structure. He could focus his thoughts at a moment he selected himself during the day, with the result that he could sleep better in the night.

Summary

Since Orth has consistently applied the music therapy according to the described methods, or applied a combination of these methods, a number of relevant points have become more apparent. Beside being a method that makes it possible to talk about traumatic experiences within the psychotherapy, these methods offer ample opportunities to express the feelings that are linked to these experiences. Furthermore, these methods assist in dealing with these pent up feelings. In the daily practice it is very possible to apply these methods alongside one another. The attitude, respect for the needs, and initiatives of the clients and the (musical) skills of the music therapist are, however, very important to guarantee sufficient safety in this process. The individual approach toward the clients and the embedding of the music therapy in the clinical treatment setting can especially enhance the feeling of safety, because deliberation and attuning between the team members can easily take place.

MUSIC THERAPY WITH REFUGEES IN AN OUTPATIENT SETTING

In her work as a music therapist with refugees, Letty Doorschodt found that offering structure and a clear picture of the goals of the therapy were two important factors, especially important to this target group. To get more insight into the structure of the therapy and the reasons behind certain activities, she decided to describe the music therapeutical model that was developed during her work experiences with refugees.

The following description of a music therapy method with groups in an ambulatory setting has unfolded within a multidisciplinary treatment model and in a treatment program consisting of five phases (see Chapter 10 of this volume). The described methods are the strategies that form the focal point in the concerned period. Furthermore, other strategies were used to introduce or to support the central approach.

The Treatment Setting

Music therapy is part of a day treatment program where the structured group psychotherapy forms a focal point. The group psychotherapy is structured according to a five-phase model. The total treatment lasted 12 months.

The treatment is followed in its entirety by a consistent group of eight men or women speaking the same language. The group has one interpreter, who sits in on all sessions of the therapy. The group comes to the day treatment three times a week. The treatment program consists of group psychotherapy, psychomotor therapy, art therapy, and music therapy. The group has one permanent confident/sociotherapist who participates in all therapies with the group. The music therapy takes place once a week for 90 minutes. Through the diversity of the therapy offered, the client has various possibilities to shape the therapy process. The various parts of the therapy supplement each other greatly.

The music therapy in this model runs parallel to the group psychotherapy phases. In every phase a specific approach to the music therapy has a central role. The music therapy is divided into the following five phases (see Chapter 10 in this volume), as also outlined in Table 17.1:

1. Getting acquainted
2. Stabilization
3. Looking back
4. Looking to the present and the future
5. Farewell

Music therapeutic strategies within the five-phase model focus on the following routines:

TABLE 17.1 Overview of the Five-Phase Model and the Music Therapeutic Approaches in the Five Separate Phases

	Phase	Central Strategy	Goal
Phase 1	Getting acquainted	Rhythm exercise in 4/4 time	Introduction offer safety Musical skills
Phase 2	Stabilization	The orchestra (musical role play)	Inventory of the musical skills of each client Extending his or her strong points
Phase 3	Looking back	Musical story supporting verbal exposure	Focus on emotions in the story
Phase 4	Looking at the present and the future	Musical life story	Integration of the past and the future in the actual self-image
Phase 5	Farewell	Exercises to say farewell Own choice of repeats of previously used routines	What experiences were important? What can I say about: my way of playing music; my own choice of musical forms; my position in the group? How can this be useful for me after the treatment?

Phase 1. Rhythm exercise in 4/4 time
Phase 2. The orchestra (musical role-play)
Phase 3. The musical story
Phase 4. The musical life story
Phase 5. Practices to say farewell

Phase 1: Getting Acquainted

The group consists of eight people. These are asylum seekers and refugees with a complex PTSD and the psychopathology linked to this disorder. Their feeling of safety is often severely damaged. Therefore, it is of utmost importance that the participants experiencing the therapy feel they are in a safe environment.

During their treatment, many asylum seekers are still unsure about their status. At that moment it is not yet decided whether they will get a status that grants them permission to stay in the Netherlands or not.

Also, due to this, in the beginning many clients find it difficult to confide in the group and in the music therapy group approach. On the one hand, the need for help is great; but at the same time, they fear they will shortly lose this support again.

Most clients are not familiar with music therapy and the therapy takes place in what is a foreign language for them. The beginning of the treatment is aimed to create a sense of safety. After a short introduction to get to know the therapist and the group, the group members get information about what music therapy is, the goal of the music therapy, and the structure of the music therapy in five phases.

The therapist explains the various ways people could react to music. Concrete examples are given: for example, somebody can have problems with loud sounds. But it is also possible that certain music pieces (familiar melodies) or certain musical instruments (sometimes totally unexpected) can evoke painful memories from the past. There are clients who find it hard or cannot cope with these emotions.

In view of the effects of the music therapy, the therapist, with the group, agrees to some clear rules. Every participant could at any moment indicate that the music must stop. He or she could also choose to leave the room for a while, so the client unable to cope with feelings does not interrupt the music process for the rest of the group. When such situations occur, we immediately look for ways to be able to get to grips with the feelings that have arisen, sometimes with words, but often with a form of music.

For many clients the rhythm exercises in phase 1 form a safe starting point. They are simple and most clients can take part. These exercises aim to acquire basic musical skills. You get to know each other (the group), the therapist, and the music as a means of communication.

Strategies in Phase 1: Rhythm Exercises in 4/4 Time

This strategy consists of practicing various rhythms in 4/4 time. For these exercises only rhythm instruments are used, like bongos, congas, rhythm sticks, and xylophones. The session starts with practicing the 4/4 tones, rhythm c., and the whole group plays them. On the first count an accent (more forceful hit) is played. This is followed by three other variations (other rhythms in 4/4 time) practiced with the complete group (see below).

```
      Rhythm exercise 4/4 time
      1       2       3       4
a.    O   ~   ~   ~   ~   ~   ~   ~    O= beat on the drum or other
b.    O   ~   ~   ~   O   ~   ~   ~    instrument
c.    O   ~   O   ~   O   ~   O   ~    c. = basic rhythm
d.    O   O   O   O   O   O   O   O    the exercise repeats itself
```

Next the therapist plays the basic rhythm (4 quarter notes). The group members add one of the four rhythms they practiced to this basic rhythm. They may vary this when they feel like it. The group members should continuously count out the 4 quarter tones of the basic rhythm (the beat) during play, in order to harmonize their own rhythm to the basic rhythm. This can be done literally by counting (silently), or they could feel it by tapping their feet. This is an example of a rhythm exercise.

On the white board the diagram with the 4/4 rhythm exercise is drawn and in the circle various rhythm instruments are available. I start to play the basic rhythm and the group quickly joins me. The group members mainly react to me. They observe my hands on the drum. They do not look around much yet.

Hassan cannot get the accent on the first count. He tries by counting along, but still is a fraction too late. He moves the drum sticks in a very jerky way.

Mohammed has chosen a tambourine. During play he becomes more enthusiastic. For Mohammed it is not necessary to count the beat, he taps his foot and sways his body. When I ask him to vary the rhythms, he loses the rhythm.

Ali has a cymbal on a stand with a drumstick. He chooses to just play the first count with an enormous hit as an accent. He tends to increase the speed but I keep him back by continue to play the 4 quarter tones in the basic rhythm

When they stop playing, Hassan says that he could not participate very well because the hits on the cymbal frightened him. He says that it felt like he was hit over the head. In spite of our agreement, that the music could always be interrupted, Hassan did not manage to interrupt the rhythm exercise. For the next practice he indicates which instruments are less threatening. We also agree that if he cannot stop the playing he could go out.

Mohammed is very content. He experienced the rhythm exercise as a relief. By playing he temporarily did not have to worry about all of his problems.

Ali sits quietly and says that he frightened himself and feels guilty toward the group. The group says that his contribution fitted nicely in the overall atmosphere. A number of other group members would like to try again.

I tell them that music sometimes can release feelings, which could frighten you. Afterward the group is very content about the results of the exercise: "Fancy that we could already play this together!"

Experiences With the Rhythm Exercises

These are some of the experiences of the participants in a rhythm exercise.

1. Participating in rhythm exercises strengthens the harmony in the group. Harmony strengthens the feeling of safety. At the beginning of the treatment the clients do not know each other very well. Nevertheless, in a rhythm exercise they can already create a complete piece of music together, and this enhances the group cohesion.

2. Through the simplicity of the 4/4 time, everybody can cope and join in. It is possible to vary later to the 6/8 time. Most clients find the 6/8 time more difficult.
3. The measure in which a client can surrender to the group rhythm corresponds to the measure in which he can, for a while, forget dominating thoughts (e.g., about the trauma).
4. In this phase, the therapist is not yet trying to find out more about the personal background of the client, but only to get acquainted to each other, in the "here and now" through the medium of music. Taking into account the fear and the suspicion of many clients, this practice seems a good opening to the therapy.

Phase 2: Stabilization

In phase 2 of the treatment the clients mainly aim to reach a personal balance. We pay attention to the complaints of a complex PTSD. Furthermore, we now work toward experiencing positive feelings. In the next phase, we need those positive experiences to be enforced to look back at the trauma.

In this phase, experimenting plays a central role. In doing so, the client finds out which musical instruments he or she prefers and which instruments are best suited to express his or her feelings. The client will also slowly start to find out that he or she relates to some ways of playing better than to others, for instance, playing on your own or playing ensemble with others; playing loudly or softly; playing a dominating instrument or following; fast or slower music.

The music therapeutic routines in this phase aim to find out which forms of music playing the client can cope with and which he or she cannot handle and will block his or her abilities. In this way the capabilities of the client will be unearthed within the (protecting) boundaries of music.

The therapist emphasises what the client can cope with, and these will be extended upon during the treatment.

Strategies in Phase 2: The Orchestra (Musical Role-Play)

In this musical role-play the clients each get a card with the role they will play in the orchestra. These roles are: one conductor/leader; five members of the orchestra/followers; one member of the orchestra, who twice produces a musical surprise; and one member of the orchestra, who twice causes a musical disturbance.

The cards cannot be shown to one another. Everybody finds an instrument fitting their roles. Then the conductor (with or without an instrument of his or her own) starts the music. The conductor also decides when the piece is finished. When play is over, the group members guess which role the others played.

In the second attempt the group members give their cards from the first round to a member of the group whom they think can play the role well. The beginning and the end of the piece are again decided by the leader (conductor). Afterward the group members discuss how they experienced the roles they gave each other.

In the third part of the session, each group member can select a card for him- or herself with a role that he or she feels is appropriate. They can only use the existing cards and extra roles; a second leader or another follower may not be added.

At the end there is an evaluation: which role suited them best and which role did they not like to play. Also discussed is the reason why the group members passed the card/role to that special other participant. This is an example of a musical role-play.

> The group is seated in a circle. I pass out the cards. The clients read the card with their roles. Immediately you can hear reactions from the group, varying from "oh nooo!" to a satisfactory "Yesss!" The participants immediately find a suitable instrument. I will assist those who have a problem with the selection.
>
> I emphasize the informal character of the musical exercies and try to create a relaxing atmosphere. When group members make jokes, I will stimulate this and make some remarks like: "We do not have to perform in the concert building," and "It cannot be wrong what you are doing."
>
> Ali has the role of leader and acts very nonchalantly. He starts to play on the big drum. When he plays, he directs his group with his drum sticks. He waves circles in air with the sticks and hardly indicates the rhythm. The followers find it hard to play along. Now everything together sounds chaotic. After a while Ali moves a bit closer to his neighbor, who has started to play a clear supporting rhythm. By linking into the rhythm of the neighbor, the music piece has gotten a clear foundation, and a clear regular rhythm is created. Now the surprises and disturbances get a chance.
>
> Fred is the one to surprise the group. He has collected an enormous array of instruments in front of him. In the beginning his music sounds very careful, but in due time he starts to play louder and faster. He creates something like a fireworks with an explosion at the end. The second time he uses the same build-up. After this, he has lots of fun playing with the group and makes a gestures in my direction, questioning whether he really only can do this twice.
>
> Hossein can cause a disturbance twice. He happily plays along with the group rhythm. Than he looks at his card again and stops his play.
>
> Ali tells us afterward that he is disappointed in the possibilities as a leader. "In Iran I was director of a major company and now I cannot even do this anymore!" Mohammed puts him at ease and tells him that it is quite possible that he is good in other things.
>
> Fred enjoyed his role in surprising the group. "Normally I am more of a follower, but this time I could really stand out. And after that, I could rejoin the group." The others are also surprised about the way he fulfilled his role and compliment him.
>
> Hossein says that he planned to first play along for a while and then suddenly disturb the basic rhythm of the leader with a different rhythm.
>
> It did not happen as he planned. He started to play along with the group and began to enjoy this. After some doubt, he decided not to obey

his role. He said that in his country, he witnessed the destruction of many things by the resistance and the struggle for power, and that he did not want to be part of such a thing any more. He did not want to disturb the playing together of the group (harmony).

Experiences With the Musical Role-Play

1. Working with role-play cards creates enthusiasm in many clients. Suddenly everything is allowed, as long as it is on the card. In their enthusiasm the clients drop their defensive guard (inhibitions) for a short while. This results in new experiences and unexpected emotions. Many clients have forgotten good experiences from before their trauma. Through this role-play, reactions arise that are connected to the unreachable (closed off) experiences from the past. Often these are positive experiences from before the trauma: "In the past I was a good leader, I was the director of a factory." "Within my family I was active and looking for adventure." On the one hand, it is painful to find that such good experiences are lost. But there is also a positive side; namely, that there is still a possibility to activate these good aspects.

2. Another important effect of this role play is that the clients learn to overcome their own prejudices about certain roles in life. In the evaluation we found that many clients have a one-sided picture of leaders (conductors) and followers (members of the orchestra). This is founded on prejudices, which originated in the period when the trauma happened. Their own pattern of norms and values was damaged by exposure to mental and physical maltreatment. As a result, processes of power and impotence are experienced as absolute. They find it hard to modify thoughts about these concepts. Through the musical role-play the clients learn from one another that in a "normal" group process different graduations of leading and following are possible. On the whole it seems that during the treatment they learn to translate these different skills of leadership and following (working together) to their daily lives.

3. Through these role-plays, relationships within the group can be discussed in an informal way. Thus, we found that the relations in the group can be different during the various forms of therapy. Somebody might be full of initiative during psychomotor therapy, but during, for instance music therapy, he tends to sit back and wait a bit more. Discussing the relationships within the group is not a goal in itself in music therapy. During the music therapy it quickly becomes visible what group members support one another in the therapy process. And how they do this is based on the positions they hold in the group during the music sessions. Such group processes and experiences during the music therapy are part of the evaluations with (and by) the clients. By limiting these talks to music, clients are often able to discuss with one another more easily and freer. "When you lead

the improvisation on the bongos, I can play my role as follower much easier."
4. In this period, the therapist controls that the discussions after the music therapy sessions are limited to that which happened during the music. In this way negative feelings regarding the musical skills of group members can be discussed easier.

Phase 3: Looking Back

The third phase is an emotionally intensive period in the treatment. In group psychotherapy we look at the traumatic past through exposure (see Chapter 10 in this volume). During the music therapy, it is noticeable that the clients in this phase at the beginning of the therapy session tend to avoid direct contact with one another. Probably these defensive guards are erected so painful memories and feelings (which surface more quickly as a result of the exposure) can be handled again. Even though they are at this moment still quite self-centered, a feeling of involvement within the group as a whole is growing.

In this phase the clients are tired from all the impressions. This makes it harder to motivate them for active participation in the music therapy. On the other hand, in this phase it is even more important to work toward a certain musical form. In the group psychotherapy, the clients have started to talk in detail about their traumatic experiences. The story they tell has unearthed a broken soul. In this vulnerable situation, the clients are offered the possibility to share the feelings that have arisen with the group.

In their stories clients often cannot find suitable words for their feelings. In the trauma stories, feelings like grief, anger, shame, and guilt are all mixed up. In their stories, they often reach contrasting feelings. When they use music, the story does not always make sense and does not have to be explained. The emotions that have arisen can be expressed plainly, and they automatically fall into place in the music. Verbal and grammatical logic do not hamper this process.

Repeated confrontation with traumatic memories is an important part of dealing with the trauma. During the exposure phase the clients who are telling their stories in the group psychotherapy are also the main clients in the music therapy. In music therapy the client gets the opportunity to retell his or her trauma story, but now in a musical shape. The main goal is to share the feelings that have arisen after the exposure session When the client feels he or she cannot keep control over his or her feelings when playing alone, he or she can select to play the musical story together with other members of his or her group.

Strategies in Phase 3: The Musical Story

The client (the storyteller) selects on his or her own an instrument he or she will use for his or her story. Sometimes the storyteller selects more than one instrument. The storyteller is then asked to react in a musical way to his or her own trauma story, which he or she has already told in the group psychotherapy (though not in exactly the same way). Beforehand the storyteller can ask a member of the group (or the therapist) to give him or her musical support at those moments he or she needs them. Together they decide what instrument the fellow group member will use to accompany the group member and what sign the storyteller will use to indicate when he or she should start and stop again. After the improvisation, the group immediately provides a musical reaction. Definitely not a verbal reaction! The storyteller now listens to the group and after this the storyteller decides whether he or she wants to add something or not.

The storyteller can also select to do a musical improvisation with the whole group together. He or she decides what instruments will be used. The client indicates what kind of music to use (e.g., start very loudly and finish sweetly, or the music should feel sad and then angry). From the beginning he or she decides the direction of the improvisation for the whole group. Signs are agreed upon to indicate changes of speed, instruments, or loudness. The storyteller keeps control during the entire piece, in contrast to the moments of the trauma, when the client had no power. After this improvisation the group immediately provides a musical reaction. The storyteller now listens to the group. Afterward the storyteller is called upon to indicate whether the piece (and the reaction of the group) fulfilled his or her expectations and intentions. In some instances the piece is repeated. This is an example of a musical story.

> Mohammed enters the room and immediately aims for the guitar. He takes it to his chair and waits for the rest of the group to enter. He says he would like to play on his own and invites Hassan to accompany him when necessary. Together they select the drum for Hassan to play on. Mohammed will look at Hassan to signal him to help and say "stop" when he wants to continue alone.
>
> The group is perfectly silent and Mohammed starts. The guitar is an unknown instrument to him. In the beginning he is examining the possibilities of the instrument, but soon he finds a number of sounds he uses to play a rhythm and he is able to repeat a number of times.
>
> His story begins when he plays sliding tones on one string, from low to high. The music is slow and sounds as if someone is crying. Suddenly the music changes into a rhythmic beat and something that sounds like chords. Mohammed starts to increases the speed he picks the strings. The speed goes up and up. After a while he looks at Hassan. Hassan accompanies Mohammed for some time in the increased tempo, but then he slows the music to a calmer rhythm. Mohammed follows and also plays slower, in the same rhythm as Hassan. They continue for a bit in the slower speed and then Mohammed finishes the music.
>
> The other group members now each select an instrument and promptly start to play in the same calm rhythm Mohammed and Hassan have just finished in. A number of group members also choose a snare instrument and play sliding tones like Mohammed did. Others play bongos and xylophones. The whole piece stays peaceful, with a simple

rhythm and no big changes in the dynamics. The players finish one after the other.

Mohammed continues to let the music take hold of him and the group also stays quiet. Then he says that he quickly wants to explain some things.

For his music he used two feelings as starting points: sadness and anger. He thought the guitar to be a good symbol. He had not tried it before for fear that it would evoke too many feelings. At present, it was no longer a hindrance to his play. He is content about his own performance, but he could not find a satisfactory end. He could not let go of those angry feelings. That was the reason he invited Hassan. He felt that the group reaction was fitting to his own piece.

Experiences With the Musical Story

1. In practice not all clients can cope with the first approach in this phase (individual routine). They often select the alternative second approach (to play together with the whole group). They are still engulfed in their own emotions and are unable to come out with these feelings on their own. The structure of the second form leaves the client the possibility to listen to his or her feelings in music in a more distant way, then by playing on his or her own. Clients should always choose the form in which they feel they will not lose control over their feelings. When after some time they still want to tell their own story individually, this will always be made possible. In this period, the clients find it most important that every therapy sessions follows the same set structure. In due course, after more sessions, it seems that the group will guard these structures even more strongly. In each group certain rituals start to grow and become part of the weekly routine. They have to take place every week (e.g., the pauses between the pieces, shaking hands after the group finished playing their piece, etc.).

2. Within the music therapy the client is able to tell the trauma story again, after he or she has already told it in the group psychotherapy, but now in a musical shape. Contrasting feelings more easily find a place in the music. After his or her own musical story the storyteller gets a musical reaction from the whole group. In this musical shape, the story is experienced together again, because the other group members know the story already from the group psychotherapy. In this way the suffering of the storyteller is shared all over again, with the others. Every time we find that the storyteller experiences this as a major support.

3. In this phase the therapist assists the client to find a suitable musical structure, where he or she finds a safe place for all the feelings that play a role in his or her trauma story.

Phase 4: Looking at Present and Future

In the next phase the client has to integrate the past from before the trauma and the trauma experience into a new self-image. Central to this phase are the following questions: "To what extent did I become a different person by my trauma experience?" "What goals can I reach?" "How do I look at the future?"

The musical therapeutic approach in phase 4 is aimed to a reintegration of past, present, and future. In this phase every client gets the assignment to compose in some way a musical piece, namely a musical life story.

Strategies in Phase 4: The Musical Life Story

The client gets the assignment to tell his life story with the help of music. The main thread in this life story is past, present, and future. The clients are offered two possibilities to tell their life stories. The first routine uses existing music on cassette or on CD. The client makes a selection of existing musical pieces. This selection should reflect his or her life story in three episodes: past, present, and future. The clients can use music from the music collection available in the music therapy area, music from a local library, or his or her own music.

The guidelines are that they use a maximum of two pieces per episode and that they use three sessions for the preparation. During the preparatory sessions the therapist is available for assistance and consultation. When the life story is ready, we immediately plan in which coming session the life story will be presented to the group. Either before or after the presentation, the client will explain the reasons for the selection of his or her music.

In the second form the client him- or herself plays his or her musical life story. This also has three parts: past, present, and future. Here also the guideline is that the preparation should maximally take three sessions. The client can ask fellow group members to accompany him or her and assist in the preparation of his or her musical life story. During the preparatory sessions the therapist can also be asked for assistance.

Either before or after the presentation, the client will explain how he or she has structured the music pieces and the reason for the selection of the instruments. In case the client wants to listen to the life story afterward, the session is recorded on cassette. This is an example of a musical life story.

> Hassan would like to do his life story using existing music. He frequently listens to music on his Walkman. He has a lot of music available, but the selection of the final pieces is a problem (maximal two for each phase). Hassan is doubtful about the placing of the trauma. Should it be placed in the past or in the present? Or does the past have two parts; before and after the trauma?

He selects to reserve the past for a period of good memories and shows this with a song from Cindy Lauper: "Girls Just Wanna Have Fun." It is a song his mother happily used to sing along at home in Iran.

Hassan reserved the present for the flight from Iran and the period of treatment in the day treatment center for refugees. He selects two pieces. The first is by Pink Floyd : "Hey Teacher, Leave Those Kids Alone" (The Wall). With this song Hassan wants to symbolize the period of resistance against the regime in Iran and against the suppression and the torturing.

The second piece is a traditional Iranian tune Hassan has on a tape of his own. He translates the title as follows: "Do Know What Happened to Us." Hassan wants to symbolize with this piece how important it was to him to be able to tell his trauma story in the therapy in the day treatment, both to the fellow group members as well as to the therapists.

Hassan expresses the future again with two pieces. The first is again a traditional Iranian tune he has on tape. It is piano music titled "Golden Mountains." The music gives him a feeling that he has momentarily returned to the familiar landscape of Iran. And that offers a moment of peace.

The second number is a Dutch song by Klein Orkest: "Over de muur" (Over the Wall). The bird in the song can choose where it wants to fly (to East or to West Berlin), while for the people there is a wall between East and West. Hassan would like to see his future similarly: free to fly between Iran and the Netherlands.

Hassan thinks it is important that this is a Dutch number, sung in Dutch. As Hassan has started to feel more familiar with the Dutch language and he feels that Dutch will be part of his future.

Experiences With the Musical Life Story

1. Telling your life story with existing music is chosen far more often, than the second approach, where you play your own music.
2. Listening to the music from your own past often evokes memories and emotions, which the clients sometimes find hard to handle. Many clients find that this approach gives them a chance to place the music from their own pasts in their present day lives. In this way, in the protected environment of the therapy, the music of the past finds a new place in their future.
3. At the beginning of this strategy in phase 4, many clients find it extremely difficult to make a definitive selection of only one of two pieces of music per episode. At the evaluation of their life stories we find that all clients eventually were happy with the limitation of two pieces (or sometime only one) per episode. The selected pieces take on an even greater meaning for them than they had at the start. During the sessions in between the clients discuss among themselves or with the therapist the content of a certain song or musical piece and about the special meaning it has in relation to their life stories.
4. Some clients select the second possibility to play their life stories themselves. The client plays the music to his or her life story in front of the group. He or she may ask and get assistance from one or more fellow group members. One advantage of this approach is that in this

way, during play, the life story is actively experienced. Often we can see this in the body language during play.

5. In this period the therapist stimulates choices to be made. These two approaches offer the client ample opportunities for each, in their own way, to look back at their lives and look ahead at the future. As regards to the expectation of the future, large differences can eventuate, mainly under the influence of their actual status as refugee and the permission to stay in this country or not.

Phase 5: Farewell (to the Treatment)

The last phase of the treatment is assigned to the rounding off of the treatment and leaving the group. In the music therapy the theme farewell is looked at from three angles:

1. Evaluation; looking back to the treatment (music therapy).
2. Looking ahead; how will the client shortly continue under his own steam, when the day treatment has finished.
3. Physical departure from the group (and the therapist).

In this phase the therapist will look back with each client to the music therapy process of the past year (phases 1 to 4), and the way the client has developed in this period through the music therapy. We especially look at the choice of instruments, the various ways of playing together with the fellow group members, and the attitude toward the other group members and the therapist. In this period all clients in turn can select a routine that was used during the past year and they would like to do again. Furthermore, two new routines will be introduced, aimed at the physical departure from the group (during a joint music exercise).

Strategies in Phase 5: Repetitions and Practices in Leaving

The repetitions of routines from previous phases of the treatment take a central place. The clients can select any routine they would like to repeat. Afterward there is an evaluation: "Why did the client want to repeat this routine?" The goal of these exercises is that every client will evaluate his or her own music therapy process (looking back on the treatment).

Furthermore, two new practices will be used, aimed at the physical departure from the group. First, the clients each select an instrument. Player 1 begins to play a rhythm or melody. After a while Player 2 joins him or her and then a bit later Player 3, and so on until all the others have joined. So in the end all eight group members, the entire group, play ensemble for a while. Then Player 2 stops. One by one players 3 to 8 also stop playing; only Player 1 continues and plays on for a while on his or her own. Eventually also Player 1 stops playing. Next the same practice is repeated a number of times, with every time a different group member getting to play the role of Player 1.

Then an evaluation takes place: "How did you like playing on your own and ensemble with the others?" "How did you like to listen to the music made by the fellow group members when you were not participating yourself?" "How did you experience your role as Player 1, when the other group members finished one by one?" "How did you find it to eventually finish up playing all on your own?"

The clients each select an instrument. One client (volunteer) starts to play. Then the other group members join him or her one by one, until all eight group members play ensemble. Then the group members are asked to each stop twice during play. The first time the client should listen carefully to the music of the group without him- or herself. After a while, in his or her head, the client has to select one of the group as the player he or she would like to play with. When he or she rejoins the group, that client will concentrate on following this selected player. In this way he or she becomes more aware of joining the others again in their play.

When the client stops for the second time, it is the definite end and the client now has finished his or her contribution to the music of the group. One by one all group members stop play. So each group member selects his or her own moment to stop.

Afterward an evaluation takes place: "How did you like playing on your own and ensemble with the others?" "How did you like to listen to the music made by the fellow group members when you were not participating yourself?" "Which group member did you select when you rejoined the group? Why did you select him or her? "How did you experience the moment when you yourself decided to definitely finish playing?" This is an example of the farewell practice.

> Ali would like to try the first exercise. This means that he will start to play and that the group joins him one by one and then also finishes one by one. At the end Ali can finish the piece on his own.
>
> He chooses a glockenspiel as his instrument. After Ali all other group members select their instruments (instruments they feel work well together with the instrument of Ali). The instruments selected are varied, including kettledrums, rhythm eggs, rhythm sticks, and a bamboo flute.
>
> Ali starts to play. He uses two tones, which he repeats continuously in a simple rhythm. After two group members have joint him, he does find more tones and he varies the rhythm. When the kettledrums join in, Ali loses the rhythm. But after a bit he quickly falls back to the old rhythm he started with and limits himself to the two tones from the beginning. When the whole group plays ensemble Ali manages to vary his play again. Now he looks around at his fellow players and he smiles. A number of times he returns to his old rhythm from the beginning, but every time he quickly starts to look for more variations.
>
> It takes some time before the first player who joined the group stops to play. At a certain point Ali indicates that the first player should stop.

Most of the group members now stop shortly after one another, until only three are left: Ali himself, the bamboo flute, and a player with samba balls. The three players continue animated. Two players accompany Ali the soloist. From time to time Ali stops play and looks for still new variations. At one moment he uses the glockenspiel as a rhythm instrument by tapping it on the side. Then he rubs his sticks over the tubes of the glockenspiel, producing sliding sounds from high to low.

When the sound of the samba balls stops, you see Ali thinking of also stopping. He looks up to me but decides to continue. Next follows a short duet with the player on the bamboo flute. Ali returns to the old rhythm of the beginning. Shortly after the flute player also stops. Ali continues solo for a while, playing the same rhythm as in the beginning of the exercise.

In the evaluation Ali, tells us that he wanted to try to see if he could fulfill his role as leader better this time than during the musical role-play, when he was very disappointed with what he achieved in his role as leader (see phase 2 in the musical role-play above).

During the therapy process Ali changed his choice of instruments. In the beginning he mostly selected big drums like the kettledrums. Now he prefers smaller instruments and also more melodic instruments.

Ali indicates that on a smaller instrument he feels more confident, and he manages to play a set rhythm easier. That is why he selected a glockenspiel for this exercise. At the moment the kettledrum joined him with great volume in a strong rhythm, he got confused for a bit. But shortly after he regained his composure and the rhythm. This was an important experience for Ali.

At the end of happily playing together with the whole group, Ali found it difficult when his fellow players had to stop one by one. Later on, when there were only three players left a similar situation occurred.

Ali had a good feeling when he did his improvisations and he could extend his own possibilities from the firm base rhythm, laid down by the two fellow players who accompanied him.

He did not think much of his own beginning rhythm, but it was functional. All in all he found, that he played his role as leader a lot better this time. Furthermore, he now does not associate this leading role in the music any longer with his role, long ago, as director.

Experiences With the Farewell Exercises

1. The musical skills of the clients at the end of the treatment are very diverse. They have found out their possibilities and limitations in communicating through their music with the rest of the group.
2. Repeating the practices from previous phases of the treatment, actually seem quite suitable to start an evaluation process. In this manner every client will be able to look back at his or her development during the music therapy process. Often we also find points of contact with the changes taking place in their daily life during the period of the day treatment.
3. During the reduction of the number of players at the end of the improvisation (first exercise), when the players stop one by one, you can clearly hear what part/support is taken away from the group. The clients feel it is important to be able to verbalize this. Often this leads to a spontaneous look forward to the period after the day treatment:

"In the coming time I will miss your support." These prospects often start off with a look to the past and to the flight from their home country. During their flight, many clients did not get the opportunity to say farewell to their families and friends.

4. For the first farewell exercise, every time a different Player 1 is discussed separately in the evaluation. In this way every client has his or her turn to experience how it feels to continue without the support of the group. By talking about this in the evaluation, every client gets an opportunity to look ahead to the period after the day treatment. In reality this physical farewell from the group in a music exercise causes many different feelings for the clients. In this way many expectations and feelings about the period after the day treatment can be discussed.

5. The therapist says farewell to every client individually by playing together with each of them one more time. Finally the therapist and the client together do a short review of the past year of his or her music therapy.

EXPERIENCES WITH MUSIC THERAPY IN OTHER GROUPS

Working with people from all over the world is fascinating. During the years of our research there were so many surprises. At the end of our chapter we want to present you a few examples that could be useful in working with people from other cultures.

Working with multilingual international male or female groups of a supportive type or with supportive groups of Lingala-speaking clients from Africa (Angola, Congo), the therapist cannot apply the above-described model designed for trauma-focused treatment without necessary adaptations. However, some exercises from the five-phase model can be used universally and result in interesting phenomena when applied across different genders and cultures.

The rhythm exercise used in the first treatment phase was, for our clients from the Middle East, usually a brand new experience, and one not always easily handled. It appeared that making music and sounds was not something they were used to. Our clients from Africa did not have any problems with this exercise at all. "The music is in our blood," is what we there told by those clients playing instruments with a surprisingly good technique. Neither the Middle Eastern nor the African clients had any significant experiences with making music.

In the female groups the musical role-play results in a lot of pleasure. It seems that female clients handle this exercise in a more natural and relaxed way than males do, and they enjoy the exercise very much.

Finding musical symbols to describe experiences from one's past seems to be easier for clients from the Middle East (Iran, Afghanistan) than for those originating from Africa. The latter group provided much resistance during this exercise. Another form had to be developed. Memories of the past can also be reached using traditional songs or ritual songs. Religious songs are also of great value. "When I sing about my lost children, I have the feeling I can still do something for them, I don't want to think about what happened in the past anymore." And the farewell rituals are different in every group of clients. Sometimes joyful, with lots of laugh, dancing, and singing, and at other times with few words and "sounds." Using music therapy in supportive groups enables the therapist to work in a less structured way and to incorporate exercises that address more individual needs of clients.

CONCLUSION

Working with traumatized refugees demands authenticity, warmth in interpersonal contact, and genuine interest for traumatized clients and their life stories. Besides that, the therapist needs to have good basic tools — instruments and recorded music material. We described our efforts to develop a methodology and such a set of tools.

REFERENCES

Austin, D. (1999). Vocal improvisation in analytically oriented music therapy with adults. In T. Wigram & J. De Backer (Eds.), *Clinical applications of music therapy in psychiatry.* London: Jessica Kingsley Publishers.

Austin, D. (2002). The wounded healer: The voice of trauma: A wounded healer's perspective. In J. Sutton (Ed.), *Music, music therapy and trauma: International perspectives* (pp. 231–259). London and Philadelphia: Jessica Kingsley Publishers.

Bonny, H. L. (1986). Music and healing. *Music Therapy, 6A*(1), 3–12

Bruscia, K. E. (1987). *Improvisational models of music therapy.* Springfield, IL: Charles C. Thomas Publisher.

Davies, J. M. & Frawley, M. G. (1994). *Treating the adult survivor of childhood sexual abuse: A psychoanalytic perspective.* New York: Basic Books.

Drogendijk, A. (2000). *Phoenix. Verslag van een stage op afdeling Phoenix* [Account of a term of probation at Phoenix] P.C. *"De Gelderse Roos."* Wolfheze: Clinical Psychology, University of Utrecht.

Kirmayer, L. (2002, December 12–15). *Failures of imagination: The refugee's narrative in psychiatry.* Presented at the Trauma, Culture and the Brain Conference, Los Angeles.

Lang, L., & McInerney, U. (2002). Bosnia-Herzegovina: A music therapy service in a post-war environment. In J. Sutton (Ed.), *Music, music therapy and trauma: International perspectives* (pp. 153–174). London and Philadelphia: Jessica Kingsley Publishers.

Levine, P. A. (1997). *Waking the tiger: Healing trauma.* Berkeley: CA: North Atlantic Books.

Limburg-Okken, A. (1989). *Migranten in de psychiatrie* [Migrants in psychiatry]. Deventer: Van Loghum Slaterus.

Orth, J. J. (1992). Music therapy met Vietnamese refugees. In J. T. V. M. de
    Jong & R. J. M. Wesenbeek (Eds.), *Vervreemd of vreemdeling: Naar een inter-
    culturele geestelijke gezondheidszorg in Nederland* (pp. 97–104). Amsterdam:
    Koninklijk Instituut voor de Tropen.
Orth, J. J. (2001). Between abandoning and control: Structure, security and
    expression in music therapy with traumatised refugees in a psychiatric
    clinic. In M. Verwey (Ed.), *Trauma and empowerment* (pp. 189–197). Ber-
    lin: VWB, Verlag fur Wissandschaft und Bildung.
Orth, J. J., & Verburgt, J. (1998). One step beyond: Music therapy with trauma-
    tised refugees in a psychiatric clinic. In D. Dokter (Ed.), *Arts therapists, ref-
    ugees and migrants: Reaching across borders* (pp. 80–93). London and
    Philadelphia: Jessica Kingsley Publishers.
Orth, J. J. (2002). Tussen overgave en controle: verlag van een workshop op con-
    gres Culturen op de vlucht [Between abandoning and control: an account of
    a workshop at conference Cultures on the run]. In H. Bot, L. Preijde, M.
    Braakman, & W. Wassink (Eds.), *Culturen op de vlucht* [Cultures on the run]
    (pp. 141–145). Wolfheze: De Gelderse Roos.
Priestley, M. (1975). *Music therapy in action.* London: Constable and Company
    Limited.
Sears, W. (2002). *Music therapy principals.* Retrieved August 14, 2002, from
    http://www.warchild.org/projects/centre/princip.html.
Smeijsters, H. (1989). Musica Humana: Opstellen over de uitwerking van muz-
    iek op de mens. Gebundelde teksten van lezingen en colleges aan de
    Katholieke Universiteit Nijmegen, de Afdeling Creatieve Therapie van de
    Hogeschool Nijmegen, de Sector Conservatorium van de Hogeschool van
    Enschede, de Nederlandse Vereniging voor Creatieve Therapie en de Rijk-
    suniversiteit van Groningen.
Smeijsters, H. (1991). *Muziektherapie als psychotherapie.* Assen: Van Gorcum.
Smeijsters, H. (1995). *Handboek Muziektherapie: Theoretische en methodische
    grondslagen voor de behandeling van psychische stoornissen en handicaps.*
    Heerlen: Melos.
Smeijsters, H. (2000). *Handboek creatieve therapie.* Bussum: Uitgeverij Coutinho.
Sutton, J. P. (2000). *Music, music therapy and trauma.* International Perspectives.
    J. P. Sutton (Ed.). London and Philadelphia: Jessica Kingsley Publishers.
van den Hurk, J., & Smeijsters, H. (1991). Musical improvisation in the treat-
    ment of a man with obsessive compulsive personality disorder. In K. E.
    Bruscia (Ed.), *Case studies in musictherapy.* Phoenixville, PA: Barcelona
    Publishers.
van der Kolk, B. (Ed.). (1987). *Psychological trauma.* Washington, DC: Ameri-
    can Psychiatric Press.
van Dijk, R. (2001). Culture, trauma, and the lifeworld of refugees. In M. Ver-
    wey (Ed.), *Trauma and empowerment* (pp. 19–40). Berlin: VWB, Verlag fur
    Wissenschaft und Bildung. Web site: The Mostar Music Centre (2002).
    (Music Therapy Methods). Retrieved December 14, 2002.
Zharinova-Sanderson, O. (2002). Therapie in musik: Entdeckungen, problemen
    und ideen aus der musiktherapie mit folterüberlebenden und traumatisierten
    flüchtlingen [Therapy in music: Discoveries, problems and notions in music
    therapy with survivors of torture and traumatized refugees]. In A. Birck, C.
    Pross, & J. Lansen (Eds.), *Das unsagbare. Die arbeit mit traumatisierten im
    behandlungszentrum für folteropfer Berlin* [The unspeakable. Working with
    traumatized clients in Treatment Centre for Victims of Torture in Berlin].
    Berlin: Springer-Verlag.

Treatment of Special Populations: Gender and Developmental Considerations

Treatment of Special Populations: Gender and Developmental Considerations

Introduction

JOHN P. WILSON

Part V contains three chapters that focus on gender, children, and adolescents who are asylum seekers and refugees. Age, developmental status, and gender differences are important to understand when designing specialized treatment programs.

In Chapter 18, Joachim Walter and Julia Bala discuss the special needs of children and families who are asylum seekers. The needs of children are linked to the well-being of their parents. Trauma that brutalizes parents has a cascade effect on children. Likewise, children traumatized directly or indirectly by the stressors of fleeing, asylum seeking, and going on with life have a reciprocal influence on their parents, siblings, and families. These reciprocal and interactive effects of trauma and asylum seeking create unique and complex problems for families; namely, how to stay intact in healthy ways without succumbing to the overwhelming and seemingly endless demands that confront them in their host culture. This, then, is the dilemma faced by the therapist who works with children and their families.

In their chapter, Walter and Bala present a number of critical issues that must be addressed in clinical work with families and children, which include: (a) dealing with the day-to-day realities of cultural marginality; (b) framing an understanding of having been politically persecuted; (c) dealing with trauma to the family as a unit and children and siblings separately; (d) processing the traumatic aspects of migration and asylum seeking; (e) identifying adaptive and maladaptive behaviors in the host culture; (f) facing the realities of limitations in therapy, especially in light of cultural differences; and (g) jointly creating therapeutic goals. These therapeutic issues are complex and demanding, and the authors correctly point out that their enormity requires the establishment of a structured, safe therapeutic environment with clear objectives and mutually established treatment goals within a relatively short period of time.

In Chapter 19, Hubertus Adam and Jelly van Essen discuss the psychological problems of adolescent refugees in exile. The authors begin their chapter with reference to the statistics that indicate that between 1990–2000, 2 million children were killed in wars and armed conflicts throughout the world and over 1 million were orphaned. According to the UNHCR, nearly a half million people were seeking asylum in the year 2000.

The authors noted that the process of forced migration, exile, and refuge seeking is extraordinarily difficult for children, and that the stressors and trauma associated with fleeing, migrating, exile, and asylum seeking impact the naturally occurring developmental tasks and processes. For adolescents, these psychosocial tasks of development include separation from parents, identity formation, cognitive growth, cultural orientation, sexual development, and career orientation. The authors state: "refugee families, in particular, often find themselves in a position where the past is destroyed, the present is characterized by insecurity, and limitations to their range of action and the future remains unknown." The combined stressors of migration and the difficulties associated with adaptation to the host culture provide fertile ground for the manifestations of anxiety and depressive disorders in adolescents. Symptoms of traumatic exposure and PTSD are evident but can be masked in acting-out behaviors and substance abuse. In regard to diagnostic considerations, the authors suggest that at least three broad areas should be evaluated: (a) the history of traumatization, migration, and acculturation; (b) developmental strengths and coping mechanisms; and (c) the quality and availability of parental support. Following adequate assessment, treatment of adolescents involves several fundamental levels: (a) establishing stability and safety; (b) ensuring potential support and emotional well-being; (c) facilitating socialization within the host culture; and (d) attempting to normalize developmental growth trajectories and working toward resolution of the symptoms of traumatization.

It is an unfortunate truism that war, political upheavals, and the breakdown of society have differential effects for men and women. Throughout history, women have been sexually exploited in war. In the recent war in the former Yugoslavia (1991–1995), Muslim women and female children were selected to be raped and impregnated by Serbian forces as acts of domination, power, and religious degradation with long-term socioeconomic consequences for those who survive. Women are also enslaved, used as chattel, and relegated to inferior status by dominant males in the country of exile and sometimes in the place where they seek asylum, freedom, and a new life.

In Chapter 20, Marianne C. Kastrup and Libby Arcel describe *gender specific treatment* for refugees and asylum seekers. To begin, they note that there is a paucity of reliable statistical data on the prevalence and severity of psychiatric disorders among women refugees. However, clinical experience in work with refugees and asylum seekers clearly documents the presence of polytraumatization and stress-related disorders, such as PTSD. Further, many refugee women have little or no knowledge of psychotherapy and appear to be reluctant to access services for treatment. And those who are offered traditional Western-oriented treatments can be uncomfortable with "talk therapy" for fears of reprisals or that the listener will not understand what they have endured because of its horrific nature. The authors correctly note that many refugees, and especially women who have been sexually violated, are extremely reluctant to discuss such experiences and that silence is a sign of fear and feelings of vulnerability rather than repression. However, in order to make integrative gains in working through their traumatic experience, they need to experience the therapist as a consistent, trustworthy, compassionate person who connects to them as a woman. This connection of women to women is particularly critical since it provides a trauma membrane by which to insulate the psychically bruised and battered women from the traumatic legacies of her experiences and at the same time gives her models of compassion, hope, and identification.

18

Where Meanings, Sorrow, and Hope Have a Resident Permit: Treatment of Families and Children

JOACHIM WALTER AND JULIA BALA

Today's warfare and political persecution very often aim not only at combatants and political activists but usually include spouses and children as targets of repression, violation of human rights, and as victims. Destroying the enemy's future by destroying the hope that rests on children and through violating spouses has been a central aim in many historical or present-day conflicts. In this chapter we — two family therapists who have worked with refugee families in exile — want to point out the effects of political trauma on the family, to describe the interactive and intergenerational effects of man-made stresses through persecution and war, and examine the role of family in surviving, coping, or even making positive use of the experiences they lived through. The positive effects of individual trauma-related psychotherapy can be of help to families as well, but we would here summarize our knowledge on the often complex interactive processes of coping with, communicating about, or dealing with cumulative stress that often requires a family-centered approach.

Refugee families in exile often emphasize that their decision to seek refuge in another country depended on considerations concerning their families. Political activism frequently includes as one of its conscious aims the wish to create a better future for the coming generations. Political defeat is often projected onto children. An old German song of the civil revolution in 1848 points at that, saying: "Defeated we are turning home, the children will have to resolve that on their own." However, protecting the families by seeking refuge somewhere else often also causes a sense of cowardice and defeat in parents for having left the avant-garde of the fight for their own reasons. If the protection itself is endangered by refusal of the asylum request or too lengthy uncertainty about it, the wish to create a better future for children leads to new defeat.

Life in exile, as pointed out in other chapters of this book, however, deals with more stresses than persecution or the primary and secondary effects of war in the country of origin. It deals with hope, with roots and a feeling of belonging, with gaps in the history of families, and with finding new possibilities of development, of coping, and last but not least often with social systems including the possibility to make use of psychotherapy or family therapy.

THE IMPACT OF CYCLICAL DISRUPTIONS

Families Belonging and Marginality

Social crises, war, and cultural revolution — main causes of migration and flight — often, already before flight, cause the ineffectiveness of previously functional coping mechanisms within families and society. That means that we are to be aware that each conflict does not start with war or persecution, but with tensions and marginalization. Usually it has its history often running through various generations.

If we look at parents' involvement in conflict that leads to possibly traumatic stresses, we often will find a mixture between historical roots, political and cognitive decisions and reflections, and neurotic reasons, which lead to engagement in conflict. Protest against one's own parents and the need to be able to feel as an actor, agent of change, can be one of the reasons to join revolutionary groups, religious aggregations, or parties in war. Many families entering into conflict or seeking refuge from conflict already have an important history of marginality. Some of them have learned to use it as a way of looking at the world and find it even useful; others feel frustrated, full of rage, or withdraw into passivity.

A sense of belonging to one's family, to one's sociocultural network, to the soil and landscape of one's country is one of the pillars of identity. In many cultures, as Parin (1992) has pointed out in his studies in Senegal, ego functioning depends on the functioning as a member of the group. He coined the term "group-ego" to depict that. This feeling of oneness with a group, the capacity to give meaning and act within this framework, is often questioned long before the open outbreak of civil conflict, political persecution, or international war. Marginality or critical integration[1] into exile will depend on the way the family is accepted during the very first days in exile, on the cultural proximity, respectively the wish to adapt one's culture intentionally. The dominating attitudes toward newcomers, governmental policies, and the availability of community resources facilitate or hinder the possibilities to find a way to belong to a new environment. The process of integration to the recipient country depends further on the existence of capacities of bonding to persons within the new society, the availability of subcultural groups, as well as on the opportunities to meet "wise" persons, "turning-point persons" as Goffman (1963) named them in his book on stigma. *Social marginality* is always a stressor, limiting the opportunities of refugee family members to reestablish their social and professional roles. In families where parents can accept that position as a price for safety, or where it is accepted as a temporary situation, the negative consequences of marginalization could be successfully counterbalanced.

The experience of *cultural marginality* is by many families we see not necessarily experienced as stressful, especially the ones with good capacities and resources. Being in the position to belong to more then one cultural group can contribute to a wider angle of perception as we know from many people moving freely between cultures. Hybrid identity (Akthar, 1995) in our sense means the capacity to feel part of a Creole culture. At best it gives the opportunity to participate at will in different cultures and be able to select by means of continuous cognitive and affective balancing what to accept and what to reject, that is, it can allow each of us to look at society and ones life not only as participant but also from a metacognitive position. We want to stress that no individual or family shares all of its society's values, norms, or rules, but in his or her individual culture selects from the range of possibilities, depending on the amount of conflicting or coexisting cultures permitted within the frame of one constantly developing culture. As Friedman (1982, p. 522, cited by di Nicola, 1997) puts it: "Families of all cultures have a tendency to select or emphasize from their culture's repertoire of customs and ceremonies those modes of behaviour that fit their own style."

---

[1] By the term critical integration Barudy, Paez, and Martens (1980) refer to the capacity to constantly draw cognitive and affective balances and reflect about which parts of the host culture to accept and which to reject.

Families Living Through Political Persecution and Torture

Torture has many aims, not only getting information, but intimidation of the whole society, by creating a state of terror, mistrust, and atomization. In order to deter people from engaging in political activities, it has to be known that individuals run a heavy risk of atrocious treatment when engaging in activities unwanted by the dominant social group. At the same time it has to be forbidden to speak openly about it in order to avoid upheaval. Most clearly, knowing and at the same time not being allowed to utter one's knowledge is intertwined in the fact that people, fathers and mothers, are taken prisoner and made to "disappear." *Disappearing* has many effects on the family: Constant preoccupation and insecurity govern family life. Fear of being persecuted oneself hinders searching for the disappeared. Normal processes of mourning, permitting the reconstruction of a planable future like reengaging in new partnerships or finding parent substitutes, are impossible, or they lead to moral dilemmas, feelings of guilt, and betrayal. Economical means of the family are being consumed by the search for the disappeared, lawyers costs consume further resources, and little time is left for wage-earning activities of the remaining family. Remaining parents are often physically, more important emotionally, absent. Children's small preoccupations and strives of daily life become negligible as compared to the sorrow for the disappeared person. Thus, disappearance of the family member paralyzes in a certain way the family life. Few families with disappeared members seek exile while one of the members is still being looked for. The families in exile with such a story usually are heavily burdened with an additional feeling of guilt and betrayal. Leaving a disappeared person behind means acknowledging death. However, once corpses have been found, going into exile is one of the possible consequences and conclusions.

Being engaged in *illegal or semilegal activities* against dictatorial regimes means that both spouses and children are not informed about the activities, leading to a split life, or that in-family communication and social communication have to be completely separated. In order to be sure that there is no betrayal or unwilling slips of information to the outside world, families have to stick together. The "Chameleon strategy" of constant adaptation requires a persistent intellectual activation. Conflict is hampered, because it would cause fear of betrayal. Secrets bind, but they give the power of betrayal to the ones involved. Knowing means the danger to be threatened by torture oneself.

Zuhal, a 7-year-old Kurdish girl, was presented by her mother for selective mutism. In session the first thing she painted was a man waving his hand, depicting her father when he was taken prisoner by military police, never to return again. The last thing he had told her was not to talk with anybody about what she knew and what she had seen. As a loyal daughter thus she remained mute until the mission of silence she had followed was relieved in family therapy.

One of the very common means of torture is to involve threats or actual damage to family members. In studies about refugee families from backgrounds as different as Chile, Afghanistan, or Sudan, all the tortured parents we talked to told us that the perceived damage was bigger concerning threats to the family than any physical torture. Torture creates a constant moral dilemma between choice of sacrificing comrades in struggle, sacrificing moral values, or sacrificing the family. As pointed out by Shay (1995), trauma in many instances can be looked at as moral trauma, betrayal of values, and destruction of central issues of meaning previously adhered to.

Political persecution has more facets to it, influencing the further development of family dynamics in exile. If one of the members — usually the father — lives in *clandestinity* he is separated from the family, not being able to follow the development of his wife and children. However, taking children into clandestinity, as some politically persecuted parents do, means a constant threat to the survival for the parents. Developmental necessities like being allowed to play aloud might be severely hampered. Many families who engaged in political activism also have a history of *imprisonment* of one of the members. More than pure persecution and war, this means being confronted with marginalization, loss of economical income, and sorrow. The pact of silence creates doubt in the children: "Is our father a criminal?" What does it mean to be a "political prisoner," how can one explain that to small children? Anger against a persecuted or imprisoned father who has left the family is difficult or even a taboo to express. Children often feel victimized or stigmatized by their fathers when they live the social consequences of being children with an "absent father." That is one of the reasons why many political exiles from Latin America agreed to a conversion of imprisonment into exile in order to be able to rejoin their families and influence their development and future. In exile — as we saw with many refugees from Latin America — the family often reunited for the first time, being crowded together and exposed to all the mutual wishes in a situation of depending completely on one another without the support of a big family or the political substitute of family, which is constituted by the political or religious grouping. The question of pertinence is often answered in a very different way for political exiles than for voluntary migrants: going into exile is usually little planned, a sudden decision, not legated, with longstanding wishes and a life project such as in voluntary migration. For voluntary migrants or refugees, making use of the political situation in order to fulfill long-existing wishes for migration, the mourning about which has been left behind, is a taboo. However, for political exiles stopping to mourn is often a taboo that is associated with individual or group meanings of having betrayed "the cause." Forgetting about the political engagement or integrating into the new society would mean that all the suffering imposed on the individual or the family is perceived as being in vain.

War has other characteristics influencing family life in exile. Many civil wars have been lengthy. The wars of independence from colonial powers have given way to civil wars often between conflicting warlords. Long-lasting war, apart from destroying access to water, health resources, food, and education, has destroyed many cultures. In Mozambique it was not worthwhile to raise cattle or plant the fields while the harvest was being threatened by robbery. Survival was only possible by breaking former existing rules or even social taboos. Leaving agriculture means to change one's perception of time — thus far oriented toward times of agricultural activity and times of relaxation and reflection — and belonging (Igreja, 2000). Cities often provide a safer environment, adding to the already existing tendency to migrate from town to the cities. Thus, refugees very often have a history of multiple internal migration in their countries of origin, meaning multiple separations for the children and parents, uprooting, and concentration onto the family as the only remaining structuring — but usually overburdened — agent. War also assists in destroying social rituals, such as the rites of passage between childhood and adult life and previously existing power relations within families. Today's warfare is different from that of ancient times in that it depends more on young people, who make use of new killing technologies, then on experienced fighters.

Where then might be the roots of refugee families in exile?

The Impossibility to Return and the Question of Pertinence: Here, There, and Between

Each family seeking refuge carries its particular problems, as do non-refugee families, which might mark the family's interpretation of the experiences of war and persecution lived through. Patterns of coping and defense that seem to have made sense in the past or during war and flight usually are transferred to the new environment. However, these well-known patterns do not always prove valid and useful anymore due to cultural difference, changed social status, weakened individual resources, and changed modes of family interaction. Due to traumatic experiences and uprooting, flexibility, adaptability, and family identity become challenged.

Legal circumstances of residence in exile often form one of the causes of family pathology. Helplessness in dealing with authorities, circumstances of living in refugee institutions perceived as humiliating, restricted possibilities of active mastery of the environmental challenges, lack of information, and the feeling of dependence hamper the possibilities of integration. The uncertainty deprives asylum seekers of reestablishing the feeling of safety, predictability, social role identities, and commitment to the present. It aggravates existing psychological problems and triggers new ones. Families staying for a prolonged period in an indeterminate state feel as if they are being deprived from a spot to anchor, from where they can restart their disrupted lives, or from possibilities to belong to any larger social group. The refusal of a permanence permit or prolonged uncertainty about it is experienced by politically persecuted parents as a lack of recognition, or as a lack of acceptance by those who had to flee because of ethnic conflicts.

Dimitri a 12-year-old boy from one of the countries of the former Soviet Union, made a drawing and commented: "This is the soul of my life. It floats. It does not know where to belong. There is no place for us neither there, nor here." Many parents struggle with an increased feeling of powerlessness due to reduced possibilities to influence the conditions of their lives, desperate for not being able to re-create the expected opportunities and safety for their children. Overwhelmed by the shadows of the past, unresolved grief, and frustration by the present situation, many parents feel guilty for not being able to offer the necessary protection to their children.

Besides the feeling of displacement, many refugees, stranded in a long-lasting asylum procedure of unpredictable length and outcome, feel captured in "narrowing of temporal horizons" (Boscolo & Bertrando, 1993). The inability to envision alternative future perspectives makes investment in the present often meaningless. Turning back to painful memories or memories that can trigger longing could be threatening. Hopelessness, apathy, and anxiety are often the shared feeling of family members. The prolonged uncertainty about the outcomes of the procedure becomes extremely stressful when part of the family is left in the country of origin or elsewhere in illegality, while family reunion is not allowed during the period of unresolved asylum request. Worries and feelings of guilt about children or spouses left behind dominate the daily lives of fragmented families. The risks caused by prolonged separation could be continued even after the reunion, if family members feel alienated from one another after long periods of unshared experiences

Xenophobia can be perceived as a stressful real life experience, more often, however, as a basic emotional climate. Children perceive their parents as weak, left with the feeling of not being sufficiently protected. And children can find it difficult to deal with the experience of being discriminated within a peer group.

"The fact that I am an asylum seeker," said Dimitri one day, "influences my whole life — how I think about myself, my relations, my concentration, my behavior. I want to tell something, but they (some peers) don't listen to me. I feel angry and sad and I think how lonely I am. As a refugee you are different from the others. Children say to you: Fuck you asylum seekers! Go back to your carton box! You are perceived as inferior, stupid, poor. You are not seen as someone. I have friends, but sometimes they don't dare to play with me, because they feel teased when asked: 'Why are you playing with this idiot?' Sometimes it becomes so hard, so difficult that I cannot deal with it."

On the other hand, problems like feelings of rejection or supposed xenophobia can also serve as an excuse for individual or family problems. Projecting guilt only on "the system" can hamper seeking adequate active reactions to problems. Insufficient schooling of children is often caused not only by xenophobia of teachers but by lack of schooling in the country of origin, posttraumatic symptoms, preoccupation concerning the parents, or mere intellectual restrictions. Rather than going through the work of mourning missed developmental possibilities and the results of traumatic experiences on intellectual functioning, they might prefer to attribute problems to their surroundings. Thus, discrimination can sometimes serve as a kind of "secondary stigma gain."

Although the development of some families is being interfered with by the impossibility to stay, in other families the impossibility to return, when combined with nostalgic sorrow and longing for their countries of origin, blocks the efforts of parents to invest in the present. If one or both parents remains fixed in a "some day" fantasy (Akthar, 1995) or a continuous hope of return, children's efforts to become rooted in the recipient country and define the domain of their belonging can become a source of loyalty conflicts.

Differential Adaptation: Spirits of the Past, Spirits of the Present

Differential adaptation or different speed of adaptation is one of the resources, but often also problems, of refugee families. The adjustment to the new culture is a prolonged process and can take different directions within members of the family. There are many ways to enter another culture from immersion to separation (di Nicola, 1997), from clinging to old supposedly "safe" patterns or to weaving a new intercultural web of two life worlds. Some family members adjust quickly to the values and norms of the new country and integrate them, others try to stick to old, well-known traditions and try to protect other members from the frightening unknown world. The disharmonious way of adjustment of family members can, according to di Nicola (1997), threaten the internal cohesion of the family, leading to role reversals and reversal of generational hierarchies with parentification of children, or distanced marital relations. The acculturation velocity is slowed when one or both parents continue to live in the nostalgic past, idealizing the original country and denigrating the recipient one. Some family members can become captured in the painful images of their traumatic past that hinder their efforts to connect with the present reality of the new culture and a perspective of the future. The acculturation process can be blocked by the insecure future, the lack of clarity about the possibility to stay in the recipient country, or the lack of possibilities for work that would facilitate the integration into society. Children usually acculturate faster and become cultural and linguistic interpreters for parents, and they take over parental tasks that can further threaten the parental leadership and leave the children without effective adult authority (McGoldrick, 1989). If this is a prolonged process it can interfere with the fulfillment of age-appropriate developmental tasks of the child.

However, we should also be aware that being able to help one's parents can be a source of fulfillment and pride.

Different patterns of adaptation can be found. Being deprived from their active role in the society, members of the family fall back onto their primary partners, even though they often have become estranged from them. The distance between partners expands because of different experiences, silencing about traumatic stressors, or because of long-lasting (physical) separation while being combatant, imprisoned, or waiting for family reunion. Caring for the family or influencing the development of family members is one of the few supposedly possible activities during forced inactivity after flight, while moving in the orbit of insecurity during asylum procedures. Fathers can try to take up their traditional role as turning-point person toward the new society, trying to reachieve activity and the narcissistic gratification of being able to "manage" the family as they used to or wished for in their countries of origin. However, they often fail in their efforts to reestablish their intrafamily and social roles due to a variety of reasons. Language acquisition, for example, depends very much on their psychic well-being, the experience of talking different languages, the possibilities for social contacts, and the availability of work for asylum seekers.

Fathers, being heavily involved in subcultural political or religious groups, often integrate less and are stricter concerning the maintenance of traditional or subcultural values. They are especially prone to feelings of guilt for having "deserted" and reactively try to maintain supposedly "correct" values in their children. They also tend to maintain the idealized view of the past and to underestimate the social processes and changes in the country of origin, augmenting frustration and anger on returning after years of being away. A time of activism is often followed by frustration. Pressure on children or wives can be exerted either not to take up contact with a surrounding, paranoically or really perceived as a menace, or as a pressure to achieve rapidly. Broken fathers sometimes try to reestablish the diminished influence in the family by exercising rigid control over children, possibly escalating family conflict and violence.

Mothers sometimes become more active in the outside social world during war, persecution, or exile by fulfilling the vacant masculine roles. Taking over roles and tasks that were strictly divided within the culture according to gender can be experienced as an additional stress or a challenge. It might not be easy to give up the power gained through this in exile, where women might have another role, even when there might be conflictive wishes to relax, to return to the known, and to "lick their wounds" after the stressful or traumatic experience of fight and persecution. If fathers stay very actively involved in politics or religion, mothers might adapt more rapidly to the new environment, running the risk of being regarded as traitors of the political cause or of the culture of origin by their husbands. However, we should not disregard that some of the families see the restricted gender roles as one of their reasons to seek refuge in exile, especially if — like in the Afghanistan under the regime of Taliban — the sociocultural change leading to fighting and persecution included heavy changes in gender relations and roles.

Due to divergent cultural norms relating to gender issues and due to wishes to leave behind traditional gender role stereotyping prevalent in the country of origin, gender roles are often mentioned as topics in therapy. Within the Chilean population (Walter, 1983) in exile, there was a strong wish to change gender role more fitting to the moral and ideological thinking of the students revolutions of 1968, its after-effects being a certain libertinage. Equality of gender chances and of roles were also heavily favored (but not necessarily realized) within the subcultures of reference. Machismo was criticized, but at the same time sexual libertinage was idealized. This, together with the feeling of having to catch up with the joys of living after imprisonment and torture, the feeling of isolation or loneliness due to alienation of partners through the separations — typical for imprisonment and life in clandestinty, and the availability of possible sexual partners in the receiving European societies contributed to many disruptions in partnerships. Latin American women often started to work earlier and learned the language better than their husbands who, also due to feelings of guilt for having abandoned the fight, spent much of their time in political reunions. This created jealousy and role conflict.

For African women losing the big family often meant losing part of their traditional power and authority, which often reside more in the intrafamily authority and dominance. Gender roles, their adaptation, and conflicts between idealized, "ideological" gender behavior, realized and realizable changes of gender roles leading to alternation in family relations and hierarchies do play an important role in working with families in exile. However, the direction of role adaptations and the content of the conflicts can vary across cultures and families.

Especially children of the second generation often learn what Roer Strier (1996) has called a "chameleon strategy" of adaptation, characterized by a bicultural adaptation to the receiving society and the traditional culture of the parents. They often fill a position of catalyst of change within the family or scout into the new society, even if they keep intensely linked to their parents whom they perceive as weak. Many parents do not want to adapt any more. Some of them feel dead, unwillingly depriving their children from sufficient parental care and protection.

Children, living a bipartite life or the life of a changeling (di Nicola, 1997), serve to keep parents near and to comfort them. Processes of detachment in adolescence are then often accompanied by heavy feelings of guilt, as Bettelheim (1963/1977) pointed out. Aggressive forms of detachment by boys and suicidal ideations in girls are especially common when separation is necessary. Sometimes adolescents try to detach themselves by taking over missions of their parents, like leaving the parents behind in order to participate in the struggle for "liberation" of their native place. Some children of Chileans, for example, took an active part in the wars of Central America in the 1980s. (Walter, 1993). A common phenomenon in this respect is the formation of subcultural adolescent groups.

Parents' patterns of care are often influenced by the effects of the cumulative or sequential stresses lived through. They might cling to patterns of overprotection useful during persecution ("kangaroo style," Roer Strier, 1996), maintaining a self-image of parental protectiveness but exposing their children to lack of conflict-handling capacity when forced to leave home. They might hand over the children to the new society ("cuckoo-pattern," Roer Strier, 1996), especially if they are numbed and helpless after their experiences and maintain the view of the receiving society as helpful.

Parental stress due to life in exile and posttraumatic symptoms often hinders the children's development. Many refugee parents cannot bear noise and movement as part of posttraumatic symptomatology, scolding their children if they enter into playful activities. They feel the need to be alone, to have time for "licking their wounds." The diminished capacity to become engaged with children, to empathize with them, or even to talk with them creates higher risks for children with single parents. Parents might not give due attention to their children. Their capacity to live through conflict with children or spouses is often burdened by the past. "I have lived through all of this, in order to provide a good life and a safe future to you. Now you fail in school and have fights with me," an Afghani father told his children in an interview. The wish for bonding and attachment can be augmented, while the capacity for attachment and atunement is often restricted. Playfulness is especially often lacking. Parents' play with their children depends on their capacity to relax, to fantasize, to imagine. However, when the fear of being overwhelmed with traumatic fantasies leads to an incapacity to relax, play is not possible.

A Chilean father in exile said that he played with his son, celebrating the fourth birthday. When they played a game of blind-man's bluff, his son put a scarf over his father's head, covering his eyes. The father instantly had a flashback of his experience being treated with electroshock and he yelled and cried. The son was left wondering what had happened, since the father had not told him about his experiences. The father avoided playing as a consequence for a long time.

Sibling relationships in refugee families often reflect differential adaptation; although the younger siblings adapt more easily, they are often scolded by their older siblings for having lost their cultural pride. However, as in groups these "scouts" or deviants have an important role as mediators of culture and creators of social contact, even if they are treated as scapegoats within their families or subculture.

MANAGING ADVERSITIES

The interplay of disruptive processes of marginalization, traumatization, uprooting, and acculturation affect children and families differently, according to the developmental stage, stage of family life cycle, cultural background, and political attitudes in the recipient country.

Whether families find a way to reestablish the continuity and stability of their lives or become blocked in those efforts depends also on how they try to make sense of their experiences and how they cope with sequential adversities. All refugee families are confronted with a set of additional tasks and demands, besides the normative developmental ones: to make sense and organize themselves around what has happened, to find a way to "make peace with the past" (Figley, 1989), to find a spot in the new environment from where they can restart their lives and redream alternative future perspectives, to redefine family boundaries and relations, and to redistribute roles and tasks within the fragmented family. Each of these tasks opens for family members many questions and dilemmas: to talk or not to talk about the painful events, to mourn or not to mourn while overwhelmed with anxieties about the uncertain future, and to which degree they need to stay loyal to their cultural practices or adjust to the new ones.

The ways families answer these questions, their attempts to attach meaning to the painful events or organize themselves around the disruptions, determine whether they manage to deal more or less successfully with the cumulative stressors. Exploring the processes of family coping and adjustment opens up possibilities for the therapist to understand how family members try to organize themselves around what happened and to plan interventions that strengthen family resilience.

Recalling Traumatic Experiences: To Talk or Not to Talk

If we think of therapy also as re-creating the capacity to remember and work through in a conjoint effort, searching for possible meanings, then we need to focus on the memory and communication of experience first. Traumatic memory and the capacity to communicate in an adequate way about it has been found to be crucial in adaptation and even resilience within families (McCubbin, Thompson, Thompson, Elver, & McCubbin, 1998). The different forms of remembering trauma range, according to Auerhahn & Laub (1998), from not knowing, fugue states, fragments, transference phenomena, overpowering narratives, life themes, witnessed narratives, and metaphors. Remembering can also take the form of reenactment or concretization (Bergmann & Jucovy, 1982). If traumatization by war or persecution is intense, it cannot be communicated and shared and thus leads to a sense of healing. It is an experience engraved into memory through special modes that make it hard to retranslate into words. Traumatic experiences originate in a world beyond words and metaphors, sometimes destroying communication not related to the painful experiences but in other contexts as well. They are characterized by concreteness, repetitiveness, and resistance to change with experience. Traumatic experiences often remain denied, hidden behind cognitive explanations or a wish to protect the others, blocked by a feeling of guilt, even survivor guilt (Niederland, 1968). Traumatic memories can be uttered in an intrusive, unchangeable, and repetitive way, not permitting the communication about them. Thus, experiences beyond words and metaphors are silencing to the self and to others. Victims feel that their proxies are not capable or willing to listen to their stories, that listening might be a contagious experience leading to vicarious traumatization — and sometimes it is unforgettable. Silencing of traumatic memories is an interactive process leading to feelings of loneliness, of "having fallen out of the world" as Reemtsma (1997) puts it. In the proxies it creates a world of "putative facts" (Bar-On, 1999), facts that might have been, that occupy the fantasy of spouses and children. The told and the untold are intensely intertwined.

Taboos are powerful in the social world of communication. Usually they start off as small concrete experiences that are consciously taught, but they end up as unconscious rules, governing daily life, feelings, and fantasies. Taboos are cultural silencing. "Breaking" taboos (a metaphor suggesting that they can be touchable and concrete), if not as an act of willfulness of a group, an idea, and action, the time of which has come, can isolate more than free.

In Mozambique during the civil war native healers regarded traumatic symptomatology as being caused by contamination by the world of the dead. Thus, traumatized individuals, being contagious themselves, had to be kept out of the social network until "cleansed" by rituals separating them from the past. Not reacting to those rituals or reoccurrence of posttraumatic nightmares was considered an indication of still being contaminated. The rituals had to be repeated or the individual secluded from his or her social network or family. Survival then was only possible in the big cities where taboos were not so powerful and social control is less. This might seem strange in cultures where the spirits of the dead are considered to be constantly present. However, in many cultures where there are ancestral religions, the effort of constantly distancing oneself from the ancestors, pacifying them, is very time- and energy consuming. The spirits have to be constantly silenced when they appear.

The attitude within a society toward traumatic past and the cultural beliefs has an important influence on how families give meaning to their experiences. In the research on transcultural transmission of trauma, Rousseau and Drapeau (1998) found relevant differences in the way two cultural groups, Southeast Asian and Central American families, are addressing their traumatic pasts. They found that Central American parents talk more explicitly about the trauma, within a political-historical context, creating a certain risk for greater invasion into the younger child's emotional world and leading to distancing by adolescents, as a protective avoidance mechanism. The silencing of

Southeast Asians seemed to protect children at first, but indirect references to the past seemed to have an impact on anxiety and depression levels in girls in puberty. Their findings emphasize the importance for higher sensitivity to the cultural and political context, as well as the developmental status of children when analyzing the meaning given to traumatic past and the ways families try to talk about it.

Research on Iranian and Kurdish families in Sweden (Almqvist & Brandell Forsberg, 1995) showed that the main attitude to the past suffering was to forget and leave it behind, as a coping or defense strategy intentionally transferred from parent to children. Warding off the past can be seen as a temporarily adaptive mechanism in refugee families, helpful in times when family members are confronted with multiple stressors during the first period of forced migration. Asylum seekers often underline that they cannot manage to cope with stressors in the present, anticipated in the future and the painful experiences in the past at the same time. However, this certainly seems to be a way of denial that cannot be used in a therapeutic way. Being a refugee means to be constantly reminded of that, not only when traumatic memories intrude or when loneliness is felt, but also in everyday life, looking for a home, work, and in thinking about academic and social achievement of parents and children. And last but not least, traumatic experience intrudes often enough without appearing in "the right moment."

As some parents formulated it "we need to become first strong to be able to became weak." When parents choose consciously to keep the doors to the traumatic past closed as a way of temporary coping, it can have different effects on family members. The essential question is whether the difficulties to communicate about the past experience of organized violence hinder the interfamilial communication or endanger the development of children and the parents. If it is a temporary strategy in stressful times, the efforts in therapy need to be focused on helping the family to reestablish a minimum stability in the here and now, before addressing painful issues in the past. The better we understand the mechanism and function of silencing in each family, within the cultural context and context of current life circumstances, the more possibilities could be created to neutralize its potentially damaging effects. Family therapy with refugee families is almost always "talking about not being able to talk and not wanting to talk."

Repeatedly retelling stories about violence and disclosing details that are threatening or traumatizing for the child, especially if not matched in an age-appropriate way, can also become a risk for the development of children. Violent events that were heard can become fused with the child's own aggressive drives, which shape and organize the child fantasies, and "chain children to parent's resources of reality" (Auerhahn & Laub, 1998). The meaning and effects of silencing, over- and underdisclosure on family members and the family dynamic in general need to be one of the essential focuses of therapeutic issues with refugee families.

Functional and Dysfunctional Adaptations

Even though the nature and extent of the conspiracy of silence (Kestemberg, 1983) at different system levels have been seen as the most important mechanisms for transmission of trauma (Danieli, 1981), there are many other attitudes within the family that can potentially endanger the development of children at various stages of their development. The impairment of survivors' capacity for parenting, such as insecure parenting style or insecure attachment (Auerhahn & Laub, 1998), emotional unavailability, excessive control, or overprotection, has been emphasized as potentially damaging for children. Dysfunctional patterns of interaction due to shattered trust, emotional numbing, parental depression, or violence can interfere with the stabilization of the family as well with the development of the children.

When approaching a refugee family it is important to understand how the traumatic experiences affect the family as a whole and how family members are trying to organize themselves around it. Some fixed, long-lasting dysfunctional patterns of adaptation built around life adversities can create greater risk for the functioning of family members than the traumatic event itself (Bala, 2001). Danieli (1981) described four differing adaptational styles of the families of Holocaust survivors: the Victim family, the Fighter family, the Numb family, and the family of Those-who-made-it, offering a complex model for understanding the transmission of intergenerational processes. He focused on analysis of the meanings, attitudes, and rules of behavior that determine the interactions and their effects on development of children. Similar adaptation patterns are described by families of combat veterans (Harkness, 1993). Exploring and identifying in which way the refugee family tries to cope with sequential disruptions by efforts to make sense of experience, redefine relationships, restructure boundaries, reestablish roles and tasks are essential in order to understand which aspects of the dominant adjustment facilitate or hinder the development of children and the family as a whole.

Many families find a way to deal with the interlocked adversities and manage to discover a way to organize themselves in a way that helps them to continue and fulfill at least basic functions. Families that tend to cope more successfully with stress are characterized by high family cohesion and flexible family roles, family-centered problem solving, open and effective communication, and readiness to utilize external resources (McCubbin & Figley, 1983, quoted in Figley, 1989). An increasing amount of research in the past decade has focused around the processes and mechanisms that facilitate the coping and adjustment of families confronted with adversities. The Resiliency Model of Family Stress, Adjustment and Adaptation (McCubbin & McCubbin, 1993) emphasizes the interplay of stress and its appraisal with the family type, intrafamily resources and social support, problem solving, and coping skills. One of the key questions emerging in the work with refugees exposed to cumulative stress and adversities is how families regenerate and which resources remain after long-lasting exposure to adversities. Openness for exploring and discovering the existing protective processes, functional adaptational patterns, and potential for recovery are especially helpful with families convinced that their resources are diminishing under the increase of demands.

The focus on how families manage disruptive experiences leads to a shift in perspective: from discovering in which way a family is damaged to questions of how families are challenged. Searching for answers to this question F. Walsh (1998, 2003) describes protective processes, such as connection and collaboration, making meaning of adversity, hope, initiative and invention, religion and spirituality as helpful healing resources. Her assumption that "resilience can be forged even when problems cannot be solved and when they reoccur" (1998, p. 63) can be seen as an important starting point when approaching refugee families. Resilience, when seen as an "adaptive capacity " or a "capacity for recovery" (Garmezy, 1991), is not just a potential resource within the family but needs to be considered in interaction with environmental resources. Building up and strengthening the weakened social network around refugee families and supporting the efforts of family members to utilize community network and resources needs to be included in therapeutic goals.

Interactive Coping and Adaptation

We tend to look at coping as a process over time, where effectiveness lies rather in the capacity to use many strategies and activities that fit the situation and development of the family members, respectful of their present and past defenses and vulnerabilities. In original works coping was viewed mainly concerning problem-focused or emotion-focused aspects (Lazarus, 1984) of an individual. Developmental and interactive aspects have only recently entered into the focus of attention. By interactive we mean ways of coping focusing on mutuality, empathy and reflectivity, and help and problem-solving communication. Looking for meaning in the family, providing meaning appropriate to age, development, and individual resources, comforting and accompanying in joy and despair form important aspects of human coping. The concept of family coping was introduced by McCubbin and McCubbin (1989), defined as a coordinated effort of the system as a whole, including also efforts by individual family members that fit together as a synthetic whole and include mutual coping strategies. The coping strategies used by one family member may facilitate or hinder the attempts of the others or often even conflicting attempts occur.

One of the advantages of viewing coping and adjustment using an interactive rather than individual focus is that we can perceive how the family as a whole creates an interactive and interaffective network of avoidance and intrusion, through role distribution, distribution of affect, and joint and individual defense mechanisms. When the focus of observation is expanded to processes and pathways of coping and adaptation over time, we can identify various roles in refugee families.

The Reminder

One of the family members is constantly asking about losses, presenting symptomatology, reminding the family of the stresses and trauma lived through, helping them not to forget. An 8-year-old Afghani boy, son of a heavily traumatized but also traumatizing former security officer of the socialist government, used to wake up at night crying and be only consoled when he viewed the photograph of his oldest sister. He used to eat only sitting at the side of the shrine that the family had created for her, after having been killed and completely burnt by a Taliban grenade, while her father fled. "Reminders" represent the intrusive pole within families. By making the family's denial ineffective, possibilities open up to face painful issues and search for different coping modalities.

The Cheerleader

Children with a specially friendly temper, born in exile or after the family has lived through trauma, give hope, humor, and a feeling of continuity to the life of the family, at the cost of not being allowed to show sadness, aggressiveness, or anger. "Cheerleaders" represent the avoidance pole within the family.

A young Chilean journalist, son of a father killed while he was in utero, was described by his siblings and parents as "the sunshine and clown of the family," as the one who was less traumatized. Asked to tell the history of the family, however, he bursts out weeping and said: "My life and birth do not matter. What matters is that my father was killed."

The Investigator

Children or parents whose lives are dedicated to finding out what has happened to disappeared family members and possibly organizing a trial or revenge. Often they are more intellectual children with a tendency to avoid open affect, serious and somehow solemn. Some of the investigators' efforts can be projected to the future, but bring a certain degree of relief in the present for all family members — knowing that one day information would be available or actions would be taken in the direction of social justice.

The Observer

Children, seemingly unaffected, who monitor with high vigilance the well-being of the family and possible environmental threats. When actively included in family therapy, they often present impressive insight into the functioning of the members of the family and the family as a whole. Their insight can generate a search for more functional coping strategies within a family, such as staying open even to possibly bad alternative outcomes of the asylum procedure, in order to become prepared for difficult times, as concluded in an Middle Eastern family, after the 13-year-old boy analyzed the existing "frozen" reactions of family members confronting a threat.

The Care Provider

Some children plan their lives fulfilling their parents' hope that "at least the family should always stay together." They can become very efficient organizers and helpers to others, within and outside the family, but they often stay trapped by being allowed to have only narcissistic gratification within a role as a helper, not as a person of his or her own. Helpers and caregivers are usually highly estimated, liked, but not necessarily loved.

The Denier

Especially adolescent children tend sometimes to negate their own and their parents' history, feeling frustrated in their attempt to live their own life while keeping contact to the parents. They might affiliate to the dominant group in the recipient society, accepting offers of integration. They might look for new relational substitutes in religious congregations, subcultural groups, and political parties opposite to their parents. Parents often feel that forgetting about the history that socialized (and emotionalized) them means betraying them, even if "within-group-deviants" (Goffman, 1963) sometimes form an important link to the outside world and break barriers and prejudices. Fighting against them stabilizes groups, showing at the same time that divergence is possible. However, each failure of a deviant can be seen as a highly ambivalent experience, reassuring strict identities but closing doors of imagination and change.

The Perfect Representative of the Culture of Origin

Diaspora culture and exile culture are often characterized by living an exaggerated "caricature" of a former life in the country of origin when there is a strong longing to return and the past is being idealized. Some Chilean children learned, for example, to dance the national dances in exile better than in Chile itself — not only because many cultural aspects under the dictatorship had been prohibited, but also because idealization is possible in exile, since there is no constant contact with a changing social reality. Often religion becomes more central for family members and the beliefs more extreme than in the country of origin.

Returning to the country of origin means having to jump a double culture and "time gap," to adjust to the cultural change between the country of exile and the country of origin, but also the gap created by the cultural change that occurred between leaving the country and returning. Return might turn into disappointment and frustration of the long-cherished wish for belonging to a society that does not exist any more or never existed in the fantasized manner.

Taking up these roles and issues in therapy can prove to be very effective, especially when the development of children or the families as a whole has been trapped. Refugee children and parents often find their own metaphors for their roles in the family, derived from their coping and adjustment used in prolonged stressful times. Thinking in terms of social roles, social prescriptions are important in the majority of the countries of origin but also in being able to understand the functioning of recipient societies.

Intrafamily Support

Analyzing with family members what they find helpful and how they try to support one another are search processes with an attempt to discover, emphasize, and stabilize those processes that can potentially strengthen the family resilience. It also gives an opportunity to sort out those adaptational attempts that have been helpful in the past but became dysfunctional in a given situation. Exploring and broadening the coping alternatives (Bala, 2000; Walter & Adam, 2000) and strengthening those processes that facilitate family adaptation, such as encouraging open communication, joint problem-solving attempts, or mutual empathy, are becoming a structural part of the therapy process.

How Parents Help Their Children

When parents are asked what they do to help their children overcome the stresses of war, persecution, exile, and return, they usually mention first the basic tasks of families: physical nurturing, providing a house where one can live in dignity, and efficient schooling. Maintaining a bicultural identity is another often frustrated wish parents find useful for their children. Silencing usually serves the double role of a self-soothing defense and a wish to protect children from the persecutory internal world and external experiences of children. Some parents make efforts to protect their children by hiding their sorrow, upsetting information about family members left behind, or bad news about the asylum procedure. Parents often think that maintaining a religious or political belief as a foundation — something that has been useful for them in the past — might be of help for their children. Discussing the effects of parental strategies used to help children can lead to strengthening the parental competency either by stabilizing the chosen support or jointly searching for alternative possibilities.

How Siblings Help One Another

Siblings can be a strong support for one another in difficult times. They can encourage, attempt to make sense of an experience by discussing, and role-playing with one another their strategies to cope with the stressors. Each subsystem of the exiled families should be acknowledged and made use of in family therapy with refugees, including the sibling system. When meeting siblings alone, children are much more open to discuss their fantasies about their parents. Discussing openly which different roles they fulfill or in which different "ecological niches" they live within the family often relieves much of sibling struggle. Talking together they can join their memories, fears, and strengths and create their own meaning. Most often they mention that jointly they wish to help their parents to feel as effective parents, even if that means being more mature than the parents.

How Children Help Parents

All children have to be able to create parental feelings in their caretakers in order to permit them to pass the strenuous tasks of parenting. Infant research has shown that in an impressive way. Refugee children and adolescents show an amazing amount of conscious and unconscious attempts at "getting at their parents." In small children this mostly means doing everything in order to "create" a lively counterpart, as we know from the attempts of babies in the "still face situation." They move, cry, laugh, wave arms, develop (psycho-) somatic symptoms. They try to give their parents a feeling of being good parents, able to influence at least the development of their children. Directly or indirectly children often offer their parents a motivational support to go on, instead of giving up, especially in difficult times when the stressors are increasing. Adolescents sometimes take over their parents' political roles, substituting the feeling of impotence of the parents. They often create anger, challenging their families. Adolescents whose proximal development has been normal usually know well the "hot spots," the difficult parts of their parents, and they know well how to create anger or frustration in them; but they also know how to flatter using the right topics.

Puhar (translated "knowledge" from Persian), a boy who had called by telephone to the therapist asking him to "resuscitate" his heavily traumatized and depressive father, sang, played organ, taking up tunes from Afghanistan, cooked, told his brothers and sisters to be quiet, asked his father to join him for a walk. Sometimes he was hated by his brothers and sisters for asking them to do so many things for the parents. Only in therapy he could be a small boy, telling how distant he felt from his father, and how he longed for his killed uncle who had substituted the father's role while the latter was involved in the Afghani civil war.

POSSIBILITIES AND LIMITATIONS IN THERAPY

How to Tell About Family Therapy

One of the main therapeutic necessities in working with traumatized families is the capacity to maintain sympathetic distance, to be able to empathize but not be overwhelmed by the stories told and realities lived through, but also to maintain an unprejudiced openness to victims and perpetrators and their children. Our experience is that family therapy with refugee families is not more difficult than with other families. Problems lie more in access to therapists willing to deal with them than in fear of being stigmatized for seeking psychotherapy. That means that access to refugees' subcultures is essential in establishing specialized services. We would like to stress, however, that refugee families can and should be treated by every psychotherapist, with or without a specialized focus, who is willing to engage in intercultural work and to give an open eye to psychosocial frustrations in exile.

However, explaining therapy to our family clients is of utmost importance in creating a holding alliance with the family. Such an introduction should include confidentiality, take up issues of cultural difference, stress the focus on coping and resources, and be empathic when relating to questions of shame within the family. We might say:

> You have come to us to seek our help in resolving problems within your family that might be very much related to what you have been living through and are living through in exile. Somehow you have managed to survive until now and I will be eager to know how you managed that.
>
> You might feel the wish to find out if we are trustworthy. Your experience might have taught you to be cautious with strangers. You are welcome to take the time you need to find out if you can trust us. Mistrust may be one of the things that has helped you to survive. However, you possibly will find out that it helps to speak openly about your experiences and how you interpret them. We will watch that you are not going to be overwhelmed by telling your experience. We are going to guard against that for you, your children, the interpreter, and we ourselves look at everything in a way that we can tolerate and where we are sure you can leave the sessions and be quiet.
>
> We come from a different culture than you and our professional role differs from your culture. Thus, we will ask questions and give you answers that can seem alien or intrusive to you. If you feel like that, please tell us, it will help you learn about values and taboos in our society and teach us about yours. However, you can be sure that we will keep confidentiality and not contact others without your knowledge and agreement.

How to Approach Cultural Differences

In our own studies about refugee families we started with the idea that culturally sensitive therapy has to open spaces for the canonical and the individual within each family. We ask the families what "family" means in their culture and their family history. We ask about what the tasks of the family as a whole and its members in their country of origin are, and to what extent they differ from that in their own perception, intentionally or forced through the experience of cultural change, persecution, war, and exile. What we found was an astonishing diversity of definitions and tasks of families even within one cultural group of origin. First, the cultural definitions even within one ethnicity concerning structure, composition, affective, protective, and functional tasks of families differed a lot. Divergence from those cultural definitions often formed one of the motives for migration. We found an adaptive, reflective, and therapeutically functional discussion of the family here (in exile) and there (country of origin), the family of old times and of now, the wishes for family feelings of parents and the children of different developmental levels. The statements given more often than not seem to be reflections of wishes for continuity, belonging and fear of loneliness, and reflections of intergenerational family problems. These statements about families in one's culture of origin can be interpreted rather as projective tests than as culturally valid definitions. However, taking them together they show the allowed margin of divergence permitted within the culture, which is usually being restricted in times of conflict.

Definitions made by parents were often influenced either by idealized wishes for belonging, by new cultural values that formed part of the social conflict like feministic, or socialistic ideas of equality, but also by the wish to escape from the strong social control typical for countries where big families still prevail. Joining families in this open, nonintrusive way brings the therapist closer to the life world of the family and creates opportunities for understanding in which way the family wishes to progress. In order to work with refugee families successfully the therapist needs "to examine, adapt, or even discard the usual assumptions, methods and goals of therapy" (di Nicola, 1997, p. 40).

The Choice of Settings and Compositions

There is no rule of how to start, but it is important that therapists should be very alert to create a safe environment through a good joining with the family. Therapists should select a setting and composition of participants comfortable to them; however, be aware that family interactions cause, promote, trigger, and model a child's reaction to adversity. In many refugee families one child is presented as the carrier of the symptoms; however, withdrawn children or apparently good copers need our attention as well. We tend to invite the whole family for the first session, however, leaving open who comes for the next session. Regardless of who comes for the first session and who is seen as a carrier of the problem, it is essential to open possibilities from the first session for understanding in which way accumulated adversities affects all family members and their mutual relations. "Helping traumatised children," as underlined by Figley (1989, p. 136), "is both a means and the end in helping the entire family shifting the focus from the child to the entire family." However, time has to be created for individual, private, and confidential conversation. If the therapist, for reasons of convenience or differential indication, decides to do therapy in a child-centered frame, parents, siblings, and the family as a whole should regularly be invited for sessions. Individual interviews with the parents should be planned at the beginning of therapy with families. Often the most important things are told before the session, on the way to the clinic, in the pauses, or after the sessions. Scenical information is as valuable as cognitive information. Trauma questionnaires can be useful in order to give individuals possibilities of mentioning silenced traumatic experiences.

Sessions with the siblings only often permit pointing out more easily hidden events, since children in the presence of the parents feel more obliged to function in a way they perceive as solicited by culture and parents. Some basic toys, paper and pencils, and some cushions or other soft toys should be present; however, do not create a "toy shop" where children feel like playing with everything and parents possibly feel humiliated for not being able to provide the same amount of toys to their children. During family therapy with smaller children, there are phases in session when the parents are addressed more, while the children usually continue to listen and take in what the parents say in play. Therapists thus should be very aware of what is going on and take up that point in later conversation, finding out about the perception of the parents or interpreting what the children are doing and how they contribute to the topics touched upon.

Interpretation has to be done carefully, opening space for possible meaning. We tend to see our task as therapists in creating — jointly with the family and its individual members — an array of possible meanings the family can live with. Interpretation has to emphasize the need to maintain defenses. Very often interpretation is not necessary but rather mediation of meanings and interpretations offered by the individual family members. Play is the most important tool for smaller children to give meaning to their experiences. The use of play in therapy, though, has to be explained to the parents. If it isn't they will get the impression that the therapists only want to provide fun: "They only play." Creating storybooks of the family's life together can facilitate the joining of different individual stories, interpretations, and a multiplicity of meanings fitting together or even leading to a more complete view of the family.

Children should be seen in individual sessions in order to understand better their views of the problems, to allow them possibilities for communicating their experiences and fantasies; to express and master their feelings and integrate the fragmented parts of their own stories in their own symbolic way, through play, drawing or story-writing. In this way opportunities are created for a child to develop his or her personal voice, articulate his or her own meanings and feelings about him- or herself, others, and the world. It is, however, essential that the child's symbolically expressed views become shared, in agreement with the child, with family members and embedded in their narratives during family therapy sessions. Individual attention for a child is especially indicated when children's potential for verbalization is limited, when the symbolic expressions are blocked, or when the possibilities to amplify the child's voice during family meetings are reduced, usually due to parental traumatization or depression. But the limited goals of individual therapy sessions with a traumatized child require always-active involvement of parents as well as changes in the entire family system. The therapist's task is, according to Larner (1996, p. 430), "to enhance family member's potentials to make meaning of the child's behaviour in the context of their life situation."

Co-Creating Therapeutic Goals

During the first contacts with the family many expectations of family members emerge, even by those families who claim they can no longer generate hope and positive perspectives. Understanding at which stage of development the family was disrupted, which meaning family members attach to the disruptions, and in which way they would like to reestablish the stability and continuity gives some initial direction toward coconstruction of the therapeutic goals. When the preferred changes are formulated in terms of small, reachable goals, family members can regain easier the sense of mastery over some aspects of their lives. When family members feel increasingly powerless, overwhelmed by too many intertwined problems, disentangling, clarifying the problems and setting priorities (van Essen & Bala, 1995) become a starting point in initiating changes. Daily, practical problems or life circumstances that create high levels of distress in the family need to be handled with care. The meaning of each problem for family members needs to be explored. The therapist can consider the possibility of community interventions or facilitate the contact of the family members with other agencies. Practical aids can be seen as concrete steps that reduce the stressors, facilitate therapy, and strengthen the therapeutic alliance (Jaffa, 1993; van der Veer, 1998). But when these problems cover other issues, they need to be addressed.

Therapy always includes overt and hidden agendas, more so if there is reason for silencing, learned mistrust, and fear. To show concern relating to the psychic well-being of the children, while there is fear of being rejected and pushed back into exile, often forms the key into therapy. Some parents utter fear of losing their children in the new society, coming in with complaints about breaking the family rules. Developmental arrests, stuttering, bed wetting, and nightmares can have other causes such as manifesting (partial) developmental arrest. All of these reasons for entering therapy are valid wishes by parents. Only in rare cases do children call for therapy like the 12-year-old Afghani boy who on the phone said: "My parents want us children to go to therapy. But it is my father who first needs help. He is like dead, weeps and does not support us any more."

Overt agendas on the therapist's part usually also include the strengthening of the family and making use of their efforts that at least led them into therapy. However, openly uttered agendas form just one side of the coin. Behind the wish to stay in the country, to find a better house — themes often beyond the therapeutic possibilities — we often find hidden agendas. Behind the wish for a certificate we may find the wish to find a place where affects, ideas, sorrows, and fear have a "residence permit." Hidden agendas need time to evolve. They can be consciously hidden by family members or related to questions of fear, guilt, and sexuality. They are rather being manifested by interpersonal defenses, like scolding the children, telling them not to say certain things, not leaving time for an interpreter to interpret, or leaving the therapist out. Hidden agendas can be indicated by metaphors, gaps in narratives, sudden affective changes, or unusual reactions of therapists in countertransference. Children's play and artistic production often present access to hidden agendas in therapy. However, children should not be abused in therapy in order to reach the parents. Therapy has to be negotiated with them as well, by telling them about the fun that therapy sometimes is, but also mentioning its side effects like time expenditure and exposure to sadness, trauma, or loss. Many themes should be mentioned in a cautious way to the family, discussing the possibilities for addressing them and emphasizing the necessity to deal with them at a later point in life. Respect for our clients demands from therapists to be open concerning what can be dealt with in which amount of time.

Therapy with families in exile is not necessarily trauma focused, but rather usually starts with questions of here and now. That is why we need therapists who are well acquainted with the sociopolitical and legal aspects of life in exile and not merely culturally sensitive trauma specialists. Families asked about their problems usually mention more stressors concerning life in exile than posttraumatic symptomatology. Thus, our Afghani clients at the University Clinics of Hamburg, as many other clients also in the Netherlands, mention loneliness due to separation from their families of origin and the loss of work, pride, and respect as the most frequent subjective causes of distress. Only when these issues are carefully dealt with can traumatic experiences, fears concerning their children's future, insecurity concerning the legal status in exile, physical complaints, and continuous feeling of tension and inability to relax emerge as topics. The wish for or the inability to return to their country or the continuous fear of forced expulsion plays a paramount role in therapy.

The Therapeutic Use of Metaphors and Narratives

Metaphors and narratives are expressions of the way we make sense of experiences, that is, the way we provide meaning in interpreting the world we live in. By providing meaning we organize experience and try to avoid fear by making the world predictable. Used within families in family therapy, metaphors and narratives provide hints at ways of coping and of defense mechanisms. Narratives and metaphors can be used as valuable diagnostic hints, but also as a means of therapy like play or associations.

Traumatic experience has been called part of a "world beyond metaphors" (Grubrich-Simitis, 1984). Literature of the 1980s and 1990s has rediscovered metaphor as a central way of conveying individual meaning and communicating in shortcuts. By shortcuts we mean that metaphors serve as hints to individual and social shared meanings, if they permit to understand the other without having to discuss the "real fact." At the same time metaphors allow the user or receptor to have his or her own allusions and associations. It helps to assume that we understand each other in an affective way, joining fantasies. The word "trauma," as a "surgical" breaking of bodily protective layers, is just one of such metaphors. If we talk of "alive" metaphors, we want to say that a person, at least for the topic concerned, is still capable to move in a world of the "pretend mode," the "as if" relating contexts of meaning of different areas, helping to find meaning by analogy. Using metaphors introduced by family members, such as feeling as if they were trapped in a black tunnel with no way out, opens up possibilities for the therapist to explore the meaning and the effects of the blocked future perspectives on the daily lives of family members. Staying within the metaphor options for searching light or way out can be explored.

Metaphors serve other functions, too. They steer the imagination of the receptor of the metaphor, but can also shut down other interpretations of reality at the same time, by focusing the imagination of the listener on certain aspects of what is to be expressed. Therapeutic metaphors can provide new focuses of perception as "an art of lenses" (Hoffmann, 1990). Metaphors can also become petrified, "canned" statements that are not to be questioned any more. In therapy with refugees metaphors can become a bridge across cultural barriers, a possibility to introduce the unuttered, or an option to allow the coexistence or convergence of multiple meanings within a family.

Narrative is the way to tell ourselves and others about experience. Children by the age of 2 to 4 years learn that what is interesting in the narrative is the conflict between the normal and the unusual. What is supposed to be culturally known does not have to be told. Tension in narrative is created by the omissions, by contradictions between the way of telling and the affective expression and flexibility accompanying it. Traumatic experience related in narrative is usually characterized by either harsh concreteness or by "spiraling" around the omitted, putative facts. Sometimes it is characterized by self-protective or interpersonally protective lying or camouflaged memory; later memories serve as a focus for re-presenting former, repressed memory. Thus, talking about feelings of persecution in a new environment like exile can be a representation of actual stress or a hint at traumatic experience in the past. Omitted facts or supposed leaps in a story might be a hint at cultural normality, at repressed memory, or at invented, protective life stories serving the aim of adapting one's story to the social circumstances of living in exile. As all other people, refugees restyle and renarrate their stories following social rules and circumstances. Therapy provides at its best a frame to reflect on this within a family, to find a conjoint liveable story permitting a sense of family identity and flexible interpretation, permitting individual identity and divergence. The narrative approach creates space for refugee families to reauthorize their stories and link them with dominant stories of political conflicts and wider societal discourses that shaped their lives within their countries of origin and within their recipient counties.

Sexuality in Family Therapy With Refugees

Destroying sexuality as one of the most intimate links between couples has always been one of the effects or even aims of violent social conflict: fear of loss, fear of shame and expulsion following violation, and sexual dysfunction due to effects of torture, forced separation, being imprisoned, or living in clandestinity with consecutive jealousy concerning the partner whose life is not shared during that time. Metaphors like "we live together like brother and sister," hinting at a strong protective taboo preventing lived and fantasized sexuality, can help point to sexual problems. Lack of sexuality augments feelings of impotence, aggressive conflict, and negative self-esteem. Even physical tenderness can be perceived as threatening because of the fear of ending up with frustrated sexual intercourse. The consolation and rejoining of a couple in exile also by reexperiencing satisfying sexuality is sometimes hampered by the circumstances of living in a restricted and "totalitarian" environment of refugee camps.

Sexual violation and torture is usually not aimed at obtaining important information but rather one of the ways to try to destroy intimacy by the enemy and create a feeling of terror. Since making a violation of a woman known to the husband or father amplifies the gap between them and augments the feeling of not being able to protect or being protected, silencing is often the case in undisclosed abuse. A barrier of shame and fear is created within the intimate relationship. Sexuality is usually being avoided. Women fear that disclosing abuse could alienate them further from their husbands or children, or lead to forceful expulsion from their families in some cultures. Sexually abused women are looked upon as contaminated physically — aside from the fact that at least in Africa, the epidemical spread of AIDS endangered them.

Bridging the gap created between family members through sexual violence can be seen as one of the most difficult tasks in therapy, usually including first individual sessions with the abused person and then with the other family members. There is often a double wall against disclosure: one partner feels ashamed, silenced, and worthless, the other usually has undisclosed fantasies about the "putative facts," which often are more difficult to reveal than the victim's own silenced story. When the silenced story became sharable, the effects of sexual violence on the husband, his feelings, and meanings attached to it need to be explored in the context of culturally shaped meanings and expectations. Issues like fantasies about revenge, guilt, and shame need to be discussed when they emerge.

We use to bring up the topic of sexuality regularly, stressing that we know we might be touching a taboo also valid in our own societies, but that it is a topic that is to be discussed with all families in the couple setting and is open for confidential therapeutic communication. Very often individual sessions touching upon sexual torture, rape, or other causes for a loss of self-esteem are necessary before the topic can be discussed in couple therapy or even family therapy.

A., an 8-year-old son of a couple of workers from Kosova, was forced to be present when the mother was raped by Serbian paramilitary forces. The mother had lost her son on a railway station during the flight and returned the day after to look for him, when she was captured and abused. The father had gone into exile already a year before. The mother compelled the therapists and her son to avoid talking about the abuse, fearing that her husband would leave her. She avoided any sexual contact with him, leaving him with the feeling of impotence to give pleasure to his wife. The son started stuttering after the rape, which he had witnessed at the age of 5 — a type of posttraumatic symptomatology we see quite frequently in children traumatized between ages 4 and 8. Therapy had to proceed very slowly in different settings including individual sessions with the mother, the father, the son, the siblings, and the family as a whole. In societies where the community expects that the husband has to leave or even kill his wife who has been raped, the therapeutic interventions need to include the possibilities to challenge the existing sociocultural discourses.

The Question of Internal, Interfamily, and External Language

The language of the powerful and the language of the powerless play their role in family therapy with refugee families. Refugees can experience that the language they usually speak is often perceived as "inferior" in the recipient countries. While English may be a language of power, talking African languages or Asian languages often is not valued. When the first centers for refugees in Europe were built in the 1970s, the maintenance of language was a very basic topic. We think it still has to be seen as crucial, especially in family therapy with refugee children and families.

Helping children to develop a language, provided usually by parents to their children, is one of the main tools for conveying information and intentions, for developing narratives of the self and in relation to significant others. It has to be "sufficient enough" to transfer what is necessary, but at the same time to maintain individual associations that make up meaning. Language has to fit to parents' affectivity and their cultural realm. Talking to oneself is one of the tools we have to maintain identity when feeling alone, threatened, or estranged. By means of language we also learn to hide our identities, to lie, to pretend — capacities we need in order to survive under hostile circumstances. The lack of language acquisition is one of the main obstacles of refugees, limiting them to live in subcultural conditions or in close contact to "fellow subcultures," like natives of the receiving country sympathizing with the country of origin. Failing to acquire the parents' language causes not only problems in intrafamily problem solving, but also a feeling of shame, and it has very real effects if the return to the country of origin becomes a choice or necessity. Language is usually intimately associated with experience. People do not forget the sound of their torturer's voice. Refugees may feel that a language like German or Dutch sound harsh or hostile. For the capacity to integrate into the labor force in the country of reception, to prosper economically, or to be able to make use of the knowledge of the receiving country in order to plan one's future, language's importance is paramount. However, children can feel alienated from their parents' language if it is a language of the powerless, a language of sorrow and grief, or of stories that are not balanced by good emotional experiences associated with that language.

In therapy with refugee families it can be useful if the therapist shares the language used by the family and understands the subtleties. Speaking some words in the language of the family opens doors and is experienced by family members as polite or sympathetic. Being able to use or understand metaphors, to know if they are culturally linked to the experience of the individual or family, or if they reflect creativity in the use of language can be extremely helpful. Not understanding, not sharing, but questioning, can, however, also be useful especially in a context of forced cultural transition. Not understanding and not being understood are the most basic experiences of refugee families in exile, augmenting feelings of forced regression, or not being understood and heard in a victimized life in the country of origin. Talking about language and realizing misunderstandings are topics that usually open new spaces in family therapy with refugees. These issues arise usually in the first sessions or need to be addressed later.

The use of different languages by family members during therapy needs to be handled with care to avoid situations of exclusion. Children might start to talk in the language that their parents do not understand, family members might talk to each or with the translator in the language the therapist cannot follow, or parents might start to talk a third language, English for example to protect children from particular information. Most of these situations can be prevented or addressed when they occur. It is the responsibility of the therapist to make sure everything said in a session is translated and becomes understandable and sharable for all the participants.

Beyond Dichotomies

In some refugee families members tend to blame each other or themselves for being engaged in political activities, leaving the country of origin or not leaving on time, for the fate of family members left behind, or for the uncertain future they are confronting. In other families problems are placed in the outside, threatening world in the realm of sociopolitical events or in forces blocking the continuity of family life. As the problems of the refugee families are neither located in the internal nor external, intimate nor political world but at their nexus, the therapist needs to address interrelated systems (Papadopoulos, 2001) and plan interventions within the "significant system" that unites people connected to the problem (Boscolo & Bertrando, 1993). That means that therapeutic interventions can reach out to schools, refugee communities, asylum centers, or larger system levels. The systemic approach in therapy with refugees creates opportunities for contextualizing the problems, exploring the interaction between the internal and external realities and meaning systems, by understanding how the dominant cultural and political discourses and processes shape the experiences of family members, and by understanding how family members make sense of the experience. The systemic view allows the therapist to shift between the social and political realities and internal representational lives of the refugees.

If the therapist manages to create a safe space for painful experiences, losses, and longings to appear, as well as space for the hidden family strength to emerge, for internal and external resources to develop, therapy becomes a subtle art of balancing between intrafamilial, sociopolitical, and cultural processes, between sorrow and hope, between memories and alternative future perspectives.

REFERENCES

Akhtar, S. A. (1995). Third individuation: Immigration, identity, and the psychoanalytic process. *JAPA, 13*(4), 1051–1083.

Almqvist, K., & Brandell Forsberg, M. (1995). Iranian refugee children in Sweden: Effects of organized violence and forced migration on preschool children. *American Journal of Orthopsychiatry, 65*(2), 225–237.

Auerhahn, N. C., & Laub, D. (1998). Intergenerational memory of the Holocaust. In Y. Danieli (Ed.), *International handbook of multigenerational legacies of trauma* (pp. 21–43). New York: Plenum Press.

Bala, J. (1998/2000).*The interplay of stressful and protective processes in refugee families.* In L. van Willigen (Ed.), *Health hazards of organised violence in children II. Coping and protective factors* (pp. 43–53). Utrecht: Stichting Pharos.

Bala, J. (2001). *Mother does not laugh any more. Therapeutic interventions with traumatised families.* In M. Verwey (Ed.), Trauma and empowerment (pp. 157–169). Berlin: VWB-Verlag fur Wissenschaft und Bildung.

Bar-On, D. (1999). *The indescribable and the undiscussable*: *Reconstructing human discourse after trauma.* Budapest and New York: Central European University Press.

Barudy, J., Paez, D., & Martens, J. (1980). Nuestra experiencia terapeutica con expresos politicos latinoamericanos. [Our therapeutical experience with former political prisoners from Latin America]. *FRANJA, 5*(3).

Bergmann, M. S., & Jucovy, M. E. (Eds.). (1982). *Generations of the Holocaust.* New York: Basic Books.

Bettelheim, B. (1963/1977). *The ultimate limit.* Glencoe, IL: Free Press.

Boscolo, L., & Bertrando, P. (1993). *The times of time. A new perspective in systemic therapy and consultation.* New York: W. W. Norton.

Danieli, Y. (1981, September–October). Differing adaptational styles in families of survivors of the Nazi holocaust: Some implications for treatment. *Children Today, 10,* 6–10.

di Nicola, V. (1997). *A stranger in the family: Culture, families, and therapy.* New York and London: W. W. Norton.

Figley, C. R. (1989). *Helping traumatized families.* San Francisco: Jossey-Bass.

Garmezy, N. (1991). Resilience in children's adaptation to negative life events and stressfull environments. *Pediatric Annals, 20,* 459–466.

Goffman, E. (1963). *Stigma. Notes on the management of spoiled identity.* Englewood Cliffs, NJ: Prentice-Hall.

Grubrich-Simitis, I. (1984). Vom Konkretismus zur Metaphorik [From concretism to metaphorics]. *Psyche, 1,* 1–28.

Harkness, L. L. (1993). Transgenerational transmission of war related trauma. In J. P. Wilson & B. Raphael (Eds.), *International handbook of traumatic stress syndromes* (pp. 635–643). New York: Plenum Press.

Hoffmann, L. (1990). Constructing realities: An art of lenses. *Family Process, 29*(1), 1–12.

Igreja, V., Mas, J., et al. (2000). The cultural dimension of war traumas in central Mozambique: The case of Gorongosa. *Mental Health Online.* Retrieved from.

Jaffa, T. (1993). Therapy with families who have experienced torture. In J. P. Wilson & B. Raphael (Eds.), *International handbook of traumatic stress syndromes* (pp. 715–723). New York: Plenum.

Kestemberg, J. (1983). Survivor parents and their children. In M. S. Bergmann & M. E. Jucovy (Eds.), *Generations of the Holocaust* (pp. 83–102). New York: Basic Books.

Larner, G. (1996). Narrative child therapy. *Family Process, 35,* 423–440.

Lazarus, R. S. F. S. (1984). *Stress, appraisal and coping.* New York: Springer.

McCubbin, M. A., & McCubbin, H. I. (1989). Theoretical orientations to family stress & coping. In C. R. Figley (Ed.), *Treating stress in families* (pp. 3–45). New York: Brunner-Mazel.

McCubbin, M. A., & McCubbin, H. I. (1993). Family coping with health crises: The resiliency model of family stress, adjustment and adaptation. In C. Danielson, B. Hamel-Bissell, & P. Wienstead-Fry (Eds.), *Families, health and illness* (pp. 21–64). St. Louis, MO: C. V. Mosby.

McCubbin, H. I., & Patterson, J. M (1983). The family stress process: The double ABCX model of adjustment and adaptation. *Marriage and Family Review, 6*(1/2), 7–37.

McCubbin, H. I., Thompson, A. I., Thompson, E., Elver, K., & McCubbin, M. I. (1998). Ethnicity, schema, and coherence: Appraisal processes for families in crisis. In H. I. McCubbin, E. Thompson, A. I. Thompson, & J. Fromer (Eds.), *Stress, coping, and health in families* (pp. 41–67). Thousand Oaks, CA, London, and New Delhi: Sage Publications.

McGoldrick, M. (1989). Ethnicity and the family life cycle. In B. Carter & M. McGoldrick (Eds.), *The changing family life cycle. Framework for family therapy* (pp. 70–91). Boston: Allyn & Bacon.

Niederland, W. (1968). Clinical observations on the "survivor syndrome." *International Journal of Psychoanalysis, 49*, 313–315.

Papadopoulos, R. K. (2001). Refugee families: Issues of systemic supervision. *Journal of Family Therapy, 23*, 405–422.

Parin, P. (1992). *Der Widerspruch im Subjekt*. Hamburg.

Reemtsma, J. P. (1997). *Im Keller*. Hamburg: Hamburger Edition.

Roer Strier, D. (1996). Coping strategies of immigrant parents: Directions for family therapy. *Family Process, 35*(3), 363–376.

Rousseau, C., & Drapeau, (1998). The impact of culture on transmission of trauma. Refugees' stories and silence embodied in their children's lives. In Y. Danieli (Ed.), *International handbook of multigenerational legacies of trauma* (pp. 465–484). New York: Plenum Press.

Shay, J. (1995). *Archilles in Vietnam. Combat trauma and the undoing of character*. New York: First Touchstone Editi Presson; German Edition: Hamburg: Hamburger Edition.

van der Veer, G. (1998). *Counselling and therapy with refugees*. New York: Wiley.

van Essen, J., Somers, A. G., & Bala, J. (1995). Het weven van een tapijt. Vluchtelingenkinderen en — gezinnen tussen breuk en herstel. Oorlog tekent je leven. *ICODO-Info, 12*(3/4), 84–97.

Walter, J. (1983). *Das Exil der Kinder. Psychosoziale Probleme der Kinder chilenischer Exilierter in der Bundesrepublik Deutschland. Ein Beitrag zur Psychiatrie der Verfolgung und Migration anhand von Familienschicksalen* [The exile of children. Psychosocial problems of children of Chilean exiles in the GFR: A contribution to psychiatry of persecution and migration using the analysis of family destinies]. Dissertation, Freiburg, Medical Faculty of the Albert-Ludwig University.

Walter, J. (1993, December 5–9). *Twelve years after: A follow-up study of Chilean families in exile*. International Conference of Health, Political Repression and Human Rights, Manila, Philippines.

Walter, J., & Adam, H. (2000). Beyond victimology? Approaches and techniques for broadening up coping alternatives. In L. van Willigen (Ed.), *Heath hazards of organised violence in children II. Coping and protective factors* (pp. 129–139). Utrecht: Stichting Pharos.

Walsh, F. (1998). Beliefs, spirituality and transcendence: Keys to family resilience. In M. McGoldric (Ed.), *Re-visioning family therapy* (pp. 465–484). New York: Guilford.

Walsh, F. (2003). Family resilience: A framework for clinical practice. *Family Process, 42*(1), 1–18.

In-Between: Adolescent Refugees in Exile

HUBERTUS ADAM AND JELLY VAN ESSEN

In Europe it is well known that migration and flight cause psychological strains. After World War II tens of millions of expellees, refugees, and emigrants came to Western Europe. Today, still, war and persecution continue to cause great suffering for children and families. In 2001 UNICEF counted 35 million refugees worldwide, 80% of them women and children. In the decade from 1990 to 2000, 2 million children lost their lives in armed conflicts, 6 million were injured or mutilated for life, 1 million were orphaned, and 12 million lost their homes (German Committee for UNICEF, 2001).

International and national conflicts, as well as religious or ethnic differences, and socioeconomic problems and poverty can drive families from their homes. Almost all refugees settle in (displacement) or near (local resettlement) their native countries. Only few of them try to build a new life far away from home, and, of those, only few actually succeed in building a new existence in exile.

Coming from many countries and different cultures, often after a long and dangerous flight, some of these refugees try to reach safety in Europe, only to find themselves confronted with the Europeans' sober reception policy and a long waiting period for a decision as to their request for asylum. Among the refugees are adults, families, and a growing number of children and adolescents, many of them unaccompanied minors.

Approximately 6 million refugees are presently living in Europe. In recent years the largest number came from former Yugoslavia, the countries of the former USSR, the Far and Middle East, and Africa. In the year 2002 the United Nations High Commissioner for Refugees (UNHCR) counted more than 450,000 people seeking asylum in 25 European countries (UNHCR, 2004). We do not know exactly how many of these are children. The variations in the data are due to the difficulties in defining migration and flight in sociological terms on the one hand and on the other hand to the lack of detailed empirical studies that make a distinction between adults and children (Angenendt, 2000). But there is no doubt that child psychiatrists and psychotherapists as well as family therapists are faced with an enormous challenge.

Who are these youngsters and families, who, on the one hand, arrive with the idea, the dream of a new life while, on the other hand, are suffering from the excrutiating burden of trauma? As psychiatrists and psychotherapists we are dealing with individual stories of migration and flight and with the ways migrants and refugees are coping with these often very complex stories (Zeiler, 1997). Over and over again we are confronted with the dire fact that flight results in a humiliating compulsion to leave one's home and an unwanted breaking-off of relations (Brucks, 2001).

By our definition, a migrant child is one whose biography is characterized by, in many cases, a lifelong process somewhere between the poles of voluntary migration and forced flight, which, depending on the child's stage of development, can vary. If the child and/or his or her parents have lived through war, civil war, or other kinds of "organized violence" (Geuns, 1987) and the child has had to leave his or her homeland on the basis of one of these occurrences, we call this individual a refugee child.

So, different groups are to be taken into consideration and could be classified in the following ways (Adam, Lucas, Möller, & Riedesser, 2002):

• Refugee children in families, born prior to or during flight.
• Refugee children in families, born after fleeing.
• Refugee adolescents who fled with their families.
• Refugee adolescents in families who were born and brought up in exile.
• Refugee children who stayed somewhere for more than 3 months on their flight route.
• Children as perpetrators.
• Unaccompanied minors.

The rising number of unaccompanied minors can be attributed to various factors. First, there are an increasing number of refugees due to the many (inter)national and ethnic conflicts throughout the world.

Second, the increase of brutalities involved, which causes the division of families, and the loss of parents and other family members by violence and manslaughter. Third, the increasing economic problems in developing countries, which drives children away from their families or brings parents to the point of sending their children to Western countries in order to and with instructions to find a better future.

When adolescents arrive in Europe with family members it does not mean they have not suffered losses. Most adolescents have to deal with the loss or disappearance of a parent, grandparent, brother, or sister. Both accompanied and unaccompanied adolescents have one thing in common: they are disconnected from their homes, peers, and context at a most vulnerable age. At this age and stage of development it is crucial for adolescents to build up self-identity while striving for autonomy. Their uprooting, whether migration or forced flight from their homeland, seriously endangers the fulfillment of this developmental phase. At the same time, by leaving traumatic influences behind, they are given a chance for protection, growth, and development in a potentially new future. In this chapter we will focus primarily on these complex inner and outer worlds of adolescent refugees.

DEVELOPMENTAL ASPECTS

Developmental tasks are related to the demands and expectations of a certain culture and a certain age (van der Veer, 1998). Fulfilling these tasks forms a basic condition for a healthy development of adolescents and young adults. Organized violence can disturb fulfilling these tasks and can lead to severe and long-lasting psychopathology. The following developmental tasks can be distinguished:

- Separation from parents and family, striving for autonomy and independence, learning to be alone.
- Development of self-image and identity, multiplied by different cultures.
- Dealing with ambivalence, doubts, and uncertainties.
- Emotional differentiation, learning the meaning of tolerance, pain, sorrow, happiness for the manner of acting.
- Cognitive growth, understanding the context and vicissitudes of life.
- Social-sexual growth, integration of aggressive and sexual impulses into daily life.
- Orientation in a new cultural system.
- Reshaping relationships and friendship, learning to love and to form relationships.
- Learning day-to-day living abilities: housing, financing, structuring.
- Future orientation: education, choice of profession, destination.

After the first separation-individuation of the toddler, adolescence can be seen as a second phase of separation-individuation. Biological changes lead to cognitive and affective changes, which, in turn, can result in seemingly resolved conflicts surfacing once again. The adolescent is confronted with these conflicts again and forced to resist its "regressive maelstrom" (Bohleber, 1996).

According to Akhtar (1995), migration can be seen as a third separation-individuation, which creates a tremendous shock with multiple losses. From a psychoanalytical point of view it involves regression and splitting with concomitant idealization or devaluation of parents, family, countries, and cultures. Adolescent refugees, in particular, must learn to overcome the notion that family is the sole meaningful authority in their lives and endeavor to find orientation and definition in a new cultural system under difficult circumstances (Erdheim, 1988).

For adolescents, the forced separation from family and friends coincides with the loss of the parental country and culture. And the adolescent individuation is repeated in the need for finding a new home in the host country. These processes interfere and become more intense as they involve double losses and double mourning, both familial and environmental (van Essen, 1999). For unaccompanied minors it is even more complicated due to the dual loss of parents and parental land, thus rendering them, through the process of identification, vulnerable.

The lack of parental support and care, regardless of whether parents are physically absent or psychologically unavailable because of other problems requiring their attention, might influence the building of identity. The absence of trusted identification models during a life phase where an adolescent attempts to manage without daily parental support can make an adolescent feel alone and insecure as to his or her competence. When separation from the parental system comes too quickly, autonomy is forced on the adolescent. Separation as a result of losses complicates the issue of mourning for dead or missing parents.

Confrontation with human violence can also create moral dilemmas, which are very difficult to handle. Living under the disintegration of social and political structures and a collapse of the community makes it difficult to identify with cultural and moral values, even more so where moral judgments are questioned by accepted aggression occurring around the youngster.

After arriving in the host country, language problems impede expression and regulation of emotions and can lead to more acting out, less self-confidence, and lower self-esteem (Kouratovsky, 1996), thus further interfering with identity building. For these youngsters a safe and secure environment, with continuing care and support as well as positive perspectives, are preconditions for preventing serious interferences with their development.

According to Groen-Prakken (1997), very young children and adolescents are among the highest risk groups in situations of war and violence: the youngest because of the risk of separation from parents, the adolescents by the high vulnerability and higher sensitivity for traumatization and subsequent interference with phase-specific separation and identity development. Adolescents have to deal with the traumatic experiences and losses imposed upon them and with loss of familial protection and parental unavailability. At the same time they must adapt to a new culture, build a new life, and find new friends. Meanwhile, these youngsters are growing up and, like their peers, have adolescent developmental tasks to fulfill (van der Veer, 1998).

> Ali is the oldest son in a Muslim family and has an important function in replacing his father, who has been missing since the war broke out in his native country. It is a cultural matter of course that Ali is taking the responsibility in caring for the family. Occupied as he is with his own developmental process, he is still too young to bear full responsibility and is not acquainted or familiar with the traditions and rules of his host country. As a result he has developed sleeping problems and depression, and has great difficulty performing his duties at school. He fails, feels ashamed, and becomes more and more depressed.

TRANSCULTURAL ASPECTS

Migration itself can be seen as a potentially traumatic event, a disruptive process, different from the traumatization by war and violence. It refers to loss of social structures, cultural values, and loss of identity (Eisenbruch, 1991). But migration can also be considered a challenge, as it offers the possibility for growth and psychological rebirth (Akhtar, 1995). Grinberg and Grinberg (1989) describe psychological growth in terms of integration, reorganization, and consolidation of identity. It implicates a search for what is lost, but at the same time looking for what is left and can be saved.

Therapists working with refugees are in a conflicting situation themselves, torn between two extremes, as it were. One extreme is the attitude and behavior of a therapist from the same culture as the family undergoing treatment. His or her perception and understanding of the family is based on having grown up under identical sociocultural circumstances. The therapist tends to overrate traditional cultural and family patterns and neglect the process of migration and flight. The other extreme is of the belief that family-dynamic and psychodynamic processes run the same course the world over, thus reflecting similar conflicts. Neither of the two considers the profound significance migration and flight have on the biography of a family and the fact that development is a changing process. Therefore, we feel that treatment focusing on cultural specifics should be based on the following (di Nicola, 1997):

- Openness and curiosity, which does not mean adopting a neutral or unbiased attitude or substituting one's own values for a xenophobic attitude. What it does mean is incorporating cultural information in therapeutic work.
- The willingness to question and analyze one's own biases, distance oneself from the surrounding cultural norms without denying one's own cultural and ethical foundation.
- The willingness to keep questioning whether the symptoms or behavior observed are the same or, in fact, differ from the usual.

Contradictory processes frequently occur simultaneously among individuals forced to migrate and are often targeted by mourning. Positive, nostalgic illusions are handed down to children; frequently, everyday life in the host country corresponds more intensely to the culture and values of the (lost) homeland, with adjustment resembling more an idealization of the culture of origin. Oftentimes these individuals seek subcultural conditions in order to create a feeling of community. Adolescents so often join peer groups that, with their similar origin and language, seem to offer them shelter. Often, however, these groups tend to be dissocial, and in some cities they are violent gangs.

Yet at the same time adults convey an image of the homeland to their children as a place where violence and/or helplessness prevail. This is often the case in families whose identity was greatly influenced by active participation in the country's political and military conflicts (and children are liable to feel that the parents sacrificed them for the sake of their political beliefs), but who are also highly traumatized and who tend to stress the intrusive aspects of trauma-related disorders.

In refugee parents, where the avoidance of trauma-related disorders is more prominent, children often feel left out of central areas of their parents' lives and, consequently, feel alone. The "conspiracy of silence," concerning the past, becomes an unbearable burden (Bar-On, 1989; Danieli, 1981).

> A mother from a Muslim family from Iraq is raped by soldiers during the absence of her husband. The same soldiers killed their youngest son. The husband never heard exactly what happened with his family. His wife is not able to talk about it, saying men are not strong enough to bare the truth, and being afraid she will no longer be accepted as part of the family. Meanwhile, both parents suffer from severe post-traumatic symptoms and depression, and are unable to function as caring parents or as partners. Their oldest son of 14 starts to have nightmares about the events that happened to his mother. What was not spoken about returned in his fantasies and dreams.

Refugee families, in particular, often find themselves in a position where the past is destroyed, the present is characterized by insecurity and limitations to their range of action, and the future remains unknown

(Bala, 2001). These people are not only limited by their own real, external actions but also by their inner ability to develop a plan of action.

BURDENING AND COPING: THE PAST

Fleeing one's country involves a dynamic process that starts long before the actual departure and, in most cases, never really comes to an end. As early as the 1940s, reports on the psychological traumatization of children through war, flight, and persecution were published (e.g., Freud, 1949; Solomon, 1942), followed by an increasing number of publications dealing with the various impacts of disasters (man-made as well as natural) on children and adolescents (e.g., Bloch, Silber, & Perry, 1956; Eth & Pynoos, 1985; Garmezy & Rutter, 1985; Jensen & Shaw, 1993; Keilson, 1979; Kuterovac, Dyregrov, & Stuvland, 1994; Terr, 1979, 1991).

Many studies have shown that long-lasting fear and uncertainty, the experience of shell attacks and bombing, witnessing maltreatment, rape, killing, or even mass murder, to say nothing of the strains of flight and expulsion, put the developing child under severe stress and, at times, even provoked massive mental harm (e.g., Arroyo & Eth, 1985; Kinzie, Sack, Angell, Manson, & Rath, 1986; Kuterovac, Dyregrov, & Stuvland, 1994; Macksoud & Aber, 1996; Saigh, 1991; Smith, Perrin, Yule, Hacam, & Stuvland, 2002; Thabet & Vostanis, 1998).

A study of how intensely children are affected by the influence of war, carried out in Kuwait after the first Gulf War, indicated a greater number of symptoms in cases where children had been directly confronted with the experience of war and mentioned as well protective measures, for example in stable family structures (Macksoud & Aber, 1996). Bosnian children also showed high degrees of posttraumatic stress disorder (PTSD) symptoms, particularly those directly involved in war activity (Smith et al., 2002). Similar symptoms were confirmed in Bosnian children living in exile in Greece. Roughly half of the Bosnian refugee children had a tendency toward depressive behavior, over 25% increased anxiety, and more than one fourth suffered from posttraumatic disturbances (Papageorgiou et al., 2000).

The events underlying the decision to leave include both living under general repression within a violent society, as well as direct threats to one's safety by war and violence. Many adolescents have faced traumatic experiences themselves. Some have undergone detention, maltreatment, torture, and rape. Some have witnessed violence directed to loved ones, seeing their father tortured, their mother raped, or their brother or sister killed. Seeing family members rendered helpless and not being able to help or rescue them can evoke a tremendous feeling of guilt or shame. Others experienced the destruction of their homes and environment, which forced them to a sudden and unexpected flight and a stay in a refugee camp. The flight itself often involves danger, lack of safety, shelter, and food, and great uncertainty as to their immediate future. Sometimes adolescents have actively participated in war actions as child soldiers, under the pressure of threats to their families or under the influence of drugs. This might well interfere with the adolescent task of coping with aggression (van Essen, 1998). In attempting to deal with extreme violence there is a tendency to project anger toward external objects. Possible reactions include distrust, fantasies of revenge, and externalization, and can develop into destructive, opposing, or antisocial behavior.

Beyond traumatization disruption of the family brings more fear and uncertainty. Separation from parents or family and family members who are missing or staying behind in danger are extremely stressful events for an adolescent, especially in cases where a youngster has no choice, or the separation was forced or could not be anticipated. Disruption of family life influences the relationships and the ability to care for and to protect one another. Adolescents mourn for the loss of parents or family members, the loss of a cohesive and functioning family, but also for the loss of day-to-day routine, peers, and education. They suffer individual and family losses as well as cultural losses.

> A 17-year-old boy from Angola witnessed severe violent acts in his own country during civil war. In the country of asylum he has post-traumatic nightmares and flashbacks of the events. Yet these are not the reason for seeking professional help. It is the loneliness, the feeling of being completely left alone in a foreign world, the lack of daily support and care and advice that make him feel utterly desperate and depressed. "Who will bury me," he asked, "when something will happen to me here?"

BURDENING AND COPING: EXILE

The consequences of war and violence are often the cause of postwar mental and psychosomatic problems, even after years in exile. Fazel and Stein (2002), in their overview of psychological problems of refugee children, point out three kinds of strain: the traumatizing experiences and the chronic stress in the initial phase in their home countries, then the flight itself, in many cases lasting for months, with mortal danger and separation from family members, and, finally, the strains in the host country including role conflicts, difficulties with the language, and legal problems. These strains can cause symptoms like insomnia, lack of concentration, impulsive outbursts, avoidance, anxiety, and intrusive thoughts and feelings; symptoms similar to those summed up in the diagnosis of PTSD. Kinzie et al. (1986) found these similarities in Cambodian refugee children in exile in the United States, Kuterovac et al. (1994) came to similar results in examining children from Croatia, as well as Smith et al. (2002), in examining Bosnian children, and Thabet and Vostanis (1998) in examining Palestinian children.

In a U.S. study, Cambodian refugee adolescents were questioned four times over a 12-year period regarding PTSD and depression. This group consisted of refugees, on average 29 years of age at the time, who were prisoners in the Khmer concentration camps during their childhood and had been heavily traumatized (Kinzie et al., 1986; Kinzie, Sack, Angell, Clarke, & Rath, 1989; Sack et al., 1993). Despite good living conditions in the United States, PTSD symptoms persisted and, in some cases, did not manifest themselves until many years later, a factor of considerable significance (Sack, Him, & Dickason, 1999). A Swedish research group (Hjern & Angel, 2000), which studied 63 refugee children from Chile and the Middle East, discovered that 7 years after arriving in Sweden and having had their first medical checkup 20% of the children still displayed behavioral problems, according to their teachers.

Another Swedish research group, studying the mental health and social adjustment of a group of very young refugees aged 6 to 10, 3½ years after their arrival in Sweden, found that the extent of violence and war experiences in the country of origin and individual vulnerability were the primary risk factors for extended posttraumatic stress reactions. The well-being of a child's mother tends to have a positive and protective effect on the child's developmental and social adjustment and is generally correlated with the quality of a child's relationships to peers and people of the same mind (Almqvist & Broberg, 1999).

Evidently psychosocial stress reactions persist even after fleeing war-torn areas and can lead to developmental disorders and behavioral problems (Adam, 1993; Angel, Hjern & Ingleby, 2001). Refugee parents rarely seek help for the mental problems afflicting their children (Šikić, Javornik, Stracenski, Bunjevac, & Buljan-Flander, 1997). Due to the difficulty of their own situation they often underestimate the consequences of violence for their children and tend to discuss the traumatic experiences afflicting their children as little as possible, if at all.

In short, adolescents, colored by their experiences with war and violence, must learn to cope with the following problems in exile:

- personal, community, and cultural losses;
- multiple separations and need for parental and family support and care;
- familial conflicts and psychic disturbances;
- long-lasting uncertainty as to acquiring residency in the new country and starting up a normal life;
- minimal facilities and common violence in reception centers;
- limitations to education and freedom of movement;
- social marginalization and discrimination.

Due to all these problems, most adolescents feel confused, insecure, and ambivalent. Hoping to feel safe after the horror they faced, they now find themselves endangered again. And even when the whole family has fled, it does not mean parents are available. They face their own problems and often fail to give enough attention to their children. Family disruption and discontinuity in daily and social life block the adolescent in working through the traumatic events of the past and in mourning his or her losses. In addition, the process of migration adds to the creation of family conflicts, raising difficulties and multicultural differences (Punamaki, 2000). As a result tasks, roles, and communication are altered. Parents are left without a supportive extended family to raise their children by themselves. As a consequence, children are involved in the household and parentification interferes with their development.

> Jozo was 12 years old when his father was shot by the Serbs and he was forced to flee with his mother to a European country. He was brought to a psychiatric hospital with attacks of difficulties in breathing. In former examinations somatic causes for these attacks had been ruled out. He reported that his mother was very lonely and sad and he had to care for her as well as to make sure the refrigerator was filled. The most beautiful moments for his mother were when she could take a little walk with her son along the river. Ambivalent feelings took his breath: on the one hand he was afraid of growing up and being separated from his mother, on the other hand he was worried by the prospect of having to stay with her forever.

Dealing with the problems of exile without mutual support systems can lead to mental instability. This is particularly difficult for refugees originating from communities where it is common for larger groups to live together. In extended families children are raised and mutual support is given within the group, resulting in group relations rather then the one-to-one relationship typical of Western society.

These specific problems of refugees should not lead to a misunderstanding. A study of 350 refugee children in Hamburg showed that, in correlation to nonrefugees, the refugees were not "more ill" in general, but the profile of psychopathology and diagnosis was different. The difference to nonrefugees were even more pronounced than between cultural subgroups (Adam, Aßhauer, Walter, & Riedesser, 2003).

IN-BETWEEN

The world of the helpers is directly opposite to the real external world of the adolescent refugees, which is affected by the helpers' experiences and sense of burn-out as much as it is by the basic sociopolitical conditions and financial resources available for refugee aid. In the case of unaccompanied minors, helpers do not know if the story these youngsters relate is actually the truth. In most cases, they have no documents, and no family member is present to validate the stories the children report when their family history is taken.

The Immigration Office, however, asks precise questions in these cases. Their work is to assess, register, and confirm the refugees, for example, determining the region they come from by questioning them on local knowledge. Adolescent refugees tend to be somewhere "in between": public facilities take care of them (in emergencies), even if they don't know whether they are under 16 or over 18 years of age, or where exactly they came from. An underlying feeling of distrust and suspicion seems to prevail on both sides.

From an intrapsychic point of view, the adolescent refugees are also "in between." On the one hand they wish to return to their homeland because of the sociolegal problems they are experiencing in exile. More often than not, they feel unwelcome and realize their perspectives are not very promising. But returning to their homeland would jeopardize their situation entirely as they would be returning to a country and circumstances they had initially fled. There is the fear of being involved in more armed conflicts, even the risk of suffering personal injury or economic disaster.

Should adolescents return from exile, having failed the social pressure of the family who scratched together enough money to secure the adolescent's (economic) survival abroad, the consequences would be overwhelming. It is not rare for families to expel young members who have thus failed; they are left to fend for themselves on the outskirts of large cities, without the care and support of their families. There is no questioning the fact that these adolescents must feel like losers. Not only have they failed to meet the expectations of their families, they failed to live up to their own expectations in the "promised land of exile" and were forced to return to their home countries. In addition, they have nothing to show for their experience abroad, no diploma or certificate of learning, in short, they are returning empty-handed.

On the other hand, these adolescents seem to recognize that the possibility of staying in the country of exile is not a means of fulfilling their hopes and dreams. They realize they are alone regardless of whether real family is present and are living in exile with no support. Although the new country might offer better social conditions than their homeland, their chances for social development are virtually nonexistent by comparison to the average adolescent from the host society.

REACTIONS AND CONSEQUENCES

The significance of a traumatic experience differs considerably from individual to individual and is most difficult to classify in general diagnostic categories. However, it is generally regarded as a crucial factor of major consequence and highly pathognostic in that it interferes with the individual's plans and hopes for the future (Finkelhor, 1995). Any plans for a future life as well as room for playful, imaginative, or transitional phases (Herzog, 1996) are destroyed, thus impeding social experimentation and sensible adjustment to changing circumstances. This may well "contaminate" areas of the individual's life that were not primarily affected by the traumatizing situation (Maltas & Shay, 1995), a fact that becomes evident when the person is no longer able to experience or tell the story of his or her life coherently and sensibly (see also Adelmann, 1995; Rosenthal, 1995). This, in turn, impedes the backing provided by former positive experiences and supportive relationships. In the search for causality and meaning past experiences are suddenly reinterpreted within a whole new context. Basic fears might be reactivated; split off (partial separate) and unreflected experiences might be transmitted to later generations, who then put them in concrete terms (Kestenberg, 1983; Kogan, 1995).

Mental integration of traumatic experiences is most difficult following acute traumatization. Recently, neurophysiologic correlates have been discovered, permitting biological interpretations. Various mental and physical adaptive reactions to traumatization were observed, such as overexcitement and dissociation. As the developing brain organizes and internalizes new information according to its use, children who have experienced traumatization tend to develop more neuropsychiatric symptoms the greater their state of overexcitement or dissociation is. If acute adaptability conditions persist they can, as a result of the formation of neuronal control functions, develop into permanent dysfunctional characteristics (cf. overviews in van der Kolk, McFarlane, & Weisaeth, 1996; Perry, Pollard, Blakely, Baker, & Vigilante, 1995, Schepker, 1997).

The International Classification of Diseases (ICD-10) (WHO, 1991) does not distinguish between PTSD in children and in adults. In the *Diagnostic and Statistical Manual of Mental Disorders* (DSM-IV) (APA, 1994), however, a pattern of symptoms to be found in children and adolescents was described. Besides the three main symptoms observed in adults (hyperarousal, intrusions, avoidance), it includes the following symptoms:

- agitated behavior;
- repeated play expressing themes and aspects of the trauma;
- nightmares and frightening dreams without recognizable contents;
- enactment leading to a repetition of elements of the traumatic experience.

Recently a discussion arose concerning whether it is permissible to diagnose PTSD in children and adolescents (Pfefferbaum, 1997). Now most scientists agree that children can show symptoms typical of PTSD. Perrin, Smith, and Yule (2000), for example, report intrusive thoughts as to the traumatic experience in severely traumatized children, especially in calm situations and before falling asleep. The intrusions in children and adolescents differ according to their age and stage of development, but, with growing maturity of the youths, they approach those observed in adults. The clusters of symptoms "avoidance" and "hyperarousal" were also found repeatedly in children and adolescents (Arroyo & Eth, 1985; Kinzie et al., 1986; Saigh, 1991).

> Adil, 16 years old, is living through nightmares and flashbacks of the events in his country where soldiers had attacked the family and killed his father and brother. During flashbacks he relives the event in his village, becomes very anxious, and starts to scream. During the day he tries to avoid any place that might trigger a flashback. He avoids public transport because of uniformed staff and stays away from school. At night the silence and solitude force him to remember. He can hardly sleep.

Besides these symptoms the life of an adolescent is greatly affected by the events he or she experiences. Day-to-day life is altered, intellectual and social functioning lowered, and behavioral problems have social implications. The image adolescents have of themselves, other important persons, and the world around them is shattered and can remain distorted for a long time. Traumatic events damage their basic trust and beliefs in a positive attitude and integrity of people surrounding them. They learn that predictability and continuity of everyday life cannot be taken for granted.

Like children, adolescents tend to expect a repetition of traumatic events (Pynoos, 1996). Once their world has been shattered there is no reason it cannot be shattered again. Often posttraumatic reactions are provoked by uncertainty and insecurity in their present lives. Not knowing whether one can stay in the host country, or witnessing the fear of parents having to return to their country of origin, triggers the reliving of former events and highlights the possibility of repetition. The traumatic expectations can be an important reason for continuous anxiety and nightmares. And where traumatic expectations exist, there is no place for positive expectations for the future and long-term perspectives.

> Masa was suddenly struck by an attack of rebels in her village in an African country, in which her family was killed and she herself was raped. Within one day her life had deeply and permanently changed. One year later, in treatment she is still unable to form any picture of her future. Asked about future education and work possibilities she gazes without understanding. Future has no meaning for her; she is fixed in the past and present.

It is a misunderstanding that the main events in the life of an adolescent who has had to flee are traumatic events of the past. Equally, it is a misunderstanding that problems following the request for asylum and the subsequent uncertainties in the country of arrival are minor disturbing factors, mainly hindering the individual's ability to cope with traumatic events or disturbing posttraumatic therapy. More precisely, it is the accumulation of stress from the past, present, and expected future, these different levels of ongoing stress closely interwoven, that form the essence of the psychopathology of adolescents who have been forced to flee.

Real and acute stress caused by not knowing whether one can stay in the host country or will be forced to return to the dangerous country of origin is sufficient reason to recall and relive past traumatic events, whereas these events probably could have been coped with if the level of present stress had been lower. The threat of having to return to the circumstances one has fled is enough to evoke profound feelings of anxiety and sorrow, which often refer to a deeper level of former anxieties and then adds to the existing psychopathology.

During traumatization, migration, and acculturation there is a sequence of events that accumulate and interfere with one another. This sequence can do greater harm than any single event by itself. Keilson (1979) pointed this out after World War II during his research among children in Jewish orphanages who had faced three sequences of traumatic experiences: (1) occupation of the Netherlands by the Nazis, (2) separation of mothers and children and deportation to the concentration camps, and (3) postwar society with foster care of the survived children. Keilson found in his study that children in different stages of age and development show different forms of reactions on traumatic experiences. From his point of view, trauma can only be understood in an appropriate way if the three traumatic sequences are considered together. Especially an unfavorable course of the third sequence can lead to serious psychopathology. Likewise, Garbarino and Kostelny (1996) speak about the risk accumulation model, developed during research among Palestinian children in the *Intifada*. They describe how children are submitted to a great number of different experiences with war and violence over a long period of time. This type-2 trauma (Terr, 1991) or continuous traumatic stress (Garbarino, 1996) causes a broad range of developmental and behavioral problems. The presence of multiple risk factors results in an exponential rise in developmental damage, with a higher risk of permanent harm. Besides dealing with traumatic experiences, main risk factors are dysfunction of the family and disruption of the community. In particular the combination of political and family stress can have serious consequences.

DIAGNOSTIC ISSUES

During the assessment one can focus on three aspects to determine whether an adolescent is apt to develop problems after experiencing organized violence:

- The history of traumatization, migration, and acculturation, and the adolescent's reactions and psychopathology, before and after the traumatization.
- The developmental strength and coping mechanisms, such as an internal locus of control, positive self-esteem, social skills, stabile relationships, ability to use available support.
- The availability of parental support and care, and the continuity and safety of a caring family and supportive community.

During the initial contact, the presence of an interpreter is essential. It is also essential that the adolescent be made aware that all therapeutic treatment is strictly confidential, also that the presence of an interpreter can be refused without the adolescent having to state his or her reason for doing so.

Assessment of the Adolescent

In the assessment of the youngsters the following issues should become clear:

- Type and extent of stressful situations experienced prior to, during, and after fleeing homeland.
- Protective and helpful factors from their point of view.
- The culture- and family-specific coping strategies with reference to fleeing or other stress factors.
- Subjective medical history, culturally specific.

Special attention should be given to the following questions:

- How do they experience the people they primarily relate to, and how did these people react prior to, during, and after their flight?
- Are symptoms directly related to fleeing or mental strain caused by flight?
- Do previously existing symptoms recur, are there new symptoms, is there a change in existing symptoms?
- Have there been dysfunctional changes in the adolescent's development prior to, during, or after fleeing?
- Which memories are helpful, which memories cause stress?
- Are there specific, repetitive play scenes, drawings, dreams?
- What are the impacts the experience of fleeing has had on the youngster?
- Have they expressed a desire to return, or do they feel ambivalent about returning?
- Does the adolescent show signs of guilt in digesting and overcoming what he or she experienced, is there a possibility of involvement in crime (child soldier)?
- Are there psychogenic reasons (e.g., traumatic or mourning processes) that might be impeding language acquisition?

Predisposing factors relating to the need for diagnosis and therapy pose added strains to the development, particularly changes in the relationships with people closest to the adolescent in stressful psychosocial circumstances, such as parental separation, physical or mental illness of parents, or loss of close family members.

Assessment of the Family

In the assessment of the family and people closest to the adolescent, the following issues should come clear:

- Who belongs to the family? To get a culture-specific definition of family (narrative) and to create together a genogram might be helpful.
- How is family defined within the particular culture? How are differences between family members defined?
- In the event the reference person of the youngster is not one of the child's parents, how long has the person had contact with the child?
- What is known about living, parental or related circumstances concerning the child prior to, during, and following flight?
- Were parents or closely related persons physically present and emotionally available during flight?
- What are the impacts the experience fleeing has had on family members?
- How was this traumatic situation perceived by the individual family members?
- Are there unspoken, perhaps culture-specific delegations to the children?
- Was the family involved in crimes of war?
- Were they able to prepare their escape?
- Which family members fled the area and who was left behind and why?
- What meaning do violence, persecution, and escape have?
- Are there family conflicts, hierarchical problems, problems in raising the children, family secrets?
- What are the family responsibilities and differences in family life cycle in homeland/in exile?
- What interpretational patterns does the family exhibit with regard to disorder etiology?
- What is the current state of legal residency? Has there been a change of residence within the country of exile?
- How intense are the contacts to the homeland?
- Does the family have an intention of returning?

Other Sociolegal Aspects

In addition, there should be an extensive exploration of the surrounding social helper system with regard to legal, social, and somatic aspects. A somatic checkup, particularly in the case of children who are behind in their development and children who have suffered trauma with physical consequences, is highly recommendable. Questionnaires that contain standard questions on exposure, specific primary symptoms, as well as reconcilability and coping can be helpful.

The following diagnostic steps should be avoided:

- Repeated organic diagnosis, which might lead to a fixation on somatic complaints.
- Psychological tests without comprehensive cultural interpretation.
- Discussion of patient's medical history with an interpreter who is a member of the family.

If there is not a special school for refugees, language barriers are a frequent obstacle in placing refugee adolescents in appropriate grades and surmising their actual level of cognitive development, both of which can lead to sublevel placement. Although the youngster might be older than his or her classmates, specific developmental disorders resulting from language problems often remain undetected and have a contrary effect on the learning level due to a lack of assistance with schoolwork in the home. This lack of parental support results, for example, from parents' poor knowledge of the language of the host country. Parents, on the other hand, fear the school might have a "negative cultural influence" on their children, culminating in their lack of cooperation with the school as well as with other institutions.

Insurance and residential status should not negatively influence diagnosis or therapeutic measures. A therapeutic residency permit might be issued. It should be distinguished between diagnosis as such and diagnosis for medical opinion or certificate. It is essential that this be clarified with parents on the one hand and the surrounding social and educational experts on the other. One therapist cannot carry out both.

Conflicts can arise as a result of social workers or therapists being highly committed, yet sociolegal institutions can be overwhelmed with requests. Third parties have a tendency to misuse refugee children as a means of driving home their own political causes, whereas refugee children tend to be stigmatized for racist motives, thus becoming outsiders. Families and/or social workers frequently have a tendency to attribute mental abnormalities or psychosomatic symptoms solely to specific living conditions. Sociolegal topics (i.e., residency status, living conditions, work situation, need for medical certificates) can be used as "openers" in consulting the adolescent and his or her family. Conflicts often arise between patients, social workers, psychiatrists/psychotherapists, and other helpers. Doctors and therapists are often seen as having the questionable power of "saving" refugees from further persecution by issuing medical certificates. Therapeutic institutions are often involved in political conflicts, thus influencing the decision as to further treatment on an in- or outpatient basis.

These institutions need support regarding whether taking care for refugee minors could be a step toward peace. In future times these minors will play a major role for the home region. The minors of today will be parents of tomorrow, and to avoid the vicious circle of violence means a big challenge for therapists. To find ways from individual trauma to participation at a social reconstruction of the region destroyed by war and persecution could be a chance for future reconciliation and a breakthrough of the circle of violence.

TREATMENT ISSUES

External protection and the stability of parental care are essential in dealing with cumulative and ongoing stress. Developmental threats result from the experiences with war and organized violence, the unavailability of a caretaker or parent, the disruption of a normal, functioning family, and a sudden change in environment as a result of evacuation or flight.

The treatment must focus on these issues, which are of concern during the assessment, whether it is dealing with traumatic experiences, coping with the recent stress, or the need for developmental support and social contacts.

In general the treatment process can be divided into three phases: stabilization, integration, and socialization. Stabilization means to reestablish a feeling of safety and security by providing structure and holding, controlling disturbing complaints like nightmares and flashbacks, and retaking a grip on daily life. Treatment during this phase will focus on restoration of a psychic equilibrium, diminishing the stress, broadening up the coping repertoire, and creating a social network as a holding environment. Most attention should be paid to here and now problems, symptom relief, and practical support.

Integration means to restore the break and discontinuities in the lifeline. To cope with the pain and the sorrow from the past, to deal with uncertainties and acute stress in the present, and at the same time to adapt to a new unknown culture. The treatment can focus on the working through of traumatic experiences and losses, the coping with the cumulative stress from past, present, and future, and the adaptation to the big changes in one's own life, in the family, and in the environment. A therapeutic residency permit can be helpful to allow the adolescent just to be there and be held in an emotionally safe environment. At least none of the items discussed will leave the therapeutic room — therapeutical secrecy is well known also by the refugees. Besides the aspects of mistrust there is a chance to develop a therapeutic relationship that can function as a corrective one in relation to former and present violence.

Socialization means to find one's place in the host society, to be able to live in two cultures rather than in between. It means to deal with issues around migration, exile, and displacement, but also with discrimination and racism; to build a new existence with orientation on education, professional career, friendships, and relations. Even without certainty about a residence permit one has to think about the short- and long-term future, find answers on questions around the cultural roots, where to belong, how his or her identity has changed, or if there will be a possibility to return. Treatment, if necessary during this phase, can be oriented on developmental and identity issues, integration, and cultural differences.

These are not separate phases. They mark a process of adaptation and coping, with ups and downs. A process modified by the specific characteristics of the youngster and the underlying psychological, familial, and environmental history.

Interventions during treatment can have an impact at the individual, familial, and community levels. They can be carried out at the same time, by different therapists or social workers, in mutual cooperation and attunement. The following interventions for treatment can be useful for adolescent refugees:

At an individual level:

- reestablish structure, safety, and predictability;
- listen to the adolescents own request for help;
- define the problems and name priorities;
- provide as much information and advice as is needed;
- reduce symptoms and focus on regaining control;
- emphasize positive experiences and interactions;
- search for identification models;
- encourage the patient to make use of internal resources and external support;
- broaden up coping styles and strengthen protective factors;
- assist in working through and giving meaning to experiences with war and organized violence;
- give emotional support for sorrow, pain, and grief;
- assist in controlling feelings of aggression, rage, and revenge;
- help to fulfill developmental tasks.

At the family and community levels, assist and support the family in:

- coping with the changes in the family, including the extended family;
- mourning for familial losses, help in finding ways to replace the lost ones;

- prevent parentification and a too great responsibility;
- dealing with family secrets and the "conspiracy of silence";
- dealing with violence within the family;
- starting procedures for family reunification or a search for missing family members;
- dealing with cultural differences in education, behavioral, and moral values;
- establishing social support and community networks;
- finding social activities;
- finding an alternative perspective for future functioning;
- dealing with long-term consequences of traumatization;
- learning to find a way to accept exile and forced migration;
- learning to deal with issues around integration, marginalization, and discrimination.

Information, Advice, and Support

The patient and his or her family or the people closest to the patient are advised and informed of the need to talk about the psychosocial consequences of fleeing. It has to be made clear to them that symptoms are not the result of an illness but of social circumstances and the experiencing of extreme stress, which could lead to a disorder in the subjective well-being of virtually any human being who had gone through similar experiences. It is crucial that the distinction between normal stress reactions and pathological reactions be consulted and explained and be clarified as to how the normal psychotherapeutic approach differs from traditional healing methods. Information for the parents about the reactions of children and youngsters can help them to understand their child and meet his or her needs. It can diminish feelings of guilt and despair of having brought their family into a situation of exile. Information on early childhood perception of stress situations and the transgenerational transmission of interpretational and coping patterns as well as mental traumatization should also be given. Besides advice about stress reactions, practical consultation is very much needed. It is important to provide information about the asylum procedure, family reunion, tracing teams for missing family members, the health policy and health system, and housing and working facilities. Not knowing about the society one is living in deprives an individual from essential coping possibilities. It is necessary to show the way to immediate and accessible help for the creation of a helping and supportive environment. The quick structuring of everyday life and the creation of "normalcy" are essential.

If it appears that during the period of consultation, therapy, or care the patient is telling "tales," this ought to be discussed among colleagues first. Accepting and discussing external realities both with the individual in question as well as with professional colleagues and coworkers help the therapist in reducing his or her feelings of being abused or betrayed and help the therapist to communicate his or her feelings of helplessness.

Reduction of Symptoms and Individual Therapy

Often the adolescent remains in a vicious circle: severe sleeping problems disturb the day and night rhythm and cause tiredness and exhaustion. The youngster is not able to function by day and has to quit school, causing him or her to feel more and more changed and thus adding to the feeling of going mad. The loss of control induces more sleeping- and posttraumatic problems.

Psychoeducation about the sleeping problems as well as antidepressive medication can help to break this circle. Many adolescents fear medication because of fantasies about intrusions during a period where their main aim is to regain control over intrusive memories. This should be discussed with the adolescent in order help him or her see antidepressive medication as making sense.

In the beginning of therapy both a supportive approach and the offer to cautiously work through the individual's experiences can be helpful. Whether it is good to talk about the traumatic events remains a topic of debate. Working through can take place in a verbal or nonverbal manner and can be very helpful in dealing with the consequences of traumatic experiences. But it has not been proven necessary and helpful for everyone. Not to talk about the content can be equally supportive in forgetting and leaving behind the memories. In the same way dissociation turns out to be for some adolescents an effective way of coping, by controlling symptoms and permitting one to continue life as normal as possible become a main goal for many adolescents. But dissociation can in other cases also coexist with severe posttraumatic symptoms and profoundly threaten normal functioning, in which case it needs to be dealt with. In all cases the issue of control is an important one; feeling that you are not in charge of your life and your body and the fear of losing control are among the main reasons to refer traumatized adolescents for treatment. A pitfall is not to talk about the traumatic content out of fear and uncertainty on behalf of the therapist.

Furthermore, it is important to assist the adolescent in coping with specific developmental phases as well as pick up symbols and metaphors that present themselves in games, narratives, or in dreams for therapeutic reframing.

> Hassan came into our hospital with a gap in his teeth thinking he was in a dental clinic not in a hospital for child and adolescent psychiatry. Although his guardian had talked everything over with him before, he insisted on getting a dental treatment, saying he could not laugh because he was ashamed of showing the gap in his teeth. It took a long time until he was able to talk about the possibility his "shame for the gap" could be a metaphor for the pains he had suffered as a child soldier and the feelings of shame connected with these pains. The gap

being real on the one hand, but on the other hand, referring to something having happened before and being lost played a crucial role in the following psychotherapy.

Encouraging adolescents to try out coping strategies in role games to lend them the feeling of control and security in new, unfamiliar surroundings is supportive, and the reference to positive relationship experiences during the flight phase allows the therapist to offer corrective suggestions for experiencing relationships. The adolescent should feel "welcome" (a "therapeutic residency permit," so to speak) and receive assistance in his or her feeling that parents are making excessive demands. The therapeutic setting creates a specific responsibility toward adolescents who are uncertain of being able to stay. Each session could be his or her last; therefore, separation and departure are ongoing themes in the sessions, and the therapist should make sure that a single topic or block of topics has been satisfactorily concluded at the end of each session. The feeling of not being able to decide about your life, being dependant on others, and out of control of your life can be devastating for an adolescent who is in need for developing autonomy and independency. It makes him or her feel helpless, and reinforces the learned helplessness (Seligman, Maier, & Geer, 1968), characteristic for coping with situations of extreme powerlessness during overwhelming traumatic experiences. Often these reactions of adolescents to a situation of uncertainty about a residence permit produce an enhancement of intrusive memories and other posttraumatic symptoms.

REFERENCES

Adam, H. (1993). *Terror und Gesundheit — Ein medizinischer Ansatz zum Verständnis von Folter, Flucht und Exil* [*Terror and health—a medical approach to understand torture, flight and exile*]. Weinheim: Beltz.

Adam, H., Aßhauer, M., Walter, J., & Riedesser, P. (2003). Patient Flüchtlingskind: Beschreibung einer Inanspruchnahmepopulation einer kinder- und jugendpsychiatrischen Universitätsklinik im Vergleich zu Nicht-Flüchtlingspatienten [Patient refugee child: description of a population of a child and adolescent psychiatry university clinic compared with non-refugee patients]. Paper presented at the Common Scientific Congress of the German Society for Child and Adolescent Psychiatry and Psychotherapy and the Austrian Society for Child and Adolescent Psychiatry and Psychotherapy, Vienna, April 2–5, 2003.

Adam, H., Lucas, T., Möller, B., & Riedesser, P. (2002). Recommendations for the treatment of child-refugees and -migrants. Theoretical and practical aspects. In B. Brandt-Wilhelmy, D. Irmler, H. Adam, T. Lucas, B. Möller, & P. Riedesser (Eds.), *Refugee children in Europe. Good practice guidelines: Psychosocial context, assessment and interventions for traumatized children and adolescents*. London: European Council on Refugees and Exile.

Adelmann, A. (1995). Traumatic memory and the intergenerational transmission of Holocaust narratives. In A. Solnit, P. Neubauer, S. Abrams, & S. Dowling (Eds.), *The psychoanalytic study of the child* (pp. 343–367). New Haven, CT: Yale University Press.

Akhtar, S. (1995). A third individuation: Immigration, identity and the psychoanalytic process. *Journal of the American Psychoanalytical Association, 43,* 1051–1084.

Almqvist, K., & Broberg, A. G. (1999). Mental health and social adjustment in young refugee children 3 years after their arrival in Sweden. *Journal of the American Academy of Child and Adolescent Psychiatry, 38*(6), 723–730.

American Psychiatric Association (APA). (1994). *Diagnostic and statistical manual of mental disorders* (4th ed.). Washington, DC: Author.

Angel, B., Hjern, A., & Ingleby, D. (2001). Effects of war and organized violence on children: A study of Bosnian refugees in Sweden. *American Journal of Orthopsychiatry, 71*(1), 4–15.

Angenendt, S. (2000). *Kinder auf der Flucht — Minderjährige Flüchtlinge in Deutschland* [Children on flight—minor refugees in Germany]. Opladen: Leske & Budrich.

Arroyo, W., & Eth., S. (1985). Children traumatized by central American warfare. In S. Eth & R. S. Pynoos (Eds.), *Post-traumatic stress disorder in children* (pp. 103–117). Washington, DC: American Psychiatric Press.

Bala, J. (2001). Mother does not laugh any more. Therapeutic interventions with traumatised families. In M. Verwey (Ed.), *Trauma and empowerment* (pp. 157–169). Berlin: Verlag für Wissenschaft und Bildung.

Bar-On, D. (1989). *Legacy of silence.* Cambridge: Harvard University Press.

Bloch, D., Silber, E., & Perry, S. (1956). Some factors in the emotional reaction of children to disaster. *American Journal of Psychiatry, 113,* 416–422.

Bohleber, W. (Ed.). (1996). Introduction to the psychoanalytical research of adolescence. In *Adolescence and identity.* Stuttgart: Verlag.

Brucks, U. (2001). Migration in die Bundesrepublik Deutschland [Migration to the Federal Republic of Germany]. In T. Hegemann & S. Salman, (Eds.), *Transkulturelle psychiatrie* [Transcultural psychiatry] (pp. 41–51). Bonn: Psychiatrie-Verlag.

Danieli, Y. (1981, September–October). Different adaptational styles in families of survivors of the nazi Holocaust: Some implications for treatment. *Children Today, 10,* 6–10.

Di Nicola, V. (1997). *A stranger in the family: Culture, families, and therapy.* New York and London: W. W. Norton.

Eisenbruch, M. (1991). From posttraumatic stress disorder to cultural bereavement: Diagnosis of Southeast Asian refugees. *Social Science & Medicine, 33,* 673–680.

Erdheim, M. (1988). *Psychoanalysis and the unconciousness of the culture.* Frankfurt: M. Suhrkamp.

Eth, S., & Pynoos, R. (Eds.). (1985). *Posttraumatic stress disorder in children.* Washington, DC: American Psychiatric Press.

Fazel, M., & Stein, A. (2002). The mental health of refugee children. *Archives of Disease in Childhood, 87*(5), 366–370.

Finkelhor, D. (1995). The victimization of children: A developmental perspective. *American Journal of Orthopsychiatry, 65,* 177–193.

Freud, A. (1949). Kriegskinder [Children in war]. In A. Freud (Ed.), *Die Schriften der Anna Freud* [The writings of Anna Freud], Bd. 2 (pp. 496–561). München: Kindler.

Garbarino, J., & Kostelny, K. (1996). The effects of political violence on Palestinian children's behavior problems: A risk accumulation model. *Child Development, 67*, 33–45.

Garmezy, N., & Rutter, M. (1985). Acute reaction to stress. In M. Rutter & L. Hersov (Eds.), Child and adolescent psychiatry: Modern approaches (2nd ed., pp. 152–176). London: Blackwell Scientific Publications.

German Committee for UNICEF [Deutsches Komitee für UNICEF] (Ed.). (2001). *Zur Situation der Kinder in der Welt* [The situation of the world's children]. Frankfurt/M.: Fischer.

Geuns, H. (1987). The concept of organized violence. In Ministry of Welfare, Health and Cultural Affairs (Eds.), *Health hazards of organized violence* (pp. 7–10). The Hague, Netherlands: Ministry of Welfare, Health and Cultural Affairs.

Grinberg, L., & Grinberg, R. (1989). *Psychoanalytic perspectives on migration and exile*. New Haven, CT: Yale University Press.

Groen-Prakken, H. (1997). Traumatisering en ontwikkelingsinterferenties bij kinderen in en na de Tweede Wereldoorlog [Traumatisation and developmental interferences in children during and after World War 2]. In T. de Ridder & S. vd Veen (Eds.), Oorlogskinderen toen en nu. Aspecten van problematiek en behandeling (pp. 10–26). Utrecht: Icodo.

Herzog, J. M. (1996). Übermittlung eines Traumas: Unbewußte Phantasie und deren Auslösung durch die äußere Realität, mit besonderer Berücksichtigung auf den Holocaust [Transmission of trauma: fantasy and external reality in view of the fact of the Holocaust]. *Psyche, 6*, 548–563.

Hjern, A., & Angel, B. (2000). Organized violence and mental health of refugee children in exile: A six-year follow-up. *Acta Paediatrica, 89*(6), 722–727.

Jensen, P., & Shaw, J. (1993). Children as victims of war: Current knowledge and future research needs. *Journal of the American Academy of Child and Adolescent Psychiatry, 32*, 697–708.

Keilson, H. (1979). *Sequentielle Traumatisierung bei Kindern* [Sequential traumatization of children]. Stuttgart: Ferdinand Enke Verlag.

Kestenberg, J. (1983). Survivor parents and their children. In M. Bergmann & M. Jucovy (Eds.), *Generations of the Holocaust* (pp. 83–101). New York: Basic Books.

Kinzie, J. D., Sack, W. H., Angell, R., Clarke, G., & Rath, B. (1989). A three-year follow-up of Cambodian young people traumatized as children. *Journal of the American Academy of Child and Adolescent Psychiatry, 28*, 501–504.

Kinzie, J. D., Sack, W. H., Angell, R. H., Manson, S., & Rath, B. (1986). The psychiatric effects of massive trauma on Cambodian children: I. The children. *Journal of the American Academy of Child and Adolescent Psychiatry, 25*, 370–376.

Kogan, I. (1995). Listening to the sound of mute children. In Stiftung für Kinder (Ed.), selected and compiled by H. Adam, P. Riedesser, H. Riquelme, A. Verderber, & J. Walter, *Children — War and persecution* (pp. 95–102). Osnabrück: Secolo.

Kouratovsky, V. (1996). Migratie- en etnisch/cultuur-specifieke aspecten bij de diagnostiek en therapie van kinderen en jeugdigen [Migration and ethnic/cultural specific aspects in diagnosis and treatment of children and youngsters]. In J. Joop & M.vd Berg (Eds.), Transculturele psychiatrie en psychotherapie (pp. 185–203). Lisse: Swets en Zeitlinger.

Kuterovac, G., Dyregrov, A., & Stuvland, R. (1994). Children in war: A silent majority under stress. *British Journal of Medical Psychology, 67,* 363–375.

Macksoud, M. S., & Aber, J. L. (1996). The war experiences and psychosocial development of children in Lebanon. *Child Development, 67,* 70–88.

Maltas, C., & Shay, J. (1995). Trauma contagion in partners of survivors of childhood sexual abuse. *American Journal of Orthopsychiatry, 65*(4), 529–539.

Papageorgiou, V., Frangou-Garunovic, A., Iordanidou, R., Yule, W., Smith, P., & Vostanis, P. (2000). War trauma and psychopathology in Bosnian refugee children. *European Child and Adolescent Psychiatry, 9,* 84–90.

Perrin, S., Smith, P., & Yule, W. (2000). Practitioner review: The assessment and treatment of post-traumatic stress disorder in children and adolescents. *Journal of Child Psychology and Psychiatry, 41*(3), 277–289.

Perry, B. D., Pollard, R., Blakely, T., Baker, W., & Vigilante, D. (1995). Childhood trauma, the neurobiology of adaptation and "use dependent" development of the brain: How "states" become "traits." *Infant Mental Health Journal, 16*(4), 271–291.

Pfefferbaum, B. (1997). Posttraumatic stress disorder in children: A review of the past 10 years. *Journal of the American Academy of Child and Adolescent Psychiatry, 36*(11), 1503–1511.

Punamaki, R. L. (2000). Personal and family resources promoting resiliency among children suffering from military violence. In L. van Willigen (Ed.), *Health hazards of organized violence in children (II). Coping and protective factors* (pp. 29–42). Utrecht: Stichting Pharos.

Pynoos, R. S. (1996, March). *The transgenerational repercussions of traumatic expectations.* Paper presented at the 6th IPA Conference on Psychoanalytic Research, London.

Rosenthal, G. (1995). *Erlebte und erzählte Lebensgeschichte. Gestalt und Struktur biographischer Selbstbeschreibungen* [Lived and told life history. Form and structure of biographical narratives]. Frankfurt: Campus.

Šikiĉ, W. H., Clarke, G., Him, C., Dickason, D., Goff, B., Lanham, K., & Kinzie J. D. (1993). A 6-year follow-up study of Cambodian refugee adolescents traumatized as children. *Journal of the American Academy of Child and Adolescent Psychiatry, 32*(2), 431–437.

Sack, W. H., Him, C., & Dickason, D. (1999). Twelve-year follow-up study of Khmer youths who suffered massive war trauma as children. *Journal of the American Academy of Child and Adolescent Psychiatry, 38,* 1173–1179.

Saigh, P. A. (1991). The development of post-traumatic stress disorder following four different types of traumatization. *Behaviour Research and Therapy, 29,* 213–216.

Schepker, R. (1997). Posttraumatische Belastungsstörung im Kindesalter — Diagnose, Verlaufsprädiktoren und therapeutische Strategien [Posttraumatic stress disorder in childhood—diagnosis, predictors and therapeutical strategies]. *Zeitschrift für Kinder- und Jugendpsychiatrie, 25,* 46–56.

Seligman, M. E. P., Maier, S. F., & Geer, J. (1968). *Helplessness: On depression, development and death.* San Francisco: Freeman.

Šikiĉ, N., Javornik, N., Stracenski, M., Bunjevac, T., & Buljan-Flander, G. (1997). Psychopathological differences among three groups of school children affected by the war in Croatia. *Acta med. Croatica, 51,* 143–149.

Smith, P., Perrin, S., Yule, W., Hacam, B., & Stuvland, R. (2002). War exposure among children from Bosnia-Hercegovina: Psychological adjustment in a community sample. *Journal of Traumatic Stress, 15*(2), 147–156.

Solomon, J. (1942). Reactions of children to blackouts. *American Journal of Neuropsychiatry, 12,* 361–362.

Terr, L. (1979). Children of Chowchilla. *Psychoanalytic Study of the Child, 34,* 547–623.

Terr, L. (1991). Childhood traumas: An outline and overview. *American Journal of Psychiatry, 148,* 10–20.

Thabet, A., & Vostanis, P. (1998). Social adversities and anxiety disorders in the Gaza Strip. *Archives of Disease in Childhood, 78*(5), 439–442.

UNHCR, United Nations High Commissioner for Refugees. (2004). http://www.unhcr.de/pdf/355.pdf (3.5.2004).

United Nations. (1969). United Nations Treaty Series (translation). *Convention concerning the powers of authorities and the law applicable in respect of the protection of infants* (concluded at The Hague October 5, 1961). Translation as published in the United Nations Treaty Series, 1969, pp. 145ff.

van der Kolk, B. A., McFarlane, A. C., & Weisaeth, L. (Eds.) (1996). *Traumatic stress: The effects of overwhelming experience on mind, body, and society.* New York: Guilford Publications.

van der Veer, G. (1998). *Counseling and therapy with refugees. Psychological problems of victims of war, torture and repression.* New York: John Wiley & Sons.

van Essen, J. (1998, April 15–20). *Of fatherland and motherland: Love and hate in adolescent refugees.* Presented at the IPA Conference at the Threshold of the Millennium, Lima, Peru.

van Essen, J. (1999). The capacity to live alone: Unaccompanied refugee minors in the Netherlands. *Mind and Human Interaction, 10*(1), 26–35.

World Health Organization (WHO). (1991). Tenth revision of the International Classification of Diseases, Chapter V (F): Mental and Behavioural Disorders (including diorders of psychological development). Clinical Descriptions and Diagnostic Guidelines. H. Dilling, W. Mombour, & M. H. Schmidt (Eds.). Bern: Hans Huber.

Zeiler, J. (1997). Psychiatrische Diagnostik bei Migranten — Typische Fehlerquellen [Psychiatric diagnosis of migrants—typical sources of error]. *T-&-E-Neurologie-Psychiatrie, 11,* 889–891.

20

Gender-Specific Treatment

MARIANNE C. KASTRUP AND LIBBY TATA ARCEL

According to the UN High Commissioner for Refugees (UNHCR, 2001), there is an estimated population of 19.8 million refugees worldwide. Out of these 48.6% are women. These figures include asylum-seekers, returnees, internally displaced persons, and war victims.

Some refugees receive more media attention, and their experiences are better documented (Kinzie & Jaranson, 2001), others remain for years in refugee camps. The gender perspective as to the visibility of the problem is challenging.

In all aspects of the integration process we have to take gender into account. Many refugee women come from societies where women's role is primarily centered around the home, and these women need particular attention when trying to cope and integrate into new environments. On the other hand, women who take the primary responsibility for the family and cling to their traditional attachments can experience neglect in the host country when it comes to integration initiatives.

Women and men differ in lifestyle, life conditions, and biology, and women on a global level are disproportionately highly represented among the poor, the illiterate, and otherwise disadvantaged groups. Findings also demonstrate that there are valid reasons to focus on gender-specific problems in relation to refugees and asylum seekers as women and men face different life situations and have different social roles. They cope in different ways with their new lives and receive different treatment to alleviate their suffering. As pointed out by Arcel (2002b), mainstream theories have not until recently recognized that women, besides being violated by the same methods and for the same reasons as men, are often subjected to other severe forms of abuse such as rape and other forms of sexual assault, forced impregnation, forced abortion or sterilization, forced maternity, and sexual slavery. This chapter provides an overview of the gender aspects related to the mental health problems of refugees and asylum seekers.

The particularities of gender in relation to symptomatology, need for treatment, and response to treatment will all be seen from a rights perspective. This approach is chosen as it is our experience working with this population both in country of origin and in exile that: (a) too little attention has been paid to the close connection between the human rights perspective and gender and (b) this tends to get lost in the discussion of treatment models. Special attention will be paid to clinical experiences with this population with the hope of being of use for therapists of both sexes in their daily clinical practice.

REFUGEES VERSUS ASYLUM SEEKERS

Persons who are asylum seekers live under particular stress due to, among other things, the uncertainty of their destiny, the fear of repatriation, and frequently the lack of access to adequate care while awaiting asylum. The situation of refugees and asylum seekers differs dramatically from one country to another due to, among others, differences in work and housing possibilities and willingness of the host country to use refugees' potential.

Information on gender is essential in planning and evaluating interventions for refugees and asylum seekers. In many refugee reports there is reference to the proportion of women and children, seldom explaining why these groups are analyzed separately, but suggesting that all women are vulnerable, which can be difficult to reconcile with today's notion of gender equity and the empowerment of women (UNHCR, 2001). It is noteworthy that gender profiles are more widely available for refugee populations in developing countries where UNHCR is directly involved in the registration and collection of data than in the industrialized world where apparently the gender focus is less dominant.

From a sociological perspective it is interesting that gender composition (UNHCR, 2001) is related to the stage of the displacement process. Populations that are displaced in total reflect a balanced demographic structure, but secondary movements tend to be more gender selective with a lower participation of women among asylum seekers in great parts of Europe and North America. It is first through family reunification that the gender balance is restored.

Further, gender plays a role in terms of location as a refugee because males are predominant in urban centers, whereas refugee camps have a more balanced gender distribution (UNHCR, 2001).

HUMAN RIGHTS ASPECTS

Inquiry into the meaning of being a female refugee is now a growing area of concern. According to UNHCR (global consultations on April 25, 2002), refugee women are disproportionately affected by physical and sexual violence, they have unequal access to asylum procedures and might not receive individual identity documents. These women run a particular risk of sexual assaults of various kinds, and many might also feel forced to render various sexual services in order to ensure their families a minimum of survival.

Muecke (1992) pointed to the fact that the issue of female refugee health primarily has focused on her reproductive ability and ignored the impact of gender as an organizing principle of life in asylum. Refugee women are often subject to specific norms of gender-related abuse despite the fact that both sexes could face the same problems. The risk of rape, of being constrained to practice prostitution to secure survival, of being excluded from training or development programs are a fact of life for these women.

Guidelines already exist on protecting the rights of refugee women; the problem is that they might not be implemented. The situation is aggravated by the fact that perpetrators of violence often receive no punishment, as the women have no access to legal aid.

There is an increasing recognition that gender aspects are important when considering refugee laws (e.g., in relation to trafficking), because women can have special reasons for applying for asylum, but also because women can face receiving no protection from authorities for their abusive partners.

Many nation-states have started to take up this challenge and work for improving the conditions of female asylum seekers in terms of their claims, availability of interpreters, and so forth, but still many nation-states have not adopted gender-sensitive safeguards in the interpretation of refugee laws. Isolated or overcrowded camps, poor services, and poorly lit and unlocked sleeping areas facilitate sexual violence. Further, a lack of police protection and a general lawlessness leave women in such camps without real protection (Arcel, 2002b).

In 1980 WHO established a system of focal points for women with the aim of promoting, coordinating, and monitoring activities and collecting, processing, and disseminating information on women's health, recognizing the complex interrelationship between the health of women and their social, political, cultural, and economic situations.

The concept of "women, health, and development" developed by WHO aims specifically at benefiting women's health and enhancing their participation in development and health and signals that we cannot consider the treatment of traumatized women without grasping the complexity of the social context in which they live. An example can be seen in the reports from Afghanistan (e.g., Rasekh, Bauer, Manners, & Jacopino, 1998) where the combined effects of war-related trauma and human rights abuses profoundly affect the mental health of the Afghani women.

LITERATURE REVIEW OF MENTAL HEALTH CONSEQUENCES

Prevalence

[F]There is no indication that males and females have different lifetime prevalence in exposure to traumatic events (ISTSS, 2000), but the two sexes experience different traumatic events. Research on the role of gender with respect to the experience of disaster has tended to focus almost exclusively on individual vulnerability. It is characteristic that there is a scarcity of studies with a focus on gender particularities, despite the fact that refugee women face multiple difficulties in exile.

We see a higher prevalence of posttraumatic stress disorder (PTSD) in women, and in the *Guidelines for Treatment of PTSD* (ISTSS, 2000), developed by the International Society for Traumatic Stress Studies, it is stated that women have a lifetime prevalence of PTSD that is twice as high as for men. Several groups report similar findings, and large-scale studies of Holocaust survivors find that women are significantly more likely to report psychological distress (85%) compared to men (65%) (Carmil & Carel, 1986). Despite such findings it is noteworthy that the existing literature (Gerrity, Keane, Tuma, & Oritz, 2001) have few referrals to gender/women and refugee status.

Women exposed to a given trauma are four times as likely to develop PTSD (ISTSS, 2000). Neither the character of the event nor how the event was perceived can account for the differences in prevalence that are also reported in disaster-stricken communities (Norris, Foster, & Weisshaar, 2002). The gender difference is reported to increase if the trauma exposure occurred in childhood (Blehar, Cuthbert, & Magruder, 2002). Women tend to exhibit a more chronic course of the condition, and referring to the report on world mental health (Rupp & Sorel 2001) the disability adjusted life years (DALYs), as a proportion of all years lived with disability among women with PTSD, were 6.6% compared to the 3.2% found in men.

Findings of gender differences in the prevalence of PTSD among non-Western adults exposed to political violence are inconsistent (Norris et al., 2002). Some studies have revealed no sex differences, for example, Thulesius and Hakånsson's (1999) work among Bosnian refugees and Sweden and Cheung's (1994) study of Cambodian refugees. Others have reported that women run a greater risk of getting a war-related PTSD, for example, Reppesgaard's (1997) sample of Tamil refugees.

A study of Kosovar refugees in the United States (Ai, Peterson, & Ubelhor, 2002) showed that 60% of these showed PTSD and that higher PTSD scores were associated with women. Westermeyer and

Williams (1998) found among Southeast Asian refugees that victims exposed to deliberate violence were more apt to be older males in leadership positions, and that the wives of some of them were also traumatized but allowed to remain in their homes after their husbands were captivated, which can be seen as a reflection of the different worlds of the two sexes.

Mollica, Wyshak, and Lavelle (1987), on the other hand, found among a sample of Cambodian refugees that women without spouses showed the most severe psychiatric and social impairment compared to other Indonesian groups. The women had higher levels of depressive symptoms and perceived themselves as socially and culturally isolated and living in a hostile social world. Further, they were overwhelmed by the effort to find work, as they had to support their children.

Comorbidity

Frequent misdiagnosis of pathology occurs with refugees. A large proportion of persons with PTSD suffer from another clinically defined mental disorder, and somatic complaints are among the most frequently presented symptoms. Very often PTSD accompanies a major depressive disorder, a combination suggesting a more serious clinical picture and less favorable outcomes than either disorder occurring alone.

Comorbid conditions seem gender-related. Males are more likely to have a history of alcohol or substance abuse, women to have a past history of depression or anxiety (Blehar, Cuthbert, & Magruder, 2002). In a Norwegian study (Lavik, Hauff, Skrondal, & Solbjerg, 1996) of refugees, a multiple regression analysis using the general level of functioning (measured as a Global Assessment of Functioning [GAF] score) as a dependent variable showed that gender was not a predictor for functioning, but women were more at risk of developing anxiety/depression. Similarly, women had higher anxiety scores among asylum seekers in Australia (Silove, Sinnerbrink, Field, Manicavasagar, & Steel, 1997).

Suicidal ideation and suicide attempts have been reported in significantly higher proportion among women who have been victims of assault, and assault is also found to lead to substance abuse, in particularly alcohol abuse (Kilpatrick & Koss, 2001). These findings are not based on refugees, and the issue of abuse among female refugees is still in its infancy.

Physical Symptoms

A large proportion of women presenting with PTSD exhibit a variety of physical symptoms. Women might complain of symptoms related to the part of the body exposed to traumata, especially in cases of exposure to physical violence. Others might have problems in the form of sexual dysfunction, sexually transmitted diseases, musculoskeletal problems, chronic pain, and functional disturbances. Rape victims in particular report symptoms in the form of chronic pelvic pain, headaches, and gastrointestinal disorders, and menstrual problems. The pain and tension influences the functioning of these women, who might further suffer from a distorted body image. It is important that any therapeutic intervention adequately addresses the physical needs of these women.

Marital Roles

Inadequate attention has been paid to the relation between marital adjustment and posttraumatic symptoms among refugees. The different social roles and expectations of the two sexes are reflected in a study among Bosnian refugee couples in United States (Spasojevic, Heffer, & Snyder, 2000) where women's marital satisfaction was predicted by their husbands' PTSD, whereas the opposite was not the case for the husbands' marital satisfaction, which the authors suggested might indicate that women are more oriented toward.

Women fulfill the role of nurturers and providers of emotional support. Consequently, exposure to disaster for the household can overload women's capacity to cope. Solomon, Smith, Robins, and Fischback (1987) found that women living in satisfactory spousal relations had worse outcomes than women with weaker spousal ties. This was in contrast to that of disaster-stricken males who had an outcome that was positively related to the degree of spousal relationship.

Pearson, Lopez, and Cunningham (1998) write that they as female professionals and caregivers have a "gut" feeling that men and women cope differently with the consequences of trauma and thus heal differently. Women tend to be the person responsible for caregiving, and they frequently have no time to consider their own needs due to their preoccupation with the needs of their immediate family.

It is well established that gender role conflicts and adverse life events can precipitate anxious and depressive disorders in women with young children. Refugee women can be particularly vulnerable to such stress, and consequently have a heightened risk of affective disorders (Matthey, Silove, Barnett, Fitzgerald, & Mitchell, 1999). Among Cambodian mothers taking refuge in Australia, the number of trauma events experienced prior to birth was associated with psychological morbidity following childbirth, but the number of support people did not predict the level of symptoms.

The link between child and maternal mental health among refugees has among others been studied in Central American refugees where the presence of the mothers' PTSD symptoms predicted the children's mental health (Locke, Southwick, McClosky, & Fernandez-Esquer, 1996).

Disaster can disrupt the role of family provider. Thus, those with the expectation of fulfilling this role can find the traumatic experiences most debilitating. On the other hand, those who are expected to fulfill the nurturing role can experience psychological problems if traumatic events intensify nurturing demands beyond the person's capacity. Single mothers who fulfill both roles, if this theory holds true, are particularly likely to experience stress.

Resilience

Interestingly enough, there is little research recorded in the field of healthy refugees, in the mechanism of defense styles, coping processes, social involvement, and cognitive styles permitting refugees to adapt into a new context. The study of resilience factors is important and still lacking in sufficiency in order to understand the positive aspects, not just focusing on the negative impact, of trauma on different populations.

The interest in the concept of resilience is rapidly expanding as not all those exposed to trauma develop PTSD. Among the protective coping mechanisms elucidated are political involvement, preparedness for torture, spirituality, emotional disclosure to others, reality orientation, step-by-step planning behavior, distraction by work, flexibility in coping, motivation for survival, and the existence of an inner locus of control and self-reliance during torture and imprisonment (e.g., Arcel, Folnegovic-Smalc, Tocilj-Simunkovic, Kozaric-Kovacic, & Ljubtina, 1998).

GENDER-SPECIFIC AND CULTURALLY SENSITIVE TREATMENT

According to the ISTSS (2000), gender differences in relation to treatment are not so systematically studied, and we do not have thorough data whether gender is predictive of treatment outcome. The literature seems to suggest that women are more responsive to treatment than men, but several differences make comparisons difficult. Among them is that women are faced with different traumata but also that other factors have to be controlled for including chronicity/severity of the condition and the presence of comorbid disorders.

Professionals should have a realistic view of the gender-based social roles and cultural expectations for women in their current situations when considering possible outcome of care (Magruder, Mollica, & Friedman, 2001). Refugee women in a mental health setting in a host country often share common denominators that challenge therapeutic systems and create contradictions and dilemmas in assessment and treatment. The following case example will illustrate some of these denominators.

> A refugee woman, 38 years old, shopkeeper, former student of law in her country of Iran is referred to a psychological counseling center by her general practitioner because of constant headaches that referring person believes are psychogenetic.
> Medical examination showed no organic reason. Back home, she had belonged to a students' resistance group, had been arrested, and been held in prison for half a year. Defloration of virgin female political prisoners was at that time routine in Iranian prisons. After abuse she was bleeding a long time without receiving any medical care, which left

recurring problems in her reproductive system. After her parents bribed the prison official to let her go, she fled with her sister first to Turkey and then through several European countries to Denmark where she has been for 12 years. She has not seen her parents or the rest of her family since then. She is currently living with another Iranian refugee, an extremely jealous man who controls every movement of her. They are both unemployed. With her somatic symptom as the beginning point, she was offered treatment in order to trace the background for her headaches. After the second session, where she related about how burdening her couple relationship was, she left treatment as her friend created problems for her every time she left home. Our follow-up contacts were not answered.

The denominators of this case are listed in the sections that follow.

Polytraumatization

Many women will have been subjected to numerous human rights abuses and traumatic experiences. We have above documented that conditions for women in refugee camps in non-Western countries are detrimental for physical and mental health. A number of them will have reproductive health problems with hormonal difficulties, bleeding, or pains as sequelae following extreme stress or prolonged stays in refugee camps during transition (Mattson, 1993; Arcel, Folnegovic, Tocij-Simnhovic, Kozavic-Kovacic, & Ljubtina, 1998). All have lost their countries, cultures, and many also family members, and the losses are reflected in their symptomatology. Consequently, they will suffer not only from one traumatic experience but from several acting cumulatively.

Referred by Third Person After Chronic Somatic and Psychological Problems

The majority do not address themselves to a psychotherapist but to a "doctor" whom they hope will alleviate their somatic problems. Usually, they are referred by a third person, typically another health or social personnel who, after the woman's somatic problems have been exhaustingly investigated and addressed, finds this woman's problems mainly of a psychological nature and refers her to a mental health service. There is often a discrepancy between the problems as perceived by the referring professional and the referred person herself. Her concern about her somatic symptoms for which "there *must* be a treatment" convinces her to accept the referral, but she will in most cases have unclear expectations.

Lack of Knowledge About Psychotherapy

The woman most often will not know what psychotherapy is and will often have resistance in talking with a psychiatrist/psychologist because of fear of stigmatization. Accordingly, a difference might exist in the two parties' expectations on self-disclosure about trauma, especially sexual trauma. The Western therapist has been trained on the necessity of self-disclosure, whereas the woman would rather practice, at least initially, silence, about the most traumatic experiences.

Expectations on Rapid Improvement

The woman's long journey in the medical system makes her impatient concerning the results of treatment, and she will often be expecting if not an immediate but at least a rapid improvement of her symptoms. An assessment period that is longer than two sessions during which she does not experience any improvement or at least hope that something will improve will undermine the credibility of the therapist and can lead to her leaving the mental health setting.

Initial Skepticism to Commit Herself to a "Talking Cure"

Even if she accepts the "talking cure," she will evaluate very carefully from the first session whether the therapist understands what she presents as her problems and whether the therapist's suggestions are compatible with the reality of her life. Convincing the women of the possibilities of a treatment where medicaments need not play a role is a major challenge in itself (Mattson, 1993).

The Woman's Social Context Can Question Psychotherapy as a Legitimate Method

The physical mobility and social independence of the refugee woman will often be restricted by her social network, which eventually can lead to her viewing treatment for psychological problems as a nonlegitimate method of treatment. Literally a family member would wait for the woman in the waiting room and would have an influential opinion on whether this kind of treatment is necessary for the woman or not.

Familial Social Control of the Refugee Woman Increases During Exile in the Host Country

Our clinical experience from working with traumatized women from many different nationalities in Denmark tells us that the social control of women in refugee groups is exaggerated in the process of acculturation in the host country. Males in the family network can feel threatened in their social role and feel responsible for keeping females in the "right" lifestyle, as they are afraid the women might be inspired by the Western ideology of self-determination for females.

Cultural and Social Distance Between Therapist and Client

The distance between therapist and client can be big due to language, education, socioeconomic status, or religion. Even when qualified interpreters exist, educational differences, as in a case where the woman is illiterate or has religious differences, or where the (nonpsychotic) woman believes she is possessed by a demon that causes her to act immorally, will be a challenge for the well-educated and often irreligious professional.

Current Stresses Are in the Foreground

Immigration and acculturation in a new country put all kinds of stresses in the refugees lives. Insecurity in their refugee status, housing, separated families, unemployment, poverty, stresses at work and schooling of children, bad news from home, racism among the indigenous people, lack of integration in society and work can all reactivate traumatic symptoms or create additional ones. The client experiences the mental health person as someone of high-status in the host country and can initially seek to obtain the therapist's support to solve her acute material and practical problems rather than talking about trauma. This case example explains this type situation.

> A war-traumatized woman 45 years old with a refugee status in Denmark, a former bank accountant in her country, divorced, came for the first time to the treatment center, referred by her general practitioner because she had been tortured and had many somatic and psychological complains. She was accompanied by her son of 25. She insisted that the son be present during the first session, as he could help her explain her situation. Although she had been severely abused, she declared initially that she did not need any treatment, but it would help her condition if the center could help her son to immigrate to Australia. We discussed her wish and its consequences extensively. It appeared that the son had developed an alcohol problem in Denmark sitting in the bars throughout the whole day with his unemployed refugee compatriots. His mother hoped that emigration to a country that gave greater working possibilities to her son would save him. However, as the center could not meet her main expectations, she interrupted contact after two sessions.

All the conditions in this case example put challenges on therapeutic system to cover the refugee woman's primary needs. We agree with Kinzie (2001) that the primary needs of traumatized clients are physical and emotional safety, predictability of relationships, reduction of symptoms, and reestablishment of social relationships.

Leaving their country and arriving in another strange country deprives refugee women of their usual means to secure their survival. They are initially disempowered, and some of them become even more disempowered through the acculturation process. It follows that all therapeutic treatment of refugees and asylum seekers must have *empowerment as a goal* defined (McWhirter, 1994) as the process by which a marginalized person becomes aware of power dynamics and develops skills to gain control over his or her life without infringing on others' rights.

This means that we in assessment and therapy begin by taking seriously the women's own problem definitions and supporting their proposals to solutions, even if they fall outside our defined systems. In many instances we will not be able to comply with their wishes, but we can discuss their solutions in a therapeutic and clarifying manner, presupposing that we can understand their cognitive and emotional worldview by building a bridge over cultural incongruence.

We have been treating traumatized refugee women (and men) from Latin America, the Middle East, and lately Bosnia for the past 20 years. We will in the following section discuss some specific issues in assessment and treatment of refugee women that take into consideration their status as women in a cultural context.

TREATMENT OF REFUGEE WOMEN: CULTURAL ATTUNEMENT OF CULTURAL INCONGRUITIES

Certain basic methodological approaches are necessary for empowering treatment of refugee women. They are not attached to any specific theoretical orientation, but concern mainly how to understand the cultural incongruities that emerge in problem definition and goal setting.

A prerequisite in order to stay in therapy with the client is the establishment not only of *empathic attunement* (Chapter 6 in this volume), but additionally of a *cultural attunement* defined as the process during which a therapist and a client from two different cultural contexts search for establishing (a) a common ground in understanding, defining, and redefining the problems of the client and (b) negotiate for an agreement concerning goals for treatment. We emphasize the terms *process* and *negotiation*, implying that the endeavor demands greater effort from both parts than when client and therapist are from the same culture. It is the task of the therapist to facilitate the process.

If the cultural attunement is to empower refugee women it has to avoid negative stereotypes about women from non-Western countries. Cultural attunement is not an easy task. It aims specifically to:

• reduce the power balance between therapist and client, which requires the therapist mainly to listen and hear the views of clients, especially when those views do not correspond with his or her own personal view;

- respect diversity, which requires nondefensiveness, avoidance of over-generalizations and overpersonalization, avoiding withdrawal and resentment in case clients who do not behave in the culturally prescribed way;
- overcome oppression in the client's life through supporting empowerment but without adding further oppression by disparaging the client's own values.

Cultural incongruities concerning views on legitimate suffering, health and illness, life and death are deeply embedded in both therapist and client. To meet the client in his or her world without the therapist losing integrity in his or her own professional and private world demands cognitive flexibility, warmth, empathy, human attitude, and constant challenging of our own majority cultural prejudices when we do not understand the reactions of clients. The therapist and the refugee woman belong to different cultures with accompanying values, norms, and what is more important, differences in understanding what constitutes the self and the most dignified mode of suffering of the self.

On the other hand, it is of great importance not to leave the client without tools to integrate into the new host culture. Therapists have a significant task in helping to increase the empowerment of refugee women. This can be done in many ways, taking into consideration the cultural and educational background of the client.

The refugee woman and her family are confronted with a new culture with gender role expectations, marital habits, gender socializations, and so forth that can be foreign and sometimes frightening. But the family has to survive in this new and frequently hostile setting and any education about the implications of role change or interpretation of the meaning of strange, unknown lifestyles and patterns of the host society can facilitate this process.

Legitimate Suffering Versus Nonlegitimate Suffering

Collective modes of suffering shape individual expressions and perceptions of how to suffer under stress, and these modes are taught and learned sometimes openly, sometimes indirectly (Kleinman & Kleinman, 1997). Interactions in the social network enter in the trauma and influence the experience of suffering. An example of how individual suffering is formed by the collectively prescribed way of suffering is the way refugee widows and widowers are expected to behave in traditional societies. A widow must demonstrate loyalty to her late husband, her behavior is monitored, and she must remain in the suffering position. On the contrary a widower's movements and social contacts are not monitored, nor does he have to stay outside the public life, a behavior that is expected of widows in many cultural groups (Ramphele, 1997).

Kleinman and Kleinman (1997) use as an example the transformation of a violated person into a "victim" in the Western societies, with accompanying moral and financial benefits attached to the status of the "victim." To know that a person is a victim of rape, of torture, of violence, or of war elicits empathy with her pain and authorizes her suffering as morally understandable. Interventions to help the victim are morally mandatory. Inherent in the conception of, for example, the victim of war rape in Western society is that the person has no complicity to violence so she expects sympathy, care, and forgiveness from her social network. Following is a case example of this situation.

> A Bosnian refugee family of mother, father, and three grown children had suffered atrocities of war and ethnic cleansing. A son was missing during combat but not confirmed dead, which created simultaneously massive anxiety and hope in the whole family. The family received medical and psychological help from a psychosocial project, and family sessions were held at their home with the medical team. Slowly a rumor reached the team that the family comprised one more member, one daughter who had allegedly been raped by the enemy. The team had never seen this daughter or heard any mentioning of her. It showed after some weeks that the family had hidden this daughter of 20 years in a small room every time the medical team, who belonged to their own cultural group, or other strangers visited them. When the team convinced the family to reveal the daughter, it it became obvious she had great uncovered medical and mental health needs. Their explanation for hiding her was their fear that she would reveal her sexual traumatization, thus stigmatizing herself and thus prevent her from ever marrying.

When parents act this way they exclude and oppress the violated girl, adding additional stress to her traumatization, but it is not because they are evil or they want to damage their daughter. In their cultural reality they share the "shame" of their daughter and believe that they protect her by hiding her. Their conception of what their daughter is entitled to after her traumatization is very different from the helpers conception. Patriarchal/traditional societies might not understand or view the sexually assaulted woman as a "victim," deserving sympathy and moral restitution, but in many instances view her overtly or subtly as an "accomplice," "damaged goods," and in all instances she represents social "stigmatization" for the whole family. In very traditional societies (i.e., the Afghani) she could be excluded from the moral community of the group, if not physically then socially and psychologically.

Not only males contribute to the stigmatization. One of the authors has interviewed Croatian war-rape victims that felt stigmatized by their female neighbors in their village. One of them related, "They tell me, why did they rape you and not us? There must be a reason," implying that she must have sexually encouraged the enemy. This client became unhappy, anxious, and isolated. Many sexually traumatized refugee women report feelings of isolation and fear when they have to leave the home environment (Arcel, Folnegovic, Tocij-Simnhovic, Kozavic-Kovacic, & Ljubtina, 1998; Mattson, 1993). The lack of identifying with the woman's position is embedded in the fact that women in many cultures are at the bottom of the ladder of power. For the same reason it is extremely important that the therapist supports the refugee woman's own sense of reality and own understanding of her situation.

Coping of Self-Assertiveness Versus Coping of Endurance

Clinicians assessing and treating refugee women are often caught in dilemmas between their wish to respect the values and norms of the clients culture on one side and their wish to empower the female client by supporting her to be more assertive against oppressive practices on the other side.

What is a particular challenge in therapy of refugee women is the incongruity between the *coping of self-assertiveness* and *giving voice to your pain* for Western women in order to change things that bother you and the *coping of endurance* of suffering, prominent in many cultures especially for women. Endurance coping for life adversaries is considered a virtue.

Root (2001) points out that many cultures have normalized the suffering and sacrificing of its women through many generations and made this a prescription consistent with being a "good" woman. Attached to this valued coping is the *coping of silence* and *strategy of "forgetting"* the traumatic experiences. As Das (1997) remarks about Indian war-raped women:

> As one woman warned me it was dangerous to remember [and talk]. These memories were sometimes compared to poison that makes the inside of the woman dissolve, as a solid was dissolved in a powerful liquid. At other times a woman would say that she is like a discarded exercise book in which the accounts of past relationships were kept — the body, a parchment of losses. (p. 84)

During the Bosnian war (1991–1995) numerous well-meaning European and North American psychotherapists traveled to Bosnia with the aim to support the war victims and to talk about their trauma. They met silence and left frustrated. According to our experience we must not confuse silence with repression of the traumatic events or resistance to therapy. Silence can mean many things, and we have to clarify what the functions and meanings of silence are in the client's culture and why this woman is silent. The culture decides whether voice can be given to certain forms of pain or whether this pain should be silenced in public and instead expressed through the body (Morris, 1997). Silence can be a defensive position out of fear and oppression or an active cognitive position as is speaking out. Is the client silenced by others, fearing their threats or is she silent by her own decision? Silence can be politeness in order to give space to an authority. It can be a dignified mode to suffer and show strength in the cultural context. It can be strategic in order to protect yourself. To endure in silence can mean hiding your innermost feelings with humiliating conditions, rather than bring them forth in public and suffer victimization as a consequence (Schweickart, 1996).

Or the refugee woman can "size up" the therapist first and then decide whether he or she is credible enough to share freely private accounts of her life with. So we have to listen to the silence as we listen to the voicing and remind ourselves that even in our Western cultures the culturally accepted speaking out on formerly private "shameful" oppressive practices as wife-battering, rape, or incest has only come about in the past 20 to 25 years.

Self-Concept Embedded in Family Relations Versus in the Individual

Individualists or idiocentric individuals give priority to personal goals over the goals of collectives. Collectivists or the allocentric either make no distinction between personal and collective goals or if they do make such distinctions, they subordinate their personal goals to the collective goals.

Landrine (1995) introduces the concepts of the Western "referential self" and the "indexical self" of sociocentric societies. The Western referential self has cross-situational and longitudinal traits: it has abilities, preferences, needs, desires, and a style of its own that describe it, refer to it, and differentiate it from other selves. The referential self is presumed to be a free agent that does what it wishes. Thereby the self has rights. Rights to privacy, autonomy, and to be protected from intrusion from other beings. The self in Western culture is assumed to be morally responsible and is the final explanation for behavior.

The indexical self (Gaines as cited in Landrine, 1995) is the self of sociocentric cultures, where the self is perceived as constituted or indexed by the contextual features of social interaction in diverse situations. The indexical self, according to Gaines, has no traits and desires or needs of its own in isolation from its relationships and contexts. The self includes other people, and moreover, the roles that the self occupies are presumed as synonymous. Although roles are understood in our culture to be occupied by choice rather than by necessity, in sociocentric cultures the person *is* the role — rather than individuals having goals, desires, or needs. Consequently, the failure to perform one's role as wife, mother, father, husband, or daughter is a failure to be a person at all. It can be the existential, social, and psychological death of the individual to fail in its role.

The above theoretizations contribute greatly to our understanding of the individual refugee person. Their limitation is that they do not focus on the substantial differences of degrees of freedom for women and men in fulfilling their roles. The understanding of suffering of women will not be uniform in all members of a given cultural group but will depend on the roles ascribed to generation, education, social class, and social status in their social groups. The assumption of cultural in-group

variability is essential here and is valid also for group variability in attitudes, values, and behaviors. What all members of an ethnic group
share, what is likely to be different, and to what degree varies greatly
(Jones & Thorne, 1995).

We have observed that sexual traumatization after war rape in individuals from the same culture (i.e., the Bosnian) can be overcome to a
great degree in a tolerant family relationship of a well-educated and
enlightened middle-class family or be continuously perpetuated in a
low-income uneducated traditional family that consciously or unconsciously stigmatizes the violated woman. In the first case the lack of
complicity in the violation and the capacity for a broader political analysis gives the refugee woman greater space to keep her dignity as a person. In the latter case the violated woman is considered to have failed as
a person even if the violation was against her will. Although both
women are Bosnian, they do not share the same "culture." This calls for
an assessment of the woman's cultural self-concept.

Identification With Versus Differentiation From the Cultural Self-Concept for Females

Understanding the cultural self-concept for females and oppressive
practices is not exhaustive for understanding the single individual. The
refugee woman's own understanding will reflect the cultural female role
in general but also a specific one attached to her in the particular social
context she is embedded in. The client's own *subjective elaboration* of
her role is the beginning point for our empowerment endeavors. Does
she accept discriminative practices as self-integrated cultural norms and
thus part of her self-concept, or does she question them and differentiate herself subtly or strongly?

In the first case it is not precluded that she might suffer under
oppression. Many refugee women will indeed suffer from unwanted
restrictions, but the *coping of endurance* supports them to adjust their
feelings to the situation rather than change the situation. They will
often say: "What can be done? This is how things are. There is no use in
talking about things that cannot change."

If she feels in opposition to the cultural values she will feel strongly
supported if the therapist acknowledges her differentiation and supports
her to oppose the discriminative practices and change her role toward
greater self-assertiveness in the family and the new community. Thus,
the culturally sensitive treatment of the refugee woman is assisting her
to find a new social identity, a new self *in* the family — a new self *in* the
host culture community, exhausting the family's or the community's
possibilities for a change of role. This treatment goal works within the
culture rather than against the culture (Landrine, 1995).

So the female refugee brings with her in counseling not only PTSD,
her traumatic experiences, and her current stresses but the whole context of her social relationships as *determining conditions of her forms of*

expressing trauma and her coping with trauma. The therapist in his or her assessment must *differentiate* between suffering from the original traumatization and suffering as the result of gender discrimination that this context of social relationships exerts on this particular woman in her attempts to overcome trauma.

This could be particularly true for feelings of helplessness and hopelessness stemming from the refugee woman's futile attempts to cope in a strongly controlling family context that restricts her mobility and undermines her self-worth by virtue of a status she is born into (Root, 2001).

As concerns clinical expressions of anxiety, powerlessness, apathy, loss of concentration, and confusion or numerous somatic complaints, it is important to differentiate whether these behaviors belong to pathology attached to the traumatic experiences themselves or if they are normal, situation-specific responses to current stresses of social alienation and lack of personal control from conditions of poverty and racism in the host country or in refugee camps during their transition (Arcel, Folnegovic-Smalc, Kozaric-Kovacic, & Marusic, 1995).

A therapist who is not taking into consideration what gender discrimination, poverty, or racism and the devalued status following these conditions in the host country mean for the expressions of suffering in the female/asylum seeker will not be able to establish a dialogue about the traumatic experiences either.

Somatic Complaints Versus Psychological Complaints

There are a number of ways in which traumatic experiences can be inscribed on the body: enduring psychophysiological changes, scars, disfigurements or tissue changes causing chronic pain, changes in body posture, changes in the body image and body self-esteem, changes in attention to the body or distancing from it, the creation of images or metaphors that become crucial for experience of the body-self. Kirmayer (1996) differentiates between the individual body and the social body. If the significance of a traumatic event is to be understood in biological terms, he points out, it must be a biology that encompasses not just the nervous system but also relationships, commitments, social position, and the wider systems of cultural meaning and value. Symptom expression or self-report, illness conceptualizations, and help seeking are embedded in larger social systems and cultural schemas, and researchers must be cautious to isolate one from another. Many somatic symptoms including those occurring with the PTSD can represent cultural idioms of distress (Kleinman & Kleinman, 1997). Focusing on somatic symptoms rather than on psychological symptoms can be based on cultural values that prescribe control of emotions as the dignified form of suffering in mature individuals.

Telling stories of trauma can be healing for the individual in the long term in our culture, but can be ignored or actively suppressed in other cultures. Attention to the body has unfortunately not been central to the psychotherapeutic treatment of trauma and PTSD despite that somatic symptoms can be used as metaphors for speaking about trauma.

However, it is a known fact that traumatized refugee women with a high degree of somatization can be plagued by these somatic symptoms and address themselves repeatedly to primary care seeking relief and somatic treatment when there is none. Body awareness can be a tool for helping the client connect not only with forgotten traumatic memories but also with forgotten resources and positive body sensations. We will need more research in somatopsychic therapies in order to prove their validity; however, they fulfill the principle of the importance of respecting the problem definition of the client.

ROLE OF THERAPIST

Many investigators have stressed the critical role of the therapist variable and therapeutic credibility (Fuertes & Gretchen, 2001; Sue & Zane, 1995; Tyler, Susewell, & McCoy, 1995). Kinzie (2001) focused on the therapist variable rather than techniques and stresses the importance of flexibility in adjusting her roles over time to meet the changing needs of the traumatized refugee. Interchange in the roles of therapist/ advisor/confidant/doctor are required in order to stay with the client.

To stay with the client means that the therapist must secure a *consistency* in contact, seek to *reconfirm trust and faith* — by being at the side of the client, *contain* the chaotic experiences she has been through and create *cognitive clarity* around these experiences, *show respect* for her views and her picture of the world, even it is distal to our own, support her, and help her reach *reconnection* to her inner world as opposed to the outer strange world she has been "thrown" into. Knowledge of her culture is helpful but not enough. Sue and Zane (1995) mention credibility and giving as particularly relevant considerations in working with culturally diverse groups. Credibility refers to the clients perception of the therapist as an effective and trustworthy helper, which has to be established within two to three sessions. Incongruities in problem definition and problem resolution automatically reduce the credibility. We as therapists need to reexamine our treatment strategies if our credibility has been diminished. As we have stressed above, being observant to the in-group variability will prevent us from confusing the values of the cultural group with the values of the single woman.

Giving is the client's perception that something was received from the therapeutic encounter. We cannot invest solely on the long-term benefits of the therapeutic process. Gift giving is therefore important in reversing this process. The refugee client needs to see a direct result from the treatment even from the first session. Sue and Zane (1995) mention examples of "gift" giving: anxiety reduction, depression relief, normalization (to reassure clients that their reactions are common), reassurance, hope and faith, skills acquisition, a coping perspective, and goal setting.

PITFALLS

The stories of refugees and asylum seekers are told in many different ways, and the complexity of their experiences can render their stories unstructured or confusing. Caregivers have a responsibility in helping to structure the observations in order for them to make sense (Kinzie & Jaranson, 2001). But caregivers also have a responsibility to establish caregiving institutions where people act from a human rights as well as gender sensitive perspective (Pearson, Lopez, & Cunningham, 1998). Such principles include awareness of self-empowerment and self-management and autonomy in structuring daily activities and psychosocial activities that foster coping and resiliency (Pearson, Lopez, & Cunningham, 1998). Traumatized female refugees carry a load of experiences of disempowerment, helplessness, and lack of self-determination. Encounters with Western services can be an experience that adds to such feelings if they focus on pathology and reduced functioning instead of promotion of health and recovery. As a consequence, women might find little if any relief when referred to care. This is in line with Muecke (1992) who in her look for new paradigms proposes a shift in focus from pathology to health with an exit from the medicalization of problems.

We as therapists should focus on how to develop strategies to overcome such feelings of helplessness and lack of self-determination. Refugee women should recognize their own strength and be encouraged to overcome any fear of independence as they frequently have to become self-reliable economically, taking care of themselves and their children in a new society. In the host society the prevailing gender role expectations usually imply that women strive for economic independence, and that any step in that direction is seen as a positive value. It is crucial that refugee women confronted with such challenges learn how to find a balance where they on the one hand retain the moral values they adhere to, but on the other hand manage to cope in the new environment.

CONCLUSIONS

Gender is one way of defining a hierarchy that assigns entitlement and superiority to one group over another, and the particular problems related to the rights of refugee women need further attention. We have to ensure that refugee women are participating as equals in decision making regarding their own life and destiny. Instead displacement can increase violence against women, and the breakdown in norms and social structures can have a negative impact on the security of women refugees. Further, a large number of women have to strive as single providers of the family and take on roles that are unfamiliar to them in order to protect their children.

Social networking is important in the new environment and might replace the role of the extended families in the country of origin. Many possible solutions to facilitate this transformation to empowered women could be presented. Among them could be mentioned the identification of key female persons in the community to serve as role models, the establishment of mentor relations between immigrant women and women of the host community, or the creation of self-help groups in the community.

Authorities have to be encouraged to ensure that women are provided possibilities to use their capacities, as empowerment can benefit them in contributing to their own protection and thereby prevent violations of their rights and ultimately the appearance of and need for treatment of mental health problems. But from a pragmatic point of view working in the community to try to set up any of the above mentioned initiatives could turn out to be a more feasible and efficient solution than lobbying for the introduction of new legislation on refugee women's rights.

This is being said in recognition that we have to focus on and try to understand the gender-specific aspects of the refugee and asylum problems if we are to estimate the need for treatment initiatives due to post-traumatic disorders and how they should be planned and implemented.

It is for us clear that we must methodically adjust mental health services to the needs of the group of refugee women that wishes to talk about psychological and relational problems. This means improving our services through the whole course of treatment from the referral process to the follow-up treatment. Better cooperation between the responsible systems are required, so expectations are clarified in advance; culturally sensitive services are improved; professionals are better trained; and our attitudes toward what treatment means with this client population is changed and becomes increasingly necessary with the migration to the Western countries.

Several scholars have discussed models for multicultural counseling that take ethics and professional issues, race, counselor roles, psychological measurement of multicultural constructs, counselor supervision and education, therapy and mental health services for PTSD into consideration (Marsella, Friedman, Gerrity, & Scurfield, 1996; Ponteroto, Casas, Suzuki, & Alexander, 2001). It is, however, the rule that therapeutic models do not elaborate on the connection between gender and therapy, presupposing that same model can be applied to both genders.

Language difficulties, ambiguities, existing negative stereotypes, misinterpretations of behavior, and differences in priorities of treatment dictated by the health system and not only by the therapist all contribute to a negative therapeutic process with ethnic clients. One crucial issue for the therapist in order to combat a negative process is grasping the cultural differences in what constitutes suffering.

Each gender is expected to suffer in a prescribed mode in order for its suffering to be acknowledged as legitimate. The socially accepted mode of suffering is absorbed not only in the self-concept of the single individual but also in its body-self, containing often contradictory needs, norms, rights, and obligations expressed in somatic complaints. There is often a discrepancy between the degree of self-determination the individual refugee woman is allowed to achieve in her cultural/family context and the degree the therapist finds necessary to support or encourage in order for the client to achieve a better coping and symptom reduction. Complaints may be tolerated, but attempts to change the situation radically with following consequences for others will meet strong resistance in the family context.

Refugee women, in addition to their traumatization, will be subjected to constrictions, overt or subtle, of their personal mobility and role expectation, that produces additional suffering and decreases their ability to cope. Ultimately, constraints in their fight for survival in exile increase their marginalization. This is especially true for lower-status women.

The cultural group will simultaneously offer her ways of maintaining endurance, through social support, social control, or frequently through religion. Some patients, even after suffering and spiritual crises, are able to lead a spiritual life in the fullest sense of the term (Kinzie, 2001). The sociocentric self-concept is also determined by fate, God, gods, or spirits and should not be misunderstood as delusions or as backward, superstitious, and unintelligent. Treatment of these clients demands considerable cognitive flexibility in the therapist and an openness to the idea that immaterial entities such as fate, God, and so forth can be as real to the client as material things. One need only remember how the ideas of God, Devil, Jesus Christ and His Resurrection, and the Holy Spirit in Christianity are a deep reality for many Christians in order to understand the reality of spirits in other cultures. Attempts from the client to revise well-integrated cultural values, even if oppressive, will create conflicts in her self-concept.

In any case clinicians treating refugee women have to be alert against two tendencies. First, a tendency to classify oppressing or even violent practices in the woman's social life on the shelf of "cultural norms," as such practices cannot be questioned in the name of cultural relativism. Second, a tendency to experience the woman as solely oppressed, thus disregarding the kind of power ascribed to her status in her cultural context.

It is true for all treatment approaches that psychological problems cannot be assessed and treated without a fundamental respect for the person and the experiences of this person. However, contact with people from other cultures can reveal to the therapist oppressing structures that blame the victim and are very difficult to accept. The therapist is left with the task to work with the refugee family in such a way that the woman does not lose credibility on one side and yet manage her feelings of indignation on the other side.

Pearson and coworkers (1998) point to the fact that we have to be aware of certain principles if we want to develop gender-sensitive services. Among them are the need for a vision of what a gender-sensitive service should look like. Strategies are needed to identify the organizational structures that prevent empowerment of women and how to integrate the social networks of men and women. We have to ask ourselves what the specific ways are in which the services offered to women differ from services offered to males and how we measure whether the services offered are culturally acceptable for women and whether they fulfill their needs.

RECOMMENDATIONS FOR FUTURE RESEARCH

From an epidemiological perspective we need studies on the prevalence of PTSD in women. There is an increasing body of knowledge on the neurobiological aspects of PTSD. Gender differences are demonstrated in animal models in relation to stress, and the literature indicates that women are more sensitive to painful stimuli. This field of research is still in an early stage, and the interrelation between gender and neurobiology needs further investigation.

Mollica and coworkers wrote in 1987 that little is known about the cultural and emotional factors that inhibit refugee women to seek treatment for help of trauma as well as the coping styles they use to overcome the problems, and that the development of culturally sensitive therapeutic approaches with this focus is in its infancy.

Psychopharmacology has in recent years got a more prominent role in the treatment of PTSD, but little research has focused upon the gender and cultural differences in response to medications (Gerrity et al., 2001).

Further, we need research on the impact of mental health services to traumatized women — what are the advantages and drawbacks? And what are the outcome of gender-specific services? We have to work across disciplines to answer questions like how to measure the impact of initiatives to increase empowerment of women, and how to measure the cultural sensitivity of services.

The field is in progression and a strong collaboration between researchers in the health professions — anthropologists, judiciary professions, and sociologists — are to be strongly recommended to search for a comprehensive approach to this important issue.

REFERENCES

Ai, A. L., Peterson, C., & Ubelhor, D. (2002). War-related trauma and symptoms of posttraumatic stress disorder among adult Kosovar refugees. *Journal of Traumatic Stress, 15*, 157–160.

Arcel, L. T. (2002a). The tortured body as part of the psychotherapeutic dialogue. *Torture, 12*(1), 25–27

Arcel, L. T. (2002b). Torture, cruel, inhuman, and degrading treatment of women psychological consequences. *Torture, 12*(1), 5–16

Arcel, L. T., Folnegovic-Smalc, V., Kozaric-Kovacic, D., & Marusic, A. (Eds.). (1995). *Psycho-social help to victims of war: Women refugees from Bosnia and Herzegovina and their families.* Zagreb: Nakladnistvo Lumin.

Arcel, L. T., Folnegovic-Smalc, V., Tocilj-Simunkovic, G., Kozaric-Kovacic, D., & Ljubtina, D. (1998). Ethnic cleansing and post-traumatic coping. In L. T. Arcel (Ed.), *War violence, trauma and the coping process* (pp. 45–78). Copenhagen: IRCT.

Blehar, M. C., Cuthbert, B., & Magruder, K. M. (2002). Mental health policy and women with PTSD. In R. Kimerling, P. Ouimette, & J. Wolfe (Eds.), *Gender and PTSD* (pp. 434–452). London: Guilford Publications.

Carmil, D., & Carel, R. (1986). Emotional distress and satisfaction in life among Holocaust survivors. *Psychological Medicine, 16*, 141–149.

Cheung, P. (1994). Posttraumatic stress disorder among Cambodian refugees in New Zealand. *International Journal of Social Psychiatry, 40*, 17–26.

Das, V. (1997). Language and body: Transactions in the construction of pain. In A. Kleinmann, V. Das, & M. Lock (Eds.), *Social suffering* (pp. 25–45). Berkeley: University of California Press.

Fuertes, J. N., & Gretchen, D. (2001). Emerging theories of multicultural counseling. In J. G. Pontenero, J. M. Casas, & C. M. Alexander (Eds.), *Handbook of multicultural counseling* (2nd ed., pp. 509–541). London: Sage.

Gerrity, E., Keane, T. M., Tuma, F., & Ortiz, D. (2001). Future directions. In E. Gerrity, T. M. Keane, & F. Tuma (Eds.), *The mental health consequences of torture.* New York: Kluwer Academic Publishers.

International Society for Traumatic Stress Studies (ISTSS). (2000). Guidelines for treatment of PTSD. *Journal of Traumatic Stress Studies, 13*, 539–588.

Jones, E. E., & Thorne, A. (1995). Rediscovery of the subject: Intercultural approaches to clinical assessment. In N. R. Goldberger & J. B. Veroff (Eds.), *The culture and psychology reader* (pp. 720–740). New York: New York University Press.

Kilpatrick, D. G., & Koss, M. (2001). Homicide and physical assault. In E. Gerrity, T. M. Keane, & F. Tuma (Eds.), *The mental health consequences of torture.* New York: Kluwer Academic Publishers.

Kinzie, J. D. (2001). Psychotherapy for massively traumatised refugees: The therapist variable. *American Journal of Psychotherapy, 55*(4), 475–490.

Kinzie, J. D., & Jaranson, J. M. (2001). Refugees and asylum seekers. In E. Gerrity, T. M. Keane, & F. Tuma (Eds.), *The mental health consequences of torture.* New York: Kluwer Academic Publishers.

Kirmayer, L. J. (1996). Confusion of the senses: Implications of ethnocultural variations in somatoform disorders for PTSD. In A. J. Marsella, M. J. Friedman, E. T. Gerrity, & R. M. Scurfield (Eds.), *Ethnocultural aspects of posttraumatic stress disorder* (pp. 131–163). Washington, DC: American Psychological Association.

Kleinman, A., & Kleinman, J. (1997). The appeal of experience, the dismay of images: Cultural appropriations of suffering in our times. In A. Kleinman, V. Das, & M. Lock (Eds.), *Social suffering* (pp. 1–23). Berkeley: University of California Press.

Landrine, H. (1995). Cultural implications of cultural differences: The referential versus the indexical self. In N. R. Goldberger & J. B. Veroff (Eds.), *The culture and psychology reader* (pp. 744–766). New York: New York University Press.

Lavik, N. J., Hauff, E., Skrondal, A., & Solbjerg, Ø. (1996). Mental disorder among refugees and the impact of persecution and exile: Some findings of an outpatient population. *British Journal of Psychiatry, 169,* 726–732.

Locke, C. J., Southwick, K., McClosky, L. A., & Fernandez-Esquer, M. E. (1996). The psychological and medical sequelae of war in Central American refugee mothers and children. *Archives of Pediatrics and Adolscent Medicine, 150,* 822–828.

Magruder, K. M., Mollica, R., & Friedman, M. (2001). Mental health services research. In E. Gerrity, T. M. Keane, & F. Tuma (Eds.), *The mental health consequences of torture.* New York: Kluwer Academic Publishers.

Marsella, A. J., Friedman, M. J., Gerrity, E. T., & Scurfield, R. M. (1996). *Ethnocultural aspects of posttraumatic stress disorder.* Washington, DC: American Psychological Association.

Matthey, S., Silove, D. M., Barnett, B., Fitzgerald, M. H., & Mitchell, P. (1999). Correlates of depression and PTSD in Cambodian women with young children: A pilot study. *Stress Medicine, 15,* 103–107.

Mattson, S. (1993). Mental health of Southeast Asian refugee women: An overview. *Health Care for Women International, 14,* 155–165.

McWhirter, E. H. (1994). *Counseling for empowerment.* Alexandria, VA: American Counseling Association.

Mollica, R., Wyshak, G., & Lavelle, J. (1987). The psychosocial impact of war trauma and torture on SouthEast Asian refugees. *American Journal of Psychiatry, 144,* 1567–1572.

Morris, D. B. (1997). About suffering: Voice, genre, and moral community. In A. Kleinman, V. Das, & M. Lock (Eds.), *Social suffering* (pp. 25–45). Berkeley: University of California Press.

Muecke, M. A. (1992). New paradigms for refugee health problems. *Social Science Medicine, 35,* 515–523.

Norris, F. H., Foster, J. D., & Weisshaar, D. L. (2002). The epidemiology of sex differences in PTSD across developmental, societal, and research contexts. In R. Kimerling, P. Ouimette, & J. Wolfe (Eds.), *Gender and PTSD* (pp. 3–42). London: Guilford Publications.

Pearson, N., Lopez, J. P., & Cunningham, M. (Eds.). (1998). *Recipes for healing.* Manila: PST/CIDS and Copenhagen: IRCT.

Ponteroto, J. G., Casas, J. M., Suzuki, L. A., & Alexander, C. M. (2001). *Handbook of multicultural counseling* (3rd ed.). London: Sage.

Ramphele, M. (1997). Political widowhood in South Africa. The embodiment of ambiguity. In A. Kleinman, V. Das, & M. Lock (Eds.), *Social suffering* (pp. 99–117). Berkeley. University of California Press.

Rasekh, Z., Bauer, H. M., Manners, M. M., & Jacopino, V. (1998). Womens health and human rights in Afghanistan. *JAMA, 204*(5), 449–455.

Reppesgaard, H. (1997). Studies on psychosocial problems among displaced people in Sri Lanka. *European Journal of Psychiatry, 11,* 223–234.

Root, M. P. (2001). Women of color and traumatic stress in "domestic captivity": Gender and race as disempowering statuses. In A. J. Marsella, M. J. Friedman, E. T. Gerrity, & R. M. Scurfield (Eds.), *Ethnocultural aspects of posttraumatic stress disorder* (pp. 363–387). Washington, DC: American Psychological Association.

Rupp, A., & Sorel, E. (2001). Economic models. In E. Gerrity et al. (Eds.), *The mental health consequences of torture.* New York: Kluwer Academic Publishers.

Schweickart, P. P. (1996). Speach is silver, silence is gold: The asymmetrical intersubjectivity of communicative action. In N. R.Goldeberger, J. M. Tarule, B. McWickir Klinchy, & M. S. Belenky (Eds.), *Knowledge, difference, and power.* New York: Basic Books.

Silove, D., Sinnerbrink, I., Field, A., Manicavasagar, V., & Steel, Z. (1997). Anxiety, depression and PTSD in asylum seekers: Associations with pre-migration trauma and post migration stressors. *British Journal of Psychiatry, 170,* 351–357.

Solomon, S. D., Smith, E., Robins, L., & Fischback, R. (1987). Social involvement as a mediator of disaster-induced stress. *Applied Journal of Social Psychology, 17,* 1092–1112.

Spasojevic, J., Heffer, R. W., & Snyder, D. K. (2000). Effects of posttraumatic stress and acculturation on marital functioning in Bosnian refugee couples. *Journal of Traumatic Stress, 13,* 205–217.

Sue, S., & Zane, N. (1995). The role of culture and cultural techniques in psychotherapy: A critique and reformulation. In N. R.Goldberger & J. B. Veroff (Eds.), *The culture and psychology reader* (pp. 767–788). New York: New York University Press.

Thulesius, H., & Håkansson, A. (1999). Screening for posttraumatic stress disorder symptoms among Bosnian refugees. *Journal of Traumatic Stress, 12,* 167–174.

Tyler, F. B., Susewell, D. R., & McCoy, J. W. (1995). Ethnic validity in psychotherapy. In N. R. Goldberger & J. B. Veroff (Eds.), *The culture and psychology reader* (pp. 789–807). New York: New York University Press.

United Nations High Commissioner for Refugees. (2001). *UNHCR statistical yearbook.* Geneva: Author.

Westermeyer, J., & Williams, M. (1998). Three categories of victimization among refugees in a psychiatric clinic. In J. Jaranson & M. K. Popkin (Eds.), *Caring for victims of torture* (pp. 61–88). Washington, DC: American Psychiatric Press.

Medical, Surgical, and Clinical Issues in the Treatment of Refugees and Torture Victims

Medical, Surgical, and Clinical Issues in the Treatment of Refugees and Torture Victims

Introduction

JOHN P. WILSON

It is unfortunately true that broken spirits can also suffer from broken bodies. Many asylum seekers and refugees have been subjected to extreme physical hardships ranging from torture to rape to deprivation of food, clothing, and shelter. Physical trauma and psychological trauma are "conjoined twins" that often require special medical and psychiatric attention. Part VI addresses these three interrelated aspects of these medical needs. First, what types of medication are useful for asylum seekers and refugee patients who are suffering from psychiatric difficulties as a result of their experiences? Second, are there special considerations relating to medical and psychiatric difficulties that should be taken into consideration in surgical approaches to victims of torture and PTSD? Third, what are the psychosocial rehabilitation needs of asylum seekers and refugees?

In Chapter 21, J. David Kinzie and Matthew J. Friedman present a condensed and highly useful review of psychopharmacology in the treatment of refugees. Research evidence in the treatment of PTSD has shown that patients suffering from PTSD manifest varying responses to pharmacological aspects prescribed to help alleviate debilitating symptoms. Moreover, as Kinzie and Friedman note, patients with different cultural backgrounds respond differently to medications. Thus, despite a patient having the same diagnosis of a psychiatric disorder, for example PTSD or PTSD and major depression, clinical trials are often necessary to determine what medications work best for which patient under which conditions. Kinzie and Friedman review the use of different types of medication for PTSD including antidepressant, antiadrenergic, benzodiazepines, and antipsychotic medications. They also review studies of psychopharmacological treatments of refugees. Overall, the results show mixed results in terms of symptom alleviation. However, antiadrenergic and antidepressant medications show positive clinical outcomes. The differential response to psychopharmacology can reflect ethnic differences in how drugs are metabolized by the body, and the authors review recent research evidence that demonstrates this fact. Complicating the question of proper psychopharmacology is the fact that among some refugee groups studied in treatment, there are complex diagnostic pictures, since diagnoses revealed various combinations of PTSD, major depression, psychosis, schizophrenia, and alcohol dependence. The authors provide a set of guidelines to assist in decision making about prescribing medication to asylum seekers and refugees. These guidelines cover nine primary decision-making criteria and should be taken into account when considering the use of medication to alleviate debilitating symptoms associated with the stressors of trauma, migration, and resettlement in a foreign culture as an asylum seeker or refugee.

In Chapter 22, Marianne Juhler discusses surgical approaches to victims of torture and PTSD. Since torture victims have been subjected to physically injurious treatments (e.g., suspension, beatings of body and extremities, electric shock, severe deprivations, etc.) there results in some cases the development of significant medical problems that can require surgical intervention in order to provide relief and correction for pathology or disease.

Marianne Juhler, a neurosurgeon with extensive experience working with torture victims, explains the intricacies of diagnosis and surgical interventions with torture victims. The "intricacies" refer specifically to differentiating PTSD-related symptoms and their somatic sequela (i.e., psychosomatic manifestations) from the objective, medical evidence of a disease process (e.g., degenerative cervical spondylosis of the spinal cord resulting from torture). Moreover, even after successful surgical intervention, victims of torture can continue to complain of pain, discomfort, or report that it has worsened, despite medical evidence to the contrary. The patient's complaints of continued or increased pain and discomfort reflect the operation of posttraumatic stress disorder conditions in its complex forms. For example, in being tortured, many victims are "supervised" by physicians who oversee the process of torture to ensure pain but without death and minimally traceable scars. Thus, torture survivors have a fear-based conditioned response to the benevolence of physicians and, where PTSD exists, a rekindling of these traumatic memories and other PTSD symptoms. As Juhler points out, the issue of medical versus psychiatric diagnosis is tricky because the loci of psychosomatic complaints associated with PTSD (e.g., back or shoulder pain) can also be the same bodily places where torture was inflicted. Moreover, the matter gets more complicated since the surgical procedure itself (i.e., an "intrusive" medical procedure) can stimulate pre- or postsurgical flashbacks to torture. In my own professional experience, victims of torture and those suffering from severe, chronic PTSD are also prone to anesthesia-related "flashbacks" in postoperative recovery, which can be confusing to medical staff unfamiliar with PTSD and the subtle but evident manifestations of exacerbated stress responses to surgical procedures and hospitalization.

In Chapter 23, Solvig Ekblad and James Jaranson discuss the psychosocial rehabilitation of asylum seekers and refugees. The authors begin by noting UNHCR statistics that worldwide there were 40 million refugees and displaced persons. Among this population of refugees, there is a substantial percentage who suffer from PTSD, depression, anxiety, substance abuse, and other problems of adjustment. Keeping these facts in mind, the authors establish a framework of understanding the context of psychosocial rehabilitation, which necessarily includes the concepts of stress, culture, acculturation, socioeconomic, and political factors. In essence, these concepts circumscribe and define the domain of relevant areas for focusing treatment programs and developing programs of psychosocial rehabilitation.

The authors present a holistic-ecological model of psychosocial rehabilitation. In a very useful and simple matrix table, they identify five systems of health care concerns and five areas of psychosocial interventions. The five systems of health care include: (1) psychological attachments (e.g., family, spouse, children, significant others), (2) security and safety concerns, (3) identity and roles in society/culture, (4) human rights, and (5) existential search for meaning. Similarly and correspondingly, the five areas of psychosocial rehabilitation include: (1) threats (e.g., separation, loss, traumatic bereavement), (2) reactions (e.g., anxiety, grief, home sickness), (3) pathology (e.g., PTSD, traumatic bereavement), (4) levels (e.g., individual, family, institutional), and (5) levels of intervention (e.g., family, psychosocial programs, individual psychotherapy, etc.). Thus, by employing a matrix of health system functions and areas of psychosocial rehabilitation efforts, the authors create 25 separate areas in which psychiatric, psychological, psychosocial, social welfare, and social policy/organizational responses can be developed to aid asylum seekers and refugees. They also review such efforts and the existing literature that documents the various needs in each of the 25 areas of focused resource allocation on behalf of refugee and asylum seekers.

21

Psychopharmacology for Refugee and Asylum-Seeker Patients

J. DAVID KINZIE AND MATTHEW J. FRIEDMAN

The pharmacotherapy of patients with PTSD has been influenced by the greatly increased knowledge of the neurobiology of severe trauma and the increasing sophistication of drug trials for treatment of traumatic conditions. The expanded scientific knowledge will briefly be reviewed below. However, a critique of these studies will indicate a limited relevance to highly traumatized refuges. The clinical complexity of these patients, emphasizing their cultural aspects of treatment, will be reviewed. Based upon broad clinical and empirical treatments, suggested pharmacological approaches to traumatized refugees from various cultures will be given.

NEUROBIOLOGY OF PTS

Multiple neurobiological symptoms are associated with stress and some are probably involved directly in symptom formation in PTSD. The evidence for these has been summarized elsewhere (Bremner, Southwick & Charney, 1999; Friedman, 2001b). Adrenergic mechanisms, especially those mediated by norepinephrine, have shown heightened reactivity in

PTSD. The evidence is strongest when subjects are exposed to laboratory stressors or traumatic memories, where elevated heart rate, blood pressure, and skin conductance have been found (Pitman, Orr, Forgue, de Jong, & Claiborn, 1987). Altered norepinephrine function is also indicated by other biological abnormalities such as response to yohimbine, depressed platelet MAO activity and MHPG response (Southwick, Bremner, Rasmusson, Morgan, & Arnsten, 1999). Abnormalities have also been detected in the hypothoramic pituitary adrenal (HPA) system including increased corticotrophin-releasing factor supersuppression with the glucocorticoid dexamethasone, increased density of lymphocytic receptors, and mixed results with urinary and plasma cortisol. Decreased serotonin uptake and binding has been found in platelets. In one study, PTSD patients exhibited platelet-poor plasma concentration of serotonin levels and elevated norepinephrine levels (Spivak, Vered, Graff, Blum, Mester, & Weizman, 1999). PTSD, anxiety, and flashback symptoms have been provoked with both adrenergic (e.g., yohimbine) and serotonergic (e.g., mCPP) agonists (Southwick, Krystal, Morgan, Johnson, Nagy, Nicolaou, et al., 1993). Recent studies on brain imaging indicate that PTSD is associated with both structural and functional abnormalities (Pitman et al., 2002). As we learn more about neurobiological alterations associated with PTSD, there is reason to hope that new medications might be designed to ameliorate symptoms caused by the unique pathophysiology of PTSD (Vermetten & Bremner, 2002; Friedman, 2000).

DRUG STUDIES IN PTSD

Antidepressants

There have been an increasing number of clinical trials with medications for treatment of PTSD in the past 10 years. The ones on nonrefugee populations will be summarized below. An early study on veterans indicated improvement in PTSD symptoms with the MAO inhibitor, phenelzine, and the tricyclic antidepressant imipramine in veterans (Kosten, Frank, Dan, McDougle, & Giller, 1991). A dual effect on both depression and PTSD symptoms was also found with the tricyclic antidepressant, amitriptyline (Davidson, Kudler, Saunders, Erickson, Smith, Stein, et al., 1993). The SSRI, sertraline, is the first medication to have received FDA approval for use in PTSD based on results in two large multisite trials with a total of approximately 400 subjects (Davidson, Rothbaum, van der Kolk, Sikes, & Farfel, 2001). In a longer (24-week) study with sertraline, it was shown that remission of PTSD symptoms continued over time (Londberg, Hegel, Goldstein, Goldstein, Himmelhoch, Maddock, et al., 2001). When sertraline treatment was extended to 64 weeks, the quality of life improved for those kept on the medication, while symptoms worsened for subjects randomly switched to placebo treatment (Rapaport, Endicott, & Clary, 2002). In addition to successful PTSD trials, Brady, Sonne, and Roberts (1995) found that sertraline also decreased alcohol consumption while PTSD symptoms improved. Another SSRI, paroxetine, has also received FDA approval based on three successful 12-week randomized clinical trials; it was found to improve all symptom clusters of PTSD (Tucker, Zaninelli, Yehuda, Ruggiero, Dillingham, & Pitts, 2001). Fluoxetine, a selective serotonin reuptake inhibitor (SSRI), was found to be effective in reducing PTSD in nonveteran, mostly female patients who responded better than veterans receiving treatment in a Veteran's Affairs (VA) clinic (van del Kolk, Dreyfuss, Michaels, Shera, Berkowitz, & Fisler, 1994). A recent multisite randomized clinical trial confirmed these early results and indicated that fluoxetine is a very effective treatment for PTSD that is well tolerated (Martenyi, Brown, Zhang, Prakash, & Koke, 2002). Citalopram (another SSRI) has also been found to be useful in adults and children with posttraumatic stress disorder (Seedat, Stein, & Emsley, 2000). A different antidepressant, nefazodone, which enhances serotonergic function through different mechanisms than SSRIs, has been shown to promote PTSD improvement in several open-label trials (Davidson, Weisler, Malik, & Connor, 1998; Zisook, Chentsova-Dutton, Smith-Vaniz, Kline, Ellenor, Kodsi, et al., 2000). Finally, an open trial with the antidepressant bupropion, which enhances adrenergic and dopaminergic (but not serotonergic) activity, has also been successful with PTSD subjects (Canive, Clark, Calois, Quells, & Tuason, 1998).

Antiadrenergic Agents

Because of known abnormalities in the adrenergic system in PTSD, it was thought as early as 1984 that the antiadrenergic agents such as propranolol and clonidine would be helpful (Kolb, Burris, & Griffiths, 1984). Propranolol is a postsynaptic beta-adrenergic antagonist, while clonidine is a presynaptic apha-2 agonist that inhibits the activities of the adrenergic system by reducing the amount of norepinephrine released presynaptically. As such, it is an effective antihypertensive agent. Clonidine has been used extensively with traumatized refugees and our experience with this medication will be discussed later. A recent report from Argentina regarding emergency room patients prescribed medication immediately after trauma exposure suggests that those who received clonidine or propranolol exhibited marked improvement 6 months later, whereas those who received antidepressants (such as venlafaxine, sertraline, and citalopram) or the benzodiazepine, alprazolam, showed no improvement (Mosca & Muro, 2002). Recently, the adrenergic postsynaptic alpha-1 blocking agent and antihypertensive medication, prazosin, has been found to reduce traumatic nightmares and global PTSD symptoms in combat veterans and in civilians (Raskind, Thompson, Petrie, Dobie, Rein, Hoff, et al., 2002; Taylor & Raskind, 2002).

Benzodiazepines

Although anxiety seems to be a major component of PTSD, and PTSD is included in the anxiety disorder section of DSM-IV, benzodiazepines have not proven effective against core PTSD symptoms (Friedman, 2001a).

Antipsychotics

Although antipsychotics have not been considered the recommended treatment for PTSD (Cyr & Farrar, 2000), psychotic symptoms can be associated with PTSD (Mueser & Butler, 1987; Mueser, Goodman, Trumbetta, Rosenberg, Osher, et al., 1998). Kinzie Boehnlein (1989) discussed it as a fairly common phenomenon in traumatized refugees. It would be useful to have studies on these difficult patients, particularly with atypical antipsychotics, which affect both the dopaminergic and serotoninergic systems and are fairly well tolerated. Although randomized trials have not been carried out on the efficacy of atypical antipsychotics for PTSD, preliminary data on veterans indicate that olanzapine can ameliorate SSRI-resistant PTSD (Stein, Kline, & Maltoff, 2002), and risperidone has been shown to reduce comorbid psychotic symptoms with PTSD (Hammer, Faldowski, Ulmer, Frueh, Huber, et al., 2003), and be useful for irritable aggression (Monnelly, Ciraulo, Knapp, & Keane, 2003). Theoretically, risperidone could reduce nightmares due to its strong alpha-1 and apha-2 blockade, the highest blockade of all atypical antipsychotics (Bezchlibnyk-Butler & Jeffries, 2000, p. 80). Although it currently appears that antidepressants affecting the serotonin system SSRIs have performed better than those affecting the norepinephrine system (e.g., buproprion and desipramine), there have been too few clinical trials with adrenergic agents to support such a conclusion. Given the recent FDA approval of two SSRI medications, and the consistent success of these medications in treating all PTSD symptom clusters, these agents must be considered first-line treatment for PTSD at this time (Friedman, Davidson, Mellman, & Southwick, 2000).

STUDIES RELEVANT TO REFUGEES

The populations in the above studies, usually Vietnam veterans and Caucasian female victims of civilian traumas, are very different from refugees. Indeed, there have been few studies conducted either in war-torn countries or with refugees themselves. A report from the Indochinese Psychiatric Clinic in Boston, with Indochinese survivors of trauma, suggests that the efficacy of monoamine oxidase inhibitors for PTSD can be independent of their beneficial effects in depression (Demartino, Mollica, & Wilk, 1995). This report also raises appropriate concerns about using MAOIs with refugees, given the dietary practices of Southeast

Asians. The Intercultural Psychiatric Program in Oregon has treated refugees for 25 years and reported the successful use of clonidine and imipramine in a prospective study with 9 Cambodian patients (Kinzie & Leung, 1989). There was a marked improvement in depression and nightmares for 7 of these patients. Although there was global improvement in PTSD reexperiencing and arousal symptoms, avoidance was not affected. In an all-night polysomnographic study with 4 Cambodian patients, clonidine was extremely effective; it produced almost complete suppression of nightmares and the patients reported better sleep and less irritability (Kinzie, Sack, & Riley, 1994). This effect appears to have been restricted to PTSD improvement since depression symptoms were not affected. A report on Bosnian refugees found sertraline and paroxetine to produce statistically significant improvement in PTSD symptoms in 6 weeks (Smajkic, Weine, Djuric-Byedic, Boskaulto, Lewis, & Pavkovic, 2001). Venlafaxine produced improvement in PTSD but not depression and was associated with a high rate of side effects. All 32 patients still met PTSD diagnosis at 6 weeks.

Clinical Aspects of Refugees and Political Asylees

There are important aspects of refugees lives that greatly influence their clinical status and need to be accounted for in the management of these patients. First, the amount of trauma endured by refugees often is catastrophic and much greater in severity and duration than that reported among patients from Western countries. Cambodian survivors of the Pol Pot regime endured 4 years of concentration camp experience, starvation, forced labor, indiscriminate executions, and sometimes were forced to witness the execution of family members. Most of the Cambodian refugee patients had some family members killed and often lost their entire families, including children. After the regime fell, there was mass confusion, victimization by bandits, and they were forced to live for 3 to 5 years in a refugee camp with unsafe and unpredictable conditions. In Somalia, after the overthrow of the government in 1992, refugees were exposed to mass and indiscriminate murder by warlords; the complete lawlessness associated with fighting by rival tribe clans resulted in mass starvation. Those who made it out of the country were subjected to robbery and beatings in refugee camps and faced an unknown future. Rural farmers in Guatemala were often caught between government militia, paramilitia, and the guerrilla forces, all of whom would come at night to attack villages, kill and kidnap men, and leave the village in utter ruin. The Aethnic cleansing, with the blockade and shelling of entire towns in Bosnia, is well documented. In addition, reports of torture of Muslim men in concentration camps and the discovery of mass graves indicate the extent of the brutality inflicted on people exposed to the many wars in the former Yugoslavia.

Second, because of the trauma, refugees are confronted with massive losses, which include death of family members, loss or separation from other families, loss of their society and culture, and loss of vocation and income because their skills are not needed in the host countries. There is a total breakdown in the social and cultural fabric of their lives. Within the family there is a disruption of the dynamics, with loss of parental authority because parents often cannot provide appropriate guidance to their children who now see them as irrelevant in a techno-logical society. Often there is a disruption of the religious practices of the traditional Muslim and Buddhist cultures. The result is a loss of cultural continuity. Additionally, refugee families are often strapped with poverty and unable to find employment. Further, since fathers are often missing or killed, single mothers must struggle with the daunting challenge of raising children in a foreign country. Most refugees have very limited language ability in the host country so that basic activities — shopping, housing, and transportation — are often huge problems.

A special group are the asylum seekers who arrive in a country without legal status and who cannot receive services until asylum is granted. They live in an unpredictable world and have a high rate of psychiatric morbidity (Silove & Kinzie, 2001).

Cultural Considerations

A major theoretical and clinical issues concern the influence of culture on symptoms following trauma, especially massive psychological trauma. Clearly, the culture of a patient, as well as his or her resilience, personality, social supports, and posttraumatic environment, will influence the expression of symptoms. Several examples from diverse non-Western cultures will demonstrate some of these factors. Tradi-tional Buddhists, who believe in karma, often will show an acceptance of terrible events that are unacceptable to most Westerners. Islamic patients, who believe that their fate is in Allah's hands, may feel less of a need to actually strive for any relief. The animus Mien tribesmen from rural Laos subjectively feel that Western medicine is not compatible with their bodies or their yin-yang understanding of disease. Cultural factors need to be understood and often addressed if therapy is to succeed. A more comprehensive discussion of cross-cultural treatment of PTSD is beyond the scope of this chapter but can be found elsewhere (Kinzie, 2001). Based on 25 years' experience treating refugees at the Intercultural Psychiatric Program (IPP), with patients from 17 cultures and languages by one of us (JDK), we offer the following personal observations on cross-cultural issues relating to trauma.

The expression of the symptoms depends largely upon the skill, tact, empathy, and experience of the psychiatrist and the ethnic mental health counselor. The Intercultural Psychiatric Program has never used interpreters, but has trained counselors of each culture to work and provide translation both linguistically and culturally between the psychiatrist and the patients. Additionally, as counselors gain experi-ence, they begin to serve as case managers and group leaders. The patient's recounting of his or her symptoms, and especially the traumatic experiences, changes and is reinterpreted as trust and safety issues as the therapeutic relationship grows. Thus, the expression of symptoms and their treatment is a dynamic process involving patients, counselors, and psychiatrists.

After massive trauma, which most refugees have experienced, the core symptoms among all refugee groups are much more similar than different. All groups have described reexperiencing, particularly, nightmares and intrusive thoughts; and hyperarousal, including poor sleep, poor concentration, and irritability. Avoidance symptoms are also common, especially those involving memories and reminders of the past and violence. Numbing and social withdrawal, however, can vary depending on individual or situational differences. Many Cambodians and Somalis in the clinic setting display overt numbing, while in the nonclinical context of their own group activities and social therapy can be more overtly emotionally expressive as long as the focus is not trauma-related. Depressive symptoms seem to be universal in all the cultural groups.

Medication needs to be part of a total program in which the major therapeutic ingredients are safety and long-term continuity. In the Intercultural Psychiatric Program, the three senior psychiatrists have been associated with the program for 20 or more years each, and 10 of the 25 counselors have been with the program for 10 or more years. This stability provides confidence for the patient who receives psychotherapy with the psychiatrist and case management and counseling with the ethnic mental health counselors. Socialization and activity groups, in which about half the patients participate, reduce social isolation and provide a good forum for medication education.

For Western-trained mental health professionals who work with PTSD patients, there are several notable differences with refugees. The small number of alcohol- and substance-abusing patients is in marked contrast to U.S. veterans. Prohibited by both Buddhist and Islamic religions, substance dependence is rare but not absent in these groups. It is more prevalent in Bosnian and Latin American refugees. Suicide and suicide attempts are very uncommon. There have been about five successful attempts in the 25 years, all of which have occurred with schizophrenic patients. Personality disorder symptoms, especially cluster B, are not common. Most of the patients have had a stable childhood and their forced migration occurred during adulthood. This lack of traumatic exposure or interpersonal violation during childhood seems to have provided most refugees with a stable identity so that destructive interpersonal behaviors or frank antisocial traits are uncommon. The long-term effects of children exposed to trauma have not been extensively studied, but a 6-year follow-up of Cambodian children exposed to massive trauma showed few personality or antisocial disorders (Sack, Clarke, Him, Dickason, Goff, Lanham, et al., 1993).

This contrasts greatly with what has been reported in Americans with PTSD caused by childhood abuse. Dissociative symptoms are not common. Most patients present in a straightforward manner, once trust is established, without the disturbances and identity problems, memory impairment, altered reality testing, or fragmented cognition, which is often present in Western patients with dissociative symptoms.

Refugee patients are both pragmatic and genuinely hopeful about Western medicine. They already have seen the obvious benefits of antibiotics, trauma surgery, good obstetrical care, cancer screening, and how effective control of blood pressure prevents cardiac death. Psychiatric medicines, providing symptom relief in the context of a relationship in which side effects are explained, are well accepted by most groups. Involving families, who often are exposed to the nightly screaming, irritability, or profound sadness of the PTSD patient, helps to ensure further compliance. If the medicine benefits the patients' perceived symptoms or needs, they will take it. A problem has been in maintaining patients on medication after symptoms have been relieved. There are similar problems getting refugees to continue to take medicine for tuberculosis treatment or for the asymptomatic treatment of hypertension.

CLINICAL CONSIDERATIONS

Ethnopsychopharmacology

Although transcultural psychiatrists have felt clinically that different ethnic groups respond to psychiatric agents differently, it was only in the 1990s that ethnic differences in psychobiology were scientifically studied, led by Keh-Ming Lin (Lin, Poland, & Nakasaki, 1993). Since that time, a number of authors have raised issues regarding the different effects of the same medications when administered to different ethnic groups (Jaime & Maharaja, 2000; Lin, Smith, & Ortiz, 2001; Pi, 1998; Ramirez, 1996; Sramek & Pi, 1996). It is now recognized that there are substantial differences in the metabolic capacity of different ethnic groups. For example, the frequency of mephenytoin poor metabolizes in different populations has been found as follows (Kinzie & Ediri, 1998b):

African Americans	1.7%
African Caucasians	2.6%
Chinese	14.6%
Japanese	22.6%
Vietnamese	22.0%

The clinical significance of this information is difficult to evaluate since there are many factors (individual genetic enzyme pathways, diet, smoking, and presence of other medicines) that also contribute to these differences in psychotropic drug response.

Compliance

One of the largest problems in evaluating medicine effectiveness is the high noncompliance rate among psychiatric patients. This seems especially true for refugees who have little understanding of the reasons why they should take medicines or little tolerance of side effects. In an early study on compliance with tricyclic antidepressants, marked noncompliance was found among Asian patients (see Table 21.1) (Kinzie, Leung, Boehnlein, & Flick, 1987).

Overall, no blood tricyclic levels were detected in 61% of patients, with the highest noncompliance observed among Vietnamese and Mien patients. After discussing this matter with these patients, the total noncompliance (e.g., zero blood levels) dropped to 22% and 27% among Cambodian and Vietnamese, respectively. However, the Mien were not influenced by this intervention since their noncompliance remained high at 67%. After a more thorough patient evaluation there was a further increase in compliance among Vietnamese and Cambodians, but little improvement occurred among the Mien, a hill tribe people from Laos. Clearly, the issue of medication compliance and the related issue of patient acceptability of pharmacotherapy must be considered when evaluating the effectiveness of medicines among refugees.

DIFFICULTY IN DIAGNOSIS IN REFUGEES

Among refugees from some countries, such as Cambodia, where the severe trauma is documented, making the PTSD diagnosis seems straightforward. For other refugee groups, it might be more difficult to elicit a history of trauma because of factors such as shame, amnesia, and poor interviewing or interpreting skills by clinicians. In addition, an accurate history of pretraumatic mental illness might be overlooked because of the dramatic presentation of the brutal events. Even in the Intercultural Psychiatric Program, a diagnosis of PTSD was sometimes missed during the initial evaluation and was only determined subsequently after structured reinterviewing (Kinzie, Boehnlien, Leung Moore, Riley, & Smith, 1990). Equally important is consideration of other psychiatric disorders that exist with PTSD among refugees

TABLE 21.1 Routine Check of 41 Asian Patients for TCA Blood Levels (N = %)

	None	Subtherapeutic 25–180 µg/ml	Therapeutic > 180 µg/ml
Cambodian	7 (39)	7 (39)	4 (22)
Vietnamese	9 (81)	1 (9)	1 (9)
Mien	9 (75)	2 (17)	1 (8)
Total	25 (61)	10 (24)	6 (15)

exposed to massive trauma. Below is a review of psychiatric diagnoses among 199 refugees from major war zones in Cambodia, Bosnia, and Somalia seen in the Intercultural Clinic during August 2002 (see Table 21.2).

Clearly, PTSD rarely exists alone; in only three people out of 199 was PTSD the sole diagnosis. PTSD was comorbid with depression in 57% to 79% of the cases. It was comorbid with psychotic symptoms in 5% and 13% of Bosnians and Somalis, respectively. Schizophrenia, with its long-term deterioration in function, was associated with PTSD in all groups. In contrast to U.S. veterans, Buddhist and Muslim refugees rarely exhibited alcohol problems. In summary, it can be difficult to make a diagnosis of PTSD with refugee patients and when PTSD is present, it is usually associated with depression and often with psychosis or schizophrenia.

THE COURSE OF TRAUMATIC SYMPTOMS

Our clinical experience and a long-term study of Cambodians in the community indicate that, as with other chronic disorders, PTSD has a long course with exacerbations and remissions. In an earlier report on Cambodian refugees (Kinzie, Frederickson, & Ben, 1984), PTSD was first described. A follow-up study indicated that the symptoms were greatly reduced at 1 year (Boehnlein, Kinzie, Ben, & Fleck, 1985). All these patients, however, had a clinically significant exacerbation of their symptoms over the next several years. Sack, Clarke, Him, Dickason, Goff, Lanham, et al. (1993) followed Cambodians in the community and initially found a 50% rate of depression and PTSD. After 12 years, the rate of PTSD dropped to about 30%, while depression almost completely disappeared. Several subjects who did not meet PTSD diagnostic criteria at one time did so at another time, indicating a fluctuating clinical course. In a reactivation study, Cambodians exhibited a marked

TABLE 21.2 Diagnosis in 2002

	Cambodians	Bosnians	Somalians
N =	110	58	31
% PTSD + depression	79	57	58
% Depression	6	19	3
PTSD	0	0	3
PTSD + psychosis	0	5	13
Schizophrenia	7	12	7
Schizophrenia + PTSD	4	5	16
Alcohol dependence	2	0	0
Total with PTSD + another diagnosis	82 (91/110)	67 (39/58)	90 (28/31)

increase in pulse rate when exposed to traumatic stimuli (that were not limited to war or Cambodian scenes) in comparison to control and Vietnam veteran subjects (Kinzie, Denney, Riley, Boehnlein, McFarland, & Leung, 1998). In all refugee patient groups, stressful personal experiences such as assaults, surgeries, and accidents exacerbated the original symptoms. Community stress, such as televised scenes about the Gulf War and World Trade Center attacks, greatly increased PTSD symptoms among all of our refugee groups.

In a recent study on the effects of viewing the 9/11 events on television, it was found that Somalis and Bosnians reported the greatest increase in subjective distress and symptoms (Kinzie, Boehnlein, Riley, & Sparr, 2002), whereas Cambodians and Vietnamese refugees exhibited surprisingly little intensification of symptoms. This probably was related to the warfare in Bosnia and Somalia being more recent than in other groups. Their Muslim religion also might have given them a sense of vulnerability in America. A chart review of 25 Cambodian patients treated for at least 10 years indicated that half (13) still had abnormal elevations in PTSD symptom severity, whereas only 4 had elevated depressive symptomatology. In summary, it is clear that for many if not most refugees, PTSD is a chronic disorder subject to stress-induced exacerbations when there is perceived risk of threats or danger. Clearly, all therapy must be aimed at chronic treatment with the expectation of periodic exacerbations in symptom severity. Follow-up studies limited to a 6-week, 12-week, or even 1-year follow-up are not adequate for evaluating longitudinal outcome.

PATIENT DEMOGRAPHICS AND EXPECTATION

The vast majority (70%) of the 1,000 refugees who participate in the Intercultural Psychiatric Program are female, varying 84% among Somalis to 69% of Bosnians. Many refugee women have not been educated so there is a high level of functional illiteracy even in their own language. Less than 4 years of education, but usually none, was present in 66% of Cambodians, and 58% of Somalis, but in only 20% of Bosnians. Many Cambodians and Somalis could not read medical instructions even in their own language, and therefore were even more confused by instructions written in English. In addition to patient education, the cultural beliefs about mental illness and expectations about medical treatment have a major influence on acceptance of medicine, tolerance of side effects, and compliance.

Many patients originally complain of multiple somatic symptoms (headache, backache, weakness, poor sleep), and even after sensitive interviewing have difficulty focusing on psychological symptoms such as depressed mood, anxiety, irritability, nightmares, poor concentration, or anger outbursts. If the patient's symptomatic concerns are not acknowledged and alleviated there is little chance for continued engagement in therapy. The implication is that many patients for whom it is difficult to understand current medical diagnosis will also have difficulty following written instructions (or even remembering oral ones) and will have very different concepts about the goals of treatment.

GUIDELINES

The above information, summarized from a large, growing database about several different refugee groups, underscores the biopsychosocial complications associated with pharmacotherapy for traumatized refugees. The guidelines presented here should serve as a preliminary list for the treating psychiatrist. Two points must be emphasized. First, treatment with medicine can only succeed if it is part of a total program, which includes supportive psychotherapy, medical evaluation, guidance regarding financial security, attention to housing needs, and opportunities for vocational rehabilitation. Second, the treatment team must include a trusted, competent, and ethical mental health counselor (or at least an interpreter) who provides both linguistic and cultural continuity for the patient and doctor.

- Take a full history of the patient including his or her life before and after the trauma, the trauma itself, the symptoms of PTSD, depression and psychosis, and the presence of other medical conditions and medicines taken.
- Determine from the patient and family (when available) what are the most disturbing symptoms or behaviors. Develop a mutual agreement on the target symptoms, such as insomnia, nightmares, irritability, depression, and pain, which are often common concerns.
- Use medicines that directly or indirectly alleviate the target symptoms of the patient complaints.
- Keep medicines very simple. Remember patients often cannot read and easily get confused. It is good to show patients the pills so they can recognize the color and shape.
- Carefully explain the benefits and some possible side effects and the need to continue medicine.
- Prepare the patient for long-term treatment. The ideal therapeutic stance is to both expect improvement and that treatment will continue.
- Do frequent evaluations, weekly at first, since there is almost universal confusion and misunderstanding with starting medicine. Always ask about compliance and get blood levels if they are available.
- Expect exacerbations, making adjustment to give symptomatic relief as needed, but don't fine-tune the medicine too often. Provide an accepting and predictable presence to the patient.
- Consider cost if there is no health insurance or third-party payer, as is true with many refugees and with all asylum seekers.

SPECIFIC MEDICINES BASED ON CLINICAL EXPERIENCE WITH THE ABOVE GUIDELINES

The use of psychotropic medicines among refugees has rarely been addressed in the published literature, but there is a large experimental clinical base on which to base these guidelines. The Intercultural Psychiatric Program has treated over 4,000 refugee patients in 25 years and currently has 1,000 adults in treatment. In a review a conducted a few years ago concerning the actual clinic practice patterns of five faculty psychiatrists who had collectively treated 240 refugee patients, it was found that 41% received tricyclic antidepressants; 42% received an SSRI; and 17% received trazodone. This represented the personal preference of the physicians rather than any special clinical or economic considerations. Indeed, the use of SSRIs varied from 17% to 79% by specific physicians. Of the 77% of refugees taking SSRIs, 74% were taking another psychotropic medicine for insomnia; the secondary medicines included a low dose of trazodone, a sedative tricyclic, or benzodiazepine. A major concern for patients has been poor sleep, for which SSRIs are often ineffective. Almost no patients on TCAs were on a secondary medicine for insomnia.

Antidepressants

SSRIs

Since depression often occurs conjointly with PTSD in traumatized refugees, and since SSRIs are effective for both depression and PTSD, they are a good choice for initial treatment. As stated earlier, two SSRIs (sertraline and paroxetine) have received FDA approval as indicated treatments for PTSD. They have been considered the first drug of choice in both practice guidelines reviews (Friedman, Davidson, Mellman, & Southwick, 2000) and by international consensus groups on treatment of PTSD (Ballenger, Davidson, & Lecrubier, 2000). SSRIs have a broad spectrum of action on all three PTSD symptom clusters, have a high safety profile, are effective against most comorbid conditions (e.g., affective and anxiety disorders), relieve clinically significant symptoms associated with PTSD (e.g., impulsive, aggressive, irritable, and suicidal behavior), and only need to be taken once a day. Fluoxetine (now sold as a generic compound) has a long half-life so that missing a day or two of dosage is not as crucial as with other medicines. In our experience, SSRIs usually have modest effects on refugees' nightmares and insomnia. Approximately 75% of patients on SSRIs also receive clonidine, primarily for control of nightmares. The sexual dysfunction side effects of SSRIs are frequently mentioned by Latin American and African patients, but are rarely considered a problem by Asian patients, even when such information is directly asked about.

TCAs

The tricyclic antidepressants have probably been overlooked as an effective first-line treatment (Diamond, Holden, Rotonda, & Tobey, 2002). The tertiary amines, imipramine, amitriptyline, and doxepin, have sedative/hypnotic actions that effectively induce sleep, especially at the usual therapeutic doses of 100–150 mg at night. They also can be given once a day at bedtime, have analgesic properties, and the anticholinergic properties can help with some gastrointestinal symptoms. Doxepin has an antihistaminic (H2) blocking capacity equal to that of cimetidine. The side effects of dry mouth, constipation, and postural hypertension are sometimes disturbing to some. Concerns about fatal overdose with tricyclics has been exaggerated among refugees. Patients with Buddhist and Islamic traditions where suicide is strongly prohibited have a very low rate of suicide. In 25 years of treating several thousand refugees we have had no depressed PTSD patients commit suicide. The five suicides that have occurred, occurred among our schizophrenic, not PTSD, patients and were not due to an overdose. A final consideration is the ease of blood level monitoring to determine compliance. This has been an extremely valuable clinical strategy when noncompliance is found, which generally facilitates a productive discussion of the patient's problem with the medicines.

Antiadrenergic Agents

Clonidine and the related compound guanfacine and probably prazosin should be considered a mainstay of treatment along with an antidepressant. Clonidine is a medicine with a long and successful record as an effective treatment for hypertension; it is safe and cheap. Given once at night it can help promote sleep because of its sedative properties. It can greatly reduce nightmares. We have increased the nightly dose until nightmares have been reduced in frequency to once every one or two weeks. Clonidine also helps ameliorate symptoms of intrusive thoughts and hyperarousal. A common starting dose is .2 h.s., and many patients have needed a maintenance dose of .2 in the morning and .4 h.s. at bedtime. Since many patients have hypertension (40% in our clinic), it is also an effective medicine for the comorbid PTSD and hypertensive combination. It can be combined well with an antidepressant (75% of our patients receiving an antidepressant are also on clonidine). It is important to emphasize that, since TCAs interact with clonidine to block its antihypertensive effects, a non-TCA antidepressant should be used in combination with clonidine for hypertensive patients. Clonidine comes in a transdermal patch, which can be applied once a week. This sometimes causes a local rash and is more expensive. There have been anecdotal reports that patients sometimes become tolerant to clonidine, so that the medication loses its effectiveness. In our experience, however, we found no loss of efficacy in patients who have received such treatment for over 15 years. If and when tolerance to clonidine does occur, guanfacine, which has a similar pharmacological action, has proven an effective replacement (Friedman, Davidson, Mellman, & Southwick, 2000). In our experience, when patients choose to decrease the number of medicines they are taking, they will prefer to discontinue antidepressants rather than clonidine. Consequently, many of our refugee patients are now taking clonidine alone.

PTSD With Psychosis

PTSD with psychosis is a surprisingly common problem among refugees. It usually presents with auditory hallucinations or delusions of thought control in addition to PTSD symptoms and sometimes clinical depression. Often it is accompanied by agitation and aggressiveness. The first goal of treatment is to control the psychotic symptoms and agitation. Risperidone has been useful, usually in the 1 to 4 mg nightly dose range. Clonidine for PTSD symptoms, as above, is started at the same time although risperidone alone sometimes controls nightmares by its adrenergic blocking action. Adding an antidepressant is delayed to determine if it is needed. Starting out with three different medicines is often very difficult for both patient adherence and clinical management.

Schizophrenia With PTSD

Several patients have presented with the entire schizophrenic syndrome including delusions, hallucinations, bizarre behavior, and limited functioning. By history, some symptoms were present before the trauma, and some clearly resulted from the trauma. When combined with PTSD, the syndrome can be a challenge to treat. The goal is to first control the psychosis, which often requires a moderately high level of an atypical antipsychotic; 20 mg of olanzapine has been helpful but the weight gain and tendency toward diabetes is a disadvantage. Ziprasidone and risperidone have been useful alternatives. Several cases have also required the administration of a conventional antipsychotic agent, such as perphenazine, to help control the symptoms. Clonidine is usually added to the antipsychotic medication for PTSD control. Because compliance has been a problem for some, approximately half of the refugees with schizophrenia receive a monthly injection of Prolixin or Haldol decanoate rather than oral antipsychotic treatment.

Mood Stabilizers

Because bipolar disorder has been rarely diagnosed among refugees, there has been little experience with mood stabilizers. Lithium treatment for several patients has been complicated by their refusal to permit venipuncture required for monitoring serum lithium levels; as a

TABLE 21.3 Summary of Clinical Experience on Pharmacotherapy on Refugees With PTSD

Medicine Class	Specific Medication	Dose Range	Comments
SSRI	Fluoxetine	20–60 mg	Generally effective in a wide range of symptoms
	Sertraline	50–200 mg	Fluoxetine has a longer half-life and missing a dose
	Paroxetine	20–40 mg	doesn't affect response
	Citalopram	10–20 mg	Fluoxetine is generic and less expensive
			Many patients complain of sexual dysfunction, and modest effect on nightmares and sleep
Tricyclic antidepressant	Imipramine	50–200 mg	Tertiary TCA help sleep and hyperarousal–amitriptyline too sedative for most refugees
	Doxepin	50–200 mg	Very sedative, initially useful for sleep disturbance; constipation, dry, mouth and hypotension are side effects; blood level easily obtained for checking compliance; analgesic properties help pain symptoms (efficacy for desipramine has not been shown)
	Amitriptyline	50–200 mg	
	Desipramine	50–200 mg	
Antiadrenergic agent	Clonidine	2–16 mg	Very effective for nightmares, reexperiencing, and agitation
alpha-2-agonist	Guanfacine	1–3 mg	Useful with coexisting hypertension (not with a TCA, however)
alpha-1-antagonist	Propranolol	40–160 mg	Prazosin useful in veterans; clearly clinical experience indicates effective in Cambodians
B-Blocker	Prazosin		

TABLE 21.3 Continued

Medicine Class	Specific Medication	Dose Range	Comments
Atypical antipsychotic	Risperidone Olanzapine	1–4 mg 2.5–20 mg	Effective for coexisting psychosis and agitation and may control nightmares; olanzapine; tendency for type II diabetes; a problem in refugees with high tendency to diabetes
Antidepressant	Carbamazepine Valproate	750–1750 mg 400–1600 mg	May be effective in some PTSD symptoms and hyperarousal Strict adherence to medicine and blood draws is a problem for many refugees
Mood stabilizers	lithium, lamotrigene gabapentin, topirimate		Not shown to be effective in PTSD at this point; no experience in refugee populations

Source: Modified from Friedman, Davidson, Mellman, & Southwick (2000).

consequence, such patients are on a low dose, 600 mg or less a day. Lithium does seem to help some patients with irritability. A trial with lamotrigine is currently under way in the general population; given its capacity to elevate depressed mood, it might prove to be a useful drug for refugees.

Benzodiazepines

Benzodiazepines generally are not helpful and can disinhibit patients who already fear a loss of control. Short-term use may be indicated, however, during extremely time-limited anxiety/stress provoking situations, such as deportation hearings.

Table 21.3 provides a summary of medicines useful for traumatized refugees. It represents clinical guidelines rather than findings in controlled studies since there is a paucity of such studies on multicultural refugees. This table is modified from Friedman, Davidson, Mellman, and Southwick (2000).

REFERENCES

Ballenger, J. C., Davidson, J. R. T., Lecrubier, Y., Nutt, D. J., Foa, E. B., Kessler, R. C., McFarlane, & Shalev, A. Y. (2000). Consensus statement on posttraumatic stress disorder from the International Consensus Group on Depression and Anxiety. *Journal of Clinical Psychiatry, 61*(Suppl. 5), 60–66.

Bezchlibnyk-Butler, K. Z., & Jeffries, J. J. (2000). *Clinical handbook of psychotropic drugs* (10th ed.). Seattle: Hoysefe & Huber.

Boehnlein, J. K., Kinzie, J. D., Ben, R., & Fleck, J. (1985). One year follow up study of post traumatic stress disorder among survivors of Cambodian concentration camps. *American Journal of Psychiatry, 142,* 956–959.

Brady, K. T., Sonne, S., & Roberts, J. M. (1995). Sertraline treatment of comorbid posttraumatic stress disorder and alcohol dependence. *Journal of Clinical Psychiatry, 56,* 502–505.

Bremner, J. D., Southwick, S. M., & Charney, D. S. (1999). The neurobiology of posttraumatic stress disorder: An integration of animal and human research in posttraumatic stress disorder: A comprehensive text. In P. A. Saigh & J. D. Bremner (Eds.), (pp. 103–143). Boston: Allyn & Bacon.

Canive, J. M., Clark, R. D., Calois, L. A., Quells, C., & Tuason, V. B. (1998). Buproprion treatment in veterans with posttraumatic stress disorder: an open study. *Journal of Clinical Psychopharmacology, 18,* 379–383.

Cyr, M., & Farrar, M. K. (2000). Treatment for posttraumatic stress disorder. *Annals of Pharmacotherapy, 34,* 366–376.

Davidson, J. R., Kudler, H. S., Saunders, W. B., Erickson, L., Smith, R. D., Stein, R. M. et al. (1993). Predicting response to amitriptyline in posttraumatic stress disorder. *American Journal of Psychiatry, 150,* 1024–1029.

Davidson, J. R., Rothbaum, B. O., van der Kolk, B. A., Sikes, C. R., & Farfel, G. M. (2001). Multicenter, double blind comparison of sertraline and placebo in the treatment of posttraumatic stress disorder. *Archive of General Psychiatry, 58,* 485–492.

Davidson, J. R., Weisler, R. H., Malik, M. L., & Connor, K. M. (1998). Treatment of posttraumatic stress disorder with nefazodone. *International Clinical Psychopharmacology, 13,* 111–113.

DeMartino, R., Mollica, R. F., & Wilk, V. (1995). Monoamine oxidane inhibitors in posttraumatic stress disorder. Promise and problems in Indochinese survivors of trauma. *Journal of Nervous and Mental Disease, 183,* 510–615.

Diamond, M., Holden, D. J., Rotondo, D. L., & Tobey, E. W. (2002). Exploring the advantages of tricyclic antidepressants. *Neuro Psychiatry Review,* (Suppl. Oct.), 2–11.

Friedman, M. J. (2000). What might thepsychobiology of PTSD teach us about future approaches to pharmacotherapy? *Journal of Clinical Psychiatry b,* (Suppl. 7), 44–51.

Friedman, M. J., Davidson, J. R., Mellman, T. A., & Southwick, S. M. (2000). Pharmacotherapy. In E. B. Foa, T. M. Keane, & M. J. Friedman (Eds.), *Effective treatments for PTSD: Practice guidelines from the International Society for Traumatic Stress Studies* (pp. 84–105). New York: Guilford Publications.

Friedman, M. J. (2001). Allostatic versus emperical perspective on pharmacotherapy for PTSD. In J. P. Wilson, M. J. Friedman, & J. D. Lindsey (Eds.), *Treating psychological trauma and PTSD* (pp. 125–138). New York: Guilford Press.

Friedman, M. J. (2001). *Posttraumatic stress disorder.* Kansas City, MO: Compact Clinical.

Hammer, M. B., Faldowski, R. A., Ulmer, H. G., Frueh, B. C., Huber, M. G., & Arana, G. W. (2003). Adjunctive risperidone treatment in post-traumatic stress disorder: A preliminary controlled trial of effects of comorbid psychotic symptoms. *International Clinical Psychopharmacology, 18,* 1–8.

Jaime, L. K., & Maharaja, H. (2000). Psychopharmacology research in the English-speaking Caribbean. *Drug and Metabolism Interactions, 16*(1), L69–81.

Kinzie, J. D. (2001). Cross-cultural treatment of PTSD. In J. P. Wilson, M. F. Friedman, & J. D. Lindy (Eds.), *Treating psychological trauma and PTSD* (pp. 255–277). New York: Guilford Publications.

Kinzie, J. D., & Boehnlein, J. K. (1989). Post traumatic psychosis among Cambodian refugees. *Traumatic Stress, 2,* 185–198.

Kinzie, J. D., Boehnlein, J. K., Leung, P., Moore, L., Riley, C., & Smith D. (1990). The prevalence of post traumatic stress disorder and its clinical significance among Southeast Asian refugees. *American Journal of Psychiatry, 147,* 913–917.

Kinzie, J. D., Boehnlein, J. K., Riley, C., & Sparr, L. (2002). The effects of September 11 on traumatized refugees. Reactivation of posttraumatic stress disorder. *Journal of Nervous Disease, 190,* 437–441.

Kinzie, J. D., Denny, D., Riley, C., Boehnlein, J. K., McFarland, B., & Leung P. (1998). A cross cultural study of reactivation of post traumatic stress disorder symptoms. *Journal of Nervous and Mental Disease, 186,* 670–676.

Kinzie, J. D., & Ediri, T. (1998b). Ethnicity and psychopharmacology: The experience of Southeast Asians. In S. Okpaku (Ed.), Clinical methods on transcultural psychiatry (pp. 171–190). Washington, DC: APA Press.

Kinzie, J. D., Frederickson, R. H., Ben, R., Fleck, J., & Karls, W. (1984). Posttraumatic stress syndrome among survivors of Cambodian concentration camps. *American Journal of Psychiatry, 141*, 645–650.

Kinzie, J. D., & Leung, P. K. (1989). Clonidine in Cambodian patients with post traumatic stress disorder. *Journal of Nervous and Mental Disease, 177*, 546–550.

Kinzie, J. D., Leung, P., Boehnlein, J., & Flick, J. (1987). Antidepressant blood levels in Southeast Asians: Clinical and cultural implications. *Journal of Nervous and Mental Disease, 175*, 480–485.

Kinzie, J. D., Sack, R. L., & Riley, C. M. (1994). The polysomnographic effects of Clonidine on sleep disorders in post traumatic stress syndrome: A pilot study with Cambodian patients. *Journal of Nervous and Mental Disease, 182*, 585–587.

Kolb, L. C., Burris, B. C., & Griffiths, S. (1984). Propanolol and clonidine in treatment of posttraumatic stress disorders. In B. A. van der Kolk (Ed.), Posttraumatic stress disorders, psychological and biological sequelae. Washington, DC: American Psychiatric Press.

Kosten, T. R., Frank, J. B., Dan, E., McDougle, C. J., & Giller, E. L., Jr. (1991). Pharmacotherapy for posttraumatic stress disorder using phenelzine or imipramine. *Journal of Nervous and Mental Disease, 179*, 366–370.

Lin, K.-M., Poland, R. E., & Nakasaki, G. (1993). Psychopharmacology and psychobiology of ethnicity. Washington, DC: American Psychiatric Press.

Lin, K.-M., Smith, M. W., & Ortiz, V. (2001). Culture and psychopharmacology. *Psychiatric Clinics of North America, 24*, 523–538.

Londberg, P. D., Hegel, M. T., Goldstein, S., Goldstein, D., Himmelhoch, J. M., Maddock, R., et al. (2001). Sertraline treatment of posttraumatic stress disorder: Results of 24 weeks of open-label continuation treatment. *Journal of Clinical Psychiatry, 62*, 325–331.

Martenyi, F., Brown, E. B., Zhang, H., Prakash, A., & Koke, S. C. (2002). Fluoxetine versus placebo in posttraumatic stress disorder. *Journal of Clinical Psychiatry, 63*, 199–206.

Monnelly, E. P., Ciraulo, D. A., Knapp, C., & Keane, T. (2003). Low dose risperidone as adjunctive therapy for irritable aggression in posttraumatic stress disorder. *Journal of Clinical Psychopharmacology, 23*, 193.

Mosca, D. L., & Muro, M. R. (2002). Presented at the World Psychiatric Association meeting in Yokohama, Japan. Pharmacological and psychotherapeutic approach of the pertraumatic situation. *WPA Abstracts*, FC-27-4.

Mueser, K. T., & Butler, R. W. (1987). Auditory hallucinations in combat-related chronic posttraumatic stress disorder. American Journal of Psychiatry, 144, 299–302.

Mueser, K. T., Goodman, L. A., Trumbetta, S. L., Rosenberg, S. D., Osher, F. C., et al. (1998). Trauma and posttraumatic stress disorder in severe mental illness. *Journal of Consulting and Clinical Psychology, 6b*, 493–499.

Perlstein, T. (2000). Antidepressant treatment of posttraumatic stress disorder. *Journal of Clinical Psychiatry, 61*(suppl. 7), 40–43.

Pi, E. H. (1998). Transcultural psychopharmacology: Present and future. *Psychiatry of Clinical Neuroscience, 52*(Suppl. S), 185–187.

Pitman, R. K., Orr, S. P., Forgue, D. F., de Jong, T. B., & Claiborn, J. M. (1987). Psychophysiologic assessment of posttraumatic stress disorder imagery in Vietnam combat veterans. *Archives of General Psychiatry, 44*, 970–975.

Pitman, R. K., Shin, L. M., & Rauch, S. L. (2001). Investigating the pathogeneses of posttraumatic stress disorder with neuroimaging. Journal of Clinical Psychiatry, 62(Suppl. 17), 47–54.

Putnam, F. W., & Hulsmann, J. E. (2002). Pharmacotherapy for survivors of childhood trauma. *Seminars in Clinical Neuropsychiatry, 7*, 129–136.

Ramirez, L. F. (1996). Ethnicity and psychopharmacology in Latin America. *Mt. Sinai Journal of Medicine, 63*, 330–331.

Rapaport, M. H., Endicott, J., & Clary, C. M. (2002). Posttraumatic stress disorder and quality of life: Results across 64 weeks of sertraline treatment. *Journal of Clinical Psychiatry, 63*, 59–65.

Raskind, M. A., Thompson, C., Petrie, E. C., Dobie, D. J., Rein, R. J., Hoff, D. F., et al. (2002). Prazosin reduces nightmares in combat veterans with posttraumatic stress disorder. *Journal of Clinical Psychiatry, 63*, 565–568.

Sack, W. H., Clarke, G., Him, C., Dickason, D., Goff, B., Lanham, K., et al. (1993). A six-year follow-up study of Cambodian adolescents. *Journal of American Academy of Child Psychiatry, 32*, 431–437.

Seedat, S., Stein, D. J., & Emsley, R. A. (2000). Open trial of citalopram in adults with posttraumatic stress disorder. *International Journal of Neuropsychopharmacology, 3*, 135–140.

Silove, D., & Kinzie, J. D. (2001). Survivors of war trauma, mass violence, and civilian terror. In Gerrity, E., Keane, T. M., & Tuma, F. (Eds.), *The mental health consequences of torture* (pp. 159–174). New York: Kluwer Academic/ Plenum Press.

Smajkic, A. W., Weine, S., Djuric-Byedic, Z., Boskaulto, E., Lewis, J., & Pavkovic, I. (2001). Sertraline, Paroxetine and Venlafaxine in refugee posttraumatic stress disorder with depressive symptoms. *Journal of Traumatic Stress, 4*, 445–452.

Southwick, S. M., Bremner, J. D., Rasmusson, A., Morgan, C. A., III, Arnsten, A., & Charney, D. S. (1999). Role of norepinephrine in the pathophysiology and treatment of posttraumatic stress disorder. *Biology of Psychiatry. Nov 1, 46*(9), 1192–1204.

Spivak, B., Vered, Y., Graff, E., Blum, I., Mester, R., & Weizman, A. (1999). Low platelet-poor plasma concentrations of serotonin in patients with combat-related posttraumatic stress disorder. *Biological Psychiatry, 45*, 840–845.

Sramek, J. J., & Pi, E. H. (1996). Ethinicity and antidepressant response. *Mt. Sinai Journal of Medicine, 63*, 320–325.

Stein, D. J., Zungu-Dirwayi, N., van Der Linden, G. J., & Seedat, S. (2000). Pharmacotherapy for posttraumatic stress disorder. *Cochrane Database System Rev* (4) CD002795.

Stein, M. B., Kline, N. A., & Matloff. J. L. (2002). Adjunctive olanzapine for SSRI-resistant combat-related PTSD: A double-blind, placebo-controlled study. *American Journal of Psychiatry, 159*, 1777–1779.

Southwick, S. M., Krystal, J. H, Morgan, C. A., Johnson, D., Nagy, L. M., Nicolaou, A. et al. (1993). Abnormal noradrenergic function in posttraumatic stress disorder. *Archive of General Psychiatry, 50*, 266–274.

Taylor, F., & Raskind, M. A. (2002). The alpha1-adrenergic antagonist prazosin improves sleep and nightmares in civilian trauma posttraumatic stress disorder. *Journal of Clinical Psychopharmacology, 22*, 82–85.

Tucker, P., Zaninelli, R., Yehuda, R., Ruggiero, L., Dillingham, K., & Pitts, C. D. (2001). Paroxetine in the treatment of chronic posttraumatic stress disorder: Results of a placebo-controlled, flexible-dosage trial. *Journal of Clinical Psychiatry, 62,* 860–868.

van der Kolk, B. A., Dreyfuss, D., Michaels, M., Shera, D., Berkowitz, R., Fisler, R., et al. (1994, December). Fluoxetine in posttraumatic stress disorder. *Journal of Clinical Psychiatry, 55,* 517–522.

Vermetten, E., & Bremner, J. D. (2002). Circuits and systems in stress. II. Applications to neurobiology and treatment in posttraumatic stress disorder. *Depression and Anxiety, 16,* 14–38.

Zisook, S., Chentsova-Dutton, Y., Smith-Vaniz, A., Kline, N. A., Ellenor, G. L., Kodsi, A. B., et al. (2000). Nefazodone in patients with treatment-refractory posttraumatic stress disorder. *Journal of Clinical Psychiatry, 61,* 203–208.

22

Surgical Approach to Victims of Torture and PTSD

MARIANNE JUHLER

Victims of previous traumatic incidents are referred for a surgical opinion or for treatment of a known surgical disease just as other patients with no such previous history. Often the relationship between prior trauma and well-defined somatic dysfunction is a straightforward case for surgical correction. These situations are not the focus of this chapter.

However, in some cases, there is also a history of torture or PTSD. Particularly in victims of torture, "simple" somatic symptoms from physical trauma coexist with psychosomatic symptoms. In some victims of torture and in most cases of PTSD, psychosomatic symptoms are dominant. Both situations can be very difficult to assess in regard to the amenability to surgical treatment, and the history of previous traumatic events of both physical and mental nature is highly relevant in order to address the indication and outcome of surgical intervention.

To make things even more complicated, a history of PTSD or torture might not even be known to the surgeon at the time of referral, either because it unknown to the referring physician, or it might not have been noted on the referral. In addition to this, most surgical clinics are not geared toward — or even aware of — the particular needs and problems of this group of patients.

- All of the above-mentioned reasons make surgical treatment of victims of torture and PTSD a difficult challenge. Meeting this challenge with qualified surgical expertise requires a rational approach to each step of the surgical patient pathway.

A CASE STORY

The following case presentation has been slightly modified for the sake of anonymity. The essential contents are unchanged and illustrate many points where things can go wrong even if the surgical procedure in itself was performed correctly and without surgical complications.

> The patient was a 50-year-old man of Arabic origin with a known history of severe physical and mental torture several years ago. He had diffuse symptoms of pain and psychological distress for which he was being treated at a treatment facility for torture victims. The reason for referral to the surgical clinic was a clinical suspicion of spinal disease due to sensory complaints of hands and feet bilaterally and difficulties with fine motor movements and gait. The condition had been progressing over approximately 6 months. A physical exam revealed moderate spasticity, hyperreflexia, and ataxia of all four extremities. In perfect accordance with symptoms and signs, cervical spondylosis and stenosis with spinal cord compression was diagnosed by MRI.

> Statistically, it is known that one third of patients operated on for this condition improve; one third stay unchanged, but progression of symptoms is halted; and the remaining third still progress despite adequate decompression. In addition in this particular case the symptoms that were not caused by cervical stenosis (diffuse, chronic pain, and mental distress) would of course not improve by the recommended surgical procedure.

> The patient was informed of the condition and the possibility of surgery with spinal cord decompression (laminectomy) at the affected levels. He was extremely anxious about postoperative pain and discomfort and also expressed fears concerning complications to surgery, but agreed to surgery.

> The surgical procedure was uneventful, and postoperative MRI showed a good decompression at all levels. After discharge, the patient underwent relevant physiotherapy. He was seen once in the surgical outpatient clinic with the assistance of an interpreter. His functional status was preserved (i.e., progression of spinal cord symptoms was successfully stopped).

> The patient was re-referred later because of "recurrent symptoms" — but no objective change was found, and MRI still showed satisfactory decompression. The patient was dissatisfied, unhappy, and angry about the treatment result. He felt even worse than before surgery.

In this case story, there is clearly a significant discrepancy between the surgeon's perception of uneventful, technically well-performed surgery and relevant postsurgical rehabilitation on one hand; and the patient's experience of the surgical procedure and his unfulfilled expectations on the other hand. Clearly, the differences of perception between patient and surgeon were neither communicated nor bridged by the preoperative consultation. Many things could have gone wrong. The sections below describe milestones on the surgical patient pathway where attentiveness to the special needs of victims of torture or PTSD could change a history of treatment failure to one of successful treatment and an outcome perceived as satisfactory by both patient and surgeon.

DISTINGUISHING SYMPTOMS OF SURGICAL RELEVANCE: THE CHALLENGE OF PSYCHOSOMATIC SYMPTOMS

The first and maybe most important challenge in surgical treatment of torture or PTSD victims is recognizing these cases among all the other patients referred for surgical evaluation and treatment.[1] The existence of psychological mechanisms as an important background or even as a major part of the symptoms is hardly ever obvious in surgical referrals. Sometimes there is a direct hint, if the background for surgical referral is previous exposure to a life-threatening accident. In other cases, the patient's origin from a country or an area of war, violent repression, or similar conditions can provide a relatively straightforward clue. In other cases, the consideration of torture or PTSD is much less obvious. "Nonorganic" or "functional" symptoms are by many surgeons regarded as "noise" obscuring the objective somatic picture of surgical disease, but in fact these can initially be the only pointer toward a torture or PTSD history.

The success of surgical treatment is dependent not only on surgical skill, but also strongly dependent on the patient's psychological constitution. In simple terms, it is often worth the effort to realize the existence of a mixed psychosomatic/somatic picture as early as possible, because the clue to changing a situation from treatment failure in an unhappy or even angry patient into a relative treatment success in a satisfied patient often lies right there. Of course, it is not the surgeon's job or obligation to go deeply into the psychological context, but rather to distinguish the surgically treatable symptoms from others and to gain the patient's acceptance of this interpretation of his or her symptoms.

Extracting the history of physical exposure and trauma mechanisms after torture or major accidents is of course important in order to define the resulting physical damage, which the surgeon can treat. It is equally important to be aware that obtaining such history is often emotionally stressful to the patient — and in the worst case it can provoke a flashback situation, where the patient relives the traumatic incident. If this situation occurs, it might be impossible to obtain any history at all, and the mutual understanding between patient and surgeon necessary for a successful treatment can be precluded. This risk is greatly reduced when the patient feels safe and trustful; for example, if he or she is either accompanied by somebody well known to the patient or if he or she is given the opportunity of a first visit with the sole purpose of introduction and initial contact, followed by a second visit more directly aimed at his or her surgical disease and related history.

The possibilities of surgical disease in victims of previous traumatic events are complex,[2] including direct sequels from the traumatic event, indirect sequels (e.g., overstraining of noninjured parts), and surgical diseases, which are either not or very unlikely related to the previous violent exposure. All of these possibilities are almost invariably mixed with psychological and psychosomatic symptoms. Unfortunately, I know of no easy rules of thumb on how to distinguish the surgically treatable symptoms in this complexity. Patience in obtaining history and physical exam, a profoundly good clinical knowledge of the involved surgical specialty, including various presentations of how psychosomatic symptoms can mimic organic disease, and at least some psychological insight into long-term effects after life-threatening experience are all essential parts of making a useful analysis and classification of the symptoms in a surgical perspective. This process is clearly also necessary to define symptoms that cannot be helped surgically, and thus also to identify the purely psychosomatic patients, in whom surgery should of course be avoided.

PREOPERATIVE INFORMATION: CLOSING THE GAP BETWEEN PATIENTS AND SURGEON'S EXPECTATIONS

Once the surgical assessment of the patient has been made and a strategy for a surgical procedure has been chosen, the patient is informed accordingly. Just as in other "nontorture/non-PTSD" cases, the expected outcome and risk of complications are explained to the patient.[3–6]

In addition, it is important to pay attention to the patient's expectations of the surgical result. There can be very large differences between these and the professional opinion of the expected or acceptable surgical outcome. The patient often hopes for or expects that surgery will miraculously remove many or all of his or her symptoms — and especially in cases of torture and PTSD, in whom symptoms are almost always complex and mixed, this is hardly ever the case. It must thus be made clear to the patient exactly which symptoms and signs the surgery is aimed at. It cannot be assumed that the patient for him- or herself then deducts that other symptoms that he or she may have are left unchanged by the surgical procedure. Therefore, the preoperative information should also include an explanation of which symptoms are not alleviated by surgery and why this is so.

Victims of torture are almost invariably refugees, and this might also be the case in some victims of PTSD. Frequently there are large cultural and educational differences. The discrepancy is often of a fundamental nature concerning even basic norms and general verbal expression. It should thus be expected as the rule rather than the exception, that surgeon's and patient's perception of disease, surgical procedures, and the patient-doctor roles are fundamentally different. The aid of an accomplished interpreter is very important in overcoming such basic difficulties of communication.[7]

The preoperative information should also prepare the patient for the postoperative course of events in order to reduce the risk of anxiety-provoking situations. The expected normal reactions during the postsurgical hospital stay, postoperative mobilization, and postsurgical treatment and nursing procedures should be mentioned so that the patient can cope with unavoidable postoperative discomfort. In this way, the situation can be optimized for the patient's cooperation in postsurgical rehabilitation, which is important to ensure a good final surgical outcome.

A major purpose of one or two preadmission appointments with the surgeon is also to create an atmosphere of trust in which the patient feels safe and well understood,[8] as this is useful for prevention of anxiety and bad treatment experience, which both carry the risk for a poor treatment result.

CONSIDERATIONS IN THE PRE- AND POSTOPERATIVE PERIOD: REDUCING STRESS AND ANXIETY

All surgical procedures are painful. In almost all victims of torture and many victims of PTSD, pain has been a central part of this life-threatening experience. Consequently, a setting is very easily created where the surgical/postsurgery experience reminds the patient so much of previous traumatic events that it results in uncontrollable anxiety. In the worst case, a psychotic flashback can be provoked, where the patient believes that he or she is back in the torture chamber and as a natural consequence sees the medical and nursing staff as torturers. This of course makes postoperative pain management particularly important in these patients.

In addition to pain, there are many other postsurgical situations that entail discomfort and anxiety. For the torture survivor, the environment in a postoperative recovery room can seem frightening, and monitoring equipment can resemble torture instruments (e.g., ECG electrodes and electrodes used for electrical torture). For PTSD patients, the recovery room can provoke memories from a life-and-death struggle during intensive care treatment after major trauma. In fact, this can be prevented if the preceding evaluation before admission and the psychological preparation of the patient have considered these possibilities. If the patient has presented his or her history and made a preparatory visit to the recovery room facilities in advance to define key issues for anxiety, these situations may also be avoided.

POSTSURGICAL FOLLOW-UP AND REHABILITATION: SECURING THE EXPECTED OUTCOME

A good functional outcome after surgery often requires some form of rehabilitation after discharge from the hospital. In surgical cases of torture or PTSD, this preferably takes place with a physiotherapist, who is well acquainted with torture- or PTSD reactions in general, or who might even know the particular patient and his or her history from previous treatment. If this is not possible, it might be prudent to obtain advice from institutions or individuals with experience in treating torture or PTSD cases.

Just as in nontorture/non-PTSD cases, follow-up visits in the surgical outpatient department are scheduled to check the surgical result and to diagnose and treat complications. An important additional purpose is to keep a mutual understanding between patient and surgeon about a satisfactory outcome. It is a well-known observation that after a surgical treatment that has been uneventful from the professional point of view, patients often have "forgotten" or repressed disagreeable information concerning side effects and limitations of the treatment. In the patient's mind there is still the perception and hope that the performed surgery will remove all symptoms. This is true in many patients even without a psychosomatic complex of symptoms due to prior traumatic experiences and despite meticulous preoperative information. Because of this, postoperative "reinformation," repeating the preoperative information, is frequently required and should be seen by the surgeon not as irritating repetitions but as an essential part of obtaining optimal surgical results.

REFERENCES

1. Apitzsch, H., Eriksson, N. G., Jakobsson, S. W., Lindgren, L., Lundin, T., Movschenson, P., et al. (1996). A study of post-traumatic stress reactions among war refugees based on medical records. A standard model may support the treatment. *Lakartidningen, 93*(47), 4285–4288, 4291–4294.
2. Lie, B., & Skjeie, H. (1996). Torture-related injuries — a medical challenge. Diagnosis and treatment of Falanga victims. *Tidsskr Nor Laegeforen, 116*(9), 1073–1075.
3. Bates, T. (2001). Ethics of consent to surgical treatment. *British Journal of Surgery, 88*(10), 1283–1284.

4. Lavelle-Jones, C., Byrne, D. J., Rice, P., & Cuschieri, A. (1993). Factors affecting quality of informed consent. *British Medical Journal, 306*(6887), 1273.
5. English, D. C. (2002). Valid informed consent: A process, not a signature. *American Surgeon, 68*(1), 45–48.
6. Finkelstein, D., Smith, M. K., & Faden, R. (1993). Informed consent and medical ethics. *Archive of Ophthalmology, 111*(12), 1604.
7. Sondergaard, H. P., & Ekblad, S. (1998). Traumatic stress in adult refugees: When ill-health is silent or speaks broken Swedish. *Lakartidningen, 95*(13), 1415–1416, 1419–1422.
8. Weinstein, H. M., Dansky, L., & Iacopino, V. (1996). Torture and war trauma survivors in primary care practice. *Western Journal of Medicine, 165*(3), 112–118.

23

Psychosocial Rehabilitation

SOLVIG EKBLAD AND JAMES M. JARANSON

Psychosocial rehabilitation of refugees and asylum seekers is an urgent issue in host societies, often combined with challenges and complications, and no template applies to everyone affected by posttraumatic stress symptoms or posttraumatic stress disorder (PTSD). The context of any rehabilitation, albeit in war affected and displaced areas, in refugee camps, in countries of final resettlement, or in postconflict societies after repatriation, dictates to a large extent how efforts should proceed. However, we must be concerned about ethical issues and we, as "experts" in the Western world, should "constantly examine our own accepted ways of thinking about the world and question the assumptions from which our practices spring" (Bracken, Giller, & Summerfield, 1997, p. 441). This viewpoint is especially needed in the area of rehabilitation for the mental health of asylum seekers and refugees. Since another chapter in this book (see Chapter 7) describes psychosocial programs in war-affected areas, this chapter will concentrate on rehabilitation programs in resettlement countries. The terms "migrants" and "immigrants" will be used interchangeably to refer to refugees and asylum seekers in the following discussion.

In 1948, the World Health Organization put forward the well-known holistic definition of *health* as "a state of complete physical, mental and social well-being and not merely the absence of disease or infirmity"

(WHO, 1946); that is, it gave somatic, psychological, and social factors equal importance. However, lay definitions usually consider a wide range of factors. Health, especially mental health, is impaired by conditions that can degrade the functional ability, lifestyle, preventive health practices, and sociocultural constructions of particular health risks. For asylum seekers and refugees, conditions that have an impact on perceived health include globalization and movements (due to collective violence, such as terrorism, war, and its consequences), poverty, illiteracy, lack of access to health care, forced dislocation from home and community, and chronic restrictions of freedom or violations of human rights. The realities of encountering such psychosocial stress can be perceived quite differently, especially if the individual neither speaks the host country's language nor is familiar with the context of that country.

In general, the mental, social, and behavioral health problems represent overlapping clusters that are connected to the recent wave of global change and new illnesses, and this interaction intensifies the effect on overall health outcomes. Due to wars and terrorism in different parts of the world, the numbers of refugees and internally displaced people (IDPs) continue to increase. By January 1, 2003, UNHCR estimated that the number of persons of concern who fall under the Mandate of UNHCR were 20.6 million refugees, and additionally about the same number were displaced persons worldwide. The effects of disaster, torture, and war on the mental health problems of refugees and IDPs are shown in different ways, for example, aggression and other adjustment problems, anxiety disorders, depression, PTSD, alcohol and other drug dependence, and psychosomatic symptoms. Such stressful conditions, which can be chronic, could also influence any underlying mental disorders, including psychotic illnesses (Saraceno, Saxena, & Maulik, 2002), and this will be a challenge for psychosocial rehabilitation. These clusters are more prevalent and psychosocial rehabilitation more difficult under conditions of high unemployment, low income, limited education, stressful work conditions, gender discrimination, unhealthy lifestyles, or human rights violations (Desjarlais, Eisenberg, & Kleinman, 1995), particularly in a multicultural society. Further, the presence of an interpreter can have an impact, according to Bolton (2002), on the following three core tasks of a healing performance: "establishing a basis of trust, understanding the patient's problems and trying to make a difference" (p. 97).

Cultural, socioeconomic, and sociopolitical factors influence to a great extent the reaction to psychosocial stress, the epidemiology of illness, and the availability and quality of services (Ekblad, 2002a). These factors also operate on the individual, familial, and more complex levels. There is increasing attention among researchers as well as clinicians to the need for an ecological and resilient view to understanding the cultural variants of forces causing psychosocial stress and the reactions to it. This chapter aims to review the components of an ecological perspective and, using this context, to highlight psychosocial rehabilitation for the treatment of PTSD among asylum seekers and refugees in a host society.

PSYCHOSOCIAL REHABILITATION FOR PTSD: THE SCIENTIFIC LITERATURE

There seems still to be considerable room for research and the development of psychosocial rehabilitation approaches (i.e., "best practices" in the discipline), even though the field of transcultural assessment and treatment of the psychosocial effects of conflict-related traumatic life events in the scientific literature has gained increasing attention (Bolton, 2000).

Reviews of the scientific literature tend to be limited in scope, focusing on particular techniques that have been validated as effective for individuals. The content of these reviews seldom includes the broader social context in which these techniques are used or assesses the usefulness for refugees and asylum seekers, whose PTSD has often been caused or exacerbated by repeated and prolonged criterion A stressors. According to DSM IV (American Psychiatric Association, 1995), a diagonstic criteria for PTSD is "The person has been exposed to a traumatic event in which both the following were present.

the person experienced, witnessed, or was confronted with an even or events that involved actual or threatened death or serious injury, or a threat to the physical integrity of self or others.
the person's response involved intense fear, helplessness, or horror. Note: in children, this may be expressed instead by disorganized or agitated behavior" (pp. 427–428).

PSYCHOSOCIAL REHABILITATION APPROACHES AND ECOLOGICAL LESSONS LEARNED

An increase in debate about interventions for health promotion began after the signing of the Ottawa Charter for Health Promotion (1986) and later charters (Jarkarta, 1998; Sundsvall, 1991). Health promotion, according to Raeburn and Rottman (1998), is empowerment and improved health, well-being, and quality of life defined by seeing the individual participate in a developing and strengthening context. Bailis, Segall, and Chipperfield (2003) studied two views of self-rated general health status and found that the effect of several predictors on respondents' self-rated health varied according to whether respondents intended to improve specific health-related behaviors in the future. These authors concluded that "self-rated health may be regulated by efforts to achieve one's relatively important health-related goals" (p. 203).

Newly arrived asylum seekers and refugees who relocate to an environment where unfamiliar information, behaviors, and social norms prevail are likely to feel a need to reevaluate their health. The meaning of these self-evaluations can dictate a variety of adaptive responses. Life situations, pre-, during, and after migration are often turbulent and include many important events, which coincide with the individual needing the strength to create a new life. On the other hand, protective psychological mechanisms exist. Acccording to Bailis et al. (2003), "self-ratings of general health may be driven less by bodily or environmental feedback than by an individual's prior beliefs about him- or herself as a healthy or unhealthy person" (p. 203). All of this has an impact on the individual's well-being during the period of introduction and will, in turn, most possibly have an impact on the individual refugee's abilities, self-sufficiency, and participation in society. Goodkind and Foster-Fishman (2002) concluded that the promotion of well-being and integration among refugees in the United States is influenced by how the society values diversity and gives possibilities to participate meaningfully in the community. However, in their study on Hmong refugees, who valued the capacity to participate very highly, the majority were excluded due to barriers such as language differences, time constraints, and discrimination. There were no options for reducing these barriers.

Palinkas et al. (2003) found that the mobilization to wellness among Somali and East African refugees in San Diego, California, involved a series of steps designed to facilitate refugee confidence, comprehension, and compliance with prevention efforts through community-provider partnerships and negotiation between refugee and organizational explanatory models of disease causation and prevention.

The first author (SE) coordinates a 4-year ongoing (2001–2004) research project in Sweden, financed primarily by the Integration Board and European Refugee Fund called "Health Promoting Introduction" (www.psychosocialmedicine.se). Its primary goal is to understand more about the possible contributions of health promotion to the field of refugee mental health. From the beginning of the project the concept of health among refugees was examined. Two doctoral students are working on the project, Karin Johansson Blight and Fredrik Lindencrona. A qualitative interview study (Lindencrona & Ekblad, 2004) assessed the understanding of health among 28 professionals in different sectors (introduction services, employment services, language schools) working with newly arrived refugees in four different municipalities in Sweden. The results showed that, in their view, health is a positive and multifaceted construct described as an ability to relate to other people, the capacity for acting as an agent, and emotional balance and positive self-image. Therefore, professionals paid attention to the need for understanding health as a multilevel, interactive phenomenon. Consequently, the identified threats to health are at the personal and contextual levels and the appropriate unit of analysis is person-in-program and community-context. As a part of this 4-year project, Broström (2002) interviewed, in the Stockholm community reception program, recently arrived refugees who saw health as a balance among basic life needs. During the interviews, the refugees perceived that important factors for health were absent in their daily lives. The refugees were, for example, insecure, unemployed, and marginalized.

Thus, a more systematic study of psychosocial rehabilitation among asylum seekers and refugees, especially newcomers, would be of interest to host countries faced with the challenge of providing mental health care to large numbers of these groups.

THE CONTEXT OF PSYCHOSOCIAL REHABILITATION

When discussing psychosocial rehabilitation the following concepts are relevant and will be described in detail below: stress, culture, acculturation, socioeconomic, and sociopolitical factors.

Stress

The concept of stress is derived from a Latin word, *stringere*, which involves compressing and drawing tightly. This describes the personal experience of being subjected to extreme hardships in life, resisting physical, psychological, and social health and well-being, and coming back into balance. Traumatic life events are stressors with which we occasionally have to cope and adapt to more or less constructively.

Culture

The concept of culture is about the process of being and becoming a social creature, about the rules of a society, and about the ways in which these are enacted, experienced, and transmitted. Culture is not static because interpretation of rules changes over time and under different circumstances (Helman, 1994). Spirituality and religion in each cultural context are important for providing meaning to life as well as a means to deal with death, suffering, pain, injustice, tragedy, and stressful experiences (Pargament, 1997). According to Kirmayer (2001), "individuals use the resources available in the social world to construct durable and socially valued selves" (p. 22), and cultures differ in the way they perform nonconscious and conscious ways of handling distress. Kirmayer (1996) suggests that the collective meaning attributed to traumatic life events shapes the construction of memories around them. Consequently, perceived distress becomes an intimate part of the person's social sense of coherence according to the rules of behavior, which are influenced by context of culture. A Swedish pilot study about the relationship between traumatic life events, symptoms, and the sense of coherence (SOC) subscale among a group of refugee and immigrants patients showed that lack of meaningfulness was associated with mental distress and impaired function (Ekblad & Wennström, 1997). The sense of coherence was inversely correlated with traumatic life stress events and mental symptoms. In another study of asylum seekers in Sweden by Ekblad and Shahnavaz (2003), there was a strong positive correlation between suicidal thoughts, posttraumatic stress symptoms, depressive symptoms, and a negative correlation with sense of coherence.

It has been stated that expression of sickness has two aspects: the disease aspect and the illness aspect. On the one hand, "disease" is the malfunctioning and maladaptation of psychological and biological processes in the individual; whereas "illness" represents the personal, interpersonal, and cultural reaction to the disorder (Kleinman, 1978). Bäärnhielm and Ekblad (2000), in a study of somatization and the meaning of illness among Turkish migrant women in Stockholm, noted that, although psychological attribution was rarely acknowledged, verbalizing coherent links between bodily symptoms and emotional distress was valued as a tool for recovery. Somatization is one common idiom of distress, that is, expression of mental distress in terms of physical suffering. In DSM-IV (APA, 1995), common idioms of distress have been recognized as culture-bound syndromes. Depression is related to the loss of significant interpersonal relationships, social status, or incentives; while anxiety is related to the anticipation of threats of safety and integrity of body or self. There are cultural variations in the regulation and expression of emotions, and culture usually sets limits of tolerance of specific and strong emotions and provides lay theories and strategies about handling emotions. For example, Asians such as Chinese and Japanese can express their emotions in accordance with the balance of yin and yang. Besides that, it is quite common that disturbances of mood, affect, and anxiety are not viewed as mental health problems, but as social or moral problems (Kirmayer, 1989).

Thus, culture is not only a patient's characteristic but also an intercultural encounter between staff, patient, and relatives. Staff also has their own ethnocultural backgrounds, professional training, and specific work contexts. Much of the evidence-based knowledge in the field of culture and psychopathology comes from qualitative research (Kirmayer, 2001). An approach that has guided considerable research in clinical anthropology is Kleinman's (1980) explanatory model, which posits that people hold ideas and concepts that give meaning to their distress, help them express and shape their illness experience, and influence the particular forms of treatment they seek. In addition, it is not uncommon that clinicians in health services do not have the knowledge of an asylum-seeker's or refugee's language, culture, or attitudes about illness (Ekblad, Kohn, & Jansson, 1998).

The access of counseling, that is, talking with a stranger as a way of solving problems in communication or of exploring the self, highlights the individual as separate from other people, which can be extremely alien culturally. Further, culture not only defines pain and suffering but also what is seen as private and public pain (Helman, 1994). A nonuniversal cultural value that is deeply embedded in northern societies is that of individualism. The individual-oriented society insists that everyone must achieve personal status first, resulting in a devaluation of the importance of the family, especially the mother.

Cultural differences between the old and new countries can result in delayed psychosocial rehabilitation for mental health problems, noncompliance with psychiatric treatments, and premature termination of treatment, all of which can result in more severe psychopathology.

Human rights violations can be a more general threat to the asylum seekers' future psychosocial existence and extend beyond threat to life, the DSM-IV (APA, 1995) definition of a trauma, and postmigration stress experiences (Silove & Ekblad, 2002). This finding alerts health professionals to attend to psychsocial rehabilitation in health screening, to human rights violations causing suicidal thoughts, and to the importance of follow-up for diagnosis of mental disorders, assessment of functional disability, and suicide prevention.

Acculturation

Berry (1991) defines factors influencing the relationship between acculturation and stress: (a) modes of acculturation: integration, assimilation, separation, marginalization; (b) phases of acculturation: contact, conflict, crisis, adaptation; (c) nature of larger society: multicultural versus assimilationist, prejudicial, discriminatory; (d) characteristics of acculturating group: age, social status, social support; and (e) characteristics of the acculturating individual: appraisal, coping, attitudes, contact.

The majority of immigrant groups experience the phenomenon of intergenerational conflict during the acculturation process. According to deSantis and Ugarriza (1995):

> The conflict evolves when parents, as the main socializing agents of children, tend to retain traditional values related to appropriate role behaviors and standards of conduct for their children. Children, on the other hand, tend to adopt the norms and values of the new host culture more rapidly than parents because of their enrollment in school, greater language facility, and friendship with children who are members of the new culture. (p. 354)

Research literature indicates that asylum seekers, refugees, and other immigrants progress through the same stages of adaptation to the host culture, but the outcome of this adaptation can vary considerably. Therefore, the issue should not be whether migrants have more mental breakdowns than native residents, or poorer mental health, but why. This is of special concern for newcomers acquiring new lifestyles in their host country (Ekblad, Ginsburg, Jansson, & Levi, 1994).

Socioeconomic and Sociopolitical Factors

To understand the sociocultural milieu in which the asylum seekers and refugees function, it is important to distinguish psychopathology from expected or culture-bound responses. In assessment and treatment, excessive reliance on models of cultural determinism would be as unproductive as totally disregarding cultural factors (Jaranson, Forbes-Martin, & Ekblad, 2001). Asylum seekers can have difficulties in adapting to a different environment, and both language difficulties and cultural sensitivities can limit access to a full range of health services. Differing expectations of both the quantity and quality of available health care can also compound these limitations. An interim report of health needs of asylum seekers in Sunderland and North Tyneside by Blackwell, Holden, and Tregoning (2002) found much heterogeneity by country of origin, religion, previous employment, and language backgrounds within the sample. They identified a range of health needs with implications for provision of psychosocial rehabilitation. Vaccination rates were low, as was screening for tuberculosis and cervical cancer. Many asylum seekers identified symptoms related to mental health and requested help in this area. Access to dental treatment was an area of high priority for many of the respondents in the study. According to Lewis and Araya (2002), "globalization of the world economy is likely to affect socio-economic inequalities and differences in the social roles occupied by men and women" (p. 60).

Lindencrona, Ekblad, and Charry (2001) studied 670 medical records of psychiatric clinic outpatients in an immigrant southern suburb of Stockholm. Many patients, especially newly arrived refugees, had various unmet social, psychological, and medical needs, were the poorest, often unemployed, and not able to speak Swedish. Many young parents caring for their children were at risk of transgenerational symptom effects, and they also had to attempt to establish themselves in a new society, a process made more difficult by prior traumatic life events.

In sum, migrants often undergo changes in socioeconomic position, experience shifts in gender relations, and confront disparate ideas about health. Symptoms can become chronic if not rehabilitated by effective early prevention. Further factors that may impact health status include, according to Ekblad (2002b):

> 1) conflict between traditional and new norms and values, such as gender roles for young women, leading to stress between their own aspirations and the values of their parents, 2) unfamiliarity with the role of women in the host population, and 3) poor employment opportunities or entrapment in unsatisfactory work environments. (p. 251)

From these concepts, reports in the literature support the need for a holistic or an ecological model of psychosocial trauma and will be described.

HOLISTIC OR ECOLOGICAL MODELS OF PSYCHOSOCIAL TRAUMA

Harvey's (1996) ecological model of psychosocial trauma postulates that reactions and recovery are related to person, event, and environment. More specifically, "the efficiency of trauma-focused interventions depends upon the degree to which they enhance the person-community relationship and achieve 'ecological fit' within individually varied recovery contexts" (p. 3). According to Moos (2002), "we need a fundamental paradigm shift in how to construe and examine the aftermath of life crises" (p. 79), which means that theories of posttraumatic development and maturation differ from theories of learned helplessness and posttraumatic stress disorder.

An ecological framework (Silove, 1999) identifies in Table 23.1 five fundamental "systems" of health potentially threatened or disrupted: (1) attachment, (2) security, (3) identity/role, (4) human rights, and (5) existential/meaning. Specific threats, reactions, pathology, and interventions are identified for each level in Table 23.1.

Attachment

Loss and separation from close attachment figures can influence health and the need for help, and the literature shows that a high level of social support reduces the risk for psychiatric disorder and impairment among migrants.

Security

Refugees have often experienced threats to the physical safety of themselves or their families and can have their security threatened by economic stress or material deprivation.

Identity/Role

The refugee experience involves a major threat to the sense of identity of both the individual and the group. Loss of land, possessions, and professions divests individuals of a sense of purpose and status in society. As mentioned above, a sense of control over one's situation and one's role in a social network affects perceptions of health.

Human Rights

Many refugees have experienced assaults upon their human rights, including arbitrary and unjust treatment, persecution, brutality, and, in some instances, torture. The literature (Jaranson et al., 2001) shows that tortured survivors are often unwilling to tell their stories of

TABLE 23.1 Systems of Health: Threats, Reactions, Pathology, and Interventions for Refugees and Asylum Seekers

Systems of Health	Threats	Reactions	Pathology	Levels	Interventions by Level
Attachment	Separation from significant others, material goods, and culture	Anxiety; grief; home sickness; nostalgia	Unresolved grief reactions	Individual	Compensation for lost bonds
				Family	Compensation for lost bonds
				Organization	Membership in social groups
				Community	Re-creating community systems
				Society	Family reunification
Security	Postmigration events; ongoing threats	Anxiety; insecurity; alertness to danger	Anxiety; PTSD; depression	Individual	Reduce anxiety; protect basic needs
				Family	Normalization
				Organization	Meaningful activities
				Community	Develop infrastructure
				Society	Access to school, work, and health care
Identity/ Role	Aimlessness; loss of hope, purpose, and identity	Uncertainty about individual and cultural roles	Suicidality; role confusion; cultural bereavement	Individual	Normalization
				Family	Family interventions
				Organization	Normalization
				Community	Community membership
				Society	Human right protection; Social Security

TABLE 23.1 *Continued.*

Systems of Health	Threats	Reactions	Pathology	Levels	Interventions by Level
Human rights	Human rights violations	Anger; hostility; lack of trust; resentment; bitterness	Traumatic anger; paranoia	Individual Family Organization Community Society	Trust redevelopment Family trust redevelopment Engagement Truth and reconciliation Human rights protection
Existential/ Meaning	Loss of faith, hope, and self-esteem; network of bad memories	Search for meaning	Suicidality; alienation; incoherent belief systems; transgenerational transmission	Individual Family Organization Community Society	Testimonial approach Re-creating meaning Meaningful social activities Linking with culture and religious traditions Protection of human rights

Source: Modified from training material of D. Silove, D., with permission April 5, 2003.

trauma before basic needs are met and trust is developed. Refugees can be unwilling to talk about their trauma experiences due to lack of confidence in health care staff, a feeling of shame, fear of increasing their symptoms, or a lack of knowledge about available help (Jaranson et al., 2001).

Existential Meaning

Traumatic life experiences pose threats to a person's sense of coherence and meaning. The loss of meaning that a stable community previously provided can leave a migrant in a state of bewilderment and uncertainty, perhaps questioning the meaning of life. Historical continuities linking past, present, and future tend to be radically disrupted by the upheavals associated with traumatic life events. Commitment to the social ideology of the threatened or oppressed group can be protective. Clinical observations show that hope is positively related with health (Nekolaichuk, Jevne, & Maguire, 1999). According to Bracken (2001), PTSD is now understood to arise from a destruction of meaning within the victim's world.

EPIDEMIOLOGY OF MENTAL DISORDERS FOLLOWING TRAUMA

Theoretical models of the relationship between traumatic stress and mental health are difficult to test because they involve complex interactions of various factors. Mental, behavioral, and social health problems are an increasing part of the health burden globally. According to the World Health Report 1999 (WHO, 2001b), neuropsychiatric conditions constitute an estimated 11.5% of the global burden of disease. Globally they account for 28% of the total years lived in disability. A large proportion of the burden of disease and social disability is attributable to major depression, both in developed and developing countries, and to increased mortality in crisis settings, since the majority of about 800,000 suicides per year result from depression. According to Ballinger (2001), "despite the variations in prevalence and symptom presentation, considerable disability and burden associated with psychiatric illnesses are observed in different cultures" (p. 3). The Global Burden of Disease Study (Murray & Lopez, 1997) has identified that, by 2020, major depression will be second only to ischemic heart disease as a cause of disability worldwide. Importantly, in developing countries, unipolar major depression is projected to be the leading cause of disease burden (Lépine, 2001).

Cross-national epidemiological research such as the Cross-National Study (Weissman, Bland, Canino, et al., 1996) has confirmed that different perceived mental illnesses such as depression and anxiety occur worldwide, but the symptomatic expression, interpretation, and social response to these symptoms as mentioned above vary across cultures (Kirmayer, 2001). Symptoms most commonly experienced in all the countries studied are insomnia, loss of energy, and thoughts of suicide (Weissman et al., 1996). The current evidence-based knowledge shows significant variation in the prevalence of these disorders among different countries (Ballinger, 2001). Besides differing levels of awareness and recognition of psychiatric illnesses and disorders due to cultural issues, there can also be variation in the methodology and population sampling of these epidemiological studies, in the clinical assessment methods, and in the collection and processing of data.

Epidemiology of Posttraumatic Stress Disorder (PTSD)

PTSD is one of the mental disorders diagnosed in the aftermath of severely traumatic events, along with other anxiety disorders and depression (Saraceno et al., 2002). However, despite an increase in knowledge about the mental health problems and methods of intervention, the magnitude of the problems remain unknown. Female gender has emerged as a risk for PTSD after civilian trauma (Breslau et al., 1998). Lifetime prevalence rates of PTSD are twice as high for women as for men (10.4% versus 5%), and women are four times more likely to develop PTSD when exposed to the same trauma. Yet, gender differences in reactions to treatment have not been studied systematically (Foa, Friedman, & Keane, 2000). Recent epidemiological evidence indicates that PTSD can be identified across cultures, and the figures are higher in psychiatric samples than in community samples. PTSD occurs in only a minority of persons exposed to mass conflict, with prevalence rates varying between 4% and 20% according to reviews by Silove (1999) and Silove, Ekblad, and Mollica (2000) and between 9% and 37% according to Modvig and Jaranson (see Chapter 3 in this volume).

Resilience and Coping

The psychological dimensions affecting health, according to Antonovsky (1987), include a "sense of coherence": (a) "comprehensibility" or the extent to which a person can make sense of internal or external stimuli; (b) "manageability" or the extent to which one perceives that resources are available; and (c) "meaningfulness" or the perception that life is meaningful and worth living despite its hardships. Migrants can also experience a sense of loss on a more personal level than other groups. Marks, Murray, Evans, and Willig (2000) review dimensions of personality and illness and demonstrate that "stress is only likely to have a strong effect on susceptibility to illness among individuals who score low on internal locus of control, self-efficacy, hardiness, and sense of coherence and who have a low level of perceived social support" (p. 116).

Major social and personal resources for migrants include strong identity, ethnic pride, empowerment, and sense of control. The support from family and ethnic organizations, as well as a positive attitude among the staff in reception programs in the host society, are important social resources for migrants. This type of contact can be a source of strength and coherence in the new environment, but, if excessive and exclusive, could also be a source of distress, marginalization, or even retraumatization. A new kind of social resource is access to cell phones and the Internet, which can facilitate contact with relatives around the world. This again can be limited by one's social position, economic status, and gender.

A range of factors that provide protective functions in the face of hardships after migration have been identified:

1. Extended family: The availability of an extended family as a unit of mutual support;
2. Employment: Access to employment during the "transit" phase and upon arrival in a host country;
3. Human rights organizations: the visible presence of human rights organizations among refugee populations, especially in camps;
4. Self-help groups: The emergence of self-help groups that empower the refugees and provide opportunities for catharsis and shared memories;
5. Small camps: The distribution of refugees into small rural camps rather than large agglomerations;
6. Cultural practices: The opportunity for refugees to freely practice their traditions, beliefs and customs, as well as to recreate their social institutions (e.g., religion);
7. Situational transcendence: The ability of individuals and groups to frame their status and problems in terms that transcend the immediate situation and give it meaning (e.g, ethnic identity, cultural history). (Jablensky et al., 1994, pp. 333–334)

Although there are the ranges of protective factors when life events appear, we should look at the other side of the coin as well, that is, challenges to rehabilitation of health.

CHALLENGES TO REHABILITATION OF HEALTH

Overview

Rehabilitation of the individual person starts with monitoring special needs by reducing or minimizing the arousal within or without, illuminating the meaning of the traumatic life event/s, applying exposure techniques to attend to the traumatic memories, and teaching how to cope (McFarlane & Raphael, 2001). The aim of the rehabilitation is to normalize the person's symptoms and processes, to guide the person from living with unintegrated past traumatic memories to integration, and to reduce anxiety by increasing a sense of personal control and supporting positive relationships. Management can include the patient's present stressors, for example, postmigration stress such as family and resettlement issues (Silove & Ekblad, 2002). Developing a management plan jointly with the patient and staff is important for recovery. This usually empowers and supports the patient in developing a sense of control over his or her perceived health. Reasons for noncompliance should be addressed as early as possible with the patient. Especially in mental health care, Watters (2001) has developed "a three-dimensional model for the analysis of the interrelationship between 'macro' level institutional factors in the mental health of refugees and the individual treatment of refugees with mental health services" (p. 1709). A relevant obstacle to rehabilitation is the person's resistance to take the risk of confronting past traumatic life events.

PTSD can occur many years after the traumatic life event, often triggered by another stressful event. This shows the importance of staff awareness and confidence in initiating a referral to relevant rehabilitation services on different levels (i.e., individual, family, organizational, community, and societal), especially for asylum seekers and refugees who do not speak the host country's language and may have greater difficulty accessing appropriate care.

The Individual Level

It is common that asylum seekers and refugees experience a threefold challenge to their health and well-being: (a) psychiatric disorders, precipitated or exacerbated by the refugee experience, (b) infectious and parasitic diseases endemic to countries of origin (e.g., tuberculosis, malaria, hepatitis, HIV), and (c) increased susceptibility to chronic diseases endemic to host countries, including cancer, diabetes, hypertension, and coronary heart disease and mental illness. The causal relationship between migration and those chronic diseases has been found through a number of mechanisms describing the asylum-seeking and refugee experience of acculturation to the dominant society of the host country. These mechanisms include acculturation stress, obesity, and changes in health-related behaviors such as alcohol use, diet, cigarette smoking, and lack of access or utilization of modern health services (Palinkas et al., 2003).

Language can be the mirror and map of a society. To learn a second language, especially as an adult, is a long process. Traumatic memories can prevent refugees from learning a new language faster, in part because they have been deprived abruptly of what was most meaningful in their lives. Language plays a major role in influencing the expression and personal perception of psychopathological conditions. These difficulties can be compounded by cultural background and educational attainment. Refugees might also fail to effectively utilize health care services for the above reasons.

The Family Level

The literature shows that family support is a crucial determinant of adjustment. Traditional interpersonal family relationships and lifestyles usually change to the dominant communication styles in the host country. Family size and relationship patterns present another source of psychosocial and cultural challenges. Migrant women carry a triple burden because of their sex, class, and ethnic origin, and often experience psychosocial challenges due to prejudice and discrimination (see Chapter 20 in this volume).

For instance, in Eastern cultures, social integration is emphasized more than autonomy (i.e., the family, not the individual, is the unit of society). Traditional Arab cultures, for instance, deal with issues of illness as a family matter. Thus, the decision-making style might be best described in Eastern cultures as family-centered. It is the responsibility of the family to hear bad news about diagnosis and prognosis and to make difficult decisions (Okasha, 2002). However, allowing patients to choose a family-centered decision-making style does not mean abandoning Western-centered commitment to individual autonomy or its legal expression in the doctrine of informed consent. Rather, it means broadening the Western-centered view of autonomy so that respect for persons includes respect for the cultural values they bring with them to the decision-making process.

It is frequently seen in clinical experience that migrant women come from cultures where it is desirable and necessary to have several children due to lack of birth control, high infant mortality, and as "insurance" in their older years to compensate for the lack of a social pension system. Such traditions can result in stress and confusion in the host culture, where family planning and limited family size can be ideal. Young family members might identify with the host country's values and prompt the parents to redouble emphasis on traditional beliefs, widening even further the gap between children and parents. Among the positive effects are greater individual freedom and economic or educational opportunities. On the other hand, negative aspects among immigrants can include a consequent change in self-concept (Tabora & Flaskerud, 1994) and increased risk for psychopathology.

The Organizational Level

Migrants are often confronted with psychosocial challenges in the workforce. They can have inadequate educational and skill levels for special types of jobs and be exploited, underemployed, or unemployed. Lack of skills or language proficiency, poor school grades, and few employment opportunities often result in poverty. In a 20-year perspective (1975–1995) of living conditions and inequality in Sweden, it was shown that women from non-Nordic countries, compared with women from the Nordic countries and Sweden, more frequently have physically demanding, hectic and/or monotonous low-status jobs (Häll, 1997).

The Community Level

One of the first challenges that the new immigrant must meet in the host country is finding a shelter in an unfamiliar setting. This is often complicated by changes in dwelling and community density, technical equipment, and pollution compared with the home country (Ekblad, Ginsburg, Jansson, & Levi, 1994). Immigrants can reside in overcrowded and substandard accommodations with limited access to fresh water, adequate nutrition, or medical care, resulting in increased vulnerability to poor health. Often they lack financial resources and, in fact, can barely manage. These housing accommodations might subject immigrants to increased social marginalization and ultimately violence. In Sweden, for example, newly arrived migrants have been concentrated to poor and deprived areas of the major cities (Socialstyrelsen, 1997).

The Societal Level

Although equity in health care systems is a key objective of the World Health Organization, many European countries have made little progress toward health equity during past decades (Bollini & Siem, 1995). Kirmayer and Minas (2000) have reviewed some salient differences in cultural psychiatry and mental health services in several countries, which they argue reflect the country's history of migration and models of citizenship. Sweden, for instance, with a strong public health sector and history of immigration, has developed and implemented comprehensive mental health services for refugees. However, the few studies in Sweden concerning ethnicity and utilization of health services indicate major challenges ahead for the health care system to meet the mental health needs of the immigrant population.

In 1997 the Swedish Integration Office published guidelines for municipalities to assist the integration of refugees by using individualized plans. The purpose was to provide the individual with the prerequisites needed to become economically independent and part of Swedish society. This and later documents stated that any health problems experienced by newly arrived adults or children should be identified and treated through health care and/or social provisions.

However, where asylum seekers and other foreign citizens are not registered as residents of Sweden, county councils (or the equivalent) have only a limited obligation to provide health care (Ekblad, 2003). There is no charge for maternity care, preventive child, and care for the mothers under the Swedish Communicable Diseases Act. Any adult taken ill during the waiting period is entitled to free emergency medical and dental care. When considering asylum applications for children, the migration board takes into consideration the UN Convention on the Rights of the Child and the Swedish Aliens Act for the best interests of the child. Asylum-seeking children, including gömda children, are entitled to health care in the same way as other children living in Swedish society. County councils receive government grants to ensure the physical and mental well-being of children, including a medical examination before they start day care, preschool, or required school (www.migrationsverket.se).

Another example for a specific target population from Australia is STARTTS (Service for the Treatment and Rehabilitation of Torture and Trauma Survivors), established in late 1988 in Auburn, New South Wales. This rehabilitation service leads in providing for the needs of refugees in their area. The mission of STARTTS, according to their fact sheet, "is to develop and implement ways to facilitate the healing process of survivors of torture and refugee trauma, and to assist and resource individuals and organizations who work with them to provide appropriate, effective and culturally sensitive services." These services include:

• culturally appropriate counselling and therapy (for individuals, families and groups);
• physiotherapy, and bodywork, including individual sessions, pain management groups and hydrotherapy programs;
• group work, including self-support groups, English language, and craft classes;
• activities for young people, including camps, excursions and groups;
• assistance in seeking employment and training;
• referral and case management;
• community liaison and consultation;
• community development projects;
• training of mainstream service-providers in awareness of refugee issues and strategies to work with this client group;
• lobbying and advocacy on refugee issues; and
• research (STARTTS Information Fact Sheet).

BARRIERS TO HEALTH CARE

Newcoming immigrant people in any society can have difficulty understanding and accessing care. Cultural beliefs and values can influence perceptions of the need for care, particularly mental health care. Stigmatization of mental health and the related perception of privacy with the desire to hide mental health problems are other common barriers. Thus, barriers among migrants seeking mental health treatment are often correlated with help-seeking behavior, mistrust, stigma, cost, and clinician bias.

This perspective gives support to the lack of awareness of culture-specific symptoms in many of the epidemiologic studies that have employed diagnostic critiera developed in Western settings. The result has often been underrecognition or misidentification of psychological distress. On the other hand, underdiagnosis of depression and anxiety is a common problem in primary care in many countries (Ballinger, 2001).

In addition, cultures might use traditional medicine or religious/traditional ceremonies for treatment and be less familiar with Western mental health interventions. Western approaches tend to emphasize the individual and minimize the importance of the sociocultural context or social networks. Of the Western approaches, the authoritative view of the doctor is more active or directive and often more acceptable (Jaranson, 1991). In group-oriented cultures, intervention-based group activities can be more relevant than individual therapies. Thus, culturally rooted traditions of religious beliefs and practices can determine people's willingness to seek mental health services.

Bäärnhielm (2000) compared the meaning of illness for Turkish and Swedish-born women with those of health professionals, concluding that "Different interpretations of illness meaning by patient and caregiver constitute a situation of different realities according to the significance and social reality of the illness" (p. 4). The Turkish women rarely accepted psychiatric attribution, nor did they value psychiatry as a tool for recovery or find it helpful to link bodily symptoms to emotional distress. The results of the study point to the mutual need to explore meaning in the clinical encounter to help patients make sense of differing perspectives of illness and healing (Bäärnhielm & Ekblad, 2000).

In focus group interviews, Bäärnhielm and Ekblad (unpublished manuscript), by evaluating the clinical experiences of health professionals in a multicultural district of Stockholm, explored how patients communicated mental ill health and social problems via physical symptoms. These professionals reported that patients commonly expressed emotional distress through bodily symptoms, but the professionals found it difficult to communicate with patients or to decode their language of suffering. These professionals tried to create coherence between their Western medical model and the patient's understanding of suffering. They lacked both organizational support and shared models for adapting their work to the multicultural population and for treating mental ill health outside of psychiatry. Such shortcomings in primary care make "somatization" a coping strategy by which immigrant patients receive attention and medical care.

FUTURE CHALLENGES AND RECOMMENDATIONS FOR PSYCHOSOCIAL REHABILITATION, PREVENTION, RESEARCH, AND POLICY

Barriers for Communication Between Scientists, Service Providers, and Policymakers

Despite an increase in knowledge among health professionals in the field of migration and its mental health issues, there are still many barriers to applying this knowledge and to improving reception policy and mental health programs. In part, such barriers can reflect failure of communication between scientists, service providers, and policymakers. These barriers also reflect basic realities in the delivery of needed services for migrant groups (Jaranson et al., 2001). Improvement requires actions at several different levels. Multicultural training, research, and service efforts in the field of mental health promotion should be given priority. Guiding principles for health promotion are, according to Rootman (2001), empowering, participatory, intersectoral, equitable, sustainable, and multistrategy. According to Ekblad (2002b), basic prevention strategy for migrants includes a gender perspective:

- Recognition of human trafficking of women as an important social and health problem.
- Policy formulation and program development to protect human rights.
- A psychosocial orientation to understand mental health behavior and experience from a gender perspective in the context of society and culture.
- Partnerships and collaboration with a greater concern of newly-arrived immigrants in host societies resulting in a greater emancipation and changing roles.
- Increasing efforts to match and access mental health care to the needs and expectations of immigrants.
- Training and preparation of all staff with responsibilities in the reception program and health service of host countries to address the psychosocial needs of migrants. (p. 257)

Mainstream professionals often confront challenges without the benefit of training, supervision, and experience when treating newcomers, especially traumatized refugees. They need to draw upon a range of interventions including standard Western treatments and traditional healing, as well as health promotion strategies in the community. In selecting the appropriate intervention, it is useful to consider the major psychosocial stress systems (Silove, 1999), which are influenced by the refugee experience at the individual, group, and societal levels. The model (Table 23.1) can help to identify protective and risk factors for intervention using the "smorgasbord" approach.

PSYCHOSOCIAL REHABILITATION: COPING WITH DEPRESSION, SOCIAL DISABILITY, AND HEALTH-PROMOTING ACTIVITIES

The literature shows the importance of emphasizing support in the community, rather than symptom reduction alone. The combination of required medical, psychological, social, and legal actions depends upon intersectoral collaboration on the organizational and community levels. In addition, focusing on depression is most relevant because its prevalence is likely increased in a crisis setting. Level of social function, as a dependent variable, should be considered since it "is supported by evidence that social productivity (i.e., returning to work) probably helps to prevent depression and has some effect in alleviating depression" (Bolton, 2000, p. 2).

Even though survivors of refugee traumatic life events have similar symptoms, cultures differ in the meaning ascribed to the key concepts of traumatic life events, such as torture. In some cultures there is reluctance to express emotions or to reveal traumatic experiences, such as sexual torture, until trust has been established (Jaranson et al., 2001). Consequently, pressuring refugees to tell their stories can be counterproductive. In such circumstances, indirect methods might be more useful (Mollica, 1988). Cultural attitudes toward suffering also play an important role in help-seeking and treatment response. Belief that suffering is inevitable or that one's life is predetermined can, for example, deter some Muslims or Buddhists from seeking health care (Jaranson et al.. 2001).

Therefore, it would be constructive to integrate clinical and research staff responsible for asylum seekers and refugees, together with relevant social and employment service staff in the community, in the provision of psychosocial rehabilitation interventions. The ongoing 4-year project, Health Promotion Introduction, mentioned above has such a scope.

IMPLICATIONS FOR CLINICAL INTERVENTION

Health professionals working with asylum seekers and refugees need:

1. knowledge of their own ethnocultural identity and the implicit biases this brings to encounters with patients, relatives, and colleagues;
2. careful consideration of the cultural bases and biases of contemporary psychiatric practice;
3. ability to work with a holistic team in the community together with asylum seekers and refugees, trained interpreters, and culture-brokers who can provide the missing social and cultural context; and
4. consideration of the refugee's own position in the health care system, as well as the cultural context.

PREVENTION

In the literature, there are three preventive activities that can improve health for asylum seekers and refugees as well as for the general population: prevention of disease (primary), reduction of impairment and disability (secondary), and treatment of disease (tertiary). All of these are important and merit consideration.

Better reception conditions for asylum seekers and other migrant population groups are needed. Blackwell et al. (2002) have shown that a questionnaire administered in the initial contact with asylum seekers can be used by health care professionals in new locations, thus avoiding the necessity of completing another health needs assessment and facilitating appropriate interventions.

RESEARCH

Transcultural studies of the affect of trauma and gender on mental health promotion, health, illness, and health care gaps are needed to facilitate communication and understanding of the mechanisms and systems of healing among different cultural, ethnic, and religious groups. Transcultural research suggests that assessment of reactions to psychosocial stress should begin with phenomenological descriptions of folk diagnoses or culture-specific syndromes (Mollica, 2000). A main goal of transcultural and international mental health research is the valid comparison of mental illness around the world. Achieving this goal entails meeting several methodological challenges that arise from the need to mesh the process of inquiry with the cultural characteristics of the groups studied (Rogler, 1989). A basic problem is how to develop research approaches that search for outcomes in different cultural contexts. The paradox, according to Draguns (2001), is the global spread of psychology (as well as other relevant disciplines [authors' comment]) decontextualized from cultural and linguistic settings but mainly using English language in publications, conferences, workshops, and so forth.

Although most countries in Europe, North America, and Australia receive large numbers of refugees and asylum seekers, individual research projects have usually focused on a single group, a single setting, and a single point in time. In an article about research on the mental health effects of terrorism, North and Pfefferbaum (2002) recommend caution because of the difficulty separating normal stress reactions from psychiatric disorders. There are few studies of other catastrophes for comparison, and the effects differ by subpopulation. Unlike other fields, there are yet no multicenter, cross-national or even cross-regional research studies. Management of data across sites in future multicenter studies will be of critical importance. A computerized approach will probably provide the most economical transfer and collation of data for joint analysis. A computerized questionnaire should assess demographic information, health history, general symptoms, use of medication, and current health care needs. The public health implications of establishing a common database across countries is enormous. Thus, for the first time, policymakers and administrators would be able to draw on common data to assess the mental health needs of refugee groups to inform both national and international practice and policy.

Second, multiple measures (quantitative as well as qualitative) need to be used more often to assess trauma, diagnostic categories, and variation in the properties of the measures. In an integrative review of current quantitative research of the mental health status of refugees in 12 studies published between 1987 and 1998, Keyes (2000) found negative mental health status (PTSD, depression, anxiety, psychosis, and dissociation) in the refugees sampled in all those studies. This review revealed a lack of culturally sensitive understanding and diagnostic measures in the majority of current published quantitative research of refugees.

Third, services provided for refugees and asylum seekers vary substantially across resettlement countries. It is imperative that we establish common methods for assessing disabilities and needs, as well as methods for dealing with these needs. Hollifield et al. (2002) state:

> the majority of articles about refugee trauma or health are either descriptive or include quantitative data from instruments that have limited or untested validity or reliability in refugees. Primary limitations to accurate measurement in refugee research are the lack of theoretical basis to instruments and inattention to using and reporting sound measurement principles. (p. 611)

Further, new researchers in the field find it difficult even to determine how to initiate research. They are faced with a plethora of methods and approaches to measurement and can spend an inordinate amount of time making decisions about which instruments and procedures to use. It is likely that innovative methods, for example, for encouraging employment or providing torture and trauma services, are being implemented, but their relative effectiveness compared to other sites/countries cannot be evaluated since there is no common method for doing so.

POLICY

The World Health Organization's (2001) commission *Macroeconomics and Health* recommends that the rich countries increase fivefold their economic investment in health for the poorest countries. The underlying argument is that an investment in health is fundamental and can be a prerequisite for economic development. The investment will be repaid by saving millions of lives each year and by strengthening global peace and security. However, for example, Swedish policy stresses emergency care for adult traumatized asylum seekers, despite the fact that counseling for violent traumatic life events can help prevent the development of psychiatric disorders and impairment.

Since Western approaches emphasize the individual and minimize the importance of the sociocultural context and social networks, public health should stimulate mechanisms of adaptation and self-help to reduce and minimize helplessness. Examples include providing regular health information and recognizing the social context of migration stress symptoms and coping strategies (Ekblad, Klefbeck, Wennström, & Pietkäinen, 1997; Wennström, Klefbeck, & Ekblad, 2000). In dealing with interventions on the five levels according to the Systems of Health (Table 23.1), primary, secondary, and tertiary prevention are of great importance.

REFERENCES

American Psychiatric Association (APA). (1995). *Diagnostic and statistical manual of mental disorders*. DSM-IV (4 suppl.). Washington, DC: Author.

Antonovsky, A. (1987). *Unrevealing the mystery of health. How people manage stress and stay well*. San Francisco: Jossey Bass.

Bäärnhielm, S. (2000). *Clinical encounters with different illness realities. Qualitative studies of somatization and illness meaning among Swedish and Turkish-born women encountering local health care services in Western Stockholm*. Licentiate thesis. Karolinska Institutet, Department of Public Health Sciences, Division of Psychosocial Factors and Health, Stockholm, Sweden.

Bäärnhielm, S., & Ekblad, S. (2000). Turkish migrant women encountering health care in Stockholm. A qualitative study for somatization and illness meaning. *Culture, Medicine and Psychiatry, 24*, 431–452.

Bäärnhielm, S., & Ekblad, S. *In unfamiliar territory: Caregivers' encounter with somatic communication of mental ill health in a multicultural community*. Unpublished manuscript.

Bailis, D. S., Segall, A., & Chipperfield, J. G. (2003). Two views of self-rated general health status. *Social Science and Medicine, 56*, 203–217.

Ballinger, J. C. (2001). Introduction. Focus on transcultural issues in depression and anxiety. *Journal of Clinical Psychiatry, 62*(suppl. 13), 3.

Berry, J. (1991). Managing the process of acculturation for problem prevention. In J. Westermeyer, C. Williams, & A. Nguyen (Eds.), *Mental health services for refugees* (DHHS Publication ADM 91-1824, pp. 189–204). Washington, DC: Government Printing Office.

Blackwell, D., Holden, K., & Tregoning, D. (2002). An interim report of health needs assessment of asylum seekers in Sunderland and North Tyneside. *Public Health, 116*, 221–226.

Bollini, P., & Siem, H. (1995). No real progress towards equity: Health of migrants and ethnic minorities on the eve of the year 2000. *Social Science and Medicine, 41*, 819–828.

Bolton, J. (2002). The third presence: A psychiatrist's experience of working with non-speaking patients and interpreters. *Transcultural Psychiatry, 39*(1), 97–114.

Bolton, P. (2000, August 12). *The psychosocial effects of conflict-related trauma.* Technical Advisory Group Meeting Report. Washington, DC. Johns Hopkins University.

Bracken, P. J. (2001). Post-modernity and post-traumatic stress disorder. *Social Science and Medicine, 53,* 733–743.

Bracken, P., Giller, J. E., & Summerfield, D. (1997). Rethinking mental health work with survivors of wartime violence and refugees. *Journal of Refugee Studies, 10*(4), 431–442.

Breslau, N., Kessler, R., Chilcaot, H. D., Schultz, L. R., Davis, G. C., & Andreski, P. (1998). Trauma and posttraumatic stress disorder in the community: The 1996 Detroit area survey of trauma. *Archives of General Psychiatry, 55,* 626–632.

Broström, E. (2002). *En kvalitativ intervjustudie om upplevelser av hälsa och hälsofrämjande faktorer hos introduktionsdeltagare i Stockholm* [A qualitative interview study regarding perceptions of health and health promoting factors among participants in the refugee reception introduction in Stockholm]. Master in public health, Department of Public Health Sciences, Karolinska Institutet.

de Santis, L., & Ugarriza, D. N. (1995). Potential for intergenerational conflict in Cuban and Haitian immigrant families. *Archives of Psychiatric Nursing, 6,* 354–364.

Desjarlais, R., Eisenberg, L., Good, B., & Kleinman, A. (1995). *World mental health: Problems and priorities in low-income countries.* New York: Oxford University Press.

Draguns, J. G. (2001, November). Toward a truly international psychology: Beyond English only. *American Psychologist, 56*(11), 1019–1030.

Ekblad, S. (2002a). Ethnopolitical warefare, traumatic family stress and mental health of refugee children In C. E. Stout (Ed.), *The psychology of terrorism. Vol. 2. Clinical aspects and responses* (pp. 27–48). Westport, CT: Praeger.

Ekblad, S. (2002b). Gender and mental health in a multicultural society. In S. P. Wamala & J. Lynch (Eds.), *Gender and social inequities in health.* (pp. 233–264). Lund: Studentlitteratur.

Ekblad, S. (2003). Swedish perspective on refugee adjustment, resettlement, acculturation and mental health. In F. Bemak, R. Chi-Ying Chung, & P. Pedersen (Eds.), *Counseling refugees. A psychosocial approach to innovative multicultural interventions* (pp. 178–187). Westport, CT: Greenwood Press.

Ekblad, S., Ginsburg, B.-E., Jansson, B., & Levi, L. (1994). Psychosocial and psychiatric aspects of refugee adaptation and care in Sweden. In A. J. Marsella, T. Borneman, S. Ekblad, & J. Orley (Eds.), *Amidst peril and pain: The mental health and well-being of world's refugees* (pp. 275–293). Washington, DC: American Psychological Association.

Ekblad, S., Klefbeck, E.-L., Wennström, C., & Pietkäinen, A.-L. (1997). Help for refugees. *World Health Forum, 18,* 305–310.

Ekblad, S. Kohn, R., & Jansson, B. (1998). Psychological and clinical aspects of migration and mental health. In S. O. Okpaku (Ed.), *Clinical methods in transcultural psychiatry* (pp. 42–66). Washington, DC and London: American Psychiatric Association Press.

Ekblad, S., & Shahnavaz, S. (2003, September 10–14). *Trauma, postmigration stress and suicidal thoughts among asylum seekers.* Abstract to XXII IASP Congress in Stockholm.

Ekblad, S., & Wennström, C. (1997). Relationships between traumatic life events, symptoms, and sense of coherence subscale: Meaningfulness in a group of refugee and immigrant patients referred to a Stockholm psychiatric out-patient clinic. *Scandinavian Journal of Social Welfare, 6,* 279–285.

Foa, E., Friedman, M., & Keane,T. (Eds.). (2000). *Effective treatments for PTSD.* New York: Guilford.

Goodkind, J. R., & Foster-Fishman, P. G. (2002). Integrating diversity and fostering interdependence: Ecological lessons learned about refugee participation in multiethnic communities. *Journal of Community Psychology, 30*(4), 389–409.

Häll, L. (1997). Invandarnas levnadsförhållanden [Immigrants' living conditions]. In *Välfärd och ojämlikhet i 20-årsperspektiv* [Social welfare and inequity in a 20 years' perspective] *1975–1995* (pp. 467–489). Stockholm: Statistics Sweden, Report 91.

Harvey, M. R. (1996). An ecological view of psychological trauma and trauma recovery. *Journal of Traumatic Stress, 9,* 3–23.

Helman, C. G. (1994). *Culture, health and illness.* Oxford, U.K.: Butterworth Heineman.

Hollifield, M., Warner, T. D., Lian, N., Krakow, B., Jenkins, J. H., Kesler, J. et al. (2002). Measuring trauma and health status in refugees. A critical review. *JAMA, 288*(5), 611–620.

Jablensky, A., Marsella, A. J., Ekblad, S., Jansson, B., Levi, L., & Bornemann, T. (1994). Refugee mental health and well-being: Conclusions and recommendations In A. J. Marsella, T. Bornemann, S. Ekblad, & J. Orley (Eds.), *Amidst peril and pain: The mental health and well-being of world's refugees* (pp. 327–339). Washington, DC: American Psychological Association.

Jaranson, J. (1991). Psychotherapeutic medication. In J. Westermeyer, C. L. Williams, & A. N. Nguyen (Eds.), *Mental health services for refugees* (pp. 132–145). Washington, DC: National Institute of Mental Health, DHHS#(ADM)91-1824.

Jaranson, J., Forbes-Martin, S., & Ekblad, S. (2001). Refugee mental health. In R. W. Manderscheid & M. J. Henderson (Eds.), *Mental health, United States, 2000* (pp. 120–133). Rockville, MD: U.S. Department of Health and Human Services, Substance Abuse and Mental Health Services Administration (SAMHSA), Center for Mental Health Services.

Keyes, E. F. (2000). Mental health status in refugees: An integrative review of current research. *Issues in Mental Health Nursing, 21,* 397–410.

Kirmayer, L. J. (1989). Cultural variations in the response to psychiatric disorders and emotional distress. *Social Science & Medicine, 29,* 327–339.

Kirmayer, L. J. (1996). Cultural comments on somatoform and dissociative disorders: 1. In J. Mezzich, A. Kleinman, H. Fabrega, & D. Parron (Eds.), *Culture & psychiatric diagnosis: A DSM-IV perspective* (pp. 151–158). Washington, DC: American Psychiatric Press.

Kirmayer, L. J. (2001). Cultural variations in the clinical presentation of depression and anxiety: Implications for diagnosis and treatment. In N. Sartorius, W. Gaebel, J. J. López-Ibor, & M. Maj (Eds.), *Psychiatry in society* (pp. 22–28). New York: John Wiley & Sons.

Kirmayer, L. J., & Minas, H. (2000). The future of cultural psychiatry: An international perspective. *Canadian Journal of Psychiatry, 45,* 438–446.

Kleinman, A. (1978). Concepts and a model for the comparison of medical systems as cultural systems. *Social Science and Medicine, 12,* 85–93.

Kleinman, A. (1980). *Patients and healers in the context of the culture.* Berkeley: University of California Press.

Lépine, J-P. (2001). Epidemiology, burden and disability in depression and anxiety. In N. Sartorius, W. Gaebel, J. J. López-Ibor, & M. Maj (Eds.), *Psychiatry in society* (pp. 4–10). New York: John Wiley & Sons.

Lewis, G., & Araya, R. (2002). Globalization and mental health. In N. Sartorius, W. Gaebel, J. J. López-Ibor, & M. Maj (Eds.), *Psychiatry in society* (pp. 57–78). New York: John Wiley & Sons.

Lindencrona, F., & Ekblad, S. (2004). *The meaning of health in a health promoting introduction for refugees and other immigrants — An explorative qualitative study of the view of professionals.* Under revision.

Lindencrona, F., Ekblad, S., & Charry, J. (2001). *Kartläggning av levnadsomständigheter, behandlingskontakter och samverkansinsatser för patienter på Fittja psykiatriska öppenvårdsmottagning* [A study of living conditions, clinical contacts and collaboration interventions towards patients at Fittja psychiatric outpatient center] *1998–1999.* Stockholm: Statens Institut för Psykosocial Miljömedicin (IPM), Sektionen för stressforskning, Karolinska Institutet, WHO's Psykosociala Center, Stressforskningsrapport # 296.

Marks, D. F., Murray, M., Evans, B., & Willig C. (Eds.). (2000). *Health psychology. Theory, research and practice.* London: Sage.

McFarlane, A., & Raphael, B. (2001). Trauma and its effects. In S. Bloch & B. S. Singh (Eds.), *Foundations of clinical psychiatry* (2nd ed., pp. 149–161). Melbourne: Melbourne University Press.

Mollica, R. F. (1988). The trauma story: The psychiatric care of refugee survivors of violence and torture. In F. M. Ochberg (Ed.), *Post-traumatic therapy and victims of violence* (pp. 295–314). New York: Brunner/Muzel.

Mollica, R. F. (2000). Special problems. In M. G. Gelder, J. J. López-Ibor, & N. Andreasen (Eds.), *New Oxford textbook of psychiatry* (pp. 1595–1601). Oxford: Oxford University Press.

Moos, R. H. (2002). The mystery of human context and coping. An unravelling of clues. *American Journal of Community Psychology, 30*(1), 67–88.

Murray, C. J., & Lopez, A. D. (1997). Alternative projections of mortality and disability by cause 1990–2020: Global burden of disease study. *Lancet, 349,* 1498–1504.

Nekolaichuk, C. L., Jevne, R. F., & Maguire, T. O. (1999). Structuring the meaning of hope in health and illness. *Social Science and Medicine, 48,* 591–605.

North, C., & Pfefferbaum, B. (2002). Research on the mental health effect of terrorism. *JAMA, 288,* 633–636.

Okasha, A. (2002). The new ethical context of psychiatry. In N. Sartorius, W. Gaebel, J. J. López-Ibor, & M. Maj (Eds.), *Psychiatry in society* (pp. 101–130). New York: John Wiley & Sons.

Palinkas, L. A., Pickwell, S. M., Brandstein, K., Clark, T. J., Hill, L. L. Moser, R.J., et al. (2003). The journey of wellness: Stages of refugee health promotion and disease prevention. *Journal of Immigrant Health,* 5(1),19–28.

Pargament, K. I. (1997). *The psychology of religion and coping: Theory, research, practice.* New York: Guilford Publications.

Raeburn, J., & Rootman, I. (1998). *People-centered health promotion.* Chichester: John Wiley & Sons.

Rogler, L. H. (1989). The meaning of culturally sensitive research in mental health. *American Journal of Psychiatry, 146,* 296–303.

Rootman, I. (2001). Introduction. In I. Rootman, M. Goodstadt, B. Hyndman, D. V. McQueen, L. Potvin, J. Springett et al. (Eds.), *Evaluation in health promotion. Principles and perspective* (pp. 4–5). Copenhagen, Denmark: WHO Regional Publications, European Series, No. 92.

Saraceno, B., Saxena, S., & Maulik, P. K. (2002). Mental health problems in refugees. In N. Sartorius, W. Gaebel, J. J. López-Ibor, & M. Maj (Eds.), *Psychiatry in society* (pp. 193–220). New York: John Wiley & Sons.

Silove, D. (1999). The psychosocial effects of torture, mass human rights violations and refugee trauma: Towards an integrated conceptual framework. *Journal of Nervous and Mental Disease, 187*(4), 200–207.

Silove, D., & Ekblad, S. (Eds.). (2002). How well do refugees adapt after resettlement in Western countries? *Acta Psychiatrica Scandinavica, 106,* 401–402.

Silove, D., Ekblad, S., & Mollica, R. (2000, April 29). Health and human rights. The rights of the severely mentally ill in post-conflict societies. Invited commentary. *Lancet, 355*(9214), April 29, 1548–1549.

Socialstyrelsen [National Swedish Board of Health and Welfare]. (1997). *Public Health Report 1997.* Stockholm.

Service for the Treatment and Rehabilitation of Torture and Trauma Survivors (STARTTS). *Information fact sheet.* Australia. http://www.swsahs.nsw.gov.au/areaser/startts.

Sundsvall Statement on Supportive Environments for Health. Third International Conference on Health Promotion, June 9–15, 1991, Sundsvall, Sweden. http://www.phs.ki.se/whoccse/Sundsvall.htm.

Tabora, B., & Flaskerud, J. H. (1994). Depression among Chinese Americans. A review of the literature. *Issues in Mental Health Nursing, 15,* 569–584.

UNHCR (2003). http://www.unhcr.ch.

Watters, C. (2001). Emerging paradigms in the mental health care of refugees. *Social Science and Medicine, 52,* 1709–1718.

Weissman, M. M., Bland, R. C., Canino, G. J., Fararelli, C., Greenwald, S., Hwu, H. G., et al. (1996). Cross-national epidemiology of major depression and bipolar disorder. *JAMA, 276,* 293–299.

Wennström, C., Klefbeck, E-L., & Ekblad, S. (2000). Samverkansmodell mellan flyktingmottagandet och psykiatrin [Collaboration modal between refugee reception center and psychiatry]. *Journal for Social Workers, 6,* 54–56.

World Health Organization (WHO). (1946). Preamble to the constitution of the WHO as adopted by the International Conference, New York, June 19–22, 1946; signed on July 22, 1946 by the representatives (Official Records of the WHO, No. 2, p. 100) and entered into force. The Definition has been amended since 1948 (http://www.who.int/about/definition/en).

World Health Organization (WHO). (2001a). Macroeconomics and health: Investing in health for economic development. Report of the commission on macroeconomics and health. Geneva: Author.

World Health Organization (WHO). (2001b). *The world health report 1999. Mental health: New understanding, new hope.* Geneva: Author.

Legal, Moral, and Political Issues in the Treatment Process

Legal, Moral, and Political Issues in the Treatment Process

Introduction

JOHN P. WILSON

Part VII of the book contains two chapters that focus on legal, moral, and ethical issues in the treatment of asylum seekers and refugees. In Chapter 24, Jane Herlihy, Carla Ferstman, and Stuart W. Turner present a discussion of legal issues in working with asylum seekers and refugees. In this chapter, the authors trace the process of what happens to an asylum seeker from entry into the host country to negotiating the maze and web of bureaucracies, which create hurdles, rules, procedures, and criteria for determining whether an asylum seeker will eventually be granted the legal status of refugee, resident alien, or some other designation. For the asylum seeker the process is typically fraught with frustration, confusion, and difficulty in understanding what is legally required by the host country, in determining their status, and, perhaps, future well-being.

Herlihy, Ferstman, and Turner break down the various component processes that an asylum seeker must face when interfacing with the bureaucracy governing their ultimate fate and disposition. The component processes include: applying for asylum, detention, credibility of claim and basis for seeking asylum, forensic evaluation and preparation of reports for authorities, issues of adequate psychological assessment for PTSD and allied comorbidities, and the role and limitations of the clinicians in the legal process.

In Chapter 25, Zachary Steele, Sarah Mares, Louise Newman, Bijou Black, and Michael Dudley discuss the politics of detaining asylum seekers and the political-legal issues regarding official national policy, which often create moral and ethical dilemmas for mental health care providers who work with persons seeking asylum, often in desperation, destitution, and life-and-death struggles for survival. But what if the host country where the asylum seekers arrive, or in some cases, simply "land" in primitive boats crafted for exile from the oppressive country and political regime from where they sought to escape, flatly rejects their pleas for asylum and assistance? Such scenarios exist in many countries in the world, including the United States, Australia, and Germany. For example, these authors, all Australians, describe their involvement in cases in which asylum seekers from Indonesia, Papua New Guinea, the Island of Nauru, and other Southeast Asian locales. As noted in the previous chapter on legal issues, asylum seekers are typically detained in barren, remote conditions with minimally adequate provisions of their basic needs. The issue of detention and its environmental conditions raises psychological, ethical, and moral questions. Are the asylum seekers' basic human rights being met in accordance with international laws? Are the conditions sufficient to ensure the physical and mental well-being of the asylum seekers? Are women, children, and families being afforded adequate care? Are the mental health and medical needs being properly met? Are the detainees being subjected to extreme or cruel conditions of living in detention centers?

The answers to these questions are not often as sanguine as would be ideally desired. As the authors document in their chapter, the Australian government's treatment of asylum seekers detained at the Woomera Reception and Processing Centre were subjected to harsh environmental conditions of extreme temperature, socially and psychologically isolating detention living units, and extremely severe treatment by "prison" guards. Indeed, the severity of the conditions eventually led to a protest riot among the asylum seekers and commanded international and national attention, controversy, and debate about Australia's policy toward illegal immigrants and asylum seekers. Thrust in the middle of this set of controversies and harsh realities of conditions of detention is the mental health professional who seeks to provide ethical care and treatment to traumatized persons seeking a better way of life. And yet, the government that authorizes their role can also act as an oppressor rather than a liberator, creating more difficulties for the asylum seekers. The authors state: "our role as health care professionals exposes us to the harsh and brutal contest being played out between powerful first world countries seeking to protect their borders and individuals seeking protection at any cost — we encounter firsthand the resulting shattered lives and broken spirits. In this contest, our ethics require us to prevent what harm we can and to document what we cannot prevent."

24

Legal Issues in Work With Asylum Seekers

JANE HERLIHY, CARLA FERSTMAN, AND
STUART W. TURNER

One of the prerequisites of working with asylum seekers and refugees is an understanding of the legal framework that gives definition to their situation. After all, it is this context in which their status is defined and through which they have to journey in a search for sanctuary.

The usual experiences of asylum seekers and refugees involve serious violations of human rights and the loss of everything that is familiar — home, family, social status, job, identity. Article 14 of the Universal Declaration of Human Rights provides that "Everyone has the right to seek and to enjoy in other countries asylum from persecution," but the disorienting process of leaving everything behind and undertaking the painful journey to somewhere new is often difficult and fraught with uncertainties.

This chapter examines the progress of the individual through the legal process of seeking and gaining asylum. First, we consider the process of arriving in a host country and claiming asylum: What does the individual have to do to obtain permission to live in a new country? We will consider the role of the clinician in this process. We will then look at the rights accorded to individuals, both while they are seeking asylum and once they have been granted the right to remain in the country as a refugee. Finally, for some, there might be a process of reparation — seeking forms of justice from the perpetrators of human rights abuses.

THE LEGAL AND POLICY CONTEXT FOR ASYLUM SEEKERS

Refugee Conventions

The UN Refugee Convention defines a refugee as a person who: "owing to well-founded fear of being persecuted for reasons of race, religion, nationality, membership of a particular social group or political opinion, is outside the country of his nationality and is unable or, owing to such fear, is unwilling to avail himself of the protection of that country" (Article 1(2)). This definition has been broadened in respect of Africa, where the term "refugee" has been extended in a more recent Convention (1974) to apply also:

> to every person who, owing to external aggression, occupation, foreign domination or events seriously disturbing public order in either part or the whole of his country of origin or nationality, is compelled to leave his place of habitual residence in order to seek refuge in another place outside his country of origin or nationality. (Article 12)

Similarly, the 1984 Cartagena Declaration extended the definition of refugees in the Americas to: "persons who have fled their country because their lives, safety, or freedom have been threatened by generalized violence, foreign aggression, internal conflicts, massive violations of human rights or other circumstances which have seriously disturbed public order" (Conclusion 3).

Refoulement

The principle of *nonrefoulement* is defined in Article 33(1) of the 1951 Convention: "No Contracting State shall expel or return ("*refouler*") a refugee in any manner whatsoever to the frontiers of territories where his life or freedom would be threatened on account of his race, religion, nationality, membership of a particular social group or political opinion." This principle applies not only to refugees, but to asylum seekers whose status has not yet been determined, and those seeking entry at a border (UNHCR, 1977a). It also relates to the practice of sending a refugee to another country that then sends them back without a fair and satisfactory assessment of their asylum claim. The principle of nonrefoulement is also enshrined in Article 3 of the Convention against Torture, the European Convention on Human Rights, the American Convention on Human Rights, and the African Charter on Human and Peoples' Rights.

Determination

While the definition of refugee is a product of the international and regional texts referred to above, the decision to recognize an asylum seeker as a refugee is a legal decision for the host country. The 1951 Convention, therefore, does not stipulate the criteria for determining the status of refugees. This is left to each state to establish the appropriate procedures taking into account the particular legal traditions and constitutional and administrative arrangements in their respective country. However, there have been some attempts to develop common standards for the determination of refugee status. Significantly, the European Union is working to develop common standards for member states (European Commission, 2000) and the UNHCR has issued a number of nonbinding policy and interpretive documents based on "best practices" to assist the competent national bodies with this task. For example, the determination of whether an individual has a "well founded fear of being persecuted" has been interpreted by the UNHCR (UNHCR, 1992, para. 37) as including a subjective element — as well as the objective appraisal — that persecution is "reasonably possible" (UNHCR, 1998) in their country of origin.

Applying for Asylum

There are different systems in place across the world for the determination of refugee status. There are countries that rely on extraterritorial assessment by the UNHCR and do not accept people who arrive illegally seeking asylum. There are countries where large numbers of people arrive, perhaps during a neighboring civil war, who have to be accommodated in large camps without a great deal of checking. However, in many Western countries, there is the opportunity for an individual to apply for asylum and for that application to be considered in detail under due process of law.

Usually, before anyone can make an asylum application under this system, they do need to be in a place of safety. Many countries have erected legal frameworks designed to deter asylum seekers. Visa requirements, imposition of financial penalties on carriers, and detention policies all have some deterrent properties. Unfortunately, rather reminiscent of the days of "prohibition" in North America, there has been a growth in "people smuggling" as legal and policy restrictions have increased.

It is the responsibility of the individual seeking asylum to make an application in which they set out their reasons. Depending on local policy and legal system, this can take the form of a statement, a written application form or an interview, or some combination of these. The initial interview can take place at the port, immediately upon the individual's arrival in the host state. They may or may not have any understanding of the procedures, or their rights within it, such as expressing concerns with their allocated interpreter or the gender of the interviewers. Subsequent interviews can be held, or statements taken, particularly if an initial negative decision is appealed against. Those seeking asylum should always be encouraged to seek legal advice.

Although the process can initially seem straightforward, the legal implications of each stage of the process are huge, not only for eventual outcome of the asylum application, but also for benefits and other associated issues.

Although the standard of proof required in asylum cases is not high, the burden of proof does fall to the applicant. This can be difficult for some people, and the UNHCR recognizes that people with a severe mental illness, for example, can require special methods of assessment. If an initial application is rejected, there might be grounds of appeal, and in some settings the whole process can drag on for months or many years.

Detention

It is becoming more and more common for asylum seekers to be detained on their arrival in host states, often for indeterminate periods. Sometimes this is used explicitly as a deterrent, and sometimes detention is restricted to undocumented applicants and/or rejected asylum seekers. Of course, many people with legitimate reasons for seeking asylum cannot access legal documentation, so this is an approach with significant risks. In extreme cases, detained asylum seekers are held with common criminals. The UN Working Group on Arbitrary Detention has noted that: "[A]rticle 14 of the Universal Declaration of Human Rights guarantees the right to seek and to enjoy in other countries asylum from persecution. If detention in the asylum country results from exercising this right, such detention might be 'arbitrary'." (UN Working Group on Arbitrary Detention, 1997). Detention can contribute to secondary traumatization and have harmful effects on asylum seekers' physical and emotional well-being. Moreover, the practice can reinforce the feelings of helplessness and isolation associated with previous experiences of torture or abuse in detention (Silove, McIntosh, & Becker, 1993; Summerfield et al., 1991). UNHCR, in its revised guidelines on applicable criteria and standards relating to the detention of asylum seekers, reminds states that any restrictions in liberty must be prescribed by law, exercised in a nondiscriminatory manner, and subject to review "to ensure that it continues to be necessary in the circumstances with the possibility of release where no grounds for its continuation exist" (UNHCR, 1999, para. 5). Particularly, in recognition of the devastating effects detention can have on the psychological well-being of those detained, UNHCR has recommended that alternatives to detention be actively sought for, among others, unaccompanied elderly persons, torture or trauma survivors, and persons with a mental or physical disability (1999, Guideline 7).

Credibility

For many people that seek asylum, there is a lack of objective evidence. States that undertake systematic persecution of their citizens typically deny such actions in public and rarely issue documentary evidence. So an application often rests on a combination of "objective" country information and the credibility of the history. Even "objective" evidence is not always accepted, and there can be different accounts of the context in the country of origin — for example, those given by investigative nongovernmental organizations such as Amnesty International and governmental agencies.

There are two common problems facing the asylum seeker, which we will consider here. The first is simply that their account might not qualify them as refugees. For example, fleeing from civil war does not necessarily mean that the individual, whatever they have experienced or witnessed, has a well-founded fear of future persecution. This is not uncommon. Indeed many of the people described pejoratively in some of the media as "bogus" asylum seekers can be entirely genuine in looking for respite from conflict — but, not being legally trained, they do not know that they are not refugees under law.

The second common problem follows from the lack of corroborative evidence. The credibility of the individual is key. In order to assess the credibility of asylum seekers, the national officials processing the asylum claim will need to assess the "reasonableness" of the facts as alleged by the claimants. This will be a challenge given that the harrowing experiences of some applicants might not appear reasonable or obvious to anyone who has not undergone them. Judgments have to be made based on the consistency and coherence of the story, any corroborative evidence, and the claimant's demeanor. In the United Kingdom, national guidelines state that "discrepancies, exaggerated accounts, and the addition of new claims of mistreatment may affect credibility" and that such discrepancies can be used as a reason for refusal of asylum (UK Immigration and Nationality Directorate, 1998). However, consistency and coherence cannot be the typical responses of those who have suffered extensive trauma.

Discrepancies and Memory

There is now an extensive literature demonstrating that individuals' memories of traumatic events are often fragmented and sensory, rather than held in a coherent narrative (Brewin, Dalgliesh, & Joseph, 1996; Foa & Riggs, 1993). This may well follow from different brain storage mechanisms for emotional (traumatic) memories versus narrative memories. Literature investigating the testimony of eye-witnesses indicates that autobiographical memory is subject to distortion by subsequent knowledge and questioning (Lipton, 1977). Furthermore, clinical studies of memory demonstrate that mood disorders, such as depression, also have an impact on what is remembered (Williams, Watts, MacLeod, & Mathews, 1997). Depression is one of the more common psychiatric problems experienced by refugees (Silove, Sinnerbrink, Field, Manicavasager, & Steel, 1997; Turner, Bowie, Shapo, & Yule, 2003). There are many other factors that can affect individuals' ability to recall accurately or consistently, such as head injury, chronic pain (both common to asylum seekers who have survived detention or torture), and sleep disturbance (a common feature of PTSD and depression).

Two studies in particular have looked at the stability of autobiographical memories of traumatic war experiences. Southwick, Morgan, Nicolaou, and Charney (1997) gave veterans of the Gulf War a checklist of 19 significant experiences, 1 month and 2 years after their return. Fifty-two of the 59 subjects changed their response to at least one item. The most commonly changed item was "Extreme threat to your personal safety." This was changed by 36% of subjects (interestingly, as many moved from "yes" to "no" as from "no" to "yes"). This clearly has implications for judicial processes that aim to judge claimants' levels of fear based on their past experiences. The number of changes was significantly associated with the level of symptoms of PTSD. Later researchers have not found this link (Bramsen, Dirkzwager, van Esch, van der Ploeg, 2001); however, they still found that a mere 12% of respondents answered with identical answers on the first and second occasions.

Herlihy, Scragg, and Turner (2002) reported a study in which repeated interviews were performed, eliciting details of traumatic experiences from refugees from Bosnia and Kosovo who had permission to stay in the UK. Up to 65% of the details provided by the refugees changed between the interviews, which were between 4 and 30 weeks apart. The longer the delay between interviews, the more the details changed for those who had high levels of PTSD. Those suffering most distress following traumatic experiences are therefore systematically most likely to be inconsistent — and thus be judged as fabricating — if there are long delays between interviews or court appearances. This empirical evidence and modern psychological understandings of memory processing and trauma have not necessarily filtered into the practice of those assessing asylum claims at national levels.

Disclosure

UNHCR has recognized that:

> claimants who have suffered severe trauma may experience difficulties in recalling the details of painful events. Individuals who feared authorities in their own countries because of what they endured may be nervous and apprehensive before any authority, inhibiting a full and accurate explanation of the case. Due to the trauma and the shame, claimants may be reluctant to reveal the true extent of the persecution suffered or feared. (UNHCR, 2002, paras. 35–36)

Oppression and torture engender strong feelings of humiliation, which can inhibit the retelling of the experiences. In particular, Ramsay, Gorst-Unsworth, and Turner (1993) found a significant relationship between sexual torture and the avoidance criteria of PTSD. They relate this to shame and point out the difficulties of disclosure of such material. These results were replicated by van Velsen, Gorst-Unsworth, and Turner (1996). Although guidelines for immigration officials can recommend that only women interview female applicants, we hear repeatedly that women are interviewed by men, and with male interpreters. Of course ensuring that interviewers are of the same gender still cannot guarantee disclosure of sexual torture, and neither does it address the disclosure of sexual torture by male applicants. Where there is a reliance on an interpreter from the same country of origin, there can be additional worries about information leaking back to the community.

The "addition of new claims" can give rise in particular to adverse judgments as to a claimant's honesty. By this is meant the later mention of a new experience of persecution, not previously disclosed. The view might be taken that the applicant is adding a "new claim of mistreatment" merely in order to avoid deportation, in other words that there is fabrication. However, this may fail to recognize the reasons for not disclosing at the outset. For example, in some cultures the social consequences of disclosure for a woman who has been raped are sufficient to inhibit survivors. A woman may risk the loss of husband and family. In these circumstances it might only be the imminent threat of being returned to her home country that makes her decide to take that risk.

Refusal

Regional human rights mechanisms have for the most part recognized the applicability of human rights principles to the refugee determination process. Article 6 of the European Convention on Human Rights (the right to a fair trial) does not appear to apply to refugee determination proceedings (ECHR, 2000). However, Article 1 of Protocol No. 7 does offer protection. It guarantees that aliens will only be expelled pursuant to a decision reached in accordance with law and shall be allowed to submit reasons against the expulsion, to have the case reviewed, and to be represented for these purposes before the competent authority or a person or persons designated by that authority. The American Convention on Human Rights (1978) provides procedural protections to aliens "lawfully in the territory of a State Party" in expulsion proceedings (Article 22(6)), whereas the African Commission on Human and Peoples Rights (1997) has recognized that the rights enshrined in the African Charter apply to all persons in the jurisdiction of a state party.

THE ROLE OF THE CLINICIAN IN THE LEGAL PROCESS

Other chapters in this book have dealt with the common mental health problems faced by refugees. It is also obvious that the legal process itself stands to affect mental health — especially in people already vulnerable because of past traumatization.

Asylum seekers have the right to be treated with dignity throughout the refugee determination process. Not only should they benefit from the basic rights and protections afforded to all people within a state, they will usually be in a vulnerable position and will need compassion and guidance from those receiving them in helping them to understanding their rights and the procedures they are required to follow (UNHCR, 1977b).

Immigration officials should be sensitive to the need to avoid revictimization or added trauma. Additional and flexible measures to meet the special needs of female asylum seekers, victims of torture or sexual violence, and traumatized persons are warranted. The European Parliamentary Assembly made such a recommendation in 1995, and UNHCR, noted in respect of the amended proposal by the European Commission for a council directive on minimum standards on procedures in member states for granting and withdrawing refugee status, the need for measures including "an entitlement for female asylum-seekers to be heard by a female interviewer and interpreter, and the assurance of in camera interviews in all cases to ensure full confidentiality and privacy, unless the applicant seeks otherwise" (UNHCR, 2002). However, as already noted, such measures are not always observed. As such, directives that require individuals to claim asylum within short time periods can be inconsistent with the needs and realities of trauma victims, who will need time to process the psychological and emotional consequences of their abuse and to establish the necessary levels of comfort to reveal the painful and often humiliating details of their experiences.

The prolonged state of anxiety while awaiting a decision has been noted by a number of authors as a significant factor in the maintenance of symptoms of PTSD and depression. In Australia, Silove et al. (1997) interviewed forty asylum seekers attending a community center. They found that a diagnosis of PTSD was associated not only with exposure to premigration trauma, but also with delays in their asylum applications and conflict with immigration officials. They concluded, "Current procedures for dealing with asylum-seekers may contribute to high levels of stress and psychiatric symptoms in those who have been previously traumatised" (p. 351).

Similarly, in a comparison of Tamil refugee and nonrefugee groups in Australia, premigration trauma exposure accounted for 20% of the variance of trauma symptoms; postmigration stress contributed 14% of the variance (Steel, Silove, Bird, McGorry, & Mohan, 1999). In the United Kingdom, Gorst-Unsworth and Goldenberg (1998) have also pointed to the importance of social support and current context in relation to the severity of psychological distress.

These studies are part of a growing literature demonstrating the role of the exile and asylum process itself in individuals' distress, despite many clinicians' assumptions that the sole cause of asylum seekers' problems lie in their experiences in their countries of origin. A prolonged process of determination can lead to deterioration in mood and, therefore, can also add to individuals' difficulties in presenting a coherent claim.

Report Writing

Clinicians can be involved in the preparation of forensic reports on asylum seekers. It is not possible to offer a great deal of specific advice since different countries operate under different policies and procedures for clinical evidence. However, there are some general principles.

There are two circumstances in which the clinician can be asked to prepare a report. The first of these concerns a clinician who is involved in treating an asylum seeker. They may be asked to prepare a professional report (in legal terms, a report as to the facts of the assessment and treatment plan). The second circumstance concerns a clinician brought in to prepare an independent, expert report purely for the purposes of determining the asylum application. These roles are quite different, although there can be a tendency to blur them.

A clinician who is treating an asylum seeker will usually have made a therapeutic alliance with that person. This alliance is helpful in treatment, but it will make it hard for the clinician to be fully independent in his or her opinions. Indeed, it could be argued that a clinician involved in treatment should not be impartial or independent. If this is the case, then it is a self-deception to attempt to prepare an independent report. The submission of obviously partisan material by clinicians will, over time, tend to undermine the acceptability and usefulness of their opinions. Our recommendation in the professional context is to restrict the report to matters of fact. Examples might include the fact of the diagnosis or psychological formulation that has been made, the treatment plan and progress, and a risk assessment. These are matters that a clinician will have dealt with and should have been recorded in a case file.

An expert report, on the other hand, will usually be prepared by a clinician with specialized training and experience in the preparation of reports. The clinician will not be involved in the treatment of that individual and can take an independent-minded approach. They will often have less contact with the asylum seeker (perhaps a single assessment interview) than a treating clinician, although they can request access to other notes and records. They will usually be expected to present a diagnostic formulation, to comment on consistency between history and current state, to advise on treatment and risk, to consider fitness to give evidence or to be interviewed, or to offer an opinion about the effects of return. These are common questions designed to assist the authorities in their determinations — in other words to address specific legal questions. Good experts will maintain an interest in the legal framework as well as in current knowledge in their own field.

There are clear limitations to the contribution of a mental health expert. We cannot decide if someone is at risk of future persecution. We usually cannot even state with certainty that they have been subjected to past persecution. It is possible to look for characteristic diagnostic or symptom profiles, but even here there can be difficulties. A diagnosis of PTSD, for example, requires that there has been a past history of major trauma. On the other hand, the legal question being asked often deals with the degree to which current diagnosis proves the past history. There is a circularity of argument here. Fortunately, there is some guidance. Those working with adult survivors of childhood sexual abuse have had to grapple with this problem already. Guidelines for use in clinical and legal settings have been developed. In brief, a clinical diagnosis of PTSD, based on the individual's history of trauma and current characteristic symptoms and signs, does not prove that the trauma took place, although it can be described as being consistent with the alleged trauma experience. In other words, the diagnosis adds weight to the account, but, on its own, does not prove it.

Questions about credibility are probably the most difficult. The key here is to ensure that the clinician restricts the opinion to clinical issues. The first principle for the clinician, in the legal arena, is always to stay within the bounds of clinical knowledge and expertise. It might be tempting to add extra comments about countries of origin or about the legal system, but the clinician is very unlikely to have sufficient knowledge in these areas. There is nothing that undermines a report by a health professional more than making additional statements. In this context, there are clear questions that can be answered that deal with credibility, but many that cannot. Moreover, the decision on the facts of the case will rest with the judge, not with the expert. Experts need to make an effective contribution where their knowledge makes this appropriate and to avoid comments when they have nothing of substance to add.

Working with asylum seekers, it is also important to resist the view that anyone who has been tortured or seriously persecuted will have PTSD. The evidence simply does not support this. Probably only a minority have this diagnosis (Turner et al., 2003). The absence of a diagnosis should therefore not be seen as undermining the credibility of an application.

Circumstances in which an expert mental health report can be especially useful include (among others): delayed reporting of allegations of rape or other sexual torture; provision of discrepant information in the setting of a severe depression, PTSD or a history of head injury; in the assessment of suicide risk; where there is evidence of serious mental illness (such as schizophrenia); and in people with learning difficulties. In other words, a clinical assessment as a general tool has clear limitations, but in specific settings it can be very important indeed.

Reference has already been made to the strong avoidance response, mediated by the emotion of shame, associated with sexual assault. If this pattern of response is clearly present, this adds considerable weight to the claim being made. Reference has also been made to the issue of discrepant information. Empirical data now exist and should be interpreted in individual cases — especially where there are strong symptoms of PTSD or depression, associated in any event with problems of concentration and memory. Similarly, a culturally appropriate neuropsychological assessment in the aftermath of severe head injury can be of enormous value.

Clinicians can be asked to give an opinion on the effect of forcible return to the country of origin. This is not a question for a professional report. A treating clinician could only ever give one answer — not to return. It is hard to see how this could always be an objective view. It is a reasonable question for an expert. Here, it is relevant to consider the significance of triggers for anxiety and panic in PTSD. It is certainly relevant to consider the effect of different levels of social support (Brewin, Andrews, & Valentine, 2000; Gorst-Unsworth & Goldenberg, 1998). However, the main issue has to do with risk of suicide, and standard risk assessment approaches should be followed.

Where there is a psychotic disorder, it might be necessary to undertake the assessment differently or to advise that it should be delayed until an active psychosis has been treated. Here the clinician will be able to advise on standard treatment approaches and the time scales for recovery.

Difficulties can arise where there are delusions of persecution. Of course, an individual can have both genuine and delusional beliefs about persecution. There is the aphorism, "Just because you are paranoid, it does not mean that they are out to get you." Indeed, the fact is that some people who are deluded are more likely than others to be persecuted. They are more likely to have difficulties appraising threat appropriately and can lay themselves at increased risk of persecution. Delusions can lead them to challenge people in authority or to pester security forces, both potentially dangerous actions in some settings.

It is possible that some have been given refugee status on the basis of entirely delusional persecution histories. However, equally, some may have been rejected on the grounds that they had some delusions — when the experience of persecution was, in fact, accurate. Great care is needed in this setting and experienced clinical input into the legal process is essential.

Delusions cannot only be relevant to understanding past experiences. They can represent a risk factor for future persecution. Probably the most obvious example of this is in people who have manic episodes. Grandiose delusions of a political or religious nature may, in some countries, lay the individual open to some of the most serious consequences. A common grandiose delusion would involve a belief that the individual was destined to be a religious leader — the next pope, ayatollah, and so forth. Their behavior is often disinhibited and considered risk-taking. To express such ideas or to behave in this way in some countries would be to court persecution, especially if there was limited knowledge of mental health issues.

People with learning difficulties can also present special issues in assessment. In safe countries, there are often special mechanisms to protect vulnerable adults, being interviewed in connection with criminal allegations. They can be more vulnerable to pressure to conform or agree with the interviewer. There can be an overreliance on factual material — going beyond what is safe in the context of their intellectual ability. Indeed, it is seldom that people are even asked about basic literacy, and yet this can be crucial to understanding their appraisal of the factual evidence. Others might present with evidence of cognitive impairment following traumatic brain injury; careful assessment can be vitally important. A mental health professional should be able to describe the nature of any vulnerability and to quantify it for the benefit of the assessment and judicial processes.

It is always appropriate to comment on treatment issues. Quite often, the expert clinician is the first mental health practitioner to have seen the asylum seeker and to be able to offer advice to those responsible for day-to-day treatment (through the report). Similarly, those making the legal decision can find this information important and can be inclined to dismiss an opinion if no treatment recommendations are made.

Fitness to give evidence can pose difficulties. Most asylum seekers have the capacity to understand the legal process and to instruct their lawyers or representatives. The problem arises when dealing with issues such as the likelihood of the individual having a panic attack, the effects of dissociation on quality of evidence, and the additional risk of suicide that can follow vigorous cross-examination. Often it is a matter of describing a circumstance clearly so that this can be taken into account by those making the final decision on this question.

Both expert and professional witnesses might have to give oral evidence. There is no substitute for practice, and we strongly advise that anyone in this situation investigates training options before taking part in a real case.

Integration

The 1951 Convention relating to the status of refugees outlines the minimum rights to which refugees are entitled, including basic civil and economic rights, and the UNHCR has developed these rights in a number of other texts (UNHCR, 1981, 2001). Many states differentiate between the entitlements of asylum seekers and confirmed refugees. Some tie the provision of assistance to the time when individuals claim asylum, disallowing "late applicants." However, the Universal Declaration on Human Rights (Article 2(1)), the International Covenant on Civil and Political Rights (Article 2(1)), and the International Covenant on Economic, Social and Cultural Rights set out basic human rights standards that apply in all circumstances, including an adequate standard of living. In its General Comment 15, adopted in 1994, the Human Rights Committee explained that, "the rights set forth in the Covenant apply to everyone, irrespective of reciprocity, and irrespective of his or her nationality or statelessness. ... The general rule is that each one of the rights of the Covenant must be guaranteed without discrimination between citizens and aliens" (Para. 1). According to UNHCR:

> best state practice addresses these concerns by providing asylum-seekers with accommodation — be it in reception centres or with host families — until the end of the procedure, and financial assistance if their access to employment is restricted. Such financial assistance may be based on the minimum social welfare allowance granted to nationals so that essential living expenses, including food and clothing, are covered. (UNHCR, 2001, para. 12)

The UN Committee on Economic, Social and Cultural Rights (2002) registered its concern in 2001 that policies relating to the reception of asylum seekers can be contrary to Article 11(1) of the International Covenant on Economic, Social and Cultural Rights, which recognizes the right of all individuals to an adequate standard of living. In this respect, the Committee commented on Venezuela's failure to issue personal documentation to refugees and asylum seekers and the impact this had on their ability to exercise the right to work, health, and education (UNCESCR, 2002). It also noted with concern the impact of the delay on determining refugee status on access to basic social services, in the cases of Senegal (para. 359) and Germany (para. 658). In a number of countries, legislation has denied some asylum seekers access to social benefits pending determination of their claims, leaving them destitute and dependent on charity. In other countries, particularly in the developing world, large numbers of refugees are given no means of sustenance.

In its General Comment on the right to health, the UN Committee on Economic, Social and Cultural Rights describes health as a fundamental human right "indispensable for the exercise of other human rights," which is "closely related to and dependent upon the realization of other human rights," including "the rights to food, housing, work, education, human dignity, life, non-discrimination, equality, the prohibition against torture, privacy, access to information, and the freedom of association, assembly and movement" (UNCESCR, 2000, paras. 1 and 3). States are obligated to ensure that the right to health is guaranteed without discrimination of any kind, in particular, by

> refraining from denying or limiting equal access for all persons, including prisoners or detainees, minorities, asylum seekers and illegal immigrants, to preventive, curative and palliative health services; abstaining from enforcing discriminatory practices as a State policy; and abstaining from imposing discriminatory practices relating to women's health status and needs. (para. 34)

Asylum seekers can face a number of other barriers to integration as a result of their experiences of flight and involuntary exile, and the physical and mental health problems relating to their past trauma. The importance of integration programs that take into account these special needs is therefore underscored. Asylum seekers can require material assistance and other support pending a final decision on their claim, and this can pose a number of challenges for the host state (UNHCR, 2001, paras. 7–9). For example, the UNHCR Executive Committee conclusions have recognized the importance of childhood education (Executive Committee Conclusion No. 47 of 1987 and 59 of 1989) and refugee employment (Executive Committee Conclusion No. 50 of 1988) in promoting durable solutions and enhancing dignity and self-respect (UNHCR, 2001).

Where the responsibility for providing social care lies with the normal statutory bodies, there can be a role for clinicians in educating such bodies in the needs of individuals with a traumatic history. The psychological sequelae of trauma, for example, can interact with accommodation that is noisy, unsafe, mixed gender, and so forth. Workers whose main role is to provide social housing to the general population might not understand this. Writing letters in support of asylum seekers applying for more appropriate accommodation can facilitate this process.

Another barrier to receiving health and social care is of course language. Interpreting and translating are costly, and statutory bodies in many areas are still reluctant to fund such services. However, equal access to care for individuals who do not speak the host language adequately is only achieved by the use of professionally trained interpreters and the translation of material such as information and letters.

These rights still need to be incorporated into policies and strategies for integration of new refugee communities. Here, different approaches have been taken including the laissez-faire, accommodation of refugees within groups from the same country of origin or attempts (usually unsuccessful) at early integration into the host community. A lot rests on the approach taken to accommodation and policies of dispersal. At this point, there is no very good model of practice on which to draw.

REPARATION FOR SERIOUS VIOLATIONS OF HUMAN RIGHTS

Quite apart from the process of seeking asylum in a host country, the path to integration and finding durable solutions will normally require the survivor to come to terms with his or her traumatic past. Obtaining closure for the events of the past can facilitate psychological recovery or instill greater confidence and a sense of the future, thereby contributing to the overall well-being of the asylum seeker. In some cases this can refer to the recovery of lost possessions or the tracing of dispersed family members. Most often, victims who were forced to flee their homes will want to know what led to the abuses that made them flee and what happened after they left. They will also want to know that the leaders and perpetrators of these abuses have been made accountable and are being prevented from perpetrating further abuses on other potential victims.

Under international law, survivors of violations of human rights and humanitarian law are entitled to reparation, which can include: restitution, compensation, rehabilitation, satisfaction, and guarantees of nonrepetition (United Nations, 2000). Invariably this will be comprised of the right to know the truth about past events and about the circumstances and reasons that led to the perpetration of heinous crimes, and the right to pursue justice, including the criminal responsibility of perpetrators and other forms of reparation such as civil claims for damages and/or administrative claims through fair and impartial proceedings. It will also include collective measures such as formal public recognition by the state of its responsibility, or official declarations and/ or commemorative ceremonies aimed at restoring victims' dignity, rehabilitation for victims, and guarantees of nonrepetition, which can include legal or administrative reform, dismantling of units, training, and public advocacy (United Nations, 2000). In some cases, it might be possible to bring a criminal prosecution or a civil claim for damages in the host state directly — this will usually necessitate the presence of the perpetrator or some other connection with the host state. For example, the Convention against Torture and Other Cruel, Inhuman or Degrading Treatment or Punishment (1987), Article 5(2) requires state parties "to take such measures as may be necessary to establish its jurisdiction over such offences in cases where the alleged offender is present in any territory under its jurisdiction and it does not extradite him."

Given that reparation is usually sought at the first instance from either the government whose official inflicted the torture and/or by pursuing a claim against the individual perpetrator, asylum seekers in a host country might need specialized advice in order to determine how best this might be achieved. Not only will there be legal hurdles, but the process is not guaranteed to lead to a positive result. Taking into account that asylum seekers have felt the need to flee from their countries of origin for fear of persecution, it is unlikely that these countries will exhibit the requisite political will to ensure that justice is done and seen to be done. There can be substantive or procedural barriers to bringing such claims, such as operable immunities for perpetrators of the worst crimes, delays and inefficiencies in the administration of justice, and difficulties in obtaining the forensic evidence necessary to support the claim. Often, successful claims will be predicated on the extent of external pressure and other leverage that is put to bear.

CONCLUSIONS

In this chapter, we have drawn on material illustrating the legal and policy context for refugees and asylum seekers at different stages of their journey. Any simple explanatory model for understanding the mental health needs of refugees is likely to be wrong, and more sophisticated explanations need to take full account of these and other contextual issues.

REFERENCES

African Commission on Human and Peoples' Rights. (1997, October). *Rencontre africaine pour la défense des droits de l'homme v.* Zambia. Comm. No. 71/92.

American Convention on Human Rights. (1978). O.A.S. Treaty Series No. 36, 1144 U.N.T.S. 123 entered into force July 18, 1978. In *Basic documents pertaining to human rights in the inter-American system.* OEA/Ser.L.V/II.82 doc.6 rev.1 at 25 (1992).

Bramsen, I., Dirkzwager, A. J. E., van Esch, S. C. M., & van der Ploeg, H. M. (2001). Consistency of self-reports of traumatic events in a population of Dutch peacekeepers: Reason for optimism? *Journal of Traumatic Stress, 14*(4), 733–740.

Brewin, C., Dalgleish, T., & Joseph, S. (1996). A dual representation theory of posttraumatic stress disorder. *Psychological Review, 103*(4), 671–686.

Brewin, C. R., Andrews, B., & Valentine, J. D. (2000). Meta-analysis of risk factors for posttraumatic stress disorder in trauma-exposed adults. *Journal of Consulting and Clinical Psychology, 68*(5), 748–766.

Cartagena Declaration on Refugees. (1984). Adopted at a colloquium entitled Coloquio Sobre la Proteccíon Internacional de los Refugiados en Américan Central, México y Panamá: Problemas Jurídicos y Humanitarios [Colloquium on the International Protection of Refugees in Central America, Mexico and Panama: Legal and Humanitarian Issues] held at Cartagena, Colombia, November 19–22, 1984.

European Commission. (2000). *Communication from the Commission to the Council and the European Parliament on the common asylum policy, introducing an open coordination method — First report by the Commission on the application of Communication.* COM(2000)755 final of November 22, 2000/COM/2001/0710 final/.

European Court of Human Rights (ECHR). (2000, October 5). *Maaouia v. France* (Application no. 39652/98).

Council of Europe. (1995). Recommendation 1261 on the situation of immigrant women in Europe, text adopted by the Standing Committee, acting on behalf of the Assembly, on March 15, 1995. See Doc. 7251, report of the Committee on Migration, Refugees and Demography, rapporteuse: Ms. Guirado.

Foa, E. B., & Riggs, D. S. (1993). Posttraumatic stress disorder in rape victims. In J. Oldham, M. B. Riba, & A. Tasman (Eds.), *American Psychiatric Press review of psychiatry* (Vol. 12, pp. 273–303). Washington, DC: American Psychiatric Press.

Gorst-Unsworth, C., & Goldenberg, E. (1998). Psychological sequelae of torture and organised violence suffered by refugees from Iraq: Trauma related factors compared with social factors in exile. *British Journal of Psychiatry, 172*, 90–94.

Herlihy, J., Scragg, P., & Turner, S. (2002). Discrepancies in autobiographical memories: Implications for the assessment of asylum seekers: Repeated interviews study. *British Medical Journal, 324*, 324–327.

Lipton, J. P. (1977). On the psychology of eyewitness testimony. *Journal of Applied Psychology, 62*(1), 90–95.

Organisation of African Unity. (1974). *Convention governing the specific aspects of refugee problems in Africa*, 1001 U.N.T.S. 45, entered into force 20 June 1974.

Ramsay, R., Gorst-Unsworth, C., & Turner, S. (1993). Psychiatric morbidity in survivors of organised state violence including torture. *British Journal of Psychiatry, 162*, 55–59.

Silove, D. M., McIntosh, P., & Becker, R. (1993). Risk of retraumatisation of asylum-seekers in Australia. *Australian and New Zealand Journal of Psychiatry, 27*(4), 606–612.

Silove, D., Sinnerbrink, I., Field, A., Manicavasagar, V., & Steel, Z. (1997). Anxiety, depression and PTSD in asylum-seekers: Associations with pre-migration trauma and post-migration stressors. *British Journal of Psychiatry, 170*, 351–357.

Southwick, S., Morgan, C. A., Nicolaou, A., & Charney, D. S. (1997). Consistency of memory for combat-related traumatic events in veterans of operation Desert Storm. *American Journal of Psychiatry, 154*(2), 173–177.

Steel, Z., Silove, D., Bird, K., McGorry, P. D., & Mohan, P. (1999). Pathways from war trauma to posttraumatic stress symptoms among Tamil asylum seekers, refugees, and immigrants. *Journal of Traumatic Stress, 12*(3), 421–435.

Summerfield, D. A., Gorst-Unsworth, C., Bracken, P. J., Tonge, V., Forrest, D. M., & Gillian, H. (1991). Detention in the UK of tortured refugees [letter]. *Lancet, 338*(8758), 58.

Turner, S., Bowie, C., Shapo, L., & Yule, W. (2003). Mental health of Kosovan Albanian refugees in the UK. *British Journal of Psychiatry, 182*, 444–448.

UK Immigration and Nationality Directorate. (1998) Assessing the Claim (Part II, Section 11). *Asylum directorate instructions.* http://www.ind.homeoffice.gov.uk/default.asp?PageId=3792.

United Nations. (1951). Convention relating to the status of refugees. Adopted 28 July 1951, entered into force 22 April 1954.

United Nations. (1987). Convention against torture and other cruel, inhuman or degrading treatment or punishment. Adopted by General Assembly resolution 39/46 of December 10, 1984 and entry into force June 26, 1987.

United Nations. (2000). The right to restitution, compensation and rehabilitation for victims of gross violations of human rights and fundamental freedoms. Final report of the Special Rapporteur, Professor M. Cherif Bassiouni, submitted in accordance with Commission resolution 1999/33, UN Doc. E/CN.4/2000/62, 18 January 2000.

United Nations Committee on Economic, Social and Cultural Rights (UNCESCR). (2000). General comment 14. The right to the highest attainable standard of health: 11/08/2000. E/C.12/2000/4.

United Nations Committee on Economic, Social and Cultural Rights (UNCE-SCR). (2002). Report on the 25th, 26th and 27th sessions (23 April–11 May 2001, 13–31 August 2001, 12–30 November 2001), Economic and Social Council Official Records. Supplement No. 2, E/2002/22, E/C.12/2001/17.

United Nations High Commissioner for Refugees (UNHCR). (1977a). Conclusions of the Executive Committee No. 6 (XXVIII).

United Nations High Commissioner for Refugees (UNHCR). (1977b). Conclusion of the Executive Committee No. 8 (XXVIII).

United Nations High Commissioner for Refugees (UNHCR). (1981). Executive Committee Conclusion 22.

United Nations High Commissioner for Refugees (UNHCR). (1987). Conclusions of the Executive Committee No. 47 (XXXVIII).

United Nations High Commissioner for Refugees (UNHCR). (1988). Conclusions of the Executive Committee No. 50 (XXXIX)

United Nations High Commissioner for Refugees (UNHCR). (1989). Conclusions of the Executive Committee No. 59 (XL).

United Nations High Commissioner for Refugees (UNHCR). (1992). Handbook on procedures and criteria for determining refugee status under the 1951 convention and the 1967 protocol relating to the status of refugees. Geneva: HCR/IP/4/Eng./Rev. 1/reedited.

United Nations High Commissioner for Refugees (UNHCR). (1998). Note on burden and standard of proof in refugee claims.

United Nations High Commissioner for Refugees (UNHCR). (1999). Revised guidelines on applicable criteria and standards relating to the detention of asylum seekers.

United Nations High Commissioner for Refugees (UNHCR). (2001). Reception of asylum seekers, including standards of treatment, in the context of individual asylum systems, global consultations on international protection. EC/GC/01/17, 4 September.

United Nations High Commissioner for Refugees (UNHCR). (2002a). Guidelines on international protection, gender-related persecution within the context of Article 1(A)2 of the 1951 convention and/or its 1967 protocol relating to the status of refugees. HCR/GIP/02/01, 7 May.

United Nations High Commissioner for Refugees (UNHCR). (2002b). Summary observations on the amended proposal by the European Commission for a council directive on minimum standards on procedures in member states for granting and withdrawing refugee status. COM 2000, 326 final/2, 18 June.

United Nations Human Rights Committee. (1994). General Comment 15. The position of aliens under the Covenant (Twenty-seventh session, 1986), Compilation of general comments and general recommendations adopted by human rights treaty bodies. UN Doc. HRI\GEN\1\Rev.1 at 18.

United Nations Working Group on Arbitrary Detention. (1997). Question of the human rights of all persons subjected to any form of detention or imprisonment. E/CN.4/1998/44.

Van-Velsen, C., Gorst-Unsworth, C., & Turner, S. (1996). Survivors of torture and organized violence: Demography and diagnosis. *Journal of Traumatic Stress, 9*(2), 181–193.

Williams, J. M. G., Watts, F., MacLeod, C., & Mathews, A. (1997). *Cognitive psychology and emotional disorders* (2nd ed.). Chichester: John Wiley & Sons.

25

The Politics of Asylum and Immigration Detention: Advocacy, Ethics, and the Professional Role of the Therapist

ZACHARY STEEL, SARAH MARES,
LOUISE NEWMAN, BIJOU BLICK, AND
MICHAEL DUDLEY

Increasingly a number of Western democratic countries appear to be turning away from their commitment to universal humanitarian principles. This is particularly evident following the events of September 11 and the associated introduction or attempted introduction of laws substantially infringing the rights and civil liberties of the general citizenry. The neglect of humanitarian principles is seen in the creation of extra-judicial detention zones, such as in the U.S. military prison at Guantanamo Bay, originally used to house Cuban and Haitian refugees, and in the refugee camps established by the Australian government on Manus Island in Papua New Guinea and the Island Republic of Nauru. A withdrawal from internationalism and associated commitment to international law is particularly evident in the United States and

Australia where there is a refusal to ratify or to translate into domestic law international human rights treaties and obligations.

The retreat from the humanitarian enterprise has been most marked in the manifest response to asylum seekers. Policies of deterrence have been variously pursued by the majority of Western democratic countries (Silove, Steel, & Watters, 2000). At the most fundamental level this has involved the implementation of visa and travel restrictions, preventing asylum seekers from making refugee protection claims at or within the border of Western countries. These strategies have been further augmented by stringent departure and transit document inspections with sanctions and fines leveled against companies transporting persons without valid travel documents. In late 2001, the Australian federal government further strengthened border protection initiatives by implementing a naval blockade of northern Australia, interdicting asylum seekers traveling from Indonesia and returning boats, or where this failed, transporting them to the aforementioned detention centers on Manus Island and Nauru. Accompanying legislation excised a number of Australian island territories from the Australian migration zone to ensure that any asylum seekers who managed to reach Australian shores would be unable to trigger Australia's protection obligations under the 1951 Refugee Convention and 1967 Protocol. Although the right of every country to protect the sovereignty of their borders is enshrined in international law, the UN High Commissioner for Refugees (UNHCR) has noted that such measures to restrict the movement of people have not only prevented the movement of illegal and irregular migrants, but have almost certainly obstructed the flight of people who have a genuine fear of persecution (UNHCR, 1997, p. 196).

Despite such strategies some 9 million asylum seekers have requested refugee protection within Western Europe, North America, and Australia over the period 1985 to 2002. The pressure posed by asylum seekers has led to a differentiated response by industrialized countries with the Anglophone countries of the United States, the United Kingdom, and Australia appearing to be at the forefront in the development and implementation of stringent asylum procedures (Silove, Steel, & Watters, 2000). These have variously included: restricted or no permission to work; restricted or no housing support; restricted or no access to welfare support; restricted or no access to health care; restricted or no access to legal services; through implementation of a narrow interpretation of the refugee convention, limited rights of independent judicial review; financial penalties for appealing negative refugee decisions; the issuing of temporary protection visas; and the detention of certain categories of asylum seekers in immigration facilities or state prisons.

The policies of deterrence pursued in response to spontaneous asylum seekers raise important practical and ethical issues that must be addressed by health practitioners. Governments pursuing such policies are in effect manufacturing difficulties and hardships for displaced and war-affected populations with the aim of ensuring that asylum seekers do not trigger protection obligations incurred as signatories to the Refugee Convention. The consequence of such "get tough on asylum seeker" policies are at least in part health related. The burgeoning research among refugee and postconflict populations has repeatedly documented ongoing risk to mental health problems, particularly depression and posttraumatic stress reactions (Cardozo, Vergara, Agani, & Gotway, 2000; de Jong, Mulhern, Ford, van der Kam, & Kleber, 2000; de Jong, Komproe, van Ommeren, El Masri, Araya, & Khaled, 2001; Modvig, Pagaduan-Lopez, Rodenburg, Salud, & Cabigon, 2000; Mollica et al., 1993, 1999). Research undertaken in Australia, one of the lead countries in the implementation of policies to deter asylum seekers, has demonstrated that postmigration stressors, most of them deliberately manufactured as part of the deterrence regime, are directly associated with deteriorating mental health (Silove, Sinnerbrink, Field, Manicavasagar, & Steel, 1997; Steel & Silove, 2000; Steel, Silove, Bird, McGorry, & Mohan, 1999).

The ethical problems arising from this policy approach are particularly acute with regard to use of indefinite nonreviewable mandatory detention of asylum seekers. The remainder of this chapter will focus on the professional, clinical, and ethical issues associated with the detention of asylum seekers as they have emerged within the Australian context.

DENYING THE SELF-EVIDENT: THE MENTAL HEALTH COSTS OF IMMIGRATION DETENTION IN AUSTRALIA

The conditions — the environment — is particularly harsh. It's a moon scape. It's dust and rubble. There's no grass inside the compound. There's sparse brush on the red desert outside the compound. There's one tree in the main compound, double palisade fencing around the entire perimeter with razor wire top and bottom. There are different compounds divided up by fences. Quite often there are barriers between the compounds so that detainees can't see, or hear, one another speaking or see each other. It's particularly hot in summer. The main compound: there was a temperature of 61 degree Celsius [142° Fahrenheit] recorded the summer that I was there and it's bitterly cold at night in winter.

Mark Huxstep, former nurse, Woomera Immigration Reception and Processing Centre. Evidence provided to Human Rights and Equal Opportunity, Public Hearing, National Inquiry into Children in Immigration Detention, August 5, 2002

In 1992 the Australian federal fovernment passed legislation enforcing a policy requiring the mandatory detention of all persons arriving in Australia without valid entry documents. Since then the vast majority of unauthorized asylum seekers and accompanying children have been detained for the full duration of the refugee determination process or until removal procedures have been enforced. Many asylum seekers are held in detention for indefinite and often considerable periods of time. A report into the conditions of detention in 1998 (Human Rights & Equal Opportunity Commission, 1998) identified over 80 detainees who had been held in detention between 2 and 5 years. A case is cited of two Cambodian brothers aged 16 and 19 years who were detained for 5 and a half years before being released without a final decision regarding their status being made. The most recent departmental figures (April 12, 2002) indicates that there were 346 individuals held for between 12 to 18 months and 256 individuals held in excess of 18 months.

Throughout the 12-year history of this policy, the detention centers have been plagued by controversy. Riots, damage to property, hunger strikes, acts of self-harm, and attempted suicides have gained national and international media attention. Statistics obtained under freedom of information legislation revealed that during an 8-month period from March 2001 to October 2001, 264 incidents of self-harm requiring medical attention came to the attention of authorities in a population comprising approximately 2,000 persons. Using these figures, Dudley (2003) estimates that the annual self-harm rates for men and women held in detention are 41 and 26 times the male and female national suicide attempt and self-harm rates respectively.

The policy of mandatory detention and the operation of the detention facilities in Australia has attracted widespread criticism from national and international human rights bodies and organizations such as the United Nations High Commissioner for Refugees (1997), the United Nations Commissioner on Human Rights (OHCHR, 2002), UNICEF (2002), the Australian Human Rights and Equal Opportunity Commission (HREOC, 1998), the Australian Commonwealth Ombudsman (Commonwealth Ombudsman, 2001), Amnesty International (2002), Human Rights Watch (2002) and the U.S. Committee for Refugees (2002). A key issue raised to the Australian government from these bodies has been the poor mental state of detainees and particularly children held for protracted periods.

Annie Sparrow, a senior registrar in pediatrics who worked in one of the remote detention centers during 2001 and 2002, stated that:

> Of particular concern to us [i.e., health care staff] are the specific problems related to children in detention. There are a number of children who have been born in detention and who often appear to be developmentally delayed. They have no grass, no dedicated area, no space to be with other infants, play and interact, and hence no stimulation. Other pressures facing children in detention are: the ongoing exposure to trauma of parents and siblings, witnessing acts of violence between officers and detainees, self-harm, mutilation and attempted hangings. Many of them show signs of significant post-traumatic stress disorder and are clingy, withdrawn, quiet and difficult to engage. Secondary nocturnal enuresis is a common problem in child detainees, for which the only current solution is the provision of nappies. Children are commonly known to be sleeping with their parents again out of

fear and anxiety. (Professional Alliance for the Health of Asylum Seekers and Their Children, 2002)

Similar concerns have been raised by key members of the immigration detention advisory group established by the Australian federal government to provide advice on the appropriateness and adequacy of detention services, accommodation and facilities. On May 8, 2002, Paris Aristotle, a member of IDAG and a mental health professional, told a media program regarding the Woomera Detention Centre in South Australia that:

> a culture of self-harm and the extent to which depression and anxiety are dominant within the population at the detention centre has now really become endemic and had reached quite a staggering degree. And what was obvious to us was that no matter how hard people were going to try, … it's now reached a point where, I think, it's actually impossible for them to prevent harm occurring within the centre at Woomera, and particularly in the case of children. (Lateline, 2002b)

On another occasion Harry Minas, a psychiatrist sitting on the same committee, stated that:

> Prolonged detention is psychologically harmful to children, particularly when the prolonged detention is in circumstances such as those at Woomera. Children are exposed to all kinds of behavior, all kinds of problems. In Woomera at various times there have been episodes of self harm, some of which have been witnessed by children, there have been some episodes of violence again witnessed by children. But I think also being in prolonged detention can seriously distort family relationships so that the parents of those children don't have the opportunity to look after them properly. (Lateline, 2002a)

In addition to these anecdotal reports, systematic evidence documenting severe mental health conditions among long-term detainees has emerged from a number of health surveys undertaken within the detention environment. The Victorian Foundation for Survivors of Torture (Paris Aristotle, personal communication, November 16, 2001) carried out a file audit of clinical assessments undertaken with 46 Cambodian asylum seekers, representing the majority of Cambodians held in Villawood and Port Hedland detention centers from late 1993 to mid-1994. At the time of interview a significant number had been detained in excess of 2 years. Clinical interviews indicated that the majority of the Cambodians had histories of trauma or multiple trauma, with 62% meeting diagnostic criteria for posttraumatic stress disorder and all displaying clinically significant symptoms of depression. The clinicians undertaking this survey concluded that the major factor that appeared to be contributing to the severity of the clinical conditions encountered was the duration of detention.

Maritza Thompson and colleagues (1998) reported the findings of a survey of 25 detained Tamil asylum seekers held at Maribyrnong Detention Centre in Melbourne during 1997 and 1998, using the Harvard Trauma Questionnaire (Mollica et al., 1992) and the Hopkins Symptom Checklist (Mollica, Wyshak, de Marneffe, Khuon, & Lavelle, 1987). Detainees exhibited a significantly higher level of depression, posttraumatic stress, anxiety, panic, and physical symptoms, compared to 62 compatriot Tamil asylum seekers residing in the community. A third study undertaken by Sultan and O'Sullivan (2001) reported that 32 of 33 detainees surveyed at an immigration detention center in Sydney displayed symptoms consistent with a major depressive illness, with 16 persons showing severe emotional distress. As with the Cambodian study the authors documented a significant deterioration in the mental health of detainees as the length of detention increased.

THE CASE OF SHAYAN BADRAIE

The plight of asylum seekers in detention was vividly brought to the attention of the broader Australian and medical community in Australia when the investigative journalist Debbie Whitmont screened a video secretly filmed in one of the detention centers on the Four Corners program in August 2001. The video contained footage of a 7-year-old boy, Shayan Badraie, who had been held in detention for 14 months. The footage showed a boy who was cradled in his mother's arms, he was mute, refusing to eat and was too weak to walk. He was being wheeled about the detention center by his parents in a wheel barrow. Shayan was 6-years-old when he first presented to a children's hospital emergency department having stopped eating and talking. During an 11 month period in a remote detention center Shayan had witnessed acute distress among detainees, riots, and self-harming behaviors, including attempted self-immolation. He had been distressed since this time with chronic sleep disturbance, nightmares, and bed-wetting. After transfer to an urban detention center he witnessed a man attempting suicide by wrist cutting and had become withdrawn and mute. Shayan was found to be dehydrated and underweight and was admitted for rehydration. He began talking and eating while in the hospital. He described nightmares about suicidal behavior and ongoing features of posttraumatic stress disorder. He was fixatedly drawing the same picture over and over again, consisting of a man with a line on his wrist and drops of blood coming down. He and his father, stepmother, and sister were depicted behind wire with tears flowing down from their eyes (see Figure 25.1).

On discharge the treating clinicians recommended that Shayan and his family be removed from the physically restraining environment of the detention center and advised that if Shayan remained in detention he would likely relapse. This advice was ignored and as predicted Shayan re-presented 6 days later, refusing to eat or drink. For the hospital staff

Fig. 25.1   Drawing by Shayan Badraie

this triggered a discussion with the detention center provider, Australasian Correctional Management, the Department of Immigration, and the detention center medical services. Hospital staff argued that returning Shayan to detention could only result in a repeat of this situation, and that this was clearly against his best interests. The children's hospital saw itself as having a duty of care to protect Shayan from retraumatization, and this put them in direct conflict with the detention center and the Department of Immigration. After 8 weeks, and significant clinical improvement, he was discharged to the detention center as no resolution about community release had emerged, despite appeals to the responsible minister. Over the following month Shayan repeatedly re-presented to the emergency department with food refusal, dehydration, and weight loss. It was only after the public airing of this case by the Four Corners program that the Minister of Immigration decided to act, removing Shayan from his family and placing him in foster care, against the advice of the hospital. Shayan became extremely distressed at the separation from his family, expressed suicidal ideation, and had ongoing symptoms of posttraumatic stress disorder. The placement remained tenuous and Shayan's mother, sister, and subsequently his father were granted visas and released from detention. He continues to receive trauma counseling.

WHEN MEDICAL ADVICE IS NOT APPRECIATED

The case of Shayan Badraie raised complex clinical and ethical dilemmas for all clinicians involved. A key concern was the need to protect the child from harm and the immediate opposition this set up with the Department of Immigration and the policy of mandatory detention. Clinicians raised their concerns that "treatment" became meaningless or was undermined when the child was returned to the same environment linked to his trauma and ongoing symptoms. For some this signified a fundamental erosion of the clinical role and highlighted issues of clinical decision-making. Clinicians essentially became advocates for the rights of the child for protection and care within a highly politicized context, raising questions regarding the boundaries of the clinical role.

This case sent shock waves throughout peak medical and allied health organizations in Australia. At no time in recent Australian history had the extreme mental suffering of a child been so vividly juxtaposed against a governmental response of indifference. In responding to the Four Corners revelations, the Minister for Immigration, who persistently referred to Shayan as "it," suggested, in contrast to the findings of all the treating clinicians, that his mental condition was due solely to premigration experiences or because he was being cared for by a stepmother.

Shortly following the public airing of the Shayan story, the Royal Australasian College of Physicians (RACP), and Royal Australian and New Zealand College of Psychiatrists (RANZCP), issued a press statement expressing their concern for the welfare of children held in detention and called on the government to undertake an independent, expert review of the impact of detention on children at the earliest possible opportunity, a view endorsed by the president of the Australian Medical Association, Dr. Kerryn Phelps. The lack of an appropriate governmental response to these concerns led to the development of the Professional Alliance for the Health of Asylum Seekers and Their Children. The alliance brought together all medical colleges and guild organizations across Australia as well as other allied health organizations comprising over 50,000 doctors and health professionals. This represented the single largest alliance of health professionals formed on a social issue in Australian history. In May 2002, the alliance submitted a comprehensive review of the best available evidence about the effects of detention on the health and well-being of children and adults (Professional Alliance for the Health of Asylum Seekers and Their Children, 2002), calling for the immediate release of children and their primary caregivers from detention and concluding that "Current practices of detention of infants and children are having immediate effects on their development and their psychological and emotional health which are likely to extend to the longer term."

Nevertheless, despite the expert health opinion reflected in the health alliance statements and submissions; the concerns raised about mental health by independent investigations (Commonwealth Ombudsman, 2001; HREOC, 1998; OHCHR, 2002; UNHCR, 1997); the body of testimonial evidence provided by health staff in direct contact with detainees; and the research evidence reviewed above, a representative of the Department of Immigration stated in April 2003 that:

> While the Department is aware that some detainees may experience difficulties in immigration detention, it is not aware of any independent, scientifically rigorous Australian or comparable overseas data or research to support claims that mental illness is endemic among detainees held in immigration detention.

And concluded: "Unfortunately mental health is an area that attracts a number of allegations. Without verification, these remain no more than hearsay" (Mason, 2003, p. 5).

In response key members of the aforementioned health alliance released the findings of research conducted with 10 families comprising 14 adults and 20 children held in a detention center for over 2 years (Steel, 2003). The study was based on a near complete sample of families from the same ethnic group held in a single detention facility in remote Australia. Structured psychiatric telephone interviews were administered to assess lifetime and current psychiatric morbidity. Findings indicated that exposure to trauma, including witnessing riots, assaults, and serious self-harm attempts was routine within the detention environment. All adults and the majority of children reported being regularly distressed by memories, intrusive thoughts, and nightmares about traumatic experiences that had occurred in detention. The results from the structured diagnostic interviews indicated that all adults and children met diagnostic criteria for at least one psychiatric illness with the majority of adults (12/14) and children (16/20) meeting criteria for more than one psychiatric disorder. The most commonly diagnosed conditions were major depression and posttraumatic stress disorder, although high rates of separation anxiety disorder, enuresis, and oppositional defiant disorder were identified among the children. Comparison with the lifetime and current diagnoses indicated a threefold and tenfold increase in psychopathology among adults and children, respectively, subsequent to detention. The official response from the Minister for Immigration was to dismiss the findings of this study out of hand:

> The *Study of Asylum Seekers in Remote Detention Centres* by University of New South Wales researchers has received wide yet unquestioning media coverage, but it is seriously flawed. It is apparent that it is based on preconceived ideas of the researchers who have been advocates of the dismantling of mandatory detention and who followed a particular line of questioning and reasoning to ensure a result satisfactory to themselves. (Ruddock, 2003)

Another strategy used in the Australian context to minimize issues related to mental illness among detainees has been to reinterpret the definition of mental illness excluding depression.

> *Reporter* (SBS, Insight Program): The World Health Organisation, the Royal Australian New Zealand College of Psychiatry, the Federal Health Ministry says that depression is a mental illness. Does it

concern you that the Department is not classifying depression amongst detainees as a mental illness when those figures are asked for?

Philip Ruddock (Minister for Immigration): Not really. I think I mean as long as you can deal with the various conditions and describe them — as I say, depression is quite significant in the Australian community and people are treated for it and I'm not sure that everybody would regard depression as being a mental illness. Now, you, look you may have some colleges and World Health Organisations that will describe it that way, but I'm not sure it would be seen that way more broadly in the Australian community. (Insight Program, 2003)

This exchange and the departmental decision not to classify depression as a mental illness when reporting on the health of detainees are deliberate and self-evident attempts to prevent information regarding the extent of mental illness within detention from being known.

"Moving the (scientific) goalposts" and forays by the minister into areas beyond his expertise are indications that "science" and "evidence" are terms that have become overtly politicized in this context. These statements are also in contradiction with major health initiatives of other arms of government (Dudley, 2003) and demonstrate the extent to which those responsible for the implementation and management of mandatory indefinite detention will go to hide the suffering of those under its care. However, the systematic attempt on the part of the Australian federal government, to minimize, trivialize, and deny the alleged mental health harms associated with protracted immigration detention might be necessary to maintain the legality of mandatory detention. The putative reasons advanced for the use of mandatory detention are essentially administrative, to ensure that individuals are available for processing and removal from Australia, should that become necessary or possible. Officially detention is not punitive, and if it was shown to be punitive, the practice would likely be unlawful under Australian Constitutional Law. Nevertheless, the Australian government does accept that it has a high level of duty of care to detained asylum seekers and argues that it meets its duty of care obligations to psychologically affected detainees by providing access to mental health care (Ruddock, 2002).

CAUGHT IN THE MIDDLE: CLINICIANS CARING AND ADVOCATING FOR DETAINEES

A therapeutic process of any client is long term, developing a relationship, getting to know the person's story, getting to know what's happening with that person and then making appropriate treatment recommendations, etcetera. As I said, I think and I believe that I did a good job in Woomera while I was there. I have to believe that for my own well being but I also have to acknowledge, that I was working in a no win environment because I couldn't change the environment.

No matter how much I worked with the clients, I couldn't change the cause of the behaviour, the course of their stress, it's like having a patient coming into the hospital with a nail through the hand and you are giving them Pethidine injections for pain but you don't remove the nail. That's exactly what is happening in Woomera. You've got people down there with nails through their hands, we're holding them, we're not treating the cause. So, the trauma, the torture, the infection is growing. We are not treating it, we're just containing it. Eventually when those people return to their homelands, if they don't get temporary visas, they are going to carry that with them.

> Harold Bilboe, former psychologist, Woomera Immigration Reception and Processing Centre. Evidence provided at Human Rights and Equal Opportunity Public Hearing into Children in Detention, July 16, 2002

Clinicians working with detentees are in contact with severely distressed and traumatized children and adults, whose trauma is in no small part due to their indefinite detention under Australian law. Initial optimism on the part of clinicians and a belief in being able to make a difference is replaced over time by a sense of powerlessness, anger, and guilt akin to that experienced by detainees. This is not simply vicarious traumatization or empathy for their plight. Rather, it arises as a consequence of engaging with and advocating against the legal and political framework that makes up current immigration law in Australia, in circumstances where clinically based recommendations are ignored, adequate access to services is denied, and detention, in its various forms, continues.

Empathy and Vicarious Traumatization

Vicarious traumatization is a term used to describe the effect on health workers and other professionals of exposure to the stories of traumatized patients (McCann, 1990). This occurs in many contexts and is recognized as a consequence of clinical work with survivors of torture and trauma. The impact can be due to the severity or volume of the traumatic accounts and occurs in large part because of the therapist's empathy with and concern for the person recounting the story. In making a clinical assessment the therapist aims to listen and empathize, to understand the experience behind the words. This exposes him or her to the experience and the feelings of the adult or child even if distress is indirectly expressed. Sometimes the poignancy of the actual words also carries great weight. A 13-year-old girl in detention said to one of us (SM) "My brother (aged 3 years), doesn't know what flowers look like. What has he done that is so wrong?" The family had been in a remote detention center since the boy was an infant. Later she said, "I feel worst in the evenings when the sky is dusky, like my mood it gets darker. I have no life here. I wish to be dead."

When a traumatic story is told by a child, either in words, or drawings, or enacted in play, the impact can be particularly intense. A child can make great efforts to draw his or her "best picture," carefully coloring it in. Great distress is conveyed in the incongruity of the simple colored drawing and the horror of the content. Figure 25.2 is a picture drawn by a 9-year-old girl after she witnesses riots.

Usually the trauma encountered by torture and trauma survivors has occurred in the past. The clinician is therefore able to use the relative safety of current circumstances as part of containing the patient's distress and beginning a process of working through and managing the impact of past abuses. In work with traumatized children, the parents, school, and community can be mobilized as resources to support recovery. Asylum seekers held in detention have not only experienced past trauma, abuse, and loss, but are living in a situation of entrapment, faced with constant uncertainty about their future safety. Significantly, all detainees, including children, report ongoing traumatic experiences within immigration detention. The events and the trauma is not past, but present, and extends indefinitely into the future. The clinician hears the stories and is unable to act protectively or therapeutically.

All the children interviewed by us in remote detention centers, amounting to in excess of 50 children, have witnessed repeated acts of self-harm by adults, including cutting, attempted hangings, self-poisoning, and jumping onto razor wire. Many children had also harmed themselves and were troubled by intrusive thoughts of suicide or images of self-harm and violence. The therapist is confronted with terrible stories of distress and trauma about current, ongoing events. There is a reversal of what is taken for granted about parenting and child protection anywhere else in Australia.

Fig. 25.2   Drawing by 9-Year-Old Girl Following Riots in Detention

In this world of "noncitizens," children believe they carry responsibility for their parents' and siblings' safety and for sexual assault. Infants remain in circumstances of high risk. Parents are incapacitated by guilt and grief as they witness the impact of events upon their children. Recommendations by child protection workers are ignored, as are those by clinicians (Layton, 2003). The clinician can do little but conclude that the setting is a major source of the children's distress and contributes significantly to the parents' inability to adequately protect and nurture their children. Assessments to this effect arise out of clinical observation and experience but are politicized by their inherent conflict with immigration policy. Recommendations that the child and family cannot be adequately treated or cared for in detention have almost universally been ignored. The individual clinician confronted with such devastating outcomes, powerless to act, experiences more than vicarious traumatization as they experience the ongoing trauma of the asylum seeker, they are directly exposed to ongoing trauma.

Naivety and Politicization

Clinicians are not usually trained in politics or sociology. They operate professionally within a system where their expertise is acknowledged and remunerated. They are used to listening and being listened to. They regularly advocate, with effect, for their patients at individual and policy levels. The patients and families they see, whatever their level of disability or disadvantage, are citizens of their own country. They are operating within the "social contract" conferred by citizenship.

In early 2002 a number of us (SM, MD) visited remote detention facilities in south Australia. We went at the request of lawyers representing families whose initial claims for refugee status had been refused and who were psychologically distressed. The aim of our visit was twofold: first to undertake medico-legal assessments that could, if appropriate, be used to support individual families' legal applications, to enable them to live in the community while their asylum claims were processed, and second, to recommend access to mental health treatment for those families. Adults and children were introduced to us by number not name. In small ways we were intimidated and bullied by detention center officers. We saw the harsh and pitiless environment within which children and young adults wandered aimlessly in the sun without hats or shoes. We visited the air conditioned, clean toilet for detention and immigration staff and also saw the dusty, blood-spattered filthy toilets available for detainees. More than this, we heard and felt the despair of the adults and children interviewed. We were motivated to help. We wrote reports and papers and made recommendations. We believed, and so did the people we spoke to, that we could make a difference, that our recommendations would be acted on and that as medical specialists, our words would count.

When we enter the world of detention, despite physically remaining on what appears to be Australian soil, we cross a border that puts us and the adults and children we talk to outside of Australia's legal and political system. We enter a zone where usual conceptions of human rights and obligations to others do not apply. Asylum seekers in immigration detention are officially "unauthorized noncitizens." In a letter to one of us (SM, Phillip Ruddock, personal communication, April 28, 2003), the Minister for Immigration wrote: "the state has the sovereign right to determine which non-citizens can enter the country, those that can remain, and the conditions under which any may be removed. ... While deterrence is not a primary purpose of detention, it is an important incidental factor."

The unauthorised noncitizen is not just "them" or "other" by virtue of their statelessness, their nationality, their cultural and religious affiliation, but most importantly by virtue of their "noncitizenship." Aspects of difference or "otherness" have been used to politicize the national debate and "dehumanize" the public image of these vulnerable individuals. At an administrative level, the naive and well-intentioned clinician encounters a system within which not only those they advocate for, but they themselves have no currency and little power. The role of doctor and clinical advocate is altered by "crossing over" into the jurisdiction of immigration law. The social contract, as we usually experience it, does not operate here. As a consequence, our words have no power. At a legislative level in Australia, immigration law overrules federal and state health and child protection legislation. This takes time to understand for the naive clinician who embarks on the process of advocacy for this group with an expectation of making a difference and with little awareness of the obstacles to be encountered. This is echoed at a service level. Some state governments have signed a Memorandum of Understanding with the federal government concerning the health and welfare of detainees. The implications of this for children in immigration detention and state child protection services (in this case in south Australia) are discussed in detail by Layton (2003), who writes:

> Most importantly the Memorandum of Understanding does not recognise the serious systemic abuse of children in detention and that the most serious abuse does not come from individuals, but arises from the circumstances of detention itself. ... The State government is being placed in an impossible legal and moral position." (Ch. 22, p. 14)

COMPROMISING CLINICAL CARE AND THE INTEGRITY OF THE CLINICIAN

> A doctor [sic health professional] must have complete clinical independence in deciding upon the care of a person for whom he or she is medically responsible. The doctor's fundamental role is to alleviate

distress of his or her fellow men, and no motive, whether personal, collective or political, shall prevail against this higher purpose.

The Declaration of Tokyo, 1975 (29th World Medical Association)

Health professionals engage with the detention regime, either on the outside as consultants, advocates, or critics, or on the inside as health staff employees. Those employed on the inside face particular threats to their clinical integrity. In earlier manifestations of immigration detention, such as in the closed refugee camps of Hong Kong in the 1980s and early 1990s, health care services were provided by the Red Cross, or other NGOs and were administratively independent from the management of the detention centers. This enabled health staff to be clearly delineated from those responsible for the security and daily operational management of the centers. The psychological importance of this distinction for the health professional and for the detainees cannot be overstated. Independent health staff can be seen as confidantes and advocates who can sympathize and identify with the plight of detainees and speak out on their behalf.

In contrast, in Australia, health and mental health professionals are employed by the detention center provider, currently Australasian Correctional Management, a subsidiary of the U.S. company Wackenhut Corrections Corporation. It is fanciful to believe that incarcerated asylum seekers can reconcile the anomaly that the organization responsible for overseeing their incarceration and thus their mental and psychological distress is also responsible for providing a service that aims to treat their mental health needs. The despondency, anger, and feelings of injustice of detained asylum seekers is palpable and increases as the period of detention continues. This anger is directed at all staff associated with the system that holds them against their will, and it is unlikely that health staff will be immune, especially as it becomes apparent to detainees that health professionals are unable to resolve the main threat to their mental health (i.e., continued incarceration). This is only compounded by the fact that Australasian Correctional Management has required health staff to wear a uniform that is virtually indistinguishable from the general uniforms of other detention center officers.

Health care practitioners are caught in a highly charged political environment, regardless of their own personal views on the matter. The culture of security, coercive management, and violence existing in Australian detention centers has created a gulf of misunderstanding, mistrust, and resentment between detainees and staff. Health staff are also not immune from such a culture. A majority of detainees we have spoken to have stated their belief that health staff have a promanagement and antidetainee bias, with complaints that all health conditions are treated with general advice to drink more water or by the administration of paracetamol and sedatives. Whether or not such claims are accurate is immaterial, as the mere perception that health staff are working in the interest of the detention center provider and not in the interests of the detainees is problematic and highlights the major difficulties that face clinicians in these settings. Moreover, regardless of the personal commitment and competencies of an individual health care practitioner, the provision of care is often compromised by the structure of the detention centers. This is well illustrated in the following testimony provided by Mark Huxstep, a former nurse at the Woomera Immigration Reception and Processing Centre, in a statement to Human Rights and Equal Opportunity Public Hearing into Children in Detention on August 5, 2002:

> There was a child who presented to the medical centre and it just so happened that her mother was a qualified doctor in her country of origin, and the child had a painful ear, so the child was given a simple pain killer that evening and referred to the doctor the next morning, who diagnosed an ear infection and put the child on regular pain killers and antibiotics. It was a liquid antibiotic that had to be refrigerated. The detainees aren't allowed to take medications back to their rooms for fear that they will overdose or collect them or whatever the rationale, and so therefore they had to come to the medical centre four times a day to get their medications. That meant coming every six hours with a small child with a sore ear who was crying in the middle of winter at night time, waiting for two hours in a queue at the gate in the freezing cold and it just happened to rain one night, and the mother was terribly distraught. She said, "I'm bringing a sick child to stand in a queue in the cold and the rain for two hours to get treatment," and I had no answer because it was true.

Julie's Story

Julie was pregnant at the time she and her husband fled Iran due to fear of persecution. After a traumatic journey by boat, they arrived in Australia and were held in detention. Julie was transferred to a hospital to give birth to her child, Nadi, but according to her testimony was distressed by the fact that detention center guards were present in the delivery room throughout her labor. Julie's husband was not allowed to attend during the delivery and did not see his wife and child until 5 days after the birth. Julie rejoined her husband in the detention center, but experienced ongoing gynecological problems relating to the birth. She became depressed and anxious. Repeated presentation to the health care staff at the detention center did not result in any effective treatment for these problems. Concerns about Julie's and Nadi's health prompted visitors to the detention center to present Nadi as a child at risk to the state child protection agency. In February 2002 the responsible department assessed the family and found that:

> The information obtained from Julie and her husband regarding her physical and mental health contrasted significantly with that obtained

from the medical clinic staff at the detention centre. The clinic staff reported that Julie was not withdrawn in any way, had never at any stage been depressed and had bonded well with baby.

In contrast Julie and her husband stated that "she has had a poor appetite for at least six months, is not eating much and feels depressed. She cries every day, sometimes three or four times. Her weight has gone down from about 51 to 45 kg since having the baby." The report concluded that "From her history it is likely that Julie is depressed and has been so for about nine or ten months. It is possible, and could readily be checked up, that she has a gynaecological infection. ... Nadi is exposed to significant risk resulting from her mother's depression." The report made three clear recommendations:

1. release of the whole family into the community pending the processing of their documentation;
2. referral of Julie and Nadi to a community baby clinic;
3. urgent referral of Julie to a gynaecologist and a psychiatrist in the community.

These recommendations were not acted upon and Julie's condition continued to deteriorate despite further representations and requests for treatment to the medical staff at the detention center. Two further interventions by the state child protection agency were made stressing the need to act on earlier recommendations.

In crisis, Julie's husband contacted visitors to the detention center who organized for two independent medical practitioners to visit Julie. On arrival these doctors were informed that they were unable to examine Julie without obtaining formal permission from the Department of Immigration. After considerable negotiation, permission to visit Julie informally was obtained, and the Department of Immigration agreed to facilitate contact with her treating physician. However, the primary care physician employed by the detention center was advised not to speak to the outside doctors by the private detention center provider. It was possible to speak to the clinic nurses in the presence of the detention center manager, who stated that Julie had been treated for the past few weeks with sedation but had commenced an antidepressant 2 days previously. They did not know if Julie was taking adequate fluids or eating, as they could not monitor this in the detention center. Julie herself arrived in a wheelchair. She presented as severely depressed, emaciated, and appeared acutely unwell, with obvious signs of sepsis, dehydration, sedation, and altered affect. A letter recommending urgent hospitalization was written but ignored.

A subsequent formal visit by independent paediatric and psychiatrist specialists was organized 3 days later through Julie's lawyers. Assessment indicated that Julie had a combination of major depression, physical compromise, and infection, which was potentially life threatening and required urgent hospitalization along with her baby, Nadi. Julie was admitted to a local hospital that evening. Her acute medical condition was treated and she was transferred to an inpatient psychiatric unit. After further representations and media intervention, her baby, Nadi, joined her several days later. Julie and Nadi were subsequently transferred to an acute adult psychiatric unit for treatment of severe postnatal depression, where she was continuously guarded by two officers from the detention center. Julie could not be moved to an appropriate mother-baby facility due to the fact that the detention center officers did not have appropriate child protection clearance for such a transfer, and permission could not be obtained from the detention provider to have her moved without the officers. Despite this Julie and Nadi both showed substantial clinical improvement while in the hospital. Julie's treating psychiatrists felt that they could not in good conscience release her back into detention as this retraumatization would be potentially life-threatening to Julie and possibly Nadi. This put them in direct conflict with the detention center and the Department of Immigration, and delayed discharge. Despite representations made by a wide variety of agencies, an impasse remained. Julie and Nadi remained in the hospital for over 5 months until she was eventually granted leave by the Minister for Immigration to remain in Australia, possibly reflecting a compromise solution to the impasse between hospital staff and the Department of Immigration.

This case highlights a number of complexities involved in the provision of health care to immigration detainees. The detention environment in this case did not allow health professionals employed by the private detention operator to adequately discharge their duty of care. This is clearly indicated by the discrepancy between the findings of the detention clinic health staff and the subsequent six physicians and specialists who assessed Julie and her baby. It was extremely difficult for all of those involved on the outside to establish a clear line of responsibility between the Department of Immigration and the detention center operator for the welfare of Julie (for example, the department gave permission for the doctor employed by the detention center operator to speak to independent medical practitioners but the detention operator did not). The inability of other lead agencies involved in the welfare of families, such as the child protection agency and the hospital, to have their treatment recommendations acted upon was undermined. The fact that detention guards who regularly deal with children (including unaccompanied minors in detention) do not require the same child protection clearance as other workers in the community is another example of the different standards of care for immigration detainees compared with the general community. The conflict of interest between the Department of Immigration and the detention center operator's charter to detain people and their responsibility to provide humane and appropriate care is also a primary reason for the failure of care highlighted in this case.

More direct threats to the clinical integrity of health care practitioner arise in respect to the management of detainees engaging in self-harm, suicide attempts, or hunger strikes. Australasian Correctional Management employ the high-risk assessment team (HRAT) approach developed in prison settings to manage suicide risk and self-harming behavior (Dudley, 2003). People who have engaged in acts of self-harm or who are considered to be at risk of future self-harm are placed on periodic observations from every 2 hours to every 2 minutes. In practice those placed on HRAT are generally placed in isolation to reduce the risk of completed suicide, with testimonial evidence suggesting that removal is often to a management block with cell-like rooms, sometimes without toilet facilities or may even involve removal to a police lockup (Four Corners, 2003). The HRAT alert will be maintained until the risk of self-harm is considered to have subsided, a decision that will often depend on assessment by health or mental health personnel. The HRAT regime appears aimed at avoiding liability for breaches of duty of care, which can result in suicide, and is not informed by notions of clinical care (Dudley, 2003). Individuals can be kept in effective isolation for days or week as a result of this approach. A psychiatric problem is recharacterized as a behavioral management program, with good behavior rewarded by release to the open detention compound. As argued by Dudley (2003), because the HRAT model does not address the contextual reasons driving self-harming behavior, it creates an environment of emotional escalation that leads inevitably to an endemic institutional culture of self-harm. The health care practitioner faces the dilemma of whether or not to identify a detainee under their care as being at risk of suicide or self-harm, knowing that the HRAT approach is aimed at the prevention of self-harm but not at the alleviation of the symptoms driving the behavior.

The management of hunger strikers also poses particular dilemmas for medical staff in detention, who are invested with the authority to request medical intervention to provide involuntary nourishment under the Australian Migration Act (Silove, Curtis, Masor, & Becker, 1996; Kenny, Silove, & Steel, 2004). General declarations relevant to the practice of all physicians emphasize respect for the autonomy of the individual and the right of the hunger striker to determine what shall be done with his or her own body. The 1975 Declaration of Tokyo, articulated at the 29th Congress of the World Medical Association, reinforces this principle: "Where a prisoner refuses nourishment and is considered by the doctor as capable of forming an unimpaired and rational judgment concerning the consequences of such a voluntary refusal of nourishment, he or she shall not be fed artificially." The Declaration of Tokyo (World Medical Association, 1975) has been, since its adoption in 1975, the most comprehensive statement produced by the medical profession on the question of torture and cruel, inhuman, or degrading treatment of detainees (Amnesty International, 2000). More detailed ethical guidelines on the management of hunger strikers have been articulated in the Declaration of Malta (World Medical Association, 1992) adopted by the 43rd assembly of the World Medical Association. While acknowledging the extreme difficulties faced by the physician in the management of hunger strikers the declaration reiterates the principle that:

> It is the duty of the doctor to respect the autonomy which the patient has over his person. A doctor requires informed consent from his patients before applying any of his skills to assist them, unless emergency circumstances have arisen in which case the doctor has to act in what is perceived to be the patient's best interests.

There appears to be little evidence that principles articulated in either the Tokyo or Malta Declarations are adhered to or even considered in the management of hunger strikers in Australian detention centers as reflected by the following exchange with the Australian Minister for Immigration on this issue.

> ***Damien Carrick:*** I also asked Phillip Ruddock if he was concerned that Australian doctors might be acting inconsistently with directives from the World Medical Association when it comes to the treatment of hunger strikers.

> ***Phillip Ruddock:*** Well I haven't got the faintest idea what some medical directions from overseas might be, and quite frankly, I don't care whether or not there is some international body that has a view about when you should force people to undertake certain procedures. We're not dealing with the sorts of situations where people would be making sensible decisions in relation to their own future, as they might if they were in the community, we're dealing with people who believe that they can manipulate government decision making by behaving in a way which may have quite adverse consequences for themselves, and that needs to be taken into account. (Law Report, 2002)

During 2001, 40 requests for the provision of involuntary nourishment to hunger strikers in Australian detention centers were authorized by the Immigration Department. The provision of a standard pro forma letter for such an intervention (see Figure 25.3) by the detention center provider creates an administrative framework that encourages and enables the treating physician to regard the provision of involuntary nourishment as a routine, ethically unproblematic, medical procedure. While the treating physician is not compelled to seek such an order, the provision of a pro forma letter encourages the doctor to act in a way that facilitates the control of the asylum seeker by the state.

Discussion of ethics generally focus on the individual practitioner as an autonomous moral agent, who must adhere to a set of ethical principles and guidelines (Beauchamp, 1999). However, it is the establishment of systems that undermines the independence and autonomy of the clinician

AUSTRALASIAN CORRECTIONAL MANAGEMENT
CURTIN IMMIGRATION RECEPTION & PROCESSING CENTRE
HEALTH CLINIC
PO BOX 1210, DERBY WA 6728
Tel: 08 9193 3804 Fax: 08 9193 3825

I, being the undersigned registered medical practitioner am responsible for the care of the following detainee who is held at Curtin IRPC under the Migration Act 1958:
Name_____DOB:_____Curtin ID number_____

This detainee has been on voluntary starvation for_____days and his/her condition is now such that I have serious concern for his/her health and well being. He/She continues to refuse any food or fluids orally and if medical treatment is not given there will be serious risk to his or her life or health. Furthermore the detainee fails to give or is not capable of giving consent to medical treatment.

I am requesting Ministerial Instrument under Migration Regulations, Section 5.35, whereby medical treatment as defined by the Regulations may be given to this detainee, without his/her expressed consent for the shorter period of one week or the duration of this hunger strike. The need for any ongoing ministerial authority will be reviewed after one week.

Yours sincerely,

_____

Date:_____

Fig. 25.3   Copy of Pro Forma Letter Provided to Doctors to Authorize Involuntary Treatment for Hunger Strikers

that have historically seen the greatest abuses of health care practice (Chodoff, 1999). It should be noted that virtually all of the acute ethical dilemmas that face health care staff discussed above are a direct consequence of the coercive nature of the detention center environment. Participation in hunger strikes by asylum seekers living in the broader Australian community is virtually nonexistent (Silove et al., 1996). Similarly, while self-harm and suicide attempts undoubtedly occur in the community, setting the evidence is that the rate is substantially lower than that manifest among immigration detainees (Dudley, 2003).

TOWARD A BLUEPRINT FOR ETHICAL PRACTICE IN DETENTION

> Be sure that you do not find yourself providing relaxation training to a patient who experiences panic attacks while the storm troopers kick down the door of their neighbour.

> Dr. Chris Clarke, School of Psychology, University of NSW, 1993

The best mental health practice incorporates a biopsychosocial approach to assessment, management, and intervention. The application of such a model is not possible in immigration detention as it has been practiced in Australia, despite the extraordinary high level of mental illness among detainees. Clinicians experience pressure to prescribe medication in the absence of a comprehensive intervention and are encouraged to ignore the impact of the environment on the ongoing trauma resulting from indefinite detention.

This raises significant questions about the clinician's role in a situation, where treatment planning, and intervention are unsuccessful for complex political and administrative reasons, predominantly the inability of clinicians to impact the detainee's psychosocial circumstances. The federal government has received advice from both mental health and child protection experts that for those adult and child detainees assessed, continuing indefinite detention is medically contraindicated. This raises a number of questions, for example, is it appropriate to continue to offer interventions when the detention context has been identified as the source of the current distress and clinically based recommendations have not been implemented? What is our responsibility, as individuals and as service providers, to these "unauthorized noncitizens" who we know to be in need, living on our soil but outside the structures that protect the rest of us from neglect, abuse, and degradation? Does "treatment" in this context amount to collusion or is it appropriate provision of support? If all your recommendations are ignored, should you keep making them?

Any answer to these questions must acknowledge that the detention of asylum seekers will continue to be practiced by a number of Western countries, at least in the short to medium term, and might expand in the near future. Government authorities or their detention contractors will continue to attempt to employ mental health professionals to ensure that they are seen to be meeting their duty of care obligations to detainees. Some mental health professionals, regardless of their own personal beliefs about the appropriateness of detention, will continue to work in these settings. Indeed it could be argued that the extreme mental distress of the detainees requires that mental health professionals play some active role in providing care. Consequently, it is important to attempt to examine how a blueprint for ethical practice in detention can be established and maintained. At the outset it must be acknowledged that some of the ethical dilemmas confronting the mental health professional in the detention center environment are not dissimilar to those facing clinicians in other custodial settings, for which detailed ethical guidelines have already been developed and which are recommended to the reader (Prison Health Care Practitioners, 2003; Weinsetein et al., 2000;). Nevertheless, there are important differences that make the ethical dilemmas in detention considerably acute. Detainees have not committed or been alleged to commit any offense. They are detained indefinitely. There is no suggestion that immigration detention should involve any kind of correctional or rehabilitative component, often a major contextual factor influencing the rationale for the involvement of mental health professionals in other custodial settings. Most important, while the indefinite detention of asylum seekers is lawful in Australia, it is clearly in breach of international human rights commitments and obligations to which Australia is a signatory.

From the outset the clinician should be prepared to acknowledge that the asylum seekers for whom they care, particularly those who have been detained for protracted periods, can experience profound psychological deterioration and that they will be able to do little to prevent this process. They need to acknowledge the limitations of their own professional ability to care for and to treat detainees and to be careful that they do not inadvertently become yet another instrument of control. Many standard psychological treatments are based on the assumption that the negative emotional reactions being experienced by a patient are disproportionate to the real environmental circumstances in which they live. In the case of those being held in detention, however, this assumption is probably not warranted, and the appropriateness of such treatments is highly problematic, as is reflected in the above quote by Chris Clarke.

At a conceptual level consideration of the adaptational framework proposed by Silove (1999) for understanding the threats faced by survivors of mass trauma provides a theoretical framework for understanding the clinical role and associated limitations that face a clinician working in detention. This conceptual model identifies five broad domains: security and safety, attachment, justice, identity and role, and existential meaning, which can variously be affected by complex trauma including the trauma caused by indefinite detention. Pathology arises when a breakdown in one of the domains occurs. For example, a breakdown in security and safety is argued to pose a serious threat to the integrity of an individual and manifest pathologically as PTSD. Threats to the attachment domain, through the murder or disappearance of family or friends, is argued to lead to complicated grief reactions and violation of the justice domain. This can be caused by exposure to systematic human rights abuses and manifests as ongoing pathological anger reactions. The focus of any intervention would thus reflect the system where evidence of the breakdown exists. For example, to ameliorate symptoms of PTSD restoration of the security/ safety system would be the focus of any intervention.

This model provides useful insights into understanding the preconditions for effective clinical work within the detention environment. The model would suggest that if clear and ongoing threats to one or more of the domains, as proposed by Silove, continue to exist in detention, then attempts to provide a therapeutic intervention for the resulting pathological outcome without addressing the threats associated with the genesis of the symptoms will not lead to clinical improvement. Thus, attempts to treat the symptoms of PTSD using standard treatment interventions without addressing the core issue of security and safety could face unexpected difficulties. For example, treatments such as imaginal exposure or testimony therapy appear to rely on, at least in part, a core assumption of safety as a precondition for treatment, with exposure leading to a form of habituation to salient trauma cues that are dependent on those cues not being linked to real life salient threats. Detainees are kept in a state of chronic anticipatory stress regarding their futures. They are likely to have witnessed significant trauma within the detention center, and they face the ever present possibility of forced repatriation to a situation that can be life threatening. Although positive treatment outcomes with asylum seekers have been noted in other contexts (Chapter 10 in this volume), it is our experience that the trauma encountered in detention renders such treatments ineffective.

While helping to identify those clinical domains that are unlikely to be responsive to treatment, Silove's model also provides a framework for understanding why interventions that, for example, attempt to promote the empowerment of asylum seekers or that acknowledge the reality of their situation of entrapment and ongoing exposure to human rights abuses are important. The palpable feelings of anger and resentment experienced by detainees result from a profound sense of injustice at being indefinitely imprisoned by the very country that they fled to for protection. Interventions aimed at empowerment seek to provide detainees with the tools and abilities to seek redress against the injustices they are subject to. The extreme feelings of betrayal experienced by asylum seekers who naively believed that Western countries were committed to upholding humanitarian principles can provide a serious threat to the existential life-world of the asylum seeker, fundamentally threatening core beliefs in the benevolence and very capacity for goodness in people. The clinician, by forming a protective and caring alliance with the asylum seeker, helps to provide a counter to these ongoing threats.

At a practical level the clinician should be aligned with and advocate for the best interests of those under his or her care and resist at all times the temptation to adopt any antidetainee sentiments that exist in the broader cultural milieu of the detention center. The role of the clinician in providing accurate and competent documentation of the mental state of detainees is often critical, both for refugee claims and in subsequent requests and appeals for community release. The clinician should not only keep accurate records but be certain that the detainees know that these records exist and that they are informed about the necessary procedures to obtain copies that could assist their claims for protection. Advocacy can also include encouraging detainees to keep their own records if possible (writings, drawings, etc). The clinician must be careful that the thresholds for reaching appropriate diagnoses are not modified to compensate for the environment of detention. The temptation of every clinician is to use diagnosis to differentiate the most unwell from the broader community of persons. However, it is possible, and previous research (Steel, 2003; Sultan & O'Sullivan, 2001; Thompson et al., 1998) would suggest, that the majority of those in detention can meet the criteria for psychiatric diagnosis. This is often best achieved by employing standardized diagnostic assessment instruments.

A key role that the clinician should play in detention is to help detainees negotiate their complex legal and administrative environments, which can often involve collaboration between legal and medical services in order to render the unintelligible intelligible and make the hidden transparent. This can include advising on and even encouraging acts of appropriate resistance to ensure their legality and to maximize their effectiveness. In short clinicians should help detainees to out-think the system that imprisons them. This could include informing detainees how they can lodge formal complaints regarding perceived breaches of their rights. There is nothing radical in these suggestions, in short they are all strategies to empower our clients to take control of their lives. It could be argued that a key clinical threat to those held in detention is that they are rendered powerless by the state. Any activity that the clinician can do to reempower them is a substantive clinical intervention. Perhaps the most important role of the clinician is to stand with and to unflinchingly testify to the suffering experienced and the culpability of the system that is producing this harm. We are not suggesting that clinicians act in a covert or secretive manner, but rather that they publicly position themselves as a clinical defender and advocate for detainees' rights and well-being. In comparison to the asylum seekers, health practitioners working in detention come from a position of acknowledged rights as citizens, employees, and professionals that they can draw on to provide as much protection to the asylum seekers as possible.

Unfortunately, it must be acknowledged that at times our ability as health professionals to form a protective and caring alliance with those subjected to indefinite detention become ethically too complex, and then even we become estranged from those we try to help, as is illustrated by the case study outlined in Figure 25.4.

The case concerns a baby, Ben, and his mother, Sonia. Sonia traveled to Australia on a valid visa and lodged a claim for refugee protection due to fears of being targeted by persons involved in criminal activities in her Eastern European home city. Because of the authorized manner of her travel to Australia, Sonia was allowed to live in the Australian community while her claims for refugee protection were assessed. During this time she formed a relationship with an Australian citizen and gave birth to Ben. Shortly after the birth, Sonia's application for refugee status in Australia was rejected at the final administrative level on technical grounds. She received notification that she had to leave Australia within 28 days and her failure to do so would result in Sonia being placed in immigration detention under threat of deportation. Ben, however, was afforded Australian residency by virtue of his father and was not detained, resulting in a 5-month-old child being forcibly separated from his mother.

Sonia and Ben's case attracted considerable media attention. Various refugee advocate groups and politicians became involved and prominent Australians wrote letters on her behalf. Sonia's lawyer approached two of us to prepare reports on Sonia's behalf. The case raises conflicting issues of law, psychiatric practice, and public health advocacy. Sonia's enforced separation from Ben meant that she could not continue breastfeeding. She received no support with this. The pregnancy had been unplanned, and she had developed a postpartum depression that required a mother-baby unit admission and medication. After Sonia was detained, the Family Court awarded Ben's father custody, because Sonia was in detention.

Ben's father could only bring Ben to the detention center 1 to 2 times weekly for approximately 1 hour each time. Sonia could not stop crying. This improved when a refugee advocacy group set up a volunteer transport roster. Ben had colds and persistent eczema and Sonia feared Ben's father did not attend to these. When Ben was sick, he was kept away from her. Sonia and Ben were both distressed by this.

We wrote to the Minister of Community Services indicating that family relationship assessments had not been considered in determining custody. Sonia's lawyer sought a "bonding and attachment report" regarding interim residence and contact, Ben's relationship to Sonia and his father, and whether if Sonia was deported, Ben should go with her or not. We observed a good attachment between Sonia and Ben, with Ben reaching out for his mother, settling easily with her, and using her as a secure base from which to observe us as strangers. We indicated that regular positive contact was of paramount importance to Ben's development, and recommended that contact increase, but stopped short of recommending that Ben stay in immigration detention with his mother overnight.

Sonia wanted Ben to stay overnight and Sonia's lawyer increasingly insisted on obtaining a report supporting this. However, it was the view of all the clinicians involved that this would send a contradictory message that could establish a precedent, potentially undermining the plan to remove all children in detention. We asked whether it was legal to have an Australian citizen in immigration detention overnight, and noted that the minister had varied immigration law to suit specific circumstances, for example, stating that women and children could be detained in the community. We suggested Sonia and Ben be admitted to a residential mothercraft hospital that could assess the mother-infant relationship and could facilitate overnight access outside detention, but the hospital declined to have asylum-seekers attended by guards on its premises. Sonia told us she would welcome overnight access some nights per week out of detention, but after further conversation with her lawyer, declined this proposal, and again insisted on overnight access in detention. Sonia hung up the phone while talking to us after we reclarified our position. Contact has now broken down. Sonia and some refugee advocates saw our position as "hardline." The lawyer made further attempts to get reports from another child psychiatrist to support Ben spending overnight periods in detention, but without success.

Fig. 25.4   Solomon's Choice

CONCLUSION

Our role as health care professionals exposes us to the harsh and brutal contest being played out between powerful first world countries seeking to protect their borders and individuals seeking protection from persecution at any cost. We encounter firsthand the resulting shattered lives and broken spirits. In this contest our ethics require us to prevent what harm we can and to document what we cannot prevent.

REFERENCES

Amnesty International. (2000). *Ethical codes and declarations relevant to the health professions* (4th ed.). London: Author.

Amnesty International. (2002). *Submission to the National Inquiry into Children in Immigration Detention*. Retrieved February 20, 2003, from http://www.hreoc.gov.au/human_rights/children_detention/submissions/index.html.

Beauchamp, T. L. (1999). The philosophical basis of psychiatric ethics. In S. Block, P. Chodoff, & S. A. Green (Eds.), *Psychiatric ethics* (3rd ed., pp. 25–48). Oxford, UK: Oxford University Press.

Cardozo, B. L., Vergara, A., Agani, F., & Gotway, C. A. (2000). Mental health, social functioning and attitudes of Kosovar Albanians following the war in Kosovo. *JAMA, 284,* 569–577.

Chodoff, P. (1999). Misuse and abuse of psychiatry: an overview. In S. Block, P. Chodoff, & S. Green (Eds.), *Psychiatric ethics* (3rd ed., pp. 49–66). Oxford, UK: Oxford University Press.

Commonwealth Ombudsman. (2001). *Report of an Own Motion Investigation into the Department of Immigration and Multicultural Affairs' Immigration Detention Centres.* Canberra: Commonwealth of Australia.

Declaration of Malta 43rd World Medical Assembly. (1991, November). *Guidelines adopted by the World Medical Association.* Valletta, Malta.

de Jong, J. T., Komproe, I. H., Van Ommeren, M., El Masri, M., Araya, M., Khaled, N., et al. (2001). Lifetime events and posttraumatic stress disorder in 4 postconflict settings. *JAMA, 170,* 351–357.

de Jong, K., Mulhern, M., Ford, N., van der Kam, S., & Kleber, R. (2000). The trauma of war in Sierra Leone. *Lancet, 355,* 2067–2068.

Dudley, M. (2003). Contradictory Australian national policies on self-harm and suicide. *Australasian Psychiatry, 11* (suppl.), S102–S108.

Four Corners. (2001). *Inside story. August 8, 2001.* Retrieved June 6, 2003, from http://www.abc.net.au/4corners.

Four Corners. (2003). *About Woomera.* Retrieved June 6, 2003, from http://www.abc.net.au/4corners/content/2003/20030519_woomera/default.htm.

Human Rights and Equal Opportunity Commission (HREOC). (1998). *Those who've come across the seas, the report of the commission's inquire into the detention of unauthorised arrivals.* Commonwealth of Australia.

Human Rights Watch. (2002). *By invitation only: Australian asylum policy.* Retrieved May 2, 2003, from http://hrw.org/reports/2002/australia.

Insight Program. (2003). *Mohammed and Juliet — A modern tragedy.* Retrieved June 1, 2003, from http://www.sbs.com.au/insight/index.php3?day-sum=2003-05-08#.

Kenny, M. A., Silove, D. M., & Steel, Z. (2004). Legal and ethical implications of medically enforced feeding of detained asylum seekers on hunger strike. *Medical Journal of Australia, 180*(5), 237–240.

Lateline. (2002a). *Australian doctors concerned over detention of children.* March 19, 2002. Retrieved June 6, 2003, from http://www.abc.net.au/lateline/archives/LatelineMonthIndex2002_May2002.htm.

Lateline. (2002b). *Woomera Detention Centre getting worse: IDAG.* May 8, 2002. Retrieved June 6, 2003, from http://www.abc.net.au/lateline/archives/LatelineMonthIndex2002_May2002.

Law Report. (2002, July 17). *Force feeding and the law.* Retrieved June 6, 2003, from http://www.abc.net.au/rn/talks/8.30/lawrpt/stories/s606948.htm.

Layton, R. (2003). Best investment: A state plan to protect and advance the interests of children. Adelaide: Government of South Australia. Retrieved May 20, 2003, from http://www.dhs.sa.gov.au/childprotectionreview/cpr-report.asp.

Mason, B. (2003, April 2–3). *The management of immigration detainees: health services and human rights.* Paper presented at the Human Rights, Human Wrongs, Human Costs—Health of Prisoners and Detainees in the 21st Century conference in Brisbane, Australia.

McCann, L. I. (1990). Vicarious traumatization: A framework for understanding the psychological effects of working with victims. *Journal of Traumatic Stress, 3,* 131–149.

Modvig, J., Pagaduan-Lopez, J., Rodenburg, J., Salud, C. M., Cabigon, R. V., & Panelo, C. I. A. (2000). Torture and trauma in post-conflict East Timor. *Lancet, 356,* 1763.

Mollica, R. F., Caspi-Yavin, Y., Bollini, P., Truong, T., Tor, S., & Lavelle, J. (1992). The Harvard Trauma Questionnaire: Validating a cross-cultural instrument for measuring torture, trauma, and posttraumatic stress disorder in Indochinese refugees. *Journal of Nervous and Mental Disease, 180,* 111–116.

Mollica, R. F., Donelan, K., Tor, S., Lavelle, J., Elias, C., Frankel, M., et al. (1993). The effect of trauma and confinement on functional health and mental health status of Cambodians living in Thailand-Cambodia border camps. *JAMA, 270,* 581–586.

Mollica, R. F., McInnes, K., Sarajlic, N., Lavelle, J., Sarajlic, I., & Massagli, M. P. (1999). Disability associated with psychiatric comorbidity and health status in Bosnian refugees living in Croatia. *JAMA, 282,* 433–439.

Mollica, R. F., Wyshak, G., de-Marneffe, D., Khuon, F., & Lavelle, J. (1987). Indochinese versions of the Hopkins Symptom Checklist-25: A screening instrument for the psychiatric care of refugees. *American Journal of Psychiatry, 144,* 497–500.

Office of the United Nations High Commissioner for Human Rights (OHCHR). (2002). *Report of the working group on arbitrary detention visit to Australia.* Geneva: Author.

Prison Health Care Practitioners. (2003). *Medical ethics in the prison context.* Retrieved June 8, 2003, from http://www.prisionhealthcarepractitioners.com/Topic_2.shtml.

Professional Alliance for the Health of Asylum Seekers and Their Children. (2002). *Submission to the National Inquiry into Children in Immigration Detention.* Retrieved June 6, 2003, from http://www.hreoc.gov.au/human_rights/children_detention/submissions/index.html.

Ruddock, P. (2002). Matters arising: Asylum seekers and healthcare. *Medical Journal of Australia, 176,* 86.

Ruddock, P. (2003). *Border protection information sheet: Mental health of detainees — The government's response.* Retrieved May 22, 2003, from http://www.minister.immi.gov.au/borders/detention/mentalhealth.htm.

Silove, D. (1999). The psychosocial effects of torture, mass human rights violations and refugee trauma: Towards and integrated conceptual framework. *Journal of Nervous and Mental Disease, 187,* 200–207.

Silove, D., Curtis, J., Masor, C., & Becker, R. (1996). Ethical considerations in the management of asylum seekers on hunger strike. *JAMA, 276,* 410–415.

Silove, D., Sinnerbrink, I., Field, A., Manicavasagar, V., & Steel, Z. (1997). Anxiety, depression and PTSD in asylum seekers: Associations with pre-migration trauma and post-migration stressors. *British Journal of Psychiatry, 170,* 351–357.

Silove, D., Steel, Z., & Watters, C. (2000). Policies of deterrence and the mental health of asylum seekers in Western countries. *JAMA, 284,* 604–611.

Steel, Z. (2003, May 12–15). *The politics of exclusion and denial the mental health costs of Australia's refugee policy.* Paper presented at the 38th Congress Royal Australian and New Zealand College of Psychiatrists, Hobart.

Steel, Z., & Silove, D. (2000). The psychosocial cost of seeking asylum. In A. Y. Shalev, R. Yehuda, & A. C. McFarlane (Eds.), *International handbook of human response to trauma* (pp. 421–438). New York: Plenum Press.

Steel, Z., Silove, D., Bird, K., McGorry, P., & Mohan, P. (1999). Pathways from war trauma to posttraumatic stress symptoms among Tamil asylum seekers, refugees and immigrants. *Journal of Traumatic Stress, 12*(3), 421–438.

Sultan, A., & O'Sullivan, K. (2001). Psychological disturbances in asylum seekers held in long term detention: a participant-observer account. *Medical Journal of Australia, 175,* 593–596.

Thompson, M., McGorry, P., Silove, D., & Steel, Z. (1998). Maribyrnong Detention Centre Tamil survey. In D. M. Silove & Z. Steel (Eds.), *The mental health and well-being of on-shore asylum seekers in Australia* (pp. 27–31). Sydney, Australia: Psychiatry Research and Teaching Unit.

U.S. Committee for Refugees. (2002). *Sea change: Australia's new approach to asylum seekers.* Retrieved May 20, 2002, from http://www.refugees.org/world/countryindex/australia.cfm.

UNICEF. (2002). *Submission to the National Inquiry into Children in Immigration Detention from Unicef Australia — United Nations Children's Fund.* Retrieved June 2, 2003, from http://www.hreoc.gov.au/human_rights/children_detention/submissions/subs_index.html.

United Nations High Commissioner for Refugees. (1997). *The state of the world's refugees: A humanitarian agenda.* New York: Oxford University Press.

Weinsetein, H. C., Burns, K. A., Newkirk, C. F., Zil, J. S., Dvoskin, J. A., & Steadman, H. J. (2000). *Psychiatric services in jails and prisons: A task force report of the American Psychiatric Association* (2nd ed.). New York: American Psychiatric Press.

World Medical Association. (1975). Guidelines for medical doctors concerning torture and other cruel, inhuman or degrading treatment or punishmnet in relation to detention and imprisonment. Adopted by the 29th World Medical Assembly, Tokya, Japan, October 1975. Geneva: WMA.

World Medical Association. (1992). Declaration of Malta on hunger strikers. Adopted by the 43rd World Medical Assembly in Malta, November 1991, and revised at the 44th Medical Assembly in Marbella, Spain, November 1992, Geneva: WMA.

INDEX

A